The Authority of the Bible and the
Rise of the Modern World

The
Authority of the Bible
and the Rise of the
Modern World

Henning Graf Reventlow

FORTRESS PRESS   PHILADELPHIA

Translated by John Bowden from the German
Bibelautorität und Geist der Moderne,
Die bedeutung des Bibelverständnisses für die
geistesgeschichtliche und politische Entwicklung in England
von der Reformation bis zur Aufklärung,
© Vandenhoeck and Ruprecht, Göttingen 1980,
with additional material supplied by the author.

Translation © John Bowden 1984

First Fortress Press edition 1985

Library of Congress Cataloging in Publication Data

Reventlow, Henning, Graf.
  The authority of the Bible and the rise of the modern
world.

  Translation of: Bibelautorität und Geist der Moderne.
  Includes bibliographical references and index.
  1. Bible—Criticism, interpretation, etc.—England—
History. 2. England—intellectual life. I. Title.
BS500.R4713   1984   220.6'0942   83–48921
ISBN 0–8006–0288–9

K895184   Printed in the United Kingdom   1–288

Hermann Schüssler (1929-1975)

in memoriam

Contents

Preface   ix

Preface to the English Edition   x

Foreword by James Barr   xii

Abbreviations   xv

Introduction: The Task   1

PART I

Preparatory Developments

1 Arriving at the Starting Point. The Cultural Situation in the
   Centuries before the Reformation   9
     (a) The problem of the Renaissance and Humanism   9
     (b) Late mediaeval Spiritualism   21
     (c) John Wyclif   31
2 Erasmus   39
3 The 'Left Wing of the Reformation'   49
4 Martin Bucer   73

PART II

The Crisis over the Authority of the Bible in England

1 The Age of the Puritans   91
     (a) Problems for research   91
     (b) The history of the Puritan struggles   99
     (c) The understanding of the Bible among Puritans and
         Conformists down to the beginning of the seventeenth
         century   105

(d) The century of transition   147

2 Lord Herbert of Cherbury: his Epistemology and
Philosophy of Religion   185

3 Thomas Hobbes: the Philosophical Presuppositions of his
Biblical Criticism   194

4 The Latitudinarians   223
    (a) Preachers and theological writers from the Restoration
    to the Glorious Revolution (1660-1689)   223
    (b) John Locke   243

PART III
The Climax of Biblical Criticism in English Deism

1 The Beginning of the Deistic Debates   289
    (a) Charles Blount   290
    (b) John Toland   294
    (c) Shaftesbury   308
    (d) Matthew Tindal, *The Rights of the Christian Church Asserted*   321
    (e) Party politics and the authority of the Bible at the
    beginning of the eighteenth century   327

2 Forms of Apologetic   335
    (a) Isaac Newton and his school   335
    (b) Rationalist apologetics: Samuel Clarke and Joseph Butler   341
    (c) At the opposite pole: Jonathan Swift   350

3 The Heyday of Deism   354
    (a) Anthony Collins   354
    (b) William Lyons   360
    (c) Anthony Collins and the Whiston Debate   362
    (d) Woolston and Annet   369
    (e) Tindal, *Christianity as Old as the Creation*   374

4 The Late Phase   384
    (a) Thomas Chubb   384
    (b) Thomas Morgan   396
    (c) Anti-deistic apologetic   406

Conclusion   411

Notes   415

Index   627

Preface

I have been preoccupied with the subject of this book for more than ten years. However, the preparatory work would never have led to the production of a manuscript had not the Volkswagen Foundation made it possible for me to have leave from my teaching duties and therefore a year of relative peace to work on it by providing a grant from 1 October 1973 to 30 September 1974. I am grateful not only for this help, but also for the provision of a further grant which has made possible the publication of my work.

Numerous assistants have helped me over the many years the book has been in preparation and without them I would hardly have been able to cover the literature it takes into consideration: Frau Beate Balzer; Pastor Gerrit Funke, Herr Bernhard Grafe and Frau Grafe; Pastor Hans-Joachim Hustadt, Frau Dr Gudrun Müller, Pastor Hartmut Neumann, Herr Gerhard Otto and Frau Elke Otto-Sanio, Pastor Dr Jean-Marcel Vincent, Pastor Matthias Weissinger.

Bochum, 29 October 1979

Preface to the English Edition

In many respects the English edition of this work amounts to a second edition. Since it is now a number of years since I finished work on the German version, I felt obliged to work through the text again thoroughly, above all supplementing the bibliographical references as far as possible, particularly with the secondary literature on the various sections of the book which had appeared in the meantime. Only a few alterations were needed to the body of the text; usually the situation described has been confirmed by most recent literature. By contrast, in many places the notes have been substantially expanded.

The English reader may find an indication of my own position helpful. I have not just been concerned to describe the way in which understanding and criticism of the Bible were an inextricable strand in the fabric of the general cultural background in the centuries between the Reformation and the Enlightenment, with its views of church and state and the typical philosophical systems during the many and varied developments in intellectual, political and social life. I also wanted to show how strongly patterns of thought stemming from the Middle Ages and a revived interest in the ancient world found their way into the general awareness of modern times. The effects of these patterns of thought can be traced right down to the present, where Christianity is largely understood as a system of moral action. Above all in Western Europe and the United States, which has been shaped by Western European thought, the consequences of the basic Reformation insight of justification not through works, but through faith alone, have largely faded from the modern mind, though this insight was also alive in the Reformed churches of the Netherlands, Scotland and England. The developments described in the following chapters will make clear how this could happen. That is why I also found the events on the Continent leading up to what happened in England important, because they determined the decisive direction. To this extent I hope that my book will also prompt critical reflection.

The translation was made possible by a grant from the Inter Nationes Foundation in Bonn, for which I am grateful. I must also thank the translator, Dr John Bowden, the publishers and printers for their admirable work in producing the English version. In Bochum, Frau Ulrike Liebau, Fräulein Heike Lengenfeld and Herr Friedbert Fellert helped with the preparation.

Bochum, October 1983

Foreword
by James Barr

People often suppose that biblical criticism is a German innovation or invention, and those in the English speaking world who are hostile to it have often cited its supposed German origin in order to frighten people away from it. It is more true, however, to say that the cradle of biblical criticism lay in the English-speaking world: only from near the end of the eighteenth century onward did Germany become the main centre for its development. Before that time England was the chief locus in which new ideas of the nature and authority of the Bible were fostered. In these respects Graf Reventlow's book redresses the balance in a striking way. He is well-known and highly respected as an Old Testament scholar, having written numerous monographs on particular books or strata of the Hebrew Bible and also having surveyed the major general issues such as the problems of Old Testament theology. It is a striking testimony to the width of his interests and knowledge that this present book lays its entire emphasis upon the development of thought about biblical interpretation in England from the Reformation to the Enlightenment. The work displays a remarkable grasp of the sources, the details and the wider distinctive outlines of those debates which brought about a gradual change in general attitudes to the Bible.

The author is certainly right when he says that modern histories of biblical scholarship, in so far as they give any attention at all to the period of English Deism and early biblical criticism, have done so only tangentially: they have noted here and there various points at which these early days showed an anticipation of later critical ideas or results. But on the whole they have not tried to enter into the profounder setting in life in which these new ideas came to birth: the reasons why new questions were asked, the nature of the problems which were encountered, the concerns which animated the scholars as they thought and wrote. It is into this entire world of concern for the Bible, rather than into the particular views about one passage or another, that Reventlow seeks to enter. He guides the reader into the total context of life and thought in which new notions about the Bible came to birth.

This total context was not solely theological or purely academic in the sense in which these terms may be understood today. Church and state formed a single continuum, and political and theological questions were seen as interdependent. Questions about power and legitimacy rested in high degree upon exegetical and interpretative ideas. In this the Old Testament – Reventlow's own specialism – was of primary importance. Even if the New Testament was the document of the earliest Christianity, the way in which it might be understood depended in remarkable degree upon the way in which the other collection of books from a yet older age, the Old Testament, was related to it. For it was the Old Testament, as it seemed, that offered guidance about king and state, about a commonwealth organized under divine statutes, about law and property, about war, about ritual and ceremony, about priesthood, continuity and succession. All of this was a disputed area from the Reformation onwards: because these were controversial matters in church and state, they generated deep differences in biblical interpretation. It was precisely because the Bible was assumed on all hands to be authoritative that it stimulated new notions about its own nature. It was because men sought answers to problems of life and society, as well as of thought and belief, that the Bible itself stimulated 'critical' modes of understanding itself.

When we look back upon this time, it is important to discern the essentially theological and exegetical involvement in almost all the currents of ideas. Seen from a later perspective the writers of the time have been perceived as if they were 'pure' philosophers or 'pure' scientists, because it was in that way that they were later understood and applied. But if the men are to be properly understood, the deep theological interest underlying their work – the work, for instance, of Isaac Newton, to cite the supreme example – must be followed out. But much, or most, of that theological interest was not that which counted before, or since, as orthodoxy: on the contrary, it was highly experimental, looking in new directions, even at the same time at which we can discern its deep indebtedness to earlier times such as the Middle Ages.

The importance of this book is, first of all, historical, in that it uncovers and sets in order a current of thinking that has been determinative of much of the history, not only of England, but of the English-speaking peoples generally. But for the development here reviewed, after all, the Constitution of the United States, or the United States herself in the form in which she exists, could hardly have come into being. But, secondly, the work is not only historical: it offers us deep insights into the way in which biblical understanding is achieved. Today the history of scholarship and interpretation is coming to be considered increasingly important. This is valuable, but only where the purposes and interests of scholarship are profoundly known. Otherwise we fall easily into abuses, as when an interpretation is rejected not because it fails to fit the text but because it can be labelled as belonging to this or that past school or tendency, or when half-baked theories of hermeneutics are allowed to override the realities of both text and scholarship. Thirdly and finally, however, a book like this may help us to understand how we ourselves work and think. The circumstances indeed cannot be identical and need not even be similar. But the scholar of today, like the man in the pew today or the reader of today's daily newspaper, thinks and operates under the impingement of forces and drives that are technological, political, economic and social. The message of scripture is heard in relation to these forces. Change in interpretation, and the evocation of new modes of understanding, is not only the likely, but the highly probable consequence for us to expect.

Christ Church, Oxford, July 1983

Abbreviations

AEcR	*American Ecclesiastical Review*
AeR	*Atene e Rome*
AES	*Archives européennes de sociologie*
AGP	*Arbeiten zur Geschichte des Pietismus*
AHR	*American Historical Review*
AIHI	*Archives internationales d'histoire des idées*
AIHS	*Archives internationales d'histoire des sciences*
AJP	*American Journal of Philology*
AJT	*American Journal of Theology*
AKG	*Arbeiten zur Kirchengeschichte*
AKuG	*Archiv für Kulturgeschichte*
AKWG	*Archiv voor kerkelijke en wereldlijke geschiedenissen in zonderheit van Utrecht*
ALKGMA	*Archiv für Literatur- und Kirchengeschichte des Mittelalters*
AmPolScRev	*American Political Science Review*
AmQ	*American Quarterly*
APh	*Archiv für Philosophie*
APG(F)	Abhandlungen zur Philosophie und ihrer Geschichte
APSR	*American Political Science Review*
ARG	*Archiv für Reformationsgeschichte*
ARG.E	*Archiv für Reformationsgeschichte Ergänzungsband*
ARSP	*Archiv für Rechts- und Sozialphilosophie*
AUSS	*Andrews University Seminary Studies*
AzTh	Arbeiten zur Theologie
BAB.L	*Bulletin de l'académie royale de Belgique. Classe des lettres et des sciences morales et politiques*
BAGB	*Bulletin de l'association Guillaume Budé*
BAGB.S	*Bulletin de l'association Guillaume Budé, Supplément critique*
BBGW	*Basler Beiträge zur Geschichteswissenschaft*
BDLG	*Blätter für deutsche Landesgeschichte*

BG	*Bijdragen tot de gescheidenis bijzonderlijk van het oud hertogdom Brabant*
BHR	*Bibliotheque d'humanisme et renaissance*
BISI	*Bollettino dell'istituto storico italiano per il medio evo*
BJHS	*British Journal for the History of Science*
BPfKG	*Blätter für pfälzische Kirchengeschichte und religiöse Volkskunde*
BPTF	*Bijdragen van de philosophische en theologische faculteiten der nederlandsche Jezuiten*
BQ	*Baptist Quarterly*
BRN	*Bibliotheca reformatoria Neerlandica*
BSHST	*Basler Studien zur historischen und systematischen Theologie*
BVGO	*Bijdragen voor vaderlandsche geschiedenis en oudheidskunde*
BZRGG	*Beihefte der Zeitschrift für Religions- und Geistesgeschichte*
CambJourn	*Cambridge Journal*
CChrCM	Corpus Christianorum. Continuatio mediaevalis
CH	*Cahiers d'histoire*
ChH	*Church History*
ChW	*Christliche Welt*
CJEPS	*Canadian Journal of Economic and Political Science*
Conv.	*Convivium*
CR	*Corpus Reformatorum*
CV	*Communio Viatorum*
CSSH	*Comparative Studies in Society and History*
CTM	*Concordia Theological Monthly*
DA	*Deutsches Archiv für Erforschung des Mittelalters*
Daed.	*Daedalus*
DNB	*Dictionary of National Biography*
DtPfrBl	*Deutsches Pfarrerblatt*
EcHR	*Economic History Review*
EHR	*English Historical Review*
EHS	Europäische Hochschulschriften
ELH	*English Literary History. A Journal of English Literary History*
ErJb	*Eranos-Jahrbuch*
ET	English translation
ETL	*Ephemerides Theologicae Lovanienses*
Fil.	*Filosofia*
GCFI	*Giornale critico della filosofia italiana*
GSLI	*Giornale storico della letteratura italiana*
GuL	*Geist und Leben*

Her.	*Hermanthena*
HeR	*Humanisme et Renaissance*
HibJ	*Hibbert Journal*
Hist	*History*
HistJ	*Historical Journal*
HJ	*Historisches Jahrbuch*
HTh	*History and Theory*
HTR	*Harvard Theological Review*
HUCA	*Hebrew Union College Annual*
HWP	*Historisches Wörterbuch der Philosophie*
HZ	*Historische Zeitschrift*
IJRS	*Internationales Jahrbuch für Religionssoziologie*
IMU	*Italia medioevale e umanistica*
Int.	*Interpretation*
JAAR	*Journal of the American Academy of Religion*
JCS	*Journal of Cuneiform Studies*
JEGP	*Journal of English and Germanic Philology*
JEH	*Journal of Ecclesiastical History*
JHI	*Journal of the History of Ideas*
JHP	*Journal of the History of Philosophy*
JMH	*Journal of Modern History*
JP	*Journal of Philosophy*
JR	*Journal of Religion*
JTS	*Journal of Theological Studies*
JTVI	*Journal of Transactions of the Victoria Institute*
JWKG	*Jahrbuch des Vereins für westfälische Kirchengeschichte*
JWCI	*Journal of the Warburg and Courtauld Institute*
KHÅ	*Kyrkohistorisk Årsskrift*
KIG	Die Kirche in ihrer Geschichte
LCL	Loeb Classical Library
LM	*Lutherische Monatshefte*
LÜAMA	Leipziger Übersetzungen und Abhandlungen zum Mittelalter
LuJ	*Luther-Jahrbuch*
LuthQ	*Lutheran Quarterly*
MennEnc	*Mennonite Encyclopaedia*
MennLex	*Mennonitisches Lexikon*
MennQR	*Mennonite Quarterly Review*
MFCG	*Mitteilungen und Forschungsbeiträge der Cusanus Gesellschaft*
MGB	*Mennonitische Geschichtsblätter*

MLR	*Modern Language Review*
MPh	*Modern Philology*

NAkG	*Nederrlands(ch) archief voor kerkgeschiedenis*
NEBrit	*New Encyclopaedia Britannica*
NEQ	*New England Quarterly*
NF	Neue Folge (New Series)
NS	New Series
NSchol	*New Scholasticism*
NZST	*Neue Zeitschrift für systematische Theologie*

PACPA	*Proceedings of the American Catholic Philosophical Association*
PaP	*Past and Present*
PAS	*Proceedings of the Aristotelian Society*
Phil	*Philosophy*
PhJ	*Philosophisches Jahrbuch der Görres-Gesellschaft*
PhQ	*Philosophical Quarterly*
PhR	*Philosophische Rundschau*
PhRev	*Philosophical Review*
PHSL	*Proceedings of the Huguenot Society of London*
PL	J. P. Migne, *Patrologia Latina*
PMLA	Publications of the Modern Language Association of America
PolQ	*Political Quarterly*
PolSt	*Political Studies*
PPR	*Philosophy and Phenomenological Research*
PQ	*Philological Quarterly*
PVS	*Politische Vierteljahresschrift*

QFRG	Quellen und Forschungen zur Reformationsgeschichte
QGT	Quellen zur Geschichte der Täufer

RCSF	*Rivista critica di storia della filosofia*
RE	*Realencyklopädie für protestantische Theologie und Kirche*
Ref.	*Reformation*
RELit	*Review of English Literature*
RESt	*Review of English Studies*
RExp	*Review and Expositor*
RF(T)	*Rivista di filosofia, Turin*
RFNS	*Rivista di filosofia neo-scolastica*
RFS	*Revue française de sociologie*
RGG	*Die Religion in Geschichte und Gegenwart*
RH	*Revue historique*
RHE	*Revue d'Histoire Ecclésiastique*
RHLF	*Revue d'histoire littéraire de la France*

RHPR	*Revue d'histoire et de philosophie religieuses*
RIFD	*Rivista internazionale di filosofia del diritto*
Rin.	*Rinascita*
RIPh	*Revue internationale de philosophie*
RLC	*Revue de littérature comparée*
RKZ	*Reformierte Kirchenzeitung*
RMM	*Revue de métaphysique et de morale*
RMS	*Renaissance and Modern Studies*
RomF	*Romanische Forschungen*
RP	*Review of Politics*
RPFE	*Revue philosophique de la France et de l'étranger*
RR	*Review of Religion*
RRAL	*Rendiconti della Reale Accademia dei Lincei. Classe di Scienze Morale, Storiche e Filologiche*
RSFil	*Rassegna di scienze filosofiche*
RSIt	*Rivista storica italiana*
RSPT	*Revue des Sciences Philosophiques et Théologiques*
RTAM	*Recherches de théologie ancienne et médiévale*
SAMH	*Studies in Anabaptist and Mennonite History*
SGSG	*Studi gregoriani per la storia di Gregorio VII*
SHCT	*Studies in the History of Christian Thought*
SMRT	*Studies in Mediaeval and Reformation Thought*
SP	*Studies in Philology*
SR	*Studies in Religion*
SSLL	*Stanford Studies in Language and Literature*
STKAB	*Schriften des theologischen Konvents augsbürgischen Bekenntnisses*
STPh	*Studia Philosophica*
StRen	*Studies in the Renaissance*
SVRG	*Schriften des Vereins für Reformationsgeschichte*
THS	Transactions of the Royal Historical Society
ThStKr	*Theologische Studien und Kritiken*
TLZ	*Theologische Literaturzeitung*
TP	*Tijdschrift voor philosophie*
TQS	*Theologische Quartalschrift*
Tr	*Traditio*
TRE	*Theologische Realenzyklopädie*
TZ	*Theologische Zeitschrift*
UTQ	*University of Toronto Quarterly*
VF	*Verkündigung und Forschung*
VIHG	*Veröffentlichungen des Instituts für europäische Geschichte*

WA	Martin Luther, *Werke*, Kritische Gesamtausgabe (Weimarer Ausgabe)
WdF	*Wege der Forschung*
WestfZ	*Westfälische Zeitschrift*
WissWeltb	*Wissenschaft und Weltbild*
ZDP	*Zeitschrift für deutsche Philologie*
ZdZ	*Zeichen der Zeit*
ZfG	*Zeitschrift für Geschichtswissenschaft*
ZKG	*Zeitschrift für Kirchengeschichte*
ZNW	*Zeitschrift für die neutestamentliche Wissenschaft*
ZPol	*Zeitschrift für Politik*
ZRGG	*Zeitschrift für Religions- und Geistesgeschichte*
ZST	*Zeitschrift für systematische Theologie*
ZTK	*Zeitschrift für Theologie und Kirche*
Zwing.	*Zwingliana*

Introduction: The Task

Any attentive observer will note a considerable decline in the significance of biblical study within the general framework of Protestant theology as it is practised in universities and church colleges and as it affects
the work of local church communities. This contrasts with the period
immediately after the Second World War, when as a result of the
influence of dialectical theology the Bible was the centre of interest for
teachers and students alike. Given a predominant concern with the
present and its seemingly urgent practical problems, which claim almost
exclusive attention, historical criticism and exegesis have come to take
very much a back place. At the same time, the unity of theology, in the
outward form in which its classical disciplines are still presented, has
been increasingly lost sight of: this is not only because increasing specialization continually prevents the individual from seeing beyond the
confines of his specialist area, but above all because the inner centre on
which biblical interpretation, the study of church history, systematic
theological thought and the life of the church should be oriented, seems
virtually to have disappeared. If we are to deal with this situation, we
must first take account of the developments which have led to it. As is
always the case in the history of ideas, the external situation is simply
the expression and consequence of internal developments which began
long before their consequences became evident, and which have un-
dermined the apparently secure foundation of theology as a discipline.

Furthermore, we may recognize that one of the most important
reasons for the vanishing role of biblical study in the wider context of
theology is a failure of exegetes to reflect adequately on their methodology and the presuppositions, shaped by their view of the world,
which they bring to their work. This may sound astonishing, given the
intensity with which an extended discussion on hermeneutics has been
carried on right down to the most recent period.[1] However, for the
most part this discussion moved in the realms of esoteric theological
reflections, to some degree forming a 'superstructure' to the tacitly

accepted foundation of an exegesis which has been taken to be 'historical-critical' and therefore scientific. Reflection on the presuppositions of historical criticism appears only by way of exception, as in the well-known study by G.Ebeling, 'The Significance of the Critical Historical Method for Church and Theology in Protestantism'.[2] As soon as that happens, however, it immediately becomes clear that this method cannot be detached from a quite specific understanding of the world and of reality.[3] Only a few years ago it was possible simply to identify the view of the world thus defined with modern thought.[4] Now, however, when we can see the intrinsic fragility of these presuppositions, and theology is presented with new tasks precisely because of the problems with which we are faced, it is desirable that we should dig deeper and uncover the ideological and social roots to which more recent biblical criticism owes its origin, its deeper impetus and the direction of the answers which it gives.

In this study I have set myself the task of looking back at the beginnings of biblical criticism (in which the Old Testament plays an important part) to uncover the motives, the intellectual presuppositions, the philosophical assumptions, and last, but not least, the developments in church politics, which have led to the conclusions at which it arrived. My aim has been to produce an inter-disciplinary study. In its earliest stages, biblical criticism was by no means an esoteric business, confined to professional scholars in tranquil studies. Carried on by theologians, philosophers and a group of authors whom we would now describe as political journalists, it attracted widespread public interest, had far-reaching political consequences and claimed to be a decisive influence on all areas of public life. Nowadays, however, despite the importance of this area of thought, which had an influence on all the significant battles between the rise of humanism and the Enlightenment, whether these were in the realm of argument or in the context of politics and church affairs, biblical criticism is ignored by the non-theological disciplines like the history of philosophy, secular and constitutional history, political science and even to some degree by church history. But in many cases this of itself leads to the obvious difficulties which stand in the way of arriving at a generally acceptable solution to the complex problems of understanding.

It would be wrong to see this book simply as one more contribution to a series of histories of the interpretation of the Bible. There are, for example, many histories of the interpretation of the Old Testament; the best-known ones in Germany are probably L.Diestel, *Geschichte des Alten Testaments in der christlichen Kirche*, 1869, reprinted 1981, and H.J.Kraus, *Geschichte der historisch-kritischen Erforschung des Alten Testaments*, [3]1982.[5] However, these histories of interpretation are primarily concerned with the results of the critical observations on the Old Testament made by earlier generations, in a kind of stocktaking of the history of interpretation, and only take into account the theological and cultural background which was instrumental in producing these results in so far as it seemed to be of significance for the way in which the results were gained.[6] The only work which adopts another methodological procedure and aim is that of K.Scholder, *Ursprünge und Probleme der Bibelkritik im 17. Jahrhundert*, 1966.[7] Following the 'deductive' approach of his teacher, G.Ebeling,[8] Scholder seeks to grasp *a priori* 'that intellectual process which ends in the dethronement of the Bible as the authoritative source of all human knowledge and understanding',[9] and he acutely points out that 'the beginnings of biblical criticism present at first much more of a philosophical than a theological problem', so that any investigation of them in the context of church history must take place in the frontier territory between theology and philosophy.[10] However, Scholder did not provide an adequate definition of this philosophical and theological movement; on the one hand he identifies it with the modern scientific (Copernican) view of the world (56ff.), and on the other with Cartesianism (131ff.).[11] In reality, the true stimuli towards biblical criticism are to be sought elsewhere; they go much further into the past and deeper into the fabric of the history of theology.

When we look for the real roots of those first reflections which brought about a critical concern with the Bible, we come upon a large-scale cultural movement throughout Europe which must be set alongside the Reformation as the most powerful force in the formation of the modern world. There is a clear line of development in the history of theology, stages of which can be seen in late mediaeval Spiritualism, the rationalistic and moralistic trends within Humanism and the Anabaptist movement, and finally in the two great trends which dominated church politics: Puritanism and rationalistic liberalism (Latitudinarianism and Deism proper) in England. Writers have aptly spoken of the 'two Reformations' which stand in juxtaposition in the sixteenth century[12] and which were a definitive influence on later developments. This second line, which has also been sweepingly called 'Humanism', in contrast to the message of the Reformation,[13] was much more influential in the development of the cultural history of modern times.[14] It, and not the Reformation proper, also determined the relationship of more recent academic Protestant theology to the Bible; its basic views have also been largely normative for Old Testament exegesis.

However, we can pursue this line only with difficulty. It is often broken. The reason for this is partly that important periods of the past cultural history of Europe are still very obscure. Darkness often shrouds above all the transitions between periods, the decisive links which might explain the continuing influence of earlier stimuli on later developments. In what respects is a particular period new, and where do we have no more than a recurrence of old ideas? One gains an over-riding impression that the continuing influence of typical attitudes and conceptions is stronger than any new development, and that even with apparently antithetical movements (as in the relationship between Puritanism and liberalism in England) the common features are greater than one might at first assume. The whole trend is much more like a river of which it is possible to see only stretches, through dense woodland; then it is again swallowed up in the deep undergrowth, though all the time following a clear direction the course of which can be pursued easily enough despite all the interruptions.

The main course of this development is described in the following pages as a movement which goes from the Continent to England and then at a later stage back to the Continent again. I have chosen England and the period of English Deism as the climax of the development I have traced because it was in that country, with its characteristic theological and philosophical history, not to mention its distinctive ecclesiastical politics, that typical views of the world developed which were to have lasting influence in forming even the hidden presuppositions in the interpretation of the Old Testament and in biblical exegesis generally. England can claim a prominent place in the history of the interpretation of the Bible. As Scholder already recognized, Germany did not join in this development until late in the eighteenth century. In France there were trends which in some respects ran parallel, but they developed in a different cultural situation (the dominant position of the Catholic church), and furthermore, because of strict censorship by both church and state, the views held there could only be circulated, until the middle of the eighteenth century, in the form of an underground literature which was written out by hand.[15] A more decisive factor is that they do not have the Protestant understanding of scripture behind them and therefore could not contribute any basic insights to the principles of later biblical exegesis.[16] As a result, the later French Enlightenment in the second half of the eighteenth century ended up by being opposed to the church in principle, to the extent of even flaunting materialism. By contrast, in England, for all the opposition, even the most extreme representatives of Deism never lost a sense of being part of Christianity. Here the Bible remained the decisive conversation partner, though people had difficulty in reading their own views into it, deriving as these did from quite different sources. Consequently this was the place where the most characteristic norms for interpreting the Old Testament, as well as the New, were also developed.

The fact that a fundamentally different aim is pursued by previous histories of interpretation is evident from the ground that they cover. Thus Kraus devotes only a few remarks in passing to English Deism.[17] In fact, the contribution of detailed critical findings made in this period to the interpretation of the Old Testament must seem to be modest in any survey which is oriented on the history of the material. However, Scholder, too, deliberately brackets off the English development, as he does the whole political and social sphere, although in both instances he feels that there is a gap in his overall account.[18] On the other hand, it might well be asked why my account does not pay closer attention to certain famous individual exegetes of the Old Testament in Holland, like H.Grotius, J.Clericus and B. de Spinoza. Precisely because the first two became significant for the history of exegesis by virtue of their philological and historical work (which is why they must have a place in the history of the material), they do not belong here. More important might be the fact that they belonged to the Arminian church, a community which was also influenced by the ideas of the 'second Reformation'. However, this particular theological trend also belongs with those areas which recent scholarship has grossly neglected, even in the Netherlands; and for the most part, modern studies of individual figures are also lacking. Be this as it may, it is clear that in many respects the course of events in the Netherlands ran parallel to that in England, just as Dutch influence on England was wide-ranging and varied – as can be seen in the careers of many individuals. Spinoza and the background to his criticism of the Bible call for a separate account, which would also have to take into account the extensive secondary literature. As an apostate from Judaism and one whose thought was consistently within the framework of a strictly rationalistic system, he had presuppositions of his own; his influence remained small because his works were declared heretical virtually as soon as they appeared and at a later period only came into view in a spasmodic way.[19]

The immediate result of this kind of survey of the history of theology might be to make clearer the premises on which Old Testament exegesis is based. Characteristic prejudices which have hitherto prevented an open judgment on their subject-matter, the Bible, might be brought to light. In all periods the interpretation of the Old Testament is, to a greater degree than has been realized, a later spiritual legacy of its founders. Demonstrating their limitations would at the same time make it possible for Old Testament scholars to redefine their role in the general context of theology, in particular in view of the demands made on Old Testament study as a theological discipline by the changed cultural situation of the present day. Finally, Old Testament scholarship, too, is presented with the kind of alternatives which have long been evident in consideration of the Reformation and its message, in the spheres of systematic theology and the history of theology. Here two fundamentally different approaches to understanding mankind and the world are offered, and it is possible for us to make a choice between them. The result of this choice also has a decisive influence on people's prospects of being able to give an appropriate reply to the theological questions of the time. Either this reply remains a product of late humanism, in which case it will no longer find a hearing in our new concerns with the question of the meaning of life. Or it will pioneer a way out of its past, in which case it will be confronted with new possibilities. Only a careful survey of the way it has come so far can clarify existing intrinsic presuppositions and help us to overcome them by making us aware of them.

PART I

Preparatory Developments

1

Arriving at the Starting Point.
The Cultural Situation in the Centuries
before the Reformation

(a) The problem of the Renaissance and Humanism

The Renaissance and Humanism occupy an important position within the cultural development of Europe: they characterize a period which is usually regarded as the decisive transition from the Middle Ages to modern times. It is therefore clear *a priori* that this period must play a decisive role in the development which is to be sketched out in this study. Nevertheless, it seems appropriate to begin by looking carefully at the question of which phenomena within the chronological and cultural context referred to by these designations need to be considered seriously in connection with the prehistory of the developments that we are to consider.

Discussion about the nature of this period has continued to be lively ever since the publication of Jakob Burckhardt's basic work *Die Kultur der Renaissance in Italien*[1] a century ago.[2] Burckhardt's name still continues to be associated with a basic view of the significance of the Renaissance which, strictly speaking, he himself did not invent,[3] but which he made widely popular by the force of his vision and the completeness of his account. In his view the Renaissance represents a decisive stage in the cultural history of mankind: <u>it sees the accomplishment of the significant transition from the Middle Ages to modern times in which the individual discovers himself because he is free to develop himself.</u>[4]

The close alliance between the Italian popular spirit and the rediscovery of antiquity[5] opens up a new view of the world in which man, and individual man at that, for the first time occupies a central place.[6] Burckhardt gives a vivid account of the way in which this new spirit emerged in all realms of life; he develops his picture, originally formed from the experience of Italian Renaissance art,[7] into a comprehensive cultural view. Numerous of Burckhardt's successors have repeated his conception of a basically new beginning in the basic cultural attitude of the Renaissance over against the Middle Ages; it had a wide-ranging influence on the idealist perspective in the further course of the nineteenth century and to some degree in the twentieth. W.Dilthey[8] and E.Cassirer[9] should be mentioned among the most significant representatives of this view.[10] For Burckhardt the Renaissance is a unique and unrepeatable climax in the history of the human spirit: brought to life by the rediscovery of antiquity, the forces of a new individualism are to be found everywhere, in politics, art and education. Here are enthusiasm for aesthetics, independence of thought, moral earnestness and unbridled passion, the desire for bloody vengeance and the struggle for renown, the enjoyment of pleasure and asceticism – all together in inimitable juxtaposition. In Burckhardt's view, in this attitude we also have the germ of a deep-rooted alienation from traditional religion;[11] when at the turn of this century rationalistic liberalism sought to claim the Renaissance as the chief witness in its cause, many of his successors put forward a much cruder version of this notion and placed far more emphasis on it than he ever intended.[12]

The view of Burckhardt and his school has been subjected to vigorous criticism. A series of scholars, especially those with a Catholic background, have been concerned to stress the religious character of thought even in the Renaissance, in contrast to the liberal rationalistic interpretation. The account by L.Pastor in his multi-volume *Geschichte der Päpste*[13] seems to be somewhat superficial. He sought to distinguish between thinkers like Valla, Panormita and Poggio on the one hand, who because of the classical ideal throw themselves into the arms of ancient paganism, and the large number of others who combine classical and Christian ideals in a noble harmony.[14] In this way the Renaissance emerges as the period of two movements running contrary to each other, one of which followed philosophical naturalism whereas the other largely found the roots of human existence and human virtue in faith. K.Burdach[15] takes a more uniform view. He explains the nature of the Renaissance in terms of the primarily political notion of a revival of the old Roman culture in Italy, which never completely disappeared, and the awakening of an Italian national consciousness.[16] This led to developments in the realm of ethics, though the original roots in religion were never torn up. The most profound stimulus towards the Renaissance was the notion of the renewal of the Christian religion; here the elements from the ancient world also had a religious character, but in contrast to the old, dogmatically rigid forms brought to life the hope of a new, freer faith. In contrast to Burckhardt and his followers, here Burdach sees no break between the Renaissance and the Middle Ages, but a broad stream of continuity going back as far as the Church Fathers.

Even for Augustine, the synthesis between the life of the ancient world, to which he still belonged, and the doctrines of Christianity was the decisive problem. Thus the question of *humanitas* remains the basic theme which runs right through the Middle Ages. However, in the Renaissance quite a new feeling for personality evidently developed, a longing for rebirth and a deep-rooted renewal of the whole of life from the depths of religion. Burdach finds the first promptings of this among the revivalist notions of the Spiritualist mystics of the thirteenth century, associated with the invasion of neo-Platonist influences.[17] E.Walser,[18] who first investigated the problem of Christian and pagan thought in the Renaissance, posed by Burckhardt and Pastor, in a study of the figure of Poggio Bracciolini,[19] concludes that despite all the difference in individual standpoints to be found in the characteristic thinkers of the Renaissance,[20] even scepticism, sensualism and an apparent lack of religion have deep roots in the primal ground of the old faith. The new is rooted in the old, and in all the conflicts is united in a harmony in the face of which the external antitheses seem to be no more than rhetorical fireworks which remain at a superficial level.[21] One interesting variant on the Catholic view of the Renaissance is the life-work of G.Toffanin, who regards the Renaissance, with its fusion of thought from antiquity and Christianity, as the period of a reaction to and reflection on Christian values as opposed to the sectarian uprisings in the thirteenth and then again in the sixteenth century.[22]

Various judgments have been passed on the problem of the continuity between the Middle Ages and the Renaissance, and it has still not been resolved. Mention should be made of the attempts, most of which are by now quite dated, to put the beginning of the Renaissance much earlier, with the first appearance of the conceptions of man and nature which were characteristic of this period – say in the twelfth and thirteenth centuries.[23] Occasionally it is put in France instead of in Italy.[24] More important for our concern is the thesis put forward by E.Gilson[25] and J. Huizinga.[26] According to them, the main elements of the modern view of life, above all individualism, but also a concern with classical antiquity and the contrast between nature and grace, had already been quite evident throughout Europe from the thirteenth century on, and it was inconceivable to treat the late Middle Ages and the Renaissance as separate periods. Countless new insights contributed to this judgment, above all the recognition that the Middle Ages, previously denigrated in a sweeping generalization, was in reality an extraordinarily varied world. To this degree the 'revolt of the mediaevalists' is no more than the logical result of their own extensive research. If nevertheless one wants to define the character of particular periods like the Renaissance or the later Middle Ages, this will only be possible through an accurate and detailed observation of the varied phenomena of each particular sphere of life.

For the Renaissance, too, is a complex phenomenon,[27] which cannot be summed up with one particular slogan.[28] Most recent research has taken account of this. After the exaggeration of Burckhardt's view and the sharp opposition to it, scholars now try to strike a balance between the continuity of historical development from the Middle Ages on and the assertion that the Renaissance forms an independent period in cultural history.[29] In more recent discussion, reference is quite often made to the understanding which the Renaissance had of itself, in which the concept and notion of rebirth take literary form at a very early stage.[30] Those who lived in the fourteenth century were already affected by the feeling that they were standing at the beginning of a new age; it was possible for this awareness to develop at the point where people felt the historical distance between themselves and antiquity, so that they could find the goal of their own concern with their literary testimony in a rebirth of antiquity.[31] Nevertheless, we must go on to ask in detail what reality matched this claim. On the other hand, it has often been stressed to what extent even the traditions of the mediaeval philosophical schools continued to have an influence in the time of the Renaissance, despite the vigorous criticism of scholasticism made by certain humanists; this is particularly true of Aristotelianism which, imported from Paris in the thirteenth century, found a permanent home in many Italian universities and above all in Padua.[32] However, Platonism too had remained a living force in the Middle Ages, though in this connection a powerful new movement was brought to Italy only under the influence of Plethon.[33]

In this connection it is particularly important to see how Burckhardt's theory of the 'rediscovery of the world and man' at the Renaissance is an apt characterization of this period, in that individualism and moralism, basic attitudes which are normative for subsequent periods, begin in this period. A.Buck points out: 'Only those who can distinguish between different varieties of individualism will be able to understand the character of Renaissance individualism.'[34] It is wrong simply to apply the modern concept of individualism to the Renaissance if we look more closely at the sources in connection with the famous theme of the 'worth of man'.[35] Here it must first be noted that this theme in no way arose first at the Renaissance; it could already be traced back to the biblical tradition, in that Gen.1.26 has the key phrase 'the image of God' and Ps.8, for example, contains praise of man's special, God-given worth. Similar notions can also be found in ancient poetry and philosophy, for example in the Prometheus saga. Cicero celebrates man's unique position as the only being endowed with reason: *sunt enim ex terra homines non ut incolae atque habitatores sed quasi spectatores superarum rerum atque caelestium, quarum spectaculum ad nullum aliud genus animantium pertinet.*[36] Motives from the Bible and from antiquity are combined in the patristic literature: the worth bestowed on man at creation, which is therefore proper to his nature, is none other than the splendour of the *imago dei*, which is renewed through the incarnation of Christ. We find such notions in Lactantius and in Augustine, in Gregory of Nyssa and Nemesius of Emesa,[37] and also in mediaeval theologians down to William of Saint-Thierry[38] and Thomas Aquinas.[39] It should be noted that the latter, arguing against Averroes, stresses the personal spiritual worth in man; what raises man above all other creatures is the link with God which is peculiar to him. It is not at all easy to distinguish from this mediaeval Christian tradition the way in which this theme is treated in Renaissance literature. At all events, it is impossible to establish a radical break, as we can also recognize from the fact that the theme of the *miseria conditionis humanae* or the *contemptus mundi* (also a traditional reproach which has antecedents in both the Bible – Ecclesiastes – and in classical antiquity) continues alongside that of the *dignitas hominis*: di Napoli has given an illuminating account of the way in which the two are closely connected and really only represent two sides of the same system of thought.[40] This double-sidedness already emerges with Innocent III (Lotario di Segni), who in the dedication of his work *De contemptu mundi sive de miseria conditionis humanae* can refer directly to the outline of a second work on the *dignitas humanae naturae*.[41] We can also find the same contrast between the heights and depths of human life, between its misery and its worth, in Petrarch, who even wrote a *De contemptu mundi*. Round about 1450 Bartolomeo Fazio could still compose a treatise along quite traditional Christian lines entitled *De excellentia et praestantia hominis*,[42] in which man's grandeur is celebrated as that of the image of God.

And yet it does appear that from the beginning of the Renaissance the treatment of the theme takes on another colouring. This can be seen most clearly in the work by G.Manetti, *De dignitate et excellentia hominis*, in which we find not only the traditional themes from classical antiquity and the Christian tradition – on beauty and the purposefulness of body and soul and their interplay, on the eternal life of the soul and the image of God as man's highest worth[43] – but also the creative acts in the history of the human spirit as indications of its excellence.[44] These additional themes (which do not completely suppress the traditional ones) are without doubt connected with the special features of the political situation to which H.Baron has directed his attention.[45] He sees the 'crisis' in the early Italian Renaissance round about 1400 in Florence, in which the Humanists who were in responsible political positions (the 'bourgeois Humanists')[46] played an active role defending the Republican freedoms of the city against the hegemony of Milan under the tyranny of the Visconti, as being one of the most decisive roots of the altered attitude of the Florentine Humanists to history and their neo-classicism in all areas;[47] in the religious sphere this also includes the defence of ancient polytheistic mythology in poetry by Salutati in his work *De Laboribus Herculis*.[48] The researches of R. von Alberti[49] have shown that the influence of this political thinking continued until well into the sixteenth century.

Another even more penetrating cultural force which also brought about a change in the climate was that of Humanism. In using this term I must recall its real and quite specific technical significance[50] as opposed to its often confused and imprecise usage – sometimes it is used virtually as a synonym for 'Renaissance'. This significance is connected with the vocational designation *humanista*, which was itself already coined in the Renaissance, and which in turn is to be understood in the sense of the *studia humanitatis* as literary education in the *artes liberales*.[51] It is therefore essentially pedagogy, a grammatical, rhetorical, historical education based on the classics.[52] But seen from the standpoint of education it opens up a new perspective: education has a deliberate aim which culminates in the adoption above all of Stoic material from antiquity,[53] in the education of man towards the good, and in morality.[54] Thus the moral trait which marks out humanism from this point on and differentiates it from the use of ancient literature in the late Middle Ages[55] develops to a large extent in the context of practical and pedagogical work. It is in no way a goal aimed at as a contrast to prevailing theological views. In support of this line appeals were made above all to Augustine and thus to the patristic tradition![56]

The basic features of this attitude can already be found in Francesco Petrarch, generally regarded as the 'father of Humanism'. In the history of the study of Petrarch, verdicts have differed markedly over this poet philosopher; he has been seen as an ardent admirer of classical antiquity and 'the first modern man', an inward-looking introvert and a prophet proclaiming action.[57] The divergence is without doubt due to the dialectical character of Petrarch's thought, in which both traditional and original material are combined within the framework of a marked individuality. One scene which has become famous comes in the poet's letter to Francesco Dionigi of Borgo San Sepolcro after his ascent of Mount Ventoux, where he describes the moment when, overcome by the beauty of the panorama which opens up before him, he takes Augustine's *Confessions* from his pocket and there reads the sentence: 'Men go to marvel at the heights of the mountains, the mighty waves of the sea, the course of the rivers, the width of the ocean, the movement of the stars, and lose themselves.'[58] Petrarch describes how he shut the book and rebuked himself for still marvelling at earthly things when he could already have learned from pagan philosophers[59] that nothing is great but the human soul.[60] Patristic and ancient pagan traditions are taken up here, and yet something quite new begins in a kind of conversion experience,[61] giving some intimation of a personal goal in life. However, it is hard to describe in a sentence what Petrarch's life says to us. For G.Voigt, Petrarch is the first 'individual man' and as such the 'ancestor of the modern world'. 'In him individuality and its claims emerge for the first time, boldly and freely, with a claim to great significance.'[62] At the same time he censures the boundless vanity that is constantly to be found in Petrarch: '... he relates everything to his person.'[63] More recent scholars have qualified and revised this judgment: thus E.Garin stresses the 'social character of a true humanity' such as Petrarch sensed: 'In Petrarch's view, love of the neighbour is the driving force and the aim of the *studia humanitatis*.'[64] 'For Petrarch, to withdraw into solitude meant the rediscovery of all the riches of his own inwardness, restoring contact with God and paving the way for an effective contact with his fellow men.'[65] However, this social character is again seen as being utterly elitist: only a small group of friends, the *litterati*, and not the *multi* or the *vulgus*, are in a position to live up to the ideal of virtue which is striven for in the *imitatio* of the ancients.[66] This is also the purpose of the contemplation of history: *apud me nisi ea requiruntur, que ad virtutes vel virtutum contraria trahi possunt.*[67] The ethical strain, taken over from antiquity, is quite clear in Petrarch; individualism is less clear, and in any case is meant philosophically more in the sense of Platonic social philosophy.[68] We should not forget the polemical orientation of this view which reflects man and his position in a Platonizing sense and which is directed against Averroism; Petrarch expresses it in a letter to Luigi Marsili in which he commends both Lactantius and Augustine as guides on the way to a *pia philosophia* which combines *studia humanitatis* and *studia divinitatis*.[69] Averroism as it was taught in Italian universities during the immediately preceding period[70] was felt by its opponents to be anti-Christian because it considered man in his natural creatureliness to be distinctive only by virtue of his rational intellect, and was also inclined to deny the immortality of the soul. The anti-Averroistic approach which was sometimes extended to the whole of Aristotelianism, i.e. Scholastic philosophy which had descended to the level of purely formal syllogisms, from which the Humanists had dissociated themselves,[71] also made a considerable contribution to the development of humanistic philosophy. Here we should note E.Garin's comment in passing, that the view 'according to which man's becoming and his action seem to be an essential part of his nature' is 'fundamentally a Christian view'.[72]

Despite all the differences which become manifest in individual details, we find a similar general picture when investigating the thought world of the other well-known authors of the early Renaissance, above all Coluccio Salutati and Lorenzo Valla. They too attempt a synthesis between ancient educational material and the Christian heritage, but in so doing their basic attitude remains governed by the Christian image of man, which is mediated to them in a special way by Augustine.[72a]

We must also keep this background in view when considering the later famous Renaissance philosophers like M.Ficino and G.Pico della Mirandola, if we are to arrive at a proper assessment of their view of man. P.O.Kristeller has observed[73] that the explicit concern with philosophical themes which we find with figures like Ficino and Pico in addition to the general background of their humanistic education is to be differentiated as an extra element, the content of which also has a stamp of its own. Although in the work of Kristeller this conception is also connected with rather too narrow an understanding of the term 'humanism', which also has the features of a world-view from as early as Petrarch,[74] he is still right to see that later Renaissance Platonism is a special phenomenon which developed in a very limited context and that its content was also formed in a quite separate way.[75] The political circumstances of the time also played a considerable role here. An early stage of preoccupation with Plato in the Italian Renaissance,[76] which made his *Republic* the centre of interest, caused his thought to be set completely in the general context of the ethical and political interests of Florentine 'bourgeois humanism'.[77] By contrast,[78] the crisis over the republican form of the state[79] which began with the rule of the Medici in Florence introduced a change in the humanistic perspective. There was now a move towards abstract speculations about the place of man in the universe, in the system of religious Neoplatonism. The influence of Plethon[80] and other Byzantines after the Council of Florence and the fall of Constantinople was significant for this new phase of Platonism: they introduced a powerful new impulse into concern with the master's thought.[81] However, the resumption in particular of the basic elements of the Neoplatonic system – the doctrine of ideas, the division of being into a hierarchy of spheres, brought about by emanation, and the conceptions of the soul and its ascent to God was the personal work of Marsilio Ficino, who must be given pride of place here as head of the Florentine Academy.[82]

If we want to attribute the development of the modern anthropocentric view of the world to Ficino (1433-1499), we can do so only with considerable qualifications.[83] It is true that we can find in his works remarks which make the human soul the mid-point of the world, the centre of all things,[84] but these comments must be put in the context of the whole of his philosophical system, which is influenced not only by an Aristotelian ontology[85] and the Neoplatonic doctrine of the spheres which produced the pattern of a hierarchy of being, but also by a strong Augustinian[85a] and mystical tradition. His stress on contemplation as the only attitude worthy of a philosopher and the one which really brings happiness is part of a legacy from antiquity,[86] as too is the ideal of exaltation from the lower world of the senses into a higher sphere of the spirit, and the Christian notion of union with God in which the soul first achieves its real nature is a legacy from mysticism.[87] So if man is given a more exalted position than in the Neoplatonic system, indeed a central position in the world, this is not because of an anthropocentric view but because here a marked feature of mediaeval Christian spirituality finds its way into the deeply syncretistic thought of the Renaissance philosopher. Man's position is taken to be exalted not *per se* but because this position incorporates in itself a relationship to the source of all being, to God – again simply a transformation of the doctrine of the *imago Dei*. However, at this point we already find a feature which will be important to us later on: the decisive position occupied by an inner relationship with God as opposed to all outward forms of religion.[88] True, these are simply an expression of man's inner relationship with God,[89] and to this degree we can see no direct rejection of external forms; nevertheless, the opposition between outward and inward is already there, nurtured by the two sources of ancient dualism and interiorizing mysticism. The juxtaposition of rationalism and mysticism, which will be characteristic of later developments, can also already be noticed in Ficino.

We obtain a similar picture to that of Ficino when we investigate the conception of the status of man in the work of his famous pupil Giovanni Pico della Mirandola (1463-1494). Since Burckhardt described Pico's discourse *On the Worth of Man*[90] with its culminating statements as 'one of the most noble legacies of that cultural epoch',[91] it has been customary to see the culmination of the Renaissance itself in these statements. But it would be wrong to understand Pico, too, as an idealist in the nineteenth-century sense. Rather, only a careful examination of his abundant literary remains can balance his manifold dependence on different traditions over against the importance of his independent contribution to the anthropology of the Renaissance.[92] We should make distinctions even within the work of Pico, since the *Oratio* (1486) is separated by a profound crisis from the later works. These, e.g. the *Heptaplus* and above all the late work *De ente et uno*, were written after Pico had been censured by the Curia; by contrast the *Oratio* is an early work of the philosopher, written when he was not yet twenty-four.[93] In the later works we can see a more marked move towards the Christian tradition and an inclination towards belief which also emerges in his personal life. Nevertheless, through the whole work there runs a basic unitary character which also makes it possible to give a systematic account of Pico's thought-world, of the kind that can be found in Monnerjahn and di Napoli. One thing above all is characteristic of this

thought-world: it is the most striking example of a consistently syncretistic attitude. For Pico, philosophy is not the opposite of theology; he
seeks to present the one by means of the other.[93a] Above all, a harmony
of opposites makes up his basic programme: Plato and Aristotle, the
Hermetic literature, Neoplatonic speculation and the Jewish Kabbalah,
Averroistic mysticism and the Stoic view of the microcosm in man, all
this is brought together into the great unity of all reality, both human
and divine, united in the *pax philosophica*, and here, in this comprehensive system, man too has his place, which is celebrated in hymns.

The first important thing about the conception of man in Pico is that
his position is considered against the background of the whole cosmos.
Therefore in the *Oratio* Pico begins with the work of creation;[94] he gives
a detailed cosmology in the *Heptaplus*, while the *Commento alla canzone
d'amore* (by G.Benivieni) presents a cosmology with Neoplatonic colouring.[95] Man, a microcosm containing within himself the varied fullness of the universe,[96] is put at the centre of the world; he is *terrestium
et caelestium vinculum et nodus*.[97] This cosmological background, corresponding to the ancient and especially the Neoplatonic view of the
world, is vital to the correct understanding of Pico's anthropology: what
he says in this connection 'applies in the first place to man in himself,
the "eternal man" as he is conceived of by God as an idea, but not
directly the specific man in the solitariness of his fragile earthly existence'.[98] The Platonic conception of the primal image should not in any
way be confused with modern conceptions. The description of man as
occupying an intermediate place between earth and heaven is simply
the revival of an old, much-discussed theme.[99] The statement that man
receives freedom to determine himself[100] is also by no means new: it
already occurs often in the patristic tradition.[100a] As over against interpretations which understand this and similar statements in terms of
a Fichtean idealism, as though here man were being given an absolute
creative power,[101] it must, however, be pointed out that the *Oratio* is
written in a rhetorical, enthusiastic mood and thus the praise of man is
given an exalted, hymnic tone.[102] A more important point is that when
he is talking about the divinity of man, Pico interprets this in terms of
the traditional *imago Dei* doctrine,[103] as a dialectical juxtaposition of
identity and difference between God and man.[104] A decisive feature,
however, is the recognition that Pico introduces the worth of man into
the framework of his whole view of the world, which has neo-Platonic
colouring and is full of emanatory themes: the place of man in the
cosmos is dynamic in that man has the possibility of either rising or
descending in the hierarchy of entities. Thus it is significant that the
discourse of the creator God to Adam in the *Oratio* begins with the
sentence: *Poteris in inferiora quae sunt bruta degenerare; poteris in superiora
quae sunt divina ex tui animi sententia regenerari.*[105] Thus man's freedom

of choice does not rest on the fact that it would be possible for him to make his own hierarchy of values; rather, he has the alternative of rising or descending in the existing order of the world.[105a] Now the goal of rising is clearly fixed, and in this Pico sees the real task of man: if man is to become *vinculum et nodus mundi*, he will do so through contemplation.[106] The object of contemplation is the divine spirit, towards which the human spirit is directed in pure, intellectual knowledge, by virtue of the divine illumination which is granted to the human intellect by the divine intellect.[107] This vision of the divine, by way of a vision of the self, the intuitive self-knowledge which man gains, finally leads him to the third stage, the consummation of the vision in love.[108] In respect of Pico's anthropology we may note that it is clearly dualistic: it lays strong stress on the difference between the body, which is of less value, and the spirit, which is the only important element.[109] However, his epistemology is mystical and intuitive; it is 'not solely a process of thought but at the same time an experience of God'.[110] Monnerjahn rightly stresses that here Pico is 'in the camp of the mystical thinkers who look back to Dionysius as their father'.[111] The third degree of vision, too, in which love and peace, i.e. the last universal unity of the world, is accomplished[112] is to be understood in this dualistic and mystical fashion as an ascent of the soul through the spheres, through detachment from the sensual to participation in ideal beauty.[113] From what has been said, we can understand how Pico rediscovered a system related to his own in the Jewish Kabbalah.[114] In addition to it, however, he also took over traditional Christian dogmas, like original sin,[115] christology[116] and even the doctrine of creation,[117] though this was mixed with conceptions drawn from the neo-Platonic doctrine of emanation.[117a]

What I have said should be enough to establish that even Pico is not to be understood as a modern thinker in the sense which has often been intended. Rather, his mode of thought is determined in many ways by traditions which are already in existence. His real contribution consists in his attempt to build a unitary system out of such different worlds, a reconciliation of predominantly Platonic philosophy with predominantly mystical theology. His work can be seen as a climax of the Renaissance in that it continues the course begun by Petrarch and draws the ultimate philosophical and systematic conclusions from it, making man the focal point of contemplation and seeing him as the hinge of history.[118] However, this man is not understood in individualistic terms, but rather as an ideal type; his status is embedded in a world event which takes on its dynamics from the force which derives from God. Nevertheless, this anthropocentricity contains important stimuli which had their effect after Pico. Furthermore, the second component which we considered, the moralistic one, is not stressed particularly either in

Ficino or in Pico. Pico, too, puts forward the ideal of *virtus*, but for him it signifies also the incorporation of human action into the harmony of the universe, an action which finds its culmination in thought, in which wisdom leads to harmony and peace. *Pie philosophari*[119] is a slogan which contains the nucleus of Pico's ethical concern.[120] However, it also includes the hidden dualism, the spiritualistic view, which has affinities in Neoplatonism and mysticism. In addition, above all in the late Pico, perhaps under the influence of Savonarola, we find a stress on good works, on love of the neighbour, which hopes for its reward. We also find the occasional remark that it is in man's own hands whether he achieves victory through his action.[121] However, these ethical elements are largely covered over by the aesthetic and intellectual ones. Pico's attitude to the visible church, its ceremonies and its sacraments remains largely obscure. We may see at least one reason for his often divergent remarks to be his perilous position, his persecution by the Curia. On the other hand, Pico always felt himself to be a faithful son of the Catholic church.[122] However, it is correct to note that his spiritualist intellectualism could not lead to any real understanding of the sacraments and outward forms. As a result he consistently spiritualized them.[123]

If we look back at the end of these considerations of the period of the Italian Renaissance, we must note that the picture gained from its best-known representatives looks different from what we might expect from the popular conceptions put forward by Burckhardt and his followers. Critical investigation of the sources in recent decades has also brought to light here a complexity which prevents us from passing judgment on this period in a few words. In respect of the theme which concerns us, we might rather speak of a modest result. A.E. van Gelder, who coined the formula 'the two Reformations',[124] finds in 'humanistic religion' a third way between Catholicism and Protestantism: what he sees as a more radical Reformation, characterized by rationalism, the beginning of humanistic thought and the establishment of moral aims.[125] In the Renaissance we can already find a stress on the second; the third is already there strongly in the 'active' period, but has less of an effect on theory. Insofar as we can talk of rationalism at all, it has quite a different complexion here from that which is typical of the rationalism of the Enlightenment. The anti-scholastic attitude of Petrarch, the anti-Averroism of the Platonists, show that clearly enough. If we look at the systems of Ficino or Pico della Mirandola, we are impressed more by the mediaeval features in them than by the beginnings of 'modern' thinking. However, these can be no more than beginnings; in fact here we have a move towards a development the real consequences of which only become evident much later. Van Gelder's view forgets a point which is also very important as a characteristic of the spiritual attitude I have described: anthropocentrism and moralism are often connected with a spiritualistic and mystical subjectivism. This spiritualistic view is very significant for the period which follows. It is already strongly developed in Ficino[126] and Pico, and brought with it its strong affinity with Neoplatonic thought-forms. These forms of expression point backwards, not forwards; however, this should not hinder us from seeing the further influence of this spiritualistic approach in the period which follows.

(b) Late mediaeval Spiritualism

The Italian Renaissance, then, can only be of limited help in showing us the prehistory of the intellectual developments which will concern us later. So we are directed to other areas which show to a much greater degree the characteristics which are typical of them. In this connection, mention should be made above all of late-mediaeval Spiritualism.[127] This term may be used to denote a varied cultural movement which may be noted partly within, and partly outside the Catholic Church in the West from the eleventh century onwards and which reaches a climax in the fourteenth century.[128] The character of the sources (most of our knowledge of the writings of the heretical groups comes from refutations by their opponents in the church, and we can obtain only sporadic information about the spiritual figures who remained in the church) and critical research into the background, which is still largely in its infancy, make it difficult for us to obtain an accurate view of details of this trend in spirituality. However, the information that we do have allows us to recognize certain common features, the frequent recurrence of which among the various groups lets us infer a common cultural background.[129] First of all, it is important to note that the appearance of this Spiritualist movement is an independent Western phenomenon;[130] in contrast to the Cathari, whose emergence goes back to direct Bogomil missionary activity from the East.[131] Even in its sectarian forms it lacks the characteristic Manichaean and dualistic view of the world,[132] just as the Cathari, conversely, do not display many of the features which are typical of Spiritualism.[133] However, Spiritualism, too, is fed by a dualistic approach in all thought and feeling: the opposition between spirit and matter, between the outer and the inner, between institution and personal faith, between mediated salvation and immediacy towards God, permeates all the statements and actions of its representatives.

H.Grundmann tends to see the most important impulse towards the rise of a heretical movement engaged in critical discussion with the church and its priestly-hierarchical structures in the Investiture Struggle and Gregory VII's propagandist efforts against simony.[134] Against this interpretation, however, we must first put the fact that similar heretical movements also appear as early as the first half of the eleventh century, and secondly, internal observations which show that the heretical programmes and actions which are all so similar, separated though they may be in time or space, signal the dawn of a time of common concern, the background influence of which Grundmann himself has noted in a variety of ways: 'A historical understanding of the heresies can therefore only be gained in connection with the general religious movements of their time, from which the new Orders also emerged, and in the controversy over developments in theology and the church.'[135] By temporarily allying himself with the 'heretical' movement, Pope Gregory VII was simply using it in his power struggle, a policy which was not without risk, as we can see from subsequent developments.

Even from the first half of the eleventh century we have reports of the emergence of heretics whose doctrines already contained features typical of the whole Spiritualist movement. The repudiation of marriage and the sign of the cross and the rejection of the Old Testament by the peasant Leuthard of Champagne (d. 1004)[136] seems to show Bogomil influence; that is not so certainly the case with his attack on the clergy, to whom he refused to pay tithes. The independence of a Spiritualist clergy active in Orleans in the entourage of king Robert I (996-1031) is much clearer;[137] as well as rejecting everything material, which in addition to marriage and eating meat also includes the sacraments of baptism, the eucharist and penance, along with opposition to the hierarchy, they manifest a doctrine of the gift of the Spirit produced by laying hands on the individual believer: this brings him forgiveness of sins, but also a personal illumination and knowledge which opens up the scripture to him.[138] The group of nobility who assembled on Mount Monteforte near Turin in 1028 was similarly influenced.[139] On the other hand, the heretics of Arras in 1025 have a different basic attitude, though it is equally oriented on the future: all externals, the sacraments, the church and its ceremonies, houses of God and the priesthood are said to be useless for man's salvation; the only important thing is action, a radical, ascetic morality with a stress on the simple life. All dogmatic teaching, even that of the Bogomils, is a matter of indifference.[140] Moralism and a kind of rationalist attitude directed against all sacramentalism is in no way alien to spiritualism, as one might at first suppose; rather, the association of spiritualist and rationalist-moralistic attitudes are typical of this whole movement.

The forces at work inside and outside the church were given new stimulus in the second half of the eleventh century by the Investiture controversy and the attitude of Gregory VII, who countered simony with the dual principle of legitimate ordination and the moral worth of the priesthood.[141] That in so doing he was simply lending his authority to certain tendencies which were also to be found elsewhere can be recognized from his association with the revolutionary Patarene movement based on Lombardy, which was aimed at combatting the immorality of the priesthood,[142] and also the burning of the priest Ramihrdus in Cambrai in 1077. Ramihrdus had refused to receive the sacrament from any abbot or bishop, because they might be unworthy. Gregory deeply lamented this execution when he heard of it.[143]

From the beginning of the twelfth century the ideals of the *vita apostolica* and Christian poverty emerge in the appearance of travelling preachers, especially in France. These call their followers out of the world to a monastic existence and thus produce the first wave of newly-founded Orders, in which an accomodation is made with the ordinances of the church.[144] H.Grundmann[145] has shown how from the beginning of the twelfth century the ideal which was originally connected only with monastic communities, expressed by the phrase 'the apostolic life' or 'the life of the gospel', also extended to wandering preachers, lay people and heretics, thus becoming a serious problem for church authorities, especially since the new Orders, who soon became an end in themselves, were no longer a channel for popular movements.

In what follows we must distinguish the ideal of poverty as a specific attitude, determined by ethical concern, from the Spiritualist trends. At the same time, however, it is clear that the two are closely connected and are prompted by the same spirit, and often by the same movements. Both are directed against the institutional church in its existing form; common to both is the same assurance that they are in possession of true knowledge.[146] However, each develops in a different way because to a great extent the church was able to find a place for the poverty movement within its framework, whereas the cruder forms of Spiritualism were excluded as being sectarian. Beyond question this is also connected with the fact that from the early church onwards, Catholic piety generally contained a world-negating, dualistic element, combined with an intrinsic feature of righteousness by works, which was concentrated in the monastic ideal. So generally speaking we must assume that a basic Spiritualist attitude often remained under a veneer of dogmatic adaptation, the influences of which then often came to light only at a much later stage.

In the twelfth century, too, the heretics were again only expressing the general concerns of the time in a crude form. One of the characteristic figures is Peter de Bruis,[147] the founder of the sect of Petrobrusians, who was active between about 1119 and 1139.[148] His opponent in the church, Petrus Venerabilis, not only gives a vivid account of the violence of the onset of these sectarians upon churches, crosses and priests, but also gives us a good idea of Peter's teaching.[149] Its chief characteristic is an exclusive concern with the New Testament, especially the Gospels, rejecting the Old Testament and the church's tradition. He regards as worthless not only the sacraments, but also the mass, prayer and good works; they are a priestly fraud. Church buildings must be destroyed, since God can be worshipped everywhere; veneration of the cross is senseless. Even hymns are regarded as a mockery of God, who does not allow himself to be influenced by beautiful sounds. This is a rejection of the whole outward form of the church and any formal worship; its place is taken by the vision of a purely spiritual church with stress on the personal faith of the individual and his direct relationship with God. The specific polemic against the veneration of the cross and the express rejection of the Old Testament presumably show the influence of the Bogomils on Peter de Bruis; generally speaking, his teaching is typical of the Spiritualist heretics of his time. It is certainly no coincidence that the second leader of the Petrobrusians, Henry of Lausanne (died *c.* 1145),[150] did not take over these two specific teachings of Peter, though on the other hand he sharpened considerably the attacks on the hierarchy of the church. One of the teachings typical of the Spiritualists is the rejection of infant baptism, shared by Peter de Bruis and Henry of Lausanne and also by other groups, including the Waldensians;[151] this was because children still have no personal faith, a factor which is made a precondition of baptism. This is matched by the high value attached to man as it emerges in a twofold way in the work of the Lombard jurist Hugo Speroni:[152] it is a critical standard for the *meritum vitae* over against the priests, who are unworthy because they are not *spirituales et mundi et perfecti*, and a positive dogma, in that the 'inner purity', the goodness of the true Christian, is derived from a personal predestination.[153] In a similar way, right at the beginning of the century the Fleming Tanchelm[154] contrasted personal purity with the corrupt church of the priests and their sacraments: he ended in a blinkered self-apotheosis. Presumably we have the same delusion in the mentally deranged Eon of Stella, who appeared in Brittany in 1145 and regarded himself as God.[155] However, we must recognize that these extremes are only exaggerations of a widespread principle which deeply influenced the spirit of the age. The high estimation of man is also the hidden background to Waldensian preaching: man's complete dedication to the work in hand, to be required of him after penitence, following the spiritual way of the complete fulfilment of faith by works with a concern for eternal salvation, directs man back to himself: his fate lies in his own hands.[156] However, this teaching is not too far removed from the conceptions put forward in the mainstream church: the theme of James 2.26, that faith without works is dead, is a view current in scholasticism and also shared by the Popes.[157] Waldes and his colleagues originally carried on their preaching activity exclusively within the church; Waldensianism was finally forced into a sectarian existence in 1215.[158] At the same time as some Waldensian groups returned to the church as 'Catholic poor',[159] kindred movements concerned for religious poverty were started in many other places. These Pope Innocent III was able to incorporate into the hierarchical church with considerable diplomatic skill:[160] the Humiliates in Northern Italy, and above all the communities formed by Francis of Assisi and Dominic in the early thirteenth century, for whom the Pope was able to find a place by giving permission for the formation of new Orders.

Of course this success in church politics would not have been possible had there not for a long time been an existing basis for the acceptance of these patterns of life and their underlying ideals among wide circles of Catholic laity. This took the form of an awareness of faith oriented on the norms of the gospel which stressed man's responsibility for his own salvation. Of course the consequence of this changed attitude could not be seen immediately. Thus Grundmann is probably right in pointing out[161] that even heretical polemics were not anti-sacerdotalistic[162] in principle to begin with; rather, the requirement for the absolute moral purity of the priest was the cause of the criticism.[163] Similarly, the rejection of the sacraments only developed gradually. However, both positions are simply the logical consequences of a basic underlying attitude which sees man himself, his spiritual quality and his ethical conduct, as the decisive factor for salvation.

About the end of the twelfth century, spiritualistic thought takes on a new, eschatological dimension in the system of Joachim of Fiore (died 1202).[164] At the same time, many ideas in circulation in this period take radical form in this thinker, who characteristically also founded an order.[165] First of all, it should be noted that Joachim cannot in any way be put on the same level as the heretics of the twelfth century and the champions of the *vita apostolica*.[166] On the contrary, there are some features in his system which show him as an orthodox figure faithful to his church, and a whole group of scholars interpret him in these terms.[167] However, on closer inspection this observation is not as un-expected as it might seem at first sight, since Spiritualist thought was quite possible in the church provided that it was not bound up with dogmatic heresy. The apparently contradictory character of Joachim's conceptions is best explained by the subjective concern of the abbot to remain within the framework of orthodoxy, to see how he can also legitimate the system concerned in terms of the previous history of the church up to the present.[168] He did not even invent his apocalyptic division of world history into three stages, following the pattern of the Trinity: it is already prefigured in Rupert of Deutz (though for him the third stage, the age of the Spirit, coincides with the age of the church after Christ)[169] and in Anselm of Havelberg, for whom the three stages represent an inner development taking the form of transitions within the process of salvation history.[170] This kind of thought could claim the authority of no less a figure than Augustine and his scheme of six ages in the history of the world, together with the triad *ante legem – sub lege -sub gratia*[171] which sometimes appears (though with Augustine, apocalyptic thought is forced into the background).[172] Nevertheless, Joachim's system has a fundamentally different character from that of his apparent models.

A first important factor is the theme which Grundmann sees as Joachim's decisive starting point:[173] he is concerned with perfect knowledge which he hopes to gain from Holy Scripture, the content of which will correspond completely with Scripture.[174] However, this is to come about through a new perfect vision of divine truth in a spiritual revelation which he expects in the third stage of salvation history. In connection with Rev.14.6, Joachim describes this new form of knowledge as the *evangelium aeternum* which is obtained through a direct illumination of man by the Holy Spirit in an *intelligentia spiritualis* and which breaks through the outward veil of the letter as that is to be found in the written form of the Old and New Testaments.[175] A reference to such an inner illumination is the shibboleth of the Spiritualists: with surprising ease it can also take on rationalistic features (cf. the key word 'enlightenment', *illuminatio*), even if in Joachim it is directed against scholastic knowledge.[176] Joachim evidently claims this spiritual illumination directly for himself and his understanding of the scriptures; one main difficulty for earlier scholars,[177] that Joachim expected this gift only in the third stage, while he himself was still living in the second, is removed by Töpfer's observation that Joachim makes the two transitional generations (the forty-first and forty-second), in which the third stage is already intimated, begin with himself and his own order.[178]

The consequences which result from this spiritual epistemology are already abundantly clear in Joachim. First of all, that in the time of the spirit, the advent of which is imminently expected, Holy Scripture will become superfluous and any exegesis unnecessary, however much it is stressed that its content is identical with the *evangelium aeternum*.[179] This is because an open and unveiled knowledge of all its *mysteria* will be given in the time of the *abundantia spiritus*. As outward signs[180] which concealed the spiritual meaning, not only will the letters of scripture be done away with; the sacraments, too, will cease to be a spiritual sign, because their real content will become directly accessible.[181] Another logical consequence of this universal direct illumination in the third stage is that at that time the role of the clergy, which was constitutive of the second stage, will also be at an end. Scholars have for a long time discussed whether the *Ordo clericorum* (i.e. the secular priests, in contrast to the *ordo monachorum*, for the status of which in the third stage see below) will continue to exist in the third stage, as Joachim's remarks are particularly obscure on precisely this point. Alongside clear statements about the imminent end of the clergy[182] stands the twelfth table of the *Liber Figurarum*, in which, in the context of an ideal constitution for the Order, alongside five oratories forming the real monastery there is an oratory each for *sacerdotes et clerici*, and there is a provision for married clergy with their children, so that both states claim their legitimate, albeit subordinate place. There is discussion as to whether this implies an ordinance for the third stage of history, which would amount to an irreconcilable contradiction with Joachim's remarks elsewhere. Töpfer, who makes a thorough examination of passages relevant to a solution of the problem from various other of Joachim's writings,[183] finally comes down, with some hesitation, on the side of an answer already put forward by Grundmann,[184] that this ordinance is only a transitional regulation and that at the end all states will be caught up in a condition of pure contemplation in which marriage is transcended. Thus in Joachim, too, the basic dualistic principle represented in monasticism also comes through in connection with the unmarried state. In its inner system, described metaphorically, the *ecclesia spiritualis*, his ideal conception of the church, which was not far off, corresponded exactly to these requirements. But that also sealed the fate of the priesthood, which was no longer needed as an intermediary at the time of spiritualistic immediacy to God. Only the monks are left, who finally incorporate the whole of humanity.[185] A whole series of scholars has stressed the fact that Joachim was originally a Cistercian;[186] in addition, the influence of Byzantine monasticism has been conjectured.[187] Eremetical ideals are the real driving-force in his thought.

Some of the characteristic features of Joachim's views seem rather to point backward; however, monasticism in the thirteenth and fourteenth century was to experience a new heyday. At the same time, with Joachim a view of the world which had been long latent in the West again becomes virulent: an anti-materialist spiritualism, the effect of which came alive through and after Joachim in a new way. Most of the positions are already to be found in his views in theory; because of his personal, contemplative attitude and careful way of life they remained concealed at this stage, but with his heirs, the Spiritualists, they took on powerful explosive force. The sacraments become superfluous, the priesthood is unnecessary, the significance of the scriptures is in fact evacuated, even if the *evangelium aeternum* is to fulfil them in their most secret sense: the first of these two themes has a hidden connection with the last, which follows consistently from the basic approach. When the ideal of the *vita apostolica*, which had already come alive among his followers and among other twelfth-century groups, was added to this, all the elements had been gathered which were to prove significant for later developments.

We can see how close spiritual illuminism of a contemplative kind, such as we find in Joachim, can come to a fundamentally rationalist approach appealing to a higher form of knowledge in the heresy of the Amalricans of Paris in 1210,[188] who combine a learned Neoplatonic pantheism with the awareness of a knowledge which has been achieved through the Spirit; here too all the sacraments are devalued – in contrast to the *vita apostolica* movement or monastic asceticism, however, the pantheistic approach leads to boundless libertinism in the moral sphere which can be observed over a number of centuries in various forms in 'free-thinking' sectarian movements, including certain trends among the Beguines and Beguards.[189]

We need not be concerned further with these phenomena in the present context. Nor can it be our task to pursue in detail internal developments within the Franciscan Order during the first centuries of its existence.[190] Their founder himself showed the Franciscan Order the principle of apostolic poverty, but in the first instance this was not put forward in uncompromising opposition to the existing church, since in his own piety Francis himself was bound in word and sacrament to the specific saving order of the Catholic church,[191] in the context of which he saw his own personal mission. Furthermore, by means of a wise policy the official church was able to incorporate the saint and his group into its existing forms, to begin with on the personal initiative of the Pope and certain cardinals,[192] and later by official documents down to Gregory IX's canonization bull of 1228.[193] However, what Francis himself had already taken to be a special divine revelation given to him,[194] his personal history and the formation of his Order, was interpreted in later legends in terms of a special gift of the Spirit which sees the Order in terms of a spiritual church and also contains such features as the notion that anyone who, as a member of the Order, possesses *intelligentia spiritualis*, as Francis himself did, already has complete knowledge of the gospel and therefore has done with books.[195] The division of the Order into the lax majority, which was inclined to accept adaptations of the Rule, and the strict advocates of the ideal of poverty[196] is directly connected with this attitude, since the latter group was at the same time the chief vehicle of the Spiritualist approach.

A visible revival of extreme Spiritualism takes place towards the middle of the thirteenth century in phenomena which demonstrate the direct influence of Joachimitic ideas. Mention should be made here of the pseudo-Joachimitic writings, including above all the commentary on Jeremiah.[197] There is controversy as to whether this commentary was produced in Franciscan circles or is even more directly connected with Joachim through pupils of his in the monastery at Fiore.[198] At all events, while in other respects there are close connections with the thought-world of Joachim here, there is also a clear intensification of criticism of the state of the church, especially the hierarchy and also the papacy, which is made responsible for the church's decline.[199] There is also a lively expectation of an imminent purification of this church in which the kingdom embodied in Frederick II appears in the role of the oppressor who overcomes the old corrupt order, while the real future lies with the two monastic orders of the third stage (which are here evidently identified with the Dominicans and the Franciscans).[200] There are fewer contemplative and mystical features than in Joachim and an increase in political topicality: at the same time the ideal picture of the future is changed in that the ideal of poverty, which in Joachim himself is secondary, comes to the fore. At about the same time there is clear evidence of the influence of Joachimitic thought in the Franciscan Order: above all the Chronicle of Salimbene of Parma[201] is a much-quoted eye-witness account of this.[202] Salimbene's narrative is somewhat adventurous, but accords closely with the attitude of expectation which had blown up.[203] It tells how, on the approach of Frederick II (1241), an abbot from a monastery of the Fiore order between Lucca and Pisa takes flight, rescuing all Joachim's writings and bringing them to safety in a Franciscan monastery in Pisa. Joachimitism seems to have spread rapidly among the Franciscans from Pisa. By 1247/48 it had already been carried by Italian brothers to France. In Provence Salimbene meets two brothers with Joachimite inclinations, one of whom, Gerhardus of Borgo San Donnino, will appear again soon.[204] In addition, a famous brother Hugo (of Bayola or Montpellier), active in the same area, is 'one of the most famous clergy in the world, a renowned preacher'[205] – at the same time he is a 'doughty Joachite'.[206] He is in turn connected with the Magister General of the order, John of Parma. Evidently Joachimitism has already spread widely among the Franciscans in a short space of time.

One unmistakable sign of this is the publication of the *Introductorius ad evangelium aeternum*, an introductory writing which Gerhardus of Borgo San Donnino attached to an edition of the three main works of Joachim which was known in Paris in 1254.[207] Unfortunately this introduction itself has not survived,[208] but we have glimpses of its content first through the extracts prepared by the professors of the University of Paris who wanted to exploit the occasion in their fight against the growing influence of the mendicant monks at the university,[209] and secondly through the protocol of the commission appointed by Pope Alexander IV in Anagni to consider the complaints of the professors from Paris.[210] As over against Denifle, who had described the excerpts as 'caricature and malicious distortion of more or less harmless remarks',[211] Benz has pointed out that the attacks on the Catholic concept of the church were already contained in the work of Gherardino himself;[212] this is confirmed by the manuscript that we now have. On the whole, as we can see at a glance especially from the sentences excerpted by the professors of Paris, Gherardino's position represents a clear radicalization of Joachim's ideas. First, Joachim's three main works are themselves regarded as the *evangelium aeternum* which will abolish the validity not only of the Old Testament (first stage) but also of the New.[213] Furthermore, the dawn of the new age, the three decisive figures for which are taken from Dan.12.7; Rev.14.14; 7.2 and identified with Joachim, Dominic and Francis,[214] is firmly set in 1260, after a twofold persecution, and therefore in the near future;[215] at this point the church of the clergy will be abolished and give place to the spirit church. In the latter the care of the *evangelium aeternum* is entrusted to an *ordo nudipedum*;[216] this is clearly to be seen as a reference to the stricter elements among the Franciscans, whose *sacerdotium* will do away with the old *sacerdotium*.[217]

Here again the sectarian exaggeration accentuates the contours of the spiritualistic material, whereas the broader trend of Spiritualists in the Franciscan orders perpetuated the same basic attitude, only in a more cautious form. The outcome of the conflict is significant in this connection. It ended with the condemnation of Gherardino by the commission of Anagni and the papal command for the destruction of his work, but at the same time prevented the professors of Paris from exploiting their victory over the mendicant Orders.[218] Whereas the radical theories of Gherardino disappeared after his condemnation, Joachimite ideas of a more moderate stamp were preserved among the Franciscan Spiritualists.[219] In the years after 1270 we see a clear split between the Spiritual wing, which takes its stand on the ground of the radical ideal of poverty and through all persecutions clearly stresses this against the external consolidation of the Order and above all against the Curia, and the group which remains faithful to the church.[220] The history of this struggle and the ultimate failure of the enthusiastic hopes of the Spiritualists cannot be considered further here.[221] It is important for us to note that precisely in the period of the utmost oppression, the expectations of the Spiritualists once again reach a climax, shortly before 1300. We have significant evidence of this in the writings of Petrus Johannes Olivi (1298),[222] above all his *Postilla super Apocalypsin*,[223] which follows the Joachimite pattern in announcing that in the imminent future the clerical church will be replaced by the Spiritual church, which is being realized among the Franciscans. However, not only is Olivi more ready to compromise over the attitude of the Spiritualists to the Orders and the Papacy;[224] in accordance with this he also thinks of the third stage in christocentric terms.[225] However, with Olivi as with Joachim it proved that subsequent disciples were far more radical; their admiration for

Olivi quickly took on sectarian features. These notions continued to have an influence in Beguine circles even after the suppression of the Olivi cult by Pope John XXII.[226] It is enough for our purpose to point to this continued survival; it would take too long to pursue all the developments in detail. We need not even give a further account of the fate of the so-called Fraticelli,[227] whose groups continued down into the fifteenth century.

The most important thing is the final conclusion which we may draw from this short survey for our main theme: the basic oppositions which are to prove normative for the later periods which will concern us are already prefigured in late-mediaeval Spiritualism. It is characteristic of the Spiritualist systems that despite apparent outward humility, they begin from a high estimation of the individual or the group filled with the spirit, on whom possession of the spirit bestows a higher form of knowledge which makes superfluous both the letters of Holy Scripture and all external forms of the communication of salvation. Indeed these outward forms, above all the sacraments and the clergy, are contested in the sectarian accentuation of the Spiritualist position as a feature standing in the way of direct knowledge of God brought about through the Spirit. Where inner and outer, the world and the spirit, are opposites, the world cannot be the bearer of salvation. In Joachim, clerical church and spiritual church, the second stage and the third stages, are brought together in an apocalyptic succession: the visionary expects the dawn of this new time. The Franciscan spiritualists believe that it has already dawned in the Franciscan church. In the ideal of poverty they put forward an ascetic form of morality, the dualistic form of which is unmistakable.

(c) John Wyclif

We now jump forward and for the first time move on to English soil. With John Wyclif (c.1330-1384)[228] we not only take a step forward in time but also find in the presuppositions of his thought a foretaste of some of the groupings and typical perspectives, the further influence of which will be characteristic of the period between the sixteenth and eighteenth centuries in England.

Only in very recent years has it become possible to arrive at a real understanding of Wyclif's position, and especially his attitude towards the Bible.[229] Before this, a number of false impressions were predominant, including not least the enthusiastic claim that he was the 'morning star of the Reformation'.[230] However, a view which sees him still largely as a Catholic thinker, for whom scripture and tradition are a unity, has also been attempted and defended.[231] It is possible to understand his real position only if we put him in the spiritual and ecclesiastical context in which he worked; in that case, however, his figure loses much of its singularity, and we recognize him again as one of the figures who thought through to the end in a particularly consistent way some of the widespread basic conceptions of their time and precisely in so doing found themselves in the role of outsiders. Of course we are not concerned with the point over which Wyclif became a heretic to his contemporaries, his doctrine of the eucharist in which (in his work *De eucharistia*, 1379) he rejected transsubstantiation because of his extreme philosophical realism, though without being able to arrive at a considered view of his own.[232] We are concerned, rather, with the two themes which have already guided us so far, with his attitudes to the Bible and to the church. Compared with the usual understanding of scripture in his time,[233] Wyclif seems to have adopted a singular position, the special character of which lies in quite a different area from what one might surmise at first glance. The starting point for the enthusiasm of all those who would see Wyclif as a forerunner of the Reformation is his principle of *scriptura sola*, i.e. the principle to which he tenaciously adhered, that only what was in accord with the words of scripture could also be right in the church of his time. However, use of this formula is dangerous because it can all too easily be understood in terms of the Reformation in the sixteenth century, and above all in terms of Luther. That, however, would be to misunderstand Wyclif's attitude completely. It is also false to assume that the special significance of Wyclif lies in the fact that he stressed the *sensus literalis* of scripture in contrast to the usual fourfold sense of scripture as found in mediaeval exegesis.[234] On the contrary, with him we always find the usual method; the 'mystical' sense of scripture is significant for theological statements as well as the literal sense, and allegorizing exegesis is generously employed.[235] Similarly, it cannot be said that Wyclif set the authority of scripture up in exclusive competition with the value of the church's tradition, since in his best-known work *De veritate sacrae scripturae*, among others he quotes a good deal of Augustine, his favourite church father, and with him other theologians old and new.[236]

Rather, his principle *scriptura sola* is meant in the sense of the *lex evangelica*: the whole Bible – not only the Old Testament (here above all the Decalogue, and not the time-conditioned ceremonial commandments) but even the New – is understood in a legalistic sense. As with Nicolaus of Lyra, who is Wyclif's chief authority here, in this approach the action of Christ occupies a central place and serves as a moral example for Christian action: *omnis Christi accio est nostra instruccio* is a central principle which describes the doctrine of the discipleship of Christ.[237] As to content, a central theme is the requirement of humility as the most important Christian virtue, in which one follows Christ's humility.[238] Alongside humility there is poverty, which forms the content of the call to discipleship.[239] Here, of course, one immediately thinks of the old demands of the *pauperes Christi* and the Franciscans; in fact frequent references have been made to the possible connections and the originally good relationship between Wyclif and the mendicant monks, above all to his defence by four *fratres* at his first summons in 1377. Really, in his work *De civili dominio*, Wyclif found words to recognize the Minorites,[240] though on the other hand he rejected the private 'religions', especially vows and habits. However, as Benrath has shown,[241] objections to the mendicant Orders can be found as early as his commentary on the Bible, which was begun in the 1370s. In his late writings Wyclif lumps monks and brothers together in his comprehensive condemnation.[242] But it is not these external positions which are decisive so much as the spiritual legacy which one can trace in Wyclif from the Spiritualistic tradition embodied in some Franciscan theologians.[243] Because he rejects the separatist course of realizing his ideals in the Orders, like the radical sectarians from the eleventh century on he becomes the advocate of revolutionary demands on the whole church. The nucleus of his programme becomes its return to apostolic poverty through a comprehensive surrender of its possessions (in the writing *De civili dominio*). With this programme Wyclif takes a decisive step beyond the usual moralizing exegesis of his time.

If we want to understand the cultural context of this demand it is not enough to point to the external circumstances which justified a criticism of the contemporary church, particularly in England.[244] There were in fact such causes, and Wyclif is by no means alone in his criticism of specific conditions in his church. On the other hand, if we are to understand further developments in subsequent centuries it is not unimportant to look rather more closely at the general state of the church in England in the fourteenth century.[245] One of the most important causes for contemporary criticism was the close interweaving of church and state, which was particularly prominent in England. In England, as in other mediaeval feudal states, from Norman times the crown had found the episcopacy to be one of its most important supports. It was not only that the bench of bishops in Parliament often occupied a key position in politics generally as well as in church matters; in addition bishops' thrones, like less exalted positions in the church, were largely occupied by men in the service of the king, as a result of the prescriptive right of the crown to have a say in their tenancy. That is how they gained their income. It explains why bishops held a series of important state positions. In the matter of the tenancy of positions in the church a *modus vivendi* was worked out between the elective right of the ecclesiastical collegial bodies, as in the case of the bishops of the chapter, the royal rights of patronage and the Pope's right of confirmation.[246] This allowed the king to find a position for his own candidates, while it was possible for the Pope to provide for cardinals and members of his household, if not at episcopal level (that was against the national interest) at least at the next level down (as canons, prebends and arch-deacons). Furthermore the Curia derived financial advantages from each confirmation as the newly appointed officials had to pay tithes from the income of their first year in office – in the case of bishops and abbots this amounted to as much as a third of their income (the so-called *servitia* and *annates*). This financial gain was also the reason why the custom of moving bishops already installed to other sees (transla-tion) was favoured by the Popes; this in turn was connected with the difference in the financial resources of the dioceses. In some cases income hardly exceeded expenditure (certainly not during the prepara-tion for the election and the subsequent year). Of course we should not use modern standards to judge this whole system, which arose because income was derived from particular localities and there was no central system of taxation and remuneration. McKisack[247] rightly points out that the earlier Protestant tendency to take contemporary complaints literally and to condemn root and branch, say, the Popes in Avignon has given way in more recent times to a more objective approach. Of course there were constant complaints about the outflow of money from the country because of the taxes paid by the clergy to the Pope, the provisions from confirmations and the positions of the cardinals and members of the Curia, and there was dispute between the Crown and the Curia over the taxation of the clergy for extraordinary expenses (for example, in times of war), but all his life Edward III (1327-77) was ready to compromise in such matters.[248] In the context of the system there was also a good side to the Pope's right to confirmation and nomination: it prevented local favouritism, brought better financial support for theo-logians active in the universities (as we can see in the case of Wyclif himself), and also gave capable candidates without influence a chance of betterment.[249] Only the disadvantages of these conditions are men-tioned in contemporary complaints; they were, however, aggravating. The chief words which keep occurring are pluralism, i.e. one person occupying a number of positions and prebends at the same time, and absenteeism, the absence of an official from his place of work as a result of this, or also because positions in the church were conferred on members of the Curia and other foreigners, or on people who were really occupied in the state or in the universities. They arranged for their functions to be carried out there by representatives of the lower ranks of the clergy, often with minimal education, whom they paid (most frequently only a pittance). Of course this caused a threatening decline in the practice of preaching and in the general level of piety; that is why a reproof to the bishops for withholding true preaching from the people plays such a prominent role in the polemical writings of Wyclif as well.[250]

However, as I have already indicated, external circumstances are not the main background to Wyclif's concept of the church and the criticism which results from it. Indeed, it could even be said that to begin with he himself practised absenteeism and pluralism,[251] partly with a dispensation and partly without; on the other hand his enemies soon expressed the suspicion that Wyclif had been led to his heretical position only by the numerous promotions to rewarding posts offered him by Gregory XI![252] Both these views, however, ignore his already long-standing attitude, which is determined by an inner consistency in his whole theological and philosophical approach. Criticism of the outward manifestations of the church was more or less widespread in the century in which Wyclif lived; his reasons went much deeper.

First of all, his ecclesiology is governed by his moralistic view of the Bible, the *Christus humilis* as a model for the church, with whose form he is identical.[253] Wyclif adopts the Franciscan ideal of poverty, but rejects the monasticism in which it took shape. Connected with this is the contrast between the *lex Dei* embodied in scripture and the *tradiciones humanae*, the human traditions devised by the Popes. Anything not contained in Holy Scripture is sin and against the will of God.[254] There is, however, a further more important reason why the Bible can be opposed to human traditions in so absolute a way. G.A.Benrath is chiefly responsible for having drawn attention to this important point.[255] The Bible derives its absolute authority from the fact that with unprecedented consistency, and in contrast to the nominalistic approach which had previously been taught in Oxford, Wyclif adopted realistic philosophy and its Platonic Augustinian understanding of the world and of reality[256] and applied it to the Bible: the Bible belongs to the eternal world of ideas, indeed it is the primal image of all eternal truth (*prima veritas*) and the book of life. For that reason it is sufficient (*sufficiens*) in itself. All universal concepts and the eternal moral laws are contained in it; indeed it is identical with the Logos, with Christ himself.[257] This idealistic view at the same time carries with it firm trust in human reason: the eternal truths of universal concepts and morality can already be discovered in the earthly sphere by reason, and the truths of faith are similarly demonstrable *aposteriori* by reason; thus the Bible cannot contain anything which would not be in accord with reason.[258] However, the identification of scripture with the Logos in turn allows an abundance of allegorical modes of interpretation.[259]

Wyclif's position over the Bible and the church is of central importance in this context. It shows how an idealistic, dualistic philosophy, a spiritualistic theology and a rationalistic epistemology can be combined with a strong stress on moralism to form a systematic unity and how this gives rise to an attitude to the Bible which, while formally according it the highest authority, brings to it so one-sided a prior understanding of its content that decisive theological statements[260] fail to be seen; in general, people with this approach read out of scripture what they read into it. Consequently, scripture, interpreted in moral terms, is elevated to become the standard for criticism of the church which in this way is measured, via this undisputed formal authority, by the criterion of the individual's own philosophical and theological views. For the 'realist' theologian (using the term in the scholastic sense) scripture enjoys a status incomparable with anything else on earth; consequently the attack on the institutions and doctrines of the church is supported in a highly impressive way.[261] The identification of the *lex evangelica* in scripture with natural reason already foreshadows the later standpoint of the Enlightenment, the biblical criticism of which is intensified by the same sense of being in possession of absolute truth, though at this later stage it is also used against all the contents of the Bible itself which stand in the way of a moral understanding. It is remarkable that in the sphere of dogmatics this attitude can bolster up quite orthodox positions, indeed can give them special support;[262] the fact that it was Wyclif's understanding of the eucharist which brought him into open conflict with the church should therefore be seen almost as an accident which could easily have been avoided.

It is also worth paying special attention to Wyclif's judgment on the relationship between state and church, above all because ideas are expressed here which are also to play a significant role later on in the history of England.[263] His attitude to this problem demonstrates one particularly strange consequence of his philosophical and theological system as a whole. In the fundamental elements of his thought on church and state Wyclif is fully dependent on mediaeval tradition, and here he follows the earlier Augustinian line.[264] In the one *ecclesia*, which as *ecclesia militans* embraces both those predestined to salvation (the *corpus Christi mysticum*) and those marked out for condemnation, and which in practice is thus identical with the members of a Christian state (specifically England:*ecclesia sive regnum*), there are the two 'swords' of spiritual and secular power. Nor is Wyclif an absolute innovator in the subordination of the church to the state in the exercise of all secular power; in his *Defensor pacis*,[265] Marsilius of Padua had already assigned all legal and material jurisdiction to the state, including jurisdiction over the church, and including the installation of priests.[266] However, not only does Wyclif deny the Pope spiritual and secular jurisdiction; as the predestined are at the same time those living in accord with the *lex Christi* (the possibility of temporary error does not affect this), they do not need the mediation of Pope, bishops and priests at all.[267] Already at this point we can see the consequences of the moralistic understanding of faith, which also shapes later constructions. The functions of king and 'authority' are defined in a similar way: the decisive factor is that the virtuous king, as vicar of God, also has secular power over the church; he has to watch over the morals of priests and in so doing to see that they wield the spiritual sword only in accordance with the ideal of original Christian poverty (if need be, in some circumstances also through dispossession). The king can here make use of the help of bishops, who must obey him in this respect. As a result, Wyclif has been said to be 'Erastian', a fact which will be of later significance in the English church. However, the content of this task shows that according to Wyclif's understanding the king also has a 'spiritual' power – he rejects any division between 'spiritual' and 'secular', precisely because of his moralistic understanding of the term spiritual.[268] On the other hand, the king's claim to rule, which is derived directly from God, is dependent on his moral attitude and the divine grace connected with it; in this respect the king is at the same time always the representative of the whole community.[269]

The fact that the two 'kingdoms' are identified on a moralistic basis also has a further momentous consequence in connection with Wyclif's understanding of the Bible as it has been described above: since state and church coincide, and since the Bible *qua lex Christi* has absolute validity, the Bible, Old and New Testaments,[270] understood legalistically, is the principal basis for the whole of life, including political life. Only the presence of sin makes human law and civil politics also necessary.[271] Here we see the foreshadowing of a programme which will have a central role in later Puritanism; it is impossible to overlook the connections between this movement and the moral Spiritualism of the late Middle Ages.

In Wyclif, as in Joachim of Fiore, we can also see that while the teacher hands on the system in its purest form, with all its elements connected in an indissoluble theoretical whole, his disciples only take up and popularize certain themes and use them for their own practical ends. In Wyclif's case, these disciples are the so-called Lollards. There is some doubt as to whether Wyclif created this movement himself;[272] at all events, it took his ideas further, beginning from academic circles in Oxford. After Archbishops Courtenay and later Arundel drove out leading members of the University in 1382,[273] and after further persecutions, some of them bloody, the movement, which originally had also been supported by members of the nobility, increasingly became diverted to the lower classes, though traces of it still seem to have remained down to the period of the Reformation.[274] Even now the Lollards[275] are more or less Cinderellas of academic research;[276] least of all is there any detailed study of their teachings in a historical cultural context. A large number of these teachings are contained in anonymous documents.[277] We can gain some impression of them from the content of the twelve conclusions[278] which the Lollard leader handed to Parliament in Westminster on 27 January 1395 and which were nailed to the doors of St Paul's and Westminster Abbey.[279] A summary[280] of these conclusions shows that here Wyclif's ideas have been transmuted into the small change of church politics, a development we have already noted with early Spiritualist sectarians: 'our usual priesthood' is not 'the priesthood which Christ handed on to his apostles': 'signs, rites and episcopal benedictions' do not have a model anywhere in the New Testament and therefore cannot bestow the Holy Spirit, 'for he and all his noble gifts cannot be reconciled in any person with mortal sin' – here, then, the efficacy of priestly actions is associated in Gnostic fashion with the sinlessness of those who give and those who receive (Thesis 2). Thesis 5 condemns church exorcism as 'necromancy' and Thesis 7 condemns prayers for the dead; Thesis 8 declares: 'Pilgrimages, prayers and gifts to blind crosses and dumb images from wood and stone are akin to idolatry': Thesis 9 rejects aural confession. Thesis 3 is directed against celibate priesthood (and thus explicitly above all against 'private orders'), and Thesis 11 is similarly directed against women's vows of abstinence. Thesis 6 requires the strict separation of spiritual and worldly rule. Thesis 4 puts forward Wyclif's particular view of the eucharist. Thesis 10 forbids the killing of men in war 'without a special spiritual revelation', a necessary addition to save the inerrancy of scripture (in the Old Testament). Thesis 12 is particularly illuminating: it is directed against the 'abundance of unnecessary crafts in our kingdom', and requires that 'goldsmiths and armourers and any craft of this kind which in the view of the apostle is unnecessary, shall be abolished for the increase of virtue.' We can see the later Puritan programme already prefigured in many points. Later we also occasionally find sabbatarianism and a requirement for the prohibition of eating pork among the Lollards; there is also hostility to infant baptism.[281]

It is unnecessary for us to follow the further fate of the Lollards in detail. It is enough to note that the basic attitudes which emerge here can be found a century later in very similar forms.[282]

2

Erasmus

The figure of Erasmus of Rotterdam must be included among those thinkers who helped to prepare for biblical criticism in the Enlightenment, although it is particularly difficult to arrive at a balanced judgment of his basic attitude to the Bible and the church.[1] A modern author concedes, 'The task of an exhaustive presentation of Erasmus' hermeneutics is an enormous one.'[2] This task is made more difficult by the equally enormous extent of the literature on Erasmus[3] and its diffuse character; by contrast, there is still no comprehensive investigation of Erasmus' understanding of the Bible which takes in all his work,[4] nor is there a general account of his theology.[5] Significantly, in this situation a variety of verdicts have been passed on Erasmus in recent times; it is no coincidence that we find the same kind of alternatives as with Joachim and Wyclif. The time is not yet completely past when Erasmus has been claimed as the father of liberal Protestantism or as a forerunner of the Reformation;[6] more recently, on the one hand attempts have been made to see in his work an 'existential *theologia vitae*, almost tending towards a Reformation theology of Scripture',[7] while on the other hand Catholic authors have been concerned, for apologetic reasons, to demonstrate his absolute orthodoxy in terms of the doctrines of the Roman church.[8] Many attempts have been made to provide a psychological explanation of the apparent twilight character of this man;[9] people have talked of his 'Janus face' and quoted Hutten's comment on him, *Erasmus est homo pro se.*[10] However, a close evaluation of his hermeneutical approach and his theological 'system'[11] shows that his theological thought, especially his understanding of the Bible, is quite consistent, and by no means as arbitrary as it might have seemed to some observers, who did not pay sufficient attention to the background to his time and his theology. It also seems that Erasmus (perhaps apart from an early stage) remained faithful to his basic views all his life.[12] There is some dispute about the influences which determined his spiritual starting point: it has long been a common view that he was already deeply influenced by the movement of the Brethren of the Common Life in the Lowlands, the *Devotio Moderna*,[13] during his stay at the school in Deventer (c. 1478-83) and s'Hertogenbosch.[14] Recently, doubt has been cast on such direct influences.[15] Another problem which has been much discussed is whether Erasmus was made to change his mind during his first stay in England, in 1499-1500, by the Humanist theologians there and especially John Colet,[16] so that he turned to theology for the first time, or to a much more marked degree.[17] However, that is by no means evident, and it might be better to say that his realization of the need to learn Greek and his plans to produce an edition of the original text of the Greek New Testament which were connected with that, go back to Colet's preoccupations above all with the letters of St Paul, which Erasmus encountered during his stay. However, these biographical problems[18] are not crucial for our concern. The basic presuppositions of Erasmus' thought are more important.

First of all, it may be said that all those who have argued for Erasmus' orthodoxy have been on the right lines. The fact that Erasmus did not join the Reformation but remained faithful to the old church[19] is not, as has often been claimed, a sign of weak character; there is a profound objective reason for his view. The theological principles of Erasmus, like his hermeneutics, do not derive from the Reformation; they are governed by an ancient theological heritage. At all events, it is vital to see where he locates his theological forebears: not among the scholastic theologians of his time (whose syllogisms and quibbling he notes with biting scorn),[20] but among the fathers of the early church, Jerome (and through him the Greek fathers, above all Origen, who was branded a heretic) and Augustine.[21] Kohls sees three reasons why Erasmus prizes Origen in particular: 1. his exegetical theology; 2. his philological concern for Holy Scripture; 3. 'the conception of the law as a law fulfilled by Christ which the Christian now encounters in a new form as the *lex evangelica* and *lex caritatis*. This opens up the way and makes it easier for the Christian to fulfil the law.'[22] Kohls recognizes a further theme: 'The conviction of the incarnation of Christ in scripture, in which he continues to live and work.'[23] Kohls' judgment errs in the next sentence, because he defines these comments as 'scriptural theology and theology of the word', evidently seeing these expressions as synonymous; here the scriptural theology of the Reformation is introduced into a total theological system which is basically remote from the thought of the Reformers, as Kohls himself shows clearly enough in discussing the later controversy between Luther and Erasmus.[24] We may also follow Kohls to the degree that he points to the Neoplatonic elements in Erasmus' understanding of revelation[25] and, connected with this, the high estimation which he had of corresponding elements in the thought of Augustine. However, this Neoplatonic approach is not a marginal phenomenon but lies behind the whole of Erasmus' theology, including his understanding of scripture. J.B.Payne has rightly stressed this[26] again recently.[27] Another fundamental feature, though because of Erasmus' predominantly practical concerns this does not develop into an explicit philosophical system, is the distinction between flesh and spirit, between visible and invisible, *mundus visibilis* and *intelligibilis*; this cosmology is[28] matched by an anthropology in which there is a contrast between *anima* and *corpus*, *spiritus* and *caro*, *homo interior* and *exterior*, though a trichotomistic view of man can also occur.[29] The phrase *hominem veluti tertium quendam mundum utriusque participem (imaginemur)*[30] is reminiscent of Pico's view of the place of man in the cosmos as *terrestrium et caelestium vinculum et nodus*,[31] though it appears in a practical rather than a speculative context.[32] It is important to note that this dualistic view[33] also plays an important role in Erasmus' understanding of the Bible: it is not just that he similarly misunderstands Paul's anthropology, in Platonic terms, in a dualistic sense;[34] the basic features of his hermeneutics are themselves dualistic. In distinguishing between letter and spirit and thus interpreting the Bible along the lines of a principle of a multiple sense of scripture he is following the old exegetical tradition from the time of Origen.[35] This fact is less remarkable than his special attention to the literal sense which logically led to his work on a critical text of the New Testament and the provision of a new Latin translation. At this point we must clearly point to the humanistic background to Erasmus' motivation, which also plays a part in his numerous editions of the church fathers and the editions of early writers.[36] It already leads Erasmus in another direction when, as has often been stressed, in the *Paraclesis*, which was one of the three introductory writings with which he prefaced his New Testament,[37] he made a passionate appeal for the translation of Holy Scripture into the vernacular.[38] Here, as K.A.Meissinger has observed,[39] we find a completely different attitude from that in the adjacent *Methodus*, which in true humanistic fashion argues for scholarly preparation for the study of theology.[40] However, these two approaches are only apparently opposite ones. It is much more important to see what aim Erasmus has in mind in popularizing the Bible; he is concerned with the *philosophia Christi* (or *philosophia Christiana*, *doctrina Christi seu evangelica*; Erasmus uses various synonymous terms).[41] In other words, following Augustine's *De doctrina Christiana*,[42] Erasmus is concerned with a form of faith and life with an ethical slant, also built on ancient sources, the focal point of which is the theme of a *devotio moderna* with a stress on simplicity.[43] The important point here is not so much whether or not Erasmus was influenced in his schooldays by the Brethren of the Common Life; rather, in this aim he follows the broad Spiritual trend which we have already been able to trace through a number of stages, and which was able to find a place in the mediaeval church, although it could easily incur the suspicion of heterodoxy (as, for a while, did Erasmus himself). In retrospect it is remarkable how we find in Erasmus positions which are very similar to those of Wyclif;[44] he, too, is on the one hand familiar with dualistic Platonist ethics and anthropology and on the other hand stresses the ethical significance of the *lex Christi* which he finds in the New Testament, above all in the Gospels. In fact, if we note this twofold starting point, we can talk of a christocentrically based scriptural theology in Erasmus.

However, in these questions judgments should be carefully differentiated. When Erasmus says that Christ is the centre of scripture,[45] he has in view the notion of the *Christus Redemptor*. A.Auer in particular has rightly protested against a view that was predominant earlier, namely that Erasmus was purely a rationalist and moralist.[46] But even if the notion of redemption through Christ is not fully absent from Erasmus' work,[47] the role of Christ as teacher and model is by far the most important.[48] To illustrate how the basic theological attitude of Erasmus differs from that which finds expression in the Reformation it is appropriate to introduce here the controversy which flared up between Luther and Erasmus over the question of the *liberum arbitrium*.[49] Here it now became evident that the opposition between Luther and Erasmus lay in their fundamentally different views of man: in Luther man is directed solely to God's grace, which is won on the cross of Christ and experienced in the forgiveness of sins; in Erasmus, too, man is directed toward grace, but he is left a remnant of freedom, the possibility of good works, and here the teaching of Christ, especially the Sermon on the Mount, can be a guideline, the way up from the sphere of the flesh to that of the spirit, in which man's real home is to be sought. For Erasmus, the ethical doctrines of antiquity can be used to a large extent at this point; he clearly shares the legacy of Stoic morality not only with the humanistic tradition but also with that of the church.[50] Schottenloher has produced an important corrective to Kohls, to the effect that the *aequitas naturae* also plays a major role as a hermeneutical principle for Erasmus;[51] characteristically, it too emerges among the arguments for the authority of scripture, and plays a prominent part.[52] Erasmus is firmly convinced that remnants from nature, which was created good, are still present in man, and that redemption and rebirth in the spirit can link up with them. This gives shape to Erasmus' paraenesis: he is concerned with discipleship in the steps of Christ, who in his life and his teaching (the *lex Christi*) has set before us what we must now realize in our own lives; what began in redemption is completed in *imitatio*.[53] Granted, this is not sheer moralism but piety[54] – however, the difference from Luther is clear.

Erasmus' hermeneutic is in line with this devout humanistic ideal of piety. It is not just that, of the two spiritual senses of Scripture which Erasmus distinguishes, he puts chief stress on the tropological;[55] he is also predominantly concerned with the Gospels and in them with the words and teachings of Jesus.[56] As we have observed, in Paul he sees above all the dichotomistic view of man, which he misinterprets in dualistic terms; he regards him as the most important authority against 'superstition' and the 'law', but above all interprets him in ethical terms.[57] This concentration on the *lex evangelica* (or *lex spiritus*)[58] at the same time leads to a certain lack of emphasis on the Old Testament (here Erasmus again follows the line of the earlier Spiritualists and is substantially different from Wyclif). However, here too our judgment must be balanced. In essentials, the comment 'Il lui manquait un sens de l'autorité de l'Ancien Testament'[59] may be correct, but here again Erasmus is influenced by the church tradition which begins from a unity of the canon, so that he sees the continuity of the *lex evangelica* (as is already evident from his choice of the terms) going back to the law of Moses, though only to one of its two sides: *...in una Mosi Lege, quae sunt duae Leges, altera crassis et carnalis, altera spiritualis.*[60] He finds in the *lex Christi* the spiritual fulfilment of what was already presented as the will of God in the *lex Mosaica.*[61] The law of Moses is abrogated in so far as it was a ceremonial law. On the other hand, it is of abiding value – and here the technical use of the term *lex* for the Old Testament comes into play – as a prophecy of Christ.[62] The use of the allegorical method for the interpretation of the Old Testament,[63] which Erasmus commends in principle (thus finding himself in agreement with the mediaeval tradition of interpretation) corresponds to this basic approach. It follows his general principle, *necubi in rebus temporariis restitemus, sed inde veluti gradu facto ac amorem...assurgamus aut prae his, quae sunt invisibilia, id quod est visibile contemnere incipiamus.*[64] He continues: *Idem observandum in omnibus litteris, quae ex simplici sensu et mysterio tamquam corpore atque animo constant, ut contempta littera ad mysterium potissimum spectes.* This is true above all of the Holy Scriptures, which *sub tectorio sordido ac paene ridiculo merum numen claudunt.*[65] Following on from this he then considers Genesis and other Old Testament stories; comparing them with the sagas of classical antiquity he makes the comment: *Fortasse plusculo fructu legetur fabula poetica cum allegoria quam narratio sacrorum librorum, si consistas in cortice.*[66] This is also true of the historical books of the Old Testament: *Quid interest Regum aut Iudicum libros legas an Livianam historiam, modo in neutra spectes allegoriam? Nam in illa multa insunt, quae mores communes emendent, in hac nonnulla etiam absurda in speciem, et quae summa cute intellecta moribus officiant.*[67] The examples he goes on to give are the murder committed by David, his adultery, Samson's immoderate love and the story of Lot's daughters. As we can already see here, Erasmus is methodically following the

course of customary allegorical interpretation, but he has his own ends
in view: positively, he seeks to interpret the Old Testament in moralistic
and didactic terms (which can only succeed through the use of allegory),
while negatively he seeks to devalue its literal statements which as
historical narratives cannot mean more to him than Livy. This also
follows from his ethically oriented christocentricity, which is also related
to the Old Testament: this is again a principle of interpretation which
Erasmus takes over but uses in his own way. For example, when in the
Ratio (Theological Methodology) he says in traditional phraseology,
'*Non quod in veteris instrumenti libris quicquam sit, quod ad nos non pertineat,
sed quod pleraque pro tempore tradita ad typum et adumbrationem futurorum
perniciosa sint, nisi trahantur ad allegoriam, veluti circumcisio, sabbata, delec-
tus ciborum, victimae, odium inimici, bella hoc animo suscepta gestaque, turba
uxorum aliaque his consimilia...*',[68] we recognize that he is less interested
in typology than in the occasion for saying something negative about
morality, cult and customs in the Old Testament.[69] In Erasmus, we
already find the broad outline of the juxtaposition of two elements on
which his verdict is negative and which later are to form a constantly
recurring pair in the biblical criticism made by the Deists: ceremonies
as the embodiment of externalization and the 'law' and the characterization of them as typically Jewish, so that for Christians to observe
them is branded as 'Judaizing'. This is his main concern, and not the
Old Testament as such; we may assume with a good conscience that
Erasmus accepts the Old Testament insofar as it can be interpreted
along christological lines in the usual way.[70] Here again we see his
dogmatic orthodoxy, which is possible for him because dogma is not
his central concern.[71] His real concern lies elsewhere, and this is a
logical consequence of his ethical and spiritualistic presuppositions: the
dualistic alternative of 'the visible and the invisible' (see above) brings
with it a fundamentally negative assessment of ceremonies, and along
with them of the 'law of the flesh', and with both of these, of Judaism.
It is equally indicative of the future that Erasmus draws his legitimation
for this alternative (alongside passages like John 6.64[72]) above all from
Paul, whose main assertions he considers to be those involving the
contrast of 'flesh' and 'spirit' (he can also identify the latter term with
'love', 'peace' and 'freedom');[73] now 'freedom' ('spirit') is the alternative
to the Mosaic law,[74] and this (along with quarrelsomeness and other
vices) is identified above all with ceremonial worship, which in turn is
identified with the Jewish way of life. There is significance in a statement like, *Ob hoc potissimum (Christus) natus ac mortuus est, ut nos doceret
non iudaizare, sed amare.*[75] Erasmus makes clear in many places what is
meant by 'Judaizing'; I shall quote just one (on Jesus, *praeceptorem
nostrum*): *in gloria Iudaeorum, quod essent filii Abrahae, in muneribus offer-
endis, in precationibus, in phylacteriis dilatatis...contemnit carnem legis et*

superstitionem eorum, qui malebant esse Iudaei in manifesto quam in occulto.[76]
Here we find the keyword which is to play such a prominent role
throughout the Enlightenment: *superstitio* – 'superstition'. Jewish superstition (this direct connection is made in other places[77]) is the same
thing as 'Jewish ceremonies';[78] Erasmus understands this to refer to all
forms of outward ceremonies in worship, and not just the veneration
of saints and relics, on which he makes some particularly biting comments. At all events, at this point the defenders of his orthodoxy have
stressed that Erasmus in no way rejects all outward forms in principle,
but only castigates the manifest misuse which could be noted in his
time.[79] In fact we can already find statements in the *Enchiridion* in which
Erasmus seems to concede the right of external practices of piety. Thus
in one passage he asks, 'So what should the Christian do? Should he
neglect the commands of the church? Should he condemn pious customs? No, but if he is weak he will regard them as necessary, and if he
is strong and perfect he will observe them all the more, so as not to
harm his weaker brother with his knowledge...' However, the passage
goes on, 'Corporeal works are not condemned, but the invisible ones
are preferred. The visible cult is not rejected, but God is assuaged only
by invisible piety.'[80] Thus here again (note yet again the reference to
Paul), Erasmus does not argue with conviction for church customs but
merely accepts them as a concession for the weak. The reason which
he gives elsewhere is also illuminating: '*me nequaquam taxare corporales
caerimonias Christianorum et studia simplicium, praesertim ea, quae ecclesiastica comprobavit auctoritas. Sunt enim nonnumquam tum indicia tum admin-
icula pietatis.*'[81] Piety is the decisive thing; it is fundamentally dependent
on the cult. This may be tolerated as a means towards its furtherance.
A negative verdict on the question follows from the Neoplatonic presuppositions: '*...in ulla... re corporali audebimus perfectam pietatem sta-
tuere?*'[82] Even a staunch defender of Erasmus' ideal of poverty like
A. Auer (there are quite a number of Catholic authors!) must concede:
'Erasmus has an unmistakable bias towards Spiritualism.'[83] The allusion
to 'the authority of the church' in the quotation above shows clearly
enough the sense in which Erasmus understands his concessions; he
certainly wants to remain in the bosom of the church – out of real
conviction (in reality the church had long since taken to itself the Spiritualism which he shared!).[84] We must also understand in the same way
the later assertions in which from 1522 onwards he keeps declaring his
loyalty to the Roman church and also his readiness to make considerable
concessions over the question of ceremonies.[85] As far as the *Enchiridion*
is concerned, one of his letters makes it plain that he wrote the work
'*ut mederer errori vulgo religionem constitutentium in ceremoniis et obserua-
tionibus pene plusquam Iudaicis rerum corporalium, earum quae ad pietatem
pertinent mire negligentium*'.[86] However, in his later writings, too, the

theme keeps recurring, above all in the *Colloquia*,[87] and not just in those works which seek to mock various church customs through satirical treatment, as in 'Of Over-hasty Vows',[88] the 'Shipwreck',[89] or in the relatively later 'Eating Fish',[90] but also in the completely serious *Convivium religiosum*.[91] It has been rightly observed that 'Les Colloquia sont de la même veine que l'Enchiridion'.[92] However, we also find a frequent preoccupation with the same theme in the *Ratio*, in which Erasmus developed his theological principles in the most systematic way.[93]

We are to understand both his attitude to Judaism and his attitude to the Old Testament in connection with this main theme. Writers have referred to the theological antisemitism in Erasmus, which is hard for us to understand today.[94] However, the term 'antisemitism' does not really do justice to his position, since in a large number of instances Judaism is no more than a synonym for 'outward worship, superstition, servitude to the law', and 'Jew' is used as a counterpart to the Christian who is truly pious in the spiritual sense[95] – and here the tradition goes back to Paul and John understood spiritualistically. Only relatively seldom do we find explicit comments made about the Jews as such; here the section from the *Ratio* seems particularly important in which there is a portrayal of the enmity of the Jews towards Jesus,[96] with evidence from the Synoptic Gospels, but using the term 'Jew' for the opponents of Jesus from the Gospel of John. Here, then, emerges that description of the Jews as a 'criminal, stubborn and rebellious people'[97] which is to play so prominent a role in the Enlightenment.

In connection with the interpretation of the Old Testament it is interesting to note that Erasmus can also choose evidence for his spiritual, anti-ceremonial viewpoint from the Old Testament. The passage from the *Convivium religiosum*, quoted above,[98] comes from a section in which Erasmus begins from Isa.1.11-17, one of the best-known passages of prophetic 'anti-cultic' polemic.[99] Hosea 6.6 plays a similar role.[100] Isaiah 1.11-17 was already long familiar to Erasmus in this sense; he already uses it in the *Enchiridion*[101] alongside Isa.58.1ff.; Ps.50.19, etc.[102] However, Prov.21.3 can also be introduced,[103] not far from the passage where the naive judgment of one of the conversation partners leads into a discussion, saying that he likes the 'wise Hebrew' better than the advocate of celibacy for his comment (Prov.18.22) that the man who has found a good wife has had an excellent find.[104] When we compare this use of selected passages from Old Testament prophecy in the fight against ceremonies in the church with the allegorical and moralistic reinterpretation of the creation narratives and the historical books, it is evident that here the spiritualistic presuppositions brought to the text are predominant and that the text itself is not allowed to speak in any way. In fact, the Old Testament itself was of minor significance for Erasmus: when in the controversy over Reuchlin the Jewish convert

Johann Pfefferkorn really would prefer to have the old Jewish writings destroyed, Erasmus can write: 'I would prefer the New Testament to be left untouched and that the whole of the Old Testament should be destroyed rather than that peace should be shattered among Christians because of the Jewish books.'[105]

It is particularly important to have an accurate view of the theological attitude and hermeneutics of Erasmus because his views on the history of the interpretation of the Bible, and especially of the Old Testament, were to have a far-reaching effect. In many respects the basic view which he puts forward has remained normative for general understanding and above all for the interpretation of the Bible down to the present day, to a greater degree than the Reformation. It is not enough to discuss whether the adjective 'orthodox' is the right one to apply to it, since in fact this approach could virtually ignore the dogmatic views which were put forward in the Catholic church at that time. It also corresponds to a spirit which had long been native to particular circles in the Catholic church and also continually tended to appear in sectarian form. In fact, at the same time we must ask[106] whether Erasmus did not also have radical disciples in wider areas of the Reformation camp. Various elements belong to this approach: a dualistic view of the world and man as a starting point and therefore a devaluation of the 'flesh', the corporeal, the real world in favour of the invisible. From this there consistently follows a rejection in principle of the visible cult, of 'ceremonies', which at best can be tolerated as aids to a piety which has not yet come of age.

In terms of the history of philosophy we can recognize Neoplatonic influences behind the dualism, whether these are taken over directly by the Renaissance or whether they are communicated (as is predominantly the case with Erasmus) by way of the church tradition (especially the church fathers). Corresponding to this dualistic starting point is the character of his piety, which has a clear spiritualistic trend and in this respect is able to strike a note of warmth. However, it contains yet another element: the ethical foundation which proves on the one hand even more clearly to be a legacy of humanism, this time of Stoic origin (this corresponds with Erasmus' early and continuing concern with a large number of writers from antiquity, and their propaedeutic function) but is also at home in the tradition of the church. Thus the humanist influence did not have any difficulty in making itself felt in the church. The result of this influence on the character of the piety propagated by Erasmus is that if it is christocentric – as is clearly the case to a considerable degree – it understands Christ above all as teacher (*praeceptor noster*), his teaching as *lex evangelica* which must now be followed, though only after Christ has made this possible for men through grace.

It is obvious how reduced a place the sacraments will occupy in an approach of this kind!

Luther clearly recognized the ominous side of this attitude and spoke out clearly against Erasmus in the case of the *servum arbitrium*. His attitude here has found many echoes right down to the present. However, he was not born to create a different kind of systematic hermeneutics on the basis of his principle, which would have been capable of asserting itself in the long run against that of the Humanists and the Spiritualists. So in the interpretation of the Bible, as we shall soon see, over the course of time the followers of Erasmus have triumphed, and down to the present day have persistently dominated the understanding of both Testaments.

It is worth mentioning one last point in connection with Erasmus, which was equally to play a major role in the subsequent period. He is the first figure to have put forward in the debate about the toleration of heretics the theory of the need to distinguish between essential and inessential principles of faith, between the *fundamentalia* and the *adiaphora*.[107] Bainton discovers this in the preface to the edition of Hilary which Erasmus published in 1523.[108] Erasmus also coined the description of doctrines 'by which the church stands and falls'.[109] Here too there is a fundamental distinction from the Lutheran Reformation, in which this statement is applied to the nucleus of the message of the Bible, justification through faith alone, around which all other dogmatic statements are grouped. Again, the reductionist way which seeks to further efforts at unity between churches by a limitation to a few fundamental articles was to be taken much more frequently in future. However, these questions lie outside the narrow focus of our investigation and therefore can be touched on only in passing.

3

The 'Left Wing of the Reformation'

The 'left wing of the Reformation' is a further significant link in the chain of development of the Spiritualistic understanding of the Bible and of a concept of the church, pointing in the same direction, which is closely linked with it.[1] Over the last twenty years, and even before that, a considerable amount of research has been devoted to trends running parallel to the Reformation. This began with the discovery of new sources[2] and led to a more accurate understanding of the whole phenomenon arrived at through a more thorough and objective evaluation of the original evidence.[3] A summary verdict, centuries old, which dismissed the whole left wing of the Reformation lock, stock and barrel with the derogatory term 'enthusiasts'[4] has here been replaced by the recognition of the great variety of theological views and practical concerns which in fact make it difficult to arrive at a well-founded description of the best-known representatives of the Anabaptist movement without careful examination of detailed evidence. In particular, it is right to object that there is a methodological error in viewing the 'enthusiasts' only from Luther's perspective.[5] On the other hand, however, attempts to arrive at a strict grouping of the various camps within the radical Reformation must be held to be only partially satisfactory. In the last resort, they go back to Ernst Troeltsch, who wanted to make a distinction between the great groups of the 'churches' and the 'sects' and within the latter between 'Anabaptism' and 'mysticism' ('Spiritualism') – from the perspective of the sociology of religion.[6] Other divisions, which go further, are those of G.Williams, who distinguishes between Anabaptists, Spiritualists and 'Protestant Rationalists'[7] and H.Fast, who distinguishes between Anabaptists, Spiritualists, Enthusiasts and anti-Trinitarians.[8] These interpretations certainly stress important differences in the spiritual approach and also in the attitude of the various groups to scripture, without doing away with the intrinsic connection between the various trends. On closer inspection, in fact, the phenomenological distinction claimed by Troeltsch between the

Anabaptists, the 'sect-formers', and Spiritualism, which he alleged to be free and individualistic, cannot be sustained, since almost everywhere[9] we may note a tendency towards forming communities, even if sometimes these are only loose groups.[10] And in essentials, the groups introduced by Williams and Fast are not so very different in their spiritual attitude that we could not speak of one general phenomenon, albeit with a great many different manifestations.[11,12]

Questions have also long been asked about the origins and historical context of those trends which appear alongside the Reformation.[13] In the nineteenth century it was L.Keller in particular who drew a line of 'old evangelical brotherhood' from the Donatists in the early church through the mediaeval Cathari, Waldensians and Bohemian brethren down to the Anabaptists,[14] a theory which had too little foundation to serve as anything but a powerful stimulus for thought. The same may be said of A.Ritschl's attempt to connect the Franciscan lay movement with the Anabaptists.[15] It was easy to object that a single movement of this kind could not be traced through church history and that there was no recognizable connection between the leaders of the Anabaptists and the mediaeval sects.[16] Instead of this, a different explanation was given, especially for the Swiss Anabaptist group which came into being in Zurich, one which has been widely accepted since. This group was said to have grown directly out of the Zurich Reformation, led by men like Konrad Grebel, who were first followers of Zwingli before they parted from him because of his gradually emerging readiness to take into account religious and political conditions in the city, which had not yet been adequately prepared for a sudden change, and to slow down the reforms.[17] In addition to this, Mennonite research on the subject is making great efforts to demonstrate that the whole Anabaptist movement, with all its different branches, was the 'real fruit of the Zurich Reformation': 'The Anabaptist community in Zurich became the starting point for the whole Anabaptist movement.'[18,19] The derivation of the Anabaptists from Luther has been stressed by both the free churches and by Lutherans;[20] without question there was some justification for this to begin with, because not only were countless representatives of the left wing of the Reformation originally disciples and followers of Luther,[21] but they also felt that they could help his original intentions of reformation to win through only by carrying them out consistently.[22]

Nevertheless, it can be shown that while some common features are shared by Luther and the radical Reformers, among the latter the Anabaptists more than the Spiritualists,[23] it was logical that the latter should soon part company with the Lutheran and Zwinglian Reformation, since in the decisive points of their understanding of themselves they were on quite different grounds from that of the all-embracing *sola fide*.[24] This is evident above all in their ecclesiology, their understanding of scripture and their ethics (with an anthropology in the background which is markedly different from that of Luther), though these three areas are simply three aspects of the same intrinsically coherent basic attitude.

We can already see the connection between this basic attitude and the phenomena described above from the fact that the same cultural and spiritual influences which affected Erasmus can also be noted in connection with the 'third Reformation'. Erasmus himself is regarded by a whole series of scholars as normative for Anabaptist views, and in addition as a mediator of the humanistic traditions which he took up, from the *devotio moderna* piety.[25] However, there is some question as to the ways in which this influence was transmitted;[26] in the case of the Zurich Anabaptists we might suppose that it came down through Zwingli,[27] while in any case there was also a small group of Anabaptists in Basle.[28] A whole series of the most significant Anabaptists of the first period were theologians with a humanistic training.[29] However, if we regard Humanism only as a phenomenon concerned with education,[30] this comment does not get us very far; but if we think in terms of a Christian Humanism with an Erasmian stamp, made up of biblicism, the ethics of discipleship and a spiritualistic concept of the church, we can in fact see a significant horizon of thought which is characteristic of the whole movement, independently of individual developments and conflicting individualistic views. In this connection, the question of the roots of the Anabaptist movement in mediaeval mysticism also gains a new significance, and is again thought to be important by a whole series of scholars.[31] In 1940 W.Pauck already pointed to the need 'to examine more carefully than has been done so far their roots in medieval sectarian and mystical groups'.[32] However, mystical influences were evidently a determinative factor only within a limited area of the movement; above all since the findings of K.R.Davis,[32a] the Anabaptist movement proper, which emerged from Zurich, is to be seen as a successor to the ascetic movements of the Middle Ages. Anyone inclined to see the Radical Reformation as a pioneer of modern attitudes[33] should not forget an insight which H.J.Hillerbrand hinted at when he remarked that the Anabaptist movement is nearer to Catholicism than to the Reformation;[34] the radical Reformation looks not only forwards, but also backwards. In fact, here we rediscover many of the typical attitudes which we already found in the late mediaeval movements we have considered, both inside and outside the church.[35]

As I have already indicated, the quest for dependent relationships which can be pointed out immediately has not as yet led to any satisfactory result. This situation is not at all surprising, given the difficulty of delimiting a cultural movement of the kind with which we are concerned. However, it is quite possible that further detailed research might reveal connections between individual figures and sources in this area which hitherto have been unknown to us. One instance of this is the career of Bernardino Ochino, who moved from the Franciscan and Capuchin Orders through the Geneva Reformation to the rationalist wing of the radical Reformation in an intrinsically consistent way.[36] However, demonstrations of this kind by means of external facts are not decisive for this investigation, which is phenomenological and concerned with the history of particular themes; the important thing is the emergence of characteristic views of the church, of the meaning of scripture, of 'ceremonies' and the central position of ethics, which enable us to assign the radical Reformation its place in the context with which we are concerned.[37] H.Bender has designated three basic views as the focal points of the Anabaptist attitude: 'First, a new understanding of the nature of Christianity as discipleship; secondly, a new conception of the church as the brotherhood of believers; and thirdly, a new ethics of love and defencelessness.'[38] The central role of the concept of the church for the Anabaptist movement has been stressed, after F.Heyer,[39] e.g. also by R.J.Smithson,[40] F.Krahn[41] and F.Littell.[42] In his book Littell puts forward the thesis that the typically Anabaptist attitude to history is evident particularly in the concept of the church which he calls 'primitivism', i.e. the conception of an ideal state in the primitive church which can be restored in the present.[43] Goertz, *Täufer*, passim, regards anticlericalism as the basic attitude which unites all Anabaptists despite the differences between the various trends (cf. also Clasen, *Anabaptism*, 77ff). By contrast Bender[44] would assign pride of place to the notion of discipleship.[45] However, both go together when we recognize the New Testament, and in it specifically the Sermon on the Mount, as the exegetical context from which the Anabaptists derived their ethics of discipleship. Thus it becomes clear that here too a consideration of the history of exegesis can provide a decisive key to the understanding of the movement as a whole.

Precisely because of the relatively large amount of material which we have about the early history of the Anabaptists, another difficulty arises. This is rooted in the nature of this evidence, in which we frequently hear the words of simple members of the movement (in the protocols of trials, and so on), often only as presented by their opponents, so that clearly thought-through theological statements are relatively rare. Hence, too, the dilemma,[46] in which research into the Anabaptists often finds itself today. Systematic investigations of their understanding of the Bible and their hermeneutics have so far been very isolated, a situation which arises again because the leaders of the radical Reformation, largely preoccupied with practical concerns, seldom made theoretical statements about their views on hermeneutics.[47] A practical and topical concern dominates even the systematically composed works of the Anabaptist and Spiritualist theologians, some of which appeared in print; but here at any rate the presuppositions of their hermeneutical thinking can be more easily demonstrated.

At one point the misinterpretations of the Anabaptist attitude arising from the earliest polemic against them,[48] which have continued to have their effect even down to the modern period,[49] may be said to have been finally refuted: the authentic Anabaptists in no way devalued scripture and put the Spirit in its place. On the contrary, they in fact had a much more rigorous principle of scripture than the mainstream Reformation.[50] That is already clear from the causes which led to the separation of the Swiss Brethren from Zwingli and is also evident in the later disputations in 1532 in Zofingen and in 1538 in Berne: the Anabaptists were concerned to carry through consistently the demands of the New Testament, and especially of the Sermon on the Mount, as they understood them.[51] There is much evidence to show that the Anabaptists, and not just the Swiss group, were intensively concerned with the Bible: the whole of their argumentation against the charges against them is based on biblical texts.[52] However – and this has clearly been shown by the vigorous scholarly discussion which has been carried on over this point -[53] the reference to scripture was made in direct association with reference to the Spirit. Among the authentic Anabaptists the two cannot be separated (and in this respect the old identification with Spiritualists has proved inaccurate), but in such a way that the 'inner word' provides the legitimation for reference to the outward word. God's Spirit, which the Anabaptists believed themselves to possess, is the ultimate authority which first gives authority to the written word of the Bible. Here, however, was a danger of making the principle of the Spirit so independent that as with the extreme Spiritualists (say Sebastian Franck), scripture can in fact become completely superfluous.[54] One person on the verge of this position is Hans Denck, whose remark in the so-called *Widerruf* of 1528 has become the best known: 'I hold Holy Scripture above all human treasures, but not so high as the Word of God, which is living, powerful and eternal...; for it is as God himself is, Spirit and not letter... Therefore salvation, too, is not tied to scripture, however useful and good scripture may be to that end. The reason is that it is not possible for scripture to make an evil heart better, though it may become better informed. But a pious heart, that is, a heart with a true ray of divine zeal, is improved by all things... Thus a man chosen by God may find salvation through preaching and scripture.'[55] For us, the interesting thing about this text is not the feature that is usually noted in it, the relationship between letter and spirit[56] – in this respect the hermeneutic legacy which we find with Erasmus is also normative for the Anabaptists, in that the concept 'word of God' is taken as the inward word of mysticism – but rather the view of

justification which underlies it: the possible use of scripture is for man's
blessedness, but this can also be achieved directly through election or
the Word of God : 'blessedness' is then defined ethically in terms of the
opposition between 'pious' and 'evil'. We can see this by the further
qualifications: to the 'pious heart' belongs the 'ray of divine zeal'; this
is a characteristic definition of the mystical 'spark of the soul' following
moral lines, as becomes even clearer by the use of the words 'made
better' immediately afterwards.

In their use of the scriptures the Anabaptists are in fact very close to
Erasmus, particularly when one understands him in terms of a christocentric 'theology of scripture'.[57] Following the insights gained by Erasmus, this theology of scripture culminates in an ethic of discipleship
modelled on the example and the teaching of Jesus[57a] (the *lex Christi*).
Modern Mennonite theologians also stress that the focal point of Anabaptist doctrine lies in discipleship:[58] 'The Anabaptist view of discipleship seeks a return to the earliest and therefore normative form of
Christianity. It is that form incorporated in the person and work of
Christ.'[59] This general ethical orientation is also expressed in the conception of baptism which stands out as a strikingly distinctive doctrine:[60]
for example, there is the statement in the Schleitheim articles, 'Baptism
is to be given to all those who have sufficiently learnt repentance and
a changed life and believe in the truth that their sins have been taken
away through Christ... that in our general opinion they desire it and
ask it of us...'[61] The requirements for baptism are instruction, repentance and voluntary resolve.[61a] Granted, baptismal grace, redemption
through the blood of Christ, is not denied: however, in the understanding of baptism as a sign and the distinction between inward and outward baptism we can see marked Zwinglian elements, and the
synergistic component comes through again in the significance attached
to the believer's own contribution.[62] Here again the opinion of Hans
Denck marks out the limit of the transition to pure Spiritualism: starting
from the distinction between inward and outward baptism, on one
occasion he can say, 'Outward baptism is not needed for blessedness,'[63]
thus denying the necessity of the sacrament itself.

We also find quite a large degree of variation on the left wing of the
Reformation with respect to 'ceremonies'. On the one hand is someone
like Pilgram Marbeck, whose view of the sacrament with its combination
of 'sign' and 'nature' comes very close to that of Luther, while being
distinct from the symbolic understanding held by Zwingli[64] – and on
the other is his opponent Kaspar Schwenckfeld,[65] who certainly started
from the Lutheran doctrine of justification but was soon disappointed
in the Reformation because of the failure of any renewal of Christianity
to develop along the humanistic lines that he hoped for,[66] and whose
thinking otherwise was utterly dualistic, and couched in timeless, me-

taphysical terms.[67] In him we find to a marked extent the fight against ceremonies characteristic of the Spiritualist tradition;[68] he feels compelled to regard them as the greatest hindrances to the religious immediacy for which he strives. So the eucharist is fully spiritualized, seen to have outward significance only with reference to the true inward food of the soul – hence the well-known recommendation that there should be a complete interruption of the celebration of the eucharist, a 'standstill'.[69] That is necessary because its indicative character is such that the sign can be received for salvation only by those who are truly born again. Similarly, baptism is simply an act of confession on the part of those who are already changed and as an external event is not necessary for salvation. Here too we can distinguish Hans Denck from Schwenckfeld, as in his view of the sacrament, though the two of them come close in their basic attitude to ceremonies: we have some strongly critical comments from Denck[70] about the use of the sacraments.[71] In his last programme of theological principles, the Widerruf, he certainly adopts a generous attitude to the use of the sacraments, but he makes it quite plain that he regards them as superfluous;[72] it is the same in the Micah commentary, in which baptism and the eucharist are described as customs usually practised only for the sake of the weaker ones, which can be observed or disregarded without harm.[73] Here, however, Denck stands in contrast to the sacramental practice of the Anabaptists proper, among whom visible baptism is of central importance, even if the element is understood only as a sign,[74] whereas in the celebration of the eucharist, interpreted as a memorial and a fellowship meal with a strong denial of the real presence, the tendency towards complete spiritualization emerged much more strongly.[75] On the other wing is Sebastian Franck,[76] with whom Spiritualism makes a complete breakthrough. He already expresses his understanding of the church in an appendix to his Chronica-Abconterfayung und entwerffung der Türkey ('Chronicle-portrait and sketch of Turkey') which appeared in 1530: 'Furthermore in our time three notable faiths have emerged: Lutheran, Zwinglian or Anabaptist. The fourth is already on the way, in which people will remove all external preaching, ceremonies, sacraments, prohibitions and vocations as being unnecessary and will simply set up an invisible, spiritual church, assembled from among all peoples and ruled only by the eternal, invisible word without any external means...'[77] Franck developed his basic view of the church as reflected in history in the third Chronicle of his Chronica, Zeitbuch und Geschichtsbibell.[78] There he puts his rejection in principle of any external form for the church in the context of a view of history with an eschatological orientation,[79] in a vigorous criticism of the primacy of Peter,[80] the Councils,[81] the 'orders and sects',[82] images of saints and the mass (the sacrament of the altar),[83] the apostasy of the elevated papacy,[84] and benefices.[85] Here the anti-

Catholic polemic of the Reformation is directed in disguised form against the churches of the Reformation themselves,[86] and consistently developed to amount to a complete spiritualization of the church.[87] Franck is particularly interesting because he is not an independent, creative figure but rather a collector of a variety of spiritual and religious traditions of his time and a point of crystallization for them;[88] although he is a solitary, he does stand in a stream which embraces Gnosticism, mysticism and the heretical mediaeval philosophy, material from Humanism and Stoicism, and Anabaptist Spiritualism.[89] The division between the inward and the outward, the basic principle of Franck's thought[90], is critical for his rejection of ceremonies and the cult;[91] in this respect he occupies the same ground as the mediaeval Spiritualists, and also the same ground as Erasmus and – to a large extent – Zwingli, except that his thought is more consistent than theirs is. Closely related is the attitude of Johannes Bünderlin,[92] for whom the rejection of ceremonies was so important a concern that within his scant writings he devoted a whole book to it.[93]

Characteristic of the Spiritualists on the 'left wing of the Reformation' is the stress that they place on the ethical action of the Christian. Here they differ from contemplative mysticism of the Dominican type and are closely related to the Anabaptists proper.[94] With them, too, we find in developed form the ethics of love and discipleship which we observed in the case of Erasmus. Sebastian Franck can again serve as an example here; many sayings of his which are very much in the spirit of Erasmus point in this direction.[95] In his *Paradoxa* 109-14,[96] under the heading *Christus sacramentum et exemplum* there is a close conjunction of Christ-mysticism and Christ as example: 'So now Christ is flesh and spirit, God and man. After the flesh he is sent to us by God as sacrament and example. As sacrament and holy mysteries, a sign of grace, so that we may grasp God in him... In short he is Spirit, so that he has shown us a trace of the divine nature... Again he is also flesh. Thus he has shown us and given us a picture of how we should behave towards God... In the life of Christ you truly find a perfect model of all action, all ministries, and so on, how you should expect to behave towards God and how you should expect God to behave towards you.'[97] But more is at issue here than with Erasmus: 'Therefore only one thing is needed for the kingdom of God... Namely, to come to God, to encounter, hear, follow and be subject to God; through his hand we are established in Christ and made to be good trees. Then all the good fruits follow automatically, without any commandment.'[98] Rebirth at the same time leads to the state of moral holiness. Discipleship is of equal importance in Denck's writings;[99] he speaks of 'Christ whom no one can truly know unless they live in discipleship with him.'[100] The writing *Vom Gesatz Gottes, Wie das gesatz auffgehaben sey: und doch erfüllet werden muss* ('Of the Law of God; how that Law is done away with and yet must be fulfilled', 1526)[101], important testimony from Denck's Anabaptist period, begins expressly from the theme which proved the decisive reason why the Anabaptists separated from the Wittenberg Reformation: namely, what they thought to be the moral failure of the Lutheran preaching of justification.[102] '... he who thinks that he is of Christ must be in God's eternal abode. He who does not walk on this way shall be lost for ever...'[103] The real centre of this train of thought is Christ's saying about the Law in Matt.5.17,[104] which is interpreted in constant discussion with the objections of his (Lutheran) opponents in terms of mystical and spiritual inwardness: 'Every commandment, all morals and law, in so far as they are composed and written in the Old and New Testaments, are abrogated for a true disciple of Christ, for he has a law written in his heart that he love God alone, according to which he can direct all his actions, though he has nothing in writing.'[105] The mystical-ethical autonomy which breaks through here as it does with Franck and makes scripture superfluous[105a] for the perfect does not mean that the commandments are done away with[106] (in fact, in the next sentences they are again qualified in favour of the general Anabaptist principle that the scripture must be opened by the Spirit – 'the key of David'[107] – if it is to be of any use): 'To the degree that a man has it, so the written law is done away with. To the degree that a man lacks it, so he will be subject to it.'[108]

The Old Testament is devalued more strongly among most Anabaptists and Spiritualists than is evident in the case of Erasmus. This aspect of their general approach, too, is closely connected with their other views.[108a] To illuminate this connection we can begin again from Franck. He has a remarkably full doctrine of the Old Testament, which he has evidently developed as a result of a keen apologetic interest.[109] His *Paradoxa* 86-89 are particularly illuminating.[110] In this section, too, Franck's concern is to defend his ideal of an invisible, purely spiritual church. In Paradox 89 there is a sharp repudiation of all outward worship and all ceremonies. Now it is worth noting that this opposition is carried on into a sharp contrast between the Old Testament and the New: 'The people of the New Testament is a free people, whose religion is completely one of freedom of spirit, good conscience, pure heart, belief in Christ, blameless life and simple love and faith.'[111] By contrast, the world does not know 'God as he is. It knows of no other religion than external, ceremonial Jewish religion with singing, saying the Paternoster, going to church, fasting, images and all kinds of ceremonies.'[112] Outward religion is 'Jewish': here we find the catchword that already came up with Erasmus.[113] However, Franck has already given extensive reasons for it. Paradox 86 takes up Ezek.20.25 and connects the 'not good' ordinances there with all 'outward ceremonies': ark, sacrifice, tabernacle, temple and even secular government: 'Israel saw such things among the heathens and wanted to have them, so God gave the child the rattle or a bell and let it play with its doll until he led it further on.'[114] God who is spirit and wills to be worshipped only in Spirit was compelled to take a step towards meeting the people: 'So that they did not begin to act by themselves and practise idolatry, to avoid worse, God added to all this child's play his word, so that it might all be done in faith and obedience.'[115] However, in his eyes these commandments were not good. 'So at last, when he thought that there had been enough playing with dolls, he did away with this religion once for all, with its kingdom, priesthood, temple, sacrifices, etc. and established a new religion of the heart ... and a new covenant.'[116] However, God also had some positive incidental aims with the ceremonial and judicial commandments in the Old Testament: 1. He wanted to compel the Jews to lead a holy, blameless life before the heathen, to show them his goodness and in so doing to attract them until the time when in the new covenant he 'appointed a new people and law in their place, gathered round Christ in the Holy Spirit';[117] 2. he gave the commandments in this way to make it possible for the figures of the Old Testament to have typological significance.[118] We have to realize that in this second point Franck is not representing any special view but is merely following one of the usual methods of interpretation for his day, albeit the one which best coincides with his general spiritualistic attitude;[119] 3. God expressly limited this external religion to Jerusalem and prohibited it elsewhere, so that at a given moment he could again remove it by the destruction of the city.[120] It is interesting to see that here Franck is explicitly taking up an argument put forward by Chrysostom in his *Adversus Judaeos*.[121]

The same view of the Old Testament also finds expression in the first Chronicle of the *Geschichtsbibel*, in which Franck, retelling Old Testament events skilfully mixed in with events from the secular history of antiquity, sets before the reader's eyes an important period of world history as he sees it.[122] K.Räber, who has made a study of this account,[123] demonstrates by means of various examples that a quite definite polemical tendency aimed at the present underlies it: 'inexorable identification of the misuses and excesses of Jewish religion with the cult of the mediaeval church.'[124] In a didactic and moralizing approach which is essentially quite timeless,[125] Franck selects certain Old Testament narratives from which it is possible to derive a rejection of the cult as mediation between the divine and the world. These include the story of Gideon's ephod (Judg.8.27),[126] and the story of the ark (I Sam.4), from which Franck concludes that the sons of Eli were only killed because they were 'popes' of the ark, like those today who reverence images of the saints or the monstrance carried in a procession.[127]

From these and similar passages Räber rightly concludes that 'at least in one stratum of his manifold being', Franck was a dualist: 'he felt that the world was remote from God and removed people from God, much as on the other hand he thought he could see a presence of God in the world and in history.'[128] Räber has also hit on what was the decisive question for Franck here: 'the point of contact between God and man, the question of a possible mediation...There is no mediation, but only direct contact which passes by and goes beyond everything that is created.'[129] A twofold and at first sight contradictory result follows from this chain of argument, though the Spiritualist thinker finds it quite consistent: the Old Testament is certainly not rejected as such; for spiritualistic exegesis it can be used just as much as the New.[130] Of course an extremely negative judgment is passed on the Israel of the Old Testament ('Judaism'); in the end the wish for an external religion rebounds on Israel: Israel is the 'fleshly, outward people' which forced God to make such concessions by its idolatry; at best it is a child whom he allowed to have its 'rattle' for a while, whereas the world has long since come of age.[131] This polemic was to recur two hundred years later in very similar form in the Deistic, Enlightenment criticism of the Old Testament; also, as we shall see, in a comparably basic controversy over the authority of the Bible.

Furthermore, in Franck too we sense something of the struggle which broke out between the Anabaptists and a large proportion of the Spiritualists on the one hand and the Reformers on the other over the authority of the Old Testament. One piece of evidence for this is Franck's letter to J.Campanus, already mentioned,[132] with the illuminating title: *Contra totum post apostolos mundum*. Here we find roughly the same arguments against sacraments and ceremonies that we already came across in the *Paradoxa*, but embedded in a general view of church history in which the development of the outward church since the time of the apostles is depicted as one long period of decay and devastation because of the advent of the Antichrist, whereas the true church since then has been scattered and hidden. Strikingly, the significance of the sacraments for the New Testament and apostolic period is not denied,[133] but since then they are thought to have become hopelessly tainted and corrupt.[134] Therefore no man on earth can gather together the church 'again and restore its sacraments without a special call from God'.[135] But this is what his opponents want – and here Franck refers to the church fathers and 'their descendants today': 'many of those who call themselves evangelical': they base their arguments on the Old Testament, from which they want to derive their requirements for contemporary church and politics: 'They confuse the New Testament with the Old... and if they have no means of defending their causes they run straight to the empty quiver, to the Old Testament, and use it to demonstrate war, oath, government, rule or authority, tithe, priesthood... They think that they have escaped the snare of the Pope and the devil splendidly, yet all they have done is to exchange and confuse the Pope's priesthood with the Mosaic realm. Now it remains a firm principle that if one cannot reintroduce priesthood from the old law, one cannot establish any realm or external form of government in accordance with the law of Moses.'[136] Franck's most significant opponent at the time this letter was written – during his stay in Strasbourg in 1531 – is well known to us: Martin Bucer.[137] The writing is evidently directed against his doctrine of church and state which was largely based on the Old Testament.[138] In fact the attempt to base contemporary institutions of church and state on Old Testament models lay at the heart of the original dispute betweeen the first Anabaptists in Zurich and Zwingli, who wanted to justify infant baptism on the analogy of the Old Testament prescription for circumcision.[139] However, this theme had wider implications than just for baptism, since fundamentally what was involved here was the whole relationship between church and state, the ordering of the two, and the role of the Old Testament in them, which also meant the problem of the unity of scripture itself.

The basic attitude of the Anabaptists towards the New Testament in the context of their ethics of discipleship was evidently further strengthened in the controversy with the Reformers. C.Bauman stresses: 'The question of the relationship between the two Testaments is fundamental to the whole controversy between the Anabaptists and the Reformation'; the main theme here is the question of violence or non-violence[140] – and therefore basically the doctrine of government.[141] According to the evidence we have,[142] the attitude of the Anabaptists to the Old Testament was largely analogous to that which we can see in Franck, and has the same ambiguity. The Anabaptists, too, stress that they in no way reject the Old Testament,[143] but they value it only in its typological significance as a prophecy of Christ and – here preparing for the beginnings of a historical approach – as a preparatory[144] period; furthermore, they never weary of stressing that it has been abrogated by Christ. The starting point of the *nova lex Christi*[145] leads to a contrast between Christ and 'Moses', between being a slave and being a child, between old covenant and new, and although the most subtle Anabaptist theologians sought to make it clear that the difference between 'flesh' and 'spirit', between the law in 'the letter' and the doing of the divine will made possible by the Spirit ran through both parts of the Bible, so that even the law of Moses is not done away with if it is observed in the Spirit,[146] in practice there came about a devaluation of the Old Testament which was interpreted by the Reformers as its abolition.

The Anabaptist attitude to the Old Testament is given particularly pronounced expression in the writings of Pilgram Marbeck and his group, to which considerable attention has been paid in most recent times: in the Strasbourg Confession of 1531 which he helped to frame,[147] in his response to Schwenckfeld,[148] in the *Vermanung* ('Admonition')[149] and above all in the *Testamenterleütterung* ('Elucidation of the Testaments'),[150] the specific theme of which is the relationship between Old and New Testaments. The reasons for writing this book, a kind of Concordance to the Bible with evidence for 118 themes from the Old and New Testaments, are given in the Foreword: at the centre we have the question of the 'faith of the fathers', a point of dispute between Anabaptists and Reformers, and a key issue[151] in the controversy between Marbeck and Bucer, and also in that with Schwenckfeld. This concerned the problem whether the pious Israelites in the Old Testament, above all Abraham, the model of faith, had received justification and the forgiveness of sins through the retroactive working of Christ's passion – against this Marbeck produced the clause from the Apostles' Creed about Christ's descent into hell which brought the patriarchs redemption only subsequently; closely bound up with this was a sharp rejection of the legitimation of secular authority in Christendom from the Old Testament which was derived from the Reformers' identification of Old and New Testaments. This related both to the authority of princes and magistrates to decide in matters of faith and to the revolutionary experiment in Münster. Fundamentally, then, the real theme is the alternative between a popular church and a free church, for which the Old Testament has decisive significance.[152] The on-going pattern in the *Testamenterleütterung* is the contrast between 'yesterday', the time of the Old Testament, and 'today', the time of the new covenant. Between them there emerges as a third category 'yesterday's promise'; here there is room for the familiar pattern of promise and fulfilment applied to the Old Testament in respect of Christ (and alongside it also the eschatological perspective on Christ's return).[153]

J.Kiwiet describes Marbeck's theology in terms of the basic notion of 'God's ordinance', which is made specific in the notion of the covenant.[154] As the old covenant, the time of the Old Testament, made up of various covenants, is contrasted with the new covenant and said to be essentially different. The difference is defined by the use of a variety of pairs of terms: the terms 'outward' and 'inward' denote on the one hand external obedience towards an external law, while in the new covenant, to serve God demands the whole man, inward and outward. This characterization of the new covenant corresponds to the ethic of the law of Christ, which we have already come across: however, with Marbeck the opposition between the Old Testament and the New is brought out essentially more sharply than elsewhere: the Old Testament is law, the law of the letter, which makes sin manifest (II Cor.3 is a central proof text); as such it has essentially negative significance.[155] A further keyword for the devaluation of the Old Testament in Marbeck is the contrast between 'temporal' and 'eternal'. The Old Testament promises and the faith of the fathers were temporal in character; their hopes were directed to temporal things and they received a temporal reward for their outward allegiance to the law;[156] that behind this, promises of eternal benefits were occasionally also concealed, points to the traditional ways of using the Old Testament which also remained in force for Marbeck.

It is not possible here to describe the whole range of Marbeck's theology. It is different, say, from that of Schwenckfeld, but in certain ways also from that of some of the Reformers by virtue of the absence of metaphysical dualism. Therefore the polemic against ceremonies, which is so widespread among the Spiritualists, is also absent. For Marbeck, too, there is a contrast between the inward and the outward, but the outward is there as a means for the inward, and the man consisting of both an outward and an inward side is one undivided unity.[157] Here, then, word and sacraments have their place in relation to the whole man; they are not signs but 'co-witness' for the nature which is directed through Christ to those who are renewed in faith and which shines forth on the outward man.[158] In his doctrine of the sacraments, as in his anthropology, Marbeck comes closer to Luther than to Zwingli; the difference is that he does not share Luther's understanding of the *sola fide*, but joins all Anabaptists in regarding the decision of faith and discipleship as constitutive, and makes the prevenience of faith the condition for the effectiveness of witness.

In contrast to the old covenant, for Marbeck the new covenant can only mean a completely new beginning. There is no continuity between the two, as the Reformers thought, but an absolute break.[159] Therefore with his covenant theology Marbeck chooses as his starting point the same ideas as Zwingli and later the Reformed representatives of federal theology,[160] but the character of his theology is fundamentally different.[161]

The result of our investigations so far may be summed up as follows. The attitude of the 'left wing of the Reformation' to the Old Testament is predominantly negative and does not correspond with the popular picture, which is largely shaped by events in Münster. Granted, the Old Testament is not repudiated as part of the canon, but in its character as prophecy and typology it is valued precisely as it is by the accepted interpretative tradition of the whole church. In controversy with the Reformers, the 'left wing' strongly contests that the Old Testament is a directly binding force in the shaping of the life of the church and of politics. For ethical action it is the *lex Christi* from the New Testament rather than the Decalogue that is normative. Furthermore, among the

Spiritualists there is a basic polemic against all outward forms of the church, against 'ceremonies', against the whole of the cult, sacraments, temple, even including preaching and prayer, the sharply contested model for which is found in the cultic forms of the Old Testament. In the fight against the 'Jewish' cult, the Spiritualists of the time of the Reformation take over the old legacy of the Spiritualist movement which reached them through Erasmus and certainly also through a broader tradition.

Only a relatively narrow group within the 'left wing' adopted another attitude to the Old Testament. Little is known about the so-called 'Sabbatarians', a small group of Anabaptists[162] whose most important leader was Oswald Glait.[163] As his writing on the sabbath is lost, we know of his views only through their refutation by Schwenckfeld.[164] Evidently the Sabbatarians took the commandments of the Decalogue, and especially the sabbath commandment, as being binding even on Christians, in a similar way to the modern Seventh-day Adventists and along the same lines as we shall note among the English Puritans.

More important for the attitude to the Old Testament among the radical groups of English Puritans is that trend which is well known as a result of the events in Münster between 1532 and 1535. However, the theological motives for their revolutionary attitude has hardly been investigated at all. The most important representatives of the trend are Thomas Müntzer, Bernhard Rothmann and Hans Hut. It has become increasingly clear in recent years[164a] that here we have a group which is clearly to be distinguished from the Anabaptist movement proper, differing from it above all in its basically apocalyptic attitude and a correspondingly different use of scripture. Only in the last few years has the basis for a reliable investigation of their theology been laid by the new critical editions of the writings of Müntzer and Rothmann.[165] Particularly in connection with Müntzer, it is also known more widely how differently the motives behind his actions have been assessed. If we leave aside the Marxist judgment that Müntzer's activity is to be set against the background of the class struggle,[166] there are still widely diverging views about the nature of his theology and the connection between his theological enterprise and his revolutionary drive.[167] However, the difficulties in understanding him which emerge here are considerably eased if we see Müntzer in the Spiritualist tradition which I have outlined above. The essential elements of the enterprise characteristic of this tradition also appear with Müntzer: his conception of revelation ultimately deriving from a Neoplatonist world-view which, like mysticism, postulates the 'inner word' of God in man and a gift of the spirit[168] which leads to union with God in the framework of a way of salvation understood as 'inner order'.[169] Indissolubly connected with this is the ethical orientation of his understanding of faith which, as

Goertz rightly stresses, should not wrongly be understood as autonomous morality.[170] Even the outward activity of the Christian also involves a 'co-operation of man with God'.[171] There are patterns of thought in Müntzer which have strong points of contact in the German mystical tradition: as for example when the notion of discipleship, which is also there, is understood above all in terms of a mysticism of the cross,[172] or the concept of mortification determines his understanding of the law. There are clear differences here from the understanding of faith in the discipleship ethics of Christian Humanism and the Anabaptist movement.[173] Therefore familiar notes occur again in his anticlerical attitude: the 'popes' are regarded as the seducers who are also capable of involving secular power in their service,[174] and as 'scribes' lead the people astray into a false faith.[175] Also characteristic of Spiritualism is the idea of apostasy which sees the existing situation in the people's church as a falsification of true Christianity and seeks to draw a sharp distinction between the elect and the godless. Connected with this is the dualistic view of the 'world' as the chief of the powers which are hostile to God.[176]

On the other hand, as Ullmann has shown,[177] Müntzer can see the world, undialectically, as a unity: the saving activity of God also embraces the material world in the framework of the *ordo rerum*,[177a] so that this automatically produces political activity. Here we can once again see Müntzer's special position as over against the cosmological spiritualism of Gnostic descent.

Accordingly, the answer which Goertz gives towards the end of his investigation to the question which is his main concern is unsatisfactory.[178] In demonstrating how Müntzer's revolutionary demands for the changing of society by force derive from the mystical and Spiritualist approach in his theology, he declares that the fusion of a mysticism of the cross and revolutionary agitation are 'Müntzer's independent contribution'.[179] This reference back to the person of Müntzer leaves the real problem unanswered. This dilemma is without question caused by too one-sided an assessment of Müntzer as a mystic. If, however, he is seen in the Spiritualist tradition, we can go considerably further at this point; Müntzer's attitude to scripture seems to provide the real key here.[180] First of all in this connection it should be pointed out that along with the extreme Spiritualists – and in controversy with Luther's understanding of scripture – Müntzer separates the spirit from the letter: in the *Ausgedrückten Entblössung*[181] it is polemically asserted against the 'scribes' (the Lutheran theologians who refer to scripture) that one could come to faith very well without scripture, and only through the spirit: 'If someone all his life long has neither heard nor seen the Bible, he can have a true Christian faith through the right teaching of the Spirit, such as was held by all those who wrote the holy scriptures without any books.'[182] About this faith, 'tried in the fire of the supreme suffering of the heart', he must also bear witness before such men 'as also had a tried and unfeigned faith'.[183] Authentic faith is legitimated not by scripture but by confirmation from brothers in the faith (the 'alliance' which Müntzer founded in Allstedt). In another passage[184] Müntzer speaks of the 'protection of the Holy Spirit which teaches us faith with the pure power of God... in the impossible work of faith... for it is discovered through action or by penetrating to the depth of souls'. The mystical terms[185] denote clearly enough the character of the process which belongs to the mystical union in which man comes into contact with the eternal spirit. Only at a second stage does scripture then come into play: the Son of God said that scripture bears 'witness': a confirmation of faith as it is experienced 'to such a degree, that if a Christian said among a crowd of the poor, that he had learned belief in Christ from God himself, people would not believe him (as we still contrive to), unless he agreed with scripture in his account.'[186] However, here the phrase in brackets expresses the proviso that such a confirmation could also be superfluous, seeing that the remark just cited about the way to faith without scripture follows directly in the context.[187] As J.Rogge has demonstrated very well,[188] in this connection we cannot separate word and spirit in Müntzer. Faithful to the mystical tradition, Müntzer begins from an understanding of the word which first expects the word as spoken by God into the individual soul, and then finds an example of it in scripture. However this contemporary 'inner word' always has priority, in that the scripture always points beyond itself. The presupposition of the right understanding of scripture is the possession of the Spirit; therefore the godless cannot understand scripture.

It is only in the light of the remarkable ambiguity of the thought-pattern of ethical Spiritualism that we can understand that on the other hand the law again plays a central role for Müntzer, and that the whole of scripture, both Old and New Testaments, provides the material principle for this.[189] The law first of all plays a central role in the inner way of salvation understood in Spiritualist terms: in suffering the penalty of the law man is led on the way of faith to Christ, through the cross to grace – but in contrast to Luther the law is not abrogated through grace but is instituted anew in a quite remarkable way. 'I set Christ with all his members as the fulfiller of the law..., for the will of God and his work must be completed utterly by observation of the law.'[190] On this Hinrichs comments: 'In Müntzer, rather, law and grace stand side by side in what is to some extent a dialectical tension.'[191] Here one could again see Müntzer as being very close to the other Spiritualists and Anabaptists, were it not that for him, in contrast to them, Old and New Testament stand on the same level, and he even accords the Old Testament law a clear pre-eminence.[192]

There is a hidden background to this remarkable position to which Hinrichs has already drawn attention:[193] it begins above all from the quotations from the prophets in the title and on the reverse of the title page of the *Ausgedrückten Entblössung*:[194] 'Thomas Muntzer, with the hammer' is given as the author, with a reference to Jer.23(29), and on the obverse Jer.1.9f. and 1.8f. are quoted in a very free translation. Thus Müntzer understands himself as a prophet who conveys the word of God as given by the spirit.[195,196] The Spiritualist beginnings are maintained, but kept within an Old Testament framework. And although the *Entblössung* sets out to be an interpretation of Luke 1, and in it Old Testament citations are interspersed with those from the New, the emphasis lies on the Old Testament. Hinrichs points to the special biographical significance which the reference to Gideon (Judg.6.13; 7.7) acquired for Müntzer: 'Gideon had such a firm strong faith that with it he conquered an enormously great world with three hundred men.'[197] Müntzer regarded himself as such a hero of faith and it was in this capacity that he bore the sword at the head of his small group in the battle of Frankenhausen.

The charismatic self-understanding is matched by a view of history which is developed from Old Testament apocalyptic. Hinrichs has discussed the question why Müntzer made Daniel 2 (and not Rom.13) the text for the 'Sermon before the Princes' and argues that for Müntzer the central notion of the chapter is the 'connection of regular periods of human history with the prophetic notion of the final kingdom', together with the significance of the appearance of the true 'Spirit' as a sign of the dawning of the end time.[198] Of course today we would be more restrained in our assessment of the role of apocalyptic material for Müntzer.[199] The significance of the Spirit is also stressed in the fourth section of the sermon[200] in which there is mention of dreams and visions (again with an abundance of Old Testament examples). The pouring out of the spirit over the whole of Christianity is a decisive sign of the dawn of the end time, as Müntzer explains with a quotation from Joel 2.11f.; 3.1-4 (Vulg.2.27-32).[201]

Thus it is his special predilection for the Old Testament which marks out Müntzer's Spiritualism and distinguishes it from the Spiritualists and Anabaptists who take the Erasmian line. As we have seen, the latter too move towards a concrete realization of the reform of existing conditions in the church, but their ideal is the primitive church, the demands of Jesus according to the New Testament, and as a result they take the route inwards, with the principles of non-violence, refusing oaths and so on. They cut themselves off from society, for these forms of life cannot be realized in public life. As a consequence the free church with its character as a minority is the necessary manifestation of this faith. Müntzer differs: his thought, oriented on the Old Testament, recognizes the world as a unity. But in contrast to Luther, who is the only one of the three great Reformers who also takes this view, he sees this unity in an undialectical way. Since on the other hand, in view of his Spiritualist heritage, he also introduces absolute dualism between good and evil as the two moral powers which determine the world, it follows for him that evil, in the form of those who perpetrate it, the godless, must be rooted out with military power.[202] Both the content of his remarks and his actions in the last months of his life are expressions of this view.

This attitude should not be confused with an approach in terms of class struggle. Hinrichs has shown how Müntzer originally understood his local rulers, the authorities, as the sword which was to wage war against the ungodly powers, and this follows particularly from the 'Sermon before the princes'. Only when he recognized that the princes were inclined towards Luther did he see the whole people as those who waged the holy war and himself as the prophet or Gideon, who had to go before them in this battle.[203] He also had a relevant Old Testament text for his original hope for the princely power: the narrative of Josiah's making of the covenant (II Kings 22; 23); he mentions it briefly in the Sermon before the princes[204] and even chooses it as the text for another important sermon.[205] The same group of problems was also to occur again in later developments in England, and there again the Old Testament background played a decisive role.[206]

In view of the starting point of Müntzer's theological thought his turning towards the Old Testament is not an inconsistency but one possible move. The typological-allegorical interpretation of the Old Testament, its 'spiritual' or 'mystical sense', also claimed a place in the Spiritualist tradition, as we have seen. Only the addition of the apocalyptic element was needed to bring out the specific reference to the present. Within the Spiritualist tradition a teleological eschatological view of history was possible in different ways: in Joachim in the scheme Old Testament – New Testament – age of the Spirit,[207] and in Franck similarly in the direction of the kingdom of the Spirit. In both, the Old Testament is produced as evidence; that the New Testament can basically follow it is the logical consequence. Müntzer finds the Spirit in Old Testament prophecy and thus in real history itself. That is why he develops his programme of political revolution. We can see from a comparison with Melchior Hoffmann[208] how little the apocalyptic orientation itself must have had such a result. Like the other Spiritualists,[209] Hoffmann stresses the contrast between Old and New Testament as between the corporeal and the spiritual, the outward and the inward fulfilment of the law, 'night' and light. He expects the great change from the return of Christ and his supernatural intervention, which is imminent, so that his final view has a purely spiritual character, which made Hoffmann seem a pure fantasist even to his contemporaries. In fact he starts from the Revelation of John and interprets the Old Testament imagery contained in it in purely allegorical terms.[210] After his arrest we see his followers split into two groups, of which the milder trend (under Obbe Philips) adopts an attitude akin to the Anabaptists and like Hoffmann himself waits passively and without violence for the return of Christ, while the militant faction under Jan Matthijs and Jan van Leiden sets up the rule of violence in Münster.[211] Here again we find a reversal which we can best follow in the theological development of Bernhard Rothmann.[212] For the early theology of Bernhard Rothmann it is worth noting W.J. de Bakker's reference to the Reformed background in his approach.[213] That also explains the stress which Rothmann lays from the beginning on doing the law. In Müntzer, too, the Old Testament is the basis on which the criteria of the law must be created. In the 'Restitution of true Christian doctrine'(ch.3) he stresses against the often-heard judgment, well, it is not the concern of Christians, what need have we of the Old Testament', that the Old Testament is valid and by no means obsolete.[214] On the contrary, he thinks that he can presuppose that any one knows what is 'in principle undoubted scripture, since all judgment must be based on the scripture, namely Moses and the prophets.'[215] Now as God's commandments must be fulfilled completely,[216] and the kingdom of Christ must be established really and truly here on earth,[217] the Old Testament laws apply completely here.[217a] True, as 'prefigurements' of Christ, the ceremonial laws are abrogated by his coming,[218] but otherwise God's will is inviolably proclaimed in scripture, and that is what the community in Münster observes.[219] In a way which we find hard to understand but which was quite normal in the hermeneutics of the time, typological and legal understandings go hand in hand, when Rothmann finds the five books of Moses to be 'the foundation and the true summary of all divine truth', on the one hand as a testimony to Christ and on the other hand as a direct source of the commandments that are to be followed in the present.[220] However, as J.W.Porter has shown,[220a] this does not mean that Rothmann in principle favours the Old Testament over against the New; rather, for him the whole Bible is a unity, with the New Testament as its focal point. But since the 'key' to scripture is the fulfilling of God's commandments as taught by Christ,[220b] despite the stress on the difference between the Testaments, that difference is in fact levelled out in a legalistic way.[220c] Whereas Rothmann's aims, like those of the other Anabaptists, were originally completely religious, their apocalyptic aspect[220d] opened up a political dimension, so that in the particular situation of Münster Rothmann could assent to the immediate realization of the kingdom of God, with Old Testament colouring. Once Rothmann is convinced by the radical Melchiorites that the kingdom of Christ has already dawned in Münster, he is ready to support the regulations which are literally to be the implementation of Old Testament ordinances in the city. Thus it is announced in the 'Precept articles'[221] in which Rothmann certainly had a hand,[222] that 'all those who love and cherish the truth and divine righteousness... where and to what degree the Christians and men of honour stand under the banner of righteousness as true Israelites in the new temple in the present kingdom... should now send, go and pay homage to John the Righteous, king on the seat of David'.[223] The new Israel is called to the seat of David under the banner of its king Johann; following this, two score commandments are proclaimed for daily life. Very similar is the 'Report of the Vengeance'[224] addressed 'to all true Israelites and followers of Christ scattered here and there, through the community of Christ at Münster'. The announcement in Jer.30.8f. that the Lord will raise up a new David is now fulfilled;[225] now vengeance will be wreaked on the godless! Therefore all Christians are summoned to come to Münster under the banner of God and all Israel.[226] These writings give an impression of the utterly Old Testamental atmosphere which dominated Münster during the Anabaptist years;[227] unfortunately the extant traditions of Rothmann are too fragmentary for us to be able to recognize the full extent of his participation.[228]

The Münster period of terror remained an episode. Nevertheless it was not to be the only attempt to impose the Old Testament ordering of life on the present.[228a] In England ,too, a hundred years later, radical Spiritualists were involved in the same thing. However, they could not have aimed at successes going beyond the narrow circle of an individual city like Münster had not the Reformation in the main church taken a similar direction. We shall consider this later.

First of all we must look again briefly at the group within the 'left wing of the Reformation' whose basic attitude was to be particularly significant for the later period: the rationalists or anti-trinitarians.[229] Strikingly the pioneers of this movement almost all come from the same area, from upper Italy (some also from southern France), and largely took the same course on their flight from the Inquisition in their homeland: first of all to Switzerland and from there, after they had almost all come to oppose the Zurich and Geneva Reformation, partly further into the areas in which at that time there was the greatest possible toleration of heretics: to Poland, Transylvania or Moravia.[230] At first glance it seems hard to find a hidden centre between the theoretical speculations about the Trinity put forward by these strongly individualistic solitaries or their mystical views and their specific demands for a radical transformation of the church and its social power, together with their criticism of the sacraments;[231] but the ingredients of this thought which according to Cantimori also included 'anti-trinitarian ideas, Neoplatonist conceptions, Anabaptist doctrines, rationalist and moral endeavours in a humanistic direction',[232] are for the most part well known to us and belong in the Spiritualist tradition that I have described above. The difference between the heretics of Italian origin and the German Spiritualists I have already discussed evidently lies in the strongly rationalistic basic attitude of the former, which is connected on the one hand with the intellectual climate of their native land,[233] and on the other with the position of their supporters, who for the most part belonged to an intellectual elite of priests, monks, and a few of the nobility. This attitude, connected with a humanistic training, led to some consequences of the basic Spiritualist attitude being thought through more radically in theory in these groups, most strikingly in the doctrine of the humanity of Jesus.

However, this is not the centre of their thought, nor even is the much noted and often praised idea of tolerance.[234] The centre is to be found in the approach which ultimately puts man at the centre, which devalues the sacraments, which must regard moral action as decisive but can also produce such different doctrines as those of rebirth through the spirit or the divinization of man in the mystical union. It is the two latter in particular which necessarily lead to the rejection of Luther's doctrine of the *servum arbitrium*, of man as *simul iustus ac peccator* and the decisive significance of the atoning death of Christ for salvation.[235]

The rationalistic heretics similarly developed a characteristic understanding of scripture clearly demarcated over against the biblical interpretation of the Spiritualists and Baptists. On the other hand their attitude has so many features in common with the basic Spiritualist tendency that there is no way in which, as so often happens, we can regard it as a singular phenomenon for its time. This can be demonstrated best by the well-known example of Sebastian Castellio.[236] Biblical interpretation occupies an important role in his life work. However, we shall not be concerned here with the reasons for his extensive translation work;[237,238] rather, we shall be interested in his hermeneutical approach which H.Liebing in particular has investigated in more detail.[239] We can recognize that Castellio, too, belongs to the Spiritualist tradition from the portrait painted by R.H.Bainton, who sees two main influences at work in him: the ethical-rational and the mystical-spiritual.[240] But he says, 'The first and dominant approach of Castellio was ethical.'[241] It is illuminating to note how the moral usefulness of an article of faith is decisive in the distinction between fundamental doctrines and adiaphora which do not divide the faith[242] which is so fundamental to Castellio's notion of tolerance; H.Liebing has collected a whole series of quotations from Castellio's writings in this connection.[243] Especially characteristic is the statement from *Contra libellum Calvini*[244] which he puts at the beginning: *Sanam doctrinam vocat Paulus eam, quae reddit homines sanos.* It is not surprising that Castellio, like Erasmus before him, could retreat to an orthodox confession when pressed;[245] dogmatic questions did not bother him; his concern was ethics. That is also true of his understanding of scripture: 'Morality as the essence of Christianity becomes the hermeneutical principle for the content of scripture.'[246] The distinction between spirit and letter within scripture is only in apparent contradiction to this[247] along with the stress on the 'Spirit' as the superior principle in which both the 'content' of scripture is expressed and also the one true authority over it is grounded.[248] In regarding the possession of the spirit bestowed by God as a precondition for understanding the spirit of scripture,[249] Castellio is apparently very close to the Spiritualism of Denck and Sebastian Franck. But in Denck and Franck, too, the 'Spirit' was a moral category: its possession is at the same time an autonomous criterion of moral action and a criterion over against all aspects which run contrary to the sole dominance of ethics: over against both cultic forms and dogmatic teaching which claims to be binding. So if moralism is Castellio's basic attitude, this shows that he belongs clearly to the Spiritualist, Humanist trend. The understanding of Christ as the exemplar bringing the new law of love and the physician healing the moral frailties of men also belongs in this sphere, as does a similar evaluation of the apostle Paul.[250]

Castellio's special contribution to the development of ideas lies in the fact that he now also clearly brings out in theory the Stoic background to the moral attitude which had been alive since the Renaissance in humanistic and religious attitudes and thus introduces a rationalism which prepares for the deistic period. That comes about on the one hand through the concept of *justitia* as a generally binding norm to which even the will of God is subject[251], the binding character of which lies in the fact that it is natural and therefore clear to all.[252] The idea of an autonomous morality runs through the whole movement, as a presupposition which is usually unexpressed, though at certain high points it is also formulated clearly, after Castellio and Lord Herbert of Cherbury also, at a later stage, by Shaftesbury and finally by Kant.[253] Secondly, a double definition of *ratio* is developed in a passage of the posthumous writing of Castellio *De arte dubitandi*,[254] in a eulogy of reason: on the one hand it is a natural human capacity to be able to distinguish between truth and falsehood by senses and understanding even in theological questions (what is *contra sensus* is wrong – the empiricist approach should be noted);[255] on the other hand reason is identical with the 'word'. (*sermo*[256]) of God, which not only speaks from outside but is also given to men as an 'inner word'.[257] The originally mystical doctrine of the *verbum internum* or inner light is thus identified[258] with a kind of common sense;[259] it is this which, together with morality, can serve as a criterion for judging the statements of scripture. Both principles are self-evident as such, and as such are prior to scripture; H.Liebing rightly stresses that this is a decisive step in the direction of the criticism of the authority of scripture.[260] The direction that this criticism will take can be seen not only in general by the combination of the two principles of morality and reason; it is even said directly in the 'praise of reason': ratio is *ante literas et ceremonias omnes*, it is *tum literis tum ceremoniis et antiquior et certior*: letters and ceremonies are the embodiment of a lower stage of religion which is to be transcended by reason. There are also references to the Jews who *plus quam rationis tribuebant*. Here we can detect the well known tones of Erasmus and his followers.[261] We shall consider later how they were handed on further by moralistic-spiritu-alistic religious humanism, leading to Deism; beyond question Castellio is one of the essential figures in this development.[262]

4

Martin Bucer

We cannot understand either the key role of the Old Testament for church life and political life in England or the polemic unleashed by the Deists against the Bible because of this central position without the decisive influence of the Strasbourg reformer Martin Bucer (or Butzer). Scholars are only very gradually beginning to realize the significance of this theologian and church politician who has been virtually forgotten over this long period; even the pioneering investigation into his theology by A.Lang[1] did not lead to any immediate sustained further study. Yet this is the man of whom H.Bornkamm says, 'after the Wittenberg friends Luther and Melanchthon he can claim the next most important position within the German Reformation.'[2,3] Even more striking is his influence on the whole of Europe; directly or indirectly the basic approach of his thought has put its stamp above all on the churches of Western Europe.[4] Thus in recent years interest in Bucer has deservedly grown considerably;[5] not least, this has been helped on by the critical new editions of his works, published and unpublished, which have appeared in the meantime[6] and which are beginning to supply a lamentable need.[7]

With Bucer we meet for the first time a supporter of the Reformation in the mainstream church; the decisive impulse which made him join the Reformation derived from his personal meeting with Luther in Heidelberg in 1518,[8] and his unwearying efforts to bring about an agreement between the various branches of the Reformation movement, between Luther, Zwingli and the Upper Germans,[9] are evidence of the cause to which he felt himself allied.[10] The fact that nevertheless the basic approach of his theology is characteristically different from that of Luther[10a] and that a series of features emerge in it which connect Bucer with the Humanist and Spiritualist tradition indicate how fluid the transitions are and how powerfully the external influences made their impact even in the heart of the Reformation. The complexity of this movement and the 'ongoing effect of spiritual ideas' in it[11] is evident, for example, paramountly in a figure like Bucer, whom we must describe, insofar as we see him as a successor to Luther, as a 'disciple of Luther with a distinctive stamp',[12] a typical man of the second generation for whom originality is less characteristic than the recurrence of many traditional ways of thinking.[13]

So far there is no comprehensive account of Bucer's theology: such an account will become possible only when his extensive work is completely accessible.[14] However, the investigations of partial aspects of his work which have been produced so far show the basic features of his attitude clearly enough. H.E.Weber has coined the evocative description 'christocentric ethical spirit mysticism'[15] for Bucer's theology and in so doing has given a series of key words to describe a general attitude the features of which we encounter to a considerable degree – and this is no coincidence – in the religious Humanism and the humanistic Spiritualism of the time. Our observations so far also make it easy for us to understand what needs to be done if we are to understand Bucer, which is to comprehend the unity of themes in his theological thought which are at first sight opposed. It is no coincidence that Bucer research has only seen the oppositions, either one-sidedly stressing one element at the cost of the others[16] or attributing his many-sidedness to his adaptable, mediating character.[17] We often also find a reference to the incompleteness of his theological views.[18] In reality, however, they belong together and are typical of the Humanistic religious feelings of the time, the characteristic representatives of which we have already encountered.

From the beginning Bucer's career was moulded by Humanism. The Schlettstadt Humanist school,[19] his intensive preoccupation in the monastery with the works of Erasmus,[20] his lively dealings with the Humanists in his immediate surroundings and further afield,[21] had basically inclined him towards an Erasmian and humanistic attitude which he never gave up[22] even after his decisive meeting with Luther.[23] In contrast to Erasmus, however, Bucer took up central ideas of the Reformation: above all the principle of justification *sola fide*, the rejection of the *liberum arbitrium*, the totality of sin, and redemption solely through the cross of Christ.[24] However, these themes appear in his writings with a characteristic colouring: already in his very first writing we have the beginnings of a twofold justification. Here, in contrast to Luther, for whom the event of justification is concentrated solely on the Christ event as grasped in faith, and any human collaboration is excluded, the process of justification is seen as a progress from faith understood intellectualistically as *persuasio* and *assensus*[25] to sanctification which fulfils justification and the good works which emerge from it.[26] After the Commentary on the Gospels of 1527, Bucer developed a regular doctrine of an *ordo iustificationis* which in the Commentary on

Ephesians (*Bibliographia Buceriana*, ed. Stupperich, 1952, no.17) is built up into a fourfold pattern which progresses from election, through the spirit-given knowledge of God and good works to the glorification of God.[27] The decisive modifications over against Luther lie in the effective version, and the focus on ethics in which human action again assumes its determinative place.[28] Thus the trend towards ethics has already long been recognized as the characteristic feature of Bucer's theology.[29] Here once again we can see the close proximity of Bucer to Erasmus, in whom similarly we can find the doctrine of a twofold justification and the same stress on good works,[30] though there is also the possibility of a regression to Thomistic scholasticism in which the notion of the concursus of *causa prima* and *causae mediae* is already present.[31] Closely connected with this is Bucer's attitude towards the Lutheran formula 'Law and Gospel': it has already been asserted in a variety of ways[32] that Bucer rejects this distinction as sophistical inventiveness contrary to scripture,[33] because for him the whole of scripture is *lex*.[34] Now Müller makes it clear that this is in no way introducing a legalistic feature into ethics;[35] rather, by deriving the concept on philological and exegetical grounds from the Hebrew word *torah*[36] Bucer is identifying 'law' with 'teaching'; it is *doctrina et vitae institutio* which teaches people *pie atque salubriter vivendum*,[37] a *doctrina pietatis*.[38] The twofold effect of the law in accordance with the Pauline scheme is preserved; but although in this context some of Paul's statements from Rom.3 emerge, that the law does not justify[39] but brings down God's wrath (Rom.4) and contributes to the knowledge and increase of sin,[40] these notions quickly end up in the use of the law as a goad, to hasten people into the arms of Christ the physician.[41] Now the real office of the law is, as in Erasmus, the *lex spiritualis*, which is written in the hearts of those who are chosen by Christ. K.Koch observes: 'Bucer's concern is not so much to distinguish law and gospel as to see them together. The expression which combines the two as it were as a common denominator is that of *doctrina*. For him the whole of scripture is teaching, both law and gospel.'[42] However, J.Müller's view that in all this Bucer did not give up the evangelical position[43] and did not leave the biblical line[44] is a questionable one. Christ plays a central role for his understanding of the law, but when we note how he considers Christ 1. as a teacher of the law; 2. as a model; 3. as giver of the Spirit to his followers so that they can live in accordance with the law, we see the line of the Reformers overshadowed by that of Erasmus which culminates in the notion of the *nova lex Christi*.[45]

Another feature which is characteristic of Bucer is his Spiritualism, which also occurs at various places. Scholars have already noted quite emphatically the central role of pneumatology for Bucer's theology.[46] J.Müller has pointed out how Bucer's conception of the role of the spirit is closely connected with the intellectualizing of his concept of faith in which *fides* is rendered by *persuasio*, faith as being convinced of the goodness of God, the mission of Christ and the validity of the promises.[47] It is the Spirit which gives this *persuasio*. Complete blessedness is achieved where there is complete knowledge of God and Christ.[48] It is evident that for Bucer 'the Spirit works mainly on the level of the intellect', though the fact that the Holy Spirit cannot be controlled guarantees that God's approach is completely grace.[49] This understanding of the Spirit also had a decisive influence on Bucer's hermeneutics. Luther's indissoluble identification of word and spirit is expressly rejected by Bucer;[50] by themselves the outward scripture (the 'letter') and the proclaimed word are useless, unless inner illumination through the Spirit given by God discloses their true understanding.[51] In this division between Spirit and letter we can clearly see the legacy of dualism in Bucer.[52] On the other hand, in contrast to the extreme Spiritualists Bucer did not give up scripture but explicitly related the knowledge given by the Spirit to the understanding of scripture. This again leads to a two-stage pattern: the first thing needed is illumination by the Holy Spirit; understanding of the word of scripture then follows from this.[53] In Bucer's life-work holding fast to scripture occupies so exalted a place that he has been rightly described as a scriptural theologian or biblicist.[54] Without question, in his emphatic return to scripture we have an expression of the conviction of the humanistic call *ad fontes*; the normative character which Bucer ascribes to scripture corresponds with the similar aim of Erasmus.[55] In his biblicism Bucer goes far beyond the Wittenberg Reformers; however, he also gives a material definition of the content of the norm of the Gospel.[56] This is also matched by his doctrine of inspiration: Müller has stressed that in Bucer there is 'some degree of objectification of the notion of inspiration', to the degree that in Holy Scripture the divine revelation is at our disposal in an objective way.[57] Therefore normative instructions for all the spheres of human life can also be derived quite directly from scripture and conversely, doctrinal precepts which are not in accord with scripture can be shown to be false.[58] However, his dualism between spirit and letter prevented Bucer from putting forward a doctrine of verbal inspiration.[59] The lack of clarity in his standpoint between the heritage of spiritualism and humanistic enthusiasm for the sources is evident from the fact that on the other hand he energetically put forward the demand for a historical exegesis of scripture, fought against allegory and in particular attempted to regain the original significance of biblical concepts.[60]

Over everything stands the principle *Nam et sacra doctrina proprie moralis est.*[61] As Müller has shown,[62] tropological exegesis, i.e. the essentially timeless application of any biblical statement to practical piety on the grounds that it is said *propter nos*, is the most striking feature of Bucer's whole exegesis. Hence his considerable proximity to Erasmus, especially in the idea of *imitatio*. The ethical background to his thought also provoked his particular views about natural revelation, which have been closely marked. The quotation I have just given comes from a section of the introduction to the Commentary on Romans[63] in which Bucer presents his view at length, culminating in the fact that everything needful for salvation has already been revealed to the heathen.[64] Bucer argues that the truth to be found among the pagan philosophers[65] was communicated to them not by natural illumination,[66] but through a divine revelation granted to all the elect from the beginning of the world. The reason he gives is that the corruption of human nature by original sin means that man cannot find his way to the image of God and the supreme virtue of loving his neighbour unless this is brought about by God in the spirit.[67] Here Bucer in a bold piece of spiritual speculation can take up John 1.9 and find in this verse a statement about the Logos as the inner light which has always illuminated the elect.[68] Thus Bucer strictly maintains the view that human beings are directed towards God's gracious action;[69] at the same time, however, he develops an overall spiritualistic conception which now allows him to find the same truth in ancient philosophy as in the Bible, only not so completely and so clearly.[70] *Omnia condita esse a Deo, certaque eius prudentia regi... eius vero restitutionem atque felicitatem omnem in eo consistere, ut naturae, hoc est Dei, de se voluntati, consentanee et congruenter vivat... sic vivens, ut sit omnibus bono, nemini malo...Deum sibi esse placatum...*[71] Thus here elements of Stoic popular philosophy[72] are incorporated almost without a break into a Christian system conceived in Spiritualist terms.[73] By a stress on the idea of revelation conceived of in christological and pneumatological terms[74] these statements are apparently assimilated for the moment; however, subsequent developments will show how quickly they can become independent and could turn into the real content of the Deistic system. Krüger has made it clear[75] that Bucer finds the focal point of this universal divine revelation less in the epistemological sphere than in that of ethics: *tam multa praeclara, quaque eximium ad probam uitae institutionem, momentum habent.*[76]

We should also see Bucer's understanding of the Bible, and above all his evaluation of the Old Testament, against this background.[77] In Bucer there is a far-reaching identification of the two Testaments: both are *idem in substantia*,[78] for both are testimony to the one eternal divine covenant[79] with the one people of God[80] and contain the one law. We also find in Bucer the traditional line of the typological exegesis of the Old Testament and the christological pattern of promise and fulfilment.[81] The Old Testament people of God and its destiny are a type for the conditions of Christianity in the present day;[82] furthermore – in a very traditional way – the return from the Babylonian exile is a type and shadow of the liberation brought about by Christ.[83] Nor did Bucer despise the usual prediction typology in the exegesis of particular passages of the Old Testament, though he also extended the fulfilment beyond the unique Christ event down to the present day in the church.[84] However, the special characteristic of Bucer's view lies in the Logos christology which is also applied to the Old Testament saving event in a way quite analogous to the universalism of revelation demonstrated in the question of ancient philosophy: Christ was already active in person in the time of the fathers: *Sunt enim ipsi per Christum servati,*[85] indeed, he was identical with Yahweh![86] Thus in essentials the whole Bible is seen along the same lines and both Testaments are accorded the same binding quality; there is an essential difference here between Bucer's attitude and the Spiritualist tradition which is embodied in Erasmus.

On the other hand his judgment is on quite a different level from that of the typical Spiritualist: we can see this from the important place which the antithetical scheme *externa/spiritualia* occupies in his thought.[87] The division between outward and inward which already emerges in his early understanding of baptism[88] and which also permeates the rest of his theology[89] is applied above all in exegesis, where it is used as a fixed hermeneutical rule[90] in order to arrive at the tropological application of a passage of the Bible from its historical meaning. Here it is a matter not only of dimming the individual fortuitous historical circumstances: *ut est locus, tempus, persona, numerus..., ad quod tum reliquum fuerit fidei et caritatis... ut proprie Dei praeceptum et ad nos pertinens, prona mente cuncta amplectendum est;*[91] here, an evaluation of the content is also undertaken: *Tum etiam uidere dabitur, quid sibi uoluerit in lege sua Deus, non certe externa illa, et infirma atque egena elementa mundi, ceremonias scilicet illas, ritusque de rebus corporalibus...*[92] Instead of this we have to work out the *nucleus verae pietatis*[93] in which the real abiding significance of the law (the Old Testament commandments) lies. *Ea (lex) in tribus sita est, ut Deo fidamus, ipsum ex animo timeamus et amemus, deinde ut proximum perinde atque nos ipsos diligamus, tertium ex utroque gignitur, ut continenter ijs, quae corporis necessitas requirit, et cum decoro utamur.*[94] Here already we find almost the same characteristics of a rational and ethical religion from the ancient Stoic heritage as will later become common currency in the Enlightenment. So we find the same devaluation of everything cultic, which is peculiar to the whole of the Spiritualist tradition, albeit with the important nuance that Bucer retains the ceremonial commandments as the sign of an inward attitude which is intended by them.[95] Elements of this view which are to be criticized are not only the fact that it has a tendency to devalue the historical[96] but also that it stems from a dualistic understanding of the world which could not in any way do justice to the Old Testament if it were looked at from this perspective.

The Spiritualist legacy in Bucer becomes a stage clearer from the fact that he even takes over the scheme of the three ages of the Spirit (alleging it to be Pauline) which we first found in Joachim of Fiore:[97] *triplicem esse aetatem populi Dei, pueritia formata est ut par erat multis ceremonijs, adiectis externo verbo, plene virilis aetas ista omnia missa faciet... At media aetas quae Euangelij Verbo regitur, ut spiritualior est, quam pueritia, ita non est tota spiritualis..., igitur Verbo utitur, ut huius causa externa quoque societate, et signis potissimum duobus, altero, quo eam societatem auspiciamur, altero quo renovamur et confirmamur.*[98] The development which is denoted here runs from the time of the Old Testament when the Israelites still needed ceremonies because of the rawness of their spirit and their childlikeness[99] down to the time of full manhood in which the full lordship of the Spirit will make completely superfluous the *externa* - ceremonies and the outward word – and the Spirit itself will take the place of the law.[100] The time of the new covenant, i.e. the present, is at the centre: it is manifest in the outpouring of the Spirit (in accordance with Jer.31.31ff.) through which the law is written in men's hearts[101] and in a reduction of the ceremonies to two, baptism and eucharist, both of which, like the outward word, still remain as a 'figure' of community and rebirth.[102] Even the law maintains its validity in the way mentioned above. The difference between old and new covenant is only relative: 'But the difference was that God further revealed and powerfully demonstrated his grace in Christ our Lord after his exaltation, and now not only among the children of Abraham after the flesh but among all nations and therefore with few outward ceremonies, as those of old will have had.'[103]

Therefore by applying the methodological canon mentioned above, Bucer can declare that the precepts of the Old Testament are directly binding in respect of their timeless content as *institutio vitae*: *per legem itaque et Prophetas intellegimus Dei doctrinam scripturis sacris comprehensam, qua ad pie et salubriter vivendum homines instituuntur.*[104] From the scheme of *externa/spiritualia* it also follows that what is required is the attitude aimed at by the ceremonial law rather than its outward fulfilment.[105] Of the three groups in the law the sacrificial laws relate to the *fides Dei*, the civil law to the *amor proximi* and the regulations for purity to the *decentia vitae*.[106] *Nam et in externis illis hanc Deus quaesivit, in sacrificijs fidem, in iudicijs charitatem, in ritibus alijs, uitae decentem modum.*[107] As also the old Israel and the church of the present are the one people of God,[108] the Old Testament commandments apply to all Christians in the sense of the *lex charitatis*.

Hence, too, their sphere of application. This sphere is primarily the church.[109] 'In Bucer the idea of the church is at the focal point of theological thought. All his views come together here.'[110] Evidently the doctrine of the church in Bucer underwent a detectable development in the successive periods of his activity. To begin with it was very strongly determined by the Spiritualist elements in his teaching; later, after the split with the Anabaptists and Spiritualists and the negotiations for the Wittenberg Concord, the external church with the administration of the sacraments, ministry and church discipline comes more into the foreground; finally, in *De regno Christi* (1551), the work of his old age, a development already introduced in the Strasbourg revolution comes to its conclusion. Here the state is put in an increasingly close relationship to the church and combined with it in one sphere of rule under the concept of the kingdom of Christ.

Even in Bucer's early writings, election is a constitutive element for the church[111] – along with the doctrine of predestination, which is important to all Reformers but is understood in most absolute terms, through Bucer and Calvin, in the Reformed churches, Bucer takes up the tradition of the early church and especially Augustine. The omni-efficiency of God is stressed[112] and the co-operation of men is strictly excluded. The church is founded through the word,[113] but as we have already seen,[114] an understanding of the truth in the word and its embodiment in scripture is possible only through the spirit which is given from above. Thus Bucer replies to the question, 'Who will tell you whether it is God's writing or man's writing?', by saying, 'The Spirit, the comforter, he tells me... If anyone asks us to believe something in the name of the churches, we see through the spirit of God and his word which is contained in scripture whether it is God's word or not.'[115] This also leads to a Spiritualist concept of the church: the true members of the church are the elect to whom the Spirit is given: 'If anyone really wants to speak of the community of Christ who build on Christ... it will certainly be only those who are chosen by God and elected to life.'[116] As such the church is invisible and can only be believed;[117] it is visible in so far as one can see the good works of Christians.[118] However, the external church embraces not only the elect, although only these are members of the true church,[119] but also 'the whole heap of those who are regarded as Christians and hold themselves to be such, cannot be separated from the community of Christ even through open vice.'[120] That Bucer wants to tolerate such people and does not want a separate church of pure bearers of the Spirit distinguishes him essentially from the Anabaptists and Spiritualists even before his public arguments with them. 'But if one wants to speak according to what we might be able to know, a community of Christ would be called where one hears his word and lives it out, although under the same roof there may be some Judases and mangy sheep.'[121] In the course of his activity, above all in his struggle against the Anabaptists, Bucer recognized the task of preserving the existing church as the place of God's institution of salvation:'We must esteem most highly the church as the bride of Christ.'[122] Therefore Bucer writes in his Memorandum for the Reichstag at Speyer in 1543:' Then although the kingdom of Christ is not of this world and our religion is a heavenly thing, a new life of rebirth in the Holy Spirit, we are still in this world and this whole world is the field in which the good seed of the divine word shall be sown.' Therefore Christ's command is to gather all people 'into his kingdom of the present community of the holy gospel, sacraments and his discipline and then also to provide seemly teachers and shepherds, overseers and pastors...'[123] Proclamation of the word, the sacraments as a visible sign of community, and above all the appointment of ministers for church discipline, teaching and pastoral care are the concerns which Bucer had during his activity in church politics in Strassburg,[124] in Hessen,[125] and elsewhere.

One piece of evidence for Bucer's views in his middle Strasbourg period is his writing *Von der waren Seelsorge* ('Of true pastoral care', 1538).[126] It is particularly important in our context because in it for the first time there is a systematic search for a strict biblicist basis for the outward form of the church, its ministries and services.[127] The starting point for Bucer's ecclesiology, with which he immediately begins,[128] is the idea of community; he had already developed this theme in the Ephesians Commentary of 1527[129] and remained faithful to it; it is also an important stimulus to his lifelong efforts at union between the confessions. The unity of the church has a christological basis: Christ is the head, the Christians are his members: community with Christ is also constitutive of the fellowship of believers among one another.[130] However, also characteristic for Bucer is the feature already included as an essential element in the definition of the church, that it is a community for education;[131] the ethical orientation of his theological thought also emerges here. In the context of this community Christians not only have to serve one another in all spiritual and physical things;[132] it is essential, since Christians still err and sin, 'that there must be a fixed doctrine, discipline and direction in the churches and community of Christ, that is a government through which Christians are constantly furthered and directed so that they learn of themselves to go forward, to let Christ be their head and surrender to him.'[133] These tasks are essentially provided for by two offices in the service of Christ, who himself has the government of the church:[134] the office of shepherd as the pastoral office and the office of deacon for 'bodily provisions'.[135] In a strictly biblicist way Bucer uses the designations 'elders' and 'bishops' for this office, but the two are synonymous and denote clergy, not laity.[136] A further concern is the choice and appointment of ministers of the church and the main tasks of pastors and church servants, whose role is above all that of seeing 'How the lost sheep are to be sought', 'How the stray sheep are to be restored.'[137] Here there is consideration of the task of mission brought about by the spiritual idea of predestination.[138] The section on 'How the injured and wounded sheep are to be bound up and healed'[139] deals with the penitence of sinners; it later also goes on to deal[140] with the institution of the ban.[141]

Bucer himself asserts in the Foreword that in all this his principal concern is to see to the ordering of the church in strict accord with biblical institutions: 'We have always presented the language of scripture, that the Christian reader will above all consider, weigh up and take to heart the foundation of scripture. For there are not a few people who, when one talks of church discipline and order, cry out that an attempt is being made to bring in the devices and interests of men. So we do not want to introduce anything anywhere which is not manifest and certain teaching and the clear and undoubted command of our Lord Jesus Christ.'[142] In accordance with the theme, the quotations almost all come from the New Testament; however, the institution of penance can be traced from Adam down through the whole history of Israel to the apostles.[143] But all these examples are on the same level and the thought is completely unhistorical. This unhistorical character of the biblicist approach is the real cause of the transfer of New Testament institutions and ministries to the present without the slightest awareness of a historical interval. Both biblicist theologians and church politicians and their opponents think in unhistorical terms until well into the eighteenth century. Only on this presupposition can we understand the fighting over the Bible which flares up in the time of the Enlightenment, above all in the Anglo-Saxon sphere.

A further theme in this work calls for our attention: the role which Bucer assigns to authority in relationship to the church and its tasks.[144] The whole work is addressed to the magistrate from whom the Strasbourg preacher vainly hoped for support for the needs of the church.[145] In a brief excursus[146] Bucer goes into the tasks of authority which as a 'Christian authority', in accordance with contemporary understanding,[147] it has to fulfil not only for the temporal good but also for the salvation of the souls of its subjects. These are as follows: 1. to seek out the 'lost sheep';[148] 2. the institution of faithful pastors; 3. the endowment of schools and the education of the young; above all, however, the authorities have to fight the sects vigorously ('root out false doctrines'): 'Also to let no one perish who is marked with the name of Christ, so that he departs from the community of the churches and the holy sacraments.'[149] Here Bucer refers to Augustine: *Cogite intrare!*, which he defends against the objection that no one should be forced to believe.[150] 'One should not force anyone to say that he believes what he does not believe, still less to go to the table of the Lord if he has no desire, as the

Pope does. But also one should not allow anyone who is born and brought up among Christians not to hear the doctrine of his Christ and live in accordance with it...'[151] Thus whereas the authorities are given the task of protecting Christians even to the extent of church government, in the closing chapter, 'On obedience to Christ',[152] with a reference to the Roman emperors Constantine, Valentinian and Theodosius, they are also told that they must be obedient to Christ in his servants. The authorities are also bound by the instruction for church and state which the servants of the word communicate from scripture in their teaching. Here again a subordination of secular to spiritual government is envisaged, which, arising out of biblicist motives, would have had immediately divisive consequences for church politics. We have to assent to Koch's[153] judgment that Bucer did not arrive at any clear demarcation of both forms of government.

The same basic attitude in theology and church politics can also be seen in the writings on the reformation of the community from the last years in Strasbourg (1546-1549), which recently have become widely available again thanks to the progress of the critical edition of Bucer's works.[153a] In these Memoranda to the Council, which Bucer intended to be normative,[153b] the main thought is that a 'second Reformation' is needed in which the fruits of the renewal of the community must be made visible in doctrine and the renewal of life in mutual love and penitence. Church discipline understood in this sense[153c] is to be achieved (since the institution of the 'churchwardens' was not effective enough) in two ways: first of all by gathering together all those who seriously want to be Christians and subject themselves to an appropriate test of their faith and way of life, to form an inner core within the churches (the 'Christian fellowship'), and secondly by the intervention of the authorities, who are to see to the shaping of public life in a Christian way, e.g. by the institution of monthly and even weekly days of prayer and specific police measures, through the imposition of the observance of the ten commandments.[153d] The pastors, too, are to censure public misdemeanours from the pulpit.[153e] Bucer could not achieve much more in Strasbourg in the direction which he desired. Above all the general political situation in Germany after the Augsburg Interim claimed the energies of all those involved in another direction.[153f] However, towards the end of his life he was once again to have the opportunity to make his ideas known abroad: that happened during his stay in England[154] in 1549-1551.[155] The result of these efforts is the great work *De regno Christi*(1550),[156] according to Anrich[157] 'the most mature and complete summary of his views on the Christian state, which works in the closest collaboration with the church in realizing the rule of Christ on earth.' The idea of the *regnum Christi*, which already forms the starting point for Bucer's pastoral writing, is here developed into a wider-ranging general picture. In it Bucer's basic theological ideas are once again expressed in their most divergent consequences. People have often been amazed at Bucer for his immediate sensitivity towards conditions in England and his insight into the political and economic situation of the country, which was arrived at in the briefest possible time.[158] Beyond question, in important issues like the role of the absolute monarch and the episcopal constitution of the state church, and above all in external matters like the retaining of ornaments,[159] with his practical instinct Bucer adapted to the English tradition.[160] However, his real intentions do not lie here but in the implementation of the Reformation in this country in accordance with the principles which had already guided him in his earlier church-political activity.[161]

The concept of the *regnum Christi* is developed to its greatest extent in the work of Bucer's old age. However, as Koch above all has shown,[162] this extension is already there in Bucer's basic approach. In the last resort, this Spiritualist approach which has grace coming to men directly through the Spirit that arouses faith (albeit also on the basis of scripture) in the last resort makes the church dispensable as a mediator of salvation, or rather sees that it merges into the *civitas Christiana*. The division of the two regimes as carried out by Luther, who sees their dialectical juxtaposition realized in the existence of every Christian, is transcended in Bucer's monistic thought by the notion of the one *regnum Christi*; in the *respublica Christiana* we simply have the two sides of this rule in which Christ reigns in church and society through his Spirit and his law. Here again Spiritualism and legalism go together. Precisely because Bucer maintains that as the church of the elect – and this is none other than the *regnum Christi* – the true church is a heavenly invisible entity, he not only stresses the need for the kingdom of Chist to be incarnate in a visible church but also requires that the whole of the life of society be shaped in accordance with his will.[163] The task of seeing to this devolves above all on the authorities, and therefore in England on the sovereign: Bucer begins the final chapter of his work with the admonition: *ut aeterno et solo salutari Dei verbo doceremur, Serenissima Maiestas Tua, Christianique reges, principesque rerumque publicarum moderatores et possint et debeant beatum filii Dei et unici sospicatoris nostri regnum populis suis solide restituere, hoc est, cum religionis, tum reliquae reipublicae uniuersae administrationem ex Christi seruatoris nostri et regis summi sententia reuocare, instaurare et confirmare.*[164] The authorities are equally responsible for both realms: the life of the church and that of politics and society; Bucer's ideal is the harmonious collaboration of the two regimes. He deals at length in one particular chapter[165] with what the two realms have in common and what is peculiar to each of them. Common to both of them is above all their aim: *Commune habet regnorum mundi et Christi administratio, ut et reges mundi eo omnia instituere et referre debeant, quo ciues suos efficiant pios et iustos, qui Deum suum rite agnoscant et colant, sintque proximis suis in cunctis actionibus suis uere salutares.*[166] Concern for worship and love of neighbour, the two tablets of the Decalogue, are also transferred to the earthly authorities. The degree to which the concepts have a strong ethical colouring is striking, as is also the way in which the task of both the church and the authorities is understood in terms of education and government. The difference between the *regnum Christi* (or the *regnum Dei*) and the *regna mundi* lies above all in the fact that this kingdom of Christ has its own goods in a fuller and more perfect form than the kingdom of this world.[167] The other common tasks – punishment and the excommunication of the wicked, and care for bodily needs (*ne quis omnino inter suos his egeat*[168]) – make it clear just how fluid the boundaries are. Finally Bucer stresses the mutual subjugation of the two kingdoms in order to emphasize their close collaboration.[169] The subjugation of the church to the state is limited to the obligation of even the clergy to pay taxes and levies (with a reference to Rom.13), in accordance with mediaeval tradition.[170] More important is the subordination of the authorities to the kingdom of Christ; the basis of this is baptism: as all the inhabitants of England including the king are baptized, they are all incorporated into the kingdom and obliged to hear the teaching proclaimed by its servants and to subject themselves to its discipline.[171] The latter is illustrated by the penance of the emperor Theodosius after the massacre of Saloniki.[172]

Using baptism as a basis makes it possible to understand the church as a people's church and to identify it *de facto* with the state, although this really produces an irresolvable conflict with the idea of predestination and the invisible church of the elect which follows from it. However, from the fact that everyone is baptized is also derived the right and indeed the duty to preach Christ's teaching to all.[173] Thus the Reformation in England is to be carried out above all by sending preachers into all areas.[174] Everyone is to be obliged to hear the sermons, even though state pressure is needed to compel them to.[175] The system of the state church in Bucer's programme, in which Bucer, too, accepts the situation prevailing in England since the Law of Supremacy of 1534, is evident not only in the fact that the king has the task of restoring the *regnum Christi* (since this cannot be expected from the bishops),[176] but also in the way in which the half-yearly synods are to be composed half of laity called by the king and that if possible they are occasionally to be led by the king himself.[177] With their task that *uitia corrigantur et pietas omnium instauretur*, they participate in the church's penitential discipline, which is the task of the church alongside doctrines and sacraments as the third *nota ecclesiae*.[178,179] The royal officials also have the same task; they are entrusted with the education of the whole people *ut eius scilicet populi et ciues a puero per prudentem et fidelem edu-*

cationem , optimas leges... instituantur, adsuefiant atque impellantur ad uerum Dei cultum, ad omnimodam uitae sanctimoniam, ad omnem charitatem, humanitatem et beneficentiam...'[180] As we see from the themes which are discussed individually, the whole of public and private life is subject to a fixed system of institutional control which again in practice transcends the readiness presupposed at the beginning in the fulfilment of the *lex charitatis*.

In his description of the *regnum Christi*, Bucer[181] bases himself on two models: the Platonic idea of the state[182] and the Bible, or more precisely the Old Testament. In the establishment of the kingdom of Christ in England Bucer again calls to life the ordinance of the covenant which was the model at the time of the Old Testament. Therefore the rulers of England are reminded of the Old Testament kings David, Solomon, Ahaz, Hezekiah, Josiah and so on in the solemn invitation to carry out the Reformation in their country.[183] Consequently the ten commandments of the Decalogue are mentioned as the basis not only of church ordinances but also of civil law.[184] It is characteristic that this is immediately explained on the principles of Plato and Cicero;[185] in conclusion it can be said of them that *Haec iuris sunt naturae, non tantum Euangelii!'*[186] For Bucer the Old Testament is the model and norm for the shaping of all circumstances; however, the criterion for the parallelism is largely humanistic ethical thought drawn from ancient sources.[187] It is striking how often Bucer can refer, for example, to Deuteronomy.[188] He often reverts to the commandment to keep holy the seventh day;[189] here the Old Testament regulations for the sabbath, transferred to the Christian Sunday, are declared to be binding in the strict sense.[190] However, the Old Testament regulations are also normative for secular law; this happens, for example, in the case of those guilty of conduct incurring the death penalty, which includes blasphemers, sabbath breakers, children who rebel against their parents, adulterers and those who bear false witness, with reference to the relevant Old Testament regulations.[191] A closely knit system of authority for guarding over the life-style of all citizens is to be set up, the model for which is the appointment of judges by King Jehoshaphat of Judah according to II Chron.19.4ff.[192]; this is an inappropriate model, like the citation of the appointment of judges according to Ex.18 and Deut.16.18ff.[193] for an institution which in reality imitates the Platonic *phylakes*.[194] However, Bucer does not have in mind a mechanical adoption of Old Testament institutions and customs, but follows here the principles which are mentioned above:[195] *Fateor, Mosi legibus ciuilibus sicut et caeremonialibus datis ueteri populo nos libertate Christi donatos non teneri, quod quidem ad externas attinet circumstantias et mundi elementa, tamen, cum multae possint leges magis esse honestae, iustae ac salutates, quam quas Deus ipse tulit, aeterna sapientia et bonitas, eo modo ex Dei sententia nostris rebus atque actionibus applicentur, non uideo, cur Christiani in rebus, quae ad ipsorum quoque usum pertinent, non debeant magis Dei, quam ullorum hominum leges sequi.*[196] It is interesting that in his later extended comments about marital questions Bucer to a large extent applies Roman law;[197] after the Old Testament period, he sees his ideas about the formation of the kingdom of Christ already prefigured in the Constantinian period.[198]

PART II

The Crisis over the Authority of the Bible in England

1

The Age of the Puritans

Bucer's ideas about the ideal form of the English state as expressed in his work *De regno Christi*, dedicated to Edward VI, already bring us right to the heart of the problems connected with religious and cultural trends involved in the English Reformation and further internal and external developments in the Church of England in the sixteenth and seventeenth centuries. In the history of theology this period is indissolubly linked with the name of the 'Puritans'.

(a) Problems for research

1. Those who use the term 'Puritans' immediately find themselves confronted with a mass of questions and a vast amount of research which in many respects seems to lead nowhere. Even the term 'Puritan' itself is hotly disputed and at first sight seems to need some definition unless, like the Georges,[1] who use it only in parentheses, one dismisses it as irrelevant.[2] Behind this rejection is the notion that the distinction between 'Anglicans' and 'Puritans' as two theologically opposed parties in the English church from as early as the time of Elizabeth I,[3] long taken for granted, is unfounded and that rather the whole of earlier English Protestantism displays a basic Calvinistic approach.[4] In fact in the sphere of doctrine the common ground between the Conformists and the Nonconformists is considerable even as late as the time of Laud; despite the special characteristics of the English Reformation,[5] the state church under Elizabeth and the first Stuarts is a Reformation church.[6] Nevertheless, the Georges' verdict must be rejected as being too sweeping and too one-sided, and Puritanism must be allowed an existence as an independent entity. But this means that its character must be sought in other areas than that of basic doctrines which it holds in common with its opponents in church politics. Its activity seems above all to appear in the various public actions, declarations and manifestos which its representatives presented at different times between 1550 and 1604

– the dates which mark out the first main period of the development. It was therefore natural that quite a number of historians should have dealt with Puritanism by depicting the outward course of events. It was the impressive consistency and decisiveness of Puritan action which first succeeded in attracting the interest of modern observers.[7] W.Haller took things a step further with his work *The Rise of Puritanism,*[8] by referring to the widespread preaching activity of the Puritans as the real centre of their action and the deeper cause of the fact that despite all opposition, in the longer term they gained the upper hand in the church. However, this again brings us back to the question of the central content of this preaching and of how it differed from the message of the conformist church. One important point on the way to an answer seems to be that for the Puritans the implementation of preaching in general and in all places was a basic requirement which they also sought to fulfil with a particular method of organization.[9] With its argument that a clergy 'such as can read the scriptures and homilies well unto the people'[10] is quite enough, and the ordinance that the number of preachers for each county should be limited to three or four,[11] the queen's reaction to these concerns[12] shows not just the effect of domestic political considerations but above all a fundamentally different view of the church.

2. However, before we can concern ourselves with this theme we must consider a basic problem of research connected above all with the fact that in the last decades as well as historians, or rather, often within their ranks, social and economic historians in particular have been preoccupied with the Puritans. No one can deny that as a result we have gained many valuable insights into the economic and social situation of England in the sixteenth and seventeenth centuries and into the connections between social developments and the situation in the church politics of the time.[13] The nature of this research was a necessary reaction to the one-sided orientation of nineteenth-century history writing on the history of ideas.[14] The question is, however, whether at this level it is possible to see the nucleus of the phenomenon of Puritanism as a movement directed from the depths by the impulse of faith.[15] By contrast, modern secularized thought-patterns often lead to complete incomprehension of the deeper motives of the thought and action of a period in which faith and the world were still closely connected and theology could assert its central position unassailed.[16]

In its origins, the treatment of Puritanism in terms of the sociology of religion, the history of culture and later secular economic history is closely associated with the name of Max Weber.[17] From him derives the well-known and extremely influential theory that the ethics of 'ascetical Protestantism'[18] played a decisive role in the rise of the spirit of capitalism as a result of its 'inner-worldly asceticism'.[19] This was because by virtue of its doctrine of predestination Calvinism called for the 'need to prove faith in one's worldly profession',[20] 'thus providing a psychological starting point for a systematic and rational ethical formation for the whole of life'[21] and by attaching greater value to work and the profit motive 'directly influenced the development of the capitalist lifestyle'.[22] At about the same time[23] this approach was pursued further by E. Troeltsch in the large-scale phenomenological treatment of his *Social Doctrines of the Christian Churches*[24] and also extended to the various subsidiary trends of Protestantism, to which Weber himself had already directed his attention in his article on the sects.[25] Since then he has influenced a large number of historians, church historians and economic historians, including scholars who, like R.H.Tawney[26] and M.Walzer,[27] are inclined to take a diametrically opposed view to that of Troeltsch, namely that Puritanism represented a repressive ideology which (at least in its original form) had first to be overcome before the liberal spirit of capitalism could develop. However, we have to ask how far the development of this whole trend of research[28] is not the history of a misunderstanding, at least in terms of Max Weber's own intentions. The misunderstanding had already arisen during his lifetime among his first critics[29] and was expressly rejected by Weber himself in his counters to these criticisms: Weber was in no way concerned to derive capitalism in a straight line from 'ascetical Protestantism';[30] he was merely concerned to demonstrate a way of life which had a religious determination and which, along with other components, produced the prior conditions for 'the development of humanity'[31] which was later to prove to be the supporting element of the capitalist system.[32] People were virtually standing his intentions on their head when they ignored the particular state of the discussion to which Weber wanted to make a contribution. He sought to put forward an alternative theory directed in particular against the Marxist interpretation of capitalism: not just the economic factors but also the personality structure of the people involved seemed important to him, and in his article he wanted above all to draw attention to the significance of the religious elements for the development of the psychological frame of mind which made it possible for man to play his role in the growth of capitalism.

Had people taken Weber at his word, they would have had to recognize that although his first article was conceived with inadequate methodology and partially erroneous presuppositions,[33] it represented a bold attempt to demonstrate the significance of a *theological* factor for the development of modern intellectual attitudes. He himself shows that questions from the sphere of theology were of fundamental importance to him in a small note to his first reply to H.K.Fischer: 'I would expect such criticism (in contrast to Fischer's, rejected as being inappropriately 'psychological') which many people would perhaps find to be extremely "retrograde" from the theological side because that is the most competent.'[34]

3. Despite the extensive literature about the external forms of Puritanism as a phenomenon, produced as a result of the 'Weber syndrome', a theological discussion about it has hardly as yet begun. That is certainly connected with the enormous difficulties in the way of an adequate understanding of its context in the history of theology.[35] There are beginnings of this kind above all in the question of the influence of various forms of continental Protestantism on the thought of the Puritans and their episcopal opponents, in attempts to define the difference between the concern of the Puritans and the thought of the 'Anglicans',[36] and also in terms of the position of Puritanism generally in the history of ideas. For this last point the decisive initative comes from the life work of Perry Miller.[37] His very first work, *Orthodoxy in Massachusetts* (1933), is deliberately opposed to the predominant approach: 'I have attempted to tell of a great folk movement with an utter disregard of the economic and social factors.'[38] Instead of this he tries to describe the thought world of the American Puritans in terms of the various historical influences which shaped it. He defines four main sources of these traditions:[39] 'One was European Protestantism, the reinterpretation of the whole Christian tradition effected by the reformers.' He can also define this basis by deriving it from the Augustinian type of piety.[40] The second element is made up of particular thought-patterns and interests of the time. In this connection reference has to be made above all to the logic of Petrus Ramus, whose antithetical scheme provided the basic figuration for Puritan rhetoric and Puritan thought.[41] Whereas here a thinker shaped by the Renaissance stands in the foreground,[42] the third element mentioned by Miller is the force of Humanism as the new form of learning and the rediscovery of ancient culture. The fourth, not to be forgotten, is the power of scholastic thinking, which continues unbroken. In this context Miller refers among other things to the use of the two great contemporary encyclopaedias, those of J.H.Alsted and B.Keckermann, by the New England theologians.[43] Piety and rational reason: these are the two basic elements from which in Miller's view the Puritan understanding of the world is built up. The tension can also be expressed by the poles of 'understanding' and 'mystery', the antinomy of which gives Puritan thought its depth precisely because the contradiction cannot be resolved. Miller deliberately oriented his account on the 'New England Mind', on American Puritan thinking; that is why the usefulness of his conclusions for the problem of Puritanism in general is limited. But in the first half of the seventeenth century the young colonies were still so closely bound up with the mother country[44] that we can largely transfer his remarks to the English Puritans.[45] From the time of Miller it has been beyond dispute that the

Puritans paid tribute to the thought forms of their time.[46] Nevertheless, Miller's approach also has its limitations. These are directly connected with the impetus which moved him to his lifelong and committed preoccupation with the American Puritans: his discontent with the American way of life dominant in his time, the optimistic rationalistic line following on from the Enlightenment, made him look to the Puritans for an alternative picture which he could present to his contemporaries as America's real spiritual home. In reality, he himself was a child of his time and place, and his capacity for understanding the Puritans was limited.[47] Thus he underestimated the importance of biblicism which was so central for the Puritans, though he registered it as a fact,[48] because such 'brutal authoritarianism'[49] inevitably seemed unattractive both to his readers and to himself. Therefore, as one critic has pointed out,[50] the origin of even the best-known biblical conceptions in their system escapes him. Nevertheless, his insights into the presuppositions of Puritan thought in the history of ideas are an indispensable basis for a considered judgment, particularly in the question of their dealings with the Bible, which he neglected, since these beginnings play a decisive role in their attitude to scripture. Specifically as interpreters of scripture, the Puritans are by no means an isolated phenomenon, as will become clear in the context of the history of exegesis presented here; they stand in a clearly recognizable succession to the various influences which were at work in their time.

One famous theme in the discussion about the Puritans is the question of the influence of Calvin. In most recent times, the older view which was accustomed virtually to identify Calvin and Calvinism because of what was usually an almost exclusive concern with the two main Reformers, has rightly given way to a more differentiated approach.[51] Even the Puritans of England were, to use Haller's phrase,[52] 'Calvinists with a difference'. It is, of course, impossible to deny the influence of Calvin on Reformed theology even in England, although as an element in church politics Calvinism could develop much less there than in neighbouring Scotland.[53] In fact at the time of Mary Tudor a series of exiles came to Geneva, including the famous Thomas Cartwright.[54] The most famous product of the English exiles who fled to Geneva is the so-called Geneva Bible, produced by William Whittingham and others, with its strongly Calvinist prefaces and notes, which for a time had wide currency in Puritan circles.[55] Nevertheless it is now widely recognized that it was not only Calvin, nor even primarily Calvin, nor even exclusively influences from continental Protestantism which contributed to the rise of Puritanism. Not only Geneva but also the centres on the Rhine and not least Zurich helped to shape the face of Puritanism through the circulation of the works of their Reformers and their successors, and also through personal connections and correspondence.[56] A.Lang,[57] W.Pauck[58] and later C.Hopf,[59] among others, have already stressed how important a role Bucer played for England. Impulses from the Reformation also combined with Christian Humanism in the anti-papal campaigns under Henry VIII and later among the Reformers under Edward VI.[60] In his famous article 'The Origins of Puritanism',[61] L.J.Trinterud has referred to people like William Tyndale, John Frith and John Bale,[62] who already in the early phase of the English Reformation developed certain basic ideas of Puritanism which, as he thinks, are 'authentic expressions of the English spirit and heritage'. One important factor is 'the heritage of medieval English thought and life',[63] in which Wyclif and the Augustinian form of piety play a decisive role.[64] Here, beyond question, is an important insight, though this heritage is in no way something specifically English.[65] To a certain degree the Lollards are evidently also mediators between the mediaeval anticlerical sectarian tradition and the Puritan trends in the English Reformation church, as more recent investigations show with increasing clarity.[66] The anti-ceremonial criticism of the church together with the demand for preaching instead of sacraments and the use of the Bible in the vernacular by laity also are important Lollard themes which also established themselves among the Puritans as well, but they received new impetus through Humanist trends and their link with the Continental Reformation.

It is certainly true that we cannot make a sharp distinction between the influence of men like Bucer and Bullinger and that of Calvin. 'These men were not Calvin's rivals but his heralds.'[67] Nevertheless, it is not unimportant that Bullinger and not Calvin was the Reformer with the highest reputation in England in the time of Edward VI.[68] The Zurich Reformation had quite a different character from that of Geneva, which was represented by Bullinger as Zwingli's successor. As has been shown in particular by H.Kressner in a pioneering investigation[69] (in this connection Kressner mentions above all Whitgift's sympathy for Gualther and W.Musculus), the fact that the influence of Zurich was predominant in England had significant consequences for the form of the established church. These consequences are again closely connected with a different way of using the Bible, as will be demonstrated in due course. Generally speaking, it was less the two main Reformers themselves than the people of secondary status belonging to the second generation whose thought became influential among Anglicans and Puritans,[70] especially – as I. Breward has again recently stressed – since the English church itself largely lacked original figures who could have developed a school of their own.[71] Here Breward recalls the exegesis and theology of G.Zanchi,[72] in which despite an emphatic biblicism, a return to Thomistic thought and Aristotelian philosophy can clearly be seen. In arriving at a balanced judgment on the theology of Puritanism we must remember

that the development towards scholastic thought and a form of Protestant orthodoxy which can also be noted on the Continent can be
established both among the English Anglicans and the Puritans, each
with a different focal point. This explains both the rationalist features
of Puritan theology and the return of certain mediaeval, sectarian and
indeed Anglo-Catholic forms of thought.

4. If we want to arrive at an open assessment of the character of
Puritanism we may not overlook the strongly humanistic traits which
are to be found in a movement which lays such strong stress on piety.
L.Trinterud has recently[73] put this above all other considerations. The
real driving force of Puritan activity, its criticism of the church and the
demand for reform which it addressed towards that church, was not so
much Calvinistic theology as exemplified in the doctrine of predestination. Rather, these zealots were motivated by the humanistic call *ad
fontes*, the idea of a restoration of the church in accordance with the
pure model which was found embodied in the Bible and above all in
the New Testament; the verdict on the most recent past, the Middle
Ages (still embodied in the Catholic Church, which was feared right
down to the end of the seventeenth century as a constant threat both
without and within – it was really only the Glorious Revolution of 1688
which brought an end to the danger), as a time of depravation and
uncleanness. In particular the emergence of ethics as their central concern shows that the Puritans continued the concerns of Humanism. The
legacy of Erasmus proves to be stronger than the legacy of the Reformation. The continental Reformers who were able to make their influence felt in England, the Zurich figures of the second generation and
people like Bucer, Martyr and Oecolampadius, were themselves at least
as strongly moulded by Humanism, as we have seen in the case of
Bucer. To this degree it is possible to follow a quite unbroken line of
Humanist tradition in which the Spiritualist heritage also plays its part.
The summary judgment of G.Mosse runs: 'It became evident that many
Puritans were humanists as well as evangelicals, that they were an
intrinsic part of the sixteenth century revival of classical thought as well
as continuators of much of medieval scholasticism.'[74]

In addition, E.C.E.Bourne[75] has drawn attention to the largely un-
conscious view of the world which lies behind all the individual positions of the Puritans: the dualistic attitude which had come down to
them in a trend extending from Gnosticism and the Manichees through
the mediaeval sects down to the Reformation period. The antithesis
between matter and spirit also underlies the whole of Puritan polemic,
and 'it is not too much to say that in this sense at any rate Puritanism
was more Manichean than Christian'.[76] Bourne sees his judgment that
the roots of Puritanism are to be limited to the three key words, 'bibliolatry, Manichaeism, papophobia',[77] confirmed by the observation that

the fight against ceremonies and the hierarchical ordering of the church is based on these three principles: 'The ceremonies were survivals of the pre-Reformation church and therefore remnants of Popery; they had for the most part no clear and explicit warrant in Scripture, and were therefore by implication forbidden; and they were outward, material signs, and therefore inimical to the true spiritual worship of God. Similarly with the monarchical Episcopate. The Roman Church had Bishops; therefore a Reformed Church should not. Episcopacy as practised in the Church of England was not (so they claimed) to be found in the Bible; therefore it was unlawful. In addition, the acknowledgement of an ecclesiastic superior was an external check upon the free play of the spirit.' Even if this passage only mentions partial aspects,[78] the connection of the Puritan movement with the development depicted so far can be clearly seen. The special form of restlessness which has been observed among the Puritans is also connected with the Spiritualist feature which in turn connects the Puritans with the later period of Pietism that developed after them.[79,80] The Puritans were always on the move; on the way to a goal of which they were ignorant and which was therefore unattainable because it was dualistically separated from the real world. Often they were borne along by a tense eschatological expectation, the negative consequences of which must have been all the more vigorous when the hoped-for change still did not come, even if (as in the Puritan revolution), it seemed to be close enough to touch. Even with power in their hands they could not bring about this change, because they were tied by their dualism.

The problem of the opposition between Puritanism and Anglicanism is often tacitly presupposed and rarely treated as a theme. It lies in the tension between the thought and life of the great church with its mediaeval tradition, which had already undergone changes as a result of humanism and also, in part, of the Reformation, and an opposite attitude which similarly was by no means free of tradition, but derived its themes in part from the Spiritualist and rationalistic sectarianism of the late Middle Ages (Lollardry) and in part from trends with a humanistic colouring, stemming in particular from the Reformation in Switzerland and southern Germany. J.F.H.New has produced the first systematic account of the various theological positions of both parties.[81] The criticism to which his work has been subjected[82] is above all connected with his static view, which does not take sufficient account of the development of the two differing standpoints over a long period, and his view of Calvinism, which is too narrow and does not allow him to see the strains of Reformed theology which are also to be found in Anglicanism. Nevertheless all those who see the anti-Puritan struggle waged by J.Whitgift (Archbishop of Canterbury 1583-1603) and the Cambridge Anglicans as an 'anti-Calvinist' trend in the English church have a significant degree of right on their side;[83] this was evidently a fight for the *via media* against a militant Reformed theology which was felt by the episcopacy and the crown to be a threat to the *status quo* in the church.

Only if we note the juxtaposition of rationalistic and spiritualistic elements can we also recognize those elements in Puritan and Anglican thought which prepared the way for the deistic approach and the biblical criticism which it produced as they were continued or argued against. The portrait of Deism has remained so fragmentary not least because so far scant attention has been paid to the continuity between the views typical of it and earlier developments in theology and the history of ideas. That is true particularly in the case of English Deism, which is the only branch of this very disparate movement to show a reasonable degree of coherence.[84] In fact numerous lines link Deism not only with the rationalistic branch of the 'left wing of the Reformation'[85] but also with the main trends within the dominant church against which its polemic was directed.

It is no coincidence that the formula which defines the character of Puritanism is best put negatively. For example, C.Hill says in a very general way: 'Puritans in Church polity and religion I shall take... to be those who remained within the State Church but wanted a cleaner break with popery'[86]; Breward comments: 'It included wide varieties of opinion and practice, but can broadly be applied to those who by reason of their religious experience and theological convictions were dissatisfied with the government and worship of the Church of England, but who nonetheless refused to separate.'[87] Still, M. van Beek has rightly observed: 'The problem of definition is largely a linguistic one.'[88,89]

(b) The history of the Puritan struggles

We can best see what the Puritans wanted and what their real motives were from their criticism of existing circumstances in the church and from events illustrating their basic attitude towards a particular form of conduct required by church and state or the specific demands which they addressed to the church at various times – that is why these events have been described regularly. The demands were not always the same, but changed over the course of time; they were always interspersed with lengthy periods of less proclamatory activity, though during these periods Puritan propaganda continued from the pulpits.[90] Later they became more wide-ranging than they were at the beginning, when what offended them seems to us to be less important and the conflicts easier to remove.[91]

1. The first occasion on which an explicitly Puritan attitude can be seen, though the name 'Puritan' was not yet current, is the conflict with

John Hooper, a refugee from England under Henry VIII who lived for a long time in Zurich and there came under the influence of Bullinger and John à Lasco.[92] After his return to England in 1549 he became a particularly radical zealot, as soon emerged on the occasion of his nomination to be Bishop of Gloucester in 1550.[93] Hooper refused to be consecrated bishop with the ordinal recently produced by Cranmer, because in it the oath of supremacy was formulated with an appeal to the saints and evangelists; and when this cause for offence was removed at a stroke by the king who, like the privy council, was well disposed to Hooper, he long persisted in his refusal to wear the vestments prescribed for the bishop at his consecration. It is interesting that Bucer replied to an enquiry by Cranmer that while vestments might not be desirable, they were not sin and could therefore be enjoined by authority;[94] this was also Luther's standpoint and that of most of the Reformers as well as the Anglicans, whereas only the Zurich Reformers urged the radical abolition of all the old liturgical forms.[95] The affair was settled relatively quickly by the submission of Hooper, who was in principle loyal to the state; he declared himself ready to wear the prescribed vestments at his consecration, but not in exercising his office, and as a result this remained an isolated episode. As early as in his fast sermons before the king in 1550,[96] Hooper had produced typically Puritan objections to vestments: all priestly vestments had slipped into the church as relics of the obsolete Aaronic priesthood and were moreover papist insignia; kneeling at the communion was forbidden because it could indicate an idolatrous veneration of the sacraments. Like Hooper and à Lasco,[97] John Knox argued two years later in a court sermon against kneeling to receive the host as provided for in the 1552 Prayer Book; thereupon the famous 'Black Rubric' was inserted as a marginal note in the text, saying that kneeling did not signify any adoration of the host, since that would be idolatry, because Christ is in heaven and cannot be in two places at the same time.[98] The dispute over the adiaphora which had broken out in Germany through the Augsburg (and Leipzig) Interim (1547-55) also came into the discussion: the position advocated in particular by Melanchthon[99] which was expressed in both the Interims worked out by theologians with Erasmian and Humanist inclinations in a formula to the effect that ceremonies and church government are adiaphora and therefore can be regulated by the authorities through ordinances, and that the *status confessionis* applied only in connection with statements of faith, was challenged above all by the South Germans and the Zwinglians on a national level (and also by the Gnesiolutherans in Saxony). As we can see, there were advocates of other positions both among the refugees from the Augsburg Interim, who came from the continent, and the returning English exiles who had fled from the persecutions under Henry VIII; both came across like-minded people in the English church, so that in these controversies we may rightly recognize the birth of the two parties of Anglicans and Puritans.

2. The confrontation which began under Edward VI continued in different circumstances during the reign of Mary among the English Protestants who had again been driven into exile. Events in the community of exiles in Frankfurt am Main in 1554 have become famous.[100] The radical group under Whittingham and Knox radically transformed the 1552 Prayer Book by the abolition of vestments, the sign of the cross, the litany, the responses and other parts of the liturgy and then, driven out by a political ploy, had to give place to an opposed party led by Richard Cox which stood for consistent observance of the forms provided for by the Prayer Book. Dickens rightly stresses that even this moderate group, which elsewhere, e.g. in Strasbourg and Zurich, included yet others, held to a completely Reformed theology, although it refused to adopt the strict Geneva order for England.[101] This too is a sign of the complexity of events and the breadth of the spectrum of theological trends to be found in the Church of England in the sixteenth and seventeenth century, factors which must be kept in mind if we are not to succumb to inadmissible simplification. It is again illuminating to see that Calvin himself, when summoned as an arbitrator over the Prayer Book by Knox and Whittingham, recommended that in the long run it should be replaced by a purer version, but still counselled concern for the weaker brethren.[102]

The same dispute over liturgical vestments flared up once again to a greater degree in the first period of the reign of Elizabeth I, in 1565.[103] The new ordering of conditions in the church under Elizabeth, on which great hopes had been set by the Protestant exiles at her accession, had disappointed those who were concerned for a far-reaching reform.[104] The Elizabethan Prayer Book of 1559 was more conservative than the book of 1551: the real presence was presupposed at the eucharist, the 'Black Rubric' was omitted, and a regulation about vestments was introduced. This laid the foundations for the new controversy which was prepared for in subsequent years by the formation of various attitudes and came to open conflict in 1565 as a result of a letter from the Queen to Archbishop Parker,[105] in which the bishops were required to impose uniformity in the question of vestments with all means at their disposal. Above all the ministers in London, led by R.Crowley, J.Philpot and J.Gough, firmly opposed this and defended their refusal to wear the prescribed vestments in a work, edited by Crowley, which became famous: *A Briefe Discourse against the Outwarde Apparell and Ministering Garments of the Popishe Church.*[106] The subsequent pamphlet war also produced A.Gilby's satirical: *A Pleasaunt Dialogue betweene a Souldier of Barwicke and an English Chaplaine* (first printed in 1581), in which the typical concerns of the Puritans were circulated for the first time in popular and sarcastic tones. The last printed work from the controversy, the collection *The Fortress of Fathers*,[107] deserves particular notice. Here a whole gallery of the ancestors of radical Puritanism appears in the form of extracts from a series of 'Fathers': after Ambrose and Theophylact we find 'Erasmus, the pearl of this age' before Bucer, Martyr, Epinus, Placius, Melanchthon, à Lasco, Bullinger, Musculus and Gualter.[108] As Trinterud observes,[109] this clearly denotes the character of this trend: 'The Genevan influence in the conflict was insignificant. The anticlerical and anticeremonial attitudes of the Christian Humanists and of Erasmus in particular, on the other hand, were clearly reflected.'

These controversies, too, came to an end relatively quickly because the main spokesmen of the Puritans were soon silenced by being carted off to the provinces. They were no separatists, but were ultimately ready to dispose themselves in one way or another, and this later contributed to the charge of vacillation which was levelled against them. This charge is certainly not justified in view of their limited aims.

3. L. Trinterud has divided his collection of texts *Elizabethan Puritanism*,[110] in such a way that he calls this group 'The Original, Anti-Vestment Party'. He distinguishes it from a second group, 'The Passive Resistance Party', in which he includes above all the famous preachers like E. Dering, R. Greenham, W. Perkins and J. Preston. It is clear that here we have an obviously independent group; however, the characterization attempted by Trinterud according to which this party too shared with the first an antipathy to vestments, ceremonies and 'popery' and in addition wanted to reform episcopacy and church government but sought to achieve this end by passive resistance rather than by force, does not seem to do justice to their character. Rather, we can recognize that the intentions of these men were in an essentially different direction; they were concerned above all with the personal piety and the life-style of the individual in the community, whereas political and church-political themes hardly concerned them, and not just for tactical reasons. Stoeffler's proposal that this movement should be called 'pietistic Puritanism'[111] is very illuminating, as we shall see in due course.

The third group is made up of the active Presbyterians like T. Cartwright, W. Fulke, J. Field and T. Wilcox, who emerged with their demands between 1570 and 1572. These men anticipated much that was then in fact changed in the Puritan revolution of the seventeenth century.[112] This group too failed to achieve its aims because of the opposition of the Crown, although it enjoyed support in lay circles and above all in Parliament. Its first champion Thomas Cartwright, who in his famous lectures on Acts given in Cambridge in 1570 declared that the Presbyterian order was the only one legitimated by the Bible,[113] was shortly afterwards removed from his chair, and even the various parliamentary moves between 1566 and 1585 led nowhere because of the Queen's intervention. We can get a good idea of the programme of this party from the characteristic manifestos which are now easily accessible in the reprint of the edition by Frere and Douglas.[114] The first and most important in the series, 'An Admonition to the Parliament'(1572),[115] contains a masterpiece of Puritan polemic against the organized church in which the principles and their biblical basis emerge very clearly. Another important work from this movement is W.Travers, *Ecclesiasticae disciplinae... explicatio*, soon translated as *A Full and Plaine Declaration of Ecclesiastical Discipline* (1574). However, there is some disagreement over its significance.[116] The anonymous Marprelate texts of 1588[117] are an example of satirical propaganda from this period; they again simply show a flare-up of the underground fires which were continuing to rage, a flare-up which was quickly suppressed. Even further out on the left wing were the early Separatists like Robert Harrison and Robert Browne.[118] The foundation of a Separatist community in Norwich in 1580 and the subsequent emigration of the sectarians to Middleburg in Holland has been noted carefully by the historians of Congregationalism. Despite the short-lived nature of the undertaking that is right, since here the principles to be found in the Puritan approach, above all the reference back to the apostolic period as the binding norm for church organization, are for the first time maintained with the utmost consistency in connection with the outward form of the church and the relationship between church and state.

4. After a short resurgence at the beginning of the reign of James I (in 1604-1607),[119] Puritan forces then emerged into full public view in the portentous years shortly before and during the Civil War, from 1638 onwards. They were in full view, after the abolition of all censorship in November 1640, in a flood of longer and shorter writings. A large number of these publications from 1640 onwards down through the time of the Commonwealth and Cromwell's rule have been preserved for us by the activity of the London bookseller George Thomason.[120] The discussion of the 1640s has also become widely known in the history of literature as a result of the part played in it by Milton and his early prose writings. These years first saw a final Presbyterian renaissance with the victory of this party through the summoning of the Long Parliament and the petitions and pamphlets that went with it. Then soon afterwards came a change in favour of the liberal wing in Puritanism, first of all the Independents and then the movements standing even further to the left, including the Diggers and Levellers. It came about through the failure of the Presbyterians in church politics, confronted as they were by Cromwell's army and the religious trends represented in it.

The sects in Cromwell's army, especially the so-called Levellers, have been much noted and celebrated in idealist and political historiography as the real or supposed ancestors of the modern democratical principles of tolerance and free thought.[121] More rarely is reference made to the religious background of their thought and the Christian origin of the concept of freedom even in people like J.Lilburne and R.Overton; on the other hand, a programme like that of the Levellers is particularly suitable for making clear the juxtaposition of Christian and Stoic thinking in Puritan views[122] and thus giving some indication of the development to be expected. This was to be characterized by the further incursion of Rationalism into the theology of the various parties represented in the English church. Of course the Levellers were 'radical' and their concepts about the ideal system of government were a reversal of the accepted notions of 'democracy from above'. However, the counter position which they also represented was shown to be one possible consequence, with the juxtaposition of ancient and Christian thought in contemporary theology.[123]

5. On the other side, it is impossible to draw a direct line from the Levellers to the thought of the eighteenth century, although they share rationalistic traits with the theology of the Enlightenment period. However, the English Deists will make it clear that the Enlightenment entered into the heritage of a whole breadth of theological thinking of the kind to be met within the church of the sixteenth and seventeenth centuries, and that there is no way of drawing a line between 'left' and 'right'. Furthermore, we should in no way limit our attention to the Puritans; among the Anglicans, too, we can find a juxtaposition of ideas from Christianity and from antiquity, except that with them the point of convergence comes on a different level. In the course of developments in the history of ideas and church politics it so happened that the Anglican position similarly became sharper and clearer in the decade before the Puritan revolution, through the dominating figure of Archbishop William Laud (1573-1643),[124] whose activity in church politics led to the immediate outbreak of revolution. He attempted to impose, by force and in direct association with the royal absolutism of Charles I, the Anglican standpoint on hierarchical government in the church and the use of ceremonies in worship. Only in more recent times have people come to see Laud in a more objective light and to recognize that his restrictive action in no way goes with a dogmatically rigid form of theological thinking. Rather, in many features, like his rational approach and the idea of tolerance, he comes very close to the spirit of the time. The position which can only be seen in embryo, theoretically, with him, because he was principally a man of action, is developed into a consistent system by his protégé William Chillingworth,[125] in his well-known work *The Religion of Protestants a Safe Way to Salvation* (1637). The

basic arguments of this book directly prepare the way for the deistic standpoint of the time of the Enlightenment.

When we consider the English Puritans, it is useful also to cast a glance at New England, at the first Puritan settlements on American soil. The writing of the New England Puritans in particular has become far better known above all through the works of Perry Miller, but now also through other American scholars,[126] and in part is also already better edited than the literature of the mother country. In the well-known Cotton-Williams controversy,[127] the separatistic background of Williams' demand for tolerance and above all the use of scripture as a basis for argumentation by him and his Presbyterian opponent Cotton becomes very clear.[128] On the whole, however, in America the development took a different course from that in England, where the collapse of the Puritan experiment and the restoration of the Stuarts in 1660, along with the Glorious Revolution of 1688, indicated marked changes in the cultural situation as well. In the Colonies and on the American continent, however, the Puritan tradition continued to be effective right down to the middle of the eighteenth century.[129]

(c) The understanding of the Bible among Puritans and Conformists down to the beginning of the seventeenth century

In all these controversies over the church and its forms, corresponding to the aspect of the Reformation from which they start, the relationship of the various parties to the Bible played a decisive role. Hitherto, there has been little study of the close connection which exists between church-political attitudes at that time and the understanding of the Bible among Puritans and Anglicans. There are a number of reasons for this, which are basically connected with the historical accounts presented in most recent research into Puritanism. Both political historiography and the more recent social and economic history which supplement it tended to underestimate the part played by intellectual developments in the context of the external course of events, and the history of ideas usually misunderstands the enormous part played by theology at this time, while the history of theology seldom looks at biblical hermeneutics because hitherto the history of exegesis has regarded this period as a pre-critical age and therefore found it somewhat unattractive.

1. However, we can already recognize with William Tyndale (c.1495-1536),[130] who has been called 'the founder of English Puritanism',[131] the particular role which the understanding of the Bible was to come to play in English theology. For a while[132] Tyndale was strongly influenced by Luther. He followed Luther closely in the way in which he translated the Bible and clearly presents his doctrine of law and gospel in the Prologue to the New Testament of 1525.[133] However, after

he began the translation of the Old Testament in 1528 (in 1530 he published *Five Books of Moses, Called The Pentateuch*[134]) another approach gradually established itself in his writings in which the law took on a new positive significance on the basis of the gospel. In the prologue to the *Pentateuch* Tyndale can describe the usefulness of scripture in two ways: 'So now the scripture is a light and sheweth vs the true waye, both what to do, and what to hope.'[135] As early as the second edition of the Prologue to the New Testament, printed separately in 1531,[136] a series of passages are inserted in which he explicitly refers to the significance of 'actions' for Christian life[137] and invites people 'to follow the steps of Christ'.[138] His translation of Jonah appeared in the same year,[139] and in the Prologue there is a passage which Clebsch[140] cites as the clearest statement of a new understanding of the law in Tyndale: 'The scripture containeth three things in it: first the law, to condemn all flesh; secondarily, the gospel, that is to say, promises of mercy for all that repent and acknowledge their sins at the preaching of the law, and consent in their hearts that the law is good, and submit themselves to be scholars to learn to keep the law...'[141] In *Pathway* we read: ' And thus repentance and faith begin at our baptism and first professing the laws of God...'[142] In much the same way as we have seen in Erasmus, the law is internalized: we also find clear expressions of this in the version of the Prologue to the New Testament of 1534: 'The gospell is glad tydynges of mercie and grace and that oure corrupt nature shalbe healed agayne for christes sake and for the merites of his deseruinges onlye: Yet on the condicion that we will turne to God, to learn to kepe his lawes spiritually, that is to say, of loue for his sake, and wyll also soffre the curynge of oure infirmyties.'[143] Or in the Prologue to Romans:[144] 'To fulfill the lawe is, to do the workes therof and what soeuer the lawe commaundeth, with loue, lust and inward affeccion and delectacion: and to lyue godly and well, frely, willingly, and with oute compulcion of the lawe, euen as though therewere no lawe at all.'[145] For this the Holy Spirit is necessary, which is given through faith. Clebsch speaks of a 'bifocal theology of gospel and law',[146] which is expressed in these remarks, since Tyndal retains the central Lutheran message of law and gospel; faith in the gospel becomes the presupposition of fulfilling the law in a new way. In principle it keeps its binding character; what has changed is the motivation towards it. Clebsch can sum up in a few sentences the basic ideas of the *Pathway*, which he calls the *magna charta* of later Puritanism because in it the attitude of later Puritanism is prefigured in a remarkably clear way:[147] it contains two ideas from the Reformation: justification comes about through faith and not by works; scripture is the possession of Christians. The direction is a thoroughly moral one : 'the Christian life consisted in adhering to a moral system that looked to the Bible for a sufficient guide to all ethical decisions; the true Christian society was a commonwealth of saints living singly and together according to scripture.'

It is also significant that given his view of the law, Tyndale can see the Old Testament and the New Testament as standing on the same level. Tyndale's preface to the New Testament contains noteworthy remarks about the relationship between the law in the Old Testament and the gospel in the New: 'And because the lawe (which is a doctryne thorow teachynge euery man his dutye, doth vtter our corrupt nature) is sufficiently described by Moses, therfore is lytle mencion made therof in the new testament, save of love only wherin all the lawe is included.'[148] Naturally even according to Tyndale's view the ceremonial regulations, above all in the Book of Leviticus, are no longer valid; by contrast the moral commandments remain in force unaltered. According to the Prologue to the Book of Exodus Moses is 'an ensample vnto all princes and to all that are in authorite, how to rule vnto goddes pleasure and vnto their neyghbours profette'.[149] The chief significance of the New Testament is that it provides the motivation for keeping the commandments that are materially present in the Old Testament.[150] The fact that the Old Testament largely remains in force – *qua* law – in a literal sense at the same time stands in the way of the typological understanding of Moses and Aaron as figures of Christ.[151] Tyndale's overall judgment on the usefulness of the whole of scripture can therefore be summed up in an early statement which has already been mentioned: 'So now the scripture is a light and sheweth vs the true waye, both what to do, and what to hope.'[152] This move towards the *de facto* identification of the Old Testament with the New in a legalistic understanding sets a course which in many respects is to become significant for the later development of English Protestantism.

The incorporation of the idea of the covenant into the overall conception I have described is characteristic of the last period in Tyndale's activity.[153] The idea of the covenant is the clamp by which he finally succeeds in holding together two sets of ideas: redemption through Christ in faith without the law and the validity for Christians of moral obligations on the fulfilment of which salvation depends. Tyndale inserts a comment into the revised Prologue to the 1534 edition of the Five Books of Moses: '...all the promyses thorow out the hole scripture do include a couenant. That is: god byndeth him selfe to fulfil that mercie vnto the, onlye if thou wilt endeuore thy selfe to kepe his lawes.'[154] The Preface to his new edition of the New Testament of November 1534 immediately starts to discuss the covenant: 'The generall covenaunt wherin all other are comprehended and included, is this. If we meke oure selves to god, to kepe all his lawes, after the ensample of Christ: then God hath bounde him selfe vnto vs to kepe and make good all the mercies promysed in Christ, thorowout all the scripture.'[155]

In this last period as it were a change has taken place over against Luther's doctrine of the free grace of God and the justification of the sinner without the works of the law: of course there is still mention of grace in Christ, but the way in which God is bound by the promise is clearly conditioned by the fulfilment of the law and made dependent on it. As a consequence the fate of those who reject the covenant, or first believe and then do not offer the obedience that is required of them, is vividly depicted in colours drawn from the Old Testament curses.[156] The new edition with marginal glosses and prologues to the various individual writings is, as Tyndale already declares in the Preface, oriented on the notion of the covenant understood in this way: 'For all the promyses of the mercie and grace...are made vpon the condicion that we kepe the lawe.'[157]

A second line which can also be observed in Tyndale is his open hostility to the ceremonial and institutional heritage of the mediaeval church. One sign of this is the way in which he constantly renders the New Testament *presbyteros* as 'senior' (in 1531 changed to 'elder')[158] instead of the 'priest' required by More. Tyndale also wrote the strongly anti-hierarchical writing *The practyse of Prelates...* (1530),[159] the larger part of which contains an example of the typically humanistic and spiritualistic understanding of history: the assumption of an ideal period of Christianity in the earliest church with a subsequent falling away, which for Tyndale begins at the moment when the priests take control in the church. The polemic is openly directed against the papacy as the source of centuries of idolatry in the church; underlying this is an attack on the episcopal system in general. For Tyndale, it also follows that he regards the New Testament form of the community, which he naturally believes to be clear and obvious,[160] as being also the normative model for the reform of the present constitution of the church which he requires. Similarly, he always renders the word *ekklesia* as 'congregacion'. In a sphere which was to be characteristic of later English theology, Tyndale still did pioneering work in a special way: he was the first to conceive of what has been called a national covenant theology.[161] He developed his thinking on this theme above all in the Prologue to Jonah, which has already been mentioned. There we have a pronounced expression of the view that England has an obligation to observe its own temporal, national laws, like the covenant people of Deuteronomy, who in Deut. 28 are confronted not only with the blessing but above all with the curse if they should break the covenant law. The catastrophes in their own national history become examples of the way in which nations who break their temporal, national covenant law are summoned to repentance by crises. This leads to an appeal to people in the present to have a concern for the prosperity in all material things which has been promised on these conditions, by showing penitence and new obedience to the laws (this is how Tyndale understands the task of the Reformation). Thus the Old Testament, and especially Deuteronomy, takes on the character of a direct model for contemporary English politics.[161a] The long-term effect of these ideas was tremendous and will continue to occupy us at length.

There is a second element which is closely connected with this first one: Spalding[162] indicates that in his coronation sermon for Edward VI, Archbishop Cranmer described the young ruler as a new Josiah who, like the reforming king of the Old Testament, will put aside idolatry and the tyranny of the papacy, guard against vice, reward virtue and practise righteousness.[163] However, this notion is already older than the reign of the young king, since even under Henry VIII theologians and humanists had transformed the mediaeval pattern of the hierarchical ordering of society in a national sense, and in so doing had given the king a central role.[164] Already at that time (mixed up with other motivations) we find an endorsement of the peerless position of the king which is derived from the Old Testament;[165] at the same time, as early as this period we have the development of the theory of an obedience which is unconditionally owed to the king even if he is a tyrant.[166]

One can read from the development of Tyndale's theology how at a very early stage the moral and anticeremonial tendencies already establish themselves in the face of the legacy of the Reformation; both of these, like rational thinking, represent trends deriving from the Middle Ages. In this connection we should not be deceived by the vigorous polemic against the Roman church, 'popery', since this it is presented according to the conventions of the old opposition, that of Humanism and Spiritualism, not least in its references to scripture. This is why at a later stage this polemic could so easily be transferred to the institution of the episcopal Church of England, while the Reformed doctrine remained intact in dogmatic terms. This course of events is not limited to England; as has long been recognized, a similar pattern can often be found in the Reformed churches on the Continent. So Tyndale's theology has been compared with that of Zurich, though no direct connection can be established between Tyndale and people there.[167] Evidently these are parallel developments, though in the long run they are much more marked in England.

During the whole of the heyday of Puritanism confrontation with the Catholics remained the breeding ground on which anti-ceremonial and anti-hierarchical propaganda developed and always found a ready hearing among the public. As early as the time of Henry VIII, when it was not yet possible to talk in terms of a Reformation in the evangelical sense, the anti-ceremonial weapon was wielded by the first fighters who had been influenced by Humanism and the Reformation. Under

Thomas Cromwell the state itself made use of certain iconoclastic writings in implementing the royal claim to supremacy and appropriating church property for the crown, which in this way found iconoclasm extremely useful.[168] During Henry's last years, when his politics had again shifted in a clearly Catholic direction and a series of prominent Protestants fled to the continent, vigorous anti-Roman polemic thundered out from the ranks of the exiles. William Turner's work *The Huntyng and Fyndyng Out of the Romish Foxe*,[169] which we shall be discussing shortly, combines criticism of priests and criticism of the cult with hostility to Rome by attempting to demonstrate to Henry VIII that the treacherous clergy are concealing the Pope and his works, which have just been driven out of England, in the customs of the English church. Fears of a re-Catholicizing of England, which came to a climax with the papal ban and Bull of Deposition dated 25 February 1570 against Elizabeth I, were quite justified throughout the greater part of Elizabeth's reign. Abroad there was confrontation with Spain, and at home there was opposition to the Reformation, and temporary reassurance came only with the defeat of the Armada in 1588.[170] The fears revived again to a lesser degree under Charles I: he was suspected of having pro-Catholic sympathies because his French wife was a Roman Catholic. They were more widespread during the long-drawn-out attempts to regain the throne made by the Catholic James II and later his son, the Pretender, after the former's deposition and flight. These religious struggles in fact extend down to our own time in the tragedy of Northern Ireland.

In essentials, the writings of those who were exiled under Henry continue the line begun with Tyndale. In R.Barnes' *Vitae Romanorum pontificorum*[171] there is a new example of the view of history with which we are already familiar, contrasting the purity of the original church with the periods of decay which inexorably set in soon afterwards. Here the innovations introduced by the Popes in the mediaeval church are continually the dark undertone to the description of the lives of the Popes which are drawn together from all kinds of material. Even more important is the work by Turner mentioned above, *The Huntyng and Fyndyng Out of the Romish Foxe*,[172] for in a way which has still not been noted sufficiently it contains the hermeneutical principles of later Puritanism. The logical starting point of all its criticism of the church is a legalistic biblicism. The Bible has to take the place of the canon law which hitherto has governed the outward form of the church: 'for the law of Christes chirche, of which englōd (England) is on(e) part is the new testamēt & the old / that is to wit the doctrine that the /Prophetes / the Apostelles & Christ taught...'[173] The earliest church was the ideal church: 'But in Christes tyme and the Apostelles tyme and in the tymes of the holy martyres was the most perfit chirch.' It follows from this:

'therfor then was the perfitest law of the chirche / then the law of Christes chirche / was in the Apostelles tyme all ready made & so perfit that no man could make any thing more perfit.'[174] The humanistic conception of the ideal primal period is bound up with a legalistic understanding of scripture. This belongs in the context of a way of thinking which still lacks the chronological and historical dimension; that becomes clear in Turner's observation: 'The word of god which is the law of the chirch lasteth for euer & is not changed / so that the chirche of Christ at all tymes hathe no other law but Christes word.'[175]

The conciusions which Turner draws from this principle are, however, only indirectly connected with it. His line of thought runs in another direction, as we can see from the overall construction of his writing. To begin with[176] he gives a long list of church customs and practices in England which in his view still perpetrate 'the popes doctrine and traditiones'. The list begins with the sign of the cross (as we saw, an age-old stumbling block[177]), mentions blessing of water and salt, churches and vestments, the traditional form of the sacrament (the chalice, and also the mixing of elements, vicarious receiving for the dead, and so on) and also the canon of the mass, its Latin form, fast times and oaths, the celibacy of the priests. Some of these are features which all the Reformers wanted to have abolished, but there is also much evidence of a basically polemical attitude towards ceremonies which can also be noted in all the accentuation on scripture. In the case of each individual feature to be discussed we are given the Pope (and in some instances the Council) through whom it was introduced; the author is concerned above all to demonstrate that a particular feature is popish, and only in a later part of the work[178] does he also go on to demonstrate that it is not in accordance with scripture either.

In addition to its main content, Turner's writing also contains some further features which are characteristic of later Puritan theology. Mention should be made of the Exodus typology which appears in Turner's interpretation of Henry VIII's Declaration of Supremacy: the action of the king, who drove the Pope out of England, 'intended suche a thynge as all myghty god dyd when he delyuered the chylder of Israel from the bondage of Pharao / and drove the chanaanites of theyr lande that the true Israelites myght haue that land and succede them.'[179] Referring to Lev.18(1ff.), he goes on to declare: 'So learned men whom the kyng apoynted to delyuer hys subiecties from the bondage of the Romish Pharao the pope / ought to haue sweped the chirch & dryuen quite out of it all that euer any pope had made...'[180] The negative type, Pharaoh/ the Pope, is established even more directly than the positive, in which Henry's role is deliberately left vague. In connection with Turner's attitude towards the Old Testament it should be observed that among the proof texts used in examining ceremonies the Old Testament quotations are profusely mixed up with those from the New. The central, basic conclusion about the use of the sign of the cross ('I haue proued now by sufficient witnesses of the scripture / that to worship before an image is to worship it'[181]) is justified by Ex.20(4); Lev.20 (1f.); Deut. 4 (15-19); 27 (15); 5(8).[182] On the other hand, there is a clear distinction between the 'Law of Moses', which was only for the Jews, and the 'law of the gospel'(sic!) which is valid only for Christians.[183] In this respect Turner is still very close to the attitude of the Erasmians.

2. A basic humanist trait can also be followed through the later statements of the 'Anti-Vestment Party'. One interesting document which above all illuminates the relationship of the radical Puritans to the Bible is the *Notae* of Hooper to the State Council of 3 October 1550. Here he gives reasons for his rejection of vestments.[184] Right at the beginning Hooper puts the demand: *Nihil est Ecclesiae in vsu habendum, quod non aut expressum Dei verbum habeat quo se tueatur, aut alioqui res sit ex se indifferens, quae facta, et vsurpata, nihil prosit, infecta vero, et praetermissa nihil obsit.* One postulate of the Reformation as a whole was that scripture (*verbum Dei*) must be the basis not only of doctrine but also of church life. However, Luther and his followers argued that in external forms of church life anything was permissible that was not expressly forbidden in scripture. This position is the starting point for the doctrine of adiaphora developed by Melanchthon,[185] which distinguishes between the sphere of dogmatics, where only *pura doctrina* may count, and the sphere of ceremonies and church government, which is neutral and which may be regulated by the authorities. At first glance Hooper's introductory sentence seems to follow this division between what is commanded by scripture and the adiaphora. The syllogism which continues it, however, *Priuata et pecularia vestimenta in Ministerio, non habent verbum dei quo praecipiuntur, neque sunt res ex se Indifferentes. Ergo non sunt in vsu habenda*, cannot be understood on Melanchthon's presuppositions. Evidently he deliberately does away with this distinction between the two spheres of doctrine and outward church forms: these, too, are not indifferent, but must be regulated by scripture as the supreme authority. That is true not only in respect of Hooper's second condition, in which he declares that things commanded or prohibited by God include not only those for which there is an explicit command or prohibition but also those which can be derived from the general tenor of scripture (examples may be infant baptism or the admission of women to the eucharist). More important is the fact that his first *Nota* stands Melanchthon's attitude to the adiaphora on its head: *Res Indifferentes, originem suam et fundamentum in verbo Dei habere debent. Nam quod ex verbo Dei probari non potest, non est ex fide, fides autem ex auditu verbi Dei. Rom.10(17).* On closer examination Hooper is not caught here in a logical contradiction to his opening sentences, since even according to his view

the adiaphora do not have the *expressum Dei verbum*. But they do have *originem et fundamentum* in the Word: there is no sphere within the church which is not to be regulated by the norm of scripture.[186] This comment corresponds exactly with the attitude which Hooper also took consistently and emphatically elsewhere. As W.M.S.West has shown,[187] it is the result of his early contact with the writings of Bullinger and above all the fruit of his lengthy stay in Zurich. West quotes from the contemporary work by Lavater about church praxis in Zurich, *De Ritibus et Institutis Ecclesiae Tigurinae*,[188] the central statement: 'Nothing is done in the church of Zurich which was not the practice of the church at the time of the apostles.'[189] In Zurich Hooper had had the opportunity of seeing the churches stripped of all decoration and of all superfluous ceremonies and returned to a form of worship which in the view of Bullinger and others there corresponded to the earliest Christian customs, the chief characteristic of which they believed to be the utmost simplicity. For them simplicity was at the same time purity, and Hooper also based the rest of his activity in England on this postulate. As it was in reality a humanistic ideal, so too Hooper's most important theological presupposition was the legalistic conception of the covenant:[190] for him the covenant signified first of all the offer of divine grace to all men, but it could be realized only through unconditional obedience to God's commandments. Here the statements of the Decalogue were normative as being basic conditions of the law.[191] Against this background it is also not surprising that for Hooper there is only one covenant and that the church of the Old and New Testaments is one and the same.[192] The covenant concluded with Adam after the Fall (Gen.3.15)[193] still holds today, but it binds God in his offer of grace only insofar as people respond to him by being obedient to the commandments. The area which is to be governed by scripture is therefore extended enormously, so that we can arrive at the position which Cranmer, the representative from the established church, puts ironically: 'It is not commanded in the scripture to kneel, and whatsoever is not commanded in the Scripture is against the scripture and utterly unlawful and ungodly.'[194] Now what determines what has its *originem et fundamentum* in Holy Scripture? Evidently there is need for some additional criterion if something is not supported by the *expressum Dei verbum*. At this point the whole weakness of Hooper's position becomes evident. He attempts to provide a criterion in his third demand: *Res Indifferentes, manifestam, et apertam vtilitatem cognitam in Ecclesia habere debent, ne videantur frustra recipi, aut fraude ac dolo in Ecclesiam intrudi*. The key word here is *vtilitas*, the use that something must have if it is to be introduced into the church, even though it is only an outward form.[195] However, in itself the term is vague, and the other expressions like *fides*, which appears in the same context in the first and second *Notae*, or truth, which appears in the third, are not much more help. The most concrete is *aedificatio* in the third: the term 'edification' denotes an important aim of the Puritans. But the rejection of vestments and ceremonies is a purely negative matter, and the fact that Hooper cannot cite any clear reasons for it nor even indicate why it does not contribute to edification but is rather directly opposed to it is connected with the fact that there are no such obvious reasons. In reality, 'not in accordance with scripture' is only the label for a rejection which stems from quite different, emotional reasons. These also underlie the observation in the second *Nota*, that things in accordance with scripture must be in accord with nature. Vestments and ceremonies are rejected because of old feelings against ceremonies. Hooper cannot say this, presumably because he was not clearly aware of it.

3. The point of dispute between Conformists and Puritans becomes clearer in the controversy carried on between Whitgift and Cartwright. While it took place considerably later in time – and in this respect we must anticipate somewhat – its subject-matter is largely parallel to the argument between Hooper and Cranmer over the Puritan *Admonition to the Parliament*.[196] After D.J.McGinn had depicted its outward course and brought together the elements of the controversy, J.S.Coolidge made a perceptive investigation of it, though his judgment on the Puritan approach must be examined more closely.[197] In the controversy between Whitgift and Cartwright, too, what is at stake is the role of the authority of scripture, and Coolidge rightly asserts that the character of the Puritan attitude can only be understood by a grasp of the various attitudes of the Puritans and Conformists to scripture.[198] The starting point of the discussion between Whitgift and Cartwright is also approximately similar to that in the encounter between Hooper and his interpreter Cranmer. On the statement 'those things only are to be placed in the church which the Lord himself in his word commandeth', Whitgift comments, 'As though they should say, nothing is to be tolerated in the church... except it be expressed in the word of God.' Cartwright retorts in a rage: 'Many things are both commanded and forbidden, for which there is no express mention in the word, which are as necessarily to be followed or avoided as those whereof express mention is made.'[199] Thus in addition to what is mentioned expressly in scripture or is to be derived from it by comparison (Hooper's *Nota* 2), there is a further group of things the regulation of which is bindingly subject to the effects of the authority of scripture. This corresponds exactly to Hooper's first *Nota*. Whitgift cannot understand that: he thinks, 'there is nothing necessary to eternal life which is not both "commanded" and "expressed" in the scripture.'

Evidently the Puritans have a still further criterion which they apply to the church and make the basis of their demands in all specific points in dispute between them and their Anglican conversation partners. In connection with the 'Admonition to the Parliament', where this background is particularly obvious, J.C.Spalding has recently established that in addition to the two *notae ecclesiae* established by the Reformers, the Puritans have a third *nota* of the church, namely that its order is shaped on the biblical pattern; this is as binding for them as the right administration of word and sacrament.[200] It is illuminating that this third *nota* does not appear in either Luther or Calvin (nor even in Bullinger). As Spalding observes, it occurs, rather, among the first theologians to be influenced by Humanism (as we might add): Erasmus, Sarcerius, Bucer and Melanchthon.[201] Through the exiles who fled in the reign of Mary it made a later mark on English Puritanism under Elizabeth I. In this way influences which had played an important role in the shaping of the English church under theologians like Bucer and P. Martyr Vermigli brought from the Continent for the Reformation in the time of Edward VI were taken up and further strengthened. As to possible influences from Geneva, a decisive point is that Calvin himself kept strictly to the two Reformation *notae* and is not responsible for the ideas developed in this direction under the English exiles in Geneva at the time of Mary.

He follows Melanchthon's view of the adiaphora. Like Hooper, Cartwright establishes four basic rules for the authority of Scripture, 'which St Paul gave in such cases as are not particularly mentioned of in the scripture':

'I Cor.x.32 The first, that they offend not any, especially the church of God.

I Cor. xiv.40 The second is... that all be done in order and comeliness.

I Cor. xiv.26 The third, that all be done to edifying.

Rom.xiv.6-7 The last, that they be done to the glory of God.'[202]

Generally speaking, in Cartwright's view also, by no means all ceremonies are laid down in scripture; indeed the church has freedom to change them depending on circumstances; yet, 'all things in the church should be appointed according to the word of God', i.e. in accordance with the rules above.[203] Here we evidently arrive at the same point as Hooper in his first *Nota*, that the indifferent things would also have to have their origin and basis in the Word of God. In the second *Nota* this is described in terms of the demand that there should be agreement with the *proportio fidei ac Scripturae*; in the third there is reference to the concept of 'edification', which is apparently to be identified with 'usefulness' in the community. It is striking that in his third rule Cartwright uses the same concept: evidently this sums up what is said in the first and second rules. It is only the fourth rule which adds a new, typically Calvinistic perspective.

Thus, as we can see, in their demand that all forms of the church's life should be in agreement with scripture the Puritans take a decisive step beyond the position of the Conformists. Their standpoint is addressed many times by Whitgift in the controversy: 'In matters of order, ceremonies, and government, it is sufficient if they "be not repugnant to the scripture". Neither do I think any great difference to be betwixt "not repugnant to the word of God" and "according to the word".'[204] It is enough for the Conformist if something, in negative terms, is not *against* scripture; from a logical point of view he cannot see any difference in the positive formulation. Evidently the Puritans do not succeed in expressing the real background to their particular demands in a way which makes sense to their conversation partners. The deeper cause of this dilemma lay in the fact that, as one modern observer has put it,[205] the Puritans had no 'philosophy': their arguments 'sprang from a deep inner conviction and an attitude of mind' and therefore could hardly be put forward as rational arguments.

4. The position of the Conformists was first developed in principle, in a way which was not just limited to practical aspects, by Richard Hooker in his *Laws of Ecclesiastical Polity*.[206,207] This work has rightly become famous, since in it Hooker was able to pursue to its roots the epistemological problem which underlay the controversy between the two parties within the English church. Moreover, from the attitude of the anti-Puritans, which hitherto had been put forward more on an emotional basis, he was able to develop a clear system incorporating the normative presuppositions of the time which was to have an influence extending far beyond the later revolutions in knowledge.[208] The question of the authority of scripture was a central point in the discussion as carried on between, say, Whitgift and Cartwright. 'But Hooker saw that the issue went even deeper and that it involved the nature of all authority, in religion, politics, and social life, and man's intellectual freedom.'[209] Therefore Hooker began a whole stage earlier and in the first book of his *Laws* concerned himself with the forms of the law as the ultimate authority which underlies all human action. It is easy to see that the ideas which he develops are a resumption of Thomism with its basis in Aristotelian philosophy;[210] as on the Continent, so too in England, with Hooker scholasticism returns to the theology of a Reformation church.

As with Thomas, so too with Hooker an ethic with an eudaemonistic bent is the real starting point for theological systematics: 'Man doth seeke a triple perfection: first a sensuall, consisting in those things which very life it selfe requireth...; then an intellectuall... lastly a spirituall and divine...'[211] As in Thomas, the combination of the Aristotelian picture of the world and Platonic spiritualist dualism leads to the distinction between nature and supernature: since the ultimate goal of perfection cannot be attained in a natural way because of Adam's fall, God has opened up the 'supernatural way'[212] which leads by redemption through the cross of Christ to the three goals of faith, love and hope.[212a] The division of the *Laws* is based on this foundation. For Hooker, as for Thomas and Plato, the law was a basic pillar of the ordering of the world; to begin with, he distinguishes in an original way between three stages of the law: the 'law of nature', the orderly activity of creation in its various naturally given functions,[213] the 'celestial law' in accordance with which the angels judge themselves,[214] and the forms of the law intended by God for man. Man, too, is inspired by the wish for perfection; reason is the capacity which shows him what the good is: 'For the lawes of welldoing are the dictates of right reason.'[215] For these reasons man can follow the Law of Reason: 'there is nothing in it but anie man (having naturall perfection of wit, and ripenes of judgement) may by labour and travayle finde out.' For this law 'comprehendeth all those thinges which men by the light of their naturall understanding evidently know, or at leastwise may know, to be beseeming or unbeseeming, vertuous or vitious, good or evill for them to doe.'[216] State law and international law belong in this sphere; the role of authority consists essentially in codifying the law of reason, administering reward and punishment and thus strengthening its position.[217] Thus positive law is added to natural law.

However, as perfection cannot be attained by the means of the state either, at this point the significance of the 'supernatural way' begins. For earthly happiness cannot be man's ultimate goal; if this goal is unlimited goodness, then it is God alone, and infinite happiness is complete union with God.[218] 'Laws therefore concerning these things are supernatural';[219] an ultimate distinction is that between 'natural laws' and 'supernatural' laws. This provides the reason why a scriptural revelation is necessary alongside the light of reason, by which man already recognizes the good of his own accord: the distinctive character of scripture lies in the metaphysical sphere.[220] However, we can see how narrow is this sphere in which faith, hope and love have their place from the fact that according to Hooker the laws of nature and of reason also appear in scripture.[221] The use of this is twofold: 'for they are either such as we of ourselves could not easily have found out, and then... the evidence of God's own testimony added to the natural assent of reason concerning the certainty of them.'[222] Moreover, according to Heb.4.12 they have the capacity to penetrate the innermost corner of the heart which is hardly ever reached by the law of nature, and never by human laws.[223]

At the end of these considerations Hooker introduces a last definition which is decisive in his controversy with the Puritans: all four kinds of laws – those of individual ethics, the state, international law and finally the natural and positive laws laid down by God – contain natural and positive laws.[224] 'Lawes that concerne supernaturall duties are all positive.'[225] But whether man or God himself is the author of these positive laws, 'alteration they so far forth admit, as the matter doth exact.'[226] If their aim remains the same (as e.g. the teaching of redemption through Christ) they too are eternally valid; however, if they relate to transitory circumstances of human life in state or church, they are changeable (for example, the whole of the Old Testament ceremonial law).[227] At this point we find Melanchthon's doctrine of the adiaphora again, which distinguishes between the sphere of dogmatics and external institutions.

On the basis of these presuppositions Hooker can then go on in the second book of his *Laws* to discuss the question of the authority of scripture with the Puritans. He thinks that the dispute about it would soon be ended if only the Puritans would concede two things: 'the first is, not to extend the actions whereof they speak so low as that instance doth import of taking up a straw,[228] but rather keepe themselves at the least, within the compasse of morall actions, actions which have in them vice or vertue; the second, not to exact at our hands for every action the knowledge of some place of scripture... but rather... to acknowledge, that it sufficeth if such actions be framed according to the lawe of reason; the generall axiomes, rules, and principles of which law being so frequent in holy scripture...'[229] Otherwise scripture and the law of nature can supplement one another in the happiest of ways: 'It sufficeth therefore that nature and scripture doe serve in such full sort, that they both joyntly and not severallye eyther of them be so complete, that unto everlasting felicitie wee neede not the knowledge of any thing more then these two, may easily furnish our mindes with on all sides.'[230] The moral-legalistic understanding of scripture is common to both Puritans and Conformists.

We can see from the example of Hooker to what extent the moral rationalism of scholasticism has asserted itself in the theology of the English state church towards the end of the sixteenth century, though the Reformation doctrine of sin and grace has still found a place in his description of the 'supernatural way'.

The picture of man which underlies Hooker's view is not that of the Reformation, in which the recognition of the totality of sin is the dominant motive. Rather his work is dominated by the mediaeval Thomistic picture of man, according to which human reason is not completely corrupted by the Fall; though it is weakened, it is still in a position to follow the natural law created by God.[231] On the other hand, the arguments reproduced here are so strongly reminiscent of later Enlightenment ways of thinking that the continuity of the ancient heritage becomes much clearer than it does against the background of the usual division into a sequence of periods in the history of ideas and of theology.[232] This will become even clearer when we turn to the period of Deism.

5. But what is to be said about the Puritan approach? Evidently their theology is of a monistic kind: they seek to orientate the centre not only of their faith but of the whole of church life, including the ceremonial organization of the liturgy and church order, directly on the Word of God (scripture). Cartwright cannot concede 'that there is some star or light of reason or learning or other help whereby some act may be well done, and acceptably unto God, in which the word of God was shut out and not called to counsel.'[233] So should one conclude from their opposition to the Conformists and their reference to scripture that Puritans are to be said to have a Reformation theology in the strict sense?[234] The observations of Perry Miller in his report *The Marrow of Puritan Divinity*[235], which has meanwhile become a classic, prevent us from drawing such a conclusion. Miller describes the use of the idea of the covenant in Puritan theology at the beginning of the seventeenth century, and this gives us a clear view of the systematic philosophical presuppositions of Puritan thought. From his findings we get the impression that these are closest to the models of thought used by the Conformists; indeed at root they are identical with them. J.Möller, who takes Miller's investigations further, recalls the origins of the Reformed covenant theology with Calvin on the one hand and Zwingli and Bullinger on the other. At the same time he makes clear the different colouring which distinguishes the Zurich understanding of the covenant from Calvin's covenant theology.[236] In Zwingli and still more clearly in Bullinger the ethical demands stand at the centre of the idea of the covenant: the covenant is given by God's free grace, the sacraments are signs or seals of the covenant, but the emphasis lies on the sanctification which is required by the covenant: the obligation for Christians to serve only God, to trust him and to follow his commandments.[237] A second important viewpoint is continuity: the covenant which according to Gen.17 God already concluded with Abraham applies to the church, since it has been confirmed and established by Christ; furthermore, it is the link which binds together salvation history from the Old Testament down to the present. Calvin, too, stresses the continued validity of the covenant[238] in the well-known statement: *Patrum omnium foedus adeo substantia et re ipsa nihil a nostro differt, ut unum prorsus atque idem sit...*, but he continues: *administratio tamen variat.*[239] Through Jesus Christ the covenant has taken on a new quality, it is a covenant of grace. It is grounded on the free grace of God alone; its obligations are fulfilled by the satisfaction of Christ on the cross; and sins are forgiven. On man's side nothing is required for his salvation but believing in the promises of the covenant. Calvin finds the way back to the Old Testament through christological typology: according to Rom.10.4, the 'law' (here

= Old Testament) has its goal in Christ; Abraham was already directed towards Christ as the way to salvation and the content of his hope in the covenant which God concluded with him (Gal.3.6-9). The Jews lived only for this future, whereas we issue out of the redemption which has already taken place. In this way, a unity between the scriptures of Old and New Testament was found, but within them the distinction between law and gospel in the Pauline sense still holds: the *nuda lex* is the law that kills; as *lex per se* it keeps its place in the economy only as the law which convinces of sin, as outward proclamation, whereas it is the efficacy of the spirit in Christ which brings life.

Covenant theology has already reached a more progressive stage of development among the Puritans of the second half of the sixteenth century. Various more recent observers have pointed out that these theologians cannot be separated from the contemporary representatives of continental Reformed scholastic theology whose writings were evidently well known to them.[240] The distinction between a 'covenant of works' made with Adam before the Fall[241] and a covenant of grace made with Abraham first appears in the Heidelberg theologian Z. Ursinus.[242] The Puritans Cartwright, Fenner, Perkins and others speak of a covenant of works and a covenant of grace. With this older generation we find the covenant idea essentially still in the form sketched out by Calvin. Thus the line of argument put forward e.g. by Perkins in his well-known *Golden Chain,* [243] chs. XIX, XXX, XXXI,[244] still seems to be in accord with Calvin's view of the covenant despite the Ramistic form of the logic: the covenant of works is the 'law' in its Pauline sense; the covenant of grace is the content of the gospel. Perkins has put discussion of it in the context of the problem of election.[245] In his Short Catechism,[246] Cartwright similarly also distinguishes between the covenant of works = law and the covenant of grace = gospel, and of the latter it is said in a quite orthodox Calvinist way, 'Beleeve in Jesus Christ & yu shallt be saved.'[247]

Yet among these Puritans the basic attitude has changed almost imperceptibly, but decisively, in comparison with the Reformers. A.Lang hinted at the distinction in this attitude for the first time in his pioneering work *Puritanism and Pietism*[248] with his account of Perkins as the 'Father of Pietism';[249,250] F.E.Stoeffler makes a thorough investigation of the context in his work *The Rise of Evangelical Pietism*.[251] Perkins, whose orthodoxy in dogmatic matters is indubitable,[252] is a good example from the group of 'pietistic Puritans'; a series of more recent commentators has agreed in establishing a changed perspective in Perkins' real concern. He stresses the personal experience of assurance and the sanctification of life as the Christian's confirmation to himself that he belongs to the host of the elect. This also appears among other Puritans of the same period, but noticeably cannot be discovered on the continent in this form.[253] One important goal for Perkins is a moral life in which the conscience provides the elect with a reliable criterion insofar as it accords with scripture. This is evident from his pioneering casuistical writings, *A Discourse of Conscience* and *The Whole Treatise of Cases of Conscience*,[254] in which he has in view not only believers but a wider public, since he regards the conscience as a God-given organ which also recalls those standing outside the church to their divine destiny.[255] Evidently casuistry of this kind filled an urgent practical need at the time, particularly in the face of Catholic polemic which could point to the absence of a Protestant ethics that could compare with developed Roman moral theology.[256] Beyond question Perkins here takes up the Aristotelian heritage, albeit with a clear concern to adopt the basic insights of the Reformers according to which only those who are reborn are capable of fulfilling the will of God, which is known only in the Spirit. On the other hand Perkins decisively rejects a simple appeal to the Spirit after the manner of the Anabaptists, 'for they condemn both human learning and the study of the scripture, and trust wholly to revelations of the Spirit; but God's Spirit worketh not but upon the foundation of the Word.'[257]

Holy scripture is the source for true living in accordance with God's commandment. Perkins begins his *Golden Chain* with this basic rule: 'The Body of Scripture is a doctrine sufficient to live well.'[258] 'Theology is the science of living blessedly for ever.'[259] The sphere which is accorded to Christian life in the whole of theology is clearly visible in the construction of the *Golden Chain*, which contains dogmatic theology only up to p.31 of the original edition,[260] whereas from p.32 onwards practical questions are discussed.[261] In this context the Decalogue has direct relevance even for the actions of the redeemed, although it is treated in the context of the covenant of works. In answer to the question whether Christ has not fulfilled the law for us, so that we are no longer bound to observe it, we read elsewhere:[262] Not at all! 'For Christ performed obedience to the law for us as it is the satisfaction of the law; but the faithful they are bounden to obedience, not as it is satisfactory, but as it is a document of faith and a testimony of their gratitude towards God, or as a means to edify their neighbours.' This is an exact account of the Puritan concern, 'witnessing to the faith', a testimony to which Perkins, his fellow disputants and pupils devoted so much zeal.

Some years ago E.F.Kevan made a thorough study of the understanding of the law among the Puritans.[263] In it he arrives at a very positive judgment on their view of the law, which he places between antinomianism and legalism; he himself is ready to identify with it to a considerable degree.[264] This work is helpful for its clear account of the various aspects which account for the high value attached to the law by the Puritans. A superficial look at the countless catechisms shows that here the Decalogue occupies a central place; it forms the focal point of reflection, as for example in the Catechism by Cartwright mentioned above,[265] in another by Richard Greenham,[266] or in John Dods' *Plain and Familiar Exposition of the Ten Commandments.*[267] The grounding of the law on God's honour, his sovereign nature as creator,[268] the relation which it has with natural law in connection with human reason,[269] are at the same time characteristics of Puritan theology, while being closely related to the thought patterns of scholasticism.[270] Another scholastic conception is that the law is eternal[271] because it accords with God's holiness and righteousness,[272] and that the knowledge of the law, albeit obscured, is not completely quenched in fallen man.[273] Hence, too, the significant role of conscience[274] – in these presuppositions a broad agreement is evident everywhere within the different theological parties of the sixteenth century.[275] However, the most important thing as far as we are concerned is that for the Puritans the law of Moses is identical with the natural law,[276] in so far as it represents a new promulgation of the natural law which has become necessary as a result of the Fall. The law of Moses is likewise to be identified with the law of Christ only to the degree that Christ proclaimed the old law afresh but in a purified form. Here we can see the typical Puritan view of the law according to which the law is not abrogated through the Fall and the justification which has taken place in Christ; that while the pardoned sinner is no longer under the condemnation of the law, the law still continues as a moral obligation.[277] Of course the view that justification must be earned through evangelical works is decisively rejected,[278] but a reference to the justification that has taken place in the form of sanctification in good works seems all the more necessary to the Puritans.[279] If we add the strictly biblicistic basic attitude which distinguishes them from the Anglicans, the reference to the Old Testament with the Decalogue at its centre as the binding form of the revealed law is the logical conclusion. If one speaks of 'pietistic Puritans', this of course includes the role of the Holy Spirit which they presuppose specifically in the observance of the law, their stress on spontaneous free will in its observation,[280] and the warm tones of the awareness of freedom which keep echoing among them.[281]

Nevertheless, we should recognize – and this is where a proviso is necessary in connection with Kevan's enthusiasm for the Puritans – that in their case there has been a clear shift of stress compared with the Reformers when it comes to ethics and specifically to the 'law'. This is closely connected with the general situation of the time, especially in England, where scholastic thought continued basically without interruption and was only partially limited by the influences of the Reformers. If anything, Humanism (from which biblicism above all derives) strengthened it even more. Evidently this trait established itself even more among the next generation of Puritan theologians. Despite all the corrections to detail which are necessary as a result of the progress of research,[282] the article by Perry Miller which I have already mentioned several times, 'The Marrow of Puritan Divinity',[283] is still valuable here. It is above all important that Miller was able to demonstrate the motives which inevitably led to this shift from the concern of the Reformers and especially Calvin: the need which emerges in scholastic theology to rationalize at least God's action, if not his being, provided the idea of the covenant by which it seemed possible to bind God's will to rules which he himself had determined and which from then on were binding on human conduct, along with corresponding divine promises. There was an obvious further step, that of identifying the law based on the covenant with the law of nature. In fact – and here we must correct Miller's comments on their biblicism – the Puritans came near to taking this last step but did not in fact take it. Some Puritans came close to it above all through the beginnings of a natural theology, in that they attributed an appropriate knowledge of God and the moral virtues to fallen man even before his redemption.[284] In this connection it is illuminating that Miller recognizes a close connection between some remarks of Preston's and the position of Herbert of Cherbury;[285] in fact there is in no way the deep division between Puritanism and Deism which people have thought to discover between the two trends.

However, for the moment the line of tradition deriving from Humanism had a still stronger influence and concentrated attention on the Decalogue as the biblical documentation of the law par excellence. The most famous instance of an indication that the precepts of the Decalogue are to be taken literally as instruction for everyday life in the present is the Puritan fight over the sabbath commandment. Since at this point, moreover, one can see a characteristic influence of Puritan views on typically English patterns of life, this feature has long attracted particular attention.[286] Sabbath teaching[287] was in no way a concern of the Reformation: Luther had protested against the late mediaeval Catholic casuistry over the sabbath.[288] In Geneva Calvin had played bowls on Sunday afternoon, and even Tyndal in England had asserted emphatically: 'We be lords over the Saboth; and may yet change it into the Monday, or any other day at all, if the people might be taught without it.'[289] It was more the policy of the established Anglican church to maintain in its legislation the sabbath precepts which had come down from Catholic times;[290] on the other hand, an increasingly strong interest of Puritan clergy in ethical questions is expressed in the various complaints about 'abuses' which take place on the sabbath, it being presupposed that the day is to serve only for religious edification.[291]

However, this is in no way limited to the Puritans: the most illuminating writing, *The Anatomy of Abuses*,[292] in which dances, card-playing and other entertainments are attacked as a blasphemous abomination and are condemned as profaning the sabbath if they take place on Sunday, comes from Philip Stubbs, who is reckoned more among the 'Anglicans'. Systematic accounts explaining that the sabbath commandment still continues to be valid for Christians only appeared at the turn of the century;[293] the discussion flared up once again when in 1618 James I enacted the *Book of Sports*,[294] in which recreations were expressly allowed on Sunday. This ordinance was revised by Charles I in 1625,[295] but was expressly confirmed again in 1633.[296]

Whether the sabbath commandment still continued to be valid depended above all on the question whether the fourth commandment has a ceremonial or a moral content. The Reformation was agreed that Jewish ceremonial legislation and also the popular laws of Moses had lost their validity; only the moral law continued to remain in force.[297] So anyone who wanted to claim that the sabbath commandment was still binding had to regard it as a moral commandment. According to Ex.20.11 the sabbath was connected with creation; it was regarded as being ordained before the Fall and before the Law of Moses, but in the Decalogue it was confirmed along with the other binding commandments which are cited there.

It is worth noting Collinson's argument that although the hallowing of the sabbath is so typical of the English scene, it is not an exclusively British invention,[298] but goes back to the theological tradition characteristic of Zurich: Bullinger and following him Hooper, and also Bucer, can be mentioned as advocates of it, and from Reformed orthodoxy Beza and Ursinus.The shift of accent over against Calvin's attitude, as indicated above, is clear. The law, here in its specifically Old Testament form, takes on a much more strongly positive and independent function because the Decalogue is understood to be a codification corresponding with the *lex naturalis*. This can be extended to so distinctively Jewish a feature as the sanctification of the sabbath. The rigorous implementation of the sabbath regulations in England did not, of course, have any parallels on the Continent and is connected with certain social factors peculiar to Great Britain.[299] Their effects were so far-reaching because they extended over a long period of time, since as the material collected by Cox[300] and newly edited by Levy shows, the real climax of the strict implementation of the rules governing the English Sunday lies only in the eighteenth century,[301] when the Puritan standpoint had thoroughly permeated the people. Indeed, with the 'Lord's Day Observance Act' of 1781,[302] a Sunday law was adapted which has still not been repealed. All this explains why a powerful opposition developed so early in Deism, which had to look for its starting point in the Bible itself and above all in the Old Testament, since pious popular opinion, and state legislation which served popular opinion in the resolutions of Parliament, referred to the Bible and specially to the Old Testament. Even the crown had to take account of this popular opinion, though Charles II, with his great zest for life, had a very different attitude. As we shall see, this opposition had its basis above all in the educated classes, though some intellectual climbers from the petty bourgeoisie, like Chubb,[303] also shared in it. We shall also see in due course how on the other hand it again adopted intellectual presuppositions from the Puritan tradition against which it fought.

It follows from these observations that the basic structures of theological thinking among the Puritans were in many respects not so different from those of Hooker. Though certain central insights of Reformation theology still asserted themselves among the Puritans, we may doubt whether these really continued to occupy the centre of their thinking.

J.S.Coolidge has ventured to argue for such a conclusion with his reference to the Puritan usage of terminology with a strong Pauline stamp.[304] We find it, for example, in Cartwright's four rules cited above, each of which is drawn from a passage in one of Paul's letters. Similarly, Hooper too will take over Pauline conceptuality to a considerable degree. Coolidge concludes from this that the Puritans are Paulinists in a specific sense and indeed that the character of their standpoint is to be sought in precisely this Pauline way of thinking: 'a Pauline understanding of scripture is in fact the matrix of Puritan thought generally.'[305] He concedes that the Puritans, too, share with their opponents the kind of arguing characteristic of Greek thought in their search for an abstract truth.[306] Alongside this, however, we are also to find the dynamic side of Pauline thought in their system, in 'organic' relationship to the community in a church ordered in a particular way (in contrast to the individualistic understanding, which only comes much later).[307] This includes the idea of Christian freedom held in tension with 'edification' in the community,[308] though centrally oriented on a christocentric point of reference: 'In sum, the idea of participation through the Bible in the new life of Christ underlies the Puritan's appeal to scripture... This dynamically Christocentric apprehension of the Bible is the originally distinctive element of Puritanism.'[309]

Any modern observer is in danger of judging witnesses belonging to a far distant past from theological or intellectual perspectives which are only valid for today – this is evident in the case of Perry Miller also, although with converse results. At all events, the presence of a Pauline terminology cannot in itself justify such far-reaching conclusions. A tiny observation is enough to make us think: even in the official agenda of Edward VI, authorized by Archbishop Cranmer, the abolition of certain liturgies and the preservation of others is supported by the same quo-

tations from I Cor.14.26 and 40 with the keywords 'order' and 'edification'. So these are traditional proof texts![310] We should ask in what
sense the 'Pauline Renaissance in England', as Coolidge entitles his
book, is to be understood, since there had already been a Pauline
renaissance under Humanist auspices before the beginning of the Reformation in 1510 as a result of the lectures of John Colet, which had
made such a great impression on Erasmus.[311] We would therefore have
to look closer to see how the Puritans in fact understood Paul and the
characteristic terms like *fides* and *aedificatio* (or their Greek equivalents)
which they drew from his vocabulary. That in fact can only be done by
way of their specific demands.

At all events, anti-ceremonial polemic – the rejection of sacral vestments and liturgical customs (like kneeling at the eucharist) in the
'Anti-Vestment Party' are not motivated by Paul but by humanistic
Spiritualism. We can trace something of this background in Hooper
when in his *Notae* he makes an identification between accord with
'nature' and the *proportio fidei ac scripturae*.[312] Equally illuminating is his
first *Nota*, in which the term *fides* is used in connection with 'demonstration' (of a custom or ordinance) from scripture. The reference, then,
is not to the justifying faith of the Reformers but to the obligation
required by a binding regulation.[313] His attitude is not substantially
different in this question from the line which is represented in the many
examples already available. He is nearest to Wyclif's view of the Bible:
to his moralism and the legalistic understanding of scripture, and especially to his principle that whatever is not contained in scripture,
being *traditiones humanae*, is sin, and is to be attributed to the corruption
of popery.[314] In a letter of June 1566[315] Beza can describe the attitude of
the Anti-Vestment party in a very similar way: 'For there be some of
opinion, that nothing at all should be added to the simplicitie of the
Apostolike church, and therfor that (whythout exception) all things are
to be done by us which the Apostels did, and whatsoever the Church
that succeeded next after the Apostels, hathe added to yet former
things, they thincke they must be abolyshed at once.' As in Wyclif, so
too in Hooper the reference is above all to ceremonies. In a well known
direction there is also added the one specific repudiation of vestments
which takes a well known direction: they are *Aaronici sacerdotij umbrae*,
which *cum Christi sacerdotio consistere non possunt*. At God's command,
Aaron's priesthood was once marked out from among the people by
means of them: anyone who now wears them as a servant of the word
is seeking to differentiate himself in an illegitimate way from the community in which Christ's priesthood has brought about the end of
human priesthood.[316]

6. For the purpose of grouping the various stages of Puritanism, the
second 'party' within Puritanism, the group which held out against the

existing order of the church for a constitution corresponding to an ideal typical form of the earliest church to be discovered from the New Testament, can of course be distinguished from the anticeremonial party. However, it is closely connected with it.[317] We can see this very clearly in the 'Admonition to the Parliament'[318] mentioned above, which gives Parliament as a task 'to employ your whole labour and studie; not only in abandoning al popish remnants both in ceremonies and regiment (the two are mentioned in the same breath), but also in bringing in and placing in Gods church those things only, which the Lord himself in his word commandeth'.[319] Here, too, the New Testament appears as a law book from which divine precepts are to be derived for the binding form of the church. We also find in the 'Second Admonition', often, though wrongly, attributed to Thomas Cartwright,[320] some echoes of the polemic against vestments[321] and against the fixed forms of prayer laid down in the ordinances of the Book of Common Prayer, the responses, the sung parts of liturgy, kneeling and so on.[322] It immediately becomes clear how dangerous it is to speak of a 'dynamic christocentric understanding of the Bible' in connection with the Puritans – with inevitable associations with the conceptuality of modern dialectical theology – when we recall the models in Erasmian Humanism for the view of the Bible visible in the 'Admonition'. The tendency of the memorandum is also evident from the numerous biblical references which appear in the margins:[323] passages from Acts are particularly frequent, and in addition to all kinds of references to the authentic Pauline Epistles and the four Gospels, the Pastoral Epistles also appear surprisingly often. When one recalls that the real impetus to the Presbyterian movement arose from Cartwright's Cambridge lecture on Acts in Spring 1570, in which he presented the example of the early church in Acts 1 and 2 as a model for the present,[324] it is impossible to mistake the continuity of the Puritan demands in the sphere of the constitution of the church with the biblical humanism of the 1520s and 1530s. In the Admonition, long comparisons are developed betwen the ancient church and the Church of England in which there is an ongoing contrast between a stereotyped 'then' and 'now'.[325] However, one should not overlook the fact that in addition, passages from the Old Testament are also adduced as evidence for the 'then'; e.g. Ezek.44; Jer.23 for the fact that 'in those dayes no idolatrous sacrificers or heathnish priests were appointed to be preachers of the gospel', just as in the first sentence of the manifesto the need for a restitution of true religion and a reformation of the church is argued primarily on the basis of II Kings 23 (Josiah's reform) and II Chron.17;29, which have a similar content – and 'in bringing in and placing in God's church those things only, which the Lord himself commandeth', with a reference to Deut 4.2; 12.32 (as usual, Deuteronomy is a favourite book of the Puritans).[326] Thus here too in the background we have a presupposition of the unity of the Testaments understood in legalistic terms, however much the 'Jewish' rites are supposed to have been superseded.[327]

The whole of the background to this view can only be understood if we take into account the perspective of the time, which was still completely unhistorical. That was particularly the case with the history of the church: in the comparison between the pure original church and the whole of later church history, which appears against this backdrop as one single movement of decay, there is still no perspective whatsoever of a context of development into which even the early church must fit. On the other hand the hermeneutic is equally unhistorical: the Bible is treated superficially, and is everywhere equally remote.[327a] Hence the attempt by the Puritans to transfer what they thought to be clearly recognizable ordinances of the earliest church directly to the church of the present.

In addition, the Puritan criticism of the existing church order was conceived of in the light of the same Spiritualist presuppositions which supply the criterion in liturgical questions. One can see this clearly, for example, in the 'An hundred pointes of Poperie, yet remayning, which deforme the Englishe reformation', from the *Plesaunte Dialogue*[328] which E.Arber has edited.[329] Here the ministries of the church hierarchy are condemned in the same breath as choral singers and organists as a popish survival; among the 'grosse pointes of poperie', liturgical vestments and things like the ringing of bells and doffing of hats at the mention of the name of Jesus appear alongside real abuses such as the large number of unworthy members of the clergy; there is also mention of the need for baptism, the laying on of hands, the use of oblates, and kneeling at the eucharist.[330] So it is quite impossible to separate out the various concerns. We are not made any the wiser even by the *Marprelate Texts*,[331] since although the most important document, the Epistle, begins by clearly formulating the principle that the office of a *pastor pastorum* is against God's law,[332] it gets carried away with its own satire in the long-drawn out enumeration of past instances of misuse of power by the bishops and abuses of all kinds in the church which they have either caused or tolerated. Nowhere are we given a theoretical account of Presbyterian principles apart from the ongoing undertone that only a preaching ministry is tolerable in the church – one of the legitimate chief concerns of the Puritans: the whole Marprelate literature thrives on polemic and satire. Its wide resonance in public and the sharpness of the measures taken against it are connected with the degree of general dissatisfaction with existing circumstances.

The systematic presuppositions of a good deal of Puritan writing are very difficult to interpret because it essentially offers criticism, criticism of conditions in a church whose structures, in many respects inadequate

or obsolete, offered plenty of occasion for this. The inadequate education of the clergy, the fact that numerous positions were occupied by
readers instead of preachers, pluralism and the absenteeism of ministers
(caused by the mediaeval financial system which had not been
superseded even in the sphere of the state), and above all the ecclesiastical jurisdiction which in many everyday matters was all-powerful
and often corrupt,[333] were constant scandals through which anticlericalism in lay circles constantly received new nourishment. As Trinterud
observes,[334] the hierarchy was prevented from making real reforms not
least by the fact that since the 'Supplication' of 1532 and the other
statutes of Henry VIII[335], it had largely been robbed of the power of
jurisdiction, so that it was compelled to defend its status by polemic.

However, we can obtain important insights into the hermeneutical
principles of the Presbyterian party from the work of W.Fulke, *A Brief
and Plain Declaration*[336], presumably written in 1572, printed in 1584 and
newly edited by Trinterud[337], in which both the biblical foundation and
the conclusions for the normative structure of the church drawn from
it by the Presbyterians are summarized in the briefest form. The definition of the church and its biblical foundation (put first, with ramistic
logic) already contains all the relevant principles in a nutshell: 'The
church of God is the house of God, and therefore ought to be directed
in all things according to the order prescribed by the Householder
himself; which order is not to be learned elsewhere, but in his holy
word.' The Puritan extension of the principle of scripture to the ordering
of the church is closely connected, as we can see from the very next
sentence, with the moralist understanding of scripture, for scripture is
'a perfect rule of all our life, and able to make the man of God perfect,
prepared to all good works.'[338] Following from this the author and his
readers are then faced with the task, 'diligently and reverently to search
the holy Scriptures, that we may find what order our saviour Christ...
hath set forth in them'.[339] With reference to quotations from the letters
of Paul and Acts, after excluding those ministries which were specific
to the times of the earliest church, there is a call for the four remaining
offices of pastors, doctors, 'governors' and deacons in the English
church. This is similar to the fourfold ministry which had already been
introduced under Calvin in Geneva.[340] There are far-reaching parallels
to the Geneva model in other remarks about the nature and tasks of
these ministries, the synodical government of the church and the relationship between the church and the secular authorities. However, this
similarity should not lead us astray so that we misunderstand the
difference of approach between Calvin and the Puritans: given the
problem of the understanding of the law in Calvin, discussed often and
a matter of controversy, we can judge that for Calvin the law is subordinate, governed by the gospel.[341] Of course there is also a hidden

Humanist motive in Calvin in the presupposition that scripture must also be binding on the outward ordering of the church.[342] This could very quickly regain the upper hand in another context, as we can see from the Puritan position.

7. As the state church was not ready to accede to such demands at this or a later time, separatist communities soon came into being.[343] However, a theory of Congregationalism was not put forward until the three-part work by the famous Robert Browne,[344] printed in Middelburg in 1582. The first and third parts of this, named respectively 'A Treatise of reformation without tarying for anie' and ' A Book which sheweth the life and manners of all true Christians',[345] contained the principles which the most radical Puritans of the time wanted to implement without further delay. C.Burrage points out that Browne did not want separation as a final goal, but only as a temporary means of compelling the state church to embark on the reforms he desired.[346] However, his ideal of the church contains features which inevitably went directly against the system of the national church and were closer to the pattern of the 'sect', which was first given this name by Troeltsch.[347] Chief of these features was the view that only committed Christians and not just the baptized should *ipso facto* belong to the church, and further, that each individual community is the church, which orders its affairs independently and is not subject to any general hierarchy in the church. In connection with this he stresses the priesthood of all believers and the need to put into practice the consequences for organization which follow from this principle: the choice of all ministers by the community, and the implementation of church discipline through the elders chosen from among the members of the community.[348] We are not interested specifically in those institutions which long continued to exist in many Reformed churches even outside the later congregationalist type and after the nineteenth century even in Lutheranism, but in the way in which they are justified by Browne. In this connection the *Treatise of Reformation* is particularly significant, because here for the first time there is a strict dividing line between the spiritual authority which applies in the church and the secular authority of the civil government. The magistrates have no spiritual power in the church; rather, as the kingdom of Christ this is a spiritual kingdom in which the power of the keys is exercised by the preaching of the word. Therefore one may not look to the secular sword in connection with the needs of the church: 'in all things wee must firste looke, what is the Lordes will and charge, and then what is the will of man'.[349] Insofar as they are members of the community, the secular authorities, too, are subject to the spiritual authority: 'They must bee vnder a Pastorall charge: They must obeye to the Scepter of Christe, if they bee Christians.'[350] In view of the absolutism of the time that is an extraordinarily bold idea! However, Burrage

has pointed out[351] that at one point in his 'Treatise' Browne has accorded
the secular authorities a competence for regulating church matters: 'We
knowe thath Moses might reforme, and the Iudges and Kings which
followed him, and so may our Magistrates: yea they may reforme the
Church and commaunde things expedient for the same. Yet may they
doo nothing concerning the Church, but onelie ciuillie, and as ciuile
Magistrates... onelie to rule the common wealth in all outwards Iustice,
to maintaine the right, welfare and honor therof, with outward power,
bodily punishment, & ciuil forcing of mē.' Nevertheless this outward
power over the church is limited: 'but to cōpell religion to plant
churches by power, and to force a submission to Ecclesiastical gouvern-
ment by lawes & penalties belongeth not to them... neither yet to the
Church.'[352] Thus a complete break between state and church is not in
prospect.

The same principles occur yet again in classic form and without visible
connection with Browne,[353] in Henry Jacob's,[354] *Reasons Taken Ovt of
Gods Word and the Best Human Testimonies Proving a Necessitie of Reforming
our Churches in England*, which appeared more than twenty years later,
in 1604.[355] On the reverse of the title page he gives four theses which
he seeks to justify: '1. It is necessary to reforme the Churches of England, their Ministerie, and Ceremonies. 2. For the space of 200. yeares
after Christ the Visible Churches vsing gouvernement were not Diocesan
Churches but particular ordinary Congregations only and the Bishops...
were only Parishionall not Diocesan Bishops, differing from other Pastors only in Priority of order not in Maioritie of rule. 3. The Scriptures
of the New Testament do cōtain & set forth vnto vs (besides the
government by Extraordinary Offices, Apostles Prophetes Evangelistes)
an ordinary forme of Church-gouvernement vsed then. 4. The ordinary
forme of Church-gouvernement set forth vnto vs in the New Testament,
ought necessarily to be kept still by vs; it is not changeable by men,
and therefore it only is lawful.' Already in the dedication to the king
we find the stubborn affirmation 'that we beleeve Gods written Word
ought to be our sole warrant for all things Ecclesiasticall'. Here Jacob
refers to the royal promise that everything which goes against the word
of God in the church is to be removed and everything that is necessary
according to God's word has to be established in it.[356] At the same time
there is the characteristic qualification: 'I say, meerely Ecclesiasticall.
For in matters any way Civil no man doubteth but God hath left liberty
unto mans judgement and liking.'

The first thesis introduces the existing church government, the ministries and particular ceremonies, as contrary to God's word in the
Church of England.[357] It is particularly striking that the second commandment is mentioned as the first of all foundations of scripture
(whereas elsewhere the New Testament is abundantly cited as the proof

of scripture). While the first commandment forbids the worship of alien gods alongside the true God, in the case of the second commandment: 'But heere he forbiddeth all Meanes being Human Invētions whereby men would giue honor to the true God.' 'As all Ecclesiasticall Rites, Actions, Ministeries, & Formes of Visible Churches... and being meerely the inventions of men, must needs by this Commandement be all simply vnlawfull.'[358] The shaping of human freedom applies only 'touching meere Circumstances, which are nothing else but Occasionall or Accidentall things therin'.[359] All unwritten traditions in the church are directly against God's word.

In what follows[360] there is first of all an attack on the government of the English church with its hierarchical structure. This is contrary to scripture. Christ appointed only one kind of church in his word, the local church.[361] The development of the office of bishop in the ancient church (a brief account is given) is contrary to God's word. One interesting feature is the differentiation carried out with delicate interpretative skills between conditions which are indifferent and traditions which are not.[362] Circumstances can be natural necessities or civil occasions: in both instances they are indifferent. For example, it does not matter whether a service is held in the temple or the synagogue. Because it is a house, and the only important thing about it is that it is an appropriate (comely) place both for worship and for living in, a temple is a mixture of civil and church property and therefore indifferent. People can decide about their place of worship and its appearance. By contrast, liturgical vestments are purely a church concern: as they are not provided for in scripture, they may not be introduced. The prejudices in respect of content implied by these positions stand out all too clearly through the casuistry.

The typically Separatist position is also adopted towards the relationship between church and state: the fear that the decentralized church government called for, and above all the basic choice of pastors by members of the community, might have an influence on the form of the civil state form and could be anti-monarchical,[363] is rejected out of hand. Church and state are two clearly distinct realms.[364] On the one hand it is stressed that government by diocesan bishops reduces the threefold ministry of Christ to the priestly ministry (redemption through the crucifixion) and removes both his prophetic ministry, to teach 'the outward forme, nature and constitution (which is but one) of all his visible churches'[365] and his royal ministry, to govern these churches through his servants (the local clergy) and ordinance, and transfers these to men;[366] on the other hand, the king is to be conceded a *ius circa sacra*. 'Howbeit always *politikōs, non pneumatikōs*: Civilly, not Spiritually or Ecclesiastically.'[367] People are neither schismatics nor rebels, far less forgetful of their duties to the king.[368]

The writing ends with a letter from Jacob to his brothers in office, a striking feature of which is the author's awareness of an apostolic mission which is evident from the opening modelled on the form of Pauline letters;[369] its content can be summed up in the formula that salvation is to be assured only through exercising the full office of pastor, including responsibilities for church government, in accordance with scripture and as commanded by Christ.

The same thought-world also appears in Jacob's later writings, like the volume *The Divine Beginning of Christs Church*, published anonymously in Leiden in 1610;[370] its basic idea is that Christ regulated once and for all the details of both the inward and outward forms of the church; this was a church government based on a free consensus[371] and strictly to be distinguished from secular government. This form is authorized by the prophetic and kingly office of Christ as it appears in the New Testament;[372] even the apostolic form of the church itself is visible in the New Testament and is binding in the form proclaimed by Christ as prophet and ordered by him as king, and confirmed by Paul.

In the confession of faith of the separatist community of exiles at Middelburg, which appeared in 1616 and which similarly goes back to Jacob,[373] the whole system is again finally described in detail in 28 articles, 'wherin onely wee dissent from the publique Ecclesiasticall order, and doctrine in England'.[374] Here again Christ's prophetic and kingly office comes first, followed by the all-sufficiency of scripture and the 'true, visible and political church'. This is followed by numerous articles about the system of ecclesiastical organization in detail, about the ministries of the church, and about dogmas and customs. The basic statement is that these external forms, too, are spiritual and religious and that their pattern was ordered in a binding way by Christ himself.[375] Here there is an analogy between the ordering of the old and new covenants: 'We believe that Christ in these things (no lesse than matters inward concerning religion) is the foundation to the whole building even of his visible and political Church now under the Gospell, as well and as throughly as he was under the Law.'[376] The outward forms of worship are not accidental, but substantial, and therefore they too are not indifferentia, but, if they are to be legal, must be ordained in scripture. All unwritten human traditions are illegal and therefore unreliable: all ordinances about the practice of religion are either true or false, corresponding to the second commandment of the Decalogue.[377] From here the supporters of this confession move to a view fixed down to the last detail, about what is true or false. Thus e.g. marriage and burial are not recognized as tasks of a minister: as such ministerial actions are not mentioned in either Old or New Testament, they are not spiritual but purely secular matters.[378] Elsewhere there is also a mass of the usual Puritan demands which are discussed in a similar way.

The work in which Jacob bases his demands explicitly on the second commandment of the Decalogue, *A plaine and cleere Exposition of the Second Commandement*,[379] is particularly interesting in the present context. For Jacob the ten commandments are of central significance: they contain not only what is literally said in them but are 'generall Heads of fundamentall grounds and Principles, vvhereunto all Duties either tovvards God or man, are truly referred, and vvhereon all the Scriptures besides do depend'.[380] All commandments are to be understood synecdochically.[381] Not only the Old but also the New Testament hangs on the two tablets of the Decalogue;[382] not only are all sins prohibited in the law, but all duties are commanded. The evangelical duties, too (like faith, hope, penitence, the preaching of hope, the holy signs or sacraments), are ordained in the law of the ten commandments.[383] The difference between the law of works and the law of faith consists only in the fact that works cannot justify (Rom.3.27) – to this extent Jacob still takes over the message of the Reformation.[384] Is the gospel not part of the law? No, insofar as the forgiveness of sins through Christ happens by faith – but it is law insofar as the gospel similarly contains duties for us towards God and men.[385] Faith too, insofar as it is regarded as a duty which we have to perform, is not opposed to the law of works; rather, in this respect the law of faith is contained in the law of works, like a part in the whole.[386] The ten commandments remain unaltered for all time (in contrast to the changing ceremonial commandments);[387] that is also true of the second commandment.

Now as this commandment too must be understood in the broadest sense ('synecdochically'),[388] in general it rules out all human authorship in matters of religious practice. Rather, on the positive side, all external forms of the church, even down to details, are arranged by God himself.[389] In what follows,[390] the author then justifies all the congregationalist demands with a wealth of scriptural passages from Old and New Testaments, which for him are a development of the second commandment.

This work is a particularly illuminating instance of a kind of thinking which in essentials underlies the whole Puritan position, but which is developed here in an unusually clear and uncompromising form. Only at the central point of justification is the Reformation insight maintained, at least formally; otherwise, the whole life of Christians and the church is completely legalized, with the result that both Old and New Testament come to stand on one level (leaving aside the ceremonial precepts of the Old Testament, which are, however, essentially replaced by New Testament 'regulations').

Browne's *Treatise* deserves special attention in connection with our theme because it adopts a position over the question of the relevance of the Old Testament for the relationship between state and church in the present in a quite special way. This aspect of the polemical work has not hitherto been investigated; moreover it only becomes understandable once we have considered the usual form of scriptural proof for the monarch's *cura religionis* in the established church.

8. H.Kressner, in his short study of the 'Swiss Origins of the Anglican State Church',[391] deserves credit for having been the first to note the role of the Old Testament in providing a basis for the episcopal party's theory of the state church. He refers back to the opposition which existed between Geneva and Zurich over the nature of the relationship between state and church; here Zurich stressed that conditions in the early church were influenced by the circumstances of the time, whereas Geneva regarded the New Testament constitution of the church as being normative for the present also. Zurich derived from its view the right to vary the role of authority depending on local circumstances. Rudolf Gualter provided the theoretical basis for this.[392] In the present context it is particularly significant that the people of Zurich, too, based their view on a biblical foundation. In contrast to the people of Geneva, however, they did not see the circumstances in the New Testament as an actual parallel to the present, since at that time the church represented an enclave within a pagan state and therefore also had to protect its external customs. They found the parallel in the Old Testament: ancient Israel, and especially the Israelite monarchy, provided them with the model for the role they assigned to the Christian authorities. However they did not look to Israel as the Calvinists looked to the New Testament: as the source for an ideal order which was also to be introduced into the present-day church; they maintained the principle that the specific circumstances of the time would have to determine the shape of external ordinances.

In that case, what role was played by the Old Testament model? Kressner did not give an answer to this question. It can only be resolved satisfactorily if we take into account the principles of traditional hermeneutics as they had been handed down from the Middle Ages and had not in any way been displaced by the Reformation. Whereas the view of the Bible, and especially the New Testament, as a legal norm from which one can directly derive valid regulations for the ordinances of one's own time, derives from Humanist thought with a background in antiquity, the character of the Old Testament, and especially the Israelite monarchy, as a model is derived by way of typology.

In discussing Bucer's book *De regno Christo*, which was so important for the English Reformation, we already noted that Bucer pointed to the pious kings mentioned in the Old Testament, like David, Solomon, Hezekiah and Josiah, as models for the task of renewing the English church which was faced by Edward VI.[393] As we also saw,[394] this was a concept already developed under Henry VIII by the court theologians as a justification for the English national church in its separation from Rome. To begin with, the typological expectation of the king was also very much alive in Puritan circles; we can see this to a considerable degree at the accession of Elizabeth I and again to a lesser extent when James I took the English crown. An example of the way in which royal typological thought does not collapse even after disillusioning experiences with a queen who acts only in terms of real politics can be found in the well-known sermon delivered by the Puritan Edward Dering before the Queen on 25 February 1570.[395] The choice of text alone, Ps.78.70-72, which recalls the election of David, reveals the intentions of the preacher, who wants to show with the Psalmist in the person of David 'both how mercifully God hath dealt with him, and how obediently David walked before the Lord'.[396] The Psalmist presented three perspectives in order to urge Judah not to misuse God's grace, which should also move 'us':[397] 'The first is of God's mercy whence he had called David. The second is of God's intent and purpose whereunto he called him. The third of David's own person, how faithfully and how truly he did execute that whereunto he was called.'[398] In the first part, after lengthy general remarks about the gratitude which Christians should have for their calling, there is a direct reference to the duty of the Queen to be grateful, and she is called upon to repent.[399] The grace which God once granted to Judah is seen as corresponding closely with the acts of benevolence which he now heaps upon England: 'Let us behold ourselves how plentifully at this day are God's mercies and benefits pured out upon us, both upon our Queen and upon her people. How mightily doth he defend us in so many dangers? How sit we here in safety, when all the world is on an uprear?'[400] But this security, the preacher continues, should not lull 'us' into a false sense of ease: as examples of such deceptive self-confidence he mentions, to some degree as negative types, King Sennacherib, who, as II Kings 18.13-19.37 reports, was later slain in Nineveh by his sons after his arrogant outbursts against Jerusalem and its God, and, characteristically from the classical tradition, the way in which Agamemnon met his death.

The second perspective is the purpose for which God called David: 'to feed his people in Jacob, his heritage in Jerusalem', is immediately applied to any authority, 'Whether he be prince or emperor, duke, earl, lord, counsellor, magistrate, whatsoever, for this purpose he is called.'[401] The direct application to the Queen follows from this: 'kings must be nursefathers, and queens must be nurses (cf.Isa.49.23) unto the church of God.'[402] Not only concern for the outward prosperity of the people is meant here: 'It is true that the prince must defend the fatherless and widow, relieve the oppressed...But this is also his duty, and his greatest duty: to be careful for religion, to maintain the gospel, to teach the people knowledge and build his whole government with faithfulness.'[403] Nothing less than the direct *cura religionis* of the Queen is called for, on an Old Testament typological basis.[404] At this point we can see that the separation of state and church is in no way part of the Puritan programme; rather, they begin by taking for granted the identity of people and church. Therefore immediately afterwards it can be said that one of the most important duties of the Queen is a care for justice and the punishment of evildoers; and here, there is a literal quotation of the commandment and promise to the Old Testament king in Deut.17.18-20. The names of numerous kings like Asa, Jehoshaphat, Hezekiah, Josiah and Solomon are mentioned as examples of the reforming zeal which pleases God. Attention is particularly drawn to the concern for the priesthood, and for the welfare of the Levites, which were seen by the pious kings of Judah as their prime tasks. This forms the basis for an invitation to the queen to care in the same way for an improvement in conditions for the clergy and to remove the gross abuses in the ministry. An important postulate in their ranks is: 'Take away your authority from the bishops'[405] – they are the ones primarily responsible for the intolerable conditions in the church. The protest of the Presbyterians is not directed against the authority of the crown but only against the rule of the episcopate.

A sermon so pregnant with Old Testament typology is not an isolated instance, but only one of numerous examples in which the institutions of ancient Israel were similarly applied, quite as a matter of course, to establish the relationship between state and church in the present.[405a]

There are a number of admirable examples of this kind of rhetoric, like the typological sermons of the Puritan William Leigh, *Queene Elizabeth, paraleld in her princely Vertues* (which was only published after the death of the Queen, in 1612).[406] A quotation from the first of these sermons will make this clear;[407] at this point the preacher begins to speak of the tribulation undergone by Elizabeth before and after her accession.

Dauid was the least and last of his fathers house,
so was Elizabeth of her fathers familie
Dauid persecuted from his youth, so was Elizabeth.
David contemned of his brethren, Elizabeth of her sister,
Saul a King persecuted Dauid, Marie a Queene was wroth with Elizabeth.
Dauid an exile in the holdes of Engeddi, the close prisoner in the holds of Wodstocke.
Doeg reuiled Dauid vnto Saul, so did Gardiner Elizabeth vnto Mary,

Dauid declared his innocencie ynto Saul, so did Elizabeth vnto her sister...

Saul in his spirit of furie purposed to haue killed Dauid playing vpon his harpe.

Winchester in his spirit of poperie purposed to haue murthered Elizabeth at her deuotion by Paul Peny and Iames Basset.

Dauid relieued and pitied by Achish King of Gath, a stranger to his person, and an enemie to his religion.

Elizabeth pitied by Phillip of Spaine, a friend to her person, yet not friend to her profession...

Throughout the whole sermon David becomes the type of the Queen: 'Dauid brought the Arke into his Citie by the hands of the Leuites. So doth Queen Elizabeth the Religion of her Christ, into the bowels of al her kingdomes, by a beautifull ministry.'[408] Just as David was the one beloved of God, so Elizabeth's rule is the rest promised to the people of God.[409]

While in the first sermon the ruler is compared closely with the biblical king David, in the second (on Josh.10.11), she is compared with Joshua (who is similarly designated 'prince' of Israel);[410] this admonishes the Queen not to forget effective prayer which will bring England deliverance from her foes. Here type and antitype, Israel and England, almost come together: 'For so good a God, so gracious a Prince, so great plenty... of all Gods blessings, both heauenly and earthly is not for Moab, Ammon or mount Seir, but for the hill of Gods holiness, Israel, England, and mount Sion.'[411]

The third sermon (on II Kings 18.5-6) chooses the pious king Hezekiah as a type whose struggle against idolatry it compares with Elizabeth's struggle against the papists ('our adversaries'). The popish conspiracy, which is felt to be the severest threat, is described as 'conspiracy against Moses, and the prophets'. 'Moses and the Prophets are beaten back with Romish Institutions': the hated Romans want to replace scripture with their own lying traditions. However, even angels are accursed if they 'preached any other Gospell than that which was deliuered by Moses and Christ'.[412] Moses and Christ as preachers of the Gospel: this and the law (which the pious Hezekiah observed) are on the same level: that is authentic Puritan tradition. In addition there is a fantastic typology which identifies England's enemies with Sennacherib, king of Assyria, with Ammon, Gebal and Edom, the 'Romish Edomites', over whose cry of annihilation (according to Ps.137.7) against Jerusalem/ England Hezekiah/Elizabeth triumphed with God's help.[413] But not only Puritans used typological arguments with a vengeance. That is the case among the representatives of the established church even more than among the Puritans; the former think that they can most clearly demonstrate the supremacy of the crown over the church by referring to the Old Testament kings and their efforts to support the temple in Jerusalem and the purity of belief in Yahweh. Thus in his defence of the English church against the Pope's claim to supremacy[414] Bishop Jewel begins with Moses and his instructions to Aaron in Ex.32, and goes on to mention David, Solomon and the well-known reforming kings as monarchs who on each occasion pointed out the limits to be observed by priests within their realm.[415] He then moves on to the Christian emperors since Constantine who summoned the famous councils of the early church by their own decrees.[415a] This juxtaposition is no coincidence, as we shall see, but rests on old tradition. We may recall that we came across the same sequence as early as Bucer.[416] The first volume of the *Convocation Book* of John Overall[417] contains a thorough exegesis of the Old Testament aimed at demonstrating the right of the divinely appointed prince to rule. The Anglican bishop Lancelot Andrewes,[418] who, having initially regarded secular rule as an ordinance which had become necessary after the Fall,[419] fully endorsed the doctrine of the divine right of kings when he became bishop, was fond of resorting to the Old Testament to justify it.[420] We can see this in the texts which he chooses to preach on at the commemoration of the 'Gunpowder Plot' (5 November 1605). They include Prov.8.15: 'Through me kings reign',[421] and Prov.24.21-23, 'My son, fear God and the king...'[422] 'By Me Kings reign': 'upon these four syllables depend all kings and kingdoms of the earth.'[423] In his work *Tortura Torti*,[424] Andrewes defends the right of kings in matters of religion (*ad res Religionis tum stabiliendas tum reformandas*) with examples from the Old Testament.[425] '*A more institutoque Israelis orditur Apologia;*[426] *inde enim vim habet, atque nervos suos quaestio haec omnis. In Israele enim populo suo regnum instituit Deo, et Ecclesiam in Regno, ex mente sua. Exemplum inde nobis sumendum est, cum in Testamento Novo nullum habeamus.*'[427] At that time state and church were separate. As nothing can be inferred on the subject from the New Testament, in these circumstances reference to the Old Testament is the legitimate way of providing a biblical justification. In the Old Testament we can see how God wanted a divinely appointed monarchy and the church in the state: '*Ab illo igitur fonte Israelis arcessimus hanc causam, et ab eo exemplo... Ecclesiae, Regnique nostri regimen informamus.*' In Israel, a change in religious matters was always brought about by the kings and not by the priests: Andrewes demonstrates this from the example of King Jehoshaphat (according to II Chron. 19), from David's concern for the ark, from Solomon's building of the temple, from the reforms of Josiah, Hezekiah, Ahaz and so on, all examples which had already become traditional. The king has the right to reform the church, to appoint and depose priests and judges, to decide church matters, to enact laws against blasphemy, to consecrate and purify the temple – and in accordance with the principle of analogy all these rights can be transferred directly to the circumstances of the English church. The priestly offices proper, however, are not to be performed by the king, as Andrewes explicitly maintains: *Nec Regi quidem Nostro licet, nec ulli, aut Sacra administrare, aut attrectare quicquam, quod potestatis sit mere Sacerdotalis, ut sunt liturgiae, Conciones, Claves, Sacramenta.*[428] *Nam nos quidem hic in Gubernando Primatum ponimus, non docendo; et Regem non Doctorem summum, sed Gubernatorem dicimus.*[429]

The examples given should be enough to illustrate the great importance attached to the Old Testament in Anglican theology of the sixteenth and seventeenth century as a basis for the order of the established church, and in particular for royal absolutism in matters of religion. N.Sykes has demonstrated what a substantial role was played by the theory of 'godly princes', not only in Reformation theology but also in sixteenth-century Anglican theology, and how significant the Old Testament was for that: 'There can be no doubt that the rediscovery in the historical books of the Old Testament of the "godly prince", and the argument therefrom a fortiori to the authority of the Christian sovereign, was one of the most important and significant themes of the Reformers, alike Lutheran, Calvinist, and Anglican.'[430] Of course the Anglicans also made a distinction in respect of the royal primacy between the invisible church and the visible church; however, in connection with the latter there is no doubt that for them the ruler of the country is the supreme authority.[431] Old Testament typology provides the biblical basis for this view, a basis which at all events was necessary in the century of the Reformation. Conversely, the Puritans could occasionally assert that no one was obliged to obey the godless princes Jeroboam, Ahab, Joram and Ahaz or any other kings who commanded superstition.[432]

However, this use of the Old Testament was in no way an innovation in the Reformation period, but a legacy which had come down from the early church. R.W.Hanning has been able to show the special kind of typology which was developed by Eusebius of Caesarea in his *Church History*.[433] In Eusebius there are two forms of typology: spiritual typology (taken over from Origen) which begins from the pre-existence of Christ at the time of the Israel of the Old Testament and sees the kings of Israel as mystical types who offer earthly models of his heavenly rule,[434] and historical typology, which can see the events of the Exodus as related in Ex.15 repeated in the account of the battle at the Milvian bridge,[435] thus laying the foundation for a Christian view of history which finds the type and realization of heavenly salvation embodied in the Christian emperors and the visible course of the ongoing history of the empire. Over against this, Augustine again limits typology to the spiritual realm and firmly rejects the identification of the progress of the kingdom of God with external history, particularly that of the Roman empire. In the long run, however, the Eusebian form of typology finds a firmer footing in mediaeval historiography: in accordance with his specific aim, Hanning discusses the instances of this from mediaeval Britain. We can see how long the typological approach to history persisted through the centuries from the widespread continuation of typological forms of thought among the Puritans of New England throughout the seventeenth century; considerable attention has been paid to this recently.[436] The Puritans in America were aware of their particular experiences in history: the dangerous journey over the ocean after leaving their old homeland, the struggle with nature and the Indians in the New World, which was similarly depicted along typological lines drawn from the Old Testament: the exodus from Egypt (from persecution by the state church) or of Abraham from Babylon, the crossing of the sea (or through the wilderness) or the ark (a traditional image of the church, but easily brought up to date in terms of the Puritan community in New England), the fight with the Indians (the serpent in the wilderness), the transformation of the wilderness into fertile land (the manna, Ex.16.14ff.) and many other typological comparisons permeate the abundant New England literature.[437] The fact that here too a vigorous future expectation is bound up with typology and that the book of Revelation was read with an eye to people's own millennial hopes is a legacy of the English Puritan tradition[437a] and also puts a special stamp on the American attitude in a later age.

We can see the extent to which the struggle between various forms of typology could influence the basic understanding of the relationship between state and church from the *Treatise of Reformation without tarrying for anie* by Robert Browne, which has already been mentioned.[438] Browne puts very clearly the understanding of the church which distinguishes the first Congregationalists from the theology of the established church and also from the non-Separatist Puritans. The starting point is the Johannine saying of Jesus, John 18.36, and the key passage for Zwingli, I Peter 3.22, that the church is a 'spirituall kingdom'. From this it follows directly that the authorities have no say in spiritual matters: 'howe then shoulde his kingdome tarie for the Magistrate...' 'for they haue not the Keyes of the Kingdome of heauen to binde and lose, and to retaine or pronounce remitted the sinnes of men...'[439] 'The Magistrates haue the ciuill sworde'[440] – Browne defends himself against the charge of a lack of loyalty towards queen and country by 1. along with the whole of the English church rejecting the papal claim to supremacy, and 2. stressing that the queen has authority throughout the sphere of secular law, even over members of the church.[441] However, he turns the tables in the spiritual realm: 'They must obeye to the Scepter of Christe, if they bee Christians.'[442] The limitation of authority to the secular sphere goes hand in hand with a Spiritualist ecclesiology: Luke 17.21 in the translation: 'The kingdome of God shoulde be *within* you' provides the starting point for the definition: 'The inwarde obedience to the outwarde preaching and gouernement of the Church, with new-ness of life, that is the Lordes kingdome.'[443]

Significantly, this controversy, which begins from the direct applica-tion of New Testament quotations, is continued with a reference to Old Testament types. The position of the opponents of the state church appears in an allusion: 'They say, beholde we haue a Christian Prince, and a mother in Israel...' – evidently when applying their argument to a woman ruler they combine the role of the king with the type of Deborah (according to Judg.5.7). Browne, the separatist, firmly denies the relevance of the analogy of Old Testament ruler figures to providing a basis for the royal claim to supremacy over the church; but we should note the way in which this comes about! The argument is clearest in a section which begins with the statement 'The Lordes kingdome is not by force...' and then continues: 'Neither durst Moses, nor anie of the good Kings of Iuda force the people by lawe or by power to recieue the church gouernement, but after they receuied it, if then they fell awaye, and sought not the Lorde, they might put them to death.' After this there is a discussion of the 'covenant' which according to II Chron. 15.10ff. was concluded under king Asa in Jerusalem; there is special mention of v.13, in which the death penalty is threatened for all those who do not seek God.[444] Thus this is certainly a type, but a type so evaluated as to provide a basis for the Congregationalist conception of the role of the ruler: the *ius in sacra*[445] is not for the ruler, but rather for the punishment of the apostates! In reply his opponents referred to the type of Moses and the 'good kings of Judah' in order to legitimate the direct supremacy of the crown over the English church. They argue that 'Moses and the kinges of Iuda did reforme the Church, and they were taried for, therefore we also must tarie for our Magistrates.' That is further rejected with another important argument: his opponents, Browne declares, act against their conscience, for they 'make our Mag-istrates prophetes with Moses, yea high Priestes as he was and figures of Christ, as both he was and the Kings of Iuda also.'[446] If we first look at the second part of this statement we can note that here the Origenist form of typology is employed as opposed to that of Eusebius: the Old Testament rulers (including Moses, who takes on various roles), are purely spiritual types whose antitype is Christ, and not secular kings of the present. The same typological understanding is used immediately afterwards against the argument put forward by the other side that Haggai and Zechariah enlisted the help of the civil authorities in the rebuilding of the temple and looked towards them: 'Therefore we aun-swere, that Zerubabel being a *figure of Christ*, as appeareth in Zacharie the 4.(6b-10a) he was to be chiefe in the worke. Neither were they in that worke as ciuill Magistrates nowe a dayes, but as Spirituall guides, representing Christe and his spirituall kingdome.'[447] We can only understand this remark if we are aware of the Spiritualist form of typology, for which the temple, along with all Old Testament ceremonies, serves as a type for the spiritual reality of the kingdom of Christ. This rejects a historical analogy for the *ius in sacra* of the English crown.

It is interesting that Browne similarly prepares a type for the specific task of the church. It is already echoed in the passage cited above, which addresses Moses as a prophet, but becomes even clearer at another point: 'Yet Christ him selfe saieth, that the Preachers nowe in his kingdome, have greater authoritie than Iohn Baptist greater then the Prophetes before him. Therefore if Ieremie was set ouer the Nations & ouer the Kingdomes, to plucke vp and to roote out, and to destroye and throwe downe, to builde and to plante, Then haue we also an authoritie against which if the Kings and Nations doo sett themselues, we maye not be afraide of their faces, not leaue our calling for them.'[448] A type is found for the Puritan preacher through the direct translation of a New Testament statement[449] and the typological use of an Old Testament prophetic passage.[450] He is like the Old Testament prophets, and as their authority was greater than that of the state, the same is true for the preachers of the present, whom the author can therefore invite: 'But ye the Lords faithfull seruantes trusse vppe your loins as Ieremie which in your charges have greater avthoritie than Ieremie, as we proved before. Arise and speake vnto them, all that I commaunde you, sayeth the Lorde...'[451] At another point, with a reference to II Cor.3, it is said 'that the ministration of the spirite committed to all faithfull teachers at this time, exceedeth in glorie the ministration by Moses and the Prophetes before time'.[452] The course of the argument is the same everywhere: a New Testament quotation is taken as a starting point in order to form the point of contact for an Old Testament type: the office of preacher is understood as a heightening of the Old Testament model and at the same time it is shown to transcend the office of king. The sacral status of the king is stripped of its typological support in that the Old Testament kings are exclusively regarded as spiritual types who have already found their antitype in Christ.

The ensuing result is confirmed when we recall the insights which S.Bercovitch has gained into the basis of the argument in the long-drawn-out controversy between the famous American separatist Roger Williams and John Cotton, the representative of New England orthodoxy.[453] Whereas Perry Miller removed the earlier misunderstanding which regarded Roger Williams as the founder of the idea of democracy and so stylized him as an American national hero,[454] Bercovitch asserts that both parties, Williams and Cotton, make extensive use of typological arguments; indeed the dispute is quite simply a clash between two different forms of typology. Here the separatist Williams takes his stand on the spiritual form of typology: the types of the Old Testament are merely to be related to the spiritual mission of Christ, to his spiritual sword,[455], whereas Cotton tends towards the historical form: the events of the political history of the present are foreshadowed typologically by similar events reported in the Old Testament: here, in the way already indicated, the specific experiences and hopes of the settlers are reflected in the choice of parallels.[456]

Not only the monarchy but also the episcopal structure of the church was justified by Anglican theologians with a reference to the Old Testament as well as the New.[457] An interesting example of this is Andrewes' sketch[458] 'A Summary View of the Government both of the Old and New Testament; whereby the Episcopal Government of Christ's Church is Vindicated.'[459] In the form of a tabular survey of the form of 'ecclesiastical government' by means of key phrases, first in the various periods of the Old Testament (under Moses, Joshua, David and Nehemiah) and then in the New Testament, this outline aims to derive the hierarchical organization of the Anglican church, including its head in the office of archbishop, directly from the New Testament ministries, at the same time making use of particular Old Testament parallels. Nowhere does it become clearer than in this double approach how strongly the traditional models of thought determine the argument. Of particular note are some methodological comments which Andrewes inserts at two points. The author finds the hierarchical structure of the Old Testament very convenient for basing the office of archbishop on an Old Testament model. However, there is a difficulty: the person of Aaron is already being used as a type of Christ. As a substitute, there is the possibility of moving to Eleazar, who as high priest can be a model for the superiority of the archbishop: 'This is here worth the noting, that albeit it be granted that Aaron was the type of Christ, and so we forbear to take any argument of him; yet Eleazar, *who was no type*, nor ever so deemed by any writer, will serve sufficiently to show such superiority as is pleaded for...'[460] Thus only the typology pointing towards Christ is regarded as a 'type' in the technical sense: the Old Testament ministries, on the other hand, are taken to be directly binding examples by means of a historical connection which is assumed to be unbroken. The Old Testament institutions are to be continued, by way of their New Testament successors, right down to the present. Andrewes himself only has a vague feeling that this is a different form of 'typology'; he tackles the problem at another point. Against the objection, 'Christ being as well King as Priest, was as well foreresembled by the kings then as by the high priest; so that if His coming take away the one type, it must also the other', he puts forward the consideration:

'If it be said, there was in the king *somewhat else* beside the representation (as a type of Christ), the like is and may be truly said of the high
priest' – there follows a reference to the obedience which Paul according
to Acts 23.5 showed to the high priest, whose office had been accorded
the only significant function before Christ, as a type of Christ.[461] From
this he derives the justification for using both Old Testament ministries
as a model on the other level: both the typological perspectives depicted
meet at one point. As the result of his reflections on the Old Testament,
to end with Andrewes produces a table in which the correspondences
between ministries of Old and New Testament are summed up:

Aaron	Christ
Eleazar	archbishop
princes of priests	bishops
priests	presbyters
princes of levites	archdeacons
levites	deacons
nethinims	clerk and sextons.[462]

The intertwining of Old and New Testament ministries and their
binding character, which extends down to the present, is asserted even
more clearly in the *Convocation Book* by J.Overall.[463] Two quotations
show this clearly enough: 'Our Saviour Christ having made the external
government of his catholic church suitable to the government of his
universal monarchy over all the world, hath by the institution of the
Holy Ghost ordered to be placed in every kingdom... archbishops,
bishops and inferior ministers, to govern the particular churches therein
planted... according to the platform ordained in substance by himself
in the Old Testament.'[464] These high churchmen do not differ from the
Presbyterians in their hermeneutical principle: they too regard the ordering of the church ministry instituted by Christ in the New Testament
as a law directly binding on the present. The difference is that they
succeed in finding the hierarchical structure which they advocate in the
New Testament, just as the Presbyterians find theirs. Against the Old
Testament background already indicated, Overall explicitly states elsewhere: 'We do verily think that if our Saviour Christ or his apostles had
meant to have erected in the churches amongst the Gentiles any other
form of ecclesiastical government than God himself had set up amongst
the Jews, they would have done it assuredly in very solemn manner.'[465]
On the other hand it has often been noted that the Anglicans in no way
regarded the episcopal order as a requisite condition for recognizing
other churches: its absence is noted as a defect, but in practice, if need
be, it can be passed over.[466]

All these arguments do not in any way have merely academic significance, as an observer today might suppose after such an interval in

time. Rather, the decisive battles over the relationship between state and church, over the outward forms of the church and the inward content of its message, were fought on the ground of Holy Scripture, and thus, because of the indissoluble unity between church and society, which was taken for granted by all parties at that time, the point in contention was the very form of society itself. The methodological heritage of the ancient church in connection with understanding the Bible, as it had been worked out by Origen, Eusebius and the other church fathers, played an important role here. With the help of typology the ancient church had succeeded in preserving both the Old and the New Testaments as normative for the church, against the background of a Hellenistic world-view. The epistemological presuppositions had not changed decisively since then; even when the Renaissance and Humanism set new accents, the scholastic methodology continued to be valid even in the sixteenth and seventeenth centuries. As a result, on the presupposition that scripture as a whole was binding, the various trends within the Reformed churches in England too could base their positions not only on the New Testament but also on the Old. Typology has an essential part to play here; we have been able to establish that the historical form of typology which presupposed a direct correspondence between Old Testament types and events and the institutions and events of the present was used not only by the Anglicans but also by the Puritans, insofar as they remained in the state church and saw their aim as being to transform it further in accordance with their ideas. This approach was also used by the New England Puritans, when they were able to transfer their principles to American soil. Only the separatist groups, which advocated a strict division between state and church and a Spiritualist view of the church, rejected such a parallel, restricting typology to the Spiritualist christological kind. Through the example of Browne, however, we can see that they were not consistent here when it came to supporting the pillars of their own conviction: thus they discovered the type for the central ministry on which they saw the church founded, the preacher, in the prophets of the Old Testament. In what Browne says about the relationship of the prophets Haggai and Zechariah to Zerubbabel and what he deduces from Jer.1.10 for Jeremiah's attitude to the royal *king*doms, we can see the way in which attempts were made to resolve the contemporary controversy with the state church by recourse to the Old Testament. The Old Testament, interpreted with the help of the typological method, was a norm binding on both sides.

(d) The century of transition

This detailed account of the positions of Puritans and Anglicans in the sixteenth century has brought out the presuppositions common to both parties in the English church and the basic attitudes which divided them. It has also demonstrated that the decisive point of difference between them consists in their different attitudes to the authority of the Bible and especially of the Old Testament. This different evaluation of the authority of scripture is the starting point for all Puritan demands relating to the outward form of the church; underlying it is not so much a greater degree of Reformation theology as rather the origin of Puritanism in the Humanistic and Spiritualist traditions, whereas it is the scholastic, rationalist line which continues among the Anglicans. One basic moral attitude is common to both and becomes stronger about the turn of the century in the scholastic development of their system. Here Hooker on the one hand and Ames on the other offer the most complete examples. To a considerable degree rooted in tradition, albeit at a completely different level, is the typological use of the Old Testament, which is completely dissociated from other ways of approaching scripture. However, one reason why this part of the Bible was held in such high esteem by both parties was that it offered them the possibility of transferring the Old Testament model directly to the circumstances of church and state politics in the present.

It must next be our task to trace further developments in the seventeenth century, which in many ways deserves to be called a century of transition. The same cultural traditions also continue in this new century, but in the course of the controversies between the various parties in the church, significant shifts take place which direct developments along new lines and thus contribute to a basically different situation.

1. Before these changes took full effect, the rational school of Anglican theology[1] produced the best-known testimony to their understanding of the Bible in the work of William Chillingworth, *The Religion of Protestants A Safe Way to Salvation*.[2] Chillingworth (1602-1644)[3] belongs with John Hales(1584-1656)[4] to the much discussed circle which from 1635-39 gathered around Lucius Cary, second Viscount Falkland (1603-1643),[5] on his estate Great Tew, and to begin with discussed principally poetical themes.[6] Later these became increasingly theological and political; the dominant tone in the religious sphere was a rational liberalism and in politics a moderate royalism.[7] In earlier accounts, above all those which were devoted to the development of the idea of tolerance as a celebrated achievement in the history of ideas,[8] the round table of Great Tew seemed to have been something like a basic group of progressives, who optimistically held high the banner of religious freedom at a time of deep intolerance and dogmatic regression. Historical reality looks rather

different. The observations collected here demonstrate clearly that Chillingworth and those of like mind are to be understood much more strongly in terms of the dominant tradition of their time and the Anglican party in which they are to be included: connecting links also exist, remarkably enough, with Archbishop Laud,[9] who is almost always regarded as their chief opponent, and backwards above all to Hooker.[9a] However, Orr has also shown that in his approach Chillingworth goes beyond Hooker's position in two important points: in the appeal to reason as a critical authority which is ultimately decisive for truth, and in the postulate of an autonomous ethics which does away with the principle of authority hitherto regarded as valid.[10] However, these two points seem to be merely nuances, rather than a real new beginning, in the evaluation of the humanistic rational tradition, in which Chillingworth is influenced by people like Erasmus, Acontius and Zanchius.

Chillingworth is particularly important in this context because at the centre of his chief work *The Religion of Protestants* he puts the principle that the Bible, and the Bible alone, is the complete rule for the faith and action of Protestants.[11] This statement is in and of itself quite inoffensive and still does not reveal anything of its author's special concern. One could also understand it on Puritan lines, though as we can see from the example of Cheynell, they were vigorous opponents of Chillingworth. However, Chillingworth means it rather differently. The direction of his thought becomes clear when we take into account his earlier personal development before the composition of his main work. This has been done recently by Orr. It is certainly no coincidence that *The Religion of Protestants* is also a work of anti-Catholic apologetics.[12] In his youth Chillingworth had gone over to the Roman church because he saw realized there the ideal of the one all-embracing church. Following the example of Humanists like Erasmus, he thought that there was nevertheless room for intellectual freedom in the Catholic church, while on the other hand he recognized that the teaching authority of the church was an indispensible authority in dubious questions of faith.[13] However, it would be wrong to assume that Chillingworth was a sceptic who had fallen into the arms of the Catholic church in a kind of *sacrificium intellectus*; rather, he went over in the conviction that there are certain true and reasonable doctrines, that these (to a limited degree) are necessary for salvation, and that they were taught by the Roman church within the framework of its infallibility.[14] However, the same basic presuppositions also governed his speedy return to Anglicanism: the claim to infallibility, asserted in a bigoted way, now appeared to him to be the decisive hindrance to the development of that rational and moral attitude of faith which he was later inclined to accept as sufficient for personal salvation even among Turks and heretics.[15]

In its polemical aim, *The Religion of Protestants* is directed against precisely this claim to infallibility. In the present context it is important to note that the burden of the charge is that the Roman church has taken upon itself the role of an authoritative interpreter of the Bible (since it would have been impossible to do away with Holy Scripture because of the large numbers of copies in circulation), has added at will new doctrines in the guise of traditions and closer definitions, and thus has laid the foundation for its tyranny over human conscience.[16] Against the claim to infallibility he cites, first, the illegitimate use of force by which people are forced to acknowledge Roman claims,[17] and secondly also[18] Rome's ridiculous way of claiming metaphysical certainty for a truth based on historical tradition which in reality has only rational probability. As such this truth must all times be subject to testing by rational reason, just as an assent to such 'moral' truth can be expected only in terms of its rational credibility.[19] Already at this point we can see in which intellectual tradition Chillingworth is at home[20] and what future developments we can expect from him. From this perspective the Roman claim to infallibility immediately proves to be untenable: if it subjects itself to rational examination it has to abandon its own principle: if it sets out to be an axiom with a priori validity, it loses all rational credibility.[21]

More important than this polemical side of his system, however, is Chillingworth's view of God and the conclusions he draws from it. This view of God – and here Chillingworth agrees with the ideas dominant in the circles of Great Tew[22] – has a profoundly moral colouring. God is good: that is not a metaphysical statement, but is intended to have a reference to mankind. God requires of weak mortals no more than they are capable of giving, and adapts his demands to their imperfection.[23] In the sphere of doctrine it follows from this that there can in principle be no truths which are universally binding; for if God takes human weakness into account, in accordance with his revealed graciousness, he cannot condemn those who through error fail to reach his goal despite their earnest endeavours.[24] Thus, 'Whoever takes pain to strive' is the final consequence; generally speaking, all that holds in the sphere of doctrine is the obligation to *seek* incessantly for the truth,[25] and in the realm of action to fulfil the ethical commandments comprised in reason.[26]

If we now return to Chillingworth's central principle, that the Bible alone is the religion of Protestants, we can see how his remarks in this connection fit into the general attitude indicated above. Chillingworth – and here he was not unlike John Locke – was profoundly convinced of the truth of the Christian religion.[27] But he rejected the struggle for dogmatic infallibility among Protestants as well as Catholics,[28] and indeed was ready to restrict himself to the minimal requirement that

Christians should believe in Christ.[29] We can see that in the last resort he was not concerned with faith but that his real criteria lay in the moral sphere from his comment in passing that even the faith of Turks and heretics could well justify a person in the eyes of God provided only that he showed complete obedience towards the requirements of their faith.[30] Therefore Chillingworth did not regard even the Bible as necessary for salvation; in his eyes it contains all that is required for human salvation, but it is also possible to be saved without regarding the Bible as God's word: 'I believe, that he who believes all the particular doctrines which integrate Christianity, and lives according to them, should be saved, though he neither believed nor knew that the Gospels were written by the evangelists, or the Epistles by the apostles.'[31].

The Bible is merely a vehicle which conveys to us the content of our faith.[32] Along the lines of the distinction mentioned above, the content of the Bible is only a 'moral' certainty, but Chillingworth is quite prepared to trust the reliability of the authors of the Holy Scriptures as he is to trust the faithfulness of the tradition.[33] However, his deepest reason is again derived from his picture of God: 'This is no other than the watchful eye of Divine Providence; the goodness whereof will never suffer that the Scripture should be depraved and corrupted, but that in them should be always extant a conspicious and plain way to eternal happiness. Neither can any thing be more palpably unconsistent with his goodness, than to suffer Scripture to be undiscernibly corrupted in any matter of moment, and yet to exact of men the belief of those verities which, without their fault... were defaced out of them.'[34]

Now what is the 'content' of scripture or the gospel? Here Chillingworth seems first and foremost to share with all Humanists from the time of Erasmus their apparent concern for the central content of scripture: 'God is not defective in things necessary; neither will he leave himself without witness, nor the world without means of knowing his will and doing it.'.[35] Thus in the foreground is the view of scripture as the lawbook from which the will of God can be read most clearly. However, at the same time Chillingworth stresses – and this is his real concern – that God has given man complete freedom of choice to adopt this means or not. On the other hand he has a high opinion of everyone's capacity to make an independent decision on questions of religion: 'Now in matters of religion, when the question is, whether every man be a judge and chooser of himself, we suppose men honest, and such as understand the difference between a moment and eternity... And then we suppose that all the necessary points of religion are plain and easy, and consequently every man in this cause to be a competent judge for himself...'[36] Here is a decisive difference from secular law, which always needs a living interpreter.[37] At this point we can see clearly that for Chillingworth – and here there is a degree of difference from his remarks mentioned above about the minimal demands on Christians and heathen – there are also intellectual problems in religion, and these relate to the understanding of the Bible.

On the one hand Chillingworth can stress strongly the value of scripture as a criterion for deciding about theological controversies. He can take from the lips of his Catholic opponents the formula 'that Scripture is as perfect a rule of faith as a writing can be.'[38] But when soon after that he explains, in a closer definition, that scripture is such a perfect guideline for all who regard it as being of divine origin and as a criterion for faith,[39] we can already see a qualification: this high esteem is at all events limited to the sphere of the church, which includes Catholics and Protestants. On the other hand, another authority is set up alongside scripture: 'natural reason, the only principle, beside Scripture, which is common to all Christians.'[40]

This additional authority also opens up in principle the possibility of a conflict between reason and the content of scripture. However, for Chillingworth this possibility does not arise directly. Above all, his distinction between fundamental doctrine and doctrine which is not fundamental, standing in the tradition of Erasmus,[41] enables him to avoid this consequence. Granted, we can find more than one place in the Bible 'which is ambiguous, and with probability capable of divers senses; and in such it is no marvel, and sure no sin, if several men go several ways.'[42] Such distinctions in interpretation are conceivable, 'provided the difference be not touching any thing necessary to salvation'.[43] In this context even a criticism of the canon is possible, which raises suspicions about the canonicity and authenticity of some of the books of the Bible.[44] But it is different with the texts which 'are so plain and evident, that no man of ordinary sense can mistake the sense of them';[45] here, as it were, it is a matter of theodicy, that they are clearly revealed by God.[46] However, there is also considerable trust in reason to decide on the doctrines of scripture, 'Reason being a public and certain thing, and exposed to all men's trial and examination.'[47]

Chillingworth seldom indicates which doctrines he sees as fundamental statements, 'those particular doctrines which integrate Christianity';[48] nevertheless at one point it emerges that he is thinking of the basic statements of the Apostles' Creed.[49] If we look more closely at the formulations in this section, we can see influences from the Stoic-scholastic picture of God,[50] and above all a moralistic perspective.[51] Orr has also stressed the same colouring in a phrase which occurs at another point: 'the fundamental doctrines of faith, such, as though they have influence upon our lives, as every essential doctrine of Christianity has…'[52] and observes: 'Chillingworth cannot conceive a really important doctrine which has no bearing on conduct.'[53] It is evidently a corollary of this main interest in ethics that at another point Chillingworth can be so indifferent to dogmatic doctrines that he exclaims: 'This restraining of the word of God from that latitude and generality... is and has been the only fountain of all the schisms of the church...' He continues: 'Take away these walls of separation, and all will quickly be one... Require of Christians only to believe Christ, and call no man master but him only...'[54] If we read these remarks with Erasmus in mind, we can see that the same ethics of discipleship lies at the heart of the whole approach. The preference for the New Testament over the Old, and within the New Testament for the Gospels of Luke and Matthew with their moral tone, matches this well.[55] In addition, there is a clear rationalism, coupled with the confidence that everyone could understand the arguments, if only they were clothed in a simple form. Chillingworth shares many of these views with his predecessor Hooker. Orr has noticed a difference between them:[56] whereas Hooker regards the testimony of the Fathers and the church to the inerrancy of the biblical text as adequate, Chillingworth leaves the final examination of the testimony and teaching of the Bible to the reason of the individual Christian.[57] This was the line to be found at Great Tew: thus John Hales can also admonish his audience in his sermon 'Of Private Judgement in Religion':[58] 'That faculty of reason which is in every one of you, even in the meanest that hears me this day, next to the help of God, is your course of integrity and sanctity; you may no more refuse or neglect the use of it, and rest yourselves upon the use of other men's reason, than neglect your own...'[59] This mixture of rationalism and moralism would necessarily have an effect on the enormous significance of the Bible for Protestants in the direction of a more critical attitude towards scripture.

2. The first half of the time of great transition represented by the seventeenth century is already characterized by an abundance of intellectual trends which are juxtaposed and woven together; in various ways they were to be significant for the development of understanding the Bible. Though Anglicans and Puritans continue to represent the main trends, there are decisive inward transformations on both sides, based on their reciprocal interpenetration, provoked as it was by the acceptance on both sides of arguments in the long-drawn out controversies over church politics and literature. Puritanism, which came to power through the victory of Cromwell's cause, is already very different from the Puritan movement in the sixteenth century, and the revolutions of the time did not fail to leave their trace on Anglicans either. The increasing closeness in approach which we can observe in the second half of the century between restored Anglicanism, in which the Latitudinarian trend gained the upper hand, and the heirs of the various groups within Puritanism, is nevertheless not inconsistent, given the original Puritan motives: their hostility to culture underlying their polemics converges with the rational and moralistic line which shows the

Puritans to be heirs of Humanism and is no less clearly present among the Anglicans. So it is possible that an observer who classifies the fronts all too schematically will find that they suddenly shift in an almost inexplicable way, in that certain Anglicans operate with typically Puritan arguments, whereas a Puritan schooling (as with the Cambridge Platonists) can lead to an explicitly Latitudinarian development.

The church politics of William Laud and his followers is in many ways significant for the preparation of these developments. Under a more realistic estimate of the presuppositions and circumstances of his work, the old judgment on Laud which condemned him as the embodiment of an old authoritarianism in church politics, liturgy and dogma has given way to a rather more sophisticated approach. This extends as far as Bourne's verdict, which is meant to be thoroughly approving, that Laud's theological attitude was essentially that of a typical Anglican.[60] In fact the various sides of Laud's position can best be understood in the light of the motives of the anti-Puritan camp. The position taken against the Puritans is evidently the reason for the striking contrast between Laud's church politics and Whitgift's attitude towards Cartwright: whereas Whitgift described most rites of the church and the structure of its organization as matters which had not been laid down by a binding command in scripture and were therefore to be ordered *iure humano* in accordance with the circumstances of the time,[61] Laud sets great store by the outward forms of worship and seeks to impose them uniformly on the whole of the English church, just as he also includes the office of bishop among the basic principles of the church and seeks to derive it from Christ himself.[62] Evidently Laud's attitude is for the most part a reaction to the Puritan demand, which intensified more and more over the course of years: whereas their wishes in the 'millenary petition' of 1603 only embraced the abolition of disputed customs and renunciation by bishops of additional tithes,[63] the attacks on the bishops themselves now became louder and louder. Laud saw the church as being shaken to the foundations by their demands, and to reject these demands he referred to the tradition of the ancient church, which he sought to preserve from anarchy above all by strict stress on the outward forms of worship.[64] In his defence against the charges of the Lower House he explains the reasons which motivate him: 'I have neither urged nor enjoined any Popish or superstitious ceremonies... But all that I laboured for in this particular was, that the external worship of God in this Church might be kept up in uniformity and decency, and in some beauty of holiness. And this the rather, because... I found that with the contempt of the outward worship of God, the inward fell away apace, and profaneness began boldly to show itself... As for ceremonies; all that I enjoined, were according to law. And if any were superstitious, I enjoined them not. As for those which are so called by some men, they are no innovations, but restorations of the ancient approved ceremonies, in, and from the beginning of the Reformation, and settled either by law or custom.'[65] Here we have above all the practical man,[66] the pastor,[67] speaking. Alongside this there is also a feeling for the beauty of liturgical forms ('some beauty of holiness'). Theologically, by contrast, Laud was more broad-minded, and as we can see from his support of Chillingworth, was not far removed from the rational tendency in Anglicanism.

On the other hand, even the staunchest defenders of Laud concede that he made his greatest mistake in the way in which he acted and his choice of means, and in so doing contributed not so much to the consolidation of the church as to its collapse.[68] Among the measures which Laud took, his action against Henry Burton, John Bastwick and William Prynne in 1637, which ended with them being condemned to having their ears cut off by the executioner at the pillory in the court of the Palace of Westminster,[69] was the most notorious, and contributed most to the final failure of his policy. While the punishment was being carried out, those involved made the event a piece of large-scale propaganda for their cause, which was taken up by those who accompanied them on the way to their distant places of exile. However, this was only the spectacular result of a situation which had developed more and more to the detriment of the state church.[70] Puritan polemic had long been addressed to the 'abuses' within the church;[71] moreover, insofar as it was directed against the bishops, as a precautionary measure[72] it was usually limited to accusations that they had appropriated secular power. However, in his persecuting zeal Laud had also mistaken the intrinsic moderation which could be found among some of his opponents.[73] The situation became substantially more tense as a result of some over-zealous partisans who were championing the role of bishops (though in church politics they were considerably more liberal than Laud): in 1640/41, with Laud's specific backing,[74] Joseph Hall published a series of writings in defence of episcopacy[75] which prompted as the Puritan reaction the demand for the complete abolition of bishops.

Hall's works are significant because they indicate a fundamental change of position in Anglican apologetic: by suddenly seeking to base the divine right of the episcopate on scripture (and additionally on the testimony of the Fathers),[76] Hall moved on to the level at which the Puritans were arguing. The difficulties which the Presbyterians already had in demonstrating from the New Testament a binding model for the church order they sought inevitably proved even greater for Hall. While he could refer to the appointment of community leaders like Timothy and Titus by the apostles, who later exercised the functions which accrued to bishops, these were not called bishops, while on the other hand, in the early church 'all to whom the Dispensation of the Gospell was committed, were called Presbyters.'[77] However, he could demonstrate that the institution of the office of bishop was necessary once the communities had multiplied and their numbers had increased, in order to put an end to the differences of opinion between the presbyters and to avoid schism and disorder. For this argument he referred to the church father Jerome.[78] Patrology was still the more familiar area for an Anglican theologian.

We can see the Puritan reaction particularly clearly from Prynne's change of attitude. Whereas earlier, as an Erastian, he had revered as models the bishops of the century of the Reformation who were faithful to the kings, in his work *The Antipathie of the English Lordly Prelacie, Both to Regall Monarchy, and Civill Unity* of July 1641 he no longer attacks the bishops' claim to secular rule, but calls for the abolition of the episcopal office generally, 'root and branch'. The year 1641 is an important turning point. The committed Puritan party[79] now becomes absolutely opposed to the bishops. This becomes clear outwardly from the abundance of anti-episcopal pamphlets which were put on the market in this year. They include the work by Smectymnuus[80], *An answer to a book entituled, 'An Humble Remonstrance'* (by J.Hall), and also the anti-episcopal writings of Milton (which were barely noted when they first appeared). The Presbyterian party in (the Long) Parliament[81] took the same line: following a petition supported by the signatures of numerous London citizens,[82] a proposal was made to abolish the office of bishop completely (the 'root and branch bill'). Contrary to the expectations of its supporters, this was given a majority on the second reading.[83] One of the reasons for Laud's failure certainly lay in the fact that he had linked his fortunes with those of the absolutist king Charles and was therefore inevitably drawn into his fall. Another reason was that he did not recognize the mood of the people,[83a] which was still dominated by the fear of renewed catholicization. W.Prynne, for example, had fuelled hate against Rome over many years by his untiring literary activity. Although the only literary work by Laud of any size is devoted to a controversy with Catholicism,[84] he was condemned for high treason as a supporter of Rome.[84a]

3. Evidence for the attitude of Puritans in this phase comes in the five contributions with which Milton entered the dispute over the bishops in 1641/1642.[85,86] It is worth singling out Milton's earlier prose works from the enormously extensive pamphlet literature of this period[87] to illustrate the situation in the years 1641/1642, above all because in his open approach the various intellectual trends which determined the climate in church politics and literature before and during the Puritan revolution come together. The change between the various phases of the controversy is reflected in the surprising contrast between the periods of his prose-writing, which follow in rapid succession. It has

become increasingly clear in the history of Milton scholarship that his prose writings can only be understood in the context of the literary struggle which flared up between the different church political parties over the question of power in state and church: first between Laudians and Presbyterians, and then after a few years, on a different front, between the latter, with their basis in Parliament, and the Independents with their roots in Cromwell's army. Finally, after the Independents had seized power and thus taken over responsibility for the Commonwealth, there were disputes between them and the Levellers, who were even further on the left wing.[88] Precisely because Milton's influence on the outward course of events was small to begin with, his contributions to the discussion could develop with an intrinsic consistency in which we can see simultaneously both the reaction of an outside observer to events and quite personal developments in his own life.

More important than the reactive element[89] is the intrinsic connection which can be noted between the various aspects in Milton's comments. The most important Milton scholars have pointed out that two main trends were determinative for Milton's intellectual background: Humanism, which dominated his days as a student in Cambridge; and Puritanism, to which he was introduced by his teacher, T. Young.[90,91] We have still to see whether these two elements can be separated; it is sometimes worth considering Barker's comment that the confidence in man and human reason which emerges in Milton's *Areopagitica* was not without precedent in the pamphlets of contemporary Puritans.[92]

Some poetic passages from Milton's early works are already illuminating for our understanding of the position from which he started, as in them we already find indications of a number of elements in his basic attitude which were continually to prove normative throughout his later work. In the light of the main themes of his late works, the great epics *Paradise Lost* and *Paradise Regained*, it seems natural to regard Milton as a typical Puritan: thus e.g. Barker adduces as specifically Puritan the themes of Fall and Original Sin, the renewal of the Christian by grace and the freedom of the redeemed.[93] However, Handford's claim is legitimate: 'These postulates are the postulates not of Puritanism alone but of the total humanism of the Renaissance.'[94] They are also presupposed by Milton as traditional *loci*, though his heart is really elsewhere. Haller has already referred to *Comus* and *Lycidas*, which he describes as 'as authentic expressions of the Puritan spirit on the eve of the revolution as anything that came from the hand of Prynne'.[95] However, it is not enough to characterize Puritanism as a consistent elaboration of Calvinist theology, since the moral idealism which runs through the dramatic poem *Comus* has its roots in a soil far removed from the Reformation. In *Comus*[96] we have the embodiment of the poet's ideal in the figure of the virgin. Her attitude is interpreted by means of the figures of the 'older brother' and 'accompanying spirit', and set off by Comus, the counterpart who commends unlimited zest for life: virtue culminating in chastity beckons as the reward for ascent in a progressive spiritualization[97] into the heavenly sphere of freedom.[98] This is a Neo-platonic pattern of thought, blended with Aristotelian ethics in the notion of the balanced norm; the limitation inherent in it makes possible an enjoyment of the gifts and beauties of nature which is pure because it has been purified.[99] The sharp polemic against Christian priests is only apparently far removed from this; in reality it is closely connected with the humanistic world-view in *Comus* because it is based on the same Spiritualist principle. It comes out in the lamentation for his friend Edward King, Lycidas,[100] who died early, a lamentation richly adorned with the themes of ancient mythology and powerful imagery: the modern reader is very surprised to find in the context of a pastoral genre typical of this time such words as:

> of such as for their bellies sake,
> Creep and intrude, and climb into the fold...[101]

Evidently both the theme and the criticism of liturgical forms was in the air:

> ...their lean and flashy songs
> Grate on their scrannel Pipes of wretched straw...[102]

Looking back some years later,[103] Milton could say of *Lycidas* that it sought to announce 'the ruin of our corrupted clergy'; evidently the allusions were more than passing thoughts for him.

It was precisely as a poet that Milton felt himself called to intervene in the controversy over church politics; he returned home from his grand tour in Italy, by his own account shattered by the news from England: '*turpe enim existimabam, dum mei cives domi de libertate dimicarent, me animi causa otiose perigrinari.*'[104] However, more than a year elapsed before the literary feud between Bishop Hall and the Smectymnuus group also made Milton put pen to paper at the beginning of 1641,[105] and for long years he set aside his poetic plans in favour of political writing.

Precisely because Milton's early anti-episcopal writings contain ideas which are so unoriginal,[106] they serve well as a typical example of Presbyterian views in the first phase of the Puritan revolution. In the writings of 1641/42 Milton supports without qualification the demands of the Presbyterian party. That is already the case with the first pamphlet, *Of Reformation*,[107] of which Milton himself later said that it was 'written with the left hand'.[108] Here Milton consistently follows his earlier line of thought: right at the beginning of this work we can note how the attitude taken towards the bishops grows out of hatred against ceremonies, which for its part has its roots in the dualistic view which was determinative of the ethics in *Comus*. In the sentence with which Milton describes the significance of the Reformation, almost all the key words from *Comus* recur: '...that Doctrine of the Gospel, planted by teachers Divinely inspir'd, and by them winnow'd and sifted, from the chaffe of overdated Ceremonies, and refin'd to such a Spirituall height, and temper of purity..., that the body... were purifi'd by the affections of the regenerate Soule, and nothing left impure, but sinne; Faith needing not the weak, and fallible office of the Senses...'[109] The counterpart to the ideal of purity, conceived of on spiritualist lines, is 'sensuall Idolatry', which is embodied in the ceremonial cult that Milton calls 'the new vomited Paganisme of sensuall Idolatry'.[110] The present state of the church means, as he goes on to explain, a relapse into conditions before the Reformation; alongside *paganism* the phrase 'Jewish beggery' is also used for it; this is an indication that Milton has the same feelings against the Old Testament that we already met with in Erasmus and most representatives of the 'left wing of the Reformation'. The well-known Puritan themes put their stamp on the list of abuses which follows, among which vestments stand at the head.[111] Milton has no good word for the bishops, but only a flood of abuse.[112]

Underlying the various individual arguments in which Milton looks back on history we find the Spiritualist and Humanist view of church history, although it is concealed by the complicated structure and diction of this polemical piece. According to this, the ideal age of the time of the first church was followed by a long period of decline, until the present offers the possibility of a return to pure beginnings. Milton's attitude to the early church seems ambivalent: on the one hand he seeks to shake the credibility of Anglicans who refer to the testimony of the church fathers to justify the institutions of the church, by pointing to the differences existing between them and the past – on the other hand he uses the argument from the choice of bishops by the people in the early church[113] as a basis for his Presbyterian demands for the present.[114] In passing, he hits out at the Emperor Constantine, specifically because he is used by the episcopal party to legitimate the state church system.[115] A specific variant[116] in Milton's view of history is his retrospect on the most recent history of England, as a result of which he seeks to show the causes of the decline since the Reformation to which he refers;[117] evidently this is meant to be an answer to the defence of the office of bishop by the Anglicans, who referred to their martyr bishops like Cranmer.[118]

In conclusion, Milton can then again introduce the authority of the church fathers as a basis for his central demand that scripture alone must serve as the source of all truth. He replies to the objection that scripture is difficult to understand, and therefore must be explained by the Fathers, with the assertion that everything that is necessary to salvation is easy to understand, and anything that is obscure is unnecessary for salvation. Otherwise he trusts in the power of reason ('that intellectual ray which God hath planted in us'), which need only be wiped clean for scripture to become completely and utterly plain, even to the simplest Christian, 'foretelling an extraordinary effusion of Gods Spirit upon every age, and sexe, attributing to all men, and requiring from them the ability of searching, trying, examining all things...'[119] At this point the course from a Spiritualist to a rationalist hermeneutic becomes crystal clear, so that while later positions adopted by Milton mark a further development, they are in no way a break in his approach. The demand that every one can and should be his own interpreter of scripture, which is first meant spiritually, also concealed within itself the germ of further radicalization and secularization, as emerged in what were to an increasing degree the purely political demands of particular groups in the debates over the following years.

We can see the increasing emphasis put on the fact that the laity have come of age in the church from *Animadversions*,[120] which followed soon after, as Milton's contribution to the debate between Hall and the Smectymnuus group: 'God who hath promis'd to teach all his Children, and to deliver them out of your hands that hunt and worry their soules: hence is it that a man shall commonly find more savoury knowledge in one Lay-man, than in a dozen of Cathedrall Prelates...'[121] The stress on the laity is in turn closely connected with the moral perspective which is also decisive for understanding the Bible: 'For certainly, every rule, and instrument of necessary knowledge that God has given us, ought to be so in proportion as may bee weilded and manag'd by the life of man without penning him up from the duties of human society, and such a rule and instrument of knowledge perfectly is the holy Bible.'[122] Again the proximity to the moral biblicism of Erasmus is striking.

According to the principle expressed in the preface to the antiprelatical writing *The Reason of Church Government*, which appeared at the beginning of the following year,[123,124] one might have expected from Milton a new attempt to establish Presbyterian church order as the binding form prescribed in the New Testament. However, Milton is not up to this task,[125] and instead of this he is soon distracted by the polemic against the bishops, with whom he is also arguing in this work.[126] We need not concern ourselves further here with the usual charges which appear, against 'superstition', against vestments and other forms, and against episcopal jurisdiction, nor even over the poetic programme in the Preface to Book II, which is usually noted particularly by those Milton scholars who have a literary orientation.[127] On the other hand, in this connection it is important to note the explicit rejection, formulated in the controversy with Andrewes,[128] of the view that the hierarchical order of the church can be based on the Old Testament. Instead of this, Milton argues 'that ordinance must be evident in the Gospell. For the imperfect and obscure institution of the Law… cannot give rule to the compleat and glorious ministration of the Gospell, which lookes on the Law, as on a childe, not as on a tutor.'[129] And, on the slogan hurled into the debate by Ussher that the apostles partly 'imitated' the Old Testament model in the order of bishops: 'if it cannot be prov'd that it was done of purpose in imitation, as having the right thereof grounded in nature, and not in ceremony of type, it will little avail the matter.'[130]

The last observation in particular shows that here a fundamentally new hermeneutical criterion is brought into play: natural law takes the place of the old typology. This criterion is also evident in Milton's subsequent remarks, in which he takes up the well-known distinction between the political and the moral 'Jewish'[131] law. Because the latter alone 'containes in it the observation of whatsoever is substantially, and perpetually true and good, either in religion, or course of life', one can say of the gospel that 'from her own authentick hand-writing, and command', this teaches everything that is moral in this sense, 'besides what we fetch from those unwritten laws and Ideas which nature has ingraven in us.'[132] In this hermeneutic, the Humanist background comes through at various points: in addition to the notion of innate ideas and their moral tone, which has a Platonic colouring, this is the confidence in the ultimately unbroken goodness of man and the power of his reason to judge of its own accord in matters of good and evil.[133] Already at this point Milton takes a considerable step beyond the Presbyterian position which at the moment he thinks he is still defending when, in respect of the ordering of the church, he poses the demand that, as the church has a special concern for 'those inner parts and affections of the mind where the seat of reason is', it has the task and obligation 'to demand from us in Gods behalfe a service entirely reasonable.'[134] What he says in an excessively long chapter[135] about the rights of the laity in the church goes with this: church government 'ought to be free and open to any Christian man though never so laick, if his capacity, his faith, and prudent demeanour command him', 'and not excluded from such place of spirituall government as his Christian abilities and his approved good life in the eye and testimony of the Church preferre him to…'[136] For the laity are 'no servants, but all sons in obedience',[137] and so in respect of ceremonies 'the weakest Christian hath thrown off the robes of his minority and is a perfect man,[138] as to legal rites.'[139] It follows from this that the laity – now evidently in opposition to the claims of the Presbyterian clergy – are to be described in accordance with I Peter 2.9 as 'the rightfull Clergy of Christ'.[140]

At two points in the *Reason of Church Government* Milton's further conclusions already begin to become evident: first his arguments for the toleration of sects which can serve to preserve the firmness of faith, but which he also can describe in eschatological expectation as the 'throws and pangs that got before the birth of reformation',[141] and secondly the charge against the prelates that they have suppressed civic freedoms in England – an echo of the similar debates in Parliament[142] in which there is a prelude to the demand for the separation of church and state. Wolfe notes that even at this stage Milton is already beginning to become an Independent.[143]

In his reply to Hall, *An Apology against a Pamphlet* published soon afterwards,[144] Milton defends the rights of the laity in the church even more resolutely, being goaded on by his opponents. Against Hall's argument that the people is not in a position to judge the qualification of a minister, he appeals to a series of biblical passages in which it is said of the community 'that they were call'd in Christ to all perfectnesse of spirituall knowledge and full assurance of understanding in the mystery of God.'[145] In connection with the endowment of every Christian with the Spirit Milton asserts that even the simplest member of the laity knows the Bible well enough to be able to decide 'when he is wisely taught, and when weakly'. 'And who almost of the meanest Christians hath not heard the Scriptures often read from his childhood, besides so many Sermons and Lectures more in number then any student hath heard in Philosophy...'[146] This last observation leads him into a long attack on the universities and their urge for learning.[147] It is no coincidence that this recalls the hostility of the mediaeval Spiritualists to scholastic theology and the stress on the ideal of the simple life in the *philosophia Christi*, as put forward by Erasmus.[148] In Erasmus, too, immediately alongside this one could find the complaint that university teachers wrote and spoke in barbaric Latin, usually understood no Greek, and 'In the Hebrew text, which is so necessary to be understood except it be some few of them, their lips are utterly uncircumcis'd.'[149] Thus the 'democratic tone' in these writings of Milton is purely theoretical, a literary motive along the lines of the Humanist tradition, whereas Milton's own ideal is that of the lover of antiquity and aristocratic artist, educated in the old languages and the 'native latinisms of Cicero'. And the original Hebrew text seems indispensable to him for a proper understanding of the Bible. So it is no wonder that Milton's enthusiasm for the simple man has disappeared again a few years later.

4. Milton's writings on divorce similarly represent an important stage in the development of his understanding of the Bible.[150] Not only his audience[151] but also his approach so far compel him to provide a biblical basis for his subject, the right to divorce. Here the problem he had to deal with was that the absolute prohibition of divorce in the canon law of the Church of England, which had so far prevailed,[152] could appeal

to an explicit command of Jesus (Matt.19.3-9). Here only a reference back to an Old Testament precept (Deut.24.1-2) could help. It was possible for Milton, on the basis of his previous presuppositions, to demonstrate that a specific precept from the Old Testament like the permission for divorce was still in force only by pushing the bounds of morality a stage further into the realm of what had previously been regarded as 'political' law. Within this he had to distinguish between a 'political' law (in the narrower sense, which only held for the Jews) and a 'judicial' law, which also had something of a moral content and therefore continued to be valid.[153] Here he was taking a further step in the direction of natural law as the central criterion for judging the content of a biblical statement. Moreover, he cites Gen.2.18, which mentions the purpose of marriage: 'It is not good for a man to be alone, I will make him a help meet.' If the chief meaning of marriage is that the wife should be a 'help' to the husband, then it is impossible to forbid her dismissal, where she is not.[154] Even canon law allows the dissolution of a marriage for sexual impotence; how much more does it accord with man's worth that marital union should serve his spirit![155] As a consequence, if there is no spiritual harmony, a marriage can be dissolved just as it can be in the case of a physical defect.[156]

At first glance, by referring to the Old Testament Milton seems to be going a long way to meet his Puritan interlocutors. The reaction of his audience, dismay and rejection (for Milton the occasion for the decisive break with the Presbyterians), shows that the normative points on both sides were not a formal scriptural principle but the presuppositions on which the Bible was approached; here, in the sphere of rigorist ethics, any understanding of Milton's idealistic arguments was excluded.

Milton deals wisely and casuistically with the command of Christ which apparently stands in his way, namely that divorce is permissible only in cases of adultery. He explains the saying on the basis of a further exegetical principle to the effect that every passage must be understood in the light of its specific occasion,[157] and on the principle presupposed as Christ's real motive in all his words and actions. Christ is acting in accordance with his 'fundamental and superior laws of nature and charitie';[158] however, when according to Matt.5.18, Christ says he will not abolish a jot or tittle, Milton explains the saying as a rejection of the Pharisees, who in their immorality exploited a permission intended for good men in genuine need, dismissing their wives for no reason, by making excessive demands.[159] Christ allowed the law of Moses to stand in cases of real need; it was not his purpose 'to cut off all remedy from a good man who finds himself consuming away in a disconsolate and uninjoi'd matrimony, but to lay a bridle upon the bold abuses of those over-weening Rabbies.'[160]

In the second edition of his *Doctrine* Milton developed this argument from natural law. Here for the most part he could take up the legalistic rationalization of the understanding of law which had already found a way into Puritan orthodoxy with the adoption of the covenant;[161] that becomes particularly clear in the reference to the revealed will by which God has bound himself, a point argued against the objection that as the Lord, God can do what he wills.[162] However, Milton also regards this law – which is unalterable because it has been revealed – as unchangeable, because it accords with 'nature'.[163] In the dedication to Parliament and the Assembly with which he prefaces his work, the argument for 'indifferentia' is brought into the rationalization: marriage and therefore also divorce are now reckoned among the indifferentia,[164] and for that very reason Milton rejects the right of the church to decide on them.[165] Rather, divorce is left to the judgment of the individual as being a matter outside the fundamental truths of faith, 'being rather so clear in nature and reason, that it was left to a mans own arbitrement to be determin'd between God and his own conscience.'[166]

It is strange, then, how in his *Tetrachordon* (1645)[167] Milton incorporates the specifically Reformation doctrine of original sin into natural-law thinking. He does this by his interpretation of the expression 'hardness of heart' in Matt.19.8.[168] According to Milton, 'hardness of heart' has a twofold significance. The first[169] meaning is decisive here: according to this, the expression denotes the state of man after the fall and above all 'the imperfection and decay of man from original righteousness'.[170] 'In the beginnning, had men continu'd perfect, it had bin just that all things should have remain'd as they began to Adam & Eve.'[171] Without the Fall the permission for divorce would not have been necessary either; Christ can have had only that in mind with the 'in the beginning' of Matt.19.8. Christ obviously cannot have intended the absurd notion that before the promulgation of the law by Moses, marriage was everywhere indissoluble. But as an immediate return to the state of innocence is impossible, the situation since the Fall has changed: 'it alter'd the lore of justice, and put the government of things into a new frame'.[172] For the fallen world, there is thus a new form of natural law, 'the secondary law of nature and of nations.'[173] Insofar as it accords with this eternal morality, and not in its specific formulation, the Mosaic law is timelessly valid.

The problem of freedom also belongs in this context.[174] It is connected with the keyword 'grace' which is already mentioned in the *Doctrine*: Christ's judgment on divorce 'can be no new commend, for the Gospel enjoyns no new morality, save only the infinit enlargement of charity'.[175] This grace means, as Milton now states in the *Tetrachordon*, in respect of the Mosaic Law: 'If our saviour tooke away ought of law,... it was the bondage, not the liberty of any divine law that he remov'd.'[176] Therefore Christ could not accord Christians any less freedom than

Jews in the matter of divorce. However, arbitrariness is illegitimate either in this or in other questions: 'Christ spoke only to the conscience';[177] this is the basis of Christian freedom and at the same time its limitation. However, as Barker acutely observed, the argument leads from the sphere of Christian freedom into the freedom which can be claimed by every man under natural law.[178] Here Milton breaks through the basic Humanist attitude again, since Gen.1.27 is so important to him: 'For nothing now adayes is more degenerately forgott'n, then the true dignity of man.'[179] People must be surprised 'why in this age many are so opposite both to human and to Christian liberty.' The 'just and naturall privileges' of men must accord with his 'inward goodness'.[180]

Whereas Barker points to the proximity of this mixture of Christian freedom and the natural right of man as a rational being to the arguments within the political debate over tolerance,[181] Sirluck indicates the consequences for the interpretation of scripture.[182] Milton's postulate, 'indeed no ordinance human or from heav'n can binde against the good of man'[183] also applies to the interpretation of Christ's command: 'nothing sooner might direct them to finde his meaning, then to compare and measure it by the rules of nature and eternall righteousnes, which no writt'n law extinguishes, and the Gospel least of all.'[184] Utilitarian ethics are extended as a criterion from the permission for divorce to all commandments: 'The General end of every Ordinance, of every severest, every divinest, even of Sabbath is the good of man, yea his temporal good not excluded.'[185]

The mention of the sabbath illuminates in a flash the shift which took place about the turn of the century towards the Puritan attitude.[186] However, Milton's observation is in no way the comment of a solitary: Barker has pointed out that Milton repeats ideas which played a role in general Parliamentary debates at the same time; in particular, *Scripture and Reason*, which serves as a defence of Parliamentary politics,[187] should be mentioned as a model.[188] With his theme of divorce Milton had isolated himself from public opinion; with the principles which he applied to this theme he was well up with the times.

In this connection only two things are important in connection with Milton's *Areopagitica* (autumn 1644), which has been noted so much in the extensive literature about the history of the idea of tolerance, though its effect at the time was so slight.[189] First, the principle of reason has acquired yet more weight. Milton attacks the preliminary censorship of all kinds of writings, including those with bad contents, since the decision between good and evil can only be an act of free resolve for which human reason provides the criterion.[190] Man cannot live in a state of innocence in the world and cannot be shut off from it as in a monastery: 'That which purifies us is triall, and triall is by what is contrary.'[191] True virtue displays itself in the voluntary choice of the good; as this is not possible without knowledge of evil, 'how can we more safely, and with lesse danger scout into the regions of sin and falsity then by reading all manner of tractats, and hearing all manner of reasons?'[192] From the demand for the toleration of what may even be bad literature, so that the truth can show itself in being tried by reason, there follows in the further course of the tractate a conclusion which has since become famous, on the toleration of sects. Outward conformity brought about by force is useless for the truth;[193] therefore even if Milton does not want to deny the noxious agitation by some sects,[194] he asks that they should be tolerated. The possibility of a progress to new positions, to 'some new enlightn'd steps in the discovery of truth',[195] lies in debating with them, not in suppressing them.

The other fact worth noting in *Areopagitica* is that Milton has moved further from his original position on the Presbyterian side, over against the bishops. He now adopts the same hostile attitude towards the Presbyterian clergy in the Westminster Assembly that he once did towards the Bishops: the presbyters are now the same tyrants as the prelates once were: this tyranny 'will soon put it out of controversie that Bishops and Presbyters are the same to us both name and thing.'[196] This change of position is not only to be explained by Milton's bitterness at being rejected by his former allies over the question of divorce; he also follows the tenor of the propaganda of the Independents, who established themselves around the turn of the year 1644/45 as an independent movement over against the Presbyterians.[197] Here, too, Milton's changing attitude is a subtle barometer for the development of the political situation in the church as a whole.

And yet, if we look back on all Milton's prose writings published before 1644, all the elements which hold them together are more important than the development which is to be noted between the earliest and the latest. This is true despite the masterly analysis by Barker, which has rightly formed the basis for all subsequent scholarship. In particular the poetic works of Milton's youth, which Barker has with good reason taken into account in his judgment, indicate that Milton's basic attitude developed very early and that even before his intervention in the discussion over church politics, he had already formed the criteria which subsequently lay behind his judgments on topics current at the time. The ethical idealism of *Comus*, the hostility to priests and worship in *Lycidas*, the belief in reason and human worth, are all part of the legacy of Humanism. Even his temporary enthusiasm for the Presbyterian cause does not alter any of this, for in his anti-prelatical writings Milton in no way argues for an authoritative scriptural principle along the lines of Cartwright, but for the spiritual moralism that was characteristic of the Humanist understanding of scripture at least from the time of Erasmus.[198] In fact he did not develop any detailed pattern of church order even in the *Reason of Church Government*. Despite this, it is not nonsensical that from the beginning Milton should have put himself in the Puritan camp; as we have seen, the Puritans were just as much heirs of Humanism as they were of the Reformation; their morality could on occasion refer as readily to 'nature' as it could to the Bible, but even more often it tacitly lay behind their implacable opposition to the outward forms of the church, on which they increasingly poured scorn.

One problem remained unresolved within Puritanism: the insuperable opposition between the struggle for a comprehensive and all-embracing Reformation, along with the reordering of the national church in accordance with the authoritative model presented in the New Testament, and the unshakable belief that they had principles for this Reformation which were so immediately illuminating that they could directly be understood by any Christian. For this conviction inevitably led to a demand for freedom of conscience which, in its conflict with the call for general church reform in accordance with scripture, produced the 'Puritan dilemma'. It was this dilemma that Barker recognized as the origin of the incurable divisions which began after the victory of the Puritan cause. The rationalist element had directed Puritan thought secretly for a long time: now on the liberal wing of the movement the high estimation of reason and the consequent pressure for tolerance and freedom in individual belief emerged as an increasingly powerful force.

5. In which of the two parties, among the Anglicans or the Puritans, did reason play a greater role? This question is still hard to answer. However, in this respect the years of the 'Long Parliament' evidently brought a decisive shift of fronts. For Hooker, the 'law of nature' or 'law of reason' was the decisive source of knowledge alongside and in scripture,[199] and this rationalistic tradition in Anglicanism lasted until the time of the men of Great Tew and Jeremy Taylor. On the other hand, Joseph Hall veered round to the authority of scripture, formerly the basis appealed to by Puritans like Cartwright, as a basis for the office of bishop, additionally appealing to the testimony of the church fathers whom Laud regarded so highly. By contrast, liberal Puritanism increasingly became the stronghold of rationalism.

A man who very definitely provided the impulse for this development, though his literary activity was limited to two works because of his early death in the Civil War in 1643, is Robert Greville, Lord Brooke.[200] His significance would be unmistakable even if Milton had not paid permanent homage to him in the *Areopagitica*.[201] It is particularly important in understanding his viewpoint to know that before his anti-prelatical polemical work, Brooke wrote a short philosophical book on the nature of truth.[202] Here he shows himself to be a 'Christian humanist'[203] of high standing, with an extensive education including a knowledge of classical and scholastic literature and philosophy, and above all of the Renaissance philosophers, who brought together in their work the legacy of Plato as transformed by Plotinus, along with Aristotle, Thomas Aquinas and Augustine. Already in this work he has a respect for reason, like the young Milton; not in the sense of modern rationalism, but along the lines of Neoplatonist idealism.[204] Nor does he set reason over against belief, but simply sees them as different degrees of knowledge.

On these presuppositions Brooke could give a new direction to the Puritan attitude in various respects when he entered the debate about bishops with the work *A Discourse opening the Nature of that Episcopacie, which is exercised in England* (1641)[205].

This is evident above all from his treatment of the indifferentia. The Puritans of the old school like Hooper and Cartwright had virtually done away with the indifferentia when they required that even the external forms in the church which were not explicitly prescribed in scripture were to be ordered in the light of the authority of scripture, on the principle of 'edification'.[206] The difficulty was that this principle could not be defined more closely, and therefore functioned in an esoteric way, since among the Puritans there was unspoken agreement over a particular view of its content which could not be demonstrated to outsiders like the Anglicans, who therefore made church authorities, i.e. the bishops, responsible for the ordering of the indifferentia.

This is the point at which Brooke begins, on the basis of his understanding of reason.[207] The fifth and sixth chapters in the first part of his *Discourse*[208] are devoted to the clarification of the term 'Indifference'.[209] He begins with the etymology of the word and explains it as a term of relationship: the preposition 'in' does not denote absolute negation: 'not purely non differens, but in such, or such a respect, it Differeth not.'[210] In natural circumstances, like black and white, hot and cold, there is a true mean between the extremes which is different from each of them and yet shares in them both, just as lukewarm is not distinct from hot, since both are warm, yet is different, since at the same time it is cold.[211] However, there cannot be such indifference in moral matters: as evil is only the vitiation of the good,[212] no passions, still less individual attitudes, can be good and bad at the same time: if an action is bad in any respect it can no longer really be called good.[213] It follows from this that the indifferent must be completely good; if it has anything bad in it it is completely bad, and therefore not indifferent. So it must be good and therefore lawful. But as indifferent cannot mean lawful at one time and unlawful at another, it can only be the case that in a particular situation a person must choose between two extremes: to act or not to act. Now in respect of the circumstances of the time only one of these alternatives can be the better one. In such a case the person concerned must choose the better – and in that case it is lawful to adopt this better course, and at the same time useful.

At this point 'right reason' has its place: since only reason can decide what is the best at the moment, and therefore the most useful and for that reason also lawful, only reason can decide what is to be done. Take, for example, the question 'To marry or not to marry?'[214] Only one of the two can be the best in a given situation, so we have to do one of two things. Now it follows from this that nothing is indifferent. 'No Thing, No Act, is Indifferent in Se, in Re...; but either necessary to be done, (if Best) or unlawfull to be done, if Bad, or lesse Good, pro hoc statu.'[215] Something can be indifferent only beause of our lack of understanding,[216] as in the case of the quack who holds good medicine in one hand and poison in the other but cannot distinguish between the two: if he gives one to the patient he errs, because it is poison.

In Chapter 6 Brooke explains where the authority lies to decide on actions in the sphere of indifferentia. As all things are either good or evil and nothing is indifferent, it is clear that it is not in the power of the church to *make* anything indifferent. Insofar as it is a matter of things which are *indifferent* because neither scripture nor reason has made them clear in us, the church does not have the authority to decide on an extreme. However, if one of the two is necessary, the church decides; it does so like any individual or group of people, by means of right reason. Now the church is the sum of its members;[217] but what if I diverge from the decision of the majority in my judgment? Should I leave the church and found a schism or party? 'God forbid; no' – I must wait, 'Read, pray, discourse, and conferre, with all humility submitting my selfe to the Reason of any man that will teach me,' and if unsuccessful, 'I must suspend till my judgement be cleared'. In the last resort, however, violence may no more force my action than my judgment. Obviously the church must decide on matters of ritual which are not prescribed in scripture ('We must use some Place, some Time, some Gesture'), but it may do so only 'by her Rule, which is Right Reason'. If anyone believes that she is wrong, he only owes her passive obedience. But the church may not compel him by force, still less the bishops.

Barker has already indicated a far-reaching consequence of these considerations of Brooke's: 'Complete freedom of conscience is the inescapable result.'[218] This appears in Chapter 7 of Part Two of the *Discourse*, when Brooke speaks of the toleration of sects, not only in the actual demand for it but also in the open sympathy with which he reports the spiritualist doctrines of the sects.[219] On the other hand, Brooke's remarks have some continuity with the earlier stage of the Puritan approach: for Hooper and Cartwright, too, it is clear that essentially there are no indifferentia, and they too pass moral judgment on the sphere of ritual actions which are usually included under this heading. For them, too, there were only the alternatives of good or evil, which Brooke now brought into a clear system with Ramistic logic and the apparatus of ancient philosophy. The difference with Hooper and Cartwright was that in the light of their Spiritualism they thought they knew *a priori* that all ritual was bad and therefore also knew how the outward ordering of the church should be shaped. Here Brooke is more sceptical, more individualistic in respect of individual reason, and therefore more open. But this scepticism is only directed against man's temporary weakness in knowledge and capacity for error, and not against the possibility in principle, indeed the duty, to decide everything in accordance with the rational criterion of good or evil – a criterion which, though conditioned by situations, was valid unconditionally. The characteristic juxtaposition of moralism, spiritualism and what was now an increasingly powerful rationalism is closer among the Puritans than among the Anglicans, even if it could not always be recognized equally clearly among them.

6. There are connecting links between a Puritanism with philosophical colouring like that of Lord Brooke and what at first sight are quite different phenomena: on the one hand the philosophical school of the 'Cambridge Platonists' and on the other the Puritan groups, from the Independents to the religious and political sects of the Levellers and kindred trends. With their political activism on the one hand and their philosophical and contemplative attitude on the other these groups are certainly worlds apart. However, as philosophy and theology in the seventeenth century were no more separated than faith and politics, they have much in common, and that is particularly true of their cultural presuppositions.

In the following account the only possible approach is to tackle the various trends and individual thinkers of the seventeenth century in succession, although moving backwards and forwards in time is unavoidable here. The century of transition has far more varied phenomena than the preceding century, and although here my purpose is only to illuminate the cultural background to the change in the understanding of the Bible in this period, this can no longer be done with a unilinear account.

Given the presuppositions which emerged with Milton and Brooke, it makes sense first to look at the 'Cambridge Platonists',[220] though the years in which the most important leaders of this school died are in fact as late as the ninth decade of the century, and a great deal of their activity lay in the period after the Carolingian Restoration.[221] However, the decisive period of their education was in the years of the Puritan revolution: thus Henry More entered Christ's College, Cambridge, in the very year that Milton left it.[222] The attitude of the Cambridge Platonists is also quite specially representative of the intellectual situation in England about the middle of the century. In contrast to the under-estimation of their significance which was customary at an earlier date, in more recent times there have been plenty of scholars who have pointed to the worldwide influence which the Cambridge school exer-cised on subsequent developments. However, they are by no means so isolated a phenomenon, given their starting point, as the title of Cas-sirer's book, *The Platonic Renaissance in England*, would suggest.[223] That is immediately evident when we put their main ideas in the context of the developments which I have described so far.

Strider has referred to the affinity between the aims and the world-view of Brooke and those of the Cambridge Platonists.[224] The young Milton should also be compared with them. The view that with the Cambridge Platonists the Renaissance suddenly revived again unex-pectedly and began to blossom on the barren soil of a predominantly strict Calvinistic Puritanism has long been shown to be misleading. Our survey so far has shown that at no time did the Puritans have absolute cultural domination in England, but quite independently of this the traditions of humanism would not have gone under, as they had long since won their place even in Puritanism.[225] In particular, the two uni-versities in England were largely the spiritual home of an academic class who to a considerable degree were more or less open supporters of humanistic ideas, where they did not still cherish scholastic forms of thinking.[226] In 1651, when Whichcote, who in the meanwhile had be-come Provost of King's College and Vice-Chancellor of the University, was at the height of his influence in Cambridge, the Calvinist Anthony Tuckney, Master of Emmanuel College, who had once been his tutor, wrote a retrospect on his formative years between 1633-43, when he was a Fellow of Emmanuel. He commented that at that time he had fallen 'into the company of very learned and ingenious men; who, I fear, at least some of them, studied other authors, more than the scrip-tures; and Plato and his scholars, above others...'[227] Henry More had been brought up in a strict Calvinistic spirit,[228] against which he had already rebelled during his three-year stay in Eton (1628-31). In 1631, when, with his views already changed,[229] he entered Christ's College, Cambridge, he found himself immediately entrusted to the supervision of a tutor who was completely to his taste: *viri pii pariter atque docti, & qua de re haud parum sollicitus fueram, minime Calvinistici.* His first question to his pupil was: *an discrimen haberem honestorum & turpium?*[230]

Thus the attitude of the Cambridge Platonists was by no means an isolated phenomenon in the cultural world of this university and in educated academic circles in England. Although their eirenic attitude may also have differed from the disputatious trends in Puritanism, which almost simultaneously with their greatest display of power were approaching the failure of their experiment,[231] in their ethical humanism they shared a large number of presuppositions with them. It is particularly instructive to look at them more closely, since as a school of philosophers (albeit with varying success from a modern perspective) they sought to bring together into a system elements of the thought of earlier humanists like Erasmus, of which these were less conscious because they were unexamined presuppositions.

However, such an enterprise is made more difficult by the baroque style which the leading figures of the Cambridge school tended to adopt in their writing. Cudworth's voluminous *True Intellectual System of the Universe*[232] is a famous – or rather, notorious – example of the almost infinite prolixity of their writing,[233] but More's work, too, is extensive, vast and full of repetitions.[234] On the other hand, for all the individual differences between the chief representatives of the school,[235] there is so much agreement in the basic approach of their work and their most important views that we can gain a relatively uniform picture of them.

One widespread view of the significance of the Cambridge Platonists goes back to Tulloch; as the first part of it accords with a powerful present-day ideology, it has found a number of followers.[236] According to Tulloch,[237] the Cambridge Platonists are chiefly important as pioneers of the idea of tolerance, and at the same time of a theological rationalism which was to gain a dominant position after the Restoration in the form of Latitudinarianism. However, the attitude of tolerance is only a concomitant phenomenon to their approach, which is oriented on morality and hostile to dogma, and their concept of reason does not have much in common with what is usually understood by 'rationalism'. Of course, the thought of the Latitudinarians, as of the Enlightenment which follows, can be misunderstood in the same way, so it is certainly not wrong to see the Cambridge Platonists as pioneers. Others rightly stress the close connection of the school with earlier developments.[238] And indeed, for example the Puritan Brooke already anticipates much of what later was to be seen as the characteristic doctrines of the Cambridge Platonists. Against this background it is no longer so striking that most of them were educated in the 'great nursery of Puritan thought',[239] Emmanuel College.

Much of the characteristic quality of the thought of the Cambridge Platonists can be seen in the works of Henry More, though he was not the founder and real head of the school. This honour goes to Benjamin Whichcote, the small amount of whose writing hardly reflects the breadth of his personal activity.[240] More was probably their most fertile writer, and he also published the most during his lifetime. The valuable work of A. Lichtenstein[241] has provided a view of the basic problems of his approach which substantially deepens earlier views and in some way corrects them. Where Lichtenstein's investigation takes us further is above all that he establishes a basically dualistic view in the much-noted concept of reason among the Cambridge Platonists in general and More in particular (this is the *recta ratio* of the humanist tradition which we already found in Brooke)[242] – the dichotomy is characteristic of Platonic thought.[243] The favourite scriptural passage of the Cambridge Platonists, Prov.20.27, 'The Spirit of man is the candle of the Lord',[244] already indicates the nature of their understanding of scripture: they do not mean purely intellectual, theoretical thought (their chief attack is indeed directed against this), but a form of living in which two forces in man are involved, intellect and will (reason and faith). This approach proceeds along two ways, knowledge and experience, and aims at a twofold goal: truth and virtue.[245] The significance of reason for religious life is continually stressed by the Cambridge Platonists; however, they are not rationalists, but develop their ideas on the basis of a lively religious experience. This again lies decisively in the moral sphere, in the development of an ethical will in the face of a God understood as the embodiment of ethical perfection and in the implementation of practical moral action.

The feature in the thought of the Cambridge Platonists which numerous modern observers have regarded as 'mystical'[246] is in reality an expression of their Greek idealistic religious sense. 'Being in the image of God' is the highest goal of religion, as More never tires of stressing; this goal is striven for in the context of an understanding of God in which God is not just the embodiment of supreme wisdom and omniscient understanding,[247] but also the embodiment of unlimited goodness. Here it is inconceivable that for all his omnipotence he could rationally be guided in his actions by anything other than the best that is conceivable.[248] Similarly, the important thing for man is to shape himself in accordance with the image of God through moral renewal,[249] so that he achieves a state of moral perfection: 'the perfecting of the Humane nature by participation of the Divine.'[250] However, this is not only the fruit of human endeavour but – in accordance with Neoplatonic emanationist thought – the 'divine life' or 'the Divine Vertues... are proper to a Creature to whom God communicates his own Nature so far forth as it is capable of receiving it.'[251] Thus here we could discover the 'mystical' element which makes this attitude a kind of 'faith' in contrast to a purely moral form of life.[252] The difference from a mere rationalism is on the same lines: it becomes clear in the fact that More postulates a higher principle over against normal reason, which he calls *divina sagacitas*. He stresses its special character: at the same time it is both divine and a property of the morally divinized man.[253]

Beyond question, at this point we can see a vividly sensed spirituality which marks out all the Cambridge Platonists. Here, too, are the roots of their resistance to all pure intellectualism, which in More issues in a special form of the humanist hostility to dogma and the doctrine of fundamentals: precisely because they keep reason and faith close together,[254] understanding this as an ethical attitude, they can dispense with dogmatic truths without a direct moral reference: 'Wherefore he that is arrived to this Substantiality of life will be fixt in all useful Divine Truths, and the Reasons that grow on such a Root will be found solid and permanent by him that has the Root.'[255] There are only a few essentials for truth in religion.[256] Therefore all higher intellectual knowledge and concerns for the happiness of man which lie in true virtue are in the end completely superfluous; they are more a form of mental acrobatics.[257] That immediately has similar consequences for the consideration of the Bible: More shares the view that only a few truths are important to salvation, and that they are all clearly contained in the Bible.[258] The ideal – and this More shares with his Humanist predecessors from Erasmus onwards – is simplicity. This ideal is conditioned not only by a hostility to dogma, but also by an antipathy to all ceremonial, as More already explains in the Preface to the *Mystery of Godliness*: 'My onely solicitude therefore was to corroborate that Faith that is plainly propounded to us out of the Scripture, which is sufficient to Salvation, and to exalt that Life which has lyen dead and buried for these so many Ages under a vast heap of humane Inventions, useless and cumbersome Ceremonies, and unpeaceable Opinions.'[259]

Among the Cambridge Platonists, the removal of the numinous from the understanding of God follows along the same lines.[260] John Smith devotes a short essay[261] to superstition and in it declares by means of a quotation from Cicero:[262] 'the true cause and rise of superstition is indeed nothing else but a false opinion of the Deity, that renders him dreadful and terrible, as being rigorous and imperious.' The appropriate attitude to the rational, 'good' God is a relationship which is purified from fear, one might almost say from reverence. In his *Aphorisms*,[263] Whichcote introduces a catchword which is typical of the terminology of the later Deists: he uses 'mystery' with the same negative connotations. 'The more Mysterious, the more Imperfect...: As Darkness is, in compare with light, so is Mystery, in comparison with Knowledge.' Instead of this, the relationship with God is directed by a rationality which consists chiefly in the cultivation of an ethical motivation and culminates in moral action. Here the Spiritualist tradition still shines through most strongly in the intensity of the sense of the possibility of divinization, which is still visible among the Cambridge Platonists, in contrast to their Latitudinarian disciples of the next generation. Lichtenstein is right to differentiate this attitude sharply from the belief in the 'inner light' which lives on among the Quakers.[264]

Ralph Cudworth deserves special mention, because in his work we find a detailed attempt to provide the theoretical basis for an autonomous ethics.[265] The central thesis of his *Treatise*, criticized by Tulloch as a tautology,[266] but representing the attempt to express such an autonomy, is 'that Moral Good and Evil, Just and Unjust, Honest and Dishonest... cannot possibly be Arbitrary things, made by Will without Nature, because it is Universally true That things are what they are not by Will but by Nature.'[267] This conception is new only as a theoretical postulate: in reality, as a basic attitude it already underlies the whole position within the Humanistic tradition which is critical of the teaching and cultic forms of the church. Of course, the explosive force which this statement was to have over the question of biblical criticism only emerged in a later period. For it is clearly thought by Cudworth to be the answer to the theory that an action becomes good or bad by God willing it to be so: 'For though the Will and Power of God have an Absolute, Infinite and Unlimited Command upon the Existence of all Created things to make them to be, or not to be at Pleasure; yet when things exist, they are what they are, This or That, Absolutely or Relatively, not by Will or Arbitrary Command, but by the Necessity of their own Nature.'[268] This is directed both against Hobbes and against the Puritan scripturalists. Its critical significance is accentuated by the further distinction between the positive good of a specific action (corresponding to a law or occasioned by a promise) which does not display any moral quality in itself, and the 'natural' good, which is prior to all law and represents an absolute criterion.[269] For according to this theory, the authority to promulgate a specific law and the obligation which others feel to behave in accordance with it can only lie in 'the intellectual Nature of him that is commanded', i.e. in the possibility of seeing the natural goodness which stands in the background. Now in so far as the question is concerned with indifferent things, these become good or evil by being related to a superior natural good (e.g. a promise which has to be kept). This provides a criterion which is also relevant in judgments on the content of the Bible, since they too must be capable of being measured by natural goodness, which according to Cudworth binds even God himself. Of course Cudworth himself did not yet draw this consequence, and the Cambridge Platonists generally are not important as interpreters of the Bible but as philosophers who in their own way press on with the intellectual development which in the end saw a fundamentally different relationship between the Bible and the forces by which it was supported.

A number of signs indicate that the Cambridge Platonists themselves had not yet arrived at a critical standpoint over against the Bible. Some members of the group are immediately ready to assent quite uncritically to the old legend[270] that Pythagoras was influenced substantially in his philosophy by Moses, who was the first philosopher, and therefore that the origin of philosophy is really to be sought in the Hebrew scriptures.[271] But the opposite relationship to the Old Testament, which was to be found in the humanist tradition, also has its supporters. A good example of this is the *Discourse on Legal Righteousness and on the Righteousness of Faith* by John Smith.[272] Here, with abundant references to Jewish exegesis,[273] there is a contrast between righteousness through the law in the Old Testament, which has as its basis a law coming from outside, based on the acceptance of human freedom of the will[274] and putting merit in place of grace,[275] as a lower, external form of religion,[276] and the 'righteousness of the gospel'[277] in the New Testament, as it is read out, primarily, of Paul understood in an idealistic way. The definition of 'gospel' which is taken as a starting point here is a prime example of Neoplatonist emanationist thought: 'the gospel is set forth as a mighty efflux and emanation of life and spirit, freely issuing forth from an Omnipotent source of grace and love, as that true godlike vital influence, whereby the Divinity derives itself into the souls of men, enlivening and transforming them into its own likeness, and strongly imprinting upon them a copy of its own beauty and goodness.'[278] Whereas the 'legal righteousness' of the Jews 'was but from the earth, earthly; consisting merely in external performances',[279] the gospel is 'an internal impression, a vivacious and energetical spirit and principle of righteousness in the souls of men whereby they are inwardly enabled to express a real conformity thereto.'[280] Smith knows how to impress the reader by brilliant formulas in pictorial language, when he depicts the longing of the soul to ascend from the lower spheres to union with the divine love and goodness[281] – in content he reproduces the view which is characteristic of the whole school.

For this approach the New Testament as a book must also become a problem. Smith comments on this in so many words: 'Though the history and outward communication of the Gospel to us in scriptis, is to be always acknowledged as a special mercy and advantage, and certainly no less privilege to us Christians than it was to the Jews...; yet it is plain that the apostle, where he compares the law and the Gospel... doth, by the Gospel, mean something which is more than a piece of book-learning, or a historical narration of the free love of God...For if this were all that is meant properly by the Gospel, I see no reason why it should not be counted as weak and impotent a thing, as dead a letter as the Law was...'[282] Smith deals with the difficulty at this point by contrasting the 'righteousness' of which Paul speaks in Gal.3.21 with the Old Testament law('to that old law which was administered only in scriptis... only externally promulged, and wrapt up, as it were, in ink and parchment') as something basically different, 'whereas this new covenant is set forth in living characters imprinted upon the vital powers of men's souls.'[283] Of course this is simply an evasion of the problem of scriptural revelation. Smith adopts another course in the discourse

Of Prophecy: here he follows the form of the condescension theory which was always the expedient for scriptural exegesis influenced by the Greek world: divine wisdom condescends to scripture, 'to assume our rude conceptions, that so it might converse more freely with us... truth is content, when it comes into the world, to wear our mantles, to learn our language... it speaks with the most idiotical sort of men in the most idiotical way, and becomes all things to all men, as every son of truth should do, for their good.'[284] According to the old methodology one possible solution is the doctrine of the fourfold sense of scripture; however, Smith does not go into these possibilities but breaks off from the theme with the enigmatic comment:'I might instance in many more things of this nature, wherin the philosophical or physical nature and literal verity of things cannot so reasonably be supposed to be set forth to us, as the moral and theological.'[285] B.Willey points to the remarkable difficulty in which the Cambridge Platonists were entangled as Christian philosophers in a century in which by general consent scripture occupied so central a place: 'It was a queer stroke of historical irony which compelled these philosophers to accept, as the repository of necessary Truth, a book which needed so much interpreting before it would yield up its precious burden.'[286]

7. However, the Bible had in no way lost its central position in public, even political discussion. We gain an illuminating insight into this if we follow the debates which took place within the leading circle of officers in Cromwell's victorious army during the years 1647-49 about the planned new ordering of politics.[287] In our context, however, the much-noted discussions in Putney in November and December 1647 are by no means as interesting as the conversations of officers in Whitehall, which have tended to be left more in the shade[288] because of the predominantly secular interests of scholars.[289] The argument of 14 December 1648 over the question 'Whether the magistrate have, or ought to have, any compulsive and restrictive power in matters of religion?',[290] the only one of which we have a fairly complete stenographic account, is particularly interesting.[291] From it we can see that in the conflict which broke out at the height of the triumph of the army over King and Parliament[292] between the various groups represented in it, the relationship between state and church played a decisive role, and that here above all the question of the role of the Old Testament was still a subject of burning interest. A century after Bucer's appearance in England, the themes which he introduced were still topical!

The basis of the debate was the '(Second) Agreement of the People', a kind of constitutional sketch for England, the original version of which was produced at the beginning of December by a committee of Levellers under the leadership of John Lilburne. Contrary to their intentions it was presented to the army leaders for further examination.[293] The section over which there was the most heated dispute contained the first of the explicitly formulated provisos respecting the rights of the representatives of the people to be chosen (in accordance with a procedure which had earlier been described in detail): they are not to be allowed to compel anyone in matters of belief by punishments or by any other constraints or to hinder the practice of religion in any place – on the other hand, however, 'the instruction or direction of the nation in a public way for the matters of faith, worship, or discipline' is to be put within their jurisdiction.[294] Behind what is at first sight an ambiguous requirement[295] there lies the fundamental division between a sphere of inwardness to which individual faith belongs and a public sphere.[296] However, the boundary between the two is not, or at least not *a priori*, identical with that between state and church,[297] but on the one hand leaves the sphere of religious spirituality which by nature is inward (though it can also be expressed in outward worship) and on the other hand the visible reality which in addition to the rest of secular life also includes the public worship of the state church.

In the discussion of 14 December concerned with this principle, the various trends represented in the army make their points through prominent spokesmen. The range extends from the relatively conservative Independents on the right to the Levellers, the authors of the Outline Agreement, on the left. John Goodwin represents the view of the separatist Congregationalists, standing close to the sects: as religion is a matter of conscience, God has given the magistrates no authority in questions of religion. For this reason no observation should be included in the Agreement on any powers of the authorities whatsoever, however limited, in this sphere.[298] Henry Ireton, the most significant of the moderate Independents and at the same time the most powerful man alongside Cromwell and majority spokesmen in the officers' council, calls for the omission of the clause, but for essentially different reasons. First, because of a fundamental trust in the representatives who will be voting,[299] and secondly, because even for Ireton, the distinction mentioned above, between an inward and an outward man, still holds;[300] this leads to the parallel differentiation between a 'compulsive' and a 'restrictive' power of the authorities in spiritual matters.[301] He, too, shares the view that in questions of conscience and thus of inward faith the authorities have no contribution to make.[302] However, they do have a 'restrictive power' in respect of the outward man,[303] related also to the commandments on the first tablet of the Decalogue:[304] 'to restrain them [though they were] to practise idolatry, to practise atheism, and anything that is against the light of God.'[305] If, then, the majority faction of the Independents argues for a certain degree of tolerance, there are limits to it. There are things – and here again we come up against the arguments from natural law which are common to all Puritans – which

have a 'perpetual ground in relation of the duty to God, a perpetual
rule by the law written in men's hearts, and a [perpetual] testimony
left in man by nature':[306] this also includes the 'religious' commandments like the prohibition of idolatry, of images and of breaking the
sabbath. Specifically, also in these matters contained on the first tablet,
the authorities must have the power to intervene 'for peace' sake', since
the most necessary thing, 'that which necessarily leads all men into
civil agreements or contracts, or to make commonwealths, is the necessity of it for preserving peace.'[307]

    An additional argument of Ireton's in addition to the derivation from
natural law, is a foundation in scripture – and this makes the discussion
significant in our context. He first produces it at an advanced stage of
the conversation, but from then on it occupies a significant place there.
Ireton first refers to the clear testimony of the Old Testament, as it was
one of the tasks of the Jewish authorities to fight against such things.
'This is clear through the current of the Old Testament.'[308] Against the
expected objection that they had to do this only as spiritual authorities
and that the death sentences at that time should be regarded as being
similar to excommunication by the church, he points out that the authorities were required to exterminate idolatry even when it was practised by the former inhabitants of the land, and they could not have
tolerated those who worked on the sabbath, broke oaths or were idolatrous, even among the 'strangers at the gate'.[309] '[I argued], that in the
state of the Jew the magistrate there... as a magistrate not of the church
only but as a magistrate of a nation, had [the] power and [the] right [to
restrain such things] – nay, it was a duty upon him.'[310] Against the
second possible objection that what was their rule under the law is no
longer valid under the gospel, he refers to natural law:[311] 'that was sin
before is sin still,... what was the duty of a magistrate to restrain before
remains his duty to restrain still.'[312] 'There are some things of perpetual
and natural right, that the scripture of the Old Testament doth hold
forth, wherein it does bear a clear witness to that light that every man
hath left in him by nature, if he were not depraved by lust. There are
some things of perpetual right in the Old Testament, that the magistrate
had a power in before the coming of Jesus Christ in the flesh. And
unless you can show us that those things are not a perpetual right...
you must give us leave to think that the magistrate ought according to
the old institution to follow that right.'[313] If we weigh the importance
of the arguments, we can see that among this group, which in some
respects stands close to the Presbyterians, the proof from scripture has
maintained its role, and along with it the Old Testament still has a
central position, but natural law still provides the real standard by
which the statements in the Old Testament are measured. We can see
very clearly how in the end this provides an unsatisfactory inter-

mediate position, from the reaction of the Levellers, who were represented in the discussion by Lilburne, Overton and Wildman. Thus
Wildman counters: '[You cannot deduce that power from the Jewish
magistrate unless you can prove] that it was not merely typical. The
question was whether it were [also] moral. If it were not moral, it were
[not] perpetual. If it were moral, it must go to all magistrates in the
world.'[314] From a rational and moral standpoint there is no legitimate
reason for taking the arguments specifically from the Old Testament.

The Levellers were the most extreme trend within Puritanism, so
much so that we can even ask how far they can still be designated a
Christian sect. W.Haller observes: 'The Levellers indeed, alone among
the contending groups of the time, were not a church or a sect but a
party. If they joined with the Independents and the sects to oppose
persecution, it was not because they desired as a group to propagate
any particular religious faith or to establish any special form of religious
organization. Their methods and objects were political and secular...'[315]
Natural law occupied a prominent place in their thought, the secular
origin of which from antiquity had impressed itself increasingly on
them. However, the way in which this happened is remarkable. We
can see it particularly well in the inner development of John Lilburne:[316]
as we can infer from his early writings,[317] in his youth he was decisively
influenced by enthusiastic spiritualism and then became familiar with
works like C. St Germain's *Dialogus de fundamentis legum et de conscientia*
(in an English translation) and Henry Parker's *Observations upon some of
his Majesties late Answers and Expresses* (1642),[318] in which natural law is
popularized and applied to the English constitution. Concern with constitutional history, and in particular with Magna Carta,[319] supplemented
this education. This gave rise to a paradoxical shift in that the charismatic capacities which had been promised to the individual in the
context of Spiritualism, in the light of the 'Law of grace', were now
transferred to the 'law of nature', and reason was given the same
'enlightened' authority that the Spirit had possessed earlier.[320] However, this mixture of the two forms of the 'law' was now combined with
the division between the realm of grace and the realm of nature which
was established in Puritan tradition and also represented by the other
trends in Puritanism;[321] this led to a development in which the secular
sphere, ruled by reason in accordance with the law of nature, could
become increasingly independent. The consequence is the absolute
equality of all men *by nature*, which Lilburne characteristically derives
from Gen.1 so that it is grounded in creation; this is a decisive stage
removed from Christian equality before God.[322]

The Whitehall discussion permits us to make a clear distinction between the various diverging trends within Puritanism.[322a] The Millenarians (represented by Harrison and Joshua Sprigge) play the part of

outsiders; they will not allow the authorities any jurisdiction to proceed against heresies and idolatry because this is solely the task of Christ, who will find his place in the heart through the Spirit.[323] The separatist independent Goodwin is more matter-of-fact: he applies the principle of the separation of the two 'governments', combines the argument from the Old Testament which was introduced into the conversation by Ireton with the argument that law and gospel are two different and exclusive periods in the history of salvation, and arrives at the conclusion that the Old Testament institutions could no longer be used as a model today because now the government is a purely secular institution, imposed by men. It is even more remarkable that Goodwin counters Ireton's arguments, in which we saw the historical (Eusebian) form of typology in the background (the Old Testament structures of government are a direct model for present society) with the Spiritualist (Origenistic) form: 'Canaan is the Kingdom of Heaven, as we all generally know': in this kingdom, which was to serve spiritually as the type of the churches of Christ, 'of the purity of them and holiness of them', ordinances were needed to keep everything as pure as possible for worship. 'Otherwise the visage, the loveliness of the type, would have been defaced.' The character of the Old Testament ordinances as types excludes the possibility of using them as direct models for the present: 'Now unless we shall suppose [that] the lands and state[s] under the Gospel are typical also...' – so it is now a question of purely secular government. It is no coincidence that we found the same kind of arguments used by the founder of Separatism, Robert Browne;[324] they can similarly be found in Roger Williams,[325] and, although they stem from quite opposite motives, in a way they prepared for the largely secular perspectives of the Levellers.[326] However, in an inflammatory sermon[327] on the limitations of the New Testament commandment I Peter 2.13 (which he acknowledges to be valid),[328] this same Goodwin could also refer to Old Testament examples of rebellion against royal despotism, like that of Elisha against Ahab, when he wanted to kill him (II Kings 6.32),[329] or of David against the persecution by Saul (I Sam.21.8-9; 22.2).[330] The actions of Old Testament kings, like Solomon's orders for the murders of Joab and Shimei (I Kings 2),[331] could be turned into an undisguised criticism of the contemporary monarchy, to which it was possible to make direct allusions in Old Testament statements like I Sam.8.11ff.,[332] which made it possible to outmanoeuvre the New Testament command in Rom.13.[333] We already found the same partisan eclecticism with Robert Browne![334]

For a moment, the Whitehall discussion of 1648[335] opens the curtain on a development within Puritanism which otherwise we can only follow by means of the pamphlet literature, which in later years becomes very thin. We get the impression that the Bible, particularly the Old

Testament, still had a central place in the arguments about the shaping of political realities in the Puritan camp. Its authority seems unassailed, and yet we recognize that the decisive criteria come from other spheres: from natural law, from a conception of the right relationship between church and state which would differ from time to time. This is matched by a predilection for one or other of the two forms of typology.

However, underneath all this a conclusion seems to be in the making which sooner or later would inevitably emerge in this situation: an attack on the relevance of the Bible to the present situation and a criticism of holy scripture itself. There is remarkable testimony to the fact that this is not far off in the polemical pamphlet which John Price, a close acquaintance of Goodwin, directed in the name of seven Baptist and Independent clergy against William Walwyn, the influential leader of the Leveller movement,[336] entitled *Walwins Wiles* (1649).[337]

In the pattern of his education[338] Walwyn is a typical example of the class from which the supporters of the Leveller movement were recruited, shaped partly by popular humanist education and partly by the spiritualist religion of the left wing of Puritanism. In his *Just Defence* he speaks of the antinomianism at which he arrived at an early stage: 'I, through God's goodnesse, had long before been established in that part of doctrine (called then, Antinomian) of free justification by Christ alone; and so my heart was at much more ease and freedom, then others, who were entangled with those yokes of bondage, unto which Sermons and Doctrines mixt of Lawe and Gospel, do subject disstressed consciences.'[339] Like Lilburne, he too made the change from religious to secular concerns, that then put him in the centre of the political struggle for natural rights. So there might be a grain of truth in the suspicion which Price voiced against Walwyn in *Walwins Wiles*, that in a conversation with a close friend on the question what he thought of scripture, whether it was God's word or not, he gave the paradoxical answer, 'I beleeve it is not the Word of God, and I beleeve again it is the Word of God': scripture is so contradictory in itself that it makes him believe that it is not the word of God – and yet, 'all those passages therein that declare the nature of God, viz., his Grace and Goodness to men, I beleeve are the Word of God'.[340] Characteristically, there is a deep mystical experience behind the knowledge that scripture is the Word of God: 'I rather find by experience... I beleeve them through an irresistible perswasive power that from within them (like unto the soft still voyce wherin God was) hath pierced my judgment and affection in such sort, that with aboundance of joy and gladness I beleeve.'[341] In the remarkable declaration of his faith, *A Still and Soft Voice*, in which this confession about scripture occurs, on the other hand he sharply attacks all the average Christians who are not adherents of true faith but of superstition because, since they have come to their religious practice only through education and outward circumstances, they are 'deadly enemies to examination and tryall of things'. If they are asked, 'how they come to know there is a God, or that the scriptures are the word of God', they tend to retort in inquisitorial fashion: 'Do you deny them: it seemes you doe? otherwise why doe you aske such questions?'[342] – evidently a situation in which Walwyn has found himself more than once with his Socratic questions. We can see how strongly doubt in the authority of the Bible was in the air elsewhere on the left wing of the Puritans from the writing by J.Goodwin, *The Divine Authority of Scripture*, which appeared shortly beforehand (1646). Here Goodwin (touching on some similar remarks in the Cambridge Platonists)[343] notes: 'The true and proper foundation of Christian Religion is not ink and paper, not any book or books, not any writing, or writings whatsoever, whether Translations or Originalls; but that substance of matter, those gracious counsells of God concerning the salvation of the world by Jesus Christ.'[344] Complementary to the mystical and rationalistic elements in Walwyn is his view that the real focal point of true faith is to be sought in ethics, where the average Christians whom he censures reveal their decisive failings.[345]

Given these presuppositions, can Price's charge against Walwyn be plucked entirely out of thin air, to the effect that on occasion he compared King James and King David, and said of them that they were 'a couple of crafty Foxes,and cunning Knaves, that by their subtilty and policy, under religious pretences, acted all things with a design of abusing and cozening their people over whom they were set'[346], even if Walwyn resolutely denied these and other charges in his *Just Defence*?[347] In that case we would have an early occurrence of this theme which was so popular in the Enlightenment.

We must note that the moralism which emerges here is closely bound up with an 'antinomian' Spiritualism. The attitude of Spiritualist preachers in the army like Dell and Saltmarsh, who proclaimed the grace of the Holy Spirit which frees men from all the bonds of the law,[348] was different in emphasis, but in no way separate in principle.[349] Their message inevitably led still more to opposition to the Old Testament, bolstered by the old Spiritualist mistrust of all outward forms, and finally also to opposition to the whole Bible as a codified norm of faith.[350]

Another feature of the thought of the extreme left is the demand for an absolute separation of church and state.This is connected with the consistent Spiritualist individualism which recognizes no authority between God and the believer, and if it does stress scripture as such a rule of faith, it subjects it completely to the conscience of the individual as the only competent judge. This position appears once again in Milton's work of 1659: *A Treatise of Civil power in Ecclesiastical causes*,[351] in which we see the poet now completely on the left wing of Puritanism: 'First it cannot be deni'd... that we of these ages, having no other divine rule of authoritie from without us warrantable to one another as a common ground but the holy scripture, and no other within us but the illumination of the Holy Spirit so interpreting that scripture as warrantable only to our selves and to such whose consciences we can so perswade, can have no other ground in matters of religion but only from the scriptures. And these being not possible to be understood without this divine illumination... it follows cleerly, that no man or body of men in these times can be the infallible judges or determiners in matters of religion to any mens consciences but thir own.' It follows from this that 'it is the general consent of all sound protestant writers, that neither traditions, councels nor canons of any visible church, much less edicts of any magistrate or civil session, but the scripture only can be the final judge or rule in matters of religion, and that only in the conscience of every Christian to himself.'[352] The secular authorities have no right to use their power in matters of religion, for 'Christ has a government of his own, sufficient of it self... in governing his church', in which he rules without force, for 'it deals only with the inward man and his actions, which are all spiritual and to oudward force not lyable'.[353] And then Milton characteristically produces a wealth of quotations from Paul as evidence for the Christian freedom which frees from the law by the spirit,[354] not only from the bondage of those ceremonies, but also from 'the forcible imposition of those circumstances, place and time in the worship of God'[355] – and thus, according to previous understanding, in the realm of indifferentia. Therefore it is important 'to distinguish rightly between civil power and ecclesiastical'.[356]

Milton's anti-priestly tendency now comes to a head: in the work 'Considerations Touching the likeliest means to remove Hirelings out of the church'[357] he not only calls for the abolition of the tithe and any payment of the clergy arranged by the state,[358] but also rejects all the university-trained clergy[359] in favour of those servants of the gospel 'in the first evangelic time', who 'were by nothing distinguished from other Christians but by thir spiritual knowledge and sanctitie of life', 'for the Gospel makes no difference from the magistrate himself to the meanest artificer, if God evidently favor him with spiritual gifts.'[360] In comparison with the 'hireling crew together with all the mischiefs, dissentions, troubles, warrs', he reminds Christians of 'thir libertie, thir adoption... thir spiritual priesthood, whereby they have all equally access to any ministerial function whenever calld by thir own abilities and the church, though they never came neer commencement or universitie.'[361] It is an error 'to think that the universitie makes a minister of the gospel' – 'the inward sense of his calling and spiritual abilitie will sufficiently tell him.'[362] Here we have an expression not only of the typical humanistic

antipathy to scholastic training,[363] but also of the fundamentally anti-
clerical attitude of Spiritualism, combined with the view that there is
no need of any special training for knowledge of the Bible, as it is
'translated into every vulgar toungue, as being held in main matters of
belief and salvation, plane and easie to the poorest'.[364] It therefore calls
for no special training, no 'school-divinitie', so that the future clergy
'were trained up in the church only, by the scripture and in the original
languages therof[365] at schoole, without fetching the compas of other
arts and sciences, more than what they can well learn at secondary
leasure and at home'.[366] Milton's demands, utopian for the time in
which they were made, were not realized: but they are an indication of
how unbroken anti-clerical forces were on the eve of the Restoration.
They were now directed not just against bishops, but against the whole
of the clergy.

2

Lord Herbert of Cherbury:
his Epistemology and
Philosophy of Religion

Edward Herbert, Lord Cherbury (1582-1648), to whom we now turn, belongs to an earlier generation than Milton and was already past the peak of his public activity when Charles I ascended the throne. The embodiment of Renaissance man, he had many interests: in the Julian-Cleves war of succession in 1610 and 1614 he strove, albeit in vain, for military honours; his chivalry towards women and his marked sense of honour involved him in a number of duels; he ventured on the fashionable paths of poetry-writing with varied success. Despite devoted service as English ambassador to the court of Louis XIII in Paris (1619-1624), he failed to gain any token of thanks from his monarch; his release followed a year-long struggle for adequate compensation for services rendered, which was beset by many disappointments. He spent the last years of his life, increasingly ill, at his family seat or in his London house.[1] We also have historical works which he had been commissioned to write, including a by no means inconsiderable history of Henry VIII.[2]

However, the name of Herbert of Cherbury has become famous not because of these achievements in a varied life, but because of his significance for the history of philosophy, specifically the philosophy of religion. Still, that he emerges in modern accounts as the founder of English Deism is, as Rossi observes,[3] mostly a matter of second-hand report about him. It is much more serious that this judgment is usually arrived at on the basis of insufficient familiarity with the background of the intellectual atmosphere in England during the time of his activity and the religious and philosophical trends dominant there. The consequence has often been an overestimation of his significance and above all his originality;[4] on the other hand, for the same reasons for a long time he was numbered among the ranks of the almost forgotten authors.[5]

Herbert can claim a place in the history of ideas because the specific movement called Deism has in him a first representative on English soil. [6] But in England as a Deist he is a lonely figure at this period,[7] though Deism is an undercurrent which occasionally comes to the surface with certain individuals in various European countries from the second half of the sixteenth century onwards,[8] above all in France. Whereas Herbert's views are quite distinct from many of the contemporary attitudes in England, there is an obvious danger in isolating him too much from the dominant views around him if we want to arrive at a true assessment of him. Thanks above all to Rossi, we can now see clearly the background of his thought and the influences at work on him, though precisely because of this, earlier hypotheses about direct dependence on well-known thinkers in the history of philosophy have now proved untenable.[9] Herbert's education was that of a typical British nobleman: he received it partly from study at Oxford (1596-1600) and partly from widespread private reading. A typical Humanist characteristic of this education is its thoroughgoing eclecticism,[10] coupled with polemic against Scholastic school philosophy.[11] In reality Herbert never went essentially beyond the forms of philosophical thinking with which he had become acquainted at Oxford: he was virtually untouched by the 'modern philosophy' of Bacon, Descartes or Hobbes;[12] instead of this, Aristotelianism formed the real basis of his thought.[13] However, he also dissociated himself from some of Aristotle's main theories, e.g. from the conception of the *tabula rasa*, for which he substituted the Stoic theory of the *notitiae communes* or (in Platonic fashion) the *ideae innatae*.[14] The influence of Stoicism, which we also came across to an increasing degree among the Puritan theologians and politicians, occupies a central position in Herbert's thought. This is true above all of his philosophy of religion. He learnt this particularly from the popular philosophy of Cicero[15] as well as from other writers of the Stoic school. The Neoplatonic influences are hard to distinguish from the Stoic ones; they give Herbert's gnoseology, and not just his view of religion, that 'mystical' flavour which might easily be felt to be irreconcilable with the rationalism of his thought.[16] However, our dealings with the Humanist tradition, which is especially clear with the Cambridge Platonists,[17] have shown how inextricably Rationalism and Spiritualism are linked together. It is particularly important to notice this if we are going to be aware first of all of the common ground between many of Herbert's presuppositions and the thought-world around him, since only against that background can his specific characteristics emerge in a true light.

So first of all we must note that when in his main theological work *De Veritate* Herbert embarks on the task of defining the concept of truth, he is only apparently tackling an abstract epistemological problem. Even in the introductory remarks to his work it becomes clear that the heuristic character which he claims for it has an eminently practical aim: the human capacities (*facultates*) whose conformity with objects comprises the nature of truth[18] are part of that *instinctus naturalis* which is active even in inanimate nature, in plants, and still more in man: *praesertim in iis* (in the things) *quae ad nostram spectant conservationem.*[19] They indicate a clear hierarchy: the highest *facultas* is the one which strives for eternal blessedness; all the lesser *facultates* only achieve intermediate aims along the way which leads to this supreme goal.[20] At this point, however, after only a few steps, we find ourselves in the realm of religion. The fideism on which the whole edifice of Herbert's gnoseology is constructed already has so to speak a religious touch, for when Herbert begins by declaring, *Quod igitur in omnium est ore, tanquam verum accipimus, neque enim sine Providentia illa Universali momenta actionum disponente fieri potest quod ubique fit,*[21] he presupposes that all men have an intuitive possession of the capacity to know the truth; the *consensus universalis* is enough to guarantee the truth without further argumentation. Now this *consensus* is predetermined by 'general providence' (*providentia universalis*), a harmony indwelling the whole, which like the *providentia particularis* given to an individual by God derives directly from God (whom Herbert, following humanistic fashion, regularly calls *Deus Opt.[imus] Max.[imus]*).[22] Methodologically speaking, we can already see a fundamental weakness of Herbert's philosophy in this beginning, and in fact Gassendi's contemporary criticism[23] began at this very point. However, Herbert's optimism that all men can arrive at the truth[24] ultimately has a moral rather than an epistemological foundation. Rossi first made this clear by comparing the Catholic apologist Mersenne, who was influenced by Aristotelian epistemology, with Herbert: the intellectualist conception of Thomism which Mersenne follows sees the axioms as epistemological principles, starting-points for deductive thought, whereas the *notitiae communes* in Herbert's sense are rules of life which in terms of eudaemonistic ethics serve for self-preservation, leading to eternal blessedness.[25] Now by regarding this universal possibility of the knowledge of the truths necessary for eternal life, open to all men and immanent in the *instinctus naturalis*, as basic, Herbert takes a decisive step beyond the Christian Humanist thinkers of his time, and it is right that, as a deist, he should be seen as starting a specific school in England. On the other hand, he also has a good deal in common with the theologians who are more or less strongly influenced by Stoicism and Neoplatonism: this is true above all of the basic approach of his thought through reason understood in terms of inspiration, of the moral aim of his system, and of the optimistic view of man which stands out from all his thinking.[26]

In these circumstances it is important that Rossi has already put an end to the notion which still influenced the anti-deistic polemic of Herbert's contemporaries, to the effect that his thought was anti-religious or even atheistic.[27] In fact it can be distinguished from Christian Humanism only in degree, and in one sense it is even quite centrally religious. The best indication of this is that in *De Veritate* his epistemology issues directly in the sphere of religion: among the *notitiae communes*, the *notitiae communes circa Religionem* occupy the most prominent place.[28] These *notitiae*, which Herbert himself often repeats with slight variants, have become famous – and with good reason: reduced to their briefest form they represent a summary of his eudaemonistic and moral view of religion. In the original form of 1633 they run as follows: *I. Esse Supremum aliquod Numen; II. Istud Numen debere coli; III.Probam facultatum conformationem praecipuam partem cultus divini semper habitam fuisse; IV. Vitia et scelera quaecumque expiari debere ex poenitentia; V.Esse praemium vel poenam post hanc vitam.*[29] We should not be led astray into thinking that the very first statement is making an ontological point; it is deliberately left indefinite because Herbert is concerned less with asserting the existence of God than with making a religious phenomenological assertion: because, as he thinks, it can be observed that a supreme deity is worshipped all over the world, it is possible to use the fact as the basis for a natural religion which relates to all men, and this all-embracing natural religion is his concern. Originally Herbert was convinced that in fact his observation was correct;[30] later (in *De Religione Gentilium*) he felt obliged to give further explanations. The second *notitia* seems to be almost a concession to the scholastic system, in that Herbert makes a distinction between the *providentia rerum communis* and the *providentia rerum particularis* (or *gratia*)[31] and bases the possibility of prayer and worship on the latter.[32] But conversely, the fact that this worship has existed always and everywhere is proof of this *providentia particularis* or grace, and as a *notitia communis*, in reality it similarly belongs in the sphere of natural religion.[33] Moreover Herbert is almost completely unconcerned about the outward forms of worship; after observing that the priests have compounded this with a good deal of superstition (see below), he quickly moves to the third *notitia communis*, which for him bears the main weight of all his considerations.[34] Herbert asserts in a particularly direct form that the real aim of religion is to be sought in morality. Here he stands apart from the humanistic theologians of his time, but above all in his emphasis. What marks him out from the Christian humanists is that he puts almost exclusively stress on the elements from antiquity in his syncretistic view; one outward indication of this is that the name of Christ does not occur once in his works![35] And the 'Arminian' trait in his thinking is once again unmistakably clear in the fourth *notitia*: it is characteristic that while he recognizes error and even 'crime',[36] he ascribes its removal not to the forgiveness of God but to the possibility of human repentance. Only in the fifth *notitia*, where Herbert adopts apparently without question the presupposition that eternal life provides the balancing factor, which is unattainable in this life, between good or evil deeds, and their appropriate recompense, has he evidently taken up a principle of Christian dogmatics. Precisely at this point, however, we can see one of the weaknesses within his system, since in a more consistent ethical approach, which took the place of that of eudaemonism, where attention is focussed on the promise of reward as the motive for moral action, the autonomous morality which we first saw attempted among the Cambridge Platonists now had to present the higher goal.[37]

Herbert was not so consistent, and in any case, as a systematic thinker he has limitations which are clearly recognizable. This fact must also be noted in answering the question how far he could acknowledge belief in revelation. There has been much discussion of the revelatory sign from heaven which according to his autobiographical account[38] Herbert received before the publication of his book *De Veritate*.[39] We need not doubt his subjective belief in such a sign, and a prayer found in his literary remains[40] can also be taken as evidence for a personal religious sense. We may recall once again in this context that the inspiration could be a feature of humanistic moralist rationalism elsewhere, wherever there was a trace of Neoplatonic influence, as clearly among the Cambridge Platonists. The *instinctus naturalis*, the starting point for the whole of Herbert's philosophical system, is thought of as 'inspired' in this sense![41]

Some other favourite Humanist themes appear in the mode of expression characteristic of the work of this 'father of English Deism'. One of these themes occurs in Herbert's *De Religione Gentilium*, which is even better known than the *De Veritate*.[42] This work is on the one hand evidence for an academic treatment of non-Christian religions which began at this time; however, as Herbert himself recognized,[43] he was not sufficiently competent in this sphere to make his own independent contribution.[44] On the other hand, the aim of the work was to defend Herbert's main theory of the one natural religion, valid for all men, against the objections which already threatened to increase as a result of the existence of polytheism – already in antiquity and in the present day among foreign peoples. This tendency is quite alien to the repertories which he used as his model, so here too, what we have is Herbert's own completely original work.

The five *notitiae communes circa religionem*, Herbert holds, were given to all men by nature, in such a way that they could make themselves evident as a means towards good moral action and through that eternal life, without a special revelation. That made the widespread dissemination of pagan religions in antiquity, loaded with many superstitious notions and partly absurd cultic practices, a basic problem. The theory of a natural religion which could be found everywhere and was valid on the basis of this general consensus seemed to be in blatant contradiction to the evidence of the history of religion – which Herbert could not deny – and thus appeared to justify the condemnation of the heathen by the church fathers and their successors. However, Herbert supposed such an assumption to be incompatible with his conviction of a universal divine providence which had to provide all men with the necessary means for their salvation.[45] In his study of the sources and accounts of the ancient history of religion on which he embarked in connection with this question he thought that he could discover everywhere behind the polytheistic facade the worship of one God as the perfect, infinite and eternal being;[46] in accordance with his approach, he thought that he could recognize this worship above all in ethical virtues and ideals, but also in the penitence which became evident as a background to all kinds of acts of atonement and purification, and in the expectation of a future recompense for both good and evil.[47] He solved the riddle of pagan religions – and at this point he declared himself to be happier than Archimedes[48] at finding his own five articles in them!

Herbert himself could identify those responsible for the fact that nevertheless those superstitious forms and cultic practices could be noted everywhere: they were the priests, who for selfish reasons diverted their peoples by deceit and deception from their original monotheistic and ethical religion into an externalized polytheist cultic religion.[49] Here Herbert is simply expressing the same antipathy to the priesthood and the cults which we have been able to trace through the whole of the Spiritualist and Humanist tradition, and in his way he chimes in with the anti-episcopal campaign which was going on during these years. However, in accordance with his manner of thinking and his deliberately antiquarian modes of expression, Herbert's polemic against the priests is put down on paper more thoroughly and more tersely,[50] and precisely because of this he was to acquire a following in the later stages of the Enlightenment. His idea of a pattern of religious development – the replacement of what was originally a pure primal religion by the increasingly expanding depravation of polytheism, in which, however, a 'thread of truth' continued to be preserved through all the confusions,[51] and which can be taken up in order to regain man's primal state – is a line of thought which has been traditional since Joachim of Fiore.[52,53]

Herbert repeated his ideas at the end of his life in some shorter writings which were incorporated into the third edition of *De Veritate*, in 1645: the *Religio Laici*[54] is addressed to educated laity,[55] whereas the

Appendix ad Sacerdotes de Religione Laici[56] arises from the specific enquiry of a friend.[57] Herbert says hardly anything new here.[58] It is noteworthy that the beginnings of a criticism of the Bible are also evident in *Religio Laici*: the 'traveller'[59] through the world of religions and the churches, disputing with one another, also comes up against the problem of sacred scriptures, in which he encounters the claim to authoritative divine revelation. Herbert thinks that whenever he picks up a sacred book, he must decide what he supposes to be in accordance with 'right reason', and what in accordance with faith.[60] This is not a matter of the problem of the dimensions of the canon, of possible textual interpolations, mistakes in pointing and ambiguities in the meaning of the Hebrew text (though Herbert shows himself to be thoroughly familiar with this theme), or of contradictions between the various authors – all that belongs on the human side in the Bible. Rather, the decisive question is where God's word is to be found in the Bible; to discover that is similarly the task of free investigation: *Quapropter operae pretium fuerit penitius disquirere, quid tandem in Sacris Scripturis sincerum, incontroversumque Dei verum audiat. Neque enim aequali Authoritate praeditum quicquid in S.S. continetur, dixerit vel ineptissimus sacerdos.* In scripture we also have the words of criminals, women(!), animals and indeed even the devil, which could not be taken to be divinely inspired in the same way as those of the most excellent of men. Even apostles and prophets can be criticized insofar as they speak in human terms. *Quid igitur in S.Bibliis tanquam ipsissimum Dei Verbum, quid porro ad salutem maxime necessarium disquirendum manet.*[61] There is no further discussion, but here we already have a clear statement of a programme which will have its effect in the future.

Finally we must also look at a work which cannot be demonstrated with complete certainty to be Herbert's, although the reasons adduced for its authenticity seem to be stronger than those to the contrary:[62] the *Dialogue between a Tutor and his Pupil*, first printed in 1768. Herbert's five *notitiae communes* occur in this work too: here they are called the five 'Catholic articles',[63] characteristics of universal religion.[64] They are the criteria by which the claim to truth of each particular article of faith added by each positive religion must be measured; here, too, the ethical character of religion is plain.[65] The general theme of the work is very strongly reminiscent of that of the *De religione Gentilium*: the various religions are first investigated as to how far they contain the truth expressed in the five articles (pp.10-105), and then as to how far they have departed from these articles (pp.106-272). The anti-priestly attitude of the *De religione Gentilium* also appears in many passages here. On the whole the *Dialogue* seems more radical than the works printed during Herbert's lifetime, in that it comes closer to the point at which the question of the truth-content of the Christian religion itself becomes acute. The pupil in particular often points his questions in this direction. But when a problem thus becomes dangerous in this way, the tutor regularly refers his pupil to the learned theologians, from whom he can obtain information. Thus the reader is left to arrive at a tacit understanding with the questioner. Otherwise, as already in the *De Religione Gentilium*, the method is to attribute the criticism of priests and cult to non-Christian religions. (This happens, for example, right at the beginning, pp.12f.) The progressive depravation of what was originally a lofty ethical religion by the constant addition of further articles is depicted by the example of Islam.

It is striking that Judaism, too, is quite deliberately included in the group of religions presented critically in this way. The great antiquity of Judaism in comparison with other pagan religions[66] is questioned, and it is pointed out that Jews had in common with Gentiles both faith in one God and a religious practice consisting in virtue and doing good.[67] By means of similar enquiries on the part of his pupil the tutor clearly shows that the revelations given to the Jewish priests must have been as suspect to the Gentiles as vice versa.[68] The Old Testament also contains all kinds of accounts which hardly seem to accord with the nature of a *Deus Optimus Maximus*: as an example the pupil mentions the story of Micaiah ben Imlah in I Kings 22, where it is even said that God sent a lying spirit to the prophets of Ahaz;[69] furthermore we also have the anthropomorphic conception that God sits on his throne and has a right hand and a left hand. Here, too, the tutor avoids giving a clear answer.[70] Another example is the criticism of God's command to Abraham in Gen.22 to offer his son as sacrifice; here even the Tutor thinks 'that it is not credible that the Deus, Optimus, Maximus, should be the author of such a precept'.[71] Generally speaking, the principle applies to scripture as to the statements of a particular tradition of faith generally, 'that unless the intrinsick value bear it out, (i.e.) the wise and good precepts for living well, do in a sort authorize the narrative or historical part, the faith will be but little worth, and perchance be thought no better than as an holy legend or allegorical history'.[72] Many things are handed down in scripture 'which are indeed but articles founded upon reason of which kind all pious precepts in that book are', whereas other things would never have been known to us without the authority of the church.[73] Therefore in passing judgment everything depends on reason, which in the last resort has to abide by the five articles if it is to discover the universally valid religion.[74] Still, the possibility of a special historical revelation is not denied. 'Tis true I would have you begin at the five articles, whether you find them mentioned in the holy writ, or any other good book; but with all you must take notice how perfect soever they are, that faith or belief concerning things past, may be conveniently, and in some cases ought to be annexed to them, as an excellent supplement... for the goodness and mercy of God is not so limitted to any one faith or country, but that it hath heretofore been, and is at this day, more conspicious and eminent in some parts of the world, than in others.'[75] For a judgment on any alleged revelation, even that handed down in the tradition of the church, the tutor refers the pupil to the use of his reason: 'I must encourage you still in the rational way you take for the discovery of truth, not doubting also, but our divines will approve the same...; since even the most rigid theologaster among them, cannot but confess, that it behoves every man to give a reason of his faith.'[76]

Thus already in Herbert we find a developed programme which is characteristic of the later Enlightenment and its criticism of the Bible. If we can say that the work is considerably ahead of its time,[77] that is true less of its theological rationalism in itself which, as we have seen, was widespread in various forms around 1640, than of the unqualified trust in reason in all instances where a verdict is called for on a specific revelation or the tradition of a revelation (like the Bible). Even if the theory of *ideae innatae* is connected with Platonism,[78] we can easily see the specific nature of Deism through a comparison with the Cambridge Platonists: in Herbert there is no trace of the warmth of religious feeling which permeates their attitude, already shaped as it is by ethical rationalism;[79] at all points his judgment is made with a theoretical detachment which marks out all of his writings, with their pompous apparatus of the fruits of all kinds of reading and the periphrastic Latin which cannot always be clearly understood, as the work of a learned dilettante, who regards religious and philosophical themes as fields for winning literary laurels and the approval of the really great scholars of his time. In many of his judgments, as in his exclusively ethical and eudaemonistic view of religion, and in the anticlerical tendency, which grew stronger particularly in his old age, he is influenced by the traditions of humanism. In his thoroughgoing orientation on antiquity, because the Christian features fade into the background, he adds momentum to an impetus deriving from Humanism which is also to be found among many of his contemporaries. He was only to find truly kindred spirits towards the end of the century, so for its first half he remains a lonely figure.

3

Thomas Hobbes:
the Philosophical Presuppositions of
his Biblical Criticism

Thomas Hobbes, the Sage of Malmesbury (1588-1679),[1] is beyond question one of the most disputed figures in the history of philosophy. The popularity which he has regained in most recent times is evident from the large number of scholarly works concerned with him.[2] Many of them stem from the borderlands between philosophy and political science, because contemporary political thought obviously needs to make an intensive study of this thinker who stands at the beginnings of modern times. However, Hobbes seems to present extraordinary difficulties to those who attempt to depict his philosophy of the state without becoming involved in contradictions; so even now there is a series of conflicting and in part mutually exclusive attempts at explanation.[3] If we try to discover the cause of this situation, one notable factor comes into the foreground which we can observe in the majority of the literature on Hobbes: most of these works are concerned to explain Hobbes' approach and the way in which he implements it purely from within his work; only rarely is there an attempt to take into account the influences from his time which made an impact on his thought and the appearance of themes and arguments which must seem contradictory to an approach which only looks at him from within the context of his works.[4] With Hobbes, more markedly than with other philosophers, we can note how modern approaches and conceptuality play their part in interpretation (this is evidently a result of the modern political relevance which he is thought to have). This also has direct consequences for the selection of material: thus it is no coincidence that all the commentators who advocate a purely secularist approach either tone down[5] the extensive chapters in which Hobbes concerns himself with theological and biblical themes, or exclude them as a concession to the spirit of the time which is alien to his system.[5a] Moreover, even the reaction to this which has recently become stronger and which seeks to justify a perspective which is in part explicitly theological and in part one in terms of the morality of natural law, has not advanced beyond a fragmented view.[6]

Research into Hobbes is a prime example of the problems which inevitably confront any attempt at understanding a thinker from a time in which philosophy and theology together still formed the basis and presupposition of any discipline – a theology which not only gave rise to anthropology and legal and constitutional theories (here ancient tradition provided a complementary ingredient) but also introduced its own constitutive elements, not least among which were references to the relevant biblical testimony. These problems of course arise in connection with the specialization in the specific areas of particular modern academic disciplines. Thus the most obvious shibboleth by which we can recognize the unbridgeable abyss between modern interpreters and their subject-matter is their customary tacit refusal to take into consideration those sections in Hobbes which are exclusively concerned with biblical exegesis.[7] One might also point out that the historians of philosophy and political scientists could not be expected to have the relevant specialist knowledge. Subjectively that may be the case, but in fact it merely provides further confirmation of the dilemma which exists. Here only interdisciplinary study can help, study in which theologians equally accept their need to be informed. However, the same failings can also be found on the side of biblical scholarship. In so far as histories of the interpretation of the Old Testament have concerned themselves with Hobbes, they have been exclusively interested in his critical observations about the historical circumstances in which individual Old Testament books were written.[8] So far, no one has attempted to discover what thinking and concerns prompted Hobbes to make this criticism and in so doing also to discover how Hobbes understood the Old Testament. So no one can object when non-theologians do not want to concern themselves with the material.

In this chapter I shall attempt to depict Hobbes' work completely within the presuppositions of the thought of his time and the world in which he lived, and as a result bring out what his method and the content of his work has in common with many of the characteristic attitudes we have already noted. That will also indicate Hobbes' special concerns, the specific character of his thinking. In contrast to previous accounts (which of course are an indispensable presupposition for any further study of this kind, because of the careful analyses of Hobbes' work which they offer from a variety of standpoints)[9], in accordance with the main theme of this book, I shall aim at illustrating the role of the Bible as the basis for Hobbes' outline of a political theory of the state and the connections which can be noted between his critical observations on the Old Testament and his philosophical thought.

The interpretations of Hobbes which have been given hitherto (limited to his philosophical theory of the state)[10] can be classified systematically in the following way:[11]

1. The traditional understanding, which corresponds to the reception which Hobbes received from the majority of his contemporaries,[12] sees him as a materialist who, inspired by the methods of the modern natural sciences, sought to apply scientific theories about bodies in movement and the mechanical influence they have on one another to human beings and the state that they create, and to derive the origin of ethical obligation, which leads to the foundation of the state, from an egoistic psychology which in a purely rational manner weighs up the self-interest of man, whose survival is threatened in his natural state of involvement in the struggle of all against all:[13] fear of death is the basic impulse behind all action, and the effort to avoid a premature violent death leads to the recognition that only peace offers the precondition for survival. Peace is assured only when everyone transfers their natural rights and power to a sovereign. This approach inevitably regards Hobbes as a radical sceptic in his view of humanity, and indeed as a virtual atheist in his world-view.[14] That was also the judgment of many contemporaries, who, like Kortholt, counted him, Herbert and Spinoza as the 'three deceivers'.[15] However, as Q.Skinner in particular has demonstrated, he also had a large number of followers, above all on the Continent, who admired him precisely for this.[16] The main point in favour of this picture of the philosopher is that it largely seems to follow the intrinsic logic of the development of the doctrine of the state from Hobbes' anthropology and the development of the latter from the doctrine of bodies in Hobbes' own work (in fact, from the beginning Hobbes had planned his *Elementa Philosophiae* in three parts, *De corpore*, *De homine*, and *De cive*, and at a very early stage sketched out first manuscripts of them;[17] it was only the political situation which moved him to have the third part of his system, *De cive*, published first in 1642[18]); the approach seeks to analyse the work strictly within its own terms on the methodological level which emerges at the beginning. This approach still has its supporters.[19]

More recently, however, it has become increasingly evident that such an approach cannot deal with all the difficulties in Hobbes' system. One main problem it leaves unanswered is the origin of an ethical obligation. How can that arise when only the egoistic interest of the individual counts in the natural state and there is no moral criterion independent of it?[19a] Scholars have asked what guarantee there is in that case for the observance of the contract by which men delegate their power to the sovereign[19b] – at all events a true peace can only be based on the recognition of a foundation which is generally accepted as binding and not just on the power of sanctions.

2. If one begins from the virtually unlimited power of the sovereign as presupposed in Hobbes, Hobbes emerges as a champion of a totalitarian ideology. This view is above all connected with the name of J.Vialatoux,[20] but has a number of other supporters.[21] In his earlier publications, Carl Schmitt similarly accorded a central position to the idea of the state as the great machine[22] – albeit with the qualification that the freedom of thought and conscience conceded by Hobbes represents a 'flaw' in the system, a mark of death on the great Leviathan.[23] More recently, however, it has become clear that the charge of totalitarianism misses Hobbes' intention; this is expressed clearly enough in the fact that the state is thought of as a means of protection which is intended to make possible the social development of the individual.[24] Unfortunately the totalitarianism theory has also been advanced from a pronounced theological standpoint, in the work of a pupil of Karl Barth's, D.Braun *Der sterbliche Gott oder Leviathan gegen Behemoth*[25]; this has rightly been criticized severely.[26] Its main error lies in its failure to place Hobbes in the history of ideas and of theology, so that he is measured in a completely unhistorical way, by the yardstick of dialectical theology.

In contrast to the totalitarianism theory, which has long since regarded an adequate interpretation of Hobbes as a pseudo-problem,[27] Hobbes is nowadays seen more as a protagonist of modern liberalism. By securing peace in its role as a protective power, the state for the first time makes individual freedom possible, though it is restricted to the private sphere. This is the way in which e.g. M.Oakeshott understands Hobbes; in dealing with the problem of 'individualism and absolutism'[28] he explains the origin of individualism in Hobbes in terms of his nominalistic approach;[29] he ends his discussion with the comment: 'Indeed, Hobbes, without being himself a liberal, had in him more of the philosophy of liberalism than most of its professed defenders.'[30] F.C. Hood has also stressed the freedom of the subject in the state as an important element, in a section of his book, *The Divine Politics of Thomas Hobbes*,[31] which has still to be mentioned in what for him is a more central context; here he distinguishes between the abstract and hypothetical freedom of natural law and freedom in the state which, while created artificially, is nevertheless first realized in that context: 'Natural right is liberty allowed by natural law; artificial right is, for the most part, liberty allowed by civil law.'[32] Further contributions in this direction might also be mentioned.[33]

3. The investigation by C.B.Macpherson, *The Political Theory of Possessive Individualism. Hobbes to Locke*, with its neo-Marxist approach, is particularly significant in one respect: it emphatically demonstrates that

Hobbes' 'natural state' is in no way to be taken literally as a postulated primal state of human development.[33a] Rather, Hobbes was giving a quite specific description of middle-class society of England around the middle of the seventeenth century: its abysmal depths were revealed at the time of the civil war when there was no power of the state to keep the conflicts under control. The natural state is 'about social, not natural men';[34] it is a hypothesis through which Hobbes seeks to describe the relationships of men *in society*.[35] M.Bianca[35a] points out that Hobbes reckoned with the possibility that the natural state of 'the struggle of all against all' really existed in particular regions of the world and above all was a possibility which haunted England as it was torn apart by the Civil War. On the other hand, Macpherson is hindered by his own ideological presuppositions when, along the lines of 'possessive individualism', he has the individual determined only by his relationship to property, and society determined by market functions. In doing this he overlooks the significance of cultural and religious differences and the independent function of the state.[35b] Here what has already been said in connection with the 'Weber syndrome' in another context also applies.[36] In a more guarded way, M.Oakeshott classifies Hobbes' ethics as 'morality of the individual', in which human beings recognize one another, 'not in the pursuit of a single common enterprise, but in an enterprise of give and take...: it is the morality of self and other selves'.[37]

4. We thus arrive at the much-discussed problem of the basis of Hobbes' ethics. It is thought that if Hobbes has a moral theory at all it must have a basis somewhere – or does he not have one, as the traditional approach suggests? If peace is the goal towards which man strives as he escapes the state of nature by making a contract, why should he then restrain the egoism with which he is naturally endowed and keep his promise? According to Oakeshott, it is in the basis for this duty, this 'ought', that we should 'reach the obscure heart of Hobbes' moral theory'.[38]

One of the answers given to this question points to the law that obligation arises at the point when the sovereign enacts laws which are then binding on all subjects. Ethics is connected with the order established by the laws. That is the positivistic legal solution to which Oakeshott also tends.[39] One may doubt whether it really does justice to Hobbes.[40]

Over against all those who see Hobbes essentially as a modern thinker, an influential interpretation, chiefly going back to A.E.Taylor,[41] and known under his name as the Taylor theory, which has been developed further by H.Warrender,[42] has sought to demonstrate his roots in natural law thinking. Taylor's basic views, which Warrender simply expands and supports by additional arguments, are as follows: 1. Hobbes' ethical theory is to be distinguished sharply from his egoistic psychology. His scholarly philosophy is one side to him, and his moral views another; the latter rest on the foundation of the traditional theory of natural law.[43] These views, moreover, are quite different in character from what one might expect from Hobbes' scientific approach; they are not teleological, but have a completely deontological stamp (here Taylor even compares Hobbes with Kant!).[44] Taylor arrived at this view because of a large number of passages in Hobbes (in *De cive*) which cannot be reconciled with an approach by way of the egoistic psychology of man in a natural state. It follows from them that, 1. the natural laws have an imperative character even in the natural state, albeit partially only *in foro interno*, and at all events they include the obligation to observe the contract; 2. even the sovereign 'is just as much under a rigid law of moral obligation',[45] for all the freedom he has to permit and to forbid as he wills, to dispose himself in accordance with the common good. Here of course he is not accountable to man, but only to God (with reference to *De cive*, ch.13). Of course he makes the distinction between 'just' (i.e. in accordance with the law) and 'unjust' (forbidden by the law), but the more basic distinction between equity and iniquity is a given.[46] 3. The law of nature is a command, and: 'I can only make Hobbes' statements consistent with one another by supposing that he means quite seriously what he so often says, that the 'natural law is the command of God, and to be obeyed because it is God's command.'[47] Now whereas it is said in the *Elements of Law* I,18,1[48] that they have this status because they are laid down in commandments in scripture, *De cive* 15,4-5 makes a distinction between the natural and the prophetic kingdom of God; in the natural kingdom all men recognize the divine power by virtue of their rational nature, which is common to them all, whereas in the prophetic realm God's rule over the elect is based on a special contract. Taylor explains that he is not in a position to balance out these contradictory statements. But, 'A certain kind of theism is absolutely necessary to make the theory work.'[49]

This view has not gone unchallenged. First of all, objections have been made by all those who exclude any ambiguity in Hobbes' thought, as presupposed by Taylor and Warrender.[50] Thus S.M.Brown[51] stresses that Hobbes repeatedly spoke clearly enough about the basis of his ethical theory in human nature and goes on to say that the Taylor theory, cobbled together from scattered comments in Hobbes, does not itself hold together. Fetscher[52] also adds the criticism that here 'by overinterpretation of traditional elements in Hobbes' teaching its political direction is reversed'. More serious is the objection of Kodalle,[53] who follows Warrender's basic approach, that 'in any interpretation of Hobbes it is not necessary to analyse the role of the moral and political obligation of the individual *in extenso* and in doing this ruling out the historical... horizon of Hobbes and his time, to the degree that happens in Warrender.'[54] Finally, it has also been asked how the clear rejection of Hobbes by his contemporaries can be explained if in the end he was merely basing himself on widespread natural law doctrine.

In connection with the following point, one more remark should be noted which Warrender is said to have made according to Greenleaf's account at the Bochum Hobbes Colloquium in 1967: if he sees Hobbes as a representative of the natural law doctrine, he connects him less with the mediaeval Christian tradition than with the Stoa and with Roman law thought.[55] This gives an important pointer towards defining the position of the philosopher within the presuppositions of the thought of his time.

5. A series of interpreters goes one stage further than the natural law theorists: they even want to see Hobbes as a specifically Christian and religious thinker. In the English-speaking world the foremost of these interpreters is F.C.Hood.[56] For Hood, Hobbes is a 'religious moralist'.[57] Hood presents a complete exegesis of Leviathan through which he seeks to provide a decided contrast to previous interpretations. To begin with, as a diametrically opposed starting point, he puts forward the view that Hobbes was the advocate of a typically Protestant theology based on the Bible. 'Scripture was the only source of Hobbes' moral convictions', is one of the key sentences here, and it is closely connected with the estimation of Hobbes' personal religion as 'moralistic rather than devotional'.[58] His political theory also fits into this context: 'religion' and 'Commonwealth' go together from the beginning as a kind of divine politics, for the natural laws are left to private judgments and therefore are not binding until they are confirmed by the commandments of God handed down in scripture. This happens in the sphere of civil duties only through the laws which have their foundation in the constitution of the state.

Hood has his own response to the basic problem of interpreting Hobbes, the relationship between his picture of society with a mechanistic tone which, though 'scientific' and inductive, is nevertheless fictitious, and the foundations of his moral judgment. His theory is that Hobbes' belief in the divine moral law, grounded in scripture, precedes his 'science' both biographically and logically and continues to remain his decisive point of reference, and that he formed only certain parts of his system on the pattern of the scientific conceptions fashionable at the time.[59] Hobbes' political philosophy is also set against a religious background; as Hood argues from *Leviathan*, ch.12, in the realm of the Christian state, politics is part of religion.[60] For Hood, this chapter (which has no parallel in *De cive*) is a key area for demonstrating the close relationship between the Christian commonwealth and true religion.[61] For science and religion there is a common root in human curiosity; people seek the reasons for events in their beginnings, but they also look to the future, and as this is obscure, curiosity turns into fear. Whereas the search for the first cause could lead to the knowledge of the one God, fear now leads people astray into superstition (belief in invisible spirits) and polytheism. There is a seed of religion in all men, but it needs cultivating if it is to bring forth real fruits and not these false ones. This came about in pagan states depending on the specific discoveries of those who directed them and served to make their subjects obedient to the laws of earthly kings and amenable to common life: to this degree in that context it is no more than 'a part of human politics'. Only in the Christian state is it 'divine politics', as its rulers have cultivated it in accordance with God's command and direction;[62] it contains commandments for those who have put themselves at the disposal of the kingdom of God as its subjects.

All this is simply a version of the content of *Leviathan*, ch.12. The difference between Hood and earlier interpreters consists in the fact that in this chapter he finds a 'divine politics' to be the real focal point of Hobbes' philosophical-political system of the state, whereas they found this focal point anywhere but here.[63] The difficulty for Hood in the face of his critics, however, is that he cannot make sufficiently clear the advantage of this particular solution over others, so that he gives the impression of having an apologetic interest which seeks harmony all too quickly.[64] Kodalle charges him with having 'given no answer to the question of the need for religious, substantial truth in political philosophy' or to the question of its relevance 'for the intrinsic functioning of the political system which he has constructed'.[65] Of course we may doubt whether the way in which Kodalle and others put this question was the right one, but Hood was in no position to give it another direction. The reason for that is because he too approached Hobbes purely in terms of his works and failed to take the only step which promises to offer a way out of the dilemmas of research into Hobbes, namely to compare Hobbes' models of thought with the kind of political and theological argument to be found in his time: within Anglicanism, as moulded by Humanism, and within Puritanism. Certain generalizations[66] point to the absence of sufficient comparative criteria to make it possible to establish more precisely the place of the philosopher in the controversies of his time.

Other interpretations which similarly stress the theological side in Hobbes more strongly are more fragmentary, less attractive, but as a result have also remained more open in the positive sense. They include the article by W.B. Glover, 'God and Thomas Hobbes',[67] J.Freund, *Le Dieu Mortel*,[67a] and also the more recent publications by Carl Schmitt.[68] The 'Hobbes Crystal' has attracted much attention in the new impression of the *Begriff des Politischen*[69], which Schmitt himself describes as 'the fruit of lifelong work on the great theme in general and the work of Thomas Hobbes in particular'. Here his prime concern is to show that the 'much-admired system of Thomas Hobbes' leaves open 'a door to transcendence'.[70] However, these are no more than hints, and the whole enterprise ends in an open question.[71]

B.Willms goes a considerable step further[72] in his book *Die Antwort des Leviathan*, in which he recognizes the important contribution of the theological sphere for Hobbes' whole system of political philosophy and so investigates it in detail.[73] In the context of his central theory, an explanation of Hobbes' thought 'as a mediation between past and future in the actuality of the present situation',[74] he understands the theological dimension as 'an actualization of the Christian element as historical facticity':[75] in connection with his aim of giving theoretical foundation to the ordering of peace, Hobbes resolves the systematic basic problem of his approach, a demonstration of the normative binding character of action to preserve peace within the ordering of the state and society, by referring to Christianity as something which is already existing in history.[76] In the case of Christianity – in contrast to other, non-authorized religion – there was a normative tradition which 'was simply historical reality, the recognition of which was not dependent on the possibility of rational deduction, i.e. on being believed', and to this degree formed 'a dimension of historical continuity' to which Hobbes could refer ('Hobbes was a Christian').[77] Over against all interpretations which sought to exclude theological argumentation from Hobbes' system proper, Willms can refer to its firm place in the whole: 'In the outline of the Christian commonwealth, Christianity is thought of as the normative substance of the world of origin, along with the abstract sovereignty which the new age made necessary: thus without political theology, Hobbes' thought is always interpreted in too narrow terms.'[78] However, it is impossible to demonstrate the rationality of God's covenant with his people founded in the Old Testament and continued in Christianity; to this degree, with 'the incursion of the historical into theory', Willms finds in Hobbes the beginning of that 'dualism of method' which was mentioned so often in research.[79]

However, this particular catchword, 'dualism of method', also indicates the point at which Willms' interpretation lacks consistency and therefore lapses into the earlier stage of interpretation. Against Schmitt, Willms expresses his conviction 'that Hobbes' thought as a whole cannot be described as that of a theologian'.[80] Despite the way in which he 'maintains the Christian determination of origin and future', Hobbes' own political system is that of a 'modern thinker', and conditioned by the necessity 'of understanding the present as a state which is characterized by the absence of God'.[81] Thus, as Kodalle rightly observes,[82] despite everything, the connection with the theologically determined 'world of origin' looks like an addition to the system which here too is interpreted within its own terms.

However, the real cause of this weakness lies deeper: it is a result of the picture which Willms has of the character and tasks of a theologian:[83] this picture is typically conceived of in terms of the present and lacks historical perspective. For a humanistic theologian of the seventeenth century, to whom state and the church are still a unity, there can be no such professional limitation to a sphere which is 'theological' in the narrower sense: granted, Hobbes is in fact no professional theologian, but as was customary at that time, theology is naturally inherent in his thought. If we see him in connection with the history of the theology of his time, this becomes clear very quickly.

The last great attempt to illuminate Hobbes' system against the background of his theological thinking, the work by Kodalle which has already been mentioned,[84] basically suffers from the same weakness. This work gives a thorough commentary on a large number of Hobbes' remarks on theological themes and in so doing stresses their central significance for the whole of his work. Nevertheless, this approach is misleading, since criteria are applied to Hobbes which derive from a concept of theology which does not apply to him. Kodalle seeks to begin his analysis by saying that 'questions are addressed to Hobbes which he himself did not raise, and perhaps could not even have raised in this explicit form, but for which it is nevertheless thought that answers can be found in his philosophy. Such an attempt will necessarily place the accents and priorities in Hobbes' system of thought differently from Thomas Hobbes himself.'[85] However, traditional phrases of Hobbes[86] are often taken too literally, so that his thought is interpreted in terms of the Reformation, and that is certainly a distortion. Here, too, the main objection must be that Hobbes is understood too little in the context of his life.[87] His independent position can only be demonstrated in contrast to the voices of his contemporaries, who adopted a standpoint on the same theme of the relationship between church and state, which was central at that time.

Finally, what is otherwise an impressive work by U.Weiss, *Das philosophische System von Thomas Hobbes*,[87a] also ends up in dualism. What is impressive about it is his undertaking to describe the whole of Hobbes' philosophical system as theoretically a consistent programme, beginning from the physical and anthropological presuppositions and going on to the construction of the state. According to Weiss, Hobbes' approach through the claim of the individual to self-preservation as the basic natural law, which is also served by the *leges naturales* as cybernetic programme instructions[87b] for life in a state alliance,[87c] leads to a limited, purely secular system, the whole sphere of which is worked out rationally step by step.[87d] This avoids the alleged dualism between egoistic motivation and an ethical norm which possibly rests on a natural law. Weiss responds to the dispute between 'totalitarian' and 'liberal' interpretation of Hobbes by asserting that the function of the sovereign as ruler is limited to channelling the individual actions of the citizens only insofar as this is necessary for their safety; otherwise they are to be left as much freedom of action as possible.[87e]

In contrast to many of his predecessors, Weiss has also recognized the significance of the theological dimension in Hobbes.[87f] With Carl Schmitt, he recognizes that Hobbes' system is 'open for transcendence'.[87g] However, his own suggestion for a solution to the problem of transcendence now creates a new dualism: starting from religious inwardness as a free space for the individual which the system leaves open, he discovers an *additional* model for the structural description of what can also conceivably be a Christian state,[87h] through ideological criticism of religion and the church[87i] and biblical interpretation;[87j] in the last resort, he sees a central Christian and theological pattern of historical thinking behind this.[87k]

The dialectic which Weiss conjectures for Hobbes is an interesting model for his thought; however, because on the one hand it understands Hobbes as a tremendously modern thinker in terms of a theory of secularization and on the other hand interprets his theological and dogmatic statements almost in terms of a Reformation theology of history, it does not pay sufficient attention to Hobbes' spiritual home in the time in which he lived and the presuppositions of his thought.

6. Much in Hobbes' approach is traditional in a more specific sense, as was recognized earlier in the interpretations limited to the content of his work. Hood's reference to Hobbes' contact with Oxford Puritanism during his membership of Magdalen Hall,[88] reminiscent of many similar careers at the time, gives one of the most probable reasons for Hobbes' moral rationalism:[89] it was a type of thought which was also widespread in Puritanism. However, it would be foolish to seek to include Hobbes among the Puritans: if we try to place him among the church-political parties of the time, he perhaps belongs more clearly to the 'Anglican' group.[90] One feature of his life already points in that direction: Hobbes was one of the frequent visitors to Great Tew;[90a] moreover it is also possible to find other external evidence for his attitude from his own words. Thus for example in his personally written *curriculum vitae* he emphatically stressed his allegiance to the doctrine of the Church of England and to its episcopal leadership.[91] Still, such a statement could be dismissed as sheer defensiveness,[92] did not Hobbes' central concern to demonstrate the need for absolute royal supremacy over church and state[93] accord exactly with the interests of Laud's party and his supporters. (We shall also come across other quite obvious Anglican remarks.) Moreover, his aim of thus securing peace in both realms

coincides completely with Laud's efforts, except that in the light of his involvement in the new methods of natural science in Paris at the beginning of the 1630s, Hobbes undertakes to demonstrate from an anthropological perspective the need for an absolutist government of human society. The interpretation of Hobbes solely on the basis of his works was usually fascinated by this method, and indeed Hobbes' own contemporaries (not in the period of Laud, but in later decades, when the situation had already changed in many respects) no longer understood him. The close connection between Hobbes' work and the changing political situation in the first half of the century has become clear in an even more specific way. In a series of articles[93a] Quentin Skinner has drawn attention to the authors (like Anthony Ascham, John Dury and Marchamont Nedham) who, in the so called Engagement Controversy after the seizure of power by Oliver Cromwell in 1649, had argued that subjects owed obedience to the new ruler who had come to power de facto, and assigns Hobbes' *Leviathan* a place among these propaganda writings. Against this, however, it should be recalled that the *Elements of Law* and the *De cive* were already published in 1640 and 1642 respectively, and therefore served to defend the absolutism of Charles I.[93b] Even in content, much that is characteristic of Hobbes comes very close to the Anglican rationalism of the first half of the century.[93c] This becomes particularly clear from a comparison with Chillingworth.[94]

Hobbes has a great many basic ideas in common with Chillingworth. First there is his recourse to the Bible as the criterion of the rules of life, required by God, in accordance with which the moral conduct of Christians has to be shaped. Of course this is a view which almost all theological groups within Protestant England took for granted. More specific is the contact between the two thinkers in the basic question which comes before any detailed statement about the binding force of the authority which makes decisions on the doctrines of scripture, that question which Hobbes puts so frequently: *Quis interpretabitur? Quis judicabit?*[95] It was this question which for a while drove Chillingworth into the arms of the Roman church and then made him seek the solution in the reason of the critical reader of the Bible himself. Hobbes, however, appealed to the power of the national sovereign to decide, an external authority with a competence in interpretation of the will of God analogous to that of the doctrinal authority of Rome, with which it was locked in deadly rivalry at the beginning of the seventeenth century. Otherwise, both believe in the rational character and the ethical reference of faith, Hobbes moving in his characteristically gradated way between his two spheres of man's fictitious primal state and the Christian commonwealth. Faith cannot be contradicted even by the decision of the sovereign, the role of which is rather to produce a functional, external uniformity which contributes to peace.

What they have in common extends even further. If for Hobbes the basic confession of faith would seem to be 'that Jesus is the Christ',[96] a statement which Schmitt would see as the keystone of the whole inner structure of his political system of the state,[97] his reduction of the content of faith to a minimal statement denoting a consensus which all can accept resembles a quite similar statement made by Chillingworth.[98] That, for Hobbes, too, the Humanist doctrine of *fundamentalia* provides the criterion for this is shown by the appeal at the beginning of *Leviathan*, ch. 43, to 'those that can distinguish between what is necessary, and what is not necessary for their reception into the kingdom of God'. They cannot be involved in any conflict of conscience as a result of the sovereign's absolutist power of decision on all other matters.[99] What is necessary for salvation is now said even more precisely: 'faith in Christ, and obedience to laws'. The remarks which Hobbes adds to this double statement are illuminating for his innermost attitude: obedience would really be enough by itself if only it could be complete; however, original sin and the fact of personal transgressions necessitate a forgiveness of past sins; this is given as a reward for faith in Christ.[100] Here we see how the statements of orthodox dogmatics, like the need for the forgiveness of sins, are formally maintained, as is also the case with other representatives of radical Anglicanism, and moreover how this is said to happen for Christ's sake. At the same time, however, they are put in another context: obedience is necessary 'for the rest of our time', and forgiveness is a reward for faith which therefore similarly appears as merit. The remarks which follow also immediately remind us again of Chillingworth:[101] the obedience required by God, in which he takes the will for the deed, is a serious endeavour to obey him. Anyone who honestly desires to fulfil God's commandments or seriously repents of his sins has all the obedience necessary for being accepted into the kingdom of God.[102] The theory that God to some extent closes one eye is the only way in which Hobbes, the 'religious moralist', who no longer thinks in terms of the Reformation acceptance of the sinner, can deal with the problem : 'For if God should require perfect innocence, there could no flesh be saved.'[103]

Hobbes' connections with the Rationalists among his contemporaries can also be demonstrated in other areas. His acquaintance with Herbert of Cherbury, whose book he himself claims to have esteemed highly,[104] seems to have been significant for his views on religion. In *Leviathan*, ch.12, which has already been mentioned, where he speaks of the origins of religion and derives it from curiosity about the cause of things and the anxiety of men in their natural state, there are comments about the origin of superstition and polytheism which Herbert could have formulated in precisely the same way. The theories of deception by the priests turn up again, with the difference that here, in accordance with

Hobbes' special interest in explaining the foundation of pagan and Christian *states*, they are in part transferred to pagan rulers. Hobbes sees these as the 'authors' of pagan religion, though towards the end of the chapter the charges are increasingly directed against the 'stubbornness of the priests'.[105]

One of the great weaknesses of research into Hobbes hitherto lies in the fact that it virtually ignores the area of anti-Roman polemics in Hobbes, or at all events has not recognized its referential character for the general tendency of *Leviathan*.[106] A controversial discussion of Cardinal Bellarmine's work *De summo pontifice* (1586) in *Leviathan* ch.42 takes up a good deal of space, making this chapter in fact by far the longest in the whole book. With this approach Hobbes embarks on a theme which, as we have seen, runs through countless of his contemporaries, since the fear of re-Catholicization and the repudiation of papal claims was a dominant topic of discussion at this time. At all events, it is worth noting the tone of this discussion, which stands out from the usual run of things by its matter-of-fact tone.[107] Still, what matters most is not the language, but the consistent way in which the rejection of the papal claim to supremacy fits in with Hobbes' main concern: to demonstrate royal sovereignty over the state and church of England. This main concern can in fact only be understood against the background of the controversies with Catholicism, in the context of the fight by the national church against the church universal, begun by Henry VIII and continued under his successors.[107a]

One of the main reasons for the many misunderstandings in research into Hobbes is that modern interpreters are no longer aware of the continuing unitary conception of church and state which extends well into the seventeenth century and which beyond question formed the basic presupposition of most parties in the English church, of all tendencies, no matter how contrary these might be, in whatever shape they gave to the life of state and church. Bucer's *De regno Christi* stands at the beginning of this development,[108] and Hobbes' monism at the end.[109] In principle the Reformation had not basically changed this structure of the mediaeval *corpus Christianum*;[110] the territorial principle simply meant a limitation to the sphere within which the sovereignty which now accrued to each particular monarch was valid. To this extent, the controversies between the universal papal church and the English national church still took place in a sphere where to a great degree presuppositions were still shared. In the beginning, these presuppositions were challenged in principle only from one direction, by the Congregationalist Separatism of Robert Browne and his successors. However, this position, with its Spiritualist presuppositions, was to become increasingly significant over the course of the century. So it is only consistent that Hobbes should fight against the Separatists as his main opponents, the 'kingdom of darkness', whose central error consisted in their teaching that 'the kingdom of God mentioned so often in scripture is the present church or the totality of Christians now alive.'[111] Hobbes' concern to provide a theoretical foundation for the authority of the sovereign in all public concerns of state and church is in no way the isolated occurrence that the general view thinks it to be; it stands in a broad tradition characteristic, in particular, of the Anglican trend within the English church. Here too it is Carl Schmitt who has usefully referred to the German theologians Wolfgang Musculus and Thomas Erastus;[112] in addition, reference should be made to the Swiss influences on English theology[113] mentioned above.[114] However, Hobbes' immediate predecessors in the sphere of Anglican Erastianism were men like Overall and Bishop Andrewes.[115]

That is not to say that Hobbes must unconditionally and at all times have been a Royalist. As we saw, the Independents, too, were supporters of the state church, and Hobbes is known to have supported their system at the time of Cromwell's rule, seeing that he returned to England from exile in France as early as 1650.[116] Given his agreement in principle with the basic theoretical concern of the government, nothing stood in the way of this return, nor of the publication of his writings in England. In specific political matters, Hobbes could be quite restrained; indeed, he believed that in his system he had showed a way which could help towards peace on the basis of a general minimal consensus. After the Restoration he could hope for the specific realization of his aims from the restored monarchy, so we should not suppose that the shift which he then made is mere hypocrisy.[117] Hobbes indeed felt himself above all to be a philosopher, in that he kept aloof from the struggles of his day and instead wanted to develop an objective system on a 'scientific' basis, which in his view would provide each individual sovereign with a criterion for assessing his decisions. The remark mentioned above, that a Christian ruler could even transfer supremacy in religious matters over his subjects to the Pope, if he held this to be correct (in which case it would not be due him in his own right but simply by virtue of the bestowal of this right), is a sign of this concern for realistic universality. Otherwise, as Carl Schmitt has so aptly put it, his scholarly contribution belongs 'completely in the sphere of practical philosophy';[118] he felt at least as directly involved as Milton in the controversies of his time, but because of his quite different temperament he reacted to them in a quite different, philosophically detached way.

7. The use of scripture in Hobbes – and it is well known how much space biblical interpretation takes up in his works, an extent equalled by that of the confusion of most modern interpreters of Hobbes over this fact – is quite explicable given his aims and the presuppositions

which were those of his time.[118a] If we are to understand them, we must go one stage beyond an interpretation of the kind that is still attempted by Kodalle, based only on Hobbes' works; above all, we should not leave out of account the hermeneutical principles of Anglican scriptural typology, many examples of which we have already encountered. The detailed arguments from scripture which Hobbes provides for his theory of the state make sense only in the light of the Eusebian tradition of typology.[119,120] This presupposition must be remembered all the more when Hobbes's typological references are not indicated in so many words; he could start from the fact that this way of thinking was current among his contemporaries (in contrast to modern interpreters).

Given this, we can also establish a consistent pattern of thought, *more geometrico*, in the chapter in which Hobbes produces his scriptural proof for the comprehensive rights of the sovereign in matters of religion. Here the essence of the argument has remained the same from the *De cive* to *Leviathan*, even if in the latter work the subject matter has expanded considerably. The relevant chapters of *De cive* are 16 and 17.[121] Chapter 16 offers an outline of the history of the religion of Israel. Hobbes makes true worship, as distinct from the idolatry of most peoples, begin with Abraham. God made himself known to Abraham through a supernatural revelation (which at this point has a firm position in Hobbes' system, so that it is perverse to regard him as an atheist)[122] and made a contract with him (the old covenant).[123] According to Gen.17.7,8, on God's side this contract contained the promise that Abraham would inherit the land, whereas Abraham bound himself to recognize God as his ruler.[124] However, it seems important to Hobbes to stress that on making this contract, God did not give Abraham any special laws other than the natural laws which had already applied previously and the 'worship enjoined by reason'; circumcision was merely a sign given along with the contract. He concludes from this that Abraham was the 'interpreter of all laws, both sacred and secular', and his children and his house were bound by the commandments which he gave. So Abraham appears as the first ruler appointed by God, with full rights to legislate in secular and spiritual matters.

This statement gives us a valuable indication of the way in which we can fit Hobbes' typological explanations into the history of his time. In connection with research into Hobbes, it has not been observed hitherto that Hobbes is by no means alone in claiming Abraham as a ruler figure in this way. Roughly contemporaneous with his works was *Patriarcha, or the Natural Power of Kings*,[125] a work by Sir Robert Filmer (who had died as long ago as 1653) which was only published in 1680 by his son and was used by the Royalists of the time as the main support for their view. This was the work against which Locke then argued in his *Two Treatises of Government*.[126] It puts forward the argument that from the time of Adam, and therefore from the creation of the human race, royal power has derived from paternal authority; it has been exercised above all by the patriarchs as fathers of families and later nations, who from the time of the sons of Noah divided the world among themselves. In this way royal power derives from patriarchal power by succession, whereas the theory of the original freedom of peoples to choose their rulers has to be refused. Hobbes differs from Filmer in that he begins with Abraham, the embodiment of faith, introduces the idea of the contract – which Filmer has rejected – against the background of the notion of the covenant with Abraham which is characteristic of federal theology,[126a] and carries through the typological presentation more clearly. The reference back to the Old Testament patriarchs as such to provide a basis for the authority of contemporary English monarchs was a familiar idea at the time. This next statement is also made with an eye to all future rulers: 'It follows from this that the subjects of Abraham, if they obeyed him, could not sin, provided that Abraham did not command them to deny the existence of the providence of God or to do something that would expressly have infringed the glory of God.'[127] The ruler – any ruler appointed by God – has authority to establish a religious and moral order which is also valid before God; the qualification hints at the points which will then form the subject of the special closing discussion in *De cive*, ch.18. Apart from that, the moral responsibility of subjects is connected only with these commandments.

Hobbes goes on to enumerate the descendants of Abraham with whom God renews the contract: first Isaac and Jacob, who had the same authority as the 'natural leaders' of the Israelites to whom they owed 'the religious service inaugurated by Abraham' (to God himself, on the other hand, they owed only 'obedience and natural worship as his subjects'). However, Hobbes makes a completely new period begin with the contract made on Sinai: now 'the rule of God over them becomes an institution'.[128] There is now the foundation for the right to direct kingly rule by God over the Israelites. The laws given by God through Moses on Sinai are also part of this kingly rule. However, they are composed of different ingredients. Some are naturally binding, 'as they had been given by God, as the God of nature';[129] others have applied since the time of the contract with Abraham, and yet others became valid on the basis of the Sinai treaty: 'God gave them specifically as the king of the Israelites'. There then follows the division of the commandments which is already known from the Reformation trad-ition. The general moral laws in the Decalogue are natural command-ments; the first commandment and the sabbath commandment belong to the covenant with Abraham, because both refer to the special rela-tionship between God and Israel; 'to the third kind belong the laws for the ordering of the state, justice and worship, which concern the Jews alone.'[130] After a short description of what the law of God had originally been (in Hobbes' view originally only Deuteronomy had this status) there follows a discussion of the question which is important for Hobbes' system: who had the authority to interpret already existing laws and to judge whether the writings of the prophets were the word of God? Here is the problem *quis iudicabitur?* This task was first the responsibility of Moses and later, under Joshua, the responsibility of the high priest Eleazar; in the time of the Judges it was again formally that of the high priest, but in reality rested with the prophets, who had the charisma for it.

However, for Hobbes this time of immediate divine rule was only a transitional period. At the centre of his concern is the following section, which begins with the accession of Saul and lasts until the exile. Hobbes stresses very strongly that in this period the kings alone had all rights, 'including the right to interpret God's word'.[131] And this also included the right 'to issue books as God's word', as Hobbes concludes from Josiah's measures on the finding of Deuteronomy.[132] The prophets and above all the priests were also dependent on the kings. Hobbes does not allow the objection that the kings alone exercised all these rights: 'But if one would object that the kings were rarely suited to the interpretation of old books which contained the word of God because of their lack of learning, and that it is therefore illegitimate for this matter to be within their rights... the kings were very well suited to nominate interpreters of this kind under their presidency, and therefore the right of kings can quite appropriately include the interpretation of the word of God, so long as they do not interpret it themselves.'[133] The kings also fulfilled priestly roles; sacrifice was the only exception, 'because this was the inherited right of Aaron and his descendants.' The way in which these statements are presented as principles shows that here Hobbes is by no means just concerned with the kings of the Israelites but that typologically he has the present monarchs in mind here. As Hobbes stresses yet again, at the end of the chapter, there were only two exceptions to the duty of the Jews to be obedient: where the authorities had commanded repudiation of God's providence, or idolatry, since both these were lèse majesté against God. He is very careful when he talks about the time after the return from Babylonian captivity: it seems that at that time supreme authority lay in the hands of priests, but for a while their authority had been severely shaken. All that is important to him is that 'even in these times the right to interpret God's word is not separated from the supreme civil authority'.[134]

Chapter 17, 'Of the kingdom of God through the New Alliance', which follows, is illuminating for the consistency with which Hobbes pursues his concern to demonstrate the rights of the sovereign even in matters of religion. Here his main aim is to demonstrate from a mixture of quotations from the New Testament that the kingly rule of Christ had not yet dawned during his earthly activity (at that time he only had the office of a 'royal representative'[135] and only the power of a 'counsellor and teacher'[136]); it had not even dawned in the present, but: 'The kingdom of God... only begins with his second coming, namely at the day of judgment, when he will come in all his majesty, accompanied by his angels.' This is confirmed by statements like John 18.36: 'My kingdom is not of this world.'[137] If Hobbes' christology thus appears to be 'consistent eschatology',[138] that can only be as a consequence of the fact that hitherto, i.e. right down to the present, power had been transferred to the earthly sovereign not only in secular but also in spiritual matters, and it serves as an argument to this effect. Had Christ's kingly rule already been established, this claim would be impossible.[139] In *Leviathan*, ch.44, Hobbes fights against the 'greatest and most principal misuse of scripture', which consists in twisting it, 'to prove that the kingdom of God, mentioned so often in the Scripture, is the present Church, or multitude of Christian men now living'.[140] Evidently here he has the Puritans, and especially the Separatist movement, in mind. As a counter argument Hobbes immediately introduces the result of his investigations (in *Leviathan*, ch.35) into the course of the history of the religion of Israel, according to which the direct kingship of God existed only over the Jews, and only from the time of Moses; it came to an end again with the election of Saul. This deprived his opponents of the possibility of exploiting the kingly rule of God in the Old Testament as a typological proof for their views about the relationship between state and church.

We can see the major role that Hobbes assigns to the church in the problem of the correct interpretation of scripture from his lengthy discussion of this question, which already appears in *De cive*. In ch.17.16ff.[141] Hobbes begins from a definition of scripture which he describes as *verbum Dei*, in that it is *canon et regula omnis doctrinae Evangelicae*.[142] Now since scripture contains much that is political, historical, moral and physical, it must immediately be pointed out that these particular passages cannot be decisive; that is the case only with whatever relates to the 'mysteries of faith' (or 'the Christian religion'). Here a distinction needs to be made between the dead word, the letters, and the meaning: that alone can be canon in a true and authentic sense, 'For the spirit is guided only by the scripture which it understands.'[143] For the scriptures to become canon, therefore, an interpreter is needed. In that case either the word of the interpreter is the word of God or the canon of Christian doctrine is not the word of God.

There now follow lengthy thoughts on the correct interpretation of scripture. Here Hobbes stresses that knowledge of the original languages and the capacity to translate them into the vernacular is not sufficient for this art; great learning and knowledge of previous times is necessary for a balanced understanding of what someone speaking directly would add to the mere wording of his speech as a result of the time and place of its delivery, his gestures, and so on. However, the decisive element in the question of scriptural authority is not so much this as the possibility of human error; in the last resort that calls for an ultimate judge of all doctrinal matters who has unlimited authority to settle all disputes. Hobbes now goes on to deal with the concept of the church: here he makes a distinction between the church of the elect, which is still concealed till the last day, and the specific church to which all the baptized belong, though in contrast to the pluralistic Congregationalist concept of the church he sees this constituted by a 'regular authority for calling synods and assemblies of Christians', an authority which he allows only to the sovereign.[144] He then returns to the right to interpret scripture. Here he is not concerned with private comment on scripture (whether oral or written), but with authoritative decisions on disputed ethical or dogmatic questions.[145] Hobbes distinguishes two different kinds of disputed questions. Matters of human knowledge, like philosophy, in which truth depends on universal assent, do not call for any authoritative decision. However, the questions concerned with the clergy, 'i.e. the questions of belief the truth of which cannot be ascertained by natural reason; these include the questions of the nature and the ministry of Christ... of the resurrection of the body... the sacraments, outward worship and similar matters', do demand it.[146] Here, 'the right to decide on all disputed matters derives from and depends on the completeness of the power of the man or the assembly who holds supreme authority in the state'[147] (Hobbes' definition of the sovereign). However, there now follows a surprising move – in which Hobbes' profoundly Anglican way of thinking suddenly appears: 'However, divine consecration... which has been handed down from Christ onwards by the laying on of hands is needed for decisions over matters of faith, i.e. questions about God, which transcend powers of human comprehension.'[148] Thus in the matter of spiritual authority reference is made to the apostolic succession – an apparent breach in the system. So Hobbes ends with the statement: 'Therefore in the mysteries of the faith, the one who exercises authority in the state, in so far as he is a Christian, is obliged to interpret the Holy Scripture through duly ordained clergy.'[149] This particular remark is illuminating because it shows that Hobbes is in no way a consistent 'Erastian', but rather thinks along the lines of the Laudians, who stress the church's own right to regulate its concerns independently through the clergy, even under the royal supremacy.[150]

It becomes clear from these remarks that Hobbes thinks on different levels. In this respect he does not stand alone but resembles humanistic Anglicanism, as we have already seen from a variety of examples. One level is that of practical and moral existence. On this level one can first operate with the unambiguous character of the natural law, which is also expressed in the corresponding 'civil' commandments of the Decalogue. In the only dimension which is normative here, what is 'required in order to enter the kingdom of heaven' (*De cive*, ch.18; *Leviathan*, ch.43) is limited to the twin demands of obedience to the will of God (in these natural laws and the civil laws which are imposed by the sovereign) and the minimal confession that Jesus is the Christ. Alongside this there is a recognition of the possibility that there are mysteries of faith which call for a teaching ministry to decide upon them; here the way in which legal authority is rooted in the supremacy of the sovereign and church authority in the charisma of office within the framework of the apostolic succession represents the specifically Anglican solution to the problem.

However, it emerges from other of Hobbes' remarks that he does not regard these things as decisive. His comments about religion in *De homine*, ch.14,[151] are illuminating here precisely because they are so brief and were published at a relatively late stage (1658). In them Hobbes declares that matters which transcend the human capacity for comprehension need to be confirmed by miracles if we are to have faith in those who proclaim them.[152] 'Since there have not been miracles for a long time past,' religion is now dependent on the laws of the state. In the ethical sphere of religion ('that one must think reverently of God and love him, fear him and worship him') there is no difference between the nations.[153] 'The only dispute is where people have different opinions; and precisely for this reason this is not part of belief in God.'[154] Hobbes goes on to refer to I Cor. 13 (when the kingdom of God comes, only love remains): 'Now as to love God is the same as to obey his commandments, there arises the further question: how we know what God has commanded.' The answer is that God has given men reason and put his commandment in their heart. This consists in the 'golden rule'. 'Thus questions about the nature of God are all too curious,and are not to be counted among the works of piety.'[155] Hobbes goes on to add that faith would be done away with by untimely knowledge; this fact shows that his interest lies exclusively in the sphere of ethical action, so that in fact he is a typical humanist.

8. In the *Leviathan* Hobbes broadly and systematically developed his remarks about the foundations of the Christian state, 'in which much depends on the supernatural revelations of the divine will',[156] above all in Part III. One can already see from the general structure of this part that here Holy Scripture has a central place: most chapters deal with it. His concern to proceed *more geometrico*, i.e. systematically, is also evi-

dent from the fact that after ch.32, which is brief and basically deals with hermeneutics, in ch.33 Hobbes immediately has a section on questions about the canon, and goes on to proceed step by step in the following chapters. Here because the discussion in *De cive* of the questions which interest him in connection with his main concern is precisely what is called for at this point, he includes it against the background of a wider context.[157] For this reason, throughout the third part we find a wealth of individual exegetical comments which show an amazing knowledge of the Bible on the part of Hobbes the non-theologian, though some of the points are only loosely connected with the systematic background to his thought. However, all these individual comments are dominated by the point which Hobbes makes at the end of ch.32: since miracles no longer occur (see above), Holy Scripture is the only criterion for judging any doctrine, 'from which, by wise and learned interpretation, and careful ratiocination, all rules and precepts necessary to the knowledge of our duty both to God and man, without enthusiasm, or supernatural inspiration, may easily be deduced'.[158] Evidently, then, it is a matter of moral level, so that the conflict with the assertion of the necessity of the supreme authority in disputes over exegesis is only an apparent one.[159] On this level we are again reminded of the exegetical rationalism of a Chillingworth indicated by the illuminating title of his main work.[160] Hobbes begins ch.33, about the books of Holy Scripture, in an analogous way: 'By the books of Holy Scripture, are understood those, which ought to be the canon, that is to say, the rules of Christian life. And because all rules of life, which men are in conscience bound to observe, are laws; the question of the scripture, is the question of what is law throughout all Christendom, both natural, and civil.'[162] The definition of 'canon' as 'rules of life' corresponds exactly with the humanistic and moral understanding of the Bible. In the following remarks it is evident how Hobbes builds a bridge from this starting point to his basic theory that the reigning sovereign is the sole legislator within his realm. According to Hobbes' approach, that seems logical, since while the commandments contained in scripture do not exhaust the sphere of possible legislation, at all events they limit it,[163] so that the sovereign also has to decide on the extent of the canon. At first sight this accords with his well-known principle: 'According to this obligation (of subjects to be obedient), I can acknowledge no other books of the Old Testament, to be Holy Scripture, but those which have been commanded to be acknowledged for such, by the authority of the Church of England.'[164] At this point, however, his 'political science' and his Anglican traditionalism again come together, in that immediately afterwards he mentions St Jerome, and points out that these are the books already recognized by Jerome, which ultimately go back to the

Septuagint. So in practice theoretical radicalism ends up in a basically conservative attitude.

In the further course of ch.33 Hobbes goes on to develop his well-known theories about the origin and authorship of the Old and New Testaments.[165] In them we can again observe the same juxtaposition of radical questioning and traditional conclusions. On the one hand we find statements which are far ahead of their time. The Pentateuch cannot have been written by Moses, but must have been composed long after his death, and the same is true of the books of Joshua, Judges and Samuel; the Song of Songs and Ecclesiastes were not written by Solomon, and so on. On the other hand it is expressly affirmed that Moses wrote everything in the Pentateuch 'which he is said to have written'.[166] It is no coincidence that this includes the 'Book of the Law' in Deut.11-27, of which it is not only to be said that it was written by Moses himself and was given to the priests and elders of Israel to read out on the Feast of Tabernacles every seventh year, but above all also 'that law which God commanded, that their Kings (when they should have established that form of Government) should take a copy of from the priests and levites.'[167] This is the specific point with which Hobbes is concerned: the binding character of the Old Testament law and its relationship to the kings. For this reason it is very acceptable to him to be able immediately to mention the names of Hilkiah and Josiah, who 'renewed the covenant of the people with God' (II Kings 23.1ff.). After his further comments on the origins of the New Testament books as well, with his final maxim, 'but it is not the author but the authority of the church which makes a book canonical',[168] Hobbes arrives at his three-part answer to the question of the origin of the authority of scripture, which he makes more precise, again in full accordance with his legalistic understanding: 'The question truly stated is, "By what authority they are made law?"' The first part of the answer runs: 'As far as they differ not from the laws of nature, there is no doubt, but they are the law of God, and carry their authority with them, legible to all men that have the use of natural reason.' However, the precepts of reason are 'law, not made, but eternal'.[169] The second possibility is a purely theoretical one in the present: 'If they be made laws by God himself, they are of the nature of written law, which are law to them only to whom God hath so sufficiently published it...' By contrast the third point to which Hobbes' main concern is directed is a real one: 'He therefore, to whom God hath not supernaturally revealed, that they are his... is not obliged to obey them, by any authority, but his, whose commands already have the force of laws; that is to say, by any other authority, then that of the commonwealth, residing in the sovereign.' The reason why the ultimate decision over the question of the canon is reserved for the sovereign derives, according to Hobbes, from the presuppositions of his thought, and accordingly is quite consistent with what was still a predominant view in his time, given the unity of state and church: 'But the church, if it be one person, is the same thing with a commonwealth of Christians; called commonwealth because it consisteth of men united in one person, their sovereign; and a church, because it consisteth in Christian men, united in one Christian sovereign.'[170] According to Hobbes, the only conceivable challenge to the solution of the national church could derive from a universal Christianity directed by a representative of Christ. He thinks he can answer this question only by making a closer investigation of the concept of the 'kingdom of God'.[171] A discussion of this is to be found in ch.35.[172] In this chapter Hobbes mainly repeats his argument from *De cive*, according to which in ancient times the kingdom of God was the earthly kingdom of the Jews down to Saul's election as king, while in ch.38, as in *De cive*, he speaks of the re-establishment of this kingdom on earth, with Jerusalem as its centre, on the return of Christ at the last day. Between these discussions come ch.36, 'Of the Word of God, and of Prophets', in which Hobbes also discusses the problem of distinguishing between true and false prophecy (cf. also ch.32), and ch.37, 'Of Miracles'.[173] In view of the problem raised by the need to distinguish between true and false prophets (for which again he adduces a wealth of biblical examples), on the question of prophecy Hobbes already arrives in ch.32 at the answer that there are two signs by which a true prophet can be recognized: 'One is the doing of miracles; the other is the not teaching any other religion than that which is already established.'[174] On miracles, however, he observed at the end of the same chapter that they no longer occur today and therefore that Holy Scripture has taken the place of any other prophecy[175] – and that in turn, as we saw, ultimately derives its authority from that of the sovereign. The argument about miracles in ch.37, like that about prophets in ch.36, is therefore no more than a repetition of what has gone before: in both cases there is indeed first a reference to reason as the instrument for distinguishing between true and false prophecy,[176] between alleged and real miracles,[177] but in respect of miracles today it can only be a matter of whether the reports of miracles which once took place are true or false, and 'In which question we are not every one, to make our own private reason, or conscience, but the public reason, that is the reason of Gods supreme lieutenant (the sovereign), judge.'[178] The same is true of the prophets: only those are true prophets who (according to I John 4.2ff.) confess that 'Jesus is the Christ' – the Messiah has already appeared in the person of Christ – false prophets are those who dispute this, and the question of true doctrine immediately brings us back to the sovereign, who is responsible for it in the first place: 'Every man therefore ought to consider who is the sovereign prophet; that is to say, who it is, that is Gods vicegerent on earth... and to observe for a rule, that doctrine, which, in the name of God, he hath commanded to be taught; and thereby to examine and try out the truth of those doctrines, which pretended prophets with miracle, or without, shall at any time advance.'[179] Thus Hobbes' system is also coherent at this point.

In view of my comments about the argument of *De cive* above, there is not a great deal new to be said about chs.40-42. Chapter 40 demonstrates in respect of the Old Testament 'that whosoever had the sovereignty of the commonwealth amongst the Jews, the same had also the supreme authority in matter of Gods externall worship.'[180] There then follows, very much in parallel with the comments in *De cive*,[181] a discussion of the covenant with Abraham. Abraham is the central typological figure of the Old Testament for Christianity; it is therefore no coincidence that Hobbes stylizes him in particular as a ruler figure, in this way incorporating him into his pattern of royal typology. Like *De cive* 17, ch.42 stresses that the kingdom of Christ only begins with the general resurrection. This prepares for the detailed argument with Bellarmine in ch.42 about the jurisdiction of the state church, over against the papal claim to primacy.[182] At the heart of this argument there is a rejection of the twofold conception that the kingdom of God is nevertheless of this world (against this, Hobbes cites especially John 18.36) and that as representative of Christ the pope has the power of jurisdiction over all Christians.[183] Here, too, Hobbes concentrates strictly on this basic question: he rejects the usual irrelevant polemics, for example that the Pope is Antichrist, with arguments from scripture.[184]

Chapter 43 once again underlines the purely moral character of Hobbes' understanding of religion, in that he formulates the central principle as: 'All that is Necessary to salvation, is contained in two virtues, faith in Christ and obedience to laws.'[185] In Part IV, 'Of the Kingdom of Darkness',[186] Hobbes returns to his argument that the kingdom of Christ only dawns in eschatology. He is now arguing against the group which he calls 'the kingdom of darkness', and to begin with refers to it rather obscurely as 'a confederacy of deceivers, that to obtain dominion over men in this present world, endeavour by dark, and erroneous doctrines to extinguish in them the light, both by nature, and of the gospel'.[187] Here it is a question of 'this power regal under Christ, being challenged, universally by the Pope, and in particular commonwealths by assemblies of the pastors of the place.'[188] He sees its basic error as supposing that 'the present church is the kingdom of Christ',[189] and an attempt is made to demonstrate this by twisting scripture, in Hobbes' judgment 'the greatest, and main abuse of scripture, and to which almost all the rest are either consequent, or subservient'.[190] This leads not only to the pope's claim to power but also to the distinction between clergy and laity generally and the privileges claimed by the priests, above all in the financial sphere.[191] We can see how influential typological arguments also are in this discussion from Hobbes' reference to the fact that for a long time the pope and his subordinate clergy everywhere demanded the tithe by divine right, after the model of the levites. It is, too, a further example of the way in which in Hobbes everything, including this basic humanist characteristic and his fundamentally anti-clerical attitude, appears in the specific garb of his theory of the state church. The other errors discussed in this chapter, the turning of consecration into conjuration, and the doctrine of the immortality of the soul,[192] can be passed over here. Chapter 45, 'Of Demonology and Superstition', and ch.46, 'Of Vain Philosophy and Fabulous Traditions', also exude the spirit of the Enlightenment. In the latter chapter there is also vigorous polemic against Aristotelian scholastic philosophy.

Chapter 47, 'Of the Benefit that proceedeth from such Darkness, and to whom it accrueth', sums up the discussion of the previous chapters and presents it under the question '*Cui bono?*'. Here Hobbes finally strikes out in a concentrated attack on the priesthood. The papacy primarily profits from the error 'that the present church now militant on earth, is the kingdom of God'.[193] 'But' – and now Hobbes discloses that he has in mind an audience closer to hand – 'in those places where the presbytery took that office, though many other doctrines of the Church of Rome were forbidden to be taught; yet this doctrine, that the kingdom of Christ is already come... was still retained. But cui bono? What profit did they expect from it? The same which the Popes expected: to have a sovereign power over the people.'[194] He fights for the royal claims over the church against Presbyterians and against Rome, as he clearly indicates in the following aims: 'For what is it for men to excommunicate their lawful king... and with force to resist him, when he with force endeavoureth to correct them?' The author of the 'kingdom of darkness' can therefore be mentioned clearly by name: 'The authors therefore of this darkness in religion, are the Roman, and the presbyterian clergy.'[195] There follows a list of predominantly Roman customs, which Hobbes derives from this origin. At the end we have 'the metaphysics, ethics, and politics of Aristotle, the frivolous distinctions, barbarous terms, and obscure language of the Schoolmen, taught in the universities.'[196] Thus the humanistic front against scholastic theology is unbroken even in Hobbes (his enthusiasm for the new science is complementary to this). There is even a retrospective survey of history (a brief one), in which earlier emperors are charged with having first tolerated the seizure of power by the clergy; the rise of the presbyters to power is traced from the time of the early church down to the papal claim to primacy. Hobbes then asserts that the way back to original purity began with the Reformation in England: first with the dissolution of papal power under Elizabeth I, then with the overthrow of bishops by the Presbyterians, and finally, most recently, by the Presbyterians' fall from power. Thus Hobbes now thinks that he can once again see the possibility of freedom as in earliest Christianity. However, once again he lapses into invective against the priests: clergy and spirits are compared in ironical series of parallels: the spirits have only one king, King Oberon, and the clergy have the pope; the clergy have their cathedrals and the spirits their castles, and so on. Apparently this polemic is now directed exclusively against Rome again, but at the end of it Hobbes asks whether, after Elizabeth had driven out these spirits, they could not return in another form. And so we are back at a favourite theme which also motivates others than Hobbes.

9. If we compare Hobbes' remarks in those parts of his work which are concerned with religious themes and the relationship between state and church with the positions of the various parties in England in the first half of the seventeenth century, as we discussed them earlier, the impression given by the political scientists, that Hobbes was a quite independent and solitary figure, increasingly fades away. Certainly his attempt to ground the sovereignty of the monarch *more geometrico* in the notion of a natural condition makes him an original philosopher of the state, and the fascination exercised by his system is as understandable as the misunderstanding of it by his younger contemporaries, which turned to hate. Real parallels to the presuppositions of his world view cannot in fact be found among them; they occur, rather, among some of the companions of his youth and in the traditions of the cultural trend to which he must be assigned, rational and ethical Humanism, as its influence was carried over from the sixteenth to the seventeenth century. In the narrower sense, he belongs to the group of rationalistic Anglicans who supported the absolutist monarchy and the system of the state church under Charles I, amidst the anti-Roman disposition which this produced, and also continued the antipathy to priests characteristic of Humanism. That produces an ambivalent attitude towards the episcopal church[197] and its forms of worship, both of which, like dogmatic statements, are classed rather as externals and are relativized by being made completely dependent on the free jurisdiction of the sovereign, while an impregnable safe area is preserved for private belief. This also determines the positions adopted – in addition to the traditional hostility to Rome, hostility to the Presbyterians, whose Puritan notions of reform, introducing a presbyteral ordering of the church, inevitably posed a threat. At first this threat was directed, if not against the state church as such, at least against the supremacy of the crown; later, when Puritanism turned into separatist groups, the whole structure of the church was threatened. It is therefore understandable that at the time of Cromwell Hobbes should have found his allies above all

among the Independents, with their basically conservative attitude. At this time Hobbes had already outlived his own presuppositions (he was already well advanced in years); they had originated among the group of young liberal intellectuals, encouraged by Archbishop Laud, which had been broken up at the beginning of the Civil war, which also destroyed their protector.

All Hobbes' basic theological statements are typical of Humanism. The creed necessary for salvation is limited to a central statement that Jesus is the Christ; the further explication of this, namely, that he is the king announced by the Old Testament prophets,[198] ties this firmly in with the structure of his royalist system. In addition, there is his indifference to outward forms,[199] and his almost exclusively moralistic understanding of religion as obedience owed to God and to his laws, direct and indirect (promulgated through the sovereign). His understanding of the Bible is connected with this: he sees the Bible above all as the sourcebook for the law and additionally as testimony to a history of Israel, the ancient people of God, represented by its leaders beginning with Abraham, a people whose obligation to obey the commandments contained in the covenant was communicated by these leaders. The legalistic relationship to God was not done away with even by the coming of Jesus Christ, since the forgiveness gained through Christ relates only to past sins, whereas from now on ('for the rest of our time') obedience to the law is once again required of all Christians. Also closely bound up with this legalistic understanding is the typological interpretation of the Old Testament rulers as the model for the role of the sovereign in the present commonwealth which unites state and church: limited only by the immutable principles of natural law, the sovereign is authorized to regulate all external forms along with those dogmatic statements which lie outside the basic confession necessary for faith, even in the sphere of the church. A possible restriction of this authority by the kingly rule of Christ is avoided by the interpretation of the beginning of this rule as a strictly eschatological event. Of course in practice the ecclesiastical jurisdiction of the ruler is a representative one, as we saw how Hobbes is well aware of the need for the king to carry out these duties through the ecclesiastical organs which are in fact at his disposal. Whereas worship and external forms are regarded as being unnecessary in the context of the system, and are therefore seen to be adiaphora in the Erasmian sense, we can see even in Hobbes, on the periphery, a hint of the antipathy to the cult and the priesthood, particularly in his attacks on Rome, which is equally an indication of the tradition in which we should place him.

So if Hobbes towers above the circle of his intellectual contemporaries as an original thinker, and his efforts towards strict rational consistency have produced an impressive system providing a basis for sovereignty over the state and the state church, in his intrinsic presuppositions and his religious attitudes, which are also the basis of his entire thought, he is completely a child of his time. He can clearly be included in an overall cultural development, namely, Christian humanism of the sixteenth and seventeenth centuries, and in a trend within church politics, i.e. the Anglicanism of the time of Laud, liberal in doctrine and royalist in politics. To this extent Hobbes is a new element in the cultural mosaic of the century of revolution, though he does not make any significant change to the overall pattern. Furthermore, biblical interpretation with a humanistic stamp is not essentially modified by Hobbes, except that with his consistent thinking he developed the basic legalistic line more clearly and uncompromisingly than any of his contemporaries whom we have considered.[200] His rational matter-of-factness also lies at the heart of his opposition to the Cambridge Platonists,[200a] whose Spiritualism was alien to him though he shared their moralism. A basic feature of his biblical interpretation, which lies at the centre above all of his use of the Old Testament, is the hermeneutical method of royal typology, which hitherto has been left completely out of account; this he uses, extending it, with his characteristic consistency, as far as the figure of Abraham.

4

The Latitudinarians

(a) Preachers and theological writers from the Restoration to the Glorious Revolution (1660-1689)

Benjamin Whichcote died in 1683, on a visit to the house of his colleague and friend Ralph Cudworth, in Cambridge. His funeral address was given by John Tillotson (1630-1694),[1] who was later to become Archbishop of Canterbury. Tillotson, a pupil of the two Cambridge Platonists, was a famous preacher and the best-known representative of the so-called Latitudinarian movement.[2] In some respects the Latitudinarians were evidently the heirs of the Cambridge school, above all in their basic rationalist and moralist attitudes and the breadth of their doctrinal sympathies, albeit with the one distinctive difference that they did not have the basically Neoplatonist and spiritualizing attitude of this group of philosophers, who are a unique phenomenon in the history of ideas. The Latitudinarians were not philosophers at all but churchmen, practical people, who had practical aims even in their theological work: the homiletical edification of their audience and an apologetic defence of the Anglican church.

It is no coincidence that the first statements from Latitudinarian circles begin immediately after the Restoration of 1660 (and thus before the Cambridge Platonists had finished their work); however, their wider public influence can be seen only after the Glorious Revolution of 1688. It then lasted well into the eighteenth century. Both political revolutions also meant profound changes in the cultural situation in England, which meant that they had direct consequences for church and theology.[3]

To begin with, for all the king's personal liberalism, the Restoration inevitably brought with it a counter movement in favour of the Anglican system, breaking the previous monopoly of Puritanism. After the failure of the historical possibility of compromise between Presbyterians and Episcopalians at the Savoy Conference in early 1661,[4] the 'Act of Uniformity'[5] obliged all clergy who wanted to remain in office to swear an oath of submission to the hierarchical order of the Church of England, to accept the Book of Common Prayer with its liturgical regulations, and to reject the Solemn League and Covenant of 1643. The effect of this was for a great many Puritans to give up their posts either voluntarily or under compulsion; the requirement of proof of episcopal ordination as a condition of appointment for all clergy and the claims of the incumbents driven away under the Commonwealth to reinstatement increased the number of new appointments.[6] However, many of the deposed clergy managed to slip into other positions, partly through powerful private patrons, while others of a Puritan inclination found a way to conform outwardly and remained at their posts.[7] The end-result of these measures was not the hoped-for restoration of the unity of the church ('comprehension') but its final division into the two blocks of Conformists and Non-Conformists, the latter of which again split into an increasing number of sects.[8] Under the cover of outward conformity a far-reaching change was developing in the intellectual situation which only needed an external factor (James II's open move towards Catholicism) to lead to a revolutionary change in every respect, namely the Glorious Revolution of 1688.[9]

One characteristic of this change was that the 'third party', the rationalist and moralist trend in Anglicanism, gained increasing influence; as early as 1661 their aim was the greatest possible 'comprehension' by a reduction in demands for liturgical and doctrinal unity. Their eventual formation as a separate party in church and politics is closely connected with the fact that because of the High Church majority in the Convocation of Canterbury they could not even carry through this aim in 1689, and instead had to be content with the Act of Toleration, which, while tolerating the Free Church groups, did not bring their members complete equality of civil rights. A second more important reason lay in the implications of the change of dynasty: the High Church clergy for the most part felt themselves bound to the legitimate royal house even after the expulsion of James II, and some of them even refused to swear the oath of allegiance to the new ruler (the so-called Non-Jurors), so that William III found himself compelled to turn chiefly to the Latitudinarian trend in the church for support. Consequently this wing was completely pressed into the role of defenders of the established church and of the political system (in close conjunction with the Whig party, whose influence was now increasing) – and particularly of the Protestant heritage.[10] The fact that after 1689 and (after the interlude of Tory rule under Queen Anne) under the first rulers of the House of Hanover the Whigs were for decades the majority party in church and state is something that they owe much more to the change of climate which began as early as 1661 than to external circumstances.

On the other hand, Puritanism, too, did not disappear at the time of the Restoration. The successive defeats of the more moderate Puritan trends, first the Presbyterians under Cromwell and then the Independents with the failure of the Commonwealth experiment, had eventually favoured the left wing among the broad spectrum of its groupings. This development can also be traced in the careers of various individuals who emigrated from the Presbyterians, through the Independents, to the Baptists or Quakers, until sometimes they eventually ended up in a state of complete scepticism.[11] The left wing of Puritanism was characterized by an extreme Spiritualism, sometimes combined with a strong mystical tone. Typical of this is the work of Sir Henry Vane, one of the most prominent representatives of this trend,[12] the obscurities of which continually presented almost insuperable difficulties to his readers.[13] The leading role which Vane already played in the Long Parliament of 1640 and then again in the Rump Parliament after the resignation of Richard Cromwell also shows the political influence of the extreme Puritan left wing during the period of the Civil War. Another example is that of the Quakers, who, growing out of the 'Seekers',[14] had at the heart of their system the doctrine of the 'inner light' as the source of a direct revelation accessible to all human beings. Otherwise the movement was marked by its well-known code of ethics and even outward modes of conduct (they refused to take off their hats as a greeting, and addressed everyone, even the most distinguished, with 'Thou' instead of 'You'), all of which followed from taking the New Testament literally. They are particularly prominent representatives of the mystical trend in Puritanism, and are thus witnesses to a legacy which derives from the Spiritualists within the 'left wing of the Reformation', like Sebastian Franck.[15,16] Similarly, however, they are also extreme representatives of the legalism typical of Puritanism, and W.S.Hudson has again drawn attention to the close connection between this and particular forms of Spiritualism.[17] Some of the characteristic features of the Spiritualists of the late Middle Ages reappear with the early Quakers:[18] they include above all the view that the present time is the eschatological age of the Spirit, in which the previous structures of the church are abolished and even the existing priesthood has to yield in favour of a new ministry inspired by the Spirit. Because they rejected the existing church, the Quakers refused to pay the tithe;[19] occasionally Quakers even caused disturbances in services held by the state church.[20] Despite the king's concern for clemency, their refusal to take the oath and the general public disapproval they incurred by their determined and eccentric behaviour led to a vigorous persecution of the Quakers by the courts and to numerous excesses against them from 1660 onwards. A number of them were even martyred: generally speaking they suffered the severest persecution of any religious group at the time of the Restoration.[21]

Their hostility to the church and the priesthood was also expressed in a series of their early writings: among these[22] reference should be made to the work of Edward Burrough,[23] who was one of the first martyrs of the persecution of the Quakers in 1662, dying in London's Newgate prison.[24] He was a barely educated but enthusiastic member of the community,[25] and what he says is a characteristic example of the enthusiasm with which Quakerism launched its attack on the existing church. The author's lofty sense of mission already emerges in the introductory *Epistle to the Reader*[26]. Here he addresses the whole world and all nations in the name of Quakerdom, using the colourful imagery of a language with a marked apocalyptic tone,[27] in order to present the dispute which exists 'between the Priests, and Professors, and all Sects in these Nations, and Us, who are in scorn called Quakers, shewing that the Controversie on our part is just and equal against them all'. He challenges these 'to prove according to the Scriptures, their Ministry, Church and whole Religion, that it is in and by the Spirit and Power of God, or otherwise to renounce and deny all their Religion, and the Profession and Practice thereof.' There follows a self-portrait of the Quakers in which they describe themselves (following Rev.7 and Ps.23) as the people of the end-time, gathered from out of all nations and through many persecutions by the Good Shepherd, having come 'out of the World, and out of great Babylon, and out of spiritual Sodom, and Egypt'. They despise all riches and crowns of this world because their spiritual (re-)birth gives them a share in another kingdom which is not of this world. They are the seed of Jacob, blessed by God. Through them the Lord does his eschatological work, 'for Sion shall rise out of the Dust, her beautiful Garments shall be put on, and Mourning and Sorrow shall flee away', and so on: the language is full of biblical messianic and apocalyptic allusions.

The penitential preacher then turns to the people he is really addressing and says to them (with a combination of Joel 1.13; Hos.2.10,5 and other Old Testament references): 'Hear this ye priests, and howl, and lament for the misery that is coming upon you; the Lord hath laid you naked, and made you bare...' He accuses them with words from Jer.23.16,28 of proclaiming their own dreams and visions and not the word of the Lord, and thus representing the apostasy of the churches since the time of the apostles. So here we find the typically Spiritualist view of church history: the contrast between the priests as the 'false Apostles, which went out from the true Apostles, and run for Gifts and Rewards, and preached for filthy Lucre', with the Quaker preachers of the spirit as the true apostles and true servants of the word – 'for they were led by the Spirit of the Father which dwelt in them, and they preached the Gospel by the Spirit, and spake as the Spirit gave them utterance' – heaps up the blame for this apostasy on clergy past and present and identifies the existing official church root and branch with 'Babylon' (see above). They, the priests, are the chief opponents who have to be fought: 'I do hereby declare unto you, in the Name and Authority of the Lord, that we have a controversie with you, and a great charge against you in all these things, in your Call, in your Practice, and in your Maintenance, and in your Doctrines.' In their call, since the apostles were called by the gift of the Spirit; in their practice, since they proclaimed what the Spirit inspired in them, whereas in the case of the priests 'what you have studied for out of Books and old Authors you preach to people' (here we meet the characteristic hostility of Spiritualists to academic study); in their manner of life, because they live on tithes and other offerings, and not like the apostles on voluntary gifts from those who hear them.

They, the Quakers, are now the recipients of the Spirit, the 'light in us that Christ has given us', which has informed them of the sorry state of the church (the woman who was once clothed with the sun and had the moon under her feet [according to Rev.12.1] but has now fled into the wilderness [Rev.12.6]). 'And we found this Light to be a sufficient Teacher, to lead us to Christ, from whence this Light came.' This possession of the spirit, however, means a departure from all dogmatic teaching and all previous forms of worship,[28] so that the Quakers go out as followers of the Lamb in the struggle against the powers of darkness and against the official church, 'the Beast and false Prophet, which have deceived the Nations', against the great whore (Rev.17) from whose cup all the world has drunk the wine of whoredom. For 'the Antichrist was set up in the Temple of God (according to Dan.9.27; 11.31; 12.11; Matt.24.15), ruling over all' since the days of the apostles and the earliest church :the clergy ('the Ministry') is this Antichrist, and the priests are not the servants of Christ but false prophets and apostles, 'wholy degenerated from what the true Ministry of Christ once was'.

The prophet of the Spirit also indicates what the true task of the secular authorities was: to punish the wicked, to protect the good, and otherwise, 'that mens Consciences are to be left free, and to be ruled by the Lord alone, and guided by his Spirit'. The state has no control over the conscience. But the authorities have far outstripped their competence in this respect by persecuting the Quakers. There follows a detailed description of all the oppressions by which the brief history of the Quakers has so far been characterized. Here one only has to compare the fruits of the Quakers with that of the priests! For they should have been given the freedom to criticize the priests openly in all the respects mentioned. Indeed the supporters of the churches should choose the time, the place and the conditions for a debate on the question whether they have not been deceived and should not renounce their whole faith. In that case, the Quakers would enter into negotiations with them! The Protestants rightly do not want to recognize the church of Rome as a church – but by themselves continuing Roman practices they demonstrate that their church, their worship and their clergy are basically the same as those of Rome, 'that the Protestant church, and Worship, and Ministry, is of the Romish Church sprung as a branch out of her, not contrary to her, and against her.' The redeployment of anti-Roman polemic against the Church of England is another typical theme of the Spiritualist position.

The *Epistle to the Reader* is an impressive compilation of the polemic against worship and the priesthood which is developed in other writings contained in the *Works*. These include in particular the 1657 pamphlet, *A Just and Lawful Tryal of the Teachers and professed Ministers of this Age and Generation by a perfect proceeding against them*,[29] and Ch.XI, 'Concerning the true Ministry of Christ and the false Ministry, and the difference between them'[30] from the Catechism (printed in 1667) *A Standard lifted up, and an Ensign held forth to all Nations*.[31] The pamphlet *The True Christian Religion again Discovered, After a long and dark Night of Apostacy*[32], which similarly comes from 1657, ends up in an invitation, given with similar prophetic solemnity, to all sects and confessions to appear at a trial which will decide who can claim to belong to the true religion. The formal criterion for this is that common to all Puritans: 'Whatsoever is professed and practised for Religion, for which there is neither command nor president (=precedent) in Scripture, is not according to the Scripture.' The content of true religion is then defined; it thus takes on characteristic ethical and Spiritualistic colouring. 'The true religion is a walking with God in purity and holiness, a performing of good to him, and not doing any evil; a belief in Christ, and receiving of him, and a living in him, and through the operation of his Spirit to be changed into his Image... and not a living to this vain World in any thing, but in all things to be guided by the Spirit of Christ...'[33] This is the typical Puritan position; the following polemic against all external forms of the church is simply a conclusion which is drawn more radically by the Quakers than by the more moderate Puritans. Detailed points of condemnation are infant baptism (since it is not in accordance with scripture, it does not bestow real membership of the church), the singing of Psalms (which is not in the New Testament), worship in 'temples' (which is against Acts 17.24), payment for ministers and the taking of tithes. What is proclaimed in the *Epistle* is also said here: such clergy are no servants of Christ, therefore it is also true of all adherents of churches and sects that 'none of you are of the Christian Religion'.[34]

It is also part of the Quakers' awareness of their mission that they regard their own time as the eschatological time of fulfilment and the return of the days of the apostles, and they themselves appear as the Spirit-guided witnesses to the truth.[35] The Spiritualist background which also underlies the legalism in the use of scripture is already clear in these remarks; however, it also comes out explicitly in the remarks about the Gospel of Christ in *A Standard*, ch.XII, in which there is a marked distinction between 'letters' and Gospel,[36] and in Ch.XIII 'Concerning the Word of God, and concerning the Scriptures', in which the eternal Word, which was from creation and (in accordance with the biblical imagery) is as sharp as a two-edged sword, is described as the force standing behind the development of scripture, which is also indispensable for the right understanding of scripture.[37]

If the early Quakers represented the extreme wing of Puritanism (and their successors soon spoke in milder tones), they were by no means an isolated phenomenon; the thoughts which they express reproduce feelings which are also widespread elsewhere. At the time of the Restoration (Burrough's works were printed in 1672) the legacy of Spiritualism was evidently still not dead. This should be carefully noted when immediately after the Glorious Revolution polemic against the established church emerges which takes up many of the arguments which had been used against it by the Spiritualist sects. The first Deists seem to have quite a different starting point: reason takes the place of the spirit, and Shaftesbury,[38] who in many respects is very close to them, argues against 'Enthusiasm'.

Nevertheless, there are striking common features indicating an intrinsic connection between the phenomena which so far has been little noted. In reality, as we were continually able to observe, Spiritualism and Rationalism go closely together: once the inner light as a charismatic force has been made a sure possession, it has only to be turned into the light of reason which all human beings have at their disposal as creatures and later as autonomous subjects, for the transition to the 'Enlightenment' to have been made.

One step on the way there is the programme of the Latitudinarians, which was outlined in *Irenicum. A Weapon-Salve for the Churches Wounds, or the Divine Right of Particular Forms of Church-Government*,[39] by Edward Stillingfleet (1635-1699). At the end of his life Stillingfleet was to become Bishop of Worcester, but at that time he was a young vicar and a former Cambridge student.[40] Among the basic ideas of this work is the distinction between a limited number of precepts, the observance of which is binding on the Christian church, and the broad sphere of indifferentia, which can be freely left to the circumstances of the time and are not constitutive of the true church. He is also hostile to the Puritans, who claim that biblical precepts are normative for the whole of the outward form of the church. Here we can recognize the legacy of the Anglicans from the first half of the century. However, there is one new development in comparison with the Laudians, which Stillingfleet in part again derives from the position of Whitgift[41] or even Ussher: his whole work is devoted to proving that apart from certain basic elements the outward organization of the church is in no way prescribed by Jesus or the apostles, but can be ordered in each age in accordance with contemporary circumstances. The rather baroque title of the work is meant to convey that in future, differences of opinion over church structures need no longer be a reason for division and discontent. Rather, if there is no divine right for the outward form of the church, there is room for a compromise on the basis of the present situation: 'For then all parties may retain their different opinions concerning the Primitive form, and yet agree and pitch upon a form compounded of all together as the most suitable to the state and condition of the Church of God among us: That so the peoples interest be secured by consent and suffrage, which is the pretence of the congregational way, the due power of Presbyteries asserted by their joynt-concurrence with the Bishop... and the just honour and dignity of the Bishop asserted, as a very laudable and ancient constitution for preserving the Peace and Unity of the Church of God.'[42]

However, it is not enough to praise the spirit of peace and tolerance in which the ideal of the church is depicted by Stillingfleet in his preface;[43] rather, we must note the kind of reasons he offers for his view in the substance of his work. Here it is striking to what degree he constructs his argument on Stoic foundations. After the introductory remark in Part I, Chapter I, that things necessary for the peace of the church must be revealed clearly, but that in respect of church government no particular form was planned by Christ as the only one to preserve peace, in the very same chapter he goes on to reflect on the nature of law. A distinction must be made between things that are permitted and those which are a duty. What is not forbidden is allowed; an explicit command is the precondition of a duty. However, that presupposes legislation and promulgation. A distinction must be made between the law of nature and positive commandments of God. 'The Law of Nature binds indispensably, as it depends not upon any arbitrary constitutions, but is founded upon the intrinsecal nature of good and evil in the things themselves, antecedently to any positive Declaration of God's Will.'[44] Now if on the basis of the law of nature positive divine commandments are decreed, like the first three commandments of the Decalogue, the formal reason for the obedience offered them by men is their agreement with the divine nature and goodness, but the efficient cause is the will and command of God, so that this law can be called a law of nature in respect of its immutability, and divine law in respect of its promulgation and origin. For the sanctioning of the law of nature also comes only from God, and therefore the obligation to obey it must equally come from God.[45] Alongside the law of nature, the second source of divine law consists in God's positive commandments as they are contained in scripture. Now the mistake of the Jews lies in the fact that they believe that all the commandments of God are immutable as such: but this is only the case when it is expressly said that they are to be immutable. There are things which are good and therefore commanded, and others which are commanded and therefore good. In all cases, however, the validity of laws ceases if the reason for their promulgation also ceases to exist.[46]

This definition already provides the basis for the remarks which follow about the way in which positive commandments of God are binding in questions of church structure and church government. In respect of the ordering of the church, as was explained in ch.II, the law of nature has absolute authority: neither human law nor God himself can change good and evil and the resultant moral obligation. Whatever accords with the law of nature can be practised in the church, in so far as more specific conditions are not laid down by positive divine laws. Whatever is determined neither by the law of nature nor by a positive divine law can be duly ordained by the supreme authority in the church. This is in principle the sphere of indifferentia, in which as it were the freedom of the individual can be limited and his conscience can be bound, in so far as it is a matter of the public practice of religion and not religion itself, which is solely an internal question for the conscience. These ideas will not seem new to us; they were already expressed by Hobbes in a very similar way.

In the following chapters there is then a discussion of how far the forms of church government are based on the law of nature. This includes the following points: 1. that there must be a human community to worship God;[47] 2. that this community must be maintained and governed in the most appropriate way. As a subsidiary point it is stated that some persons in the church must be superior to others, and only the existence of a church order in itself is a matter of natural law, not the form of this order, and moreover that special respect is due the one responsible for worship. Further, 3. that all rites and ceremonies must be solemnly performed – at the same time it is stressed that the worship of God is rational and does not do away with the use of reason. At this point the Laudian heritage again becomes clearer. 4. That there must be a way of settling disputes which threaten the peace of the community. The question here is when separation from the mainstream church is legitimate (only if further communion with it were sin, if corruption is noted; mere suspicion of corruption is no reason for establishing new churches). There is also a discussion of basic articles, freedom of conscience, possibilities and ways of ending disputes. 5. That all those who are admitted into a community must agree to be governed by its laws and regulations. Here – and again there is a striking similarity to Hobbes – the consensus theory is expressly transferred from the state to the church: secular communities are grounded in mutual consent, explicitly when they are constituted by entry into them, and implicitly when people are born into already existing communities. In the church, implicit consensus is arrived at through baptism and explicit consensus through the express confession of the gospel by adults. 6. That anyone who violates the laws of the community must give account of this to its leaders and must be subject to the penalites that they impose.

It is typical that Stillingfleet uses instances from pagan religions, and sometimes from Judaism, to support most of these natural laws for the church (in the case of the fourth and fifth laws he draws parallels between state and church); they apply not only to the Christian church but to all human religious communities – in a quite neutral sense.

In the second part of the book, Stillingfleet is occupied with the other possible source of divine law for the church, God's positive commandments. Here he is concerned above all to demonstrate that while there must be a church government, and that it must be administered by divinely appointed servants, in other respects – in contrast to the Puritan view – no specific forms for this church government have been prescribed by Christ, appointed by the apostles, or handed down in the ancient church. Rather, the few valid laws for church government which occur in scripture (they are concerned with the qualifications which people need for the office of government, call on them to exercise their ministry appropriately and establish rules to this effect)[48] are equally applicable to various specific constitutional forms. In principle, every minister has the same rights over against the whole church, which the church can establish and restrict in accord with specific needs. In particular, a hierarchical church order is permissible, but not necessary.

Generally speaking, then, Stillingfleet is a defender of the Anglican position, albeit with the important qualification (itself in no way alien to the nature of Anglicanism) that he has sympathies wide enough to embrace those who hold other views of the church, especially the Presbyterians and the forms they ordain.[49] He is willing to accord a place to features of their church order, above all the synods, lay elders and presbyteries, within an inclusive national church in which they will exist alongside the dioceses, based on episcopal principles: the functions of each will be mutually delimited. Here only the principles of utility and 'wisdom' will apply.[50]

Latitudinarianism is a true child of Anglican theology. Its thought-patterns are shaped by Stoic rationalism to such a degree that it is only a very small step from here to the rational thought of the Enlightenment. The Stoic heritage in Stillingfleet is easy to recognize from the central place occupied by the 'law of nature' in his work. In this respect he in fact presents more of a closed system than most of his predecessors.

The Latitudinarians themselves revered rationalism in a 'mild' form; this is true particularly of the chief representatives of the trend, who were principally occupied in preaching. With the systematic theologian Stillingfleet, however, one can already suspect the direction that a more critical reason will take in the future. This is particularly clear from the role accorded to Holy Scripture in his *Irenicum*.

This role can only be understood dialectically. First of all, we must note that a few years later Stillingfleet produced the large-scale work *Origines Sacrae*,[51] which was to prove a very important tool for apologetic against Jesuits and Deists because of its comprehensive argumentation.[52] In the *Irenicum*, too, the truth of scripture is not questioned as such.[53] However, the significance of scripture in matters of church order is decisively weakened when compared with the central position which it occupied among the Puritans. The main contribution to this is made by the arguments in Part II, Chapter II, which are concerned with the problem raised by the partner in the conversation here, who argues that the positive laws in scripture have immutable validity,[54] and in chapters III and IV, where it is asked whether Christ appointed the form of church government by positive commandments.[55] In both cases the answer is 'No'.[56] A central position is occupied by a detailed demonstration that Christ did not give such commandments in respect of church government. The mere fact that the existence of an ongoing clerical ministry in the church is there by divine right is undeniable;[57] Stillingfleet defends it against the Spiritualists with a reference to Matt.28.20; Eph.4.12. But the New Testament does not show that either episcopal or presbyteral church order is binding. Even the examples of Timothy and Titus cannot change that; what this shows is that particular ministers in the earliest church could have authority over more than one community, but since it is unclear whether these were evangelists for a limited time or duly appointed bishops, no final conclusion can be drawn from their functions. In practice the authority of the New Testament in matters of church order is limited to a few basic principles: 'All things to be done decently and in order. All to be done for edification. Give no offence. Do all to the glory of God.'[58]

This group of arguments also contains a discussion of the significance of the Old Testament. In Part II, ch.III, the question whether an Old Testament law continues to be valid for Christians is focussed on the specific problem, 'whether any formal Law of God concerning a form of government for his Church, either by persons acting in an equality of Power, or subordination of one Order to another, under the Gospel, doth remain in force or no, binding Christians to the observing of it.'[59] In other words, it is focussed on the alternative of a hierarchical episcopal or a presbyterian system. The reference to the tribe of Levi indicates that in fact there was inequality there, between Aaronic priests and Levites, and in both cases between their *n^esī'īm* and the ordinary members of the clan. However, as the latter is something which the tribe of Levi has in common with secular tribes, conclusions can be drawn for any church order under the gospel only from the superiority of the priests to the Levites and the exalted status of the High Priest. From the first point it can be argued that there was inequality among ministers under the law which also should exist under the gospel; it can be found in the superiority of priests to deacons. From the other point one can argue either too little or too much: too little, if Aaron's office was only typical or ceremonial, because in that case it would not signify any special authority over men (Eleazar was appointed head of the clan during Aaron's lifetime); too much, if the continuation of the same authority is called for in the church, since that is the argument of the Papists.

However, all these considerations are ultimately otiose, since Stillingfleet comes to the conclusion: 'All that can be inferred then from the Jewish pattern, cannot amount to any obligation upon Christians, it being at the best but a judicial Law, and therefore binds us not up as a positive Law, but only declares the equity of the things in use then. I conclude then, That the Jewish pattern is no standing Law for Church-Government now, either in its common or peculiar form of Government.'[60] The mere fact that superiority and subordination must exist in church government does not prove in any way contrary to the law, as it was also to be found under the law. 'The Jewish pattern then of Government, neither makes equality unlawfull, because their Laws do not oblige now; nor doth it make superiority unlawfull, because it was practised then. So that notwithstanding the Jewish pattern, the Church of Christ is left to its own liberty for the choice of its form of Government, whether by an equality of power in some persons, or superiority and subordination of one order to another.'[61]

In the following chapter (Part II, ch. IV), the view is then rejected that Christ must have established a particular form of church government in his church, just as Moses did for the people of the old covenant, because of the typological correspondence between Moses and Christ. This does not follow, because a distinction must be made between an outward and inward régime, and Christ was entrusted with the 'internal Mediatory power over the hearts and consciences of men'.[62] Moreover, in that case all the ritual forms of Jewish worship would have to be adopted, down to the smallest detail. However, only the four general principles can be transferred;[63] in other respects a whole series of characteristic differences between gospel and 'Jewish state' can be demonstrated.[64]

In almost every point Stillingfleet's position is fully in line with Anglican tradition. That includes his rejection of the view, held by the

Puritans, that the Old Testament ordinances are normative for forms of church government. Interestingly enough, Stillingfleet makes his case with the help of the spiritual form of typology (Moses/Christ), which was equally familiar to the Puritan left. On the other hand, his recourse to the 'law of nature' as the ultimately valid criterion for church order leads him to spiritualize revelation and the New Testament in a way which is becoming clear in his characterization of the rule of Christ cited above. The division in Hooker's system, as noted by Hillerdal,[65] begins with his heirs. The problem of having to give reasons for the necessity of a special revelation, which then becomes acute in the deistic struggles, is already making itself felt.

The sermons and other writings of the rest of the Latitudinarians are also governed by the same basic rationalist and moralist attitude; as a preacher, here Tillotson, later to become archbishop, towers above the rest.[66] G.Burnet, himself a Latitudinarian by conviction, says in his funeral oration that it had been Tillotson's view that 'the great design of Christianity was the reforming men's natures, and governing their actions... and raising their minds above the interests and follies of this present world, to the hope and pursuit of endless blessedness. And he considered the whole Christian doctrine as a system of principles all tending to this.'[67] We also find the goals of morality as the chief content of the Christian religion, furthered by the prospect of eternal blessedness, addressed in his sermons.[68] Here, as was already the case with Stillingfleet, there emerges again the juxtaposition of 'natural' and 'instituted' or 'revealed' religion. The Sermon in Birch, no.101 (on Micah 6.6-8), treats 'of the great duties of natural religion, with the ways and means of knowing them',[69] in the specific form of a discourse in which the preacher develops in five points the way in which 'God has made known these duties to us, and the goodness and the obligation of them:

1. By a kind of natural instinct.
2. By natural reason.
3. By the general vote and consent of mankind.
4. By external revelation.
5. By the inward dictates and motions of God's Spirit upon the minds of men.'[70]

The preacher enters upon long discussions, carefully divided into subsections, of the first three points; this is evidently where his heart is, as he seeks to make clear to his audience in impressive words that as the embodiment of all duties towards God,[71] righteousness and mercy are quite natural, given to all men by an innate instinct, but also capable of being arrived at by natural reason, as the pursuit of these virtues is only to our own advantage.[72] The notion of consensus emerges as an additional argument;[73] the foundations for it are the general approval with which virtue meets; shame after an evil action, which makes the perpetrator fear the judgment of his fellow men; and the fact that laws everywhere are promulgated against vices and never against virtues. Here, however, there is a quite different mood from that among the Cambridge Platonists;[74] moral rationalism has suppressed any mystical and spiritualist traits. At the same time we can see very clearly in Tillotson the causes which led to this development.

It is evidently the homiletic and pedagogical concern of the Archbishop to attract his audience with arguments which carry their own conviction; hence his appeal to common sense and what he believes to be the natural preponderance of good. In addition to this apologetic concern, there is above all his own conviction that the real content of religion is ethical;[75] in fact he has very little more than this to say.[76] In the sermon I have discussed, there is only a short section on the role of revelation; the essence of it is that the content of the revelation which has taken place through the Son 'as to the matter of duty, is the same in substance with the law of nature', for 'the gospel teacheth us the very same things which nature dictated to men before; only it hath made a more perfect discovery of them'.[77] Evidently it is not the intention of the Latitudinarians to devalue the Christian religion; on the contrary, they feel themselves to be its defenders. Moreover, it is clear (as we can already see from the choice of text) that there is an explicit antipathy to external forms which the relevant prophetic sayings of the Old Testament are made to support; thus Tillotson ends his sermon on Micah 6.6-8 with a literal quotation from Isa.58.5-9 to establish that 'that which God chiefly expects from us, is reformed lives'.[78] In comparison with this, 'external devotion' is secondary. Here Tillotson adopts a very eirenic tone,[79] but the way in which he thinks is evident enough. If the church ritual in which people are involved descends into being a mere matter of form, it is at the same time devalued. Here, too, the insights of the Reformation are seen to be a stage which surpasses 'the Jewish Religion': 'the Christian religion hath set us free from those many positive and outward observances, that the Jewish religion was encumbered withal; that we might be wholly intent upon these great duties, and mind nothing in comparison of the real and substantial virtues of a good life.'[80]

This last feature becomes a theme of other sermons by Tillotson. Principal mention should be made here of a sermon on Matt.9.13 [Hos.6.6] (Birch, no.102),[81] which in the printed version has the title: 'Instituted Religion not Intended to Undermine Natural'. It, too, has a didactic character: the preacher is concerned to develop two basic statements:

First, That natural religion is the foundation of all instituted and revealed religion.

Secondly, That no revealed or instituted religion was ever designed to take away the obligation of natural duties, but to confirm and establish them.[82]

The first maxim corresponds to the scheme with which we are already familiar. As a basis for the second, Tillotson develops considerable acuteness in exegesis: the saying of Jesus (quoted from Hos.6.6) means that 'in comparing the parts of religion and the obligation of duties together, those duties which are of moral and natural obligation are most valued by God, and ought to take the place of those which are positive and ritual. "I will have mercy, and not sacrifice;" that is, rather than sacrifice, according to the true meaning of this Hebrew phrase, which is to be understood in a comparative sense, as is evident from the text itself, in Hosea' – with reference to the parallel member, which reads: 'and the knowledge of God rather than burnt-offerings'. The comparative sense of the passage in Hosea is recognized more accurately than it is by some modern exegetes; at the same time it corresponds exactly with the preacher's own estimation of outward forms: he tolerates them but does not think much of them.[83] However, the full significance of the decision emerges only when the second principle is made into a generalized statement, in which (in conjunction with the first) 'instituted' and 'revealed' religion are compared, and their roles are considered in relationship to natural duties: this identity makes revealed, or at any rate institutional, religion no more than a servant of the natural obligations with which it is really concerned. So the preacher can also stress that: 'The great design of the Christian religion is to restore and reinforce the practice of the natural law, or, which is all one, of moral duties'[84] – this is already the case, as he goes on to explain, under the Jewish religion, but also applies under the gospel: 'And now, under the gospel, the preceptive part of it is almost wholly made up of moral duties.'[85] 'Positive rites and institutions of revealed religion', by contrast, are always of subordinate significance and must yield the moment they come into conflict with moral duties.[86] Here, too, the Papacy is again adduced as a horrifying example of 'a blind and furious zeal for some imaginary doctrines and rites of the Christian religion'[87] – the traditional opponent still has a part to play even in the time of the Jacobins.

The sermon on Rom.12.1,[88] under the title 'Holiness of Life the Most Acceptable Sacrifice to God', points in the same direction. Here, alongside a powerful penitential sermon on the bodily sins of the time (prompted by the word 'body'), the well-known prophetic and other Old Testament passages about the lesser worth of sacrifice and the New

Testament passages about 'spiritual' worship are quoted to demonstrate that 'the moral purity and virtue of sincere Christians'[89] are the 'living sacrifice' mentioned in the text. A section in this sermon in which Tillotson defends Old Testament sacrifices against the evidently widespread charge that they were not worthy of God sheds light on Tillotson's apologetic position, and consequently on the transitional role of the Latitudinarians in an 'age of transition':[90] as God has created all animals and intended that they should provide nourishment for men and one another, no objection can be made to using them as sacrifices. Nevertheless, God accepted them only for a time, as a sign of the penitence of sinners and as a type of the sacrifice of Christ.[91]

The sermon on Matt.22.40,[92] 'Of the Nature of Moral and Positive Duties', proceeds in a similar way, arguing 1. that all moral duties are summed up in the two principles of love of God and love of neighbour; 2. that all positive and ritual commandments, 'though in their proper place they ought not to be left undone',[93] are subordinate to the moral commandments and support them. For 'In the perfection of virtue and goodness, consists the image of God; and in the same likewise is placed the chief happiness of man.'[94] Ritual celebrations are only useful insofar as they 'truly increase our devotion towards God; if they enlarge our charity and good-will towards men';[95] that also holds for the Christian sacraments like baptism and the eucharist. 'The love of God and of our neighbour are qualifications which will remain and be perfected in heaven; but all ritual observances are appointed only for the assistance and improvement of our religion here upon earth.'[96] These remarks, too, indicate that concern for the *status quo* which allows the Latitudinarians to maintain a mediating position, though their real preferences are clear enough. Thus Tillotson also speaks as one who occupies high positions in the church and as a responsible pastor in a church which, at least externally, lives by its traditional forms. But whereas his predecessor in the see of Canterbury, William Law, could still defend these norms on purely aesthetic grounds,[97] Tillotson evidently does so only out of loyalty to an existing order, a position which he finds easier to adapt to his own easy-going attitude than the sharp polemic which was to emanate from the Deistic camp.

Tillotson also commented on the role of scripture in a series of sermons; one is on II Tim.3.16, with the title 'The Scripture a sufficient Rule of Religion'.[98] Initially this is about the inspiration of scripture (which is direct inspiration only in the case of the prophets; with the writers of the historical and moral books it is to be understood simply as concomitant guidance by the Holy Spirit).[99] It then goes on to discuss the sufficiency of this inspiration as 'a rule both of faith and practice in matters of religion'.[100] The starting point of the argument here is the distinction between the two ways by which God's will is made known to men: reason and revelation. Reason is the only adequate rule in things which are to be judged by reason, and scripture in all things which are to be judged by revelation. Scripture deals with things which are 'conditions of salvation': as such, if they are not to lead to absurd consequences, they must be expressed so clearly and simply that people with the simplest intellectual capacities can understand them as soon as they are taught.[101] In the continuation of the sermon, those things which are necessary for salvation are then defined further (in an argument against Roman challenges to the Protestant principle of scripture): 'namely, repentance from all wicked works, and faith towards God and our Lord Jesus Christ; the belief of resurrection from the dead, and of a judgement to come; and a life of virtue, or suitable obedience to our Lord's express commands in the Gospel.'[102] All these things are expressed so clearly in scripture that the simplest person can understand them. By contrast, 'whatsoever, I say, is of so abstruse a nature, that a person of mean capacity can neither of himself, nor by means of any instruction given him, be able clearly to understand it; such a thing cannot possibly be necessary to be understood.'[103] Therefore all ordinary Christians can make the scripture their rule of life; specialists can concern themselves with more difficult questions if they have a mind to.

If we compare these remarks with Chillingworth's *Religion of Protestants* on the one hand and Toland's *Christianity not Mysterious* on the other,[104] we can note a consistent development. In all three the basic attitude is the same, and the humanistic basis is unmistakable. That is not surprising, when we hear that during his study at Cambridge Tillotson was deeply moved on reading Chillingworth's work.[105] By contrast, he evidently took in virtually nothing of the subtler thought of his immediate teachers, the Cambridge Platonists.[106] The line goes from the rational Anglicanism of the Great Tew group to the Latitudinarians. But only some finer points distinguish the Latitudinarians from Deism proper, though as defenders of the *status quo* in church politics terms they adopt a different attitude towards its further critical development. The weakness of the later anti-deistic apologetic which was recruited from the Latitudinarian camp lies in the fact that it shares the majority of its opponents' fundamental moralistic principles, therefore in the sphere of dogmatics can defend only territory which has already been evacuated.

That becomes even clearer if in conclusion we consider some sermons in which Tillotson is expressly concerned with the meaning of the Old Testament. The sermon on Gal.2.15-16, 'The End and Design of the Jewish Law',[107] is particularly illuminating. The theme of these Pauline statements, justification through faith and not through the works of the law, could have put in question the customary moralism and set the preacher on a new course. However, nothing of the kind happens, although even Rom.3.28 is to hand. Rather, here too the starting point is the usual definition of the gospel, 'that most perfect revelation of his will, which he has made to mankind by our saviour Christ', whereas the second part of Rom.3.28 is rendered as 'without observing the ceremonies of the Jewish law'. The law is not abrogated as a way to salvation, but the Jewish ceremonial law is no longer valid for Christians. Generally speaking, however, Rom.3.31 still holds! Instead of doing away with the law, 'by introducing Christianity we establish, confirm, and perfect the moral and immutable part of the law much more effectually, than the Jewish ceremonies were able to do'.[108] The distinction between ceremonial law and ethical law is traditionally a Reformation insight, but the conclusions which Tillotson draws from it go in a fundamentally different direction: granted, there is a small section which takes up what the text says, with the observation that 'Christian religion teaches us to expect salvation not from our own merits but from the grace of God',[109] but at the central point we have the principle: 'The summ and essence of all religion is obedience to the moral and eternal law of God.'[110] The difference between the duties of the Christian religion and those of the Jewish religion are seen simply in the fact that these 'are almost wholly moral and spiritual, respecting the inward disposition of the heart and mind; whereas on the contrary the ceremonies of the Jewish law were for the most part external.'[111] This is precisely what is meant by the terms 'flesh' and 'spirit', 'law' and 'grace', 'faith' and 'works' in the Pauline epistles. Jewish religion had proved inadequate for making men really holy, so it had to be replaced by Christianity, which in this respect was more effective (as in any case was natural religion at an earlier stage). The reason why God nevertheless gave the Jews ceremonial commandments first is explained by the theory of condescension: 'The Jewish law was an institution of religion adapted by God in great condescension to the weak apprehensions of that people.'[112] But these commandments are merely meant to prepare for obedience to the moral and ethical law. Paul did not in any way want to replace works by faith, but to introduce the perfection of Christian (inward) virtues in contrast to the outward (ceremonial) works of the Jewish law. To this degree there is also no contrast between James and Paul.

In a similar way, the two sermons on Matt.5.17 (Birch, nos. CIII-CIV)[113] also depict the relationship between Christianity and the law of Moses: in the first sermon Tillotson is concerned to show that in accordance with his words in Matt.5.17, Jesus did not destroy the law of Moses: the civil or judicial law had only been intended for this people and came to an end with its political existence; and while as a shadow of the perfect law, the ceremonial law was abrogated with the death of Jesus as the beginning of the new covenant, the moral law continued to be valid. It was also the aim of the 'law and the prophets' (the Old Testament) 'to engage men to the practice of moral duties',[114] but the Mosaic law was too weak and imperfect adequately to fulfil this task. Christianity compensated for all the weaknesses of the old order. In the second sermon this last point is again endorsed with a detailed comparison with Jewish religion, in which the essential points of comparison are: external ceremonies on the one hand, intrinsic virtues on the other; the possibility of attaining true forgiveness of sins on the one hand instead of more perfect atonement; the limitation of rewards and punishments to temporal things on the one hand, the prospect of immortality on the other; and finally the promise of support through the Holy Spirit on the way to virtue and perfection.

Beyond question this way of describing the advantages of Christian faith also has a eudaemonistic trait which is partly connected with the apologetic aim of the sermons;[115] however, it does correspond to a basic feature of their rationalistic and moralistic approach. Associated with this is the optimistic confidence that is placed in the possibilities of human reason to recognize truth when presented convincingly and also to draw logical conclusions for behaviour from it, in that guilt appears as mere error which can be removed by relevant teaching.[116]

This basic structure of the Latitudinarian approach also emerges very clearly in the popular work *Of the Principles and Duties of Natural Religion*, by John Wilkins, Bishop of Chester (died 1672), who was Tillotson's friend and his wife's stepfather.[117] This was first produced in 1675 by Tillotson, who wrote a Foreword.[118]

John Wilkins was one of the founder members of the Royal Society, a well-known mathematician and natural scientist, and one of the most prominent adherents of the 'new philosophy', which since Francis Bacon had become increasingly influential on the spiritual life of England. As a result of the new discoveries in the natural sciences, above all in the realm of astronomy, which had produced a completely different picture of the world, natural theology had taken on a new lease of life within the ranks of the so-called 'virtuosi'.[119] A whole series of these scholars who believed themselves to be convinced Christians, saw it as their task to fight against the danger of atheism and to utilize their newly-won insights into a miraculous ordering of the universe which they regarded as the most important proof of the existence of God as a wise and omnipotent creator. Latitudinarian preaching was only the popularized form of the ideas presented by these people on the pretext of being the most modern science. A whole series of such works appeared,[120] in which the same ideas (with a few variations) were presented again and again. Wilkins' work gives a good view of the thought-world of this literature.

In his short foreword, Tillotson himself mentions the three main aims which are striven for in the work: 'First, To establish the great Principles of Religion, the Being of God, and a Future State... Secondly, To convince men of the natural and indispensable obligation of Moral Duties; those I mean, which are comprehended by our Saviour under the two general Heads of the Love of God and of our Neighbour. For all the great Duties of Piety and Justice are written upon our hearts, and every man feels a secret obligation to them in his own Conscience... Thirdly, To persuade men to the practice of Religion, and the virtues of a good life, by shewing how natural and direct an influence they have, not only upon our future blessedness in another World, but even upon the happiness and prosperity of this present Life.'[121] After a short epistemological introduction and account of principles,[122] this programme is started on with an extended doctrine of God, beginning with proofs for the existence of God[123] (here the consensus argument has pride of place[124]) and continuing with an account of God's perfections. Both this doctrine of God and the transition to religious duties are typical of Greek thought, according to the title to Chapter XII,[125] 'naturally flowing from the consideration of the Divine Nature and Perfections'. This is then further explained by the remark that the consideration of the divine perfections is not to be exhausted in mere speculation (though it begins with that!), but 'must derive an influence upon the heart and affections; it being natural for men to proportion their esteem of things according to that worth and dignity, which they apprehend to be in them.' Following this, worship, faith, love, the reverence and fear of God and finally active and passive obedience towards the law and the will of God are discussed as the elements of natural religion (chs.XII-XVII). Book II, in which 'the Wisdom of Practising the Duties of Natural Religion' is depicted in all spheres from health,[126] outward security[127] and material possessions[128] to the happiness of the inner man[129] and blessedness in the world to come[130], carries out the eudaemonistic justification of religion systematically in a paradigmatic way.[131] Only the final chapter[132] then goes on to discuss the significance of Christian religion, the advantage of which over natural religion is seen in its greater clarity and the reward promised for doing one's duty: 'For notwithstanding all that hath been said of Natural Religion, it cannot be denied, but that in this dark and degenerate state into which Mankind is sunk, there is great want of a clearer light to discover our duty to us with greater certainty, and to put it beyond all doubt and dispute what is the good and acceptable Will of God; and of a more powerful encouragement to the practice of our duty, by the premise of a supernatural assistance, and by the assurance of a great and eternal reward.'[133] This took place in the most perfect way through the revelation in Christ, whom we now obey 'as our Lord and Lawgiver'.[134] This doctrine of Christianity was first communicated through the Old Testament, which, as the oldest document in the world, is taken to be the origin of the first speech, the alphabet, of all other languages, and of the tradition of the earliest history of the world. It is still accepted uncritically: 'And though this Book were written in several Ages and Places, by several persons; yet doth the Doctrine of it accord together, with a most excellent harmony, without any dissonance or inconsistency.'[135] Similarly, the facts about the career and activity of Jesus as recorded in the New Testament (which stands in a close reciprocal relationship with the Old) are indubitably true, as is attested by the universal testimony of friend and foe. Nor would it accord with the nature of God to work such miracles in favour of a lie or a deception. Moreover, the uniqueness of the Christian religion lies in the goals it puts before us (eternal happiness) and the means it prepares to achieve them (the duties of the first and second tablets of the Decalogue). The Christian virtues are the chief examples of lofty ethics;[136] moreover, they accord with the rules of purest reason.[137]

(b) John Locke

Although all these Latitudinarian preachers and writers were widely known in their time and, like Archbishop Tillotson, achieved the highest positions in church and state, they are now largely forgotten, known only to specialists. It seems right that this should be so, since the principles which they express have not been worked out by individual thinkers; rather, they are typical features, illustrating a basic attitude which was felt to be quite obvious and taken for granted in wide circles of the Anglican clergy. This attitude also corresponded to the mood generally among the educated classes in England, who were exhausted by the controversies from the Puritan revolution onwards, disappointed by the rule of the 'saints' and weary of the far-reaching theological debates. Thus liberal Anglicanism, which in the 1630s was represented only by a small group of people, could gain a dominant public position and was to have an enduring effect on intellectual developments in the next century.

This development can again be demonstrated particularly clearly in the person of a significant individual, the famous philosopher John Locke (1632-1704).[137a] Locke, whose immediate influence can be traced only towards the end of the eighteenth century, was important to more recent scholarship in the history of ideas down to the Second World War almost exclusively for his epistemological theories as developed in the *Essay Concerning Human Understanding* (1690), which was therefore regarded as his main work. The unsatisfactory state of the sources also contributed to this: a critical edition of his works has begun to appear only in very recent times,[138] and for long years the extensive Locke manuscripts were not generally accessible.[139] In the last two decades, however, the situation has changed fundamentally: the sources which have newly appeared in print, revealing to us early unpublished works by Locke and preliminary stages of his main works (which were completed late), thus making it possible for us to have a view of the whole of his intellectual development, have produced a wealth of secondary literature[140] and disclosed many sides to his thinking. This new approach demonstrates that Locke's thinking was very much more universal and complex than could ever emerge from the earlier perspective, which knew only parts of his work. However, the interest of scholars usually still tended to be a partial one, even in more recent times: in addition to a series of works which continued to be concerned mainly with Locke's epistemology and the problems which arise from it,[141] the political science which has developed over the last few decades has discussed Locke's theories of the state and society selectively, apart from the theme of tolerance, considering above all his relationship to the theory of natural law.[142] There are unmistakable parallels to the phases in research into Hobbes; in part, too, the same authors have included both Hobbes and Locke in their general approach.[143] Here, too, we again have an attempt to stress factors relating to social history as the most important key to understanding the presuppositions of the philosopher's thought.[144] In Locke, too, largely because of the predominant perspectives of modern scholars, the theological dimension of his thought was usually regarded as being of more or less secondary importance, although it runs through his whole work like a scarlet thread; moreover, in *The Reasonableness of Christianity*, towards the end of his life he gave a comprehensive final account of his theological thinking, as a keystone to his life work.[145] Where Locke's theology has been discussed, this has been more in connection with the attacks which followed the publication of *The Reasonableness of Christianity*, accusing its author (who was as yet unknown to the public) of being a Socinian.[146] This charge is no longer thought to be tenable in the strict sense by modern observers,[147] but the view that Locke was a Unitarian has still not died out.[148] It might be difficult to arrive at a final answer to this problem, but it touches only on a marginal question which, moreover, takes us into the area of dogmatics, a sphere in which the real decisions were not made at this period. Few authors have recognized that the religious side in Locke's thinking is in a particular way constitutive of his whole philosophical system: in addition to previous approaches,[149] that is also true for his views on politics.[149a]

The real handicap of research into Locke again lies in the fact that for a long time it has sought to understand his work in isolation, without paying enough attention to the intellectual situation in England generally at the time of his activity; much that had to be said about research into Hobbes could usefully be repeated here.[150] If such connections are observed, they are again for the most part concentrated on a general line in the history of philosophy and again applied to epistemology; or – since Locke lived abroad for many years or went on journeys – he has been studied purely in biographical terms – and decisive influences on his thought from Holland and France have been noted.[151] Now it is true that a lively cultural exchange between the scholars of Europe was still possible at this time because of the dissemination of Latin as a scholarly language, and Locke's participation in this exchange is shown by his correspondence with the leading Dutch Arminian Philip van Limborch and the entries in the diary of his journey through France in 1675-1679. But as a result of all this, the real home of the philosopher and the intellectual trends dominant in it have faded too much into the background, and when again selective comparisons have been attempted between Locke and his older fellow-countryman Hobbes,[152] this has come to grief on the fact that the two figures have been contrasted in isolation.[153]

The real significance of Locke, the features of his thought corresponding to views widespread in his time and the conceptual advances which he attempted and which took him some way beyond earlier developments, only become clear against the more comprehensive and at the same time more specific background of the contemporary situation in England; here we need in particular to note the lesser-known secondary figures, since they represent much more clearly the spiritual climate of England. That is particularly the case with contemporary sermons, so for example we can learn very clearly the unspoken presuppositions for Locke's systematic considerations from the ideas which Tillotson presented to his hearers. Occasionally the affinity of Locke's approach to Latitudinarianism has been noted,[154] and he is certainly most aptly termed a Latitudinarian. He belongs in this movement not only because of his general religious views but also because his particular conceptions of the relationship of state and church, of natural law and revelation, of the key phrase 'true religion',[155] which for him consists in confessing Christ,[156] and the wide sphere of indifferentia, which include above all outward liturgical forms, largely follow the liberal Anglican tradition. His own contribution in this sphere is very much smaller than is generally supposed, and it is certainly no chance that where, at the height of his creative powers, he was most convinced that he could offer a new epistemology, in the gnoseology of the *Essay Concerning Human Understanding*, in his old age at least he returned to clearly traditional ways for the foundation of his ethics.

Now that his early works are also known, it has become even easier to put his thought in the framework of contemporary trends. So it is no longer surprising – as it was in fact surprising to scholars researching into Locke – to find two early tractates from Locke's hand in which he deals with the problem of indifferentia and here in a very 'Hobbesian' way argues for the right of the state to determine these external features of worship.[157] This view is by no means as 'conservative' as it might seem,[158] but corresponds exactly with the liberal Anglican tradition, which counters the Puritan claim to totalitarian control over the whole of religious life by relegating outward forms of worship to the sphere of indifferentia and leaving them for the state to order.[159] A series of Locke's remarks in this connection immediately makes clear his indebtedness towards that tradition, as when in the 'Preface to the Reader' of the First Tractate he begins a section with the sentence: 'As for myself, there is no one can have a greater respect and veneration for authority than I', and then gives as the reason for this his expectation that the new regime will bring 'the substantial blessings of peace and settlement in an over-zealous contention about things, which they themselves confess to be little and at most are but indifferent'.[160] He then continues: '...I have no less a love of liberty without which a man shall find himself less happy than a beast.' Abrams' description of the young Locke in the year of the Restoration as being deeply uncertain and looking for a new authority 'that could override private men's judgments'[161] corresponds exactly with the starting point of Chillingworth, who sought law and order in the Bible.[162] As the newly-edited *Essay on Infallibility* shows, as with Chillingworth, the argument with the Roman 'teaching office' played an important role here.[162a] We will rediscover in Locke other presuppositions of liberal Anglicanism.[163] His conversation-partner E.Bagshaw[164] is to be located on the separatist wing of the Puritans: for him the state has no right to legislate on indifferentia in the sphere of religious actions; insofar as they are not laid down in scripture by the law of God, they are a matter for the individual conscience.[165]

Now it would be wrong to describe Bagshaw as an individualist and Locke as the opposite. The two are not so far removed in respect of their individualism; where they differ is over the sphere in which they accept its validity. We can see this particularly clearly from the way in which Locke introduces the role of scripture into the discussion. Positively, it can be said of scripture that it is a perfect rule *quatenus generales morum normas tradit a quibus reliquae omnes emanant et deduci possunt*; it is *regula morum perfecta* both for every authority[166] and also in respect of the life-style of the individual.[167] Here for the first time we encounter the role of scripture as a source of moral norms, which was later to acquire great significance in Locke: the theme of the *Reasonableness of Christianity* is already intimating its presence.[168] On the other hand, however, the sphere in which scripture is allowed to speak is limited; it contains no instructions on all the individual actions and decisions in life – *qualis nulla unquam perfecta fuit regula vitae nec esse potuit* – so that the churches themselves are left to regulate ceremonies in accordance with particular circumstances.[168a] The reason for this is illuminating: were scripture a perfect rule in every respect, the consequence would be *perfectionem scripturae hoc argumento tollere magistratus authoritatem in rebus civilibus quam ecclesiasticis.'*[169] Thus in his early writings Locke is concerned to reserve to the state its own sphere of legislation, which includes not only civil ordinances but to a limited degree church ordinances as well. To make this possible he draws a distinction between two different kinds of worship: if the scripture is also (*si malint*) to be regarded as *perfecta regula interni et necessarii cultus* (*veri cultus* in *versio A*) *divini*, it would be necessary to require a uniform official ordering of the outward forms of worship (as already in King Edward VI's agenda,[169a] with Laud the reference is to I Cor. 14.40).[170] In the sphere of moral interiority,[171] however, the right to individualism is reserved. So Bagshaw and Locke are not so far removed in their individualism; the difference is that Locke limits this, at least at one stage, more markedly in favour of the rights of the state.[172]

What Locke says in the two *Tracts on Government* about the role of scripture and the norms of natural law basically already reproduces the view which, with only slight changes, he preserved throughout his work. The long-drawn-out discussion of the significance of traditional natural law in Locke[173] demonstrates that modern interpreters find it difficult to arrive at an appropriate understanding of the combination of aspects of the Christian humanistic tradition from which Locke descends. One contributory factor is still the debate with John Edwards over Locke's orthodoxy,[174] in that L.Strauss and R.Cox develop the theory of 'The Cautious Mr Locke'[175] to the point of asserting that Locke only put forward the statements contained in his works from the traditional theory of natural law as a cover for his real revolutionary theory, in which man and his right to self-preservation have a central position.[176,177] On the other hand, questions from modern political research, stamped by the social sciences, are introduced to show that Locke was, say, a collectivist majority democrat,[178] or that he was a theoretician of 'bourgeois society',[179] whose 'theory of property, which is almost literally the central part of his political theory',[180] is 'directly understandable today if we see it as the classical theory of the "spirit of capitalism'" or as a theory of the main task of politics'.[181] In addition, there are a number of interpreters who regard Locke's theory of natural law as a continuation of the classical system.[182] Yet others, above all the editor of the *Two Treatises of Government*, P.Laslett,[183] regard Locke's natural law theory generally as contradictory: philosophical system and political theory fall apart irreconcilably.[184]

The discussion is by no means at an end; on the contrary, it has been made more complicated by the fact that the earlier view, that Locke did not in fact comment on the problem of natural law has been ruled out by W.von Leyden's edition of the *Essays on the Law of Nature* from the years 1663/64.[185] Here Locke presents substantially a traditional view of natural law.[186] However, the most interesting aspect of the *Essays* is that they anticipate the line of questioning in the *Essay Concerning Human Understanding*, in so far as Essays II-V discuss the epistemological problem of the possibility of recognizing the natural law explicitly, and the others implicitly. This makes the theme of natural law one of decisive significance for Locke, too, although in the *Essay* it is only touched on in passing.

In his recent work *Naturrecht und Politik bei John Locke*,[187] W.Euchner has attempted to resolve the controversy between scholars who claim that Locke puts forward a traditional theory of natural law and those who see him as a pioneer of modern bourgeois social philosophy by demonstrating that Locke's thinking on natural law is ambivalent: 'In Locke's political philosophy ingredients of classical natural law and modern bourgeois social philosophy stand side by side unreconciled.'[188] In intention Euchner's work follows the socio-economic line represented on the one hand by Macpherson and on the other by L.Strauss: 'It sees itself as a contribution towards illuminating the genesis of the bourgeois political and social view of the world.'[189] Against the background of an ideal and typical structural model of the classical system of natural law, which Euchner understands as a 'heuristic expedient' by which he can measure particular agreements and deviations in Locke's theory of natural law,[190] he demonstrates three points which make Locke stand out: 1. his modern epistemology,[191] 2. the motivation for human action, where Locke has adopted a hedonistic and utilitarian position,[192] and 3. the reinterpretation of the position of the individual in the system of rights and duties. Here Euchner, continuing the perspective of L.Strauss,[193] stresses the right to property (connected with a modern theory of the value of work) as a central theme of Locke's theory of society and state.[194] As to the origin of the second element, Euchner thinks that he can demonstrate that Locke, like Hobbes, was dependent on an Epicureanism which was revived by the French scholars P.Gassendi, F.Bernier and others; Locke came across this specifically on his journey to France in 1675-79.[195]

Not all these ideas are new: however, in Euchner's work the results of a whole perspective of research are brought together into a compact, impressive system based on a thorough use of the sources.[196] Nevertheless, the limitations of this view quickly emerge. On the one hand this is because of the way in which the questions are put: the central concern with the relatively few passages dealing with property (specifically this means Chapter 5 of the *Second Treatise on Government*[197]), which is already taken over from Macpherson and Strauss, gives the subject overwhelming importance and consequently leads to a basically anachronistic picture of the philosopher.[198] To this extent the method (a feature of the Weberian school) has already prejudiced the result.

On the other hand, Locke's originality in respect of the hedonistic and utilitarian motivation which he brings to bear on moral action is largely overestimated, because there is no comparison with his English contemporaries; and it is nonsense to limit the consideration of rewards and punishments, especially in a future life, to special influence from the French Gassendists – it is far too general in English philosophical literature and indeed in contemporary sermons. From the texts we have already investigated, we should also recall Herbert of Cherbury's fifth *notitia communis circa religionem;*[199] the aim of Chillingworth's work *The Religion of Protestants a Safe Way to Salvation,*[200] which already becomes evident in the title of the book; Tillotson's sermons; and above all the programme which John Wilkins carried through in his work *Of the Principles and Duties of Natural Religion.*[201] Thus the idea is widespread in the rationalistic Anglicanism of the seventeenth century.[202] We saw that a eudaemonistic note is already struck with Hooker, who is often mentioned as a characteristic advocate of a traditional natural law;[203] however, among the Latitudinarians of the second half of the century, among whom Locke is also to be included in this respect, Hooker became unduly important because of the apologetic interests which were predominant.

By contrast, one independent contribution made by Locke which was to be of further influence was his epistemology. Over the question of authority as such, though, Locke similarly adopts a traditional approach,[204] and we can only assess the true significance of his answers if we recognize the combination in them of traditional patterns of thinking and newly-won insights. The *Essays on the Law of Nature* already demonstrate the decisive points: Locke accepts the existence of a natural law as the basis of an ethical system for human action, but rejects the earlier theories about its origin and the possibility of recognizing it. These include above all the theory of the *ideae innatae*[205] and the derivation of the *lex naturae* from the general consensus on basic ethical questions.[206] Instead, Locke develops his own argument for the existence of the *lex naturae* and the possibility of recognizing it, which in a remarkable way is again derived from both traditional and original elements. In Essay VII the binding character of natural law is at one point categorically asserted in a Thomistic way;[207] the ethnographic observation that the customs of many nations contain grossly immoral features[208] is unimportant, as the absolute commands of the law of nature apply to all men[209] and only deeply rooted customs and bad examples lead people astray into following their passions and not their reason.[210] The connection between the law of nature and men lies in man's rational nature: as there is a harmony between this law and rational nature, the latter can also be recognized by reason.[211] However, Locke in Essay II is not content with this traditional statement: rather, he is concerned with the question of the way in which the law of nature can be recognized on the basis of a discursive concept of reason: *Ratio autem hic sumitur pro facultate animae discursiva quae a notis ad ignota progreditur et unum ex alio certa et legitima propositionum consecutione deducit. Haec est illa ratio cujus ope gens humana in cognitionem legis naturae pervenit.*[212] However, this reason, which can also be called the 'light of nature',[213] in accordance with the rationalistic tradition, arrives at the knowledge of the law of nature by the senses alone – here there are already intimations of Locke's empiricism – since *ideae innatae* and tradition are excluded as means.[214] This does not come about through direct perception but is a discursive conclusion: and here the physico-theological proof for God finds a place. From what the reasonable man observes with his senses, from their visible movement and order he concludes that all these things have an author; as he arrives at the knowledge that this must be a God, there necessarily follows the existence of a law of nature which is binding on all mankind.[215] This argument is developed in more detail in Essay IV: *An ratio per res a sensibus haustas pervenire potest in cognitionem legis naturae? Affirmatur.*[216] This essay is particularly illuminating because in it on the one hand there are already intimations of Locke's epistemology, later developed in the *Essay Concerning Human Understanding*, on the principles of the natural sciences of the time, and on the other a development of a voluntaristic conception of natural law. Through sense perception we learn that there are things in the world that can be known, i.e. bodies that actually exist, and their properties, which can all in some way be derived from the principle of motion;[217] we recognize the marvellous regularity of the construction of this world, to which we also belong as part of it. From this, our understanding argues back to the author of so admirable a work: this can only be an omnipotent, wise creator, who has also made men as the most perfect part of this world. It follows from this that he has the power to preserve us or to destroy us, to raise us up or cast us down, to make us happy or wretched. Consequently reason, starting from sense experience, can lead us to the recognition of a legislator, a supreme power, on which we are dependent.[218] For, Locke goes on to explain, if we recognize the existence of a Creator who is not only omnipotent but also wise, we cannot assume that he created the world without a firm goal, for nothing and with no purpose. It is evident that God intends that men should do something. The will of a superior power in respect of what we have to do is the second presupposition for the recognition of any law.[219]

Most of the features in this argument have a traditional origin: both the physico-theological proof of God and the theological argument, along with the associated voluntaristic concept of God, derive from Scholasticism. The most novel element, the empiricist epistemological principle, does not have a supporting function but is merely used as the starting point for a stage of the argument, the physico-theological proof of God. Moreover, it has to be said that Locke later abandoned the physico-theological argument and replaced it with a form of anthropological proof.[220] The focal point of the controversy with tradition does not lie here but at another point. The significance of Locke's move against Innatism becomes clear when we recognize that (whether consciously or unconsciously) in his approach he revives the natural law theory of Nominalism in an uncompromising form and thus rejects the Thomistic theory dominant in the English universities, which for the most part was based on a Realist metaphysic: whereas in the Thomistic natural law theory the law of nature was an ordinance inherent in the cosmos itself, and in man as part of this cosmos, unchangeable and only in principle dependent on the original will of a creator, the will of God now comes more markedly into the centre.[221] With the rejection of Innatism and the consensus theory the epistemological principle in connection with the lex naturae now shifts: essentially, it can now no longer begin with what exists in the cosmos, but must itself derive from the Lord of creation and have in view his purposes with mankind and his action. This also gives a completely new status to the problem of revelation, which in the sphere of the immanentism of natural law could play little more than a formal role (though in the *Essays* Locke first deliberately brackets off revelation, as he is concerned with natural law).[222] We do not have to look too far in search of the roots of this position: in Locke, too, as we shall see, we finally come upon the traces of the biblicism which predominated in the English church.

We do, however, have to maintain – as a great variety of Locke's interpreters have seen – that Locke is not at all consistent in his understanding of natural law in the *Essays*: unlike Essays II and IV, Essay VII moves largely on Thomistic lines. In particular, the idea of the rational nature of man and its harmonious accord with the rational character of the law of nature, lies outside the framework marked out in the other essays and indicates an epistemological theory which is alien to them.[223]

Locke's own method of solving the problem of natural law becomes clearer only when we move from the *Essays on the Law of Nature* to the earlier stages of the *Essay Concerning Human Understanding* which as a result of the early outlines to be found in Locke's posthumous papers (and which have been published meanwhile), go back as far as the years 1670/71.[224] There is also external evidence for an intrinsic connection between the two works: the circumstances of the origins of these outlines have now been largely explained. According to a marginal note by Locke's friend J. Tyrell (one of those present) in his copy of the Essay which is now in the British Library,[225] the meeting of the five or six friends which, according to Locke's own, much noted, account in the 'Epistle to the Reader'[226] which introduces the *Essay* gave the first impetus to his concern with the epistemological main theme of the *Essay*, began with a 'discourse about the principles of morality and revealed religion'. Moreover, in a detailed comparison between the *Essays* and the outlines W.von Leyden has shown the way in which Locke referred back to the latter for the former.[227] In the drafts Locke for the most part discusses his general epistemology, in Draft A beginning with his famous semi-empirical principle of sense perception and the simplest ideas of the properties of physical things which are gained from it as the basis of human knowledge.[228] Moral ideas about virtue and vice are only touched on briefly here, though there is the interesting distinction between two possible ways of defining virtue and vice. One can follow the terminology of the particular country in which one happens to live, and whose language contains terms for good and evil actions in accordance with the standards valid there,[229] thus arriving at a moral system. However, since these are human creations they are uncertain. Alongside them are the rules not made by us but for us, 'and these are the rules set to our actions by the declard will or laws of another who hath power to punish our aberrations'. Even here there is an indication of the possibility that Locke could be forced to go beyond the limits of his narrower epistemological system to provide the grounds for an absolute morality. However, at this point Locke observes that as he must first demonstrate such a lawgiver and show 'how he hath declard his will and law', he must postpone this question to a more favourable opportunity.[230] In Draft B this passage is put at the end and extended in two ways: first, at its conclusion by a more detailed explanation of how human actions relate to a law by which they are described as good or evil – therefore he calls them 'moral relations' – and secondly, by the attempt undertaken in an inserted comment to see the love commandment as being rather like a summary of this law.[231]

Locke concerned himself again with the problem of morality some years later, in some random remarks. These give new importance to an idea which stands in isolation in Essay VII of the *Essays of the Law of Nature*, where Locke had spoken of the possibility of demonstrating morality which can be derived from the rational nature of man in the same way as the angle of a triangle in mathematics. For a man is obliged to love and honour God and to fulfil other demands in accordance with the rationality of nature, i.e. to observe the law of nature.[232] The diary entry of 26 June 1681[233] also stresses the difference between the sciences of mathematics and morality as the two spheres based on the knowledge of true ideas, and physics, politics and experiential wisdom which are based only on the history of facts. He thinks that in morality we can only arrive at 'demonstrative certainty' if we have a true idea of God, of ourselves as his creatures, and of the relationship in which we stand to God and our fellow creatures, as also of righteousness, goodness, law and happiness – for like the truths of mathematics these are neither *aeternae veritates* nor dependent on history and facts. 'For that the three angles of a triangle are equall to two right ones is infallibly true whether there be any such figure as a triangle existing in the world or noe and it is true that it is everymans duty to be just whether there be any such thing as a just man in the world or noe.'[234] As a being endowed with reason, man can understand his relationship to his creator in analogy to the obedience owed a father by his son. This also leads to the obligation towards other people which sustains society.

The problem of natural law in Locke becomes more complicated as a result of the incorporation of the eudaemonistic (or Neo-Epicurean) principle into ethics. The psychological considerations about 'joy' and 'sorrow' as impulses to human action which first appear in a diary entry under 16 July 1676[235] and anticipate Chapter 21 of the Second Book of the *Essay concerning Human Understanding*[236] play a part here. The earliest evidence for their influence on ethics appears in the paper 'Of Ethick in General'.[237] On the basis of psychological presuppositions, to begin with, good and evil present themselves to the individual in connection with the direct effect of his actions as pleasure or pain.[238] However, here – as with, for example, a hangover after drinking too much – we have only natural good and evil, according to a distinction which Locke now introduces, in agreement with a widespread tendency.[239] Moral good and evil, however, are denoted by the intervention of a higher power who distributes rewards and punishments in accordance with the laws which he decrees.[240] And now Locke repeats the passage already contained in Draft A of the *Essay* which in the new context now receives a different status: 'But there is another sort of morality or rules of our actions... and these are the rules set to our actions by the declared will or laws of another, who has power to punish our aberrations; – these are properly and truly the rules of good and evil, because the conformity or disagreement of our actions with these, bring upon us good or evil.'[241] So here God's reward and punishment from the repertoire of the traditional ingredients of Christian moral theory are combined with the eudaemonistic approach to ethics in order to make the leap to the theory of the law of nature. Even here, however, we can see how unconvincing Locke is in his attempt.

Locke goes on to say that in order to know these rules, it is necessary, 1. to make known this legislator for all men, who has the power and will to reward and punish; and 2. to show how he has declared his will and law, i.e. to speak of God and the law of nature. However, this (again) he must postpone to an 'appropriate place'. At the end of the fragment he again begins such an attempt,[242] but breaks off without continuing it.

In the *Essay concerning Human Understanding*, Locke attempts to find a place in his epistemology as a whole for the theory of the possibility of deducing moral principles and norms.[243] Here he takes up again the approaches from Essay VII of the *Essays on the Law of Nature* and the diary entry of 26 June 1681, when at several points he indicates that man can gain clear and true ideas of the concepts of morality in the same way as he can those of mathematics.[244] Locke's epistemology[245] makes a distinction between 'simple' ideas which are developed 'passively' by the spirit through sensation and reflection on the qualities of things communicated by the senses, and 'complex' ideas which are gained 'actively' through the combination of a number of different kinds of simple ideas.[246] The 'mixed modes'[247] arise when the spirit combines different simple ideas from different spheres. 'Mixed modes' are generally related to the sphere of human action, especially thought, movement and power,[248] and form the conceptuality for the norms of which laws and morality are composed. In detail they are enormously different.[249] It is important that the 'mixed modes' have no relationship to an immediate reality: '*Mixed Modes and Relations*, having no other *reality*, but what they have in the Minds of Men, there is nothing more required to this kind of *Ideas*, to make them *real*, but that they be so framed, that there be a possibility of existing conformable to them.'[250] Precisely for that reason – and now Locke's Nominalism makes an appearance – the morality formed from such concepts enjoys the advantage of being a demonstrable science: 'Upon this ground it is, that I am bold to think, that *Morality is capable of Demonstration*, as well as Mathematicks: Since the precise real Essence of the Things moral Words stand for, may be perfectly known; and so the Congruity, or Incongruity of the Things themselves, be certainly discovered, in which consists perfect Knowledge.'[251]

However, in carrying out this programme in practice Locke immediately runs into considerable difficulties. Various commentators have already pointed out that the statements which Locke produces as examples of the possibility of demonstrating morality are either very banal,[252] or are largely taken from the traditional theory of the law of nature.[253] If we look more closely, a large number of them, like the love commandment, unmistakably come from scripture.[254] Of course, that is not to say that in this context Locke felt that they belonged to scripture: primarily they are no more than general principles of natural law. However, the epistemological problems connected with the law of nature again become clear in the passage from *Of Ethick in General*, section 10, which has already been quoted,[255] where Locke, reproducing the passage from Draft A, § 26, word for word, repeats the distinction between the man-made moral system and the rules made 'not by us but for us'.[256] Here, moreover, there is a reference to the lawgiver and the will which he has made known to all men (with the key words 'God' and 'natural law'), along with a comment that this relationship can as easily be recognized as any other. Compared with Draft A, Locke has made an addition on the basis of his epistemological approach: 'that we have moral ideas as well as others, that we come by them the same way, and that they are nothing but collections of simple ideas.'[257] Nevertheless, he wants to maintain the distinction between the twin points of reference of moral actions: as 'generosity, modesty and contentment' they are at first only *modes*, i.e. concepts which consist of a collection of simple ideas, in the context of a man-made morality. Only: 'As they refer to a law with which they agree or disagree, so are they good or bad, virtues or vices.'[258] Given his previous remark, however, it still remains the case that, as this law is known or presumed to be known, agreement with this rule can be recognized as easily as any other connection, without the further explanation which is promised at the end of the fragment. In the chapter of the *Essay* in which Locke attacks innate ideas (I, 3), too, he presupposes that the majority of mankind acknowledges the existence of God and therefore also natural law,[259] but 'what Duty is, cannot be understood without a Law; nor a Law be known, or supposed, without a Law-maker, or without Reward and Punishment'; the very idea of God which is necessary here is not innate.[260] Evidently Locke continues to suppose that this morality, too, can be deduced, as emerges above all from Essay IV, 3, 18,[261] which repeats the earlier remarks to this effect; here it is worth noting that this deduction about the 'idea' of an omnipotent supreme being is attempted by establishing a parallel with the idea of man himself as a rational being. There is no direct way to natural law in contrast to purely human moral conceptuality. However, this means that, given Locke's epistemological approach, such a derivation is impossible in principle. Euchner aptly observes: 'Locke's radical Nominalism, which prevents the reason pressing on beyond the world of conceptuality to the reality of things, already blocks his epistemological attempt to arrive at the law of nature...'[262] There is also evidence that after the publication of the *Essay Concerning Human Understanding*, Locke himself doubted whether such a proof could really be given: Locke writes in a letter to Molyneux in 1692: 'I thought I saw that morality might be demonstratively made out; yet whether I am able so to make it out, is another question.'[263]

But how are we to judge this limitation of Locke's epistemology in respect of the reality of things (Locke is not a genuine empiricist, because there is an abyss between the 'ideas' and the real being of things which is ultimately unknown[264]) and in respect of the principles of a morality which is binding in the strict sense? D.G.James has given a definite verdict by entitling the first of the two chapters about Locke in his book *The Life of Reason* 'The Humble Heart'.[265] He stresses the passages in the *Essay Concerning Human Understanding* in which Locke speaks of the limitation of human knowledge, and comments in a pointed way: 'His essay is an Essay concerning Human Understanding; it is also an Essay concerning Human Ignorance.'[266] Locke deals with the limits of knowledge in Essay IV, 3, and with the magnitude of ignorance in IV, 3,22ff.[267] The limitation of human knowledge follows on the one hand from a limitation to the real world of things indirectly accessible to the senses; but even these are felt by our weaker senses to be incomplete, and we progress only to its secondary properties, capable of being experienced by the senses, and not its primary properties. Secondly, our knowledge does not even extend as far as our ideas, since the connection between them is often unknown. However, all knowledge on the one hand stops at the limits of the physical world which can be grasped by the senses and on the other at the systems which can be constructed from the 'mixed modes'.

At this point there should next be an enquiry into the role of revelation. D.G.James has pointed out the significance of Essay IV, 16,[268] where Locke discusses the 'degrees of assent'[269] which, in view of the frequent lack of absolute certainty, correspond to the degrees of probability of a thing in accordance with the weight of our own and others' experiences and the credibility of testimonies of various kinds. Now while in respect of such testimony from the tradition it follows 'That any Testimony, the farther off it is from the original truth, the less force and proof it has',[270] there is still a sphere where mere testimony can claim the highest degree of assent, because this testimony derives from a supreme authority, and that is God himself.[271] This testimony is called 'revelation', our assent to it 'faith'. However, there is not even certainty for this in the absolute sense,[272] but only 'assurance beyond Doubt'.[273]

In IV.18 Locke goes on to speak of the relationship between 'faith' and 'reason'. Important principles consistent with Locke's epistemological approach are here: first, that no recipient of revelation inspired by God can communicate new simple ideas which his fellow-men have not already had by sensation or reflection, since otherwise these would be outside the framework of conceivable experience and conceptuality and therefore be quite incomprehensible.[274] Secondly, all things could also be communicated by revelation which could already be discovered by reason and the ideas naturally at our disposal: 'In all Things of this Kind, there is little need or use of *Revelation*, GOD having furnished us with natural, and surer means to arrive at the knowledge of them.'[275] In all things which rest on clear perception, the correspondence of ideas or the evident deduction of reason, we do not need the support of revelation; should God nevertheless reveal something directly, our certainty cannot be greater than the knowledge that it is a revelation from God. In that case, at all events the criterion holds: 'But yet nothing, I think, can, under that Title, shake or over-rule plain Knowledge; or rationally prevail with any man, to admit it for true, in a direct contradiction to the clear Evidence of his own Understanding.'[276] 'And therefore, *no Proposition can be received for Divine Revelation*, or obtain the Assent due to all such, *if it be contradictory to our clear intuitive Knowledge.*'[277] This assertion then turns into the epistemological principle: 'Whether it be a divine Revelation, or no, *Reason* must judge; which can never permit the Mind to reject a greater Evidence to embrace what is less evident, nor allow it to entertain Probability in opposition to Knowledge and Certainty.'[278]

Now of course there are also 'many things, wherein we have very imperfect Notions, or none at all'; as examples Locke mentions the 'fall of the angels', or the resurrection of the dead. These are the specific sphere of faith,[279] about which revelation has to inform us. Thus we have here the kind of theology which has been called 'rational supernaturalism';[280] the object of faith is 'supernatural things' in the sphere of dogmatics.[281] As far as the *Essay* is concerned, the observation by D.G.James holds, that 'Locke is, first and last, a Christian philosopher',[282] and his philosophy for the most part 'a preparation for assent'[283] primarily only in this sphere: if we remember that Chapter IV, 19, 'Of Enthusiasm', only made an appearance with the fourth edition, the remarks about the limits of the realization of human knowledge and revelation as the surest source of certain truth in IV, 16 are contrasted with a relative strong confidence in reason in IV, 18, which severely limits the realm of 'assent'. Things change only in IV, 19. The ambivalent nature of this chapter, which significantly was written about 1695, is misunderstood by James when along the lines of his thesis he calls it 'Locke's great (and inconsistent) retraction'.[284] Rather, here the perspectives are shifted to quite a different level: to begin with, the chapter seems only to take further the line of IV,18, certainly also forced into heightening the argument in a quite specific direction as a result of the polemic against 'enthusiasm' which has been inserted here. James quotes the introductory sentences of this chapter, in which Locke states the principle that in the search for the truth, no lover of the truth can give his assent to a statement for which he does not have sufficient proof.[285,286] The enthusiasm against which Locke (like his pupil Shaftesbury) argues in this chapter, which has been added later,[287] is the extreme Spiritualism the representatives of which claimed direct personal inspiration. Locke in particular criticizes their favourite term 'light': 'light' can only be 'the evidence of the truth of a statement'.[288] On this first level of argumentation we have a clear form of rationalism which rejects Spiritualism. However, Locke does not leave things at that. It is striking that in IV,19,15 he mentions two criteria for the truth of a remark: 'If this internal Light, or any Proposition which under that Title we take for inspired, be conformable to the Principles of Reason or to the Word of God, which is attested Revelation, *Reason* warrants it, and we may safely receive it for true, and be guided by it in our Belief and Actions.'[289] The two factors, reason and scripture, are also expressly juxtaposed in IV, 19, 16 as criteria whether a revelation is genuine and derives from God or not: 'Nothing can do that but the written Word of GOD without us, or that Standard of Reason which is common to us with all Men. Where Reason or Scripture is express for any Opinion or Action, we may receive it as of divine Authority...'[290]

In IV,19 Locke evidently already begins from a juxtaposition of reason and scripture on the same level, a position which was not yet to be found in IV, 18 in this form. It was not in IV, 18 because his rational supranaturalism formally kept apart the spheres of competence of the two factors. According to IV, 18, revelation can be dispensed with wherever natural ways to certain knowledge are at our disposal. Only where reason does not go further than probability is it possible that an evident revelation can determine our assent, even against probability. 'For where the Principles of Reason have not evidenced a Proposition to be certainly true or false, there clear *Revelation*, as another Principle of Truth, and Ground of Assent, may determine; and so it may be Matter of *Faith*, and be also above *Reason*.'[291] But what is 'clear Revelation'? If it is valid, 'whether it be a divine revelation or no, reason must judge',[292] and moreover, 'There can be no evidence, that any traditional Revelation is of divine Original, in the Words we receive it, and in the Sense we understand it, so clear, and so certain, as that of the Principles of Reason',[293] revelation itself would have to be measured by the criteria of reason. In the original version of the *Essay* Locke avoids this, by dividing, as he supposes, the 'provinces of faith and reason' by clear boundaries.[294] It is otherwise in IV, 19: there he says (IV, 19,16) in respect of the claim to revelation of 'inspired' who appear without any further outward credentials: 'But in such cases too we have Reason and the Scripture, unerring Rules to know whether it be from GOD or no.'[295] In IV, 19,14 Locke had said that it was not his view that one must test by reason whether a statement revealed by God can be grasped by natural criteria and if not, reject it, but one must test whether it is a revelation from God or not.[296] In IV, 19,15 he refers to miracles as possible confirmation for a revelation that has been given and recalls that the recipients of biblical revelation would have received outward signs as confirmation for themselves and their hearers that the revelations they received came from God.[297] Nevertheless it is not the case that miracles are directly necessary as a confirmation of the divine quality of scripture;[298] they would, however, be able to confirm the claim of someone who appeared now as a bearer of revelation. Otherwise scripture is presupposed as 'attested revelation' without further inquiry; alongside reason and with the same status, it is a 'rule free of error' and in the sphere where 'knowledge and certainty' do not have the pre-eminence it holds that 'Whatever God hath revealed, is certainly true.'[299] If, then, reason temporarily seemed to occupy a place quite independently of scripture, at this stage Locke has returned to a clear recognition of the authority of scripture. The year 1695 is also the date of the composition of *The Reasonableness of Christianity*. Locke's attitude to scripture in the last years of his life will concern us in more detail in connection with this work.

R. Ashcraft calls the *Essay concerning Human Understanding* a 'testament of Locke's dilemma'. Personally Locke is convinced of the absolute truth of Christianity and the simple demands of faith from scripture, but he knows that those who have defended it hitherto have done so inadequately, only with arguments from authority and not with arguments from reason.[300] This does not seem to have convinced Locke either. In the *Essay* he embarks on a long epistemological course which is meant to bring him nearer to his aim of a rational basis for faith and morality. These methods fail in both areas, and as Locke cannot abandon faith and morality, he is compelled to return to an argument from authority. Here he keeps morality in mind as the most important aim: 'For 'tis rational to conclude, that our proper Imployment lies in those Enquiries, and in that sort of Knowledge, which is most suited to our natural Capacities, and carries in it our greatest interest, *i.e.* the Condition of our eternal Estate. Hence I think I may conclude, that *Morality* is *the proper Science, and Business of Mankind in general.*'[301]

The problems left open in the *Essay* all focus on the answer which Locke has given in his last substantial work *The Reasonableness of Christianity*.[301a] Ashcraft observes: 'If the Reasonableness of Christianity has been less misunderstood than the Essay, it is only because less attention has been paid to it.'[302] That this work has been so little noted in the history of philosophy[302a] is understandable in view of the surprising impression which one has of it at first glance: here we seem to be meeting quite a different Locke. The most amazing thing is the comprehensive knowledge of the New Testament which he shows in the detailed arguments for his central theses: the philosopher has been replaced by an exegete who is quite remarkable by the standards of his time. The surprise would, of course, be less if one had remembered the consistency with which, in reflecting on a reliable basis for ethics, Locke was increasingly thrown back on the authoritarian solution of seeking it in the Bible, or one had noted sufficiently how in the seventeenth century all the problems of the time were indissolubly bound up with theological questions, and particularly those connected with understanding the Bible. It was therefore only consistent for Locke to occupy himself explicitly with biblical themes in the years of leisure in Oates. However, this intensive preoccupation with the Bible did not develop all of a sudden; as Viano points out,[303] it can be demonstrated from diary entries from as early as 1676. Locke was particularly interested in the works of John Lightfoot and other exegetes who from the middle of the century had been occupied with the problems of a harmony of the Gospels;[304] here in turn he followed Le Clerc, who had rejected R.Simon's critical hesitations over this form of rationalizing the Bible.

In a letter of thanks to Samuel Bolde,[305] who had hastened to his defence, inserted into the preface to the *Second Vindication* of his work, Locke indicated the occasion for it: this was the controversy over justification which flared up at the beginning of 1695 between some orthodox theologians and Dissenters, and which one day he came upon by chance.[306] 'The Scripture was direct and plain, that it was faith that justified: The next question then was, what faith was that justified; what it was which, if a man believed, it should be imputed to him for righteousness. To find out this, I thought the right way was, to search the Scriptures.' Locke's subsequent report on the results of his research into scripture is certainly no surprise in the case of a rationalistic thinker: he was amazed at the 'reasonableness and plainness' of the doctrine of justification he had found in scripture, and even more amazed that it was not universally seen and accepted.[307]

This personal testimony makes it clear that Locke wrote *The Reasonableness of Christianity* chiefly for his own information, in an attempt to solve the key question of the basis for ethics, which still remained open. The answer which he gives towards the end of his life points to the Bible as the source of morality, especially to the New Testament, and in this context specifically to the teaching of Jesus. In that connection, in the letter to Bolde which I have already quoted, Locke again recalls: 'That which added to my satisfaction was, that it led me into a discovery of the marvellous and divine wisdom of our Saviour's conduct, in all the circumstances of his promulgating this doctrine; as well as of the necessity that such a lawgiver should be sent from God, for the reforming of the morality of the world.'[308] Jesus as the lawgiver and moral reformer: here already is the basic tenor which is characteristic of the whole of *The Reasonableness of Christianity*. It is clearly in line with the rationalistic Humanist tradition and because of the tightness of its argument can be seen as a high-point in the development of that tradition. It is even more surprising to find Locke as its author; however, even this fact is understandable and logical if we note his own way of posing the problem which is evident from the works we have discussed.[308a]

We can see how rarely these connections are noted from the sparse verdicts passed on *The Reasonableness*; these include the particularly obtuse regrets of F.Bourne 'that Locke did not, in discussing "the reasonableness of Christianity" treat more fully of its ethical aspects'.[309] Locke himself perhaps made some contribution to the misunderstandings which have dogged his work down to modern times when at various points he says that the morality and religion taught by Jesus are the easier and simpler way, 'suited to vulgar capacities'[310] – this already prompted the view that Locke wanted the simple Christianity which he propagated to act as a useful stimulus to morality for the working and uneducated class, whereas for himself and the educated class he had claimed the higher way of the rational deduction of ethical principles,in accordance with his remarks in the Essay.[311] This view, which has a Marxist colouring, is in fact simply another version of the earlier view that the whole work is simply a concession to official Christianity worked out by Locke, an expression of his 'caution',[312] whereas he kept to himself quite different ideas. If we read *The Reasonableness* in the context of the *Essay*, carefully weighing up all the remarks, we may arrive at another verdict. At first glance we are in fact struck by those statements in which Locke specifically speaks of the working classes: 'Where the hand is used to the plough and the spade, the head is seldom elevated to sublime notions, or exercised in mysterious reasoning. It is well if men of that rank (to say nothing of the other sex[!]) can comprehend plain propositions, and a short reasoning about things familiar to their minds, and nearly allied to their daily experience.'[313] And in respect of the possibility (discussed in the Essay) of a morality which can be deduced like mathematics: 'The greatest part of mankind want leisure or capacity for demonstration... And you may as soon hope to have all the day-labourers and tradesmen, the spinsters and dairy-maids, perfect mathematicians, as to have them perfect in ethics this way.'[314] On the other hand there are some 'men of parts, and studious of virtue (who had occasion to think on any particular part of it [the law of nature])',[315] endowed with 'leisure and the capacity for argument'[316] – one may note that Locke certainly includes himself in this privileged group. But we are then struck by the hypothetical way in which Locke speaks of the conceivable possibilities for arriving at a well-grounded ethics which would be open to those who had sufficient gifts and sufficient leisure to reflect. For while these people can even discover as it were individual points of ethics quite appropriately, they are not capable of establishing their binding nature 'from the true principles of the law of nature, and foundations of morality'.[317] Obviously it is an error of method to single out the apparently sociological terms from a context in which Locke is concerned to demonstrate that before the mission of Jesus 'a clear knowledge of their duty was wanting to mankind'.[318] When he speaks of the 'majority of mankind'[319] who in this world are destined to 'labour and toil',[320] he has mankind itself in mind: 'the frailty of man, apt to run into corruption and misery'[321] which is usually unsuccessful at arriving at a basis for morality of its own accord. So Locke evidently includes himself here. The aim of the *Reasonableness* can be understood in the light of the dilemma of the *Essay* and a remark which occurs in Locke's letter of 30 March (5 April) 1696 to W.Molyneux who, like others, had urged him to write a 'Treatise of Morals': 'But the Gospel contains so perfect a body of ethics, that reason may be excused from that inquiry, since she may find man's duty clearer and easier in revelation than in herself.'[322] For the background of the references to the mass of workers who do not have the leisure for difficult considerations, we should recall not only its function as a rhetorical illustration in which in the contrast with the philosophers of antiquity it is applied by a kind of merismus to the whole of mankind,[323] but also that simplicity of doctrine is a Humanist ideal of the kind that we have already found repeatedly in the course of our investigations from Erasmus to Henry More.[324] Locke's observation that the simple men of the working world are seldom inclined to look on 'sublime notions' or to be 'exercised in mysterious reasoning', but could understand 'plain propositions',[325] recalls similar remarks made by his predecessors, influenced by Humanism, who like him reject the scholastic urge for learning. Finally, he also goes against his own earlier efforts in the *Essay*, the lines of argument in which now seem to him to be too complicated for the majority of people, who have nevertheless to be led to a well-founded morality.

However, over and above the earlier Humanists, in these remarks we also find a fundamental attitude which A.Lovejoy has stressed as being one of the characteristic marks of all Enlightenment philosophy:[326] in Locke it is quite clearly implied in his rationalistic approach and at the same time present in the specific form of his natural law thinking. This attitude is characterized by the *a priori* assumption, which had consequences extending from the subsequent period down to the present, that because they are beings endowed with reason, all men are basically the same (Lovejoy calls this 'uniformitarianism').[327] Thus differences in opinion and taste are signs of error, and truth must be of such a kind that it can be understood by all men. But as Locke the perceptive observer notes from a look at reality that the majority of men are incapable of complicated efforts of thought, the truth must be gradated in such a way that there comes a point when it is adapted to the understanding of even the most unpractised. This takes him back to the Bible, which he welcomes as an 'Elementary book' of this kind,[328] which can give even the manual worker everything needful for his life and eternal salvation. In this respect Locke is moved by a real pedagogical concern, and this is expressed at the end of his work, in a passage which he once again quoted in his *Vindication* as central to his considerations.[329] There he writes: 'I could not forbear magnifying the wisdom and goodness of God (which infinitely exceeds the thought of ignorant, vain, and, narrow-minded man) in these following words: "The all merciful God seems herein to have consulted the poor of this world, and the bulk of mankind; these are articles that the labouring and illiterate man may comprehend."'[330]

In his work *The Reasonableness of Christianity*, Locke sets himself two closely connected goals: in the dogmatic sphere to demonstrate that a minimal confession (that Jesus is the Messiah) is enough for salvation; however, this is bound up with the demonstration that Holy Scripture provides the only reliable authoritative morality, which is decisive in providing a basis for ethics.[330a] Locke is moved by a strong personal faith in the truth of Holy Scripture, as he himself writes to Stillingfleet (at that time Bishop of Worcester) in January 1697: 'The holy scripture is to me, and always will be, the constant guide of my assent: and I shall always harken to it, as containing infallible truth, relating to things of the highest concernment.'[331] As many commentators have noted, the central dogmatic statement that Jesus is the Messiah comes very close to the decisive statement in Hobbes: 'Jesus to be the Christ.'[332] Nevertheless, we are not to assume Locke to be dependent on Hobbes; rather, both thinkers are rooted in the Anglican Latitudinarian tradition, which can reduce the fundamental element of doctrine to a single sentence. On the other hand, we can be amazed at the way in which Locke produces his argument that this is the central statement of Christianity, from all four Gospels, Acts and some other New Testament passages (he is particularly fond of the Gospel of John), offering a wealth of skilfully chosen quotations and thus producing a classical argument from scripture of considerable length.[333] Within this argument, which gives rise to Locke's exegetical comments on the Gospels, we find the famous observation (misinterpreted by Strauss), similarly supported by numerous examples, that Jesus kept his status as Messiah secret until the last stage of his activity and spoke of it only in a veiled way[334] – this is a clear anticipation of Wrede's theory of the messianic secret in the Gospel of Mark. Locke produces many reasons why Jesus acted so 'cautiously':[335] had he openly declared himself to be Messiah not only the Jews but also the Romans would have done away with him before the appointed end of his mission, and the people would have proclaimed him their king at the wrong time,[336] which could have led to a rebellion with the most disastrous consequences. Even on his last journey to Jerusalem and in Jerusalem itself Jesus avoided calling himself Messiah in order not to appear a criminal and to obtain a formal declaration of innocence from Pilate.[337] Among other things, the preaching of the 'kingdom of God' or 'kingdom of heaven' is such a means of concealment, a way of hinting at the kingdom of the Messiah.[338]

Now, although they occupy by far the greatest amount of space, these statements about Jesus and his role as Messiah are not the real aim of the work. For this one must recall, rather, Locke's own declaration that he wrote *The Reasonableness* in order to clarify the question of justification which had emerged in a topical discussion. In using Paul's statement that justification comes about through faith, Locke has only taken up one side of the issue, by defining the content of this faith as recognition of the statement that Jesus is the Messiah. It is typical of his rationalist moralism that he does not repeat the Pauline formula 'faith without the works of the law' (see below); on the contrary, he takes it for granted that justification takes place through works. Now he has to clarify what law provides the criterion for these works. Because faith is understood purely intellectually as holding a dogmatic statement to be true, Locke can make room for this basic decision: as always, rationalism and moralism are closely connected.

Locke embarks on this all-embracing question by beginning with Adam:[339] 'It is obvious to any one, who reads the New Testament, that the doctrine of redemption, and consequently of the gospel, is founded upon the supposition of Adam's fall.'[340] '...what Adam fell from (is visible), was the state of perfect obedience, which is called justice in the New Testament.'[341] The punishment for this was the loss of immortality, and Adam's descendants were also affected by this. Locke rejects original sin (and the eternal punishments of hell as its consequence) as being unworthy of God.[342] The second Adam, Christ, brings the whole of humanity back to life (II Cor.15.22), which it receives again in the resurrection.[343] Now this does not mean that the unrighteous will attain eternal life;[344] that would be irreconcilable with the 'eternal and established law of right and wrong'. It is quite clear: 'Immortality and bliss belong to the righteous; those who have lived in an exact conformity to the law of God, are out of the reach of death.'[345] Now according to Rom.3.20-23, all have sinned and therefore no one could be justified by the works of the law. Locke himself answers the possible objection, 'Why then did God give so harsh a law that at the time of the apostles none of the descendants of Adam had kept it?' 'It was such a law as the purity of God's nature required, and must be the law of such a creature as man; unless God would have made him a rational creature, and not required him to have lived by the law of reason.'[346] If therefore all sinners must die, even the possibility of life regained by the resurrection would not have been much use, as it would be closed to these people – unless God had given another law, 'the law of faith' (Rom.3.27), which is opposed to the 'law of works'.

The subsequent definition of the 'law of works' and the 'law of faith' contains both traditional and original elements. The statement that 'the law of works' is the law given by Moses is traditional (following John 1.17 and other biblical passages cited by Locke); to this Locke adds, referring to the classical proof text Rom.2.14, the theory 'that under the law of works, is comprehended also the law of nature, allowable by reason, as well as the law given by Moses.' For without a law not even the Gentiles could have been sinners (according to Rom.3.9,23).[347] This association of the law of nature with the law of Moses under the law of works is central to the further development of Locke's thought: he goes back to it in the closing part of his discussion. First, however, he goes on to speak about the 'law of faith'. Again, a statement from Rom.3 (v.31) serves as a basis for his assertion that the law of works is in no way done away with by the law of faith; rather, the law is indispensable as a guideline for righteousness, and only for that reason is there need of faith which can be reckoned as righteousness. A traditional legacy of the Reformation is the division of the law of Moses into the civil, ritual and moral law, of which only the moral law is binding on Christians.[348] Now – and at this point the artifice with which Locke assigns an unexpected place to the 'law of faith' becomes evident – what matters is a complete fulfilment of the law: 'righteousness without works' (according to Rom.4.6) means 'without a full measure of works, which is exact obedience.'[349] Where human obedience falls short of the law and does not fulfil it, God helps out with the 'law of faith': 'The rule therefore, of right, is the same that ever it was; the obligation to observe it is also the same: the difference between the law of works, and the law of faith, is only this: that the law of works makes no allowance for failing on any occasion... But, by the law of faith, faith is allowed to supply the defect of full obedience: and so the believers are admitted to life and immortality, as if they were righteous.'[350] Jesus also saw it like this: 'He did not expect, it is true, a perfect obedience, void of slips and falls: he knew our make, and the weakness of our constitution too well, and was sent with a supply for that defect.'[351] Faith is thus merely an extension of obedience and fills in the gaps in our obedience to the law; through faith, men who because of their incompleteness and weakness (and that holds for all men) cannot arrive at perfect obedience towards the whole law on all occasions, and therefore would have fallen victim to death, are still allowed to live.[352] For this it is necessary to accept the statement 'that Jesus is the Messiah', but not just that. Locke himself answers the objection that this is only historical belief and not belief which saves and justifies,[353] and that the devil could have had such faith: that is not possible, since repentance is as necessary as faith for the 'covenant of grace'.[354,355] Now repentance is not only remorse over sins committed but (according to Acts 3.19; 26.20) 'a turning from them into a contrary life'.[356] We see from the Sermon on the Mount how

Jesus confirms and again brings into force all the moral commands of the Old Testament.[357] As a king he requires obedience to his commands from his subjects, and if there were no punishments for the transgression of his commands, he would not be king.[358] In this connection Locke recalls among other things the golden rule (Matt.7.12),[359] and after surveying all kinds of passages from the Gospels in which there is mention of the commandments of Jesus, he concludes: 'Thus we see our Saviour not only confirmed the moral law... but moreover, upon occasion, requires the obedience of his disciples to several of the commands he afresh lays upon them; with the enforcement of unspeakable rewards and punishments in another world, according to their obedience or disobedience.' 'They were required to believe him to be the Messiah... but righteousness, or obedience to the law of God, was their great business... But their past transgressions were pardoned... and their future slips covered, if, renouncing their former iniquities, they entered into his kingdom, and continued his subjects with a steady resolution and endeavour to obey his laws.'[360] Locke thus also chooses his key sentence 'Jesus is the Messiah' because for him, dogmatics and morality belong directly together in this confession of faith; New Testament faith, too, is a legalistic religion. This becomes quite clear at the point where Locke refers to the last judgment as the decisive event for Christians, too: '... and that they may not be deceived, by mistaking the doctrine of faith, grace, freegrace and the pardon and forgiveness of sins, and salvation by him... he more than once declares to them, for what omissions and miscarriages he shall judge and condemn to death... when he comes at last to render to every one according to what he has done in the flesh.'[361] Locke recalls that in the statements about the Last Judgment there is mention only of doing or not doing, and never of believing or not believing (though the reckoning of faith in the sense indicated would not be excluded).[362] His view can be summed up in a two-membered statement: 'These two, faith and repentance, i.e. believing Jesus to be the Messiah, and a good life, are the indispensable conditions of the new covenant, to be performed by all those who would obtain eternal life.'[363]

In the last part of his discussion Locke, starting from usual objections to the necessity of the New Testament for salvation, arrives, very much along the lines of the apologetic tradition, at the relationship between the New Testament law and the law of nature. There is, for example, the objection concerning the generations of mankind who lived before the time of Jesus and therefore could not believe in him: that these pre-Christian generations could not be saved if the faith that Jesus is the Messiah were necessary for filling the gap in perfect obedience towards the commandments of God.[364] And there is the related question, extremely topical at the time of the discovery of distant peoples, as to what the position was over the rest of mankind who had never heard anything of a saviour and Messiah. Locke replies to this that what God requires of every man is only in accordance with what he has and not in accordance with what he does not have,[365] and points in the direction of the law of nature: 'The law is the eternal, immutable standard of right.'[366] In this connection, one particular side of this law is decisive: through the light of reason God has revealed to all mankind that he is good and gracious. So whoever makes use of this 'candle of the Lord'[367] will find the way to forgiveness even without belief in the Messiah.

In that case, was Jesus' work superfluous? At this point, where in view of the statement in Acts 4.10,12 of the unconditional need for faith in Jesus on the one hand and the accordance of the law of nature with reason on the other hand, his whole edifice is threatened with collapse, Locke does not content himself with a reference to the unsearchable wisdom of God,[368] but once again embarks on a large-scale apologetic argument for the necessity of Jesus' mission. This last part of *The Reasonableness* represents the continuation, in the strict sense, of the problems left open in the *Essay*.

In principle Locke continues to assert that human reason could have arrived at a natural knowledge of God of its own accord. However, the inward and outward make-up of man before Christ had prevented this: 'Though the works of nature, in every part of them, sufficiently evidence a Deity; yet the world made so little use of their reason, that they saw him not, where, even by the impressions of himself, he was easy to be found.'[369] Locke derives the reasons for this hindrance partly from the traditional arsenal of rationalism: in the first place he mentions the priests, who had excluded reason from religion and replaced it with false notions of God and 'foolish rites'.[370] Just as it lacks knowledge of God (on which, according to Locke's model,[371] the knowledge of the law of nature also depends), so too mankind also lacked a clear knowledge of its duty.[372] The priests are mainly responsible for this, too: 'the priests made it not their business to teach them virtue.'[373] Therefore the change brought about by Jesus was urgently necessary: 'The outward forms of worshipping the Deity wanted a reformation. Stately buildings, costly ornaments, peculiar and uncouth habits, and a numerous huddle of pompous, fantastical, cumbersome ceremonies, every where attended divine worship.' Jesus brought a cure for this 'in a plain, spiritual and suitable worship'.[374] If we can clearly recognize a Puritan legacy here,[375] this is presumably also the case, though in a characteristically twisted form, with Locke's second argument: that despite the theoretical possibility, in practice human reason did not gain adequate knowledge of God and its duties without external help. Some clear thinkers, like the pagan philosophers, certainly arrived at the knowledge of the one supreme God,[376] but from the scattered comments of the best-known philosophers of all countries on ethical questions it is impossible to arrive at a consistent moral system, nor do they have real authority unless one also seeks to take over the erroneous remnant of their teachings.[377] 'Experience shows, that the knowledge of morality, by mere natural light (however agreeable soever it be to it) makes but a slow progress, and little advance in the world.'[378] This experience, which Locke contrasts *more geometrico* with his own earlier attempts at a derivation of the law of nature, leads him to concede: 'It is true, there is a law of nature: but who is there that ever did, or undertook to give it us all entire, as a law...? Who ever made out all the parts of it, put them together, and showed the world their obligation?'[379] It has now become clear to him that 'Natural religion, in its full extent, was no-where, that I know, taken care of, by the force of natural reason. It should seem... that it is too hard a task for unassisted reason to establish morality in all its parts, upon its true foundation, with a clear and convincing light.'[380]

In addition to the hindrances to a natural knowledge of the law already mentioned, Locke sees above all a pedagogical problem. The ancient philosophers who arrived at a true knowledge of God could not hand on this knowledge: 'They kept this truth locked up in their own breasts as a secret, nor ever dust venture it amongst the people; much less amongst the priests... Hence we see, that reason, speaking ever so clearly to the wise and virtuous, had ever authority enough to prevail on the multitude.'[381] Even apart from outward obstacles, the derivation of the law of nature in moral instruction is difficult and complicated: 'The teachers are always but upon proof, and must clear the doubt by a thread of coherent deductions from the first principle, how long, or how intricate soever they be.'[382] The working population (and this is how all the statements mentioned about them are to be understood) would have neither the time nor the leisure to be concerned with such difficult problems. Even if all the duties of mankind were clearly de-monstrated, one would arrive at the conclusion 'that method of teaching men their duties would be thought proper only for a few, who had much leisure, improved understandings, and were used to abstract reasonings. But the instruction of the people were best still left to the precepts and principles of the Gospel.'[383]

We must see these pedagogical considerations above all if we are to define appropriately the place of *The Reasonableness of Christianity* in Locke's works. As in the *Essay*, he is concerned with the communication of knowledge, in the first place with the basis of morality, but the approach through a theoretical epistemology has proved impossible: therefore he returns to authority, that of the New Testament and the teaching of Jesus. Here, too, is the answer to the central point at issue, whether or not Locke recognized the law of nature as an adequate basis for morality (and thus also for the righteousness of God): in principle, and indeed in practice, human reason, hindered by all kinds of circumstances, is not in a position to press forward to a comprehensively based morality, and is therefore directed towards the 'law of grace' which is contained in the message of Jesus.[384] 'And it is at least a surer and shorter way, to the apprehensions of the vulgar, and mass of mankind, that one manifestly sent from God, and coming with visible authority from him, should, as a king and lawmaker, tell them their duties, and require their obedience, than leave it to the long and sometimes intricate deductions of reason, to be made out to them.'[385] The philosophers had no real authority for their doctrines – the authority of Jesus is decisive, especially as it is also supported by miracle. Healings of the sick, raisings of the dead are facts which also impress ordinary people:[386] Locke had already given the miracles a prominent place as a proof of the messiahship of Jesus.[387]

The same pedagogical concern motivates Locke to stress as one of the essential advantages of the teaching of Jesus over against that of the ancient philosophers 'the great encouragement he brought to a virtuous and pious life'.[388] There then follow some apparently grossly eudaemonistic (or Neo-Epicurean) remarks: 'Mankind, who are and must be allowed to pursue their happiness, nay, cannot be hindered' was little attracted by the doctrine of the ancient philosophers: 'the chief of their arguments were from the excellency of virtue; and the highest they generally went, was the exalting of human nature, whose perfection lay in virtue.'[389] True, they showed the beauty of virtue, 'but leaving her unendowed, very few were willing to espouse her'![390] The teaching of Jesus overcame this lack of power to convince by presenting life and immortality as its reward. 'But now there being put into the scales on her side, "an exceeding and immortal weight of glory", interest is come about to her, and virtue now is visible the most enriching purchase, and by much the best bargain.'[391] In the post-Kantian period one may laugh at such remarks, but it must be remembered that they were written even before Shaftesbury's moral idealism.[392] Locke writes them with a burning pedagogical concern: the display of the heavenly prize will finally impress virtue on mankind as a goal worth striving for, which one cannot take amiss if one's own happiness proves to be the supreme goal. Here once again it should be pointed out how close Locke is to the Latitudinarian preachers who similarly presented heaven and hell to their audience in order to motivate them to accept their moral teachings. Locke also sees the remarks in the middle section of his treatise about a confession of the Messiah being the only fundamental doctrine necessary for salvation in the same light;[393] in his retrospect in the *Vindication*, which has already been quoted,[394] he praises the wisdom of God precisely by virtue of the fact that he has produced such a minimal confession which can be understood by the working and the uneducated man.

It is striking that in *The Reasonableness* Locke argues almost exclusively from the New Testament: even the fact that he begins from Adam does not conflict with this, since, as soon emerges, Adam is viewed in the perspective of I Cor.15.21f., i.e. in the perspective of the New Testament.[395] The revelation of the Old Testament to the patriarchs already contained the knowledge of the one invisible God, but 'that revelation was shut up in a little corner of the world', in a people which had few connections with the other nations and was despised by them. Jesus broke through these limits, and with his message went beyond the region of Canaan.[396] And if the law of Moses, too, is identical in its moral part with the law of nature, as the 'law of works' it is still ultimately inadequate as the way to salvation, and needs to be confirmed and instituted anew by Jesus as the 'law of grace'. Moreover, it is remarkable that Locke exclusively refers to the teaching of Jesus in the Gospels (and that of the apostles in Acts). This approach becomes easier to understand when we put it in the context of contemporary efforts to make a harmony of the Gospels, in which Locke had been interested since 1676.[397] This is in turn connected with the rationalistic and legalistic attempt to derive statements of basic doctrine from the Bible and make it into a moralistic law book; the Gospels seemed particularly suitable for this, and with it the interest in reconstructing *ipsissima verba Jesu*. This doctrine is only the 'Law of faith'.[398] Locke also clearly sets himself apart over the New Testament Epistles. He denies that the truths contained in the New Testament Epistles are fundamental.[399] This argument serves to confirm Locke's basic theory that only the teaching of Jesus and the apostles (in Acts!) that Jesus is the Messiah are necessary for salvation.[399a] Of course one can find fundamentalia in the Epistles, but there they are mixed with other truths[400] which are not necessary for salvation,[401] since the Epistles are occasional writings.[402] On this point Locke arrives at some insights which sound amazingly modern: as occasional writings, the Epistles are not intended to proclaim basic truths to outsiders but to strengthen Christians, who were already believers, by additional instructions.[403] One must remember their historical conditioning.[404] In addition, Locke attacks the proof-text method of producing dogmas from isolated statements in the Epistles; rather, one must on each occasion discover the main purpose of an epistle and the context of the arguments.[405] Apart from using it in *The Reasonableness*, Locke has also made this principle the starting point for his own interpretation of the Epistles of Paul,[406] the significance of which for the history of exegesis is far from being recognized.

In this whole attitude, the similarity to Erasmus and his relationship to the two Testaments is unmistakable: it is striking that, like Erasmus, Locke bases his *lex evangelica* centrally on the teaching of Jesus, understood in moral terms.[407] Alongside this, the attitude of the two to the law and thus to the two Testaments is again clearly different: the Spiritualist basis in Erasmus is not visible in Locke in this form, although there is an attack on ceremonial and criticism of the priests. In addition, we should also remember Chillingworth, for whom a similar fixation on the New Testament and the moral teaching of Jesus went hand in hand with a basic rationalistic attitude closely related to that of Locke.[408] On the whole it is amazing – and this should be stressed against the widespread interpretation of Locke as a radical modern thinker – to what a substantial degree the Humanist legacy still continued to influence him; and it is through this, and not through his epistemology, that he was to be an influence on the philosophy of the English Enlightenment in the first half of the eighteenth century: on the Deists and their moral view of religion, from which also a radical biblical criticism emerged which is not yet evident with Locke.[409]

Locke's two *Treatises of Government* are welcome evidence for his involvement in the discussions which used the Old Testament as relevant support for a particular view of authority in the contemporary controversies of the time over state politics, different examples of which we have already encountered.[410] As P.Laslett has demonstrated[411] in the introduction to his edition,[412] now to be regarded as definitive and for the first time again complete,[413] Locke wrote these two treatises (the second of them first[414]) in the years 1679-81 and not, as would seem to emerge from the Preface which he added to the impression of 1690,[415] in the year 1689 to justify the Glorious Revolution. The occasion was the strong public reaction produced by the republication of the works of Sir Robert Filmer, including in 1680 the first appearance of his hitherto unpublished *Patriarcha*.[416] These were used by the Tory Party in support of their propaganda for male descent which would favour the Catholic James II.[417] Filmer had died in 1653; the composition of his *Patriarcha* falls into the period around 1640[418] and belongs in the context of the discussions between Royalists and the Parliamentary party in the years before the outbreak of the Civil War. That his ideas again became topical in the Restoration period is only one of the indications of the way in which intellectual and political developments were linked with those in the first half of the century, carrying over the period of the Commonwealth. Filmer's arguments seem far less removed from the intellectual background of the seventeenth century than a present-day observer might imagine.[418a] The many examples which we have already encountered show us that his method of taking the Bible, and especially the Old Testament, as the starting point for an argument for the contemporary form of politics, is very much the usual way of going about things. As Laslett stresses,[419] the presupposition that the Bible contains God's true, only and complete will for all things, was so generally recognized that it called for no special defence. In particular, both the Puritans and the Anglicans were fond of referring back to the Old Testament, and we saw how central a role was played here for the High Church Party by the derivation of the prerogatives of the monarchy directly from the Old Testament. To this degree Filmer is by no means isolated; his work is just one among many with a similar direction. However, he is original (though by no means without any model[420]) in his method: in contrast to the usual connection between the Old Testament and contemporary institutions by way of typology, Filmer seeks to demonstrate a direct, genealogical descent of contemporary forms of rule throughout the world, and all structures for the ordering of human society, from the beginnings reported in the Old Testament.[420a] Human society takes its departure from Adam, who was intended at his creation to be ruler over his descendants.[421] After Adam, the other antedeluvian patriarchs had royal authority over their descendants through their paternity. This provides Filmer as it were with a basic rule for human society: all the children of Adam, i.e. all men, are by nature subject to their fathers. 'And this subordination of children is the fountain of all regal authority, by the ordination of God himself.'[422] This theory, which was later called 'patriarchalism',[423] immediately provides Filmer with an unexceptionable basis for the divine authority of kingship in the form of the hereditary monarchy, in which the oldest son has the right to succession and the claim to the absolute obedience of all members of his family, i.e. his subjects. The bridge between Adam, who had lordship over the whole world through creation,[424] and the rights of modern kings to rule, is provided by the time of Noah and the flood. Noah took the decisive step, by dividing the world among his three sons, and all the peoples scattered around the world after the confusion of languages stem from the sons and grandsons of Noah. However, they were not disorganized masses, but always families who were subject to their patriarchs, i.e. their rulers. All the kings who now rule on earth derive their rule from these first kings.[425] Of course all kinds of specific difficulties arise here as a result of the variety in the forms of rule in the large and smaller states of Filmer's time, as he well knows. However, Filmer deals with these difficulties which stand in the way of a natural descent of all kings from the patriarchs and by them from Adam, and also the extinction of ruling houses, their suppression by usurpers, and so on, by asserting that in this case such a change of rule corresponds to the will of God and restored the natural relationship which had been confused by human error.[426] Filmer bases this obligation of subjects to obey their rulers on the fifth commandment, in a characteristically changed form, 'Honour thy Father'[427] – a manoeuvre on which Locke immediately based his criticism. However, Laslett makes it clear that the patriarchalism which Filmer represented in theory corresponded closely to the political and above all the economic conditions of his time: in particular, it also corresponded to his own circumstances as a country gentleman and head of a large family and clientele.[428] The political principle which he contested most strongly was the consensus theory: that the people originally had sovereignty and delegated it by common assent to a ruler from whom in certain circumstances they could get it back again.[429]

For Filmer, too, it was quite obvious that the Old Testament was normative for the true form of a divinely willed monarchy. The monarchy runs through the whole history of Israel as a divinely willed form of government.[430] Even in the time before the monarchy the Israelites were ruled by monarchs, since the elders in the time of the judges were patriarchal heads of families.[431] The unlimited authority of kings in law is already clear from Samuel's description of a king (I Sam. 8); at the same time this shows what a subject must tolerate without having the right to rebel against it.[432] However, the king must remember that the law of nature compels him to put general security and well-being above all else – the only resource that subjects have against tyrants is prayer to God.[433] The well-known New Testament sayings about tax in Rom.13; I Peter 2.13 are quoted in order to justify the duty of Christians to be subject to their rulers. In addition to the Bible, Filmer also goes through the history of the later kingdoms; he is particularly concerned to demonstrate that the monarchy and the empire were also the ideal form for the history of the Roman empire. The people returned to these in times of danger, whereas democracy was only a relatively brief interlude, full of unrest at home and abroad.[434] Disorder is generally the characteristic of any democracy: 'such mischiefs are unavoidable and of necessity do follow all democratical regiments. The reason is given: because the nature of all people is to desire liberty without restraint.'[435] It is interesting that in addition to the Bible at one point Filmer also refers to Aristotle's *Ethics* and quotes the statements of the philosopher to the effect that monarchy is the oldest, natural and divine form of rule, the best form of the state, and that popular rule is the worst.[436] However, Laslett rightly stresses[437] that Filmer is in no way a crude absolutist: he has certainly a place for Parliament[438] and is generally interested in justifiying the *status quo*. His remarks about kingship have a hidden focus in the history of the monarchy in England; it is important to him to stress that since the Norman conquest England has had no tyrants.[439]

Filmer can base not only political but also economic conditions in England on the Old Testament. Against Grotius' theory of an original communism[440] and a kindred view of John Selden, he attempts to demonstrate the original absolute control of the patriarch Adam and Noah over all possessions; they had assigned spheres of rule to their sons of their own accord, through gift and renunciation.[441]

Locke attacks these theories of Filmer in his *Two Treatises*.[442] The impression which the modern reader gets, 'two hundred unreadable pages introducing an essay which is lively and convincing if a little laboured and repetitive',[443] and which in printed editions has often led to the omission of the first treatise, misunderstands the polemical starting point of the whole work and overlooks the pressure of the situation to which Locke had to react in all his remarks:[444] the persuasive power of the derivation of political demands for the present from models in the Old Testament was still unbroken around 1680, and the Tory propaganda campaign, carried on with Filmer's argument, for the Catholic succession of James II was so dangerous that the Whig party[445] and its leader, the First Earl of Shaftesbury, supporting Locke, could counter it only by attempting to refute Filmer on his own ground, that of the Old Testament. The first of the two treatises is devoted to this destructive method: only after the destruction of Filmerism could Locke present his own views of state and society in the second treatise.[446]

The present-day reader finds it difficult to see the significance of this first treatise because it is so directly concerned with Filmer in its criticism. For Locke's contemporaries this was far from being the case to the same extent,[446a] and in fact there is justification in P.Laslett's[447] criticism that Locke did much less justice to his opponent than did, say, his friend J.Tyrell.[448]

At a superficial level Locke found his opponent easy game: in his constructions Filmer was so far fetched that it was easy to point out the disagreements and logical gaps in his argument. Locke's method was to point out these absurdities and in an often ironical tone to refute them by giving the literal meaning of the biblical passages he quoted: this corresponded to a widespread form of controversial and pamphlet literature. Thus he makes it clear from Gen.1.26, 28 that what is meant in Gen.1.28 is not the rule of Adam over other men, his descendants, but the subjection of animals to mankind as a whole.[449] Gen.3.16 is not the basis for a domination of Adam over Eve, i.e of men over women, but merely indicates the natural dependence of a wife on her husband. This would also have affected e.g. Queens Mary and Elizabeth had they married a subject, but not their political sovereignty. Moreover this saying is a curse to Eve at the moment of the expulsion from paradise – not a moment when Adam could expect privileges to be bestowed on him.[450] Against the assertion that through his paternity Adam had received royal sovereignty over his children Locke argues, first, that it is not the father by procreation but God who is the creator of each individual,[451] and secondly, that the cause of the act of procreation is the temporary satisfaction of lust and not a far-reaching plan;[452] finally, that if the parents give their child life, here the role of the mother is far more important, so that she must have at least an equal share in controlling her children.[453] What Locke says in rejecting Filmer's abbreviation of the fifth commandment, about the honour owed by their children to both parents, is connected with this; here he produces a whole series of examples from various parts of the Old Testament and once again reveals a remarkable knowledge of the Bible.[454] Here, too, Filmer gave him an easy target to aim at. If the children have a claim to appropriate sustenance from their parents as long as they are weak and small, then after the death of these parents they have a right to the legacy which is brought to them by the natural succession of generations.[455] That happens even more with the argument by which Filmer wanted to demonstrate the transmission of the monarchical power originally given to Adam to contemporary kings. Here Locke's most important argument is that, given the Fall, such a right to rule was in fact bestowed on Adam by God, and that this right was handed on to all his descendants.[456] If one goes through the whole of this succession, which is assumed to extend from Adam to present-day monarchs, then, as Locke convincingly shows, there are so many gaps, so many jumps, that it is impossible to derive royal from patriarchal power. If in fact a man as heir of Adam had inherited in primogeniture the right to rule over the whole world, then the first task would be to find him, so that all the other kings could lay their crowns at his feet.[457] But in that case all these kings would have no reasonable claim to rule. 'If there be more than one Heir of *Adam*, every one is his Heir, and so every one has Regal Power.'[458] If there is a paternal right bestowed by procreation, this cannot be handed down to the oldest son as heir in the form of the right to rule over his younger brother;[459] rather (presupposing this paternal authority), it can be asserted that every father on earth has the same paternal authority on the basis of his claim at law which he has by virtue of procreation.[460] The exclusive right of the oldest heir to entire possession and sole rule cannot be demonstrated as early as the patriarchs,[461] still less after the division of the world among the descendants of Noah.[462] Moreover, the transition from the law of possession to the right to rule is a logically illegitimate jump: the monopoly of possession of land and thus of the whole production of the means to live does not either allow one to leave fellow men hungry – the brother in need has a claim to a gift from superfluity – or to enslave them.[463] It should be noted that this context of Locke's provided by Filmer provokes particular preoccupation with the theme of 'property' – not the 'ideology of the bourgeois age'! In particular, Locke attacks Filmer's theory that in founding the Israelite monarchy, God restored the original line of succession which had been broken in the meantime[464] – the significance of this particular argument only becomes clear when we recall that the kings of Israel were used in a special way by the Loyalists as types of the privileges (and duties) of the kings of England!

Essentially, however, our interest is not in these individual arguments but in the hermeneutical approach expressed in them, – though at some points Locke's basic attitude already comes through, above all when he refers to the rights of all men, all fathers, and women as well as men, to the heritage of Adam. We can see this first in the little asides which regularly occur, where Locke makes it clear that the view of his opponent is so different from general human understanding that it cannot be taken seriously. Sometimes he even says this in so many words: 'God, I believe, speaks differently from Men, because he speaks with more truth, more Certainty; but when he vouchsafes to speak to Men, I do not think, he speaks differently from them, in crossing the Rules of language in use amongst them.'[465] Thus Locke does not recognize other than the simple literal meaning, in terms of common sense or, as we can see in his example of the role of the wife in bearing children, from empirical scientific observation. At another point he says, 'The Prejudices of our own ill grounded Opinions, however by us called *Probable*, cannot Authorize us to understand Scripture contrary to the direct and plain meaning of the Words.'[466] On the other hand, Locke himself certainly has his own prejudices. He already makes clear his concern in the introductory paragraphs of the first treatise: he accuses Filmer of arguing for the slavery of mankind with his theory of the absolute monarchy as an order of creation, and of supporting those forces which have refused it 'a Right to natural Freedom'.[467] 'Men are not born free' ('Men are not naturally free'): in this statement he sums up Filmer's position which he challenges.[468] At another point he formulates his own view: 'If all this be so... then Man has a *Natural Freedom*... since all that share in the same common Nature, Faculties and Powers, are in Nature equal, and ought to partake in the same common Rights and Priviledges, till the manifest appointment of God... can be produced to shew any particular Persons Supremacy, or a Mans own consent subjects him to a Superior. This is so plain, that ...'[469] That, then, is the theme which he makes the real starting point of his much noted political theory in the second treatise. It is quite evident – and L.Strauss has rightly referred to this point[470] – that the natural state which Locke postulates as a kind of *tabula rasa* wiped clean of any power and thus as an ideal which in reality has already dawned, by the recovery of which any politics is to be measured, in no way rests on a biblical basis. Here Locke stands firmly on the ground of modern theories of natural law, in the realm of which the natural state is a central model of thought, as it is in Hobbes – though Locke is of a less radical stamp.[471] The Whig ideals of freedom and equality, closely akin to the postulate of the Levellers, albeit on a rather different level,[472] are as alien to the actual social conditions of the Old Testament as is the idea of Adam's absolute monarchy over the world in Filmer. If we ignore Filmer's exaggeration, we can ask whether in his patriarchal model he is not considerably closer to the Old Testament than Locke – despite his apt comments on individual details, e.g. in respect of the word *'ādām* as a collective designation for men in general, or of the status of the wife as mother which is becoming evident in the fifth command-ment[473] – which in no way does away with this patriarchal system but can be directly derived from it. Laslett draws attention to the important point[474] that Locke does not note Filmer's apt counter-criticism, above all of the assumption that such a natural state in fact existed, and of the theory of a general consensus underlying all political institutions.[475] It was Filmer's fear that a consistent individualism as the basis of a democ-racy, as presupposed by Locke, would inevitably lead to anarchy and result in the rule of violence, and he attempted to demonstrate this above all from the history of Rome.[476] If we reduce his ideas to the basic theory that any political order develops in freedom on the basis of natural communities, which are also the basis for authority and subor-dination and domination, we cannot assert that this is void of any truth content. The position which Locke represented had an incomparably greater political influence – though its consequences in the French Revo-lution may hardly have been what Locke intended. In Locke, freedom in the natural state is governed by the fact that even then the law of nature applies, and that as a being endowed with reason man is capable of discerning it at any time,[477] even if in practice there are always people who allow themselves to be guided by error or passions and therefore break the peace[478] of the natural state. For Locke it is a basic presup-position, which subsequent disciples are increasingly less ready to grant, that all men are God's creatures, at whose command and in whose service they are sent into the world and whose possession they remain.[479] Even if this belief contains a recognition of the mysteries of creation,[480] it is profoundly full of trust in the capacity of reason to recognize God's will completely.

Therefore reason is also the ultimate criterion for the exposition of scripture. This is also expressed clearly in the first treatise, in those passages in which Locke sometimes mentions 'Scripture and Reason',[481] and sometimes even 'Reason and Revelation'[482] as the decisive criteria for the correctness of an assertion (rejecting Filmer's theories). In his description of the 'natural state' in the second treatise Locke still puts forward the view that reason in the natural state at least generally has the capacity to recognize the law of nature, even if in reality the dis-ruptive exceptions of irrational conduct govern actual conditions. In *The Reasonableness* this optimism has disappeared, and the negative reality which is already a pressure in the treatise has gained the upper hand. Nevertheless, Locke does not give up his basic view that the will of God corresponds with reason. In theory, it also continues to be recognizable in the form of the law. In practice, at this point the law of God revealed in scripture tends to appear, and here Locke takes up the understanding already offered by the Puritan tradition. However, he does not take over the authoritarian biblicism of the Puritans: even the law communicated through the proclamation of Jesus is rational; it accords with the rules of reason and can be made plausible according to rational principles (including the rewards which are promised in return for its fulfilment). Locke is an acute observer of reality, who therefore increasingly contradicts his rationalistic presuppositions the more he progresses in his experience. Nevertheless, he cannot detach himself from them completely. His New Testament hermeneutics is twofold: the beginnings of historical thinking, which prove successful when he is dealing with the New Testament epistles, do not affect his evaluation of the Bible as a whole, since when it comes to the Gospels he does not go beyond the ideas of his time, which remain stuck in the timeless-normative thinking in the tradition of classical rationalism.[482a] As we shall see more clearly in due course,[483] as with many rationalist Anglicans, the Old Testament remains completely in the shade.

In his views of the tasks of state and church Locke remained much more faithful to his starting point than the usual interpretation has generally recognized. This is clear from a look at what is probably Locke's best-known 'unknown' writing, the *Epistola de Tolerantia*.[484] As early as 1957,[485] and again in 1966,[486] J.Ebbinghaus commendably attacked the 'cult of which this letter... has become the object', and fought against the impression 'that Locke is now finally condemned to the role of a pioneer on the way to religious tolerance.'[487] Particularly in the case of the *Letter on Tolerance*, interpreters have fallen victim in abundance to the temptation to read a large number of conceptions from the present into a document of the past. However, for all the acuteness with which Ebbinghaus brings out the obvious contradictions in the thought of the *Letter on Tolerance*, he in turn has succumbed to the danger of beginning from an abstract concept of man's right to conviction in this letter, which not only removes it from the circumstances in which it was written but in turn must make it seem incapable of reconciliation with any conceivable real conditions in which the church must exist in any state.[488] However, his criticism of Locke is helpful insofar as it clearly demonstrates the rationalistic basis of Locke's position and the perplexity of such rationalism in the face of any authentic claim to revelation in view of its imposition of boundaries between fundamentals which are allegedly necessary for salvation and indifferentia which are to be imposed by the state, even against the conviction of those affected that the external forms of worship are equally necessary for salvation. He thus warns us to put the *Letter on Tolerance* back in the context of Locke's work, and relate it to the conditions of the time.

The prehistory of the *Letter on Tolerance* is now also well known thanks to the publication of the *Two Tracts on Government* of 1660/61,[489] the *Essay concerning Toleration*,[490] written in 1667 and other texts from Locke's literary remains, and its real intention can now be understood in relation to these earlier works.[490a] Certain basic presuppositions have remained unchanged for Locke at all three stages: these include the distinction between inward fundamental convictions of faith, necessary for salvation, which are ultimately the individual's responsibility and on which no external pressure may be exercised, and external liturgical forms. Here the realm of morality is characteristically assigned to the sphere of inward convictions (which come about through rational knowledge), though it makes itself known in outward actions. Moreover, there is a particular view of the duty of the state to supervise the church, albeit limited to the sphere of its specific competence, and finally a special opinion on Catholics and atheists: these are refused toleration in principle, though it can be exercised towards sects. The obvious starting point here is the existence of a state church which even the ruler acknowledges: the idea of tolerance is developed from an Anglican position.[491] The decisive change in approach from Locke's views on the rights of the state in the years 1660/61 can already be noted in the Essay of 1667: religion now appears as a completely private affair. Private concerns include not only speculative views on the Trinity, hell-fire, transsubstantiation and the Antipodes,[492] but also 'the place, time, and manner of worshipping my God, because this is a thing wholly between God and me'.[493] The reason is a changed view of the church, which we already find in the two diary entries of 1661, 'Sacerdos' and 'Ecclesia':[494] there Locke understands the church as an association in which individuals compact to worship God together.[495] In principle this provides the right for a number of churches to exist. In these churches, apart from what reason teaches, the only binding liturgical forms are those which are made so by 'revealed law'; all the rest are based on the free agreement of church members and are only valid for the individual in so far as he is a voluntary member of the church concerned. Therefore neither the secular authority nor any other power can compel anyone to belong to a particular church. However, *de facto* Locke begins from the existence of a state church, since in the *Sacerdos* he still allows the secular authority, insofar as it is itself a member of the church, power of administration in the indifferentia 'for decency and order',[496] although he expressly comments here that the state is a purely secular society. In the *Essay concerning Toleration* this division of state and church is stressed even more strongly. In an insertion[497] in the final version of this essay, Locke again considers the matter of the indifferentia and now expressly stresses that the state also has no power of direction even in external forms of worship which are usually regarded as indifferent, as the individual is subjectively of the opinion that these particular forms which he uses are well-pleasing to God, even if of themselves they are completely indifferent. It is then the case in this subjective sense 'that in religious worship noething is indifferent.' This observation shows how near and yet how far Locke is from the Puritans: they held the view that, quite objectively, there are no indifferentia because God's will in scripture has regulated everything in a binding way – for Locke, on the other hand, everything ends up in complete subjectivism.[498] Now the reason for the difference in his view of the church also becomes clear: since Locke has taken over the consensus theory of more recent natural law for his understanding of the nature and task of the church, and accordingly describes the church as an assembly based on the free agreement of the people[499] (in so doing, at the same time he rejects the absolute authority of the king *jure divino*) – which is why he also limits the ruler's task closely to the preservation of the external existence, the possessions and the peace of his citizens[500] – he transfers the same conception to the church, which he now thinks came into being in a similar way by a kind of primal contract (and continues to come into being in the form of particular specific communities).[501] The individual, too, is always a member of a specific church only by virtue of his own free decision: 'No one is born a member of a church. Otherwise the religion of parents would pass over to their children by the same right of inheritance as their worldly goods...'[502] Of course it is easy to contrast this with reality: then as now, church membership was usually a consequence of birth;[503] at this point the remoteness of Locke's rationalism from reality becomes particularly clear. In the end Locke arrives almost at the same position as the Independents and the separatist Puritans in respect of the rights of the church to regulate its outward liturgical forms by its own will. Of course, in his case it is based on completely different presuppositions and ends up in an even more radical individualism, since here one can press the question to the point of asking how, in any such fundamentally free association of any particular number of individuals, these associations as a whole would be able to arrive at general rules which would be binding on its members over a longer period.[504]

This is also evident from the fact that in practice Locke in no way achieves the complete separation of state and church for which he strives. In the *Essay concerning Toleration* the focus on the interests of the state is abundantly clear: here Locke is above all concerned to demonstrate that tolerance can be granted to all sects as long as they do not become dangerous to the established state order by turning into a political party.[505] This aim is not only necessitated by what was probably a specific political purpose of the memorandum (as we may understand the Essay to be),[506] but is also the consequence of Locke's fundamental perspective. Despite his generalized argument, he still speaks as a citizen of England who belongs to the state church and who attempts to solve the religious and political problems of his country from that perspective.

If we read the *Epistola de Tolerantia* in the light of previous discussions in the seventeenth century and even in the age of Elizabeth I, we will find a repetition of the large number of themes which are endlessly discussed in them: the rights and wrongs of an episcopal constitution for the church;[507] the forms of worship, including rites and liturgical vestments;[508] indifferentia and the right of the state to order them. However, on all these points Locke adopts his characteristic position, which has been developed step by step since 1661; here the trend already broadly developed in the *Essay concerning Toleration* can still be recognized clearly (we have been able to note repeatedly this way of working, which is typical of Locke).[509] Locke has maintained his principles: separation of the tasks of church and state; the church as a voluntary assembly for the purpose of the common worship of God,[510] and the state as such a body for the preservation of earthly goods.[511] From this division there follows the duty of the state to tolerate religious communities, the inner speculative and practical (moral) convictions of its members, and whatever liturgical forms it may subjectively regard as well-pleasing to God, where they are not expressly ordained by God. Locke always sees a case of conflict only when religious convictions come into conflict with the common good, for the preservation of which the state is responsible. In the sphere of worship there is the famous example of Meliboeus, who believes subjectively that God requires him to offer a calf in his honour. In normal circumstances this is an indifferent action: no authority can prevent him from doing in the temple what he could also do at home at a normal festival. But if the cattle are decimated by a drought and the state has provisionally to forbid all slaughter of calves to guarantee more stock, Meliboeus may no longer offer his sacrifice unpunished.[512] In the sphere of morality, possible conflicts are even more easily conceivable; here, too, Locke attempts to mark out the rights of the state in respect of its tasks: it is responsible only for the earthly prosperity of society and may only order or forbid things which serve this end, whereas the private individual is responsible for the salvation of his soul and must do what he believes is pleasing to God and will secure his salvation.[513] If the state orders something which is against his conscience, he must leave it undone and accept the legal punishment. If the lawgiver believes that an ordinance is for the common good and his subjects believe the opposite, a dilemma arises which Locke leaves to the decision of God at the last judgment.[514] The final section, which deals with the toleration of churches (especially the Roman Catholic Church), atheists and sects, is governed only by the perspective of the consequences which follow from possible tolerance for the state and thus for the earthly good of its citizens. Thus tolerance which is otherwise to be extended in principle is refused to Catholics because they have obligations to a foreign ruler (the pope); and to atheists, because no human society is possible for them, since if one removes God as the guarantor of all oaths, society loses its basis.[515] By contrast, tolerance is commended towards the sects because they are only a danger to the state if they are suppressed by force, whereas granting tolerance to them would make an end to wars of faith and transform their adherents into faithful subjects.[516]

What role does the Bible play in the *Letter of Tolerance*? There is a comment in principle about the significance of scripture as *regula fidei* in the postscript to the letter in connection with the definition of heresy and schism.[517] According to Locke a religion is defined by its *regula fidei (et cultus divini)*. Not only are Islam and Christianity different religions because the Moslems have the Quran and Christians the Bible as their rule, but so too are Papism and Lutheranism, Johannine Christianity[518] and the Geneva Reformation, because Papists and Johannine Christians accept further traditions outside the Bible, which Lutherans and Reformed Christians recognize as the sole rule of faith. By contrast, heresy arises when a division comes about among those who accept only Holy Scripture as a rule, over doctrines which are not contained in explicit words of scripture.[519] That is the case both if a majority or a part of the church favoured by the authorities[520] excludes others, or if anyone separates himself from the church because particular doctrines are not publicly taught in it which Holy Scripture does not present in clear words. In both cases heretics deliberately and stubbornly commit an error in respect of fundamentals, since although they have established scripture alone as the foundation of faith, they regard other doctrines as fundamental which are not found in scripture. Here, too, it is no help if someone asserts that his doctrines are derived from Holy Scripture, since no one can seriously put forward such interpretations, even if they are supposed to be capable of reconciliation with the *regula fidei*, to be divinely inspired, and therefore as binding as scripture itself. Otherwise the person concerned would also have to recognize as binding the different contradictory doctrines of Lutherans, Calvinists, Remonstrants, and Anabaptists. Locke ends by observing that he can only wonder at the arrogance of those who thought they could communicate the things necessary for salvation more clearly than the Holy Spirit.[521] He deals with the problem of schism in a very similar way, defining it as a division in the church community over part of services or church order which is not necessary, i.e. not prescribed explicitly in scripture.[522] Anyone who denies nothing that is laid down explicitly in the words of holy scripture and does not bring about any division on the basis of things which are not explicitly mentioned in it cannot be called either a heretic or a schismatic.

These remarks correspond precisely with what Locke explicitly expounded as his basic attitude to the Bible in the *Reasonableness*. They can be taken as the briefest definition of the position which rational Anglicanism adopts towards Holy Scripture. It is striking that Locke thinks that he has taken over the doctrine of scripture expressly as a legacy of the Reformation: he also stresses the *sola scriptura* as the unexceptionable foundation, and it is particularly interesting that in this respect he explicitly mentions both Lutheran and Reformed as adherents of this doctrine. At the same time, however, the significance of this *sola scriptura* is twisted decisively if (as also happened in a way with the Puritans) the New Testament appears as the lawbook of Christ the lawgiver, from which one can derive the normative instructions for dogmas, liturgical forms and church order, while the literal sense is seen to provide abstract statements, valid for all times and needing no further interpretation. Locke's idea of tolerance is also shaped by the distinction between fundamentals (which can be demonstrated from scripture) and indifferentia (which cannot); he certainly does not have in mind a general toleration of any conceivable religious conviction, but clearly presupposes the rationalistic form of Christianity with a moral colouring as the norm, by broad-mindedly allowing a wide range of subjective convictions and their corresponding confessional expressions, from the episcopal structure of the state church to the Independents and Congregational Puritans, above all in respect of the interest of the state.[523] The *Epistola de Tolerantia* will inevitably be misunderstood without any consideration of the Latitudinarian understanding of the Bible. Hardly anywhere else does it become clearer to what degree the history of philosophy needs the history of biblical exegesis as a presupposition for understanding.

This is also true in a special sense of that section of the letter in which Locke comes to speak of the relevance of Old Testament statements for the politics of religion in his time. Here he is concerned particularly with the commandment in the law of Moses that idolaters are to be exterminated.[524] Against those who claim that this commandment is binding even in his day and that heathen in America and adherents of sects in Europe should be dealt with accordingly,[525] Locke denies that it binds Christians in any way. Here, as Ebbinghaus rightly points out,[526] he is attacking the viewpoint put forward by Cartwright in his controversy with Whitgift,[527] that even the Mosaic judicial laws continue to be valid. However, he does take a decisive step beyond the points made hitherto. While Locke does not want to do away with the traditional tripartite division of the Mosaic law into the moral, judicial and ceremonial law,[528] he says that it is insignificant in this context. For him, none of the law of Moses is valid for Christians any longer! He is led to this conclusion by applying his principle, that positive laws obligate only those to whom they are given,[529] to the Old Testament laws as well. The Law of Moses is addressed only to the people of whom it is said, 'Hear O Israel' (Deut.5.1; cf.4.1), or, as he significantly goes on to put it, the 'Jewish state'.[530] In what follows Locke explains his view with the comment that the Jewish state, in contrast to all other states, was constituted[531] as a theocracy, so that there was no difference there between church and state.[532] Therefore the laws among this people which related to the worship of an invisible God were civic laws and part of the political regime. Now there is no Christian state under the gospel. The countless cities and kingdoms which have gone over to Christian faith have kept their old forms of state and government, about which Christ did not say anything in his law. Therefore in a Christian state, too, no man can be forced to observe the faith prescribed by the authorities or be kept from practising an alien religion. In this respect, too, Locke's demand for tolerance follows logically from his basic principle of the separation of church and state, the separation of civil commandments which relate to the civic sphere from commandments of Christ which relate to the realm of morals. The conditions in Old Testament Israel cannot be a model for this in any way. Locke demonstrates this in a second argument,[533] by means of the fact that strangers within Israel and foreigners outside the land of Canaan were not forcibly compelled to observe the Mosaic faith. Granted, the Canaanites were to be rooted out of the promised land, but this was because God was king of the Jewish people in a special way, so that serving another God in his kingdom would have been high treason, *hujusmodi aperta defectio cum Jehovae imperio istis in terris plane politico*.[534]

Given the typological argument for the monarchy which had been prevalent hitherto, this argument is revolutionary. There is a precedent for it, as for the requirement of a strict separation betwen church and state, only in the attitude of the radical Separatist Puritans. In contrast to Henry Jacob, Robert Browne and others, however, in Locke there is no longer any mention of the Spiritualist form of typology, which looks to Christ in the light of the Old Testament. If he does not put this so radically and still allows the Mosaic law to stand in *The Reasonableness* as his expression of the 'works of the law' (though it is binding only by virtue of its agreement with the law of nature),[535] in practice he regards the Old Testament as finished with, as far as being part of the Christian Bible is concerned. Here, too, Locke is a consistent Erasmian. In this way he was decisively to predetermine the attitude of almost the whole of the Enlightenment period, and moreover of a number of Christian theologians down to the present.

The whole of Locke's scriptural exegesis is a further example of the way in which at this period exegesis is not done for its own sake but because of the normative validity of scripture for quite specific questions of political life or in the associated search for the foundations of social ethics which would serve as a criterion in current controversies over the form of state and society in England. In the *Epistola de Tolerantia*, as already in its earlier stages, the political aim is the hidden scarlet thread which runs through all the individual arguments and culminates in a commendation of the toleration of the sects, above all on grounds of political expedience. The considerations of scripture also contained in this letter serve the same purpose. In addition, in Locke's comments about the origin and validity of Christianity which are made most systematically in *The Reasonableness*, there is a systematic attempt to overcome the fundamental problem of religion which presented itself to Humanist rational thought as it was to be found in the tradition of the English church among Anglicans and Puritans, in different forms which nevertheless derived from a common beginning. With Locke the systematic thinker we find a particular clear expression of the dilemmas in which this kind of thinking inevitably became involved in view of the historical form of biblical revelation. The contradictions which many observers have noted in his system arise, not from his person, but from the contradictions inherent in the traditions which he takes up. Particularly in his principles of social ethics and ecclesiology, alongside his forward-looking approaches we can also find numerous elements which go back far into the past (the same could also be said of his epistemology, which has been usually celebrated as modern, because of its nominalistic presuppositions). In the case of Locke himself, much remains ambivalent because of the contradictions in his basic attitude, which in matters of religion was conservative. These then emerged in a more pronounced and one-sided way among the more radical spirits who followed him. This led to the vigorous controversies of which Locke had only a foretaste in the debate during the last years of his life.[536]

PART III

The Climax of Biblical Criticism in English Deism

1

The Beginning of the Deistic Debate

According to a phrase of E.Troeltsch's which has become famous, Deism is the 'Enlightenment philosophy of religion'.[1] Deism and Deist 'were originally self-designations of those who stood by the confession of natural religion (without always challenging the possibility of faith in revelation)'. It was 'the conviction of the Deists that there is a natural religion and that this precedes all religions of revelation... in it they saw contained the objective conditions of the good pleasure which God can take in men. They therefore declared that it was sufficient, and that to follow the precepts of natural religion, which together and individually had moral character, qualified a man for eternal salvation.' This definition by G.Gawlick[2] characterizes a movement which underwent a relatively closed development in the first half of the eighteenth century in England,[3] a fact which indicates that this was the country most conducive to the public dissemination of its standpoint. Here we should think not so much of the relatively great freedom for expressing opinions which had prevailed in England since the Glorious Revolution (in marked contrast to the strict censorship in authoritarian Catholic France). Even more important is the fact that the general cultural situation, which is evident from the Latitudinarian attitude of certain of the clergy and the church people who were moulded by their preaching, provided an appropriate breeding ground for the Deistic attitude. Deism was an extreme but by no means isolated phenomenon; even its orthodox opponents shared a series of its fundamental presuppositions. It was precisely that which made it so difficult to challenge the Deistic arguments successfully, though as a rule these were presented by mediocre thinkers and not with any brilliance. Some Deists apparently went only a little way beyond already familiar standpoints (in small steps, often arguing on adjacent territory and also differing among one another). That is evident from the purely external fact that a number of English Deists felt themselves to be Christian writers,[4] in contrast to the Libertines in France,[5] and this is indicated by the titles of their writings;

their attitude seems only gradually to become distinct from that of the Latitudinarians.

(a) Charles Blount

The first Deist to emerge with a series of publications after several decades of Puritan rule and the Restoration, during which we hear nothing of the existence of a Deistic movement in England,[6] is a resolute defender of the sufficiency of natural religion and a sceptic about belief in revelation. Here, apart from references to pagan religions which are made very much from the outside, the discussion is almost undisguisedly concerned with Christianity. Charles Blount,[7] who still largely appears as an isolated figure, is very reminiscent of the French Libertinists in his attitude;[8] otherwise, his direct link with Herbert of Cherbury is evident.[9]

It is hard to appreciate completely today the stir caused by one of Blount's first[10] publications, a translation with commentary of the two first books of the work of Philostratus on the ancient miracle-worker Apollonius of Tyana.[11] At that time, however, the enterprise of producing a new edition of the life of this Pythagorean social reformer, whose miracles had once been compared polemically by Hierocles in the fourth century with the miracles of Christ, was understood as an affront against Christianity. Above all, however, in his extensive notes, filled with a profusion of learned material from all areas of contemporary science and history, Blount had tucked away a series of concealed ironical and critical hints which for example put in question the miraculous birth of Christ,[12] or lashed out at Elisha, 'that hot angry Prophet, who cursed the poor little Children, and made them be destroyed with Bears, only for calling him Bald-pate, 2.Kings 2,23',[13] or enumerated the reasons against a mediation between God and man, which 'prevailed with many of the wisest of the Heathens'. Here, while on the surface the mediating function of the Catholic saints is being compared with the lower gods of ancient polytheism and 'our blessed Intercessor Christ Jesus' is clearly excepted, it is quite evident that the reasons against any mediation[14] apply quite generally and can convince not just 'the most wise and honest among the Heathens', whereas belief in a mediator is intended 'for the vulgar, who were subject to the Idolatry of their Priests... and swallow'd without chewing those pills of Faith, which were accommodated to the Sentiments of Mankind.'[15] From the 'Summary Account of the Deists Religion' in Blount's last work, the *Oracles of Reason*, it furthermore becomes clear that in fact he excludes mediation from his religion quite generally.[16] In other of Blount's writings, sarcastic criticism of biblical figures like David[17] is extended to various biblical stories as such, though he skilfully hides behind orthodox authors, as when in a letter to his friend Charles Gildon which is included in the *Oracles of Reason*,[18] he defends the work of the geologist Thomas Burnet, *Archaeologiae Philosophicae* (ET 1692), and in particular chapters VII and VIII,[19] in which the worthy natural scientist wrestles rationalistically with the biblical creation story.[20] Blount had found this explicable only by means of patristic allegory, and in the letter which he includes refers to similar doubts which occur in the writings of the profoundly speculative mystic and doctor Sir Thomas Browne.[21,22]

These more sporadic attacks on the Bible, especially the Old Testament, are supplemented by a thematic recapitulation of the rationalist and Spiritualist criticism of the cult and castigation of the priesthood in the pamphlet *Great is Diana of the Ephesians*.[23] Here Blount (using the slogan taken from Acts 19.28 as a title) concerns himself particularly with the origin of sacrifice, which in his view goes back to the self-interest of the priests, who introduced superstition, rites, ceremonies and above all sacrifices,[24] because they thought that they would get more out of common people by sacrifices and expiatory gifts than through their virtue and knowledge.[25] Here Blount is evidently continuing Herbert of Cherbury's criticism of religion.[26] He shares with him the view that in the beginning of its history, before the clergy introduced cultic religion, religion consisted in a purely rational form of worship on the part of all human beings (above all as presented by the ancient philosophers).[27] At the same time he thus provided a slogan for the whole of the Deistic and rationalistic debate which followed. On the whole he understands the term 'religion' only in this depraved sense.[28] In this writing, too, Blount is concerned *expressis verbis* only with pagan religion, but for all his caution he makes it evident that indirectly he here has the clergy of his own church in view.[29] In another passage[30] he says explicitly: 'The ancient Jews, and modern Christians, have many Rites and Ceremonies common with the Gentiles, which is more than our vulgar Divines do imagine.'

In connection with the Jews and ceremonies in the Old Testament, in Blount we have the first traces of another instructive example of the way in which Deism could take up the result of research in the history of religion, which to begin with was still contained within an orthodox framework: it is the thesis first developed by John Spencer,[31] who belonged to the Cambridge school, that (in contrast to the view widespread until that time,[32] that pagan philosophy and religion took over their truths directly or indirectly from the revelation to Moses) the origin of the religious institutions and ceremonies of the Old Testament are to be derived from Egyptian customs. His extensive investigation (1504pp. of text and several indexes), carried through with great learning, not only derives almost every individual cultic custom in the Old Testament from Egyptian models, but also provides a well-thought-out theological explanation for the development which is assumed to have taken place in this way. The most important aim of the Law of Moses which God gave his people was to counter the idolatry of the Israelites.[33] During their long stay in Egypt, the people of Israel had become so accustomed to Egyptian customs and serving Egyptian idols,[34] that God could only lead it from false religion to true religion by a burdensome ceremonial law.[35] Moreover, God intended certain customs as a sign of the exclusive relationship which his people was to have with him as their only God.[36] Now when the idolatrous ceremonies gained the upper hand and God resolved to restore the faith of the fathers in his people, he excluded idolatry and all rites opposed to faith and good morals from the law and the cult.[37] On the other hand, he took over many other customs which had become familiar through long practice, and which he regarded as tolerable or suitable for symbolic use; had he suddenly forbidden all previous rites, the Israelites would have immediately lapsed into paganism. So he was careful to dissuade them gently and gradually from pagan idols and ceremonies.[38]

A fleeting glance is enough to show that Spencer's background, with his concern for apologetic, is also to be found in a basically rationalistic attitude. He explicitly affirms that God could not possibly have taken delight in a cult which was established arbitrarily, with countless details of an external nature. *Absit, ut vel per somnia quis rem tam ridiculam cogitaret.*[39] With the aid of a brilliant idea, the whole learned construction simply serves to make sense of what by his own standards is absurd, by supposing that God has a pedagogical concern. The idea of education helped the Enlightenment – up to Lessing – to cope with the problem posed by historical phenomena to their basically static concept of reason. It is less well known that Lessing was by no means the first to have this idea, and that it can already be found in apologists of the seventeenth century like Spencer.

Spencer also presupposes a second prejudice in his system: in his works we keep finding the statement that in Egypt the Jews had been a 'rough' people, corrupted in Egypt and prone to idolatry.[40] The antisemitism taken over by the Humanists from the Middle Ages is the starting point for all his considerations. He could only make sense of the ceremonial law of this people – and thus rescue the Old Testament as Holy Scripture – by introducing the idea of condescension (*synkatabasis*)[41] as a theme of the divine legislation. With another aim in view, this antisemitism could easily turn into a rejection of the Old Testament itself in principle, and that is in fact the development which we can note among the later Deists.

Although Blount mentions no names, in two passages we can see that he is familiar with Spencer's theory of the Egyptian origin of Jewish customs: in the letter to Major A,[42] mentioned above, he states that

Abraham and Moses were 'well skill'd in Egyptian Learning' and recalls those (evidently Spencer and Marsham) who thought that Moses and the Jews had taken over various of their customs from the Egyptians.[43] Of course the accent is fundamentally different from that in Spencer, and it is no longer God, but Moses, who is called the lawgiver, and he is anything but honoured by the adoption of Egyptian customs. The link with Spencer is stronger in Blount's remark about the Egyptian origin of sacrifice in *Great is Diana*; here, in a reference to Theodoret, he observes that 'whereas the Aegyptians sacrificed either to Daemons or Idols, the Israelites through the Divine permission were allow'd to offer them to God'. He goes on to quote Jer.7.21 as evidence that God allowed the custom of sacrifices to himself so that the Israelites should not offer them to false gods, and moreover says that Moses had never ordained sacrifices, 'but by the way of tolerating them after the Israelites were come out of Aegypt'.[44] There follows the rationalistic explanation that the sacrifices were useful to the Israelites in Egypt not only for their bellies but also for their backs, since at that time garments were made out of animal skins! Similarly, in *Great is Diana* he supposes that sacrifices will also have spread from Egypt to Greece, Italy and to remoter areas.[45]

These are not the only themes in which Blount already prepares for the later Deistic debate. In his work the *Summary Account of the Deists Religion*,[46] mentioned above, we find a brief summary of what a Deist formulates as his creed. Much of this is familiar from Herbert and has a marked Stoic flavour: God as 'one Supream infinite and perfect Being',[47] worshipped not through images, sacrifices, mediator, but 'Positively, by an inviolable adherence in our lives to all the things *phusei dikaia*, by an imitation of God in all his imitable Perfections'.[48] God 'hath but one Affection or Property, and that is Love', so there is nothing fearful in his nature.[49] He created the world for the greatest good of his creatures: 'So our Religion must necessarily be this, to do good to his Creatures.'[50] Here, then, against the background of an optimistic view of God and the world, we find a self-understanding not too far removed from that of liberal Anglicanism, in which, as also among many Latitudinarians, religion almost amounts to moral action.[51] A definition of Deism as faith in the adequacy of natural religion without mankind in addition being directed towards a revelation (as understood by Gawlick),[52] is clearly expressed for the first time in the letter 'Of Natural Religion, as opposed to Divine Revelation',[53] also included in the *Oracles of Reason*. However, this does not come from Blount himself but from a correspondent denoted only by the initials 'A.W.'. This states quite clearly: 'Natural Religion is the Belief we have of an eternal intellectual Being, and of the Duty which we owe him, manifested to us by our Reason, without Revelation or positive Law.'[54] The seven points for the main tenets of this natural religion which follow (the existence of the infinite eternal God as the Creator who directs the world by his providence; our duty to revere him in praise and prayer; 'That our Obedience consists in the Rules of Right, the Practise whereof is Moral Virtue'; reward and punishment after this life; penitence after error, with trust in God's forgiveness) are largely reminiscent of Herbert, though he never spoke out so clearly against any need for revelation. It is no coincidence that Leland prized this letter particularly highly. It is striking that hardly any of the English Deists in the hey-day of this school distinguished themselves so clearly from a religion of revelation; they all began from the existence of Christianity as a given fact and sought to reconcile its characteristics, and in particular its relationship to the Bible as the basis of Protestant belief, with their rational, anti-sacral moralistic views. Remarkably, to some degree the Deists have one basic feature of their apologetic in common with their orthodox opponents. Both groups, albeit in different ways, are heirs of the liberal Anglicanism of the seventeenth century; thus vigorously though they may have carried on their controversies, these were for the most part a dispute within a rational Christianity, which was to be concerned more with the extent of the critical conclusions to be drawn from the premises held in common and with a consistent application of them than with justifying them; the basis for the premises was to be put in question only much later, and from a very different direction.

(b) John Toland

The continuity with this tradition emerges immediately in the first significant work of the second main period of Deism, the beginning of which is marked by John Toland's *Christianity not Mysterious*.[55] L.Stephen and, following him, E.C.Mossner[56] have divided Deism into a 'constructive' and a 'critical' phase, the division between which is marked by Locke and the adoption of him by the Deists.[57] In fact it is the deliberate reference to Locke, whose admirer Toland already unmistakably[58] shows himself to be here (to Locke's immediate distaste),[59] which is unmistakable in this early work by Toland.[60] The epistemological investigation which opens the book,[61] in which Toland is concerned with the role of reason for human knowledge, is largely oriented on Locke's *Essay concerning Human Understanding*. 'However, Toland drew conclusions from Locke's premises which Locke either did not draw or did not express openly.'[62] Moreover, it is important that although Toland only published his work a year after the appearance of the *Reasonableness* (1695), he took no notice of the change in Locke's views[63] which had become clear in this work,[63a] but picked up the threads of the Essay where Locke had let them lie, having come to doubt the possibilities of reason. Though this represents a decisive new step, the proximity of Toland in his early work to Locke is an important fact, which saves *Christianity not Mysterious* from being wrongly estimated merely as a book which is directed against Christianity. G.Gawlick's comment should be noted here: 'In *Christianity not Mysterious* Toland presupposed the truth of the Christian revelation instead of questioning it or even denying it.'[64] The apologetic concern of which I spoke is evident: Toland's work is meant seriously as a defence of Christianity, albeit as a defence before the forum of reason, which is now no longer just one authority among others but the absolute standard before which Christian doctrine, too, must justify itself. 'Whereas Locke was content to show that Christianity is reasonable, Toland proved that nothing contrary to reason and nothing above it can be a part of Christian doctrine.'[65] The basis of his definition of evidence is provided by a definition of reason and its functions for human knowledge which is taken from Locke even down to points of detail (the distinction between the receiving of ideas in the spirit through the impressions of the senses and reflection by the soul on its own patterns of thought,[66] the description of its activity as 'perceive the Agreement or Disagreement of any Ideas' and the theory of the 'intermediate ideas' and the definition of reason which follows from this as 'That Faculty of the Soul which discovers the Certainty of any thing dubious or obscure, by comparing it with something evidently known',[67] and also the distinction between primary and secondary properties,[68] accurately reflects the epistemology of the Master, which Toland extensively repristinates). He describes this evidence as 'the exact Conformity of our Ideas or Thoughts with their Objects, or the Things we think upon'.[69] From here his next step is the use of reason as a critical standard of judgment about all things: 'what is evidently repugnant to clear and distinct Idea's, or to our common Notions, is contrary to Reason.'[70] However – and this should not be overlooked – the last important component for his assertion that there is nothing mysterious in Christianity is the distinction between real and nominal being, which Toland also takes over from Locke: in this respect he is quite ready to concede the limitations of human knowledge: 'As we know not all the Properties of things, so we can never conceive the Essence of any Substance in the World.'[71] Now these limits are divinely willed: 'because knowing nothing of Bodies but their Properties, God has wisely provided we should understand no more of these than are useful and necessary for us.'[72] However, it is precisely this knowledge which opens up the possibility of the claim that nothing in religion can be a mystery if it is the case 'That nothing can be said to be a Mystery, because we have not an adequate Idea of it, or a distinct View of all its Properties at once; for then every thing would be a Mystery.'[73] This is followed by the trivial statement which in fact reflects all the epistemological optimism of the Enlightenment, that people can begin by assuming that human education and knowledge can constantly progress: 'The Knowledge of finite Creatures is gradually progressive, as Objects are presented to the Understanding.' The limits of knowledge mentioned here are no hindrance to this: man need not worry about what is useless or impossible to know,[74] while on the other hand it is the case that : 'It is improper therefore to say a thing is above our Reason, because we know no more of it than concerns us.'[75]

When applied to the Christian religion, these epistemological considerations give rise to two conclusions: 1. 'That no Christian Doctrine, no more than any ordinary Piece of Nature, can be reputed a Mystery, because we have not an adequate compleat Idea of whatever belongs to it.' 2. 'That what is reveal'd in Religion, as it is most useful and necessary, so it must and may be as easily comprehended.'[76] With this theory that the fundamental elements in religion are easy to understand, Toland is again very close indeed to Locke, and it is almost an echo of his considerations when in the Foreword he comes to speak of 'the Vulgar', who could equally be judges of the meaning of things, and refers to the poor who, without being expected to understand anything about philosophical systems, 'soon apprehended the Difference between the plain convincing Instructions of Christ, and the intricate ineffectual Declamations of the Scribes'.[77] When in his Foreword Toland dissociates himself from patristic and scholastic theology,[78] and instead of this refers to the 'concepts and doctrines of the Gospel',[79] and the 'clear convincing instructions of Christ', he is precisely following the line of the Humanist tradition in the English church. His explanation that 'In the following Discourse... the Divinity of the New Testament is taken for granted'[80] is therefore not at all surprising, and when he announces as the aim of the third part of his work which was originally planned in three parts (though only the first part appeared), 'And in the third, I demonstrate the Verity of Divine Revelation against Atheists and all Enemies of reveal'd religion,'[81] his attitude is completely consistent in this context.

In that case, is *Christianity not Mysterious* a Deistic work at all? Is it, as was generally assumed at an earlier stage,[82] a main work of Deism? G.Gawlick first had considerable reservations about this view.[83] However, the disagreement vanishes if we follow Gawlick[84] in distinguishing two different trends within Deism, of which the less radical, which 'with diminishing exceptions is characteristic of English Deism',[85] while beginning from a doctrine of God oriented on Stoicism and the natural law, nevertheless leaves open the question of recognizing a religion of revelation.[85a] But it is also characteristic of this kind of Deism that it measures revelation throughout by critical reason, and a static morality and an equally static supranaturalist concept of God provide the standard. 'Religion is always the same, like God its Author, with whom there is no Variableness, nor Shadow of changing', Toland explains in the preface to *Christianity*;[86] hence the guiding thread of his investigation, 'that the true Religion must necessarily be reasonable and intelligible'.[87]

The decisive difference in methodological approach between the critical Deists and the rational supranaturalist trend in liberal Anglicanism which preceded them thus arises from a difference in perspective. The Latitudinarians, too, distinguish between the ethical commandments of the Christian religion which correspond with the natural law on the one hand and external liturgical forms (ceremonies) on the other. In the sphere of dogmatics, from the rationalist point of view they remained at a half-way stage, in that they continued to require the recognition of a few statements as fundamentals necessary for salvation, but pushed to one side the question of the reasonableness and general comprehensibility of the other statements contained in the Bible. In the sphere of ceremonies their position was even more unsatisfactory, in that they regarded these as a matter of indifferentia and quite inessential for faith, thus ruling out *a priori* a discussion of their content. Here the Puritans with their radical requirements about ceremonies were more consistent. The critical Deists were much more the heirs of the Puritans. Despite a different epistemological starting point for their criticism, they had more in common with the Puritans than is usually acknowledged: in their moralism and antipathy to the cult they proved to be stepbrothers from the same household, the wider sphere of Humanism. This also becomes clear from the fact that the world-view presupposed by the most varied trends undermining the same heritage, not least among them the English Deists, is a Stoic system brought up to date.[88] However, for the Puritans the Bible as such was a given authority in the sense of the Humanist cry, taken up by the Reformation, 'Back to the sources!' Methodologically they were unaware that they were reading it through moralistic, anti-ceremonial spectacles. In Toland's *Christianity not Mysterious*,[89] we can see how the critical period of Deism, trained in Locke's epistemology, now reflects these presuppositions.

Toland expresses his presuppositions clearly:'...we hold that Reason is the only Foundation of all Certitude; and that nothing reveal'd, whether as to its Manner or Existence, is more exempted from its Disquisitions, than the ordinary Phenomena of Nature.'[90] The basis for any conviction is rational judgment. Of course the authority of God in the form of divine revelation has its place, but only as a 'means of information' alongside the moral certainty which can be claimed by a trustworthy human testimony which is either direct or mediated by unbroken tradition.[91] But, 'I believe nothing purely upon his word without Evidence in the things themselves.' This evidence consists in

the 'clear conception I form of what he says'.[92] Here we should think
of the definition of evidence quoted above,[93] which corresponds to
Locke's system. Even revelation has to prove itself before this court. Of
course Toland to some degree already anticipates the result by already
declaring in the Foreword: 'Scripture or Reason... I'm sure, agree very
well together';[94] in another passage he justifies this from his understanding of God: 'The Authority of God, or Divine Revelation, is the Manifestation of Truth by Truth itself, to whom it is impossible to lie.'[95] In
this passage an attentive observer will register the critical point at which
the two different systems of thought clash: the supranaturalistic view
of the world with a Stoic stamp in which the entity 'God' (even if
understood in more personal terms than with the Epicureans)[96] occupies
a place which has already been established *a priori*, and the alleged
openness of reason as it makes a methodical test. When faced with a
revelation, reason must also remind people of the qualification 'that
God should lose his end in speaking to them, if what he said did not
agree with their common Notions'.[97] A decisive weakness in the Enlightenment position is that the *a priori* given by their world picture
remains.[97a] Another lies in the rigidity of the epistemological scheme,
according to which even God's action must accord with the conditions
of what is conceivable within the framework of the common notions
(or, according to Locke's system, 'usual ideas'): 'When we say then,
that nothing is impossible with God, or that he can do all things, we
mean whatever is possible in it self, however far above the Power of
Creatures to effect.'[98]

In this context Toland also goes on to speak about the significance of
faith. 'All Faith or Perswasion must necessarily consist of two Parts,
Knowledg and Assent.'[99] In the light of the rationalist presuppositions
of Deism, here faith too is intellectualized; it is a form of knowledge
which must be supported by reasons.[100] Faith is distinguished from
knowledge only by the form of the information: it is not direct knowledge, but an understanding which is arrived at by reflection on its
object, which is communicated through revelation.[101]

Miracle, too, is assigned its place in the same context. Gawlick stresses
that Toland 'does not indicate the slightest doubt in the miracles of
Jesus as proofs of his divine mission'.[102] That is possible because he also
rationalizes them. According to Toland a miracle cannot be contrary to
reason;[103] therefore miracles which are contradictory in themselves and
serve no clear higher purposes, and which cannot be performed in
public, cannot be recognized as such.[104] A miracle occurs when it transcends all human capacities, and when the normal laws of nature could
not bring it about.[105] It may not be impossible according to the criteria
of reason. So as miracles are thus possible, the miracles attested in the

New Testament are a prominent support for the divinity of the message of Christ.[106]

Generally speaking, however, Toland does not spend a great deal of time on miracles, but resolutely goes on to demonstrate the aim already mentioned in the title of the second main section of his work, 'That the Doctrines of the Gospel are not contrary to Reason',[107] with an argument from the method and style of the New Testament. Here he is guided by the presupposition that 'all the Doctrines and Precepts of the New Testament... must consequently agree with Natural Reason, and our own ordinary Idea's'.[108] This produces an important hermeneutical principle: the only rules which can apply to the interpretation of scripture are those which apply to all other, purely secular literature.[109] The significance of this statement for the history of interpretation must be stressed strongly, although Toland does not really carry it through himself. He is content, as a consequence, to stress the simple, natural style of the gospel[110] and to indicate that the aim of the apostolic message is 'Piety towards God, and the Peace of Mankind'.[111] The chapter in which Toland discusses the theory that human reason is too corrupt as a result of original sin to be able to recognize the truths of the gospel[112] sheds a good deal of light on the theological background to his thought. Reason as a capacity[113] is given with humanity itself. Man may not use it, and be led astray by error and false passions, but that is not his inescapable doom. 'We lie under no necessary Fate of sinning.'[114] Rather, it is up to man whether or not he uses his reason. So we are called to account if we do not keep God's commandments. "tis the perfection of our Reason and Liberty that makes us deserve Rewards and Punishments.'[115] In the face of the general proneness towards evil, which Toland does not ignore, he commends to everyone his own striving to free himself from uncertainty: 'We should labour to acquire Knowledge with more confident Hopes of Success.'[116] In this passage we can see how closely the answer to the epistemological problem in Enlightenment theology is bound up with the legalistic approach of humanistic ethics. Here, too, Toland is so 'modern' because he clearly states already existing tendencies and thus anticipates much that is often repeated by later representatives of the Enlightenment. At the same time we can clearly see the central opposition to the Reformation doctrine of justification.

In the third and longest part of his book, Toland carries through the main aim of his investigation, to demonstrate that there is nothing mysterious or beyond reason in the Gospel. In this part we once again come across much from the well-known arsenal of the Humanist tradition.[117] Toland is original in combining these notions with a concept of reason shaped by Locke. According to Toland, by 'mystery' we are to understand two sorts of thing: 1. Things which are comprehensible in themselves but are so concealed by images, types and ceremonies that this veil must be removed before reason can penetrate to them. 2. Things which are incomprehensible of their own nature, however clearly they may be revealed.[118] In contrast to ancient paganism, in which the 'cunning priests'[119] disguised religion with ceremonies, sacrifices and rites[120] – as usual the criticism of the priesthood is predominantly directed against paganism – in the gospel there are no mysteries,[121] since in the New Testament only those things are called mystery which previously were concealed and have now been made generally known by revelation. They include above all the gospel itself, certain special doctrines (the calling of the Gentiles, the resurrection and so on), and finally what is told in parables, which was only mysterious for those to whom it was not explained.[122] Thus there are 'mysteries' in the gospel only in the first sense; that is, they are really no longer mysteries, since they were only mysterious until revelation unveiled them. In the second sense they cannot be the object of revelation, for their nature consists in the fact that they accord with reason, i.e. with common notions.

If only we allow reason a role in the interpretation of scripture, from the veils which the word 'mystery' at first seems to cast over revelation in the New Testament there emerges a pure, rational gospel. Toland finds this gospel in the message of Jesus understood completely according to Humanist and Puritan ideals: '...he fully and clearly preach'd the purest Morals, he taught that reasonable Worship... which were more obscurely signifi'd or design'd by the Legal Observations. So having stripp'd the Truth of all those external Types and Ceremonies which made it difficult before, he rendred it easy and obvious to the meanest Capacities.'[123]

Unfortunately things did not stay like that in the post-apostolic period. In the last chapter of his book,[124] Toland gives a survey of the history of the corruption of Christianity which is modelled on the theory of depravation, typical of the Spiritualists. While Jewish Christianity is thought to be little at fault in this development,[125] the penetration of paganism into the church is said to be the chief culprit in it. Philosophers, emperors and the clergy were mostly to blame for this takeover of an alien ideology into Christianity. The mysteries added to the two simple sacraments of baptism and the eucharist clearly had pagan characteristics. These newly introduced mysteries in particular contributed to this development. At this point Toland now expresses quite openly his conviction that 'so divine an Institution [as Christianity] did, through the Craft and Ambition of Priests and Philosophers, degenerate into mere Paganism.'[126] At the end of his investigation he stresses emphatically once again that 'priestcraft' is the real cause of the corruption in the church,[127] and in this connection he thinks that he can appeal to the Reformers Luther, Calvin and Zwingli.

Christianity not Mysterious is not just chronologically the beginning of the Deistic debate. In this small book we also find an almost complete presentation of the most important themes which are discussed again and again in this debate. Above all, however, Toland gives voice to all presuppositions and basic judgments which the Deists subsequently used as established criteria for their verdicts on the Bible and the church, for all their individual differences. Among Toland's successors we often find a concern with particular problems and also often extensive remarks which are merely criticism of the existing situation. In various points this criticism will also incorporate the themes which, like the problem of miracle, were treated by Toland in a more restrained way or were not seen as problems at all. Here, however, it is simply a matter of a gradual progress along a way which is already firmly marked out. The basic presuppositions remain unaltered: rationalism, belief in an autonomous morality (which is also independent of revelation and already prior to it) and the criticism of all external forms of religion, adopted as part of the Spiritualist heritage.

Toland himself made a further significant contribution to these themes. His *Letters to Serena* are particularly important in this connection.[128] The first three letters,[129] addressed to Queen Sophie Charlotte of Prussia,[130] discuss classical themes of the Enlightenment like the origin and power of prejudice (Letter I[131]), the history of belief in immortality (Letter II[132]) and the emergence of idolatry (Letter III[133]). Toland himself was personally of the opinion[134] that the first letter was not only a kind of preface to the letters in the collection but so to speak a key to all the rest of his works. In this letter he is concerned to show that a normal member of human society is so stuffed full of prejudices by his education, from the nursery to the university,[135] and above all, too, by the world view and customs of the society in which he lives, that severe disciplining of the reason is needed for him to free himself from them. The men of the Enlightenment suspect matured, inherited views, like everything that has been handed down through history, including all external authority. Their ideal is the free man who constantly disciplines his reason, 'giving law to his own actions as a free and reasonable man'.[136] The consistent implementation of this programme inevitably brought about a different relationship to the biblical revelation from that which had been largely current up to the time of Locke: the fact that in Toland's *Christianity not Mysterious* revelation continues to appear only as a means of information[137] represents the decisive step towards autonomy on the part of the man who no longer means to follow God-given ordinances but proposes to take on himself the law of his actions.

However, in practice this theoretically free man of the Enlightenment was by no means the *tabula rasa* depicted by Toland and his successors in this context. For they too followed a pre-existing system, though they deliberately reflected its content less than the generation preceding them, whose starting point was still natural law. This is the remarkable reverse effect which grew out of post-Lockean epistemology, in presupposing that certain things were a matter of course and were immediately evident to common sense. Locke himself, as we have seen, was very much aware of the problems arising here, but his successors no longer took them into account. Despite Toland's protest in his first letter to Serena, the pre-critical model of thought was in no way superseded by Locke's contradictory epistemology. Natural religion continued to be the presupposition – and in this way the system of natural law was continued in the changed form arrived at by Locke, though still in continuity with the earlier form. This was the ideal to be restored (and conversely, the source of the theory of depravation). For apologetic reasons, revealed religion was made to coincide with it, or it was applied as a critical criterion to the Bible and the church either in matters of individual detail or as a whole.

The second and third letters of Toland to Serena are an interesting example of this; they have been called a 'natural history of religion' in outline.[138] Spencer's influence can again be seen in the argument in the second letter, derived from ancient sources, that the doctrine of the immortality of the soul and kindred doctrines like those of heaven and hell had been invented by the Egyptians ('the Fountains of Learning to all the East, the Authors of the Chaldaean and Greek Religions'[139]); that they had done this without divine revelation, but rather on the basis of their funeral rites,[140] is a further – and extraordinarily clear-sighted – natural explanation. From there, Toland argues, these doctrines had spread to the other pagan religions, including those of the Greeks and the Romans. Toland also goes on to introduce all those witnesses who spoke out against the immortality of the soul, and accepts their reasons. Should we in that case take seriously the assertions which are occasionally thrown in, that the Christian revelation can nevertheless provide an assurance of immortality?[141] Gawlick[142] argues emphatically to this effect. His judgment is probably correct, in which case we would again be on the track of one of those hidden breaks in logic which allows Toland (and other Christian Deists) to presuppose the authority of revelation while asserting on the other hand that at all events its content must be capable of reconciliation with the standards of human reason ('not mysterious').[143] Their practical attitude of faith is rather different from that suggested by Toland's theoretical definition of the concept of 'faith'.[144] The fact that revelation is given *a priori* is the real reason for their approach, which is essentially that of subsequent apologetic.

Even more typical of Deistic argumentation is the third letter, in which Toland gives an account of the origin of ancient polytheism, its superstitious cultic customs and its credulous conceptions of the world and the beyond. Here too the theory of depravation predominates, with belief in a pure primal religion, without idolatry or stereotyped cultus, of the kind which Toland presupposes among the earliest Egyptians, Persians, Romans and the first Hebrew patriarchs, 'the plain Easiness of their Religion being most agreeable to the Simplicity of the Divine Nature.'[145] In contrasting the superstitious and idolatrous forms of ancient and modern pagan religion with this ideal, Toland is not driven by a neutral phenomenological interest in religion. It is more than a guess that he is not really so much concerned with paganism, but that his criticism is in fact directed towards Christianity.[146] This is demonstrated by the concluding section, in which Toland points out 'that almost every Point of those superstitious and idolatrous Religions are in these or grosser Circumstances reviv'd by many Christians in our Western Parts of the World, and by all the Oriental Sects',[147] and the attached list of ceremonies could come from a fiery Puritanical sermon. Toland does not write for the sake of writing; in no way, he explicitly observes, is 'the gratifying of mens Curiosity a sufficient Recommendation to any Disquisitions, without some general Instruction naturally conducing to Wisdom or Virtue.'[148]

Toland expressed his views about what Christianity should be and what he also thought that it had originally been in other books. In this connection his writing *Nazarenus* is particularly important.[149] In the first part of this work Toland is concerned to demonstrate not only – as is generally known – that there were two groups in earliest Christianity, Jewish Christians and Gentile Christians, but that both would have the right to exist side by side in the present, had not those who went over to Christianity from paganism falsified it by countless pagan ceremonies and contradictory doctrines. Indeed, the Jewish Christians (who had originally called themselves 'Nazarenes',[150] as Toland indicates in the title of his work, though he is also familiar with the designation 'Ebionites') really come much closer to the ideal of Christian life; and by remaining faithful to the Law of Moses had never detached themselves from their own origins. The Jewish Christians were wrongly suspected by their fellow believers from the Gentile world, excluded from the community and in the end completely suppressed.[151] In this respect, Toland believes that they could serve as the model for the restoration of the original pure church which inspired him in his task of reform. He puts this clearly in the preface to *Nazarenus*; there is virtually no passage in which the Spiritualist legacy of the Enlightenment emerges more clearly than here: 'Now, this Gospel consists not in words but in virtue: 'tis inward and spiritual, abstracted from all formal and outward performances: for the most exact observation of externals, may be with-out one grain of religion. All this is mechanically done by the help of a little book-craft, whereas true religion is inward life and spirit.'[152] Moralism is closely connected with Spiritualism.[153] Referring to the 'Apostolic Decree' (Acts 15.19f.),[154] Toland first explains that only the Noachite commandments were binding on Gentile Christianity, whereas Jewish Christians had to observe the whole of the law of Moses (including the ceremonial law!). Now this is valid for them only because it is a national law, expressing the Jewish identity which derives from Moses.[155] Common to all mankind (in addition to faith, which is valid for all Christians[156]) is the obligation of the moral law, for which 'sound Reason, or the light of common sense' is the criterion.[157] That is what holds all of society together, quite independently of whether or not there is a revelation, and it is confirmed by the most contrasting revel-ations and human groupings. Now the Jews provided the best presup-position for the restoration of a moral law, for the original Mosaic law came very close to this, and even though it had been corrupted for the Jews by their own priesthood, Jesus' own purpose was none other than to restore it in its original purity.[158]

Nazarenus contains yet other arguments in which we can also see something of the polyhistorical interest of its author: thus alongside the reference to a lost Ebionite Gospel 'of the Hebrews', attested by quo-tations in the church fathers,[159] there is an account of an apocryphal Gospel of Barnabas, a copy of which he himself found in Amsterdam,[160] and which he believed to be the original gospel of the Moslems.[161] Here too we find a theological concern in that Toland wants to accord Islam, as one of the heirs of earliest Christian thought, a place as an embodi-ment of the universal rational and moral religion, thus denying church Christianity its claim to exclusiveness.[162] An appendix[163] claims (again through the discovery of a book) that originally pure Christianity lasted several centuries longer in Ireland than elsewhere, and further append-ices are concerned with the 'Mohammedan' Gospel of Barnabas, with Mohammedans generally (Christians living in their countries are to ask them about the details of their religion), and with the special fate of the Jews. In a few pages this pamphlet[164] offers interesting evidence of the fascination which Judaism exercised on Toland all his life.[165] Two prob-lems concerned him: 1. how the Jews could have maintained their religious and national characteristics from the end of their statehood to the present, since the great empires of antiquity had long since passed away, and 2. why during the time that they existed as an independent state they were constantly inclined toward idolatry, whereas since then they had not only stubbornly preserved their characteristics, but had also firmly rejected any form of idolatry. Toland seeks the reason for this in the predominant character of the Mosaic law in its original form and the quality of the statehood ordained by this law in its initial purity, which far surpassed the work of ancient lawgivers like Solon, Lycurgus and so on. Even if he did not carry out his intention, announced on numerous occasions,[166] to write a separate work on the *Respublica Mosaica*, it is clear that for him ideal Judaism is an embodiment of purely rational religion.[167] He therefore thinks that if the Jews, who in his day are more numerous than, say, the Spanish or the French, were to settle again in Palestine, 'which is not at all impossible', because of their ideal constitution they would be more powerful than any other people in the world. 'I would have you consider, whether it be not both the interest and duty of Christians to assist them in regaining their country.'[168] Toland also expressed his inclination towards Judaism in other writings, as in his *Reasons for Naturalizing the Jews in Great Britain and Ireland* (1714),[169] in the *Origines Judaicae*, printed as an appendix in *Adeisidaemon*(1709).[170] The themes of both works are closely connected: they deal with superstition, *Adeisidaemon* being devoted to proving that when Livy reports miracles and signs at length in his account of Roman history he simply wanted to note them as a conscientious historian of everything worth knowing, but did not in any way believe in such things.[171] Motzo Dentice[172] points out that here for the first time, in contrast to his account of the detrimental effect of superstition on state and society,[173] Toland depicts the atheist as a citizen serving the common good, even though he does not fear God's vengeance on crime and the flames of hell, and is restrained not by holy reverence for oaths, but only by civic respect for promises given.[174] By contrast, Locke still withheld tolerance completely from atheists and papists. In *Origines Judaicae*, Toland is polemical against the *Demonstratio evangelica* (1679) of the famous Catholic apologist P.D.Huet. Huet cites the ancient geographer Strabo; Toland responds by quoting verbatim, at length, an account by Strabo on his journey to Palestine and the Jews, in order to clear earliest Jewish religion of the charge of superstition (this is analogous to the theory which he later puts forward in the *Nazarenus*). He also does this to establish that Strabo's report agrees with the Pentateuch in demonstrating that Moses founded a monotheism free from superstition and any cultic rites, based only on the ten commandments, which correspond to the laws of nature.[175] He explains the sacrifice and ceremonies which occur in the Old Testament, with a reference to Ezek.20.24f., as the consequence of commandments which God gave the Jews later as a punishment, because of their proneness to idolatry.[176] Here we find the beginnings of a criticism of the Bible, though at the same time we can see how much this is twisted to confirm a preconceived judgment. Anyone who feels this to be a curiosity from the distant past might well consider whether the pattern of the history of

Israelite religion in J.Wellhausen's *Prolegomena to the History of Israel* is not still based on the same model.

His love of the Jews makes Toland an exception among the Deists, and his special position has often been assessed accordingly.[177] However, on closer inspection the fact that he seems to be so individualistic in his predilection is merely the consequence of the way in which literature about Deism isolates this movement from its historical background and its setting. Conversely, Toland's favourable attitude towards the Jews is one of the clearest signs of the relatively close connection between this early Deist and certain trends deriving from Puritanism, which had an influence long beyond the end of the century, even in orthodox Anglican circles. We can find a close parallel to Toland's basic ideas as expressed in *Nazarenus* in the extensive work by Theophilus Gale, *The Court of the Gentiles*.[178] Here, with vast use of literary evidence from Josephus and the early church fathers to modern orientalists like Isaac Vossius and John Selden, it is argued that the wisest philosophers among the Gentiles derived their knowledge from Holy Scripture. In the third volume of this work, which appeared in 1675 with the sub-title *The Vanity of Pagan Philosophy*, the depravation theory is applied to the history of the church in a variant form. Pagan religion and philosophy (which are identical) are nothing but a corruption of Judaism, and in the sphere of the church Popery has preserved the most abominable practices of the idolatrous ancient world. Only the Jewish revelation in its original form (in the later distortion contained in the Kabbalah it had been corrupted by Pythagoreanism) is to be associated with Puritan Protestantism. We can see to what extent such a view was still normative in influential circles even within Anglicanism down to the eighteenth century from the equally extensive labours of Newton on the Old Testament: Genesis he understood as a historical work providing a chronology for the history of the world, the only reliable authority for which he believed to be the tradition of Old Testament Israel.[179] The volte-face followed with the later Deists, who now resolutely fought against this authority.

Among the four writings collected together in *Tetradymus* (1720), the first, *Hodegus*, which is concerned with the pillars of cloud and fire which guided the Israelites through the wilderness, is of special significance for the history of the interpretation of the Old Testament.[180] Here Toland is one of the first exegetes[181] to explain a miraculous process reported in the Old Testament in quite radical terms by assuming that it was quite a natural event: a beacon which was carried before the people on their journey through the wilderness in a container and which by day directed them with its cloud of smoke and by night with its glowing fire.[182] His aim with these interpretations – this is the only one that he carried through – was to rescue the Pentateuch, and Moses as its author, as he says,[183] from superstitious interpretations on the one hand and from rejection as being fictitious on the other. 'The discoveries I made of this sort created in me a higher veneration for Moses, than even was instill'd by my instructors, and on better grounds.' As we can see, this purpose is closely connected with his general argument that the original religion of Moses was a particularly pure expression of a religion free from superstition and cult which corresponded with the law of nature. It indicates the direction in which the biblical criticism of the Enlightenment was to go on developing, though Toland's idealization of the Old Testament tended not to be followed; the Old Testament was assessed in negative terms. Furthermore, it should be noted that Toland treats the miraculous narratives in the Old Testament in quite a different way from the miracle stories of the New Testament: his supernaturalism is limited to the key statements of the New Testament (so that he finds the miracles of Jesus quite credible), whereas he wants to understand the Old Testament in as natural terms as possible.[184]

He similarly approaches the canon of the New Testament with a critical eye, as is evident[185] above all in his *Amyntor*.[186] Here he gives an extensive list of apocryphal writings ascribed to Christ and his apostles which are mentioned in a wide variety of church fathers or other extant writings,[187] and were not incorporated into the New Testament when the canon was formed. He does this in connection with the challenge to the authenticity of the book *Eikon Basilike*, attributed to the executed King Charles I, which had already been made in *The Life of John Milton*: we can see how this theme still had a burning topicality for the Whigs, of whom Toland was a passionate supporter, in the time of the Jacobites.[188] Not content with this, however, Toland goes on to raise the question why in that case the writings of the Apostolic Fathers (like the letters of Barnabas and Clement) were not incorporated into the canon, when by contrast pieces now in the New Testament, like II Peter, James and Jude, were not generally recognized until the time of Eusebius.[189] He repudiates the charge that he is now rejecting writings in the New Testament as suspect, but on the other hand expresses the suspicion that there could be another series of writings kept out of the canon (above all further gospels, for which the number four is by no means essential), which are to be accorded the same authenticity as those which are now included.[190] Toland is not satisfied with the authority of Eusebius, to which his opponents refer, since Eusebius overlooked a whole series of important witnesses. Finally, it is also very difficult to judge the resolutions of the Council of Laodicea, at which the decision was taken about the final form of the canon, since there too reference is made exclusively to the traditions of the Fathers which he, Toland, can similarly advance for the writings which he would defend as authentic.[191] In conclusion, as an argument for his observations on the need to be clear about the extent of the canon and to have authentic criteria for it,[192] he points out that a number of sects down to the time of Augustine, like the Manichaeans, the Ebionites and the Marcionites, had quite a different canon from the one now officially accepted.[193] Though he does not raise any objections against parts of the canon itself, Toland's references are still effective in the way in which they radically question the certainty with which all parties felt that they could refer to the New Testament as a fixed entity.[194] This, however, is to attack at a central point the scriptural faith dominant in Humanist Protestantism of a Calvinist stamp, above all among the Puritans.

We need not go further here into Toland's other writings. In particular, his move towards pantheism towards the end of his life[195] had no influence on the further development of Deism. With his many-sided interests, more than any other writer in England he reflects the revolutionary situation giving rise to the spiritual constellation of the eighteenth century. Here positions were adopted which proved decisive for the understanding of the Bible in modern Protestantism. This is also the context of Toland's rich activity as a political writer; we need to see it as more than an expression of the extravagant personal interests of this many-sided man.[196] Rather, with Toland it becomes clear to what extent, even at the beginning of the eighteenth century, state politics and church politics in England form a whole, and how as a result political parties (which now for the first time emerge in that role) and basic theological positions closely influence one another. However, we shall return to these connections later.

(c) Shaftesbury

No investigation into the origins of the modern understanding of the Bible can omit a consideration of the Third Earl of Shaftesbury,[197] whose attitude to the Bible ushers in the dawn of a completely new age of dealing with the Bible, though it is only hinted at and is often left completely open. There is some question as to whether he is to be reckoned among the Deists at all.[198] However, the answer to this question becomes less important if we see Shaftesbury's position in the wider context of the legacy of Humanism. Here one can find a series of the main elements of his thought which have already been touched on regularly in the course of this investigation. The same thing is true of the old disputed question as to whether Shaftesbury goes back to the (Neo-)Platonic tradition or the Stoic tradition. E. Cassirer, above all, attempted to demonstrate that the former was the case by asserting that Shaftesbury had been influenced by the Cambridge Platonists;[199] since B.Rand's edition of a collection of reflections on various themes in two of Shaftesbury's notebooks drawn largely from the Stoic philosophers Epictetus and Marcus Aurelius, under the name *Philosophical Regimen*,[200,201] E.A.Tiffany has argued for the latter position, in a noteworthy article which is based above all on this material.[202] In reality, as has recently been rightly recognized,[203] both Platonic and Stoic conceptions influenced Shaftesbury's thinking, partly through his own considerable reading of ancient works,[204] and even more through the contemporary trends which influenced him; among these should be mentioned both the rationalistic and moralistic Latitudinarians[205] and the spiritualist Cambridge Platonists.[206]

In the intellectual climate of his time Shaftesbury is a quite independent thinker; his character as a 'Moralist'[207] and philosophical writer[208] with predominantly practical intentions produced the distinctive literary form which can be seen in the *Characteristics* and explains the wide acclaim and general popularity which Shaftesbury's work enjoyed throughout the eighteenth century, far beyond the frontiers of England.[209] In addition to the central interest in ethics which he shares with other Humanists there is a further characteristic emotional feature in his view of the world and his literary mode of presentation which people have tried to characterize by means of the keywords 'enthusiasm'[210] or even 'irrationalism',[211] seeking in this way to describe a deliberate directness in his view of the role of human beings in moral action and in the incorporation of nature into his world. Here people thought they could detect the recapitulation of certain elements of the Renaissance, and an anticipation of the later Romantic movement. That explains the importance which has been attached to Shaftesbury in particular in connection with the history of aesthetics, although in this respect we need to be careful of erroneous interpretations. In this respect E.Tuveson, in his article 'The Importance of Shaftesbury',[212] which is a valuable contribution to the understanding of the special significance of Shaftesbury for the English Enlightenment, has brought precision to a number of issues. In contrast to the indeterminate Pelagianism which was already predominant in the sermons of the Latitudinarians, the starting point for which was a capacity still present in human nature, despite the Fall, for good actions directed by reason, he believes that the decisive new step taken by Shaftesbury in his ethical theory is that he propagates the human disposition towards the good to which he directs his attention as a capacity to live in accordance with the harmony present in the ordered universe as taught by the new philosophy (Newton and the Newtonians[213]), in accordance with the natural ordinances of life in this world.[214] His decisive statement is that it is 'natural' for human beings to act well; this introduces a new stage of modernity insofar as now there is no need either of a divine inspiration (as among the Christian Neoplatonists) or of the grace and forgiveness of God (as in the elements of Christian doctrine which are still present among the Latitudinarians) in order to develop this capacity. Given this approach, we can understand that Shaftesbury found kindred conceptions in particular among the Stoic philosophers of late antiquity; in fact his approach has traits of an even more marked revival of antiquity than could be found in previous Humanist thought.[215] It has been aptly observed that Shaftesbury thus regarded himself as a Reformer in the moral sphere;[216] here one might recall Locke's love of pedagogy. However, Tuveson points to Locke in another connection: once the old confidence in the *ideae innatae* had finally been destroyed by Locke's criticism, the famous 'moral sense', which students of Shaftesbury had long regarded as the central keyword for his ethical approach,[217] acquired its epistemological basis through the application of Lockean epistemology to the sphere of ethics: now the objects of reflection were not only the ideas obtained from sense experience, but also human actions and affects;[218] the concepts of virtues (and vices) are 'natural', 'instinctive', in such a way that Shaftesbury can again term them 'innate', in deliberate opposition to Locke.[219] This is a decisive step forward from the whole of seventeenth-century thinking: 'with Shaftesbury we begin to see conduct in terms of what we should now call "normal" instead of in terms of obedience to divine or natural law...'[220] – ethics has become independent of any form of normative revelation as a criterion applied to people from outside, even in the form of natural law, much less in the form of a divine will communicated in the Bible. Of course Shaftesbury is not areligious;[221] but his form of religion, which he designates the true form of enthusiasm in contrast to superstitious fanaticism, is itself an immanent phenomenon.[222] It is the enthusiasm which has its place in any human life, in the encounter with higher goals in the elemental movements of our make-up: 'all sound love and admiration is enthusiasm: The transport of poets, the sublime of orators, the rapture of musicians, the high strains of the virtuosi – all mere enthusiasm! Even learning itself, the love of arts and curiosities, the spirits of travellers and adventurers, gallantry, war, heroism – all, all enthusiasm!'[223] Grean[224] stresses above all the keyword 'love', and recalls that in this way the eros doctrine of Plato and Plotinus takes on new life, as had already been the case in the Italian Renaissance with Ficino[225] and happened later with the Cambridge Platonists. Here there is also a close connection with ethics: good and beautiful are basically the same,[226] so that in another passage Shaftesbury can describe in an all-embracing philanthropical gesture a movement of the heart which is at the same time supremely good and thus godly: 'To love the public, to study universal good, and to promote the interest of the whole world, as far as lies within our power, is surely the height of goodness, and makes that temper which we call divine.'[227] Here we have almost reached the limits of belief in a personal God. Grean notes a dissolution of the concept of God in the process of progressive enthusiastic self-transcendence which is depicted: 'The process itself is not only the means to Deity, but is Deity.'[228] 'God is the symbol of man's true good or true interest.'[229] This, too, is not completely new, but a further development of the Neoplatonic idea of emanation coupled with elements of Stoic cosmology against the background of the modern scientific view of the world. In this way Shaftesbury can establish what he terms the 'devoutest part' of religion on purely this-worldly traits which find transcendence in the midst of immanence: 'for if there be divine excellence in things, if there be in Nature a supreme mind or Deity, we have then an object consummate and comprehensive of all which is good or excellent... Now that there is such a principal object as this in the world, the world alone...by its wise and perfect order must evince.'[230] However, these truths do not correspond to the external world of experiences but to the inner form of being itself;[231] this 'general body' goes with a 'general mind', closely connected to the whole as the 'particular mind' is to the individual: 'What are you yourself but a part of nature and united by nature to other parts...?'[232] And to this degree it is the case that the ideas of divinity and beauty (both are similarly synonymous!) are innate in man 'or such as men were really born to and could hardly by any means avoid'.[233]

Fundamentally there is no legitimate place here for the biblical revelation. In his *Inquiry concerning Virtue or Merit*, Shaftesbury reflects on the relationship between morality and belief in God,[234] and decides against the voluntaristic solution: before any acquaintance with the simplest form of knowledge of a God, one can already detect even in a primitive man a feeling of good and evil and an attitude which is by nature friendly.[235] By worshipping a God who acts cruelly or immorally (Shaftesbury makes explicit mention of Jupiter with his love affairs), man can mislead himself into cruel or immoral actions and be confused in his natural feeling for good and evil. In this passage Shaftesbury seems to be alluding directly to official Christianity:[236] 'If there be a religion which teaches the adoration and love of a God whose character it is to be captious and of high resentment, subject to wrath and anger, furious, revengeful, and revenging himself, when offended, on others than those who gave the offence[237]... favourable to a few and cruel to the rest' – then a similar attitude is required of his followers.[238] Given his general position, Shaftesbury cannot have anything at all to do with the God of the Bible; his contingency is irreconcilable with Shaftesbury's idea of order. Conversely, however, 'whoever thinks there is a God, and pretends formally to believe that he is just and good, must suppose that there is independently such a thing as justice and injustice, truth and falsehood, right and wrong, according to which he pronounces that

God is just, righteous, and true.'[239] Thus such a God is *a priori* bound
by the pre-existing moral order, which is independent of any revelation
and valid in itself, and his existence is conceivable only in accordance
with these criteria. The idealistic view of God on the Greek model is
simply the other side of the absolute system of ethics which Shaftesbury
is the first to put forward consistently.[240] However, it also follows from
this that a biblical revelation which contains additional ethical norms is
superfluous: 'If the mere will, decree, or law of God be said absolutely
to constitute right and wrong, then are these latter words of no signi-
ficancy at all.'[241] In respect of his ethics, in complete contrast to Locke,
Shaftesbury is a clear realist; he decisively rejects the Nominalist tradition which sought the roots of all ethical norms in the sovereign will
of God.[242] But revelation is no longer used even for the announcement
of rewards and punishments in the beyond (hitherto one of the pillars
of moral Christianity, even in the form of early Deism put forward by
Herbert of Cherbury): in carrying through the ethical idealism which
he requires, Shaftesbury consistently attacks the widespread view that
the announcement of future rewards or punishments could be a real
stimulus to moral action.[243] Such eudaemonism would do away with
the ethical character of action. On the other hand, Shaftesbury's ethic
is in no way free of Utilitarianism: he is never tired of stressing that
ethical action brings satisfaction, though this satisfaction is similarly
immanent in action: to do good automatically brings satisfaction and
therefore happiness.[244]

The regular ordering of natural laws which can be observed in the
world argues for the existence of a just governor of the world. Only
someone who thus has found his way to first belief in God can ascend
to a second stage: 'He can then hearken to historical revelation, and is
then fitted... for the reception of any message or miraculous notice from
above, where he knows beforehand all is just and true'.[245] In practice,
however, Shaftesbury shows little inclination to listen to the historical
revelation. Instead of this, he assembles a whole series of observations
which can shed a critical light above all on Old Testament institutions
and events. A section in the *Miscellaneous Reflections*[246] demonstrates the
popularity of Spencer and Marsham among all the critics of Jewish-
Christian belief: Shaftesbury also eagerly takes up the material presented by both scholars about the Egyptian derivation of most of the
cultic institutions and their demonstrations that the Israelites took over
many of these.[247] In this connection he mentions the circumcision introduced by Abraham, a custom taken over from Egypt,[248] and points
to the servile dependence of the Israelites on their oppressors, who
were within a hairsbreadth of returning to their old dependence even
after the exodus (on which they did not embark willingly[249]), with
detailed quotations from Spencer, about the 'stubborn habit and stupid

humour of this people'[250] which was subsequently governed by the superstitious customs and rites of the Egyptians. Moreover the exodus is morally offensive as 'the retreat of a Moses by the assistance of an Egyptian lone',[251] just as the behaviour of Joseph in Egypt, when he allied himself with the priestly caste and as a result came to possess the whole land, gives rise for critical comments.[252] There is also passing mention of the massacre brought about by Moses (Ex.32.27ff.; Num.16.41), which was also occasioned by this same stubbornness of the people, since otherwise he was 'the meekest man on earth' (Num.12.3).[253] In this kind of moral criticism of figures of the Old Testament Shaftesbury resembles Bayle, who was also personally known to him after his stay in Holland in 1698/9; however, he is not just attacking individual figures, but is arguing as a matter of principle, as is evident from a section in *Advice to an Author*[254] in which Shaftesbury rejects biblical themes and characters as subjects of literary description. He thinks that as heroes in poetry, figures like Moses and Joshua, would not match up to the usual standards of heroism and generosity, because for all our understanding of the situation of the chosen people in the midst of Gentile nations, fellow feeling must prevent us from regarding with any satisfaction the punishments inflicted by human hands against such strangers and idolaters.[255] The warlike mercilessness of Israel depicted in the Old Testament cannot be reconciled with normal moral and idealistic principles. This corresponds exactly with the maxims which Shaftesbury had earlier[256] designated the 'philosophy' or 'science' through which 'religion itself is judged, spirits are searched, prophecies proved, miracles distinguished: the sole measure and standard being taken from moral rectitude, and from the discernment of what is sound and just in the affections.' It is interesting that on these principles Shaftesbury came to comment critically on Milton, who is so esteemed elsewhere. He looks on the famous epic *Paradise Lost* with some reservations, as the contents, from Genesis, are 'so abstrusely revealed and with such a resemblance of mythology, that they can more easily bear what figurative construction or fantastic turn the poet may think fit to give them'.[257] Though this kind of poetry is not to his taste, in his view it would be ominous for a poet 'should he venture farther into the lives and characters of the patriarchs, the holy matrons, heroes and heroines of the chosen seed; should he employ the sacred machine, the exhibitions and interventions of divinity according to Holy Writ to support the actions of his piece...'[258] He seeks to leave everything that is Christian theology in the narrower sense, that concerns the personal being and becoming of the deity, to the clergy, 'to whom the State has assigned the guardianship and promulgation of the divine oracles', the official interpretation of scripture. Scholars have puzzled over how this Hobbesian sounding remark could be intended; it can be set alongside others, according to which Shaftesbury willingly promises to submit to the Christian religion 'as by law established'.[259] However, the contradictory character which a modern observer thinks he can see in such passages becomes understandable when we take into account the situation of an intellectual Anglican of the time, who at one level of consciousness and action can follow the official customs of the state church,[260] whereas at another he gives expression to his elitist literary scepticism.[261] As we shall see, there is also an eminently political side to this position: during the years in which Shaftesbury was active as a writer, it was the official line of the Whig Party, of which Shaftesbury was a supporter, to advocate Erastianism against high-church claims for the self-government of the church; however, that line was quite in accord with the Anglican liberal heritage, for as we have seen, the liberal Anglicans, too, had never thought a separation of state and church necessary. Leaving the state to order the outward form of the church made room for the personal sphere of religion.[262]

For example, any critically thinking Christian must be sceptical about the biblical tradition. Shaftesbury is the first to develop this principle as a theoretically formulated methodological postulate. Shaftesbury's scepticism, which he quite generally acknowledged,[263] is directed in particular towards revelation, for anyone who has never personally experienced the receiving of divine revelation or has never been witness to a miracle, 'being destitute of the means of certainty depends only on history and tradition for his belief in these particulars' and is therefore 'at best but a sceptic Christian. He has no more than a nicely critical historical faith, subject to various speculations, and a thousand different criticisms of languages and literature'.[264] The keyword 'historical faith' for the first time gives open expression to the dilemma which historical Christianity was to pose for the whole of the Enlightenment right down to Lessing. The debate about miracles is connected with this. Here Shaftesbury's position still represents a transitional stage. For the Latitudinarians, the miracles in the Old and New Testaments were still one of the main supports for the divinity of Jesus Christ and the Christian religion generally; Locke's discussion of the problem was still carried on in this context.[265] Shaftesbury goes a step further: in a discussion in *The Moralists* about spirits, appearances and so on,[266] he expresses doubts as to whether belief in such things[267] does not rest on self-deception rather than on deliberate deceit. He replies to the question which this provokes from his fictitious conversation partner, as to whether in that case he can believe in any miracles at all, along the lines of his basic Anglican position as sketched out above: 'No matter, said I, how incredulous I am of modern miracles, if I have a right faith in those of former times by paying the deference due to sacred writ.'[268] However, this is a return to the argument that has been usual hitherto, for whereas in apologetics so far miracle had been the most powerful proof for the divinity of Jesus' mission and thus for the authority of scripture, the present situation is now the reverse. Existing 'legal' authority has to vouch for the credibility of miracle. Shaftesbury goes on to say that the most appropriate standpoint for an orthodox Christian (and he thinks he has more right to this title than modern believers in miracles) is to expect no further miracles, since the best maxim is the customary one: 'That miracles are ceased.'[269] However, after this completely orthodox observation,[270] the discussion goes a stage further. Now his conversation partner is made to assert that miracles really could not contribute anything to the vindication of faith since, on the grounds that only miracles in the present could provide conclusive proof of the existence of God, and not those which were reported by merely human tradition,[271] it is only right to assume that God reveals himself to reason and submits himself to its judgment. But that happens by way of natural theology: 'The contemplation of the universe, its laws and government, was... the only means which could establish the sound belief of a Deity.'[272] By contrast, the introduction of miracles by orthodox theology runs directly counter to the course of nature and introduces disorder into the world. It therefore even leads to atheism, particularly among the critical youth, when having discovered pure order in nature they are taught that God is to be sought only in the disruptions of this order. Faith in a traditional (biblical) revelation can be built up only on the recognition of the divine origin of this order (as has been noted above).[273]

Shaftesbury seems to approach large stretches of the Bible with a gentle humour, as he does other objects of his wit. Here his true judgment – assent or concealed rejection – remains doubtful in view of his argument for 'good humour' as a desirable attitude, even in religion. This is the case above all in the section in the *Miscellaneous Reflections*,[274] where he adds by way of qualification to his observation in the *Letter concerning Enthusiasm* that the Jews were 'naturally a very cloudy people'[275] all kinds of examples of humour and witty description in the Old Testament to show, as he says, 'how readily the inspired authors had recourse to humour and diversion as a proper means to promote religion and strengthen the established faith'.[276] In addition to David's dance before the ark he mentions Jonah as the example of a pupil who tries in vain to avoid his schoolmaster; the bad temper which Jonah also shows in his afflictions is looked back on with humour. Shaftesbury also recalls the 'popular pleasant intercourse and manner of dialogue between God and man' (Gen.3.9), between man and beast (Num.22.28), or even between God and Satan (Job 1; 2 etc.), along with the sharp, humorous and witty style of Jesus in his various sayings, stories and parables, and even in his miracles; here Shaftesbury places particular emphasis on the miracle of changing water to wine (John 2.11).[277] In view of their apologetic function in connection with his verdict on the Jews, it must remain questionable whether Aldridge is right in saying[278] that Shaftesbury simply wanted to make fun of the Bible in these remarks, even if immediately afterwards[279] Gen.22 and Judg.11.30ff. are cited as examples of the dark superstition predominant at the time.

Shaftesbury also adopts a critical attitude to the textual problems of the biblical tradition and the difficulties in interpreting it. He makes his worthy conversation partner ('our gentleman'[280]) first respond to the maxim 'that the Scripture, the Scripture was the religion of Protestants'[281] with a question about the extent of the canon: 'whether it were the apocryphal Scripture or the more canonical? The full or the half-authorised? The doubtful or the certain?', and this question directly leads into the associated question of the textual tradition: 'The singly-read or that of various reading? The text of these manuscripts or of those?' Given the partisan character of the church fathers, which can also be seen from their suppression of all heretical writings against which they fought, one cannot have a great deal of confidence in their fidelity to the biblical tradition which was entrusted to them.[282] Shaftesbury puts forward the basic principle that any historical truth handed down in writing (in contrast to moral or – and this is almost a synonym – aesthetic truth, which is immediately evident as common sense) has first to undergo a thorough testing of the character and genius of its author and the capacity of the historian who handed it down to make an unbiassed judgment before anything can be accepted on its authority. In addition to this, there is the methodical examination of the text which he calls 'critical truth', 'or the judgement and determination of what commentators, translators, paraphrasts, grammarians and others have, on this occasion, delivered to us; in the midst of such variety of style, such different readings, such interpolations and corruptions in the originals; such mistakes of copyists, transcribers, editors, and a hundred such accidents to which ancient books are subject.'[283] Shaftesbury is up with the literary criticism of his time, represented in particular by Dutch scholars like Jean Leclerc, with whom he was acquainted, and he is ready to apply these methodological principles, for which the critical reader must not only be an 'able linguist' but also apply other sciences like chronology, natural philosophy and geography,[284] not only to ancient secular texts but also to the Bible itself.[285] ''Tis indeed no small absurdity to assert a work or treatise, written in human language, to be above human criticism or censure... there can be no scripture but what must of necessity be subject to the reader's narrow scrutiny and strict judgement, unless a language and grammar, different from any of human structure, were delivered down from heaven, and miraculously accomodated to human service and capacity.'[286] Shaftesbury compares the Bible with certain old church pictures which are said to have been painted by a supernatural hand and with a sacred brush: he ventures to assert 'that if the pencil had been heaven-guided it could never have been so lame in its performance'.[287] Here again Shaftesbury first refers to his Anglican loyalty: if the authority authorizes a particular sacred writing, 'it becomes immoral and profane in any one to deny absolutely or dispute the sacred authority of the least line or syllable contained in it'. But if (as is the case with the Bible), this scripture is 'multifarious, voluminous, and of the most difficult interpretation', such an ordinance is impossible to carry out and cannot hold its ground against much well-founded criticism and public opinion. Still less is this the case for the repeated translations of the text of the Bible into the vernacular which only enthusiasts and fanatics claim to be sufficient, whereas thoughtful ministers of the established churches are far from basing their faith on the common text, or even describing the original text as a literary masterpiece. They seek to defend only the substance of the narrative and the main facts as confirmation of the authority of the revelation.[288] Here there is a need for historical- critical examination, as there is in the case of secular texts.[289] In defence of the right of the reader to criticize the authors of even the biblical writings, Shaftesbury argues that neither Jesus himself nor Moses, to whom the Pentateuch is attributed, were authors of these accounts, in which for example even Moses' death occurs (Deut.34.5ff.)[290] – an observation already made by Karlstadt and often repeated.[291,292]

We can see how decisively views on the validity of scripture have changed in comparison to the seventeenth century from the way in which Shaftesbury quotes sections from the writings of the two liberal Anglicans Jeremy Taylor and J.Tillotson.[293] A.O.Aldridge has pointed out[294] that here he deals in a very arbitrary way with his witnesses and only seeks to support his own view; in particular, in Taylor's remarks about the obscurity of scripture he passes over the key statements, made at the beginning of his discussion, to the effect that all the fundamentals in scripture are expressed clearly and simply, and only takes up for his own ends the subsequent incidental remarks that numerous other passages are veiled in obscure imagery. This approach is no coincidence; it shows that Shaftesbury had no real authorities for his attitude to the Bible. Apart from Blount, the outsider, and in contrast to Toland's *Christianity not Mysterious*, which indeed sought in its own way to strengthen the authority of the Bible, he is the first one to base his Christianity (if we can call it that; despite his frequent claim to be a legal Christian, he himself preferred the designation 'theist'[295]) on natural religion. The development which has taken place is particularly clear if we contrast Shaftesbury with Chillingworth, who throughout the seventeenth century had been the chief witness for liberal Anglicans;

those who still refer to him are now classed as 'enthusiasts' and accused of blind bibliolatry.

This produced a new relationship to the Bible in the Enlightenment both in England and outside it – the influence of Shaftesbury in the first half of the eighteenth century in England and in the second in Germany was great[296] – and decidedly changed the character of later Protestantism. In his basic approach to ethics Shaftesbury remained faithful to the Humanist tradition; by abandoning its Nominalist roots in the will of God and thus in the Bible, making absolute the Realist line of natural law which similarly went right back to Scholasticism, with the generally accepted criteria of good and evil, and transferring it to the nature of mankind itself, he ushered in an age in which the relationship to Holy Scripture was understood in a different way. For the liberal theology of the seventeenth century, with its humanistic stamp, and even for the Puritans, the Bible was principally a formal authority – formal to the degree that in reality each group read its particular view into the Bible and divided it by their own criteria into fundamentals and peripherals, or even claimed it in its entirety. However, we can see precisely from the way in which the Bible was manipulated at that time just how intact its authority was and how every party (including the Deist Toland) could gain authority for its doctrine only by demonstrating that it was in accordance with the Bible. With Shaftesbury things were basically different. By detaching the autonomy of ethics, first postulated by the Cambridge Platonists, from all previous compromises and emotionally connecting it with the idea of a harmony within the world as established by Newton, he showed that the revelation contained in the Bible and handed down by historical tradition could be dispensed with. Consistently with this, we do not find in him the beginning of an attempt to demonstrate from the Bible the ethics which are evident to mankind from nature; he even explicitly rejects this course by repudiating the Nominalist derivation of ethics from the will of God.

We also find in Shaftesbury the characteristic Spiritualist theory of depravation in respect of the history of the early church.[297] He speaks of the apostle Paul with great respect; what he finds particularly laudable in Paul is that, although he had personal experiences of miracles outside and communications within, he was sceptical and cautious about the certainty of such divine communication. Earliest Christianity was 'set so far apart from all philosophy or refined speculation, that it seemed in a manner diametrically opposed to it'.[298] Just as dogmatic theology with its claim to absoluteness only invaded the church at a later stage, so too it was with superstition. According to Shaftesbury, this is directly connected with the adoption of what were once items from pagan temples by Christian clergy after Constantine's rise to power; as a result, the church was corrupted, and at the same time there was a dissolution of the ancient schools of philosophy whose former sophistical teachers now became teachers within the church,[299] thus introducing partisanship and bigotry into theology, along with every possible pagan and Jewish mystery tradition and speculation. And as if Blount's work were well known to him, he takes as an example of the self-interest of the priesthood, which is the cause of all this, the story of Diana of the Ephesians from Acts 19.23ff. As an example of the continuation of the apostasy of the church, once begun, into superstitious ceremonies there is also the Roman Church, which exploited the superstition and enthusiasm of the people, using a wealth of pomp in order to bring the masses under its spell to the advantage of its growing hierarchy; it adopted this course since the mob can best be won over by scenes and ceremonies, by chalices and candles.[300] The section about Egypt (II,181ff.), a passage which I have already quoted in connection with Shaftesbury's judgment on the Egyptian origin of Jewish customs, also has the same underlying intention.[301] However, its main purpose is to stress the role of priests 'in this motherland of superstition'[302] and in particular to point to the abundant estates which they were able to appropriate over the course of time.[303] Shaftesbury can adduce other examples than Egypt, where the priesthood threatened to swallow up the whole state with its possessions. From this he draws the general conclusion: 'Nor is it possible... for any state or monarchy to withstand the encroachments of a growing hierarchy...'[304]

Evidently these veiled observations, which for the sake of caution are concerned with so distant a culture as the paganism of ancient Egypt, were in reality made with a direct interest in the present. As in the earlier periods of theological controversy, so too in the first decades of the eighteenth century, these controversies were closely connected with the situation in church and state politics. A.O.Aldridge has impressively drawn attention to the importance of these connections for Shaftesbury.[305] He points to the controversies between High Church and Low Church which reached a climax above all in the years between 1700 and 1711, though their origin is to be sought in the Glorious Revolution of 1688[306] and its long lasting consequences. With the flight of James II, which put an end to the strife over his pro-Roman religious policy, and was brought about by the intervention of William of Orange, the year 1688 produced a severe crisis over the question of legitimacy: the Archbishop of Canterbury, William Sancroft, head of the Church of England, and five bishops, along with about 400 other clergy, refused to take the oath of allegiance to the new ruler as he had not ascended the throne by divine right of inheritance (they were known as the Non-Jurors).[307] Even more serious than the secession itself were its immediate consequences for the church as a whole: in the Synod controlled by the lower clergy, the lower chamber of the Convocation of Canterbury, which had the right of assent to the Crown's ecclesiastical legislation (the upper house of the Synod consisted of the bishops), an orthodox attitude prevailed which was opposed to any compromise with the Nonconformists. It was already evident in the rejection in 1689, in the Lower House of Parliament, which still included Tory members from the time of Charles II, of the proposed reforms of the Book of Common Prayer and Canon Law, which was intended to make possible a return of the Dissenters into the bosom of the church (the so-called 'Comprehension Bill'), and in the Synod of the Act of Toleration, which Parliament had already passed. The synod was thereupon suspended *sine die*. Theological convictions for the most part corresponded to political ones, given expression in the parties of the Whigs and the Tories. William III had filled the places of the Jacobite bishops who had resigned or died with Latitudinarians like Tillotson or Whigs like Gilbert Burnet,[308] a policy which Queen Anne was also for the most part compelled to continue in the first years of her reign, albeit against her personal conviction. This led to a confrontation between the lower clergy of an orthodox stamp, mostly with Tory inclinations, and an episcopate which for the most part consisted of Whigs or moderate Tories who were theologically liberal and supported a parliamentary monarchy and the Hanoverian succession.[309] For an understanding of the attitudes of both Toland and Shaftesbury it is important to know that they both belonged to the Whig party; his financial independence made it easier for the latter to be more faithful to his principles.[310]

In the period after 1700, a series of events led to opposition in the church developing even more clearly between the High Church group, now so named, which brought together the radical Orthodox (the 'high flyers'), Jacobites and Non-Jurors, and the Low Church group, which argued for tolerance and which sympathized politically with the Whigs. To justify their attitude the Non-Jurors had developed a theory of the church as the perfect society which postulated a complete independence of the church from the state, and freedom for it to regulate its own concerns (this was only loosely connected with the question of the oath). On this point it therefore came very close to the requirements of the extreme Puritans,[311] although these were arrived at from opposed presuppositions and were bound up with 'Laudian' elements like a stress on the liturgy and the rights of the episcopacy standing in the apostolic succession. A remarkable situation arose from the fact that this programme was now advocated above all by members of the lower clergy, since after the departure of the Jacobite bishops there were virtually no High Churchmen on the bench of bishops.

The programme gave rise to vigorous polemics which were intensified by the fact that William III kept preventing a recall of Convocation and thus deprived the lower clergy of their voice. In his *Letter to a Convocation*

Man of 1697 the well-known High Churchman F.Atterbury[312] already warned of the danger threatening the clergy from the state and was even more demanding that the Synod should have the right to independent legislation in the sphere of the church, analogous to the rights of Parliament in secular matters.[313] By contrast, the traditional polemic against the priesthood now found a new goal in the hands of the Low Church supporters: it was now directed against the High Church trend and its claims, and thus was at the same time a form of party propaganda for the Whigs against the Tories.[314] Despite its rationalistic starting point, it was in no way limited to the Deists in the narrower sense. On the other hand, it did not take in broad areas of the people: D.Ogg observes that anticlericalism has never been as popular in England as it has been in France and Italy;[315] in particular this was a consequence of the position of parish priests, above all in the country. As Aldridge has demonstrated,[316] Shaftesbury's anti-priestly passages are directed above all against the High Church party. They are just one of the examples of the anti-High Church Whig polemic which arose in the first years of the reign of Queen Anne. One of the first attacks of this kind appeared as early as 1702: E.Hickeringill, *Priestcraft its Character and Consequences*, and from then on the slogan contained in the title of this pamphlet became the watchword of all those with Whig or Deistic inclinations.

(d) Matthew Tindal, The Rights of the Christian Church Asserted

A particularly controversial piece of Whig propaganda was Matthew Tindal's *The Rights of the Christian Church Asserted* (1706, published anonymously), in which this writer,[317] who later became well known as a result of *Christianity as old as the Creation* (1730)[318], a deistic work written in his old age, challenged at length the claims of the High Churchmen and Non-Jurors of Atterbury's school.[319] As he already makes clear in the Foreword, he seeks above all to reject the claim of the High Churchmen that the church, as an institution by divine right, should be independent of the state: 'that the Doctrine of Two Independent Governments, one belonging to the Clergy by Divine, the other to the King and Parliament by Human Right, is inconsistent with the Constitution of the Establish'd Church.'[320]

Even in the Foreword Tindal develops his main argument, which first of all culminates in an emphatic reference to existing constitutional realities. For him there is no way past the existing ordinances. It is interesting that here he refers principally to the constitutions of Henry VIII, which have created the binding system of England's established church. This Low Church politician now seeks to defend the system against the High Churchmen![321] 'It was to defend the Church of England against the Papists, Jacobites, and other High-fliers',[322] he explicitly declares, and in fact above all in the Foreword, one is amazed at the legalistic nature of the argument coming from the pen of a Whig. However, this attitude is obviously connected with the important change of course in the politics of the party to which J.H.Plumb in particular[323] has drawn attention: whereas the Whigs who under Charles II had still defended the constitutional principles against the Crown, which had tended towards absolutism, and the parliamentary majority supporting it, the party leaders now saw a way to power only through an alliance with the Court and the influence they could exercise on it, above all in financial respects; by contrast, as representatives of the nobility and the small towns, the Tories increasingly embodied the independence of Parliamentary freedoms over against the Executive and royal centralization.[324] We can also see a similar shift of position in the attitudes of the political groups in the church: the High Churchmen now fought for a church founded on its own, divine right, whose nature it was to order its own concerns independently of state control while the Low Churchmen, the successors to the liberal Anglicans and Latitudinarians, argued for far-reaching church control by secular authorities. As a defensive reaction against the 'high-flying' High Church ideology, anti-priestly polemic gains new strength: Tindal stresses explicitly that when he uses the term 'clergy' as a generic term he does not mean the loyal clergy,[325] but 'that Popish, Eastern, Presbyterian, and Jacobite Clergy (who are infinitely the Majority)'.[326]

However, further reading of Tindal's book quickly shows that there has not been a real break with the old Whig principles in the party, even in this phase.[327] In a striking way, right at the beginning of the book, in the introduction, where he goes into the secular political presuppositions of his position, he writes polemically (though without explicitly naming names) against Filmer's patriarchalism[328] and stresses that even in the primal state,[329] men were not only free,[330] but also equal.[331] He accepts the consensus doctrine in connection with the origin of all state legislative power, and stresses that even the present government rests on a consensus, which in principle can be revoked at any time.[332] However, the necessary consent to the legislative authority on the part of the individual citizen now happens only tacitly, and publicly by way of the parties.[333] The ideal form of the state is party democracy, in which the will of the majority rules.[334] The state constitution advocated by the Whigs thus continues the ideals first propagated by the Levellers. However, at least officially, it no longer calls for republicanism,[335] but supports a monarchy which, however, since the Bill of Rights has changed its character substantially, and has become constitutional.[336] The real sovereign is no longer the sacral Crown on the basis of an inherited *jus divinum*, but the representatives of the people.

These political principles are also the basis for regulating relationships between state and church. In this respect, too, the continuity between Tindal's views and those of earlier liberal Anglicanism is unmistakable.

Tindal rejects one limitation on the rights of the authorities in the secular sphere (their task is seen, in an old-fashioned way, in terms of the office of the sword[337]) because their responsibility of seeing to the welfare of their subjects[338] cannot stop short at the realm of religion. As a consequence, for example, they even have the duty to punish an atheist because the denial of the existence of God undermines the moral basis of society.[339] On the other hand, however, the right of the state in church matters is limited to those issues which affect the prosperity of human society. Above all, in principle they may not intervene in the freedom of the individual conscience,[340] in respect either of the outward forms of worship or of dogmatic speculations, so long as this does not do wrong to others, 'because as to these matters Men are still in a state of Nature, without any Sovereign Representative to determine for them what they shall believe or profess'.[341] Therefore the authority of the state does not extend to the indifferentia, for that would decisively limit the freedom of the individual. Again arguments emerge which originally came from the left wing of Puritanism but have a different basic approach as a result of their secularization.[342] In the background we have a completely individualized concept of the church which is analogous to the consensus theory as applied to the state: like an association,[343] the church does not come into being through tradition but through the voluntary entry of its members.[344] Now this voluntary character also extends to the doctrines of a church and its outward forms of worship, and even after joining it, each individual must judge them for himself and cannot submit to any majority decision; anyone whose judgments differ can found a church of his own with those of like mind, even if there are only two or three of them (Matt.18.20).[345] There is only one reason for the state to interfere: religious persecution. Here, at least, it must intervene and energetically punish those who persecute others in matters of conscience, as if they were robbers, murderers or others violating the common good. The basic principle is that the power of the authorities 'is confin'd to such religious Matters as are likewise Civil, that is, where the Publick has an Interest'.[346]

As in Locke (and often clearly in dependence on him), in Tindal we also find a demand for tolerance towards the various church groupings which differ from one another. He allows Dissenters an existence independent of the state, as happened with earliest Christianity under a non-Christian authority.[347] Otherwise, however, he wants to see the Anglican Church valued. At this point, of course, he gets into consider-

able difficulties, as it is hard to see why the same claim to self-government should not be allowed for the Anglicans as for the Dissenters. For
Tindal, however, the claims of the High Churchmen lie on quite a
different level. The decisive factor is evidently the concept of the 'Christian nation': his main argument is that it is unthinkable for a Christian
nation that God has appointed two governments independent of each
other, one for church matters and the other for secular matters, each
with both legislative and executive functions.[348] Here he is concerned
above all with the claim of the clergy that they have an unchangeable
divine right, deriving from Christ and the apostles, to legislation over
indifferentia like rites and ceremonies, in other words, their claim that
their synods can lay down a binding *status confessionis* for all their
members and compel these members to observe it by the power of the
keys, which can lead through ecclesiastical courts to excommunication.[349] So in the first place he seeks to demonstrate that there cannot
be two independent authorities in the same *society*.[350] The most important principle is that of the indivisibility of power: 'that all Supreme
or Independent Power must be indivisible'.[351] All the individual reasons
which are given for this[352] show that the argument here suddenly has
to be based on quite different principles, largely corresponding to the
specific English situation. Here (if we exclude the Dissenters and Catholics) the power over both spheres is in fact exercised by the one existing
authority, which consists of Crown, Government and Parliament, and
which since Henry VIII has had the state church firmly in its grasp.
Thus far the reference developed in the preface to the decrees of this
king relating to the church is quite relevant: the whole book is one long
vindication of the *status quo*. By contrast, the opposed claim of the High
Churchmen disputed here is pure ideology; it has no parallel in reality
and is represented by those who no longer hold the reins of power.[353]
Although on these principles we would expect a form of Erastianism in
Tindal,[354] and the preface says a good deal about the supremacy of the
Crown over the church even in ecclesiastical matters (*jus in sacra*), it is
clear that in fact he wants to defend the right of Parliament to legislate
for the church, since 'As her Majesty has no Power in Ecclesiasticals
except by the laws of the Land, and can't divest her self of any part of
it without Consent of Parliament; so both must be equally concern'd in
this Charge.'[355] From this he derives the final conclusion that these
rights of Parliament in fact confirm the church in its privileges,[356] since
the church, i.e. not its hierarchy but all its members, is the people. As
the church in view is no longer a free church, which is understood in
each case as a separatist association, but the Church of England, there
is automatically a kind of identity between the English people and this
church; however, the people is represented by Parliament. The fact that
the secular Parliament and not the Synod has the *jus in sacra* means 'the

Power relating to these things to be fundamentally lodg'd in the People'.[357] And of course it is the law of nature which gives the people this right.[358] In this transference of authority over the church from the Crown to Parliament we have an exact reflection of the change in the constitutional situation which had come about through the Revolution: C.Garbett[359] in fact speaks of a form of Erastianism which now triumphed,[360] except that 'It was in the future Parliament, and not the Crown, which controlled the Church.'[361] If we are to assess these remarks rightly, however, we must not forget that in the English Constitution Crown and Parliament were in fact always understood as a unity;[362] except that now the emphasis had noticeably shifted in the direction of Parliament. In individual details the competence of the secular power in church matters now extended to the determination of the boundaries of communities and districts, to church buildings, their construction and maintenance, to the control of every detail of the liturgy,[363] and above all to the appointment and dismissal of clergy:[364] 'It can belong only to the People to appoint their own Ecclesiastical Officers'.[365]

According to Tindal's views the latter authority is closely connected with the character of the tasks of the church itself. For him the church is above all a moral institution,[366] and therefore the authorities have the duty to appoint clergy with the task 'publickly to instruct his Subjects to avoid all such things as he has a Right to restrain by preventing Force, and to practise all such as he ought to encourage by suitable Rewards'. It would be absurd if they were excluded 'from a Right of authorizing Persons publickly to mind him of what he owes to his Subjects, and them of those Dutys they are to render to him and one another'.[367] Excommunication because of heterodoxy is so damaging because in some circumstances it excludes a man of the highest moral standing from society whereas one who is immoral but orthodox enjoys the highest esteem.[368] If priestly powers ('priestcraft') were removed, the virtues propagated by Christianity would lead human nature to supreme perfection.[369]

The manifest contradiction in Tindal's way of arguing derives from the fact that he puts two basically irreconcilable concepts of the church side by side. One is partly a congregationalist legacy, which has been stamped by the modern idea of contract and sees the church as an association which arises through the voluntary assembly of its members. However, Tindal only applies this concept of the church to the Dissenters; for them, on the basis of this definition, inner autonomy in relationship to the state follows, with the right to control their outward forms of worship; the Anglican church and its members are required to tolerate their separate existence. However, he firmly rejects this claim to autonomy for the Anglican church on the part of the High Churchmen (although he clearly recognizes that it corresponds to the demands of the Presbyterians).[370] Here, rather, he begins from the mediaeval notion of unity which sees the *Corpus Christianum* as an indivisible whole and does not know any division between the secular and the spiritual sphere, a presupposition which was also shared by Erastus, whom he so esteemed, and which was maintained on a national basis in the specific reality of the established church of England right down to his own day (and continues formally even now in the position of the Crown!). Thus there can be no question of equal treatment at law; what the Free Churchmen had long since achieved is denied to the Church of England. The High Churchmen could easily have discovered the contradictions in the arguments of the Low Churchmen had they not found themselves in a similar dilemma: for they, too, followed an ideal of unity which had absolutist colourings, began from the divine right of the Crown, and required only collaboration between the episcopate and the synod, as the organ by which the church, led by a hierarchical clergy, governed itself. However, this ideal did not in any way correspond to reality since (with a few exceptions, like the reform of Canon Law in 1603/4 which simply took its departure from the Synod authorized by the king) from the time of Henry VIII the Crown usually exercised its rights over the church with the help of Parliament.[371] This led to a conflict of principles which could not be resolved logically, and which has continued down to the present day in all forms of national church in Europe. Theoretically Tindal's position was untenable; in practice, however, it corresponded to existing circumstances and was therefore successful in the long run.

One of the most important arguments against the inalienable right of the clergy to legislate for the church which was claimed by the High Churchmen is the recognition that there cannot be such an unalienable right, since the external forms of the church must adapt themselves to the circumstances of the time.[372] It follows from this that the conditions expressed in the Bible cannot in any way be binding in the long term. 'The Circumstances of a few private Christians, form'd into particular Congregations, independent of one another, as at first, and those of the now National Churches, being so very different, must require a very different Polity.'[373] Now one can learn from the New Testament itself that the earliest Christians changed their church order depending on circumstances: the abolition of certain sacred customs (the brotherly kiss, the footwashing), conversely the practice of sacraments like baptism by the laity,[374] the abolition of offices (like that of deaconesses) or the changing of their tasks (as in the case of deacons), or even the repealing of strict prohibitions (consuming blood, eating sacrificed animals) show their great freedom in these things.[375] The same is also true of the laws of the Jews (in the Old Testament); these, too, were adapted by God to the special circumstances of Judaism and also regularly changed (as can be seen, say, in the varying attitudes of Moses and the prophets to sacrifice, or also in the laws 'which were not good', mentioned in Ezek.20.25), until they were finally abandoned altogether.[376] Merely moral principles are unalterable by nature, and therefore eternally binding.[377]

This attitude shows that in relation to Holy Scripture (as with Shaftesbury),[378] a new position has been reached. If every church order is changeable and time-conditioned, then the biblical ordinances can no longer be a model and scripture cannot even be binding in the limited sense that it still was for the liberal Anglicans. Shaftesbury then takes the last step towards the autonomy of moral awareness. If we are to understand Tindal's late work *Christianity as old as the Creation* as a Deistic work in the true sense, we cannot overlook the preliminary steps towards it which already become evident in the earlier church-political writings of the same author.[379] In the triangular relationship between presuppositions based on a world view, theories about the relationship between state and church, and the understanding of scripture, it is impossible to remove any of the angles without the whole system becoming incomprehensible.

Tindal's *The Rights of the Christian Church Asserted* caused a considerable stir among his contemporaries, above all through its vigorous attacks on the priesthood. The term *Priestcraft* appears repeatedly,[380] and despite the way in which it is explicitly limited to certain members of the clergy, everyone felt that the author adopted a basically hostile attitude to all priests. 'And Priestcraft is so rank a Weed, that it will not suffer a Plant of any Virtue to grow near it':[381] this statement is probably the best expression of where, for Tindal, the alternative lies. So we also find in the book all the usual associations of 'priestcraft' and 'superstition',[382] and also the traditional comparison with the pagan temple priesthood[383] (bringing out the negative parallels). There is even the charge that the Jews brought superstition out of Egypt, and a reference to their proneness to idolatry.[384] All this is not original, however, and could hardly direct attention to the work, were it not caught up in party political propaganda.

(e) Party politics and the authority of the Bible at the beginning of the eighteenth century

Tindal evidently expresses attitudes which are characteristic of wide areas of the Low Church.[385] However, we should be wary of thinking that the whole cultural situation has changed at a stroke since the Revolution. The opposed ideology of the High Churchmen and Jacobites is only one of the pieces of evidence to the contrary, and even the

Jacobites were to be a long time in losing their significance.[385a] That is also the case with the specific theme of the divine right of kings, which underlies Jacobite notions of legality.

G.Straka[386] has demonstrated how this theme was also taken up by the Anglican theologians who supported the accession of William III and Mary. They did so, in their own way, because they thought that it was the only way of making plausible to the mass of believers the legitimacy of the adoption of power by the foreign liberator. The possession of the crown was still attributed to the direct guidance of God, albeit by way of conquest, and this adoption of power could not be legitimated in any other way. The notion of contract among the supporters of the 'modern law of nature' for the moment represented only a minority view. Among the numerous writings and sermons in support and glorification of the new rulers which are quoted in Straka, one is struck by the reference to the Bible, which is natural in the sermons, but stands out even in the theoretical works: just as the fact that the King of England reigned by divine right was already traditional, so too the take-over of power in 1688 was legitimated above all from the Old Testament. One particularly interesting example of the transition to the thought forms of 'Parliamentary Erastianism' in this connection is R.Fleming's *The Divine Right of the Revolution*,[387] in which the transference of the crown to William III by the declaration of Parliament[388] is compared with the choice of David by the elders of the people, and thus declared to be divinely willed: the principle 'The voice of the people is the voice of God'[389] is legitimated by the Old Testament itself. However, it is also possible to justify events, like the new appointments by the king to the vacancies caused by the deposition of the Non-Juror bishops, by the Old Testament: evidence for this is the pamphlet of a certain Mr Hill: *Solomon and Abiathar: Or the Case of the Depriv'd Bishops and Clergy discuss'd*.[390] Here the events after Solomon's accession (II Kings 2.26f.) are made to serve as a type for contemporary church politics. The still-powerful High Church group refers to the Old Testament even more, above all in the years of Tory reaction under Queen Anne. In 1702, the year of her accession, when the right wing of the Tories enthusiastically celebrated the end of the 'alien rule' of Orange and the accession of a ruler who was English-born and loyal to the Church of England,[391] the High Church clergyman Henry Sacheverell preached a sermon (which was later printed) in which he called on people to go back to the old model of the state church, excluding the Dissenters, and to a sacral government which supported the throne with the altar; as a model for this he cited the rule of David, which was supported by God's counsels.[392] We can see how popular this attitude was from the famous trial of Sacheverell in 1710 because of a sermon similarly presenting the High Church position, which had been delivered in the previous year. The trial ended with what amounted to an acquittal, stirred up a mass of feelings, and contributed to the temporary end of Whig predominance.[393]

Through their sermons, the parish clergy, most of whom were ortho-dox and many of whom had high church leanings, continued without interruption to exercise an influence on the mass of people, above all in the country, throughout the first half of the eighteenth century. The role played by Holy Scripture, and especially the Old Testament, in the kind of thematic preaching which was then current, is the real back-ground to the struggle over the Bible which was waged over many decades by Deists and 'Freethinkers'.[394] Here the presuppositions of their thinking (the identification of religion and morality, the theory of the sufficiency of natural religion, and the subsidiary role of revelation, along with the hostility to the cult deriving from the Spiritualist trad-ition) and external circumstances grounded in the church and party political fronts of the time came together in the composition and pres-entation of their polemical writings.

In the controversies over religion in their time, the Deists were by no means so isolated a phenomenon as most of the specialized accounts of their theological and philosophical ideas suggest.[395] Rather, they were directly caught up in the party disputes of the first decades of the eighteenth century. Already in the cases of Toland and Tindal we have seen that both 'philosophers' were Whig supporters and directly in-volved in the politics and propaganda of the party. That is also true of Anthony Collins, whose work *Priestcraft in Perfection*[396] is also opposed to the High Church claim, discussed by Tindal, that the church has the right to make independent decisions about its own internal concerns. I have already mentioned that the third Earl of Shaftesbury was the most prominent 'deistic' Whig theoretician.

To put it in an exaggerated way, there were political reasons for the origins of biblical criticism in England: the Whig ideologists were con-cerned to deprive their opponents, the High Church Tories, of their support in the Bible. By denying its status as the source of revelation and pointing out the human elements in its composition and its all too human content, they sought to strike at the roots of Tory thinking.[397] They thus took an important step forward beyond the arguments of the early Whig propagandists from the time of William III, who themselves had maintained the biblical basis of a theory of divine right, albeit in a changed form. The mode of their procedure is clearly matched by the motives of the French Oratorian Richard Simon, who by no means undertook his criticism of the Bible in an unprejudiced zest for know-ledge, but with the controversialist's zeal to deprive the Protestants of the basis of their faith, the infallibility of the Bible.

The connection between the Deistic movement and the programme of the Whig party, and also the differences of opinion possible here, become even clearer when we look at the abundant pamphlet literature which comes from the pen of the Dioscuri John Trenchard and Thomas Gordon, whose self-chosen nomenclature already indicates their programme.[398] They became particularly well known as a result of the weekly *The Independent Whig*, which[399] originally appeared from January 1720 to January 1721 in the form of a series of self-contained discussions and in the end ran to seven steadily expanded issues.[400] Gordon, who wrote the first issue (of 20 January 1720),[401] mentions his principles right from the start: he seeks to fight against 'blindness and prejudice', against 'ignorance', for 'reason and common sense',[402] and sees his goal in an attempt 'to reform Mankind'.[403] He seeks his opponents in 'Priestcraft and Tyranny,[404] i.e. in a particular form of clerical claim to rule in which are to be found the roots of all evil, and the most dangerous threat to freedom as the supreme good. It is illuminating that in the second number (of 27 January 1720), Gordon, like Tindal,[405] asserts that he is not attacking the honourable clergy who do duty to their office; his aim is 'to illustrate the Beauty of Christianity, by exposing the Deformity of Priestcraft; to distinguish the good Clergy from the bad...'[406] In other words, the plan of the undertaking is a series of polemical writings against the High Church party (as is already hinted at in the sub-title, which is expanded after the fifth issue: 'A Defence of Primitive Christianity, And of our Ecclesiastical Establishment, Against the Exorbitant Claims and Encroachments of Fanatical and Disaffected Clergymen'); the argument takes the well-known form of the depravation theory: it is demonstrated that Christianity, which was originally disseminated only by miracle and gentle persuasion, without any claims to power on the part of the apostles ('the meek Spirit of the Christian Religion'), was soon turned by the priests in their desire to rule into a religion of blind obedience, superstitious ignorance and mindless church discipline against any clear-thinking Christian, leading a pious life and thus putting the immoral clergy to shame.[407] This negative development in the church extended as far as the Reformation; it is the aim of the *Independent Whig* to warn against the danger of the recurrence of the same development through the demands of the English High Churchmen.[408] In a series of passages there are attacks on the illegitimate privileges of the clergy which they have secured for themselves;[409] the High Church priests are presented as enemies of the Reformation[410] and are designated the most morally corrupt of all men.[411] There is an attack on their cruelty (in the persecution of those who do not share their views),[412] and indeed on their atheism,[413] 'Priestcraft' as a constant attack on reason is widespread not only in the temples of ancient paganism and the Roman Curia, but unfortunately also among the Jacobite High Churchmen of England;[414] their claim to power is the severest enemy of religion.[415] Religion is none other than morality,[416] ceremonies are superfluous and shameful; nor were they originally part of Christianity.[417] The same thing can be said, for example, about the institution of penance; fasting and mortification are superstitious actions which stand in the way of true religion.[418] Similarly, in the *Creed of an Independent Whig*, a pamphlet which also appeared in 1720,[419] we find that the supreme article of faith is that 'I believe no Bishop nor Presbyter, Priest or Deacon... can remit Sins.'[420] The established state church is justified:[421] a church authority independent of the state is absurd and impossible.[422] Rather, the ministers are 'Creatures of the Civil Power'!'[423] Furthermore, the priesthood is not seen as a special condition in the Gospel, since the Jewish priesthood was abrogated: rather, Jesus Christ is the only priest.[424] Priestly power generally cannot be reconciled with the Gospel and is rejected by it.[425] How much all this belongs in the context of the contemporary church political struggle is evident, among other things, from the sermon inserted anonymously into the fifth edition of the *Independent Whig*[426] (it was given on 30 January 1732, the anniversary of the execution of Charles I, who was celebrated in countless memorial sermons as a martyr by the High Church preachers[427]). This attacks the high church claim by rejecting commemoration of Laud, the second famous martyr, and asserting that 'Laud and his Adherents were notorious Persecutors'.[428] It describes the reign of Charles I as a 'continued Series of Oppressions', which 'had abolished Liberty and Law, and established universal Slavery'.[429] In all this we can also recognize a strong Puritan heritage. This is clearest in the sketch *The Character of an Independent Whig*,[430] where there is a contrast between the moral blamelessness to be required of a minister and the false respect which is paid to priestly vestments; the author declares: 'This consecrating of Garments, and deriving Veneration from a Suit of Cloaths, is barefac'd Priestcraft. It is teaching the Practice of Idolatry to a Gown and Cassock.'[431] Particularly striking here is the invective against games of chance and above all against masked balls, which are described as 'schools of vice'; the reintroduction of them into England is even suspected of being the insidious ploy of the French ambassadors, who aim at corrupting and enslaving the English.[432] The verdict against the universities and theological seminaries can also be found in this Whig confession.[433]

However, in respect of the Bible the *Independent Whig* of 1720 still maintained Locke's standpoint: 'The Scriptures are justly stiled the Revealed Will of God; they are addressed to all Mankind, and given to remain as a Rule of Faith and Manners to the End of the World', we are told, in the style of seventeenth-century liberal Anglicanism.[434] 'To fear God, and keep his Commandments, is the Summary of the Old Testament; and to believe that Jesus Christ is come in the Flesh, is the

Compendium of the New.'[435] Thus Locke's minimal confession also appears in the second part of this sentence.[436] It is expressly stressed that in these central points Scripture is clear and evident.[437] Confessions of faith are therefore superfluous (as is stressed above all against Rome):[438] 'We contend that the Scripture alone is a sufficient Rule of Faith and Practice.'[439] Reason alone is in a position to test the correctness of the claim of revelation.[440] However, in content the will of God communicated in the Bible is none other than the law of nature: 'The Decalogue, or the Law of the Ten Commandments, delivered by God himself from Mount Sinai... was little else but the Law of Nature reduced into Tables, and expressed in Words of God's own chusing.'[441] Similarly, it is the case that reason, which had already been man's only guide towards finding the will of God when he was in a state of nature,[442] must also pass judgment on revelation. For the biblical revelation also consists of words, and it is left to reason to determine what sense these have, whether in the original language or in translations. 'The Spirit of God has invented for us no new ones... but must infallibly be the same to every man.'[443] 'To conclude, Scripture, and Reason, without which Scripture can have no Effect, are the only Tests of every Falsehood and Imposture, and every Superstition.'[444]

Nevertheless, in these years there was already considerable unrest over the Bible, even if it never came to full expression. The freedom to express opinions which already existed to a greater degree than ever before since the Glorious Revolution, was nevertheless not great enough for direct critical work on scripture to be possible without consequences for the author. One instance of this is the work *The Difficulties and Discouragements which attend the Study of the Scriptures in the way of private Judgement* which first appeared anonymously, and which according to the ten editions cited in Trinius,[445] was enormously popular. It should also be put in the context of Whig propaganda. Here, on the pretext of well-meaning advice to a minister and another who has taken up serious study of the scriptures in order to understand them better, there is a sharp criticism of the contemporary practice of the church, which disregards the Bible (so that closer concern with it, quite apart from all the technical difficulties that are bound up with it, does no good to anyone who aspires to a good position in the church). Extended study of the scriptures is of little use because the orthodox confession of faith does not rest on any critical knowledge of holy Scripture. For example, even in the time of the ecumenical councils in the first centuries, at which the decisive directions were laid down for the development of doctrine, the Old Testament was not understood at all in its original language (except by Origen, and he was regarded as a heretic). As a critical judgment on scripture was unnecessary for the formation of the creed, such knowledge on the part of the modern observer would only damage his high respect for the Fathers. Moreover, only tradition, and not the scripture on which it is supposedly based, is normative for the orthodox creed. Therefore 'an exact and careful study of the Scripture, is not a safe and profitable study. 'Tis a much safer, as well as more compendious way to make a man orthodox, to study the tradition of the church.'[446] In the same sarcastic tone as is evident in this comment the author goes on to say that the equally laborious study of the whole tradition is unnecessary since 'the established church, you will allow, is orthodox in all necessary points... therefore you need only her opinions to make you orthodox.'[447] For this one need only read the liturgy and the (Thirty-Nine) Articles, and even the uneducated person can do that in a short space of time in his own mother tongue. In that case he will have time for other studies without running the risk 'of falling into any dangerous opinion'.[448]

Moreover, even if it were necessary to study scripture, 'in the last place I say, and I am sure the world will say it with me, that they have been sufficiently studied already' – in which case, who, even if he discovers something new, will want to oppose his private judgment to such significant men who are familiar with the tradition of their church, men who in addition had a piety and humility which can no longer be found among the scholars of today?[449] (The reference is to patristic exegesis, which was still normative for orthodoxy.) And if there is no result at all, in other words, it is not worth anything? Above all, however (and this is the decisive obstacle): 'That a painful, exact, impartial study of the Scriptures, will by some be thought not only to do no good, but also a great deal of hurt, both to the public and to yourselves.'[450] Later this is said even more clearly: it is the lack of freedom which despite their best intentions has kept so many admirable teachers and good Protestants from venturing on such a study. 'They found that it was dangerous to examine impartially, and speak freely'; for fear of their safety they had to gloss over the greatest errors which were contained in the traditional interpretation of scripture.[451] Therefore the most eminent people preferred to devote their life's work to the pagan writers and emended and explained more there than in the whole canon of scripture over two centuries. Hence the advice, 'turn yourself to the study of the heathen historians, poets, orators, and philosophers. Spend ten or twelve years upon Horace or Terence. To illustrate a billet-doux or a drunken catch; to explain an obscene jest; to make a happy emendation, on a passage that a modest man would blush at...'[452] Bitter irony? Evidently the expression of the impotent rage of the oppressed, sacred zeal for the Protestant ideal of scripture – and precisely in that respect a marvellous example of the art of satire. It is satire that makes such effective propaganda; that Shaftesbury inscribed on his banner as being the most acute means against 'enthusiasm'; and that

Swift, standing on the other side, brought to inimitable literary consummation.[453]

2

Forms of Apologetic

It needed only another short step for criticism of the Bible to be opened up, and this is what in fact happened with the Deists who followed.

(a) Isaac Newton and his school

Alongside (and not unconnected with[1]) the party-political background to Deistic biblical criticism, we should also recall the predominant influence of the 'new philosophy' which we have already encountered in the person of John Wilkins. Since this 'new philosophy' had found an effective academic organization in the Royal Society,[2] in 1660, it had become increasingly popular. In the last decades of the seventeenth century and the first decades of the eighteenth it had found its towering academic and philosophical leader in Isaac Newton.[3] If we want to make a proper assessment of the significance of Newton for later developments, we must distinguish between the various spheres to which he devoted his attention. Only recently has the full extent of Newton's intensive personal preoccupation with theological themes and above all those of biblical exegesis become fully known (the focal points are chronology and the apocalyptic of Old and New Testaments – Newton calls Daniel and Revelation 'prophecy'). The reason why this preoccupation remained hidden for so long and so could not exercise any direct influence on the history of exegesis is that Newton did not intend his investigations in this sphere for publication, and his manuscripts have only been made fully accessible to research in recent years.[4]

It is hardly surprising that Newton was so intensively preoccupied with theological problems, even though this may seem offensive to modern historians of science. His predecessors like Francis Bacon, John Wilkins and Robert Boyle still began from a unity of thought which quite naturally included theological aspects. Even the disciples of Newton, like W.Derham, W.Whiston, A.A.Sykes and S.Clarke, continued this tradition in their own way (it is no coincidence that most of them were clergy of the Church of England). The views of Newton in the more traditional spheres of theology are in no way unique, but fit into the picture with which we already have become familiar. A good deal of attention has been paid to the fact that Newton advocated a form of 'Arianism'.[5] However, in view of the accusations against Locke to this effect[6] and a unitarian tendency widespread elsewhere in the rationalistic theology of the time,[7] this is in no way a striking detail. Manuel has classified it appropriately in a lecture in his most recent published series entitled 'Corrupters Ancient and Modern',[8] in which he quotes from Newton's unpublished manuscripts his arguments about the falsification of what he assumes to have been a pure undogmatic form of Christianity which has come about in the course of church history; they are of a form which we have kept meeting among the representatives of rationalistic Anglicanism. According to Newton, in the time of the apostles there was only a short, simple confession of faith, 'easy to be understood and remembered by the common people'.[9] The way in which he blames the Papists, the ancient philosophers (metaphysicians) and the enthusiasts for the corruption of Christianity is as unoriginal as his theory that love for God and love for the neighbour are the two basic commandments for religion, which are also common to Jews and Christians.[10] The intensity of his preoccupation with the Bible, especially with the Old Testament,[10a] which even increased in his later years, and also with the early Church Fathers (whom he later regarded as being corrupted by the influence of ancient philosophy) is in accord with the imagery and ideals of the time and certainly shows traces of the Puritan education which Newton had in common with many other significant people of his generation.[11] Some other striking features in his work also belong in this context: in his concern above all to exalt the Israel of the Old Testament and to declare that its culture is the oldest in the world, on which the whole of antiquity was dependent, he takes up old Puritan convictions which had been developed to a large degree above all by Gale in his *Court of Gentiles*.[12] In giving expression to this concern in the form of detailed chronological calculations based on the figures given in the Bible,[13] he also follows an academic method of the time, of which James Ussher's *Annales Veteris Testamenti* (1650) is the best-known example. Even Newton's method of introducing astronomical calculations here is not a new one, since Joseph Scaliger had already done the same thing.[14] All this, and even his concern with prophetic predictions (Daniel and the Revelation of John), in which along with many contemporaries he follows the example of Joseph Mede,[15] would not in fact assure Newton any special place in the history of theology were it not for his scientific research and the revolutionary consequences which followed from it for the whole of the intellectual history of modern times.

To the wider public, who did not know his private theological works,

in his lifetime Newton was purely a scientist. His pre-eminent achievements in the sphere of the exact sciences made him an unparalleled
authority here;[16] above all his position as President of the Royal Society
(from 1703) gave him immense influence on the whole of English
intellectual life, including the court and the politically influential circles
of the aristocracy. It was not just that in exercising his office Newton
was careful enough to avoid offending the tradition of society, to occupy
himself exclusively with scientific themes, and in no way to make room
for theological issues[17] – even in his own academic publications he first
of all limited himself strictly to the immanent features (thus in the first
edition of his *Principia* the word God occurs only once, in passing).[18]
His conception of the world, built up on mechanical causalities which
can be calculated in completely mathematical terms, and in particular
his theories of the existence of absolute space and absolute time, make
it easy to understand the charge laid against him that his system had
dangerous atheistical consequences.[19] Only as a result of this criticism
did Newton see fit to add to the second edition of the *Principia* a detailed
Scholium Generale in which he draws lines from his mechanical system
of the world and his views of an absolute space and an absolute time
to a conception of God which these presuppose and which for him
personally continues to remain intact.[20] In fact, as emerges from his
posthumous papers, Newton had long been occupied with the connections between natural knowledge and knowledge of God; for him too,
both spheres were closely connected in accordance with the tradition of
the 'Christian Virtuoso'.[21] In the *Scholium Generale*, Newton stresses that
the order of nature could not have come into being without an intelligent creator: 'This most elegant system of the sun, the planets and the
comets could not have arisen without the plan and the rule of an
intelligent and powerful being. And if the fixed stars are the centres of
similar systems, all these, constructed on a similar plan, are subject to
the rule of One.'[22] He had also come to similar conclusions in the second
English edition of the *Optics*, in Query 31[23] about the ordering of the
material world by its Creator: '... all material things seem to have been
composed... by the councel of an intelligent Agent. For it became Him
who created them, to set them in order. And if he did so, it is unphi-
losophical to seek for any other origin of the world, or to pretend that
it might arise out of a chaos by the mere laws of Nature; though being
once formed, it may continue by those laws for many ages.' The whole
of creation, from the eccentric, yet ordered paths of the comets to the
miraculous physical construction of the smallest animal, bears witness
to the wisdom and skill of an omnipotent and eternal agent.[24]

If there is an indication here of a line which is to find an immense
following among Newton's disciples, one can refer for Newton himself
to the famous, albeit isolated testimony from the *Scholium Generale*, in

which he impressively – and explicitly to ward off the misunderstanding that God is none other than the *anima mundi*, but also in opposition to the view which concedes him only the role of First Cause – stresses the Lordship of God.[25] God is also called Pantocrator; the name 'God' is a relational term which refers to the servants of God, and when the relationship of man to God is expressed in phrases like 'my God, your God, God of Israel', and so on, we can see that this is a personal, not a metaphysical God.[26] Newton also stresses the distance and sovereignty of God in relationship to his concepts of absolute space and absolute time.[27] In addition, as H.Metzger[28] and more precisely H.Guerlac[29] have shown, in his letters to Bentley (1692/3)[30] and above all in the Latin edition of his *Optics* of 1706, as R.Cudworth had done before him,he assigned God the role of mover (for gravity and attraction) in his atomistic view of the world, which at that time had only matter and empty space.[31] By contrast, the hypothesis of an ether filling all the intermediary spaces, which he later adopted (in the second English edition of the *Optics*, 1717), allowed a purely mechanistic theory of the world.

So what determined Newton's subsequent development[32] was not his personal confession of faith, in which we can still see the influence of the Puritan heritage, but the inner consistency of the mechanical and mathematical system of the world which he worked out and which at the same time he made enormously popular.[33] Of necessity the way led from him to the positivistic view of the world held by the French Enlightenment and in the nineteenth century, which in the end could dispense with God even as *prima causa*.[34] This certainly came about contrary to Newton's own intentions,[35] but not without his complicity, since the One who initially was celebrated with enthusiasm by countless of Newton's followers[36] was not the personal Lord in whom he privately believed and whom he had encountered in his preoccupation with apocalyptic prophecy, working for the benefit of human beings towards a consummation for this world, but God, the Governor of the world system, ordered in a perfect way. (Here they saw their need for natural theology fulfilled.) These followers then fell victim to the criticism of Hume, the radicals and Kant, so that there was nothing left but materialism, the basis of which was already present in Newton.

This development goes beyond the period of English Deism which we are discussing here. However, its first stage, the so-called 'Physico-theology', already reached an amazing climax among the Newtonians in Newton's lifetime, evidently encouraged by him. Richard Bentley[37] made a start to this in his famous Boyle Lectures of 1692,[38] in which he was the first to fulfil the commission given in Boyle's Testament,[39] 'for proving the Christian Religion, against notorious Infidels, viz. Atheists, Theists, Pagans, Jews, and Mahometans...' Thus in accordance with the intentions of the founder, the enterprise pursued an explicitly apologetic aim;[40] its main argument was the teleological proof of the existence of God. Bentley conducted it in two areas: by means of the miraculous construction of the human body[41] and by means of the origin and ordering of the cosmos.[42] Whereas the first theme was soon afterwards developed at length in John Ray's *Three Physico-Theological Discourses* (1693), for the second, especially in the last two sermons, Bentley mainly took as his basis the results of Newton's work. Consequently there has been much discussion as to how far Newton was not only involved personally in the choice of the preacher,[43] but also shared his teleological and apologetic concern. The beginning of the first of his four letters to Bentley is regularly cited in this connection.[44] Some observers doubt whether the words, 'When I wrote my treatise about our Systeme I had an eye upon such Principles as might work with considering men for the beliefe of a Deity & nothing can rejoyce me more than to find it useful for that purpose', are meant completely seriously, as the first edition of the *Principia* reveals no such attempt.[45] However, the trend of Bentley's sermons corresponds so closely to what Newton himself later said about the way in which his observations of the world were a pointer to God as the one who acts purposively in the world[46] that one would do better to presuppose the full assent of the master.[47] In fact Manuel is right in saying that despite his partial concern that the spheres of natural science and theology should not be confused, Newton himself was largely responsible for this confusion.[48]

A large number of similar, and sometimes fantastic, physico-theologies followed in Bentley's wake. In 1774, Herder knew of fifty such systems.[49] A series of them was first presented in the Boyle Lectures: among them are the eight sermons of 1704, which S.Clarke published in the following year under the title *A Demonstration of the Being and Attributes of God*.[50] Here, in close conjunction with Newton, he demonstrated the existence of God as an eternal, unchanging and omnipresent being, endowed with freedom, unlimited power and boundless goodness, from the origin of matter and its movement and from the perfection of creation (in particular against Hobbes and Spinoza – as the expanded title says, the notorious atheists). In conclusion (as a transition to the theme of the next year's sermons, which were to deal with ethics) he spoke of the moral perfection of this God.[51] Another representative of the approach is W.Derham, *Physico-Theology: or a demonstration of the Being and Attributes of God, from his works of creation* (1715, the Boyle Lectures for 1711/12).[52]. An example of Newtonianism in theology is John Craig's *Theologiae Christianae Principia Mathematica* ([1]1699).[53] The correspondence between Samuel Clarke and Leibniz in 1715-16 has attracted special attention.[54] Here we can note that Clarke was a very faithful advocate of Newton's cause, above all stressing God's freedom and his dynamic role, over against a progressive world-event which will ultimately come to an end, in opposition to the purely static world-view of Leibniz.[55] So we can say that the Newtonians, along the lines of their master, sought to retain the personal God in the framework of a moderate voluntarism;[56] or, in other words, they wanted to leave room for special providence over against general providence, thus guarding against consistent rationalism. (This is probably the most important issue in Clarke's correspondence against Leibniz.) On the other hand, however, 'For Clarke and Newton, undoubtedly, the created universe is ultimately and completely a manifestation of total providence.'[57] So here we have only a transitional position which cannot be maintained in the long run. We can recognize that very clearly, for example, in the framework of what is probably the most significant account of Newtonian physics: in the work of C.MacLaurin: *An Account of Sir Isaac Newton's Philosophical Discoveries*[58]; he finds it much easier to make clear how the order which can be observed in all parts of the world points almost automatically to the one who brought it about, who created these structures and set these movements in motion, than to make plausible his second statement, that this God still intervenes actively in the world.[59]

In the last resort a rearguard action was also the further concern which moved Newton and his school to harmonize the account of creation in Genesis with this new scientific view of the world. In addition to Thomas Burnet's *Telluris Theoria Sacra*,[60] special mention should be made here of William Whiston's *A New Theory of the Earth*,[61] which treats the account by Moses as being historically reliable in the literal sense down to the last detail. Whiston made use of Newtonian astronomy to demonstrate that the Flood was caused by the passing of a great comet on 27 November of the 1700th year after the creation.[62] Even were it thought unhistorical to laugh at such attempts, such a form of apologetics could not be convincing for long, and in its own way it contributed towards intensifying the Deistic criticism of the Bible.

We can see immediately where things were heading from an episode recorded by Whiston. He reports 'a certain Club of Persons not over religiously dispos'd, who being soberly asked, after Dr. Bentley's remarkable Sermons at Mr. Boyle's Lectures, built upon Sir Isaac Newton's Discoveries, and levell'd against the prevailing Atheism of the Age, What they had to say in their own Vindication against the Evidence produc'd by Dr. Bentley? The Answer was, That truly they did not well know what to say against it, upon the Head of Atheism: But what, say they, is this, to the Fable of Jesus Christ?' Whiston adds: 'And... it may, I believe, be justly observ'd, that the present gross Deism, or the Opposition that has of late so evidently and barefacedly appear'd against

Divine Revelation, and the Holy Scriptures, has taken its Date in some Measure from that Time.'[63] In practice, in the long run the Newtonians only played into the hands of the Deists, against whom they wanted to fight, and the Atheists (who at that time were more a chimaera than a real danger, though their time came in the second half of the century).[64] The Arianism widespread among them (which was accepted e.g. by Newton himself, Clarke, and most naturally by Whiston)[65] is an indubitable sign that the view of God held by these people was primarily oriented on the 'book of his works'.[66] Above all, however, moralistic ethics, already a living issue as a legacy of humanistic theology, gained an additional foundation in the 'new philosophy', which made it increasingly independent of the Bible and thus more and more independent of theology generally.

(b) Rationalist apologetics: Samuel Clarke and Joseph Butler

The most significant champions of ethical rationalism among the Newtonians were Samuel Clarke[67] and – in friendly alliance with him but belonging to a younger generation, and therefore already somewhat removed from Newton's influence – Joseph Butler, who to some degree introduced the whole legacy of rationalism into his work. We can best see the real influence of Newtonian thought on theology, and in particular on ethics, from Clarke's Boyle Lectures of 1704 and 1705. The *Demonstration* of 1704 (published in 1705) and the 1705 title, *A Discourse concerning... Natural Religion*[68] are conceived of as a connected whole: Clarke wanted to develop his ethics consistently from his natural philosophy and his doctrine of God. However, the way in which he carries through this undertaking already shows at first glance the fatal dilemma in which the Newton school is inevitably trapped with its attempt to reconcile the legacies of Christianity and antiquity on the basis of a mechanistic and dynamic view of the world. E.Albee, the only one to have made a thorough analysis of both of Clarke's works,[69] has already seen the profound dualism which runs through them. However, he was not fully aware of the extent of this dualism, evidently because he was still unaware of Newton's theology and therefore the degree of Clarke's dependence on it. Albee sees the *Demonstration* as still being essentially coherent; for the most part it is dominated by the notion of the freedom of God and the theory that the present ordering of the world is created by his arbitrary decrees, and as such bears witness to the existence of its creator. Hence Proposition XII, in which from the principle that as *suprema causa*, God must be a being of infinite goodness, righteousness and truth,[70] Clarke draws the conclusion that his action must necessarily always be determined by what corresponds with these criteria on any given occasion,[71] must seem to him to be a complete reversal by Clarke in his approach.[72] In reality, this is an internal contradiction, which arises throughout the Newtonians' argument. At an earlier stage, Clarke had already spoken of the perfection of God along the lines of the ontological concept of God: God is not only infinitely good and just, but also infinitely wise;[73] his unlimited power[74] and unbounded freedom[75] are also formed as infinitesimal conceptions within the framework of the thought of this ontological approach. However, because freedom as a possibility of action that cannot be determined beforehand breaks apart this ontological system, there arises an antinomy which Clarke cannot master, even by the formula which he coins, 'the Fitness of Things'. For him the 'Fitness of Things' is a criterion of both divine and human action; by means of it he attempts to develop ethics directly from cosmology. An excursus attempts to connect God's freedom and his obligation: God was in no way compelled to create the world, as he was infinitely happy and all sufficient in himself; nor need he have maintained it after its creation. 'But it was Fit, and Wise, and Good, that Infinite Wisdom should Manifest, and Infinite Goodness Communicate it self: And therefore it was Necessary... that Things should be made at such Time...' 'And when and whilst Things are in Being, the same Moral Perfections make it Necessary, that they should be disposed and governed according to the exactest most unchangeable Laws of eternal Justice, Goodness and Truth...'[76] At this point the ontological argument then creeps in: 'Because while Things and their several Relations are, they cannot but be what they are; and an infiniteley Good Being, cannot but choose to act always according to this Knowledge of the respective Fitness of Things...'[77]

We now move on to the *Discourse*, in which Clarke develops his system of ethics. This shows the same lack of balance between two basic presuppositions which conflict with one another as in the *Demonstration*, except that they do so with a kind of mirror effect. For Clarke, his basic thesis on ethics follows first of all directly from the considerations which appear at the end of the *Demonstration*: 'The same consequent Fitness or Unfitness... with regard to which, the Will of God always and necessarily does determine it self, to choose to act only what is agreeable to Justice, Equity, Goodness and Truth, in order to the Welfare of the whole Universe; ought likewise constantly to determine the Wills of all subordinate rational Beings, to govern all their Actions by the same Rules, for the good of the Publick, in their respective Stations: That is, these eternal and necessary differences of things, make it fit and reasonable for Creatures so to act.'[78] It is well known that in this argument Clarke is influenced by the natural law approach of R.Cumberland,[79] who similarly stresses the rational, mathematically ordered structure of the cosmos, and assigns to the laws of moral action their place in the ordering of the whole.[80] The antique Stoic heritage which is present in Cumberland's[81] view of God and his ethics also plays a decisive role in Clarke, coming through the changes of the Newtonian world-view which attaches yet more importance to the cosmological ideas of order in a modified form. However, after this argument, surprisingly enough Clarke now embarks on a further one: 'Prop.III. That the same eternal Moral Obligations, which are of themselves incumbent indeed on all rational Creatures, antecedent to any respect of particular Reward or Punishment; must yet certainly and necessarily be attended with Rewards and Punishments.'[82] Were we perfect rational creatures, no other form of moral obligation would be necessary, but at this point Clarke sees the limitations of human moral existence, that we are delivered over to feelings which provoke irrational behaviour, and in this way he arrives at this distinction between a 'primary' and a 'secondary' moral obligation – a dualistic theory, which Albee[83] rightly finds highly problematical. The doctrine of reward and punishment and the assertion that these are to be expected in a 'future state'[84] are traditionally Christian statements, but they represent a complete break with the approach which has been followed hitherto. The traditional Christian doctrine of original sin which has a role here[85] allows Clarke to criticize the Stoic doctrine that virtue is a reward in itself,[86] but this would follow the lines of his original argument. Over against Shaftesbury, who resolutely takes the step towards autonomous ethics, Clarke beyond question remains at the half-way stage. His attempt to bring together the philosophical and the biblical concepts of God cannot have any convincing result. The God of the Bible is in fact introduced as a *deus ex machina*, and in view of that, the whole argument which follows must seem authoritarian and arbitrary. On this second level of argumentation Clarke goes on to introduce the argument for the necessity of a revelation, in which one feels Locke's influence strongly[87] when Clarke asserts that while all the obligations of natural religion can in general be derived from true reason, in view of man's state which for the moment is corrupted, only very few people are in a position personally to recognize these things clearly for themselves. So they were very much in need of special instruction:[88] the best pagan philosophers were not in a position really to reform mankind,[89] and therefore a divine revelation was absolutely necessary.[90] This is in fact the weak point of the apologetic argument, in that it seeks to introduce historical propositions into a deductive argument which cannot be proved to be consistent in this connection. All the other arguments which Clarke goes on to put forward cannot get over this decisive flaw since they are *a posteriori*, to the effect that only the Christian religion among the religions of the world 'has any just pretense or tolerable appearance of Reason',[91] that the practical duties taught by it for the most part coincide with our natural knowledge of God and at their strongest are in a position to contribute to human happiness;[92] that the motives with which the Christian religion inculcates these duties[93] and the way in which it does so[94] are very closely parallel to natural conceptions; and finally, that all Christian doctrines are in accord with unbiassed reason and directly serve to improve morality.[95]

In this context Clarke also introduces a theory of miracles,[96] which is directly derived from Newton's dynamic cosmology: since the normal guidance of the world, as a constant overcoming of the inertia of matter, represents continuing divine action, even miracle is not impossible in itself; it is not in fact harder to achieve than the normal divine action, but is merely a 'work effected in a manner unusual, or different from the common and regular Method of Providence, by the interposition either of God himself, or of some Intelligent Agent superiour to Man, for the Proof or Evidence of some particular Doctrine, or in attestation to the Authority of some particular Person'.[97] Since, as is evident from this definition, in this hierarchically arranged world not only does God himself perform miracles, but can also commission an angel to do so, or can delegate power to creatures,[98] in principle a miracle does not even lie outside the natural capabilities of created beings.[99] Indeed even miracles performed by evil powers are not mere deceptions.[100] Therefore one can only distinguish miracles performed by God from those performed by evil spirits with an intent to deceive by the doctrine which they serve to endorse: if this doctrine is godless or leads to blasphemy, we have the deception of evil spirits; conversely, the other miracles come from God.[101]

From Clarke's Boyle sermons one can recognize the forced situation in which rationalistic apologetic finds itself in this period. It could not overcome the intrinsic contradiction between the philosophical approach, which it also wanted to follow, and the traditionally Christian doctrines which it sought to defend (subjectively one cannot deny Clarke this purpose in any way). As natural religion was an integral part of its system, at best it could accord the revelation in it a secondary function, that of a pedagogical expedient which was in a position to bring the principles of morality closer to the weakened reason of the average man, though in principle they should have been able to recognize these rules.[102] At all events, we must say that these problems are particularly evident in Clarke precisely because he was known as a predominantly clear thinker (which is why Newton transferred his discussion with the brilliant Leibniz to him). Garin has stressed the proximity of Clarke to Deism,[103] particularly referring to the role of revelation in his work.[104] In fact Clarke's view in this connection is very similar to that of Tindal in his book *Christianity as old as the Creation*,[105,106] and Tindal did not fail to exploit this situation extensively.[107] On the other hand, Clarke did not conceal his sympathy for the sort of Deists 'who, if they did indeed believe what they pretend, have just and right Notions of God and of all the Divine Attributes in every respect';[108] if one does not share his view that to be consistent, such Deists would also have to arrive at the recognition of the Christian revelation, in fact he largely paved the way for them.[109]

The dilemma in which rationalistic apologetic finds itself through its line of thought based on the two 'Books', natural and revealed religion, appears in another, equally illuminating way in Joseph Butler's *The Analogy of Religion, Natural and Revealed to the Constitution and Course of Nature* (1736).[110] However, chronologically Butler's work belongs at the end of the period we are considering and his argument already presupposes the heyday of deism, against which it is directed. Still, precisely because there is hardly a thought in the *Analogy* which had not already been expressed often in the Boyle Lectures or the anti-deistic literature immediately preceding it,[111] a look at the *Analogy* by way of example can illuminate the pattern of thought among the official defenders of the church.[112] Although it had been provoked by a need to ward off the Deists, in its approach this apologetic nevertheless shows so many features in common with its opponents that we can understand why it made so little impression on them. Indeed, in view of a work like Butler's *Analogy*, the question which is often asked, whether because of the fragility of its arguments this apologetic did not help to hasten on the decline of the Christian religion which it sought to defend, cannot easily be brushed aside. This uncertainty is evident today, so we can understand why Butler, who was highly respected during his lifetime and in part well into the nineteenth century,[113] still arouses considerable attention today, at least in the history of ideas.[114] However, the rise of radical biblical criticism among the later Deists and their successors[115] only becomes understandable when we consider the place which Butler assigns to revelation and know the arguments with which he sets out to defend its role.

A survey of the construction of the *Analogy*[116] already shows the course which Butler plans to adopt: he means to demonstrate the significance of revealed religion (or Christianity) by means of natural religion, in accordance with the principle of 'Analogy'.[117] In content, his picture of natural religion, as he develops it in the first part of the book, corresponds largely with the Humanist model (thus, for example, the similarity with Cherbury's principles is striking);[118] in terms of method, however, he is governed by the empiricist principles of Locke and the Newtonians. Butler takes his starting point from the demonstration of the existence of eternal life deduced by analogy (Part I, Chapter I): this proves to be above all a moral requirement.[119] For the rule of God is a moral rule (Part I, Chapter III), which is exercised through reward and punishment (Part I, Chapter II). Now – and this is the old problem of the Psalmists – as the fate of the morally wicked in this world is often undeservedly favourable, whereas the righteous must often renounce the reward they are due, a future life is absolutely necessary to provide the possibility of restoring the balance of justice which does not come about on earth. In the light of this, the temporal existence of man represents a time of trial in which he is put to the test in respect of his future status by all kinds of difficulties and dangers, in an analogous way to his testing in respect of his earthly destiny in the sphere of the natural government of God (Part I, Chapter IV). This state of testing serves moral discipline and improvement, in that man can prepare for his future state of eternal blessedness, just as, by analogy, he can arrange his circumstances here on earth (Part I, Chapter V). In this sense, life can be regarded as a school for eternity, just as youth can be regarded as a stage in education for maturity.

The concluding chapter of the First Part (Chapter VII[120]) is important for the method of argumentation in the Second Part. Here Butler takes up a principle of Locke's epistemology,[121] albeit with a characteristic shift; as is already clear from the introduction, this has guided him as a basic presupposition throughout his investigation: it is the distinction between certain and probable knowledge. Whereas according to Locke certain knowledge is to be gained in the realm of abstract ideas and also in the sphere of theoretical ethics, particularly in the *Essay Concerning Human Understanding* IV, 3 and IV, 16, he stresses that in the context of the experimental sciences knowledge is to be gained only on the incomplete level of probability (which, particularly in Essay IV, 19, he later extends to the 'supernatural' statements of Christian dogmatics).[122] Butler transfers Locke's thesis to the sphere of man's practical behaviour in the world, and thence by way of 'analogy' to the statements of 'natural religion'. In this way he consistently avoids theoretical abstract arguments: for his procedure, as he makes clear at another point, he deliberately chooses the practical anthropological starting point.[123] He expects his conversation partner to ask practical and utilitarian questions: How am I to establish in the world? What basic insights of 'natural religion' must I take into account in order to provide for my future in eternal life in the right way? He is an apologist to such an extreme degree that in his argumentation *ad hominem* he is prepared to accept all the principles of his conversation partner.[124] This readiness leads him to make excessive use of the argument from probability: even in the introduction he indicates that both (natural) religion in general and (revealed) Christianity in particular are concerned with matters in connection with which one can in practice act according to analogous principles of greater or lesser probability, as people also do in everyday matters. Butler's basic argument has a certain similarity to Pascal's

'Wager';[125] he attempts to demonstrate to his unbelieving or sceptical reader that not only natural religion but also revealed Christianity has at least so high a degree of probability that even according to the lights of the sober considerations of utility, it is worth following in practical life and action. The *Analogy* has an eminently practical and ethical aim – this is typical not only of Butler personally but of the whole religious approach of his time: 'His main aim is to show that this probability is sufficient for it to be reasonable to use Christianity as a guide of life.'[126] In the sphere of 'natural' religion, which Butler deals with in the first part of his work (up to and including Chapter V), he proceeds in such a way as to make plausible certain doctrines which he supposes to be part of natural religion (in reality the expectation of eternal life and of rewards and punishments in the beyond are Christian statements, even if the humanistic tradition claims that they are a consensus on the part of all mankind) on the basis of the similarity (analogy) between the known course of nature[127] and Christianity as a whole. The background to this is the Newtonian view of the world as a totality set in motion by God in accordance with particular laws;[128] in Butler's view there are analogous laws to this in the general principles of natural religion which we can also recognize without revelation.[129] In addition to some other objections which can be passed over here,[130] attention has been drawn particularly to the fact that the argument from probability is quite weak, simply because, as Butler himself expressly says,[131] all degrees of probability are conceivable, down to a mere possibility which in no way can be an adequate ground for the devotion of a person's whole life. However, we have to admit that Butler in fact believes that he has demonstrated a higher degree of probability than mere possibility for 'natural religion'.[132]

In the second part, which is concerned with revealed religion, the principle of probability which Butler also applies here[133] becomes one stage more dangerous. In respect of the content of this revealed religion Butler is not at all original: it is 1. 'a republication, and external institution, of natural or essential religion, adapted to the present circumstances of mankind'.[134] The almost verbal agreement of this formulation with the sub-title of Tindal's work *Christianity as old as the Creation* is striking: 'or, the Gospel, a Republication of the Religion of Nature'. On this point we can hardly see any difference between the argumentation of Butler and the thinking of the Deists.[135] At first things seem to be different with the second point: 'containing an account of a dispensation of things not discoverable by reason'.[136] Here Butler, following the usual line of rational supernaturalism, includes above all the traditional doctrines of the saving of fallen mankind by Christ as the mediator, of his incarnation, of the Holy Spirit, and so on (Ch. V). For the first point he continues to rely on the demonstration of similarities ('analogies') between natural and revealed religion (both stress the same truths, like the existence of God, a future life, reward and punishment, etc.).[137] His most significant weakness emerges first when he goes on to the justification for the second sphere, since here he refers to another form of argument which, while he subsumes it under the general concept of analogy, is in reality purely external proof, proof from a history understood as an arsenal of facts.[138] Against the background of his general approach, that there cannot be a compelling argument for the truth of Christianity, the metaphysical doctrines of which go beyond the arguments of reason,[139] there are then such things as above all the various miracles and prophecies which must be adduced as 'its direct and fundamental proofs'.[140] The whole biblical tradition is seen on this level: 'This revelation, whether real or supposed, may be considered as wholly historical. For prophecy is nothing but the history of events before they come to pass; doctrines also are matters of fact; and precepts come under the same notion. And the general design of Scripture, which contains in it this revelation, thus considered as historical, may be said to be, to give us an account of the world, in this one single view, as God's world.'[141]

Miracles and prophecies, for which there is evidence in scripture, together with other concomitant signs, 'amount to a much higher degree of proof, upon such a joint review, than could be supposed upon considering them separately, at different times'.[142] However, these are only 'probable proofs',[143] which only attain a higher degree of probability through their accumulation. Neither individually nor taken together are they compelling in the sense of being certain knowledge, since in conclusion Butler does not venture to claim more than a moderate degree of probability for them: 'In the next place, with regard to Christianity, it will be observed; that there is a middle between a full satisfaction of the truth of it, and a satisfaction of the contrary. The middle state of mind between these two consists in a serious apprehension, that it may be true, joined with doubt whether it be so.'[144]

In respect of the way in which Butler uses these 'historical arguments',[145] in accordance with contemporary terminology one would describe him as a fundamentalist: 'Scripture history'[146] is demonstrated by reliable witnesses, the venerable age of the traditions, and so on, to be a chain of demonstrable facts.[147] This provided the opponents of revelation with the drift of their argument: they only needed to remove the main pillars of this edifice, miracles and prophecy, and the credibility of the whole of Christianity would inevitably collapse, because it was based on what was supposed to be a facticity capable of being demonstrated rationally. In fact, as an apologist Butler had gone a decisive step even beyond Locke: while Locke towards the end of his life put his trust, again unfounded but provoked by insight into the limitations of human reason, in the biblical tradition, Butler, although he similarly speaks of the limits of reason, does so in purely quantitative terms. For him the act of faith is not an existential event but an exclusively intellectual process, based on the evaluation of grounds for and against the reliability of external witnesses to facts.[148] Thus essentially he occupies the same ground as the Deists; so the refutation born of rational scepticism which meets him on his own ground, as expressed by Hume, inevitably dealt him an annihilating blow. In fact his philosophical arguments are extremely weak; he was not in a position to produce genuinely theological ones.

Now it will be noted that Butler's work comes almost at the end of the Deistic debate. The reason why the Deists did not triumph over the official apologetic of which he was a representative was that in their intellectual presuppositions they were hindered by similar weaknesses, and lacked Hume's consistency. Their arguments were not more profound; they simply took a different course: they attacked the credibility of miracle and the fulfilment of prophecy with negative, rational arguments; they doubted the truth of the supernatural content of the Christian revelation and only accepted natural religion; they believed that the moral ordering of the world was in principle intact, and therefore that the traditional statements about the Fall, the mediation of Christ and redemption were outdated beyond rescue since they believed in the goodness in man and the power of his reason even to recognize the law of his moral actions.

Butler's position in the sphere of ethics[149] is on the one hand very similar to the attitude of the Deists. His meta-ethical standpoint, for which we find formulae in his work which are almost identical to those of Clarke, even in points of detail,[150] has been called ethical intuitionism or 'a non-naturalistic objective analysis'.[151] In this respect he seems to occupy a place in the development of ethical theories which starts with Cumberland, and already takes a decisive new step with Shaftesbury. He now goes one stage further. A far-reaching autonomy of ethics seems to emerge in his work in two directions: first, in the derivation of ethical norms from an immutable ordering of the world to which even God himself is subject (here, like his Humanist predecessors, Butler follows the Stoic tradition[152]), and secondly in the central role of conscience, which we have to understand as an innate capacity in human beings for rational judgment about good and evil.[153] If we take this side of his ethical system we must accept that A.Duncan-Jones is right in speaking of the characteristically non-theological structure of Butler's ethics.[154] Here the idealistic belief in the natural goodness of men stands at the centre.[155] However, Butler does not represent this standpoint in a pure form; alongside this we have his moral theory, the character of which is determined by the content of specifically Christian doctrine which Butler has portrayed in his *Analogy* as at the same time both natural and revealed religion, on the assumption of a divine rule over the world and the expectation of a future life and reward and punishment in the beyond.[156] At this point the two lines of ethical theory deriving from antiquity, eudaemonism and altruism, again meet: in secondary literature this has led to an on-going discussion about the role of benevolence and self-love in Butler's ethics.[157] If Butler's remarks on all these matters are ambiguous and often obscure, the reason for this may be his place in the history of tradition between the Humanist ethical tradition, Lockean-Newtonian psychological epistemology and supranaturalistic Christian apologetic. In his work these are mixed up in an amalgam which is only comprehensible in the light of this special situation. Here, as we can see from the close identification of the most important elements of natural and revealed religion in the *Analogy*, the Christian substance has already been largely evacuated so as to become a general world-view; the role of the biblical tradition becomes a mere archive providing historical authentification on which depend only a number of special doctrines of purely secondary importance, which Hobbes and Locke were already prepared to surrender in favour of a minimal consensus. The combination of moral laws with biblical ethics, or more exactly the ethics of the New Tetament, even if this was already presented before Locke in more of an *a posteriori* way, is now totally dissolved; such a way of verifying ethical norms is now completely abandoned.[158] To this degree Butler's system is a testimony to the far-reaching changes which had taken place in the understanding of the Bible in the first decades of the eighteenth century even in the official Anglican camp. The development which Bacon, Boyle and Newton had introduced in their honourable enthusiasm for furthering Christian belief by using the results of their scientific knowledge about an amazing physical and regular ordering of the cosmos to support religion was almost changed into its opposite: 'Natural religion was supposed to be the sure defender. Yet in the end the defender turned out to be the enemy in the gates. In theory natural religion was meant to supplement Christianity, to provide it with a rational foundation; in practice it tended to supplement it.'[159]

(c) At the opposite pole: Jonathan Swift

We would, however, be taking too one-sided a view of intellectual development of the time were we to overlook the influence which the established Church of England – in its basic doctrine one of the Reformation churches – continued to exercise on wide areas of the population.[159a] One of its representatives was the Dean of Dublin, Jonathan Swift. But in the dominant climate of ethical optimism there was need for remarkable sensitivity to the depths of human existence, countering this optimism with a view gained from the foundations of Christian anthropology. It was similarly almost as inevitable that such an attitude would make Swift an outsider and largely spoil the chances of a career as that he would encounter misunderstanding and misinterpretation on the part of his contemporaries. However, we need to go further into the reasons which until very recently largely prevented even his modern interpreters from arriving at an appropriate understanding of his real intentions. One of the main reasons is beyond question the literary form in which Jonathan Swift[160] clothed the best known of his works; he thought that he could appropriately describe the problems which he observed only in the indirect language of satire,[161] and by means of allegory compel his reader to reflect on prevailing conditions in state, church and society.[161a] Now it was precisely this form which led to the misunderstandings that obscured his significance above all in the nineteenth century and even now have not been fully removed, even if in the meantime we can see the beginnings of a more appropriate judgment.[162] The interpretation of Swift, too, has been flawed because of the insufficient attention paid to the perspective from the history of theology in many more recent interpretations from the pens of literary critics, which isolate the literary aspects. Only in most recent times have voices been heard pointing out that Swift was a clergyman of the Anglican church and took his calling seriously;[163] theological motives above all governed him in his most famous satirical works and in accordance with the thought patterns of the time they are indissolubly bound up with political, moral and literary perspectives.[164] Swift's specifically and earnestly theological writings are little known, like the few extant sermons of his[165] which can shed further light on the true attitude that is also concealed behind the satires.

So far, scholars have failed to note what can be learned from a comparison between his early satire, *The Tale of a Tub*,[166] and his late work *Gulliver's Travels*:[167] that in the decades during which he observed his world, Swift underwent a considerable intellectual development. In the basic story[168] of *The Tale of a Tub*, about three brothers each of whom receives as a legacy from his father the same garment with the instruction not to change it in any way if they do not want to take harm, we find a new example of the well-known Humanist Protestant depravation theory of church history.[169] Here Swift proves to be a faithful pupil of moderate rational Anglicanism; it is striking that Jack, the representative of the Scottish Reformation, seems much more ridiculous in his conduct, which is depicted as irrational, than Peter, who embodies the Roman Church.[170] In the fight against 'Enthusiasm' Swift here stands in the same line as Shaftesbury (this is also particularly clear in the 'Digression' in Section IX). But even in the 'Digressions' in which he argues for the

'Old'[171] against the confusions of the 'Moderns', we have a lively Humanist legacy which maintains the classical foundations of thought against the claims of modern natural science.[172] The same theme, which also occurs in the 'Battle of the Books', recurs in *Gulliver's Travels*, in the journey to Laputa, where Swift again expresses his concern at the totalitarian claim of the Newtonians in the form of his caricature of the astronomers, possessed and working with flappers.[173] The anthropology is different: here Swift, the incorruptible observer of behaviour who is growing steadily more disillusioned, has an experience to which he gives impressive artistic expression by means of classical satire, in particular in the fourth of Gulliver's journeys.[174] Precisely at this point, nineteenth-century Idealism understood Swift least, making him out with every sign of abhorrence[175] to be a misanthropist and solitary.[176] In the meantime it has become clear that, as in his serious[177] and ironical[178] ecclesiastical and theological writings, so in Gulliver's position between the rational, fabulous Houyhnhnms, far removed from being human, and the animal Yahoos, Swift draws a picture of man which comes to be diametrically opposed to the rationalistic claims of the Humanist tradition: the cold Stoic rationality of the Houyhnhnms is similarly a caricature which gets in the way of any real human relationship,[179,180] as too is the brutal animalism of the Yahoos, which nevertheless corresponds much more closely to the reality of human existence. It has become increasingly clear that in Gulliver's fourth journey Swift seeks to reject the human arrogance which presents itself in the general intellectual attitude of his time, in particular in Latitudinarian theology.[181] Over against the general confidence in human rationality he recollects with impressive vividness the basic assertion of Christian belief that man is sinful and, in the conditions of his creaturely existence, fallen.[182] Swift's letter of 29 September 1725 to Pope is often quoted;[183] here Swift rejects the current definition of man as an *animal rationale* and instead of this allows only the definition *animal rationis capax*.[184] Man is capable of a modest degree of reason only when he has experienced the beginning of the renewal of his life through the acceptance of forgiveness: Swift is concerned to present this Christian truth to his readers, conditioned by the Enlightenment, in parable form.[185] We must also see in this context the episode with the Struldbruggs, whose senility in their eternal earthly life provides the contrast between self-seeking human worth and the eternity beyond, which can only be achieved through God's help.[186] The Glubbdubdrib episode teaches Gulliver, who had just boasted of the pre-eminence of the English nation, and especially its nobility, to the king of Brobdingnag, the insight that even among the famous dead there is hardly one who has not gained his position through doubtful means.[187] The whole narrative, especially after the third journey, is the account of a progressive disillusionment.[188] In all this Swift has progressed far beyond the Humanist influence of his youth[189] (though he largely remained a moralist in connection with the themes of his time).[190] His definition of man, which finds a series of critics[191] depicted in Gulliver's fourth journey, that he has an existence midway between the animal and the rational, and that it is important for him to attain a balance between the two elements, does not affect matters. Swift's true intent – and this is also served by the introduction of the Houyhnhnms as rational animal beings[192] – is rather to destroy man's self-assertion[193] and to leave him in the uncertainty which is the fruit of apt satire,[194] at the same time serving the pastoral aim of making the reader receptive to true modesty.[195]

So if we hear Swift as a voice which energetically contradicts the powerful Stoic and rational mood of the age,[196] at the same time we must note that he was a crass outsider and owes the hearing that he found,[197] then as now mostly misunderstood, chiefly to his satirical skill and less to the cause which he represented.[198] The general trend went beyond him, and that after his few years of also being able to exercise indirect influence in major political issues during the episode of Tory rule under Queen Anne,[199] he had to spend the rest of his life in distant Ireland is only an outward sign of the ineffectiveness of his profound criticism in an age which, after the fashion of Shaftesbury and Bolingbroke, had moral optimism inscribed on its banner.[200]

3

The Heyday of Deism

(a) Anthony Collins

In the meantime, the Deistic movement continued with the emergence of Anthony Collins.[1] There is much in the life and the character of Collins and his writings to confirm the lines of development which we have noted so far. It is no coincidence that his acquaintance with Locke in the last years of Locke's life[2] prompted Collins to his own writing, and Locke's influence is also evident from the content of many of his works. That is already true of his first book, the *Essay concerning the Use of Reason in Propositions, the Evidence whereof depends on Human Testimony* (1707).[3] The definition of the concept of reason with which Collins begins,[4] 'By Reason I understand the faculty of the Mind whereby it perceives the Truth, Falsehood, Probability or Improbability of Propositions', is as much conceived of in the spirit of Locke as is the closer definition of the truth, falsehood, probability and improbability of statements as 'the necessary or probable agreement or disagreement of the Ideas of which the extremes in Propositions consist.'[5] Thus Collins' starting point is closely related to that in Toland's *Christianity not Mysterious*;[6] like Toland, Collins began from Locke's epistemology in the fourth book of the *Essay Concerning Human Understanding*, but drew consequences from this approach which Locke had deliberately avoided.[7] He gives as a criterion for the distinction between statements to which assent can be given and those to which it cannot that these 'are adequately divided into Propositions agreeable or contrary to Reason; and there remains no third Idea under which to rank them.'[8] This is particularly true of all statements which are to be accepted as historical facts on the basis of men's outward convictions, and above all of revealed religion.[9] Credibility in this area can be claimed only for statements of which it is true 'That the words made use of in the Relation stand for known Ideas, or Ideas that we are capable of forming'.[10] As will be clear from the following remarks,[11] this relates in particular to the sphere of mysteries, which must remain as incomprehensible as talk of colour is to a blind man. Even reports of a divine revelation must be adapted to our human capacities for understanding.[12] Statements about faith may not contradict one another, nor must they go against statements which we can derive through formal deduction from ideas (in the Lockean sense).[13]

These principles call for a special kind of application in connection with Holy Scripture. For in order that even the simplest of ordinary people could understand that he was concerned for them, God had to make use in a revelation of such words 'whose literal meaning is False, but whose real meaning is consistent with the justest Notions of Reason and Philosophy'.[14] Scripture must therefore be read in such a way as to investigate 'whether the Words under any Construction bear a reasonable Sense'. 'It is most evident that the Authors of the Holy Scriptures had not principally in view Speculative-Instruction.' Rather, they adapted their expressions to the capacity of the majority of people to understand. 'No doubt, had Moses or any of the inspired Writers been to write a Treatise of Metaphysicks wherein they had treated of God, they most certainly would have spoken of him with exactness, and have elevated their Minds above all created Beings, and put nothing to appearance into their Idea of God but what belong'd to an infinitely perfect Being.'[15] However, in their writings they had a moral purpose. Anthropomorphic concepts and conceptions about God go with this form of accommodation. Therefore the Bible cannot be understood in the literal sense, but (with its spiritual statements about God which are found in other places) their meaning has to be rendered according to the principles of reason and philosophy.

In these remarks we find a good many of Locke's ideas of education. It is also characteristic, however, that Collins can twice explicitly quote remarks of Tillotson's to support his argument;[16] in many respects his thought is closely related to that of the Latitudinarians.[17] In this early work we even find some explicitly apologetic features, as when Collins, with some comments on Ex.16.35; Deut.3.14 which are also taken from D.Huet,[18] explains these two passages as later additions to the Pentateuch, thus saving its Mosaic authorship.[19] Here he clearly expresses his aim: it is 'to prove the necessity of the use of Reason to distinguish Falsehood from Truth in matters of Revelation', even when he adds as his declared apologetic intent: 'in order to give all possible Authority to that which can with any reason be suppos'd to be a Revelation'.[20]

Collins next[21] concerns himself with 'Things above, and Things contrary to Reason'. In these remarks (which are not always very clear) he is concerned[22] among other things with the doctrine of the Trinity. At least it is clear that Collins puts forward the view that no one need believe anything that is 'beyond reason', i.e. that cannot be grasped by reason. He firmly rejects the usual view that there are also things which can only be partially grasped by human reason, if at all. Even in the apparently difficult cases of the ideas of God's infinity and eternity and the relationship between his foreknowledge and man's freedom the contradictions can be removed by clear definitions.[23] For the second problem he arrives at the solution of determinism, a theory which he developed further three years later (arguing against a sermon by W.King, the Archbishop of Dublin)[24] and finally established in 1717 in the work which O'Higgins describes as by far the best of his purely philosophical works:[25] the *Philosophical Inquiry concerning Human Liberty*.[26] In this context, however, we need not go further into this question and can make only a passing reference to the debate between Collins and Clarke in 1707-8 on the question whether the soul is material and whether matter can think.[27]

Collins' activity as a writer, too, is closely connected with the events of his day in church politics (and thus of course also with politics in general). We can see this particularly clearly in the appearance of a pamphlet that he wrote in connection with the Sacheverell debate of 1709-10.[28] Here he has a detailed discussion of the statement in the twentieth of the Thirty-Nine Articles of the Anglican Church, 'The Church hath power to decree rites and ceremonies, and authority in controversies of faith', and undertakes to demonstrate that this is a later addition to the text.[29] As is already clear from the sub-title of his work,[30] he sees the insertion of this clause as a piece of deception on the part of the senior clergy.[31] It is illuminating, however, that by his methodological approach (in interpreting the passage as an addition to the text) he clears the Convocation of 1562 under Archbishop Parker, which originally passed the Thirty-Nine Articles, and that of 1571, which revised them, of any deliberate intent: evidently he wants to show those who were really responsible for the Reformation under Elizabeth I in a positive light and therefore attributes the fraudulent insertion, which he thinks that he has first discovered in the printed Latin edition of 1563,[32] to an unknown person.[33] This tendency is matched by the content of a detailed note[34] with an anecdote about Queen Elizabeth. She is said to have discovered that legends of saints and martyrs had been slipped into her personal copy of the Book of Common Prayer by the Dean of St Paul's and had censured this as a severe infringement of her declared intent to remove 'all such Relicks of Popery'. The origin of this way of thinking becomes quite plain when in addition we find an attack on the use of organs and images in churches and 'Placing the Communion Table Altarwise', bowing towards the east and putting candles on the communion table:[35] clearly here the old Puritan charges against the liturgical formulae of the mainstream church are taken up! The hidden connection between the Deistic approach and the legacy of the

Puritan hostility to ceremony is very evident at this point.[36] In this context there also belongs the polemic against Archbishop Laud, who is accused in ironical fashion of deliberate untruthfulness;[37] on the other hand, the worth of the Bible is deliberately stressed: here Collins significantly refers to the tradition of Anglican rationalism in the form of Chillingworth's authority.[38] In the year 1713 there followed Collins' most famous book, the *Discourse of Free Thinking*.[39] Though the hypothesis that other authors than Collins were involved in the *Discourse* cannot be maintained,[40] nevertheless the book is not the isolated work of an individual, but is connected with the organized 'Freethinkers', who are also mentioned in the title. For a time this movement also had its own weekly journal, *The Free-Thinker*,[41] and during these years met in a London coffee house.[42]

The famous definition of 'freethinking' with which Collins begins his remarks[43] can only be understood in the general context of his intentions. His most important opponent Bentley[44] criticized him for merely stating the obvious.[45] However, Collins is evidently concerned with the right to free thinking independently of any given authority[46] and on any possible theme.[47] He very quickly comes to the opponents whom he has in view, the priests,[48] and the object of their central concern, the Bible.[49] The whole outline of the work[50] is determined by these two poles. The area in which free-thinking is most urgently desirable, and where this right is refused to people, namely over religious questions, is introduced in the second section. Here he deals with the nature and properties of God and the authority and meaning of those scriptures which are regarded as holy.[51] Man is refused the right to think in this sphere by the 'enemies of freethinking': these enemies are the priests. Of the seven arguments with which Collins justifies the duty of free-thinking in the second section[52] – they include the catchphrase 'superstition'[53] and the reference to the gospel for its own sake,[54] both integral elements of the legacy of Humanism and Puritanism, to which Collins also comes very close in this work[55] – it is the last,[56] 'The Conduct of the Priest... makes Free-Thinking on the Nature and Attributes of God, on the Authority of the Scriptures, and on the Sense of Scriptures, unavoidable'[57] that is disproportionately extended by no less than ten instances of their conduct. Here, too, it is again striking that a whole series of these instances is concerned with scripture. Collins takes a disproportionate amount of space to discuss the difference of opinion between the priests of the various religions of the world over their particular sacred scriptures, and within the Christian churches and sects over the extent and nature of the canon;[58] and also the various views which are to be found among the priests of the church in connection with the meaning of scripture; here he refers both to text-critical problems and to the obscurities of its content and problems of interpretation.[59] The same theme recurs in the form of charges against 'the priests', more exactly against particular theologians. One example of their conduct is that they made the canon uncertain (by indicating its relatively late formation)[60] and that they substantially damaged the cause of Protestantism over against the Papists by drawing attention to the numerous textual variants in the New Testament.[61] The final conclusion which Collins draws from this conduct runs: 'That since the Priests, not only of different Religions and Sects, but of the same Sect, are infinitely divided in Opinion about the Nature of God, and the Authority and Meaning of Scriptures...since they render both the Canon and Text of Scriptures precarious and uncertain...; we have no way of setling our selves in a right Notion of God; in the Reception of the present Canon of Scripture, and that Sacred Greek Text of the New Testament which is commonly printed; and in the Belief of the Doctrine and Practice of the Discipline and Worship of the Church of England as founded on that pure Text..., but by ceasing to rely on them, and thinking freely for our selves.'[62]

While the aim of these remarks, the invitation to dare to be wise, *sapere aude*, the motto of the Enlightenment, is very clear, Collins' attitude to scripture cannot be defined quite so simply. Lechler's comment that as soon as examples are introduced, everything that is said about the right and obligation to free-thinking becomes ambivalent,[63] is particularly true of Collins' observations on scripture. Indeed Collins gives the impression that he wants to preserve 'this pure text' intact and safeguard the reliability of the canon by branding as doubtful the scientific investigations of the theologians he has quoted as being lamentable consequences of the doubtful behaviour of the 'priests', and instead of this pointing to the private judgment of each individual layman as the way to rescue an authentic scriptural authority. It looks as if this was intended to be a tacit rejection of Christianity in general, or at least of revelation, and this is the way in which contemporary polemics immediately understood Collins. However, another interpretation is possible if we take him literally. This would be an attitude which is markedly hostile to the High Church movement and in this sense to the clergy,[64] continuing the tendency in *Priestcraft in Perfection* which again develops the line in Tindal's *Rights of the Christian Church* and other writings from the dispute against the High Churchmen during the Tory rule under Queen Anne. In that case a direct repudiation of scripture as such cannot be found here. In support of this view, which also seems to me to fit in best with the circumstances, O'Higgins has also cited a letter which Collins wrote to the Geneva theologian B.Pictet,[65] in which he expressly guards against an abbreviated quotation by Pictet of the passage just cited and points out that we may well have a way of avoiding the difficulties caused by theologians, namely by free-thinking. O'Higgins describes Collins' purpose in his *Essay on the Use of Reason* with the words 'that his aim was not to discredit Scripture but to produce instances that he considered requisite "to prove the necessity of the use of reason to distinguish falsehood from truth in matters of Revelation" and at the same time to throw an implied slur on the clergy.'[66] This is similarly true of the *Discourse of Free Thinking*. The list of Collins' intellectual forebears, which he himself provides,[67] and the authors to whom he refers,[68] put him in the Humanist and rationalist tradition which extends from the Puritans on one side[69] to the Deists on the other.[70] Obviously – and this is particularly evident from the frequent references to Chillingworth – Collins personally continues to value the Bible, above all the New Testament,[71] which he thinks that he can save by commending freedom of judgment. However, the effect of his comments was quite the opposite: his argument about the uncertainty of the canon and the textual tradition of the New Testament inevitably shook the authority of the Bible. It could not be foisted on to the theologians he incriminated, though this was probably Collins' real intention: in this respect he was a 'fundamentalist'.[72]

However, even in this connection his attitude was not completely straightforward. In the third section of his book in particular, there are all kinds of remarks which inevitable give the impression that he is basically against Christianity, or at least against Revelation. This is the case, for instance, when he again gives morality a central position in a humanistic theology which again thinks in strict alternatives, making all peace and order in society dependent on the fulfilment of moral obligations and branding all that detracts from this, including speculative opinions (theological doctrines) as evil.[73] Or there is the passage where he regards as superfluous the presence of priests and provisions for them: 'For it is manifest that all Priests, except the Orthodox, are hir'd to lead Man into Mistakes.'[74] However, all these remarks must be taken more as flashes of polemical rhetoric than as weighty insights, and this is how his contemporary opponents understood them.[75] Moreover, it must be pointed out that in his later writings Collins expressed himself with more moderation;[76] like Locke, all his life he remained a practising member of the church.

Furthermore, we should not overlook Collins' Whig background which also motivates his writings with a strict concern for church politics. His correspondence bears witness to the interest with which he pursued politics in the interest of this party and local records show how he put them into practice in the country area where he had influence.[77] The anti-priestly polemics in his early writings, up to the *Discourse*, are coloured by party politics, as is the case with many of his contemporaries, but as with the kindred catchword 'superstition',[78] they also take up the old Humanist ideology. Cultural developments are also consistent at this point; contemporary political events are indissolubly connected with it and governed by the themes of the most prominent controversies. The *Discourse* shows once again that even in this period the Bible still played an important role in these discussions, and that an author who contested the criteria for judging it could be certain of attracting widespread public attention.[79] In his later years Collins once again entered this discussion; we must consider that in more detail in due course.

(b) William Lyons

Before that, however, we should also look at a work in which 'freethinking', the strict implementation of Locke's epistemology, is made into a programme with the utmost consistency. This is *The Infallibility of Human Judgment*, a work which appeared anonymously in the same year as Collins' *Discourse* from the pen of W.Lyons.[80] Here it is said of reason that as the supreme human capacity, it is infallible and has to be regarded as the sole criterion of truth and falsehood in all spheres: 'The Reason of Man doth as infallible judge of Wisdom and Folly, Justice and Injustice, and the like, as of Colours; and any disputable Proposition, Religious, Moral or Political, may thus be brought to the Judgement, and try'd.'[81] It is ominous when an authority other than reason is established under the cloak of an honoured name, since even true authorities are subject to change and falsification. Therefore every authority has to be tested to see whether it is good or evil.[82] The judgment of reason is now determined by its objects (e.g. a colour) and cannot be falsified by the will.[83] One particular danger in this respect is a revelation which has been given beforehand. True knowledge of God follows from consideration of the ordering of the universe – here we can see the powerful influence of the Newtonian view of the world – from which we arrive at the existence of God as the embodiment of unlimited wisdom, perfection and power.[84] The claim of a revelation to belief without proof, associated with threats of extreme punishment if faith is withheld, is in direct contradiction to the wisdom and righteousness assumed by God. 'Therefore when any Reveal'd Religion offers itself to our consideration, it ought to be examin'd by Reason; stedfastly asserting, That the general Reason of Mankind (that is to say, Light of Nature and Conscience) is a competent judge of what is just and wise, good and bad; and 'tis impious and blasphemous to affirm any thing of God that is foolish or unjust.'[85] The aims of revealed religion, like total subjection to the will of God, correction of one's own behaviour, contempt for all honours and advantages in this world, expectation of future fulfilment, are not to the detriment of mankind and can therefore be allowed. By contrast, corruption is caused by the honours and values which the representatives of religion may attain by their authority, if in so doing they forget the rules of morality. The greatest difficulties come about through the lack of clarity in the laws laid down in revelation when these, as so often, are obscure sayings and allegories. Here reason could help, but the claim of its representatives that these are direct divine revelation and therefore that those who undertake to prove them by reason merit eternal damnation, gets in the way of this, and leads to reciprocal persecution of those who think otherwise and to hatred and contempt, particularly among the most pious, as they believe that their eternal salvation is at stake.

Even if a new infallible religion, based on undoubted revelation, were now introduced, in the course of time this would degenerate, since in the material revealed errors would arise through mistakes in copying and the like, and the claim to authority would hinder their examination by reason. Moreover, the people who advocated such a reason would feel themselves to be above questioning by reason, since their authority was supported solely by the authority of divine revelation.

Reason, for which there is a series of synonymous designations,[86] leads people to nothing but truth and goodness. It is present among all men as a capacity to judge good and evil, no matter how much or how little experience they possess.[87] 'And all Errors, both in Opinion and Practice, are in the Will only, in not chusing as the Judgment dictates.'[88] The reason why nevertheless the most different views are to be found side by side must be that additions or deletions come about in the process in which the conceptions follow one another in the spirit; however, they can be avoided if we follow the process of thought back to its origin. Faith cannot be played off against reason, since 'Believing is an Assent of the Judgement, or knowledge of a Thing being true on a due apprehending and judging it.'[89] Scepticism is simply a product of laziness in thinking and cowardice. The sin against the Holy Ghost which cannot be forgiven (Mark 3.29) is sin against the light of nature, i.e. if people do not take up the possibility of judgment. From all religions we can learn something about the immortality of the soul, about the rewards and punishments which await us in the beyond – perhaps these relate to such unthinking action without the use of reason. In this sense all people have a tendency towards natural religion: enemies of religion are fools, no-goods, and enemies of mankind.

However, all religion which is practical in this way is in danger of being cluttered up with abuse. This whole 'superstructure' must be pulled down, and practical religion must be set on its true foundation of reason. 'One person'(Jesus) criticized these deceptions, 'our Royal Moralist';[90] he preached pure truth in a royal way. It is important to have clear apprehension; when this is applied, on closer consideration many things which seemed to be mysterious no longer appear so.

Thus revelation is left a place, if only in terms of practical religion, of exclusively moral teaching; Christianity, and in particular the teaching of Jesus, is given a prominent albeit not unique position (one can also learn something from other religions!). Lyons characteristically absolutizes reason and the direct use of it for practical and moral action along the lines of Locke's epistemology;[91] moreoever, he limits real theological knowledge to natural theology.[92] All authority must submit to reason, and what it offers for assent must be subjected to the epistemological process which embraces apprehension, judgment and will. If the demand is in opposition to what is seen in apprehension, the judgment establishes this; if the apprehension sees nothing, there is no basis for a judgment. In both cases it is to be noted that in the case of the person who has elevated the claim to a proposal (who presents revelation) there is no prior judgment either because he himself does not believe it, or because only a will and not the reason is involved in the matter which he presents.

Lyons' work displays incomparably greater consistency of thought than most of the other works of English Deism, even the better known among them. It is beyond question most consistent in pursuing its theme: the central role of reason for religion understood essentially in practical and moral terms. However, fixation on this one theme has led to its leaving many questions open; thus the role of historical revelation is merely hinted at. However, it is evident that in this respect Lyons thinks unhistorically, in the fashion typical of Deism: as man can judge good and evil in accordance with the criteria which are always present in his own reason (errors are based only on laziness and scepticism, or a lack of determination to make the judgment), revelation can basically only repeat those things at which reason can also arrive of its own accord. This very point would be made explicitly a few years later (by Tindal).

(c) Anthony Collins and the Whiston Debate

The traditional role of scripture was shattered by a further debate in which Collins similarly played a part. Characteristically, it was set in motion by the apologetic, though also eccentric, efforts of a disciple of Newton who was later made an outcast because of his Arianism. This was the original and many-sided W.Whiston, whose acquaintance we have already made.[93] It is also worth noting that he first presented his thinking on the theme in the context of the Boyle Lectures;[94] to begin with they came fully within the framework of official apologetic.

In the sermons of 1707 Whiston was already occupied with the predictions in Old Testament prophecy and their fulfilment in Jesus Christ. According to the text of the first sermon, II Peter 1.19,[95] the prophecies in the Old Testament are an indisputable proof of the truth of the Christian religion. Here Whiston already makes a resolute attack on any twofold and above all typological interpretation of the prophecies: this is the only way in which they can be used as a compelling argument with the Jews, to whom it must be demonstrated that all their prophecies have been fulfilled in the Messiah Jesus of Nazareth.[96] Moreover, if prophecies had more than one meaning, we could not be certain whether they did not have further meanings in addition to this second one. In that case they could apply to even more events, and then we could only give fantastic rather than rational explanations.

At all events, the difference between historical reports and prophecies (the former refer to past events and the latter to the future) is that the one type uses a simple style which is understandable to all, whereas the other uses mysterious language so that at first prophecies are veiled and are only disclosed when the time has arrived for their fulfilment. There is also a series of prophecies which was already fulfilled during the time of the Old Testament. If we Christians think that we can also claim these for Jesus Christ, we lose any advantage of convincing people with them as proofs of our religion. Whiston, the mathematician, is also fond of speculation: those prophecies which relate to the Old Testament period are also clearly understandable in that they use the term 'year' of the period of time to which they refer, whereas those which refer to Christianity, the Messiah and the church among the Gentiles use the enigmatic term 'day' for a year. Furthermore, all the calculations of days, months and years in prophecy are meant to be quite exact, and allow an exact meaning to be found soon enough. The same is also true of the beasts in Daniel, which always denote world empires; we are to assume that the plague of locusts in Joel has an analogous meaning.

When it refers to Old Testament prophecies, the New Testament never begins from a twofold sense of scripture. Thus in Acts 2.25ff., St Peter never says that one of the psalms he mentions can also be interpreted secondarily, in terms of Christ, though they originally spoke of David; on the contrary, he says that David spoke of Christ. The main goal of prophecy was the coming of the Messiah. This must be maintained against modern interpreters, who have in view only the historical events themselves, like Solomon with his Temple and Zerubbabel with his, and so on. Instead of this, we should keep to the church fathers, who constantly thought only of the Messiah, his coming and his kingdom. With this view, Whiston is fully within the Anglican tradition, for which patristics always had great significance.[97]

The prophecies of the Messiah are of two kinds: some, less numerous,

relate to his first coming, with the way to the cross and the destruction
of the Jewish nation because of its rejection of the Messiah. The others
relate to his second coming, the establishment of the kingdom and the
restoration of the Jews. The Jews understood the prophecies about the
glorious coming of the Messiah, but overlooked the less numerous ones
about his first coming to suffer. Conversely, most of the more recent
Christian exegetes have misunderstood the simple statements about the
millennium, the new Jerusalem, Ezekiel's temple, and so on, and therefore deny the second coming of Christ before the end of the world to
restore the Jewish nation and establish his kingdom.

Already within this framework Whiston expresses hesitations as to
whether the prophecies have always been preserved intact in the present text of the Old Testament. At least in the way in which the books
are now arranged, their style is abrupt, short, and disrupted by the
frequent appearance of things from quite a different context. But 'I must
be so free and fair as to confess, I cannot every where look upon the
present Order either of the Histories or Propheties of the Old Testament
to have been the original one.'[98] Where such disruptions are clearly
visible, they can be removed and the original text can be restored.
Whiston gives some examples of this, including the double date in
Ezek. 1, the first occurrence of which really belongs before ch.30, where
there is no date, and two verses in Deuteronomy (Deut.10.6,7) which
have obviously been inserted in the wrong place, as we can see from
a comparison with the Samaritan Pentateuch.[99]

His apologetic zeal later led Whiston to make a detailed investigation,
following these considerations, which appeared in 1722 under the title
An Essay Towards Restoring the True Text of the Old Testament and which
was the stimulus towards a lengthy debate about the predictions. In it
he attempted to demonstrate that both the Hebrew text of the Old
Testament and the present text of the Septuagint are not preserved in
the form which they had in the time of Jesus and the apostles, but were
considerably altered by the Jews at the beginning of the second century,
in both Hebrew and Septuagint versions.[100] As far as the Pentateuch is
concerned he regards the Samaritan Pentateuch as a still uncorrupted
version of the text as it appeared in the time of Jesus and the apostles.[101]
Similarly, the psalms in the Septuagint version and the Roman psalter
are a still uncorrupted text from this time.[102] The quotations in the New
Testament from the Old which diverge from the present wording are
a faithful reproduction of the Hebrew and Septuagint wording of that
time.[103] Moreover, one can refer back to quotations from the Old Testament in Philo and Josephus, each of whom uses the text of the
Septuagint or the Hebrew text normative in their time.[104] If one were to
restore the original text at all the questionable places, one would find

many great predictions by the prophets fulfilled literally and could give up altogether the assumption of a twofold meaning.

These assertions by Whiston were the occasion for Collins to write a work of his own about prophecy, the *Discourse of the Grounds and Reasons of the Christian Religion*(1724).[105] This work has various different parts: an elegantly written Foreword in which Collins again demands the right to free discussion, albeit within defined limits[106] (he also defends Whiston in this connection),[107] and two main sections, a second, detailed one in which he presents a lengthy criticism of Whiston's arguments, and a first in which he puts forward his own view. Only the first is worth detailed consideration. One could well say that while the appearance of Whiston's work was the stimulus to the publication of the *Discourse*, Collins had evidently thought for some time about the problems in question. He deliberately joined in the discussion of the significance of Old Testament prophecy for Christian faith. To reject the adventitious theories of Whiston was relatively easy for him. Whiston's falsification theory was untenable in this crude form; a deception of the Jews of this magnitude could never have been accepted by Christians in the second century. Now if such a falsification had in fact taken place, there would be no serious possibility of regaining the original text: a Bible restored in accordance with Whiston's methods would be simply a Whiston text, which would falsify the original form as much as any other reconstruction.[108]

Collins' own view is primarily built up to some degree on Whiston's position. Right at the beginning he stresses that 'Christianity is founded on Judaism, or the New Testament on the Old.'[109] With his theory that the Old Testament and not the New is the Christian canon,[110] Collins is going back to a long tradition in the English church, though only to its positive aspect, not its negative one. He steers towards the conclusion of his argument with great consistency: according to him, the only touchstone for the truth of Christianity is that the prophecies of the Old Testament are fulfilled in Jesus. In the New Testament the predictions from the Old are used by the apostles as the main argument for the truth of Christianity. According to Collins there are no other solid arguments; if this particular one does not hold water, then Christianity is false.[111] Collins concentrates his argument on five proof texts from the Old Testament in the Gospel of Matthew[112] and shows that they are used in a typological ('mystical' or 'allegorical') sense – he claims to have tested this by all the prophecies quoted by the apostles.[113] For Collins, however, as for Whiston, legitimately there is only one fulfilment for a prophecy, the literal one; if it can be shown that this already took place in the Old Testament period, the claim of Christianity to a second fulfilment by Jesus is clearly refuted. Thus Collins for example goes into great detail over the announcement in Isa.7.14 and believes that he can demonstrate conclusively that the promised child is Isaiah's own son.[114] O'Higgins has pointed out that for exegetical conclusions of this kind Collins bases his work on that of the Dutch Arminians, above all Hugo Grotius.[115] In fact his later work, *The Scheme of Literal Prophecy Considered,*[116] has a whole chapter in defence of this theologian.[117] He was probably also of the opinion that Grotius had already explicitly endorsed the view that the prophecies of the prophet were fulfilled in his own time and had rejected the spiritual typological fulfilment in Jesus from the start. However, this was a misunderstanding, already introduced by Grotius' earlier critics.[118] In reality, Grotius himself and the other exegetes who followed him had assumed that some prophecies were literally fulfilled in Jesus; others were first fulfilled in Old Testament times, but this did not exclude a second typological fulfilment in Christ.

The kind of typological thinking which had its heyday at the end of the century was basically alien to Collins. Locke's epistemology had done its work so thoroughly that for Collins, as for many of his contemporaries, there could only be 'clear and lucid ideas' along the lines of empiricism.[119] Collins understands the typology and allegory in the New Testament as an adaptation on the part of the apostles to the thought patterns of the Jews and Gentiles of their time;[120] the church fathers, too, had engaged in wild allegorizing.[121] The Jews began to allegorize only after the exile.[122] In the Old Testament itself there is not the slightest trace of a typological or allegorical intent; rather, the books of the Old Testament are the simplest and most easily understandable of all the writings of antiquity.

Now what follows from the assertion 'that Christianity is wholly reveal'd in the Old Testament, and has its divine Authority form thence; that it is not literally, but mystically and allegorically reveal'd therein'?[123] Evidently, that if this only possible argument does not hold, there is no basis for Christianity. One must really conclude from this that at the time when he composed the *Discourse*, Collins was an open opponent of Christianity. However, he remained a practising member of the Anglican church.[124] It must also be said that he never expresses this negative conclusion in his work, but limits himself to asserting that the argument from prophecy in the New Testament equally has an allegorical stamp.[125] The problem can hardly be solved in this form, but for the men of this time, as today, there were evidently different levels of awareness, between which contradictions were not excluded. At all events, one can note that the move against New Testament Christianity is an extreme effect of a high estimation of the Old Testament, of a kind which is quite clearly evident in Collins. The Puritan heritage which lives on in him in a remarkable way makes itself felt at this point with a consistency which is quite appropriate to Puritanism, but is rarely carried through with the degree of consistency to be found here. The lack of historical perspective leaves open the possibility of deciding either for the New Testament in contrast to the Old (that was the solution of many Spiritualists) or for the Old in preference to the New. The Puritans usually stopped at this preponderance; it is Collins who first sees a strict alternative.

It is easy to point out in detail how many exegetical errors he committed. His Arminian authorities like Grotius and Clericus were far better exegetes.[126] Nevertheless, he drew attention to an important dilemma within the customary orthodox apologetic of his time. As a result he set in motion a considerable debate about Old Testament prophecy,[127] which only ended with his death in 1729. Of the refutations of his work, that by T.Bullock[128] is an example of the continuation of an exclusive interest in the New Testament. In diametrical opposition to Collins, Bullock stresses that Christianity is in no way based on the Old Testament. Rather, Christianity is a new law which was given by Jesus, to whom was given the true spirit of God in all fullness and who abrogated the law of the Jews in the Old Testament. This law of Christ can be confirmed by rational arguments. The frequent references by the apostles to the Old Testament in the New merely have an apologetic aim; they wanted to demonstrate to the Gentiles that their religion was an imposture and therefore had to be abandoned, and to the Jews that their religion could be changed and turned into Christian faith.[129]

If we look more closely, these arguments, too, are by no means new, but continue the attitude of that wing in Puritanism which, from a Spiritualist starting-point, based itself entirely on the New Testament and therefore came largely to reject the Old.[130] The legalistic conception of the significance of the New Testament also belongs completely in this context.

Other opponents, like A.A.Sykes[131] and E.Chandler,[132] accepted Collins' presupposition that Christianity was based on the Old Testament predictions. All in all they were true pupils of Locke to the degree that they saw as the basic confession of Christianity (and its only fundamental principle) that Jesus was the Messiah. With often profound learning they sought, like Chandler, to demonstrate the literal fulfilment in Christ of a large number of prophecies, understood in messianic terms; Chandler relied especially on the apocryphal literature from between the Testaments for his argument that the Jews at the time of the New Testament had a widespread messianic expectation. Moreover, they also sought to legitimize the use of typology.[133] Thus S.Chandler produces a mass of arguments from the post-exilic writings of the Old Testament and from the New Testament with which he seeks to show that at that time the typological approach was widespread.[134] Over against this, Whiston persisted in his view that prophecy could not have two meanings.[135] Collins responded in the work *The Scheme of Literal Prophecy Considered*.[136] In its first part he follows the structure of Chandler's work closely, and shows that in all the predictions from the Old Testament relating to Jesus Christ produced by Chandler, twelve literal and four typological, on each occasion the reference is to an object or a person from the history of the time. Here he arrives at some insights worth noting. One particular result which has become famous is his judgment on the authenticity of the book of Daniel;[137] he was the first to date it in the period of Antiochus Epiphanes, a conclusion which has meanwhile proved to be accurate.[138]

As far as hermeneutical principles were concerned, the debate inevitably remained barren. Both parties, Collins and his opponents, had a very one-sided view of prophecy, which they understood almost without exception in terms of prediction.[139] However, the effect of Collins' attacks was that the application of the traditional argument from prophecy in apologetics became very uncertain, and this method of argumentation seemed increasingly to be antiquated.[140] The many learned refutations did not make much difference in this respect, as the general mood tended very much towards Collins' attitude. Some of the subsequent developments are also already evident with Collins. He carried on a brief debate about the meaning of miracles with J.Green[141] and T.Lobb[142] as his opponents.[143] In this book there is also a short list of objections to Judaism: God's command to Abraham to sacrifice his son, the death of Jephthah's daughter, God's command to Israel to steal the Egyptians' jewellery when they leave Egypt and so on – the well-known moral objections which recur among various Deists.[144]

Somehow – and this is a last sign of the Puritan influences which continued to affect him – Collins retained a high opinion of 'the excellency of original primitive Christianity; Christianity as deliver'd in the Scriptures'.[145] It remains an open question how he could reconcile this with the tendency of the *Discourse*, with which he had really taken away the ground from under any form of Christianity. Perhaps he simply needed an ideal picture, in order to be able to contrast it with the Christianity of the present, distorted by 'some modern priests'.[146] We may concede that O'Higgins is right in speaking of a degree of inconsistency in Collins in view of this discrepancy.[147] At another point he refers to the principles which Collins himself proclaims in a section of his *Scheme of Literal Prophecy*.[148] With slight differences, these are the well-known principles of Humanist Christianity which we have already come across on numerous occasions: a eudaemonistic ethic which strives to know the will of God and to obey it, with the aim of happiness in this world and above all in the world to come. Freedom and tolerance are to be granted to those in search of this will. The author will show what is true and original Christianity and what additions have been made to it. The state has to carry through the law of nature by civil sanctions only because its observance is absolutely necessary for society. None of this is surprising. In many respects Collins was not at all original. The recognition that Deism did not come from outside but in fact developed within Christianity can well be demonstrated from his work.[149]

Collins made his last comments[150] in a dispute with J.Rogers, who in a foreword to eight published sermons on the necessity of divine revelation[151] had argued with the *Scheme*.[152] What interested Collins in Rogers' remarks was above all his attack on natural religion: his fear (supported by the experiences of the Commonwealth) was that reason left to itself will not in any way produce the ideal natural religion, but will lead to arbitrariness and confusion, as each person will be guided by his own reason and what he holds to be natural religion. This will also obscure the law of nature. In the second part of his short letter Collins defended natural religion against Rogers. To a considerable degree his reply makes use of the *via negationis* and in so doing employs widespread deistic arguments: mankind cannot be directed towards revelation, as this was originally given only to the Jews, and only at a very late stage to the rest of mankind.[153] Non-Christians (e.g. in America) led just as moral a life as Christians.[154] On the contrary, there are many people who have charged Christianity with furthering vice rather than virtue.[155] He himself is of the view that true Christian teaching contains a foredetermined moral standard, and proves the pre-eminent quality of Christianity by the fact that it 'does but republish the law of nature'.[156] But this already brings us to a further stage of the deistic debate which followed soon afterwards, in which Collins no longer played a part.

(d) Woolston and Annet

First of all, though, we must consider the debate about the miracles in the New Testament, which developed in a remarkable way from the debate about the prophecies. Lechler[157] has given a very thorough account of the details of this discussion, and as it is impossible to add anything of substance to that,[158] I can content myself here with some points which are particularly important in this context. Thomas Woolston was the protagonist here; he first entered the debate about the prophecies and then developed his position with a discussion of the miracles in the New Testament. In the eccentric way in which they were made, his contributions are a particularly instructive symptom of the intellectual attitude of the majority of rationalistic Anglican theologians. Woolston was a typical representative of this position not only in the post that he held,[159] but also in his aim, which originally was completely apologetic. The two apparently contradictory main elements of his thought can be explained only from the peculiar tradition of the Anglican clergy: a predilection for the allegorical and typological exegesis of the Bible and a gross rationalism which emerges above all in Woolston's judgments on the New Testament miracle stories. It should be noted here first of all that the patristic tradition in Anglican theology was unbroken, and one can find a deep familiarity with the writings of the church fathers among all the more important theologians, who also take for granted a knowledge of ancient philosophy. On the other hand, Lockean empirical rationalism had largely established itself in the first decades of the eighteenth century. Woolston combines both, and the apparently bizarre contours of his thought are produced by the meeting of two worlds in him: the hermeneutics of Hellenistic late antiquity, which thinks in terms of correspondences between separate levels of meaning, and the one-dimensional spirit of modern times, which presupposes a strictly limited area of reality and recognizes as possible only what can be tested by experience and reconciled with empirical, experienced reality.

In his first work, *The Old Apology for the Truth of the Christian Religion* (1705),[160] Woolston follows a model of thought which was already fading into the background in this period[161] but which, as we saw, was widespread in the seventeenth century: the Origenist form of typology.[162] The basic notion is that a divine emissary first of all has to demonstrate his authority to the ruler of the country in question.[163] So Christ had to do that towards the Roman emperors.[164] As proof that he did in fact do this, Woolston adduces the typological parallel with the miracles which Moses performed before Pharaoh: the exodus from Egypt is the typology for the redemption of the world through Christ.[165] He thinks that he can demonstrate that the exodus story in all its details was an exact typology of the history of Christ and the early church.[166,167]

However, the miracles of Jesus and in the time of the early church, performed for the benefit of the Roman emperors, were much more substantial than the miracles of Moses, which by contrast were only shadows. They convinced the emperors of the authority of the Christian cause.[168] Already in this early writing, there is also a remarkable feature intended to stress that the miracles really happened: Woolston attaches great importance to the legendary letter of Pilate to Tiberius, the content of which is confirmation that the events connected with Christ really happened.[169] In addition, there is the comment that the chest in which Moses was launched on the Nile (Ex.2) was a type of this letter![170] In order to nullify the widespread antipathy towards the typological-allegorical method, Woolston points to the numerous practitioners of this kind of exegesis in the earliest church and thinks that it must not be supposed that the venerable church fathers could have erred to this degree.[171] Especially as the ancient Jews were also allegorical interpreters![172]

At the end of the book[173] its apologetic concern is expressed unmistakably: Woolston asks the modern atheists, Deists and Jews whether the ancient pagans were not dull of sense in clinging on to idolatry so long despite such evidences of Christianity. The Jews of today, too, have every reason to follow the Christians if they still expect a messiah, since the typological argument must convince them that Christ freed his church, as Moses freed the people from Egypt.[174] Woolston also thinks that Moses and prophecy contain an exact typology of the history of the church down the ages, though he does not venture to draw conclusions from this for future events in the history of the church.[175]

The work does not seem to have had any major consequences, and Woolston spent a further fifteen years quietly in his college, occupied with an intensive study of the church fathers. Then he launched into a number of anonymous pamphlets in which he argued for allegorical interpretation[176] in the guise of a variety of fictitious characters.[177] The mixed motives which appear in these writings are interesting: his preference for the allegorical method, which seems to be a hobby-horse, is connected with the ideal of earliest Christianity (allegory was practised there, so it is also binding for today). He therefore makes a defence of Quakerism as an extreme form of Puritanism with a Spiritualist colouring, and finally shows a developing hostility to the Anglican theologians, who in the Second Letter to Dr Bennett[178] are already branded as 'servants of the letter' (in contrast to the spiritual allegorists). This hostility grows into a psychopathic hate of all the clergy after his dismissal, which came about soon after the appearance of these writings;[179] while this is of course not unconnected with the dispute over the allegorical interpretation of the Bible, Woolston soon goes on to hurl furious accusations at all the clergy.[180] Here, and in the question which appears in the sub-title, as to whether the contemporary clergy are not servants of the apocalyptic beast, we are reminded strongly of the polemic of the early Quakers[181] (it is no coincidence that Woolston defends this particular sect in his apologetic). Moreover, the attack on the priesthood is in no way to be explained as a mere personal characteristic of Woolston; it takes up themes which are living issues over a wide area and among a variety of groups.

On the basis of his presuppositions it was natural for Woolston also to involve himself in the debates on the argument from prophecy; here he put himself forward as an arbitrator[182] between Collins and Whiston. For him Collins is the unbeliever; Whiston, and all those who argue for the literal sense of holy scripture, is the apostate. Woolston shares with Whiston the presupposition that the truth of Christianity can be proved only by showing that the Old Testament prophecies have been fulfilled in it. But he argues as fanatically for typological and allegorical under-standing as Whiston does on the other side for the literal sense.[183] All other arguments for Christianity are invalid if the argument from proph-ecy is inadequate.[184] Neither the teaching of Jesus, 'who taught all in Parables, neither did he ever speak without a Parable'[185] nor miracles[186] are valid as such proofs. As Collins had questioned the validity of the miracles,[187] at this point Woolston can take over his arguments word for word, and fully agree with them.[188] And although he says that he does not want to go more closely into the miracles of Jesus, though he is quite in a position to do so,[189] he does speak of the resurrection and declares (with a reference to the theory that the body was stolen, Matt.28.13) that the objections to it are quite convincing – even he himself would have to be convinced by them did he not hold fast to the spiritual meaning of the resurrection, namely the mystical death and resurrection of Christ from the tomb of the letter of the law and the prophets.[190]

Now it is remarkable to see how, in a further series of writings,[191] while Woolston takes the ground from under a large number of miracle stories in the gospels[192] with rational arguments that they could not possibly have happened like that, he does not do so in order to chal-lenge the Bible itself but in order to suggest a mystical and allegorical meaning for all these narratives (or, as he thinks, to uncover what is hidden beneath their wording).[193] To our sensibilities the plain common sense[194] which serves as the criterion for what is possible on the level of reality denoted by the literal meaning and the burgeoning fantasy with discovers what is 'meant' allegorically at any point are simply irreconcilable. However, both are pre-existing patterns of thought, one from the age-old Spiritualist tradition and the other from modern em-piricism, the rational colouring of which is simply a contemporary expression of a Humanistic rationalism which is almost as old. Thus in one sense Woolston is a quite typical phenomenon, and his thought, which goes further in both directions, shows the characteristic features of the Anglican tradition in a particularly clear light.

In the long run an argument split in this way could not be sustained, so it is not surprising that further discussion focussed on the question whether or not the miracles in the New Testament had in fact happened, and could therefore be regarded as an argument for Christianity. In particular, it was the central miracle, the resurrection of Jesus, on which the controversy concentrated. The chief contestants were, on the apo-logists' side, Thomas Sherlock (later Archbishop of Canterbury) with his extraordinarily popular writing *The Tryal of the Witnesses of the Res-urrection of Jesus*,[195] and on the deistic side P.Annet, with his riposte *The Resurrection of Jesus considered, in Answer to the Tryal of Witnesses. By a Moral Philosopher*.[196,197]

The most important features of the debate are the epistemological principles which both spokesmen (like others who were involved in the discussion on both sides[198]) took for granted. Decisive for both is a demonstration that the miracles in fact happened. The only thing that matters is their facticity, which Sherlock seeks to demonstrate by his 'eye-witness testimony' and which Annet wants to dispute. Annet expresses himself quite clearly: 'If faith be founded on fact, let the truth of fact appear; if on reason, let reason discover the foundation.'[199] In stressing reason as the sole criterion of judgment, he is as consistent as W.Lyons.[200]: 'Reason is my only rule and the displaying truth my only aim.'[201] Restricted to these alternatives, 'true' and 'false' are also the decisive criteria for judging the Bible: 'Is it not material whether what these evangelists say, is true of false? Whether this is a true or false insinuation to countenance the history?'[202] Here, too, there is a panegyric on natural religion;[203] its opposite is any alleged inspiration, the source of all conceivable religious ills and the most scandalous enemy of virtue and reason.[204] If faith does not rest on facts or reason, but on tradition, it is important to examine the facts standing behind the tradition in order to establish whether the evangelists themselves did not succumb to deceptions, or reported things by hearsay which cannot be demonstrated; whether interpolations did not creep into the texts which in any case can hardly have come down to us uncorrupted.[205] In the further course of the investigation the author examines in detail the gospel statements about the announcements of the passion of Jesus (of which the disciples later knew nothing!), about the events at the burial (nothing points to a resurrection of the corpse), and about the alleged appearances of the risen Christ in which above all the discrepancies between the evangelists raise the gravest suspicions about the credibility of such witnesses. Against everything that is reported in the Bible about these things, it must be said that, 'God never requires men to believe things contrary to evidence, nature, and common sense';[206] but the proofs that we have in the Bible are believed only by those in whom they have been implanted by their education, before their understanding matured.[207] The only possible proof is 'the proof of the spirit' – but as anyone can talk of that, it only convinces believers and not those who ask for proofs, so that here the principle applies that 'Things not known cannot be proved by things equally unknown.'[208]

Finally, Annet stresses quite clearly that for his (static and ethical) concept of 'religion' a historical tradition like that of the Bible remains meaningless precisely because it is historical: his purpose has been 'to convince the world that an historical faith is no part of true and pure religion, which is founded only on truth and purity. That it does not consist in the belief of any history, which whether true or false, makes no man wiser nor better.'[209] Miracles as counter proofs are also rejected because they contradict knowledge, understood empiricistically in the Lockean sense:[210] 'Things asserted, which are contrary to the experience, and reason of all mankind; and to what they know of the law and usual course of nature, are, to the common sense and understanding of men, utterly impossible; because such assertions contradict all men's notions of these laws, that are known by common experience.'[211]

With Annet, criticism of the Bible has entered on a new phase. It has become more basic and more consistent. At this point a series of old and more recent traditions come together. The concept of natural religion, which Annet shares with many predecessors, is well known. We can also see time and again how he comes into tension with traditional biblical and Christian faith. A new element is the resolution and openness with which Annet pushes biblical faith to one side and declares it to be superfluous. Previously, attempts to harmonize it with natural religion or to find the statements of natural religion in the Bible almost always predominated. Whiston and Woolston also tried this, each in his own way. Annet's resolute farewell to such manoeuvres, which in each occasion resulted in a double hermeneutic, is also a consequence of his own hermeneutics, in which empiricism has now finally broken through: 'If a stone appeared to roll up a hill of its own accord to my sight, I should think I had a reason to doubt the veracity of my eye-sight, or of the object.'[212] By analogy, this empiricist insight also applies to the possibility of the resurrection of Jesus: 'As we know by experience that all men die, and rise no more, therefore we conclude, for a dead man to rise to life again, is contrary to the uniform and settled course of nature.'[213] Newtonian thought has established itself completely – though in conclusions of which its author could not have dreamed. Annet now declares tersely and clearly: 'Natural powers are fit to answer all the ends of virtue and religion; therefore supernatural powers are needless.'[214] A man of honour and good manners does not need any supernatural gifts to instruct humanity in unsullied holiness of heart and conduct and in this way to make it acceptable to God. Even God works in accordance with the unchangeable laws of things. Miracles are superfluous there. 'If God acts towards mankind, as the moral fitness of things requires, there is no occasion for miracles; for if reasonable exhortations to virtue, and dehortations from vice; if prudent persuasion, and just laws, will not make people virtuous, nothing can.'[215] Annet learnt his lesson well from Clarke!

(e) Tindal, Christianity as Old as the Creation

However, even the majority of the Deists did not go as far as Annet. For the most part they continued with attempts to demonstrate an agreement between natural religion and the Bible. The best-known work in this connection is Tindal's *Christianity as Old as the Creation*, which appeared in 1730 (thus dating from some time before Annet's comments).[216,217] The book, which aroused a good deal of attention on its appearance,[218] and provoked a mass of refutations,[219] is usually said to be a 'key work of Deism'.[220] It deserves this title. The discussion, styled in antiquarian fashion as a dialogue (modelled on Cicero) once again presents all the basic notions which played a role in rationalistic theology from the Latitudinarians down to the Deists. The book has been described as a typical work of its age,[221] and as such it represents a kind of collection of material in which the author has brought together a mass of conclusions from the discussion, which in most aspects had now been going on for several decades, with a degree of completeness which had not been achieved hitherto.[222]

The most important features of the Deistic conception of religion can also be found here; above all the assumption of the existence of a natural religion which holds for all men and is adequate for everyone, which Tindal defines as 'the Belief of the Existence of a God, and the Sense and Practice of those Duties, which result from the Knowledge, we, by our Reason, have of him, and his perfections'.[223] It is based on the law of nature, which for its part is none other than 'the Relations between Things, and the Fitness resulting from thence', as Tindal puts it, following Clarke.[224] It can be recognized by all men, because it corresponds to their own rational nature; for the law of nature 'is so call'd, as being a Law, which is common, or natural, to all rational Creatures'.[225] Religion is connected with morality even more exclusively than in all the preceding Deistic statements; it is understood in strictly legalistic terms as 'the practice of Morality in Obedience to the Will of God';[226] its aim is 'to render (man) as perfect as may be in all moral Duties whatever'.[227] In the title to Chapter II we read, 'That the Religion of Nature consists in observing those Things, which our Reason, by considering the Nature of God and Man, and the Relation we stand in to him and one another, demonstrates to be our Duty';[228] rational knowledge of the 'fitness of things' and moral action follow immediately upon one another.[229] This morality is, moreover, clearly eudaemonistic, in a way that is characteristic of the whole Enlightenment: from God's properties as an infinitely happy, all-wise Being, it follows that he can give to his creatures only commandments which are to their advantage: 'Nothing can be a Part of the Divine Law, but what tends to promote the common Interest, and mutual Happiness of his rational Creatures... As God can require nothing of us, but what makes for our Happiness; so he... can forbid us those Things only, which tend to our Hurt.'[230]

Because this religion (morality) corresponds to the nature of God (is grounded in a metaphysical theology)[231] and at the same time to the nature of things and the rational nature of men, it can also be known directly; it is distinct from outward revelation only by the way in which it is communicated: 'The One being the Internal, as the Other the External Revelation of the same Unchangeable Will of a Being, who is alike at all times infinitely Wise and Good.'[232] Reason is the organ of this inner revelation: at this point we can see once again the heritage which combines rationalism with its Spiritualist ancestry. Reason also has the same evidential value as the direct gift of the spirit: 'All men, at all Times, must have had sufficient Means to discover whatever God design'd they shou'd know, and practice.'[233]

The other pillars in the construction of Tindal's thought also correspond to the rationalist and Spiritualist tradition. These are: first, the doctrine of the perfection of natural religion, which contains everything that man needs to know about God's will for his salvation.[234] An external revelation can at best confirm what men could know by themselves if only they used their reason rightly. However, Tindal concedes (and in so doing also follows the line familiar since Locke and Shaftesbury) that in practice people do not always live up to this ideal. This is the foundation for his central thesis. We should note that this is intended as apologetic, just as much as the remarks of most of the moderate Deists,[235] whose proximity to the Latitudinarian apologists here is very obvious: Christianity is not a new religion, but is the new proclamation of the law which has been valid from the beginning and is given with human nature itself;[236] it is the 'Republication of the religion of Nature'.[237]

It is not Tindal's intention to demonstrate *a priori* that the Christian revelation is superfluous. In an ideal situation it could in fact be dispensed with. Its content cannot add anything new to the will of God as that is generally known. According to Tindal's conviction (which, however, he hints at rather than expresses clearly,[238]) it nevertheless fulfils an important role because as a 'Republication' or 'Restoration' of natural religion it once again calls men's attention to the natural law which in reality they have continually failed to follow purely, because from time immemorial they have fallen victim to superstition by following a positive religion. At this point Tindal takes up the old Humanist and Puritan classifications in a way which has seldom been formulated so thoroughly before, and incorporates them skilfully into his system: all external cultic practices are superstition;[239] they can be dispensed with by true, natural religion, which consists only in ethical knowledge and moral action, and in reality can only detract from this religion. Revelation serves to remove these hindrances and, by teaching purely moral duties, to restore natural religion.

At this point it is impossible to miss the connection with the second element of Spiritualism: its hostility to the cult. Tindal recognizes that even public worship is necessary by nature and that certain outward regulations are necessary for it.[240] But he resolutely denies that God can have given any commandments in this connection. Positive regulations of any kind, which at best can hold only for certain times and seasons, do not square with the eternal immutability of God.[241] In a familiar way, he makes the priests responsible for giving these things an increasing degree of importance in the history of the church because they have monopolized their claim to power with rites, ceremonies and popish forms.[242] Tindal supports the congregationalist solution for the indifferentia and suggests that all church affairs should be regulated by general consent.[243] Here, too, he is more systematic than his predecessors: everything that is morally insignificant is indifferent, and therefore left completely to human freedom.[244] Gawlick[245] points out that Tindal solved the long-standing dispute among the Latitudinarians about the fundamentalia and what is to be understood by them by no longer regarding positive precepts and prescriptions as divinely revealed. In this way he arrives at the sole essentials, which have this character because they are founded on the 'rational nature of things'. When he boasts that he has demonstrated religion described in this fashion in a way 'founded upon such demonstrable principles, as are obvious to the meanest Capacity',[246] we are reminded immediately of Locke and his pedagogical concern.[247]

Of course there is a basic presupposition, a general *a priori*, which underlies all this: Tindal presupposes a metaphysically formed concept of God as the perfect being in which there is a criterion, even if it remains purely related to practice,[248] by which it is possible to assess what may be seen as the content of revelation and what may not in a way that is universally binding. As he fills out the substance of this criterion of his relationship to reason and his eudaemonistic morality,[249] he takes over the same antique Stoic material which we kept meeting among his Humanist predecessors.[250] The significance of his work lies above all in the fact that he incorporated the various elements which he found in the themes discussed[251] by his rationalistic contemporaries into a logically consistent system; for the most part he thought this through to the end on the basis of his presuppositions, and avoided the obvious gaps in the thinking of the Latitudinarians. This made his approach more thorough than those of his predecessors. To this degree the attention which has again been paid to him recently is quite justified. Furthermore, he is still to be seen more as a conservative in his concern, which at least subjectively is still of a 'Christian' apologetic kind.

However, the consequences of this system were particularly evident in the sphere of the understanding of the Bible. Tindal devotes a whole, very detailed chapter to the role of the Bible, in which a number of ideas are repeated several times.[252] The starting point of his judgment about the value of the Bible is his definition of natural religion, which in this chapter, too, he regards as the only binding form. Holy Scripture – and this he takes for granted – can be significant only in respect of the divine commandments which are contained in it: the definition of religion which is exclusively identified with morality[253] does not allow of anything else. Such commandments as may find their way into the Bible must, however, *a priori* coincide with the content of natural religion if they are to have authority, since 'must not our Reason tell us, that infinite Wisdom can have no Commands, but what are founded on the unalterable Reason of Things?'[254] The will of God can only be what is in accord with the nature of things and his own unchangeable nature.[255] Nothing other than human reason can decide what is in accord with 'the eternal Reason of Things'.[256]

Now if religion is there for all mankind (for the aim of moral action is happiness, and this is intended for all men),[257] its commandments must be so simple that they can be understood even by the most ordinary people (the 'common people')[258]: 'True religion can't but be plain, simple, and natural, as design'd for all Mankind, adapted to every Capacity, and suited to every condition and Circumstance of Life.'[259] Here Tindal is taking up Locke's well-known ideas.[260] Now one has to say exactly the opposite of the Bible: understanding it is hampered in a variety of ways by the utmost difficulties. First of all, Tindal mentions the foreign languages in which it is written and which bar direct access to it to all but a few people.[261] He goes on to point to the vast number of exegetical skills which must be mastered before one can have access to it: as an example he lists a whole series of exegetical technical terms as used in contemporary scholarship.[262] In addition there are the uncertainties in the tradition which have found expression in the countless textual variants of the New Testament,[263] not to mention the differences of opinion in interpreting the content.[264] The course taken by liberal understanding of the Bible in a century can be very clearly recognized in a comment by Tindal about Chillingworth ('the greatest Champion the Protestant Cause ever had'), of whom he says 'that he was abler at pulling down than building up'. On the basis of his own arguments there is nothing left for him than the cry for which there is no justification whatsoever: 'The Bible, I say, the Bible is the Religion of Protestants.'[265]

At this point he also introduces the traditional anti-clericalism: the difficulties which bar the way to the Bible for ordinary people are the best way for priests to exert their own power over the laity. In all religions the overwhelming majority of all people, who do not understand their religious documents in the original languages, are compelled to put their trust in the priests, who have an interest in deceiving them as far as possible.[266] Here Tindal has above all his own Anglican clergy in mind.[267] He will not allow the objection of his conversation-partner, that these seek only to interpret the laws of Christ and not to make their own laws.[268] Behind this polemic there lurks a more fundamental problem: for the moralist who thinks in an absolute metaphysical framework an unbridgeable abyss opens up towards a religion which has become historical and which by nature rests on tradition. 'Natural Religion, which is of the greatest Importance to Mankind, and is a perpetual standing Rule for Men of the meanest, as well as highest Capacity, carries its own Evidence with it, those internal, inseparable Marks of Truth; but can that be said of any Religion, which depends on Tradition?'[269] A number of problems follow from this for the moralists. For example, the question of the moral integrity of persons responsible for the first dissemination of this historical religion plays a considerable role. As recipients of revelation they merit trust only if they were personally of unexceptionable morality, so that they themselves were not deceived and did not deceive others.[270] The answer to this is largely negative, as a short survey from Abraham to Paul[271] shows: the best-known biblical figures were anything but infallible men. In addition there is the reference to tradition generally: the more indirect a witness, the less convincing he is.[272]

Just as problematical, however, is the content of the biblical revelation itself. Most central is the stimulus which the biblical image of God offers for the reader oriented on the metaphysical conception of God. Tindal devotes a particularly large amount of space to this. The divine freedom of will which is already becoming evident in the Bible contradicts the postulate of the eternal changelessness of the supreme being in a way that cannot be resolved.[273] Now there are also many specific statements about God in the Bible the content of which cannot be reconciled with this conception. They include statements like God swearing, getting angry, repenting, and the many anthropomorphic descriptions[274] which attribute human limbs to him and have him communicating directly with mortal beings (although we can see some contradiction over whether people can see God face to face or not[275]); finally, the Bible says such incredible things as that God deceives or breaks his promises.[276]

It is above all in the Old Testament that offences of this kind accumulate. In this context Tindal can again quote with approval a Latitudinarian remark (this time by Tillotson) which expresses a good deal of sympathy for the Marcionite theory of the two different gods in Old and New Testaments.[277] The cruel actions of the Jews towards the Canaanites are referred to with particular abhorrence, the way in which heedlessly and without any specific reason they exterminated them along with their children (a commandment from God to this effect is nothing if it cannot be made to agree with the law of nature).[278] Moreover, here – and at this point Tindal takes up the argument that has been traditional since Spencer – the people of the Jews are particularly inappropriate as instruments of vengeance on an idolatrous people because of the idolatry that they brought with them from Egypt. However, Tindal asserts (and here we can see the beginnings of a historical approach), that 'the same Spirit... does not alike prevail throughout the Old Testament; the nearer we come to the Times of the Gospel, the milder it appear'd.'[279] Ezekiel 18.20 already represents progress from the clan responsibility for guilt of which the Decalogue speaks, and Jesus' refusal in Luke 9.54-56 to call down fire, like Elijah, on the Samaritan village which would not receive him, contrasts with Old Testament cruelty.

Thus to begin with, it seems in accordance with good Humanist tradition that the New Testament is to be given predominance over the Old. 'And if there's a Contrast between the Spirit of the Old, and the Spirit of the New Testament, ought not we Christians to stick to the latter...?'[280] In fact Tindal also seems to move towards a similar conclusion when he observes that the commandments of the gospel 'are Rules in their own Nature obligatory, which, from their internal Excellency, always bound Mankind'.[281] But in the very same sentence he connects it with his guiding principle that they must then be capable of being recognized by all people, even those with the least gifts. Only now do there follow the long sections on the sufficiency of natural religion from which quotations have already been made. The objection by the conversation partner (B) that despite the perfection of the old religion (natural religion) a new one was necessary because men had not kept the earlier one[282] is received by A with scepticism. He again points to the uncertainties of interpretation and tradition; here the need to know languages, exegetical rules and historical information are only part of the problem, for even among the theologians who have mastered these skills, as among the Councils, there is endless dispute as to what is orthodox and what is not. Now if one assumes that God has put in the hearts of all men the rules of morality in accordance with which they have to live, in a way which it is easy for them to understand, this is at the same time a criterion for judging the biblical commandments. Although Tindal in his well-tried manner now again has a quotation ready (from the Lausanne natural law theorist, Jean Barbeyrac), stressing the complete agreement of Christian morality with the dictates of true reason as one of the most convincing arguments for the divine character of the Christian religion,[283] he himself is far from claiming statements obtained from the New Testament as binding precepts after the manner of his Puritan predecessors. Rather, his reservations about the New Testament are obvious.

His observations on 'prophecy', which appear at one point in the form of an excursus, are striking in themselves.[284] Here his real theme is what is nowadays summed up under the term 'imminent expectation of the parousia in the New Testament'. The fact that the apostles (and, as is indicated, Jesus himself) were mistaken in their expectation of the imminent return of Christ leads Tindal to ask whether in that case they could be inspired in other less central things.[285] Doubts are already expressed about the apostles themselves as witnesses to the tradition. How could they have misunderstood the meaning of Jesus' mission so grossly after spending a whole year in his close presence?[286] A expressly rejects the remark made by his conversation partner that however many textual variants it might contain, scripture, and in particular the New Testament, must be free of serious errors, since it is intended by God to be a clear and unalterable rule for human action: this is true only of the law of nature, which is not dependent on any knowledge of language or on the reliability of copyists and translators.[287]

This leads to a fixed rule of interpretation which Tindal offers as a key with which one can avoid all difficulties: 'to admit all for divine Scripture, that tends to the Honour of God, and the Good of Man; and nothing which does not.'[288] Evidently this rule, which appears in other passages in the form 'that there are no Doctrines of a divine Original contain'd in the Gospel Dispensation, but what by their innate Excellency are knowable to be such'[289] is meant to show the agreement of the relevant commands with the law of nature.[290] The formulation of this hermeneutical key is an important landmark in the history of biblical exegesis, in that here the development which led to an increasing ethicization of Christianity came to a provisional conclusion. In this respect, too, Tindal's book also fulfils an important function in that it logically brings to an end, and states openly, the presuppositions of numerous predecessors which they failed to think through consistently. Tindal is also a clear thinker in that he derives his principle directly from the concept of God: 'Ought we not, in Order to prevent all Mistakes, in the first Place to get clear ideas of the moral Character of the Divine Being...; ought we not to compare what we are told of him, by what we already know of him, and so judge of what Men teach us concerning God, by what God himself teaches us' – it then follows that as God is infinitely wise and perfectly good, 'no Doctrines can come from him that have not these Characters stamp'd on them.'[291]

Turning to the New Testament, though, one is far from coming to the end of all the problems. Tindal knows very well that even the moral commands of Jesus, which are formulated in the simplest way,[292] are not to be taken literally. He recalls the forms of parables and hyperbolic and metaphorical expressions throughout the New Testament.[293] Even the commandments in the Sermon on the Mount, like Matt.5.40 or 5.39,[294] or even Matt.19.12,[295] when taken literally, lead to absurd consequences, as is shown by instances from church history or the views of particular sects. Interestingly, among these examples there also appears the biblical prohibition against interest: Tindal stresses the damaging consequences this would have for commerce were it observed.[296] Here, too, he comes to the conclusion that fatal consequences from such statements, as for example also from Matt.18.22, could only be avoided if they were interpreted 'consistently with what the Light of Nature dictates to be our Duty, in preserving our Reputation, Liberty, and Prosperity'.[297] At this point all those who see in such remarks the glimmerings of the ideology of a quite specific economic order (early capitalism) have a grain of truth![298] Tindal then explicitly establishes the principle that ethical rules must be applied in accordance with the circumstances prevailing at a particular time.[299] Furthermore, it is the motivation behind the actions which makes them good or bad: anything that furthers human happiness is good, and whatever produces the opposite effect is bad.[300] Another interesting feature is the reference to Confucius,[301] whose maxims Tindal seeks to introduce to illuminate the teaching of Jesus because their content is in full agreement with it and expressed in a simpler way.

Added to this comment is a reference to the reason why the words of Jesus are so difficult to understand: they are 'accommodated to the then Way of speaking'. This corresponds to a feature which we can trace right through Tindal's comments about the New Testament (though it is completely absent from those about the Old). It follows the same line as the beginnings of the reference to context in his ethics, which we noted above. Taken by itself, it inevitably clashes with Tindal's often repeated assertion that in judging whether a commandment is true or false it is important to see whether it corresponds with the immutable law of nature.[302] Tindal is evidently well informed about the state of New Testament exegesis in his time, and the many observations about the style and language of the New Testament which he uses as a basis for his argument why it cannot be applied directly to the present could have led him to arrive at the conclusion that not only was the New Testament a book of its time, but that it was also historically conditioned. However, his thinking does not go further at this point and therefore as a biblical critic he keeps to his acceptance of timeless and absolute values,[303] which in his ethical thinking he almost seems to transcend. Nevertheless, here we find a stress on the subject-matter itself of a kind that was to develop fully only in a much later generation of exegetes. The limitations of his thinking also appear at the point already mentioned, where he leaves to the decision of each particular age the specific forms of practising religion, with a reference to the old distinction between fundamentalia and indifferentia,[304] because he can see them only as means to an end, 'to be vary'd as best suits those Ends'.[305] The underlying dualism of Humanist Enlightenment thought, the distinction between inward and outward and the Spiritualism associated with that, which is suspicious of anything concrete and material, also runs through these remarks.

By way of summary, it can be said that although Tindal sets out to demonstrate in a large-scale system the parallel in content between the religion of nature and the Christian revelation (although the looser form of a dialogue is retained, this is merely the quite external form of a construction which has been thought through as a basic system),[306] his work has in fact demonstrated precisely the opposite. Its aim is to provide a key (or touchstone) for use in demonstrating in each individual instance which statements of the biblical revelation can claim to be an expression of the divine will and are therefore also binding on the citizens of England in the eighteenth century. The law of nature, which at the same time corresponds with the unchangeable nature of God who is pure wisdom and goodness, is this criterion. Because it is at all times clearly understandable to all men, even the simplest, it can be applied to the Bible at all points. Tindal carries through this test, but in the wider context of both Testaments which he considers, in essentials he finds nothing which stands up to it. The Old Testament is ruled out from the start, because neither its God nor its human beings are adequate to the moral claim by which they are subjected to an inexorable trial. This negative verdict is good Humanist tradition. But Tindal does not pass even the New Testament. Too much of its content, too, is offensive (the mistake over the imminent expectation of the parousia, the human weaknesses of the apostles) and there are also too many doubts about the process of tradition to which it was submitted and to the linguistic and conceptual forms of expression in which its message comes to us. In this way, what appeared central to the early Humanists and Puritans, the commands of the Gospels and Jesus' own commandments, more or less slip through his fingers. Even these sayings are not immediately usable; they need interpretation which changes their metaphorical imagery into direct statements that can also be understood by the man in the street. But in that case – though Tindal avoids this conclusion, it follows logically from his remarks – they fall under the verdict of being the kind of authority from which in fact he seeks to free mankind: professional interpreters are needed, and there is no direct access of the kind that people have to the law of nature because this is written on their hearts.[307] So while we can concede that subjectively, Tindal's intention is to salvage revealed religion, in fact he has only demonstrated the difficulties of discovering its permanent content. Thus ultimately he has shown that revealed religion is superfluous, as the religion of nature is enough for human salvation, and is so much more easily accessible to man. So we can say that Tindal largely prepared for the conclusions which Annet expressed openly a few years later.

4

The Late Phase

(a) Thomas Chubb

Lechler[1] has compared Thomas Chubb's *The True Gospel of Jesus Christ Asserted* (1738) with Tindal's *Christianity as Old as the Creation*. Chubb, the man of the people, self-taught, who engaged in the various themes of the Deistic debate out of a burning interest in theological problems which were then engaging the interest of a large public (as they do today in the United States) and who made a wealth of significant contributions of his own to them,[2] is especially interesting precisely because of his universality. We can find shorter or longer discussions by him of most of the questions topical at the time – the role of reason,[3] religion,[4] miracles,[5] and so on[6] – about which he wrote repeatedly. His *Posthumous Works* include a collection under the title *The Author's Farewell to his Readers* in which as his legacy Chubb yet again indicates where he stands over the numerous groups of problems which occupied him intensively throughout his life.

However, of all this writing, Lechler[7] regards only *The True Gospel* as 'an integrating element in the history of the development of Deism'.[8] His view that Chubb's aim is essentially that of Tindal, but approached in a different way,[9] is not in fact completely correct. Although both have points of contact in a large number of basic conceptions which were the common currency of deism, Chubb's remarks on the New Testament in this work represent a clearly earlier stage in the inner development of the movement, even if it appeared a few years later than Tindal's magnum opus.[10] For Chubb it is still obvious that 'the laws of Christ' can and must be the basis of the life of a Christian;[11] he still knows nothing of Tindal's doubts as to whether these are to be set up at all.[12] It was the purpose of Jesus on his coming into the world to save the souls of men, i.e to secure God's favour for them and to assure their blessedness in another world.[13] In the case of Chubb, too, ethical eudaemonism underlies this approach.[14] Chubb refers to the history of the life and ministry of Jesus as the source from which we can learn something about his real aims.[15]

It follows from the history of the life of Jesus that he approaches people as a free being and presents them with a series of 'doctrinal propositions' which are based on the assumption of the existence of a deity and are called evangelium, i.e. good news, because of their great significance for mankind. They are commended with the intention that a well-grounded conviction of them can become the source and principle of human action, remedy human vices and thus secure the favour of God.[16] Thus Chubb, too, understands the gospel in an exclusively moral sense: he emphasizes that 'a wellgrounded perswasion of those truths thus becoming a principle of action in men... is called believing the gospel; and believing in Jesus Christ'.[17] The truths which Jesus teaches can be summed up in three main points.[18] 1. Christ demands that we should direct our spirit and our life in accordance with the eternal and unchangeable rule of action which is grounded in the reason of things.[19] 2. He requires repentance and a change of life from all who have violated this law as the only certain basis for divine grace and forgiveness. 3. To make these truths more impressive he proclaims that God has appointed a day of judgment in which he will reward or punish men depending on whether or not they have lived in accordance with this rule.[20]

Although in Chubb's view, also, the law which Christ brought is identical with the law of reason which has always been in existence,[21] it does occur similarly in the Bible. Above all he recalls the Ten Commandments as his summary,[22] and also some of the maxims used by Jesus like the Golden Rule and the command to love one's neighbour,[23] which at the same time he can call 'the sum and substance of the moral law'. He also quotes in detail from the Sermon on the Mount, in which Christ taught what 'temper' his disciples had to have,[24] though on the other hand he observes that Christ did not present any complete moral system which is applicable in all states of life.[25] Insofar as Chubb still regards the message of Jesus as the basis of what Christian faith means to him, in his book he is closer to Chillingworth than Tindal or even Annet. His remarks are also particularly illuminating on those points which he does *not* seek to recognize as the content of Christian faith. Here the deep gulf that separates the moral form of 'religion' which he advocates from the central statements of the traditional Christian message becomes visible in an unusually clear form. At the same time, the fact that he can allow all this to be printed under his full personal name without worrying about his personal safety or even his outward prosperity[26] shows how fundamentally the climate in England has changed from the persecution experienced by Toland, Whiston and Woolston. In fact Chubb's remarks are not too far removed from what had become the convention of theology even in the dominant groups within the mainstream church, which were made up of Whigs.[27] The critical point in his work can be located fairly accurately: it is at the centre, where Christian doctrine cannot be reconciled with his moralistic system. In other dogmatic questions, although he does not conceal e.g. his Unitarian views,[28] he makes striking concessions to the church's creed. Thus he wants to leave open, for example, the question whether Jesus could have performed miracles;[29] although in another passage he speaks out against ceremonies,[30] he gives a lengthy explanation as to why Christ instituted baptism and the eucharist ('in conformity to the usages and customs of the world, and the fondness there is in the generality of men to external observances' – however this comment shows clearly enough his dislike of both sacraments!);[31] indeed he even begins from the resurrection as an indubitable fact![32] However, he can do so without any hesitation since 'The Gospel of Jesus Christ is not an historical account of matters of fact.'[33] Passion, death, resurrection, ascension: these traditional statements of the creed are not part of the gospel, for that was preached to the poor before these events.[34] The credibility of these events depends on the proofs that can be advanced for them. Even the miracles which Christ did were intended to attract the attention of his hearers and to direct it towards his message: the history of these events, which is a history of facts like any other, is not part of this message. The gospel of Jesus Christ was the teaching which he proclaimed, and that is the only thing that matters.[35] For as much as anything is important in the life of Jesus, it is his way of life, which corresponded exactly to the law of nature. 'Christ preached his own life if I may so speak, and lived his own doctrine.'[36] The moral teacher is at the same time a model: that is the logical consequence.

The proclamation of Jesus is to be distinguished sharply from the theological statements in the New Testament about his life and ministry. All these interpretations, as for example the Logos doctrine in the Gospel of John and what can also be read there about Christ's relationship to God, his pre-existence, and so on, are merely the private opinion of the author.[37] The same goes for Paul's remarks about Jews and Gentiles in Rom.11.[38] There are a whole series of traditional Christian doctrines which conflict with the law of nature (the 'moral fitness of things') and the moral perfection of God. They include above all the doctrine of vicarious righteousness and the atoning suffering and death of Jesus Christ. It is absurd and a violation of heavenly majesty if a person assumes that he is pardoning someone for the sake of the merits by which another has made himself well pleasing. That would be to presuppose that he was acting in accordance with false and evil principles. The good conduct and suffering of Christ are no more a reason for God to act in a friendly way towards another person than colour has anything to do with sound. It was simply his way of life which made Christ personally valuable. He himself never proclaimed such doctrines as that of imputed righteousness.[39] Conversely, it would be as nonsensical to claim that sinners could be commended to God as acceptable, not because they themselves provide the basis for this, but on the basis of Christ's righteous way of life, his suffering and intercession.[40] The only possibility Jesus had of saving sinners was to summon them to repentance; indeed, this was his chief concern, because mankind generally was corrupt and evil.[41] God does not approve and disapprove arbitrarily, depending on his whim 'but from the real and intrinsick valuableness or unworthiness of the object of such his approbation or dislike'.[42] Any other conduct on the part of God would be an expression of a manifest moral imperfection: it would be unworthy of God to allow anything that did not merit this approval. So the only possibility was for Christ to save men 'by his working a personal change in them', and by confronting them with such truth as could move them to change themselves, to make themselves personally acceptable to their creator, and as a result become worthy recipients of his favour. The ethical order is unexceptionable, and here God's being and action are also involved: 'God is eternally and unchangeably the same, he always likes or dislikes as the being which is liked or disliked is in itself the proper object of one or the other.'[43]

Equally nonsensical is the doctrine of the satisfaction of the righteousness of God by the death of Christ: 'Upon which I observe, that the sufferings of the innocent could not possibly be a satisfaction to justice for the fault of the guilty', for the guilty subject must also incur the punishment, and if God had punished the innocent and let the guilty go free this would obviously have been unjust.[44] However, Chubb thinks he can exonerate the Apostle Paul from such teaching, since his statement that the blood of Christ takes away sin is meant in terms of a moral example, and is intended to bring the sinner to repentance.[45] Moreover, such a form of expression is to be seen in the context of the apostles' adaptation to the ideas of their contemporaries, the Jews, and statements like those of Lev.16.21,22 were already similarly used metaphorically, since the sins of the people could not literally be collected and carried off by the scapegoat.[46]

However, there are yet other dogmas which stand in the way of the Gospel. There is, for example, the doctrine of original sin, according to which, because of the behaviour of ancestors or the influence of the devil, men are incapable of good deeds and are condemned to evil ones.[47] Although Chubb in no way sees the state of mankind in a rosy glow – on the contrary, mankind was grossly corrupt when Christ undertook to reform and save it – the awareness of the existence of a deity as the creator of the world who takes notice of the actions of men and will call each individual to account for what he has done continued to remain alive among them.[48] Christ addressed them as *free* beings,[49] who voluntarily[50] subject themselves to his commandments (as self-evident laws of nature), change their behaviour, and thus make themselves well-pleasing to God.

From this moral system other notions contained in Chubb's work follow logically. Thus he comments on the church that because of the need for voluntary assent to the doctrines of Christ, no Christian can be dependent on laws of the state or a rule within the church.[51] If a Christian wants to make another obedient to the commandments of Christ, the only permissible and necessary means of convincing him are arguments and good example. In Chubb's eyes, the mixture of Christian and secular societies is an 'unnatural coalition', which has contributed to the maintenance of the most absurd doctrines and superstitious customs over many generations.[52] Christ laid the foundation for the propagation of the gospel in 'friendly societies or families of love',[53] in which brotherly life together is to be the rule.[54] The choice between these societies is open to any disciple of Christ: he can decide personally to which particular society he wants to attach himself; here he is not responsible to any fellow Christian, but only to God.[55] The financial contribution of any Christian to his society is also left to him and is dependent on his assessment of his own situation and that of the society to which he belongs.[56] This is an indirect criticism of the tithe (which was then the current form of church tax) and other official offerings for the clergy.[57]

Chubb's work is not lacking in attacks on ritual, either. Christ's work of reform was very necessary because people had fallen victim to many kinds of superstition and idolatry.[58] The pagan religions had suggested other means of a ritual kind to their adherents in place of moral virtue, which is the only way of pleasing God; these means allowed them to perform sacrifices and ceremonies and in addition to persevere in an evil life.[59] However, in the course of its later development even Christianity was distorted in just the same way as the other religions by absurd doctrine and superstitious practices: it came to consist more and more in external matters and less and less in the inner principle which rules men's inclinations and actions.[60] There is a fundamental danger here: 'Thus the setting too great a value upon, and paying too great a regard to rites and ceremonies and positive institutions, by giving them the preference to moral duty, is highly injurious to the gospel of Christ.'[61] Similarly, however, the emergence of clergy who are useless because they are not entrusted with the immediate government of the community,[62] characterized by pluralism and absenteeism, by unnecessary riches and splendour, is a basic evil of the church.[63] Finally, even the most strenuous theological learning and wearisome study is unnecessary for a leading role in the church. For the gospel of Christ is a simple matter which has only one aim, the saving of souls.[64] Here again we come up against an echo of the theme begun by the great Locke.[65]

In the juxtaposition in Chubb's book of groups of themes which by today's standards are far removed, we can see the uninterrupted influence of the combined view of state, church and the Bible as a normative source of order which in the English cultural world extended from the time of Bucer to the late period of Deism. *The True Gospel of Jesus Christ* is also an attempt to derive binding norms from the New Testament for both the moral action of the individual and the form of the church. However, as the real criteria are not obtained from the Bible itself but from the static thought-forms of the ancient system of natural law, the result obtained can only be a caricature of the Bible from which almost everything that it says, with the exception of a tiny fragment (the supposed teaching of Christ) is omitted. This too becomes a caricature of itself, as is shown nowhere more strikingly than in the comparison of Jesus with Confucius, whose teaching is in fact given against a similarly static background. The contradiction which is becoming evident here in fact runs through the whole development of Humanism up to the Enlightenment; however, in terms of epistemology the earlier representatives of the trend in rationalism leading up to the Latitudinarians are still largely unaware of it. The chief service of the Deists is that under the tutelage of Descartes, Locke and Newton they also worked it out in a way which (with certain qualifications) was methodologically clear. But in the light of their epistemological presuppositions, they too remain at a half-way stage: they do not take the step to a complete dissolution of the Christian tradition. Nor does Chubb give up the attempt to derive his ethical maxims from a teaching of Jesus which can be demonstrated in the New Testament, and in the same work he produces principles for what he sees as the ideal form of the church. In the case of the latter it is easy to see the legacy of Congregationalist Puritanism (which in its turn is governed by the ancient idea of contract); the principle of the strict division of state and church also belongs in this context.

The negative side emerges directly from this position: for ethical rationalism, rooted in tradition, which bases itself on unhistorical norms which are universally valid, and yet moves in the sphere of a Western Christian culture which has come into being through a specific historical development, criticism of large parts of the content of this tradition becomes a necessary form of self-discovery. Criticism of the Bible and the church are the most important areas of this controversy; they both belong closely together, since they derive from the same ideals and are focussed on themes connected by the same stream of tradition. Therefore one cannot understand the background to the origins of biblical criticism in the history of ideas if one does not see it alongside criticism of the church, and justice can be done to both of them only if we consider the world-view which underlies both of them equally.

The True Gospel of Jesus Christ is the last work in which the whole of this overall view can still be seen. The final collapse of the system is already in view during the late phase of Chubb's own work. In the *Farewell* of the unwearying writer to his readers it is especially in the work *Of Divine Revelation in General*[66] that we can see a final shift in his attitude which almost takes him beyond the limits of Christian Deism.

Even if the apologist has not yet completely abandoned his old position, he has more or less turned into a sceptic. He does not deny the possibility of a revelation, but almost his first word in this connection is 'uncertainty'. It is uncertain whether a revelation which is communicated through visions, voices, dreams or other impressions is really a divine revelation, since we have no rule for distinguishing true revelation from mere deception, divine dreams from other dreams and divine impressions from other impressions.[67] If this is already true of a revelation at first hand, it is true even more of one which has only been communicated by those who think they have received one. Really there is only a negative criterion, from which we can read what real revelation cannot be: as the moral character of God, his constant wisdom and goodness, is already known without revelation, anything in expressions of an alleged revelation of God that is unworthy and attributes to him actions which fall short of this level, is a certain indication that there is not a divine revelation. Now this criterion cannot be used the other way round: even if a revelation says of God only things that are worthy of him, that is no proof that they are in fact of divine origin.[68] Nor is revelation even proved through miracles, since while an authentic revelation may be accompanied by miracles, that is in no way necessarily the case.[69] Chubb then goes on to discuss the three great religions of revelation – Judaism, Islam, Christianity – in turn; Christianity is discussed last. Here, in connection with his attitude to the archive of revelation in this religion, the Bible, we can see an attitude which, while being more precise, is at the same time also partly modified. Not a few statements are strongly reminiscent of Tindal's remarks.

If we begin from the fact that the New Testament contains the written tradition in which the Christian revelation has come down to us, we see that this is in no way identical with the whole of the New Testament. Rather, only the materials which are directly related to the message of Christ can be taken into consideration. In the first place they are to be found in the four Gospels. Acts is not relevant because it emerges that sometimes the apostles were not always clear about the content of the message of Jesus. Thus they saw Christianity as a supplement to Judaism and accordingly limited their task to the mission to the Jews.[70]

Of course, this error was remedied by Paul, but his hypocritical action in the temple according to Acts 21.20ff. makes him morally suspect in the same context.[71] On the other hand, he decidedly went too far in his remarks against the supporters of the Mosaic ritual law in Gal.5.2,4, for even if they might fall victim to such an error out of weakness, this should not mean that they forfeited any divine grace, provided that they remained upright and virtuous people.[72] A further erroneous doctrine of the first apostles is that the church only has possessions in common, which only apostles and clergy are entitled to control. The story of Ananias and Sapphira is a vivid example of the moral pressure exercised by them in this connection.[73] Chubb finds this control particularly ominous, because although it was soon given up in this form, it laid the foundation for the later claim of the clergy to property. We hear elsewhere that the Apostles only preached repentance and the forgiveness of sins (Acts 2.37f.); this decidedly restricts Christ's message and cannot be normative for us because both the main points of this preaching, the restriction of the gospel to Israel and the sharing of goods, soon proved erroneous. Still less can the letters of the apostles contain the gospel, since apart from the material for endless disputes which they provide through their manifold contradictions, they offer a good deal which is directly contrary to the gospel: for example Paul's rejection of the Jewish law, where by contrast Jesus himself and the first apostles required obedience to the law,[74] and other doctrines which Chubb does not want to go into further.[75] From this he concludes 'that those epistles, in the gross, cannot with any propriety, be considered as the Christian revelation'.[76] As the Book of Revelation, too, must be left out of account,[77] only the Gospels remain. And we must be very careful even about them. In the first place, it is questionable whether the persons to whom they are attributed were really their authors; secondly, whether these persons were sufficiently qualified to know the truth of what they were reporting; thirdly, whether they had sufficient love of the truth; and fourthly and fifthly, whether their books have been transmitted faithfully and translated accurately – this is particularly important for Chubb, who knew only English.[78] Like Tindal, Chubb has the gravest suspicions of the process of tradition to which the New Testament owes its origin;[79] it is already uncertain whether these writings come from the apostles at all, and even if they do, their authors were still mortal men who were subject to error. The choice of canonical writings from earliest Christian literature is based on arbitrary decisions which were disputed even at the time, and in its present form, the New Testament goes back to copies which were themselves already corrupted in many ways because of the relatively late date of their origin.[80] All this information, which Chubb takes from professional scholars[81] counsels him to extreme caution – and in this connection he refs to the words of Jesus in Matthew 24.4.[82] Finally, the Gospels in part contain statements the content of which contradicts the message of Jesus or is unworthy of it, as e.g. John 20.22f., which entrusts the right to forgive sins to human hands which are quite incapable of it;[83] there are also statements which are intrinsically incredible, like Matthew 4.8, a notion which is impossible because of the view of the world it implies.[84]

In connection with the last-named instance Chubb goes on to mention the principles by which one can distinguish between the credible and the incredible, between true and false: he stresses 'that not only credibility, but also a conformity to our natural notices of things, and to the eternal rules of right and wrong in the subject, ought to be the boundaries of our faith and practice'. This provides a twofold criterion which relates to two main areas: that of material statements from the realm of natural things and that of moral statements: 'whatever is repugnant to our natural notions of things, or to the eternal rules of right and wrong is, under that appearance, repugnant to the human understanding, the one in a natural and the other in a moral view.'[85] Two different philosophical traditions are combined in this double rule, which was to have far-reaching effects on the history of historical-critical exegesis: on the one hand Lockean empiricism (present in the keyword 'human understanding') and on the other ethical rationalism. For both of these Chubb also uses the term 'common sense'.[86] Here Locke's influence again becomes quite clear when Chubb stresses that such a capacity to judge on natural and moral things is a 'natural standard' which, as a 'product of nature', is open to all men irrespective of their state of education.[87]

According to Chubb, the standards mentioned above must be applied to distinguish the probable from the improbable within the Gospels and thus to arrive at what could be regarded as *ipsissima verba Jesu*. Care and concern must prevail here.[88] In the last resort, however, Chubb believes that, despite all the difficulties presented by the external tradition of these sayings, he has a sure rule in the three main statements which he developed in his earlier work as the content of the message of Jesus.[89]

All these considerations have one presupposition. Chubb replies in characteristic fashion to a question which arises right at the beginning: 'That there was such a person as Jesus Christ, and that he, in the main, did, and taught as is recorded of him, appears to be probable.'[90] The probability that Jesus in fact lived is greater than the opposite, because the expansion of early Christianity can hardly be explained on the presupposition that the story of his life and mission were a fiction. It is also more probable that Jesus received his power from God, because it served the general good and he did not use it to deceive; similarly, he was familiar with traditional knowledge which served the same ends.[91] The argument from probability, which is evidently the foundation for the whole of Chubb's system in its later phase – he himself does not venture to claim certainty on this point – is strongly reminiscent of the arguments of Butler, whose apologetic comes all too close to the frontiers of scepticism. Chubb observes that the great distance in time and space between the events and his inability to examine instances thoroughly leave him in this uncertain state; had he better information he would perhaps arrive at other conclusions.[92]

However, interest in historical facts also has its limitations. Chubb certainly sees a decisive difference between facts where it does not make a great deal of difference whether or not they actually happened (for example, whether someone like Alexander the Great or Julius Caesar really lived or not),[93] and the facticity of the activity of Jesus, which is decidedly important for us. On the other hand, he can completely relativize the importance of the question whether or not the Mohammedan revelation could be divine or not by focussing on the usefulness of any possible answer to it: 'If the revelation referred to could furnish me with such useful knowledge, or with a better rule of life, or with more powerful excitements to the practice of virtue and true religion, than at present I am in possession of, and thereby I should be made a wiser and a better man; then I acknowledge that such conviction would be beneficial to me.' Nevertheless, he would think it ridiculous to change one's religion, since to lay down one external form of religion and exchange it for another is hardly much more use than to change the colour of one's clothes.[94]

In the ultimate consistency of his approach as it became clear in his later years, Chubb is hardly an advocate of a historical religion any more. Of course Christianity is particularly important to him, because it is recognized in the part of the world in whose culture he lives and because it was presented to him in his childhood as a sacred truth.[95] He replies with the utmost caution to the question whether in that case on his own presuppositions he is a Christian: 'Thus far then I am believer, and a Christian; but whether it will be allowed that these appellations are properly applied to me, I know not, nor am I sollicitous about it.'[96] Here we can clearly find a different tone from that in the self-conscious title of the book by Tindal; it is also a more honest one, since in the course of time the apologetic presupposition of most Deists that they could save Christianity, albeit interpreted in their own terms, inevitably became increasingly spurious, the more their critical standards ate away at the substance of this Christianity. If Christ can continue to have any significance, it is above all as a moral model.[97] That is also the role which Christian moralism was long to assign to him.

Something else is striking about the system in this posthumous writing of Chubb: for him the Old Testament is already excluded from being a legitimate part of the Christian Bible. This is not only because 'in gross' he limits the positive content of the Christian message to the words of Jesus as they can be discovered from the Gospels and thus already postulates a New Testament 'canon within in the canon'. As we saw, this largely corresponds to the approach of certain Puritan movements. Now he even makes the Old Testament as a whole into an alien religion: it is the document of Jewish revelation,[98] which could only be recognized as divine with difficulty, 'because, by such admission, the most beautiful and amiable picture of the Deity, viz. God's moral character, will be sullied, if not defaced thereby.'[99] In his judgment on the Old Testament Chubb also begins from his notion of God;[100] the moral conduct of the God of Israel (say in the command to exterminate the Canaanites and Amalekites, and other cruelties) and by contrast God's familiarity with people like Abraham, Moses and so on, is irreconcilable with this ideal.[101] Moreover the Jewish revelation contains a whole series of doctrines which contradict the twofold criterion of common sense: for example, the assertion that God chose a particular people from all mankind is the expression of an intolerable favouritism, as God must treat all men equally until their conduct gives an occasion for the opposite.[102] Equally unjust was the assumption that God favoured the descendants of the patriarchs for the sake of their fathers Abraham, Isaac and Jacob; this might perhaps accord with human conduct, but would be quite inappropriate for God, who did not receive any favour from Abraham which he could return to his children but was rightly well disposed only to Abraham himself because of his virtue.[103] Relieving the twelfth part of the people (the tribe of Levi) of all work and concern for their own livelihood on the grounds that they are consecrated to God is as harmful to society as the existence of the same religious drones in popish countries[104] – here Chubb's anticlericalism finds a particularly rewarding target. He also expresses doubts about the reliability of the Jewish tradition and in particular the Jewish law in the form of the Pentateuch. Here Chubb enumerates the dangers to which the Book of the Law was exposed during the varied history of Israel: above all he takes up the traditional theme of the Jews as the 'ignorant, inactive people', in order to casts doubts on them as the ones who handed down such a tradition.[105] It is worth noting that in this context Chubb refers specifically to the remarks by Paul (and by Peter in Acts) hostile to Jewish ceremonies, which in the usual way he describes as sources of superstition and false religion.[106] Evidently, however, in contrast to his predecessors, he does not act selectively, attacking only the ceremonial law, but condemns the whole of Israel's tradition. At this point he is silent about the Decalogue, which he judged positively in his early work.

As is evident from a whole series of parallels, in his explicitly negative attitude to the Old Testament the later works of Chubb are in all probability dependent on the writer who made the Old Testament his prime object of concern and thus introduced a last round in the Deistic debate, Thomas Morgan, author of a three-volume work *The Moral Philosopher*.[107] A debate between Morgan and Chubb had already developed through a series of Morgan's publications: in the last contribution to this series,[108] Morgan's acute hostility to Judaism had already become clear.

Antipathy to the Old Testament as such is nothing new among the Deists. We have seen that it even goes back well before the period of Deism and is one of the characteristic marks of the Humanist world view. As a rule, however, it only appeared as a subsidiary theme, also implicit where the New Testament exclusively, and even more narrowly the teaching of Jesus, was regarded as the only normative order for the present. However, Tindal's work and the debate it provoked already drew attention to the Old Testament in a special way, as we can see from the various contributions which Conyers Middleton[109] made to it.[110] Although Trinius puts him among the Deists, he was impelled by serious apologetic motives,[111] for example to argue for the allegorical understanding of the story of Creation and the Fall, as they could not be taken literally. He explained circumcision as a custom of Egyptian origin (here he refers to Philo and the church fathers[112]) and above all denies that the exodus of Israel from Egypt and the lawgiving by Moses took place at the direct command of God, accompanied by miracles. Rather, Moses acted as a wise lawgiver, who, like the most important lawgivers of Greece, was driven by the awareness that God was behind him, and communicated this awareness skilfully to the people.[113]

For his plan to work, he had to foist all kinds of miracles on the people (though he himself did not seriously believe that these were real miracles). In this context Middleton also goes into the dependence of the Israelites on Egyptian customs which was pointed out by Spencer, and which is evident, among other things, in the golden calf, which was none other than the God Apis.[114] It is worth noting that for his judgment on Moses, Middleton refers above all to Josephus, from whom he produces detailed quotations for his rationalistic explanation. He stresses that he does not in any way want to cast doubt on the divinity of the Mosaic law by his arguments: because of the wisdom of Moses as a just lawgiver his claim that his laws came from God was justified (according to Josephus, too, they were much better than those of the Gentile lawgivers).[115] He calls Cicero as a witness that our faith should not rest on testimony or authority but on the weight of reason.[116]

(b) Thomas Morgan

It needed only the slightest shift of emphasis for the defence of the Old Testament on this basis to turn into a challenge to its authority. On the other hand, the vigour with which Morgan disputes the validity of the Old Testament for Christianity can be explained only in connection with the natural way in which, over the centuries, Old Testament models had been adopted by the established church and constitutional theory had been based on its theology – starting from an approach which was similarly rooted in Humanist views of origin, but which arrived at quite the opposite results where the Bible was concerned. Therefore Morgan's work also represents a landmark in English intellectual history because it denotes the definitive end of the Old Testament in this role. Though large and imaginative books appeared, to defend it against Morgan,[117] – the best of these is beyond question William Warburton's *Divine Legation of Moses*[118] – the days when it had normative validity for the contemporary forms of church and state had gone for ever.

Morgan's basic presuppositions deliberately take up the tradition of ethical rationalism. According to some principles which are already mentioned in the Preface to the first volume, it is 'the moral Truth, Reason, or Fitness of Things' which alone can demonstrate that a doctrine comes from God and is part of the true religion, and accordingly is 'the moral Truth, Reason and Fitness of Actions (...) founded in the natural and necessary Relations of Persons and Things, antecedent to any positive Will or Law'.[119] As Morgan explains on one occasion, in reply to a critic's question, he goes by the criterion of 'moral truth' precisely as defined by Samuel Clarke.[120] That 'Truth and Justice, Mercy and Charity, Temperance and Sobriety, under the Inspection and Cognizance of the supream Being, as the righteous Governor and Judge of the World', must be the will and the law of God for men, because it is 'necessary to the Wellbeing and Happiness of Mankind throughout the whole period of their existence' is as clear to Morgan as a principle of Euclid.[121] In this sense 'moral philosophy', the concept that he puts in the title of his work (which first appeared anonymously), means for him 'the Knowledge of God, Providence, and Human nature';[122] it is a world view which ends up in the justification of morality as its prime goal, issuing into a physico-theological proof of God: the recognition of the Creator from the physical and moral ordering of creation.[123] Lechler has already pointed out that in contrast to the mechanical view of the world, Morgan stresses the constant presence and the direct activity of God in his creation[124] and expressly rejects the opposite view as atheism.[125] This feature again confirms his relationship to Clarke, and beyond him to Newton, for the doctrine of God's constant intervention in the world was a religious conviction which he resolutely defended against Leibniz.[126] At yet a third point we can note Morgan's dependence on Clarke beyond what has been observed by Gawlick: we have already been able to establish in Clarke's system[127] the same sort of break from rationalism as an ethical theory as Gawlick establishes in the strongly hedonistic features of Morgan's ethics, as they appear in his physico-theology.[128] One can even point back beyond Clarke to Locke, whom Euchner believes to have been the vehicle through whom the Neo-Epicureanism of the French school around Gassendi had been introduced into English rationalism.[129] Locke's influence remained dominant throughout Deism. It is in no way accurate for Gawlick to see here a change of view on the part of Morgan in the *Physico-Theology* over against the *Moral Philosopher*, since it is one of the starting points of Morgan's criticism of the Mosaic law, that its sanctions extend only to temporal things, 'none of its Rewards or Punishments relating to any future State, or extending themselves beyond this life.'[130] The inner tensions between absolute and eudaemonistic morality which produce an apologetic stamped by ethical rationalism, but incorporating elements from the Christian tradition, also recur in Morgan. That he can write a work under the title *Physico-Theology* shows how strongly on the whole he is influenced by the Newtonian school.

Morgan is also an apologist insofar as he assigns the Christian revelation a necessary role in the development of humanity. Granted, natural religion is quite sufficient for man's salvation and in principle can be recognized by reason, but in practice it has disseminated so much obscurity and ignorance in the world that the teaching of Jesus was very necessary to put the authentic principles of nature and reason in a true light again.[131] The theories of Euclid and Newton's *Principia*[132] are also in accord with reason, but no one will claim that he could have discovered them without these teachers. Nevertheless, one basic principle, as Morgan stresses explicitly yet again in the preface to the third volume, is 'that natural and revealed Religion are essentially and subjectively the same, and that they can only be distinguished by the different Ways or Means of conveying the same truth to the mind.'[133] He also thinks it important to establish that the morality of the gospel is none other than that of the pagan philosophers like Plato, Cicero and Plutarch; as their writings show, the right conceptions of God and providence, of moral truth and righteousness, were not lost in the world.[134] In principle it is the case that each truth must be necessarily or contingently true, and cannot rest on mere authority.[135] Given this, following Tindal, Morgan can then term Christianity the 'restoration', 'revival'[136] or even the 'best rendering'[137] of the religion of nature. However, only the content of a revelation and not its manner is decisive: anyone who has to communicate a truth which is important for the eternal salvation of mankind may term it revelation whether he has acquired it through divine illumination or through the power of his own reason.[138] For there is only one criterion for deciding on divine truth: its accord with moral truth or the 'fitness of things' which demonstrates it to be such directly to reason.[139]

On the basis of these presuppositions Morgan concerns himself with the Old Testament, and the uncompromising rejection of the Old Testament as part of the Christian Bible is his particular contribution to the Deistic debate. In adopting this position he takes up a theme which had already aroused a lively echo in the discussion of the argument from prophecy sparked off by Collins. Collins' argument, with which he even put in question the validity of the Christian revelation, had begun from the presupposition that the typological view, which had been current for a long time and had been used by traditional theology to legitimate the event of Christ in the light of the Old Testament, no longer proved tenable. This had become clearest in the fact that Woolston's defence of allegorizing had no longer been taken seriously by the academic world but, quite in contrast to the situation at the turn of the century, was judged to be the abstruse fantasy of a lone individual.[140] The force of Collins' argument, that Christianity itself was more than dubious because the assertion that Christ had been foretold in the Old Testament was untenable on a literal understanding of that book, stood or fell with the presupposition that the Bible was an indissoluble unity. What if that was not in fact the case? If one could write off the Old Testament as testimony to a pre-Christian religion and vindicate the New Testament in another way (e.g. through its accord with the law of nature) Christianity could still be defended, albeit as a pedagogical means to the moral illumination of mankind. In fact Thomas Bullock had already taken this decisive step in renouncing the Old Testament in his defence against Collins.[141] In this respect too, then, Morgan follows particular patterns of apologetic. However, the resoluteness of his condemnation of the Old Testament is not tactical but the expression of a vigorous antipathy and the recognition that almost everything contained in the Old Testament is irreconcilable with his principle of 'moral truth'. With this attitude, too, he takes up an old legacy which we can pursue right through the history of Spiritualism.

The scorn which Morgan poured on the theory of the typological relationship between Old and New Testaments still presented by orthodox theologians[142] can be evaluated in the history of ideas only as a rearguard action. Typology as a hermeneutical method was already in full retreat – apart from some late survivals in the United States. Morgan believes that to suppose the prophets to have predicted the advent of Jesus as Messiah in the literal sense is even more of an error, since Jesus never regarded himself as Messiah in the Jewish sense.[143] Morgan does not spend much time on such considerations, but immediately goes over to a frontal attack on the essential content of the Old Testament. Here everything that does not accord with his purely moralistic religion is radically rejected. Above all, he attacks the law of Moses. A remarkable speculative theory[144] helps him to make the transition from the purely moral natural, monotheistic primal religion which he believes to have existed at the beginning of the historical development[145] to polytheism: a rebellion of the angels in heaven led to the fall of the rebellious angels from heaven; after their arrival on earth they took up a middle position between God and man and finally deceived men into offering them divine worship.[146] Morgan also explains the origin of sacrifice (originally supposed to have consisted only in solemn feasts) and of the clergy (first instituted by Joseph in Egypt) in the light of these events.[147] Thus Egypt became the 'Mother of Superstition'.[148] The Israelites were so Egyptianized during their long stay in Egypt that they fell victim to the same superstition and lost all true knowledge of God, religion and providence.[149] Here Morgan takes up Spencer's old theory and, like so many Deists, makes it serve his own ends. Because Moses had to cope with such a blind, hard-hearted people,[150] he was compelled to adapt himself to their condition and give them a law which was not conceived as the law of nature and therefore could not be tested to see whether it corresponded to the fitness of things, but had to be adopted by them as the direct will of God.[151]

Morgan rejects the Mosaic law in its two, traditionally different forms of ceremonial law and moral law. There is nothing special about the way in which the ceremonial law is taken to be abrogated by the gospel; a consensus to that effect goes right back to the Reformation.[152] However, Morgan goes one step further by no longer allowing even a typological significance to the ceremonial law.[153] He criticizes the ceremonial law for having favoured the priesthood as greedy eaters through meaningless sacrifices[154] and in this way is able to use the Levites as examples of his anticlericalism. In another passage he shows explicitly that here he is thinking of his own Protestant clergy (and not just the Papists).[155] In addition to this, he includes in Judaism everything in Christianity that contradicts the pure moral religion. This includes the sacraments of baptism and eucharist, both of which were retained at the Reformation: Jesus continued them merely as national secular Jewish customs, and the priests were the first to falsify their meaning and make mysteries of them. He wants to allow baptism merely as proselyte baptism, while regarding infant baptism (of the children of already Christian parents) as illegitimate.[156] In rejecting infant baptism he is again following old Spiritualist tradition. Similarly, all dogmatic statements which stand in the way of a purely legal retribution of human deeds at the last judgment on the basis of the unchanging criterion of moral truth, like the doctrine of the vicarious righteousness of Christ, are rejected as 'the corrupt dregs of Judaism'.[157]

However, Morgan cannot even recognize the Mosaic moral law as divine. In his eyes it is merely a civil, political law, which only regulates outward actions in order to secure the civil rights of society, and does not extend to the inner disposition of men and women, in which alone true virtue and righteousness can exist. Similarly, all the sanctions of this law were purely temporal and this-worldly, without prospect of rewards and punishments in another world.[158] This notion, too, is by no means original to Morgan; rather, as we have seen,[159] Locke had already anticipated him in it and his influence may be evident at this point also. As key witness for it Morgan claims none other than the apostle Paul. Paul was 'the great Free-thinker of his Age, the bold and brave Defender of Reason against Authority',[160] who not only condemned the Mosaic ceremonial law as fleshly and fatal,[161] but also condemned the moral law as weak and imperfect.[162] If we remember how long a tradition there already was of appealing to Paul, in English and especially in Puritan theology,[163] we may want to see this feature, too, as more of a conservative element. In this connection, however, the Christian Deist often has to defend his key witness against the charge that he himself often acted in accordance with the Mosaic moral law and occasionally even in accordance with the ceremonial law. The answer is that Paul only did this in the sense that he observed the law in its capacity as the civil law of his land because he was born a Jew and adapted himself to his Jewish fellow citizens and not because he regarded it as a divine law which would also have been binding on his conscience.[164]

Morgan subjects not only the Mosaic law but also the most significant figures of the Old Testament to vigorous moral criticism. Thus for example the character of David is depicted in the blackest colours: 'he had been the most bloody Persecutor that ever had been known, and his whole Life had been one continued Scene of Dissimulation, Falsehood, Lust and Cruelty.'[165] Several times he goes right through the course of Israelite history from the Exodus to the monarchy, showing other people like Samuel,[166] Elisha,[167] and the kings of Israel in an unfavourable light. They are praised only in one respect, and here the judgment is favourable particularly on people whom the author of Kings condemns, like Solomon and Jezebel: their toleration of foreign religions is praised as tolerance: they granted freedom of conscience to both natives and foreigners by refusing to exterminate the idolaters with fire and sword, in accordance with the wishes of those who were zealous for faith.[168] The whole people under the leadership of Moses and his followers offended against the law of righteousness by refusing to have any dealings with other nations and fighting with fire and sword not only the Canaanites in their own land but also the surrounding peoples, for religious reasons and with a desire for domination.[169] In his moral denigration of Old Testament figures, Morgan can already follow the example of P.Bayle, who in his *Dictionnaire Historique et Critique* vigorously criticized Abraham and above all David, but with the opposite intention of leaving room only for God's grace as opposed to the universal sinfulness of mankind.[170]

Remarkably, Morgan sees prophecy, at least in accordance with its original intention, as a counterpart to the internal constitution of Old Testament Israel, depicted as it is in such gloomy features. Samuel founded an academy of the prophets in Naioth,[171] where in addition to the classical liberal arts the prophets studied above all 'Moral Philosophy, or the Knowledge of God, Providence and human Nature', with the aim of preaching perfect righteousness and rigid virtue.[172] This they in fact did for a while, against the utmost resistance of the people, above all the priests and kings.[173] Their calling then degenerated, and in addition to the proclamation of salvation with which they sought to avoid the hatred of the people,[174] Morgan also has to censure their fanatical resistance to the tolerance of kings like Solomon and Ahab. A story like that of Micaiah ben Imlah (I Kings 22) is sufficient reason for censuring the deliberate lying prophecy of this man.[175] Despite these reservations, the claim that the prophets proclaimed morality[176] and attacked rites and the priesthood[177] has remained significant for ethical and rationalist exegesis – and for the understanding of the prophets – down to the present day – as has the caution over their proclamation of salvation. Morgan also finds the picture of God in the Old Testament offensive. The story of the exodus in which God makes a personal appearance like a man, in a visible, tangible way, and acts familiarly with Moses can only be understood as dramatic poetry after the style of Homer; Moses used this means to adapt himself to the superstitious temperament of his people.[178] Later, Morgan progresses to the statement that this God who is visible and bounded in space and time cannot have been the absolutely infinite and invisible God and Creator, but was only a local guardian deity, the God of just this people without reference to any other nation.[179] On the other hand, Morgan finds his view of the history of religion in the Old Testament: the pure primal religion which stands at the beginning, and the corruption by ceremonies and superstition which follows. To some degree the religion of the patriarchs represents this pure primal form, even if it included belief in angels as local guardian deities and intermediaries.[180] The great corruption of the religion took place for the first time under the priesthood which Joseph instituted in Egypt.[181] We can trace the way in which this view influenced Old Testament interpretation down to Wellhausen's pattern in his *Prolegomena* of three phases for the history of Israelite religion.[182]

Many detailed exegetical insights are included in all these observations, and we get the impression that Morgan is very well up in the exegetical science of his time. Already in Book II he comments that it is a well known fact among scholars that most or all of the biblical books have undergone considerable alterations and expansions at the hand of later redactors,[183] and that Moses did not write anything beyond the original book of the law; the creation stories and the patriarchal narratives, for example, come from various hands which were at work at different times long before Moses.[184] These observations are given as answers to Leland's comments;[185] in the first volume it looks as though Morgan himself still regarded Moses as the author of these stories.[186] That would accord fully with his change of mind about the authorship of Hebrews: in 1726 Morgan had still assumed this to be by Paul,[187] whereas he now censures Leland for this very assumption.[188] Evidently the work by this apologist, who was famous at that time,[189] had made Morgan pay more attention to the results of contemporary critical exegesis, which had made some progress since Spinoza, Hobbes, Simon and Grotius.

However, these matters are only of secondary significance for Morgan. He declares unmistakeably that for him historical events of any kind, especially extraordinary and miraculous ones, can never be the basis for his faith.[190] Therefore all historical religions are equally remote from him: 'I am a Christian in Contradiction to any other historical Religion; or a Disciple of Christ in opposition to Moses, Zoroastres, Confucius, Mahomet, or any other Reformer in Religion.'[191] He is a Christian only because for him the content of Christianity is identical with natural religion,[192] and in his view the duties of moral truth were expressed more clearly and with better motivation by Jesus Christ than by any other religious legislator.[193] Therefore the problem whether Moses and the Old Testament prophets possibly foresaw the events of Christ (as orthodox teaching asserts) has just as little force for him. The life of Mohammed or the pope can be prophesied beforehand, even by a godless man like Balaam. 'But, I cannot see how any of these, or other prophecies, can be taken in Evidence for the Truth of Doctrines or Righteousness of Persons.'[194] The abyss of history is in fact unbridgeable for an adherent of natural religion. This in no way excludes high esteem for Moses and the prophets as historical persons: 'but as for Moses and the prophets, though I admire them, as Politicians, Historians, Orators and Poets, I have nothing to do with them in Religion, as I cannot possibly be of their Religion.'[195] Jesus was justified in often referring back to Moses and the prophets, in that they too were not lacking in moral truth and righteousness.[196]

Philalethes, who in the dialogue is Morgan's spokesman, does not take any offence at being called a Christian Deist.[197] That he immediately adds to this remark his comment, quoted above, about Moses and the prophets, shows the deepest reasons for his polemic against the Old Testament: he rejects the Old Testament because the fact that it is included in the biblical canon shows most clearly the way in which Christianity is deeply entangled in history; he can only identify himself with it because he reduces it to the teaching of Christ, which he understands as moral law[198] and thus identifies with timeless natural religion.

His treatment of miracles in the Old Testament also belongs in the same context:[199] whereas in the first volume he was only concerned with the possible proof value of miracles and declared that they could not serve as proof for a doctrine because they are not logically connected with it,[200] while not denying the possibility of their occurrence, in the second volume he regards them as being quite impossible. As a truth can only be seen through reason, whereas on the other hand God only does miracles for an extraordinary purpose, there is no occasion for him to confirm a truth by miracle.[201] Specifically, Morgan tries to explain the miracle stories contained in the Old Testament from natural causes (as in the miracles at the sea and the events on Horeb[202]). He ends up with fundamental doubts about the credibility of miracle stories in general, since such an event is so improbable in itself that even good witnesses are not enough to confirm it.[203]

Because of his rejection of the Old Testament, Morgan has been called a 'modern Marcion'.[204] In fact Marcion's theory of the demiurge as the God of the Old Testament, who is as harsh and cruel as he is imperfect and subordinate to the true God, is very similar to Morgan's theory of the weak national guardian deity of the Israelites. Another striking feature is the reference to the apostle Paul as a witness for true Christianity against Jewish Christianity, which still maintains the obsolete forms of the Old Testament and is influential in the church down to the present day. However, Gawlick has also drawn attention to the decisive differences which separate Morgan from Marcion: in Morgan there is none of the metaphysical dualism which is charcteristic of the whole of Gnosticism: the contrast between a good and an evil principle and the separation of the redeemer God from the creator God. Rather, a monistic cosmology determines his physico-theology.[205] Gawlick is certainly right in saying that Morgan is far removed from the cosmological dualism of Gnosticism. Between the two is the gulf of two ages and cultures. Nevertheless, it is no coincidence that Morgan often refers to Gnosticism as evidence of early Christian Paulinism and a pioneer of freedom of conscience.[206] In fact Morgan stands on the shoulders of witnesses to an intellectual tradition which in the last resort goes back to ancient Gnosticism and which has preserved its dualism down to modern times, albeit transposed into different forms and on another level. The attacks on the Old Testament conceal the old Gnostic opposition between spirit and matter which, when associated with the adoption of Stoic thought and its rational and moralistic notions, must turn against the specifically corporeal nature of faith which unmistakeably emerges in the Old Testament. In his attempt to provide a basis for an ideal of Christianity which can be reconciled with his approach, the Old Testament becomes the source of all the falsifications which he believes to have come about in the course of history. The theory of depravation in the history of the church, which he shares with Gnosticism and all its successors, also compels him even to make a critical selection from the New Testament; here all that is left in addition to Paul, who is distorted for his purposes, is the teaching of the earthly Jesus, reduced to morality.

Does Morgan thus prove to be 'an heir of the Reformation' and is he a 'good Protestant' in his protest against conditions in the official church?[207] Perhaps that is the case in the psychological sense, if we take as criteria honesty and a readiness to contradict. But his contradiction is more a matter of principle than a criticism of particular conditions justified by circumstances in the church. The picture of the church which stands behind his remarks is not the legacy of Luther or Calvin but, if we reflect, that of the left wing of the Reformation. We would therefore do better to call him an heir of Spiritualism. As this investigation has shown, basic themes of Spiritualism remained influential throughout the history of rationalist biblical criticism. Even physico-theology, with its stress on the idea of creation, did not change anything, because it associated the results of the 'new philosophy', based on the results of the exact natural sciences but ideologically quite definitely going beyond them, with ethics derived from natural law, only at a secondary level, without arriving at the combination of a relationship to God and a relationship to the world grounded in human existence as this is presupposed by the biblical tradition. As we have seen in the case of Newton,[208] the 'Christian Virtuoso' remained an ethical rationalist in his basic religious convictions. This hidden difference between world-view, conception of God and ethics resulted in the later shift to pure materialism as formulated by the French Enlightenment because it could not integrate Newton's and Morgan's belief with a God who was really active in the world. For this God, as ethical rationalism postulated him, was not really free; as a metaphysically defined entity he was an abstraction who did not have anything other than his name in common with the living God of the Bible.

The much less well known[209] pamphlet by Jacob Ilive, *The Oration spoke at Joyners hall in Thamesstreet On Monday, Sept.24, 1733*, is aimed with similar acuteness and in some ways even more radically against the Old Testament.[210] This writing has fantastic and speculative features, reminiscent of Gnosticism, such as an interpretation of cosmology based on John 14.2, according to which God created the world (which in reality is hell[211]) as an abode for Lucifer and his fallen angels who, embodied in men, are to be reconciled with God through repentance.[212] Anyone who refuses this repentance will remain in darkness, in which the earth will ultimately return to chaos.[213] The fire which will punish such people is not material.[214] The doctrine of a material eternal hell fire which awaits the damned is absurd and laughable:[215] it has been invented by the clergy of all times in order to deceive people and make them pliable through fear.[216]

Ilive adduces the Old Testament as the most important evidence for his theory that from the beginning the priests deceived the people.[217] By his false example in intending to sacrifice his firstborn son (Gen.22.2), which he then immediately abandoned (Gen.22.12) Abraham, the first priest, already moved the people to sacrifice their firstborn to idols over a long period. Jacob, who deceived Esau, and Laban with his idols are further examples of lying priests whose line can be traced through all the periods before Christ.[218] However, the greatest deceiver among the priests is Moses: 'What heavy Burdens, what strange Rites, what wonderful Stories did he impose upon his Brethren under the Sanction of, Thus saith the Lord.'[219] He taught the Jews to worship God with pagan rites. He began his career with the murder (Ex.2.11f.) of an Egyptian who had done nothing but spark off a sportive boxing match with an Israelite (that is the way in which the author interprets the word 'strike'). In the service of his father-in-law Jethro, whose daughter he married after his flight, he claimed that he had received a divine revelation from a burning thorn bush – 'I think a Man may chuse whether he will believe a Murderer'. The story of how the Israelites cheated the Egyptians of their jewellery at the Exodus, claimed by Moses to be a command of God (Ex.4.21f.), is a further sign of the character of this man. Moses learnt the whole manipulation of the people from his father-in-law Jethro the priest, including the art of attracting them to a leader and imposing his laws on them on the pretext that they came from God. 'Moses imposed upon the Jewish People, under the Sanction of "Thus saith the Lord". I need only beg the Reader to look into these Four Books of Moses, viz. Exodus, Leviticus, Numbers and Deuteronomy, and as to the Truth of this Assertion, I promise him entire Satisfaction. Only I add, my single Opinion is, that these Rites and Ceremonies were not instituted by the God of Heaven, but by Jethro and Moses, and that the Words, "Thus saith the Lord: As the Lord commanded Moses": should be read: Thus saith Jethro; as Jethro commanded Moses.' The appointment of Aaron as priest by

Moses also belongs in this context.[220] After Moses had appointed a group of elders who would finally completely gloss over the law by their skill at exegesis, by segregating the tribe of Levi, Aaron continued the deception by misleading the people into making the golden calf ('I am glad it was not a Lamb, for then the Christian Divines of all Ages might have said, that it was Type of Christ').[221] As many people fell into this deception, Moses and Aaron together resolved to sort out the affair by arranging a great massacre with the help of the Levites (Ex.32.26-28).[222] Thus Moses made an end to the 'priestcraft' of Aaron.

After these comments, Ilive returns to his main theme: angelo-anthropology. He thinks that his hypothesis gives a rational explanation of the origin of sin and why we are enemies of God.[223] The author stresses very emphatically that we are all sinners and therefore are rightly subject to the same punishment (banishment to corporeality on earth).[224] His summons to humility[225] contrasts with the optimism of a Shaftesbury or Bolingbroke or indeed with the other ethical rationalists. Ilive directly addresses 'our modern Arians', whom he admonishes to repent.[226] His rejection of the Old Testament (which only circumstances prevented him from carrying on through the other books, in addition to Genesis and Exodus) is bound up with a deep and singularly Gnostic piety.[227] In the Foreword he declares himself ready to subject himself to the judgment of the clergy of his church, 'whose Skill in Theology far exceeds mine', and adds that if anyone finds his attacks on the priests too harsh he would stress that the whole of the clergy of the Church of England do not have a share in the deception.[228] So here we would seem to have a pious laymen of the church whose particular comments echo in an extreme form voices which were widespread in certain Anglican lay circles: there is a hostility to ceremonial which has developed out of a Spiritualism which is hostile to the body, bound up with hatred of everything priestly and especially the Old Testament, from which in their view all the ritualism in the church derives. This Spiritualism has a strong moralistic colouring; the most significant figures of the Old Testament are also judged in moral terms and the devastating verdict on them at the same time seals the fate of the whole of the Mosaic law. The conclusions in Ilive follow in a remarkably intensified and yet incidental form: one can only regret that he had no occasion to develop them systematically.

(c) Anti-deistic apologetic

However, testimony of this radical character remains isolated. Official theology was more sober, more rational. How close the Deists were in their presuppositions to the apologetics of the church, although they drew more far-reaching consequences from them, can be demonstrated

by countless examples from the 'Refutations' which their writings provoked. According to the treatise by the Presbyterian preacher M.Low-
man, *A Rational Ritual of the Hebrew Worship*,[229] directed against Morgan,
which seeks to illuminate the significance of Mosaic ceremonial legislation by means of perspectives gained from Maimonides,[230] this legislation indeed served wise religious ends; its imperfection is connected
with the equally wise adaptation by God to the special situation of the
Israelites who, after the exodus from Egypt, were largely surrounded
by idolatrous peoples and could only be kept from apostasy by God
himself giving them ritual prescriptions for the service of Jehovah.
Strikingly, this orthodox writer formulates the essentials of Religion
with explicit reference to none other than Herbert of Cherbury,[231] whose
five *notitiae communes* are elevated to the rank of an 'excellent rule' for
demonstrating the true value of the Mosaic laws.[232] The existence and
worship of the one God, virtue as the most important part of this
worship along with piety, abhorrence of all evil, which leads to penitence and improvement, expectation of rewards and punishments in the
future – these were in fact the principles which an apologist of this
period could regard as his own,[233] and precisely these are in his view
the aims which were also accentuated by the Old Testament precepts
of the law. After a lengthy argument he asserts with satisfaction: 'You
see here the Doctrines of the Hebrew Church well agree with the
Essentials of Religion according to Lord Herbert, taught by the best
light of Reason, and confirmed by general Consent of Men of sound
Minds.'[234] It is indeed remarkable that a century after his death the
'Father of Deism' should be cited as the key witness against the Deists
of the eighteenth century! His Stoic approach had largely established
itself, and his *notitiae* contained more dogmatics in accordance with
orthodox taste than the modern Deists would allow.

A particularly instructive example of the nature of this apologetic is
John Conybeare's *A Defence of Reveal'd Religion*,[235] written against Tindal.
Lechler has accorded it the highest praise for its logical clarity.[236] At the
same time he points out how near Conybeare's ideas are to those of his
opponent. This is because of the agreement over the philosophical
presuppositions on which both base their work.[237] In fact even without
the numerous quotations from Locke which appear in this book, we
can recognize the teaching of the great master as a leading thread which
runs through all the discussions. One basic presupposition in Conybeare, too, is that in content the law of nature corresponds to revelation.
His argument against Tindal is concerned above all that this natural law
(or – and in content this amounts to the same thing – natural religion)
is not as easily recognizable by all men in all circumstances as Locke
had assumed. The term 'law (religion) of nature' is ambiguous, 'Either,
because it is founded in the Reason and Nature of Things; or else,

because it is discoverable by us in the Use and Exercise of those Faculties which we enjoy.'[238] To be perfect, the law of nature would also have had to be capable of being recognized fully by all men. However, this is not the case, first, because mankind after the Fall (and here this traditional doctrine slips into the argument) no longer has an unclouded reason,[239] and secondly, because what mankind as a whole would be capable of knowing cannot be known in the same way by each individual. On the contrary: the intellectual capacities and the moral level of man are quite different,[240] so that a moral rule of life is not as clearly recognizable by a member of the working masses as it is by an intellectual.[241] As in the case of other scientific knowledge, the law of nature, too, was 'discoverable by Mankind gradually, and in a long Course of Years.'[242]

The idea of development which comes in at this point (and through which Conybeare advantageously dissociates himself from Tindal's timeless system)[243] also makes it possible to assign an important place to revelation. The immanent stimuli to moral action which derive from the 'fitness of things' or from the inner satisfaction which an action provides of its own accord do not add up to a real obligation,[244] which rather presupposes the declared will of a loftier being, the will of God. While the law of nature is perfect in theory, it is not so in practice, as it is not absolutely clear and simple for all men, even for the wisest.[245] Moreover, it is not associated with the clearest nor even with the most important sanctions: in view of the eternal life of the soul, these are to be expected in a future state. And this cannot be made equally comprehensible to all men (though it can be demonstrated by reason).[246] Revelation is thus necessary for twofold pedagogical reasons: first, because it communicates even to people endowed with lesser intellectual capacities and moreover to all mankind who are in principle hampered by the Fall, the knowledge about the full extent of the divine will which they lack, and secondly because it provides the necessary motivation for moral action only by communicating judgment and eternity. As we live in a fallen state, we also need divine forgiveness, and we can in no way assure ourselves of that by mere rational considerations.[247]

In a further argument,[248] Conybeare discusses the problem whether the law of nature is unchangable in such a way that it cannot be supplemented by additional commandments. Behind this question lurks the old theme of the indifferentia, i.e. the positive ordinances and customs of the church. Conybeare thinks that God can also give such positive commandments as either similarly issue in a moral purpose or do not, but at all events are not given without reason.[249] In this connection he observes 'that no Religion hath ever yet subsisted in Fact without some Institutions. Mere Natural Religion, without any thing instituted of any Kind, is nothing but Idea, and hath no existence but in the Mind.'[250] As such positive precepts can only be communicated through revelation, this also ensures its special role alongside natural religion.[251] Among the reasons for the necessity of rules established through revelation and therefore binding uniformly on the whole church for its rites and ceremonies, the argument from 'Order and Decency' is striking:[252] one is immediately reminded of Archbishop Laud. Once again the continuity of Anglican theology through all the shifts in the history of ideas is made quite plain.

If, then, natural religion (or the law of nature) needs supplementing in various points, for which mankind, with differing intellectual capacity and with natural facilities limited by the Fall, is referred to revelation, and if too it is only reward and punishment in the world to come that provide the right pressure for obedience to the will of God, it is impossible to establish a conflict in content between the law of nature and a law made known by revelation. According to Conybeare it is quite illegitimate to claim such a conflict. 'What is, in its Nature, fit and proper, must be agreeable to the will of God: What is, in its Nature, unfit and improper, must be disagreeable thereto.'[253] That is the law, or religion, of nature. Natural and revealed religion differ only in their extent. Revelation adds principles and commandments which natural reason does not recognize, or does not recognize sufficiently because of its *de facto* limitations, and positive precepts which further the appropriate form of worship or the advance of inner piety. It makes quite clear what can only obscurely be recognized in the context of natural religion, and is essentially more effective because it combines its commandments with impressive sanctions.[254]

Conybeare does not think very much about further points made by Tindal and others: the unreliability of external testimony for historical revelation, the difficulties of tradition and the uncertainty of historical facts. He contents himself with making comments like, if the facts reported in scripture were based on inadequate foundations, the authors could barely have found such widespread credence and gained so many adherents.[255] And if in that case other difficulties still remain unsolved, is it not better to assume that we still need some help to solve them rather than that they are absolutely unsurmountable?[256]

Other ordinary apologists argued in the same way as Conybeare, e.g. Edmund Gibson as Bishop of London[257] in his Pastoral Letters,[258] or the Newtonian A.A.Sykes in his *Principles and Connexion of Natural and Revealed Religion*,[259] the main idea in which is that the existence of God as the Governor of the universe and the knowledge that moral action accords with his will can be an additional and stronger motive to moral action than the fact that moral action is simply in accord with the ordering of things.[260] For Sykes, too, religion is identical with moral action;[261] the advantage of religion based on revelation over natural religion lies in the fact that it provides us with more arguments for such action than we possibly would otherwise have.[262] In what does the nature of revelation consist? First of all, if a person who has had a revelation from God only expresses such truths as can also be known through our natural capacities, we need not conclude that these rest on revelation.[263] They may be communicated by revelation, but this is not probable, since normally God does not reveal doctrines of ordinary morality like the Golden Rule.[264] In the case of true revelation of what is previously unknown to us and communicates things which cannot be ascertained through mere reason, as for example that God will judge the world through Jesus Christ, authority is the basis of assent.[265] But as the recipients of revelation were fallible human beings and did not always act in an inspired way,[266] we may note 'that no Proposition ought to be admitted as matter of Revelation, without a proper Evidence of its coming from God.'[267] Of course such truths may not contradict the rules of reason, even if reason could not have discovered them of its own accord; they must be comprehensible.[268] However, there is no proof that in fact a revelation has taken place other than a conviction based on authority. Sykes simply uses the traditional proofs for the truth of the biblical revelation: the prophecies of the Old Testament that were fulfilled in Christ,[269] and the miracles in the two Testaments.[270]

It is understandable that an apologetic working with such weak arguments could not defend its position for very long. The Deists had already launched successful attacks on arguments like those from prophecy and miracle. The fact that the debate took this turn is grounded in the attitude of apologetic: the Deists had to remove these supports if they were to carry their battle for the sole validity of natural religion to a victorious conclusion. That they nevertheless achieved only half a victory and not a complete one, as one would have expected in view of the weakness of their church opponents, is above all because they only fought half-heartedly. Even they did not want to break completely with inherited Christian religion. In their efforts to rescue at least a basic element of the Christian tradition, even if this was only a cloak for the natural religion which was all that they advocated, to some degree they even remained apologists themselves. Thus in the last resort they represented no more than a transitional situation. David Hume's acute criticism of the possibilities of reason arriving at a certain knowledge in the sphere of religion meant the end of Deism as well as of its opponents. As Gawlick aptly remarks,[271] Deism did not come to an end through a victory by the apologists of the church, but because its time was past.

Conclusion

It is beyond the scope of this investigation to discuss the period which followed Deism. Because its specific aim is to describe the significance of the intellectual and constitutional developments in England for the modern understanding of the Bible and conversely the role of the Bible in this development, it can also forgo a complete study of all those thinkers who have been designated Deists. Thus for example an account of Bolingbroke[1] would not add any essentially new elements to the picture we have obtained.

Despite its disappearance in the land of its origin, Deism remained important round about the middle of the eighteenth century because of two far-reaching effects which it had. One of these developments leads to the United States, where Deism came to be extremely important for the constitution of the new state through figures like Thomas Paine, Benjamin Franklin and Thomas Jefferson. On American soil it again came to be combined with late forms of Puritanism which continued to have a significant effect in the theology of Jonathan Edwards and his pupils. From the juxtaposition of the two there arose the typical form of New England theology. This approach, which took over from idealist philosophy the notion of harmony, has shaped American thought and theology right down to the present day. We can understand how these two trends came together and were not in opposition to each other, when we note the Humanist approach which underlies them both and which has been evident so many times in this work. The enormous influence which such thinking has also had on culture generally, as on developments in world politics in the twentieth century, need only be hinted at here. In countless areas of ecumenical theology the decisive struggle today is over the question whether, in the future of the world churches, Reformation thought along the line of Luther and Calvin or the spirit of the left wing of the Reformation will prevail.[2]

The second line leads to Germany, also in the second half of the eighteenth century. The direct and indirect influences of English Deism on the German Enlightenment, which represents a late phase in the general development of ethical rationalism, are great, especially since the German Enlightenment differed from that in France by sharing the same basically apologetic position as English Deism. The numerous translations of English Deistic literature which appeared on the German market after the publication of Johann Lorenz Schmidt's translation of Tindal's *Christianity as Old as The Creation*, 1741,[3] are testimony to this. However, the most significant work in which all the fruits of the biblical criticism of English Deism were systematically incorporated, the *Apologie oder Schutzschrift für die vernünftigen Verehrer Gottes* (Apology or Defence for the rational worshippers of God), by Hermann Samuel Reimarus,[4] was largely prevented from having any direct influence (the famous dispute over the Fragments published by Lessing took place at a time when the development of method had already progressed beyond the Deistic positions); it could only be published complete in our time.[5] However, we cannot overestimate the influence exercised by Deistic thought, and by the principles of the Humanist world-view which the Deists made the criterion of their biblical criticism, on the historical-critical exegesis of the nineteenth century; the consequences extend right down to the present. At that time a series of almost unshakeable presuppositions were decisively shifted in a different direction: for example, Puritan hostility to ceremonial provided the stimulus in later biblical interpretation for the denigration of all that was priestly and the high value attached to the prophetic element, interpreted in anti-cultic terms. Similarly, behind a widespread view of the history of Israelite and Jewish religion, we can see the Humanist pattern in which religion is thought to have declined from a pure and natural original form to a final form distorted by ritualism.[6] Although the catchword 'ethical monotheism', which was the determining principle characteristic of exegesis of the prophets above all in the age of Wellhausen, Hölscher and Duhm, has disappeared from current usage, the basic views underlying it are still as alive as ever. As in the case of Old Testament exegesis, so too the development described can also be recognized behind important trends in contemporary New Testament scholarship and the motives and views of the theologies which shape it. The central role which is played by the proclamation of Jesus on the one hand and an extreme Paulinism on the other have their model and their ultimate background in certain Puritan and Deistic notions which we have met in the course of this investigation. We must also see the far-reaching gulf between Old and New Testament theology, expressed in a widespread reserve on the part of New Testament scholars towards the Old Testament (and seldom vice versa) against this background. It can trace its ancestry back as far as Erasmus (from a more recent period Kant and Schleiermacher could also be mentioned in this connection).

A consideration of the development of Humanism and the Enlightenment in England can be useful for all these areas and thus for any Protestant theology which seeks its basis in the Bible. Moreover, the history of philosophy also appears in a different light when we see more clearly than before the close connection between philosophical systems and contemporary theology. The significant role played by the interpretation of the Bible in the thinking of Hobbes, Spinoza or Locke, to mention only the best-known names, and indeed for scientists like Boyle and Newton, threatens to be forgotten too easily in today's world, for which the Bible seems so remote. To forget the role of the Bible in their thought makes it difficult to understand all these figures and even distorts their actual intentions. Furthermore, we should remember the significance of the names mentioned above for constitutional history, which is often treated in complete isolation from its theological, not to mention its biblical and exegetical background. Nor is it possible to have precise knowledge of the politics of the time without adequate theological knowledge. In this respect the present investigation is an interdisciplinary one. One of its most important aims has been to demonstrate that the political thought of the sixteenth, seventeenth and eighteenth centuries continually sought its models and arguments within the Bible, and the approach of each particular thinker in question provided the real criterion for the analogies drawn between the reconstructed biblical model and the principles which were normative for shaping the society of his time. Even typological thinking fits in with these standpoints in its two forms, the political and the spiritual. Here, as we saw, state politics and church politics are closely connected. State and church were not seen as separate entities but as related bodies, and even the congregationalist model did not propagate a lack of connection between them: it firmly rejected the identity of the two spheres. Without this controversy over the normative form of the church and the associated question of the relationship of the state to the church, and the degree of the state's involvement in church order, it is impossible to understand the motivation and content of Deistic biblical criticism. Had the Bible not still been accepted as a norm, the dispute over it would never have flared up. The acknowledgment of scripture as a norm necessarily meant that the parties involved in controversies within politics or the church provided themselves with weapons from the arsenal of the Bible: this was as much the case in the struggles between Tories and Whigs over state power at the beginning of the eighteenth century as it was in that between Royalists and supporters of the Commonwealth ideologies two generations earlier. Only as a result of the attack by the Deists on the authority of Scripture (preparations for which were made, against their own intentions, by the Latitudinarians, Locke and Newton), an attack which they made step by step, did the legacy of antiquity in the form of natural law and Stoic thought, which since the late Middle Ages had formed the common basis for thought despite all the changes of theological and philosophical direction, remain the one undisputed criterion. This produced a basically new stage both in the history of ideas and in the English constitution. This position already contains the roots of its own failure, in that the consistent development of the epistemological principles of Locke and Berkely by Hume soon showed that its basic presuppositions were untenable. However, two irreversible and definitive developments remained, which had made an appearance with it: the Bible lost its significance for philosophical thought and for the theoretical constitutional foundations of political ideals, and ethical rationalism (with a new foundation in Kant's critique) proved to be one of the forces shaping the modern period, which only now can really be said to have begun.[7] Both of these developments were prepared for on English soil, so if we are to understand our own cultural situation it is in many ways important to pay attention to that particular historical context.

Notes

1. Introduction: The Task

1. For the Old Testament see especially C.Westermann (ed.), *Essays on Old Testament Interpretation*, ET 1963, and A.H.J. Gunneweg, *Understanding the Old Testament*, ET 1977. For the general question of hermeneutics see also V.Warnach (ed.), *Hermeneutik als Weg heutiger Wissenschaft*, 1971; O.Loretz and W.Stolz (eds.), *Die hermeneutische Frage in der Theologie*, 1968. The literature is very extensive.

2. ET in *Word and Faith*, 1963, 17-61. Cf. also E. Käsemann, 'Vom theologischen Recht historisch-kritischer Exegese', *ZTK* 64, 1967, 259-81.

3. Cf. Ebeling, op.cit., [29]: 'In its concern with the past and the interpretation of its sources it cannot simply put on one side the understanding of reality which has been gained by the spirit of the modern world.' O.Bayer, *Was ist Theologie? Eine Skizze*, 1973, 103f., has recently been critical of Ebeling. By contrast, the recognition of most recent hermeneutics that the subject is himself involved in the historical process of tradition and has his criteria shaped by the particular presuppositions of the world-view of his time is of decisive importance. Cf. also e.g. H.-G.Gadamer, *Truth and Method*, ET ²1979; K.Lehmann, 'Der hermeneutische Horizont der historischen Exegese', in *Einführung in die Methoden der biblischen Exegese*, ed. J.Schreiner, 1971, 40-80, esp.61f.; F.Hahn, 'Probleme historischer Kritik', *ZNW* 63, 1972, 1-17, esp.12ff.

4. Thus Ebeling, op.cit.; cf. also H.Blumenberg, *Die Legitimät der Neuzeit*, 1966; and e.g. T.Rendtorff, 'Historische Bibelwissenschaft und Theologie', in *Beiträge zur Theorie des neuzeitlichen Christentums*, Festschrift W.Trillhaas, 1968, 72-90.

5. Mention should also be made of T.K.Cheyne, *Founders of Old Testament Criticism*, 1893, reprinted 1971; A.Duff, *History of Old Testament Criticism*, 1910; J.Coppens, *De Geschiedkundige Ontwikkelingsgang van de Oudtestamentische Exegese vanaf de Renaissance tot en met de Aufklärung*, 1943; E.M.Gray, *Old Testament Criticism, its Rise and Progress*, 1923; H.F.Hahn, *The Old Testament in Modern Research*, 1954, ³1966; E.G.Kraeling, *The Old Testament since the Reformation*, 1955; R.Schäfer, *Die Bibelauslegung in der Geschichte der Kirche*, 1980. Sometimes these works deal only with particular periods (Cheyne; Hahn) or have specific perspectives (Kraeling); some (Coppens; Schäfer) are too sketchy to penetrate the problems at all deeply.

6. Kraus, *Geschichte der historisch-kritischen Erforschung des Alten Testaments*, ³1982, 1, rightly points out this weakness in Diestel's work, full though it is of material: 'it does not give a clear enough and deep enough account of the cultural and theological context.' However, the starting point of Kraus's own work in the history of the material gives it a similar character.

7. Cf. the review by T.Mahlmann in *TLZ* 94, 1969, cols.193-7.

8. Cf. above 415, nn.2-4.

9. Op.cit., 14.

10. Op.cit.,12.

11. Here he is imprisoned in the self-understanding of the early 1960s (see above, 415 n.4), which has since become doubtful.

12. H.A.E. van Gelder, *The Two Reformations in the 16th Century*, 1964.

13. E.Wolf, 'Reformatorische Botschaft und Humanismus', in *Studien zur Geschichte und Theologie der Reformation*, Festschrift E.Bizer, 1969, 97ff. However, the use of the term 'humanism' can only be commended with reservations, as it is a comprehensive phenomenon which cannot be clearly defined. Cf. below, Ch.1 (a), 14.

14. H.Liebing, 'Die Ausgänge des europäischen Humanismus', in *Geist und Geschichte der Reformation*, Festgabe H.Rückert, 1966, 357ff., gives a sketch which indicates the essentials of this movement.

15. Cf. I.O.Wade, *The Clandestine Organization and Diffusion of Philosophic Ideas in France from 1700-1750*, 1938, reprinted 1967.

16. Individuals like I.de la Peyrère and J.Astruc do not belong in the same historical context; R.Simon's principle of tradition and the secondary role for scripture to which it leads is typical of his presuppositions elsewhere; cf. Kraus, *Geschichte*, 68f.

17. *Geschichte*, 56-8.

18. Op.cit., 14. The false weighting becomes evident in the fact that he sees the development in England as a 'special case'. Here he rightly criticizes Hirsch's history of theology for failing to reproduce 'the real division of spiritual weight in seventeenth-century Europe' – despite his considerable recognition of developments in Western Europe, op.cit., 10.

19. Cf. the dispute between Jacobi and Mendelssohn over the alleged influence of Spinoza on Lessing.

Part One

1. Arriving at the Starting Point

1. First appeared 1860; second edition 1869. I have used the edition in the *Gesammelte Werke*, Vol.III, Basle 1955.

2. For the history of research cf. above all W.K.Ferguson, *The Renaissance in Historical Thought*, 1948. Cf. also the short sketch in id., 'The Reinterpretation of the Renaissance', in *Facets of the Renaissance* (1959), Torchbook ed. 1963, 1-18. Cf. also the supplementary contributions in the review of the work by H.Baron, *JHI* 11, 1950, 493-510. – H.Schulte Nordholt, *Het beeld der Renaissance*, 1948. Also H.Baron, 'Renaissance in Italien', *AKG* 21, 1931, 95-128; 215-39; 340-56; A.Buck, 'Italienischer Humanismus', *AKG* 37, 1955, 105-22; 41, 1959, 107-32, and the collective volume *Zu Begriff und Problem der Renaissance*, ed. A.Buck, 1969, with an introduction by the editor which has the same title, 1-36. There is a survey of the period in V.H.H. Green, *Renaissance and Reformation*, 1952; ²1964, reprinted 1974, 29-57. From the enormously varied literature on the whole subject only works directly relevant to the theme could be discussed here. Cf. especially the survey by C.Angeleri, *Il problema religioso del rinascimento. Storia della critica e bibliographia*, 1952.

3. It goes back to J.Michelet's *Histoire de la France*, Vol.7, *Histoire de France au seizième siècle. Renaissance*, 1855.

4. In Michelet, op.cit., 6, the statement is: 'L'homme s'y est retrouvé lui même.'

5. Cola di Rienzo, the Roman tribune of the people, is a famous figure in connection with the formation of the Italian national consciousness. K.Burdach has paid

special attention to him, cf. e.g. id., 'Rienzo und die geistige Wandlung seiner Zeit', in *Vom Mittelalter zur Reformation*, Vol.I, 1913-28; correspondence of Cola di Rienzo, id., Vol.II; 'Sinn und Ursprung der Worte Renaissance und Reformation', in *Reformation – Renaissance – Humanismus*, [2]1926, reprinted 1967, (1-84) 10ff. Also K.Brandi, *Cola di Rienzo und sein Verhältnis zu Renaissance und Humanismus*, 1928.

6. Michelet, op.cit., 6, already speaks of 'la découverte du monde, la découverte de l'homme'. This becomes the title of one of the main sections of Burckhardt's work (*Gesammelte Werke*, III, 190ff.).

7. Cf. his *Cicerone*, 1855 (reprinted 1939); also 'Die Renaissance in Italien', in *Geschichte der Baukunst*, ed. F.Kugler, 1867.

8. 'Auffassung und Analyse des Menschen im 15. und 16. Jahrhundert' (1891), in *Gesammelte Schriften*, Vol.II, [3]1923 ([5]1957), 1ff.

9. *Individuum und Kosmos in der Philosophie der Renaissance*, 1927.

10. Cf. also the account in Angeleri, *Problema*, 33ff.

11. Cf. e.g. op.cit., 382: 'It is unmistakable that such views of life after death partly presupposed the end of the most essential Christian dogmas and partly brought them about. The concepts of sin and redemption must have been almost completely obscured.' – For the role of religion in Jacob Burckhardt cf. A. v. Martin, *Die Religion in Jacob Burckhardts Leben und Denken*, 1942; W.K.Ferguson, 'Jakob Burckhardt's Interpretation of Religion', in *The Quarterly Bulletin of the Polish Institute of Arts and Sciences in America*, 1943.

12. There is a vivid formulation of this approach e.g. in P.Wernle, *Renaissance und Reformation. Sechs Vorträge*, 1912, 14f.: 'It is not only the complete lack of Christian values which is typical of the new type of man... the fact that man relies completely on himself and his power..., but it is the absence of moral and religious ideals generally, the limitation to given reality and individuality in good and evil.' For the popular picture of the Renaissance which has arisen since Burckhardt and the literary cult of the Renaissance around 1900 see W.Kaegi, in E.Walser, *Gesammelte Studien zur Geistesgeschichte der Renaissance*, 1932, XXVIIIff. and already W.Rehm, 'Der Renaissancekult um 1900 und seine Überwindung', *ZDP* 1929, 296-328.

13. 22 volumes, 1886-1933.

14. Other representatives of this approach are G.Guiraud; H.Bremond; R.Arnold; E.Göller; D.Bonomo; cf. Angeleri, *Problema*, 81ff.

15. Cf. the works mentioned.

16. Hence his concern with Cola di Rienzo.

17. Cf. e.g. *Reformation – Renaissance – Humanismus*, 31ff.; 100ff.

18. For him, cf. W.Kaegi in E.Walser, *Gesammelte Studien*, XIff.; Angeleri, *Problema*, 86ff.

19. *Poggius Florentinus, Leben und Werke*, 1914.

20. Cf. e.g. Walser's study *Die Religion des Luigi Pulci*, 1926.

21. In addition to Walser's *Gesammelte Studien* particular mention should also be made of his *Studien zur Weltanschauung der Renaissance*, 1920.

22. His main works are: *La fine dell'Umanesimo*, 1920; *Che cosa fu l'Umanesimo*, 1929; *Storia dell'Umanesimo del XIII al XVI seculo* (1933), [2]1964; *La religione degli Umanisti*, 1950.

23. H.Thode, *Franz von Assisi und die Anfänge der Renaissance in Italien*, 1885, introduced this movement by seeking the origins of what he thought was the characteristic individualistic spirituality of the Renaissance in the ascetic-mystical movement of the thirteenth century, especially among the Franciscan spirituals (for this theme cf. also E.Garin, 'Il francescanesimo e le origini del Rinascimento', in id., *L'età nuova*, 1969, 113-36). Similar notions also appear in the works of E.Gebhardt, *Les origines de la Renaissance in Italie*, 1879; *La Renaissance italienne et la philosophie de l'histoire*, 1887; *L'Italie mystique, histoire de la Renaissance religieuse au Moyen Age*, 1890.

For the gradual return to Burckhardt's basic view which can be noted in these works cf. Angeleri, *Problema*, 79. The title of C.H.Haskins, *The Renaissance of the Twelfth Century*, 1927, is programmatical. There is an extensive bibliography of this trend in *La Renaissance du XIIième siècle*, ed.G.Paré, A.Brunet, P.Tremblay, 1933.

24. J.Boulanger, 'Le vrai siècle de la Renaissance', *HeR* 1, 1934, 9-30; J.Nordström, *Medeltid och Renässans*, 1929 (= *Moyen Age et Renaissance*, 1933).

25. 'Humanisme médiéval et Renaissance', in *Les idées et les lettres*, 1932, 171-96; id., *Héloïse et Abélard. Études sur le Moyen-Age et la Renaissance*, 1938, etc.

26. *Herfstijd des Middeleuwen*, 1929; German *Herbst des Mittelalters*, ⁶1952.

27. J.Huizinga already pointed out (in 'Das Problem der Renaissance', in *Wege der Geschichte*, 1930, 138) that 'only a pluralistic treatment' was appropriate to the nature of the Renaissance; anyone who sought to catch it in the net of a uniform scheme 'will only entangle himself in the meshes'. Cf. also A.Buck, *Begriff*, 28. The remarks by E.Walser are also similar, cf. W.Kaegi, in Walser, *Gesammelte Studien*, XXXIII.

28. It is no coincidence that Renaissance research developed into a specialist discipline, cf. A.Buck, *Begriff*, 31.

29. Thus for example the position of H.Schulte Nordholt, *Het beeld*, and above all the important work by C.Trinkaus, *In Our Image and Likeness. Humanity and Divinity in Italian Humanist Thought*, two vols, 1970. Cf. also id., 'The Religious Thought of the Italian Humanists and Reformers: Anticipation or Autonomy', in C.Trinkaus and H.Oberman (eds.), *The Pursuit of Holiness in Late Medieval and Renaissance Religion*, 1974, (9-30) 25. He sees the Renaissance as a 'movement' rather than an era. For the question of the Renaissance as a period cf. also J.R.Hale, 'The Renaissance Label', ibid., 31-42. For the question of periodization cf. also the collection edited by W.Bahner, *Renaissance, Barock, Aufklärung*, 1976. Cf. also A. Buck, *Begriff*, 17ff.; C. Angeleri, *Problema*, 125ff.

30. The first to refer to this was K.Burdach, cf. *Reformation*, 3ff. Further literature on this question in P.O.Kristeller, *Renaissance Thought*, Vol.1, *The Classic, Scholastic and Humanist Strains*, 1961, 150f.n.3. Also B.L.Ullman, 'Renaissance – the Word and the Underlying Concept', in *Studies in the Italian Renaissance*, 1955, 11-25.

31. For this new historical consciousness cf. E.Garin, 'Il concetto della storia nel pensiero di Rinascimento', in *RCSF* 6, 1951, 108-18 = 'Der Begriff der Geschichte in der Philosophie der Renaissance', in A.Buck, *Begriff*, 245-62; M.P.Gilmore, 'The Renaissance Conception of the Lessons of History', in *Facets of the Renaissance*, ed. W.K.Werkmeister et al, 1963, 73-101; A.Buck, *Das Geschichtsdenken der Renaissance*, 1957; id., 'Begriff', in the collection of the same name, 19f.

32. P.O.Kristeller in particular has repeatedly referred to this; cf. e.g. 'The Aristotelian Tradition', in *Renaissance Thought*, Vol.I, 24-47; 'Humanism and Scholasticism in the Italian Renaissance', ibid., 92-119, esp.110ff. (also in *Studies in Renaissance Thought and Letters*, 1956, reprinted 1969, 553-83); id., *La tradizione aristotelica nel Rinascimento*, 1962. At one point Kristeller comments: 'The Renaissance is still in many respects an Aristotelian age which in part continued the trends of Mediaeval Aristotelism, and in part gave it a new direction under the influence of classical humanism and other different ideas.' *The Classics and Renaissance Thought*, 1955, 47.

33. See 16 above.

34. *Begriff*, 23. For the problem cf. especially N.Nelson, 'Individualism as a Criterion of the Renaissance', *JEGP* 32, 1933, 316-34, and more recently also M.B.Becker, 'Individualism in the Early Renaissance: Burden and Blessing', *StRen* 19, 1972, 273-97.

35. Cf most recently G. di Napoli, ' "Contemptus mundi" e "dignitas hominis" nel Rinascimento', *RFNS* 48, 1956, 9-41; A.Buck, 'Die Rangstellung des Menschen in der Renaissance: dignitas et miseria hominis', *AKuG* 42, 1960, 61-75; P.O.Kristeller, 'Ficino and Pomponazzi on the Place of Man in the Universe', *JHI* 5, 1944, 220-6 =

id., *Studies*, 279-86 = id., *Renaissance Thought* II, 1965, 102-10, and above all Trinkaus, *Image*, passim.

36. *De natura deorum* II,56; quoted by Buck, *Rangstellung*, 64.

37. Cf. E.Garin, 'La "dignitas hominis" et la letteratura patristica', *Rin.* 1, 1938, 102-46.

38. '*O imago Dei, recognosce dignitatem tuam; refulgeat in te auctoris effigies*', in *Cantica Canticorum*, cap.I., Migne, PL 180, col.494C.

39. *Summa theol.* I, 29,3: *Persona significat id quod est perfectissimum in tota natura.* Cf. also R.Javelet, *Image et ressemblance au douzième siècle de Saint Anselme à Alain de Lille*, two vols., 1967; Trinkaus, *Image*, 179ff.

40. *Op. cit.*

41. Cf. the quotation in di Napoli, op.cit., 11.

42. Printed in F.Sandeus, *De regibus Siciliae et Apuliae... epitome*, 1611. The manuscript Bibl.Vatic., Cod.Urb.lat. 227, which Trinkaus uses in *Image*, 215ff., and dates at 1447/48, has the title *De hominis excellentia ad Nicolaum Quintum*; there are extensive extracts in his notes.

43. There is a brief survey of the content in di Napoli, op.cit., 19ff.; an extensive account with numerous quotations in Trinkaus, *Image*, 230ff. For Manetti see E.Garin, *Der italienische Humanismus*, 1947, 578ff. = *L'Umanesimo Italiano*(1951), ²1958, 66f. = *Italian Humanism*, ET 1965, 56ff.; *Religious Thought*, 362ff.

44. Cf. A.Buck, *Rangstellung*, 66. For the whole question see A.Auer, 'G.Manetti and Pico della Mirandola, De dignitate hominis', in *Festschrift K.Adam*, 1956, 83-102. – One might also compare the central position of man in the philosophy of Nicolas of Cusa, of which the humanists took little notice despite their considerable parallels with it. Neoplatonic influences are also unmistakable in Nicolas. Cf. recently K.Flasch, *Die Metaphysik des Einen bei Nikolaus von Kues*, 1973, esp.122.

45. Cf. especially his works *Humanistic and Political Literature in Florence and Venice at the Beginning of the Quattrocento*, 1955; *The Crisis of the Early Italian Renaissance* (1955), ²1966.

46. Cf. also L.Martines, *The Social World of the Florentine Humanists, 1390-1460*, 1963.

47. A.Buck, 'Italienischer Humanismus' (an account of research), *AKwG* 41, 1959, (107-32) 123: 'There is no longer any doubt that for many Italian humanists participation in politics had an existential significance and was not only of an aesthetic or literary nature.' Cf. already E.Garin, 'Introduzione', in id., *Filosofi Italiani di Quattrocento*, 1942, 3-75, esp. 33ff.

48. Cf. Baron, *The Crisis*, 295ff.

49. *Das florentinische Staatsbewusstsein im Übergang von der Republik zum Prinzipat*, 1955.

50. It was coined by F.J.Niethammer in the early nineteenth century, *Der Streit des Philanthropismus und des Humanismus in der Theorie des Erziehungsunterrichts unserer Zeit*, 1808; cf. W.Rüegg, *Cicero und der Humanismus*, 1946, 1ff.

51. Cf. P.O.Kristeller, 'The Humanist Movement', in *Renaissance Thought* I, 9f.; cf. also id., 'Humanism and Scholasticism', in *Studies*; id., *Eight Philosophers of the Italian Renaissance*, 1964, reprinted 1966, 3; id., 'Humanist Learning in the Italian Renaissance', *The Centennial Review* 4, 1960, 243-66 = id., *Renaissance Thought* II, 1-19, esp. 3 etc. A.Campana, 'The Origin of the Word "Humanist"', *JWCI* 9, 1946, 60-73. P.F.Grendler, 'The Concept of Humanist in Cinquecento Italy', in *Renaissance. Studies... H.Baron*, ed. A.Molho and J.A.Tedeschi, 1971, 445-63, puts forward the same view with some qualifications.

52. For Kristeller, 'Humanist Learning', 16, the real significance of the Italian Humanists lies 'in the education program which they set forth and carried through'. H.W.Eppelsheimer can even say, with Huizinga, 'Humanism (in its temporal man-

ifestation) has nothing to do with humanity...; by *humanitas* it means education and not a higher form of man, but being a kind of virtuoso.' In A.Buck, *Begriff*, 116.

53. Cicero, who was originally read above all because of his style and then was prized because of the content of his work, especially *De natura deorum* (cf. Poliziano's remarks in E.Garin, *Geschichte und Dokumente der abendländischen Pädagogik*, II, *Humanismus*, 1966 [= *L'educazione in Europa*, ¹1957], 12f.), plays an important role in transmitting material from antiquity. Cf. T.Zielinski, *Cicero im Wandel der Jahrhunderte* (1897), ⁴1929; Rüegg, *Cicero*.

54. Cf. P.O.Kristeller, 'The Moral Thought of Renaissance Humanism', in *Chapters in Western Civilization*, ed. Contemp. Civil. Staff of Columbia College, ³1961, 298-35 = id., *Renaissance Thought*, II, 20-68. The remark by Poggio Bracciolini is characteristic: *Tempus esset jam de somno surgere ac danda opera, ut aliquid mihi prodessent ad vitam et mores illi, quos habemus, et quos quotidie legimus. Epistolae*, ed. T.Tonelli, 1832, I, 62. For E.Garin, 'the humanistic perspective in bourgeois life' is the centre of his account of Italian humanism: *Humanismus*,9 (this passage is not in the second edition and the ET). Cf. also E.Kessler, in E.Garin, *Geschichte*, 298f. In *L'educazione*, 78, however, Garin goes a decisive step further, explicitly taking up Burckhardt's formula about the 'discovery of the world and man': 'Perciò, anche se non necessariamente in polemica dichiarata con la tradizione religiosa, l'educazione umanistica si presenta come una riconsacrazione dell'uomo, della sua mondanità, della sua vita nella città terrena, delle sue passioni, di quanto è più terrestre, corporoso, naturale.' Cf. also id., *Mediaevo e Rinascimento. Studi e ricerche*, ²1961, 6f., dissociating himself from the definitions of Campana and Kristeller.

55. For the care for the tradition of ancient literature in the transition from the Middle Ages to the Renaissance cf. the literature mentioned in A.Buck, *Begriff*, 19f., nn.69,70, and id., 'Gab es einen Humanismus im Mittelalter?', *RomF* 75, 1963, 213-39.

56. Augustine, *De doctrina christiana* II, 41,62. Cf. E.Kessler, 'Geschichtsdenken und Geschichtsschreibung bei Francesco Petrarca', *AKuG* 51, 1969, 109-36; P.O.Kristeller, 'Augustine and the Early Renaissance', in *Studies*, 355-72; Trinkaus, *Image*, passim.

57. There is an extensive literature on Petrarch. The earlier verdict on the poet, from his contemporaries to Voigt and Burckhardt, is described in W. Handschin, *Francesco Petrarca als Gestalt der Historiographie*, 1964. For more recent Petrarch scholarship see above all B.T.Sozzi, *Petrarca, Storia della critica*, 1963. I have used the most recent large-scale work on Petrarch, A.Tripet, *Pétrarque ou la connaissance de soi*, 1967 (cf. 191ff. for a bibliography of editions of Petrarch). – In addition to Trinkaus, *Image*, 3ff., 190ff., etc.; Kristeller, *Eight Philosophers*, 5-18, there is also a sympathetic assessment by M.Seidlmayer, 'Petrarca, das Urbild des Humanisten', in *Wege und Wandlungen des Humanismus*, 1965, 125-73, and H.Baron, 'Petrarch: His inner struggles and the humanistic discovery of man's nature', in *Florilegium Historiale*, Festschrift W.K.Ferguson, 1971, 18-51.

58. Augustine, *Confessions* X, 8.

59. The reference is to Seneca, *Epistulae* 8,5. Cf. G.A.Levi, 'Pensiero classico e pensiero cristiano nel Petrarca', *AeR* 39, 1957, (77-101) 86.

60. F.Petrarca, *Le Familiari*, ed. V.Rossi, Vol.I, 1933 (Edizione Nazionale, Vol.X), 159. As G.Billanovich above all has pointed out (*Petrarca Letterato*, I: *Lo Scrittoio del Petrarca*, 1947, 192ff.; id., 'Petrarca e il Ventoso', *IMU* IX, 1966, 389-401), from a literary-critical point of view this letter cannot be regarded as 'genuine', but represents a later literary fiction on the part of Petrarch; nevertheless it retains its value as intrinsic testimony and as an echo of a real experience of the poet, cf. H.Baron, *From Petrarch to Leondardi Bruni*, 1968, 125-23; id., *Petrarch*, 22ff.

61. Many other 'modern' philosophers had similar experiences, including Herbert of Cherbury, cf. below 522, nn. 38f.

62. G.Voigt, *Die Wiederbelebung des classischen Alterthums* I, 12-101: 'Francesco Petrarca, die Genialität und ihre zündende Kraft', quotation 81. – Cf. also A.Buck, 'Das Problem des christlichen Humanismus in der italienischen Renaissance', in *Sodalitas Erasmiana* I,II, *Valore universale dell'umanesimo*, Naples nd. (1950), (181-92) 183: 'For Petrarch man is already the starting point and goal of all his thoughts and feelings.' – H.Baron, *Petrarch*, shows how towards the middle of Petrarch's life, above all under the influence of Augustine, there is a more marked return to mediaeval Christian views, though he did not completely give up the humanistic ideals of his youth. The combination of these two explains the ambivalence of his remarks, especially as he later worked over some of his early material in this direction.

63. Ibid. Cf. also the account in H.W.Eppelsheimer, *Petrarca* (1926), reprinted 1971, 159ff.

64. *Humanismus*, 13 = *Umanesimo*, 24 = *Humanism*, 20.

65. *Humanismus*, 14 = *Umanesimo*, 25 = *Humanism*, 21.

66. For the concept of 'virtu' as a leading theme in Petrarch cf. H.Baron, 'Das Erwachen des historischen Denkens im Humanismus', *HZ* 147, 1933, 5-20. K.Heitmann, *Fortuna und Virtus. Eine Studie zu Petrarcas Lebensweisheit*, 1958, uses these concepts to demonstrate the obscure fluctuation of Petrarch between Stoa, Peripatetics and Christian doctrine; however, in cases of doubt Christian faith seems to win through, cf. especially the summary, 249ff.

67. *De viris illustribus*, ed. G.Martellotti, 1964, 4,34ff. For the theme cf. E.Kessler, *Geschichtsdenken*.

68. Cf. also E.Garin, *Humanismus*, 18f. = *Umanesimo*, 29 = *Humanism*, 25. The significance of his own subjectivity, which as an explicit self-awareness is in fact something new in intellectual history, is rather different. Cf. M.Seidlmayer, *Wege*, 163ff. Cf. also (under the keywords indicated in the title and especially in connection with Augustine's *Confessions*) T.P.C.Zimmermann, 'Confession and Autobiography in the Early Renaissance', *Studies... Baron*, 119-40.

69. *Rerum senilium libri, Opera omnia*, 1581, XV, 6-7.

70. Cf. P.O.Kristeller, 'The Aristotelian Tradition', in *Renaissance Thought*, I, (24-47) 42f.; id., 'Paduan Averroism and Alexandrism in the Light of Recent Studies', *Atti del XII Congresso Internazionale di Filosofia* IX, 1960, 147-55 = id., *Renaissance Thought* II, 111-18.

71. For the limited extent of this antithesis see, however, Kristeller, op.cit., 42ff.

72. *Humanismus*, 32 = *Umanesimo*, 42 = *Humanism*, 36. According to Trinkaus, *Image*, XX, 'a plea for a renewal of a theology of grace' is an essential theme of the Humanists in the Renaissance. Behind the whole discussion we can also recognize the philosophical contrast between nominalism and realism, which can also be seen at a rather different level with Wyclif, who is rather earlier, see below, 432 n.256.

72a. Cf. especially the summary account in Trinkaus, *Image*, 51ff., 103ff. For the influence of Augustine on the whole period cf. already P.O.Kristeller, 'Augustine and the Early Renaissance', *RR* 8, 1944, 339-58 = id., *Studies*, 355-72.

73. 'The Humanist Movement', in *Renaissance Thought*, I, (3-23) 19f.; id., *Eight Philosophers*, 1964, 38.

74. However, Kristeller observes that by making generally accessible the writings of all the ancient philosophers, Humanism also opened up the way to the study of various philosophical systems: 'Changing Views of the Intellectual History of the Renaissance', in *The Renaissance*, ed. T. Helton, 1961, (27-52) 34.

75. Cf. also P.O.Kristeller, 'Renaissance Platonism', in *Facets*, 103-23.

76. Cf. E.Garin, 'Ricerche sulla traditioni di Platone nella prima metà del seculo XV', in *Mediaevo e Rinascimento, Studi in onore di B.Nardi*, 1955, 339-74.

77. To this phase belong the translations of Plato by Umberto and Pier Candido Decembrio and Leonardi Bruni. In Petrarch, on the other hand, we cannot yet speak of a real Platonism, cf. E.Garin, *Humanismus*, 18f. = *Umanesimo*, 29 = *Humanism*, 25.

78. With qualifications, cf. V.Alberti, *Staatsbewusstsein*.

79. Cf. F.Adorno, 'La crisi dell'umanesimo civile fiorentino da Alemanno Rinucci al Machiavelli', *RCSF* 31, 1952, 19-40.

80. For Pletho and the Platonism of Mistra cf. B.Knös, 'Gémiste Pléthon et son souvenir', *BAGB.S: Lettres d'humanité* 9, 1950, 97-184; id., 'Encore Gémiste Pléthon', *BAGB*, 4.ser., No.3, 1954, 60-5; F.Masai, 'Le problème des influences byzantines sur le platonisme italien de la Renaissance', *BAGB.S: Lettres d'humanité* 12, 1953, 82-90; id., *Pléthon et le platonisme de Mistra*, 1956. – According to Ficino's account (in the preface to his *In Plotini Epitomae, Opera omnia*, 1572, reprinted 1962, Vol.II, fol.1537), Pletho's lectures in Florence in 1438 led Cosimo dei Medici to found the Platonic Academy.

81. Alongside Pletho mention should be made here above all of Cardinal Bessarion, cf. L.Mohler, *Kardinal Bessarion als Theologe, Humanist und Staatsmann*, two vols., 1923-27. – However, it should be noted that Pletho wanted to use Platonism for political plans of reform, whereas Ficino was concerned for harmony between Platonism and the Christian tradition. Consequently he developed above all the speculative element in the Neoplatonic form.

82. For the biography of Ficino cf. above all A.della Torre, *Storia dell'Academica Platonica di Firence*, 1902, and R.Marcel, *Marsile Ficin (1433-1498)*, 1958. The standard work on Ficino's philosophy is P.O.Kristeller, *The Philosophy of Marsilio Ficino*, 1943, reprinted 1964; I have used the reprint. Cf. also id., *Eight Philosophers*, 37-53. But cf. also the more recent qualifications by Kristeller of his earlier work (particularly in connection with his former conjectures about Ficino's originality) and the areas which he mentions as the subject-matter for future research: id., 'L'état présent des études sur Marcel Ficin', in *De Platon et Aristote à la Renaissance. XVIᵉ Colloque International de Tours*, 1976, 59-77. Cf. also G.Saitta, *Marsilio Ficino e la filosofia dell-'Umanesimo*, ³1954; M.Schiavone, *Problemi filosofici in Marsilio Ficino*, 1957.

83. For what follows cf. also Garin, *Filosofi*, 59ff.; P.O.Kristeller, 'The Philosophy of Man in the Italian Renaissance', in *Renaissance Thought* I, 120-39; Trinkaus, *Image*, 461ff.

84. Cf. the quotation in Kristeller, 'The Philosophy of Man', *Renaissance Thought*, 129.

85. Cf. Kristeller, *The Philosophy of Marsilio Ficino*, 35ff.

85a. Cf. E.Garin, 'S.Agostino e Marsilio Ficino', *BSag* 16, 1940, 41-47; A.Tarabochia Canavero, 'S.Agostino nella teologia platonica de Marsilio Ficino', *RFNS* 70, 1978, 626-46.

86. Cf. Kristeller, 'The Philosophy of Man', in *Renaissance Thought*, 127f.

87. Cf. Kristeller, *The Philosophy of Marsilio Ficino*, 289ff.; cf. 262f. This is also the context for the theory of 'Platonic' love as joy in the good and the beautiful which transcends all that is sensual. Cf. ibid., 263ff., and for the theme of the metaphysic of love in Renaissance Platonism E.Garin, *Humanismus*, 137ff. = *Umanesimo*, 132ff. = *Humanism*, 114ff.

88. Hence, too, stress on prayer as the way to a union of the soul with God, cf. Kristeller, ibid., 315f.

89. Cf. Kristeller, ibid., 317.

90. Cf. the edition by E.Garin, *Pico della Mirandola, De dignitate hominis*, Latin and German, 1968, with a valuable introduction by the editor. Critical editions worth

mentioning are *De hominis dignitate. Heptaplus, De ente et uno e scritti vari. A cura di E.Garin*, 1942; *De hominis dignitate... A cura di B.Cicognani*, 1942.

91. 'Kultur', in *Werke*, Vol.III, 241.

92. The most important more recent works about Pico (apart from the introduction by E.Garin to his edition of *De dignitate hominis* – cf. already id., *Filosofi*, 59ff. – and the introduction by C.Vasoli in the reprint of the Basle edition of the *Opera Omnia* I, 1557, reprinted 1969) are G.Semprini, *La filosofia di Pico della Mirandola*, 1936; E.Anagnine, *Giovanni Pico della Mirandola, Vita e dottrina*, 1937; E.Garin, *Giovanni Pico della Mirandola*, 1937; P.M.Cordier, *Jean Pic de Mirandole ou la plus pure figure de la Renaissance*, 1957, and above all the two basic accounts of his theology by E.Monnerjahn, *Giovanni Pico della Mirandola*, 1960, and G.di Napoli, *Giovanni Pico della Mirandola e la problematica dottrinale del suo tempo*, 1965, both with extensive secondary literature. Cf. also E.Garin, 'Le interpretazioni del pensiero di Giovanni Pico: L'opera e il pensiero di Giovanni Pico della Mirandola nella storia del "Umanesimo"', *Convegno Internazionale* I, Florence 1965, 3-33. Also more recently H. de Lubac, *Pic de la Mirandole. Études et discussions*, 1974.

93. Cf. Garin, Introduction to *De dignitate hominis*, 7ff.; di Napoli, *Pico*, 274ff., is more sceptical, as recently is Garin himself, *Convegno Internazionale* I, 8,33.

93a. L.Braghina, 'Alcune considerazioni sul pensiero morale di Giovanni Pico della Mirandola', *Convegno Internazionale* II, 17-34, esp. 26, emphasizes as a new attitude on the part of Pico over against scholasticism the fact that for him philosophy and not faith becomes the basic ethical principle. G.Semprini, 'L'amore come "ascensus alla pax unifica"', ibid., II, 43-51, stresses: 'La filosofia è considerata da Pico il vestibolo della religione; la prima ci aiuta a conoscere Dio; la seconda ad amarlo'(49).

94. Latin/German edition, Garin, 26/27-28/29.

95. Cf. Monnerjahn, *Pico*, 18ff.; E.Colomer, 'Individuo e cosmo in Nicolo Cusano e Giovanni Pico', *Convegno Internazionale* II, 53-162.

96. The *Oratio* reports in mythical style that at creation God did not have at his disposal any archetype for man, 'therefore he did not give him anything of his own, but the possibility of choosing between the highest and the deepest in the world'; German/Latin edition, 28/29.

97. *Heptaplus* V 7; 7b. Commento I 11; 737.

98. Monnerjahn, *Pico*, 31.

99. Cf. especially H.Baker, *The Image of Man. A Study of the Idea of Human Dignity in Classical Antiquity, the Middle Ages and the Renaissance*, 1961; de Lubac, *Pic*, passim. Also E.Colomer, 'Das Menschenbild des Nikolaus von Kues in der Geschichte des christlichen Humanismus', *MFCG* 13, 1978, 117-43, esp. 137ff. Cf. also 12f. above.

100. As we find in the address of the Creator to Adam: *ut tui ipsius quasi arbitrarius honorariusque plastes et fictor, in quam malueris tue formam effingas, Oratio*, Latin/German edition, Garin, 28. For the differences between the *Oratio* and *Heptaplus* (the *Oratio* celebrates man for his freedom, the *Heptaplus* for his position in the cosmos), cf. di Napoli, *Pico*, 375ff. However, the two are mutually complementary, cf. 379.

100a. Cf. de Lubac, *Pic*, 170ff.

101. Monnerjahn, *Pico*, 30, quotes some comments by E.Garin which give this impression. However,in *Convegno Internazionale* I, 16ff., Garin clearly guards himself against an interpretation which sees Pico's remarks as the manifestation of an immanentist humanism which is against the church.

102. Cf. E.Monnerjahn, *Pico*, 30: 'The address is not a matter-of-fact, sober account, but a hymn of praise which flows on, ascending from notion to notion, drawing a picture of man more from a visionary approach than from rational philosophical consideration.'

103. The *Quinta exposita* in the *Heptaplus* comments on Gen.1.26.

104. Cf. *Heptaplus*, ed. Garin, 302.: '*Est autem diversitas inter Deum et hominem, quod*

Deus in se omnia continet ut omnium principium, homo autem in se omnia continet ut omnium medium.' For the problem see also G.di Napoli, 'Contemptus mundi', 24ff; id., *Pico*, 379f. Monnerjahn stresses: 'However, Pico has not left out of account particular limits, above all the essential division between man and God, at the very point where man is most "divine", in his nature as *vinculum et nodus mundi*. The predicate *divinus* is applied to man only in an analogous sense, through participation as an image. It does not mean any identification of man with God.' See also de Lubac, *Pic*, 68ff.

105. *Oratio*, German/Latin edition, Garin, 28.

105a. Cf. also Semprini and Colomer, *Convegno Internazionale*; Colomer, 'Menschenbild', 140ff.

106. Cf. *Oratio*, German/Latin edition, 33: *Si purum contemplatorem (videris)... hic augustius est numen humana carne circumvestitum.* Cf. also di Napoli, *Pico*, 386ff.

107. *Intellectum, qui est in nobis, illustrat maior atque adeo divinus intellectus, sive sit Deus (ut quidam volunt) sive proxima et cognata mens.' Heptaplus* IV, 2; 5b.

108. For the whole question see E.Monnerjahn, *Pico*, Part I, Chs.3-5, 35ff.; also Semprini, *Convegno Internazionale*.

109. 'Nothing is great in man outside the Spirit', writes Pico in the *Disputationes adversus astrologos* (Garin edition, 1946), III, 27, 109a. Cf. also Monnerjahn, op.cit., 33f.

110. Monnerjahn, op.cit., 41.

111. Ibid.

112. This is the second statement of the *Oratio*.

113. Pico depicts this ascent in the *Commento*; cf. Monnerjahn, op.cit., 66ff.

114. Cf. Anagnine, *Pico*, 75ff.; G.Scholem, 'Zur Geschichte der Anfänge der christlichen Kabbala', in *Essays Presented to Leo Baeck*, 1954, 158-93; F.Secret, 'Pico della Mirandola e gli inizii della cabbala cristiana', *Conv* 25, 1957, 31-47; id., *Les kabbalistes chrétiens de la Renaissance*, 1964, 24-44; di Napoli, *Pico*, 282ff.; H.Greive, 'Die christliche Kabbala des Giovanni Pico della Mirandola', *AKuG* 57, 1975, 141-61.

115. Cf. Monnerjahn, *Pico*, 71ff.; di Napoli, *Pico*, 416ff.

116. Monnerjahn, *Pico*, 116ff.; di Napoli, *Pico*, 427ff.

117. Monnerjahn, *Pico*, 19ff.; di Napoli, *Pico*, 350ff.

117a. For Pico's sources cf. P.O.Kristeller, 'Giovanni Pico della Mirandola and his Sources', *Convegno Internazionale* I, 35-42; for his Jewish teachers Elia del Medigo, Flavius Mithridates and Johanan Alemanno cf. G.dell'Aqua/L.Münster, 'I rapporti di Giovanni Pico della Mirandola con alcuni filosofi ebrei', *Convegno Internazionale* II, 149-68; F.Secret, 'Nouvelles précisions sur Flavius Mithridates maître de Pic de la Mirandole et traducteur de commentaires de kabbale', ibid., 169-87.

118. His world view is in any case traditional and Platonist; cf. A.Dulles, *Princeps Concordiae. Pico della Mirandola and the Scholastic Tradition*, 1941.

119. *Briefe*, ed. L.Dorez, 'Lettres inédites de Jean Pic de Mirandole (1482-1492)', *GSLI* 25, 1895, 352ff.; letter no.66b.

120. For the whole question see Monnerjahn, *Pico*, 154ff.

121. *Briefe*, ed. Dorez, no.59b. For the whole question see Monnerjahn, op.cit., 162f.

122. Cf. Anagnine, *Pico*, 287.

123. Cf. Monnerjahn, *Pico*, 147ff. However, in connection with Monnerjahn's general verdict on Pico it should be noted that the author writes from a Roman Catholic standpoint. Di Napoli, *Pico*, 463ff. argues (against Monnerjahn) even more strongly that Pico has an orthodox understanding of the sacraments.

124. Cf. above, 416 n.12.

125. *Reformations*, 8-10.

126. Cf. W.Dress, *Die Mystik des Marsilio Ficino*, 1929.

127. In one sense at this point we are back to the questions put by Gebhardt and Thode (cf. above, 417 n.23), though from quite a different perspective.

128. Cf. here above all H.Grundmann, *Religiöse Bewegungen im Mittelalter*, with the appendix 'Neue Beiträge zur Geschichte der religiösen Bewegungen im Mittelalter' (reprint), 1961 (also 1972); id., *Ketzergeschichte des Mittelalters*, Die Kirche in ihrer Geschichte, 2, G, Part I, 1963; A.Borst, *Die Katharer*, 1953, esp.71-120. Of the earlier histories of heresy, C.U.Hahn, *Geschichte der Ketzer im Mittelalter* (1845), 1968, has appeared in a new impression.

129. Cf. H.Grundmann, *Bewegungen*, appendix, 504: 'On the other hand it is striking and cannot be coincidental that some themes, motives and tendencies keep recurring, though on the basis of different arguments and with different consequences, and that they often appear in orthodox groups of the religious movement as they do among the heretics. For all the difference in the answers, however, often the same questions and problems disturb, move and divide the religious spirits of the time.'

130. A.Borst, *Katharer*, 72: 'Their concern is Western.' J.Fearns, 'Peter von Bruis und die religiöse Bewegung des 12.Jahrhunderts', *AKuG* 48, 1966, (311-335) 335, 312 and nn.3-6, puts forward opposite views about the origin of heretical ideas in the West and those who represent them. The question of the role of the Bogomils is decided in accordance with the emergence of the dualistic-cosmological speculation typical of them in the programmes of Western sectarians.

131. Cf. Borst, op.cit., 89ff.

132. Cf. Grundmann, *Bewegungen*, 479f.

133. This made possible their later formation as a church with the adoption of hierarchical and sacramental forms, a development which was strongly contested by the Spiritualists; cf. Borst, op.cit., esp.121.

134. Grundmann, *Bewegungen*, 13ff., 508. Cf. also Borst, op.cit., 81f.

135. Grundmann, *Bewegungen*, 519.

136. Cf. G.Ilarino, 'Le eresie popolari del seculo XI nell'Europa occidentale', *SGSG* II, 1947, (43-89) 46f.; Borst, *Katharer*, 73. The contemporary account of Rudolf the Bald has recently been published in J.Fearns, *Ketzer und Ketzerbekämpfung im Hochmittelalter*, 1968, 9ff.

137. Borst, op.cit., 74ff.; Grundmann, *Bewegungen*, 477 and n.6; id., *Ketzergeschichte*, 9, and the source in Fearns, op.cit.

138. Grundmann, *Bewegungen*, 479, points out that the laying on of hands is the only rite attested among the heretics; it has the same content as among the ancient Manichees, but there is no trace of dualistic speculation and mythology.

139. Cf. Borst, op.cit., 77, and n.18 (further literature there).

140. Cf. Ilarino, op.cit., 63ff.; Borst, op.cit., 76f.

141. Cf. Grundmann, *Bewegungen*, 13ff; Borst, op.cit., 80ff. – In detail, A.Nitschke, *Die Welt Gregors VII. Studien zum Reformpapstum*, Diss.phil. (typescript), Göttingen 1950.

142. Cf. Borst, op.cit., 81f. and n.4 (literature); Grundmann, *Bewegungen*, 508f.

143. Cf. Borst, op.cit., 82 and n.6 (literature); Grundmann, *Bewegungen*, 514 n.47; id., *Ketzergeschichte*, 13.

144. Cf. Grundmann, *Bewegungen*, 38ff.; *Ketzergeschichte*, 15ff.

145. *Bewegungen* (appendix), 504ff.; cf. also M.D.Chenu, 'Moines, clercs, laïcs au carrefour de la vie évangelique (XIIe siècle)', *RHE* 49, 1954, 59-89. For what follows see also H.Wolter, 'Aufbruch und Tragik der apostolischen Laienbewegung im Mittelalter', *GuL* 30, 1957, 357-69. Wolter sees the participation of the laity in the Crusades as an essential cause of their interest in the monastic ideal of the *vita apostolica*.

146. A clear sign of this is that the prohibition against owning books was also

included among the demands of the poverty movement, since theological knowledge was seen as assimilation to the church and people even believed that they had a direct knowledge of the truth hidden in the Bible.

147. Cf. R.Manselli, 'Studi sulle eresie del seculo XII', *Istituto Storico Italiano per il Medio Evo, Studi storici* 5, 1953, 1-24; J.Fearns, *von Bruis*; J.Leclerq, *Pierre le Vénérable*, 1946, 357-67.

148. For dating cf. Fearns, *von Bruis*, 313ff. The main source for Peter is the writing of the abbot Petrus Venerabilis of Cluny, *Epistola contra Petrobrusianos Hereticos*, in CChrCM X, 1968, ed. J.Fearns; extract also in Fearns, *Ketzer*, 18ff.; cf. also P.Abelard, *Introductio in Theologiam* II, c.4, PL 178, col.1056AB. For Peter cf. Leclerq, op.cit.

149. Cf. in detail Fearns, *von Bruis*, 318ff.

150. Cf. R.Manselli, 'Il monaco Enrico e la sua eresia', *BISI* 65, 1953, 1-63. Also Borst, *Katharer*, 85f. and n.15 (literature). However, Borst derives some elements of the radical aspect of the sect from Henry which had already come about under Peter; Henry, for example, evidently reverted to the cross again as a symbol.

151.Cf. Fearns, *von Bruis*, 320ff.

152. Cf. Ilarino da Milano, *L'eresia di Ugo Speroni nella Confutazione del maestro Vacario*, 1945.

153. Grundmann, *Bewegungen*, 516, differs from Ilarino in thinking that Speroni's belief in predestination was only set off by his move against the wickedness of the priests, and not vice versa. Basically this doctrine is only a further development of his anthropocentric approach.

154. Cf. H.Pirenne, 'Tanchelin et le projet de démembrement du diocèse d'U-trecht vers 1100', *BAB.L* 13, ser.5, 1927, 112-19; L.J.M.Philippen, 'De hl. Norbertus en de strijd tegen het Tanchelisme te Antwerpen', *BG* 25, 1934, 251-88. – The letter from the Cathedral Chapter of Utrecht to Archbishop Frederick I of Cologne about Tanchelm is in Fearns, *Ketzer*, 15ff. – Cf. also Grundmann, *Ketzergeschichte*, 17f.

155. Cf. Borst, *Katharer*, 87ff., and the literature mentioned there.

156. K.-V.Selge has recently developed a detailed account of the teaching of the early Waldensians from the *Liber antiheresis* of Durandus of Osca (or Huesca)(1200), cf. *Die ersten Waldenser*, Vol.I, 1967 (Vol.II contains an edition of the text of the work; there are also extracts from the *Liber antiheresis* in *Wegbereiter der Reformation*, ed. G. A. Benrath, 1967, 4ff.). See also more recently A.Molnar, *Valdenšti*, 1973 (German: *Die Waldenser*, 1980; Italian: *Storia dei Valdensi. I. Dalle origini all' adesione alla Riforma*, 1974).

157. Cf. Selge, op.cit., I, 32f. Cf. id., 317: 'The content of Waldensian preaching was from the beginning mediaeval and Catholic in its basic Pelagian feature of justification by works.'

158. For the Lateran council of 1215 and its resolutions against the travelling preachers cf. Grundmann, *Bewegungen*, 135ff.

159. Cf. Grundmann, *Bewegungen*, 100ff.; Selge, op.cit., I, 188ff.

160. Grundmann, *Bewegungen*, 70ff.

161. Op.cit., 515f.

162. Ilarino, *Ugo Speroni*, 414.

163. Ethical arguments join with economic and political conditions, as we can see particularly clearly from the work of Arnold of Brescia, who otherwise remains completely in an orthodox framework as far as dogmatics is concerned. For him see most recently G.Edelsbrunner, *Arnold von Brescia*, Graz dissertation 1965; R.Manselli, 'Arnold von Brescia', *TRE* 4, 1979, 129-33.

164. For Joachim cf. above all H.Grundmann, *Studien über Joachim von Fiore*, 1927, reprinted 1966; E.Buonaiuti, *Gioacchino da Fiore. I tempi, la vita, il messagio*, 1931; I.C.Huck, *Joachim von Floris und die joachitische Literatur*, 1938; F.Russo, *Gioacchino da Fiore*, 1959; A.Crocco, *Gioacchino da Fiore*, 1960; B.Töpfer, *Das kommende Reich des*

Friedens, 1964, 48-103; M.Bloomfield, 'Joachim of Flora', *Tr* 13, 1957, 249-311. The literature on Joachim over the last few decades has been very extensive. Bibliographies particularly in F.Russo, *Bibliografia gioacchimita*, 1954; id., 'Rassegna bibliografica Gioacchimita (1958-1967)', in *Citeaux* 19, 1968, 206-14; also B.Hirsch-Reich, 'Eine Bibliographie über Joachim von Fiore und dessen Nachwirkung', *RTAM* 24, 1957, 27-44; cf. also H.Grundmann, *Neue Forschungen über Joachim von Fiore*, 1950. – In addition to the reprint of the three Venetian impressions of Joachim's main works, *Concordia novi ac veteris testamenti* (1519), *Expositio in Apocalypsim* (1527) and *Psalterium decem cordarum* (1527), 1965/6, and the bilingual Venetian edition, *Vaticinia sive Prophetiae abbatis Joachim et Anselmi Episcopi Marsiani, cum praefatione et adnotationibus Paschali Regiselmi. Vita Joachim per Gabrielum Barium (Latine et Italice)*, 1589 reprinted 1972, there is a critical edition of the writings *Tractatus super quattuor Evangelia*, ed. E.Buonaiuti, 1930; *De articulis Fidei*, ed. E.Buonaiuti, 1936; *Adversus Judeos*, ed A. Frugoni, 1957. The important *Liber figurarum* was produced as a facsimile edition in 1953 in the second edition (two vols) by R.Tondelli. There is a selection from the three main works in a German translation in A.Rosenberg (ed.), *Joachim von Fiore, Das Reich des Heiligen Geistes*, 1955. For the biography of Joachim see now especially H.Grundmann, 'Zur Biographie Joachims von Fiore und Rainers von Ponza', *DA* 16, 1960, 437-564.

165. After he had left the Cistercian monastery of Corrazzo, he founded his own monastery of San Giovanni di Fiore in the desolate Sila hills; it is still in existence today (his Order lasted only until 1570). For the dates of the foundation of Joachim's monastery (between 1189 and 1194) cf. H.Grundmann, *Biographie*. – Cf. also id., *Forschungen*, 47ff.

166. This is rightly stressed by B.Töpfer, op.cit., 78f., 95.

167. For the two trends in modern research into Joachim, one of which stresses his orthodoxy whereas the other stresses the revolutionary character of his thought, cf. Grundmann, *Forschungen*, 64f.

168. Töpfer, op.cit., 79f. and n.161 points *inter alia* to the fact that in Joachim there is no criticism of the Donation of Constantine and that he even supports the ecclesiastical doctrine of two authorities; mention should also be made of his sharp rejection of the contemporary heretical movements, cf. Töpfer, op.cit., 95 and n.250.

169. Cf. Grundmann, *Studien*, 91.

170. Cf. Grundmann, *Studien*, 92ff.

171. Cf. Grundmann, *Studien*, 85ff.

172. Töpfer, *Reich*, 81ff., points out how Joachim is concerned to keep a careful balance with Augustine in his later writings.

173. *Studien*, 19ff.

174. Töpfer, op.cit., 56, quotes various remarks of Joachim, from which it emerges 'that the eternal gospel or the *intelligentia spiritualis* of man which corresponds to it in function cannot disclose to man any truths which are fundamentally different from the gospel of Christ...'

175. After a great deal of hesitation by scholars, Töpfer, op.cit., 55ff., has given a balanced judgment on the relationship between the *evangelium aeternum* and scripture: this is not just a symbolic spiritual sense of scripture but a new higher form of knowledge which in the end makes even the letters, i.e. scriptural revelation, superfluous. Cf. also E.Benz, *Ecclesia spiritualis*, 1934, 245f. For the *intelligentia spiritualis* cf. also Grundmann, *Studien*, 149ff. For the *Concordia* as an interpretation of history which goes beyond the typological relationship between Old and New Testaments see F.Förschner, *Concordia. Urgestalt und Sinnbild in der Geschichtsdeutung des Joachim von Fiore*, Diss.Phil.Freiburg 1970.

176. To this extent Töpfer, op.cit., 56 n.47, is to be corrected.

177. E.g. Grundmann, *Studien*, 149ff.; cf. also E.Benz, *Ecclesia*, 25: 'In the case of

Joachim, his own historical scheme, according to which he deliberately puts himself in the second age and its church, prevents the emergence of revolutionary ideas; it was only the spirituals of the next generation who had a right to draw the revolutionary consequence of his metaphysics of history.'

178. According to Töpfer, the fixing of the year 1260 for the dawn of the third age only came about with Joachim's later disciples; however, the difficulty of the mention of the year in *Liber figurarum*, tables 3/4, forces him to assume that this work was finished after Joachim, op.cit., 50 n.11.

179. Cf. *Concordia*, V, 117, f.133 ra: *huiuscemodi studia et labores cessabunt*; *Expositio* f.123r.: *quia tempus exponendarum scripturarum consumatum erit...*' Contemplation will take the place of the study of scripture in the third stage. For the relationship of the eternal gospel to the Bible see Töpfer, op.cit., 55ff. Crocco, *G.da Fiore*, 99, is right that the *evangelium aeternum* is not a new writing, but his final conclusion, 'ma il più sublime e spirituale senso del Vangelo di Cristo, anzi di entrambi i Testamenti', gives the false impression that the Bible in the previous sense will have no significance for the period of the spirit.

180. *Oportet ex toto evacuari figuras, Concordia* IV, 37f., 58rb.

181. Cf. *Tractatus*, Buonaiuti edition, 86 (corrected from Töpfer, 58 n.52): *...quantum ad ipsa sacramenta transitorium est et temporale, quod autem per ea significatur eternum,* Concordia V, 74f., 103 ra/b: *Nam neque usus panis et carnis neque potus vini et aque neque unctio olei eterna est, est autem eternum id quod designatur in ipsis.* – Grundmann, *Studien*, 114; E.Benz, 'Creator Spiritus. Die Geisteslehre des Joachim von Fiore', *ErJb* 25, 1956, (285-355) 320; Töpfer, op.cit., 58, have rightly seen that in Joachim the sacraments cease in the third stage; that follows logically from his system.

182. Cf. Töpfer, op.cit., 62.

183. Op.cit., 63ff.

184. *Forschungen*, 63ff.

185. For the two monastic orders which are to take over the twin tasks of preaching and meditation (which is rated even higher) in the third stage of Joachim's system (he describes them as *viri spirituales* – they were later identified with the two mendicant Orders) cf. Töpfer, op.cit., 66ff.; M.Reeves, *The Influence of Prophecy in the Later Middle Ages. A Study in Joachimism*, 1969, 141ff.

186. Cf. the references in Töpfer, op.cit., 96.

187. Bloomfield, *Joachim of Flora*, 182ff.; Töpfer, op.cit., 96f.

188. Cf. Grundmann, *Bewegungen*, 355ff.; also already id., *Studien*, 164ff.

189. Also Grundmann, *Bewegungen*; cf. also op.cit. (appendix), 530ff.

190. In addition to the earlier accounts by K.Balthasar, *Geschichte des Armutsstreites im Franziskanerorden bis zum Konzil von Vienne*, 1911; R.de Nantes, *Histoire des Spirituales dans l'Ordre de Saint François*, 1909; cf. especially M.D.Lambert, *Franciscan Poverty*, 1961, and E.Benz, *Ecclesia spiritualis* – unfortunately the latter work has no scholarly apparatus.

191. Cf. Benz, op.cit., 145ff.; 59f.

192. Above all Cardinal Hugo of Ostia; for these events see Benz, op.cit., 150ff., and Grundmann, *Bewegungen*, 127ff.

193. Cf. Benz, op.cit., 85ff.

194. Cf. Benz, op.cit., 58f.

195. Cf. Benz, op.cit., 128f.

196. Cf. Balthasar.

197. *Abbatis Joachim in Jeremiam prophetum interpretatio*, printed 1577. For the time of composition (c.1243) cf. Töpfer, *Reich*, 108ff.; Reeves, *Influence*, 56.

198. Cf. on the one hand Töpfer, op.cit., 108ff., and on the other M.Reeves, most recently op.cit., 151ff. n.2.

199. Cf. Töpfer, op.cit. 112f., and the instances cited there.

200. Cf. Töpfer, op.cit., 118ff., 113ff.

201. Critical edition of the Chronicles by D.Holder-Egger, in *Monumenta Germaniae Historica, Scriptores*, Vol. XXXII, 1905-13, with an introduction by B.Schmeidler, VII-XXXII; German translation by A.Doren, two vols, 1914. For Salimbene de Adam or of Parma OFM see above all M.Scivoletto, *Fra Salimbene da Parma*, 1950; also Benz, *Ecclesia*, 205ff.

202. For what follows see Benz, op.cit., 175ff.; Töpfer, op.cit, 124ff.; P.G.Bondatti, *Gioachinismo e Francescanesimo nel Dugento*, 1924, 35ff.

203. *Chronicles*, German translation I, 218.

204. Op.cit., 219.

205. Op.cit., 205.

206. Op.cit., 211. – Benz, *Ecclesia*, 177, makes a vague connection between this and the previous quotation.

207. Cf. H.Denifle, 'Das Evangelium Aeternum und die Kommission zu Anagni', *ALKGMA* 1, 1885 (reprinted 1955), 49ff.; E.Benz, 'Joachim-Studien II: Die Exzerptsätze der Pariser Professoren aus dem Evangelium Aeternum', *ZKG* 51, 1932, 415ff.; id., *Ecclesia* 244ff.; G.Bondatti, op.cit., 66ff.; B.Töpfer, op.cit., 126ff.; M.Reeves, op.cit., 60ff., 187ff.

208. But the corpus of Joachim's own three writings supplied with Gherardino's glosses has been preserved, cf. B.Töpfer, 'Eine Handschrift des Evangelium aeternum des Gherardino von Borgo San Donnino', *ZfG* 8, 1960, 156ff.

209. Cf. Denifle, op.cit., 82ff.; the excerpts themselves are published in Benz, *ZKG* 51, 1932, 415-26. The purpose of the excerpts becomes particularly clear through the writing by William of St Amour, *Liber de periculis novissimorum temporum*, 1255, directed against the mendicant monks; cf. Benz, op.cit., 449ff.

210. Printed in Denifle, op.cit., 99-142.

211. Op.cit., 84.

212. *ZKG* 1932, 443f., 452f.

213. Cf. the excerpts I-III, XI of the professors in Benz, *ZKG* 1932, 416f. Also the literal quotation in the protocol of Anagni in Denifle, op.cit., 101: *ad quam scripturam tenetur populus tercii status mundi, quemadmodum populus primi status ad vetus testamentum et populus secundi ad novum.*

214. Protocol in Denifle, op.cit., 101,131.

215. Cf. Töpfer, op.cit., 128f.

216. Cf. excerpt IV in Benz, *ZKG* 1932, 417.

217. Protocol in Denifle, 101; cf. excerpt VII in Benz, *ZKG* 1932, 417.

218. Cf. Benz, *ZKG* 1932, 453ff. Of particular significance is the sentence from Alexander IV's second bull, Chartularium Universit.Paris., ed. Denifle, 1889, nos.258, 298: *Alexander IV mandat Reginaldo episcopo Parisiensi, ut in abolendo Introductorio prudenter procedat, ne fratres Minores ex hoc ullum opprobrium incurrant.* See Benz, op.cit., 455: 'The Parisian professors had lost a victory and the Curia had won a defeat.'

219. Cf. Töpfer, op.cit., 131ff. Bonaventura, the General of the Order (1257-74), attempted to find a balance between the strict observers and the majority party: his own teaching contains Joachite-Spiritualist notions in a moderate form, see Töpfer, op.cit., 149ff.

220. Angelo of Clareno wrote the history of these controversies in his *Historia septem tribulationum* (after 1320) (partial edition by F.Tocco, *Le due prime tribolazioni dell'ordine dei minori*, 1908, 97-131, 221-36); the rest is in F.Ehrle, 'Die Spiritualen, ihr Verhältnis zum Franziskanerorden und zu den Fraticellen. 3. Die "historia septem tribulationum ordinis minorum" des fr. Angelus de Clarino', *ALKGMA* 2, 1886 (reprinted 1956), 106-64, 249-336. – H.Grundmann, *Studien*, 188ff., rightly points out that among the Spiritualists proper in the thirteenth and fourteenth century strict

observance over against the Franciscan rule represented the real aim of the struggle: the *perfectio evangelica* is primarily the *status altissimae paupertatis*, not asserted in opposition to the New Testament but understood as its fulfilment. However, that does not mean a spiritual return to Catholicism, 'where perfection means a negation of the world'(189). The wheel has come full circle.

221. After the expectations associated with the hermit pope Celestinus V were disappointed by his speedy resignation in 1294, the Spiritualists were repressed by Boniface VIII and his successors. There is also a short account of the history of this struggle in T.Manteuffel, *Die Geburt der Ketzerei (Narodziny herezji*, 1963, German), 1965, 56ff.

222. For him cf. Benz, *Ecclesia*, 256ff.; D.Douie, *The Nature and the Effect of the Heresy of the Fraticelli*, 1932, 82ff.; Töpfer, op.cit., 217ff.; Reeves, op.cit., 194ff.; F.Ehrle, 'Petrus Johannes Olivi, sein Leben und seine Schriften', in *ALKGMA* III, 1887 (reprinted 1956), 403-533.

223. R.Manselli, *La 'Lectura Super Apocalipsim' di Pietro di Giovanni Olivi*, 1955. The *Postilla* is still unpublished, cf. Reeves, op.cit., 197 n.1.

224. Cf. Töpfer, op.cit., 217; Manselli wants to understand Olivi more strongly in Augustinian terms; but cf. Töpfer, op.cit., 231, and n.115. Cf. also Reeves, op.cit., 195, 199.

225. Töpfer, op.cit., 221f. This is also matched by the shift of accent in the expectation of the time of salvation in Olivi's disciple Ubertino da Casale. In his work *Arbor Vitae Crucifixae* (printed 1485), the *renovatio evangelice vite* or *renovatio formae Christi* take the place of Joachim's *intellectus spiritualis*. Cf. Töpfer, op.cit., 235; Reeves, op.cit., 208. For Ubertino cf. also E.Knoth, *Ubertino von Casale*, 1903.

226. Cf. Ehrle, *Olivi*, 451ff.; cf. id., 'Die Spiritualen', in *ALKGMA* IV, 1888 (reprinted 1956), 28-190, 40-42; Benz, *Ecclesia*, 349f.; Reeves, op.cit., 201ff.

227. Cf. Ehrle, *ALKGMA* IV, 1888, 64ff.; Douie, *Fraticelli*; Reeves, op.cit., 213ff.

228.Wyclif's Latin works have been published since 1882 by the Wyclif Society in 36 volumes, reprinted 1966; other books to have appeared are: *Select English Works*, ed. T.Arnold, I, 1869; II/III, 1871; *The English Works... Hitherto Unprinted*, ed. F.D.Matthew, 1880; *Trialogus* and *Supplementum Trialogi*, ed. G.Lechler, 1869; *Opuscula*, ed. S.H.Thomson, *Spec.*, 1928, 248-53; of the *Summa de ente libri primus et secundus*, ed. S.H.Thomson, 1930; *Tractus de Trinitate*, ed. A.Breck, 1962. The main work not yet published is the Commentary on the Bible, cf. Benrath, see below. – The most important secondary literature is: G.Lechler, *Johann von Wyclif und die Vorgeschichte der Reformation*, I,II, 1873; S.H.Thomson, 'The Philosophical Basis of Wyclif's Theology', *JR* 11, 1931, 86-116; H.B.Workman, *John Wyclif*, two vols, 1926, reprinted 1966 (the monumental biography of Wyclif); F.Loofs, *Leitfaden zum Studium der Dogmengeschichte*, II, ⁵1953, ed. K.Aland, 529-43; P. de Vooght, *Les sources de la doctrine chrétienne d'après les théologiens du XIVe siècle et du début du XVe avec le texte integral des XII premieres questions de la Summa inédite de Gerard de Bologne (d.1317)*, 1954; cf. id., 'Wyclif et la "Scriptura sola"', *ETL* 39, 1963, 50-86; M.Schmidt, 'John Wyclifs Kirchenbegriff, Der Christus humilis Augustins bei Wyclif. Zugleich ein Beitrag zur Frage: Wyclif und Luther', in *Gedenkschrift für W.Elert*, 1955, 72-108; M.Hurley, ' "Scriptura sola": Wyclif and his Critics', *Tr* 16, 1960, 275-352; J.A.Robson, *Wyclif and the Oxford Schools. The Relation of the 'Summa de Ente' to Scholastic Debates at Oxford in the Later Fourteenth Century*, 1961; W.Mallard, 'John Wyclif and the Tradition of Biblical Authority', *ChH* 30, 1961, 50-60; L.J.Daly, *The Political Theory of John Wyclif*, 1962; J.Stacey, *John Wyclif and Reform*, 1964; G.A.Benrath, *Wyclifs Bibelkommentar*, 1966; cf. id., 'Wyclif und Hus', *ZTK* 62, 1965, 196-216; K.B.McFarlane, *John Wycliffe and the Beginnings of English Nonconformity*, 1966; E.C.Tatnall, 'John Wyclif and Ecclesia Anglicana', *JEH* 20, 1969, 19-43; F.de Boor, *Wyclifs Simoniebegriff*, 1970; W.Farr, *John Wyclif as Legal Reformer*, 1974; P.Auksi, 'Wyclif's Sermons and the Plain Style',

ARG 66, 1975, 5-23. Cf. also A.Molnár, 'Recent Works on Wyclif's Theology', *CV* 7, 1964, 186-92; G.A.Benrath, 'Stand und Aufgaben der Wyclif-Forschung', *TLZ* 92, 1967, cols.261-4.

229. G.A.Benrath, *TLZ* 92, 1967, col.264, is certainly right in observing: 'We are still a long way from being able to determine "Wyclif's place in history"... and perhaps even further still from being able to give a sure account of "Wyclif's place in theology".' In his monograph (see the preceding note) Benrath himself, however, has given us some important guidelines towards solving the problem of Wyclif's relationships to the Bible and the church, which concerns us here. R.W.H.Frederick, *John Wyclif and the First English Bible*, 1957, is less helpful.

230. R.Buddensieg in particular has criticized this erroneous judgment in the introduction to his edition of *De veritate Sacrae Scripturae* (see above). F.Loofs, *Leitfaden zum Studium der Dogmengeschichte* II, ed. K.Aland, ⁵1953, 537, calls this introduction a 'report in a marked Protestant/Reformed mode'. – Cf. also Buddensieg, *John Wyclif und seine Zeit*, 1885, esp.1ff. M.Hurley, op.cit., 333f., also goes into the differences between the German original and the abbreviated English translation. For other admirers of Wyclif, ancient and modern, cf. also J.Stacey, *Wyclif*, 12ff. He himself, however, has not escaped the dangers of a Protestant distortion.

231. P. de Vooght, *Les sources*, 168-200; id., 'Wyclif et la "Scriptura sola"', *ETL* 39, 1963, 50-86. The latter article is a reply to Hurley's criticism, op.cit., 337ff. – For de Vooght's picture of Wyclif cf. also G.A.Benrath's account of the literature in *VF* 16, 1971, (25-55) 49.

232. Cf. Workman, op.cit., II, 30-45; Stacey, *Wyclif*, 101ff.; Hurley, op.cit., 299ff. His chief critic on this point was his former friend the Franciscan William Woodford (or Wodeford; for the form of the name cf. de Vooght, *ETL* 39, 50 n.3), cf. Robson, op.cit., 190-5. It emerges from Woodford's testimony and also from Wyclif's Bible Commentary that he did not put forward this view only in 1379, but held it as early as about 1370; cf. also Benrath, *Bibelkommentar*, 269ff.; 321f.

233. Cf. also J.Leclerq, 'L'exégèse médiévale de l'Ancien Testament', in *L'Ancien Testament et les chrétiens*, 1951, 168-82; B.Smalley, *The Study of the Bible in the Middle Ages*, 1952; H. de Lubac, *Exégèse médiévale* I, 1,2; II,1,2, 1959-64.

234. Thus e.g. McFarlane, op.cit., 91. The view that 'Wycliffe does not seem to have thought any form of interpretation necessary' is completely erroneous.

235. Cf. Mallard, op.cit., 54ff.; Benrath, *Bibelkommentar*, 316f.: 'In accordance with his presuppositions Wyclif must have been well disposed to allegorical interpretation', ibid., 317. Cf. also id., *ZTK* 62, 202: 'Without hesitation he uses the traditional theory of the fourfold sense of scripture. He saw no reason to supersede it; precisely with its help he was able to disclose the manifold riches of scripture which he celebrated.'

236. Cf. Mallard, op.cit., 51f.; Benrath, *Bibelkommentar*, 22, 53, 317. In a late writing like *De eucharistia* Wyclif makes a distinction between church fathers and theologians of the first millennium (the council of 1059 under Nicolas II is a watershed for him, because there he finds an understanding of the eucharist of which he approves); at all events their authority seems to him supported by scripture, and more recent theologians, whose doctrine he will recognize only insofar as it accords with scripture, cf. Hurley, op.cit., 299.

237. This theme occurs repeatedly throughout Wyclif's various writings, cf. the survey in Hurley, op.cit., 280ff., but of course also in his Bible Commentary, cf. Benrath, *Bibelkommentar*, 184ff., cf. 325. *Lex mosaica* and *lex evangelica* are combined into a unity, ibid., 324.

238. For the *Christus humilis* as a model for Christians and the church cf. M.Schmidt, *Kirchenbegriff*, esp. 88f.; Auksi, op.cit., 9. – Benrath, *Bibelkommentar*,

236ff., mentions the excursus on Matt.11.28-30 (Latin text ibid., 354-62) as a special example. Cf. also ibid., 328ff.

239. Cf. Benrath, *Bibelkommentar*, 285ff., 326ff.

240. 3.1,4; cf. Hurley, op.cit., 293.

241. *Bibelkommentar*, 334f.; cf. also *TLZ* 32, col.262.

242. Cf. Hurley, op.cit., 304f.; Stacey, *Wyclif*, 40ff. – For the development of Wyclif's relationship to monasticism cf. already G.V.Lechler, op.cit., Vol.I, 588; M.Schmidt, *Kirchenbegriff*, 97, can even say: 'Wyclif's real opponents are the mendicant Orders.'

243. According to Workman, op.cit., II, 100, the idea of the *ecclesia spiritualis* was 'in the air'. Cf. also M.Schmidt, *Kirchenbegriff*, 78.

244. Stacey, op.cit., 29ff. does this in a very committed Protestant tone.

245. Cf. G.M.Trevelyan, *England in the Age of Wycliffe*, [3]1909 (reprinted 1948), esp. 104-69; W.A.Pantin, *The English Church in the Fourteenth Century*, 1955; McFarlane, op.cit., 41ff.; McKisack, *The Fourteenth Century 1307-1399*, The Oxford History of England V, 272-311. Similar circumstances also prevailed in other parts of the Western church. Best known are the impacts of circumstances in Germany, which are reported in the two critical accounts from the fifteenth and beginning of the sixteenth centuries, the so-called *Reformatio Sigismundi* (ed. H.Koller, 1964), cf. also L.Graf zu Dohna, *Reformatio Sigismundi*, 1960; and the book of the so-called 'Revolutionary of the Upper Rhine' (ed. A.Franke, analysis by G.Zschäbitz, 1967).

246. Cf. A.Deeley, 'Papal Provision and Royal Rights of Patronage in the early Fourteenth Century', *EHR* 43, 1928, 497-527; I.R.L.Highfield, *The Relations between the Church and the English Crown 1348-78*, Oxford Dissertation 1950 (unfortunately inaccessible to me).

247. Op.cit., 273.

248. For example it made the Parliamentary statute of provisions of 1351 and the Praemunire of 1353 in practice ineffective, cf. McFarlane, op.cit., 54; McKisack, op.cit., 280f.

249. Cf. McFarlane, op.cit., 51: 'It would not be difficult to show that the court of Rome used its powers as well, if not indeed a good deal better than, the patrons whom it superseded; for where its own material interests were not primarily at stake it was capable of applying higher and more consistent standards than any but the best of those on the spot', and other considerations, ibid.

250. Cf. M.Schmidt, *Kirchenbegriff*, 81f.

251. For his parish in Fillingham, from 1363, cf. Workman, op.cit., I, 151ff.; for his prebend in Westbury, cf. ibid., 156ff.; later for Ludgershall, ibid., 195ff., and Lutterworth, ibid., 209ff.

252. Cf. McFarlane, op.cit., 67f.

253. Cf. M.Schmidt, *Kirchenbegriff*, 88f.

254. Hurley, op.cit., 304, refers to the 'devastating effect' with which Wyclif used the *argumentum e silentio* from scripture against the whole ordering of the church. However, its effect was to have unforseeable consequences in later centuries. The principle of the sufficiency of the *lex Christi* in scripture as developed in *De civili dominio* belongs in the same context; what is not implicitly contained in scripture is 'human tradition'. For details cf. Hurley, op.cit., 286ff.

255. Cf. the works mentioned above. Also already B.Smalley, 'The Bible and Eternity: John Wyclif's Dilemma', *JWCI* 27, 1954, 73-89, and the typescript dissertation by G.Wendelborn, *Das Verhältnis von Schrift und Vernunft im Werk John Wyclifs*, Rostock 1964 (and his own account in *TLZ* 91, 1966, cols.233f.).

256. For Wyclif's philosophical ultra-realism cf. S.H.Thomson, *JR* 11, 1931, 86-115; Robson, op.cit., esp.141ff.; R.Kalivoda, 'Joannes Wyclifs Metaphysik des extremen Realismus und ihre Bedeutung im Endstadium der mittelalterlichen Philosophie', in

MISCELLANEA MEDIAEVALIA II, ed. P.Wilpert, 1963, 716-24; Farr, *Wyclif*, 7ff. – de Boor, op.cit., esp.67ff., points to the central significance of a rational understanding of order for Wyclif's concept of the church.

257. In this sense Wyclif quotes John 10.36: *Non potest solvi Scriptura quem Pater sanctificavit et misit in mundum*, with the masculine relative pronoun, cf. Hurley, op.cit., 295.

258. Cf. Benrath, *ZTK* 62, 200f.; Wyclif already presented these principles in his *Principium*, his theological inaugural lecture, cf. B.Smalley, 'Wyclif's Postilla on the Old Testament and his Principium', in *Oxford Studies presented to D.Callus OP*, 1964, (254-96) 278ff., 291; Benrath, *Bibelkommentar*, 48ff.

259. Benrath, *Bibelkommentar*, 316f.

260. E.g. the Pauline doctrine of justification; Benrath, op.cit., 263, points out 'that gospel and law are not dialectically contrasted but held together in a synthesis', and observes, op.cit., 265: 'Wyclif did not penetrate to the centre of Pauline theology.'

261. Cf. also Benrath, *ZTK* 62,202. – G.H.Tavard, 'Holy Church or Holy Writ: A Dilemma of the Fourteenth Century', *CH* 23, 1954, 193-206, shows the rift between the authority of scripture and the authority of the church which was gradually emerging in the fourteenth century. Cf. id., *Holy Writ or Holy Church*, 1959. – A subsidiary line in Wyclif's argument is the question in *De civili dominio* (in which he follows an Augustinian doctrinal tradition communicated by R.Fitzralph, cf. Daly, op.cit., 89ff.), that as men laden with sin have lost the right to rule, the sinful clergy are to be dispossessed; cf. Daly, op.cit., 73ff.; etc.

262. Here he follows the scholastic-Augustinian school, cf. Loofs, *Leitfaden*, 530f.; also Benrath, *Bibelkommentar*, 320f. It follows from his 'rational supranaturalism' that his system has a strict doctrine of predestination. It is well known that in this respect he is dependent on Thomas Bradwardine (for him cf. above all H.A.Oberman, *Archbishop Thomas Bradwardine, a Fourteenth Century Augustinian*, 1957); cf. F.J.Laun, 'Thomas von Bradwardin, der Schüler Augustins und der Lehrer Wiclifs', *ZKG* 47, 1928, 333-56; id., 'Die Prädestination bei Wiclif und Bradwardin', in *Imago Dei, Festgabe G.Krüger*, ed. H.Bornkamm, 1932, 63-84; Robson, op.cit., passim, and thus on the Ockhamite tradition.

263. For this see H.Fürstenau, *Johann von Wiclif's Lehren von der Einteilung der Kirche und von der Stellung der weltlichen Gewalt*, 1900; Daly, op.cit., 85f. (the relevant Wyclif quotations); H.Kaminsky, 'Wyclifism as Ideology of Revolution', *ChH* 32, 1963, 57-74; Farr, *Wyclif*.

264. Daly, op.cit., 81ff.

265. German-Latin edition by W.Kunzmann and H.Kusch, two vols, 1958; for the content cf. especially the Introduction, XXV, and E.Emerton, *The Defensor Pacis of Marsiglio of Padua*, 1920; H.Segall, *Der Defensor pacis des Marsilius von Padua*, 1959 (on this see S.Krüger, *HZ* 180, 1955, 660f.).

266. Mention should also be made of William of Ockham, cf. M.A.Schmidt, 'Kirche und Staat bei Wilhelm von Ockham', *TZ* 7, 1951, 265-84; R.Scholz, *Wilhelm von Ockham als politischer Denker*, ²1952. Wyclif is directly indebted to the teaching of Richard Fitzralph, Bishop of Armagh, cf. his *De pauperie salvatoris* (partial publication in Wyclif's *De dominio divino*, ed. R.L.Poole, 1890, reprinted 1966); cf. also Daly, op.cit., 89f. However, the similarity with Marsilius too is so great that Emerton, op.cit., 78-80, has thought that in writing his works Wyclif had the *Defensor pacis* open on the table.

267. Cf. esp. *De officio regis*, 226: *quilibet Christianus ubicunque fuerit formatus, fide scripture habet Christum sibi assistentem, et sine alio papa vel conversante episcopo sufficiens ad salutem*.

268. Cf. Kaminsky, op.cit., 64; E.Tatnall, *JEH*, 1969, has shown how strongly Wyclif refers back to special English traditions for the role of the king in state and

church and also for other questions connected with their relationship, cf. also Farr, *Wyclif*, passim.

269. Cf. Kaminsky, op.cit., 65; Farr, *Wyclif*, 70ff.

270. Cf. *De civili dominio* 1, 118: *Ad primum suppono ex fide quod Christus instituit unam legem, que est Vetus et Novum Testamentum ad ecclesiam catholicam regulandum.*

271. Ibid., 125; Farr, *Wyclif*, 120ff.

272. Cf. McFarlane, op.cit., 101; cf. also Stacey, *Wyclif*, 128. There is an interesting reference to the circulation of Wyclif's ideas among the Lollards through collections of sermon material in manuscript form in A.Hudson, 'A Lollard Compilation and the Dissemination of Wycliffite Thought', *JTS* NS 23, 1972, 65-81.

273. Cf. McFarlane, op.cit., 105ff.; McKisack, op.cit., 517ff.

274. Cf. A.G.Dickens, *Lollards and Protestants in the Diocese of York, 1509-1558*, 1959; id., 'Heresy and the Origins of English Protestantism', in *Britain and the Netherlands*, ed. J.S.Bromley and E.H.Kossman, 1964, 44-67; id., *The English Reformation*, 1964, 26ff.; M.E.Aston, 'Lollardy and Sedition, 1381-1431', in *PaP* 17, 1960, 1-44; id., 'Lollardy and the Reformation: Survival or Revival', *Hist* 49, 1964, 149-70; J.A.F. Thomson, *The Later Lollards, 1414-1520*, 1965; C.Hill, 'From Lollards to Levellers: Rebels and Their Causes', in *Essays in Honour of A.L.Morton*, ed. M.Cornforth, 1978, 49-67.

275. With the exception of the first usable English translation of the Bible which they completed; cf. S.L.Fristedt, *The Wycliffe Bible, Part I*, Stockholm Studies in English 4, 1953; II, Stockholm Studies 21, 1969; D.C.Fowler, 'John Trevisa and the English Bible', *MPh* 58, 1960, 81-98; C.Lindberg (ed.), *MS Bodley 959. Genesis to Baruch 3,20 in the Earlier Version of the Wycliffite Bible*, vols I-V, Stockholm Studies in English, 1959-69. The edition by J.Forshall and J.Madden, *The Holy Bible: made from the Latin Vulgate by John Wycliffe*, four vols, 1850, was reprinted in 1971.

276. D.Kurze, 'Die festländischen Lollarden', *AKuG* 47, 1965, (48-76) 48, asserts that one can still discover most about them in I.L.von Mosheim. The external information is also in McFarlane, op.cit., 121ff.; Stacey, op.cit., 128ff., and in the earlier literature, Trevelyan, op.cit., 291-352; Workman, op.cit., II, 325-404.

277. Some titles in Workman, op.cit., II, 392.

278. For the earlier places of publication cf. Workman, op.cit., II, 391 n.2. Original Middle English text in H.S.Cronin, 'The Twelve Conclusions of the Lollards', *EHR* 22, 1907, 292-304.

279. Cf. Workman, op.cit., II, 390f.

280. Cf. also Workman, op.cit., II, 396 (not quite complete).

281. Cf. the confession of a certain William Aylward, in McFarlane, op.cit., 184f.

282. Cf. the themes enumerated by C.Hill, 'From Lollards to Levellers' (n.275 above).

2. Erasmus

1. For the writings of Erasmus we are still largely dependent on the monumental edition of the *Opera Omnia*, ed. J.Clericus, Leiden 1703-06 (reprinted 1961-62 = LB); it was a significant achievement in its time, but it is uncritical. The literature often quotes the *Ausgewählte Werke*, ed. H. and A.Holborn, 1933 (reprinted 1964 = H). Of the new critical edition of the *Opera Omnia*, Amsterdam 1969ff., Vols I, 1-I, 5 + II, 5-6 + IV, 1-3 + V, 1 have so far appeared (1971ff. = K). The *Opus epistolarum*, ed. P.S.Allen et al., 1906-57 (= Allen) is comprehensive. Cf. also the selection *Briefe, verdeutscht und herausgegeben*, ed. W.Köhler, 1938, third edition, nd., ed. A.Flitner (Preface 1956). There are also individual editions, *Diatribe de libero arbitrio*, ed. J.v.Walter, ²1935; *Vom freien Willen*, verdeutscht von O.Schuhmacher (1940), ²1956; *Opuscula*, ed. W.K.Ferguson, 1933; *Inquisitio De Fide*, ed. C.R.Thompson, 1950; *Enchiridion*,

ed.W.Welzig, 1961. Also *Ausgewählte Schriften*, Latin and German, ed. W.Welzig, 1967-80 (8 vols. = W: the German translation is not always reliable). For the writings of Erasmus cf. also *Bibliotheca Erasmiana*, ed. F.van der Haeghen, ten vols, 1897-1915.

2. J.B.Payne, 'Toward the Hermeneutics of Erasmus', in SCRINIUM ERAS-MIANUM, II, 1969 (see the next note), (13-29)·16.

3. Cf. e.g. J.C.Margolin, *Douze années de bibliographie érasmienne (1950-1961)*, 1963; id., *Quatorze Années de la Bibliographie érasmienne, 1936-1949*, 1968. There is an extensive but in no way complete bibliography in particular in E.W.Kohls, *Die Theologie der Erasmus*, two vols, 1966, Vol.II, 137-74. Cf. also SCRINIUM ERAS-MIANUM, two vols, 1969, Vol.II, 621-78 (despite its length, this too is not complete!; cf. the prefatory remark, 621). Cf. also C.Augustijn, 'Erasmus, Desiderius (1466/9-1536)', *TRE* 10, 1982, 1-18 (bibliography 15-18). As this is not intended to be a monograph on Erasmus, I had to limit the quotation of literature.

4. Closer attention has been paid only in recent years to Erasmus' exegetical life work and his hermeneutical presuppositions. H.Schlingensiepen, 'Erasmus als Ex-eget auf Grund seiner Schriften zu Matthäus', *ZKG* 48, 1929, 16-57, dealt exclusively with the annotations to this Gospel, but in so doing investigated material that was typical of him. O.Kuss, 'Über die Klarheit der Schrift. Historische und hermeneu-tische Überlegungen zu der Kontroverse des Erasmus und des Luther über den freien und versklavten Willen', in *Schriftauslegung. Beiträge zur Hermeneutik des Neuen Testaments und im Neuen Testament*, ed. J.Ernst, 1972, 89-149, limits himself to this famous debate. One of the most significant recent contributions to discussing these problems is the article by J.B.Payne, mentioned above. Cf. also L.Bouyer, 'Erasmus in Relation to the Medieval Biblical Tradition', in G.W.H.Lampe (ed.), *The Cambridge History of the Bible*, 1969, II, 492-505; J.Coppens, 'Erasme exégète et théologien', *ETL* 44, 1968, 191-204; C.S.Meyer, 'Erasmus on the Study of Scriptures', *CTM* 40, 1969, 734-46; J.W.Aldridge, *The Hermeneutics of Erasmus*, 1966 (unfortunately unsat-isfactory); D.Harth, *Philologie und praktische Philosophie. Untersuchungen zum Sprach-und Traditionsverständnis des Erasmus von Rotterdam*, 1970, and (starting from the *Ratio*, but pressing on to fundamental insights into Erasmus' exegetical approach), M.Hoffmann, *Erkenntnis und Verwirklichung der wahren Theologie nach Erasmus von Rotterdam*, 1972. Cf. also H.Holeczek, *Humanistische Bibelphilologie als Reformproblem bei Erasmus von Rotterdam, Thomas More und William Tyndale*, 1975; A.Rabil, Jr, *Erasmus and the New Testament: The Mind of a Christian Humanist*, 1972, esp. 99ff.

5. Because of its limited foundation in the sources and its one-sided perspective Kohls, *Theologie*, does not satisfy this demand, cf. especially the review by O.Schot-tenloher, *ARG* 58, 1967, 250-7. However, the author's later work on this theme, especially *Luther oder Erasmus* I, 1972, II, 1978, must be taken into account for a balanced judgment. Cf. Schottenloher, op.cit., 257: 'Now of course it is the case that Erasmus hitherto has been wickedly neglected by theological literature.' In recent years Roman Catholic authors in particular have rediscovered him. One example of this, with a good description of Erasmus' basic Spiritualist position, is the study by J.Etienne, *Spiritualisme érasmien et théologiens louvainistes*, 1956, 3ff.

6. For a history of scholarship cf. Kohls, *Theologie*, 1ff. Van Gelder, *Reformations*, 173, still comments: 'Thus Erasmus, more than any other author, made important contributions to the spreading both of the "major" and the "minor" Reformation of the 16th century.' A more intensive observer of the religious development of Eras-mus, A.Renaudet (cf. above all his *Études Érasmiennes*, 1939, and his summary article, 'Le message humaniste et chrëtien d'Érasme', in *Sodalitas Erasmiana I, Il valore universale dell'umanesimo*, 1950, 44-53) speaks of a 'théologie moderne… essen-tiellement fondée sur le Nouveau Testament', and adds, 'Elle réduit la croyance à une essence très pure de spiritualisme évangelique', *Sodalitas* I, 51). 'Erasmian modernism' is characterized above all by a markedly sceptical attitude towards

theology and institutions of the church. For criticism of Renaudet cf. above all L.Bouyer, *Autour d'Érasme*, 1955, 95-135.

7. Kohls, *Theologie*, 140, 166, 189; and the review by Schottenloher, op.cit., and Payne, op.cit., 17 n.17. Cf. also Kohl's more recent positions, e.g. in *Luther oder Erasmus*; id., 'Die theologische Position und der Traditionszusammenhang des Erasmus mit dem Mittelalter in *De libero arbitrio*', in *Festschrift W.von Loewenich*, 1968, 32-46.

8. E.g. L.Bouyer, *Erasme*; G.Gebhardt, *Die Stellung des Erasmus von Rotterdam zur römischen Kirche*, 1966 (for a critique cf. C.Augustijn, 'The Ecclesiology of Erasmus', in SCRINIUM, II, (135-55) 136f.; C.J. de Vogel, 'Erasmus and the Church Dogma', in SCRINIUM II, 101-32. The pros and cons are discussed in J.Coppens, 'Erasmus, vrijzinnige of rechtzinnige theoloog', in *Erasmus plechtig herdacht*, 1969, 5-39.

9. In particular, the well-known biography by J.Huizinga, *Erasmus*, 1923: German 1928, ³ 1941, is written from this perspective; but cf. also P.Mesnard, 'Le Caractère d'Erasme', in *Colloquium Erasmianum*, 1968, 327-32, and e.g the short sketch on his physical constitution and his character in W.P.Eckert, *Erasmus von Rotterdam. Werk und Wirken*, two vols, 1967, Vol.1, 8f.

10. *Epistulae obscurorum virorum*, ed. A.Bömer, 1924, Ep.59. – W.Dilthey, 'Weltanschauung und Analyse des Menschen seit Renaissance und Reformation', *Gesammelte Schriften II*, ⁵1957, 43, seems to see him as a 'demon with a hundred faces'. Luther's comment, *Tischreden* 131 (WA, TR 1, 55,32f.) is also quoted often: 'Erasmus is an eel. No one can catch him but Christ. There are two of him.'

11. As Erasmus was not a systematic theologian but primarily what we would today call a theologically committed writer, we can only talk of his 'system' with a pinch of salt. Nevertheless, a clear theological line can be established in his thought. An attempt to work this out has been made recently above all by M.Hoffmann, *Erkenntnis*.

12. L.W.Spitz, *The Religious Renaissance of the German Humanists*, 1963, 199, observes: 'In his case, more than in that of most intellectuals, the end was present in the beginning so that his development was marked by gradualism and a high degree of consistency.' R.Bainton, 'Continuity of thought of Erasmus', in *American Council of Learned Societies, Newsletter*, XIX, 1968, 1-7, also stresses the unchanged basic attitude of Erasmus.

13. Founded by Geert Groote of Deventer (1340-84); its best known member is probably Thomas a Kempis (1380-1471).

14. Here the most important book has been P.Mestwerdt, *Die Anfänge des Erasmus. Humanismus und 'Devotio Moderna'*, 1917 (reprinted 1971).

15. R.R.Post questions whether the *Devotio Moderna* had any effect on the development of Humanism and especially questions the conjecture that Erasmus was influenced in any way by the brothers in Deventer or positively in s'Hertogenbosch, cf. *The Modern Devotion*, 1968, esp. 658ff. – Cf. already id., 'Erasmus en het Laat-Middeleeuwsche Onderwijs', BVGO 7, 1936, 172-92. – Contrast recently A.Hyma, *The Life of Desiderius Erasmus*, 1972, 17ff. Cf. also J.Henkel, *An Historical Study of the Educational Contributions of the Brethren of the Common Life*, Pittsburgh dissertation 1962, esp. 179-86. J.Tracy, *Erasmus. The Growth of a Mind*, 1972, 28f., argues for a limited but stronger influence of the brothers on Erasmus than Post supposes.

16. Cf. E.Hunt,*Dean Colet and His Theology*, 1956; L.Miles, *John Colet and the Platonic Tradition*, 1961. The biography by J.H.Lupton, *A Life of John Colet*, 1887, ²1909, reprinted 1961, is still basic. Cf. also S.Jayne, *John Colet and Marsilio Ficino*, 1963 (with bibliography); D.Freiday, *The Bible – its Criticism, Interpretation and Use in Sixteenth and Seventeenth Century England*, 1979, 13ff. *The Works, 1873-1876*, ed. Lupton, reprinted 1965-66.

17. This argument is put forward above all by O.Schottenloher, *Erasmus im Ringen*

um die humanistische Bildungsreform, 1933. – But see R.Pfeiffer, 'Erasmus und die Einheit der klassischen und christlichen Renaissance', *HJ* 74, 1955, 175-88 (= id., *Ausgewählte Schriften*, 1960, 208-21). For the significance and character of Colet's influence cf. e.g. F.Seebohm, *The Oxford Reformers: John Colet, Erasmus and Thomas More*, ²1869; K.Bauer, 'John Colet und Erasmus von Rotterdam', in *ARG.E* 5 (FS H. von Schubert), 1929, 155-87; R.Marcel, 'Les "découvertes" d'Érasme en Angleterre', *BHR* 14, 1952, 118-23; G.Santinello, 'Erasmo e Colet', in *Studi sull'umanesimo europeo*, 1969, 77-116. A. Hyma denies that Colet had a decisive influence on Erasmus, cf. 'Erasmus and the Oxford Reformers, 1493-1503', in *BVGO*, 7.R, 7.7, 1936 , 132-54; id., 'Erasmus and the Oxford Reformers (1503-1519)', *NAkG* 38, 1951, 65-86; id., *The Life*, 43ff. R.H.Bainton takes a similar view in his most recent biography, *Erasmus of Christendom*, 1969, 75 (cf. already in 'Continuity', 4f.). J.Tracy, op.cit., 84 n.4, also recalls early evidence on Erasmus' theological concerns from his letters.

18. There is a whole series of Erasmus biographies, some belonging more in the category of belles-lettres. In addition to those already mentioned by Huizinga, Eckert, Bainton and Hyma, *Life*, cf. also R.Newald, *Erasmus Roterodamus*, 1947 (reprinted 1970); P.Smith, *Erasmus*, 1923, reprinted 1962; R.Stupperich, *Erasmus von Rotterdam und seine Welt*, 1977. Cf. also the brief account by C.Augustijn, 'Erasmus von Rotterdam', in *Die Reformationszeit* I, ed. M.Greschat, 1981, 53-75, and his article in *TRE* (n.3 above).

19. For details of the proceedings cf. Bainton, *Erasmus*, ch.VII, 144ff. For the content cf. above all K.H.Oelrich, *Der späte Erasmus und die Reformation*, 1961. Underlying this is a special view of church history to which A.Friesen, 'The Impulse Toward Restitutionist Thought in Christian Humanism', *JAAR* 44, 1976, 29-45 esp. 39ff., has referred; corresponding to the carefully balanced approach of Erasmus, it is two-sided: on the one hand, in his view Christian morality has constantly declined since the time of the early church and is in urgent need of restoration in the spirit of the New Testament and the law of Christ – but on the other hand he also recognizes the hierarchical structure of the church of his time as being necessary and given because of the passage of time, and unlike the Reformation, does not want to overthrow it completely.

20. However, his attitude to early and high scholasticism, and particularly to Thomas Aquinas, differs, cf. C.Dolfen, *Die Stellung des Erasmus von Rotterdam zur scholastischen Methode*, Münster dissertation, 1936.

21. Cf. Kohls, *Luther oder Erasmus* I, 34ff. Erasmus writes at one point (*Ep.* 1700, Allen VI, 328): *Theologiam scholasticam, nimium prolapsam ad sophisticas argutinas, ad fontem divinorum voluminum et ad veterum orthodoxorum lectionem revocavi.*

22. Op.cit., 35.

23. Op.cit., 36.

24. Op.cit., 42ff.

25. Op.cit., 41.

26. As an explicit criticism of Kohls, cf. SCRINIUM I, 17 n.17.

27. *Hermeneutics*, 17ff.; cf. already the significant investigation by A. Auer, *Die vollkommene Frömmigkeit des Christen. Nach dem Enchiridion militis Christiani des Erasmus von Rotterdam*, 1954, 64ff.

28. Erasmus describes it in the Canon quintus of his *Enchiridion* (LB V, col.27, D-E; W 1, 180f.; H, 67).

29. The tripartite division into *spiritus, anima* and *caro* already occurs in the title of Ch.VII of the *Enchiridion*; Erasmus finds it in Origen and thinks that he is following Paul (*libet et Origenicam hominis sectionem breviter referre. Is enim Paulum secutus, tres partes facit, spiritum, animam et Carnem...*; LB V, Col.19 A; W I, 138; H, 52). Occasionally Erasmus is also uncertain whether man should be understood dichotomistically or trichotomistically, cf. *Enchiridion*, Ch.IV, beginning: *Est igitur homo*

prodigiosum quoddam animal, ex duabus tribusve partibus multo diversissimis compactum...(LB V, col.11, E-F; W I, 108; H, 41). For Erasmus' anthropology see most recently esp. Hoffmann, *Erkenntnis*, 147ff.

30. LB V, col.11 E-F; W 1, 182; H, 39.

31. Cf. above, 423 n.97. Also Auer, *Die vollkommene Frömmigkeit des Christen*, 1954, 69, recalls these parallels.

32. It is uncertain how far Erasmus (by way of Colet) was specially influenced by the Platonist Renaissance philosophers (an exaggerated view of this is taken by J.Pusino, 'Der Einfluss Picos auf Erasmus', *ZKG* 46, 1928, 75-96); it is more probable that the Platonist influence comes through reading the church fathers, cf. Payne, *Hermeneutics*, 18f.

33. However, this is not to be interpreted in Gnostic terms as hostile to the body, cf. Auer, op.cit., 66ff.; Payne, op.cit., 21f.; W.Hentze, *Kirche und kirchliche Einheit bei Desiderius Erasmus von Rotterdam*, 1974, 25ff.

34. Given his scriptural theology it is remarkable that Erasmus refers first of all to Paul, whom he mentions in agreement with Plato. Cf. *Enchiridion*, Ch. VI (LB V, col.15; F; W I, 126; H, 47): *Iam vero philosophorum levis sit auctoritas, nisi eadem omnia, tametsi verbis non iisdem, sacris in litteris praecipiuntur.* Payne, op.cit., 20, however, also points to statements according to which Erasmus recognizes the greater anthropological unity in Paul: 'However, he does not seem to grasp the intimate psychosomatic unity of Paul, because he reads Paul with Platonic glasses.' Bainton, *Erasmus*, 63, also regards a Neoplatonic interpretation of Paul as being possible.

35. Cf. Payne, op.cit., 24f. A.Rabil, *Erasmus*, esp.100ff., points out that in Erasmus allegorical exegesis gradually fades into the background in favour of grammatical interpretation.

36. Erasmus refers at the end of his *Apology* to L.Valla and J.Faber (LB VI, unpaginated; W III, 114; H, 174). Cf. also the preface to his edition of Valla's annotations to the New Testament, in Allen I, 182. Erasmus already called for a return *ad fontes* in the *Epistola de contemptu mundi*: '*Si quid ex ipsis fontibus libet, utriusque testamenti volumina petuntur*' (LB V, col.1260, B). Cf. also Kohls, *Theologie* I, 29. O.Schottenloher, *Erasmus im Ringen um die humanistische Bildungsreform*, 1934, has worked out that in Erasmus the humanistic principle of return to the sources is decisive at this point, though with a shift of emphasis to the Christian church fathers and above all the New Testament. Cf. also his review of Kohls, *Theologie*, in *ARG* 1967, 255f., and C.J. de Vogel, op.cit., 103, 106f.

37. Cf. H, XIV; G.Winkler, Introduction to W III, XVIIIff.

38. Here we have the phrases which are so often quoted: *Optarim, ut omnes, mulierculae legant euangelium, legant paulinas epistolas... Utinam hinc ad stivam aliquid decantet agricola, hinc nonnihil ad radios suos moduletur textor, huiusmodi fabulis itineris taedium lenet viator* (W III, 14). It has been rightly pointed out that here sacred simplicity is celebrated with the most artistic methods of Latin rhetoric, Winkler, Introduction to W III, XXV.

39. *Erasmus von Rotterdam*, ²1948, 206ff.

40. Cf. W III, 38ff. This passage was published as early as 1518 as an extended *Ratio verae theologiae* (LB V, cols.75ff.; W III, 117ff.; H,175ff.; L).

41. Cf. Winkler, Introduction to W III, XXIff.

42. Cf. also Kohls, *Erasmus und Luther*, 37ff.

43. The most famous evidence for this pedagogical concern is the *Enchiridion militis Christiani*, the aim of which is also reported in the letter to Paul Volz (prefaced to the edition of 1518; cf. now also W I, 2ff.). A. Friesen, *JAAR* 1976, esp. 34ff., rightly stresses that the moral reform of humanity is one of the main aims of Christian humanism and demonstrates this above all by means of Erasmus.

44. Cf. above, 35f.

45. Quotations in Kohls, 'Die Bedeutung literarischer Überlieferung bei Erasmus', *AKuG* 48, 1966, (219-33) 226f., and in Payne, op.cit., 28 nn.85, 86. For Erasmus' 'Christocentrism' cf. also Hoffmann, *Erkenntnis*, esp. 59ff.

46. *Frömmigkeit*, 103ff.; cf. also Kohls, *Theologie* I, 106ff. (but cf. the following note); de Vogel, op.cit., 119ff.; Payne, op.cit., 29 n.87, gives a few instances of the earlier version.

47. On the other hand Kohls, op.cit., has excessively exaggerated 'the central significance of the cross of Christ for salvation' (op.cit., 107).

48. Cf. Payne, op.cit., 29: 'For Luther Christ means essentially *Gabe*, for Erasmus both *Gabe* und *Aufgabe*, but with the stress upon the latter.'

49. As this is the best known theme of Reformation history there is an almost impossibly large literature on it. K.Schwarzwäller, *Sibboleth*, 1969, has given an account of judgments on Luther's *De servo arbitrio*. The most objective account of the dispute itself is H.Bornkamm, 'Erasmus und Luther', in *LuJ* 25, 1958, 1-20 = id., *Das Jahrhundert der Reformation*, ²1966, 36-55. Cf. also H.Dörries, 'Erasmus oder Luther', in *Kerygma und Melos*, Festschrift C.Mahrenholz, 1970, 533-70, and Kuss, op.cit.; id., n.26 for further literature. – For the events leading up to the dispute and the basic opposing positions cf. recently also Kohls, *Erasmus und Luther*. Erasmus' two polemical documents in the dispute, *De libero arbitrio* and *Hyperaspistes*, have been newly edited in W IV with an introduction by W.Leskowsky.

50. This holds even more generally for the propaedeutic function which Erasmus alredy assigns to philosophy in the *Antibarbari*; cf. Kohls, *Theologie*, 35ff. The text of the *Antibarbari* is now also in K I, 1ff. There are unmistakable remarks in this direction in the *Paraclesis*: While Erasmus first of all emphatically rejects the desire to compare Christ with Zeno or Aristotle ('*Certe solus hic e coelo profectus est doctor, solus certa docere potuit*', LB V, col.139 D; W III, 10), he can soon afterwards continue, '*Quid autem aliud est Christi philosophia, quam ipse renascentiam vocat, quam instauratio bene conditae naturae?*' (LB V, col.141 F; W III, 22), and point out that much of this can also be found in the books of the heathen. Here he goes on to mention the Stoics in first place, but also Socrates, Aristotle, Epicurus, Diogenes and Epictetus. All this eventually leads him back with no problem to the teaching of Christ (LB V, col.142; W III, 24). Erasmus explains himself even more clearly in the *Convivium religiosum* (which was first inserted into the *Colloquia* in 1522). After a quotation from Cicero, who is making Cato speak, we find: '*Hactenus Cato. Quid ab homine Christiano dici potuit sanctius?*' (LB I, col.682 C; W VI, 80 – the German translation omits the decisive sentence; K I, 3, 252). And later, on the last words of Plato's Socrates: '*Proinde quum huiusmodi quaedam lego de talibus viris, vix mihi tempero, quin dicam: sancte Socrates, ora pro nobis*' (LB I, col. 683 D-E; W VI, 86; K I, 3, 254). However, we should not overlook the rhetorical and artificial character of this appeal. Cf. also C.Augustijn, *Ecclesiology*, 148-51, on the extent and limitations of this approach.

51. Review of Kohls, *Theologie*, ARG 1967, 253ff.; cf. also Payne, op.cit., 30f.; Hoffmann, *Erkenntnis*, esp. 120ff.; also G.Kisch, *Erasmus und die Jurisprudenz seiner Zeit*, 1960. A comment by Luther from his *Table Talk*, *Erasmus nil facit cum sua theologia, quam quod Christum iuristam facit* (WA, TR 2, no.1605), is interesting because it is so acute.

52. Cf. *Enchiridion*, Ch.VIII, Can.I (LB V, col.21 F-22A; W I, 152); *Symbolum* (LB V, col.1135E-1136C); *Eccles.* (LB V, Col. 1078B-D). J.-C.Margolin, *L'idée de nature dans la pensée d'Erasme*, 1967; id., *Erasmus, Declaratio de pueris statim ac liberaliter instituendis. Etude critique*, 1966, has recently given a detailed account of the role played by the concept of nature in the Stoic sense, above all in Erasmus' educational writings. – Cf. also O.Schottenloher, 'Lex naturae und Lex Christi', in SCRINIUM II, 253-99.

53. Instances in Auer, *Frömmigkeit*, 103ff., who finds agreement here with Catholic teaching generally and identifies himself with it. – Kohls, *Theologie* I, 69f., interprets

the conception of law and grace which is already present in the *Epistola de contemptu mundi* and then in the *Antibarbari*; here human responsibility is already taken up into the 'view determined by salvation history', and freedom of decision is understood as 'will liberated by grace'. This seems to be an almost precise definition of the connection of Gabe and Aufgabe, but the decisive nuance has too much of a Reformation tone. Schottenloher, *Lex naturae*, 278: 'For Erasmus this concern was not the law but the rule of the spirit, which now took the law into itself.'

54. Auer, op.cit., 118f. The influence of mysticism after the fashion of Bernard is clear; cf. Winkler, Introduction to W III, XXIII; also de Vogel, op.cit., 123: 'It has two aspects: the one is in man's moral character, in his actions and his mentality; the other is a kind of mysticism – if "mystic" is having an inner experience of the Presence of God.' This is also matched by the understanding of the term *lex*. O. Schottenloher puts it like this: 'Erasmus' conception was theological and not conceived in terms of natural law. The *lex Christi* was not legalistic...': 'Lex naturae und lex Christi', in SCRINIUM II, 289.

55. Payne, op.cit., 48 n.193, quotes in this context two views from the exegesis of the Psalms: 1. on Ps.1: *...vel quod ea melius quadret, vel quod magis conducat ad vitae correctionem, quam praecipue spectamus* (LB V, col.174 A-B), 2. on Ps.14: *Nos tamen in praesentia maluimus tractare sensum moralem, qui, licet videatur humilior, est tamen, meo iudicio, utilior* (LB V, col. 301 B). – Cf. further Rabil, *Erasmus*, 100ff.

56. Cf. *Enchiridion*, Ch.VII, can.IV (LB V, 25B; W I, 168; H, 63): *Christum vero esse puta non vocem inanem, sed nihil aliud quam caritatem, simplicitatem, patientiam, puritatem, breviter quicquid ille docuit... Ad Christum tendit, qui ad solam virtutem fertur.* Schlingensiepen has already established a preference for the Gospels and in them for the discourses of Jesus by means of the Matthew paraphrase; from the preface he quotes the paraphrase where Erasmus says that when he is dealing with the letters of the apostles he is still dealing with men, but in the Gospels with the majesty of Christ, op.cit., 24 and n.3. Cf. also *Ratio* (LB V, 84A; H, 193; W III, 170): *Illud mea sententia magis ad rem pertinuerit, ut tirunculo nostro dogmata tradantur in summam ac compendium redacta, idque potissimum ex euangelicis fontibus, mox apostolorum litteris.* Or at another point (LB V, col.105D; H, 236f.; W III, 294): *conveniet ad omnes vitae actiones exemplum ac formam e divinis libris venari, praecipue vero ex euangeliis, e quibus potissimum nostra ducuntur officia.*

57. For example in the *Ratio* there is a long section (inserted in 1520) in which Erasmus considers *quemadmodum ad magistri formam apostolorum vita doctrinaque respondeat* and here deals in the first place with Paul, who, through his capacity to adapt to the brethren, his meekness, and also his attitude to rites and 'superstition' appears as the embodiment of the ideal of piety put forward by Erasmus (LB V, col.98 F; H, 223ff.; W III, 258). The *Enchiridion* was essentially written because of Erasmus' concern with Paul which was stimulated by Colet's lectures on him. Cf. the letter of dedication (*Epistles* 164, Allen I, 374f.) and M.Bataillon, *Erasme et l'Espagne*, 1937, 221, who refers to the significance of the Pauline simile of one body and many members. Erasmus comments on the letters of Paul: *Paulus autem Apostolus post Christum fontes quosdam aperuit allegoriarum, quem secutus Origenes, in hac parte theologiae facile primatum obtinet.* Cf. H.de Lubac, *Exégèse* II, 2, 439 n.3 (unfortunately without references). For the significance of the Gospels and apostolic writings for Erasmus as a basic theme in the *Paraclesis* because of the *philosophia Christi* they contain, cf. J.Etienne, *Spiritualisme*, 18ff.

58. Cf. Kohls, *Theologie* I, 145.

59. J. Savignac, in *Le Monde*, 2 August 1969, V, quoted by J.Coppens, 'Où en est le portrait d'Erasme?', in SCRINIUM II, (569-87) 583 n.72.

60. *Paraphr. in Rom.* 8.3; LB VII, col.556 B.

61. Cf. Krüger, *Bucer und Erasmus*, 1970, 69ff.

62. *Imo adeo non abolemus Legem aut labefactamus, ut eam etiam confirmemus, stabiliam-usque, id praedicantes factum, quod Lex futurum promiserat, eumque nuntiantes, in quem ceu scopum Legis spectabat, Paraphr. in Rom.*3.31; LB VII, col. 787 E. Cf. also Krüger, op.cit., 70f.

63. There is still no accurate study of the discussion of the Old Testament in Erasmus; provisionally cf. Lubac, op.cit., 427-53.

64. *Enchiridion*, Ch.VIII, can.V, LB V, col. 28 E; H, 69; W I, 186; cf. already the beginning of Canon V: *'Addamus quintam regulam..., ut in hoc uno constituas perfectam pietatem, si coneris semper a rebus visibilibus...ad invisibilia proficere iuxta superiorem hominis divisionem'* (LB V, col.27 D; H, 67; W I, 180). A. Auer, op.cit., 80ff., has described this statement as the 'principle of Christian piety' which Erasmus puts in the centre.

65. LB V, col.29A-B; H, 70; W I, 188. – H.C.Porter, 'The Nose of Wax: Scripture and the Spirit from Erasmus to Milton', *THS* 5, Ser.14, 1964, 155-74, has demonstrated how the division between *spiritus* and *littera* in Erasmus has had an effect on English theological understanding of the Bible down as far as Milton.

66. LB V, col.29 C; H, 70; W I, 190.

67. LB V, col 29D-E; H, 71; W I, 192 (the German translation distorts the whole meaning by separating the last phrase and making it an independent sentence!).

68. LB V, col.86 F; H, 199; W III, 184.

69. Cf. Lubac, op.cit., 444.

70. There is such an evaluation e.g. in the *Ratio* (in a passage inserted in 1520): *'Apud me certe plus habet ponderis Isaias quam Iudith aut Ester, plus euangelium Matthaei quam Apocalypsis inscripta Joanni, plus epistolae Pauli ad Romanos et Corinthios quam epistola scripta ad Hebraeos'* (LB V, cols 92 C-D; H, 211; W III, 222). Here Erasmus characteristically refers to Augustine (*De doctrina Christiana* II, 8; PL 34,40f.).

71. Therefore an emphatic demonstration of this orthodoxy, as e.g. that by L.Spitz, 224ff., by-passes the heart of this problem.

72. LB V, col.30 D; H, 73; W I, 196.

73. LB V, col.35 E; H, 82; W I, 222.

74. Therefore Erasmus can comment on Matt.5.17 with conviction: *Nequaquam in hoc veni, quo vel Legem reddam dilutiorem, vel abrogem novis praeceptis. Quin potius ideo veni, ut Legem absolvam ac perficiam. Paraph.in Mt.* 5.17, LB VII, col. 28D. For the whole passage see Krüger, 69ff.

75. Cf. *Enchiridion*, Ch.VIII, Can.V; LB V, col.30 B; H, 73; W I, 194.

76. Cf. *Enchiridion*, Ch.VIII, Can.V; LB V, col.35 D-E; H, 82; W I, 222: *Totus in hoc est Paulus, ut caro, quae contentiosa est, contemnatur et in spiritu, qui caritatis et libertatis est auctor, nos constituat.* There are countless similar remarks in adjacent passages. Erasmus refers here e.g. to Rom.8.1ff. (LB V, col.33 E; H, 78; W I, 212).

77. *Superstitio Iudaeorum*: LB V, col. 36B; H, 83; W I, 224; the opposite here is *apostolorum regula; Iudaicae superstitiones*; LB V, col.36 A; H, 83; W I, 224; etc. Whereas for Gerson the term *superstitio* only denoted obvious abuses (cf. *Oeuvres complètes*, ed. Glorieux, 1960, I, 137, 217), Erasmus extends the concept to the whole of worship. For the whole question see also Tracy, op.cit., 95ff.

78. *Ceremonia Judaica*: LB V, col. 38 D; H, 88; W 1, 238.

79. Cf. e.g Auer, op.cit., 157ff.; 173ff.; etc. Lubac, op.cit., 445 n.5.

80. *Quid igitur faciet Christianus? Negliget ecclesiae mandata? contemnet honestas maiorum traditiones? damnabit pias consuetudines? Immo si infirmus est, servabit ut neces-sarias, sin firmus et perfectus, tanto magis observabit, ne sua scientia fratrem offendat infirmum et occidat eum... Non damnantur opera corporalia, sed praeferuntur invisibilia. Non damnatur cultus visibilis, sed non placatur deus nisi pietate invisibili* (LB V, col.37 B-C; H, 85; W I, 230). Similarly also in the Colloquium *Convivium religiosum* (1522): *Dicam... me non damnare, imo vehementer probare sacramenta et ritus ecclesiae; sed quosdam*

vel improbos vel superstitiosos, vel, ut mollissime dicam, simplices et indoctos, qui docent populum hisce rebus fidere, praetermissis his, quae nos vere reddunt Christianos (K I, 3, 255; W VI, 86f.).

81. LB V, col.32E; H, 76; W I, 206.

82. LB V, col.32C; H and W I, op.cit.

83. Op.cit., 155; cf. also 151: 'It is impossible not to recognize the consistent realism of Erasmus in this question. He was unrealistic in respect of man and his constant, factitious move towards the incorporation of the spiritual and the divine.' However, he is right in saying: 'Through the incarnation the law of incorporealization is elevated with supreme impressiveness to the generally valid basic law of salvation.'

84. Cf. Bainton, *Erasmus*, 69: 'But despite all diversionary tactics his main thrust was towards making the external forms of religion superfluous.'

85. Huizinga, *Erasmus*, 197ff., depicts the return of Erasmus to conservatism in his later years, as does Bainton, op.cit., 305: 'Indisputably his tone changed.' However, Erasmus did not give up his Spiritualism as a result; Bainton, op.cit., 310ff., shows from the Freiburg writings that Erasmus generally remained true: 'A shift of emphasis they do indeed disclose, but they so far repeat the teaching of a lifetime that one finds them at times somewhat repetitious', op.cit., 326. Basically, 'All breathe the spirit of the *Enchiridion*', op.cit., 319.

86. To John Colet, *Ep.* 181, Allen I, 405. – Cf. also Tracy, *Erasmus*, 90.

87. They are published in two new editions: K I, 3, 1972; a selection in W VI (1967).

88. *De votis temere susceptis*, K I, 3, 147ff.

89. *Naufragium*, K I, 3, 325ff.; cf. also Bainton, *Erasmus*, 220ff.

90. ΙΧΘΥΟΦΑΓΙΑ, K I, 3, 495ff.; W VI, 314ff. – Cf. also Bainton, op.cit., 259f.

91. K I, 3, 221f., 231-66; W VI, 20ff. Cf. above 441 n.80.

92. K I, 3, Introduction, 9; cf. E.Guttmann, *Die Colloquia familiaria des Erasmus von Rotterdam*, 1968, 149, 161.

93. Cf. e.g. LB V, col. 106F; H, 239; W III, 302: '*Evolve testamentum omne novum, nihil usquam reperies praeceptum, quod ad caerimonias pertinet. Ubi de cibis aut veste verbum ullum? Ubi de inedia aut similibus ulla mentio? Solam caritatem suum praeceptum vocat. Ex caerimoniis oriuntur dissidia, e caritate pax.*' Or LB V, col. 113 A-B; H, 252; W III, 336: '*Non probo vero, quod humanis constitutionibus tota paene Christianorum vita caerimoniis oneratur; quod his nimium tribuitur, pietati minimum.*' Cf. also Etienne, *Spiritualisme*, 27f. For Erasmus' anticeremonialism cf. also Tracy, *Erasmus*, 90ff.; H.Treinen, *Studien zur Idee der Gemeinschaft bei Erasmus von Rotterdam und zu ihrer Stellung in der Entwicklung des humanistischen Universalismus*, 1955, 92ff.

94. G.B. Winkler, Introduction to W III, XXXVIII; cf. also ibid., 239 n.142.

95. I mention only *Enchiridion*, Can. V (LB V, col.33 C; H, 7; W I, 210): '*ut pro Christiano sis Iudaeus, mutis tantum elementis serviens... Quod si in spiritu ambulasti, non in carne, ubi fructus spiritus?*' Ibid. (LB V, col. 33 D; H, 78; W I, 212): '*...quod olim in baptismo iurasti te Christianum, hoc est spiritalem, non Iudaeum futurum?*' It should be noted that these remarks are made in a context where Erasmus is explicitly referring to Paul, Rom.8.1ff. Cf. also the evidence quoted on p. 441 nn.77,78.

96. LB V, col. 95 B- 96; H, 216ff.; W III, 236ff.

97. *Gens sceleratissima Iudaeorum et pertinaciter rebellis* (LB V, col. 97 F; H, 222; W III, 252); cf. also: *Noverat suae gentis duritiem Christus* (LB V, col. 95 C; H, 216; W III,236); and in the *Convivium religiosum*: '*Iudaeos autem aversatur Deus, non quod observarent legis ritus, sed quod his stulte tumidi, negligerent ea, quae Deus maxime vult praestari a nobis; ac madentes avaritia, superbia, rapinis, odio, livore, ceterisque vitiis, existimabant Deum ipsi multum debere, quod diebus festis versarentur in Templo, quod immolarent victimas, quod abstinerent a cibis vetitis, quod illi nonnumquam ieiunarent; umbras amplectebantur, rem negligebant*' (K I, 3, 246; W VI, 64).

98. See previous note.

99. *'Quomodo Deus aversetur sacrificia, docet ipse nos apud Esaiam cap.I'* (K I, 3, 246; W VI, 62). Cf. also *Paraphr. in Matt.* LB VII, 54 D. It emerges from this statement that the authority of the prophetic books is unbroken for Erasmus, even in non-christological matters. Cf. also 441 n.70.

100. K I, 3, 246; W VI, 61f. The passage is cited in the light of Matt.9.12f. Cf. also K I, 3, 247; W VI, 66.

101. LB V, col. 36 C-D; H, 83f.; W I, 226.

102. LB V, cols. 36-7; H, 84ff.; W I, 228ff.

103. *Convivium religiosum*, K I, 3, 247; W VI, 64.

104. K I, 3, 245; W VI, 60. It is no coincidence that here there is mention of *sapiens Hebraeus* and not of *Iudaeus*; however, the saying had a Johannine stamp.

105. *Malim ego incolumi Nouo Testamento vel totum Vetus aboleri quam Christianorum pacem ob Iudaeorum libros rescindi.* To J.Caesarius, 3 November 1517, *Ep.* 701, Allen III, 127.

106. Cf. 51 above.

107. Cf. R.Bainton, 'Erasmus und das "Wesen des Christentums"', in *Festschrift E.Benz*, 1967, 200-6; id., *Erasmus*, 225ff.

108. In Allen V, *Ep.* 1334, 172ff.; extracts in Bainton, *Erasmus*, op.cit.

109. *Ep.* 2134, Allen VIII, 111 line 111.

3. The 'Left Wing of the Reformation'

1. The term was coined by R.Bainton, 'The Left Wing of the Reformation', *JR* 21, 1941, 124-34; revised version in id., *Studies on the Reformation*, 1966, 119-29; cf. already J.McNeill, 'Left Wing Religious Movements', in *A Short History of Christianity*, 1940, 127-32, and has spread widely since then. Cf. e.g. H. Fast (ed.), *Der linke Flügel der Reformation*, 1962. In addition there is also the designation 'radical Reformation'; cf. esp. G.Williams, *The Radical Reformation*, 1962 (there is an extended evaluation of this account by A.Rotondò, 'I movimenti ereticali nell'Europa del Cinquecento', in *Studi e ricerche di storia ereticale Italiana del Cinquecento*, 1974, 5-56).

2. Mention should be made here above all of the edition of the acts of the Anabaptists: G.Bossert (ed.), *Quellen zur Geschichte der Wiedertäufer I: Herzogtum Württemberg*, 1930 (reprinted 1971); K.Schornbaum (ed.), *Quellen zur Geschichte der Wiedertäufer II: Markgrafentum Brandenburg (Bayern, I Abt.)*, 1934 (reprinted 1971); id. (ed.), *Quellen zur Geschichte der Täufer V: Bayern, II. Abt.*, 1951 (reprinted 1971); J.Adam, H.G.Rott, M.Krebs (eds.), *Quellen zur Geschichte der Täufer. Elsass I und II. Stadt Strassburg 1522-1532/1533-1535*, 1959-60; M.Krebs (ed.), *Quellen zur Geschichte der Täufer IV: Baden und Pfalz*, 1951; G.Mecenseffy (ed.), *Österreich I*, 1964; id. (ed.), *Öesterreich II*, 1972; G. Franz, etc. (ed.), *Wiedertäuferakten 1527-1626. Urkundliche Quellen zur hessischen Reformationsgeschichte*, 1951 (Täuferakten Hessen-Waldeck); L.Müller (ed.), Glaubenszeugnisse oberdeutscher Taufgesinnter, 1938 (reprinted 1971); R.Friedmann (ed.), *Glaubenszeugnisse oberdeutscher Taufgesinnter 2*, QGT 12 = QFRG 34, 1967 (but for criticism cf. G.Seebass, *Müntzers Erbe. Werk, Leben und Theologie des Hans Hut [1527]*, Erlangen Habilitationsscrift 1972 [typescript], 153; I am grateful to Herr Seebas for letting me use his own copy); L. v. Muralt, W.Schmid (eds.), *Quellen zur Geschichte der Täufer in der Schweiz*, I, Zurich 1952, ²1974; H.Fast (ed.), *Quellen zur Geschichte der Täufer in der Schweiz*, II, Ostschweiz, 1973; M.Haas (ed.), *Quellen zur Geschichte der Täufer in der Schweiz*, IV, *Drei Täufergespräche*, 1974. The critical new edition of the most important published works by the main representatives of this movement is still, however, in its infancy. With the exception of the writings of Caspar Schwenckfeld (*Corpus Schwenckfeldianorum*, Vols.I-XIX, 1907-1961, not completely critical) mention can be made here only of the works of Hans

Denck, *Schriften*, ed. W.Fellmann (G.Baring), I-III, 1955-1960; B.Hubmaier, *Schriften*, ed. G.Westin and T.Bergsten, 1962; Bernhard Rothmann, *Schriften*, ed. R.Stupperich, 1970, and Thomas Müntzer, *Schriften und Briefe. Kritische Gesamtausgabe*, ed. P.Kirn and G.Franz, 1968 (cf. also S.Bräuer, *LuJ* 38, 1971, 121-31). However, they are an indication that the task in general has been recognized and has been begun. The *Paradoxa* of Sebastian Franck has been edited very idiosyncratically by H.Ziegler, 1909; a New High German version of the edition of 1542 has been produced by H.Wollgast, 1966. The *Chronica, Zeitbuch und Geschichtsbibell*, ²1536, reprinted 1969, and *Das verbütschiert mit sieben Siegeln verschlossene Buch*, 1539, reprinted 1971, is published only as a photomechanical reprint. The planned critical collected edition, ed. J.Benzing and H.Kolb, has not yet appeared (1983). Cf. also the *Kriegsbüchlein des Friedens*, ed. V.Klink, 1929. J.Loserth, *Quellen und Forschungen zur Geschichte der oberdeutschen Taufgesinnten. Pilgram Marbecks Antwort auf Kaspar Schwenckfelds Beurteilung des Buches der Bundesbezeugung*, 1929, is a significant monograph. Cf. also the bibliography by K.Kaczerowski, *Sebastian Franck*, 1976.

3. Mennonite scholarship in Europe and America has made an important contribution here, above all in the *MennQR* edited by H.S.Bender (since 1927); cf. also the Festschrift for Bender: G.F.Hershberger (ed.), *The Recovery of the Anabaptist Vision*, 1957. The German journal is the *MGB* (since 1936). However, here the pendulum is generally swinging too much to the other side and the Anabaptists are being brought too close to the Reformers proper. It will emerge in due course that they had a fundamentally different approach. Unfortunately I had access to the general account by U.Gastaldi, *Storia dell'Anabattismo dalle origine a Münster (1525-1535)*, 1972, only during the final stages of preparing the English version of this book. There are other important general accounts in: C.P.Clasen, *Anabaptism: A Social History, 1525-1618*, 1972 (extracts also in J.M.Stayer/W.O.Packull [eds.], *The Anabaptists and Thomas Muntzer*, 1980, 33-39); R.Friedmann, *The Theology of Anabaptism*, 1973; H.-J.Goertz, *Die Täufer. Geschichte und Deutung*, 1980 (with bibliography). Cf. also W.Schäuffele, *Das missionarische Bewusstsein und Wirken der Täufer*, 1966; Bauman (see below n.7). Bibliography: H.J.Hillerbrand (ed.), *Bibliographie des Täufertums, 1520-1630*, 1962; id., *A Bibliography of Anabaptism, 1520-1630. A Sequel*, 1975. There is also a bibliography of the secondary literature in M.Lienhard (ed.), *The Origins and Characteristics of Anabaptism*, 1977, 231-42. Cf. also G.W.Locher, *Die Zwinglische Reformation im Rahmen der europäischen Kirchengeschichte*, 1979, 236-66.

4. There is a classic account in K.Holl, 'Luther und die Schwärmer', in *Gesammelte Aufsätze zur Kirchengeschichte* I, ²,³1923, 420-64; also F.Heyer, *Der Kirchenbegriff der Schwärmer*, 1939; W.Maurer, 'Luther und die Schwärmer', *STKAB* 6, 1952, 7-37; K.G.Steck, *Luther und die Schwärmer*, 1955.

5. Cf. H.J.Goertz, *Innere und äussere Ordnung in der Theologie Thomas Müntzers*, 1967, 11; in n.4 he refers to the dependence of the verdict on the particular understanding of Luther which the interpreters have.

6. E.Troeltsch, *The Social Teaching of the Christian Churches*, ET 1931, 691ff. Cf. op.cit., 742: 'The Anabaptists formed a community ruled by Christ and composed of genuine saints. The "spiritual reformers" did not recognize a visible church at all, but they looked for the Third Age.' Cf. also id., 'Protestantisches Christentum und Kirche der Neuzeit', in P.Hinnenberg (ed.), *Die Kultur der Gegenwart*, 7.1, Section IV, First Half, ²1909, 504-16. – There is also a similar division in G.Westin, 'Döparrörelsen som forskningsobjekt', *KHÅ* 52, 1952, 52-92; cf. also id., *Der Weg der freien christlichen Gemeinden durch die Jahrhunderte*, 1956, 41ff.; cf. also G.A.Benrath, 'Die Lehre ausserhalb der Konfessionskirchen', in C.Andresen (ed.), *Handbuch der Dogmen- und Theologiegeschichte* 2, 1980, 560ff. (ch. I: Die Lehre der Spiritualisten; ch. II: Die Lehre der Täufer) – K.Holl, op.cit., 424 n.1, has questioned this view: 'There is no Anabaptist movement which is not based on mysticism, however simple.' T.Bergs-

ten, 'Pilgram Marbeck und Caspar Schwenckfeld', *KHÅ* 57, 1957, 39-100; 58, 1958, 53-87; 1957, 43 n.6, observes: 'It is the mistake of both Troeltsch and Holl to simplify and generalize.' That is doubtless connected with the inadequacy of the sources known at the time. For criticism of Troeltsch cf. also M.Haas, 'Täufertum und Volkskirche – Faktoren der Trennung', *Zwing.* 13, 1970-72, (261-78) 271f.; id., 'Die Täuferkirchen des 16. Jahrhunderts in der Schweiz und in Münster – ein Vergleich', *Zwing.* 13, (434-62) 462.

7. G.Williams (ed.), *Spiritual and Anabaptist Writers*, 1957, 20ff.; cf. id., *Reformation*, also taken over by C.Bauman, *Gewaltlosigkeit im Täufertum*, 1968, 31. F.Blanke makes a distinction between the Anabaptist movement, the Spiritualist movement and the anti-trinitarian movement, but recognizes that there are transitions and mixed forms, 'Täufertum und Reformation', *Ref.* 6, 1957, (212-23) 212 = in G.Hershberger (ed.), *Das Täufertum, Erbe und Verpflichtung*, 1963, (55-66) 55 = *Aus der Welt der Reformation*, 1960, (72-84) 72.

8. In Fast (ed.), *Der linke Flügel*.

9. Sebastian Franck is an exception, cf. above, 55ff.

10. However, as T.Bergsten has shown in *KHÅ*, there are differences here between P.Marbeck, with his sense of the church, and the pietistic Schwenckfeld, who tended towards forming sects.

11. Thus B.Lohse, 'Die Stellung der "Schwärmer" und Täufer in der Reformationsgeschichte', *ARG* 60, 1969, 5-26, stresses the variety in the phenomena summed up under titles like 'left wing' or 'radical Reformation'. However, despite the many objections (cf. e.g. the review by A.G.Dickens *PaP* 27, 1964, 123-5), the view of G.Williams, who sees the 'radical Reformation' as a fourth main form which can be distinguished as clearly as Lutheranism, Calvinism and Anglicanism, is not unjustified. M.Haas also thinks that 'in place of the present hair-splitting analyses, Anabaptism is better classified as a *general tendency* within the period of the Reformation', 'Täuferkirchen', 439. H.-J.Goertz, *Täufer*, again sums up the whole movement under this term despite the explicit recommendation that 'the monogenetic view of the Anabaptist movement should be replaced by a polygenetic one'(13). For various other principles of classification cf. also H.Bender, 'The Anabaptist Vision', *ChH* 13, 1944, 3-24 = Stayer/Packull, *Anabaptists*, 13-22 (extract); id., 'Das täuferische Leitbild', in G.Hershberger (ed.), *Das Täufertum. Erbe und Verpflichtung*, 1963, 31-54 = *The Recovery of the Anabaptist Vision*, 1957, 29-54; id., 'The Anabaptist Theology of Discipleship', *MennQR* 24, 1950, 25-32; also the review by D.Smucker, 'Anabaptist Historiography in Scholarship Today', in *MennQR* 22, 1948, 116-27. Survey of the various trends in Clasen, *Anabaptism*, 30ff.

12. Following E.Troeltsch, Free Church (Mennonite and Baptist) scholars have worked on freeing the Anabaptist movement of the suspicion of enthusiasm and revolutionary and violent radicalism. Cf. e.g. B.Unruh, 'Die Revolution und das Täufertum', in *Gedenkschrift zum 400j. Jubiläum der Mennoniten und Taufgesinnten*, 1925, 19-47; H.Bender, 'Die Zwickauer Propheten, Thomas Müntzer und die Täufer', *TZ* 8, 1952, 262-78 = *Thomas Müntzer*, ed. A.Friesen/H.J.Goertz, WdF CDXCI, 1978, 115-131 = 'The Zwickau Prophets, Thomas Müntzer and the Anabaptists', *MQR* 27, 1953, 3-16 = Stayer/Packull, *Anabaptists*, 145-51 (extract): R.Friedmann, 'Conception of the Anabaptists', *ChH* 9, 1940, (341-65) 343ff. (cf. also H.Blanke, *Täufertum*), which is especially concerned with relationships with Thomas Müntzer. For the history of the theme cf. A.Friesen, 'Social Revolution or Religious Reform? Some Salient Aspects of Anabaptist Historiography', in *Umstrittenes Täufertum 1525-1975*, 1975 (²1977), 223-43. The earlier view that Müntzer was the founder of Anabaptism was wrongly advanced by H.Bullinger, cf. H.Fast, *Heinrich Bullinger und die Täufer*, 1959, 89ff. On the other hand it cannot be overlooked that even in Müntzer's early theology there is a mystical approach and a spiritualist-legalistic

ethic which can also be found in the Anabaptist movement. Cf. K.Holl, op.cit., 425, and recently especially H.-J.Goertz, *Ordnung*, 10. There are connecting links above all between Müntzer and the south German Anabaptist movement, cf. G.Baring, 'Hans Denck und Thomas Müntzer in Nürnberg', *ARG* 50, 1959, 145-81; G.Mecenseffy, 'Die Herkunft des oberösterreichischen Täufertums', *ARG* 47, 1956, 252-9 = 'The Origin of Upper Austrian Anabaptism', in Stayer/Packull, *Anabaptists*, 152-3 (extract). We have impressive evidence of the self-understanding of Mennonite scholarship in the collection edited by G.Hershberger, *The Recovery = Das Täufertum*. – However, we should ask whether it is not possible to see, precisely in this self-portrait, features which enable us to find a common approach on decisive questions within the 'third Reformation', despite the multiplicity of the phenomena within it. For more recent research into the Anabaptists cf. the surveys by W.Köhler, 'Das Täufertum in der neueren kirchenhistorischen Forschung', *ARG* 37, 1940, 93ff.; 38, 1941, 349ff.; 40, 1943, 246ff.; 14, 1948, 164ff.; E.Teufel, 'Täufertum und Quäkertum im Lichte der neueren Forschung', *TR* NF 13, 1941, 21ff., 103ff.; 183ff.; 14, 1942, 27ff., 124ff.; 15, 1943, 56ff.; 17, 1948/49, 161ff.; Friedmann, *Conception*; id., 'Anabaptists', in *MennEnc* I, 113-16; id., 'Recent Interpretations of Anabaptism', *ChH* 24, 1955, 132-51; id., 'Progress in Anabaptist Studies', *ChH* 27, 1958, 72-6; G.H.Williams, 'Studies in the Radical Reformation (1517-1618): A Bibliographical Survey of Research Since 1939', *ChH* 25, 1958, 46-69; H.J.Hillerbrand, *Bibliographie des Täufertums, 1520-1630*, QGT 10, 1962; id., 'Die neuere Täuferforschung', *VF* 13, 1968, 95-110; J.M.Stayer/W.O.Packull/K.Deppermann, 'From Monogenesis to Polygenesis: The Historical Discussion of Anabaptist Origins', *MQR* 49, 1975, 83-121; G.A.Benrath, in C.Andresen (ed.), *Handbuch* 2, 611-18.

13. T.Bergsten, *Balthasar Hubmaier*, 1961, 13-30, gives the best systematically arranged survey of scholarship on this problem, to which only the most recent literature needs to be added.

14. L.Keller, *Die Reformation und die älteren Reformparteien*, 1885, and in further publications, cf. 'Keller, Ludwig', in *MennEnc* 3, 162ff. There is also a similar view in E.H. Broadbent, *The Pilgrim Church*, 1945.

15. A.Ritschl, *Geschichte des Pietismus. I. Pietismus in der reformierten Kirche*, 1880, 1-100, esp.31f.

16. Thus already Troeltsch, *Social Teaching*, 696 (but cf. the qualifications, 699). Cf. also L.von Muralt, *Glaube und Lehre der Schweizerischen Wiedertäufer in der Reformationszeit*, 1938, 5f.; Smucker, op.cit., 123f. By contrast K.R.Davis, *Anabaptism and Asceticism*, SAMH 16, 1974, again takes up Ritschl's view, see below.

17. After this view was put forward by C.A.Cornelius, *Geschichte des Münsterischen Aufruhrs*, 2, 1860, 14f., and Troeltsch, *Social Teaching*, 703f., this process of development has been clearly demonstrated in most recent times, cf. above all L. v. Muralt – W.Schmid, *Quellen*; H.Bender, *Conrad Grebel*, 1950; J.Yoder, *Täufertum und Reformation in der Schweiz* I (= *Täufertum* I). *Die Gespräche zwischen Täufern und Reformatoren 1523-1538*, 1962; id., *Täufertum und Reformation im Gespräch*, 1968 (= *Täufertum* II); id., 'The Turning Point of the Zwinglian Reformation', *MennQR* 32, 1958, 128-40 = Stayer/Packull, *Anabaptists*, 61-65 (extract), id., 'Der prophetische Dissent der Täufer', in Hershberger (ed.), *Täufertum*, 89-100; id., 'The Evolution of the Zwinglian Reformation', in *MennQR* 43, 1969, 95-112; id., 'Der Kristallisationspunkt des Täufertums', *MGB* 29, 1972, 35-47; F.Blanke, 'Die Vorstufen des Täufertums in Zürich', *MGB* 5, 1953, 2-13; id., *Brüder in Christo*, 1955; id., *Täufertum und Reformation*; H.Fast, 'The Dependence of the First Anabaptists on Luther, Erasmus and Zwingli', *MennQR* 30, 1956, 104-19; id., "Die Wahrheit wird euch freimachen"', *MGBl* 32, 1975, 7-33; J.F.G.Goeters, 'Die Vorgeschichte des Täufertums in Zürich', in *Studien zur Geschichte und Theologie der Reformation*, Festschrift E.Bizer, 1969, 239-81; J.M.Stayer, 'Die Anfänge des schweizerischen Täufertums im refor-

mierten Kongregationalismus', in *Umstrittenes Täufertum 1525-1975. Neue Forschungen*, 1975 (²1977), 19-49; M.Haas, 'Der Weg der Täufer in die Absonderung', ibid., 50-78 = 'The Path of the Anabaptists into Separation: The Interdependence of Theology and Social Behaviour'; Stayer/Packull, *Anabaptists*, 72-84; G.W.Locher, *Zwingli und die schweizerische Reformation*, KIG 3, fasc. J 1, 1982, 36-42. Cf. also Gastaldi, *Storia*, 103ff.; J.Wenger, *Die dritte Reformation*, 1963, 14ff.; also the short biographies: H.Fast, 'Konrad Grebel. Das Testament am Kreuz', in *Radikale Reformatoren*, ed. H.-J.Goertz, 1978, 103-14; M.Haas, 'Michael Sattler, Auf dem Weg in die täuferische Absonderung', ibid., 115-24.

18. H.Fast, 'Täufer', *RGG*³, VI, cols. 601-2. Similarly F.Blanke, *Täufertum und Reformation*, 220/63/80f.: 'Anabaptism arose on the ground of the Reformation; it is a child, a self-willed child, of the Reformation movement.'

19. The attempt by J.Kiwiet to distinguish the Upper German Anabaptists from the Zurich Anabaptists because of their eschatological and spiritualistic traits and to derive these from the stimuli of H.Denck and H.Hut, especially in his *Pilgram Marbeck*, ²1958, 40ff., has come up against opposition; cf. reviews by H.J.Hillerbrand, *ChH* 28, 1959, 100f.; id., *Die politische Ethik des oberdeutschen Täufertums*, 1962; H.-J.Goertz, *Ordnung*, 8f.

20. This was already done by the historian L. von Ranke, *Deutsche Geschichte im Zeitalter der Reformation* (Gesammelte Ausgabe der Deutschen Akademie I, 7), ed. P.Joachimsen, 1925, III, 397ff.; later esp. K.Holl, op.cit., and K.G.Steck, *Luther*. The very first Anabaptists claimed that they were carrying through the Reformation consistently to an end whereas Luther had remained at the half-way stage; this view can still be found in comments from the Free Churches; H.Bender, *Das täuferische Leitbild*, 38, speaks of it as the 'line of interpretation which finds increasingly strong echoes and may presumably come to dominate the field. It is that which sees Anabaptism as the climax of the Reformation, as the fulfilment of Luther's and Zwingli's original view and thus makes it appear as that consistent evangelical Protestantism which uncompromisingly recreates the original New Testament community, the vision of Christ and his apostles.' According to H.Fast, *Dependence*, however, not much importance is to be attached to this direct influence of Luther on the first Anabaptists. – For the Marxist view of this dependence cf. G.Mühlpfordt, 'Der frühe Luther als Autorität der Radikalen', in *Weltwirkung der Reformation*, I, ed. M.Steinmetz and G.Brendler, 1969, 205-25.

21. One need only recall Karlstadt, Müntzer, Schwenckfeld; however, the Zurich Anabaptists were also influenced by Zwingli, who until the separation was himself strongly influenced by Luther.

22. This is stressed above all by Mennonite scholars. Cf. e.g. J.Horsch in numerous contributions in *MennQR* 4-8, 1930-1934 (discussed by J.von Muralt in *Zwing* 6, 1934-38, 65-85) and cf. Bender's remark, above n.20.

23. After K.Holl, op.cit., and Steck, op.cit., cf. recently e.g. H.Fast, *Dependence*; H.J.Hillerbrand, 'The Origin of the Sixteenth-Century Anabaptism: Another Look', *ARG* 53, 1962, (152-80) 154f. The Anabaptists above all took over the anti-Catholic demands of the Reformation and preserved some features of the Reformers – characteristically above all again in the sphere of dogma, as in contrast to the rationalist anti-trinitarians they kept to the creeds of the early church and, with the Reformation, to the decisive significance of grace for the act of justification. Their dissent begins over the question how the *sola fide* is to be determinative for the whole existence of Christians, and therefore in the question of ethics.

24. In the case of Müntzer, Goertz, *Ordnung*, 23f., has doubted whether his theology in fact derives from Luther's. Cf. also Lohse, 'Stellung', 9. The demonstration by M. Brecht, 'Herkunft und Eigenart der Täuferanschauung der Züricher Täufer',

ARG 64, 1973, 147-65, that Luther's view of baptism of 1519 found its way to the Anabaptists of Zurich through K.Grebel is stimulating.

25. W.Köhler in particular sees Erasmus as one of the spiritual fathers of the Anabaptists because of his moralistic 'Sermon on the Mount Christianity', cf. esp. 'Wiedertäufer', *RGG*[2], V, cols. 1915-17; Köhler says e.g. in O.Clemen (ed.), *Flugschriften aus den ersten Jahren der Reformation*, II, 1907 (reprinted 1967), 296: 'In the comprehensive character of their restoration (of the earliest community) they are closer to Erasmus than to Luther, but they popularized him and therefore interiorized him.' Cf. also L. von Muralt, op.cit., 6f.; Hillerbrand, op.cit., 157ff., mentions the associated problems of discipleship, pacifism, dualistic ethics, the contrast between outward and inward and visible and invisible, the anthropocentric understanding of justification (the principle of free decision to become a disciple) and free will; for the latter see also T. Hall, 'Possibilities of Erasmian Influence on Denck and Hubmaier in Their Views on the Freedom of the Will', *MennQR* 35, 1961, 149-70. – Cf. also Fast, *Dependence*, 109ff.; K.R.Davis, 'Erasmus as Progenitor of Anabaptist Theology and Piety', *MennQR* 47, 1973, 163-78. E.W.Kohls, *Die theologische Lebensaufgabe des Erasmus*, AZTh I, 39, 1969, 35f., however, has reservations.

26. Thus Goertz, op.cit., 6 n.4, observes that the enumeration of influences must 'to some degree seem arbitrary', 'as long as there is no investigation of the way in which they were received'.

27. Cf. Goertz, op.cit., 6; Fast, *Dependence*, 110f.; Gastaldi, *Storia*, 74. By contrast Stayer/Packull/Deppermann, 'Monogenesis', 92, deny such influence.

28. L. Keller, op.cit., 373ff., sought the origin of the Anabaptists here, regarding Humanism as one of their presuppositions.

29. That is true e.g. for Grebel as it is for Zwingli (cf. H.Bender, *Grebel*, though he limits Humanist influence on Anabaptist theology as far as he can), Hubmaier and Denck (see below).

30. See above, 419f. n.52.

31. H.Bornkamm, review of F.Blanke, *Brüder in Christo*, 1955, *HZ* 182, 1956, 387f., still does not consider the question whether preparatory stages of the Zurich Anabaptist movement are to be found in mediaeval forms of piety to be settled by Blanke's demonstration 'that the movement is a radical Zwinglianism'; similarly Bergsten, *Hubmaier*, 24, with reference to Bornkamm. For relationships between South German Anabaptists and mediaeval mysticism cf. W.O.Packull, *Mysticism and the Early South German-Austrian Anabaptist Movement 1525-1531*, 1977; cf. also id., 'Zur Entwicklung des süddeutschen Täufertums', in *Umstrittenes Täufertum*, ed. Goertz, (165-72) 167. Goertz, op.cit., interprets the theology of Thomas Müntzer, which he again puts much more markedly in the context of the whole para-Reformation movement, essentially in the light of the tradition of mediaeval (Dominican) mysticism. The still influential account by R.M.Jones, *Spiritual Reformers in the 16th and 17th Century*, 1914, is also well known. Reference is also often made to the so-called *Theologia Deutsch* as an important source of tradition for the radical Reformation; it is well known that this book was also highly prized by the young Luther, who produced two editions of it in 1515 and 1518 but then abandoned it as it was taken up by the radical Spiritualists, cf. the translations into Latin by S.Castellio and S.Franck, the introduction to the edition by H.Mandel, 1908, and the Worms edition by Denck and Haetzer, 1527; also G.Goeters, *Ludwig Haetzer*, 1957, 133ff. and the bibliography by G.Baring in H.Denck, *Schriften* I, 1955, 40ff.; cf. J.Kiwiet, 'Die Theologia Deutsch und ihre Bedeutung während der Zeit der Reformation', *MGB* 15, 1958, 29-35; C.Bauman, op.cit., 144f. Bauman describes this heritage as 'sound mysticism', op.cit., 144.

32. 'The Historiography of the German Reformation', *ChH* 9, 1940, (305-40) 339.

32a. Cf. Davis, *Anabaptism*, passim. The author has recently defended his views against objections and in some respects made them more precise, cf. id., 'The Origins of Anabaptism: Ascetic and Charismatic Elements Exemplifying Continuity and Discontinuity', *AIHI* 87, 1977, 27-41.

33. It happens in many ways; cf. e.g. the remarks by F.Blanke, *Brüder*, 82, and Gelder, *Two Reformations*, passim. The Marxist view of history takes up the radical Reformation in its own way. Cf. the collection *Weltwirkung*. By contrast the works of G.Zschäbitz already represent a first step towards a less one-sided ideological approach. Cf. Zschäbitz, *Zur mitteldeutschen Wiedertäuferbewegung nach dem grossen Bauernkrieg*, LÜAMA, RB 1, 1958, e.g. 166: '...that probably the last word has not yet been spoken about the character of the Reformation and the Peasants' War in the context of German history.' In Zschäbitz, 'Die Stellung der Täuferbewegung im Spannungsbogen der deutschen frühbürgerliche Revolution', in *Die frühbürgerliche Revolution in Deutschland*, ed. G.Brendler, 1961, 152-62, we can also trace uncertainty over the classification of the two phenomena.

34. 'Anabaptism and the Reformation: Another Look', *ChH* 29, 1960, 404-23 = Stayer/Packull, *Anabaptists* 46-53 (extract), 418-52. M.Haas, 'Täufertum', 262ff., also conjectures a continuity between Anabaptism and late mediaeval sectarianism at least in the history of ideas, if not outwardly; cf. id., *Täuferkirchen*, 461: 'I do not in any way think... that this is a continuity in persons, but it is nevertheless possible to refer to the consistency of a certain attitude towards the world.' Because of this proximity to Catholicism H.-J.Goertz, 'Die ökumenische Einweisung der Täuferforschung', *NZST* 13, 1973, (362-72) 371, has suggested the designation 'the right wing of the Reformation' as a working hypothesis.

35. G. Rupp devotes a few thoughts to the hidden connections between mediaeval and Reformation Spiritualism, 'Word and Spirit in the First Years of the Reformation', *ARG* 49, 1958, 13-26. W.Klassen, *Anabaptism: Neither Catholic Nor Protestant*, 1973 (²1981) sees Anabaptism as a third confession alongside the two great confessions of the sixteenth century. Cf. recently especially K.R.Davis, *Anabaptism*; id., 'The Origins of Anabaptism: Ascetic and Charismatic Elements exemplifying Continuity and Discontinuity', in M.Lienhard (ed.), *The Origins and Characteristics of Anabaptism/Les débuts et les caracteristiques de l'Anabaptisme*, 1977, 27-41. Davis makes it clear that it was not mysticism but an ascetical lay theology in the spirit of the *Devotio Moderna* which was normative for the Anabaptists. For criticism cf. in part Stayer/Packull/Deppermann, 'Monogenesis'.

36. The most basic biography is still that by K.Benrath, *Bernardino Ochino von Siena*, ²1892, reprinted 1968; the intrinsic elements in the development are best presented in R.Bainton, *Bernardino Ochino, Esule e Riformatore Senese del Cinquecento, 1487-1563*, Versione dal Manoscritto Inglesi di E.Gianturco, 1940.

37. Hillerbrand, *Täuferforschung*, 103, rightly comments: 'Now the lack of direct connections should not be confused with the complete absence of theological influences.'

38. *Das täuferische Leitbild*, 44. Cf. also the account in Clasen, *Anabaptism*.

39. *Kirchenbegriff*, 3.

40. R.J.Smithson, *The Anabaptists*, 1935, 14f.

41. 'Prolegomena to an Anabaptist Theology', *MennQR* 24, 1950, 5-11, 10f.

42. *Das Selbstverständnis der Täufer*, 1966 (= *The Anabaptist View of the Church*, ²1958, XXX), 11ff.

43. U.Bergfried, *Verantwortung als theologisches Problem im Täufertum des 16.Jahrhunderts*, Tübingen theological dissertation, Wuppertal 1938, 19ff., similarly sees the centre of the Anabaptist thought system as being the doctrine of their community as a community of saints.

44. Review of Littell, *Anabaptist View*, *MennQR* 27, 1953, 249ff.

45. Littell, 'Der täuferische Kirchenbegriff', in Hershberger (ed.), *Das Täufertum*,

115-29, esp.118f., again counters with the point that this is an ideal of discipleship connected with the community. H.J.Hillerbrand, 'Die gegenwärtige Täuferforschung – Fortschritt oder Dilemma?', *BZRGG* 4, 1959, (48-65) 61, points out that the idea of discipleship and the concept of the church among the Anabaptists were simply two sides of the same thing. Cf. also H.Fast, 'Variationen des Kirchenbegriffs bei den Täufern', *MGB* 27, 1970, (5-18) 9: 'Freedom... to be a disciple of Jesus is probably the innermost nucleus of the concept of the community in Anabaptism and the free churches.' For the idea of discipleship in early Anabaptism cf. Friedmann, *Theology*, 24, 44; Goertz, *Täufer*, 67ff. mentions the involvement of the connection with Menno Simons' 'improvement of life' in justification and sanctification as understood by the Anabaptists. Both Friedmann and Goertz stress that this attitude increasingly led to legalism among the later Anabaptists. The Anabaptists rejected the charge of justification by works, cf. Friedmann, *Theology*, 79. Similarly, for K.R.Davis, *Anabaptism*, Postscript 135, Anabaptism is 'an Ascetic Theology of Manifest Holiness and Relative Perfectionism'. Cf. id., 'Origins', passim.

46. Cf. Hillerbrand, op.cit.

47. Yoder, *Täufertum* II, 11, observes: 'They had neither the time nor the inclination to do professional theology, nor – with a few exceptions right at the beginning – did they have the education.' Friedmann, *Theology*, 27, 29, etc. speaks of an 'existential Christianity' (cf. also n.3 on 34 for the earlier use of this expression); nevertheless one can call this 'implicit theology' a theology too, 21, cf. 36.

48. Cf. Bauman, *Gewaltlosigkeit*, 130ff.

49. Cf. Holl, op.cit., 424, 431.

50. Cf. von Muralt, *Glaube und Lehre*; Bauman, op.cit., 125ff., 148ff.; W.Wiswedel, 'Zum Problem "inneres und äusseres Wort" bei den Täufern des 16.Jahrhunderts', *ARG* 46, 1955, (1-19) 1ff.; I. Wenger, 'Der Biblizismus der Täufer', in Hershberger (ed.), *Täufertum*, (161-72) 161ff.; J.Yoder, 'Der prophetische Dissent der Täufer', ibid., (89-100) 91f.; H.Bender, *MennEnc* I, 322f. W.Köhler, 'Die Verantwortung im Täufertum des 16.Jahrhunderts', *MGB* 5, 1940, (10-19) 19, wrote: 'The Anabaptists wanted to be good biblical Christians and by and large were so.' Cf. also E.Bernhofer-Pippert, *Täuferische Denkweisen und Lebensformen im Spiegel oberdeutscher Täuferverhöre*, 1967, 42: 'In the first place the Brethren must be seen as Bible Christians.' For this group of problems cf. also G.G.Gerner, *Der Gebrauch der Heiligen Schrift in der oberdeutschen Täuferbewegung*, Diss.theol. Heidelberg 1973.

51. Cf. Horsch, op.cit.; von Muralt-Schmid, op.cit., and recently Yoder, *Täufertum*, I and II; id., *The Turning Point*. The Schleitheim Confession (text by Köhler in Clemen, *Flugschriften* II, 305-16, and in B.Jenny, 'Das Schleitheimer Täuferbekenntnis 1527', in *Schaffhauser Beiträge zur vaterländischen Geschichte* 28, 1951, [5-81] 9-18 – also as an offprint, Thayngen 1951. Literature: F.Blanke, 'Beobachtungen zum ältesten Täuferbekenntnis', *ARG* 37, 1940, 242-9; R.Friedmann, 'The Schleitheim Confession (1527) etc.', *MennQR* 16, 1942, 82-98; J.Wenger, 'The Schleitheim Confession of Faith', *MennQR* 19, 1945, 243-53), bases its arguments for the special teaching of the Anabaptists on New Testament proof texts, cf. especially Jenny, op.cit., passim. However, the Sermon on the Mount is not central to the same degree among all the representatives of the 'left wing'; it emerges more strongly in Denck and less so among the Anabaptists, cf. Gerner, *Gebrauch*, 89ff.

52. Cf. e.g. Bernhofer-Pippert, op.cit., 41f.; Wiswedel, *ARG* 1955, 1ff.; Bauman, op.cit., 125ff.; Yoder, *Täufertum* II, 86ff.

53. Cf. already Köhler in Clemen, op.cit., 286f.; von Muralt, *Zwing.* 6, 69f. (against Horsch); Bernhofer-Pippert, op.cit., 42f.; Wiswedel, op.cit.; Bauman, op.cit., 134ff. Goertz, *Täufer*, 54-66, arguing especially against C.Bauman, points to the fundamental differences in the understanding of scripture between the Swiss and the South German Anabaptists; only among the latter is the 'Spirit' emphatically con-

trasted with scripture. The comments by Wenger, *Biblizismus*, are too abrupt at this point.

54. Cf. Bernhofer-Pippert, op.cit., 43f.; Wiswedel, op.cit., 5ff. Bauman, op.cit., 137ff. attempts to approximate this 'sound mysticism' to the 'spiritual radicalism' of Luther, referring to Steck, op.cit. This is beyond question a caricature, since Luther soon recognized the dangers of his initial Spiritualism in view of the emergence of the 'Enthusiasts' and therefore abandoned it. Cf. K.-H.zur Mühlen, *Nos extra nos. Luthers Theologie zwischen Mystik und Scholastik*, 1972. For the general character of the Anabaptist movement as a charismatic movement cf. also K.R.Davis, 'Anabaptism as a Charismatic Movement', *MQR* 53, 1979, 219-34.

55. *Schriften*, ed. Fellmann, 2, 106. For Denck cf. further Packull, *Mysticism*, 35-61; the short bibliography in id., 'Hans Denck. Auf der Flucht vor dem Dogmatismus', in *Radikale Reformatoren*, ed. H.-J.Goertz, 51-9; id, 'Denck, Hans (ca.1500-1527)', *TRE* 8, 1981, 488-90 (with bibliography).

56. Cf. O.Vitalli, *Die Theologie des Wiedertäufers Hans Denck*, Diss.phil.1932, 36f.; A.Hege, *Hans Denck*, Diss. theol. Tübingen 1942 (typescript), 79ff.; W.Fellmann, 'Irenik und Polemik bei Hans Denck', *LuJ* XXIX, 1962, (110-16) 110f.; cf. also G.Goldbach, *Hans Denck und Thomas Müntzer*, Hamburg theological dissertation 1969, 70ff.; Gerner, *Gebrauch*, 120f.

57. Cf. above, 436 n.7.

57a. Cf. more recently also G.Gerner, 'Folgerungen aus dem täuferischen Gebrauch der heiligen Schrift', *MGB* 31, 1974, 25-43. R.Friedmann, 'The Doctrine of the Two Worlds', in G.Hershberger (ed.), *Recovery*, 105-18 = id., *Hutterite Studies*, 1961, 92-102 = 'Die Lehre von den beiden Reichen', in Hershberger (ed.), *Täufertum*, 101-14, sees the division made by the Anabaptists between the kingdom of God and the kingdom of the world as the reason why for both of them the focal point lay with the Gospels instead of with Paul.

58. Cf. Bender, *Leitbild*.

59. G.Burkholder, 'Nachfolge in täuferischer Sicht', in Hershberger, *Täufertum*, (131-45) 132.

60. Cf. especially G.Mecenseffy, 'Das Verständnis der Taufe bei den süddeutschen Täufern', in *Antwort, Festschrift Karl Barth*, 1956, 642-6; R.S.Armour, *Anabaptist Baptism*, 1966; Goertz, *Täufer*, 77ff.

61. In Jenny, op.cit., 10; cf. ibid., 44ff.

61a. Cf. also Gerner, *Gebrauch*, 13ff.

62. Cf. Bernhofer-Pippert, op.cit., 45ff., and the evidence quoted there. For the synergism of the Anabaptists cf. also K.R.Davis, *Anabaptism*, 149ff. However, according to Davis, 169, the Anabaptists do not deny the decisive role of grace. Nevertheless, A.J.Beachy, *The Concept of Grace in the Radical Reformation*, has demonstrated that the Anabaptist view of grace was fundamentally different from that of the Lutheran and Calvinist Reformation. They firmly rejected the formula *simul justus ac peccator*. On the one hand according to Anabaptist teaching man even after the fall had retained the capacity to prepare for grace in a remnant of his primal state; on the other hand the grace achieved by Christ had a universal validity. In the end the radical character of sin was denied. Even after the reception of grace there remained the need for ethical action to achieve Christian existence.

63. 'Bekenntnis für den Rat zu Nürnberg', in *Schriften*, ed.Fellmann, 24, line 25; cf. also B.Lohse, 'Hans Denck und der "linke Flügel "der Reformation', in *Festschrift W.von Loewenich*, (74-83) 79.

64. Cf. Bergsten, *Pilgram Marbeck = KHÅ*, 1958, 53ff.; Armour, op.cit., 120ff.; also W.Klassen, *Covenant and Community*, 1968, 85. However, for Marbeck, too, the rebirth of the inner man comes first, whereas baptism includes even the outward

man. For Marbeck see also Gastaldi, *Storia*, 283ff; G.A.Benrath, in Andresen, *Handbuch*, 633f. (with bibliography). Cf. also below, 62.

65. For their controversy cf. Loserth, *Quellen*, and Bergsten, op.cit.

66. Cf. H.Weigelt, *Spiritualistische Tradition im Protestantismus*, 1973, 31ff. The works by K.Ecke, which idealize Schwenckfeld in terms of the Reformation, are vigorously criticized by G.Maron, *Individualismus und Gemeinschaft bei Caspar von Schwenckfeld*, 1961, 26f., 31f.

67. Cf. above all G.Maron, op.cit., 35ff., who speaks of 'biblicistic gnosticizing mysticism'. For Schwenckfeld cf. also the brief biography by H.Weigelt, 'Caspar von Schwenckfeld. Verkünder des "mittleren" Weges', in *Radikale Reformatoren*, ed. H.J.Goertz, 198-200; R.E.McCaughlin, 'Caspar Schwenckfeld', in *Reformationszeit I*, ed. Greschat, 307-21; Benrath, in Andresen, *Handbuch* 2, 587ff. (with bibliography).

68.Cf. H.Urner, 'Die Taufe bei Caspar Schwenckfeld', *TLZ* 73, 1948, cols. 329-42; Maron, op.cit., 86ff. There is a good deal of evidence there.

69. Since 1526; cf. *Corpus Schwenckfeldianorum* II, 332f.

70. In the Micah commentary perhaps also by his supporters.

71. Cf. also B.Lohse, op.cit., 79ff.; A.Coutts, *Hans Denck*, 1927, 188ff.; Hege, *Denck*, 130f.

72. 'Ceremonies in themselves are not sinful, but anyone who thinks that he can achieve anything either through baptism or breaking of bread is superstitious. Anyone who concerns himself vigorously with ceremonies does not gain much; for if one were to lose all ceremonies one would not suffer much harm...' *Schriften*, ed. Fellmann, 2, 109, lines 2ff.

73. 'Thus it is also with our ceremonies of Christ, established in the old state, baptism and eucharist. It is not that if we observe them we are as a result somewhat better before God and man, or if we are obliged to forego them because of love and to avoid causing offence, we sin against God and our neighbours. They are customs, neither commanded nor ordained, which are to be observed because love and necessity requires them,' *Schriften*, ed. Fellmann, 3, 84, lines 25ff.

74. Cf. Armour, op.cit., esp. 56f., 135f.

75. Cf. Bernhofer-Pippert, op.cit., 45ff.

76. For his writings cf. above, 443 n.2. Of the secondary literature the following books are particularly important. Basic works: A.Hegler, *Geist und Schrift bei Sebastian Franck*, 1892; also *Blätter für Deutsche Philosophie* 2, 1, 1928 (with contributions by P.Joachimsen, G.Lehmann, L.Blaschke, A. von Grolman on Franck); A.Koyré, 'Sébastien Franck', in *RHPR* 1931, 353-85; id., *Mystiques, Spirituels, Alchemistes*, 1955; J.Lindeboom, *Een Franc-tireur der Reformatie*, 1952; L.Littauer, *Sebastian Francks Anschauungen vom politischen und sozialen Leben*, Leipzig dissertation 1922; K.Räber, *Studien zur Geschichtsbibel Sebastian Francks*, 1952; E.Teufel, *Landräumig*, 1954 (the best biography, though very enthusiastic about Franck; W.-E.Peuckert, *Sebastian Franck. Ein deutscher Sucher*, 1943, is more detailed but less precise); M.Barbers, *Toleranz bei Sebastian Franck*, 1964 (in the first part there is a survey of the cultural influences on Franck and his basic religious views); H.J.Hillerbrand, *A Fellowship of Discontent*, 1967, 31-64; S.L.Verhuis, *Zeugnis und Gericht*, 1971; S.Wollgast, *Der deutsche Pantheismus im 16.Jahrhundert. Sebastian Franck und seine Wirkungen auf die Entwicklung der pantheistischen Philosophie in Deutschland*, 1972 (Marxist); C.Dejung, *Wahrheit und Häresie. Eine Untersuchung zur Geschichtsphilosophie bei Sebastian Franck*, Phil. diss. Zurich 1979; cf. also S.Ozment, *Mysticism and Dissent*, 1973, 137-67; id., 'Mysticism, Nominalism and Dissent', in C.Trinkaus/H.Oberman (eds.), *The Pursuit of Holiness in Late Medieval and Renaissance Religion*, 67-92, esp. 89f.; id., short biography in H.-J.Goertz (ed.), *Radikale Reformatoren*, 201-9. Cf. also H.Weigelt, 'Sebastian Franck', in *Die Reformationszeit* II, ed. M.Greschat, 1981, 119-28; G.A.Benrath, in Andresen,

Handbuch 2, 578ff.; A.Séguenny, 'Franck, Sebastian (ca.1500-1542)', *TRE* 11, 1983, 307-12 (with bibliography).

77. Nuremberg 1530, fol.K 3b.

78. Cf. above 444 n.2. Survey of contents in Verhuis, op.cit., 19ff. In the preface (fol.III), Franck's own verdict on this Chronicle is: 'However, this heretical chronicle may also be called a mixed theology/ since you have here... almost the best/ that with my little understanding/ I have been able to find, read and acquire...'

79. Cf. Book VIII, fol. CCLXXII-CCLXXV. Cf. Verhuis, op.cit., 25ff.; Dejung, op.cit., passim.

80. Book I, fol.V-LXII.

81. Book II, fol. LXII-LXXXI.

82. Book IV, fol. CCXIII-CCXXXVI.

83. Book V, fol. CCXXXVI-CCLII.

84. Book VI, fol. CCLIII-CCLIV.

85. Book VII, fol. CCLXV-CCLXXII. Between them, at first sight in isolation but in a deeper sense with complete consistency, there is the third book 'Of Heretics' (fol. LXXXI-CCX), an alphabetical Lexicon of heretics with which Franck is a fore-runner of Gottfried Arnold's *Unparteiischer Kirchen- und Ketzerhistorie*, 1699. He ex-presses clearly his basic attitude to the heretics: 'There you find all kinds of opinion and heresy/ blessed is the one who can read the best from it. For hardly a heretic is so evil/ who has not had some good ideas alongside his erroneous ones.' Preface to Chronicle 3, fol.II. 'You should not think/ my reader/ that I regard all these as heretics/ whom I present here... the judgment... is not mine/ but that of the Pope/ his Councils/ and his followers... in that case I would judge/ I would perhaps change the game/ and canonize many of them / and put them among the saints/ who are here arraigned as heretics...' Preface to the *Ketzerchronik*, fol. LXXXI.

86. Cf. the section on Luther, fol.CLXVII-CLXXVI (it was reprinted in Rome in 1883!). On Luther, Franck says: '... and as I can neither believe, grasp nor understand his theology, I will pass no judgment on it...' fol. CLXXVf. – For Franck's attitude to Luther cf. E.Teufel, 'Luther und Luthertum im Urteil Sebastian Francks', *Festschrift K.Müller*, 1922, 132-44; H.Weigelt, *Sebastian Franck und die lutherische Reformation*, 1972.

87. The connections between Franck's philosophy of history, his concept of the church (which on the one hand completely does away with the external form of the church in that subsequently it exists only after the spirit, and on the other hand extends to believing heathen, taking further the humanistic theme of the blessedness of elect heathen), and a spiritualization even of the Word of God, which as inner light first discloses scripture, become particularly clear in the well-known letter to Johannes Campanus: Early New High German and Middle Dutch translation in Krebs-Rott, *Quellen, Elsass*, 301-25; ET in G.Williams, *Writers*, 147-60; New High German translation in Fast, *Flügel*, 219-33. Cf. also the evocative definition of Franck's Spiritualist concept of the church, *Paradoxa*, Preface, trans.Wollgast, 12.

88. Cf. Hegler, 'Sebastian Franck', *RE³*, VI, 149: 'F. was no original thinker.' Koyré, *RHPR*, 'Il compile. Il subit toutes sortes d'influences. Il lit beaucoup... Une mosaique. Mais non sans unité. Une synthèse? Ce serait peut-être aller trop loin. Disons un amalgame.'

89. Cf. the survey in Barbers, op.cit., 17ff. The classification of Franck in Wollgast, *Pantheismus*, as a representative of 'materialistic pantheism' (for the Marxist definition of this term cf. 154f.) among the ancestors of dialectical materialism (cf. 11, 60), must be regarded as false. Wollgast himself notes that he did not succeed in this ('Franck's materialistic pantheism is inconsistent', 165). However, the book contains many individual observations which are also helpful for a different overall understanding.

90. Cf. Wollgast, Introduction to Franck, *Paradoxa*, XXIV; id., *Pantheismus*, 142ff.,

157ff.; cf. also id., 'Einige Bemerkungen zur Bedeutung und Stellung Sebastian Francks', in *Weltwirkung*, 271-86. R.Friedman, 'The Doctrine of the Two Worlds', in G.Hershberger (ed.), *The Recovery of the Anabaptist Vision*, 1957, 105-18 = id., *Hutterite Studies*, 1961, 92-102; id., *Theology*, 36ff., sees 'the heart of the implicit theology of Anabaptism' in the dualism between the 'kingdom of God' and 'world'; cf. also G.Zaepernick, 'Welt und Mensch bei Sebastian Franck', in *Pietismus und Neuzeit*, ed. A.Lindt/K.Deppermann, 1974, 9-25.

91. Cf. also *Paradoxa*, par.89 (ed. Wollgast, 148f.). Cf. also Wollgast in 'Weltwirkung', 276f.; id., *Pantheismus*, 170ff.

92. Three writings contained in a collected volume in the Dresden Staatsbibliothek (Sign.8 Theol.cath. B 862, VI) bear his name. 1. *Aus was ursach sich Gott in die nyder gelassen und in Christo vermenschet ist...*, 1529 (ET by C.R.Foster and W.Jerosch, *MennQR* 42, 1968, 262-84); 2. *Eine gemeyne Berechnung über der Heiligen Schrift Inhalt*, 1529; 3. *Erklärung durch Vergleichung der biblischen geschrifft, das der Wassertauff samt anderen eüsserlichen gebreüchen / in der Apostolischen kirchen geübet. On Gottes befelch und zeügnis der geschrifft / von etlichen diser zeit / wider efert wird*, 1530. The anonymous writing *Ein gemayne einlayttung in den aygentlichen verstand Mosi...*, new edition 1529, which appears in the same collection, is certainly also by him. A reprint of these rarities is urgently needed. – For Bünderlin cf. A.Nicoladoni, *Johann Bünderlin von Linz*, 1893; C.R.Foster, 'Johannes Bünderlin', *MennQR* 39, 1965, 115-24; U. Gäbler, 'Zum Problem des Spiritualismus im 16. Jahrhundert', *TZ* 29, 1973, 334-44; Packull, *Mysticism*, 155-63.

93. See the preceding note, no.3. Text: John 4.24!

94. A.Schwindt, *Hans Denck. Ein Vorkämpfer undogmatischen Christentums*, nd (1924), 17, observes on Denck: 'What connects him on the one hand with the mystics is faith in the ultimate unity of being of the soul with the divine being or, as he calls it, faith in the living word in the soul, but on the other hand what separates him from them is the moral impulse which he derives from this recognition.' For Denck's moralism against a mystical-humanistic background cf. also Packull, *Mysticism*, 51ff. H.J.Goertz,. op.cit., devotes his work to demonstrating how for Müntzer faith extends from inner order, understood mystically, to outward order. This type of mystical thinking corresponds much more closely to the thought-forms of Franciscan spirituality, as we established them on pp.28ff. It should be noted that the *Theologia Deutsch* has a purely contemplative and quietistic character, although it is taken up by the Spiritualists of the Reformation.

95. R.Kommoss, *Sebastian Franck und Erasmus von Rotterdam*, 1934, has devoted a special investigation to the relationship between the two, in which both differences and common features emerge clearly. For our problem cf.: 'Franck's supreme principle of divine revelation, the "inward word", clearly betrays his origin from two different intellectual movements, mysticism and humanism... For Franck the inner word is not primarily a power of knowledge but a compelling call from the most powerful religious experience, an impulse and a force for action.' Cf. also Ozment, 'Franck', 205. Weigelt, *Franck*, 57ff., rightly specifies 'moralism as Sebastian Franck's real concern'. Cf. also Wollgast, *Pantheismus*, 146ff.

96. Translation follows Wollgast, 180ff.

97. Quotation from Wollgast, op.cit., 183f.

98. *Paradoxa* 135-7, op.cit., 218f. Cf. also *Paradoxa* 217-8, op.cit., 347f.: 'Just as the fire cannot be other than hot and burn by nature without any command – so the pious man, transformed and newly born from God, becomes a divine nature so that he cannot do other than right... without necessity or command, etc.'

99. Cf. Hege, op.cit., 124ff.; Goertz, *Täufer*, 68ff.; Packull, *Mysticism*, 48ff. For the account of Denck in Franck cf. Wollgast, *Pantheismus*, 118ff.

100. 'Was geredt sei, dass die Schrift sagt', in *Schriften*, ed. Fellmann, 2, 45, lines 6f.

101. *Schriften*, ed.Fellmann, 2, 48ff.

102. For the problem from Luther's perspective cf. W.von Loewenich, 'Die Selbstkritik der Reformation in Luthers grossem Katechismus', *Von Augustin zu Luther*, 1959, 269-93.

103. Op.cit., 50, line 36 to 51, line 1.

104. Op.cit., 52, lines 8-10.

105. Op.cit., 63, lines 7-11. For the internalizing of the law in Denck cf. also Packull, *Mysticism*, 53.

105a. For Franck's struggle against the Reformation doctrine of scripture cf. also Weigelt, in Greschat, *Reformationszeit* II, 124.

106. Isaiah 22.22; id., line 16.

107. Denck distinguishes 'three kinds of law, which the scripture calls commandment, morality and justice. Commandments are what stem purely from love of God and the neighbour and may never be transgressed without sin, and to that the conscience of all reasonable men bears witness', op.cit., 62, 26-29. The identification of the love commandment, reason and conscience is remarkable! Mysticism (in the statement quoted above which follows in the text), moralism and rationalism here go into one another: 'Morals are outward order directed to the natural and daily customs of men; hereby they shall be reminded of the things which are divine and eternal. For all customs are sacrament or sign, and anyone who understands them may miss the signs.' Id., lines 31-34. The last sentence could also be read reciprocally: 'sacraments are morals or signs.' The same general view is evident everywhere. Cf. also the similar remarks in G.Seebass, 'Hans Denck', in *Fränkische Lebensbilder*, ed. G.Pfeiffer and A.Wendehorst, 1975, 107-29.

108. Id., 66, lines 13f.

108a. Cf. also Gerner, 'Folgerungen', 29ff.

109. So far there are no thorough investigations of Franck's attitude to the Old Testament, but cf. A.Séguenny, 'L'exégèse spirituelle de Sébastien Franck sur l'exemple du Commentaire de Psaume 64', in *Histoire de l'exégèse au XVIe siècle*, 1978, 179-84. Diestel, op.cit., devotes a few sentences to his doctrine of the spirit and scripture, but none to the Old Testament. There are rather more in Weigelt, *Franck*, 54f., but only on the allegorical/typological interpretation of the Old Testament, which is not a special feature in Franck. But cf. L.Littauer, op.cit., esp. 26-35. Cf. also Wollgast, *Pantheismus*, 173. K.Räber, op.cit., 29ff., makes some valuable comments simply on the evaluation of Old Testament history in Franck's *Geschichtsbibel*; cf. also Dejung, *Wahrheit*, 123-31.

110. Translation follows Wollgast, 136ff.

111. Wollgast, 153.

112. Wollgast, 148f.

113. See above, 83, 85f.

114. Wollgast, 137.

115. Op.cit., 136.

116. Op.cit., 137.

117. Op.cit., 140.

118. 'Now as God was not concerned at all with the figure and the ceremonial worship of Israel, so on the other hand he was utterly concerned for its significance, which they figured and which was later to be revealed and expressed in Christ', op.cit., 138.

119. Franck also went into the allegorical-typological exegesis of the Old Testament in other works, cf. Weigelt, op.cit., 54f.

120. Op.cit., 142-44.

121. *Huc usque ferme ad verbum Chrysostomus*, op.cit., 144.
122. *Geschichtsbibel*, fol. I-CXL.
123. *Studien*, 29-39.
124. Op.cit., 29.
125. Cf. Räber, op.cit., 30. For him it is 'a clear example of Franck's passion for drawing a moral doctrine from everything and presenting it as it were in sermon form to his contemporaries', op.cit., 37. However, it is only the history and not the doctrinal statements in the Bible which have such moral value, cf. *Geschichtsbibel, Preface*, and Räber, op.cit., 39. For moralism as Franck's real concern cf. Weigelt, op.cit., 57ff.
126. *Geschichtsbibel*, fol. XLVIIIb; Räber, op.cit., 30f.
127. *Geschichtsbibel*, fol.L a; cf. Räber, op.cit., 31f.
128. Op.cit., 32.
129. Op.cit., 33.
130. 'You find this difference (between inward and outward) in both Old and New Testaments. Both are one in spirit and meaning but different in letter. Therefore in both one must not look to the dead letter but to the spirit and meaning of Christ which makes alive, which tears down the dividing wall and makes one of the two', op.cit., 141.
131. This is an anticipation of an argument which was to play a role again, centuries later, in Lessing's *Erziehung des Menschengeschlechts*.
132. Cf. above, 453 n.87. Cf. also Lindeboom, *Franc-tireur*, 33; Wollgast, *Pantheismus*, 122ff.
133. 'Although therefore to begin with Christ did not baptize without cause...', in Fast, *Der linke Flügel*, 221 (Krebs-Rott, *Elsass* I, 304). The image of the doll is then applied to the young church instead of to Israel, as in the *Paradoxa*: 'God allowed the church outward signs in its youth, indeed he gave them like giving a child a doll', but now they have put them aside as superfluous, Fast, op.cit., 227f. (Krebs-Rott, op.cit., 316).
134. Fast, op.cit., 220 (Krebs Rott, op.cit., 303, 309f.).
135. Fast, op.cit., 225 (Krebs-Rott, op.cit., 311).
136. Fast, op.cit., 223 (Krebs-Rott, op.cit., 308); cf. also Dejung, *Wahrheit*, 189-91.
137. Cf. Teufel, *Landräumig*, 34-38. According to Wollgast, *Pantheismus*, 79, the letter to Campanus was written probably before Franck's stay in Strassburg.
138. Cf. above, 79ff.
139. Specially in his writing *Von der touff, Werke, Kritische Ausgabe*, IV, 188-337. Cf. also *Wer Ursache gebe zu Aufruhr, Werke, Kritische Ausgabe* III, 374-469; cf. R.Armour, *Baptism*, 1966, 36f.; Yoder, *Täufertum* II, 34ff., and for the dispute over baptism between Zwingli and the Anabaptists also B.Jenny, op.cit., 44-51.
140. Bauman, *Gewaltlosigkeit*, 155.
141. Problems of church and society – to put it in modern terms – are also the real background to the two other themes of the oath and infant baptism. Cf. also H.J.Hillerbrand, *Ethik*, 41ff.
142. Bauman, op.cit., 155ff. has collected some of the most typical comments by Anabaptists on the OT in various religious discussions.
143. Cf. Bauman, op.cit., 162. Cf. also the Confession of the Swiss Brethren in Hessen, in *Täuferakten Hessen Waldeck*, 187, 404-40, art. 1, 407. For the marked concern with the Old Testament in Anabaptist circles (including the first translation of the prophets from the Hebrew by H.Denck and L.Hätzer), cf. also Klassen, *Covenant*, 105f.
144. Cf. Wenger, *Reformation*, 67-70.
145. Bauman, op.cit., 169, speaks of 'christological New Testament monism'.
146. Cf. the remarks by P.Riedemann, *Rechenschaft unserer Religion*, 1565, new impression 1938, vol. II, 67, in Bauman, op.cit., 168f.

147. Ed. J.C.Wenger, *MennQR* 12, 1938, 167-202.

148. *Verantwortung über Casparn Schwenckfelds Iudicium*, ed. J.Loserth.

149. *Vermanung auch gantz klarer / grundtlicher und unwidersprachlicher bericht...* (*c.1542*) (edited by C.Hege, in *Gedenkschrift z. 400j. Jubil. der Mennoniten oder Taufgesinnten, 1525-1925*, 1929, 178-282), also known as the *Taufbüchlein*. F.Wray has shown that this writing is in fact a version of B.Rothmann's *Bekenntnisse von beyden Sacramenten* (ed. Stupperich, *Die Schriften Bernhard Rothmanns*, 139-95), in which the accentuation of the difference between Old and New Testaments by Marbeck is an important point: F.Wray, 'The "Vermanung" of 1542 and Rothmann's "Bekenntnisse" ', *ARG* 47, 1956, 243-51.

150. *Testamenterleütterung. Erleütterung durch ausszug auss Heiliger Biblischer schrift...* (no date or place of publication). Two well known copies in Berlin and Zurich. Preface reprinted in Loserth, op.cit., 579-84. All Marbeck's writings are described in J.Kiwiet, *Marbeck*, 71-81 (cf. also Bergsten, *KHÅ*, 1957, 56ff.), and Klassen, *Covenant*, 36-56, who ascribes to Marbeck two other anonymous books. For Marb(p)eck cf. also the short biography by W.Klassen, 'Pilgram Marpeck. Freiheit ohne Gewalt', in *Radikale Reformatoren*, ed. H.-J.Goertz, 146-54.

151. Bergsten, op.cit., 83ff.

152. For the Anabaptists, the rejection of the conception of authority derived from the Old Testament was a central theme. For the discussion of it by Peter Riedemann in his 'Rechenschaft', 1540/1 (cf. the article, 'Rechenschaft unserer Religion', *ME*, vol. IV, 259-61), cf. Hillerbrand, *Die politische Ethik*, 42f.

153. Cf. the preface in Loserth, op.cit., 582f.

154. Op.cit., 84ff. There is also a variety of evidence there which is referred to here. For the 'divine ordering' as a mystical thought-form cf. also Goertz, op.cit., 39ff.

155. Cf. Klassen, op.cit., 114ff. Klassen, op.cit., 124, stresses that Marbeck was practically alone in his sharp contrast between Old and New Testaments. However, it was particularly clear only in thinking through a hermeneutical consequence which was a logical sequel to the basic Anabaptist attitude.

156. Evidence in Kiwiet, op.cit., 95f.

157. Cf. Bergsten, *KHÅ*, 1957, 92ff.

158. Cf. esp. *Verantwortung* I, in Loserth, op.cit., 123ff. It is understandable that Schwenckfeld did not understand these complicated arguments, cf. his *Iudicium*, ibid. For the distinction between 'sign' and 'testimony' cf. also Kiwiet, op.cit., 134f., and for Marbeck's doctrine of baptism with its unity of 'inward' and 'outward' baptism cf., Armour, op.cit., 113-34, op.cit., 102.

159. Cf. Kiwiet, op.cit., 102.

160. For this cf. esp. G.Schrenck, *Gottesreich und Bund im älteren Protestantismus, vornehmlich bei Johannes Coccejus*, 1923. Also cf. above, 119ff.

161. For Calvin cf. H.H.Wolf, *Die Einheit des Bundes*, 1942, ²1958. The title expresses Calvin's view precisely.

162. Cf. 'Sabbatarian Anabaptists', *MennEnc* IV, 396; 'Sabbatharier', *MennLex* IV, 3f.

163. Cf. W.Wiswedel, 'Oswald Glait von Jamnitz', *ZKG* 56, 1937, 550-64.

164. 'Vom Christlichen Sabbath und Unterschied des Alten und Neuen Testaments', in *Corpus Schwenckfeldianorum*, IV, 444-518.

164a. Cf. Stayer/Packull/Deppermann, 'Monogenesis'; K.R.Davis, most recently in 'Origins', AIHI 1977.

165. Cf. above, 443 n.2. For Müntzer there are now also the two editions by M.Bensing and B.Rüdiger, *Politische Schriften. Manifeste. Briefe 1524/5*, ²1973, and S.Bräuer and W.Ullmann, *Theologische Schriften aus dem Jahr 1523*, 1975. Quotations are from the edition by Franz (despite the deficiencies of this edition, which are

indicated in the reviews; cf. Steinmetz, *ZGW* 17, 1969, 739-48; G.Bräuer, *LuJ* 38, 1971, 121-31; H.Volz, *BDLG* 105, 1969, 599ff.; R.Schwarz, *TZ* 26, 1970, 147f., it is still the fullest).

166. Cf. A.Friesen, 'Thomas Müntzer in Marxist Thought', *ChH* 34, 1965, 306-27; id., 'Die ältere und die marxistische Müntzerdeutung', in *Thomas Müntzer*, ed. Friesen and Goertz, (447-80) 461ff. For the whole area of Marxist interpretation cf. also id., *Reformation and Utopia: The Marxist Interpretation of the Reformation and its Antecedents*, VIEG 71, 1974; R.Schmid, 'Thomas Müntzer im Geschichtsbild des dialektischen Materialismus', *DtPfrBl* 65, 1965, 258-62; B.Lohse, 'Thomas Müntzer in marxistischer Sicht', *Luther* 43, 1972, 60-73. In this respect the writings of E.Bloch have become particularly famous (cf. esp. *Thomas Müntzer als Theologe der Revolution*, [1]1921, enlarged ed. 1969), though they cannot be regarded as scholarly historical research. Cf. also esp. M.M.Smirin, *Die Volksreformation des Thomas Müntzer und der grosse Bauernkrieg*, 1952; A.Meusel, *Thomas Müntzer und seine Zeit*, 1952; M.Bensing, *Thomas Müntzer und der Thüringer Aufstand 1525*, 1966, and his illustrated biography, *Thomas Müntzer*, [2]1965.

167. Most important here are the works by C.Hinrichs, *Luther und Müntzer*, [2]1962; T.Nipperdey, 'Theologie und Revolution bei Thomas Müntzer', *ARG* 54, 1963, 145-81 (also in *Wirkungen der deutschen Reformation bis 1555*, ed. W.Hubatsch, WdF 203, 1967, 236-85; revised version in id., *Reformation, Revolution, Utopie*, 1975, 38-84 with an appendix on research into Müntzer, 1961-1974, id., 76-84; English ed. 'Theology and Revolution in Thomas Müntzer', Stayer/Packull, *Anabaptists*, 105-17 [extract] and Goertz, *Ordnung*; also id., 'Der Mystiker mit dem Hammer. Die theologische Begründung der Revolution bei Thomas Müntzer', *KuD* 20, 1974, 23-53 = *Thomas Müntzer*, ed. Friesen and Goertz, 403-44 = 'The Mystic with the Hammer: Thomas Müntzer's Theological Basis for Revolution', *MQR* 50, 1976, 83-113 = Stayer/ Packull, *Anabaptists*, 118-32 (extract). Cf. also W.Elliger, *Thomas Müntzer*, 1960; id., 'Thomas Müntzer', *TLZ* 90, 1965, cols.7-18 = *Thomas Müntzer*, ed. Friesen and Goertz, 54-73; id., *Thomas Müntzer, Leben und Werk*, 1975 [[3]1976] (cf. also the reviews by S.Bräuer, *TLZ* 102, 1977, cols.215-20, and e.g. B.Lohse, *Deutsches Allgemeines Sonntagsblatt* 1975, no. 21, 25 May 1975, 10); id., *Aussenseiter der Reformation: Thomas Müntzer. Ein Knecht Gottes*, 1975; E.Gritsch, *Reformer without a Church*, 1967; G.Rupp, *Patterns of Reformation*, 1969, 157-353; H.J.Hillerbrand, *Fellowship*, 1-30; K.Ebert, *Theologie und politisches Handeln, Thomas Müntzer als Modell*, 1973; L.Grane, 'Thomas Müntzer und Martin Luther', in *Bauernkriegs-Studien*, ed. B.Moeller, SVRG 189, 1975, 69-97 = Friesen/Goertz, *Müntzer*, 74-111; R.Schwarz, *Die apokalyptische Theologie Thomas Müntzers*, 1977, and the short account by S.Bräuer and H.-J.Goertz, 'Thomas Müntzer', in *Reformationszeit* I, ed. M.Greschat, 335-52; R. von Dülmen, *Reformation als Revolution*, 1977, 63-168; G.A.Benrath, in Andresen, *Handbuch* 2, 568ff. Short biography: H.-J.Goertz, *Thomas Müntzer. Anfragen an Theologie und Kirche*, ed. C.Demke, 1977. For the contemporary state of research into Müntzer cf. the accounts of literature by M.Steinmetz, 'Thomas Müntzer in der Forschung der Gegenwart', *ZfG* 23, 1975, 666-85; S.Bräuer, 'Müntzerforschung von 1965-1975', *LuJ* 44, 1977, 127-41; 45, 1978, 102-39 (cf. also id., 'Thomas Müntzer', *ZdZ* 29, 1975, 121-9; A.Friesen, 'Müntzerdeutung'; H.-J.Goertz, 'Schwerpunkte der neueren Müntzerforschung', in *Thomas Müntzer*, ed. Friesen/Goertz, 481-536.

168. Cf. esp. Goertz, *Ordnung*, esp. 56ff., 92ff. – However, Goldbach, op.cit., 68, has objected, in my view rightly, to the classification of Müntzer's overall view as mysticism. Müntzer is not a mystic but a Spiritualist (so too Gritsch, op.cit., 179ff.); J.M.Stayer, *Anabaptists and the Sword*, [2]1973, 74, criticizes Goertz for having minimalized the apocalyptic content of Müntzer's thought.

169. Cf. Goertz, op.cit., 40ff.

170. Op.cit., 136.

171. Op.cit., 143.

172. Op.cit., 131f.

173. Op.cit., 123ff.

174. Cf. the well-known passage in the 'Sermon before the Princes' (*Werke, Kritische Ausgabe*, 241-63; for its content and the circumstances of its composition cf. C.Hinrichs, *Luther*, 5-76; G.Wehr, *Thomas Müntzer in Selbstzeugnissen und Bilddokumenten*, 1972, 58ff.; W.Elliger, *Leben*, 443ff.) with the vision of the snakes and the eels, op.cit., 256. – It is not completely by chance that Müntzer agitated for the iconoclasm of Mallerbach, cf. Hinrichs, op.cit., 11f.; Elliger, *Leben*, 417f.

175. *Ausgedrückte Entblössung*, Werke, Kritische Ausgabe, 293ff.

176. Cf.Goertz, op.cit., 134ff. W.Ullmann, 'Das Geschichtsverständnis Thomas Müntzers', in Demke (ed.), *Thomas Müntzer*, (45-63) 47, points out that Müntzer did, however, put forward the theory of decay in a moderate form.

177. Cf. W.Ullmann, 'Ordo Rerum. Müntzer's Randbemerkungen zu Tertullian als Quelle für das Verständnis seiner Theologie', *Theologische Versuche* VII, 1976, 125-40, esp. 128ff.

177a. Seebass, *Hut*, 415ff., has pointed out that Müntzer's understanding of order was based on Gen.1.28: it is concerned with the right relationship between God and his creatures. Hut's theological thought was also shaped by this 'term which is central for the understanding of his theology' (Seebass, op.cit., 416).

178. Op.cit., 14ff. W.Elliger's most important concern is also to work this out, cf. *Leben*, Einleitung, 1ff.

179. Op.cit., 144.

180. H.Gerdes, *Luthers Streit mit den Schwärmern*, 1955, has already given an acute description of Müntzer's relationship to scripture, and especially the Old Testament understood in a legalistic way (also in connection with Karlstadt's views); cf. also id., 'Der Weg des Glaubens bei Müntzer und Luther', *Luther* 26, 1955, 152-65 = Friesen/Goertz, *Müntzer*, 16-30. Cf. now the works of R.Dismer, *Geschichte, Glaube, Revolution. Zur Schriftauslegung Thomas Müntzers*, Diss. theol. Hamburg 1974; R.Mau, 'Müntzers Verständnis der Bibel', in Demke (ed.), *Thomas Müntzer*, 21-44; J.Rogge, 'Wort und Geist bei Thomas Müntzer', *ZdZ* 29, 1975, 129-38; Grane, 'Müntzer', 88ff./92ff. For what follows cf. also W.Elliger, 'Müntzer und das Alte Testament', in *Wort und Geschichte*, Festschrift K.Elliger, 1973, 57-64, and above all A.Friesen, 'Thomas Müntzer and the Old Testament', *MennQR* 47, 1973, 5-19 = 'Thomas Müntzer und das Alte Testament', in Friesen/Goertz (ed.), *Thomas Müntzer*, 383-402.

181. *Werke, Kritische Ausgabe*, 265-319. The copy intended for the censor has the title *Gezeugnus des erstenn Capitels des Euangelion Luce...*; both versions are printed in parallel in the critical edition. For the content cf. Hinrichs, op.cit., 101ff.; Elliger, *Leben*, 536ff.

182. *Werke, Kritische Ausgabe*, 277. The inspiration of the present-day believer is identified with the inspiration of the authors of the biblical writings. At one point in the 'Sermon before the Princes' Müntzer makes Paul (Rom.10.8,20) speak in a mystical sense: 'to hear words from within, in the abyss of the soul through the revelation of God. And if there is a man who does not see and accept this through the living testimony of God, Romans 8, he cannot say anything at all about God, though he may have devoured a hundred thousand Bibles.' *Werke, Kritische Ausgabe*, 251. Further instances of this relativizing of the Bible in Mau, op.cit., 28.

183. Op.cit., 278.

184. Op.cit., 273f.

185. Cf. Hinrichs, op.cit., n.44, ad loc.

186. Op.cit., 277.

187. Hinrichs, op.cit., 107, has here shifted the meaning of the rendering of the

'would' (the subject is 'the person learned in scripture') by rendering it 'should'. Goertz, op.cit., 73 n.2, quotes the passage as an absolute statement in a similar way. By contrast in the 'Schutzrede' ('Hochverursachte Schutzrede', *Werke, Kritische Ausgabe*, (321-43) 338, in his defence against Luther Müntzer can refer to his own use of scripture (similarly cited by Goertz, ibid.). Mau, op.cit., gives a very vivid account of Müntzer's ambivalent relationship to scripture after the Prague manifesto (originally Müntzer put forward a word-theology of a Lutheran kind); for Müntzer the 'inner word' is now decisive; as an external authority, the Bible bears witness to that spiritual reality, but only for the elect; in the case of the damned it only confirms their hardness of heart. The dualistic basic model is at work here in two ways.

188. J.Rogge, op.cit.

189. For this group of problems cf. Hinrichs, op.cit., 172ff.; Goertz, op.cit., 73ff.; R.F.Thiemann, 'Law and Gospel in the Thought of Thomas Muentzer', *LuthQ* 17, 1975, 347-63, esp. 357ff. The point made by Dismer, op.cit., 199, 201, that Müntzer refers to the whole Bible and not predominantly to the Old Testament, is important. The same goes for Müntzer's disciple H.Hut, cf. G.Seebass, *Hut*, 454ff.

190. 'Schutzrede', *Werke, Kritische Ausgabe*, 327. Cf. also Grane, 'Müntzer', 90-94: 'Only one thing is left for a gospel, namely the realization of the testimony of scripture, i.e. the fulfilment of the law in the life of the elect.'

191. Op. cit., 173. – W.Elliger, *Müntzer*, 1960, 17, points to the 'fulfilment of the binding demand of God' as a central postulate for Müntzer. Cf. also 20f., 39. – For the role of scripture as law cf. further Mau, op.cit., 33ff.

192. For Müntzer's orientation on the Old Testament cf. already H.Boehmer, 'Thomas Müntzer und das jüngste Deutschland', *Gesammelte Aufsätze*, 1927, (189-222) 207. There are statements like this especially in the 'Schutzrede': Müntzer expressly declares that he relies particularly on the Pentateuch for his understanding of the law ('now through the beginning of the Bible and ordering of the first sections I strive for the purity of the divine law', *Werke, Kritische Ausgabe*, 326f., and also 'Christ began from the beginning like Moses and declares the law from beginning to end', ibid., 326). Goertz points out that there is no simple biblicism here, but that the whole of the scripture is understood as a unity in the light of the 'inner word', op.cit., 73ff. This does not mean the 'law of man's primal condition' with its absence of state and possessions, justice and compulsion, nor natural law (against Hinrichs, op.cit., 174f.), nor the Anabaptist principle of the ethic of love and non-violence in the light of the Sermon on the Mount. Rather, Müntzer accepts the use of force in his programme, in the light of an orientation which is primarily on the Old Testament! Cf. esp. Friesen, *Müntzer*, 8ff., 387ff. This inner orientation on the Old Testament is not done away with by the material use of the whole of scripture, against Dismer, cf. n.189 above (cf. the correction by Grane, *Müntzer*, n.91). Müntzer's abrupt rejection of Marcionitism and the relativization of the Old Testament by the Humanists is important, cf. Ullmann, *Geschichtsverständnis*, 51.

193. Cf. op.cit., 102, 104.

194. *Werke, Kritische Ausgabe*, 267.

195. Cf. the beginning of the Vorrede, op.cit.

196. Similarly in the 'Sermon before the Princes': 'Therefore a new Daniel must arise and interpret your revelation', *Werke, Kritische Ausgabe*, 257.

197. *Werke, Kritische Ausgabe*, 273. For the significance of the Gideon pattern cf. also Elliger, *Leben*, 760.

198. Op.cit., 39ff. By contrast G.Maron, 'Thomas Müntzer als Theologe des Gerichts', *ZKG* 83, 1972, 195-225 = *Thomas Müntzer*, ed. Friesen/Goertz, 339-82, limits the apocalyptic theme in Müntzer to the idea of judgment. However, for criticism cf. Bräuer, *LuJ* 1978, 133f. For the role of apocalyptic in Müntzer cf. also Stayer, *Anabaptists*, 74ff. For the 'Sermon before the Princes', see 82ff.

199. This follows first from Goertz's investigation and secondly from Ullmann's more recent works. Cf. Ullmann, *Geschichtsverständnis*, 51ff. (on the choice of the text Dan.2 for the Sermon before the Princes); also id., 'Thomas Müntzers Lehre von Gott und von der Offenbarung Gottes', *Theologische Versuche* VI, 1975, 89-104, esp. 99. R.Schwarz, *Die apokalyptische Theologie*, by contrast again puts more stress on the chiliastic character of Müntzer's understanding of the Reformation and compares it with similar views in Taboritism.

200. *Werke, Kritische Ausgabe*, 252ff.

201. Op.cit., 255.

202. Deut.13.6; Ex.22.2 and other Old Testament texts are evidence of this for him, op.cit., 259. It is the task of the prince to wield this sword. Ullmann, op.cit., 55, attacks the 'theological absurdity' that Müntzer could have proclaimed the sword as a means of salvation. But the quotation he uses continues, 'thus the sword is also necessary to blot out the godless', op.cit., 261.

203. For Müntzer's prophetic claim cf. also F.Lau, 'Die prophetische Apokalyptik Müntzers und Luthers Absage an die Bauernrevolution', in *Gedenkschrift W.Elert*, 1955, 163-70 = *Thomas Müntzer*, ed. Friesen/Goertz, 3-15.

204. Op.cit., 258.

205. On 24 July 1524, cf. Hinrichs, op.cit.,69.

206. See above, 108f., 136f.

207. Goertz, op.cit., 148, denies that Müntzer is dependent on Joachim because of this distinction. However, influence from Joachim on Müntzer cannot be ruled out in principle, cf. Friesen, *Müntzer*, 13ff./329ff.

208. Cf. P.Kawerau, *Melchior Hoffmann als religiöser Denker*, 1954; K.Deppermann, *Melchior Hoffman. Soziale Unruhen und apokalyptische Visionen im Zeitalter der Reformation*, 1979; his writings (cf. ibid., 4f.; bibliography nos.39-61, 130ff.) have mostly not been reprinted in new editions (the *Ordonnantie*, 1530, however, is in the Bibliotheca Reformatoria Neerlandica, V, 145-70; ET 'The Ordinance of God', in Williams (ed.), *Writers*, 183-203). Also cf. W.J.Kühler, *Geschiedenis der Nederlandsche doopsgezinden in de Zestiende eeuw*, ²1961, 52ff.; C.Krahn, *Dutch Anabaptism*, 1968, 80ff.; Stayer, *Anabaptists*, 211-26; K.Deppermann, 'Melchior Hoffmans Weg von Luther zu den Täufern', in *Umstrittenes Täufertum*, ed. Goertz, 173-205; id., 'Melchior Hoffman', in *Reformationszeit* I, ed. M.Greschat, 323-34.

209. Evidence in Kawerau, op.cit., 36, 56f.; cf. also Deppermann, *Hoffman*, 59f.The double view of the Old Testament indicated above, 000 n.187, also appears in Hoffmann (this is not made clear by Kawerau, op.cit., 57 n.1).

210. Cf. Kawerau, op.cit., 75ff; Deppermann, *Hoffman*, 212ff. Hoffmann sees himself as the prophet Elijah (cf. Kawerau, op.cit., 108) who announces the end, and Müntzer as Gideon, who brings in the kingdom of God.

211. Cf. briefly Williams, *Reformation*, 355-60; Kühler, *Geschiedenis*, 69ff., 229ff.; Stayer, *Anabaptists*, 211f., and above all Krahn, op.cit., 133ff.

212. Cf. R.Stupperich, *Einleitung*, in *Schriften*, Xff. Cf. also the short biography, W. de Bakker, 'Bernhard Rothmann. Die Dialektik der Radikalisierung in Münster', in *Radikale Reformatoren*, ed. H.-J.Goertz, 167-78. The most thorough monograph on Rothmann's thinking is the investigation by J.W.Porter, *Bernhard Rothmann (1495-1535), Royal Orator of the Münster Anabaptist Kingdom*, Wisconsin dissertation, Ann Arbor Microfilm 1964.

213. Cf. Stupperich, op.cit., XIX; W.J.de Bakker, *De vroege theologie von Bernhard Rothmann*, Doopsgezinde Bijdragen n.r.3, 1977, 9-20.

214. Op.cit., 223f.

215. 'Von Verborgenheit der Schrift', *Schriften*, 302, with a reference to Luke 17.29.

216. *Restitution*, ch.9, op.cit., 244ff. The 'key' to the scriptures is the doing of the commandments, 'Von Verborgenheit der Schrift', 2, op.cit., 303ff. – For the concep-

tion of the spirit as the 'key' to scripture, which also goes back to M.Hoffmann, cf.also R.Stupperich, *Das münsterische Täufertum*, 1958, 16, who refers to the work of Hendrik Roll, 'De slotel van dat secret des Nachtmaels' (thus the full title), *BRN* 5, 1909, 1-123.

217. *Restitution*, ch.17, op.cit., 270ff.

217a. In fact a penal law was promulgated in Münster which declared that predominantly Old Testament commandments were directly binding on the present and had the death penalty as the only sanction: cf. the Latin translation of the lost original in H. von Kerssenbroick, *Anabaptistici furoris Monasteriensium inclitam West-phaliae metropolim evertentis*, ed. H. Detmer, Geschichtsquellen des Bistums Münster 5/6, Münster 1899-1900, 577-81: *Duodecim seniorum edictum publicum*. Cf. also D.Kluge, 'Die Rechts- und Sittenordnung des Täuferreiches zu Münster', *JWKG* 69, 1976, (75-100) 78ff. The so-called 'Münster articles' are a general ordering of the church and daily life: J.Niesert (ed.), *Münsterische Urkundensammlung* I, Coesfeld 1826, 160-6 = H.Detmer (ed.), 'Ungedruckte Quellen zur Geschichte der Wiederta-"ufer in Münster', *WestfZ* 51, 1893, (90-118) 115f. Cf. also D.Kluge, 'Die Vorbereitung der Täuferherrschaft in Münster', *JWKG* 68, 1975, (23-38) 34ff.

218. *Restitution*, ch.3, op.cit., 224. The typological evaluation of the Old Testament, especially the 'tabernacle of Moses', also occurs elsewhere, cf. especially *Verborgen-heit*, ch.3, op.cit., 307ff.

219. *Restitution*, ch. 2, op.cit., 222.

220. 'Von Verborgenheit', *Schriften*, 309, cf. the following remarks on the symbolic significance of the 'tabernacle of Moses'.

220a. Cf. Porter, *Rothmann*, Vf., 117ff.

220b. Cf. Porter, *Rothmann*, 111ff.

220c. Porter, *Rothmann*, 174ff. identifies 'faith and good works' as a central theme in Rothmann. It is of decisive importance to follow the law of God taught by Christ, 176ff. This is also matched by the role played by the natural law of God which is attested by every man's conscience, cf. 170ff.

220d. Like Joachim of Fiore, Rothmann is familiar with the succession of three ages of the world; the third is the kingdom of Christ in the millennium, which is still expected before the eschaton, cf. Porter, *Rothmann*, 217ff.

221. Cf. Stupperich, op.cit., XVII, XXI, 443, and already H.Detmer (ed.), 'Beken-tenisse', in *Zwei Schriften des Münsterischen Wiedertäufers Bernhard Rothmann*, 1904, 125.

222. Op.cit., 443ff.

223. Op.cit., 444.

224. Op.cit., 285-99.

225. Op.cit., 294f.-297.

226. Op.cit., 297. For the messianic mood in the *Restitution* see also W.J.Kühler, *Geschiedenis*, I, 1932, 146ff. For Rothmann's writings on the use of violence cf. also Stayer, *Anabaptists*, 239ff.

227. For the outward course of events and the measures carried through on an Old Testament pattern cf. F.Blanke, 'Das Reich der Wiedertäufer zu Münster', *ARG* 37, 1940, 13-37 = *Aus der Welt der Reformation*, 1960, 48-71, and recently K.-H.Kir-chhoff, *Utopia 1534/5*, Geschichte der Stadt Münster 3, 1979; H.Rothert, *Das Reich der 'Wiedertäufer' zu Münster*, (1947, ²1948) ³1982, ed. K.-H.Kirchhoff; G.Dethlefs, 'Das Wiedertäuferreich in Münster 1534/5', in *Die Wiedertäufer in Münster. Katalog zur Ausstellung*, Münster, 1982 (⁴1982/3), 19-36; R.Stupperich, 'Das münsterische Täufertum, sein Wesen und seine Verwirklichung', ibid., 37-54. Cf. also biblio-graphy, ibid., 62-4. Cf. also H.Ritschl, *Die Kommune der Wiedertäufer in Münster*, 1923; H. von Schubert, *Der Kommunismus der Wiedertäufer in Münster und seine Quellen*, 1919; G.Brendler, *Das Täuferreich zu Münster 1534/5*, 1966, and the inves-

tigations into social history by H.Neumann, *Masse und Führer in der Wieder-täuferschaft in Münster*, phil. diss (typescript), Freiburg 1959; O.Rammstedt, *Sekte und soziale Bewegung. Soziologische Analyse der Täufer in Münster (1534/35)*, 1966; K.-H.Kirchhoff, *Die Täufer in Münster 1534/35*, 1973; L.G.Jansma, *Melchioriten, Munstersen en Batenburgers*, 1977, 111ff. Also von Dülmen, *Reformation*, 229-355.

228. So none of his sermons has been preserved, cf. Stupperich, op.cit., 52.

228a. The Old Testament is also seen as being completely at one with the New Testament by Müntzer's disciple H.Hut, as both are understood as law and identified with the natural law. Cf. Seebass, *Hut*, 438ff., 452ff.

229. Cf. above, 445 n.7. The second designation gives a striking special doctrine, but not the core of their attitude.

230. After he had first of all produced a meditation on the sources of this group, *Per la storia degli Eretici Italiani nel seculo XVI i Europa*, 1937, D.Cantimori gave a comprehensive account of its representatives, *Eretici Italiani del Cinquecento*, 1939 = German translation *Italienische Häretiker der Spätrenaissance*, 1949. Cf. the review by G.Ritter, 'Wegebahner eines "aufgeklärten" Christentums im 16. Jahrhundert', *ARG* 37, 1940, 268-89. Their further fortunes in Eastern Europe have recently been traced by D.Caccamo, *Eretici italiani in Moravia, Polonia, Transsilvania*, 1970; cf. already id., 'Richerche sul socianismo in Europa', *BHR* 26, 1964, 573-607.

231. G. Ritter, op.cit., several times demonstrates in Cantimori's approach that for him a comprehensive definition of the thought-world of the figures he describes remains basically obscure and blurred. It is too superficial to see christological speculation as the centre of their thought (*Häretiker*, 26). Rather, Cantimori himself (ibid., 30) recognizes that the anti-Trinitarian interpretation of Jesus is a radical consequence of the *imitatio* thinking which aims at presenting Jesus increasingly as a mere exemplary man.

232. *Häretiker*, 25.

233. G.Ritter, op.cit., 270f., points out that 'that inward attitude among large areas of the upper middle class towards the Christian doctrine of salvation' which was to be found in Germany was almost completely missing in Italy.

234. One example of this is the almost effusive praise of Castellio in the judgment of R.M.Jones, *Spiritual Reformers*, 1914, ²1950, Ch.VI. Cantimori is one of the few critical commentators.

235. Here rebirth is seen completely as divine action towards man and is in no way understood synergistically, cf. e.g. the remark by Servetus, *Dialogorum de Trinitate libri duo*, 1533, fol. D 5¹r, in Cantimori, *Häretiker*, 42: *Omnino debet fieri patre trahente, et illuminante, et ex mera gratia, quos vult, vocante et iustificante, quia non est currentis nec volentis, sed Dei miserentis.*

236. The biography by F.Buisson, *Sébastien Castellion*, two vols, 1892 reprinted 1964, is still basic. Cf. also E.Giran, *Sébastien Castellion et la réforme Calviniste*, 1914 reprinted 1970; R.Bainton, B.Becker, M.Valkhoff, S.van der Woude (eds.), *Castellioniana. Quatre études sur Sébastien Castellion et l'idée de la tolérance*, 1951; R.Bainton, 'Sebastian Castellio and the Toleration Controversy of the Sixteenth Century', in *Persecution and Liberty*, Festschrift G.L.Burr, 1931, 183-210; W.Kaegi, *Castellio und die Anfänge der Toleranz*, Basler Universitätsreden 32, 1953; B.Becker (ed.), *Autour de Michel Servet et de Sébastien Castellion*, 1953 (a collection with a number of articles about Castellio); S.van der Woude, *Verguisd Geloof*, nd (Servetus and Castellio); G.Güldner, *Das Toleranz-Problem in den Niederlanden im Ausgang des 16. Jahrhunderts*, 1968, 16-31; J.B.Bauer, 'Brüderlichkeit und Toleranz bei Sebastian Castellio' in *Aspekte der Brüderlichkeit in der Theologie*, ed. J.Marböck, 1981, 115-33. Castellio's influence is discussed by R.Guggisberg, *Sebastian Castellio im Urteil seiner Nachwelt vom Späthumaismus bis zur Aufklärung*, 1956. Cf. also B.Becker, 'Coornhert en Castellio', in *Handelingen van het 18e Nederl. Philologen-Congres*, Groningen 1939, 49-51; id.,

'Sébastien Castellio et Thierry Coornhert', *Studia Bibliographica... H. de la Fontaine Verwey*, 1966 (1967), 11-25; Güldner, op.cit., 1.Exkurs: 'Coornhert und Castellio', 159-69; R.Bainton, 'Sebastian Castellio and the British American Tradition', *Het Boek*, NS 30, 1951, 347-9. J.Jacquod, 'Sébastien Castellion et l'Angleterre, quelques aspects de son influence', *BHR* 15, 1953, 15-44. For early connections between Castellio and England cf. H.R.Guggisberg, 'Sebastian Castellio und die englische Reformation', *Festgabe H. von Greyerz*, 1967, 319-38; for his stay in Basle and influences on France cf. P.G.Bietenholz, *Basle and France in the Sixteenth Century*, 1971, 122-36; for later followers in Basle itself, A.Rotondò, 'Pietro Perna e la vita culturale e religiosa di Basilea fra il 1570 e il 1580', in *Studi*, 273-391, esp. 281ff. Modern new editions of the writings of Castellio have so far been scarce; much is still unpublished. But cf. the selection of unpublished letters in Buisson, op.cit., II, 381-476, of unedited fragments, 477-500. The work *De haereticis an sint persequendi*, 1554, appeared in a facsimile edition in 1954, ed. S.van der Woude, with preface; the French translation, *Traité des hérétiques à savoir si on les doit persécuter*, 1913 (ed. P.Olivet). For circumstances of its composition and its content cf. also U.Plath, *Calvin und Basel in den Jahren 1552-1556*, BBGW 133 = BSHST 22, 1974, 128ff.; for that and other material connected with Castellio cf. E.Droz, 'Castellioniana', in *Chemins de l'hérésie* II, 1971, 325-432. The unpublished writing, *De arte dubitandi et confidendi, ignorandi et sciendi*, not complete, ed. E.Feist, is in Cantimori (ed.), *Per la storia*, 277-430, the complete text now in S.Castellio, *De arte dubitandi et confidendi, ignorandi et sciendi*, introduction and notes by E.Feist Hirsch, 1981 (SMRI,29). ET *Concerning Heretics, etc.*, ed. R.H.Bainton, 1935. Also *Conseil à la France désolée*, ed. M.F.Valkhoff, 1967 (on the content and circumstances of composition cf. also H.R.Guggisberg, 'Castellio und der Ausbruch der Religionskriege in Frankreich', *ARG* 68, 1977, 253-66) and also the French/Latin parallel text: *De l'impunité des hérétiques / De Haereticis non puniendis*, ed. B.Becker/M.Valkhoff, 1971. Bibliography of the old impressions in Buisson, op.cit., II, 341-80. Supplements also in Guggisberg, op.cit., 177ff. Cf. also H.R.Guggisberg, 'Castellio, Sebastian (1515-1563)', *TRE* 7, 663-5.

237. After he had first published *Moses latinus* (1546; Buisson, op.cit., II, 355, no.5) and other Old Testament books in Latin translation (Buisson, 355f., nos 6,7), there later followed the whole Bible in Latin, with notes as a continuous exegesis (Buisson, 357 no.8), which at the same time also appeared separately (Buisson, 362, no.11) and in French (Buisson 359, no.9). The Latin Bible and also the New Testament (Buisson, 359ff., no.10) went through many editions before the end of the eighteenth century. In 1557 he defended his translation of the New Testament against Beza in a Defensio (cf. Buisson, 104f.) – printing was possible only in 1562 (Buisson, 362, no.12).

238. Here first of all we have the truly humanistic impulse towards providing the smoothest and most elegant text possible, cf. the Preface to *Moses latinus*, and Buisson, op.cit., I, 295f. However, the *laudatio* to Moses as the master of all arts also belongs in the same context. For the French translation of the Bible cf. also O.Douen in Buisson, op.cit., I, 415ff. E.Giran, op.cit., 96ff., stresses the radical-Reformation intention of the translation over against this.

239. *Die Schriftauslegung Sebastian Castellios*, Tübingen theological dissertation 1953 (typescript); id., 'Die Frage nach einem hermeneutischen Prinzip bei Sebastian Castellio', in *Autour de Michel Servet, etc.*, 206-24 (partial printing of the dissertation; in what follows I quote from the collected volume). E.Feist-Hirsch, 'Castellio's "De Arte Dubitandi" and the Problem of Religious Liberty', in the same volume, 244-58, makes almost the same observations, but draws the opposite conclusions from them (Castellio as a pioneer of modern Western religious and political freedom).

240. *Persecution and Liberty*, 185; *Castellioniana*, 53. Whereas earlier he derived the former more directly from Erasmus and the latter from Franck and the German

mystics, later he refers to Castellio's humanistic training in Lyons for his contact with the former and his translation of the *Theologia Germanica* and the *Imitatio Christi* (Buisson, op.cit., II, 17 and 18) in connection with the latter trend. However, both translations appeared very late (1557 and 1563) and are only signs of a basic attitude which existed for much longer. Güldner, *Toleranz-problem*, 29f., recognizes the same two basic lines.

241. *Persecution and Liberty*, 186. Güldner, op.cit., 30, takes a very similar view.

242. For the extent of the problem cf. already W.Köhler, 'Geistesahnen des Johannes Acontius', in *Festschrift K.Müller*, 1922, 198-208. For Castellio cf. Bainton, in *Persecution and Liberty*, 202; id., in *Castellioniana*, 56ff.

243. *Autour de Michel Servet*, 210ff.

244. Ad No. 129, fol. Iiiij b. There are numerous similar statements in Güldner, op.cit.

245. In the letter to G.Constantin in Buisson, op. cit., II, (431-4) 434, cf. Liebing, *Frage*, 210.

246. Liebing, op.cit., 214.

247. Evidence in Liebing, op.cit., 206f.

248. Cf. again Liebing, op.cit., 207f.

249. Liebing, op.cit., 208f.

250. Liebing, op.cit., 213.

251. When God is described with Stoic terms as *bonus* and *optimus* (*De arte dubitandi*, ed.Feist, 314, 310 = ed. Feist Hirsch, 20, 14; cf. Liebing, op.cit., 215), we have formulas which appear again some decades later in Herbert of Cherbury, 'the Father of deism' (cf. below, 521 n.22).

252. Cf. Liebing, ibid.

253. These include the concept of the 'good' (which also plays a role in Thomistic scholasticism – Humanism and Scholasticism are in no way always opposites), or the Good and the Beautiful, as with Shaftesbury; in each case we can see a deliberate return to antiquity.

254. Ed. Feist, 357-64 = ed. Feist Hirsch, 59-67; there is a section with the climax of the argument in Buisson, op.cit., 495. French translation in Baudouin, op.cit., 97ff.

255. Cf. Liebing, op.cit., 216f.

256. Castellio expressly produces a comparison with Christ, *qui Graeco sermone Logos dicitur* (ed. Feist Hirsch, 65).

257. *quasi quaedam interior et aeterna semperque loquens veritatis oratio atque sermo* (ed. Feist Hirsch, 66).

258. Bainton, *Castellioniana*, 61, already stresses the difference from deductive *ratio*. Liebing, op.cit., 219f., offers illuminating instances of the equivalence of *ratio* and *spiritus* in Castellio.

259. Cf. Liebing, op.cit., 219. For the Stoic background of the concept of *ratio* in Castellio, R.Bainton, *Concerning Heretics*, 105, refers to passages in Cicero and Justin.

260. Op.cit., 223.

261. Castellio, too, is in no way the modern man that his admirers suppose; e.g. a judgment like that of J.Lindeboom, *Stiefkinderen van het Christendom*, 1929, 260, 'Here we are far from the Middle Ages, and even a long way past the end of the sixteenth century,' is quite wrong.

262. The circulation of Castellio's writings in the Netherlands and in England and their role in the dispute of the Arminians/Remonstrants and Socinians with their orthodox opponents is evidence of this. Cf. esp. Guggisberg and the articles by Becker, Bainton and Jacquod.

4. Martin Bucer

1. A.Lang, *Der Evangelienkommentar Martin Butzer's und die Grundzüge seiner Theologie*, 1900 reprinted 1972.

2. H.Bornkamm, 'Martin Bucer. Der dritte deutsche Reformator', in *Das Jahrhundert der Reformation*, ²1966, 88-112 (= *Martin Bucers Bedeutung für die europäische Reformationsgeschichte*, 1952), 88.

3. The account of research by R.Stupperich, 'Stand und Aufgabe der Butzer-Forschung', *ARG* 42, 1951, 244-59, predominantly reported the obstacles which above all the circumstances of the time had put in the way of further solid work. His verdict was: 'The hopes which people might have had sixty years ago in connection with Bucer scholarship have not been fulfilled.' – Cf. also B.Thompson, 'Bucer Study since 1918', *ChH* 25, 1956, 63-82, and the survey of research in F.Krüger, op.cit., 3-37.

4. Cf. H.Bornkamm, op.cit.; W.Dankbaar, *Martin Bucers Beziehungen zu den Niederlanden*, 1961; E.Harvey, *Martin Bucer in England*, 1906; A.Lang, 'Puritanismus und Pietismus, 1941; also id., 'Butzer in England', *ARG* 38, 1941, 230-9; C.Hopf, *Martin Bucer and the English Reformation*, 1946; also the correspondence with the Bohemian Brethren, ' La correspondance entre les Frères Tcheques et Bucer', *RHPR* 31, 1951, 102-56.

5. Cf. recently the continuation of the Bucer bibliography: M.Köhn, 'Bucer Bibliographie 1951-1974', in *Bucer und seine Zeit. Forschungsbeiträge und Bibliographie* (Festschrift R.Stupperich), 1976, 133-65, and id., '25 Jahre Bucer-Forschung', in *Horizons Européens de la Reforme en Alsace*, 1980, 161-75. Cf. also R.Stupperich, 'Bucer, Martin (1491-1551)', *TRE* 7, 1981, 258-70 (with bibliography). Of the more recent monographs the most important for our theme are: Johannes Müller, *Martin Bucers Hermeneutik*, 1965, and F.Krüger, op.cit. Cf. also K.Koch, *Studium Pietatis. Martin Bucer als Ethiker*, 1962, and most recently M.Greschat, 'Der Ansatz der Theologie Martin Bucers', *TLZ* 103, 1978, cols. 81-96; id., 'Martin Bucer', in *Reformationszeit II*, 7-28. Summary accounts of Bucer's theology are given in O.Ritschl, *Dogmengeschichte des Protestantismus*, III, 1926, 122-56, and H.E.Weber, *Reformation, Orthodoxie und Rationalismus*, I, 1, 1937, 203-17. Cf. also R.Seeberg, *Lehrbuch der Dogmengeschichte*, IV, 2, ³1920 (=⁴1954), 552ff. Unfortunately there is not yet a biography of Bucer which satisfies modern academic demands; one must still go back to the old account by J.W.Baum, *Capito und Butzer, Strassburgs Reformatoren*, 1860, which is thorough only for the years up to 1529. G.Anrich, *Martin Bucer*, 1914, is a popular account. Cf. also H.Eels, *Martin Bucer*, 1931, reprinted 1971 (and on it Stupperich, *ARG*, 1951, 250). – Cf. also the monograph by S.Looss, 'Der frühe Martin Butzer – Ideologie und revolutionäre Wirklichkeit in der Zeit von Reformation und Bauernkrieg', *Jahrbuch für Geschichte* 10, 1974, 57-119, which goes up to 1534.

6. *Martini Buceri Opera Omnia, Ser. 1, Deutsche Schriften*, ed. R.Stupperich (= DW): so far vols 1, 2, 3, 4, 5, 7, 17 have appeared (1960ff.); *Martini Buceri Opera Latina*: so far there have appeared Vol.I, 1982, XV (*De regno Christi*, 1955; cf. also Vol.XV bis: *Du royaume de Jésus Christ, traduction de 1558*, 1954). *Correspondance de Bucer*, Vol.I, ed. J.Rott, SMRT XXV, 1979; cf. also J.Rott, *Correspondance de Martin Bucer. Liste alphabétiques des correspondants*, Association des Publications de la Faculté de Théologie Protestante de l'Université des Sciences humaines de Strasbourg, Bulletin 1, 1977. From earlier there is *Der Briefwechsel des Landgrafen Philipp von Hessen mit Bucer*, ed. M.Lenz, three vols, 1880-91 (reprinted 1965). Also J.Pollet, *Martin Bucer. Etudes sur la correspondance*, two vols, 1958-62.

7. Cf. Stupperich, *ARG* 1951, 244f.

8. Cf. Bucer's account of this event in *Briefwechsel des Beatus Rhenanus*, ed. A.Horawitz and K.Hartfelder, 1886, reprinted 1966, 108ff.; also in WA IX, 160-9 – the better

text. For the event itself cf. H.Boehmer, *Der junge Luther*, 1951, ⁶1971, 173ff.; K.Koch, *Studium*, 10ff.; M.Greschat, 'Die Anfänge der reformatorischen Theologie Martin Bucers', in *Reformation und Humanismus. Festschrift R.Stupperich*, 1969, 124-40.

9. W.Köhler, *Zwingli und Luther*, two vols, 1924 and 1953, has given a detailed account of the history of these negotiations in connection with the understanding of the eucharist down to 1538. Cf. also E.Bizer, *Studien zur Geschichte des Abendmahlsstreites im 16.Jahrhundert*, 1940 (reprinted 1962).

10. H.Strohl, 'Buzer interprète de Luther', *RHPR* 19, 1939, 223-61, takes the view that Bucer preserved Luther's original intentions more purely than Melanchthon or the Gnesio-Lutherans – but did he not just misunderstand him? See below, 00 n.23. The differences between Bucer and Luther, which from the beginning were deepseated, can hardly be overlooked; cf. *inter alia* W.Holsten, 'Christentum und nicht christliche Religionen nach der Auffassung Bucers', *ThStKr* 107, 1936, 105-94, passim; J.Müller, op.cit., 25ff.; K.Koch, op.cit., 10ff.; Greschat, *Anfänge*; id., *Ansatz*, esp. cols.87f.

10a. Cf. also E.-W.Kohls, 'M.Bucer als Anhänger Luthers', *TZ* 33, 1977, 210-18, though he overlooks the differences.

11. Krüger, op.cit., 225.

12. Stupperich, in DW 1, 10.

13. Cf. R.Seeberg, op.cit., 555 (on Zwingli and Bucer): 'Both were decisively influenced by Luther's gospel and both then interpreted this in accordance with the spirit of the strong pre-Reformation trends with which they were surrounded.' For the wider influence of the Humanist attitude on the second generation of the Reformers generally cf. also L.W.Spitz, 'Humanism in the Reformation', *Studies... Baron*, 641-62. In this connection the remarks of M.Greschat about the relations of Bucer to Humanism are particularly interesting: cf. 'Martin Bucer als Dominikanermönch', in *Bucer und seine Zeit*, 30-53; id., *Ansatz*, esp. cols.83-85.

14. Cf. Stupperich, op.cit.

15. H.E.Weber, op.cit., 203.

16. As does e.g. A. Lang Bucer's mystical and spiritualistic impulse, and his 'pietism' (cf. *Evangelienkommentar* 8, 137, 377f., and the title of the work of his old age, *Puritanismus und Pietismus*), denying any Humanist influence. Ignorance of cultural history is expressed in his statement: 'Elsewhere Humanism and Pietism end up in history as opposites,' *Puritanismus*, 15. By contrast G.Anrich has strongly stressed the influence of Humanism on Bucer, in 'Die Strassburger Reformation nach ihrer religiösen Eigenart und ihrer Bedeutung für den Gesamtprotestantismus', *ChW* 19, 1905, cols.583-7 (602-6, 630-4); cf. also id., *Martin Bucer*, 121ff.; cf. 73 and 'Bucer' in *RGG¹*, I, 1372f.

17. Cf. Anrich, *Martin Bucer*, 40, 124; H.Bornkamm, *Martin Bucer*, 107: 'But Bucer attempted to say that now as a Humanist, now as a Platonist, now as a Reformer, now as an Anabaptist, now as a Catholic, as he wanted to be all things to all men.' However, Bornkamm sees the unity in Bucer's concern. – Recently Greschat, *Ansatz*, has worked this out particularly well.

18. E.g. in Anrich, *Bucer*, 121. H.E.Weber, op.cit., 216, sees a tension between 'objective system' and 'subjective appropriation'; H.Bornkamm, op.cit., finds his theology 'often complicated and barely comprehensible'.

19. Cf. E.-W.Kohls, *Die Schule bei Martin Bucer in ihrem Verhältnis zu Kirche und Obrigkeit*, 1963, 23ff., 42; Krüger, op. cit., 39f.

20. That is shown in particular by the list of books ordered by Bucer dated 30 April 1518, now in DW 1, 281-4, with numerous works of Erasmus; cf. Baum, op.cit., 101; Kohls, op.cit., n.148 on p.185; M.Greschat, 'Martin Bucers Bücherverzeichnis', *AKuG* 57, 1975, 162-85; cf. also id., *Ansatz*, n.46.

21. Cf. R.Raubenheimer, 'Martin Bucer und seine humanistischen Speyerer Freun-

de', *BPfKG* 32, 1965, 1-52; Krüger, 40ff. His correspondence with Beatus Rhenanus is particularly important evidence: Briefwechsel nos.75, 79, 95, 119, 146, 160, 162 (163), 200, 202, 232, 236, 248, 285, 382.

22. K.Koch, *Studium Pietatis*, 10-15, has shown by way of Bucer's account in the disputation in his letter to Beatus Rhenanus that Bucer partly interpreted Luther's theses in Erasmian terms and partly completely passed over statements which were central for Luther. But cf. the qualification in Krüger, op.cit., 140.

23. That was first clearly recognized by R.Stupperich, cf. *Der Humanismus und die Wiedervereinigung der Konfessionen*, 1936, 23: 'Even when Bucer had taken Luther's side, he still maintained a high estimation of Erasmus and his work. He continued to maintain Erasmus' theological views. That is not altered by the fact that their ways later parted and Bucer soon came to be sharply opposed to Erasmus.' – Cf. also id., 'Bucer', *RGG*[3], (cols.1452-57) col.1456; Kohls, *Lebensaufgabe*, 36ff. – K.Koch, op.cit., 27, gives evidence of Bucer's ongoing high estimation of Erasmus. F.Krüger, op.cit., offers a thorough investigation of Erasmus' basic approach in Bucer's writings up to 1530. N.Peremans, *Erasme et Bucer, d'après leur correspondence*, 1970, deals with the development of the relationships between the two men, which were characterized by increasing alienation outwardly, though both had fundamentally the same concern.

24. One piece of evidence for this is his work: '*Summary*' (*Martin Butzers an ein christlichen Rath und Gemeyn der statt Weissenburg Summary seiner Predigt daselbst gethon*), now in DW 1, 69-147; on this A.Lang, *Evangelienkommentar*, 94ff.; cf. also R.Seeberg, 552, and also in his first work *Das ym selbs* (*Das ym selbs niemant, sonder anderen leben soll, und wie der mensch dahyn kummen mőg*), now in DW 1, 29-67, here esp. 59.28-60.1; 63.22ff.; see K.Koch, op.cit., 20ff.; F.Krüger, op.cit., 140, and in the Opinion of 1523, DW 1, 304-44, Art. II, 316ff., and F.Krüger, id.

25. *Proinde fidem in Deum recte definiemus si dicamus esse persuasionem, Deum esse ut omnium rerum authorem, etc.: Sic fidem Christi certam persuasionem, eum esse nostrum redemptorem ac instauratorem*, sources in Koch, op.cit., n.6, 204. Cf. already Lang, *Evangeliumkommentar*, 107ff.; also J.Miller, op.cit., 22ff.; Koch, op.cit., 43ff.; Krüger, op.cit., 157ff.

26. 'Then only the divine word makes us healthy and blessed, brings faith, faith brings love, love the fruit of good work, which is followed by the eternal inheritance and divine and blessed life.' *Das ym selbs*, DW 1, 67,8ff. Cf. the introduction by J.Müller, DW 1, 39, n.19; Krüger, op.cit., 177.

27. *Notandus ordo: primum habet locum electio siue praedestinatio, proximum adoptio in filios, quae alias vocatio dicitur, dum nimiro spiritu suo donatus ad se Dominus trahit suique cognitione donat, quos ab aeterno ad hoc deputavit. Tertio demum loco succedit vitae sanctimonia et dilectionis officiositas, qua bona opera proferentur... Ut ita quartum in sanctis sit gloria Dei et iustitia...*, *Eph.-Komm.*, fol. 26b.; cf. in Krüger, op.cit., 176 n.173. Cf. also already in the commentary on the Gospels (Stupperich, Bibliographie, no.14) II, fol. 24 a-b; and Koch, op.cit., 44; Krüger, op.cit., 177 and n.174. O.Ritschl, op.cit., 139ff., has already described the remarkable structure of Bucer's doctrine of double justification. He finds its origin in Reformed theology, *Bucer*, op.cit., 148. In summary one can say of it that Bucer 'dissociated himself from distinguishing the *justificatio* from the *renovatio* of the sinner and rather asserts both as an indivisible unity', op.cit., 151. On this Ritschl observes: 'Yet with this theologumenon he virtually deprived the notion of justification in the Wittenberg Reformers of its characteristic point', cf. op.cit., 150, also 148. – Cf. further, Koch, op.cit., 43ff.; Krüger, op.cit., 174ff.

28. Cf. *Enarrationes in Sacra Quattvor Evangelia* (= *Ev.-Komm.*1), 1530 fol. 123B: *Fide iustificamur, id est, iusti efficimur, operibus ac dictis, iustificamur, id est, iusti declaramur et iudicamur*. And in the Ephesians commentary, fol. 62f: *Duplex est iustificatio, non*

una, fidei et operum. The concept of the second cause also emerges in the Commentary on Romans (Stupperich, *Bibliographia*, 55), 116 col.1, and Krüger, op.cit., 177ff.

29. Cf. already Lang, *Evangelienkommentar*, 205; H.E.Weber, op.cit., 206f.; Ritschl, op.cit., 123f.; Koch, op.cit., treats Bucer in monograph fashion as an ethicist and by way of introduction quotes a typical formula of Bucer: *Nam et sacra doctrina proprie moralis est, ars nimirum recte et ordine vivendi*, op.cit., 8. Cf. most recently again Greschat, *Ansatz*, passim; id., *Reformationszeit II*, 11ff.

30. Cf. Stupperich, *Humanismus*, 23; Krüger, op.cit., 165ff., and cf. above, 439 n.48. – The doctrine of twofold justification was also a nucleus of compromises with a humanist stamp, the result of which was the so-called Regensburg Book of 1541, cf. Stupperich, *Humanismus*, 105ff.

31. Krüger, op.cit., 179f. Stupperich, 'Schriftverständnis und Kirchenlehre bei Butzer und Gropper', *JVWKG* 43, 1950, (109-28) 113, observes: 'It is unmistakable that at this point in Butzer the Scholastic doctrine of *meritum de congruo* and *meritum de condigno* has a weakened influence.'

32. Cf. Koch, op.cit., 66ff.; J.Müller, op.cit., 207ff.; Krüger, op.cit., 75ff.

33. *Ps.Komm.* (Bibliographia, no.25), fol. 111b/112a (quoted word for word in Krüger, op.cit., 75f., n.51; cf. Koch, op.cit., 66).

34. *Ps.Komm.*fol.16a. Cf. *Eph.Komm.*, fol.90d: *Lex vel Scriptura sacra dicit....*

35. Op.cit., 209.

36. In the excursus *De lege*, *Ev.-Kom*. I, fol. 48B.

37. *Ev.-Komm*. I, fol. 48C.

38. Ibid., fol. 49C.

39. Ibid., fol. 50B.

40. Ibid., fol. 50C.

41. Ibid., fol. 50D. The same idea appears in Erasmus, LB VII, fol. 955C; cf. LB V, fol. 208f. Cf. Krüger, op.cit., 81.

42. Op.cit., 67.

43. Op.cit., 210.

44. Op.cit., 209.

45. Cf., above, 439f. n.53; Krüger, op.cit., 75ff., has rightly stressed the close proximity to Erasmus.

46. A.Lang has already virtually described Bucer's theology as a 'theology of the spirit', *Evangelienkommentar*, 120. Thus he sees Bucer in proximity to the Anabaptists: 'What prevents our assuming that Butzer's doctrine of the Spirit is influenced by the same religious moods as give Anabaptism its enthusiastic force?' For the effect of the spirit in the 'Bucerian pneumatocracy', cf. also Koch, op.cit., 78f. Cf. also Greschat, *Reformationszeit II*, 12f.

47. J.Müller, op.cit., 22ff., and the evidence there.

48. Müller, op.cit., 27.

49. Krüger, op.cit., 91.

50. 'And the outward word is not like a cart, so that the spirit of God is carried into the heart, as several now write.' *Getrewe Warnung*, DW 2, (225-58) 239.7ff. Cf. also in the Johannes-Kommentar (Bibliographie, no.20), fol. 140b, 141a, and Krüger, op.cit., 89 n.6.

51. There are numerous similar remarks made by Bucer, cf. esp. in the writing against C.Treger, *Ein kurtzer wahrhafftiger bericht...*, DW 2, 15-173, 83, 18ff.: 'Otherwise, although one already has scripture and the church, indeed Christ himself physically as a preacher, where the Spirit does not teach us inwardly we remain bereft of all understanding.' Cf. also esp. Bucer's discussion of the inner and outer word in Krebs-Rott, *Quellen VIII.Elsass* II, 193ff. = DW 5, 422-9.

52. J.Müller stresses: 'In Bucer word and spirit become completely separate',

op.cit., 44, cf. also 45. W.P.Stephens, *The Holy Spirit in the Theology of Martin Bucer*, 1970, cf. esp. 264ff., differs.

53. Cf. *Ein kurtzer wahrhafftiger bericht*, DW 2, 83.15ff.: 'That all certain and sure (knowledge) really comes from the Comforter, the Holy Spirit, who brings it about that we understand and mark scripture, what is in accordance with it and what is not.' *Joh.-Komm.*, fol. 139a: *'Non igitur cum uerbo hic spiritus offertur, sed e supernis infunditur, ut uerbum intelligatur.'* However, in his interpretation of the story of the wise men from the East Bucer wants to give an explicit demonstration that the elect can arrive at faith and thus justification even without the word of God, cf. Müller, op.cit., 44f.; Krüger, op.cit., 100.

54. Cf. inter alia Lang, *Evangelienkommentar*, 35f.; Müller, op.cit., 54; Krüger, op.cit., 92. Greschat, *Ansatz*, col.90, stresses that Bucer's 'theological approach' nevertheless 'is not primarily developed from biblical exegesis but from systematic reflection on the theological programmes that he encounters. The biblical foundation merely gives authoritative backing to this.'

55. Cf. Krüger, op.cit., 92ff.

56. Müller, op.cit., 58, quotes from the writing against Treger the remark in DW 2, 89, 10-20. Again the topic is the question of the evaluation of Bucer's attitude; for this cf. on the one hand Müller, op.cit., 59, and on the other Krüger, op.cit., 96ff.

57. Op.cit., 72.

58. Cf. *Summary*, DW 1, 83.27-84.3 :('bey der heilgen schrifft'). 'Thus all teaching and preaching is a rule which is written on the conscience by the Holy Spirit and teaches all that is good in abundance. Thus all that does not accord with divine scripture and does not have its basis in it must be offensive, superficial and misleading.'

59. This and not 'Bucer's exegetical sense' (against Müller, op.cit., 75: Krüger, op.cit., 94, is more in the right direction) is the background to the statement in *Getrewe Warnung*, DW 2, 238.30-239.4: 'Of course no one has provided the tone and the letter for the word of God but rather the sense and the meaning, such as the books of the Bible give us, and all who speak from God, that is, Paul and others, speak the word of God. But no one may grasp this and accept it with faith unless he has inward ears to hear it.' The spirit of the believer who hears its meaning and understands it matches the spirit of scripture.

60. Cf. Müller, op.cit., 94ff., 100ff.

61. *Römer-Kommentar*, 29, col.1.

62. Op.cit., 142ff.

63. P.28, cols.2ff. It has the title: *An insit Philosophia, quod cum doctrina Pauli congruat.* Originally the introduction was meant to be the preface to the commentary on the whole Pauline corpus.

64. *Nihil omnino ad salutem fuisse cognitu necessarium, quod Deus gentibus non primis etiam illis saeculis manifestavit. Röm.-Komm.*, 35.n.1. For the section cf. Lang, *Evangelienkommentar*, 335ff.; H.Strohl, 'Théologie et Humanisme à Strasbourg au moment de la création de la Haute-École', *RHPR* 17, 1937, 435-56; Müller, op.cit., 60ff.; Koch, op.cit., 36ff.; Krüger, op.cit., 98ff.

65. Bucer recognizes a clear gradation within philosophy in which Plato has a special rank; cf. Koch, op.cit., 39; Müller, 62. In other passages Bucer characteristically praises Cicero; cf. Krüger, op.cit., 101.

66. That was the aim of Erasmus, cf. Krüger, op.cit., 102, 105, 106, and see above 00 n.50.

67. *Röm-Komm.30, col.1.*

68. *Joh.-Komm.*, fol.20a; cf. Krüger, op.cit., 111ff.; Müller, op.cit., 61f.

69. 'Bucer cannot speak of a divine nature in man,' Krüger, op.cit., 111.

70. *Eadem habet Philosophia, sed nec tam clare, nec tam pure, nec tam certe, nec tam locuplete, nec denique tanta cum autoritate, Röm.-Komm.*, 35.

71. *Röm.-Komm.*, 33. Detailed extract also in Lang, *Evangelienkommentar*, 335f., and Krüger, op.cit., 124 n.228.

72. Cf. Koch, op.cit., 40.

73. In fact these ideas are not so isolated as Lang, op.cit., 336, assumes in the light of his general understanding of Bucer; but cf. Krüger, op.cit., 98ff.

74. *Unde quicquid divinitus hominibus dictum factumve est, opus fuit Verbi, quod erat in initio, per quod sunt facta omnia, Joh.-Komm.*, fol. 5B.

75. Op.cit., 119ff.

76. *Ps.Komm.*, fol. 16A.

77. Cf. Müller, op.cit., 200ff.; Koch, op.cit., 30ff.; Krüger, op.cit., 77ff.

78. *Ev.Komm.* 1, fol. 48D.

79. Here Bucer quotes the covenant formula *per suam bonitatem Deus noster, et nos eius per fidem populus*, ibid.

80. Cf. 'Bericht aus der heyligen geschrift'; DW 5, 183/38-40: '...and so they will talk of the people of God; in itself it is a people and body of all the elect of God from the beginning of the world to the end; all have one spirit, one faith...' Stephens critizies this point in the light of his basically apologetic approach (264): 'he (Bucer) does not sufficiently stress the distinctness of the New Testament'.

81. Cf. Müller, op.cit., 211ff.; cf. also Koch, op.cit., 31.

82. *Quicquid veteri populo accidit, typus est, in quo opera et iudicia Dei...delineata considerari debent*, Zephaniah commentary (Bibliographia, no.22), fol.1A.

83. *Joh.-Komm.*, fol. 11A: *Omnia rectius et plenius quadrare in liberationem factam per Christum, cuius illa per Cyrum facta, typus et umbra quaedam fuit.*

84. Cf. Müller, op.cit., 214ff.

85. *Ev.Komm.*, I, fol. 49A.

86. *Quare equidem Christum nostrum, illum* YHWH *fuisse, nihil dubito, qui patribus locutus fuit etc., Joh.-Komm.*, fol. 14A; cf. also *Röm.-Komm.*, fol. 64B.

87. Cf. Müller, op.cit., 169ff., 201ff.; cf. also Krüger, op.cit., 78f. – Müller's assertion, op.cit., 176, that this pattern is not to be understood 'on the presupposition of an alleged Spiritualism' but only in the light of the Reformation *sola gratia* has no basis in fact.

88. In the work *Grund und Ursach* of 1524, DW I, 185-278, esp. 256, 11-26, where he distinguishes outward baptism with water from inward baptism with the spirit; cf. Lang, *Evangelienkommentar*, 217ff.; Müller, op.cit., 170ff.

89. Cf. Müller, op.cit., 175. This applies above all to Bucer's characteristic understanding of the eucharist, which on the one hand stresses with Luther the effect of the *verbum externum* on the elements in the sacrament, and on the other hand connects its efficacy and the real presence of Christ with the presence of the faith of the believer. Cf. C.H.Smyth, *Cranmer and the Reformation under Edward VI*, 1926, 25, etc.; Hopf, *Bucer*, 42ff.

90. *Canon certissimus, Ev.-Komm.* I, 103D, cf. the quotation in Müller, op.cit., 179.

91. *Ev.Komm.* I, 104B; cf. the quotation in Müller, op.cit., 180 n.37.

92. *Ev.Komm.*I, fol.50D.

93. See above, 469 n.38.

94. *Ev.Komm.*I, fol. 48 B. Cf. also Krüger, op.cit., 79.

95. *Satis indicavit (Deus), quid in ceremonijs, quas populo statuit, sibi uoluerit, sane non eas sed fidem et sui timorem, quam illa significabant. Ev.-Komm.* I, fol.48 C. This judgment permitted Bucer also to accept the sacraments in church practice, and indeed to stress the validity of external church ordinances over against the Anabaptists and the extreme Spiritualists. Cf. also Müller, op.cit. 170f. n.5. This conservative attitude towards outward church ordinances developed in Bucer above all in the negotiations

over the Wittenberg Concord and from there on above all governed his actions in church politics. Cf. Lang, *Evangelienkommentar*, 250ff., 298ff.; Koch, op.cit., 53ff.

96. This criticism advanced by Müller is in danger of passing an unhistorical judgment, since a historical view of this kind was alien to the whole of the sixteenth century.

97. Cf. above, 25ff. Müller, op.cit., 176 n.24 also regards it as probable that there is a connection between Bucer and Joachim at this point.

98. *Joh-.Komm.*, fol.49b. For the theme cf. Müller, op.cit., 205f.; cf. 175f.; Krüger, op.cit., 81ff.

99. *Propter ruditatem spiritus et vitae Dei infantilitatem, Zeph.-Komm.*, fol. 561.

100. *Unde nullis externis quoque legibus illud firmat (Deus), sed donat suum spiritum, qui lex illa est, Ev.Komm.* I, fol. 151A/B.

101. *Ev.Komm.* I, fol. 150A/B; 151A/B; cf. *Eph.-Komm.*, fol.64B.

102. Cf. also 'Bericht', DW 5, 179.13-16: 'As they say it "in the figure", whereby they mean that circumcision was a figure and representation of rebirth, which we acquire through our Lord Jesus, they speak truly. Now insofar as baptism takes place outwardly, it too is a figure and model of the same rebirth.'

103. 'Bericht', DW 5, 182.16-20. Cf. also 'Dialogi', (Bibliographia, no.50), fol. 0 3B, and on this theme more recently W. van't Spijker, 'De eenheid van Oud en Nieuw Verbond bij Martin Bucer', in *Wegen en gestalten in het gereformeered protestantism*, Festschrift H. van der Linde, 1976, 47-60.

104. *Ev.Komm.* I, fol.149A.

105. *Satis indicavit, quid in ceremonijs, quas populo statuit, sibi voluerit, sane non eas sed fidem et sui timorem, quam illa significabant, Ev.Komm.* I, fol. 149B.

106. *Ev.Komm.* I, fol. 149A.

107. *Ev.Komm.* I, fol. 152A.

108. Cf. above, 471 n.80.

109. For Bucer's ecclesiology cf. esp. Lang, *Evangelienkommentar*, 176ff., 298ff.; R.Stupperich, 'Die Kirche in M.Bucers theologischer Entwicklung', *ARG* 35, 1938, 81-101; id., 'M.Bucers Anschauungen von der Kirche', *ZST* 17, 1940, 131-48; J.Courvoisier, *La notion d'église chez Bucer dans son développement historique*, 1933 (see the review by H.Strohl in *RHPR* 13, 1933, 242-9; for criticism cf. also Stupperich, *ARG* 1938, 82 n.1); Koch, op.cit., 50ff. – For the practice cf. also W.Diehl, *Martin Butzers Bedeutung für das kirchliche Leben in Hessen*, 1904; W.Bellardi, *Die Geschichte der 'christlichen Gemeinschaft' in Strassburg (1546/50)*, 1934; J.Adam, *Evangelische Kirchengeschichte der Stadt Strassburg bis zur französischen Revolution*, 1922; F.Wendel, *L'église de Strasbourg et son organisation 1532-1535*, 1942; R.Bornert, *La réforme protestante du culte à Strasbourg au XVIᵉ siècle (1523-1598)*, 1981; M.Lienhard/J.Willer, *Strassburg und die Reformation*, ²1982; B.Vogler, 'Elsass', *TRE* 9, 1982, 524-34 (bibliography). S.Ozment, *The Reformation in the Cities*, 1975, describes the intellectual and sociological background for the success of the reformation movement in the German cities.

110. Stupperich, *ZST*, 1940, 131. Similarly Koch, op.cit., 50.

111. Cf. already *Summary* DW 1,114; *Grund und Ursach*, DW 1, 206, etc.; *Ein kurtzer warhafftiger bericht*, DW 2, 48: the church is 'the Christian group of the elect who want only to be the true sheep of Christ, their one shepherd, and hear his voice.' Cf. also *Eph.Komm.*, fol.25B: *Deus ante conditum mundum nos sibi in filios elegit.* For the significance of predestination cf. also Stephens, 23ff.,261ff.

112. Cf. already Lang, *Evangelienkommentar*, 94ff.

113. Cf. *Ein kurtzer warhafftiger bericht*, DW 2, 69.38- 70.3: '...so the Christian church speaks and hears none other than its promised word. Therefore, *ad scripturas*, to scripture, to scripture... but scripture must be God's word; as we hear it so we hear the true church...' Cf. already *Das ym selbs*, Preface, DW 1, 44.15f.: 'Thus it is

certainly also the kingdom of Christ and the true church, where the word of Christ is heard with such pleasure and is kept with such zeal.'

114. See above, 470 n.53.

115. *Ein kurtzer warhafftiger bericht*, DW 2, 93f.

116. Ibid., 115.

117. 'For the Christian community is none other than the community of the saints, that is, the believers. And this is invisible, since we believe it. That would not be the case were we to see it.' Id., 113.25ff. Cf. also 115.21f., 28f.

118. 'But since those who dwell in the body bring forth their good fruit, here we know them.' Id., 113.28f.

119. 'So are all such as are not chosen by God and therefore have no right belief, but nothing other than dissembled, feigned Christians mixed in with the righteous, not members of the Christian community.' Ibid., 114.22ff.

120. Ibid., 112.37-113.2. Here Bucer often quotes the image of the net, which catches good and bad fish (Matt. 13.47); ibid., 112.30f.; 115.19ff.

121. Ibid., 115.16ff.

122. T.Schiess, *Briefwechsel der Brüder Ambrosius und Thomas Blaurer*, 1908, II, 790.

123. Lenz, *Briefwechsel*, II, 174.

124. Especially through the institution of the 'Christian community', cf. Bellardi. Evidence of this is the church order of 1534 which Bucer made normative, now in DW 5, 15-41. For this and for the events which immediately preceded and followed it, cf. F. Wendel, *L'église de Strasbourg et son organisation (1532-1535)*, 1942.

125. Cf. Diehl and above all the correspondence with Count Philipp edited by Lenz.

126. DW 7, 67-245. Cf. for the whole question also Courvoisier, op.cit., 97ff.; Stupperich, Introduction, in DW 7, 69ff. Latin translation *De vera Animarum cura* in *Scripta Anglicana* 1577, 260-356 (quoted a good deal earlier because it was more easily accessible). For this cf. Stupperich, Introduction to *Von der waren Seelsorge*, DW 7, 85ff.

127. According to G.Anrich, *Strassburg und die calvinische Kirchenverfassung* (inaugural lecture), Tübingen 1928, 21ff., here are the roots of the later constitution of the Reformed church. Lang sees them as being that 'here for the first time, as far as I know, the principle of the sole rule of Christ in the church is taken as the basis for the whole of church order', *Evangelienkommentar*, 307. For the influence of Bucer and Calvin cf. already Lang, *Evangelienkommentar*, 9f., 365ff.; O.Ritschl, op.cit., 157f.; R.Schultz, *Martin Butzers Anschauung von der christlichen Oberkeit*, 1932, 8ff.; Courvoisier, op.cit., 135ff.

128. DW 7, 98f.

129. Cf. Stupperich, *ZST*, 1940 , 135ff., and the evidence mentioned there.

130. 'That we must have one heart and one soul in Christ, and be his body and all members together in him, whererever we would be Christians', DW 7, 92.18ff.

131. The definition of the church runs: 'The church of Christ is the assembly and community of those who are gathered and united in Christ our Lord through his spirit and word from the world, that they are a body and members of one another, of which each has his office and work for the common betterment of the whole body and all members', DW 7, 98.29-99.2.

132. DW 7, 102.10ff.

133. DW 7, 103.5ff.

134. DW 7, 103.12ff.

135. DW 7, 114.18ff.

136. DW 7, 117.14ff. -121. Cf. also Courvoisier, op.cit., 101.

137. Cf. the index, DW 7, 91.

138. Cf. Courvoisier, op.cit., 104.

139. DW 7, 157ff.

140. DW 7, 219ff.

141. Bucer's legalistic thought is also expressed in these characteristics of the church; cf. also Stupperich, Introduction, DW 7, 72.

142. DW 7, 94.31-95.6.

143. DW 7, 181f.

144. Cf. the introduction by R.Stupperich, DW 7, 81ff.; also Courvoisier, op.cit., 106f. – For Bucer's ideas on the tasks and position of the authorities in general, see esp. Koch, op.cit., 152ff.; for the 'Pastoral' writing, 171ff., and more recently M. de Kroon, 'De christelijke overheid in de schriftuitleg van Martin Bucer en Johannes Calvijn', in *Festschrift H. van der Linde*, 1976, 61-74. – In his writing *De Missa* (1537), Capito goes into the same tasks of government, cf. O.E.Strasser, *La pensée théologique de Wolfgang Capiton*, 1938, 132ff. (with extensive extracts). Cf. also Luther, *Von weltlicher Obrigkeit*, WA 11, 229ff.

145. Cf. Stupperich, Introduction, DW 7, 83f.

146. DW 7, 146.6-151.27.

147. Cf. also Strasser,op.cit., 132; Wendel, *L'église*, 179ff.

148. 'They are not to preach, and dispense and order word, sacrament and discipline in the churches, for this is a special ministry and office in the churches...; but because the authorities have the supreme power over all men... So truly all authorities are responsible above all to see that no one lives among them who does not always seek with all faith and is led to Christ.' For *extra ecclesiam nulla salus*! DW 7, 147.16ff.

149. DW 7, 148.10ff.

150. DW 7, 149.3ff.

151. DW 7, 150.27ff.

152. DW 7, 230ff.

153. Op.cit., 172.

153a. DW 17, 153-345.

153b. In part other authors, like Paul Fagius, were involved. These were official submissions by preachers or part of them (cf. DW 17, 155). Usually, however, Bucer was solely or decisively responsible for content and style.

153c. Of course the idea that the community of believers must be visible in the world is a genuine feature of the Reformation (W.Bellardi, in DW 17,156); however, the basic approach and way in which the programme of discipline was carried out is in complete accord with Bucer's line.

153d. Cf. esp. the work *Erinnerung der Prediger an die Obrigkeit*, DW 17, 196ff.

153e. Cf. the document DS 7, 341ff.

153f. Bucer's failure in Strasbourg is an immediate result of the Interim (1548), cf. Bornert, *Réforme*, 208ff.

154. Bucer already had connections with England at a much earlier stage, cf. Harvey, op.cit., 11f.

155. Cf. Harvey, op.cit.; Hopf, op.cit.; also the introduction by F.Wendel, in *Opera Latina* (OL) XV, IX-XXXV; P.Collinson, *Archbishop Grindal, 1519-1583. The Struggle for a Reformed Church*, 1979, 49ff.; W.S.Hudson, *The Cambridge Connection and the Elizabethan Settlement of 1559*, 1980, 58-60.

156. For this work cf. in addition to the introduction by F.Wendel in the critical edition in OL XV: W.Pauck, *Das Reich Gottes auf Erden. Utopie und Wirklichkeit*, 1928 (for criticism cf. H.Strohl, *RHPR* 10, 1930, 571-8; A.Lang, *ZKG* 48, 1929, 122f.); R.Schultz, op.cit., 23ff.; H.Strohl, 'Un aspect de l'humanisme chrétien de Bucer', *RHPR* 18, 1938, 432-47; Hopf, op.cit., 99f.; Courvoisier, op.cit., 117ff.; T.F.Torrance, *Kingdom and Church*, 1957; Koch, op.cit., 177ff.

157. G.Anrich, *Bucer*, 115.

158. Cf. *inter alia* Pauck, *Reich Gottes*, 68f.; Schultz, op.cit., 24; Lang, *Puritanismus*,

36. However, it should be noted that in his judgments he is in full agreement with the views of a number of contemporary English politicians and theologians (cf. Pauck, op.cit., 71f.) etc., from whom he presumably derived his information, cf. Wendel, OL XV, LIII.

159. Cf. the letter in Harvey, op.cit., Appendix VII, 133ff.; also Hopf, op.cit., 131ff., and the correspondence, 148ff.

160. Cf. Schultz, op.cit., 23ff.

161. Cf. Wendel, OL XV, XXXVIIIf.

162. Op.cit., 152ff.

163. Cf. the quotation, op.cit., 154 n.148, and Wendel, OL XV, XLIV. M.Greschat has shown that in this view the understanding of the law as cosmic order, which Bucer has taken over from the Thomistic tradition, is dominant, cf. the beginning, esp. cols.87, 90. For the Thomistic understanding of the law cf. U.Kühn, *Via charitatis. Theologie des Gesetzes bei Thomas von Aquin*, 1964, 65.

164. OL XV, 293.

165. OL XV, 6-20.

166. OL XV, 7.

167. OL XV, 4.: *Quaecumque omnis regni propria bona sunt, ea in hoc regno existere exhiberique tanto plenius atque perfectius, quam in ullo unquam humano regno existere exhiberique potuerint.*

168. OL XV, 10. Here it is also a matter of seeing that no one overworks (with an allusion to Plato) and no one is idle.

169. *Conuenit inter regna mundi et regnum Christi, quod sicut regna mundi regno Christi, ita etiam regnum Christi suo modo subiiciatur regnis mundi,* OL XV,14.

170. Cf. Koch, op.cit., 170.

171. *Proinde sancto baptismate omnes regno Christi incorporantur et obedientiae eius sese addicunt, ad sacros coetus frequentes conueniunt, ut et Christi doctrinam ibi percipiant plenius et disciplinae se eius solidius accommodent. – Vere etenim reges, qui nulli quam Christiani sunt, norunt se Christum audire, cum ueros eius audiunt ministros; Christum adspernari, cum illos contemnunt,* OL XV, 14f./15f.

172. An example already produced by Bucer in *Von der waren Seelsorge*, DW 7, 163f.; indeed, the whole argument is already prefigured there.

173. Cf. Courvoisier, op.cit., 122ff.

174. OL XV, 101ff.

175. OL XV, 11ff.: *ad quod etiam S.M.T. authoritate omnes adigendi sunt.*

176. OL XV,98.

177. OL XV, 129f.

178. For Luther there are only the *notae* of word and sacrament.

179. OL XV, 70ff.

180. OL XV, 281.

181. Apart from numerous English models, among which the Utopia of Thomas More occupies a special place, cf. Pauck, op.cit., 72ff.; Wendel, OL XV, LIIf.

182. Bucer at one point expressly rejects the suspicion *meque rempublicam quandam Platonis, ut dicitur, uelle architectari,* OL XV, 294. But cf. the numerous references to Plato and Cicero in Wendel's footnotes.

183. OL XV, 99. – Cf. also 16, 17, 102, 299, 303, 309.

184. OL XV, 266f.

185. OL XV, 267, nn.11, 12, 13.

186. Cf. OL XV, 268.

187. The notes in OL XV provide abundant evidence for the indissoluble fusion of biblical and classical quotations and allusions.

188. Cf. the index, OL XV, 19f.

189. OL XV, 80ff. – 114ff.; for earlier mentions cf. 115 n.1.

190. Not only is all work and staying away from services forbidden, but *Item, solutioribus se ludis, intempestuis commessationibus et aliis uitiosis dedere uoluptatibus*, OL XV, 114f.

191. OL XV, 287f.

192. OL XV, 277.

193. OL XV, 278.

194. Cf. Koch, op.cit., 183.

195. Cf. above, 472 n.105.

196. OL XV, 156.

197. Cf. Wendel, OL XV, XLIIIf.; for the theme also Hopf, op.cit., 107ff.

198. Cf. OL XV, 17,19,36f.,82, 130-3.

Part Two

1. The Age of the Puritans

1. C.H. and K.George, *The Protestant Mind of the English Reformation, 1590-1640*, 1961. Cf. also C.H.George, 'Puritanism as History and Historiography', *PaP* 41, 1968, 77-104. J.W.Allen, *English Political Thought, 1603-1644*, 1938, 302, observes, 'Puritanism seems to be a discovery of later thought and research.'

2. Martin Schmidt, 'Die Problematik des Puritanismus im Lichte seiner Erforschung', *ZKG* 60,1941, 207-54, gives an account of the history of earlier research. Cf. also J.Bauer, 'Reflections on the Nature of English Puritanism', *ChH* 23, 1954, 99-108; C.Hill, *Society and Puritanism in Pre-Revolutionary England*, 1964, ²1967, 13ff.; B.Hall, 'Puritanism: the Problem of Definition', in *Studies in Church History*, ed. C.W.Dugmore and C.Duggan, II, 1965, 283-96; M. van Beek, *An Enquiry into Puritan Vocabulary*, 1969, 9ff.; D.Little, *Religion, Order and Law. A Study in Pre-Revolutionary England*, 1969, 250ff.

3. Cf. below, 481 n.81.

4. Cf. especially *Mind*, 70ff.

5. Cf. the recent excellent account by A.G.Dickens, *Reformation*. A series of scholars, however, points to a strong anti-Calvinist reaction in the state church, which begins in the last period under Elizabeth, cf. below 481 n.83.

6. This is also the view of A.L.Rowse, *The England of Elizabeth*, 1951. Cf. e.g. 469: And indeed the position of the church, as laid down in the Thirty-nine Articles, was that of a Reformed church, it was not Lutheran.' On the other hand Rowse's judgment on the Puritans is anything but apt and unprejudiced. For criticism cf. D.Little, op.cit., 254f., and below, 477 n.16. But cf. also Dickens, op.cit., 313ff.; I. Breward, *Introduction to the Work of William Perkins*, ed. Breward, 1970, 15.

7. A pioneer work of this kind is the book by M.M.Knappen, *Tudor Puritanism*, 1939 (²1965), who sees Puritanism as 'a chapter in the history of idealism'. The most thorough new account is P.Collinson, *The Elizabethan Puritan Movement*, 1967. It is striking that history writing has concerned itself predominantly with the Tudor period and less with the time of the first Stuarts. But cf. W.Haller, *The Rise of Puritanism*, 1938 (third impression 1957); id., *Liberty and Reformation in the Puritan Revolution*, 1955, reprinted 1967; W.Notestein, *The English People on the Eve of Colonization*, 1954, 156ff.; and the works by C.Hill.

8. For the type of the Puritan preacher cf. recently also I. Morgan, *The Godly Preachers of the Elizabethan Church*, 1965; for the style, technique and content of the sermons, J.W.Blench, *Preaching in England in the Late Fifteenth and Sixteenth Centuries*, 1964, 57ff., 100ff., 168ff., 220ff., 292ff. There is also a survey in H.Davies, *Worship and Theology in England*, Vol.I, *From Cranmer to Hooker, 1534-1603*, 1970, 294ff.; Vol.II,

From Andrewes to Baxter and Fox, 1975, 133ff. J.Chandos (ed.), *In God's Name. Examples of Preaching in England from the Act of Supremacy to the Act of Uniformity, 1534-1662*, 1971, gives an anthology of sermons.

9. The best-known example is the formation of the committee of the twelve 'feoffees' in 1626 to collect the contributions for the purchase of patronage rights, in order to be able to present Puritan preachers to the parishes; this was immediately prevented by Laud. Cf. Haller, op.cit., 80ff. C.Hill, *The Economic Problems of the Church*, 1956, reprinted 1963, 245-74; I.M.Calder, 'A Seventeenth Century Attempt to Purify the Anglican Church', *AHR* 53, 1948, 760-75; I.M.Calder (ed.), *Activities of the Puritan Faction of the Church of England, 1625-33*, 1957. The so-called 'prophecyings' were of far-reaching influence, above all the Bible conferences of the local clergy (the 'classis') modelled on Zurich 'prophesying', in which the central concern was further training for preaching, cf. Collinson, op.cit., 168ff. For the patronage of Puritan preachers cf. also K.Shipps, 'The "Political Puritan"', *ChH* 45, 1976, 196-207.

10. Above all the prohibition against 'prophecyings', cf. Collinson, op.cit., 191ff.

11. Cf. Collinson, op.cit., 191.

12. Cf. Collinson, op.cit., 194.

13. One example of this is the extensive work of Christopher Hill, esp. *Problems*; *Puritanism and Revolution*, 1958 (²1965); *Society and Puritanism in Pre-Revolutionary England*, 1967. However, despite his Marxist approach Hill is not blind to the non-economic aspects, including the specifically Christian ones. Cf. e.g. his testimony in 'A Bourgeois Revolution?', in *Three British Revolutions: 1641, 1688, 1776*, ed. J.G.A. Pocock, 1980, (109-39) 110f. For comments on Hill cf. R.Ashton, 'Puritanism and Progress', *EcHR* Ser.2, 17, 1964-65, 579-87; R.C.Richardson, *The Debate on the English Revolution*, 1977, 98ff. K.Walsh, *England under Tudors and Stuarts*, Neue Perspektiven der Forschung, Innsbrucker Historische Studien 4, 1981, 169-204, gives a survey of the most recent publications.

14. The classic representative of this school is S.R.Gardiner with his eighteen-volume history of England: *History of England 1603-1642*, 1883-1901 (1965); id., *History of the Great Civil War 1642-1649*, 1886-1891 (1965). For him cf. Richardson, op.cit., 69ff.

15. C.H.George, *Puritanism*, 97ff., has biting criticism of the whole direction of scholarship ('the Weber-Woodhouse-Haller syndrome of analytical errors', op.cit., 98), but of course goes well wide of the mark.

16. C.Hill once directed this criticism against the historian H.R. Trevor-Roper: 'For over a century before 1640 men all over Europe had been suffering, and killing for what they held to be light ideals... Professor Trevor-Roper asks us to see in all this only a reflection of the financial difficulties of a section of the English gentry. The spiritual wreathings of a Milton, a Vane, a Roger Williams are nothing but the epiphenomena of economic decline. The idea is difficult to discuss seriously,' *Puritanism and Revolution*, 1958 (²1965), 12. Rather different, but equally sweeping, is the verdict of A.L. Rowse, op.cit., on the Puritans: 'Power was – as usual – what they wanted; and therefore the issue of Church government was the important one' (486). '...for, as we all know, human egoism is the greatest motive force in the world' (488). It is then, Little observes, op.cit., 253, almost superfluous for Rowse, 479, to go on to tell us that he just can't stand the Puritans!

17. His two famous articles, 'Die protestantische Ethik und der Geist der Kapital-ismus', and 'Die protestantischen Sekten und der Geist des Kapitalismus' (1904 and 1906), have now been made easily available along with contemporary criticism and Weber's important ripostes in two Siebenstern Taschenbücher, 53/54, ²1969, and 119/20, ²1972: *Die protestantische Ethik* I and II. There is a similar collection of texts in English in R.W.Green (ed.), *Protestantism and Capitalism. The Weber Thesis and Its Critics*, 1959. The translation by T.Parsons, 1930 (reprinted 1958) was specially influ-

ential in the Anglo-Saxon world; significantly it only contained the first article and thus gave rise to many misunderstandings.

18. For Weber that is above all 'Calvinism in the form which it adopted in the main areas of Western Europe where it was dominant especially in the seventeenth century', together with Pietism, Methodism and the Anabaptist sects. *Die protestantische Ethik* I, 115.

19. Cf. op.cit., 136f.

20. Op.cit., 137.

21. Op.cit., 142.

22. Op.cit., 175.

23. Weber, *Die protestantische Ethik* II, n.3, p.54, points out 'that in the meanwhile, in a most fortunate way, my colleague and friend E.Troeltsch had taken up from his own perspective a whole series of problems which were on my route'; over against assertions of a 'Weber-Troeltsch collective' Weber also (op.cit., 149ff.) explicitly stresses the independence of the two approaches and methods. Nevertheless, in approach Troeltsch is the one who takes, as he himself often acknowledges.

24. Esp. 579ff., 625ff.

25. *Die protestantische Ethik* I, 279ff.

26. *Religion and the Rise of Capitalism*, 1926, ²1937, reprinted 1960; cf. id., 'Introduction', in Max Weber, *The Protestant Ethic*, 1930.

27. 'Puritanism as a Revolutionary Ideology', *HTh* 3, 1964, 59-90; id., *The Revolution of the Saints: A Study in the Origins of Radical Politics*, 1965. – For criticism cf. D.Little, 'Max Weber Revisited: The Protestant Ethic and the Puritan Experience of Order', *HTR* 59, 1966, 415-28 = *IJRS* 3, 1967, 101-13; id., *Religion*, 229ff.

28. For its history cf. above all the account by E.Fischoff, 'The Protestant Ethic and the Spirit of Capitalism', *Social Research*, 1944, 53-77; cf. also the collection of articles, *Protestantism*, ed. R.W.Green.

29. Cf. the contributions by H.K.Fischer and F.Rachfahl, now in *Ethik* II.

30. But cf. already Weber's first answer, *Ethik* II, 27ff.

31. 'Antikritisches Schlusswort', op.cit., 303.

32. Cf. esp. Fischoff, op.cit., 355ff. Similarly the attempt in C.Hill, *Change and Continuity in Seventeenth-Century England*, 1974, 81ff. The sketch of the Protestant attitude given there on the basis of central statements from the Reformation is impressive. Nevertheless, in my view the line determinative for the development as a whole was not the Reformation line but the other, which Hill traces back to the 'mediaeval sects' (and which I would like to set against a wider background). See below.

33. For criticism cf. Fischoff, op.cit., 361ff.

34. Op.cit., 36 n.7. There is a very objective account of Weber's views on 'the Protestant ethic' in R.Bendix, *Max Weber. An Intellectual Portrait*, 1960, especially chs. 2,7. However, this work too has been written by a sociologist!

35. G.L.Mosse, 'Puritanism Reconsidered', *ARG* 55, 1964, (37-48) 38, observes: 'The sources of Puritan ideology have made it necessary for historians of Puritanism to be as learned as the divines themselves, no mean task for a modern scholar.'

36.This term, though anachronistic (cf. Collinson, *Movement*, 13), established itself as a designation of the episcopal party under Elizabeth I.

37. His most important book is *The New England Mind: The Seventeenth Century*, 1939, ²1954 (reprinted 1967). Cf. also the continuation: *The New England Mind: From Colony to Province*, 1953, reprinted 1967. An article of Miller's which summarizes the definition of Puritan thought is 'The Marrow of Puritan Divinity', in *Publications of the Colonial Society of Massachusetts* 23, 1937, 247-300 = *Errand into the Wilderness*, 1956, reprinted 1964, 48-98 = *The New England Puritans*, ed. S.V.James, 1968, 12-42. Cf. also the General Introduction in *The Puritans*, ed. P.Miller and T.Johnson, 1938

(²1965) and the Introduction to S.V.James, op.cit., 1-11. For discussion of Perry Miller cf. inter alia *Perry Miller and the American Mind. A Memorial Issue, Harvard Review* 2, 1964; D.A.Hollinger, 'Perry Miller and Philosophical History', *HTR* 7, 1968, 189-202; G.M.Marsden, 'Perry Miller's Rehabilitation of the Puritans: A Critique', *ChH* 39, 1970, 91-105; D.D.Hall, 'Understanding the Puritans', *The State of American History*, ed. H.J.Bass, 1970, 330-49; U.Brumm, *Puritanismus und Literatur in Amerika*, 1973, 11f.

38. Op.cit., 11.

39. Cf. esp. *The New England Mind: The Seventeenth Century*, 92.

40. Cf. op.cit., 3ff. Marsden, op.cit., 92, points out that Miller deliberately goes back to Augustine as in twentieth-century America 'Calvinist' was a bad word. However, one of Miller's mistakes was that he contrasted Ramus too strongly with Aristotle: rather, the Aristotelian and Scholastic elements in English thought remained until towards the end of the seventeenth century. For criticism of Miller on this point cf. also Hall, *Understanding*, 333f.

41. Cf. *New England Mind*, 116ff., and passim; also the appendix, 493ff.

42. Cf. also K.L.Sprunger, 'Ames, Ramus and the Method of Puritan Theology', *HTR* 59, 1966, 133-51; W.S.Howell, *Logic and Rhetoric in England, 1500-1700*, 1961, 146ff.

43. Op.cit., 102f.

44. Most of the publications were still printed in London.

45. Miller himself stresses in the preface to his *New England Mind*, X: 'I have made little distinction, for the purposes of defining and illustrating the ideas, between the writers of New England and the particular English theologians and preachers of the early seventeenth century under whom New Englanders studied, whom they read and digested before their migration and continued to read for a century thereafter.'

46. Cf. also the works mentioned and G.L.Mosse, *Puritanism Reconsidered*, 38: 'It became evident that many Puritans were humanists as well as evangelicals; that they were an intrinsic part of the sixteenth century revival of classical thought as well as continuators of much of medieval scholasticism.'

47. According to Hollinger, op.cit., 199, Miller was a naturalist; he himself was not a believer, cf. Brumm, op.cit., 15. Marsden, op.cit., 92, observes: 'It is possible, therefore, to discover in Miller's Portrait of the Puritans aspects which reflect the values of twentieth-century America as much as those of seventeenth-century New England.'

48. *New England Mind*, 19f., etc.

49. Op.cit., 65.

50. Marsden, op.cit., 93f.

51. Cf. especially E.Bizer, *Historische Einleitung zu Heinrich Heppes Dogmatik*, 1958, XXVII; B.Hall, 'Calvin against the Calvinists', *PHSL* 20, 1960/61, 284-301; G.E.Duffield (ed.), *John Calvin*, 1966, 19ff. No one today would repeat without qualification the statement by M.M.Knappen, op.cit., 376: 'In fact, Calvin cast such a deep shadow over the Puritan world that he determined the tone of its entire thinking.'

52. *Rise*, 84.

53. For the problem cf. Haller, ibid.,

54. Cf. Southgate, 'The Marian Exiles and the Influence of John Calvin', *Hist(L)* 27, 1942, 148-52; cf. C.H.Garrett, *The Marian Exiles* (1938), ²1966, 23; S.Pearson, *Thomas Cartwright and Elizabethan Puritanism*, 1966, 7, 94, 158, etc., and the monograph by C.D.Cremeans, *The Reception of Calvinistic Thought in England*, 1949.

55. Cf. Collinson, *Movement*, 164f. Some dedications now in L.J.Trinterud (ed.), *Elizabethan Puritanism*, 1971, 202ff.

56. Cf. *Original Letters Relative to the English Reformation, 1531-58*, I and II, ed.

H.Robinson, 1846-47; *The Zurich Letters*, I and II, ed. H.Robinson, 1842-45. One illuminating example is the career of John Hooper, cf. 176f.

57. *Puritanismus*, 22ff.; cf. id., *Bucer in England*.

58. *Reich Gottes*, 113, and passim. For criticism on this point, however, cf. Little, 251.

59. Martin Bucer.

60. J.M.McConica, *English Humanists and Reformation Politics under Henry VIII and Edward VI*, 1965. Cf. also already Knappen, op.cit., 31ff.; van Gelder, op.cit., 328ff.; P.N.Siegel, 'English Humanism and the new Tudor Aristocracy', *JHI* 13, 1952, 450-68.

61. *ChH* 20, 1951, 37-57.

62. Op.cit., 38.

63. Op.cit., 37. Cf. also already Haller, *Rise*, 5, for a connection with mediaeval preaching and its characteristic content.

64. Op.cit., 40.

65. 'The distinguishing marks of English mediaeval piety listed by Trinterud were in fact common to most of western Europe and something markedly similar to the puritan spirit has been a recurrent phenomenon in Christian history.' Breward, *Perkins*, 17.

66. Cf. already W.H.Summers, *The Lollards of the Chiltern Hills*, 1906; also for the earlier period M.E.Aston, 'Lollardy and Sedition, 1381-1431', *PaP* 17, 1960, 1-44; J.A.F.Thomson, *The Later Lollards 1414-1520*, 1965; for the later period A.G.Dickens, *Lollards and Protestants in the Diocese of York, 1509-1558*, 1959, ²1966; id., 'Heresy and the Origins of English Protestantism', in *Britain and the Netherlands*, ed. J.S.Bromley and E.H.Kossman, 1964, II, 47-66; id., *The English Reformation*, 22ff.; id., 'The Ambivalent English Reformation', in Dickens et al. (ed.), *Background*, 43-56. In part Anabaptist groups which had come over from the continent, and who found kindred spirits among the Lollards, were also integrated into English nonconformity, cf. I.B.Horst, *Anabaptism and the English Reformation to 1558*, 1972, esp. 35f., 38ff., 55ff. – I had no access to J.F.Davies, *Heresy and Reformation in the South-East of England*, unpublished D.Phil. dissertation, Oxford 1968.

67. J.McNeill, *The History and Character of Calvinism*, 1954, ³1962, 310.

68. This is clear above all from the correspondence collected in the Original Letters. Bullinger's authority was still the same in the first years of Elizabeth, cf. Zurich Letters (see ibid.). Cf. also Cremeans, op.cit., 60.

69. *Schweizer Ursprünge des anglikanischen Staatskirchentums*, 1953. Cf. recently also G.Locher, 'Zwinglis Einfluss in England und Schottland – Daten und Probleme', *Zwing* 14, 1975, 165-209 (with bibliography).

70. Trinterud, *ChH* 1951, 37, etc. mentions above all the Rhineland Reformers: in addition to Zwingli and Bullinger these are Oecolampadius (much of whose thought is akin to Bucer), Capito and Martyr (Vermigli). Cf. also D.Hall, *Understanding*, 335f. For the whole problem cf. also G.R.Elton, 'England und die oberdeutsche Reform', *ZKG* 89, 1978, 3-11; id., 'England and the Continent in the Sixteenth Century', in D.Baker (ed.), *Reform and Reformation: England and the Continent c.1500-c.1750*, 1979, 1-16.

71. Perkins, op.cit., 18f. Cf. already Knappen, op.cit., 367.

72. For his work cf. O.Gründler, *Die Gotteslehre Girolani Zanchis und ihre Bedeutung für seine Lehre von der Prädestination*, 1965.

73. *Elizabethan Puritanism. General Introduction*, 3ff.

74. *Puritanism*, 38. For the continued influence of humanism in England under the Tudors, its social roots and its continuation of the mediaeval image of the ordering of society cf. also P.N.Siegel, 'English Humanism and the New Tudor Aristocracy', *JHI* 13, 1952, 450-68. However, it is important to see that the English humanists of

the early sixteenth century like More, Colet, Grocyn and Linacre were for the most part committed Christian humanists, and essentially different in attitude from Erasmus (cf. A.Hyma, 'The Continental Origins of English Humanism', *Huntington Library Quarterly* 4, 1940/41, 1-25), so that they cannot be regarded as the forerunners of later developments.

75. *The Anglicanism of William Laud*, 1947, 37ff.

76. Op.cit., 38.

77. Op.cit., 40.

78. Bourne himself calls his verdict 'rather unkindly'.

79. See above, 120f.

80. Cf. also A.Simpson, *Puritanism in Old and New England*, paperback 1961, 1f.; cf. also D.Hall, *Understanding*, 331.

81. *Anglican and Puritan, The Basis of their Opposition, 1558-1640*, 1964.

82. Cf. Breward, *Perkins*, 14f.

83. Cf. esp. P.M.Dawley, *John Whitgift and the English Reformation*, 1954, ch.5, 133-60; H.C.Porter, *Reformation and Reaction*, 1958, 413; Little, *Religion*, 253.

84. Cf. G.Gawlick, 'Der Deismus als Grundzug der Religionsphilosophie der Aufklärung', in *Hermann Samuel Reimarus (1694-1768) ein 'bekannter Unbekannter' der Aufklärung in Hamburg*, 1973, (15-43) 18.

85. Cf. above, 445 n.7; 69ff.

86. *Society*, 20.

87. *Perkins*, 14. Cf. already B.Hall, 'Puritanism: the Problem of Definition', in *Studies in Church History*, ed. C.W.Dugmore and C.Duggan, 2, 1964, (283-96) 290.

88. *Vocabulary*, 11.

89. Hill, *Society*, 13ff., depicts the different usages beginning with contemporaries.

90. Cf. above, 476f. n.8; Haller, *Rise*, passim, and Knappen, op.cit., 379ff.

91. For what follows see also the surveys in H.Davies, *Worship* I, 40ff.; W.R.D.Jones, *The Mid-Tudor Crisis, 1539-1563*, 1973, 71-112; and P.Toon, *Puritans and Calvinism*, 1973 (though he does not recognize the problems inherent in the title of his work).

92. For his life, his stay in Zurich and the influence that Bullinger had on him, and his activity in England see W.M.S. West, 'John Hooper and the Origins of Puritanism', *BQ* NS 15, 1954/5, 346-68; 16, 1956/7, 22-46, 67-88.

93. For these events cf. Knappen, op.cit., 82-89; J.H.Primus, *The Vestments Controversy*, 1960, 3ff.; J.Ridley, *Thomas Cranmer* (1962), paperback 1966, 308ff.; Dickens, *Reformation*, 241f.; West, op.cit., *BQ* 16, 30ff. However, there is a positive reaction to his activity as bishop, cf. F.D.Price, 'Gloucester Diocese under Bishop Hooper', *Trans. Bristol and Gloucester Arch.Soc.*, 60, 1938, 51-151; J.Gairdner, 'Bishop Hooper's Visitation of Gloucester', *EHR* 19, 1904, 98-121; Dickens, *Reformation*, 242f.

94. Cf. Cranmer's writing in *The Works*, ed. J.E.Cox, 1844-46, II, 428; Bucer's answer in *Scripta Anglicana*, 681-4. Martyr and Bucer had responded to Hooper's direct questions in a similarly decisive way: cf. Martyr to Hooper in G.C.Gorham, *Gleanings of a Few Scattered Ears during the Period of the Reformation in England*, 1857, 187-96; Bucer to Hooper, ibid., 200-9. Calvin also adopted a similar standpoint: Calvin to Bullinger, ibid., 241-3.

95. Only Bullinger and à Lasco strengthened Hooper in his attitude. Cf. Ridley, op.cit., 314.

96. Cf. Hooper to Bullinger, 5 February 1550, in *Original Letters*, 74ff.; cf. 27 March 1550, ibid., 78ff.; 29 June 1550, ibid., 86ff. The text of the sermons is in J.Hooper, *Early Writings*, ed. S.Carr, 1843, 431-558. – Cf. also West, op.cit., *BQ* 16, 26ff. On Hooper's sermons and his concept of the Bible cf. also E.R.Gane, 'The Exegetical Methods of Some Sixteenth-Century Puritan Preachers', Hooper, Cartwright and Perkins', *AUSS* 19, 1981, 21-36, 99-114.

97. In an undated letter (August 1551?) to Cranmer, *Opera*, ed. A. Kuyper, 1866, II, 655ff.

98. Cf. P.Lorimer, *John Knox and the Church of England*, 1875, 103-5, 259-63; Ridley, op.cit., 336f.; Knappen, op.cit., 96f. Text etc. in W.Muss-Arnold, 'Puritan Efforts and Struggles, 1550-1603', *AJT* 23, 1919, (345-66, 471-99) 347. The study also contains a vast amount of bibliographical information about Puritan literature in the period in question.

99. *Loci* of 1535, in *CR* 21, 510ff. – Cf. already on Erasmus, op.cit., 88, 107f.

100. Cf. the account *A Brieff Discourse off the Troubles Begonne at Franckford*, according to the traditional view written by W.Whittingham, but according to most recent research (cf. P.Collinson, 'The Authorship of A Brief Discourse...', *JEH* 9, 1958, 188-208) written by Thomas Wood, ed. J.Petheram, 1846; ed. E.Arber, 1908; C.Garrett, *Exiles* (1938), ²1966; Knappen, op.cit., 118ff.; Dickens, *Reformation*, 289ff. and most recently (with criticisms of Garrett), R.van der Molen, 'Anglican Against Puritan: Ideological Origins during the Marian Exile', *ChH* 42, 1973, 45-57.

101. Op.cit., 292ff.

102. Cf. *Discourse*, ed. Arber, 50f. Van der Molen, op.cit., 53f., makes it clear that Calvin is claimed by both parties as an authority but basically offered more support to the Anglicans.

103. Cf. R.W.Dixon, *History of the Church of England from the Abolition of the Roman Jurisdiction*, VI, 1902, 44ff.; J.H.Primus, *Controversy*; Knappen, op.cit., 187ff; Collinson, op.cit., 71ff.; E.H.Emerson, *English Puritanism from John Hooper to John Milton*, 1968, 11ff.

104. For the Elizabethan settlement cf. esp. J.E.Neale, *Elizabeth I and Her Parliaments*, I, 1953, reprinted 1964, 51ff.; id., 'The Elizabethan Acts of Supremacy and Uniformity', *EHR* 65, 1950, 304-32; C.S.Meyer, *Elizabeth I and the Religious Settlement of 1559*, 1960; Dickens, *Reformation*, 294ff.; Hudson, *Cambridge Connection*; Collinson, *Grindal*, 85ff. For the reign of Elizabeth I generally cf. also S.H.Thomson, *Europe in Renaissance and Reformation*, 1963, 703ff.

105. *Parker Correspondence*, ed. Bruce and Perowne, 1853, 223-7; the text in J.Strype, *The Life and Acts of Matthew Parker*, 1821, II, App.nr.XXIV; Dixon, *History*, 44ff.

106. Op.cit., 1566.

107. Anon., appeared 1566. Excerpts in Trinterud, *Puritanism*, 67ff.

108. In Trinterud, op.cit., 84.

109. Op.cit., 81. It should, however, be noted that here only the radical wing of Puritanism was affected; the basic Reformation attitude is much more marked among its moderate representatives (like Perkins) and no one who has read these writings can seriously claim that the influence of Calvin was insignificant. For Perkins cf. recently R.O.Stuart, *The Breaking of the Elizabethan Settlement of the Church*, Yale PhD 1976 (Ann Arbor microfilm), 102ff.

110. Op.cit., 10ff. This division follows that first made by A. Lang, *Puritanism*, 72ff.

111. F.Stoeffler, *The Rise of Evangelical Pietism*, 1965, 28.

112. The connection between the two becomes evident from the fact that the manuscript of the Book of Discipline printed for the Westminster Assembly of 1645 (under the title *A Directory of Church Government* [reprinted 1872]) came from Cartwright's papers (prepared in 1585/6), cf. Pearson, *Cartwright*, 392; Collinson, *Movement*, 295.

113. Cf. Pearson, op.cit., 33.

114. *Puritan Manifestoes*, ed. W.H.Frere and C.E.Douglas, 1907 (reprinted 1972). – Cf. also the extracts in H.C.Porter (ed.), *Puritanism in Tudor England*, 1970, 145ff.

115. *Puritan Manifestoes*, 1ff. (Also in W.H.Dunham/S.Pargellis, *Complaint and Reform in England*, 1938 [reprinted 1968], 232ff.). The authors were Wilcox and Field.

There is also a reproduction of the second edition of Field's *A View of Popish Abuses* in C.H.Porter, *Puritanism*, 122ff. Cf. most recently esp. Collinson, *Movement*, 118ff. and already Knappen, op.cit., 234ff.

116. Cf. on the one hand Cremeans, *Reception*, 86: 'After its publication Traver's Ecclesiastical Discipline became the authoritative presentation of Nonconforming Calvinism', and on the other Collinson, *Movement*, 107f.

117. M.Marprelate, *The Epistle* (1588), ed. E.Arber, 1880; *The Epitome* (1588), ed. Arber, 1885; *The Marprelate Texts*, ed. W.Price, 1911; Scholars Press Facsimile of all the texts, 1967. E.Arber, *An Introductory Sketch to the Martin Marprelate Controversy* (1895), reprinted 1964; W.Pierce, *An Historical Introduction to the Marprelate Tracts*, 1908 (for criticism cf. however the review by W.H.Frere, *EHR* 25, 1910, 338-42); G.Bonnard, *La Controverse de Martin Marprelate*, 1916. For the bibliography of the original editions and the question of authorship cf. also Muss-Arnold, *Efforts*, 484ff. and more recently, L.H.Carlsson, *Martin Marprelate, Gentleman. Master Job Throkmorton Laid Open in His Colours*, 1981 (the author is Job Throkmorton, 1545-1601).

118. Cf. *The Writings of Robert Harrison and Robert Browne*, ed. A.Peel and L.H.Carlson, Elizabethan Nonconformist Texts, Vol.II, 1953. For Browne see above, 130. P.Zagorin, *The Court and the Country*, 1969, 158f. points to the marked contrast which the Nonconformists who remained in the church felt from the Separatists. However, he concedes that Separatism itself was a branch of Puritanism, whose basic approach it shared.

119. The most important events of this period are the Millenary Petition and the Hampton Court Conference, the effects of which were largely disappointing for the Puritans. It was at this Conference that James I made his famous remark 'No bishop, no king.' For events cf. Collinson, *Movement*, 448ff.; Knappen, *Puritanism*, 317ff.; W.McElwee, *The Wisest Fool in Christendom. The Reign of King James I and VI*, 1958, 134ff.; M.H.Curtis, 'The Hampton Court Conference and its Aftermath', *Hist* 46, 1961, 1-16; B.Babbage, *Puritanism and Richard Bancroft*, 1962. The text of the Millenary Petition was reprinted in H.Gee and W.J.Hardy, *Documents Illustrative of English Church History*, 1910 (reprinted 1966), 508-ll, and in J.R.Tanner, *Constitutional Documents of the Reign of James I*, 1930 reprinted 1961, 56ff.; it contains an extract from W.Barlow's account of the Hampton Court Conference, 60ff. The writings of William Bradshaw (collected in the two reprint volumes *Puritanism and Separatism* and *English Puritanism and Other Works*, ed. R.C.Simmons, 1972) are an example of the self-understanding of the non-separatist Puritans of this period.

120. The famous Thomason Collection in the British Museum is now beginning to appear in print: R.Jeffs (ed.), *The English Revolution I: Fast Sermons to Parliament. Vol.I, Nov.1640-1641*, 1970, and is completely available on microfilm (Ann Arbor University Microfilms). Cf. also above, 504 n.87.

121. Cf. e.g. S.R.Gardiner, *History of England*; G.P.Gooch, *English Democratic Ideas in the Seventeenth Century*, 1898 ([2]1927); T.C.Pease, *The Leveller Movement*, 1916, reprinted 1965; M.Freund, *Die Idee der Toleranz im England der grossen Revolution*, 1927; W.K.Jordan, *The Development of Religious Toleration in England*, three vols, 1932-38, Vol.II 1938, reprinted 1965; id., 'Sectarian Thought and Its Relation to the Development of Religious Toleration, 1640-1650', in *Huntington Library Quarterly* 3, 1939/40, 197-223, 289-314, 403-18; P.Zagorin, *A History of Political Thought in the English Revolution*, 1954.

122. This was first explained by A.S.P.Woodhouse in the introduction to his edition of the Putney Debates (1647-49) from the so-called Clarke Manuscripts: *Puritanism and Liberty*, 1938, [2]1951, reprinted 1965, 11f. in terms of the confusion between the concept of Christian freedom and the idea of human rights in terms of the Stoic notion of natural law as popularly understood; cf. also W.Haller, 'Introduction', in *The Leveller Tracts 1647-1653*, ed. W.Haller and G.Davies (1944, reprinted

1964), 35ff.; U.Bonanante, in the introduction to his anthology of Puritan documents in Italian translation, *I puritani. I soldati della Bibbia. A cura di U.Bonanate*, Torino 1975 (Introduction, 3-34) gives the impression that this was a gradual transition from theological to more 'secular' arguments. That is incorrect.

123. Woodhouse, op.cit., 35f., points out that despite the opposition between the parties as we find them in Cromwell's army – the Presbyterians, Independents, Millenarians and Levellers – Puritanism represents an intrinsic unity or, better, a continuity within a basic approach from which various lines of development were conceivable.

124. The contemporary biography by P.Heylyn, *Cyprianus Anglicus* (1668), [3]1719, stands at the beginning of a whole series of accounts of his life. Cf. the more recent biographies by A.C.Benson, 1887; H.M.Wallis, 1890; C.H.Simpkinson, 1894; W.H.Hutton, 1895; W.L.Mackintosh, 1907; A.S.Duncan-Jones, 1927; H.R.Trevor-Roper (1940), [2]1963. Also M.Creighton, 'Laud's Position in the History of the English Church', in W.E.Collins (ed.), *Commemoration Essays on Archbishop Laud*, 1895, reprinted 1969, 3ff.; earlier bibliography, ibid., 165ff.; H.Bell, *Archbishop Laud and Priestly Government*, 1907; E.C.Bourne, *The Anglicanism of William Laud*, 1947.

125. Cf. R.Orr, *Reason and Authority. The Thought of William Chillingworth*, 1967; cf. also R.M.Krapp, *Liberal Anglicanism, 1636-47*, 1944.

126. U.Brumm, *Puritanismus*, 4ff., gives a survey of the history of American research into Puritanism. Cf. recently also L.Ziff, *Puritanism in America: New Culture in the New World*, 1973.

127. Cf. H.B.Parker, 'John Cotton and Roger Williams' Debate Concerning Toleration, 1644-1652', *NEQ* 4, 1931, 735-56; E.Feist-Hirsch, 'John Cotton and Roger Williams: Their Controversy Concerning Religious Liberty', *ChH* 10, 1941, 38-51; J.Rosenmeier, 'The Teacher and the Witness: John Cotton and Roger Williams', in *William and Mary Quarterly* 25, 1968, 408-31; S.Bercovitch, 'Typology in Puritan New England: The Williams-Cotton Controversy Reassessed', *AmQ* 19, 1967, 166-91; R.Reinitz, 'The Typological Argument for Religious Toleration: The Separatist Tradition and Roger Williams', *Early American Literature* 5, 1970, 74-110; id., 'The Separatist Background of Roger Williams' Argument for Religious Toleration', in *Typology and Early American Literature*, ed. S.Bercovitch, 1972, 107-37; Ziff, *Puritanism*, 105ff. Partial reprint of documents from the controversy in J.H.Polishook, *Roger Williams, John Cotton and Religious Freedom*, 1967.

128. Earlier, Williams' demands were usually misunderstood in terms of modern politics; only recently has the theological background to his thought been recognized more clearly (bibliography, not completely without error, in U.Brumm, *Puritanismus*, 57ff.). What has here been worked out in a limited area (with the collaboration of Perry Miller, cf. his volume of selections, *Roger Williams. His Contribution to the American Tradition*, 1953, paperback 1962) still needs to be done for the whole area of Puritanism.

129. The most significant thinker of American Puritanism, Jonathan Edwards (1703-1758), falls completely within the eighteenth century. For the role of Puritanism in America cf. esp. S.E.Mead, *The Lively Experiment: The Shaping of Christianity in America*, 1963; H.S.Smith – R.T.Handy – L.R.Loescher, *American Christianity: An Historical Interpretation with Representative Documents*, two vols, 1960-1963; S.E.Ahlstrom, *A Religious History of the American People*, 1972, esp. 124ff., 295ff.; Ziff, *Puritanism*; R.E.Richey and D.G.Jones (eds.), *American Civil Religion*, 1974; C.C.Goen, 'Puritanism and the American Experiment', *RExp* 73, 1976, 5-21. – In England, Puritanism was gradually dissolved from the time of the Restoration by a rationalist climate, cf. G.R.Cragg, *From Puritanism to the Age of Reason*, 1950, reprinted 1966.

130. Cf. M.M.Knappen, 'William Tyndale, first English Puritan', *ChH* 5, 1936, 207-25; J.F.Mozley, *William Tyndale* 1937 (reprinted 1971); W.E.Campbell, *Erasmus,*

Tyndale and More, 1949, 97ff., 189ff., 267ff.; W.Clebsch, *England's Earliest Protestants*, 1964, 137ff.; J.Møller, 'The Beginnings of Puritan Covenant Theology', *JEH* 14, 1963, (47-67), 50ff.; G.E.Duffield, Introduction to *The Work of William Tyndale*, 1964, XI-XXXVIII; Dickens, *Reformation*, 70ff.; C.H.Williams, *William Tyndale*, 1969; J.McGold-rick, *Luther's English Disciples. The Reformation Thought of Robert Barnes and William Tyndale* (West Virginia Univ. Dissertation 1974, used on an Ann Arbor Microfilm); Freiday, *The Bible*, 23ff. R.Pineas, 'William Tyndale: Controversialist', *SP* 60, 1963, 117-32, concerns himself with the stylistic means which Tyndale used in his literary controversies with More and others. The introduction by S.L.Greenslade to his collection of extracts, *The Work of William Tyndale*, 1938, 24ff., is out of date. An earlier biography is that by R.Demaus, 1886.

131. Clebsch, op.cit., 138.

132. In the house of the London merchant Humphrey Monmouth and during his visit to Wittenberg in 1524. Cf. Mozley, op. cit., 44ff.; Clebsch, op.cit., 139; Williams, op.cit., 16ff.; McGoldrick, op.cit., 44. – However, G.Rupp, *Six Makers of English Religion, 1500-1770*, 1957, reprinted 1964, does not regard the supposed stay in Wittenberg as being very probable. Duffield, in *Works*, XV, leaves the question open.

133. Prologue to the 'Cologne Fragment', facsimile edition, ed. A.W.Pollard, 1926. Cf. Mozley, op.cit., 63; Clebsch, op.cit., 144; Williams, op.cit., 127f. L.J.Trinterud, 'A Reappraisal of William Tyndale's Debt to Martin Luther', *ChH* 31, 1962, 24-45, has demonstrated from the use of the concept of the law and the covenant in Tyndale, along the lines of the remarks which follow, that he differs from Luther more than he is indebted to him and represents, rather, the South German type of Reformation with a humanist stamp, which reverted to a new form of legalism. This has recently been disputed by J.McGoldrick, op.cit., but his arguments are not very convincing. D.Freiday, *The Bible*, 23ff. is not so much interested in the question, but the passages out of Tyndale's works which he cites show the trend distinctly enough. H.Holeczek, *Humanistische Bibelphilologie als Reformproblem bei Erasmus von Rotterdam, Thomas More und William Tyndale*, SHCT IX, 1975, esp.259ff., is more restrained.

134. Facsimile ed. J.I.Mombert, 1884, reprinted 1967.

135. 'Aprologe shewing the use of the scripture', *Pentateuch*, ed. Mombert, 8 (also in *Works*, ed. Duffield, (36-41[43], 37).

136. 'A Pathway into the Holy Scripture', in *Doctrinal Treatises and Introductions to Different Portions of the Holy Scriptures*, ed. H.Walter, 1848, 1-28 (*Works*, ed. Duffield, 2-24).

137. 'Our deeds do us three manner of service. First, they certify us that we are heirs of everlasting life, and that the Spirit of God, which is the earnest thereof, is in us; in that our hearts consent unto the law of God, and we have power in our members to do it, though imperfectly. And secondarily, we tame the flesh therewith, and kill the sin that remaineth yet in us...And thirdly, we do our duty unto our neighbour therewith...' Op.cit., ed. Walter, 23f. (ed. Duffield, 19f.); cf. Møller, op.cit., 51.

138. *A Table, Expounding Certain Words in the First Book of Moses, called Genesis, Doctrinal Treatises*, 405-10 (*Works*, ed. Duffield, 43-8), 409 (47) etc. – For the 1525 revision of the Prologue cf. Clebsch, op.cit., 165ff.

139. *The prophete Jonas with an introduccion before teaching to vnderstonde him*, pro-logue also in *Doctrinal Treatises*, 447-66.

140. Op.cit., 164.

141. *Doctrinal Treatises*, 449.

142. Op.cit., 27.

143. *The New Testament. Translated by William Tyndale*, 1534, Reprint ed. by N.N.Wallis, 1938, 9.

144. Op.cit., 293ff.

145. Op.cit., 296f.

146. Op.cit., 155. According to Clebsch the focal point shifted later more clearly in the direction of the Law, cf. op.cit., 173. Williams, op.cit., 133, expresses doubts about Clebsch's view because he separates the theological periods in Tyndale too markedly.

147. Op.cit., 167f.

148. *New Testament*, ed. Wallis, 9. For the continuation of the quotation see above, 485 n.143.

149. *Pentateuch*, ed. Mombert, 162 (*Works*, ed. Duffield, 50). – Cf. also 'A Pathway', *Doctrinal Treatises*, 8 (*Works*, ed. Duffield, 4): 'The Old Testament is a book, wherein is written the law of God, and the deeds of them which fulfil them, and of them also which fulfil them not. The New Testament is a book, wherein are contained the promises of God; and the deeds of them which believe them, or believe them not.'

150. Cf. Clebsch, op.cit., 158.

151. Cf. Clebsch, op.cit., 157 and n.5.

152. *Pentateuch*, ed. Mombert, 8 (*Works*, ed. Duffield, 37).

153. L.J.Trinterud, *Origins*, 39, and J.G.Møller, op.cit., 55ff., have already drawn attention to this. Cf. above all Clebsch, op.cit., 181ff.

154. *Pentateuch*, ed. Mombert, 8, footnote (*Works*, ed. Duffield, 41).

155. *New Testament*, ed. Wallis, 4.

156. Op.cit., 7f. Cf. Clebsch, op.cit., 189f.

157. Op.cit., 8. – Cf. also the comparison with the edition of Matt.1-22 of 1525 and the other quotations from the marginalia of the NT edition of 1534 in Clebsch, op.cit., 187ff.

158. Cf. Dickens, *Reformation*, 71. Cf. also Tyndale's explanation of his use of the term 'elder' in the preface to the New Testament, ed. Wallis, 11ff.

159. Also in *Expositions and Notes on Sundry Portions of the Holy Scriptures, etc.*, ed. H.Alter (Parker Society), 1849, 237-344. Cf. also Clebsch, op.cit., 159ff.

160. Cf. *New Testament*, ed. Wallis, 11.

161. J.C.Spalding, 'Restitution as a Normative Factor for Puritan Dissent', *JAAR* 44, 1976, (47-63) 50.

161a. Cf. also W.D.J. Cargill Thompson, 'The Two Regiments: the Continental Setting of William Tyndale's Political Thought', in D.Baker (ed.), *Reform and Reformation*, 17-34.

162. Op.cit., 52.

163. T.Cranmer, in J.Collier, *An Ecclesiastical History of Great Britain*, 1840, V, 184f.; in Spalding, op.cit., 52.

164. Cf. F.L. van Baumer, *The Early Tudor Theory of Kingship*, 1940, reprinted 1966; also P.N.Siegel, *JHI*, 1952, 462ff. For the historical events cf. recently G.R.Elton, *Reform and Reformation. England 1509-1558*, 1977.

165. Cf. van Baumer, op.cit., 86.

166. Cf. van Baumer, op.cit., 94ff. For the difference between this theory and the doctrine of the divine right of kings which was first developed by James I and his theologians cf. above, 92.

167. Møller, op.cit., 51. Here Tyndale is obviously dependent on a writing 'On the old and new God', probably by Joachim Vadian of St Gall, cf. Clebsch, op.cit., 169f.

168. Cf. J.McConica, op.cit., 169ff.

169. Appeared pseudonymously in Basle, 1534; cf. Knappen, op.cit., 59. *Short-title Catalogue*, ed. A.W.Pollard, G.R.Redgrave etc., 1926 (STC), 24,353. – I have used an Ann Arbor microfilm.

170. For a summary account of events cf. J.B.Black, *The Reign of Elizabeth 1558-1603*(1936), ²1959, 166f., and above all P.McGrath, *Papists and Puritans under Elizabeth*

I, 1967. Cf. also C.Hill, *Antichrist in Seventeenth-Century England*, 1971, 1-40. For the climate of the time see also J.E.Neale, 'The via media in Politics', in *Essays in Elizabethan History*, 1958, 113-24. – L.Borinski, *Englischer Humanismus und deutsche Reformation*, 1969, 21ff., points out that there were reasons in domestic politics for polemic against popes and bishops as early as the fourteenth century, connected with the fact that the king relied on the church's support above all against the nobility and the citizens, and the Pope played a significant role as the guarantor of the system. The move by Henry VIII against the Pope modified these positions without doing away with them completely.

171. Wittenberg 1536, preface by Luther. German translation 1545, Czech 1565. For Barnes cf. Clebsch, op.cit., 42ff., and for the *Vitae*, ibid., 73f.; there are modernized extracts from his works in *Reformation Essays of Barnes*, ed. M.S.Tjernagel, paperback 1963; H.C.Porter, *Puritanism in Tudor England*, 1970, 28ff.

172. Op.cit.

173. Op.cit., 27.

174. Op.cit., 28.

175. Op.cit., 28f.

176. Op.cit., 12ff.

177. See above, 425 n.136.

178. Op.cit., 37ff.

179. Op.cit., 35.

180. Op.cit., 36.

181. Op.cit., 41.

182. Op.cit., 42f.

183. 'The law of the gospel is a mor perfit law for the Christen then the law of Moses was for the iewes. But the iewes neded no other law nor ceremonies then the law of Moses/ then the Christen men nede no other law (as touching theyr soules) but the law of the gospel.' Op.cit., 36.

184. Ed. C.Hopf, 'Bishop Hooper's "Notes" to the King's Council', *JTS* 44, 1943, 194-9. For the document and Bishop Ridley's answer (printed in J.Bradford, *Writings*, ed. A.Townsend, II, 1853, 373-95) see also Primus, op.cit., 16ff.; W.M.S.West, 'John Hooper', *BQ* 16, 33ff.

185. Cf. above, 482 n.99.

186. ...*verumetiam omnis Divinae voluntatis cognitio, quae ex scripturarum inter se collatione, et comparatione, necessario deduci et colligi potest, vim habet, et Naturam Praecepti Divini, siue ad praecipiendum, siue ad prohibendum, si modo Naturae ac proportioni fidei ac Scripturae conveniat.*

187. West, op.cit., esp. *BQ* 15.

188. 1559, reprinted 1702.

189. West, op.cit., *BQ* 15, 354.

190. Cf. West, op.cit., *BQ* 15, 356ff.

191. Cf. the introduction to his 'Declaration of the Ten Commandments', 'Unto the Christian Reader', in *Early Writings*, ed. S.Carr, 1843, 255-70; cf. also West, op.cit., *BQ* 15, 357ff.

192. Cf. *Early Writings*, op.cit., 126; cf. also West, op.cit., *BQ* 15, 368.

193. *Early Writings*, 258.

194. Cranmer to the Privy Council, 7 October 1552; in Lorimer, op.cit., 104; cf. Knappen, op.cit., 96.

195. Hooper had already suggested this in the introductory statement quoted above.

196. Cf. above, 482f. n.115.

197. D.J.McGinn, *The Admonition Controversy*, 1949; J.S.Coolidge, *The Pauline Renaissance in England. Puritanism and the Bible*, 1970, 1ff. – The controversy is reported

in detail in *The Works of John Whitgift*, three vols., ed. J.Ayre (Parker Society), 1851-53, Vol.1. For Whitgift cf. also P.M.Dawley, *John Whitgift and the Reformation*, 1955. For the controversy with Cartwright, ibid., 133ff. E.F.Kevan has also put forward a similarly 'evangelical' conception of the Puritans, cf. below, 490 n.263.

198. Op.cit., 2f.

199. *Whitgift's Works* I, 176. – Extracts from the controversy can also be found in McGinn, op.cit., 374ff.

200. Spalding, 'Restitution', *JAAR*, 1976.

201. In the *Consultatio* of the Archbishop of Cologne; cf. Spalding, op.cit., 55.

202. *Whitgift's Works* I, 195.

203. Ibid.

204. Ibid., 239f.

205. P.Munz, *The Place of Hooker in the History of Thought*, 1952, reprinted 1971, 46.

206. I have used the Folger Library edition, ed. W.Speed Hill, Vol.I, 1977 (= F); cf. also the Everyman edition, 1907 reprinted 1965 (= E).

207. For Hooker cf. esp. L.S.Thornton, *Richard Hooker. A Study of his Theology*, 1924; G.Michaelis, *Richard Hooker als politischer Denker*, 1933, reprinted 1965; A.P. d'Entreves, *Riccardo Hooker*, 1939; id., *The Medieval Contribution to Political Thought*, 1959, 117-42; E.T.Davies, *The Political Ideas of Richard Hooker*, 1946; cf. also id., *Episcopacy and the Royal Supremacy in the Church of England in the Sixteenth Century*, 1950, 41ff.; F.J.Shirley, *Richard Hooker and Contemporary Political Ideas*, 1949; P. Munz, op.cit.; G.Hillerdal, *Reason and Revelation in Richard Hooker*, 1962; J.S.Marshall, *Hooker and the Anglican Tradition*, 1963; Freiday, *The Bible*, 41ff. For Anglican theology as a whole from Hooker to Laud cf. also recently G.R.Cragg, *Freedom and Authority*, 1975, 97-126. C.J.Sisson, *The Judicious Marriage of Mr Hooker and the Birth of the Laws of Ecclesiastical Polity*, 1940, provides a biographical background to the book.

208. These effects were probably so permanent because, as Munz, op.cit., 13, observes, 'his ideas did not survive in their original purity and with their original meaning, but were transformed and became part of the living tradition of English political thought.'

209. Cf. Thornton, op.cit., 27ff.; Michaelis, op.cit., 46ff.

210. E.T.Davies, *Episcopacy*, 42; cf. Munz, op.cit., 19.

211. *Laws*, Book I, ch.XI, 4: F 114, cf. E I, 205.

212. 'A way mysticall and supernaturall': F 118, cf. E 208.

212a. O.Loyer, 'Contrat social et consentement chez Richard Hooker', *RSPT* 59, 1975, 369-98, makes it clear that Hooker is dependent on two traditions at the same time: the Aristotelian, which regards man as a political being with a positive concern for building up society, and the sceptical Stoic/patristic view which begins from man as fallen and expects the restoration of a primal state on another level.

213. *Laws*, Book I, ch.III, 2-5, F 64ff.; cf. E 154ff. For what follows cf. also Thornton, op.cit., 25ff.; Michaelis, op.cit., 34ff.;Shirley, op.cit., 77ff.; and above all Hillerdal, op.cit., 40ff.

214. *Laws*, Book I, ch. IV: F 69ff.; E 161ff.

215. *Laws*, Book I, ch. VII, 4: F 79; E 171.

216. *Laws*, Book I, ch. VIII, 9: F 89f.;E 182.

217. *Laws*, Book I, ch.X: F 95ff.; E 187ff.

218. *Laws*, Book I, ch.XI,2: F 111f.; E 202f. Cf. also Hillerdahl, op.cit., 56ff.

219. Op.cit., 209.

220. This is the context of phrases reminiscent of Greek thought: 'intuitive vision of God in the world to come', 'real and actual fruition of that which no tongue can express', and 'endless union', op.cit., 209.

221. *Laws*, Book I, ch.XII, 1 and 2, F 119ff.; E 210f. Cf. also Hillerdahl, op.cit., 80ff.

222. Op.cit., 210.

223. Op.cit., 211.

224. *Laws*, Book I, ch. XV, 1: F 130: cf. E 219.

225. *Laws*, Book I, ch. XV, 2: F 130; cf. E 220.

226. Ibid.

227. *Laws*, Book I, ch. XV, 3: F 131f.; E 221f.

228. A phrase from Cartwright.

229. *Laws*, Book II, ch. I,2, F.145; cf. E, 235.

230. *Laws*, Book I, XIV, 5, F 123; cf. E 218. Cf. also Freiday, *The Bible*, 44f., 46.

231. G.Hillerdal, *Reason*, has clearly seen the division in Hooker's thought (over against an almost unqualified reverence, as represented e.g. by B.J.Marshall, *Hooker*); cf. e.g. the comparison with Luther, 25, 33f., and the final conclusion, 148, that Hooker could not balance faith against reason. The theory of God's grace as a presupposition of right reason simply transposes this to a higher plane, without making clear the significance of 'grace'. Cf. also the metaphysical basis in Hooker, 97ff. His thought is ultimately imprisoned in a Spiritualist dualism, which is also widespread among other representatives of the time.

232. S.L.Bethell, *The Cultural Revolution of the Seventeenth Century*, 1951 ([2]1963), 13ff., has rightly pointed out the central role of reason as it was taken over directly from mediaeval scholasticism in Anglican theology as early as the late sixteenth and early seventeenth centuries. In Hooker the rational approach is particularly marked, cf. op.cit., 19ff. Reason is indispensable not only for natural theology but also for judging revelation and scripture. Bethell stresses that the Latitudinarians and Locke were not the first to assign it this significance. By contrast, G.F.Allison, *The Rise of Moralism. The Proclamation of the Gospel from Hooker to Baxter*, 1966, points to the predominance of the Reformation (anti-Tridentine) doctrine of justification among most of the earlier Anglicans (apart from Taylor); this was only broken through the advance of moralism as a result of the revolution in the time of the Commonwealth. Both positions have retained an appropriate aspect of it: whereas the earlier Anglicans were still able to maintain a balance between the heritage of the Reformation and the familiar patterns of scholastic thought, the moralism of the rationalist school in Anglicanism (within which the Great Tew group must already be included) increasingly gains the upper hand.

233. T.Cartwright, *The Second Replie of Thomas Cartwright: Agaynst Maister Doctor Whitgiftes Second Answer, Touching the Church Discipline*, 1575, 56, quoted by Coolidge, op.cit., 10.

234. It appears in this way e.g. in L.Borinski, 'Puritanische und anglikanische Lebensideale im Zeitalter der englischen Revolution', in *Festschrift T.Spira*, 1961, 197-211. He gives an apt account of Anglican thinking, but interprets the Puritans one-sidedly in a Calvinist sense and therefore misunderstands the humanistic features which they share with the Anglicans.

235. Cf. also id., *Mind*, 365ff.

236. Op.cit. For the idea of the covenant among the Puritans cf. also J. von Rohr, 'Covenant and Assurance in Early English Puritanism', *ChH* 34, 1965, 195-203; C.J.Sommerville, 'Conversion versus the Early Puritan Covenant of Grace', *JPH* 44, 1966, 178-97; J.A.McKenzie, 'The Covenant Theology – A Review Article', in ibid., 198-204; R.L.Greaves, 'John Bunyan and Covenant Theology in the Seventeenth Century', *ChH* 36, 1967, 151-69.

237. Cf. the quotations from Zwingli and Bullinger in Möller, op.cit., 47f., and already G.Schrenk, *Gottesreich und Bund im älteren Protestantismus*, 1923, 36ff. Tyndale should also be put in this line, cf. above 107f.

238. For what follows see also H.H.Wolf, *Einheit*.

239. *Institutio* II, X, 2.

240. Cf. Møller, op.cit., 58; Breward, *Perkins*, 16f., 90, etc.

241. Thus most federal theologians, including Cartwright, but not Perkins.

242. Cf. Schrenk, op.cit., 58f. Ursinus distinguishes a *foedus naturale* from a *foedus gratiae*.

243. The original Latin version is *Armilla aurea*, 1590, ET 1592. It is now most easily accessible in the extended extract in Breward, op.cit., 169ff.

244. Breward, op.cit., 210ff., who leaves out the lengthy discussions about the Decalogue which come in between. For the content see Lang, *Puritanismus*, 109ff.; Møller, op.cit., 59ff.; Stoeffler, *Rise*, 1965, 53ff.

245. Cf. the title of Ch.XIX: 'Concerning the outward means of executing the decree of election and of the decalogue', ed. Breward, 210.

246. In *Cartwrightiana*, ed. A.Peel – L.Carlson, 1951, 159ff.

247. Op.cit., 166.

248. H.Heppe, *Geschichte des Pietismus und der Mystik in der reformierten Kirche, namentlich der Niederlande*, 1879, is the first to speak of a Puritan pietism.

249. The designation comes from Heppe, op.cit. T.Merrill, *William Perkins 1558-1602. English Puritanist*, 1966, IX, says of him: 'William Perkins was the most famous and influential spokesman for Calvinism of his day, and his works provide a rewarding thoroughfare into the heart of that attitude, so basic to Anglo-American heritage, which we have come to call Puritan.' For him cf. also the biography by J.J.van Barsel, *William Perkins, eene bijdrage to de kennis der religieuse ontwikkeling in England ten tijde van Konigin Elisabeth*, 1913; R.Stuart, op.cit.

250. Op.cit., ch.3, 101ff.

251. 1965. II, 24-108. – Cf. also the careful investigations into the conditional character of the covenant of grace by J.S.Coolidge, op.cit., 99ff.

252. He defended the doctrine of predestination in a work of his own (*De praedestinationis modo et ordine et de amplitudine gratiae divinae*) and affirmed justification in the Reformed sense against semi-Pelagian attacks (cf. Breward, op.cit., 84ff.). He also had a conservative attitude in church politics, as is evident among other things from the fact that he swore the notorious *ex officio* oath (on which cf. Collinson, *Movement*, 266f.) and rejected the term 'puritan'. He himself expressly declared: 'till we separate from Christ, none should sever themselves from our Church, ministry, and service of God', Breward, op.cit., 22.

253. Cf. Breward, op.cit., 22.; von Rohr, *Covenant*, passim. For the whole theme see also N.Pettit, *The Heart Prepared*, 1966.

254. Both writings have been newly edited by Merrill, op.cit.

255. Cf. the definition of conscience put in typically Ramistic form at the beginning of the *Discourse*, Merrill, 5ff., and the introduction, 19f. Merrill gives a representative selection from the two tractates, unfortunately without indicating the page numbers of the original and without a critical apparatus.

256. Cf. Miller, *Marrow*, 53; Breward, op.cit., 58ff.

257. *Workes*, ed. J.Legate and C.Legge, III, 1618, 413; cited by Breward, op.cit., 36.

258. Breward, op.cit., 177.

259. Ibid.

260. *Workes*, ed. J.Legate and C.Legge, I, 1616.

261. Cf.Stoeffler, op.cit., 55. In Breward's extract the weight is shifted, in that the detailed comments on the decalogue (pp.32-70 in the original addition) are omitted.

262. In chapter XXXVII, about justification, Breward, op.cit., 232.

263. E.F.Kevan, *The Grace of the Law*, 1964.

264. In his summary concluding chapter he comments: 'In a great many places the present writer's own convictions are so clearly expressed by the Puritans that this concluding chapter wears something of the character of an Apologia pro Puri-

tanis and takes the form of a presentation of their views in the context of present-day thinking' (op.cit., 251). At various points in his work he himself speaks of the dogmatic interest which guided the author: against an antinomianism which is widespread in certain Protestant circles (in particular he seems to be thinking of the Barthians) he refers to G. Wingren and others for the sequence 'law and gospel' instead of 'gospel and law': in the light of creation the law is understood as natural law which is identical with the law that has been revealed (in the Decalogue). Only through this parallel does the latter receive its binding quality (op.cit., 262ff.).

265. See above 490 n.246.

266. *Short Form of Catechizing,* cf. Stoeffler, op.cit., 59.

267. J.Dod and R.Cleaver, *A Plain and Familiar Exposition of the Ten Commandments with A... Catechism etc,* 1603 (nineteen editions between then and 1635!). Cf. also Stoeffler, op.cit., 61f. – The early writing by Lancelot Andrewes, *A Pattern of Catechistical Doctrine,* also has great similarity in construction and approach to these works. On the one hand it is said (Part II, Ch.II, 2, *Minor Works,* 71): 1. The law does not create perfection, 2. it is our 'schoolmaster to Christ'; and on the other hand, within the usual doctrine of the two covenants, the covenant of grace is defined as follows: 'that Christ to God should make perfection, to us should restore that we had lost, and on our side, that we should perform perfect obedience, but by Christ' (Part II, Introduction, *Minor Works,* 62). In later remarks by Andrewes we find the Thomistic doctrine that grace fully restores nature which is of itself good and is only marred by the fall; cf. Porter, *Reformation,* 393ff. Porter stresses the differences from Perkins, but one could just as easily stress the common features.

268. Kevan, op.cit., 47ff.

269. Op. cit., 52ff. – It may be of interest in our later concern with the early Deism of Herbert of Cherbury that in a quotation from Richard Baxter cited by Kevan (op.cit., 55), he includes the knowledge of natural law among the *communes notitiae.*

270. Kevan himself points to the proximity to Hooker and Thomas Aquinas, op.cit., 55. He observes that the Puritans stood out as theologians in that they stressed the need of revelation for the full knowledge of God's will; however, it must be added that Thomas also did this. Kevan is probably right in claiming that in the biblically oriented system of the Puritans the revealed law is founded on creation alone; however, it is doubtful whether this is as irreconcilably in conflict with Stoicism, rationalism and Thomism as he supposes (op.cit., 57).

271. Op.cit., 66ff.

272. Here Baxter puts forward the opposite position, that the law is dependent on God's free will and his particular aims.

273. Op.cit., 69ff.

274. Op.cit., 73ff.

275. Op.cit., 77.

276. Op.cit., 158f.

277. Cf. Kevan, op.cit. ch.V, 'The Continuance of Moral Obligation', 167ff., with numerous examples.

278. Cf. op.cit., 206f.

279. Op.cit., 208ff.

280. Kevan, ch.VII, op.cit., 225ff.

281. The comparison with the Quakers, op.cit., 243, is not far out from this perspective. For the Puritans' own testimonies on their spiritual experience, especially their conversion experiences, cf. also O.C.Watkins, *The Puritan Experience,* 1972.

282. And also despite many misunderstandings. Miller, too, has guarded against the view that he wanted to demonstrate that the Puritans were not Calvinists, op.cit., 48f.

283. 1937.

284. Cf. Miller, op.cit., 74f.

285. Op.cit., 75.

286. M.Levy, *Der Sabbath in England*, 1933; H.Schöffler, *Abendland und Altes Testament*, 1937, 52ff.; Knappen, op.cit., 442ff.; P.Collinson, 'The Beginnings of English Sabbatarianism', in *Studies in Church History*, ed. C.W.Dugmore and C.Duggan, I, 1964, 207ff.; C.Hill, *Society*, 145-218.

287. The transference of the regulations about the Jewish sabbath to the Christian Sunday had already taken place in the Middle Ages.

288. *Auslegung der Zehen Gebot* (1528), Luther's (and Melanchthon's) *Unterricht der Visitatoren an die Pfarrherrn* (1528, 1538, 1539, 1545), WA 26, 206. Further evidence for the Reformers' view of the Sabbath in R.Cox, *The Literature of the Sabbath Question*, two vols., 1865. However, it is characteristic that A.Karlstadt, *Von dem Sabbat und geboten Feyertagen*, 1524, was a sabbatarian; cf. G.Rupp, 'Andreas Karlstadt and Reformation Puritanism', *JTS* NS 19, 1959, 308-26.

289. *An Answer to Sir Thomas More's Dialogue. The Supper of the Lord*, ed. H.Walter, 1850, 97f.

290. Cf. the evidence in Knappen, op.cit., 445f., and for the matter as a whole W.B.Whitaker, *Sunday in Tudor and Stuart Times*, 1933. C.Hill, *Society*, 159, refers to the 'Virtual unanimity of early Elizabethan times on the subject of Sunday observance.'

291. Instances in Collinson, op.cit., 208.

292. 1583, reprinted 1879 (new impression 1965).

293. Titles in Collinson, op.cit., 209 and n.4. The work by J.Dod mentioned above is one of the most influential of them.

294. Text in Levy, op.cit., 193ff.; Tanner, op.cit., 54ff., and elsewhere.

295. Text of the ordinance in Levy, op.cit., 206ff.

296. Text in Gee-Hardy, *Documents*, 528ff.

297. For Luther's conception cf. H.Bornkamm, *Luther and the Old Testament*, ET 1969, 81ff.

298. Op.cit., 210ff.

299. Cf. Collinson, op.cit., 215.

300. Op.cit.

301. Levy, op.cit., 272.

302. Wording in Levy, op.cit., 275ff.

303. See below, 617 n.2.

304. Op.cit. The work partly met with unqualified approval (cf. Seaver, *ChH* 40,1971, 490f.; Nuttall, *JTS* 22, 1971, 284-7, etc), but was also partly subjected to justified criticism (cf. e.g. Wilson, in *Int* 25, 1971, 521f., and esp. Delius, *TLZ* 96, 1971, cols 610f.).

305. Op.cit., XIII.

306. Op.cit., 21.

307. Op.cit., 147.

308. Op.cit., 148.

309. Op.cit., 145.

310. Cf. *Liturgies of Edward VI AD 1549*, 1844, 155; also in Cranmer, *Works*, ed. Cox, 518.

311. See above, 436f. n.17.

312. See above 487 n.186.

313. Ridley goes into this term 'faith' in his answer; he cannot understand it either as the conviction of conscience or as a reference to an article of faith (Bradford, *Writings*, II, 376; cf. also Primus, op.cit., 21f.).

314. See above, 432 n.254.

315. *Puritan Manifestoes*, ¹1907, ²1954 (ed. Frere and Douglas), 43-55 (there wrongly dated July), 45.

316. Op. cit., 198. Primus, op.cit., 20, points out that this is the first application of the idea of the universal priesthood to the question of clothing. However, apart from the influence of Hebrews, the familar antipathy to Judaism is predominant here.

317. Primus, op.cit., 149ff., depicts the development of Separatism and Presbyterianism out of the dispute over vestments.

318. See above, 482f. n.115.

319. *Puritan Manifestoes*, 8.

320. Printed in Frere and Douglas, *Puritan Manifestoes*, 87ff. The editors' criticism, op.cit., XXIII, of the style and unsystematic construction of the work is justified.

321. '...their rochets, hoodes, cappes, clokes, tippets and gownes, or such like implements used by the Phariseis whiche claimed highe roumes, and made large borders on their garmentes...', op.cit., 102f.

322. Op.cit., 114ff.

323. In the *Puritan Manifestoes* they are turned into footnotes, cf. XXXI.

324. Collinson, *Movement*, 112f., who points out that William Turner had already drawn the same conclusions about the ideal form of the church from the same chapters sixteen years earlier.

325. *Puritan Manifestoes*, 8f., 13ff.

326. Ibid., 8f. For the punishment of crimes 'then' and 'now' cf. also the Old Testament examples, 17.

327. 'Jewish purifyings', ibid., 11.

327a. E.R.Gane, *AUSS* 1981, treated Puritan hermeneutics in the sermons of Hooper, Cartwright and Perkins. Everywhere he detects the same characteristic presuppositions, above all an extreme literalism, legalism and blindness to historical differences.

328. 101f. above.

329. *Introductory Sketch*, 28ff.

330. Evidently this is a similar collection to the one in Turner's *Romish Fox*; probably Turner was the direct model for a number of similar undertakings (Turner's second work *The Huntyng of the Romishe wolfe*, 1554, appeared in 1565 as a reprint under a different title, cf. Collinson, *Movement*, 78). E.C.Bourne, *Anglicanism*, has not inappropriately described the Puritan world view with the terms 'bibliolatry, Manichaeism, papophobia', op.cit.; in particular the hostility to the physical in their attitude is more Manichaean than Christian, op.cit., 38.

331. I have used the edition by E.Arber, 1880.

332. Op.cit., 7.

333. Cf. C.Hill, *Society and Puritanism*, 298ff.; R.A.Marchant, *The Puritans and the Church Courts in the Diocese of York, 1560-1642*, 1960.

334. *Elizabethan Puritanism*, 232.

335. Cf. Dickens, *Reformation*, 113ff. – Texts in Gee-Hardy, no. XLVIff., 145ff.

336. Known as 'A Learned Discourse', fuller title in Trinterud, op.cit.

337. *Elizabethan Puritanism*, 239ff.

338. The quotation is II Tim.3.17. Quotations in Trinterud, op.cit. 243f.

339. Op.cit., 244.

340. In the *Ordonnances ecclésiastiques* of 1541, which in turn are dependent on Bucer's Strasbourg church order.

341. Cf. e.g. J.Bohatec, 'Calvin et l'Humanisme', *RH* 183, 1938, 207-41; 185, 1940, 71-104; id., *Budé und Calvin*, 1950; J.Boisset, *Sagesse et Sainteté dans la pensée de Calvin*, 1959; by contrast, W.Niesel, 'Calvins Ablehnung des Humanismus', *RKZ* 80, 1930, 282ff.

342. H.H.Wolf stresses: 'The particular evaluation of the law in Calvin... is now not connected with any "legality", but it is the relationship of the law to its *anima*, its inclusion in the notion of the covenant, which led Calvin to this stress on the law', *Einheit*, 42. For the theme see also W.Kolfhaus, *Vom christlichen Leben nach Johannes Calvin*, 1949, 115ff.

343. Cf. C.Burrage, *Dissenters* I, 79ff.; R.M.Jones, *Mysticism and Democracy in the English Commonwealth*, 1932, 35ff.; E.Routley, *English Religious Dissent*, 1960, 48ff.; Haller, *Rise*, 173ff.; E.S.Morgan, *Visible Saints. The History of a Puritan Idea*, ¹1963, ²1972, 33ff.; B.R.White, *The English Separatist Tradition. From the Marian Martyrs to the Pilgrim Fathers*, 1971; M.R. Watts, *The Dissenters*, I, From the Reformation to the French Revolution, 1978. Cf. also Cragg, *Freedom*, 219-44.

344. Cf. C.Burrage, *The True Story of Robert Brown*, 1906; id., *The Early English Dissenters*, 1912, I, 94ff.; F.Powicke, *Robert Browne, Pioneer of Modern Congregationalism*, 1910; D.C.Smith, 'Robert Browne, Independent', *ChH* 6, 1937, 289-349; Watts, *Dissenters*, 26-34, and the introduction by L.H.Carlson in A.Peel and L.H.Carlson (eds.), *Writings*, 4ff. – G.F.Nuttall, *Visible Saints. The Congregational Way, 1640-1660*, 1957, 8, sees Brownism as being only the preliminary to Congregationalism, which does not begin in the strict sense until 1640.

345. Reprinted in *Writings*, ed. Peel and Carlson, 150ff.

346. Op.cit., 101,104.

347. *Social Doctrine*, 328ff., 691ff. etc.

348. Cf. also H.Davies, *The English Free Churches*, 1952, 49ff.

349. *Writings*, 158.

350. Op.cit., 153f.; cf. 156, lines 4ff.

351. Op.cit., 105.

352. Op.cit., 164.

353. In the dedication to King James I (unpaginated, folio A 2), there is reference only to Cartwright; later (76) once again to Peter Martyr (Vermigli). However, a reference to Browne would have been very unwise!

354. Cf. Haller, *Rise*, 264; Knappen, *Puritanism*, 331, 333; W.Förster, *Thomas Hobbes und der Puritanismus*, 1969, 90ff.; cf. also the short version with the same title in R.Koselleck/R.Schnur (eds.), *Hobbes-Forschungen*, 1969, (71-89) 74ff. Following the contemporary judgment of Paget, Nuttall, *Visible Saints*, 10, calls him a 'Semi-separatist'. This view (which is disputed by Watts, *Dissenters* I, 53; ibid., 52f., for a further description) is confirmed by the thorough investigation made by S.A.Yarbrough, *Henry Jacob. A Moderate Separatist, and his Influence on Early English Congregationalism*, Baylor University PhD Thesis (Ann Arbor Microfilm). The most decisive fact is that Jacob wanted to maintain fellowship with the parishes of the Church of England which were organized on a congregational, presbyterian or even episcopal basis, provided that they corresponded to the New Testament ideal; this differed from radical separatism as Browne understood it. Cf. esp. op.cit., III (abstract) and the summary, 189-94.

355. The work is very rare. I have used an Ann Arbor microfilm of the copy in the library of Union Theological Seminary, New York.

356. On p.74 Jacob refers to the king's Edinburgh confession of faith of 1580, in which he condemns all rites, signs and traditions which are introduced into the church without the word of God. Similarly, p.75, on the *Basilikon Doron* of James I. Proudly quoted to the king from the Catholic edition of 1604 is the statement that the Puritans ('as they falsely and maliciously call us') are the ones who carry through the Protestant principle most consistently.

357. Op.cit., 1.

358. Op.cit., 1f. – Cf. *A plaine and cleere Exposition* (134 below).

359. Op.cit., 2.

360. Op.cit., 4ff.

361. 'Only a Particular ordinary constant Congregation of Christians in Christes Testament is appointed and reckoned to be a visible Church.' Op.cit., 5. *An Attestation of many Learned, Godly, and famous Divines..., That the Church-Government ought to bee always with the peoples free consent*, 1613 (British Library: I have used an Ann Arbor Microfilm), cites a mass of evidence from Reformation theologians (Beza, Calvin, Zwingli, Luther and so on, 21ff.), as well as modern (48ff.) and early church (64ff.) councils (64ff.).

362. Op.cit., 1ff.

363. 'For this Ecclesiastical government being popular (say they) it will require the Civill governement also to become conformed to it', op.cit., 26.

364. 'First we absolutely denie that any manner of Ecclesiastical Governement requireth the Civill Governement to becom conformed to it... The bounds of either Governement are distinct and cleerly severed the one from the other: albeit each doth ayd & succour the other', op.cit.,26.

365. Op.cit., 26.

366. Op.cit., 52ff.

367. Op.cit., 57. Cf. ibid.: 'The king is Custos & Vindex, the Keeper and Maintainer (by compulsive power) of the whole state of Religion. But he is not Author or Minister of any Ecclesiasticall thing or Cōstitution whatever.'

368. Submission to the king is also expressed in the 'humble Supplication' of 1609 ('To the right High and mightie Prince, James, etc... A humble Supplication for [Toleration and libertie...'] British Library: I have used an Ann Arbor Microfilm) and at the beginning of the 'Confession', see below.

369. 'An Exhortation. To all the godly, learned, and faithfull Pastors of the severall Churches in England Henry Jacob Minister of Gods word, wisheth grace and peace to be multiplied in Christ Iesus', op.cit., 79.

370. Again I have used an Ann Arbor microfilm.

371. Op.cit., fol. E recto.

372. Op.cit., fol. B2 recto.

373. 'A Confession and Protestation of the Faith of Certaine Christians' (British Library: I have used an Ann Arbor Microfilm).

374. Op.cit., fol. A 3 verso.

375. Op.cit., fol. A 5 recto.

376. Op.cit., fol. A 5 verso.

377. Op.cit., fol. C recto.

378. Op.cit., fol. C 5 recto.

379. 1610 (British Library: I have used an Ann Arbor Microfilm).

380. Op.cit., fol. A 2 recto. Cf. also fol. A 4 verso – A 5 recto.

381. Op.cit., fol. A 3 recto.

382. Op.cit., fol. A 6 verso – A 7.

383. Op.cit., fol. A 8 recto – verso.

384. Op.cit., fol. A 8 verso – B recto.

385. Op.cit., fol. B verso – B 2 recto.

386. Op.cit., fol. B recto – B verso.

387. Op.cit., fol. B 2 verso – B 3 recto.

388. Op.cit., fol. D 3 recto.

389. Op.cit., fol. D 4 recto – verso.

390. Op.cit., fol. D 5ff.

391. Op.cit., 73ff.

392. In his Homilies on I Corinthians: *In priorem D. Pauli ad Corinthios Epistolam Homiliae*, 1572; cf. Kressner, op.cit., 75.

393. See above, 475 n. 183.

394. See above, 109.

395. 'A Sermon Preached Before the Queen's Majesty the 25th Day of February by Master Edward Dering.' New impression in Trinterud, *Elizabethan Puritanism*, 138ff. Further examples of this royal typology in K.Schmidt, *Religion, Versklavung und Befreiung*, 1978, 22ff.

396. Op.cit., 142.

397. Initially the preacher speaks in the first person plural, and then he goes on to address the king directly.

398. Ibid.

399. Op.cit., 146: here Dering openly alludes to the decoration of the royal chapel, which was offensive to the Puritans.

400. Op.cit., 147.

401. Op.cit., 149.

402. Ibid.

403. Op.cit., 150.

404. Cf. also op.cit., 152: '...The case is clear, the prince is a spiritual magistrate. It belongeth unto him to reform religion. He is the highest judge in the church of God to establish that by law which the law of God has appointed.'

405. Op.cit., 160.

405a. As W.M.Lamont has shown (*Godly Rule*, 1969, 23ff.), the expectation (with a millenarian colouring) that the Christian ruler (Elizabeth I as the new Constantine) would bring salvation was already put forward by John Foxe and was widespread among the earlier Puritans. He can even say: 'To Puritans... the defence of the Christian Emperor was more than a political gesture. It was a central tenet of their faith' (46). The Puritans maintained this attitude until the reign of Charles I.

406. I have used an Ann Arbor microfilm.

407. Op.cit., 46f.

408. Op.cit., 55.

409. Op.cit., 56.

410. Op.cit., 83 (wrongly paginated: = 53).

411. Op.cit., 59.

412. Op.cit., 132.

413. Op.cit., 137.

414. J.Jewel, *Apologia ecclesiae Anglicanae*, 1562 (Works, III, ed.Ayre, 1848: the work was long regarded as a semi-official account of Anglican theology, cf. E.T.Davies, *Episcopacy*, 15, 18; cf. also M.Creighton, 'Jewel, John (1522-1571)', *DNB* X, 1959/60, 815-19).

415. E.g. *Josias rex diligenter admonuit sacerdotes et episcopos officii sui. Joas rex repressit luxum et insolentiam sacerdotum.*

415a. This typology could also go back through imperial themes to Old Testament themes: F.A.Yates, *Astraea. The imperial theme in the Sixteenth Century*, 1975, 29ff., 'Queen Elizabeth I as Astraea' (after Ovid), has demonstrated this for the imperialism of Elizabeth I.

416. Cf. above, 475 n.183.

417. Written in 1606 and formally accepted as an official document by the convocations of Canterbury and York, but not confirmed by the crown, this was first published in 1689 by Sancroft under the title 'Concerning the Government of God's Catholic Church and the Kingdoms of the Whole World'. Reprinted Oxford 1844.

418. Bishop of Chichester 1605-09, of Ely 1609-19, and Winchester 1619-26. Cf. P.A.Welsby, *Lancelot Andrewes 1555-1626*, 1958; recently M.Schmidt, 'Andrewes, Lancelot (1555-1626)', *TRE* 2, 1978, 683-7; for his early period see also H.C.Porter, *Reformation*, 391ff.

419. In his lecture manuscript from Cambridge which was published in 1630

(²1641) under the title 'A Pattern of Catechistical Doctrine', now in *Minor Works, The Works of Lancelot Andrewes*, ed. Wilson and Bliss, 11 vols, 1841-1854, Vol. VI, 1846, (reprinted 1967), 1ff., 198. At that time he even gave the people the right to choose their own rulers. Cf. the lecture copy printed in 1642 ('The Morall Law expounded', cf. *Minor Works*, 1846 ed., Notice), 409.

420. Cf. Welsby, op.cit., 202ff.

421. Sermon of 5 November 1613, in *Works*, IV, 1854 (reprinted 1967), 277ff.

422. Sermon of 5 November 1614, ibid., 296ff. The eight sermons on 5 August (commemoration of the Gowrie plot, 5 August 1600, cf. Welsby, op.cit., 141f.) all have Old Testament texts dealing with the anointed or the defeat of his enemies.

423. Op.cit., 279.

424. An answer to the work composed by Cardinal Bellarmine and brought out under the pseudonym Matthäus Tortus: *Responsio Matthäi Torti... ad librum inscriptum Triplici Nodo triplex cuneus*, 1608 (the book mentioned in the title is a personal work of King James I, who thus intervened in the dispute about the oath of loyalty required of Catholic subjects. Now in *Political Works of James I*, ed. C.H.McIlwain, 1918). For the controversy cf. Welsby, op.cit., 144ff.

425. *Tortura Torti sive ad Matthaei Torti librum responsio*, in *Works*, VII, 1854 (reprinted 1967), 445ff.

426. The work of James I, who rushed to the aid of Andrewes.

427. Op.cit., 446.

428. Op.cit., 449.

429. Op.cit., 554.

430. N.Sykes, *Old Priest and New Presbyter*, 1957, 3: cf. also the rest of Chapter 1, 1ff.; cf. also id., *The Church of England & Non-episcopal Churches in the Sixteenth & Seventeenth Century*, 1848, 4f. Cf. also above all Lamont, *Godly Rule*, 28ff. J.Lecler, *Geschichte der Religionsfreiheit im Zeitalter der Reformation* II, Vol. II, 1965, 412f. (French original: *Histoire de la Tolérance au siècle de la réforme*, 1955), points out that the first works which stress the royal *ius in sacra* in the 'Erastian' sense already appeared under Henry VIII. Among them special emphasis should be laid on S.Gardiner, *De vera oboedientia*, 1535 (new impression e.g. in P.Janelle, *Obedience in Church and State*, 1930, 67-170). For the analysis of the tractates cf. Janelle, op.cit., 271ff. The authority of the Bible is already adduced in these works as a basis for the rights of the king. Lecler's reference to the parallels with contemporary writings from Lutheran Germany is important.

431. Cf. Whitgift, *Works*, III, 198: 'If you mean the universal church, only Christ is the Head... But if you speak of particular churches, as the Church of England, the church of Denmark, then, as the prince is the chief governor and head of the commonwealth under God, so is he of the church likewise.'

432. Gilby, *A Pleasaunt Dialogue, betweene a Souldier of Barwicke and an English Chaplaine*, 1581, 66.

433. R.W.Hanning, *The Vision of History in Early Britain*, 1966, 25ff.

434. *Church History* I, 3,7.

435. Ibid., IX, 9,5: Constantine is the new Moses, his army the new Israel and Maxentius the new Pharaoh.

436. Cf. esp. U.Brumm, *Die religiöse Typologie im amerikanischen Denken. Ihre Bedeutung für die amerikanische Literatur- und Geistesgeschichte*, 1963; cf. also id., *Puritanismus*; S.Bercovitch, *Controversy*, 166-91; and the collection *Typology*, ed S.Bercovitch.

437. Numerous examples in Bercovitch, *AmQ*, 1967. M.L.Lowance, Jr, 'Cotton Mather's Magnalia and the Metaphors of Biblical History', in *Typology*, ed. Bercovitch, 139-60, discusses the typological use of the history of Israel and other hermeneutical methods in the well-known history of the church in America by this famous Puritan, *Magnalia Christi Americana* (1702), and other of his writings. For the

further effect of this way of thinking down to the present cf. e.g. E.F.Humphrey, *Nationalism and Religion in America, 1774-1789*, 1924, reprinted 1965; H.R.Niebuhr, *The Kingdom of God in America*, 1937; E.L.Tuveson, *Redeemer Nation: The Idea of America's Millenial Role*, 1968; W.S.Hudson (ed.), *Nationalism and Religion in America: Concepts of American Identity and Mission*, 1970; C.Cherry (ed.), *God's New Israel: Religious Interpretations of American History*, 1971; J.H.Symylie, 'On Jesus, Pharaos, and the Chosen People. Martin Luther King as Biblical Interpreter and Humanist', *Int.* 24, 1970, 74-90; R.T.Handy, 'The American Messianic Consciousness. The concept of the Chosen People and Manifest Destiny', *RExp* 73, 1976, 47-58; K.Schmidt, *Religion*, 33ff.

437a. Cf. Lamont, *Godly Rule*, passim.

438. 1582 (reprinted 1903).

439. All instances, op.cit., 155. There is already an allusion to John 18.36 in op.cit., 154.

440. Op.cit., 157.

441. 'Agayne we say, that her Authoritie is ciuil, and that power she hath as highest under God within her Dominions, and that ouer all persons and causes. By that she may put to death all that deserue it by Lawe, either of the Church or common Wealth...' , op.cit., 152. Cf. also 164: 'We knowe that Moses might reforme, and the Iudges and Kings which followed him, and so may our Magistrates: yea they may reforme the Church and commaunde things expedient for the same. Yet may they doo nothing concerning the Church, but onelie ciuillie, and as ciuile Magistrates, that is, they haue not that authoritie ouer the Church, as to be Prophetes or Priestes, or spiritual Kings...: but onelie to rule the common wealth in all outwarde Iustice, to maintaine the right, welfare and honore therof, with outward power, bodily punishment, & civil forcing of me.'

442. Op.cit., 154. Cf. also op.cit., 155. 'But they put the Magistrates first, which in a common wealth in deede are first, and aboue the Preachers, yet haue they no ecclesiasticall authoritie at all, but onely as anie other Christians, if so be they be Christians', with op.cit., 154: 'Howe then shoulde the Pastor, which hath the ouersight of the Magistrate, if he bee of his flocke...' Cf. also 156, lines 6ff.; 161, 19f.

443. Op.cit., 161. For Browne's Spiritualist ecclesiology cf. also op.cit., 163: 'our spirituall provision, as the guiftes, callings & graces of the church neede not anie worldly preparation in such outward ceremonies.'

444. Op.cit., 161.

445. For the concept (which is anachronistic here) and its origin cf. J.Heckel, *Cura religionis – Ius in sacra – Ius circa sacra* (Festschrift U. Stutz, 1938, 224ff.), reprinted 1962, (281) 58ff.

446. Both quotations, op.cit., 163.

447. Ibid., my italics.

448. Op.cit., 157.

449. Matt.11.11.

450. Jer.1.10.

451. Op.cit., 159.

452. Op.cit., 166.

453. *AmQ* 1967. For the discussion see also E.Feist-Hirsch, *John Cotton*, 38-51.

454. P.Miller, 'Roger Williams: An Essay in Interpretation', in *The Complete Writings of Roger Williams*, ed. P.Miller, VII, 1963, 5ff.

455. Examples in Bercovitch, op.cit., 173. Cf. also id., *Roger Williams. His Contribution to the American Tradition*, 1953. K.Schmidt, *Religion*, 46, quotes from Williams, 'Bloudy Tenent of Persecution', in *Complete Writings* III, 303ff. the statements according to which Old Testament Israel appears as a type only of the church. Schmidt

rightly points to Williams' spiritual affinity with the 'left wing of the Reformation', op.cit., 47f.

456. See above, 497f. n.437. – For Williams see esp. also R.Reinitz, *Typological Argument*, 74-110. He rightly stresses the connection between Williams' spiritual typology and the Separatist tradition.

457. Cf. the earlier work by A.J.Mason, *The Church of England and Episcopacy*, which is mainly based on a series of extracts from sources and is limited to its narrow theme. However, it does produce the sources. There is no investigation of the question which concerns us here .

458. On the title page we find: 'Out of the rude draughts of Lancelot Andrewes.'

459. In *Minor Works*, 337ff.

460. Op.cit., 342; cf. also 349.

461. Op.cit., 349.

462. Op.cit., 350.

463. See above, 496 n.417.

464. Op.cit., 205.   465. Op.cit., 132.

466. Here Overall can give an example: the famous case of the institution of a Dutchman with presbyteral ordination to a living without reordination, as reported by J.Birch in his *Life of Tillotson* (1753), 169ff. Cf. A.J.Mason, op.cit., 78f., and for the problem as a whole N.Sykes, *Church*; id., *Old Priest*, 85ff.

1. R.M.Krapp, *Anglicanism*, calls them 'liberal Anglicans', cf. 3. The name 'Latitudinarian', often used very loosely, will be reserved for the liberal theologians of the time of William III and his followers, who were the spiritual heirs of Chillingworth's generation, cf. below, 538f. n.2. For this school cf. also H.J.McLachlan, *Socinianism in Seventeenth-Century England*, 1951, 63ff.; I.Cotman, *Private Men and Public Causes*, 1962, esp. 135ff. M.Sina, *L'avvento della ragione. 'Reason' and 'above Reason' dal razionalismo teologico inglese del deismo*, 1976, is a comprehensive work on the rational trend in English theology. It came to my notice too late to be used in the first edition. – For developments in the Church of England as a whole over this period cf. N.R.N.Tyacke, *Arminianism in England in Religion and Politics*, Oxford DPhil thesis, 1968; id., 'Puritanism, Arminianism and Counter-Revolution', in *The Origins of the English Civil War*, ed. C.Russell, 1973, 119-43.

2. 1637, often reprinted later, e.g. in the *Collected Works*, ⁹1727; in the *Works*, 1820. Apart from the second edition of 1638 in the Marburg University Library I had available the two-volume edition (in 12°), London 1839, which unfortunately does not contain the interesting Imprimatur (cf. Krapp, op.cit., 6ff.).

3. We have an eye-witness account of his end, albeit extremely biassed, by his opponent, into whose hands he fell in his last illness: F.Cheynell, *Chillingworthi Novissima, or the Sickness, Heresy, Death and Burial of Mr. Chillingworth*, 1644. There is an early biography by the well-known P. des Maizeaux, *An Historical and Critical Account of the Life and Writings of Wm. Chillingworth*, 1725; cf. also J.D.Hyman, *William Chillingworth and the Theology of Toleration*, 1931; Krapp, op.cit.; Sina, *Ragione*, 28ff.; and above all R.R.Orr, *Reason*.

4. Cf. J.Tulloch, *Rational Theology and Christian Philosophy in England in the 17th Century*, ²1874, reprinted 1966, I, 170ff.; J.H.Nelson, *John Hales of Eaton*, 1948; Sina, *Ragione*, 40ff., and the biography, also by P. des Maizeaux, *An Historical and Critical Account of the Life of the Ever-Memorable Mr.John Hales*, 1719. *The Works of the Ever Memorable Mr.John Hales*, ed. Hailes, three vols. 1765, reprinted 1971.

5. Cf. Tulloch, op.cit., I, 76ff.; K.Weber, *Lucius Cary, Second Viscount Falkland*, 1940.

6. Tulloch, op.cit., I, 95ff.

7. However, in view of the scattered and predominantly literary conversations

among the group, R.R.Orr, op.cit., 35f., warns against overestimating its influence on Chillingworth's theological attitude.

8.These include above all J.Tulloch, op.cit.; M.Freund, *Toleranz*; W.K.Jordan, *Development*; T.Lyon, *The Theory of Religious Liberty in England, 1603-1639*, 1937. H.Kamen, *Intoleranz und Toleranz zwischen Reformation und Aufklärung*, 1967, 171f., still asserts: 'The Latitudinarians (cf. above 499 n.1) were clearly hostile to Laud's policy.' Krapp, op.cit., 1ff., has already commented that this view is unhistorical; however, he falls into the opposite mistake of caricaturing the men of Great Tew as sceptics and political opportunists.

9. Krapp, op.cit., has traced the ramifications of the relationships between Chillingworth and Laud.

9a. The group around Samuel Hartlib pursued very similar concerns, cf. J.R.Jacob, *Robert Boyle and the English Revolution*, 1977, 16ff.

10. Cf. op.cit., 203ff. In this connection we should also recall the influence of Arminianism, the expansion of which under Charles I and Laud has been noted by N.Tyacke, 'Puritanism, Arminianism and Counter-Revolution', in *The Origins of the English Civil War*, ed. C.Russell, 1973, 119-43. Calvinism was certainly the dominant official teaching in both church parties at the end of the sixteenth century, but not the real motive power.

11. *Religion of Protestants* VI, 56 (quoted by Orr, op.cit., 71).

12. The book is directed against the work of the Jesuit Edward Knott, *Charity Maintained by Catholics*, which it quotes and refutes section by section (for Catholic controversial literature of the time cf. G.H.Tavard, *The Seventeenth-Century Tradition. A Study in Recusant Thought*, 1978; on Knott [really Matthew Wilson], 87ff.). As Knott got hold of proofs of the work and replied to it even before it was published (in a pamphlet, 'A Direction to N.N.'), Chillingworth added a preface ('The Preface to the Author of Charity Maintained') which in turn answered the reply. For the role of anti-Catholicism in the period in question cf. recently R.Clifton, 'Fear of Popery', in *The Origins* (see note 10 above), 144-67.

13. For the reasons for his conversion see most recently Orr, op.cit., 11ff.

14. Cf. Orr, op.cit., 24f.

15. Wharton MSS 943, fol.859, quoted in Orr, op.cit., 41.

16. 'So the church of Rome, to establish her tyranny over men's consciences, needed not either to abolish or corrupt the Holy Scriptures...; but the more expedite way... was to gain the opinion and esteem of the public and authorized interpreter of them, and the authority of adding to them what doctrine she pleased, under the title of traditions and definitions.' *Religion of Protestants*, II,1.

17. *Religion of Protestants*, II,1,18; III, 10; IV, 16; V, 112; VI, 66; cf. also Orr, op.cit., 48.

18. Against the background of a distinction in principle between two kinds of certainty, 'metaphysical' certainty, which rests on personal observation or mathematical proof and is absolutely assured, and a 'moral' certainty which, while not supported by the statements of credible witnesses, nevertheless has a high degree of certainty; cf. Wharton MSS 943, fol.871, quoted in Orr, op.cit., 51ff. In his work *The Problem of Certainty in English Thought*, 1963, H.G.van Leeuwen puts Chillingworth's (and Tillotson's, see below) epistemology in the wider context of a movement which led to the overcoming of the radical scepticism that had emerged in the sixteenth century above all in France (e.g. with Montaigne and de la Mothe Le Vayer): the solution, already initiated by Mersenne and Gassendi and particularly widespread in England, ended in assigning different degrees of probability to knowledge, though absolute certainty could not be attained. For Chillingworth, cf. op.cit., 15-32.

19. *Religion of Protestants*, VI,7; cf. II, 139, 149, 154; quoted in Orr, op.cit., 54ff.

20. On another occasion (*Religion of Protestants*, IV, 16, footnote), he refers to his obligation to Acontius and Zanchius.

21. Cf. Orr, op.cit., 57f.

22. Cf. Orr, op.cit., 61.

23. Cf. the evidence in Orr, op.cit., 60f.

24. In *The Religion of Protestants*, II, 104, Chillingworth introduces the parable of the master who sends his servant to a distant city and cannot legitimately rebuke him if on the way he arrives at a crossroads with no signposts and cannot continue his journey.

25. *Religion of Protestants*, III, 14.

26. Id., 'Answer to the Preface', no.3 (1839 edition, I, 66).

27. Cf. Orr, op.cit., 72.

28. Cf. esp. *Religion of Protestants*, Preface, no.21 (1839 edition, I, 25f.): 'The truth is, they that can run to extremes in opposition against you (the Roman church); they that pull down your infallibility and set their own... are the adversaries that give you the greatest advantage...: whereas upon men of temper and moderation... such as require of Christians to believe only in Christ, and will damn no man nor doctrine without express and certain warrant from God's word; upon such as these you know not how to fasten...' Cf. also the comment about Luther, id., II, 82; cf. IV, 16.

29. Cf. the quotation in the previous note and IV, 16. However, Orr's observation, op.cit., 78, that Chillingworth disputed the view prevailing equally among Catholics and Protestants that the main function of religion is to bring about the assurance of salvation, is misleading. He too is concerned with the assurance of salvation, except that he refuses to connect salvation with the acceptance of particular dogmatic statements.

30. Wharton Mss 943, fol.859, quoted by Orr, op.cit., 82.

31. *Religion of Protestants*, II, 159. Cf. also ibid.: '...if a man should believe Christian religion wholly and entirely, and live according to it, such a man, though he should not know or not believe the Scripture to be a rule of faith, no, nor to be the word of God, my opinion is, he may be saved; and my reason is, because he performs the entire condition of the new covenant, which is, that we believe the matter of the gospel, and not that is contained in these or these books.'

32. Ibid.; cf. also Preface 32 (1839 ed., Vol.I, 36).

33. Preface, nos.13-14 (1839 ed., I, 18); cf. II, 24-25.

34. II, 24.

35. II, 93.

36. II, 16.

37. Here Chillingworth is responding to a comparison made by his opponent Knott, cf. Orr, op.cit., 88ff.

38. *Religion of Protestants*, II, 5.

39. II, 8.

40. II, 3; cf. also VI, 55: 'Neither do we follow any private men, but only the Scripture, the word of God, as our rule; and reason, which is also the gift of God given to direct us in all our actions, in the use of this rule.'

41. Cf. above, 443 nn.107f.

42. I, 13; cf. III, 24.

43. II, 20.

44. Cf. Orr, op.cit., 103. Luther already practised canonical criticism of this kind.

45. III, 24.

46. 'For if God would have had his meaning in these places certainly known, how could it stand with his wisdom...to speak obscurely? or how can it consist with his justice to require of men to know certainly the meaning of these words, which he himself hath not revealed?' II, 127.

47. II, 110.

48. II, 159.

49. II, 127, quoted Orr, op.cit., 100.

50. 'If any one should deny that there is a God; that this God is omnipotent, omniscient, good, just, true, merciful...'

51. '...a rewarder of them that seek him, a punisher of them that obstinately offend him; that Jesus Christ is the Son of God and the Saviour of the World; that it is he by obedience to whom men must look to be saved...'

52. IV, 2.

53. Op.cit., 94.

54. IV, 16.

55. Cf. Orr, op.cit., 104f.

56. Op.cit., 110ff.

57. *Religion of Protestants*, II, 30, with footnotes.

58. *The Works*, 1765, reprinted 1971, II, 141-66.

59. Op.cit., 156f. – Krapp, *Anglicanism*, refers to the numerous points of contact between Chillingworth's views and those of the Polish Socinians: 'Was Chillingworth a Socinian?', op.cit., 85ff. Here he can refer back to the charges made against Chillingworth by his most significant opponent, Cheynell. In fact there are numerous points of contact between the English Latitudinarians and Continental rationalism, even if their anti-trinitarian doctrine is absent in England.

60. 'The positive beliefs of Laud may be summed up in the simple statement that he was an Anglican', Bourne, *Anglicanism*, 107. Theologically Laud was essentially a Latitudinarian; there was frequent reference to his toleration towards those who differed from him in points of doctrine, as is evident above all in his attitude towards Chillingworth, John Hales, etc. Cf. the chapter 'Laud's Tolerance', in Bourne, op.cit., 144ff. Even a critical commentator like H.R.Trevor-Roper, *Laud*, 338, can concede 'that Laud, in spite of his intolerant practice, professed a more tolerant theology than his adversaries, and was not disposed to persecute those whose convictions were intellectually held and rationally defended.' Cf. also his comments for the new impression, X. For qualifications, however, cf. Krapp, *Anglicanism*, 6ff.: 'How tolerant was William Laud?'

61. Cf. above, 488 n.204.

62. Laud explains his standpoint most clearly in the letter to Joseph Hall of 11 November 1639 (*Works*, ed. Scott and Bliss, 7 vols, 1847-60, VI, 1857 [reprinted 1975], 177, 572ff. – in Bourne, op.cit., 91 n.1, wrongly numbered as 178).

63. Gee and Hardy, *Documents*, 509f. Cf. also R.Ashton, *The English Civil War*, 1978, 100: 'One of the most potent sources of misunderstanding of the nature of the Puritan challenge in the decades before 1640 is the failure of many historians to recognize that the Puritan mainstream was not Presbyterian or anti-episcopal...'

64. Cf. esp. Bourne, op.cit., 98ff.

65. *Works*, III, 1853, reprinted 1975, 407f.

66. All commentators stress that Laud was above all a practical man, for all his theological training. T.M.Parker, 'Arminianism and Laudianism in Seventeenth-Century England', in Dugmore and Duggan, *Studies in Church History* I, 20-34, stresses that the Laudians were more notable for their church politics and less so for their (Arminian?) teaching. Zagorin, *The Court*, 188f., joins others in denying Arminian influence and describes the movement as an 'Anglo-Catholic' or 'High Church' reaction to clerical circles in the church. For their cultural background cf. also Cragg, *Freedom*, 100ff.

67. Reference has been made to the intense Puritan piety as expressed in Laud's intimate diary, cf. C.H.Simpkinson, 'Laud's Personal Religion', in *Lectures on Archbishop Laud*, ed. W.E.Collins, 123ff.

68. Cf. e.g. Bourne, op.cit., 59f.

69. One contemporary report on events along the lines of Puritan propaganda is the anonymous pamphlet, *A Briefe Relation of Certain Speciall and Most Materiall Passages*, 1637 ([2]1638, [3]1641). A personal account by Prynne is his work *New Discovery of the Prelates Tyranny*, 1641. The documents are in S.R.Gardiner, *Documents Relating to the Proceedings against William Prynne in 1634 and 1637*, 1872. Cf. further Haller, *Rise*, 249ff.; Trevor-Roper, *Laud*, 317ff.

70. For political developments generally cf. J.Marriot, *The Crisis of English Liberty. A History of the Stuart Monarchy and the Puritan Revolution*, 1930 and more recently Ashton, *Civil War*. For the anti-clerical underground movements among the people and their partially economic basis cf. also C.Hill, *The World Turned Upside Down*, 1972, reprinted 1973, esp. 22ff., 70ff., 82f.

71. One of the themes was the position of the altar in the church. As Dean of Gloucester in 1615 Laud had already moved the altar from the nave to the east end of the cathedral in order to make sure it was revered 'altar-wise', an arrangement which he tried to impose on all the churches in his archdiocese after his elevation to be Archbishop of Canterbury. (Cf. the 1633 ordinance in Gee and Hardy, *Documents*, 533-5). For the proceedings see Trevor-Roper, op. cit., 151ff. From this there developed a literary feud in which both Laud's supporters (such as above all P.Heylin, *A coale from the altar...*, 1635 [[3]1637, I have used a microfilm of the copy in the Huntington Library]) and opponents (above all John Williams, Bishop of Lincoln, who contributed his own work *The Holy Table, Name and Thing*, 1636, to which Heylin responded in the following year with his *Antidotum Lincolniense*), were involved.

72. Cf. W.M.Lamont, *Marginal Prynne 1600-1669*, 1963, 41f.

73. Lamont, op.cit., made it clear that Prynne was not in any way originally a 'radical', but for years could be numbered among the moderate Anglicans with a basic royalist attitude. Cf.also id., *Godly Rule*, index s.v.Prynne. The same is true of Williams, against whom Laud waged a vigorous struggle.

74. Cf. the letter mentioned 502 n.62 above; also P.Heylin, *Cyprianus*, 398f., who reports that Laud gave Hall an outline for the planned work.

75. *Episcopacie by Divine Right Asserted*, 1640; *An Humble Remonstrance to the High Court of Parliament*, 1640; *A Defence of the Humble Remonstrance*, 1641; *A Short Answer to the Tedious Vindication of Smectymnuus*, 1641. For the content cf. D.M.Wolfe, in Milton, *Complete Prose Works*, I, ed. D.M.Wolfe, 1953, 53ff.; 76f.; 81ff. (Yale ed.). For forerunners in the defence of episcopal (jurisdiction) supremacy like Carleton, Barlow, and Downame cf. Lamont, *Godly Rule*, 36ff.

76. Cf. Barker, *Milton and the Puritan Dilemma*, 1942 reprinted 1964, 22.

77. *Episcopacie*, Part II, 20 (quoted Wolfe, op.cit., 54).

78. Cf the quotation in Wolfe, ibid., and n.7.

79. V.Pearl, *London and the Outbreak of the Puritan Revolution*, 1961, 160-76, depicts its growth among the clergy and middle classes of London after the 1630s. For the role of the middle class (including country people) in the Parliamentary party and their army in the first Civil War and the different reasons which led them to join the party, their motives being a mixture of religious and external concerns, cf. also B.Manning, 'Religion and Politics: The Godly People', in id., *Politics, Religion and the English Civil War*, 1973, 83-123.

80. S.Marshall, E.Calamy, T.Young, M.Newcomen and W.Spurstow; cf. Barker, op.cit., 341 n.5, and above all F.L.Taft and A.Baizer, 'The Legion of Smec', Appendix F in Milton, *Prose Works* I, 1001-8.

81. That the king had had to summon because of his campaign in Scotland in November 1640.

82. Reprinted in Milton, *Prose Works* I, 976-84, and in S.E.Prall (ed.), *The Puritan Revolution*, 1968, 96-103.

83. For proceedings in the 'long Parliament' cf. D.M.Wolfe, ibid., 56-76.

83a. Cf. R.Clifton, 'Fear of Popery', *Origins*, ed. C.Russell, 144-67. Cf. also B.Manning, *The English People and the English Revolution*, 1976, 21ff.

84. The discussion with the Jesuit Fisher, in *Works*, II, 1849.

84a. For the background of this charge cf. Ashton, *Civil War*, 111ff.

85. Literature on Milton is extremely extensive. A.Barker, *Milton*, is still an important and sympathetic investigation of the prose works against the background of the ideas of the time and Milton's intrinsic development. Cf. also E.M.W.Tillyard, *Milton*, 1930 (rev.ed. 1966); D.M.Wolfe, *Milton in the Puritan Revolution*, 1941, reprinted 1963; M.Fixler, *Milton and the Kingdoms of God*, 1964; M.Y.Hughes, *Ten Perspectives on Milton*, 1965; W.J.Grace, *Ideas in Milton*, 1968; H.M.Richmond, *The Christian Revolutionary: John Milton*, 1974; D.F.Bouchard, *Milton: A Structural Reading*, 1974; C.Hill, *Milton and the English Revolution*, 1977. For Milton's influence see also G.G.Sensabaugh, *That Grand Whig Milton*, 1952. Among the biographies D.Masson, *The Life of John Milton*, 7 vols, 1859-94 (reprinted 1946, 1965) is still the standard work. But cf. also K.Muir, *John Milton* (1955), ²1962; W.R.Parker, *Milton*, two vols, 1968. Editions of the works: *The Works of John Milton*, ed. F.A.Patterson, 20 vols., 1931-40 (Columbia ed.) is complete but has no notes; *The Complete Prose Works of John Milton*, ed. D.M.Wolfe, seven vols, 1953 (Yale ed.) has copious notes. The introduction by D.M.Wolfe in I, 1-210, and its continuation by E.Sirluck in II, 1-216, is itself a valuable monograph account of the historical and cultural background to the prose writing and the most important literary contributions to the church-political struggle in which Milton was involved. Cf. recently also the introduction by E.W.Tielsch in id. (ed.), *John Milton und der neuzeitliche Liberalismus*, 1980, 1-76.

86. D.M.Wolfe, in Milton, *Prose Works*, I, App. B, 961-4, has again collected evidence (following Masson, etc.) that Milton himself wrote the postscript (id., 966-75) to the Smectymnuus work: 'An Answer...' This question can be left open here.

87. It can be found in essentials in the Thomason Collection of the British Museum (cf. *Catalogue of the Pamphlets, Books, Newspapers, and Manuscripts Collected by George Thomason*, 2 vols, 1908, see above 483 n.120), and in the McAlpin Collection of Union Theological Seminary, New York (cf. G.R.Gillett, *Catalogue of the McAlpin Collection of British History and Theology*, 5 vols., 1927-30). There is a thematic selection in W.M.Haller, *Tracts on Liberty in the Puritan Revolution*, three vols. 1934 (reprinted 1965).

88. S.R.Gardiner has gone into the constitutional history of these years with exemplary thoroughness in his important accounts, *History of England, 1603-1642*, 10 vols., 1883-4, reprinted 1965; *History of the Great Civil War, 1642-49*, 4 vols., 1893, reprinted 1965; *History of the Commonwealth and Protectorate*, 4 vols., 1903, reprinted 1965. Cf. also M.Ashley, *Oliver Cromwell and the Puritan Revolution*, 1958, and the collection *The English Civil War and after, 1642-1658*, ed. R.H.Parry, 1970. Cf. also Watts, *Dissenters* I, 77-186; also P.Wende, *Probleme der englischen Revolution*, 1980. A more recent general account on a smaller scale is G.Davies, *The Early Stuarts*, Oxford History of England IX, ²1959.

89. This seems to me to be partly over-exaggerated in Barker, *Milton*. Cf. also 165f. below.

90. Cf. Barker, 'Milton's Schoolmasters', *MLR* 32, 1937, 517-36.

91. Cf. e.g. Barker, *Milton*, XXIIf.; Wolfe, in Milton, *Prose Works*, I, 1f. Whereas Barker stresses the Puritan side to Milton, J.H.Hanford, 'Milton and the Return to Humanism', in *John Milton, Poet and Humanist*, 1966, 161-84, stresses his connection with the Humanism of the Elizabethan period. Cf. e.g. op.cit., 180: 'Now Milton, throughout his life, was a humanist in both his method and his aim.' C.Hill, *Milton*, passim, e.g. 95, by contrast sees in Milton a confluence of notions from Puritanism

and from the popular radical traditions. In referring to the Waldensians, Wyclif and the Lollards (69ff., 85), he confirms the connections which I have drawn out (though from a fundamentally opposed standpoint). The otherwise very impressive investigation by H.M.Richmond, *Milton*, suffers from its obsolete definition of Puritanism as the counterpart to the idealistic rationalism of antiquity, op.cit., 21 (also 46: 'The stoic self-righteousness of the pagan ethic, which is theoretically at the opposite end of the scale to puritanism'; but cf. the better insight, op.cit., 196). It seems to me that the either/or – Humanist or Puritan – is a false alternative.

92. *Milton*, XXII.

93. Op.cit., XXIII.

94. Hanford, op.cit., 180.

95. Haller, *Rise*, 317.

96. For what follows cf. especially A.S.P.Woodhouse, 'The Argument of Milton's Comus', *UTQ* 11, 1941, 46-71; Barker, *Milton*, 9ff. W.J.Grace, 'Ideas in Milton', op.cit., 130ff. For this judgment see Richmond, *Milton*, 65ff., cf. n.99 below.

97. *Works*, Columbia ed. I,1, 102:
So dear to Heav'n is Saintly chastity,
That when a soul is found sincerely so,
A thousand liveries Angels lacky her...
Begin to cast a beam on th'outward shape,
The unpolluted temple of the mind,
And turns it by degrees to the souls essence,
Till all be made immortal...'

98. The epilogue of the 'Spirit' ends:
Love vertue, she alone is free,
She can teach ye how to clime,
Higher than the Sheary chime;
Or if Vertue feeble were,
Heav'n it self would stoop to her' (op.cit., 123).

99. Barker points to the imbalance of the two groups of ideas underlying this. The devaluation of nature by Spiritualism would cut the poet off from the living beauty of the human world, while the ascent into nature would destroy the sublime worth of the authentic poetry, op.cit., 13. Richmond, op.cit., 65ff., tones down the rigorism of the passage by rightly pointing out the fact that *Comus* is a masque which was produced for a particular occasion (the Earl of Bridgewater taking over the administration of Wales) and contains underlying allusions to this occasion. However, he cannot avoid conceding that in the end Milton cannot rid himself of the more or less Platonic ethics of his milieu.

100. Cf. Grace, *Ideas*, 139ff.; Hill, *Milton*, 49ff.

101. *Works*, Columbia ed., I, 1, 80.

102. Op.cit., 81.

103. In a preface to the edition of the *Poems* of 1645.

104. *Defensio secunda*, *Works*, Columbia ed., VIII, 124 (cf. 125). In reality Milton only sees this in retrospect, in 1654, as a motive for his return, which he delayed for several months; cf. most recently Hill, *Milton*, 56.

105. For the exact dates cf. Wolfe, in Milton, *Works*, Yale ed., I, 107, 514.

106. Barker, *Milton*, 27, observes: 'There is, in fact, scarcely a single idea in his early pamphlets which cannot be found in the Smectymnuan writings.' The lack of originality in Milton's prose works is also recognized as a generally held opinion by Richmond, *Milton*, 98. Cf. also Hill, *Milton*, 100, 461.

107. Cf. the survey of contents by Wolfe in *Works*, Yale ed., I, 108-15.

108. In *Reason of Church Government*, Yale ed., I, 808.

109. Op.cit., 519f. – An acute commentator has observed that Milton's religious

thought contrasts strikingly with his consciousness as a poet who uses the image as a means towards the realm of fantasy, 'a realm made real through touch and smell and sound... Radical Protestant that he was, religion was to him an ethical code rather than the art of communication through fusion of sense and spirit.' Wolfe, *Milton*, 115; cf. id., in Milton, *Works*, Yale ed., I, 109.

110. According to Prov.26.11; II Peter 2.22; cf. also footnote 4 ad loc., op.cit., 520.

111. Op.cit., 521ff.

112. Examples in Wolfe, op.cit., 113.

113. If he wanted to conceive of a real bishop the bishop would have to be modelled on a democratic ideal: 'But that he will mould a modern Bishop into a primitive, must yeeld him to be elected by the popular voice, undiocest, unrevenu'd, unlorded, and leave him nothing but brotherly equality...', op.cit., 548f.

114. Cf. Wolfe, op.cit., 111.

115. The church is no trembling vine which needs the state to support it; furthermore both Constantine's pro-Arian religious policy and his personal life-style provide sufficient grounds for criticism (op.cit., 554f.)! According to Hill, *Milton*, 84f., Milton thus follows the radical tradition which saw the decisive apostasy of the church in the state church which was founded by Constantine. For the Constantinian typology of the state church cf. above, 497 n.435. Milton dissolves typological thinking by a rational and moralistic approach.

116. Cf. Wolfe, op.cit., 109f.

117. Op.cit., 525ff.

118. Milton retorts: 'Not presently does it follow that every one suffering for Religion, is without exception', op.cit., 533. For Prynne the revision of his judgment was significant precisely in this question, cf. above, 155.

119. Op.cit., 566.

120. Here we can pass over Milton's controversy with Archbishop Ussher over the authority of the church fathers in the matter of episcopacy: 'Of Prelatical Episcopacy'; for the substance cf. Wolfe, op.cit., 115ff.

121. Op.cit., 690.

122. Op.cit., 699.

123. For the date cf. R.A.Haug, in *Works*, Yale ed., I, 737f.

124. Op.cit., 749.

125. Cf. Wolfe, op.cit., 199.

126. Milton is referring to the collection *Certain Briefe Treatises, Written by Diverse Learned Men, Concerning the Ancient and Modern Government of the Church*, which appeared in 1641; cf. Wolfe, op.cit., 193f.; Haug, op.cit., 738.

127. Op.cit., 801ff.; for the significance of this digression cf. Haug, op.cit., 741ff.

128. A tractate by him was included in the collection which Milton attacked, cf. Wolfe, op.cit., 195f.

129. Op.cit., 762. Here and in what follows Milton refers back to Gal.4.1-5 and other passages from Galatians.

130. Op.cit., 764.

131. At one point Milton describes the ritualistic regulations introduced by the clergy not only as 'dead judaism' (op.cit., 843) but as 'Canaanitish' ('for that which was to the Jew but jewish is to the Christian no better then Canaanitish'), op.cit., 845.

132. Id. For the further shifting of boundaries in the sphere of the 'political' law in the Old Testament in the 'Doctrine and Discipline of Divorce' cf. below, 507 n.153.

133. This high estimation breaks through particularly clearly at a point where Milton speaks of man's 'honourable duty of estimation and respect towards his own soul and body' and, taking up an image from Dante, of the 'hill top of sanctity and

goodnesse above which there is no higher ascent but to the love of God', op.cit., 842 – completely in the Neo-Platonic thought patterns of the Renaissance.

134. Op.cit., 747f.

135. Op.cit., 830-50. Cf. also Wolfe, op.cit., 199ff.

136. Op.cit., 844.

137. Op.cit., 848.

138. Allusion to Eph.4.13 as a contrast to I Cor.3.1.

139. Op.cit., 828.

140. Op.cit., 838.

141. I, 7; op.cit., 794ff.; quotation, 795. – Fixler, op.cit., 79ff., describes the utopian character of the expectations which moved the public during these years and which also underlie Milton's prose writings, when a new Reformation is thought to be immediately imminent.

142. Cf. op.cit., 852 n.9.

143. Op.cit., 201.

144. April 1642, cf. F.L.Taft in Preface, op.cit., 862ff. Here Milton is responding to Hall's *A Modest Confutation*, 1642, in which Hall had attacked Milton's *Animadversions*.

145. Op.cit., 931f.

146. Op.cit., 933.

147. For Milton's attitude to the universities cf. J.H.Hanford, *A Milton Handbook* (1926), reprinted 1961. Appendix A, 355ff. We also find a similar attack on the universities and their urge for learning among the antinomian preachers in Cromwell's army, like John Dell, cf. L.F.Solt, *Saints in Arms. Puritanism and Democracy in Cromwell's Army*, 1959, 93f. – However, we can see that the theme is much older among the Puritans from the attacks on the training of clergy in the universities already made by W.Travers, *Ecclesiasticae Disciplinae et Anglicanae Ecclesiae ab illa aberrationis plena e Verbo Dei dilucida Explicatio* (ET by T.Cartwright), 1574, 142, 143, 146. Cf. also Hill, *Milton*, 103ff.

148. Cf. 439 n.43 above.

149. Op.cit., 934.

150. The most important specialist articles are: A.Barker, 'Christian Liberty in Milton's Divorce Pamphlets', *MLR* 35, 1940, 153-61; K.Svendsen, 'Science and Structure in Milton's Doctrine of Divorce', *PMLA* 67, 1952, 435-45. Cf. also esp. Barker, *Milton's Divorce Tracts*, 63ff.; E.Sirluck, Introduction to Vol.II of the *Works*, Yale ed., 137ff.; V.N.Olsen, *The New Testament Logia on Divorce. A Study of their Interpretation from Erasmus to Milton*, BGBE 10, 1971, 128-42. Cf. also H.G.Porter, *The Nose of Wax*, 169ff.; E.W.Tielsch, 'Einleitung', 38ff.; Hill, *Milton*, 117ff.

151. The detailed dedication put at the beginning of the second edition of the *Doctrine and Discipline of Divorce* is explicitly addressed to Parliament, dominated by Presbyterians, and the Westminster Assembly.

152. Except for adultery, but in that case remarriage was excluded even for the innocent partner.

153. This distinction already occurs in the first edition of the *Doctrine and Discipline of Divorce*, *Works*, Yale ed., II, 318, where Milton says of the Deuteronomic precept on divorce: 'Yet grant it were of old a judicial Law,it need not be the lesse moral for that, being, as it is, about vertue or vice.' As it has moral content, a judicial law also continues to be valid.

154. Op.cit., 309.

155. 'From which words so plain, lesse cannot be concluded, nor is by any learned Interpreter, then that in Gods intention a meet and happy conversation is the chiefest and the noblest end of mariage.' Op.cit., 246.

156. For the whole question cf. *The Doctrine and Discipline of Divorce*, I, chs.2-4, op.cit., 245ff.

157. Op.cit., 282.

158. Op.cit., 325.

159. 'Wherin we may plainly discover how Christ meant not to be tak'n word for word, but like a wise Physician, administring one excesse against another to reduce us to a perfect mean.' Op.cit., 282f. Again the Aristotelian ideal of the 'mean'!

160. Op.cit., 283.

161. This circumstance has not yet been noted sufficently. Cf. above, 119ff.

162. 'God hath not two wills, but one will, much lesse two contrary... The hidden wayes of his providence we adore & search not; but the law is his reveled wil...; herein he appears to us as it were in human shape, enters into cov'nant with us, swears to keep it, binds himself like a just lawgiver to his own prescriptions, measures and is commensurat to right reason.' Op.cit., 292; quoted also by Sirluck, op.cit., 151.

163. Op.cit., 325 – and with reason, cf. the previous note.

164. 'a civil, an indifferent, a somtime diswaded Law of mariage', op cit., 228. Cf. op.cit., 345: 'divorce is not a matter of Law but of Charity.'

165. He addresses the threatening question to those in positions of responsibility in state and church: 'When things indifferent shall be set to over-front us, under the banners of sin, what wonder if wee bee routed...' op.cit., 228.

166. Op.cit., 318, already in the first edition! For the problem, cf. already Barker, *Milton*, 72f.

167. This work offers a thorough exegesis of the four passages in Old and New Testaments which deal with marriage and divorce: Gen.1.27f.; 2.18,23f.; Deut.24.1f.; Matt.5.31f.; 19.3-11; I Cor.7.10-16. For the date of its appearance cf. the preface by A.Williams, op.cit., 571.

168. Op.cit., 660ff.

169. The second, according to which 'hardnes of heart is tak'n for a stubborne resolution to doe evil' does not come into consideration here, for 'that God ever makes any law purposely to such, I deny', op.cit., 662.

170. Op.cit., 661.

171. Op.cit., 665.

172. Ibid.

173. Op.cit., 661. Sirluck, op.cit., 157, points out that Milton took over this distinction from the Parliamentary debate of 1644.

174. For the theme cf. Barker, *MLR* 1940; id., *Milton*, 98ff.

175. Op.cit., 330f.

176. Op.cit., 642. Cf. also op.cit., 587: 'But Christ having... interpreted the fulfilling of all through charity, hath in that respect set us over law, in the free custody of his love, and left us victorious under the guidance of his living Spirit, not under the dead letter; to follow that which most edifies...;' cf. also Barker,*MLR* 1940, 160.

177. Op.cit., 661.

178. Barker, *Milton*, 107; cf. also Sirluck, op.cit., 155.

179. Op.cit., 587.

180. Ibid. Hill, *Milton*, 268ff., points to Milton's increasing Arminianism, which corresponds to a widespread trend both on the right wing of the church and among the radical sects.

181. Barker, *Milton*, 108.

182. Op.cit., 156.

183. Op.cit., 588.

184. Op.cit., 636.

185. Op.cit., 623.

186. Barker, *Milton*, 111, observes: 'The orthodox may well have wondered at the monstrous brood hatched out of their mature positions. To make man's good the rule of divine prescript seems certainly to set the creature above God.' However, the orthodox were not so innocent over this development!

187. *Scripture and Reason Pleaded for Defensive Arms etc.*, 1643 (cf. Barker, Index of Works, op.cit., 419).

188. Cf. Barker, op.cit., 108ff.

189. Barker, op.cit., 88, observes: 'What is now his best-known prose work seemed to fall still-born from the press.' For the content cf. recently also E.W.Tielsch, 'Einleitung', 50ff.

190. 'Good and evill we know in the field of this World grow up together almost inseparably'; to be able to choose between the two God entrusted man 'with the gift of reason to be his own chooser', op.cit., 514.

191. Op.cit., 515.

192. Op.cit., 516f.

193. Cf. op.cit., 564.

194. '...'tis not untrue that many sectaries and false teachers are then busiest in seducing', op.cit., 566.

195. Ibid.

196. Op.cit., 539. Cf. also the well known ending to the sonnet, 'New Presbyter is but Old Priest writ Large.' *Works*, Columbia ed., I, 71.

197. Cf. Sirluck, op.cit., 143.

198. H.Porter, *The Nose of Wax*, has brought out this connection most clearly; on Spiritualism as a hermeneutical principle in Milton, for whom at the same time a marked trait of natural law goes along with the role of conscience ('Conscience, charity and the spirit' are Milton's three hermeneutical principles, op.cit., 172, cf. esp. op.cit., 171ff.).

199. Cf. above, 117f.

200. Cf. Haller, *Rise*, 331ff.; id., *Tracts*, 19ff.; Barker, *Milton*, 54ff.; Wolfe, in Milton, *Works*, Yale ed., I, 145ff., and above all the monograph by R.E.L.Strider II, *Robert Greville, Lord Brooke*, 1958.

201. *Works*, Yale ed., II, 560f.

202. *The Nature of Truth*, 1640, facsimile reprint ed. V. de Sola Pinto, 1969. For the content cf. Strider, op.cit., 81ff.

203. Strider, op.cit., 84.

204. This is particularly clear in his definition of reason, which comes right at the beginning of the pamphlet: 'for what is the Vnderstanding other than a Ray of the Divine Nature, warming and enlivening the Creature, conforming it to the likenesse of the Creator?' Op.cit., 3f. The term *ratio* occurs similarly among the 'Cambridge Platonists', whose thought is nearer to the Renaissance than to the Enlightenment; cf. also above, 191f. For the identification of spirit and truth in the sense of the unity of being in Plotinus as a a model for Lord Brooke cf. Strider, op.cit., 108. He also draws attention to the Neoplatonic heritage in Augustine, op.cit., 109, the significance of which for Puritanism was stressed so much by Perry Miller, cf. above, 479 n.40.

205. The second edition of 1642, which contains mainly technical improvements (cf. Strider, op.cit., 153 n.1), was reprinted as a facsimile by W.Haller in *Tracts on Liberty* II, 37-163: this edition has been used here.

206. See above, 113f.

207. 'Right Reason; The Candle of God, which He hath lighted in man, lest man groaping in the darke should stumble, and fall,' *A Discourse*, 25 (Haller, *Tracts* II, 69).

208. Op.cit., 17ff. (Haller, *Tracts* II, 61ff.).

209. Cf. Strider, op.cit., 213ff.

210. Op.cit., 18 (62).

211. Ibid.

212. On this point Brooke similarly follows the Platonic-Augustinian ontology, as already in *The Nature of Truth*, 101; cf. Augustine, *Confessions* III, 7.

213. It is interesting that here Brooke refers to the Stoic maxim *Omnia peccata sunt paria* and to Cicero, op.cit. 19 (63).

214. One assumes that this example prompted Milton to his discussions of divorce.

215. Op.cit., 26 (70).

216. 'I conceive that all the Indifference (in the world) lies in our Understandings, and the Darknesse therof... but there is none in the things themselves, or Actions...', op.cit., 26 (70).

217. 'By the Church here I meane, not onely One or Two, or a few, of what Ranke soever; but All, even every true Member of the whole Church. For I conceive every such Member hath de jure a Vote in This Determination.' Op.cit., 29 (73).

218. *Milton*, 57.

219. Here Joel 3.1 played a considerable role: 'Yea, they have heard that God promised to poure out his Spirit upon all Flesh, all Beleevers (as well Lay as Clergy)', etc., op.cit., 107 (151).

220. For them cf. above all: J.Tulloch, *Rational Theology*, II; E.A.George, *Seventeenth Century Men of Latitude*, 1909, 69ff.; R.M.Jones, *Reformers*, 288ff., 305ff.; F.J.Powicke, *The Cambridge Platonists*, 1926, reprinted 1970; G.P.H.Pawson, *The Cambridge Platonists and Their Place in Religious Thought*, 1930; J.H.Muirhead, *The Platonic Tradition in Anglo-Saxon Philosophy*, 1931, reprinted 1965, 25ff.; E.Cassirer, *The Platonic Renaissance in England and the Cambridge School*, ET 1953, reprinted 1961; W.C.de Pauley, *The Candle of the Lord* (1937), reprinted 1970; W.K.Jordan, *The Development*, IV, 94ff.; G.R.Cragg, *From Puritanism to the Age of Reason*, 1950, reprinted 1966, 37ff.; H.Baker, *The Wars of Truth*, 1952, 124ff.; R.L.Colie, *Light and Enlightenment: A Study of the Cambridge Platonists and the Dutch Arminians*, 1957; R.Hoopes, *Right Reason in the English Renaissance*, 1962, 174ff.; B.Willey, *The Seventeenth Century Background*, 1962, 133ff.; cf. id., *The English Moralists*, 1964, 172ff. Sina, *Ragione*, 64ff.; C.F.Patrides, 'Cambridge, Platoniker von', *TRE* 7, 1981, 598-601 (with bibliography). A short summary of their teaching can also be found in G.Gassmann, 'Die Lehrentwicklung im Anglikanismus: Von Heinrich VIII. bis zu William Temple', in Andresen (ed.), *Handbuch* 2, (353-409) 386ff. – Also the works on individual scholars of the school (cf. the Reading List in Patrides [see below], XXXIf.) – Two collections of excerpts from the works of the school with good introductions have appeared recently: G.R.Cragg (ed.), *The Cambridge Platonists*, 1968; C.A.Patrides (ed.), *The Cambridge Platonists*, 1969.

221. Cf. Cragg, *Puritanism*, 38. Their dates are: Benjamin Whichcote: 1609-1683; Henry More: 1614-1687; Ralph Cudworth: 1617-1688. John Smith, who was about the same age, died young: 1618-1652.

222. Cf. A. Lichtenstein, *Henry More. The Rational Theology of a Cambridge Platonist*, 1962, 4.

223. Lichtenstein's charge that for all its learning and brilliance Cassirer's work betrays a deficient knowledge of the history of English literature, op.cit., 221, tells heavily against such a famous work.

224. Strider, op.cit., 135ff., etc. (cf. Index). Cf. also D.Bush, *English Literature in the Earlier Seventeenth Century, 1600-1660*, ²1962, 358.

225. Brooke himself is the best example of the extent to which Platonism and scholastic thought had found a footing in Puritanism; the background to his views in this direction has been illuminated above all by the work of Perry Miller. Cf. 000 n.204 above. Also Strider, op. cit., 232f.

226. For Cambridge cf. W.J.Costello, *The Scholastic Curriculum at early 17th Century Cambridge*, 1958; H.C.Porter, *Reformation*; for the period in question see esp.414ff.; also M.H.Curtis, *Oxford and Cambridge in Transition 1558-1642*, 1959, reprinted 1965 (with a rather different perspective).

227. 'Eight Letters of Dr. Antony Tuckney, and Dr. Benjamin Whichcote... written in September and October, MDCLI', appendix to B.Whichcote, *Moral and Religious Aphorisms... published in MDCCIII, by Dr.Jeffery. Now re-published... by Samuel Salter*, 1753 (new edition also by W.R.Inge, 1930). Tulloch, op.cit., 59ff., gives a detailed account of the correspondence.

228. He gives an account of his youth in the *Praefatio Generalissima* to the Latin edition of his *Opera Omnia*, II, 1, 1679, reprinted 1966, 1ff. This edition (I, 1674: *Opera Theologica*; II, 1 and 2, 1679: *Opera Philosophica*) is at present the most readily accessible edition of More's work thanks to the 1966 reprint provided with an introduction by S.Hutin. Of course it does not contain the works which appeared later, and also lacks some works of the author's youth (see the list in the introduction by S.Hutin, I, Vf.). Originally More published his works predominantly in English (cf. the lists in Lichtenstein, op.cit., 227ff., and S.Hutin, *Henry More*, 1966, 208); in the *Opera*, where they were written in the vernacular they are translated into Latin by the author himself. Most recent Anglo-Saxon scholarship tends to use the English originals rather than this edition, and the relevant English translations of the Latin works.

229. *Hisce principiis imbutus firma scilicet stabilique persuasione de Existentia Dei & illibata illius Justitia perfectaque Bonitate, quod Deus Optimus perinde esset atque Maximus. Praefatio Generalissima, Opera Omnia*, II, 1, VI.

230. Ibid.

231. Cudworth delivered his famous sermon before the Lower House at the time of the Long Parliament on 31 March 1647 (reprinted in Patrides, op.cit., 90ff.). However, they rarely emerged into public view in this way.

232. 1678, reprinted 1964. There are also a number of other editions and a Latin translation by Mosheim (1733; [2]1773: re-translation of his commentary into English by J.J.Harrison, 1845). For Cudworth cf. J.A.Passmore, *Ralph Cudworth*, 1951; L.Gysi, *Platonism and Cartesianism in the Philosophy of Ralph Cudworth*, Phil.diss.Basel 1962; also the literature mentioned in Patrides, *Platonism*, XXXII.

233. Cf. the verdicts on the work quoted by Patrides, op.cit., 33.

234. Cf. the comments by Patrides, op.cit., XXV, and above all Lichtenstein, op.cit., Xf.

235. This is still presented most clearly in Tulloch, op.cit., although his verdict on the significance of the Cambridge Platonists needs to be revised. – Cf. also the short comments in Baker, op.cit., 125.

236. Lichtenstein, op.cit., 220, mentions E.A.George, Pawson and Powicke, but the list could be continued.

237. Cf. op.cit., 1ff., and esp. 456ff.

238. Bush is particularly illuminating, op.cit., 358. He points out the Platonic influence on such different men as Sir Thomas Browne, Lord Brooke, Henry More and Milton, and also on Herbert of Cherbury; on the other hand there are the Puritan theologians who applied Ramistic logic to the thought world of Calvinism.

239. Bush, op.cit., 359; but cf. also already Tulloch, op.cit., 7.

240. Cf. Tulloch, op.cit., 45f. Sina, *Ragione*, 69ff.

241. Op.cit., cf. also Sina, *Ragione*, 131ff.

242. See above 509 n.207. For the term cf. esp. R.Hoopes, op.cit.

243. Op.cit., IX, 20 etc.

244. De Pauley, op.cit., alludes to him in the title of his investigation. It is worth noting that in the original Hebrew text the elements in the noun clause appear in

the reverse order. The image of the candle which combines experience and intuitive thought is not coincidental; it is also widespread in Puritanism outside the group of the Cambridge Platonists, cf. G.F.Nuttall, *The Holy Spirit in Puritan Faith and Experience,* ²1947, 38ff.

245. Lichtenstein, op.cit., 20.

246. Cf. e.g. Tulloch, op.cit., 376f., who sees a lapse 'into mystical extravagances' in More's move against Cartesianism. There is a special investigation on John Smith by E.I.Watkin in his collection *Poets and Mystics,* 1953 (ch.X, 238-56); he says of him: 'Smith's religion is thus distinctively mystical in type'; he is 'a mystic of the middle stage, the illuminative way', op.cit., 253.

247. For the Cambridge Platonists this aspect presents itself in their Neoplatonic conceptuality, cf. More, *Annotations upon the Discourse of Truth,* 1682, 264 (quoted in Lichtenstein, op.cit., 51): 'the Divine Understanding Exhibitive, which is the Intellectual World... and Fountain of Intellectual Light. That is, according to the Platonick Dialect, of those steady, unalterable and eternal Idea's (*to gar eidos zos*) of the nature and respects of things represented there in the Divine Understanding Exhibitive in their Objective Existence.' Thus in the Platonic sense God is the *nous noetos* in which the Ideas are grounded and along with which they have an eternal existence. There is also the subordinate idea of God as the all-knowing observer of the world, op.cit., 261; cf. Lichtenstein, ibid.

248. Cf. *Divine Dialogues,* ²1713, 301f., cited in Lichtenstein, op.cit., 52f.: 'That's a thing... I could yet never understand, that the most omnipotent Power that is imaginable can ever have a right to do what is wrong... No Power, though never so Omnipotent, can claim a right to such an act, no more than any Intellect, never so Omniscient, can claim a right of authentickly thinking that true which is really false.' It follows from this, 'That to infinite, permanent and immutable Goodness of right belongs as well Omnisciency as Omnipotency... So... is there not all reason, that he that is so immutably Good, that it is repugnant that he should ever will any thing but what is absolutely for the best, should have a full right of acting merely according to the suggestions and sentiments of his own Mind...?'

249. Cf. *An Explanation of the grand Mystery of Godliness* (1660), in *The Theological Works,* 1708, I, XVI, 6 (quoted in Lichtenstein, op.cit., 47): 'the true Life of Religion, which is the renewing the Mind into the Image or Similitude of God.'

250. *Conjectura Cabbalistica* (1653), in: *A Collection of Several Philosophical Writings,* ⁴1712, 'Preface to the Reader', sec.3 (quoted in Lichtenstein, op.cit., cf. also *Opero Omnia,* II, 2, 468).

251.*Mystery of Godliness* II, XII, 2, (quoted in Lichtenstein, ibid.).

252. Lichtenstein, op.cit., 161ff., demonstrates how while More in theory draws a clear distinction between religion and morality, in practice he does not completely succeed in distinguishing them since the relationship to God, being of a moral character, is hardly different from one between men. In Whichcote we can read the succinct comment: 'The state of religion lies, in short, in this: a good mind, and a good life. All else is *about* religion and hath but the place of a means or instrument', *Works,* 1751, I, 168 (also in Patrides, 334).

253. '...*Oraculum Dei nusquam audiri nisi in sancto suo Templo, hoc est in probis sanctisque hominibus, penitusque purificatis Spiritu, Anima ac corpore. Est enim quaedam vel ipsius etiam corporis Sanctitas, ac Temperamenti... Principiumque Rationis Ratio non est sed quiddam praestantius. Quid autem Scientia praestantius esse potest, nisi Deus?*' *Opera Philosophica, Praefatio Generalis,* in *Opera Omnia,* II, 2, sec.VI, VII, 4.

254. Cf. Lichtenstein, op.cit., 69ff.

255. *Divine Dialogue,* 294f., quoted by Lichtenstein, op.cit.,74.

256. 'Truth lies in a little room, especially that of it that is most useful', *Divine Dialogues,* 306, quoted in Lichtenstein, 106. Cf. also *Enchiridion Ethicum,* Book II, X,

4, quoted in Lichtenstein, 106: *Nec magis opus est viro probo tam fideli omniaque fere retinenti Memoria. Nam pulchra illa ac Divina in quibus Beatitudo consistit pauca sunt... vel potius unum qiddam, quo, veluti oculo colores, omnia honestorum & turpium discrimina clare discernuntur... Neque enim ex praeceptorum multitudine memoriae insculptorum, sed ex intima quadam vita simplicissimoque sensu agere solet vir probus perfectaque Virtute praeditus.* Moreover here we have an explicitly eudaimonistic form of ethics.

257. Cf. *Enchiridion Ethicum*, II, X, passim (in *Opera Omnia* II, 1, 63ff.); cf. Lichtenstein, 113ff. – The same attitude is adopted by Whichcote. Among his 'six mistakes about religion' (in *Works*, 1751, 2, 387) the first mentioned is 'to think that religion lies in a system of propositions'. Cudworth makes faith of the 'vulgar sort', 'that they know Christ enough, out of their Creeds and Catechismes, and Confessions of Faith', the starting point for his famous sermon to the Lower House (printed in Patrides, op.cit., 90-127, quotation, 91). In constantly repeated phrases he stresses: 'Christ came not into the world to fil our heads with mere Speculations' (op.cit., 96). 'Inke and Paper can never make us Christians' (92), etc. Nor is there any purpose in penetrating the mysteries of election: 'We have no warrant in Scripture, to peep into these hidden Rolls and Volumes of Eternity' (94), 'to pry into these secrets'(93). Instead of this, 'Hereby we know that we know Christ, hereby we know that Christ loves us, if we keep his commandments' (95). The latter demand, constantly repeated, appears e.g. in the evocative alternative which he presents to his hearers: 'I beseech you, Let us consider, whether or no we know Christ indeed: Not by our acquaintance with Systems and Modells of Divinity; not by our skill in Books and Papers; but by keeping of Christs Commandments'(108). Here Cudworth, as a typical Christian Platonist, stresses that the 'Christ without us', or, 'the gospel, if it be only without us', could not save, 'without the real partaking of the Image of Christ in our hearts'(109).

258. 'There should be no Injunctions as indispensable in matters of Religion, but such as they (the books of the Bible) plainly determine.' *Mystery of Godliness*, V, XVII, 8, quoted in Lichtenstein, op.cit., 120.

259. *Mystery of Godliness*, Preface, sec.20; quoted in Lichtenstein, op.cit., 127. – Whichcote (see previous note) by contrast presents more the earlier Anglican attitude: 'Some men take certain images, performances and forbearances to be religion... I leave these to every man but he must not lay stress on them.' Cudworth blames the Puritans for being 'superstitiously anti-ceremonial', 'The Second Sermon', in *The True Intellectual System of the Universe*, ed. T.Birch, reprinted 1820, IV, 394.

260. Cf. Lichtenstein, op.cit., 173ff.

261. 'A Short Discourse on Superstition', in *Select Discourses*, ed. S.Patrick, 1859, 25-38.

262. He translates *Superstitio, in qua inest timor inanis deorum*, (*De natura deorum*, I, ch.XLII, quoted from LCL, 1935) as: 'an over-timorous and dreadful apprehension of the deity', op.cit., 26.

263. Aphorismus 1014 (in *Aphorisms*, also in Patrides, op.cit., 335). Cf. also Cudworth in Patrides, op.cit., 96: 'I perswade my self, that no man shall ever be kept out of heaven, for not comprehending mysteries that were beyond the reach of his shallow understanding.'

264. Op.cit., 78f. Nor can a formula like that of Cudworth (in Patrides, op.cit., 109) that Christ's saving action could not save, 'unless Christ by his Spirit dwell in us', be understood in this sense. Cudworth himself declares the 'true Evangelicall Holinesse, that is Christ formed in the hearts of the believers'(111) as 'goodnesse'(112) or 'new obedience' which at the same time means participation in the 'Image of God in Righteousnesse and true Holinesse.'

265. *A Treatise Concerning Eternal and Immutable Morality*, 1731. Reprint as appendix to *The True Intellectual System*, ed. Harrison, 1845; extracts also in L.A.Selby-Bigge,

British Moralists (1897), reprinted 1965, 2, cols.813-48. Cf. the detailed investigations by J.Martineau, 'Dianoetic Ethics: Cudworth', in *Types of Ethical Theory*, 1885, II, 396-424; Muirhead, op.cit., 57ff.; E.M.Austin, *The Ethics of the Cambridge Platonists*, Phil.diss. Philadelphia 1935, 22ff.; Gysi, op.cit.; Passmore, op.cit., 40ff. Passmore in particular has performed the useful service of taking into account the unprinted Cudworth manuscripts in the British Library (Add MSS 4981; cf. op.cit., 51, and the appendix; some extracts in Muirhead, op.cit., 63ff.) for further interpretation of Cudworth's views. Cf. also M.H.Carré, 'Ralph Cudworth', *PhQ* 3, 1953, 342-51. Nathanael Culverwel's work *Of the Light of Nature*, 1652 (it was written considerably earlier), takes a similar position; edition by J.Brown, 1857; however, Culverwel does not belong among the narrower circle of Cambridge Platonists.

266. *Rational Theology* II, 285.

267. Op.cit., I, ch.2,1; also in Selby-Bigge, op.cit., col.813.

268. Op.cit., I, ch.2,2; also in Selby-Bigge, op.cit., col.815.

269. Op.cit., I, ch.2,3-4; also in Selby-Bigge, op.cit., cols. 816ff. For 'natural' good and its priority to all 'positive' commands cf. also Austin, op.cit., 20ff. According to Cudworth, even the divine will is bound by the unchangeable Good: in that God himself embodies the absolute Good as its supreme hypostasis, which has also been made visible in the creation of all things and is present in the divine *nous* as the idea of the natural good. Cf. Gysi, op.cit., 124ff. In trinitarian speculation Cudworth transfers the Good into the deity itself, cf. Gysi, op.cit., 105ff., 123f. Therefore God cannot decree any positive commands which would contradict natural Good. – From an epistemological perspective this world-view is based on the theory of *ideae innatae*, as it is in Herbert of Cherbury (see below, 188); cf. S.P.Lamprecht, 'Innate Ideas in the Cambridge Platonists', *PhRev* 35, 1926, 553-73.

270. Patristic instances in Patrides, op.cit., 7 n.1.

271. Thus Cudworth, *Intellectual System*, 12ff. Similarly also More, cf. the instances cited in Patrides, op.cit., 7 n.2.

272. Discourse VII, in *Select Discourses*, 299-360. – For Smith, cf. in addition to Tulloch, op.cit., 117ff. (on Discourse VII, esp. 180ff.): George, op.cit., 89ff.; Powicke, op.cit., 87ff., and De Pauley, op.cit., 67ff.; B.Willey, *The Seventeenth Century Background*, 138ff.; J.K.Ryan, 'John Smith, Platonist and Mystic', in *NSchol* 20, 1946, 1-25; E.I.Watkin, *John Smith the Cambridge Platonist*, see above, 512 n.246; Sina, *Ragione*, 89ff.

273. Special note should be taken of the numerous Hebrew quotations from the Kabbalistic and Talmudic writings. We also find close acquaintance with the Jewish tradition of interpreting the Bible in Discourse VI, On Prophecy, op.cit., 171ff. This concern with Jewish literature accords with the tradition of the Christian Neoplatonists: we already found it in Pico della Mirandola, cf. 424 n.114 above.

274. Op.cit., 2, 302ff.

275. Op.cit., 2, 311ff.

276. '...we may observe what a lean and spiritless religion this of the Jews was, and how it was nothing else but a soulless and lifeless form of external performances, which did little or nothing at all reach the inward man, being nothing but a mere bodily kind of drudgery and servility', op.cit., 318.

277. 'Evangelical' or 'Gospel-righteousness'.

278. Op.cit., 323.

279. Op.cit., 325.

280. Op.cit., 327.

281. Op.cit., 353ff. Earlier exegetes like Tulloch and George could largely identify with Smith, cf. the enthusiastic judgment in George, op.cit., 94ff., and Tulloch, op.cit., 189: 'These – the eternal problems of religious philosophy (Is man essentially a spiritual being?) were the problems to which Smith directly addressed himself

with clear-sighted and admirable perspicacity. And his answers, upon the whole, go as nearly to the heart of their solution as any that have been given.' But cf. also Powicke, op.cit., 106f. There is virtually a devotional tradition as far as Smith is concerned, cf. op.cit., 94.

282. Op.cit., 327f. There are similar comments in Cudworth: 'Inke and Paper can never make us Christians', see above, 513 n.257.

283. Op.cit., 328f.

284. Op.cit., 173f.

285. Op.cit., 177.

286. *The Seventeenth Century Background*, 146f.

287. Editions of the text, C.Firth (ed.), *The Clarke Papers*, 4 vols., 1891-1901; A.S.P. Woodhouse, *Puritanism*. For the debates, in addition to the older work by S.R.Gardiner, *History of the Great Civil War*, cf. above all the admirable introduction in Woodhouse, op.cit.; in D.M.Wolfe, *Leveller Manifestoes of the Puritan Revolution*, 1944, reprinted 1967, 66f., 89ff., and e.g. H.N.Brailsford, *The Levellers and the English Revolution*, 267f., 384ff.; J.Franck, *The Levellers*, 1955, 135ff., 178ff.; W.Haller, *Liberty*, 297ff., 321ff.; G.Yule, *The Independents in the English Civil War*, 1958, 70ff.; recently also R.Saage, *Herrschaft, Toleranz, Widerstand*, 1981, 190ff.

288. Characteristic examples of this are the works of Brailsford, op.cit., and D.W.Petegorsky, *Left-Wing Democracy in the English Civil War* (with G.Wistanley as hero), 1940. An example from most recent times of an emancipatory-ideological aim with a Christian background is the work by K.Schmidt, *Religion*, which also goes into the Commonwealth period, 59ff.

289. Brailsford's judgment, 'They lack the drama and the human interest of the discussions at Reading and Putney', op.cit., 384, can be taken as typical. But cf. Watts, *Dissenters*, 124f.

290. Cf. Woodhouse, op.cit., 125; for the origin of this contemporary information about the theme of the session see the relevant note on p.484.

291. In Woodhouse, op.cit., 125-69. For the theoretical political aspect cf. also Saage, op.cit., 208ff.

292. Landmarks in outward developments are the battle of Naseby (14 June 1645), which was the decisive defeat of the Royalists in the first Civil War; the tensions which arose after the end of this war between the Army and Parliament, which led to the formation of a representative body for the Army; the second Civil War of 1648; and finally 'Pride's Purge' (6 December 1648): the expulsion of most members of Parliament by a military action and the execution of the king (30 January 1649). For these events see e.g. the brief accounts in G.Davies and Ashley. Behind them are the religious confrontations between the Anglicans on the Royalist side, the Presbyterians in the Parliamentary majority and in Scotland, and the Independents and the sects in the Army.

293. Cf. Frank, op.cit., 175. The original version is printed in D.M.Wolfe, *Leveller Manifestoes*, 293-303, and in Woodhouse, op.cit., 356-67 (with the alterations made by the leaders of the Army). It was published one day after the debate which concerns us, on 15 December 1648. The composite volume edited by G.E.Aylmer, *The Levellers in the English Revolution*, 1975, contains only the first version of November 1647 (88-96) and the third version of May 1649 (159-68).

294. Cf. Wolfe, op.cit., 300; Woodhouse, op.cit., 361f.

295. The division becomes clearest in the observation that no one may be hindered from the exercise of his belief in any place 'except such as are, or shall be, set apart for the public worship', ibid.

296. Cf. Woodhouse, op.cit., [57]f.

297. In Woodhouse, op.cit., that does not yet become quite clear.

298. Woodhouse, op.cit., 126.

299. 'Let us submit to these future Representatives, and if we be not satisfied in one Representative, it may be [we shall be satisfied] in the next.' Woodhouse, op.cit., 132.

300. 'He (the authority) hath not power to conclude your inward, but [only] your outward man', op.cit., 131.

301. In this way the question (read out by Ireton), 'Whether [the magistrate have, or ought to have, any power in matters of religion...] is expanded in the discussion to: 'Whether the magistrate have or ought to have any compulsive or restrictive power in matters of religion?', op.cit., 150-2.

302. 'All civil power whatsoever... is not able to bind men's judgments...', op.cit., 130.

303. Op.cit., 133. Here Overton objects: 'If he hath power over my body, he hath power to keep me at home when I should go abroad to serve God', op.cit., 139.

304. Op.cit., 150.

305. Op.cit., 143. For Ireton cf. also R.W.Ramsay, *Henry Ireton*, 1949.

306. Op.cit., 156. Cf. also 154 :'Those are things against which there is a testimony in the light of nature, and consequently they are things that men as men are in some capacity [to judge of], unless they are perverted.'

307. Op.cit., 130. This argument is supported by Philip Nye who asserts that God will punish a nation which tolerates such sins, op.cit., 160.

308. Op.cit., 155.

309. Op.cit., 156.

310. Op.cit., 162.

311. See the quotation above.

312. Op.cit., 156.

313. Op.cit., 146.

314. Op.cit., 160f. Repeated by Thomas Collier, 'If it is moral, it should have been given to all states as well as to the Jews', op.cit., 164.

315. W.Haller,*Tracts on Liberty*, I, 86f. – W.W.Wittwer, *Grundrechte bei den Levellern und bei der New Model Army. Ein Beitrag zur Vorgeschichte des Menschenrechtsgedankens*, 1972, 65ff., denies any connection between the Levellers' demands for human rights and any church or religious models, say the Independents' constitution for the church or other Puritan principles. Instead of this he claims that only the idea of natural law (on the basis of Magna Carta, cf. 54f.), as connected with the specific political situation, had an effect on their conceptions of the sovereignty of the people and contracts. On the one hand that is quite correct, but on the other the whole of the Puritan left wing was also influenced by secular notions of natural law in its concepts of religion and the church: people like Lilburne made similar individualist demands for the structure of the church. For the fact that the leading Levellers had usually been Separatists and the connection between their demands and non-Conformist postulates cf. Watts, *Dissenters*, 117ff. For the Levellers cf. also H.Shaw, *The Levellers*, 1968 reprinted 1971; for their political demands cf. also B.Manning, 'The Levellers', in I.W.Ives (ed.), *The English Revolution 1600 – 1660*, 1968, 144-58.

316. Cf. Haller, *Rise*, 273ff.; *Tracts on Liberty*, Introduction, 40ff.; D.B.Robertson, *The Religious Foundations of Leveller Democracy*, 1951, 13ff. Robertson gives a very thorough description of the combination of mysticism, scripturalism and natural law doctrine which is characteristic of the religious and political thought of the Levellers.

317. The writing *A Worke of the Beast*, 1638, was included by Haller in his collection *Tracts on Liberty*, II, 1ff. It is certainly no coincidence that Lilburne ended his life in 1657 as a Quaker.

318. Printed in Haller, *Tracts on Liberty*, II, 165-213. For Parker cf. M.A.Judson, 'Henry Parker and the Theory of Parliamentary Sovereignty', in *Essays in History and Political Theory. In Honour of C.H.McIlwain*, nd, 138ff.

319. Lilburne made their acquaintance through Edward Coke's *Institutes of the Laws of England*, 1628-44.

320. Cf. Wittwer, op.cit., 8: 'An individualist picture of man is the presupposition for any legal sanctioning of subjective claims to freedom.'

321. Woodhouse, op.cit., introduction [89]ff., has rightly referred to William Ames as an important representative of this theology with a Humanist colouring.

322. '...all and every particular and individuall man and woman, that ever breathed in the world since, ...are, and were by nature all equall and alike in power, dignity, authority, and majesty...' Lilburne, *The Free Man's Freedom Vindicated*, 1646, 11. The whole section is quoted in Pease, op.cit., 199ff. Cf. also in Brailsford, op.cit., 119. J.C.Davis, 'The Levellers and Christianity', in B.Manning (ed.), *Politics* (above n.79), 225-50, rightly notes the Christian origins of the idea of equality, pragmatism and the stress on moral action among the Levellers, but fails to recognize the connections with the specifically Christian and Humanist tradition. Moreover the antinomianism and the idea of universal salvation in Walwyn and others (230f.) is not the root but the expression of this attitude. Similarly already D.M.Himbury, 'The Religious Belief of the Levellers', *BQ* 33, 1954, for the connection between the Levellers and the other Puritan sects of the time.

322a. Cf. A.Woolrych, 'Puritanism, Politics and Society', in Ives (ed.), *Revolution*, 87-100.

323. Thus Sprigge, op.cit., 144: '...the only means of suppressing and eradicating them, and that is the breaking forth of him who is the Truth, the breaking forth of Christ, in the minds and spirits of men.' – For the role of the Spiritualist preachers in Cromwell's army like Peters, Saltmarsh and Dell cf. W.Haller, 'The Word of God in the New Model Army', *ChH* 19, 1950, 15-33; id., *Liberty and Reformation*, 189ff., and L.F.Solt, *Saints in Arms*. For the role of the millenarians cf. also A.Woolrych, 'Oliver Cromwell and the Rule of the Saints', in R.W.Parry (ed.), *The English Civil War and After, 1642-1658*, 1970, 59-77.

324. Above, 142f. These observations are confirmed by S. P. Fienberg's evaluation of the Independents, exemplified in the sermons of Thomas Goodwin ('Thomas Goodwin's Scriptural Hermeneutics', *JRH* 10, 1978, 32–49). Whereas the Presbyterians relied on rules for church government based on the whole of scripture, including the injunctions of the Old Testament and confirmed by reason, the Independents advocated a Christ-centred biblicism, founded exclusively on the New Testament, combined with a fervent millenarism.

325. Above, 498f. n.455.

326. Yule, op.cit., 72, inappropriately attributes this form of typology to the Levellers: it is important to make a sharper differentiation here.

327. *Anti-Cavalierisme*, 1642, reprinted in Haller, *Tracts on Liberty*, II, 219-69; cf. I, 30-32.

328. Op.cit., 6 [224].

329. Op.cit., 11 [229].

330. Op.cit., 12 [230].

331. Op.cit., 13 [231].

332. Op.cit., 7 [225].

333. Op.cit., 6 [224].

334. Above, 143.

335. The disputed regulation about the rights of Parliament in matters of religion was completely changed by the majority of the officers in the final form of the 'Agreement', cf. in Woodhouse, op.cit., 361 n.26. This paper itself was finally allowed to lie in Parliament and never had official recognition, cf. Frank, op.cit., 182.

336. For him cf. Pease, op.cit., 251ff.; Woodhouse, op.cit., [54]ff. Haller, *Tracts on*

Liberty, I, 33-45, 56-63, 92-94, 107-10, 115-18, 121-7; id., *Liberty and Reformation*, 282-7; Frank, op.cit., 29-39 etc. (cf. index).

337. Reprinted in W.Haller and G.Davies, *The Leveller Tracts, 1647-1653*, 1944, reprinted 1964, 285-313.

338. He gives an account of this in *Walwyns Just Defence*, 1649, reprinted in Haller-Davies, op.cit., 350-98 (Italian translation also in V.Gabrieli ed., *Puritanesimo e libertà. Dibattiti e libelli*, 1956, 165-229. Introduction ibid., XLII-L.), 9 (362): 'using Seneca, Plutarchs Lives, and Charon of humane wisdom, as things of recreation, wherein I was both pleased, and profited.' But: '... amongst which Lucian for his good ends... whereof I can read only such as are translated into English'! As an unlettered man, Walwyn ('I cannot construe three lines of any Latin author') had only come into contact with the popularized form of Humanist education, the wide influence of which becomes visible from his example.

339. Op.cit., 8 (361). Also quoted in Frank, op.cit., 31f. – Cf. the comment in *A Wisper in the Ear of Mr.Thomas Edwards Minister* (1646), in Haller, *Tracts on Liberty*, III, 319-36, 2f. [322f.]: 'I am one that do truly and heartily love all mankind, it being the unfeigned desire of my soul, that all men might be saved, and come to the know-ledge of truth.'

340. *Walwyns Wiles*, in Haller and Davies, 297f.

341. 'A Still and Soft Voice', in D.M.Wolfe, *Milton*, 366-74, 11f. (371f.).

342. Op.cit., 4 (367).

343. Cf. above 513 n.257; 515 n.282.

344. Op.cit., 17, quoted in Haller, *Tracts on Liberty*, I, 84.

345. '...the superstitious mans devotion costs him little... hot and fiery against heresie and blasphemy... hee is not so hasty to runn into his poore neighbours house, to see what is wanting there, hee may ly upon a bed, or no bed, covering or no covering... and all this troubles not the superstitious mans... Conscience...', op.cit., 8 (369). The anti-dogmatic approach is not lacking: Walwyn could wish for 'more of the deeds of Christians, and fewer of the arguments'!, op.cit., 15 (374). Wolfe, *Milton*, 170ff., has referred to this work of Walwyn's as 'one of the most remarkable intellectual creeds of Walwyn's generation'.

346. *Walwyns Wiles*, in Haller-Davies, op.cit., 9 (298).

347. Ibid., 20 (377f.).

348. Cf. Solt, op.cit., esp. 27ff.

349. W.S.Hudson, 'Mystical Religion in the Puritan Commonwealth', *JR* 28, 1948, 51-56, would distinguish a trend in Puritanism which was not hostile to the use of reason in religion and led to the Cambridge Platonists of the period of the Resto-ration, from the Spiritualist group represented by people like Dell and Saltmarsh, which ended with the Quakers. However, the Cambridge Platonists themselves are the best example of the way in which a particular form of rationalism goes hand in hand with moralism and spiritualism.

350. The old contrast between 'spirit' and 'letter' lives on in a comment by John Saltmarsh: 'If so to say we serve not the oldnesse of the Letter, but in the newnesse of the Spirit: If to say... We are not under the Law, but under Grace... If this be Antinomianism, I am one of that sort of Antinomians', *An End of One Controversie*, 1646, 116, cited in Solt, op.cit., 28.

351. In *Works*, Columbia ed., VI, 1-41; cf. esp. Barker, *Milton*, 217ff.

352. Op.cit., 6f.

353. Op.cit., 20.

354. Op.cit., 28ff.

355. Op.cit., 28.

356. Op.cit., 18.

357. Op.cit., 42-100; cf. esp. Barker, op.cit., 228ff. – For the background and the

prior history to this idea of Milton's cf. also Howard Schultz, *Milton and Forbidden Knowledge*, 1955, 194ff. It is particularly worth noting that the same devaluation of clergy trained in the university as a 'mercenary and hireling ministry' in contrast to true enlightenment of the spirit can also be found in Roger Williams, in his pamphlet, 'The Hireling Ministry None of Christ'(1652), now in *Complete Writings* VII, [147]-[187]; cf. also Barker, *Milton*, 231f.

358. Masson, *Life*, V, 615f., gives a vivid account of the consequences which would follow the implementation of this unrealistic request: 'Why, there will be a flutter of consternation, of course, through some ten thousand or twelfe thousand parsonages; ten thousand or twelfe thousand clerical gentlemen will stare bewilderedly for a while at their wives' faces...'

359. 'a partie, a distinct order in the commonwealth, bred up for divines in babling schooles and fed at the publick cost,' op.cit., 98.

360. Op.cit., 98.

361. Op.cit., 99.

362. Op.cit., 93.

363. In respect of the university Milton goes on to say: 'What it may conduce to other arts and sciences, I dispute not now', ibid.

364. Op.cit., 75.

365. It is significant that Milton should make this request as a Humanist!

366. Op.cit., 96.

2. Lord Herbert of Cherbury

1. There is a detailed account of the life and teachings of Herbert in M.Rossi, *La vita, le opere, i tempi di Eduardo Herbert di Chirbury*, 3 vols., 1947; cf. also the review by M.H.Fisch, *JP* 46, 1949, 195-203 (the earlier work by C.de Remusat, *Lord Herbert de Cherbury*, 1874, is out of date, cf. also the comment by Rossi, op.cit., I, VI). Cf. also C.G.Grundig, *Geschichte und wahre Beschaffenheit derer heutigen Deisten und Freydencker*, 1748, 19ff.; Lechler, *Geschichte des englischen Deismus*, 1841 reprinted 1965, 36ff.; also more recently Sina, *Ragione*, 147ff., and especially R.D.Bedford, *The Defence of Truth. Herbert Cherbury and the Seventeenth Century*, 1979; cf. also D.Braun, *De vera religione. Zum Verhältnis von Natur und Gnade bei Herbert of Cherbury und Thomas Hobbes*, Abhandlungen aus der Pädagogischen Hochschule Berlin I, 1974, 81-120.

2. *The Life and Raigne of King Henry the Eight*, 1649 (written 1634-39, cf. Rossi, op.cit., II, 474). The speech, 293-6 (also printed in H.R.Hutcheson [ed.], *Lord Herbert of Cherbury's De Religione Laici*, 1944, app.A), also touches on the problem of religions and sects.

3. Op.cit., I, VI.

4. The orthodox theologian Christian Kortholt from Kiel already contributed to that by ranking him with Hobbes and Spinoza among the 'three deceivers' (adopting a theory contained in the anonymous work of religious criticism *De tribus impostoribus, Anno MDCIIC. Von den drei Betrügern*, 1598 [edited with an introduction by G.Bartsch, translated by R.Walter, 1960] which, however, referred to Moses, Jesus and Mohammed).

5. Rossi, op.cit., I, VI, points out that his writings were not printed again for centuries. G.Gawlick has provisionally remedied this bad state of affairs with three facsimile reprints: E. Lord Herbert of Cherbury, *De Veritate, Ed.Tertia. De Causis Errorum. De Religione Laici. Parerga* (reprints of the editions of 1645), 1966; id., *De Religione Gentilium errorumque apud eos causis* (reprint of the 1663 edition), 1967; id., *A Dialogue between A Tutor and his Pupil* (reprint of the edition of 1768), 1971. However, there is a dispute between Rossi, op.cit., III, 315ff., and Gawlick, Introduction to the new impression, IXff., whether the last work should be attributed to

Herbert. Gawlick, in the Introduction to the new impression of *De Veritate*, VII, complains that since Rossi's work Herbert has again been overshadowed by an interest in the philosophy of history. The recent work by Bedford, *Defence*, is some help here. We still lack a critical edition of his works, although various editions and even preliminary stages in manuscript form have been preserved.

6. For Deism cf. recently above all the contributions by G.Gawlick, 'Deismus',in *HWP*, ed. J.Ritter, 1970ff., II, cols.44-47; id., 'Der Deismus als Grundzug der Religionsphilosophie der Aufklärung', in *Hermann Samuel Reimarus (1694-1768), ein 'bekannter Unbekannter' der Aufklärung in Hamburg* (ed. by the Joachim-Jungius-Gesellschaft), 1973, 15-43; id., Preface in G.V.Lechler, *Geschichte*, V-XXI; also the introductions to the new impressions of the main works of the Deists for which he has been responsible. There are also well-informed surveys of the Deistic debates in E.C.Mossner, *Bishop Butler and the Age of Reason*, 1936, reprinted 1971, 46ff.; G.R.Cragg, *Reason and Authority in the Eighteenth Century*, 1964, 62ff.; G.Gestrich, 'Deismus', *TRE* 8, 1981, 392-406; cf. also J.Orr, *English Deism. Its Roots and its Fruits*, 1934. Lechler's work is still basic to an account of the outward and inward developments of the movement.

7. Bedford, *Defence*, esp. 239f., guards against characterizing Herbert as a Deist, which derives from the old polemic against him. In fact his aims were quite different from those of the later Deists, although he had prepared the way for them. The first Deist did not appear until 1680, in the person of C.Blount, who rightly or wrongly appealed to Herbert, cf. below, 567 n.9; 523 n.55.

8. First mentioned in a report by P.Viret, *Instruction Chrestienne en la Doctrine de la Loy et de l'Euangile*, 1563, Part II, dedication, fol.V, recto – VI recto (wording also in Gawlick, preface to Lechler, op.cit., VIIIff. ; cf. also id., in *Reimarus*, 19f.). Cf. also 'Origo et fundamenta religionis Christianae. Eine bisher noch unbekannte deistische, antichristliche Schrift aus dem sechzehnten Jahrhundert. Mitgetheilt von A.Gfrörer', *Zeitschrift für die historische Theologie* 6/2, 1836, 180-259, discovered in Halle by J. Olearius in 1587.

9. The assumption that Herbert could be dependent on the last Italian Renaissance philosopher Thomasso Campanella seemed particularly attractive: thus above all A.Carlini, 'Herbert di Cherbury e la scuola di Cambridge', *RRAL* ser.5a, 26, 1917, (273-357) 308, for whom 'tutta la filosofia herbertiana..., specialmente per la parte metafisica, è una schierra derivazione campanelliana'. But cf. Rossi, *Alle fonti del deismo e del materialismo moderno*, 1942, 10f.; id., *Chirbury*, I, 284f. He points out above all Carlini's chronological mistakes (Herbert wrote *De Veritate* long before the appearance of Campanella's main works). The discussion has been recently taken up in an extended form: D.P.Walker, *The Ancient Theology*, 1972, 164-93, thinks he has unmasked Herbert in his work *De religione gentilium* as an adherent of the ancient Orphic-Gnostic astral religion, as were Telesio, Bruno and Campanella. But cf. Bedford, *Defence*, 178ff. It is important that Herbert in no way thought in pantheistic terms, although on occasion he came very close to pantheism, cf. Bedford, op.cit., 103. Campanella could at most have been an influence on Herbert's late work *De Religione Gentilium*, cf. Walker, op.cit., 188f., and see below.

10. Cf. esp. Rossi, *Alle fonti*, 12ff.; id., *Chirbury*, I, 289ff. In contrast e.g. to the course proposed by H.Scholz, *Die Religionsphilosophie des Herbert von Cherbury*, 1914, of drawing attention to literal points of dependence in Herbert on all possible writers, ancient and modern, he refers to the need to think in much broader terms: 'deve considerare grandi movimenti di pensiero ed i motivi permanenti che possono avere influito sui deisti di tutti le epoche' (*Alle fonti*, 12).

11. This, too, is a traditional Humanist theme and in no way simply the consequence of his experiences when studying in Oxford, as Gawlick, Introduction to Cherbury, *De Veritate*, VIII, supposes.

12. Cf. Rossi, *Chirbury*, I, 278ff.; also Gawlick, Introduction to Cherbury, *De Veritate*, XXII: 'Herbert plays hardly any part in the development of empirical knowledge prepared for and expected by Bacon; he lived as it were in the other hemisphere of the intellectual world.'

13. Cf. Rossi, *Chirbury*, I, 291: 'Aristoteles fu senza dubbio la base fondamentale del pensiero di Herbert... Potrei quasi dire senz'altro che la filosofia di Herbert, all' ingrosso, non è che una forma degenere di aristotelismo modificato qua è la dall'inserzione di testi stoiche e platoniche.' – Cf. also Gawlick, op.cit., XIX; Bedford, *Defence*, 54f.,66.

14. Cf. R.G.Kottich, *Die Lehre von den angeborenen Ideen seit Herbert von Cherbury*, Berlin diss. 1917. However, the latter conception misses Herbert's intentions: Herbert is not concerned with the *ideae innatae* as such but with capacities for knowledge innate in all men on the basis of common notions, cf. Bedford, op.cit., 74ff., esp. 78.

15. For the role of Cicero cf. e.g. T.Zielinski, *Cicero im Wandel der Jahrhunderte*, ⁴1929, reprinted 1967, specifically on Deism, 210ff.; G.Gawlick, 'Cicero and the Enlightenment', in *Studies on Voltaire and the Eighteenth Century*, 25, 1963, 657-62.

16.The Neoplatonic conception of the *instinctus naturalis* as the basis of knowledge produces an approach of which Rossi can say 'che la sua gnoseologia ha, in fondo, base religiosa... – e il suo deismo... ha qualcosa di mistico.' *Chirbury*, I, 424. Cf. also *Alle fonti*, 21ff.; Bedford, op.cit., 81.

17. See above, 292f.

18. *Veritatem inter objecta & facultates conformitatem summe conditionalem comperimus*, *De Veritate*, ed. Gawlick, 4. *Universa igitur Veritatis nostrae doctrina, ad probam facultatum conformationem reducitur quas varias in se ipso (juxta objectorum differentias) unusquisque comperiet*, ibid., 6, etc.; Bedford, op.cit., 74, recognizes one of the basic presuppositions of Herbert's system in his assumption that all men have the same understanding and the same capacity for knowing the truth.

19. Op.cit., 3. Cf. also 206: *Facultatum autem prima in omni homine (immo & in universo) sit Instinctus ille Naturalis, qui circa propriam conservationem uniuscujusque individui, speciei & generis versatur...*

20. *proinde & Facultatem illam quae Beatitudinem aeternam appetit, cum omni homine insit, frustra dari non posse*, op.cit., 4. Cf. also the continuation of the quotation in the previous note: *...objectorum autem ultimum sit Beatitudo illa aeterna, cujus gratia caetera quaecunque bona expetuntur (reliquis Facultatibus & Objectis intercedentibus)...Totis facultatibus intermediis rite conformatis, ipsa conformatur Beatitudo aeterna*. Cf. Rossi, *Chirbury*, I, 362.

21. Op.cit., 2.

22. Cf. op.cit., 122: *Impie igitur dicitur, Naturam sive Providentiam rerum communem, & Gratiam sive Providentiam rerum particularem in Antithesi positas esse, vel inter se pugnare, cum utraeque a Deo Opt.Max. proficiscantur*. In the *Appendix ad Sacerdotes* (for its origin, cf. Gawlick, Introduction to Cherbury, *De Veritate*, XXXVf.) the question is raised right at the beginning: *An alius verus, ac idem Optimus Maximusq; Deus, aut Pater Communis ab omni humano genere recte vocari possit quam qui Providentia Vniversali utens, cunctis hominibus ita consulit, ut una cum appetitione status aeterni beatioris, quam illorum animis indidit, Media poro quaedam communia, commoda, efficaciaq; ad statum illum consequendum subministret?*

23. P.Gassendi, *Ad Librum E.Edoardi Herberti Angli, De Veritate, Epistola*, in *Opera Omnia*, 1658, reprinted 1964, III, 411-19. Cf. also Rossi, *Chirbury*, I, 485ff.; Gawlick, Introduction to Cherbury, *De Veritate*, XIIf.; Bedford, *Defence*, 55. Gassendi had already been very critical in a letter to E.Diodati (printed in *Correspondance du P. Marin Mersenne*, ed. C. de Waard, 1955, IV, 337; also in Rossi, op.cit., III, app.XVI, 435ff.).

24. It is Stoic insofar as it begins from the harmony between nature and reason, and Neoplatonic insofar as it takes into account an ascent from the lower, material spheres to the highest goods. Cf. Rossi, *Chirbury*, I, 402f.

25. Rossi, *Alle fonti*, 39ff., esp. 54f.; cf. also id., *Chirbury*, I, 407: 'Quindi, base del conoscere non è la verità ma il bene. La deontologia precede la gnoseologia; o meglio, il conoscere è soltanto una forma subordinata della nostra ricerca istintiva della felicità eterna.' Cf. also Bedford, *Defence*, 77.

26. A comparison with the Cambridge Platonists is particularly instructive, cf. above, 172ff.

27. Cf. the comment quoted on 519.n.4 above. Recently G.Gawlick has repeatedly stressed in his various accounts of Deism that Herbert was in no way hostile to revelation in principle, and could certainly have accepted it, particularly in its English form.

28. In the 1645 edition (ed. Gawlick) they are on 208ff. For the original version of 1633 cf. Rossi, *Chirbury*, I, 535 n.1.

29. For the individual statements, their variations in Herbert and their implications, cf. Rossi, op.cit., 537ff.

30. For the way in which he explained polytheism in 1633, cf. Rossi, op.cit., 537 and n.3; 541 n.13.

31. Cf. *De Veritate*, ed. Gawlick, 212: *Inde Divina illa Religio... non solum ob beneficia ex ipsa providentia rerum communi collata, sed ob ea etiam quae ex gratia, sive providentia rerum particulari impendebantur, ubique gentium sancita est.*

32. Cf. ibid.: *Inde...non solum orari, sed exorari posse Numen illud coeleste ex facultatibus omni homini sano et integro insitis creditum est.*

33. Cf. op.cit., 213: *...quia tamen cultus ille Divini Numinis ab omni saeculo receptus, doctrinam illam de Gratia sive Providentia rerum particulari necessario infert, ideo doctrinam Gratiae, sive Providentiae rerum particularis tanquam Notitiam Communem proponimus.*

34. He brushes aside the external forms, like polytheism earlier, with the opening remark: *De ritibus, ceremoniis, traditionibus sive scriptis, sive non scriptis, Revelationibus etc. minime conventum est...*, op.cit., 215.

35. Cf. Rossi, *Chirbury*, I, 496, 518f.

36. It is not fortuitous that the Christian *peccata* is replaced by the ancient word *scelera*.

37. Cf. also Gawlick, in *Reimarus*, op.cit., 24f.

38. S.Lee (ed.), *The Autobiography of Edward, Lord Herbert of Cherbury*, ²1906, 133f.

39. For this see most recently Gawlick, Introduction to *De Veritate*, XIV-XVI; Bedford, *Defence*, 156f.

40. Reprinted most recently in Gawlick, op.cit., n.15 and XLIIIf.

41. Thus *providentia communis* and *providentia particularis* have a common beginning; in my view Gawlick does not take this sufficiently into account and as a result does not give an adequate definition of the role of revelation in Herbert's system: cf. also in *Reimarus*, 22-24. Bedford, op.cit., 173ff., demonstrates in detail that Herbert very much thought of himself as a Christian. However, this was a rationalistic Christianity with an 'Arminian' stamp. Central Christian doctrines like justification and redemption through the cross of Christ are alien to him.

42. Cf. above, 519f. n.5.

43. Op. cit., 181.

44. As a model he particularly used G.J.Vossius, *De Theologia Gentili et Physiologia Christiana, sive de Origine ac Progressu Idololatriae*, 1642ff. (³1675); he also presented the work to the leading humanist for his approval before publication, which was planned, but not carried out, in his lifetime. Cf. Rossi, *Chirbury*, III, 108ff.; 238ff.; Gawlick, Introduction to *De Religione Gentilium*, XIff.

45. *De Religione Gentilium*, 3f.

46. Cf. op.cit., 158: *Summum tamen aliquem extare, & semper extitisse Deum, neque apud Sapientes, neque apud ipsos insipientes dubium (puto) fuit.*

47. Cf. ch.XV, op.cit., 184ff. Rossi, *Chirbury*, III, 148, points out that Herbert took over the description of the twelve virtues from the usual classical sources, but described them in accordance with his own basic principles.

48. *Quibus etiam inventis me foeliciorem Archimede quovis existimavi*, op.cit., 218.

49. Cf. op.cit., 168: *Quum Dei summi attributa supra allata inter Gentiles recepta essent, callidum (puto) irrepsit sacerdotum genus, qui... e re sua esse putaverant, ut alios huic summo Numini adjungerent Deos... Ex pluribus quippe Diis potius, quam ex uno aliquo quantumvis maximo obstringi populares animos censebant... Plus porro utilitatis stipendiique ex variis ritibus, ceremoniis, religionumque sacris... accessurum sibi persuadebant, quam si omnes omnium hominum aetates eadem pietatis & virtutis officia exercerent.* For Herbert's move towards anticlericalism, which he dates to the years 1637-1639, cf. Rossi, *Chirbury*, III, 47ff.

50. Gawlick, Introduction to *De Religione Gentilium*, n.5, enumerates some of the typical phrases about the deception and dishonesty of priests which appear throughout the work.

51. Cf. op.cit., 2: *...animum porro ad investigandum adjeci, an e Gentilium superstitionum glomere filum aliquod veritatis extricari daretur, quo semetipsos e Labyrintho errorum illorum expedirent.*

52. Cf. above 427 n.174.

53. Cf. the inclusion of Herbert's *De Religione Gentilium* in the tradition of *prisca theologia* (cf. op.cit., 1n.1) by Walker, *Ancient Theology*, 164-93, esp. 175ff. Gawlick, Introduction to *De Religione Gentilium*, VIIIf., criticizes Herbert's thought for having wrongly defined the relationship between idea and phenomenon in religion, in that 'he regarded the idea of religion as something empirically given which stood at the beginning of history' and thus interpreted this relationship 'as a historical process which had the character of a history of decline', whereas 'the idea of God and religion is not given but enjoined' on human reason. This criticism (rightly distinguished from an attitude of wanting to know better, which overlooks the presuppositions of the thought of Herbert's time) itself comes from an idealistic starting point, as we can see.

54. Ed. Gawlick, 127ff.

55. What was evidently meant to be a preliminary study, written in English with the same title (MS 5295 E of the National Library of Wales), was published by H.G.Wright in *MLR* 28, 1933, 295-307. Blount's work *Religio Laici* is evidently dependent on this version. Cf. most recently Gawlick, op.cit., 59. For the problem of this manuscript cf. also M.Rossi, in *Transactions of the Edinburgh Bibliographical Society*, 4, 1957, 45-52; also Gawlick, Introduction to Herbert, *A Dialogue*, XXVf.

56. Ed. Gawlick, 155ff.

57. Cf. Rossi, *Chirbury*, III, 55f., and App. XXIX, 504ff.; Gawlick, op.cit., XXXVI.

58. The increasing prominence of the laity, another Humanist ideal which Herbert takes up, was also introduced in 1645 in *De Veritate*, cf. Gawlick, op.cit., XXXV.

59. For the origin of the concept, as a term for the 'man in the street', in Job 21.29, cf. Rossi, *Chirbury*, III, 53 n.10.

60. *...videndum...quid Rationi rectae, probae scilicet Facultatum Conformationi, quid Fidei porro circa praeterita existimetur congruum...*, op. cit., 134.

61. Op.cit., 135.

62. Cf. above 519 n.4.

63. Op.cit., 13, 105, 258, 271; cf.6.

64. Op.cit., 7.

65. Cf. op.cit., 8, where the teacher asks the pupil: 'Why should you require a more ample religion, when the five articles alone will give you a just exercise for

your whole life, while thus you either think good thoughts, speak good words, or do good actions; and would you not think your time thus better employed, then in studying of controversy...?'

66. Op.cit., 66f.

67. Op.cit., 67f.

68. Op.cit., 96.

69. 'Upon which one might make a syllogism thus, what soever God commands is good, just, and fit to be done; but God commended a lying spirit in the manner above recited, ergo it is good, just, and fit to be done', op.cit., 87.

70. Op.cit., 88.

71. Op.cit., 78. For the theme cf. G.Gawlick, 'Abraham's Sacrifice of Isaak viewed by the English Deists', in *Studies on Voltaire and the Eighteenth Century* 57, 1967, 577-600.

72. Op.cit., 3.

73. Op.cit., 84.

74. Op.cit., 7f. Bedford, *Defence*, esp. 211ff., points out that Herbert uses this approach as a basis for the idea of tolerance, for which he is similarly a very early witness.

75. Op.cit., 63. According to D.Braun, *De vera religione*, esp. 86f., 104ff., in his main work Herbert also wanted to allow the possibility, alongside the *providentia rerum communis*, of a special revelation, albeit subjectively limited and therefore not really capable of being handed down; cf. especially the quotation from *De Veritate*, 1, id., 87 n.14.

76. Op.cit., 104.

77. Gawlick, op.cit., VI.

78. Cf. above, 512 n.247. For Platonist metaphysics in Herbert cf. further Bedford, *Defence*, 87ff.

79. This is true of his system; for his personal religion, cf. above, 189.

3. *Thomas Hobbes*

1. For his life cf. above all J.Aubray, *Brief Lives 1669-1696*, ed. A.Clark, 1898, I, 321-403; also the more recent accounts by G.C.Robertson, *Hobbes*, 1886, and above all F. Tönnies, *Thomas Hobbes. Leben und Lehre*, ³1925, reprinted 1971, 1ff. Cf. also W.Röd, 'Thomas Hobbes (1588-1679)', in O.Höffe (ed.), *Klassiker der Philosophie*, I, Munich 1981, 280-300.

2. There has rightly been talk of a 'Hobbes renaissance': I.Fetscher, Introduction to *Der Leviathan*, 1966, LXII. Bibliographies above all in H.MacDonald – M.Hargreaves, *Thomas Hobbes. A Bibliography*, 1952; H.Mizuta, *The List of Works of and relating to Thomas Hobbes*, 1954; A.Pacchi, 'Bibliografia Hobbesiana dal 1840 ad oggi', *RCSF* 17, 1962, 528-47; R.Stumpf, 'Hobbes im deutschen Sprachraum – Eine Bibliographie', in *Hobbes-Forschungen*, ed. R.Koselleck and R.Schnur, 1969, 287-300.

3. The following surveys of research may be recommended: Carl Schmitt, 'Die vollendete Reformation. Bemerkungen und Hinweise zu neuen Leviathan-Interpretationen', *Der Staat* 4, 1965, 51-69; B.Willms, 'Einige Aspekte der neueren englischen Hobbes-Literatur', ibid. 1, 1962, 93-106; id., 'Von der Vermessung des Leviathan. Aspekte neuerer Hobbes-Literatur', ibid. 6, 1967, 75-100, 220-36; id. 'Der Weg des Leviathan. Die Hobbes-Forschung von 1968-1978', *Der Staat*, Beiheft 3, 1979; W.H.Greenleaf, 'Hobbes: The Problem of Interpretation', in Koselleck and Schnur, *Hobbes-Forschungen*, 9-31 = M.Cranston and R.S.Peters (eds.), *Hobbes and Rousseau: A Collection of Critical Essays*, 1972, 5-36. Cf. also I.Fetscher, op.cit., IX-LXIV, and the collective discussion by U.Weiss, 'Hobbes' "Rationalismus": Aspekte der deutschen Hobbes-Rezeption', *PhJ* 85, 1978, 167-96.

4. In the background is the view expressed by H.R.Trevor-Roper, that in his time Hobbes stood completely 'outside the main stream of English political thought': 'Thomas Hobbes', in *Historical Essays*, 1957 (233-8), 233. Similarly also Fetscher, op.cit., IX: 'Thomas Hobbes the political philosopher occupies a lonely position at the centre of the Western philosophical tradition.' In an earlier period of research this view was virtually all-prevailing, cf. e.g. G.P.Gooch, *Political Thought in England: Bacon to Halifax*, 1951, 23: 'No man of this time occupied such a lonely position in the world of thought.' C.Schmitt, op.cit., 53, rightly affirms against this: 'It goes without saying that first of all we must make clear what Hobbes really said. But the next question is what he really meant. That cannot be answered without a discussion of the history of his time.' The connection is seen most clearly by P.J.Johnson, 'Hobbes's Anglican Doctrine of Salvation', in R.Ross, H.W.Schneider and T.Waldmann (eds.), *Thomas Hobbes in His Time*, 1974, 102-25, cf. below. In addition to the connections mentioned below reference should also be made to the surprising dependence of Hobbes on the arguments of the propagandists who from 1649 onwards were arguing for loyalty to the new regime; this has been investigated by Q.Skinner, 'Thomas Hobbes et la défense du pouvoir *de facto*', *RPFE* 163, 1973, 131-54.

5. Thus the two last books of *Leviathan* are omitted in the German edition in Rowohlt Classics, 1965, edited by P.C.Mayer-Tasch: 'They would be of extremely limited interest for a modern edition', op.cit., 287. Fetscher is more cautious and leaves things open: 'It is extremely difficult to decide whether Hobbes himself thought his arguments based on his accounts of the history of Israel and the doctrines of the New Testament to be of fundamental importance. At all events, his contemporaries regarded him as an atheist, and were not prepared to give credit to his protestations to the contrary.'

5a. Cf. e.g. M.Missner, 'Hobbes' Method in Leviathan', *JHI* 38, 1977, (607-21) 621: 'It is generally believed that the latter half of the Leviathan was written just to convince a certain type of unphilosophically minded audience that existed in Hobbes' day...'

6. One example of this is the most fundamental work of this kind, which at the same time criticizes previous attempts and takes them further: K.H. Kodalle, *Thomas Hobbes – Logik der Herrschaft und Vernunft des Friedens*, 1972. On it see above, 204.

7. Kodalle, op.cit., 70ff., 115ff., is again quite ready to do this, but in part he lacks the grounding for an adequate judgment. On the other hand, Z.Lubieński, *Die Grundlagen des ethisch-politischen Systems von Hobbes*, 1932, clearly recognizes the significance of revealed religion for Hobbes' system, at least as a form of apologetics against Catholic and Protestant theologians: 'The fact that he gives them so much space within his system shows the great importance which he attaches to theological arguments.' Op.cit., 208f.

8. That is already true for Diestel, op.cit., cf. index s.v.Hobbes, and similarly also for Kraus, *Geschichte*, 57ff. J.Coppens, *De Geschiedkundige Ontwikkelingsgang*, does not mention Hobbes at all. Kraeling, *The Old Testament since the Reformation*, 1955, 44f., is a prime example of the way in which he can be caricatured: 'He sought a secular state, emancipated from all ecclesiastical influence and held that whatever the state sanctions is good. Religion, he taught, is fear of invisible powers whose existence is invented, or just accepted on the basis of tradition.' Cf. also the comments in the introduction, 9ff.

9. An amazing degree of acuteness and detailed study has been devoted to the riddle of Hobbes by his interpreters.

10. By contrast, little attention has been paid to his natural philosophy, which falls outside our theme. Cf. e.g. F.Brandt, *Thomas Hobbes' Mechanical Conception of Nature*, 1928; A.Pacchi, *Convenzione e ipotesi nella formazione della filosofia naturale di Thomas Hobbes*, 1965. The recently edited manuscript, *Critique du De Mundo de Thomas White*,

ed. J.Jacquot et H.W.Jones, 1973 (ET *Thomas White's De Mundo Examined*, translated H.W.Jones, 1976), belongs largely in this sphere, but also goes over into anthropology and social doctrine. For the work cf. also E.G.Jacoby, 'The "Anti-White" of Thomas Hobbes', *AGP* 59, 1977, 156-66. For the transition from natural philosophy to social philosophy see also M.Diesselhorst, *Ursprünge des modernen Systemdenkens bei Hobbes*, 1968, and T.A.Spragen, Jr, *The Politics of Motion: The World of Thomas Hobbes*, 1973 (on the relationship between the world-view of Hobbes and Aristotle and the revolution brought about in this area by approaches in political science).

11. The beginning of such a division is offered, e.g., by Greenleaf, op.cit., 9ff. – In any case, it is impossible to consider all the literature here. F.S.McNeilly, *The Anatomy of Leviathan*, 1968, 5, comments: 'One has to decide whether one is writing a book about Hobbes or a book about books about Hobbes.'

12. Cf. above all, S.I.Mintz, *The Hunting of Leviathan*, 1962; J.Bowle, *Hobbes and his Critics*, 1951 (reprinted 1962), has more reservations. There is a more general account of the cultural climate of the period in J.Redwood, *Reason, Ridicule and Religion. The Age of Enlightenment in England, 1660-1750*, 1976, 70ff. A well-known contemporary criticism by J.Lowde, *A Discourse Concerning the Nature of Man*, 1964, appeared in a reprint in 1979.

13. From a methodological perspective, this can also be described as the psychological approach, cf. Morris, 'Gauthier on Hobbes' Moral and Political Philosophy', *PPR*, 33, 1972/73, 387-92.

14. Thus e.g. Bowle, op.cit., 42: 'He was a radical sceptic, with a cynical view of human nature. If he was not an atheist, he was certainly an agnostic.' Similarly G.P.Gooch, *Hobbes*, 1940, reprinted 1978, 20: 'Though he professed to be an orthodox Christian, he was entirely destitute of religious sentiment.' Cf. also R.Polin, *Politique et philosophie chez Thomas Hobbes*, 1953, XVf.,135,140. By contrast, B.Willms, *Weg*, 115, says that there are at least the beginnings of a consensus in modern scholarship that the answer to the question whether Hobbes was an atheist 'can be passed over in connection with his philosophy'. This, however, amounts to a refusal to consider a perspective which is by no means unimportant to the understanding of Hobbes generally.

15. Cf. above, 519 n.4.

16. Q.Skinner, 'The Ideological Context of Hobbes' Political Thought' , *HistJ* 9, 1966, 286-317 = 'The Context of Hobbes' Theory of Political Obligation', in M.Cranston and R.S.Peters (eds), *Hobbes and Rousseau: A Collection of Critical Essays*, 1972, 109-42; id., 'Thomas Hobbes and His Disciples in France and England', *CSSH* 8, 1966, 153-67.

17. On this cf. Fetscher, op.cit., XIIIf.

18. Thus Hobbes himself in 'Foreword to the Reader', in the second edition of *De cive. Opera Philosophica quae latine scripsit omnia*, ed. Molesworth, II, 1839, reprinted 1966 (= *OL*), 151; cf. also *Vom Menschen – Vom Bürger*, ed. G.Gawlick, 1959, (²1966, reprinted 1977) 71f.

19. Extensive monographs from recent times on this question (in addition to numerous more general works which discuss Hobbes only in passing) are those by R.Peters, *Hobbes*, 1956, reprinted 1967, M.M.Goldsmith, *Hobbes' Science of Politics*, 1966, and J.W.N.Watkins, *Hobbes' System of Ideas* (1965), ²1973. Cf. also F.R.Hrubi, 'Leviathan und der Tod Gottes', *WissWeltb* 24, 1971, 222-30; C.H.Hinnant, *Thomas Hobbes*, 1977, and e.g. M.Karskens, 'Thomas Hobbes over vrijheid, wet en recht', *Wisg.Persp. op Maatsch. en Wetensch.* 20, 1979/80, 8-15. One example from most recent times is M.Malherbe, 'La science de l'homme dans la philosophie de Hobbes', *RIPh* 33, 1979, 531-51: he argues that Hobbes' anthropology fits perfectly into his philosophical system, so political anthropology cannot be separated from physics (547). R.M.Lemos, *Hobbes and Locke. Power and Consent*, 1978, 3, takes precisely the opposite

view. According to him, Hobbes' political philosophy and the rest of his political system are to be understood quite separately, and independently of each other. R.Commers, 'Thomas Hobbes and the Idea of Mechanics in Social Sciences and Ethics', *Philosophica* 24, 1979, 147-83, discusses the mechanistic system which Hobbes developed for social and political philosophy as the first consistent system in a series of similar modern ones.

19a. E.g. G.Schedler, 'Hobbes on the Basis of Political Obligation', *JHP* 15, 1977, 165-70, wants to limit the basis for political obligation in Hobbes narrowly to a 'self-preservation ethic'. T.F.Ackerman, 'Two Concepts of Moral Goodness in Hobbes' Ethics', *JHP* 14, 1976, 415-25, also makes Hobbes derive the conventional moral goodness of an action (if it is commanded by the sovereign) from the natural goodness which is based on self-preservation, as the sovereign acts *de jure* on the basis of the authorization of his subjects and therefore ordains only what is necessary for their self-preservation.

19b. The clarification of the terms 'contract' and 'covenant' in Hobbes' definition of cession by M.T. Dalgarno, 'Analysing Hobbes' Contract', *PAS* 76, 1975/6, 209-26, is helpful.

20. J.Vialatoux, *La Cité totalitaire de Hobbes. Théorie naturaliste de la civilisation*, 1935 (²1952). Cf. also J.Mourgeon, *La science du pouvoir totalitaire dans le Leviathan de Hobbes*, 1963.

21. For the Voegelin school cf. Willms, *Der Staat*, 1967, 79 and n.32; 82f. The dissertation by Ilting's pupil F.O.Wolf, *Die neue Wissenschaft des Thomas Hobbes*, 1969, which confines Hobbes to the friend-foe pattern, also ends up in the totalitarian theory, cf. esp. 105. Cf. also G.Manenschijn, *Moraalen eigenbelang bij Thomas Hobbes en Adam Smith*, 1979, ch.I, 5ff. According to F.Viola, 'Totalitarismo e irrazionalismo nella teoria morale di Hobbes', *RIFD* 54, 1977, 76-132; id., *Behemoth o Leviathan? Diritto e obbligo nel pensiero di Hobbes*, 1979, 53ff., 163ff., 255ff., while Hobbes himself was not a totalitarian, his system unintentionally paved the way for later totalitarianism. Cf. also A.Philonenko, 'Hobbes et la légende de la tyrannie', in O.Höffe (ed.), *Thomas Hobbes Anthropologie und Staatsphilosophie*, 1981, 143-62.

22. *Der Leviathan in der Staatslehre des Thomas Hobbes. Sinn und Fehlschlag eines politischen Symbols*, 1938; id., 'Der Staat als Mechanismus bei Hobbes und Descartes', *ARSP* 30, 1936/37, 622-32.

23. Cf. *Leviathan*, 84-97. There is a similar view in R.Koselleck, *Kritik und Krise. Ein Beitrag zur Pathogenese der bürgerlichen Welt*, 1959, esp. 29f.

24. '...such a common power, as may be able to defend them from the invasion of foreigners, and the injuries of one another, and thereby to secure them in such sort, as that by their own industry... they may nourish themselves and live contentedly...' and in which the sovereign only has to act 'in those things which concern the common peace and safety'. *Leviathan*, ch.XVII, in *The English Works*, ed. Molesworth, 1839, reprinted 1966 (= *EW*), Vol.III, 157f. = *Leviathan*, ed. Oakeshott, 1946 (²1957), 112 = paperback (1962; ¹⁴1977), 132. Cf. in this connection also K.Algouin, 'Hobbes' Citizen: His State of Mind When Keeping the Covenant', *PACPA*, 1975, 198-207. J.P.Monteiro, 'Estado e ideologia em Thomas Hobbes', *Rev.Latinoamericana de Phil.* 6, 1980, (37-45) 41, calls Hobbes' state 'proto-burocrático'.

25. 1963. Cf. esp. 160ff.

26. Cf. e.g. Willms, *Der Staat* 6, 1967, 226ff.; C.Schmitt, *Der Staat* 4, 1965, (51-69) 54ff.; Kodalle, op.cit., 21ff. The way in which God is incorporated into Hobbes' political system of the state, interpreted in an absolutist way, in Manenschijn, op.cit., 66ff., cf.88ff., is one-sided.

27. Willms, op.cit. 93.

28. Introduction to Hobbes, *Leviathan*, 1946 (²1957), LVff. = id., *Hobbes on Civil Association*, 1975, (1-74) 60ff.

29. For Hobbes' nominalism cf. above all D.Krook, 'Thomas Hobbes' Doctrine of Meaning and Truth', *Phil* 31, 1956, 3-22.

30. Op.cit., LVII/63.

31. 1964, 186ff., and passim.

32. Op.cit., 154. Cf., similarly, G.C.Kwaad, 'Thomas Hobbes en "Two Concepts of Liberty"', *Wisg. Persp. op Maatsch. en Wetensch.* 20, 1979/80, 23-9.

33. Cf. also the significance of the theme in Willms, *Der Staat*, 1962, 99ff.; *Der Staat*, 1967, 93ff. Cf. also R.C.Grady II, *Political Obligation and Individualism: Hobbes and Locke*, PhD Diss Vanderbilt 1972 (Univ.Microfilm, Ann Arbor), esp.182ff. Tönnies, *Thomas Hobbes*, 222f., understood Hobbes as a 'theoretician of the liberal state'. According to M.A.Cattaneo, 'Hobbes théoricien de l'Absolutisme Eclairé', in *Hobbes-Forschungen*, 199-210, Hobbes is the theoretician of enlightened absolutism. Cf. also Schmitt, *Der Staat*, 1965, 59f., and recently M.Bianca, *Dalla natura alla società. Saggio sulla filosofia politico sociale di Thomas Hobbes*, 1979, cf. 9ff., 43f., etc.: Hobbes' political philosophy is the theory of the liberation of man from his natural dispositions, and the state of nature which is a constant threat to him, through the formation of a society which gives him the possibility of personal development in a state of peace. This interpretation has an abstruse form in Kodalle, op.cit., 188; in the light of the 'development of the awareness of subjectivity' he settles on democracy as the ideal form of the state, following Hobbes' approach. According to F.M.Coleman, *Hobbes and America. Exploring the Constitutional Foundations*, 1977, Hobbes is the theoretician of liberal democracy and the spiritual ancestor of the American constitution, rather than Locke, who was merely the popularizer of these ideas.

33a. Therefore any interpretation which seeks to refute Hobbes by the argument that an anarchistic society could also live peacefully (thus D.B.Suits, 'On Hobbes' Argument for Government', *Reason Papers* 4, 1978, 1-16) is also wide of the mark.

34. 1962. Cf. also id., 'Hobbes' Bourgeois Man', in *Hobbes Studies*, ed. K.C.Brown, 1965, 169-83 (originally under the title 'Hobbes Today', *CJEPS* 11, 1945, 524-34). For the work cf. also I. Berlin, 'Hobbes, Locke and Professor Macpherson', *PolQ* 35, 1964, 444-68.

35. Op.cit., 16. Cf. also R.W.Alexander, 'The Myth of Power: Hobbes' Leviathan', *JEGP* 70, 1971, (31-50) 39f.; G.Hungerland, 'Hobbes' Theory of Signification', *JHP* 11, 1973, (459-82) 465. For the social approach cf. also H.Willms, *Die Antwort des Leviathan*, 1970, 43-75.

35a. Op.cit., 44f. (with examples).

35b. K.Thomas, 'The Social Origins of Hobbes' Political Thought', *Hobbes-Studies*, ed. K.C. Brown, 185-236, makes it clear that Hobbes' social standards were very complex and also included Aristotelian ideals.

36. Cf. above, 92ff. Also the criticism by Kodalle, op.cit., 36f., of Macpherson. – B.Willms, *Antwort*, 72, is much more cautious and therefore much closer to reality: 'It is impossible to give an account of the many dimensions in the intertwining of confessional positions with social interests and claims to political supremacy.'

37. 'The Moral Life in the Writings of Thomas Hobbes', in *Rationalism in Politics*, 1962, 248-300 = id., *Civil Association*, 75-131. The interpretation by B.Barry, 'Warrender and His Critics', *Phil.* 43, 1968, 117-37 = M.Cranston/R.S.Peters (eds.), *Hobbes and Rousseau: A Collection of Critical Essays*, 1972, 37-65, which finds the basis for the phrase 'having an obligation to do x' in Hobbes only formally on the assignment of a right by the person concerned. There is a famous, though disputed, interpretation by L.Strauss, *Natural Right and History*, 1953 (^{5}1965), 166-202, according to which Hobbes transformed the Epicurean tradition in an idealistic sense and in this way gave it a political significance. 'He tries to instil the spirit of political idealism into the hedonistic tradition. He thus became the creator of political hedonism...', op.cit., 169. Cf. his similar verdict on Locke, above, 247. Cf. already the earlier form of this

idea in id., *The Political Philosophy of Hobbes. Its Basis and Its Genesis*, 1936 (reprinted 1952, ⁴1963; German *Hobbes' Politische Wissenschaft* [original version of 1935], 1965).

38. Op.cit., 263/92.

39. Cf. op.cit., 266ff./95ff. Cf. also J.W.N.Watkins, *Hobbes' System of Ideas*, 1973, 129. N.Bobbio, *Introducione alle Opere Politiche di Thomas Hobbes*, I, 1959, takes a similar position, as does C.Lafer, 'Hobbes e la filosofia do direito', *Rev. latinoamer. de Fil.* 6, 1980, 17-25. Cf. also the other contributions to the Sao Paulo symposium in this journal, especially the final contribution: M.Reale, 'O legado de Hobbes a filosofia di direito e do estado', ibid., 165-9. According to A.Ollero, 'Hobbes y la interpretacion del derecho', *RIFD* 54, 1977, 45-67, also, Hobbes has a voluntaristic conception of law.

40. Willms, *Der Staat*, 1967, 222, thinks that Oakeshott has not got as far as connecting morality with the problem of politics. We shall try to illuminate this question from yet another angle. J.M. Brown has made a sharp attack on Oakeshott; he calls this theory which makes morality dependent on the sovereign 'disastrous': J.M.Brown, 'A Note on Professor Oakeshott's Introduction to the Leviathan', *PolSt* 1, 1953, 53-64; id., 'Hobbes, A Rejoinder', ibid. 2, 1954, 168-72. Cf. also the criticism by H.Warrender, *The Political Philosophy of Hobbes*, 1957 reprinted 1961, 1966, 75-8, and M.A.Cattaneo, 'Alcune osservationi sul concetto di giustizia in Hobbes', *RIFD* 39, 1962, 87-93.

41. A.E.Taylor, 'The Ethical Doctrine of Hobbes', *Phil.*13, 1938, 406-24 = *Hobbes Studies*, ed. Brown, 35-55 (with an introduction by S.M.Brown, 31-34) = *Hobbes' Leviathan: Interpretation and Criticism*, ed. B.H.Baumrin, 1969, 35-48. However, it should be noted (as Greenleaf in particular points out) that earlier publications already saw the roots of Hobbes' thought in mediaeval models. 'The ground was well prepared, then, when Taylor published his now well-known paper.' Mention should be made in this connection above all of F.Tönnies, who was the real founder of the'Taylor theory'(37). Cf. Ilting, Introduction to Tönnies, *Thomas Hobbes*, 13. Cf. there esp. 196ff.

42. Op.cit.

43. Cf. Warrender, op.cit., 213: there are 'two systems in Hobbes' theory, a system of motives, and a system of obligations. The system of motives ends with the supreme principle of self-preservation...; the system of obligations ends with the obligation to obey natural law regarded as the will of God.'

44. Cf. Taylor's well-known statement: 'Hobbes's ethical doctrine proper, disengaged from an egoistic psychology with which it has no logically necessary connection, is a very strict deontology, curiously suggestive, though with interesting differences, of some of the characteristic theses of Kant.' *Hobbes Studies*, 37. G.Bellussi, 'Considerazioni sul gius-naturalismo di Thomas Hobbes', *RIFD* 39, 1962, 719-44, also argues emphatically that Hobbes' thought is based in natural law.

45. Op.cit., 45.

46. Op.cit., 43. R.M.Lemos, *Hobbes*, above, 526f. n.19, points out that the power of the sovereign is limited to positive legislation only by the basic principle of the natural law, that all law has to contribute to the self-preservation of man.

47. Op.cit., 49. P.E.Moreau, 'Loi divine et loi naturelle selon Hobbes', *RIPh* 33, 1979, 443-51, has recently made very clear the structure in which, according to Hobbes, the natural law which can already be recognized by reason in the natural state is at the same time a divine commandment and as such, like the civil laws which follow from it, is imposed by the sovereign.

48. Thomas Hobbes, *The Elements of Law*, ed. F.Tönnies, 1928, 74 (²1969, 95). For the role of scripture in Hobbes' *Elements of Law* cf. recently also L.Roux, 'Introduction', in T.Hobbes, *Les éléments du droit naturel et politique*, ed. L.Roux, 1977, 45-50.

49. *Hobbes-Studies*, 50. E.P.Burki, *Notes sur le Léviathan de Hobbes*, Annales de

l'Université Jean Moulin. Sér.Droit et Gestion, 1976, Fasc.2, 25-62, emphatically puts forward the view that the norms of natural law are also fundamental to the order which is established by the constitution of the state. Burki stresses the significance of theological argumentation for Hobbes: natural law is grounded on a divine institution. S.R.Sutherland, 'God and Religion in Leviathan', *JTS* 25, 1974, 373-80, is much more restrained: in certain instances (in the case of an oath, in the moral obligation of the sovereign, in international law) we can at least see Hobbes' referring to the will of God. For S.R.Letwin, 'Hobbes and Christianity', *Daed* 105, 1976, 1-21, who to some degree contrasts with Burki, Hobbes' historical contribution consists precisely in the fact that he has detached his system from traditional roots in ancient natural theology, its understanding of the world and its anthropology, and instead of this has made space for a strictly Christian and biblical view of the world.

50. Cf. Warrender, op.cit., 274: 'There exists a considerable gulf between these laws and the principles upon which Hobbes' natural man is motivated to action.' It is also worth noting the solution of M.A.Cattaneo, *Il positivismo giuridico inglese. Hobbes, Bentham, Austin*, 1962, 45ff., who draws a distinction between the level of natural ethics, which is built up on the basic commandment of self-preservation and peace, and the level of the law, dependent on its enactment by the sovereign, which is to be understood in terms of 'typically English juristic positivism'. M.Oakeshott, *Moral Life*, 28ff./118, attempts to explain the division by assuming two different levels of argument in Hobbes: 'an explanation..., which recognizes Hobbes to have two doctrines, one for the initiated... and the other for the ordinary man.' D.P.Gauthier, *The Logic of Leviathan*, 1969, seeks to overcome this alleged division by referring to the eminently practical aim of Hobbes' thinking, in which rational = moral = practical, cf. esp. 28f. His final conclusion is 'that the Hobbesian "moral" system is nothing more than a system of common, or universal, prudence', op.cit., 90. Similarly, id., 'Why Ought One Obey God? Reflections on Hobbes and Locke', *CJP* 7, 1977, 425-46. This definition is quite apt if we put it in the context of Hobbes' humanistic presuppositions, which will be developed later. B.Morris, 'Gauthier on Hobbes' Moral and Political Philosophy', *PPR* 33, 1972/3, 387-92, accuses him of not paying enough attention to the realistic side in Hobbes' approach. Gauthier has recently ('Thomas Hobbes: Moral Theorist', *JPh* 76, 1979) modified his view by supposing that in having the social contract aimed at peace, Hobbes laid the foundation for a conventional egoistic morality, which limited the natural egoism of all against all.

51. 'Hobbes: The Taylor Thesis', *PhRev* 68, 1959, 303-23 = (in two parts): *Hobbes Studies*, ed. K.C.Brown, 31-34, 57-71 = *Hobbes' Leviathan*, ed. Baumrin, 49-66.

52. Introduction to *Leviathan*, LXXII.

53. Op.cit., 16: 'We fully agree with this central theory of Warrender's and the basis for it.' Cf. also 15: 'Warrender's significant book.'

54. Op.cit., 15. However, Kodalle himself hardly goes beyond what he criticizes in Warrender.

55. Cf. Greenleaf, op.cit., 14 n.24.

56. *The Divine Politics of Thomas Hobbes. An Interpretation of Leviathan*, 1964.

57. Op.cit., 100. Hobbes declares in a dedication to Charles II: 'Religion is not philosophy, but law', *EW* VII, V.

58. Op.cit., 4.

59. Hood speaks of 'the way of the conversion into science of the small part of his religious moral thought susceptible of such conversion', op.cit., 41. J.Bernhard, 'Genèse et limites du matérialisme de Hobbes', *Raison Présente* 47, 1978, 41-61, by contrast sees Hobbes being led at the limits of his materialistic system to the problem of the transcendent action of God to which only the biblical historical tradition can

give an answer, cf. esp. 50. K.C.Brown, 'Hobbes' Grounds for Belief in A Deity', *Phil.* 37, 1962, similarly already sees the starting point for Hobbes' belief in God in the 'argument from design'. It is important to recognize that no break in the system was recognizable here even for Newton and his contemporaries (see above, 337f.).

60. Here Hood, op.cit., 70, in particular cites the Latin text, *OL* III, 89: *horum politica pars religionis est.*

61. Hood, op.cit., 68ff., *Leviathan*, ed. Oakeshott, 69ff., 87ff.; *OL* III, 85ff.

62. Cf. n.60.

63. Kodalle, op.cit., 128ff., discusses the same chapter later, with other statements from the same area.

64. Cf. e.g. Greenleaf, op.cit., 16; Kodalle, op.cit., 16ff. Willms, *Der Staat*, 1967, 230ff., and Schmitt, *Der Staat*, 1965, 51ff., are more positive.

65. Kodalle, op.cit., 18f.

66. Thus e.g. 13: 'Hobbes' morality is traditional and Christian. His Scriptural doctrine of civil obedience is a traditional Christian doctrine...' Q.Skinner, Review Article, *HistJ* 7, 1964, (321-33) 330, has rightly recognized that the methodological weakness of Hood's work is to be sought here: 'It can be shown that historical and exegetical consistency cannot fairly be regarded as separate issues.' Here he himself is simply thinking of the connection with the 'discussion about the more general state of ethical and political thinking of the time', op.cit., 331, and not of contemporary theology.

67. *ChH* 29, 1960, 275-97 = *Hobbes Studies*, ed. Brown, 141-68; cf. also id., 'Human Nature and the State in Hobbes', *JHP* 4, 1966, 293-311; also R.Woodfield, 'Hobbes on the Laws of Nature and the Atheist', *RMS* 15, 1971, 34-43. Cf. recently also M.Clive, 'Hobbes parmi les mouvements religieux de son temps', *RSPT* 62, 1978, 41-59.

67a. Koselleck and Schnur, *Hobbes-Forschungen*, 33-52.

68. Especially 'Die vollendete Reformation', a bibliographical survey the title of which already betrays its perspective. For Schmitt's earlier interpretation of Hobbes cf. M.Jänicke, 'Die abgründige Wissenschaft vom Leviathan', *ZPol* NS 16, 1969, 401-15.

69. Text of 1932 with a foreword and three corollaries, 1963, 122.

70. Op.cit., 121. For Hobbes' piety cf. recently also H.W.Schneider, 'The Piety of Thomas Hobbes', in R.Ross, H.W.Schneider and T.Waldmann (eds), *Thomas Hobbes in His Time*, 1974, 84-101.

71. For criticism cf. also Kodalle, op.cit., 19f.; id., 'Carl Schmitt und die neueste Hobbes-Literatur', *PhR* 18, 1972, (116-30) 117f. On the other hand Gauthier can still put forward the view that 'the material content of Hobbes' moral and political theory is independent of any theistic suppositions', and is in principle completely secular (Gauthier, *Logic*, 204f.), though open to the contribution of theistic ideas which do not affect this basic character. The reason for that would be of a purely apologetic kind: 'Christianity is important for Hobbes only in so far as it must be reconciled with his views', op. cit., 187 n.1. M.M.Goldsmith, *Hobbes' Science of Politics*, 1966, who gives a detailed account of Hobbes' argument where it relates to religion (214-27), incorporates it in his overall system, which he believes to have a Galilean basis, and declares: '...religious conflict became so important an obstacle to civil peace that Hobbes thought it necessary to devote half of *Leviathan* to the discussion of religion. Religion could not be ignored, because to control the church was to control the main influence on the formation of public opinion', 226, cf. also 321. According to M.Gavre, 'Hobbes and His Audience: The Dynamics of Theorizing', *AmPolScRev* 68, 1974, (1542-56) 1547ff., Hobbes took up anthropological and theological arguments put forward by Calvin because he wanted to convince the Puritans (Presbyterians) of his royalist standpoint. For Lemos, *Hobbes*, 4f., the reference to

the Christian tradition provides a foundation for Hobbes' political philosophy, which is arrived at independently of it, only as an afterthought. Cf. also B.Gert, Introduction, in *T.Hobbes, Man and Citizen*, 1972 reprinted 1978, 29. Watkins, *System*, 65, is even simpler: the (egoistic) natural law is said by Hobbes to be divinely created because it is natural.

72. But also in opposition to Schmitt, cf. *Antwort*, 177.

73. Op.cit., 176-215.

74. Op.cit., 31.

75. Op.cit., 179.

76. 'Insofar as it was in fact alive in his situation', op.cit., 178.

77. Op.cit., 184. This can also be heard from a neo-Marxist perspective: 'In this situation the possibility of claiming religion as the foundation of a gift of divine grace was a welcome way of creating absolute validity for the crown... Hobbes himself clearly said that such references were to have purely pragmatic value. He regarded it as being necessary, under the pressure of circumstances, to produce a corresponding general awareness, even if subjectively he saw the manipulative element in it' (R.zur Lippe, 'Bürgerliche Subjektivität', in *Autonomie als Selbstzerstörung*, Suhrkamp ed. 749, 1975, 42). Obviously Willms does not have such a bias. P.Manet, *Naissances de la politique moderne. Machiavel, Hobbes, Rousseau*, 1977, esp. 111f., 125ff., similarly explains Hobbes' recourse to the God of the Bible by the compulsion to find a basis for the binding character of the divine commandments in history, in view of the *de facto* impotence of the theoretically almighty God of natural religion.

78. Op.cit., 209. Also in *Weg*, 119f., Willms notes a coincidence of faith and philosophy in the possibility – but Christian faith is only one of the human possibilities for providing a basis for political order, which the system leaves open. R.C.Grady II, 'The Law of Nature in the Christian Commonwealth: Hobbes' Argument for Civil Authority', *Interpretation* (The Hague) 4, 1975, (217-38), 237f., sees Hobbes' arguments for the civil authority from both philosophy and theology as complementary.

79. Op.cit., 183f. This 'fideism' on the part of Hobbes towards scripture and its picture of God, which emerges combined with some theistic approaches, contrasted with Hobbes' denial of the possibility of a knowledge of God through reason, is the theme of R.Hepburn's contribution, 'Hobbes on the Knowledge of God', in M.Cranston and R.S.Peters (eds.), *Hobbes and Rousseau*, 1972, 85-108. Probably rightly, Hepburn discovers logical contradictions in these arguments of Hobbes, but sees his basic approach as a legacy of the Christian tradition.

80. Op.cit., 177.

81. Op.cit., 79.

82. K.M.Kodalle, 'Schmitt', 126.

83. 'But the theologian concerns himself either only with specific subjects, from the exegesis of specific texts to the problem of pastoral praxis, or he concerns himself in specifically theological terms with any kind of subject, i.e. in the light of specific aims of the church or of theology, or simply as a presentation of any kind of subject to those parts of the populace who support his claim...' By contrast Hobbes is 'scientific and physical in his philosophic intent, not from a transcendental perspective, but from an immanent one', op.cit., 177f.

84. *Hobbes*. Cf. also the shorter version, id., 'Subjektivität und Staatskonstitution. Freiheit, "absolute Wahrheit" und das System more geometrico', in R.Schnur (ed.), *Staatsräson. Studien zur Geschichte eines politischen Begriffs*, 1975, 301-23.

85. Op.cit., 13. For criticism cf. also S.Gehrmann, review, *Neue Polit. Lit.* 21, 1976, (516-18) 516.

86. That holds e.g. for *Leviathan*, ch.43, Kodalle, op.cit.,63.

87. One starting-point is the excursus on the idea of the covenant, 70ff. I must retract my earlier judgment on Hobbes over this point, 'Das Arsenal der Bibelkritik des Reimarus', in *Hermann Samuel Reimarus (1694-1768) ein 'bekannter Unbekannter' der Aufklärung*, 1973, (44-65) 60 n.27.

87a. 1980.

87b. Cf. op.cit., 175ff.

87c. Cf. op.cit., 173,179,181.

87d. Cf. op.cit., 31.

87e. Op.cit., 229. Here, too, there is again a reference to the cybernetic model, cf. op.cit., 234 n.243.

87f. He criticizes a series of general accounts for mistaking this particular dimension, op.cit., 235 n.245.

87g. Op.cit., 238. A view which is expressly rejected by Manet, *Naissances*, 125.

87h. Op.cit., 241f.

87i. Op.cit., 242f.

87j. Op.cit., 243ff.

87k. Op.cit., 247ff.

88. Hood, op.cit., 3. W.Förster, *Hobbes*, 30ff., gives a more detailed account of Hobbes' time in Oxford.

89. See 530 n.57 above. Glover, *Human Nature*, 294, rightly refers to the double background of tradition to which Hobbes, like all Anglican thinkers, was obligated: 'Hobbes... is caught between two ultimately irreconcilable traditions: the classic tradition with its emphasis on the unchanging order which is the basis for understanding all flux and change; and the Biblical tradition with its emphasis on freedom, will and the dynamic quality of a world over which a living and acting God is sovereign.'

90. In the sense defined above, 499 n.1. We can find a first step towards this recognition in P.Doyle, 'The Contemporary Background of Hobbes' "State of Nature"', in *Economica* 7, 1927, 336-55, even if by being restricted to a study of the 'state of nature' in Hobbes and by the classification of his approach as 'Calvinistic', it notes only a partial aspect and therefore does not recognize the Anglican infrastructure of his work. By contrast, P.J.Johnson, *Doctrine*, fully confirms my view, which I arrived at without knowing his work (addendum to the English edition).

90a. Cf. also Johnson, 'Doctrine', 106. K.Thomas, 'Social Origins', 206, also derives Hobbes' ethical ideals from the circle at Great Tew.

91. ...*cavit, ne quid scriberet, non modo contra sensum Scripturae Sacrae, sed etiam contra doctrinam Ecclesiae Anglicanae, qualis ante bellum ortum authoritate regia constituta fuerat. Nam et ipse regimen Ecclesiae per episcopos prae caeteris formis omnibus semper approbaverat, Vita, OL* I, XVI.

92. So in fact Braun, op.cit., 35.

93. In the same *Vita* he writes of *Leviathan*: *In eo opere Jus Regium, tum spirituale tum temporale, ita demonstravit, tum rationibus tum authoritate Scripturae Sacrae, ut perspicuum fecerit, pacem in orbe Christiano nusquam diuturnam esse posse, nisi vel doctrina illa sua recepta fuerit, vel satis magnus exercitus cives ad concordiam compulerit, OL*, I, XVf.

93a. Q.Skinner, *Context*; id., 'Conquest and Consent: Thomas Hobbes and the Engagement Controversy', in G.E.Aylmer (ed.), *The Interregnum: The Quest for Settlement, 1646-1660*, 1972, 79-98; id., 'Thomas Hobbes et la défense du pouvoir *de facto*', *RPFE* 163, 1973, 131-52; cf. also id., 'History and Ideology in the English Revolution', *HistJ* 8, 1965, 151-78.

93b. Cf. J.M.Wiener, 'Quentin Skinner's Hobbes', *Political Theory* 2, 1974, 251-60.

93c. That already applies to the universal conception of order which is also put forward by Hobbes, though he is the first to do it on mechanical causal grounds, cf. R.W.Alexander, *Myth*, 33f. For the substance cf. also W.H.F.Barnes, 'The Rational

Theology of Thomas Hobbes', in *The Person Universe. Essays in Honor of J.Macmurray*, ed. T.E.Wren, 1975, 54-63. M.M.Reik, *The Golden Lands of Thomas Hobbes*, 1977, 15, stresses: 'Hobbes does belong to the end of the Renaissance period rather than to the Restoration or the beginning of the Enlightenment in England.'

94. Cf. above, 147ff. Johnson, *Doctrine*, 109ff., has a detailed discussion of it; he also recalls John Hales, see above, 152: *Doctrine*, 106ff.

95. Cf. e.g. Schmitt, *Der Begriff des Politischen*, 122, and *Der Staat*, 1965, 64ff.

96. *Leviathan*, ed. Oakeshott, 388ff./428ff. Cf. esp. 388/428: 'The *unum necessarium*, only article of faith, which the Scripture maketh simply necessary to salvation, is this, that JESUS IS THE CHRIST. By the name of Christ is understood the king, which God had before promised by the prophets of the Old Testament, to send into the world.' The key word 'king' shows the connection with Hobbes' general approach by way of royal typology. Cf. also *De Cive*, ch.18, *OL*, 424ff.

97.*Der Begriff des Politischen*, 122; cf. also *Der Staat*, 1965, 62.

98. 501 n.28.

99. *Leviathan*, ed. Oakeshott, 384/424. It is interesting that in the explanation of this principle which Hobbes gives in *De homine*, he hints at its development in the statements of the Apostles' Creed, *OL* II, 421f.n.; Chillingworth, too, seems to have the Apostles' Creed in mind. The statement is understood in terms of a consistent eschatology in *Leviathan*, ch.42: 'That Jesus was the Christ, that is to say, the king that was to save them, and reign over them eternally in the world to come', ed. Oakeshott, 338/376.

100. 'All that is *Necessary* to salvation, is contained in two virtues, faith in Christ, and obedience to laws. The latter of these, if it were perfect, were enough to us. But because we are all guilty of disobedience to God's law, not only originally in Adam, but also actually by our own transgressions, there is required at our hands now, not only obedience for the rest of our time, but also a remission of sins for the time past; which remission is the reward of our faith in Christ.'

101. Cf. above, 501 n.24.

102. 'The obedience required at our hands by God... is a serious endeavour to obey him... Whosoever therefore unfeignedly desireth to fulfil the commandments of God, or repenteth him truly of his transgressions... hath all the obedience necessary to his reception into the kingdom of God' (*Leviathan*, ed. Oakeshott, 385/425, cf. 394). Cf. also the similar statements in *De homine* 18; *OL* II, 416. The interpretation by Kodalle, op.cit., 63, who looks here for an authentic rendering of the Reformation *sola fide*, does not do justice to the tone of this passage.

103. Ibid.

104. Cf. Tönnies, *Thomas Hobbes*, 6,16.

105. Hobbes ends the chapter with the statement: 'So that I may attribute all the changes of religion in the world, to one and the same cause; and that is, unpleasing priests; and those not only amongst Catholicks, but even in that church that hath presumed most of reformation.' *Leviathan*, ed. Oakeshott, 79f./97. Here, too, the reference is explicitly to Christian priests, Catholics and above all Presbyterians(!), and not to pagans. For the polemic against the Catholic clergy cf. also the end of ch.47, with its repeated comparison of 'ecclesiastics' with spirits; ed. Oakeshott, 457/500f.

106. Carl Schmitt is one exception, with his important notes about the contrast between Hobbes' theory of the state and the monistic *corpus* doctrine of John of Salisbury with the papalistic claim to the *potestas indirecta*, *Der Staat*, 1965, 63ff. Cf. also Johnson, 'Doctrine', 105; Manet, *Naissances*, 117. Cf. also J.G.A.Pocock, 'Time, History and Eschatology in the Thought of Thomas Hobbes', in *The Diversity of History. Essays... H.Butterfield*, ed. J.H.Elliott/H.G.Koenigsberger, 1970, (149-96)

193ff. = id., *Politics, Language and Time. Essays on Political Thought*, 1972, (148-201) 177ff.

107. Kodalle, op.cit., 99 n.27, points out that Hobbes even says that it is lawful if Christian sovereigns transfer rule over their subjects to the Pope in matters of religion – though of course they do this of their own free choice. *Leviathan*, ed. Oakeshott, 360/398f.

107a. For the Catholic controversial literature of the time cf. Tavard, *Tradition*.

108. See above, 83ff.

109. In *De cive*, chs.17,21, Hobbes explicitly says: 'From what I have said hitherto it follows as a necessary consequence that a state of Christian people and a church made up of them is one and the same, which can only be called twofold for twofold causes.' *OL* II, 397.

110. Cf. Heckel, *Cura religionis...*

111. *Leviathan*, ed. Oakeshott, 398/438.

112. *Der Staat*, 1965, 57.

113. 172.

114. The reference to the 'artificial attempt at order' of the Politiques in France, which may have influenced Hobbes, is an important one: R.Schnur, *Individualismus und Absolutismus*, 1963, 56ff.

115. Cf. above, 139, 144ff.

116. For Hobbes' relationship to Cromwell and the Independents cf. J.Lips, *Die Stellung des Thomas Hobbes zu den politischen Parteien der grossen englischen Revolution*, 1927, reprinted 1970, 82ff. Cf. also 533 n.93a and the works by Q.Skinner mentioned there.

117. Cf. Lips, op. cit., 92ff.

118. *Der Staat*, 1965, 64.

118a. Thus Pocock, 'Time', 163/162 is also concerned to understand Hobbes' ideas in *Leviathan*, Books III and IV, as a historian; i.e. for him 'first, in the thought-patterns characteristic of the time, secondly, in the thought-patterns characteristic of the author.' In fact this is one of the few attempts to arrive at an adequate understanding of these usually neglected remarks as well.

119. Lack of familiarity with typological thinking leads Kodalle to his irrelevant criticism of Hobbes, op.cit., 78. Cf. already the misunderstanding in Gooch, *Hobbes*, 25.

120. In the light of this presupposition it is possible to misunderstand B.Willms' statement: 'for Hobbes it is no longer possible to legitimate any rule from a religious conviction as such', *Antwort*, 72.

121. *OL* II, 351ff. – R.Peters, op.cit., 225ff., already gives a brief but quite complete account on Hobbes' ideas on religion. However, his verdict, 'He was patently not a religious man', op.cit., 247, mistakes the rationalistic and moralistic type of Humanist religion.

122. Kodalle, op.cit., 70ff., strongly stresses the character of the covenant as gift: it is a heteronomous determination in the context of God's concern in history, which opens up the chance of autonomous freedom to those to whom this offer is made. The scheme, which derives from the nominalist conception of God, certainly plays some role in Hobbes; however, it should also be recognized that the question here – in the context with which Hobbes is concerned – is that of the autonomy of the *ruler*. The use of the idea of the covenant itself shows the influence of federal theology on Hobbes, though because of its wide dissemination we should not think in terms of any specific model.

123. Hobbes excludes the covenant with Adam and Eve as a basis for the kingdom of God because it was soon revoked again. For the significance of the covenant with Abraham for Hobbes and the continuation of the idea of the covenant through the Old Testament cf. also Förster, op.cit., 186ff.

124. Here Hobbes defines specific faith, in distinction from the acknowledgement already owed to God by nature; his starting point is that Abraham was to recognize God specially as the one who had revealed himself to him.

125. New edition: P.Laslett (ed.), *Patriarcha and Other Political Works of Sir Robert Filmer*, 1949. According to him, op.cit., 3, the work was presumably written before 1640.

126. Cf. above, 271ff.

126a. W.Förster, *Hobbes*, 179ff. (cf. id., in *Hobbes-Forschungen*, 79ff.) gives the illuminating explanation that Hobbes developed his doctrine of the covenant as a response to the idea of the covenant among the Puritans.

127. *OL*, II, 355.

128. All the quotations, *OL*, II, 357.

129. Here one should mention the discussion of natural law in Hobbes carried on by Taylor and his successors.

130. Like the previous quotations, *OL*, II, 359.

131. *OL*, II, 368.

132. *OL*, II, 368.

133. *OL*, II, 369.

134. *OL*, II, 370.

135. *OL*, II, 376.

136. *OL*, II, 377.

137. *OL*, II, 378.

138. G.Schrenk, *Gottesreich*, 185f.; cf. also Kodalle, op.cit., 98. For the eschatological dimension in Hobbes cf. esp. also Pocock, 'Time', 173ff./172ff.

139. To this degree Braun's hostility to Hobbes is understandable. Peters, op.cit., 240, already referred to this aim of the argument.

140. *Leviathan*, ed. Oakeshott, 398/438.

141. *OL*, II, 392ff.

142. *OL*, II, 392.

143. *OL*, II, 393.

144. From this follows the important definition, 'that a state of Christian men and a church are completely one and the same, and can only be called twofold for twofold causes'; this should not be taken to be extravagant, but in accordance with the normal understanding of the non-separatist theology of the time.

145. 'In that others are not justified in acting and teaching contrary to his interpretation', *OL* II, 409.

146. OL, II, 412.

147. Ibid.

148. Gawlick's German translation runs like this, op.cit., 309; the Latin text really says, 'is to be derived from Christ himself' (*ab ipso Christo derivanda*, *OL*, II, 413.)

149. *OL*, II, 413.

150. Cf. J.W.Allen, *English Political Thought*, 131ff.

151. *OL*, II, 118ff.

152. For Hobbes' remarks elsewhere about miracles cf. Kodalle, op.cit., 141-4. There are important statements e.g. in *Leviathan*, ch.32, ed. Oakeshott, 245f./274f.

153. Cf. Herbert's *notitiae communes circa religionem*!

154. *OL*, II, 120.

155. Ibid. For the question of the problem of God in Hobbes and the contradictory answers to it cf. generally Kodalle, op.cit., 105ff.

156. *Leviathan*, ed. Oakeshott, 242/271.

157. Cf. also Y.Maouas, 'Essai sur le "Leviathan" de Thomas Hobbes', *RMM* 81, 1976, 478-512.

158. Chs. 40,41 and 43 correspond to *De cive*, chs.16,17,18. Between them, in

ch.42, there is the discussion with Bellarmine, which in point of content belongs there, and before it a number of chapters on individual questions which are only touched on briefly in *De cive*. Hobbes' basic approach is the same in both works, which is important for the understanding of *Leviathan*. Cf. H.J.Johnson, arguing with McNeilly: *Ethics* 80, 1969/70, 243-5.

159. *Leviathan*, ed. Oakeshott, 246/275.

160. See above, 213.

161. See above, 147.

162. *Leviathan*, ed. Oakeshott, 246/276.

163. 'For although it is not laid down in scripture which laws each Christian king is to enact in the territories over which he rules, it is laid down which laws he is not to enact,' ibid.

164. *Leviathan*, ed. Oakeshott, 247/276.

165. Cf. above, 525 n.8.

166. *Leviathan*, ed. Oakeshott, 248/278.

167. Op.cit.

168. *Leviathan*, ed. Oakeshott, 253/282.

169. For this statement see the conclusions drawn by Warrender.

170. All these quotations and comments are in *Leviathan*, ed. Oakeshott, 254f./283ff. The definition in *De cive* sums up the unity of the argument even more evocatively: *Restat ergo, in omni ecclesia Christiana, hoc est, in omni civitate Christiana, Scripturae Sacrae interpretatio... dependeat et derivetur ab auctoritate illius hominis vel coetus, penes quem est summum imperium civitatis, OL,* II, 411f.

171. Chapter 34 contains interesting remarks about the term 'spirit' in another context; they can be passed over here.

172. Cf. also Kodalle, op.cit., 121ff., though he has not recognized the importance of the statements in the general context of the work.

173. Cf. Kodalle, op.cit., 141ff. One can only assert that 'this ultimately functioned as the keystone for the autonomy of the individual', op.cit., 141, if 'political science' is still regarded as the scarlet thread running right through the work and there is a failure to see the direct connection of the chapters ending with ch.42 with the controversial question of authority in the church.

174. *Leviathan*, ed. Oakeshott, 244/273; cf. also op.cit., 290/323.

175. Op.cit., 246/275; cf. above, 536 n.152.

176. '...Every man then was, and now is bound to make use of his natural reason, to apply to all prophecy those rules which God hath given us, to discern the true from the false', op.cit., 284/315f.

177. '...we must both see it done, and use all means possible to consider, whether it be really done; and not only so, but whether it be such, as no man can do the like by his natural power, but that it requires the immediate hand of God', op.cit., 290/323.

178. Op.cit., 291/324.

179. Op.cit., 284/316.

180. Op.cit., 315/351.

181. Cf.above, 209.

182. Cf. above, 207f.

183. Cf. esp. op.cit., 337/374.

184. Op.cit., 364f./402f.

185. Op.cit., 385/425. Cf. above, 206.

186. Cf. already J.Laird,*Thomas Hobbes*, 1934 reprinted 1968, 236ff.

187. Op.cit., 397/437.

188. Op.cit., 399/439.

189. Ibid.

190. Op.cit., 398/438.

191. Op.cit., 400/440.

192. Hobbes' struggle against this widespread Enlightenment view again shows his great knowledge of the Bible and especially of the Old Testament.

193. Op.cit., 525/494.

194. Op.cit., 526/495.

195. A comment by K.H.Ilting, 'Hobbes und die praktische Philosophie der Neuzeit', *PJ* 72, 1964, (84-102) 101, shows how one can arrive at a crass misjudgment by failing to note the background in church politics. He thinks that 'with religion and philosophy, which he denounced as the "kingdom of darkness"', Hobbes sacrificed man's spiritual existence to Leviathan. For criticism cf. already C.Schmitt, *Der Staat*, 1965, 66 n.6; Willms, *Der Staat*, 1967, 224.

196. Op.cit., 528. B.Willms rightly observes: 'It cannot be said of Hobbes that he broke radically with Aristotle. Rather, his book is related to the Aristotelisms of contemporary scholasticism.' *Der Staat*, 1967, 82. However, that is not a step which Hobbes himself takes; it corresponds with the traditional and anti-scholastic attitude of the Humanists. On the other hand, in Hobbes there is here a move against Greek metaphysical theism in favour of the demanding God who is the foundation of the deontological character of his ethics; cf. Glover, op.cit., 163ff.

197. Cf. the rather contradictory statements of Hobbes quoted above, 533 n.91 and 214.

198. See above, 534 n.96.

199. A well known instance of this is the reference to Naaman the Syrian (II Kings 5), whom Hobbes connects with the question whether false lip-service can be commanded by the sovereign: 'Lip-service is only an external matter and no more than any other gesture by which we indicate our obedience; in it a Christian who holds to belief in Christ with all his heart has the same freedom as that allowed by the prophet Elisha to Naaman the Syrian', *Leviathan*, ed. Oakeshott, 327/364.

200. Among whom More and Cudworth in particular fought against him; cf. Mintz, op.cit., 80ff.

200a. Pocock, 'Time', stresses above all that Hobbes distinguishes two levels of reference in human existence and thus also for morality and politics, and allows each one its own right: 'the one of nature, known to us through our philosophic reasoning on the consequences of our affirmations, the other of divine activity, known to us through prophecy, the revealed and transmitted words of God', op.cit., 160/159. The juxtaposition of both aspects (on which see also J.Bernhardt, 'Raison et foi chex Hobbes', in *Science, Raison, Progrès aux XVIIᵉ et XVIIIᵉ Siécle dans le Monde Anglo-Américain. Actes du Colloque tenu à la Sorbonne 2./3. Dec 1977*, 67-78) is quite typical of an Anglican of the time.

4. The Latitudinarians

1. J.Tillotson, 'A Sermon Preached at the Funeral of the Reverend Benjamin Whichcot, D.D. May 24th, 1683', also in *Sermons on Several Subjects and Occasions*, 1748, II, 108-26.

2. The term 'Latitude-men' appears first in Simon Patrick, *A Brief Account of the new Sect of Latitude-men*, 1662 (reprint ed. T.A.Birell, 1963), by which he similarly means the Cambridge Platonists, as is also the case in G.Burnet, *History of His Own Time* (ed.M.J.Routh, 1833 reprinted 1969), I, 342, cf. e.g. R.L.Colie, *Light*, 22; Cragg, *From Puritanism*, 61; Birell, op.cit., Introduction, III; Sina, *Ragione*, 64ff. But it is better for the sake of clarity to follow the terminology which developed towards the end of the century and to describe as 'Latitudinarians' the liberal theologians of the subsequent generation, who are clearly distinct from the Cambridge Platonists. This

is done by Tulloch, *Rational Theology,* and more recently again by R.Cragg, op.cit., 61ff.; id., *The Church and the Age of Reason,* 1960, ²1966, 70f.; Birell, op.cit. Cf. also N.Sykes, *From Sheldon to Secker,* 1959, 145ff. M.C.Jacob, *The Newtonians and the English Revolution,* 1976, 43, does not give a clear definition.

2. Cf. e.g. N.Sykes, *Church and State in England in the XVIIIth Century,* 1934, ch.1, 1–41; C.Hill, *Some Intellectual Consequences of the English Revolution,* 1980; D.Ogg, *England in the Reigns of James II and William III,* 1955, ²1957, 222ff.; D.Bahlman, *The Moral Revolution of 1688,* 1957, reprinted 1968; C.F.Mullett, 'Religion, Politics and Oaths in the Glorious Revolution', *RP* 10, 1948, 462-74; M.C.Jacob, *Newtonians,* 72ff.

4. Cf. Sykes, op.cit., 10f.; H.Davies, *Worship and Theology in England from Andrewes to Baxter and Fox, 1603-1690,* 1975, 365ff.

5. Cf. Burnet, *History,* I, 330ff.; C.E.Whiting, *Studies in English Puritanism from the Restoration to the Revolution, 1660-1688,* 1931, reprinted 1968, 1ff.; M.A.Thomson, *A Constitutional History of England, 1642 to 1801,* 1938, 124ff.; C.F.Mullett, 'Toleration and Persecution in England, 1660-89', *ChH* 18, 1949, 18-43; E.Routley, *English Religious Dissent,* 1960, 103ff.; J.T.Wilkinson, *1662 – and After. Three Centuries of English Nonconformity,* 1962, 44ff.; G.Gould, *Documents Relating to the Settlement of the Church of England by the Act of Uniformity of 1662,* 1862. The full text of the Act is printed there, 286-404.

6. For details cf. especially Whiting, op.cit., 7ff.

7. Cf. Sykes, op.cit., 21.

8. These are described in detail by Whiting in the work mentioned above.

9. Thus Sykes, op.cit., entitles Chapter I 'From Restoration to Revolution: Seed Time and Harvest'.

10. Cf. Sykes, op.cit., 33. It is doubtful, however, whether this role was completely 'uncongenial' when one thinks of Hooker and Chillingworth's connections with Laud, cf. 148 above. Latitudinarians and Laudians agreed within Anglicanism in their basic rationalistic and moralistic attitude: they differed in their judgment on liturgical questions and later on legitimism. Both reckoned the liturgy to be in the sphere of indifferentia, but the High Churchmen pressed for it to be ordered normatively by the hierarchical church, whereas here too the Latitudinarians tended towards minimalism.

11. Cf. the inner development of Lilburne and Walwyn, above 517. n.317; also Nuttall, *The Holy Spirit,* 13f.; W.S.Hudson, 'Mystical Religion in the Puritan Commonwealth', *JR* 28, 1948, (51-6) 54.

12. There are numerous biographies of Vane: in addition to the contemporary one by his friend G.A.Sikes, *Life and Death of S.H.V.,* 1662, cf. e.g. C.W.Upham, *Life of S.H.V.,* 1835; J.Forster, 'S.H.V.the Younger', *Eminent British Statesmen* IV, 1838, 1ff.; J.K.Hosmer, *Life of S.H.V,* 1888; J.C.Hearnshaw, *The Life of S.H.V. the Younger, Puritan Idealist,* 1910; W.W.Ireland, *The Life of S.H.V. the Younger,* 1905; J.Willcock, *Life of S.H.V. the Younger, Statesman and Mystic (1613-1662),* 1913, but (after Sykes) there is no systematic account of his theological views. However, cf.Ireland, op.cit., 436ff.; M.Freund, *Die Idee der Toleranz,* 275ff.; Jones, *Spiritual Reformers,* 271ff.

13. Burnet already reports on the private meetings for edification held by Vane: 'In these meetings he preached and prayed often himself, but with so peculiar a darkness, that though I have sometimes taken pains to see if I could find out his meaning in his words, yet I could never reach it.' *History,* I, 294f. W.Ireland observes: 'In reading Vane's theological writings, one grasps at the meaning, believes that there is a meaning, yet it escapes, or only dwells in the mind for a moment, leaving no conception behind', op.cit., 447. This obscurity is a characteristic mark of mysticism.

14. Cf. W.C.Braithwaite, *The Beginnings of Quakerism* (1912), ²1955 reprinted 1970, 25ff., 58ff., 80ff.; Whiting, op.cit., 133ff. H.Davies, *Worship,* 490f., stresses the sim-

ilarities between Quakers and Baptists and assumes that they originate with the spiritual Puritans of the time of Cromwell. Cf. esp. 495.

15. Cf. above, 55ff.

16. So too Whiting, op.cit., 133; Hudson, op.cit., 54. However, e.g. Nuttall, *The Holy Spirit*, 15, comments: 'any direct influence is far to seek'. – For the early enthusiasm of Quakerism in the period 1652-56, cf. also G.F.Nuttall, *Studies in Christian Enthusiasm. Illustrated from Early Quakerism*, 1948 (on Aldam, Farnsworth, Holme, Nayler and the Ranters). T.Sippel, *Werdendes Quäkertum*, 1937, calls attention above all to John Everard (died 1640); cf. already id., 'Über den Ursprung des Quäkertums', *ChW* 12/19/26 May 1910; id., *Zur Vorgeschichte des Quäkertums*, 1920.

17. Op.cit., 53f. Nuttall, op.cit., VIII, thinks that Quakerism 'indicates the direction of the Puritan movement as a whole'. The intellectual connection with Puritanism is also clear even if the Puritan clergy resolutely rejected the 'enthusiasm' of the early Quakers. Cf. H.Brinton, Preface to G.F.Nuttall, op.cit., 7.

18. Cf. above, 21ff.

19. Cf. Whiting, op.cit., 135.

20. Cf. Whiting, op.cit., 192f.

21. Cf. Whiting, op.cit., 186ff., who among other things refers to the contemporary reports of John Whiting, *Persecution Exposed*, [2]1791. For the persecution of the Puritans generally cf. G.R.Cragg, *Puritanism in the Period of the Great Persecution*, 1957.

22. Mention should also be made e.g. of J.Aynhoe, *A Short Description of the True Ministry and the False*, 1672; J.Audland, *The Memory of the Righteous Revived*, 1689; cf. Whiting, op.cit., 135, and the composite volume by T.Camm and C.Marshall, *The Memory of the Righteous Revived*, 1689, in which there are numerous short works by John Camm and John Audland.

23. *The Memorable Works of a Son of Thunder and Consolation, Namely, That True Prophet, and Faithful Servant of God, and Sufferer for the Testimony of Jesus, Edward Burroughs*, 1672.

24. Cf. E.Brockbank, *Edward Burrough*, 1949; also Braithwaite, op.cit., 285f., and cf. index; Whiting, op.cit., cf. index.

25. Cf. the verdict of Braithwaite, op.cit., 286.

26. Fol. a 2 – d 2, unpaginated.

27. The opening of the Epistle reads: 'To all the World to whom this may come to be Read'.

28. 'And so we ceased from the teaching of all men, and their words, and their Worships, and their Temples, and all their Baptisms, and Churches, and we ceased from our own Words, and Professions, and Practises in Religion... and we became Fools for Christ's sake...'

29. Op.cit., 223ff.

30. Op.cit., 248f.

31. Op.cit., 241ff.

32. Op.cit., 325ff.

33. Both quotations, op.cit., 326. By contrast, all the Quaker doctrines were defended at length as being in accordance with scripture, op.cit., 335ff. The oath of the Protector Cromwell to support the Christian religion, which is in accordance with scripture, is the starting point for the whole pamphlet, op.cit., 325.

34. Op.cit., 327. There are also similar remarks against the clergy in *A Faithful Testimony Concerning the true Worship of God* (1659), op.cit., 474ff.; in *A Hue-and-Cry after the False Prophets and Deceivers* (1661), op.cit., 879ff., and elsewhere. For the rejection of the tithe as not being in accordance with scripture cf. especially 'John Audland's Letter to a Priest concerning Tythes', in Camm and Marshall, *The Memory*, 176-81.

35. Cf. op.cit., 341: 'The Testimony of Truth it self, and the Way of the Lord it

self, for many Generations hath not so clearly and purely been held forth, as it is now in this Age and Generation; for now the true Light hath shined, and the Way of Salvation is evidently made manifest.' '...and the Same Power of God, and the same Truth that was in the Apostles days, and the same Ministry by the Gift of the same holy Ghost, as was in the Apostles dayes, is now witnessed.' The Quaker sense of mission is well illustrated by John Audland's work sent to the Lord Protector: 'Some Particulars concerning the Law, sent to Oliver Cromwell' (in Camm and Marshall, op.cit., 297-319). As well as protesting against the bloody persecution of the Quakers by Cromwell, which derives from the priests and makes use of laws of the Catholic Mary (298f.), and inveighing further against the priests because they take the tithes (304f., 307ff.), above all it contrasts the state law, which only has to punish law-breakers (309), with the law of God which is in the conscience (300, 302; cf. also 'the Light of Christ in the Conscience', 301), which is competent in all other matters, and with which even the Lord Protector has to conform. In details this law commands men to give tithes to the poor (so that there would no longer be any beggars in England, just as once there were none in Israel, 303), forbids swearing (302,304) and executing thieves (who must rather pay compensation in accordance with the law of God or be sold into slavery – a literal application of the Old Testament precepts), and also any respect towards men because this is due to God alone (305f.). At the end Cromwell is threatened with inexorable punishment from God if he does not hear the appeal (312).

36. 'Many have the letter which know not the Gospel, nor hath received it, and this Gospel, which is everlasting, have we received from God.' Op.cit., 249.

37. 'The Servants of the Lord handled, tasted, saw and felt the Word of Life, and from it spoke the Scriptures, as they were moved by the holy Ghost...and none can understand it without the same Spirit that gave it forth.' Ibid.

38. Cf. above, 371ff.

39. First appeared 1659; I have used the second edition of 1662 (University Library, Tübingen).

40. Cf. Tulloch, *Rational Theology* I, 411ff.; J.Nankinvell, 'Edward Stillingfleet', in *Transactions of the Worcestershire Arch. Soc.*, 1946, 16-34; M.Schmidt, *RGG³*, VI, col.381, and most recently R.T.Caroll, *The Common-Sense Philosophy of Religion of Bishop Edward Stillingfleet*, 1975.

41. For Whitgift and Laud see above, 116, 153.

42. Op.cit., 'Preface to the Reader', cf. the quotation, the orthography of which has slightly been altered, in Tulloch, op.cit., I, 423.

43. This is the tendency in Tulloch's idealistic view.

44. Op.cit., 14.

45. Op.cit., 14f. As his authority the author here mentions Selden, Molina and Alphonsus a Castro; the influence of late Spanish Scholasticism is clear.

46. Op.cit., 16f.

47. Cf. Cherbury's second *notitia circa religionem*, above, 188.

48. Op.cit., 182f.

49. Tulloch, op.cit., 443f., rightly points out that Stillingfleet excludes the Congregationalist solution *de facto*, by holding fast to the national church.

50. 'Prudence must be used in Church-Government, at last confessed by all parties.' Here he is quite ready to make the concession: 'That Prudence best, which comes nearest Primitive practice.' Except that this is not normative, but merely an image that can be used and from which deviation can be made if need be. The quotations come from the Table of Contents of Part II, unpaginated.

51. 1662, ³1666.

52. For his later attitude as an 'orthodox Anglican', as it is evident in the contro-

versy with Locke, cf. W.Dahrendorf, *Lockes Kontroverse mit Stillingfleet und ihre Bedeutung für seine Stellung zur anglikanischen Kirche*, Diss. phil. Hamburg 1932.

53. On the contrary, it is explicitly stated: 'The Word of God being the only code and digest of divine laws, whatever law we look for must either be found there in express terms or at least so couched therein, that every one, by the exercise of his understanding, may by a certain and easy collection, gather the universal obligation of the thing inquired after.' op.cit., 151.

54. Op.cit., 158ff.

55. Op.cit., 170ff.

56. In passing, in Part II, ch.II, he also takes account of the 'Enthusiasts' (Quakers), whose spiritual ancestors he perceptively finds among the mendicant monks at the time of the emergence of the Waldensians.

57. Op.cit., 158.

58. Op.cit., 178. Also cited in Tulloch, op.cit., 446. It should be noted how much the Pauline concept of 'edification' has faded here in comparison with its evocative use among the earlier Puritans.

59. Op.cit., 171.

60. Op.cit., 174.

61. Op.cit., 175.

62. Op.cit., 177.

63. Cf. above, n.58.

64. Op.cit., 79ff.

65. Cf. above, 489 n.231.

66. For thirty years (from 1664 on) Tillotson was a preacher in the church of St Lawrence Jewry in London, with enormous success, not only among the merchant class, but also among young clergy who wanted to learn how to preach from him. We can also see the popularity of his sermons from the numerous editions of his works which take up a large number of pages in the British Library catalogue. By contrast the modern secondary literature on him is sparse: apart from the uncritical earlier work by W.G.Humphrey, 'Tillotson, the Practical Preacher', in *The Classical Preachers of the English Church*, second series, 1878, 133-65, cf. G.L.Locke, *Tillotson. A Study in Seventeenth-Century Literature*, 1954 (more interested in the literary questions of style; the same is true of I.Simon, *Three Restoration Divines: Barrow, South, Tillotson. Selected Sermons* , two vols, 1967); N.Sykes, 'The Sermons of Archbishop Tillotson', *Theol* 53, 1955, 297-302; J.O'Higgins, 'Archbishop Tillotson and the Religion of Nature', *JTS* NS 24, 1973, 123-42; M.C.Jacob, *Newtonians*, cf. index s.v.Tillotson; Sina, *Ragione*, 226ff. For the influence of Tillotson's style of preaching and that of the other Latitudinarians, and the general milieu of preaching at the time, cf. also Sykes, *Church*, ch.VI, 231ff. esp. 257ff.; W.F.Mitchell, *English Pulpit Oratory from Andrewes to Tillotson*, 1932 (on Tillotson, 333ff.); Davies, *Worship*, 133ff.

67. G.Burnet, *A Sermon Preached at the Funeral of the Most Reverend Father in God, John... Archbishop of Canterbury... 30 November 1694*, 1695, 31, quoted from Cragg, *From Puritanism*, 77 (where the orthography is modernized). Tillotson, however, also makes his own comment on the aim of his addresses: 'I have made it my business, in this great presence and assembly, to plead against the impieties and wickedness of men... and I do assure you, I had much rather persuade any one to be a good man, than to be of any part or denomination of Christians whatever.' *Works*, ed. Birch (see next note), II, 58.

68. I have used the *Works*, ed. Birch, 1820 (with the editor's biographical account – first published in the folio edition of 1752), I-X, though these contain only part of Tillotson's sermons; also the edition by R.Barker, I-II, ²1717. Cf. also I. Simon, op.cit., II, 69. Op.cit., V, 273ff.

70. Op.cit., V, 281.

71. 'And this phrase may comprehend all those acts of religion which refer immediately to God; a firm belief of his being and perfections; an awful sense of him as the dread Sovereign and righteous Judge of the world; a due regard to his service, and a reverent behaviour of ourselves towards him in all acts of worship and religion, in opposition to atheism and a profane neglect and contempt of God and religion...', op.cit., V, 279f.

72. 'To begin with piety towards God. Nothing can more evidently tend to our interest, than to make him our friend, upon whose favour our happiness depends. So likewise for gratitude... for every man is ready to place benefits there where he may hope for a thankful return', etc., op.cit., V, 285.

73. Before Locke, this was one of the main arguments of all defenders of natural religion, cf. already Cherbury (above, 187). Tillotson also stresses (with a reference to Cicero's statement *Omnium consensus naturae vox est*): 'And this is an argument of great Force; there being no better way to prove any thing to be natural to any Kind of being, than if it be generally Found in the whole Kind.' Ed. Birch, V, 453.

74. Cf. Cragg, *From Puritanism*, 63.

75. Cragg , op.cit., 78, points to the justified cause for moral preaching which was given to the Latitudinarians by the moral situation of the period of the Restoration: however, this preaching also stemmed from their basic attitude. This situation becomes particularly clear with the appearance of the (anonymous) work: *The Whole Duty of Man*, shortly before the Restoration, in 1657; it is concerned only with the moral duties of the Christian, and with this in view achieved a tremendous success (twenty-eighth edition 1790 – modern reprint also in the Ancient and Modern Library of Theological Literature, nd.). For the content of the book and its role cf. especially C.J.Stranks, *Anglican Devotion*, 1961, 123-48. – Independently of that, Tillotson's personal attitude is (Locke, op.cit.,102): 'His religious thought is dominated by practicality; it is the moral and not the doctrinal part of religion with which he is deeply at heart concerned.'

76. Cf. the attacks on Tillotson because of his alleged Socinianism in *The Charge of Socinianism Against Dr. Tillotson*, 1695, a charge which Tillotson sought to counter by the publication of his christological sermons (see Cragg, op. cit., 76; cf. also I.Simon, *Three Restoration Divines*, 280). G.L.Locke, op.cit., 91, can say with a degree of justification: 'Today, since most churches have gradually become more and more liberal in their beliefs, the theology which he propounded would be regarded as ultra-conservative.' Tillotson could even accept miracles by interpreting them in rationalist terms. His position is therefore characterized by A.C.McGiffert, *Protestant Thought Before Kant*, 1913, as 'supernatural rationalism'. O'Higgins, *Tillotson*, points to the obvious division in Tillotson's attitude between natural religion and supernatural revelation and explains it above all in the light of his apologetic aims. The weakness of the Latitudinarians did not lie in heretical dogmatics but in the predominance of an ethics with a Stoic stamp.

77. Op.cit., V, 292. Revealed religion is above all the expansion and completion of natural religion (although that is its basis), in that it holds out the prospect of reward for moral action in the complete assurance of the resurrection of the dead and a heavenly life (Birch edition, VI, 19f.), thus filling the gaps in it: 'the duties are still the same, only it offers us more powerful arguments, and a greater assistance to the performance of those duties.'

78. Op.cit., V, 295.

79. 'We have now betaken ourselves to prayer and fasting and it was very fit, nay necessary we should so do; but let us not think this is all God expects from us', ibid.

80. Op.cit., V, 294.

81. Op.cit., V, 298ff.

82. Op.cit., V, 298.

83. Cf. also the following remarks: 'When moral duties and ritual observances come in competition, and do clash with one another, the observation of a rite, or positive institution, is to give way to a moral duty... it being a tacit condition implied in all laws of a ritual and positive nature, provided the observance of them be not the hindrance and prejudice of any duty, which is of a higher and better nature; in that case, the obligation of it does for that time give way and is suspended.' Op.cit., V, 301.

84. Op.cit., V, 312f. Cf. also I, 450. 'All the duties of Christian religion which respect God, are no other but what natural light prompts men to, excepting the two sacraments.'

85. Op.cit., V, 315.

86. Op.cit., V, 316.

87. Op.cit., V, 321.

88. Not in the edition by Birch. But cf. *Works*, ed. R.Barker, II, 690ff. (the title has the misprint Rom.22.1).

89. Op.cit., 697 (quotations from this edition are given with small initials).

90. Cragg, *From Puritanism*, 75.

91. Op.cit., 694.

92. Similarly only in Barker, op.cit., II, 704ff.

93. Op.cit., 707.

94. Op.cit., 708.

95. Ibid.

96. Op.cit., 709.

97. Cf. above, 153f.

98. Only in Barker, op.cit., II, 84ff.

99. Op.cit., 86.

100. Ibid.

101. Op.cit., 87.

102. Op.cit., 88. Cf. also the definition in the sermon on Matt.23.13 (Birch ed., II, 517ff., 520): 'wherein the nature of God, and his will concerning our duty, and the terms and conditions of our eternal happiness in another world, are fully and plainly declared to us.'

103. Ibid. The theory that scripture is easy to understand in matters necessary for salvation recurs in various of Tillotson's sermons, but also as an explicit definition in his early writing directed against Rome, *The Rule of Faith* (1966; Birch, Vol.X, 225f.; cf. G.L.Locke, *Tillotson*,, 22), Sect.III, 14: 'Our principle is, the Scripture doth sufficiently explain itself, that is, is plain to all capacities, in things necessary to be believed and practised.' For Tillotson's epistemology with its gradation of degrees of certainty of knowledge, which is reminiscent of Chillingworth, cf. van Leeuwen, *Problem*, 32-50.

104. Cf. above, 294ff.

105. Cf. Birch, *Life*, 1820 ed., I, V; also G.L.Locke, op.cit.,19.

106. Cf. H.M.G.Watkin, *Church and State in England to the Death of Queen Anne* 1917, 343: 'The Latitudinarians were not the men to understand the noblest parts of the Cambridge teaching – Tillotson sat in vain at Cudworth's feet.' On the other hand, to be fair to Tillotson it must be conceded that he maintained the necessity of supernatural grace; O'Higgins, op.cit., gives an impressive description of the split in his thought which arose as a result.

107. Only in Barker, op.cit., II, 307ff.

108. Quotations, op.cit., 311.

109. Op.cit., 312. Tillotson keeps to the ground of the orthodox creed at this point, as in all other dogmatic statements (cf. also Humphrey, *Tillotson*, 143f.). Cf. also the

remark in the sermon on Heb.5.9 (Birch ed., VI, 92ff. 103): 'He died for us, that is, not only for our benefit and advantage, but in our place and stead; ...and because he died, we are saved from that eternal ruin and punishment which was due to us for our sins.' However, the main aim of the sermon is to demonstrate 'what obedience the gospel requires as a condition, and is pleased to accept as a qualification in those who hope for eternal salvation,' and this is not in contradiction with the free grace of God proclaimed in the Gospel.

110. Op.cit., 313, cf. 315, where this is termed the sum of natural religion, Jewish religion and Christian religion.

111. Op.cit., 312.

112. Op.cit., 313.

113. Birch ed., V, 232ff., 339ff.

114. Op.cit., V, 332.

115. Cf. also O'Higgins, op.cit., passim. G.L.Locke, *Tillotson*, 67, defends him against the charge of a plain eudaemonism, surely with some degree of justice, but cf. below, n.131.

116. Cf. Locke, op.cit., 106f.

117. Cf. *DNB* 1959/60, XXI, 264-7; W.Lloyd, *A Sermon preached at the Funeral of the Reverend Father in God J.Wilkins*, London 1672, 1675; P.A.Wright-Henderson, *The Life and Times of J.W.*, 1910; D.Stimson, 'Dr. W. and the Royal Society', *JMH* 3, 1931, 539-63 (also separately); R.F.Jones, *Ancients and Moderns. A Study of the Rise of the Scientific Movement in Seventeenth-Century England*, 1961; B.Shapiro, *John Wilkins 1614-1672*, 1969.

118. Cf. G.L.Locke, op.cit., 25; I. Simon, *Three Restoration Divines*, 276; R.S.Westfall, *Science and Religion in Seventeenth-Century England* (1958), reprinted 1970, 120ff., 164ff.; A.Jeffner, *Butler and Hume on Religion*, 1966, 137f.; Shapiro, op.cit., 233ff.

119. This designation goes back to R.Boyle, at the same time the most significant representative of the movement. For him cf. esp. M.S.Fisher, *Robert Boyle, Devout Naturalist*, 1945; also J.F.Fulton, 'Robert Boyle and his Influence on Thought in the Seventeenth Century', *Isis* 18, 1932, 77-102; H.D.Rack, 'Boyle, Robert (1627-1691)', *TRE* 7 (1981), 101-4 (short bibliography). Also J.F.Fulton, *A Bibliography of Robert Boyle*, ²1961.

120. R.S.Westfall, *Science and Religion*, 107 n.1, gives the most important titles.

121. Preface, unpaginated.

122. Chs.I-III, 38 (Table of Contents and page headings give this wrong).

123. Chs.IV-VII, 39-99.

124. Op.cit., 40ff.

125. Op.cit., 176: according to Tillotson's Foreword this chapter was prepared for the printer by Wilkins himself (whereas the rest of the material was collected by Tillotson posthumously from his working papers).

126. Ch. II, 314ff.

127. Ch.III, 324ff.

128. Ch.IV, 330ff.

129. Ch.VII, 372ff.

130. Ch.VIII, 388ff.

131. This was not carried out by Tillotson personally, but was presumably as he intended.

132. Ch. IX, 394ff.

133. Op.cit., 395.

134. Ibid.

135. Op.cit., 400.

136. 'Whatever any Philosophers have prescribed concerning their moral virtues of Temperance, and Prudence and Patience, and the duties of several relations, is

here enjoyned in a far more eminent, sublime and comprehensive manner.' Op.cit., 406.

137. 'So exactly conformable to the highest, purest Reason, that in those very things wherein it goes beyond the Rules of Moral Philosophy, we cannot in our beste judgment but consent and submit to it.' op.cit., 406f.

137a. Cf. recently the short biography by R.Brandt, 'John Locke (1632-1704)', in O.Höffe (ed.), *Klassiker der Philosophie*, 360-77.

138. So far only *An Essay Concerning Human Understanding*, ed. P.H.Nidditch, 1975, has appeared (quotations from the *Essay* follow this edition), and Vols.I-VI of the *Correspondence*, ed. E. de Beer, 1976-81 (Clarendon Edition). Cf. the progress report by P.H.Nidditch, *The Locke Newsletter* 9, 1978, 15-19. Otherwise I have used the 1963 reprint of the 1823 edition *The Works of John Locke. A New Edition, corrected. In Ten Volumes*. In content it corresponds to the previous collected editions since 1714. Cf. also H.O.Christophersen, *A Bibliographical Introduction to the study of John Locke*, 1930, 87ff.

139. Locke's literary remains, first passed on to his cousin Peter King, were long guarded by his descendants. Fragmentary extracts were published by Lord King in his *Life of John Locke* (two vols, 1829, ²1830, with further editions in 1858 and 1884). Some scholars already had occasional access to the collection earlier (thus A.C.Fraser and B.Rand since about 1926, R.I.Aaron and J. Gibb 1935). However, only the purchase of all the material by the Bodleian Library from the estate of the Earl of Lovelace in 1947 (cf. P.Long, *A Summary Catalogue of the Lovelace Collection of the Papers of John Locke in the Bodleian Library*, 1959) made its full extent accessible to scholars, and made possible the partial editions which have appeared since in editions to be mentioned below.

140. There is a selection in W.Euchner, *Naturrecht und Politik bei John Locke*, 1969, bibliography B., 301ff. Cf. also R.Hall and R.Woolhouse, 'Forty Years of Work on John Locke 1929-1969', *PhQ* 20, 1970, 258-68, 394-6. The newest short introductions to his work as a whole are in J.D.Mabbott, *John Locke*, 1973, and I.Mancini/G.Crinella, *John Locke, Grandi ipotesi*, 1976.

141. Another study which belongs here, being also dominated by a concern to give a comprehensive account of all Locke's work, and coming near to that in its fullness of information and approach, is the monograph by C.A.Viano, *John Locke. Dal razionalismo all'illuminismo*, 1960. (On it cf. W.von Leyden, *Mind* 71, 1962, 436f.; also R.Allers, *Erasmus* 14, 1961, 142-5; G.F.Vescovini, *RF* 52, 1961, 489-91). Also the works by J.W.Yolton, *John Locke and the Way of Ideas*, 1956 reprinted 1968; id., *Locke and the Compass of Human Understanding*, 1970; J.L.Mackie, *Problems from Locke*, 1976; P.A.Schouls, *The Imposition of Method. A Study of Descartes and Locke*, 1980. The most acute investigation of Locke's epistemology in respect of the nature of the material in the context of the empirical science which was flourishing at that time is the article by M.Mandelbaum, 'Locke's Realism', in *Philosophy, Science and Sense Perception: Historical and Critical Studies*, 1964, paperback 1966, 1-60. Cf. also Yolton, *Locke and the Compass*, 5f.

142. W.Euchner in particular has made surveys of research in this area; cf. the reports, 'Zum Streit um die Interpretation der politischen Philosophie John Lockes', *PVS* 3, 1962, 283-94; id., 'Locke zwischen Hobbes und Hooker', *AES* 7, 1966, 127-57, and most recently the introduction to id., *Naturrecht*, 1ff. Cf. recently also J.Dunn, *The Political Thought of John Locke*, 1969; G.Parry, *John Locke*, Political Thinkers 8, 1978.

143. That is true both of Leo Strauss, *Natural Right and History*, and of C.B.Macpherson, *Possessive Individualism*.

144. I have already commented, 197f. above, that Macpherson's approach is one-sided. By contrast, the work by Euchner mentioned above, 248, *Naturrecht*, is significant, imaginative and original.

145. The episode which R.Ashcraft, 'Faith and Knowledge in Locke's Philosophy', in *John Locke: Problems and Perspectives*, ed. J.W.Yolton, 1969, (194-223) 194, reports is significant. When he told a new graduate in Philosophy, Politics and Economics at Oxford of his special interest in Locke's religious views, the graduate confessed his ignorance in these matters, 'explaining that it was Locke's epistemology his studies had emphasized'. The earlier work by E.Crous, *Die religionsphilosophischen Lehren Lockes und ihre Stellung zu dem Deismus seiner Zeit*, APG(F) 34, 1910, reprinted 1980, is an exception. It makes a somewhat violent attempt (cf. 83) to develop a system out of these 'doctrines'. It is also typical that of Locke's works with a religious theme the *Letter concerning Toleration* has appeared in numerous modern editions and the *Reasonableness of Christianity* in virtually none, so that we still have to go back to the text in the *Works*, VII, 1-158 (the edition by I.T.Ramsey, London 1958, is an abbreviated version; that by G.W.Ewing, 1965, offers only a reprint of the text of the Complete Works, partially modernized and Americanized, cf. XXI).

146. The most dangerous attack was made by the strict Puritan John Edwards in his book, *Some Thoughts Concerning the Several Causes and Occasions of Atheism*, 1695, 104-21. Locke replied in his work *A Vindication of the Reasonableness of Christianity* (now similarly in the *Works*, Vol.VII, 159-90). Moreover, he was supported not only by S.Bolde (see below, 556 n.305) but by an anonymous author in a pamphlet with the title: *The Exceptions of Mr. Edwards in his 'Causes of Atheism' against 'The Reasonableness of Christianity as Delivered in the Scriptures' examin'd and found Unreasonable, Unscriptural and Injurious*, 1695. Edwards replied in *Socinianism Unmasked*, 1696; in *The Socinian Creed...*, 120ff. he again rejected Locke's minimal confession 'that Jesus is the Christ' as Socinian.

147. Cf. H.McLachlan, *The Religious Opinions of Milton, Locke and Newton*, 1941, reprinted 1972, 73. However, M.Cranston, *John Locke, A Biography*, 1957, ³1966, 392 (the only reliable biography, which for the first time takes full account of the manuscript remains), points out that despite Locke's explicit assertion that he has not read the works of the Rakauans ('A Vindication', in *Works*, VII, 171f.), extracts from these writings appear in his notebooks.

148. The main representative of this approach is McLachlan, op.cit. Cf. also id., *Socinianism in Seventeenth-Century England*, 1951, 325ff. L.Stephen, *History of English Thought in the Eighteenth Century*, Vol.1,2, 1881, 1902, reprinted 1962, I, 111, comments: 'Locke, the Unitarians, Toland, form a genuine series, in which Christianity is being gradually transmuted by larger infusions of rationalism.' Cf. also Cranston, op.cit.; Viano, *John Locke*, 370. Cf. also J.Redwood, *Reason, Ridicule and Religion*, ch.7, 156-72, on the general theme of contemporary anti-trinitarianism.

149. D.G.James, *The Life of Reason*, 1949, 92ff., and R.Ashcraft, op.cit., here take Locke's epistemology principally into account. Cf. recently also S.C.Pearson, Jr, 'The Religion of John Locke and the Character of his Thought', *JR* 58, 1978, 244-62.

149a. Parry, *Locke*, is a laudable exception here.

150. Cf. above, 194ff.

151. This is particularly true of Viano and Euchner.

152. This is done above all by Strauss, *Natural Right*, esp. 202ff., and R.H.Cox, *Locke on War and Peace*, 1960, 1-7, 21ff., 142ff. P.Laslett challenges the conjecture that Locke is frequently dependent on Hobbes, in the introduction to his edition of *Two Treatises of Government*, 1960, reprinted 1963, ²1970, 71ff., as does P.Abrams, in the introduction to his edition: *Two Tracts on Government*, 1967, 75ff.

153. There are exceptions to this general verdict. The introductions by P.Laslett and P.Abrams already mentioned are particularly valuable for the way in which they locate Locke in contemporary discussions, as are the introductions by E. de Marchi to *John Locke, Lettera sulla Toleranza*, ed. R.Klibansky – E. de Marchi, 1961, and J.W.Gough to *J.Locke, Epistola de Tolerantia. A Letter on Toleration*, ed. R.Klibansky-

J.W.Gough, 1968. Sina, *Ragione*, 286ff., 307ff., 317ff., 337ff., seeks to balance influences on Locke from different sides: English and French culture generally, Le Clerc and Van Limborch specially.

154. R.I.Aaron, *John Locke*, 1937, ²1955, ³1971, 124ff.; J.W.Gough, op.cit., 26; J.T.Moore, 'Locke's Development from Conservative to Liberal on Toleration', *Int. Stud. in Phil./Studi Int.di Fil.* 11, 1979, 59-75. – E. de Marchi, op.cit., XXIff., XXVIIIff., recalls the attitude of the Great Tew group in connection with Locke's earlier writings.

155. Locke deals with this in his *Third Letter for Toleration*, adopting the term introduced by his conversation partner J.Proast, in *Works*, VI, 422.

156. Cf. below, 557 n.332.

157. These are the two discussions edited by P.Abrams in *Two Tracts on Government*: 1.*Question: Whether the Civil Magistrate may lawfully impose and determine the use of indifferent things in reference to Religious Worship?* 2. *An Magistratus Civilis possit res adiaphoras in divini cultus ritus asciscere easque populo imponere? Affirmatur.* They were composed in 1660 or 1661. Also written in 1661 was the essay recently edited from the posthumous papers, *An necesse sit dari in Ecclesia infallibilem Sacro Sanctae Scripturae interpretem? Negatur.*, by J.C.Biddle, 'John Locke's *Essay on Infallibility*: Introduction, Text and Translation', *JCS* 19, 1977, 301-27.

158. Cf. M.Cranston, op.cit., 67: 'Locke in 1660 and 1661 was thus a man of the Right, an extreme authoritarian. Within a few years his political views were to be radically changed.' Similarly also Laslett, Introduction, 19 (but cf. 20!). Cf. also N.Bobbio, *Locke e il diritto naturale*, 1963, 109f.: 'In questi due scritti giovanili Locke sostiene con accanimento, e senz'ombra di dubbio, la posizione non-liberale.' de Marchi, op.cit., XXVII, sees an impasse in Locke's intellectual development in the two writings. Abrams entitles the first section of his introduction, 'John Locke as a Conservative', op. cit., 3., and asserts: 'I can find no reason to call Locke's thought liberal (in the sense that the Letters Concerning Toleration are liberal) before 1667,' op.cit., 8. On the other hand he makes it clear that Locke's authoritarianism remains limited to the indifferentia, which as such must be ordered by the law, and is diminished by his 'love of liberty'. Moore, 'Development', also regards Locke's early writings as 'conservative', although he correctly describes the Latitudinarians as 'liberal theologians and philosophers who worked within the established Anglican tradition' (61). The attitude adopted by Locke towards the indifferentia in 1660/1 is an element from this tradition.

159. Abrams, op.cit., 36ff., gives a short survey of the history of the indifferentia debate and cites a series of relevant works; however, he does not discuss its earlier history in the sixteenth century.

160. *Tracts*, ed. Abrams, 120.

161. Op.cit., 8, cf. also 50.

162. Cf. above, 150.

162a. Biddle, 'Essay on Infallibility', 309f., conjectures that Locke could have read Chillingworth's work. However, at that time the problem of 'papism' was very much in the air; cf. also Locke's letter no.75, extracts of which are printed in Biddle, op.cit., 307.

163. Cf. below, 559 n.408.

164. *The Great Question concerning Things Indifferent in Religious Worship*, 1660; *The Second Part of the Great Question...*, 1661; *The Necessity and Use of Heresies, or the Third Part...*, 1662.

165. That in so doing he stresses his loyalty to the king and the legitimacy of state legislation in the civil sphere again corresponds exactly with the attitude of Robert Browne and Henry Jacobs, cf. op.cit., 226, 242 n.44, 227ff. Viano, *Locke*, 54f., thinks that Locke sought a *via media* in the theory of the state between the democratic

system laid down by the Levellers in their *Agreement of the People* and the authoritarian system of Grotius and Hobbes. However, the opposition to Bagshaw is in the religious rather than the political sphere; politically, Bagshaw is similarly a royalist, cf. the quotation in Abrams, op.cit., 18. Milton's position on the role of the laity in the church should also be compared, cf. above, 159.

166. 'nec aliquod vel magistratus vel parentis vel domini iustum reperiri potest mandatum quod non continetur et fundatur in scriptura'.

167. *Tracts*, ed. Abrams, 203f. (ET, 234). Similarly, the *Essay on Infallibility*, ed. Biddle, 322f., says that only those statements of scripture which concern 'praecipua christiani hominis officia, justicia castitas charitas benevolentia' are necessary for salvation and also clearly understandable.

168. See below, 263ff.

168a. Similarly *Essay on Infallibility*, ed. Biddle, 324f. Here there is a qualification that this is only 'directive, not definitive' infallibility, since the shepherds of the church can err if they lead, but not the sheep, if they follow!

169. *Tracts*, ibid. Cf. also in the first treatise: 'The scripture is very silent in particular questions, the discourses of Christ and his Apostles seldom going beyond the general doctrines of the Messiah or the duties of the moral law,' op.cit., 172. This is already a reference to the content of the *Reasonableness*, cf. below, 263.

169a. See above, 101.

170. Also in the *Essay on Infallibility*, ed. Biddle, 324/5. Abrams, op.cit., 20, stresses the central role of the argument for order in the treatises; however, we must also note the links of the argument with tradition. It was in no way central for his predecessors, either.

171. This 'true cult' consists in moral action, as already in Herbert's third *notitia communis*, see above, 188.

172. The influence of Puritan thought can be traced at this point (here reference should be made to his Puritan home, cf. Cranston, op.cit., 1, 1ff., and the Puritan atmosphere in Oxford at the time of Cromwell, cf. ibid., 32). In particular, the then Dean of Christ Church, John Owen, should be remembered. As an Independent, he held the view that people should be free to think and hold services as long as they did not disturb peace and order, cf. ibid., 41. The proximity of these views to Bagshaw is clear. Cf. further von Leyden, Introduction to his edition of *John Locke, Essays on the Law of Nature*, 1954 (reprinted 1958, 1965), 42; he draws attention to the Puritan academic teaching Locke received in the moral philosophy of H.Wilkinson and F.Howell.

173. Cf. the progress report by Euchner. Recently also W.Baumgartner, *Naturrecht und Toleranz bei John Locke*, Würzburg dissertation 1975.

174. See above, 547 n.146.

175. Thus the title in Cox, op.cit., 7. The tradition of Locke's caution already appears in earlier works, e.g. in Cranston, op.cit., passim.

176. Strauss, *Natural Right*, 202-51. For criticism cf. e.g. J.W.Yolton, 'Locke on the Law of Nature', *PhRev* 67, 1958, (477-98) 478; C.Monson, 'Locke and his Interpreters', *PolSt* 6, 1958, (120-33) 120ff.; Euchner, *PVS* 3, 1962, 287f.; id., *AES* 7, 1966, 141ff.; id., *Naturrecht*, 3f.

177. In fact there is an explicit reference in Cox, op.cit., 51, to the 'possibility that John Edwards... and others were essentially correct in stating that Locke deliberately concealed his heterodoxy by outwardly professing an orthodoxy which he was set upon undermining, and did so primarily for prudential reasons.' For criticism of this hypothesis cf. however also H.Aarsleff, 'Some Observations on Recent Locke Scholarship', in *John Locke. Problems and Perspectives*, ed. J.W.Yolton, 1969, (262-71) 264ff.

178. W.Kendall, *Locke and the Doctrine of Majority-Rule*, 1959.

179. Strauss, *Natural Right*, 228. Similarly also the investigation by R.Rotermundt,

Das Denken John Lockes. Zur Logik bürgerlichen Bewusstseins, 1976, which has a Marxist orientation, and G.Zarone, *John Locke. Scienza e forma della politica*, 1975, which has the same ideology.

180. *Natural Right*, 234.

181. *Natural Right*, 246.

182. These include R.Polin, *La Politique Morale de John Locke*, 1960; J.W.Yolton, *PhRev* 1958; Monson, ibid.; R.Singh, 'John Locke and the Theory of Natural Law', *PolSt* 9, 1961, 105-17. Cf. id., 6: '...his version of natural law is a continuation of the classical natural-law philosophy and not a deviation of it as Hobbes' certainly is.' Similarly also M.Seliger, 'Locke's Natural Law and the Foundation of Politics', *JHI* 23, 1963, 337-54.

183. Op.cit., Introduction, esp. 79ff.

184. Cf. ibid., 82: 'Locke is, perhaps, the least consistent of all the great philosophers, and pointing out the contradictions either within any of his works or between them is no difficult task.'

185. 1954 (1965).

186. Of course L.Strauss attempted to tone this down, cf. his contribution to the discussion, 'Locke's Doctrine of Natural Law', *APSR* 52, 1958, 490-501.

187. 1969.

188. Op.cit., 9.

189. Op.cit., 13.

190. Op.cit., 14. This model is characterized by Euchner in the following way: 'First, nature is not chaos but order; it has a normative structure. Secondly, there is a way of reading norms valid for human beings from the natural order, i.e. an epistemology of natural law; and thirdly, a theory of the binding nature of the natural law.'

191. Op.cit., 119ff.

192. Op.cit., 95ff.; 167; 184ff.

193. ⁵1965.

194. Op.cit., 80ff. Cf. 184: 'In private property human freedom to some degree objectifies itself for self-preservation and happiness.'

195. Cf. esp. op.cit., 11(ff.) and 234ff., n.18. Cf. also above, 000 n.151. This origin was already conjectured by R.I.Aaron, *John Locke*, 31ff., 257, and von Leyden, Introduction to *Essays*, 71.

196. Some scholars have received it with effusive praise. Thus e.g. the review by B.Tibi, *ARSP* 58, 1972, 589-91, ends with the comment: 'The recent controversy over Locke may come to an end with Euchner's work. On the other hand it is clear that the academic vanity of the numerous interpreters of Locke will not make it easy for them to recognize the insights of Euchner's work.'(!) H.Bank, *PVS* 12, 1971, 454-8, has an equally positive verdict.

197. Ed. Laslett, 303ff. One could with some justification also point to certain parts in the first Treatise (esp. I,7), but particularly at this point it becomes clear that the theme is predetermined by the work of R.Filmer which Locke is criticizing, cf. below, 560, nn.416, 417.

198. H.Speer, review in *Der Staat* 11, 1972, (102-5) 104, also comments: 'Prominent and important though Euchner's work is in its consistency and the logic of its argument, a better defence is needed of its thesis that the combination of traditional and modern natural law thinking in the work of John Locke on the one hand reflects a bourgeois ethos with its capitalistic profit motive, which has yet to come to full awareness, and on the other hand serves to defend it.' It should be noted that Locke only took up the theme of property when he saw himself compelled to do so by his argument with Filmer. Thus it has a specific context, which is occasioned by Filmer's theories. Cf. Laslett, Introduction, 68, and above, 275f.

199. See above, 188.

200. See above, 147.

201. ¹1675.

202. In F.Atterbury, *Sermons and Discourses*, II, 1740, 20, we find an extensive list of authors who give as the essential background to Christian ethics the prospect of the future life and the rewards to be expected there, or the fear of eternal punishment; cf. also A.O.Aldridge, *Shaftesbury and the Deist Manifesto*, 1951, 304.

203. See above, 116f.

204. Cf. above, 148ff. de Marchi, op.cit., XXIXf., sees in this work an acceptance by Locke of the critical principles of the Great Tew circle.

205. Cf. Essay III: *An lex naturae hominum animis inscribatur? Negatur.*, ed. von Leyden, 136ff.

206. Cf. Essay V: *An lex naturae cognosci potest ex hominum consensu? Negatur.*, op.cit., 160ff.

207. *His nequicquam obstantibus, asserimus legis naturae obligationem perpetuam esse et universalem*, op.cit., 192.

208. Op.cit., 190.

209. Op.cit., 196.

210. Op.cit., 202: cf. also 132/134. For the parallels in Thomas see op. cit., 202 n.4.

211. *Quandoquidem igitur omnes homines sint natura rationales, et convenientia sit inter hanc legem et naturam rationalem, quae convenientia lumine naturae cognoscibilis est, necesse est omnes rationali natura praeditos, id est omnes ubique homines hac lege teneri*, op.cit., 198. The exception of children and mentally ill is not allowed: *etsi enim omnes obliget lex quibus datur, non tamen eos obligat quibus non datur, nec datur iis a quibus cognosci non potest*, op.cit., 202.

212. Op.cit., 148.

213. Locke declares at the beginning of his second essay, entitled *An lex naturae sit lumine naturae cognoscibilis?*: *Sed per lumen naturae aliquid esse cognoscibile nihil aliud velimus quam hujusmodi aliqua veritas in cujus cognitionem homo recte utens iis facultatibus quibus a natura instructus est per se et sine ope alterius devenire potest*, op.cit., 122.

214. *Tertius et ultimus qui remanet cognoscendi modus sensus est, quod principium constituimus legis cognoscendi*, op.cit., 130. Cf. also 146: *nihil remanet quod lumen naturae dici posset praeter rationem et sensum.*

215. *Dico fundamentum omnis illius cognitionis hauriri ab iis rebus quas sensibus nostris percipimus; et quibus ratio et argumenti facultas... ad earum opificem progrediens, argumentis a materia, motu, et visibili hujus mundi structura et oeconomia necessario emergentibus, tandem concludit... Deum esse aliquem rerum omnium authorem; quo posito necessario sequitur universa lex naturae qua tenetur gens humana...*, op.cit., 130/132.

216. Op.cit., 146ff.

217. *...esse in rerum natura res sensibiles, hoc est revera existere corpora et eorum affectiones, scilicet levitatem, gravitatem, calorem, frigus, colores, et caeteras qualitates sensui obvias, quae omnes aliquo modo ad motum referri possint*, op.cit., 150. Here Locke refers to the atomism favoured in the Royal Society, cf. Mandelbaum, op.cit., and Viano, op.cit., 434ff.

218. *Unde liquido apparet rationem sensu monstrante viam nos deducere posse in cognitionem legislatoris sive superioris alicujus potestatis cui necessario subjicimur, quod primum erat requisitum ad cognitionem alicujus legis*, op.cit., 154.

219. *quod secundum erat requisitum ad legis cujusvis cognitionem, scilicet voluntas superioris potestatis circa res a nobis agendas...*, op.cit., 156.

220. Cf. von Leyden, op.cit., 65, and Euchner, *Naturrecht*, 47f.

221. For the distinction between the two systems of natural law cf. briefly Euchner, *Naturrecht*, sec.3, n.86, on pp.246f.; in detail H.Welzel, *Naturrecht und materiale Gerechtigkeit*, ²1955, 67–105. For Locke's Nominalism cf. further Parry, *Locke*, 28f.;

J.R.Milton, 'John Locke and the Nominalist Tradition', in R.Brandt (ed.), *John Locke Symposium Wolfenbüttel 1979*, 1981, 128-45. Epistemologically speaking this Nominalism leads to a theistic attitude, cf. G.A.J.Rogers, 'Locke, Law and the Laws of Nature', op.cit., 146-62.

222. *dum inquirimus non quid homo divino spiritu afflatus scire, quid lumine e caelis delapso illuminatus conspicere valet, sed quid naturae et sua ipsius sagacitate eruere et investigare potest homo mente, ratione, et sensu instructus*, op.cit., 122. However, it should be noted that here Locke is only attacking a direct inspiration in the present, i.e. like 'enthusiasm' later. This has no bearing on the relationship of the Bible as a source of revelation to natural law.

223. von Leyden, op.cit., 199 n.1, mentions alongside Cicero the names of Vasquez, Suarez, Grotius, Sanderson and Culverwel as representatives of this theory of harmony, and conjectures that Locke took it over from Culverwel.

224. *An Early Draft of Locke's Essay together with Excerpts from his Journals*, ed. R.I.Aaron and J.Gibb, 1936 (usually cited as Draft A); *J.Locke, An Essay concerning the Understanding, Knowledge, Opinion, and Assent*, ed. B.Rand, 1931, xerox copy 1959 (usually cited as Draft B).

225. Cf. H.R.F.Bourne, *The Life of John Locke*, two vols. 1876 (reprinted 1969), I, 248f., etc.

226. John Locke, *An Essay concerning Human Understanding*, ed. P.H.Nidditch, 1975, 6ff.

227. *Essays*, ed. von Leyden, Introduction, 62ff.

228. Draft A, 1, 3ff.

229. Euchner, *Naturrecht*, 129, points out that 'virtue' and 'vice' in Locke are not natural law concepts but those of social morality. However, Locke's terminology is not consistent (id., n.41).

230. Draft A, 25f, 37-39.

231. Draft B, 155-62; esp. 307, 303f.

232. *Essays*, ed. von Leyden, 198. E. de Marchi, op.cit., XXX, points out that from 1660 to 1670, the influence of the new science of R.Boyle and T.Sydenham on Locke makes itself felt increasingly strongly. Cf. also R.S.Westfall, *Science and Religion*, op.cit., 162ff. For the change in Locke's epistemological approach towards subjectivism in the question of God and the moral doctrine derived from it cf. also R.Brandt, 'Observations on the First Draft of the Essay Concerning Human Understanding', in R.Brandt (ed.), *John Locke Symposium*, 25-42.

233. Aaron and Gibb, op.cit., 116-18; cf. also von Leyden, op.cit., 55 n.1, and Euchner, *Naturrecht*, 147f.

234. Aaron and Gibb, op.cit., 117.

235. Printed in von Leyden, op.cit., 263-72. Cf. also the page on 'moral good' and 'moral rectitude', ibid., 72f.

236. For this chapter cf. Euchner, op.cit., 95ff.

237. For the most part printed in Lord King, *Life*, II, 122-33 – the numbering of sections 11 and 12 is missing in King, cf. von Leyden, op. cit., 70 n.1.

238. Lord King, op.cit., II, 128. A quotation from the wider context can also be found in Euchner, *Naturrecht*, sec.6, n.216 on p.271. von Leyden, op.cit., 72f., prints a passage omitted by King and later deleted by Locke as section 7 of the paper 'Of Ethick in General', and a further page in which there is an even clearer discussion of the hedonistic principle.

239. von Leyden, op.cit., 71, mentions Pufendorf, Cumberland and Parker as its advocates, but that is not to be understood in exclusive terms.

240. *Of Ethick in General*, sections 8 and 9, in Lord King, op.cit., II, 128-30.

241. Op.cit., 130f.; cf. with Draft A, sec.26, p.39.

242. 'The next thing then to show is, that there are certain rules, certain dictates,

which it is his will all men should conform their actions to, and that this will of his is sufficently promulgated and made known to all mankind', op.cit., 133.

243. Bobbio, op.cit. 150f., also recalls that the task of demonstrating morality is the main aim of Locke's epistemological investigations in the Essay. G.A.Rauche, *Die praktischen Aspekte von Lockes Philosophie. Die Bedingtheit der negativen Kritik Lockes durch den ethischen Charakter des Essay,* 1958, makes the view 'that Locke's epistemology and psychology of knowledge culminate for the most part in his second stage of knowledge, namely the ethical' (op.cit., 2), the guideline to his whole investigation. G.A.J.Rogers, 'Locke', brings out the loose connection between knowledge of nature and knowledge of morality in Locke's epistemological approach. Schouls, *Imposition,* passim, does the same thing in more detail. For all the remarks which follow cf. also, in brief, J.J.Chambliss, 'Conduct and Revelation in the Educational Theory of Locke, Watts, and Burgh', *Educ.Theory* 26, 1976, (372-87) 372-79.

244. Here the approach to the 'idea' of a supreme being and 'the *Idea* of our selves, as understanding, rational Beings' is the same in Essay IV, 3,18 (ed. Nidditch, 549), as in the diary entry and already in Essay VII of the *Essays on the Law of Nature.* The comparison with the angles of the triangle emerges again there, in order to demonstrate by means of what are supposed to be self-evident principles like 'Where there is no property there is no injustice', or 'No government allows absolute liberty', that morality is to be included 'amongst the sciences capable of demonstration' and here stands on the same level as mathematics. ('I am as capable of being certain of the truth of this proposition as of any in mathematics.') On III, 11, 16; IV, 11, 18, cf. below, n.251.

245. For what follows cf. esp. Euchner, *Naturrecht,* 149ff.

246. Essay II, 2,1-3 (ed. Nidditch, 119ff.); II, 12,1 (id., 163f.).

247. Essay II, 22 (ed. Nidditch, 288ff.).

248. Essay II, 22,10 (op.cit., 293).

249. 'These simple *Ideas,* I say, of Thinking, Motion, and Power, have been those, which have been most modified; and out of whose Modifications have been made most complex Modes, with names to them,' op.cit., 293. Were one to enumerate them all, 'That would be to make a Dictionary of the greatest part of the Words made use of in Divinity, Ethicks, Law, and Politicks, and several other Sciences,' op.cit., 294. – S.H.Daniel, 'Locke: Human Concernment and the Combination of Ideas', *Dialogue* 20, 1977/78, 20-26, but points out with reference to Essay II, 23,12 (ed. Nidditch, 302f.), that Locke limits the possibilities of forming complex ideas to what is necessary for a successful creative life.

250. Essay II, 30,4 (ed. Nidditch, 373); cf. II, 31,3 (376f.: there again we find the comparison with the triangle, the idea of which would be true even if there were not really any triangle in existence); II, 5,3 (ed. Nidditch, 429; the text printed there runs: 'these *Essences of the Species of mixed Modes, are* not only *made* by the Mind, but made *very arbitrarily,* made without Patterns, or reference to any real Existence'); IV, 34,8 (ed. Nidditch, 566): the certainty of insights rests on established ideas. This is particularly true of mathematics and, 'In the same manner, the Truth and Certainty of *moral* Discourses abstracts from the Lives of Men, and the Existence of those Vertues in the World, whereof they treat...').

251. Essay III, 11, 16 (ed. Nidditch, 516); cf. IV, 12, 8 (op.cit., 643f.): 'For the *Ideas* that Ethicks are conversant about, being all real Essences, and such as, I imagine, have a discoverable connexion and agreement one with another; so far as we can find their Habitudes and Relations, so far we shall be possessed of certain, real, and general Truths; and I doubt not, but if a right method were taken, a great part of Morality might be made out with that clearness, that could leave, to a considering Man, no more reason to doubt, than he could have to doubt of the Truth of Propositions in Mathematicks, which have been demonstrated to him.'

252. This is true of the statements cited above, 553 n.244.

253. Thus e.g. most of the statements brought together by Yolton from the *Essays* and the *Second Treatise*, *PhRev*, 1958, 487f. Cf. also Euchner, *Naturrecht*, 155f.

254. The statements collected by Yolton, op.cit., for the most part from the Decalogue; also Gen.9.6; Isa.58.7; Eph.6.4.

255. 552 n.241.

256. Lord King, op.cit., II, 130f.

257. Lord King, op.cit., 132.

258. Ibid. Cf. also Essay I, 3,6: '...the true ground of Morality; which can only be the Will and Law of a God, who sees Man in the dark, has in his Hand Rewards and Punishments, and Power enough to call to account the Proudest Offender' (ed. Nidditch, 69).

259. Essay I, 3,6 (op.cit., 69).

260. Essay I, 3,12 (op.cit., 74).

261. Cf. above, 553 n.244.

262. *Naturrecht*, 161f.

263. *Works*, IX, 294: = *Correspondence*, ed. de Beer, IV, no.1538, 523.

264. H.Aarsleff, *Some Observations*, 262, rightly supposes that Locke is better seen as a rationalist than as an empiricist, since reason plays the decisive role for him. Conversely R.I.Aaron, 'The Limits of Locke's Rationalism', in *Seventeenth Century Studies, Presented to Sir Herbert Grierson*, 1938, 292-310, has pointed out that Locke's rationalism is limited, in that reason can only be concerned with material which is obtained through sense experience and reflection upon it. 'Thus we conclude that Locke is both a rationalist and an empiricist at one and the same time, and it is possible to argue that he is both without being inconsistent', op.cit., 303. Cf. also Laslett, Introduction, 87: 'a peculiar and fertile admixture of empiricism and rationalism.'

265. D.G.James, op.cit., ch.II, 63-114. The remarks by R.Ashcraft, op.cit., 195f., end up in the same direction.

266. Op.cit., 92.

267. Ed. Nidditch, 538ff., esp. 553ff.

268. Op.cit., 547f. For this and what follows cf. also Sina, *Ragione*, 365ff.

269. Ed. Nidditch, 657ff.

270. Op.cit., 663f.

271. 'There is one sort of Propositions that challenge the highest Degree of our Assent, upon bare Testimony, whether the thing proposed, agree or disagree with common Experience, and the ordinary course of Things, or no. The Reason whereof is, because the Testimony is of such an one, as cannot deceive, nor be deceived, and that is of God himself. This carries with it Assurance beyond Doubt, Evidence beyond exception,' *Essay* IV, 16,14, op.cit., 667. For the limitation of reason by revelation cf. also Aaron, 'Limits', 304, and recently J.C.Biddle, 'Locke's Critique of Innate Principles and Toland's Deism', *JHI* 37, 1976, 411-22.

272. James, op.cit., 100, points out that in the fifth edition Locke changed the statement in the first four editions of the *Essay*, '... Faith: which has as much Certainty as our Knowledge itself...' (ed. 1690, Reprint 1970, 340) into 'excludes all wavering, as our knowledge itself...' J.T.Moore, 'Locke on Assent and Toleration', *JR* 58, 1978, 30-36, points to the connection between the individual reference of assent in questions of faith and Locke's demand for tolerance.

273. Essay IV, 16, 14, see above n.271.

274. IV, 18, 3, op.cit., 689f.

275. IV, 18, 4, op.cit., 690.

276. IV, 18, 5, op.cit., 692.

277. Op. cit., 692.

278. IV, 18, 10, op.cit., 695.

279. IV, 18, 7, op.cit., 694. This is, at any rate, the place for the existence of spirits, IV, 3, 17 and 27, op.cit., 548, 557f.

280. Cf. Lechler, *Geschichte*, 193 n.1,. and Gawlick, Introduction to Toland, *Christianity*, 12.

281. According to IV, 17, 23 (op.cit., 687), there are things 'according to, above and contrary to Reason'. Insights above reason cannot be ideas obtained through deduction by natural capabilities, but can only be attained through revelation. In this respect Locke remained true to himself all his life, for in the *Essay on Infallibility* (ed. Biddle, 322f.), we already find the mention of *profunda et quae humanum intellectum prorsus superant rerum divinarum mysteria*, among which Locke includes the doctrine of the Trinity, the doctrine of two natures, the infinity and eternity of God, etc., which must be believed but cannot be explained in other words than those of scripture.

282. *The Life of Reason*, 98. Similarly also Ashcraft, op.cit., 214.

283. Ibid.

284. Op.cit., 101.

285. IV, 19, 1, op.cit., 697.

286. James' interpretation makes Locke more consistent than he was; therefore his proposal that he should be compared with Pascal as a 'philosopher of assent', op.cit., 111ff., is only of limited help.

287. See below, 581 n.267.

288. IV, 19,13; op.cit., 703f.

289. Op.cit., 704f.

290. Op.cit., 706.

291. IV, 18, 9; op.cit., 695. R.Brandt, 'Observations', 25f., points to the traditional derivation of the distinction between natural knowledge and revelation on the basis of certainty and probability.

292. See above, 256f. and n.278.

293. IV, 18,10; op.cit., 695f. For the relationship between language and assent to the revelation laid down in scripture cf. recently also J.T.Moore, 'Locke's Analysis of Language and the Assent to Scripture', *JHI*, 1976, 707-14.

294. Cf. IV, 18, 11, ibid.

295. Op.cit., 705. Cf. also 427 and n.290.

296. Op.cit., 704.

297. Op.cit., 704f.

298. Locke recalls that scripture does not mention such signs of authentication everywhere, op.cit., 705.

299. IV, 18,10; op.cit., 695; cf. also S.C.Pearson, *Religion*, 250f.

300. Ashcraft, op.cit., 202.

301. IV, 12,11; op.cit., 646.

301a. For what follows cf. recently also Sina, *Ragione*, 370ff.; J.T.Moore, 'Locke on the Moral Need for Christianity', *Southwestern JPH* 11, 1980, 61-8.

302. Op.cit., 218.

302a. One exception here is Crous, *Lehren*, 42ff., who incorporates the content of the *Reasonableness* into the reconstruction of Locke's system of philosophy of religion without taking account of the developments in his thought (which at that time had not yet been researched).

303. *John Locke*, 354f. Note, however, the analysis by L.Zscharnack, Introduction to the translation by C.Winckler, 1914, VIIff.

304. J.Lightfoot, *The Harmony of the Foure Evangelists among themselves and with the Old Testament*, 1644; A.Arnauld, *Histoire et concorde des quatre Evangélistes*, 1669; cf. also the correspondence with N.Thoynard mentioned in Viano, op.cit., 354f.n.3.

305. His most important pamphlet in support of Locke bears the title, *Some Considerations on the Principal Objections and Arguments which have been Publish'd against Mr. Locke's Essay of the Human Understanding*, 1699.

306. In *Reasonableness*, in *Works*, VII, 158 (ed. Ramsey, 76), Locke reports that he spoke with some teachers of the Dissenters. Cf. also 264 above.

307. *A Second Vindication of the Reasonableness of Christianity*, Works VII, 181ff.; Preface, 186f. One may recall Herbert of Cherbury's satisfaction at his work, above, 523 n.48.

308. Op.cit., 187.

308a. For Locke's inner development in connection with the problems of natural law cf. recently J.O.Hancey, 'John Locke and the Law of Nature', *Political Theory* 4, 1976, 439-54.

309. F.Bourne, *Life*, 2, 289.

310. *Works*, VII, 157 (ed. Ramsey, 76), cf. 139 (ed. Ramsey, 60f.): 'And it is at least a surer and shorter way, to the apprehensions of the vulgar, and mass of mankind, that one manifestly sent from God, and coming with visible authority from him, should, as a king and lawmaker, tell them their duties...'

311. Thus with special emphasis Macpherson, *Individualism*, 224ff. Cf. also Schouls, *Imposition*, 223. For criticism cf. also Parry, *Locke*, 35f.

312. It is well known how by an illegitimate methodology Strauss derived the theory of Locke's 'Caution' from his statements in *Reasonableness* (see below) about the caution of Jesus and some ancient philosophers in communicating their message, *Natural Right*, 206ff. The position of Polin, *Politique*, 89ff., cf. esp. 90 n.4, is particularly characteristic: he rejects the *Reasonableness* as a mere work of self-defence because it contradicts his basic theory that Locke has a rational ethic based on the classical law of nature.

313. Op.cit., 157 (ed. Ramsey, 76).

314. Op.cit., 146 (ed. Ramsey, 66).

315. Op.cit., 142 (ed. Ramsey, 62f.).

316. Cf. also 157: 'leisure for learning and logic'.

317. Continuation to above, op.cit., 142 (ed. Ramsey, 76).

318. Op.cit., 138 (ed. Ramsey, 63).

319. Op.cit., 146; cf. 'the bulk of mankind', ibid. (ed. Ramsey, 66).

320. Ibid.

321. Ibid.

322. *Works*, 9, 377 (quoted in Ashcraft, op.cit.,219) = *Correspondence*, ed. de Beer, V, no.2059, 595.

323. Cf. also the closing comment in which Locke reports his conversation with representatives of the Dissenters. They are asked, 'Whether half their people have leisure to study? Nay. Whether one in ten, of those who come to their meetings in the country, if they had time to study them, do or can understand the controversies at this time so warmly managed amongst them, about "justification", the subject of this present treatise?' They had to confess that they did not understand the difference of opinions over the matter in question, *Works*, VII, 158 (ed. Ramsey, 76).

324. See above, 42, 173.

325. Op.cit., 157.

326. A.Lovejoy, *The Great Chain of Being*, 1936, 288-93; id., *Essays in the History of Ideas*, 1948 (reprinted 1965), 78-98.

327. Cf. *Treatises*, ed. Laslett, 290: 'the rule of reason and common Equity, which is that measure God has set to the actions of Men...'

328. This expression coined by Lessing in *Erziehung des Menschengeschlechtes* accurately reproduces Locke's estimation of the Bible without the elements in his development.

329. Op.cit., 175.

330. Op.cit., 157 (ed. Ramsey, 76).

330a. Cf. also O.Gauthier, 'Why Ought One...'

331. 'A Letter to the Right Reverend Edward Lord Bishop of Worcester, Postscript', in *Works*, IV, 96.

332. Cf. above, 534 n.96. In Locke, however, the sentence is fuller: (to) 'believe him to be the Saviour promised, and take him now raised from the dead, and constituted the Lord and Judge of all men, to be their King and Ruler', op.cit., 157; cf. *Vindication*, op.cit., 174f. Gough, Introduction to *A Letter on Tolerance*, 31, asserts that in his Second Vindication, for Locke this statement was abbreviated to the sentence 'Jesus of Nazareth to be the Messiah', but Locke, op.cit., 194ff., energetically rejects this as the repeated supposition of his opponent. However, the parallel to Hobbes is still evident (and here one should also recall Chillingworth, see above, 501 n.28).

333. Op.cit., 17-101 (ed.Ramsey, 32).

334. Op.cit., 34-98 (ed.Ramsey, 37f.).

335. Op.cit., 35, 40, 86 (ed.Ramsey, 38, 38f., 42).

336. Op.cit., 35ff. (ed.Ramsey, 38ff.).

337. Op.cit., 69f., 77ff.

338. Op.cit., 54, 82ff., etc. (ed.Ramsey, 39ff.).

339. Bourne, op.cit., 2, 285, sees this as the most original part of the treatise.

340. Op.cit., 4 (ed.Ramsey, 25).

341. Op.cit., 5 (ed.Ramsey, 25).

342. 'Could a worthy man be supposed to put such terms upon the obedience of his subjects? Much less can the righteous God be supposed, as a punishment of one sin...to put man under the necessity of sinning continually, and so multiplying the provocation', op.cit., 6 (ed. Ramsey, 27).

343. Op.cit., 9 (ed.Ramsey, 28).

344. 'On the other side, it seems the unalterable purpose of the divine justice, that no unrighteous person, no one that is guilty of any breach of the law, should be in paradise,' op.cit., 10.

345. Ibid. (ed. Ramsey, 28).

346. Op.cit., 11. Cf. also op.cit., 112: 'God is an holy, just and righteous God, and man a rational creature. The duties of that law, arising from the constitution of his very nature, are of eternal obligation; nor can it be taken away or dispensed with, without changing the nature of things, overturning the measures of right and wrong, and thereby introducing irregularity, confusion and disorder in the world.' Note how strongly traditional ideas of the law of nature still have an influence here!

347. Op.cit., 13 (ed. Ramsey, 29).

348. Op.cit., 14f. (ed. Ramsey, 30f.).

349. Op.cit., 15 (ed. Ramsey, 31).

350. Op.cit., 14 (ed. Ramsey, 30).

351. Op.cit., 112 (ed. Ramsey, 47).

352. Cf. also op.cit., 110 (ed.Ramsey, 45): 'God, therefore, out of his mercy to mankind... proposed to the children of men, that as many of them as would believe Jesus his Son... to be the Messiah... should have all their past sins... forgiven them: and if for the future they lived in a sincere obedience to his law, to the utmost of their power, the sins of human frailty for the time to come, as well as those of their past lives, should, for his Son's sake, be forgiven them: and so their faith, which made them be baptized into his name (i.e. enrol themselves in the kingdom of Jesus the Messiah... and consequently live by the laws of his kingdom) should be accounted to them for righteousness; i.e. should supply the defects of a scanty obedience in the sight of God.'

353. Op.cit., 101 (ed. Ramsey, 43).

354. At this point we can see how Locke's view grew out of the Puritan preaching of the law, see above, 107f., 119ff.

355. 'Repentance is as absolute a condition of the covenant of grace as faith; and as necessary to be performed as that', op.cit., 103 (ed. Ramsey, 44).

356. Op.cit., 105.

357. Op.cit., 115 (ed. Ramsey, 48).

358. Op.cit., 114 (ed. Ramsey, 47). 'For if they believed him to be the Messiah, their King, but would not obey his laws... they were but the greater rebels; and God would not justify them for a faith that did but increase their guilt...'

359. Op.cit., 116 (ed. Ramsey, 48).

360. Op.cit., 122 (ed. Ramsey, 49); cf. op.cit., 125 (ed. Ramsey, 50).

361. Op.cit., 125f. (ed. Ramsey, 50f.). Cf. also 126f. (ed. Ramsey, 50f.): the following remarks on the Last Judgment.

362. Op.cit., 127f. (ed. Ramsey, 51f.).

363. Op.cit., 105 (ed. Ramsey, 44f.).

364. Op.cit., 128ff. (ed. Ramsey, 52ff.).

365. Op.cit., 132 (ed. Ramsey, 54f.).

366. Op.cit., 133 (ed. Ramsey, 55).

367. Here Locke seems to be following the Cambridge Platonists.

368. Op.cit., 134 (ed. Ramsey, 56); this recalls the statements in Essay IV, 16, cf. above, 554 n.271.

369. Op.cit., 135 (ed. Ramsey, 57).

370. '...gave them up into the hands of their priests, to fill their heads with false notions of the Deity, and their worship with foolish rites, as they pleased: and what dread or craft one began, devotion soon made sacred, and religion immutable... Nor could any help be had or hoped for from reason...; the priests, every where, to secure their empire, having excluded reason from having any thing to do in religion', op.cit., 135 (ed. Ramsey, 57).

371. Cf. above, 255f.

372. Cf. above, 261.

373. Op.cit.,138 (ed. Ramsey, 60).

374. Op.cit., 147f.(ed. Ramsey, 67f.): '...they need not be solicitous about useless ceremonies. Praises and prayer, humbly offered up to the Deity, were the worship he now demanded.'

375. The requirement that in this worship 'all should be done decently, and in order, and to edification', contains the very same Puritan phrases (drawn from Paul) which we already found in Cartwright, cf. above 00.

376. Op.cit., 135f. (ed. Ramsey, 57).

377. Op.cit., 141f. (ed. Ramsey, 62).

378. Op.cit., 140 (ed. Ramsey, 61).

379. Op.cit., 142 (ed. Ramsey, 63).

380. Op.cit., 139 (ed. Ramsey, 60). Here it also becomes clear that Schouls' remarks about 'the adequacy of reason' for the knowledge of God's will, *Imposition*, 219ff., which at first sound plausible, in effect fall short.

381. Op.cit., 135 (ed. Ramsey, 57).

382. Op.cit., 146 (ed. Ramsey, 66).

383. Ibid.

384. P. Abrams, in *Two Tracts on Government*, Introduction, 92, here introduces the distinction between 'objective' and 'subjective' knowledge which well explains what is meant. Objectively, morality would be derived from the law of nature, but subjectively, before Christ mankind was not in a position to do this. In this way, however, Abrams contradicts what he has said earlier, that Locke did not end up

with a 'consequential idea of the law of nature as a distinct moral norm', op.cit., 89. Here, Yolton has a clearer picture in his review, *JHP* 6, 1968, (291-4) 293: 'The Reasonableness does not reject the law of nature; it merely argues for revelation through Christ's mission as a clearer and more thorough statement of that law.'

385. Op.cit., 139 (ed. Ramsey, 60f.).

386. Op.cit., 146 (ed. Ramsey, 66).

387. Op.cit., 18, 32 (ed. Ramsey, 33, 37). Moreover, towards the end of his life Locke wrote a short essay 'On Miracles' (in *Works*, IX, 256-65, ed. Ramsey, 88-99).

388. Op.cit., 148 (ed. Ramsey, 68).

389. Op.cit., 149 (ed. Ramsey, 68f.).

390. Op.cit., 150 (ed. Ramsey, 70).

391. Ibid. (ed. Ramsey, 70).

392. Cf. below, 371ff.

393. 'Though all divine revelation requires the obedience of faith, yet every truth of inspired Scriptures is not one of those, that by the law of faith is required to be explicitly believed to justification... Those are fundamentals, which it is not enough not to disbelieve; every one is required actually to assent to them,' op.cit., 156 (Ramsey, 75).

394. See above, 556 n.307.

395. Op.cit., 9 (ed. Ramsey, 28).

396. Op.cit., 137f.

397. 'What those are, we have seen by what our Saviour and his apostles proposed to, and required in those whom they converted to the faith,' op.cit., 156.

398. Cf. above, 265.

399. Op.cit., 151ff.

399a. Locke repeatedly stresses the obscurity which even Holy Scripture displays as an ancient text. This is a further reason why only the fundamentalia can be necessary for salvation. Cf. J.T.Moore, 'Locke's Analysis of Language: and the Assent to Scripture', *JHI* 36, 1976, 707-14.

400. Locke hastens to affirm: 'These holy writers, inspired from above, writ nothing but truth,' op.cit., 155.

401. 'But yet every sentence of theirs must be taken up, and looked on as a fundamental article, necessary to salvation', ibid.

402. 'that the epistles are written upon several occasions', op.cit., 152; cf. also 153f.

403. Op.cit., 155 (ed. Ramsey, 73).

404. '...they... regard the state and exigencies, and some peculiarities of those times,' op.cit., 154 (ed. Ramsey, 73).

405. '...he that will read them as he ought, must observe what is in them which is principally aimed at; find what is the argument in hand, and profit by them. The observing of this will best help us to the true meaning and mind of the writer', op.cit., 152 (ed. Ramsey, 71). Cf. also his preliminary remarks on his paraphrase on the letters of Paul ('An Essay for the Understanding of St. Paul's Epistles, by consulting St. Paul himself', in *Works*, VIII, (1-23) 7), where he laments the later division into verses which has led to people taking the verses 'usually for distinct aphorism', where the weak spirit needs 'undisturbedly' to be presented with 'the thread and coherence of any discourse'. For his method of a cursory exegesis, ibid., 13ff. Here Locke is well ahead of his time on the exegetical trail. For Locke's exegesis of Paul cf. also L.Salvateorelli, 'From Locke to Reitzenstein: The Historical Investigation of the Origins of Christianity', *HTR* 22, 1929, 263-369.

406. Cf. the previous note.

407. Cf. above, 41ff.

408. Cf. above, 150ff

409. P.Abrams is quite right in saying in distinction from the prevailing view of Locke, 'he remained committed to the ideals of the conservative, rationalist Christian world view in which he was educated', in *Two Tracts*, 97f. These connections have usually been concealed in recent discussion, because the alternative between the traditional scholastic doctrine of natural law and modern liberal ideas rules out the whole realm of Humanistic rationalism in the English world of ideas.

410. Cf. above, 135ff., 208ff.

411. It is characteristic of the interpretation of Locke that has long been dominant that for decades only the second treatise was reprinted, cf. Laslett,*Treatises*, 47f. Mabbott, *Locke*,141, still comments on the first part: 'But it is now of purely historical interest and need not concern us further.'(!)

412. 1960 (1963).

413. Op.cit., 45ff. – cf. also the summary account by Cranston, op.cit., 205ff. E.S. de Beer, 'Locke and English Liberalism: the Second Treatise of Government in its Contemporary Setting', in J.W.Yolton (ed.), *Locke*, (34-44) 35f., cf.43, is also in basic agreement.

414. Op.cit., 59, 61.

415. Op.cit., 155.

416. *Political Discourses of S.R.F.*, 1681; in Laslett, (ed.), *Patriarcha*, 47 A, no.2 – the edition also mentioned in Laslett, *Treatises*, App. B., 137, no.33; cf. also ibid., 57.

417. A new, modernized edition which is otherwised faithful to the wording is that by P.Laslett, *Patriarcha and Other Political Works of S.R.F.*, 1949. For Filmer cf. already P.Laslett, 'S.R.F.: The Man versus the Whig Myth', in *William and Mary Quarterly* 3.s.5, 1948, 523-46; W.H.Greenleaf, *Order, Empiricism and Politics. Two Traditions of English Political Thought*, 1964, 80-94; G.J.Schochet, *Patriarchalism in Political Thought*, 1975, 115ff. For the argument of the *Patriarcha* cf. also R.Crippa, *Studi sulla conscienza etica e religiosa de seicento*, 1960, 57ff.; Dunn, *Political Thought*, 58ff.; M.Henningsen, ' "Divine Right of Kings": James I and Robert Filmer', in *Zwischen Revolution und Restauration. Politisches Denken in England im 17.Jahrhundert*, ed. E. Voegelin, 1968, 17-45, esp. 37f.

418. Cf. Laslett, *William and Mary Quarterly*, 5, 531f.; id., in Filmer, *Patriarcha*, 1949, 3; Schochet, *Patriarchalism*, 116.

418a. For the place of his work in the seventeenth-century discussions between the Parliamentary party and the Royalists over the origins of law in general and the political order cf. J.G.A. Pocock, *The Ancient Constitution and the Feudal Law* (1957), reprinted 1967, 151ff., 187ff.

419. In Filmer, *Patriarcha*, 11.

420. For Filmer's forerunners and contemporaries cf. Laslett, op.cit., 27ff.; he refers in particular to Overall's *Convocation Book* (cf. op. cit., 237 n.217 and 247 n.463). Cf. also J.N.Figgis, *The Divine Right of Kings*, 1896, ²1914, reprinted 1965, 148ff., who sees the beginning with Adam as an aspect of natural law which is a peculiarity of Filmer's use of the Old Testament. However, the conclusions he draws from this are taken too far.

420a. For the argument cf. also Schochet, *Patriarchalism*, 136ff.

421. 'Creation made man Prince of his posterity', op.cit., 57.

422. Ibid.

423. Cf. Laslett, op.cit.22. For the role of patriarchalism as a political trend in the seventeenth century cf. Schochet, *Patriarchalism*, passim.

424. Op.cit., 58. This also includes domination of women, since Eve herself was made of part of Adam; cf. 'Observations on Mr.Hobbes' Leviathan', in Laslett, op.cit., (241-50) 241; cf. also 'The Anarchy of a Limited or Mixed Monarchy', id., (278-313) 283 (on Gen.3.16).

425. 'It is true, all Kings be not the natural parents of their subjects, yet they all

either are, or are to be reputed, as the next heirs of those progenitors who were at first the natural parents of the whole people', *Patriarcha*, op.cit., 60f. Cf. also *The Anarchy*, op.cit., 288ff.: '...but that in the same multitude...there is one man amongst them that in nature hath a right to be the King of all the rest, as being the next heir to Adam, and all the others subject unto him.'

426. Op.cit., 60-62; cf. also *The Anarchy*, op.cit., 288: '...all Kings that now are, or ever were, are or were either Fathers of their people, or the heirs of such Fathers, or usurpers of the right of such Fathers.'

427. Op.cit., 62; cf. also *The Anarchy*, op.cit., 289.

428. Op.cit., 20ff. Cf. also id., *William and Mary Quarterly*.

429. Op.cit., 53ff., 81f. Cf. also Laslett, op.cit., 31.

430. The kings of Israel stand in the legitimate succession of the original patriarchate of Adam: 'But when God gave the Israelites Kings, He reestablished the ancient and prime right of lineal succession to paternal government,' op.cit., 60. 'God did always govern His own people by monarchy only,' op.cit., 84.

431. Op.cit., 84f.

432. 'There is no nation that allows children any action or remedy for being unjustly governed,' op.cit., 96.

433. Op.cit., 96f. – Even kings are bound by laws, but only in so far as in their judgment these are just laws, op.cit., 104; otherwise the ruler has full prerogatives over the law, op.cit., 105ff.

434. 86f.

435. Op.cit., 89. Cf. also 90-93.

436. Op.cit., 85, cf. already 78ff. For the derivation of patriarchalism from Aristotle cf. Laslett, op.cit., 27. Filmer developed this feature in another of his writings, *Observations upon Aristotle's Politics touching Forms of Government*, ed. Laslett, 193-229. Here at the conclusion (229) we also have the programmatic six points: '1. That there is no form of government, but monarchy only. 2. That there is no monarchy, but paternal. 3. That there is no paternal monarchy, but absolute, or arbitrary. 4. That there is no such thing as an aristocracy or democracy. 5. That there is no such form of government as a tyranny. 6. That the people are not born free by nature.'

437. Op.cit., 32.

438. Op.cit., 113ff.

439. Op.cit., 94.

440. *De Jure Belli et Pacis*, 1625, 138.

441. Op.cit., 63ff.; cf. also *Observations upon H.Grotius' 'De Jure Belli et Pacis'*, ed. Laslett, (261-74) 273.

442. For the train of thought cf. Viano, op.cit., 299ff.; Laslett, in *Locke, Two Treatises*, 92ff.; Euchner, *John Locke, Zwei Abhandlungen über die Regierung*, 1967, 20ff. For the occasion and argument cf. also J.Dunn, 'The Politics of Locke in England and America', *John Locke Problems*, ed. Yolton, 45-80.

443. Laslett, in *Two Treatises*, 61. L. de Koster, *Locke's Second Treatise of Civil Government*, 1978, Preface, 6f., still expresses a similar view: 'History has consigned Filmer's treatise to the dusty shelves of obscure documents, and with it Locke's refutation in the First Treatise.' But without knowing the First Treatise, a modern reader can hardly understand the arguments of the second treatise properly. Lemos, *Hobbes*, 74, states emphatically: 'The Two Treatises of Government are just that – two treatises. The second is independent of the first, in the sense that it does not presuppose it and is intelligible independent of any knowledge of it.'

444. Originally it was only a single treatise in two books, cf. J.Gerritsen, in P.Laslett, *Further Observations on Locke's Two Treatises of Government, 1690*, 1954; also Laslett, *Two Treatises*, 50, 284.

445. The terms appeared first at the beginning of the eighteenth century, but the parties had already formed.

446. Against Laslett, in *Two Treatises*, 61. Schouls, *Imposition*, 201, rightly points out: 'the importance of Filmer's works can hardly be overemphasized in this context.' The attempt by R.W.K.Hinton, 'A Note on the Dating of Locke's Second Treatise', *PolSt* 22, 1974, 471-8 (cf. also K.Olivecrona, 'A Note on Locke and Filmer', *Locke Newsletter* 7, 1976, 83-93) to antedate this even beyond Laslett's approach by deleting all references to Filmer to arrive at what he supposes to be an early version of the Second Treatise does not alter the material connections in any way.

446a. M.P.Thompson, 'The Reception of Locke's Two Treatises of Government 1690-1705', *PolSt* 24, 1976, 184-91, points out that to begin with the discussion was almost exclusively over the First Treatise, because it was topical in connection with the controversies over the constitution down to the first decade of the eighteenth century, whereas the Second Treatise only gained its reputation much later.

447. Op.cit., 68f.

448. *Patriarcha non Monarcha* (anon.), 1681.

449. Book I, sec.30 (ed. Laslett, 179): '...that God in this Donation, gave the world to Mankind in common, and not to Adam in particular' (ibid., 180): '*Man* there, as is usual, is taken for the Species, and *them* the individuals of that Species...'

450. Op.cit., I, secs.44-49 (ed.Laslett, 189ff.).

451. Op.cit., I, sec.52 (ed. Laslett, 196).

452. Op.cit., I, sec.54 (ed. Laslett, 197f.).

453. Op.cit., I, sec.55 (ed .Laslett, 198).

454. Op.cit., I, secs.60f. (ed. Laslett, 202ff.).

455. Op.cit., I, secs.88ff. (ed. Laslett, 224ff.).

456. 'about the descent of *Adam*''s Regal Power..., that the *Line* and *Posterity* of *Adam* is to have it, that is in plain *English*, any one may have it, since there is no Person living that hath not the Title of being of the *Line* and *Posterity* of *Adam*,' op.cit., 1, sec.111 (ed. Laslett, 240).

457. Op.cit., I, sec.104 (ed. Laslett, 234f.).

458. Op.cit., I, sec.105 (ed. Laslett, 236).

459. Op.cit., I, sec.101 (ed. Laslett, 232f.).

460. Op.cit., I, sec.103 (ed. Laslett, 233f.).

461. Op.cit., I, secs.111ff. (ed. Laslett, 239ff.).

462. Op.cit., I, secs.139ff. (ed. Laslett, 260ff.).

463. Op.cit., I, secs.41-43 (ed. Laslett, 186-9).

464. Op.cit., I, secs.159ff. (ed. Laslett, 275ff.).

465. Op.cit., I, sec.46 (ed. Laslett, 191).

466. Op.cit., I, sec.36 (ed. Laslett, 183).

467. Op.cit., I, sec.3 (ed. Laslett, 161,162).

468. Op.cit., I, secs.5 and 6 (ed. Laslett, 161 and 162).

469. Op.cit., I, sec.67 (ed. Laslett, 208). As J.H.Franklin. *John Locke and the Theory of Sovereignty*, 1978, shows, Locke bases the general sovereignty of the people on this principle and thus also diverges from the Whig principle of Parliamentary rule.

470. *Natural Right*, 215f.

471. Cf. Euchner, in *Locke, Zwei Abhandlungen*, 26f. – For the character of compromise in Locke's theory of the natural state cf. also Bobbio, op.cit., 204ff.

472. Here in fact, with Euchner and others, one should point to the function of property. However, E.J.Hundert, 'Market Society and Meaning in Locke's Political Philosophy', *JHP* 15, 1977, 33-44, makes it clear that Locke still in no way presupposes a market economy as envisaged by nineteenth-century liberalism, but begins from the society of his time, with its states and hierarchial ordering, in which those who depended on wages and those in service, without land, formed a lower class.

473. Cf. above, 561 n.427 and 562 n.454.

474. Op.cit., 69.

475. Cf. also Laslett, Introduction to Filmer, *Patriarcha*, 16f., 31.

476. *Patriarcha*, op.cit., 86ff.; cf. *The Anarchy*, op.cit., 279ff.

477. *Two Treatises* II, 6: 'The *State of Nature* has a Law of Nature to govern it, which obliges everyone; And Reason, which is that Law, teaches all Mankind, who will but consult it, that being all equal and independent, no one ought to harm another in his Life, Health, Liberty or Possessions' (ed. Laslett, 289). Cf. also II, 12: 'for though it would be besides my present purpose, to enter here into the particulars of the Law of Nature...yet, it is certain there is such a Law, and that too, as intelligible and plain to a rational Creature, and a Studier of that Law, as the positive Laws of Common-wealths, nay possibly plainer...' (ed. Laslett, 293). – Cf. also R.Polin, 'Justice in Locke's Philosophy', *Nomos* 6, 1963, (262-83) 266ff.; and already id., *La Politique Morale*, 116-18. There is much to be said for E.S. de Beer's comment, *Locke*, ed. Yolton, 41, 43, that Locke above all has the actual English constitution in view.

478. II, sec.19 (ed. Laslett, 298f.).

479. II, sec.6 (ed. Laslett, 289).

480. I, secs.52-53 are more impressive in this respect (ed. Laslett, 196-7).

481. I, sec.4 (ed. Laslett, 161).

482. I, sec.60 (ed. Laslett, 202). Cf.also I, sec.56 (ibid., 199); 'the dictates of Nature and Reason, as well as his Reveal'd Command'; 'God and Nature', I, sec.90 (ibid., 225); I, sec.119 (ibid., 246); 'any Law of God and Nature', I, sec.93 (ibid., 228); I, sec.116 (ibid., 243);'God or Nature', I, sec.111 (ibid., 240); 'God by the Law of Nature or Revelation', I, sec.166 (ibid., 279f.). All these statements, however, do not correspond exactly to what is quoted in the text, as on each occasion the contrast is between the law of nature and revelation (also against Cox, op.cit., 47).

482a.P.A.Schouls, *Imposition*, 239 n.7, refers to the similarity between Locke's view of scripture and the views of present-day fundamentalism.

483. See above, 283ff.

484. The Latin original, written in 1685 and published in Gouda in 1689, was largely replaced by the English translation by W.Popple which appeared in that year and the next; it is often rather loose. Only in the last twenty years has a series of new bilingual editions appeared: *J.Locke, Lettera sulla Tolleranza. Testo latino e versione italiana. Prem. di R.Klibansky, Intr. di E.de Marchi*, 1961 (also in Polish: *J.Locke, List o tolerancji*, 1963); *J.Locke, Carta sobre la tolerancia, Intr. da A.Waismann, Prol. de. R.Klibansky*, 1962; *J.Locke, Lettre sur la Tolérance. Texte latin et traduction française. Préf. par R.Klibansky, Intr. par R.Polin*, 1964; *J.Locke, Epistola de Tolerantia. A Letter on Toleration, Pref. by R.Klibansky, Int. by J.W.Gough*, 1968 (quotations from this last edition). Cf. also *J.Locke, A Letter concerning Toleration*, ed. M.Montuori, 1963; *J.Locke, Ein Brief über Toleranz*, tr ...J.Ebbinghaus (1957), ²1966.

485. In the introduction to the first edition of his German translation.

486. In the second edition which is used here.

487. Preface to the second edition, VII.

488. For criticism cf. Gough, in *J.Locke, Epistola*, Introduction, 40ff. R.Koselleck, 'Aufklärung und die Grenzen ihrer Toleranz', in T.Rendtorff (ed.), *Glaube und Toleranz. Das theologische Erbe der Aufklärung*, 1982, (256-71) 259, still takes a similar view: 'He sought to remove all religious motivation from politics...' But cf. the more qualified comments about the content of the Letter on Tolerance which follow.

489. Op.cit.

490. In F.Bourne, *Life*, I, 174-94; also in *Scritti Editi e Inediti Sulla Tolleranza, a cura di C.A.Viano*, 1961, 81-107. For the various versions cf. Viano, op.cit., 6-12, and Gough, op.cit., 14 n.2.

490a. Cf. also Baumgartner, *Naturrecht*, 78ff.

491. Both those who celebrate Locke without qualification as a pioneer of modern ideals of tolerance and the criticism of Ebbinghaus to the opposite effect are to be faulted for having overlooked this. F.G.Gawlick, 'The English Deists' Contribution to the Theory of Toleration', in *Studies on Voltaire and the Eighteenth Century*, CLI-CLV, 1976, (823-35) 826ff., affirms that Locke's idea of tolerance was only of limited effect because Locke maintained certain truths which were to be believed as revealed as the condition for blessedness. It was first the attitude of the Deists that only natural religion and morality were to be required that made genuine tolerance possible.

492. At that time still a disputed theory!

493. Bourne, op.cit, I, 176 = *Scritti*, 83.

494. In King, *Life*, II, 82-92, 99-101.

495. Cf. *Ecclesia*, in King, op.cit., II, 99: 'That it is a supernatural but voluntary society, wherein a man associates himself to God, angels and holy men.' So it is 'a society by consent', 'the need of entering into such society being only to obtain the favour of God, by offering him an acceptable worship,' op.cit., 100.

496. In King, op.cit., 85.

497. Only in *Scritti*, 86. Cf. also Gough, Introduction, 15f.

498. For the differences between the idea of the covenant which is constitutive for forming the church among the Puritan Congregationalists and the idea of the covenant in Locke cf. also Viano, *John Locke*, 409.

499. 'There are others who affirm that all the power and authority the magistrate hath is derived from the grant and consent of the people.' Bourne, op.cit., I, 175 = *Scritti*, 82.

500. In Bourne, op.cit., I, 174 = *Scritti*, 81: 'That the whole trust, power and authority of the magistrate is vested in him for no other purpose but to be made use of for the good, preservation and peace of men in that society over which he is set.' Cf. also 175/82.

501. Locke has worked out the parallel in exemplary form in the paper 'On the Difference between Civil and Ecclesiastical Power', printed in King, op.cit., 108-19.

502. *Nemo nascitur alicujus ecclesiae membrum, alias patris avorumque religio jure haereditario simul cum latifundiis ad quemque descenderet...*, *Epistola*, ed. Klibansky, 70.

503. Gough, in Locke, *Epistola*, Introduction, 39f.

504. Ebbinghaus, op.cit., Introduction, XLf.

505. For content and criticism cf. esp. Ebbinghaus, op.cit., Introduction, XXXVIIIff.; Gough, op.cit., 14ff. (also on the various expansions).

506. Cf. already Bourne, op.cit., I, 172f.; also Ebbinghaus, op.cit., Introduction, XXXVIIIf.

507. Op.cit., 72/74.

508. Op.cit., 108.

509. Op.cit., 102-8.

510. *Ecclesia mihi videtur societas libera hominum sponte sua coeuntium ut Deum publice colant eo modo quem credunt numini acceptum fore ad salutem animarum*, op.cit., 70. Nowhere does the influence of ancient thought on the Humanist tradition which is still alive in Locke emerge as clearly as in this Latin formulation.

511.*Respublica mihi videtur societas hominum solummodo ad bona civilia conservanda promovendaque constituta. Bona civilia voco vitam, libertatem, corporis integritatem et indolentiam, et rerum externarum possessiones, ut sunt latifundia, pecunia, suppelex, et cetera*, op.cit., 64/66.

512. Op.cit., 108/110. Ebbinghaus, op.cit., Introduction, LIf., criticizes Locke for introducing an insoluble conflict of conscience in the case of poor Meliboeus.

513. Op.cit., 126.

514. Op.cit., 128.

515. Op.cit., 132/4.

516. Op.cit., 134ff.

517. Op.cit., 148ff.

518. A sect in lower Mesopotamia of which Locke is said to have known through the work by Ignatius a Jesu, *Narratio Originis, Rituum, et Errorum Christianorum Sancti Ioannis*, 1652, cf. Gough, op.cit., n.68, on 162.

519. *Quod apud illos, qui solam Sacram Scripturam pro regula fidei agnoscunt, haeresis sit separatio facta in communione Christiana ob dogmata disertis Sacrae Scripturae verbis non contenta*, op.cit., 150.

520. Even the state church can therefore become heresy!

521. With F.Bourne, *Life*, I ,169, Ebbinghaus, op.cit., 136 n.36, and Gough, op.cit., 163 n.70, think that in this statement they can find the echo of a remark by Chillingworth (*Religion*, IV, 17). That would fit in well with the proximity of the two thinkers which we can also establish elsewhere.

522. *Schisma... nihil aliud est quam separatio in ecclesiae communione facta ob aliquod in cultu divino vel disciplina ecclesiastica non necessarium. Nihil in cultu divino vel disciplina ecclesiastica ad communionem Christiano esse potest necessarium, nisi quod disertis verbis jusserit legislator Christus, vel instinctu Spiritus Sancti Apostoli*, op.cit., 154.

523. Ebbinghaus, op.cit., LIVf., has recognized most clearly that the appendix to the Letter on Tolerance shows how little Locke is capable of real tolerance, in that in this way he makes the scripture law. Of course Locke does not subjectively speak with 'total resignation in this sphere' (LIV), but with a real conviction that he has natural criteria for distinguishing heresy and schism which (if they emerge in the fundamentalia) he equally obviously regards as being intolerable. An original right of men as moral beings (of the kind that Ebbinghaus shows in neo-Kantian terms as his own *a priori*, op.cit., LXIII) would have been completely outside his line of vision.

524. Op.cit., 114ff. Here Gough's translation 'idolaters were to be driven out', op.cit., 115 distorts the sense of the Latin *idolatras exterminandas*, 114 (on p.118, on the other hand, we have *expellanda... erat idolatria*, corresponding to Locke's special interpretation, by which Gough presumably unconsciously let himself be guided in translating the sentence introduced by Locke on p.114 as a possible objection). Popple 'to be rooted out', is more correct (cf. also Ebbinghaus, 73).

525. The altered situation already emerges from the fact that Locke speaks only of the requirement to take away the property of the Indians and Sectarians for the counter-position. Of course reality in America down to the recent past looked much more literally like the Old Testament demand.

526. Op.cit., n.19, 132f.

527. See above, 114f.

528. Ebbinghaus, op.cit., points out that Popple's translation does not take account of the important *hac in re* of the Latin text. In the *Reasonableness* Locke in fact affirms the continued validity of the moral law as such, cf. 265 above.

529. *Lex enim quaecunque positiva nullos obligat, nisi eos quibus ponitur*, op.cit., 116.

530. *respublica Judaica* (or *Israelis*), ibid.

531. *in theocratia fundabatur*, op.cit., 116. Popple is again inaccurate: 'was an absolute theocracy'.

532. Popple again inaccurate: 'between that commonwealth and the church.' In both cases Gough, op.cit., 117, is exact.

533. Op.cit., 116ff.

534. Op.cit., 118.

535. See above, 264f.

536. Aaron, *John Locke*, 299, observes on Locke: 'He differed from the Deists in one most important respect. He held that whilst religion never contradicted reason,

reason itself cannot take us the whole way. Since we are finite and limited beings, reason cannot reveal to us all we need to know in order to live the religious life. We do know how to live that life, but only because God has spoken his Word to man through Christ. That event was not merely rational and not merely natural. The supernatural remains in Locke's theology; the Mysteries remain. Locke believes in the Virgin Birth and the Resurrection from the Dead. The miracles remain; they are the supernatural power and authority of Christ.'

Part Three

1. The Beginning of the Deistic Debate

1. 'Der Deismus'(1898), in *Gesammelte Schriften*, IV, 1925, (429-87) 429.

2. 'Deismus', in *HWP*, 2, cols.44f.; Preface to Lechler, *Geschichte*, XIV. Cf. also id., 'Der Deismus als Grundzug', in *Hermann Samuel Reimarus*, passim. – Cf. already the 'Deistic Confession of Faith' in P.Skelton, *Deism Revealed, or the Attack on Christianity*, ²1751, I, 34f.

3. For its scattered emergence on the continent of Europe cf. Gawlick, Preface to Lechler, op.cit., VIIIff.; id., in *Hermann Samuel Reimarus*, 16ff. Lechler's work is still the standard account of the history of the English movement, as Gawlick rightly stresses in his Foreword, XXII. Cf. recently also P.Casini, *Introduzione all'illuminismo. Da Newton a Rousseau*, 1973, II, 51-163.

4. The underground literature which developed there (cf. G.Lanson, 'Questions diverses sur l'histoire de l'esprit philosophique en France avant 1750', *RHLF* 19, 1912, 1-29, 293-317, and above all I.O.Wade, *The Clandestine Organization*), *a priori* had a much more radical anti-ecclesiastical character.

5. G.Gawlick in particular continually makes this point, cf. *HWP* 2, col.46; Introduction to Lechler, op.cit., XVf.; Introduction to J.Toland, *Christianity not Mysterious*, 111., etc. However, this self-understanding can only be justified in the light of the Humanist and rationalist content which at that time Christianity had also adopted outside Deism; considered objectively, G.R.Cragg, *Reason and Authority*, 63, is right when he writes: 'Clearly they can be regarded as Christians only if Christianity is so drastically re-defined that it forfeits all its characteristics as an historic faith.' G.E.Aylmer, 'Unbelief in Seventeenth-Century England', in D.Pennington and K.Thomas (eds.), *Puritans and Revolutionaries. Essays in Seventeenth-Century History presented to Christopher Hill*, 1978, 22-46, shows impressively that real atheism was still absent in this period. He refers above all to seventeenth-century polemic directed against alleged 'atheism'.

6. E.C.Mossmer, *Bishop Butler*, 49, recalls Stillingfleet's *Letter to a Deist*, 1677 (²1697); while it chiefly attacks Hobbes and Spinoza, it could be regarded as an indication of the existence of Deists. Cf. also Sina, *Ragione*, 204ff. However, it remains doubtful whether the terminology of the word 'Deist' was already developed precisely enough at that time.

7. Recent works on him are: U.Bonanate, *Charles Blount: libertinismo e deismo nel Seicento inglese*, 1972; cf. also J.A.Redwood, 'Charles Blount (1654-93), Deism and English Free Thought', *JHI* 35, 1974, 490-8; Sina, *Ragione*, 175ff. A bibliography of his writings is: J.S.L.Gilmour, 'Some Uncollected Authors: XVIII: C.Blount', in *Book Collector* 7, 1958, 182-7.

8. P.Villey, 'L'influence de Montaigne sur Charles Blount et sur les Déistes anglais', *Revue du Seizième Siècle* 1, 1913, 190-219, 392-443, seeks to demonstrate the influence of this French sceptic from the end of the sixteenth century on Blount (though in other respects the basic attitudes of the two writers are very different).

In fact Blount quotes Montaigne a great deal, particularly in the *Philostratus*. Bonanate, op.cit., 167, would prefer to reckon Blount among the Libertinists rather than among the Deists.

9. As we have seen, his short work *Religio Laici*, 1683 (original edition in the British Library; I have used a xerox copy in the possession of the Philosophical Seminar of the Ruhr University of Bochum), is the reproduction of a preliminary English draft of Herbert's work which was later printed in Latin with the same name, cf. above, 523 n.55. Blount undertook the work in order to refute the poem of John Dryden which appeared in 1682 under the same title, cf. Sina, *Ragione*, 178ff.

10. Earlier, in 1679, there appeared e.g. his work *Anima Mundi* (reprinted in the *Miscellaneous Works*, 1695, II). For the content and the earlier history of the theme cf. Bonanate, op.cit., 6-33. In this writing Blount, following above all the arguments of Pomponazzi (*Tractatus de immortalitate animae*, 1534), denies the immortality of the soul and all the consequences of that which are exploited by the church. In passing he takes the opportunity of making all kinds of comments about superstition and speaking sceptically about worship, cult, prayer and ceremonies (esp.122ff.). Cf. also Sina, *Ragione*, 176ff.

11. C. Blount, *The Two First Books of Philostratus, Concerning the Life of Apollonius Tyanaeus*, 1680.

12. *Philostratus*, 11: "'Tis well known to all men that have search'd into the Records of ancient Time, how necessary it hath ever been esteem'd for Heroes to have a Birth no less miraculous than their Life; as it appears by the several Histories of Semiramis, Cyrus, Romulus and many of the heathen Gods.' After retailing the gossip of the miraculous rescue of an illegitimate child which had been thrown off London Bridge and later grew up to be a thief, who was ultimately hanged, he ends by commenting that he does not doubt that in a blasphemous way Hierocles had compared the miraculous signs at the birth of Apollonius with the star and the angels' song, 'as being both equally strange, but not alike true. For to believe any Stories that are not approved of by the publick Authority of our Church, is Superstition; wheras to believe them that are, is Religion.' It is easy to see how here Hobbes' principles are ironically made use of under the pretext of preserving orthodoxy.

13. *Philostratus*, 37.

14. 'First, Thinking it unnecessary, Misericordia Dei being sufficiens Justitiae suae. Secondly, God must have appointed this Mediator, and so was really reconciled to the World before. And that thirdly, a Mediator derogates from the infinite Mercy of God, equally as an Image doth from his Spirituality and Infinity,' *Philostratus*, 42. The same reasons against mediation are also given in 'A Summary Account of the Deists Religion', in *Oracles of Reason*, (88-96) 89. Cf. also the extract in P.Gay, *Deism: An Anthology*, 1968, (47-61) 48.

15. *Philostratus*,42.

16. Cf. n.14 above. J.Leland, *A View of the Principal Deistical Writers*, 1755, 70f., has stressed this point.

17. *Philostratus*, 6: here one should recall the more extensive criticism of David's career in P.Bayle, 'David', *Dictionnaire Historique et critique*, II, [5]1748, 253-55, 908-13 (two versions).

18. 1693, in *Miscellaneous Works*, 1.

19. Op.cit., 20ff.

20. Where did Adam and Eve get needles from to sew fig-leaves together for aprons after the Fall?, in Blount, *Oracles*, 44; but there are also profound considerations in it, like the conclusion that in Gen.1 it was not Moses' intention to depict the beginning of the world 'exactly according to the physical Truth... but to expound the first Originals of Things after such a method as might breed in the minds of

Men Piety, and a worshiping of the true God', in Blount, op.cit., 74. Blount does not take these up.

21. Sir Thomas Browne, *Religio Medici*, 1642; id., *Enquiries in the Vulgar Errors*, 1646, cf. *The Works of Sir Thomas Browne*, ed. G.Keynes, new edition, Vols.1-4, 1964. In particular Blount quotes Browne's remark, 'There are in Scripture Stories that do exceed the Fables of Poets', *Oracles of Reason*, Letter, 3. For Browne cf. also J.Bennet, *Sir Thomas Browne*, 1962; J.S.Finch, *Sir Thomas Browne: A Doctor's Life as Science and Faith*, 1950; P.Green, *Sir Thomas Browne*, 1959; F.L.Huntley, *Sir Thomas Browne*, 1962; E.S.Merton, *Science and Imagination in Sir Thomas Browne*, 1949; W.P.Dunn, *Sir Thomas Browne. A Study in Religious Philosophy*, ²1950; R.S.Westfall, *Science and Religion*, 147-51.

22. For the work cf. already Lechler, *Geschichte*, 123; cf. also Mossner, *Bishop Butler*, 50. J.Orr, *English Deism*, 112, mixes together individual titles of Blount's writings in his quotations and cites as Blount's own comments what he takes over from his informants. For Burnet's work, ibid., 57f., where there is also the amusing passage from a ballad by William Pittis who mocks Moses as author of the Pentateuch, in Burnet's view.

23. In *Miscellaneous Works*, III. Cf. Bonanate, *Blount*, 38ff.

24. Op.cit., 3.

25. Op.cit., 4.

26. Cf. above, 189ff.

27. 'Before Religion, that is to say, Sacrifices, Rites, Ceremonies, pretended Revelations, and the like, were invented amongst the Heathens, there was no worship of God but in a rational way, whereof the Philosophers pretending to be Masters, did to this end, not only teach Virtue and Piety, but were also themselves great examples of it in their Lives and Conversations; whom the People chiefly follow'd till they were seduced by their crafty and covetous Sacerdotal Order who, instead of the said Virtue and Piety; introduced Fables and Fictions of their coining...' op.cit., 3. Cf. also the letter: 'To ...Major A. concerning the Original of the Jews', in *Oracles of Reason*, (128-36) 135: 'The Article of one true God, was common both to Jews and Gentiles... The Universality of Religious Worship consisting in the practice of Virtue and Goodness, we may find also common to the Gentiles, as well as to the Jews.' The dependence is clearly evident at another place (*Anima Mundi*, 122), where Blount points out that the pious Gentiles designated God by the title *Deus Optimus Maximus* (a standard formula in Herbert of Cherbury).

28. Cf. op.cit., 14: 'The Original of Sacrifices seems to be as ancient as Religion it self.' Preface, fol.F 3, is somewhat inconsistent with this: 'Not that true Religion is here to be blamed, but only those ill Constitutions, wherein the most Sacred Instructions turn sowre.' But that is probably only one of the verbal concessions to official Christianity.

29. Cf. Preface, fol.F 5: 'The general decay of Piety, hath in most Religions whatsoever preceeded from the exemplary viciousness of their Clergy; though perhaps less in ours than in others.' And, in another context: '...for I write not to Heathens, but Christians.' (ibid.).

30. 'To Major A.', op.cit., 135.

31. *De Legibus Hebraeorum Ritualibus et Earum Rationibus*, Cambridge 1685, also Tübingen 1732 (*Works*, ed. L.Chappelow, two vols, 1727); I have used the Editio Tertia, Leipzig 1705. Lechler was the first in modern times to draw attention to the significance of this work, cf. *Geschichte*, 137-9. F.E.Manuel, *The Religion of Isaac Newton*, 1974, 87, points out that this is a compendium of the Latin works of Maimonides. Mediaeval Jewish exegesis was long normative for Christian exegesis. A preliminary work is id., *Dissertatio de Urim et Thummim in Deuteronomio*, 1669. The chronicle of the world by the historian James Marsham, *Canon chronicus Aegyptiacus*,

Ebraicus, Graecus, London 1672 (I have used the edition *nunc in Germania recussus,* Leipzig 1676) connects Hebrew chronology with Egyptian: *Res Ebraeorum cum Aegyptiacis quam plurimum permixtae sunt,* op.cit., 12.

32. Cf. above, 306. Marcham, op.cit., 149ff., is also against this thesis.

33. Lib.I, Cap.I, op.cit., 29ff., 35ff.

34. Op.cit., 30ff.

35. Op.cit., 36ff. *Deum Legem Ceremonialem dedisse, ut idolatriae se passim diffundenti repagulum obiceret, & Abrahami saltem semen a peregrinis ad patrios mores, & ab idolis ad veri Dei cultum sensumque, revocaret.* Lib.I, Cap.II, 42.

36. Lib.I, Cap.IV, op.cit., 53ff.

37. *...Deo visum est, hanc rationem inire, cum Religionem in integrum restituere, & Israelitas ad patrum pietatem revocare, statuisset. Idolorum cultu, sub poena, iis interdixit; & ritus omnes, fidei vel moribus honestis adversantes, a Legis & cultus sui corpore, ...penitus amputavit,* Lib.III, Praefatio, op.cit., 761.

38. *Deus interim... ritus non paucos, multorum annorum & Gentium usu cohonestatos, quos ineptias norat esse tolerabiles, aut ad mysterium aliquod adumbrandum aptos, in sacrorum suorum numerum adoptavit...; modo Deus ritus antiquos omnes inhibuisset, in eos proculdubio & Gentium sacra impetu & desiderio calidiore fuissent ruituri. Quando itaque Deo jam res esset cum eo rudi populo...; Eorum ritus nonnullos paululum emendatos leni animo tulit; & per* synkatabasin *illam Israelitas a Gentium idolis & ceremoniis sensim & suaviter avocare studuit, quos statim & cum violentia quadam avellere non potuit.* Ibid.

39. Op.cit., 57.

40. Cf. e.g. the quotation in n.38.

41. Cf. ibid. Spencer also often uses the Latin verb *accomodare,* when he speaks of God's activity of a lawgiver to Old Testament Israel.

42. In *Oracles of Reason.*

43. *Oracles of Reason,* 134.

44. Op.cit., 38.

45. Op.cit., 14.

46. In *Oracles of Reason.* Cf. Bonanate, op.cit., 74ff. Leland, *View,* 70, already stressed this and the part of the *Oracles of Reason* mentioned next as particularly noteworthy.

47. *Oracles,* 88.

48. Op.cit., 89.

49. Op.cit., 90.

50. Op.cit., 95.

51. Cf. also Letter to Major A., *Oracles,* 135: '... the Universality of Religious Worship consisting in the practice of Virtue and Goodness.'

52. Cf. the beginning of this chapter, above, 566 n.2.

53. *Oracles,* 197-211.

54. Op.cit., 197.

55. 1696 (anonymous); a second edition with the name of the author appeared in the same year (third edition 1702). Facsimile reprint of the first edition, ed. G.Gawlick, 1964 (the additions in the second edition are in an Appendix, 177ff.); also H.F.Nicholl, 'John Toland: Religion without Mystery', *Her.* 100, 1965, No.C, 54-65; cf. also H.Swanston, 'British Interpreters VII: John (Junius Janus) Toland', *Scripture Bulletin* 12, 1981, 11-13.

56. L.Stephen, *English Thought,* I, 93; Mossner, *Bishop Butler,* 46ff., 52ff.; P.Gay, *Deism,* 12f., objects that it obscures more than it clarifies, as all the Deists were both critical and constructive Deists. What is meant, however, is the acceptance of Locke's critical epistemology which had come about since Toland, and in this sense the classification is justified.

57. Gawlick, in Toland, *Christianity,* 30 n.37, points out that Locke's relationship

to Deism has yet to be explained sufficiently (as has the way in which Locke was assimilated by later anti-Deistic orthodoxy). The difficulties in demonstrating the situation exactly rest partly on the fact that Locke, too, is not entirely an original thinker and otherwise is an exponent of a widespread world-view, see below.

58. When he was accused by Stillingfleet, *A Discourse in Vindication of the Trinity*, 1696, of being the spiritual author of Toland's ideas, he decisively rejected any connection with him, 'Second Reply', in *Works*, VI, 104. – J.C.Biddle, *Critique*, stresses the gulf between Locke's recognition of the limits of reason and Toland's rational Christianity.

59. Though first without the mention of any name, *Christianity*, 83, 87. But cf. a few years later id., *Letters to Serena*, 1704, facsimile new impression ed. G.Gawlick, 1964, 226: 'I consider his (Locke's) Essay of Human Understanding to be the most useful Book towards attaining universal Knowledge, that is extant in any Language...'

60. There is still no comprehensive modern monograph on John Toland (1670-1722). But cf. Lechler, *Geschichte*, 180-210, 463-77; J.Hunt, *History of Religious Thought in England from the Reformation to the End of the Last Century*, 1871, reprinted 1973, II, 236-62; A.Lantoine, *Un précurseur de la Francmaçonnerie: John Toland (1670-1722). Suivi de la traduction française du Pantheisticon*, 1927; C. Motzo Dentice di Accadia, 'Il deismo inglese de settecento, I. – John Toland', *GCFI* 15, 2.ser., vol.2, 1934, 69-95; id., *Preilluminismo e deismo in Inghilterra*, 1970, 175-210; F.Heinemann, 'John Toland and the Age of Reason', *APh* 4, 1950, 35-66 (for the most part already in *RESt* 20, 1944, 125-46); cf. also id., 'John Toland, France, Holland and Dr. Williams', *RESt* 25, 1949, 246-349; Casini, *Introduzione*, 67ff.; Cragg, *From Puritanism*, 136-55; C.Giuntini, *Toland e i liberi pensatori del'700*, 1974; A.Sabetti, *John Toland, un irregolare della società e della cultura inglese tra Seicento e Settecento*, 1976; Sina, *Ragione*, 439ff.; M.G.Jacob, *Newtonians*, 210ff.; H.Graf Reventlow, 'Judaism and Jewish Christianity in the Works of John Toland', in *Proceedings of the Sixth World Congress of Jewish Studies* III, 1977, 111-16; also the introductions by G.Gawlick, in his facsimile editions of Toland, *Christianity and Letters to Serena*. Unfortunately I had no access to the unpublished dissertation (Trinity College, Dublin) by H.F.Nicholl, *The Life and Work of John Toland*, 1962. Contemporary biographies are: J.L.Mosheim, *De vita, fatis et scriptis Joannis Tolandi Commentatio* (in *Vindiciae antiquae Christianorum disciplinae*, etc, ²1722, 1-184); anon. (E.Curl), *An Historical Account of the Life and Writings of the Late Eminently Famous Mr.John Toland*, 1722, 'though this is more of a panegyric than a biography' (J.A.Trinius, *Freydenker Lexicon*, 1759, facsimile edition 1966, 481); J.A. Desmaizeaux, 'Some Memoirs of the Life and Writings of Mr.John Toland: In a Letter to S.B.L', in *A Collection of Several Pieces of Mr.John Toland*, 1726, I, III-XCII (also in *The Miscellaneous Works of Mr.John Toland*, 1747, I, III-XCII). – For Toland's writings cf. G.Carabelli, *Tolandiana. Materiali bibliografici per lo studio dell'opera e della fortuna di John Toland 1670-1722*, 1975. – G.Ricuperati deals with manuscripts of Toland from the former private library of the free-thinking adjutant of Prince Eugene of Savoy, G.W.Baron von Hohendorff, which are partly sketches for later printed versions and which have been preserved in Vienna, in connection with the *Triregno* of P.Giannone (1676-1748): *RSIt* 79, 3, 1967, 628-95; for further manuscripts (especially letters) in the British Library see M.C.Jacob, 'John Toland and the Newtonian Ideology', *JWCI* 32, 1969, 307-31.

61. For the content cf. Lechler, op.cit., 182-94; Zscharnack, Introduction to Toland, *Christentum ohne Geheimnis*, 1-53; also M.Muff, *Leibnizens Kritik der Religionsphilosophie von John Toland*, Diss. phil. Zurich 1940, 8-36.

62. Gawlick, Introduction to *Christianity*, 16*. Cf. also Motzo Dentici, *GCFI* 1934, 74,77 = *Preilluminismo*, 178,181.

63. Gawlick, Introduction to *Christianity*, 10*, thinks that this writing can hardly

have influenced him because his own plan was too well matured. However, it must be said that he would not have agreed with Locke's return to an unqualified acceptance of the authority of revelation.

63a. Toland had already completed his work *before* Locke's *Reasonableness*, which thus was possibly meant as an answer to Toland, cf. M.C.Jacob, *Newtonians*, 214f. (with a reference to John Biddle).

64. Introduction to *Christianity*, 11*. This is particularly to be stressed against Sabetti, *Toland*, esp. 151ff., who will not recognize any difference in Toland's basic position between his later 'pantheistic' writings and *Christianity*, and claims that the early work already contains 'una condanna...della religione *tout court* intesa come superstizione e...come *instrumentum regni*' (156).

65. Cragg, *From Puritanism*, 141. The quotation meant is *Christianity*, 6.

66. Op.cit., 9f.

67. Op.cit., 12f. Cf. the definition, op.cit., 57: reason is 'that Faculty every one has of judging of his Idea's according to their Agreement or Disagreement, and so of loving what seems good unto him, and hating what he thinks evil.'

68. Op.cit., 18.

69. Op.cit., 16.

70. Op.cit., 23.

71. Op.cit., 83.

72. Op.cit., 76.

73. Op.cit., 75.

74. Op.cit., 79.

75. Op.cit., 78. – F.Heinemann, op.cit., 59, criticizes Toland's concept of reason: 'Toland believes in the perfection of the finite understanding and takes it as if it were infinite.' This criticism is justified, but in view of what has been said it should be noted that this is an infinity of *practical* reason in its sphere, and not of a *pure* reason limited in any case.

76. Op.cit., 80.

77. Op.cit., XXf., cf. already XIX and 147, where he speaks of the 'Poor and Illiterate', who can very well understand the unfalsified gospel.

78. He counts himself among those 'rejecting those Fooleries superadded... to such as prefer the Precepts of God to the Inventions of Men, the plain Paths of Reason to the insuperable Labyrinths of the Fathers', op.cit., XXIII, and attacks 'this Scholastick Jargon', with which the school theologians are said to have falsified the simple truth of scripture, op.cit., XII.

79. Op.cit., XIV.

80. Op.cit., XXVI.

81. Op.cit., XXVIf.

82. Thus already Lechler, op.cit., 194, and also M.Schmidt, 'Deismus.III. Englischer Deismus', *RGG³*, II, 1958 (cols.59-69), 62.

83. Introduction to *Christianity*, 111. – F.Heinemann, *John Toland*, 431, by contrast speaks of a particular radical and revolutionary character of Toland's Deism in comparison with the later English Deists.

84. Most clearly in *Hermann Samuel Reimarus*, 22ff.

85. Op.cit., 24.

85a. At any rate, C.L.Becker, *The Heavenly City of the Eighteenth-Century Philosophers*, 1932, esp.50f., generalizes far too much when he attributes quite generally to the 'philosophers' of the eighteenth century the view that traditional revelation, above all in Holy Scripture and the church, has been superseded.

86. Op.cit., XII.

87. Op.cit., XXVII. – Heinemann, op.cit., 63, calls Toland one of the fathers of

English rationalism, explaining 'rationalism' in the English sense of the word as the 'practice of explaining the supernatural in religion in a way consonant with reason'.

88. We can recognize this above all in the significant role played by Cicero as an authority, cf. T.Zielinski, *Cicero im Wandel der Jahrhunderte*, ⁵1967, esp. secs.16, 17, 210-44; G.Gawlick, 'Cicero and the Enlightenment', in *Studies on Voltaire and the Eighteenth Century*, 25, 1963, 657-82; for Toland in particular cf. id., Introduction to Toland, *Letters to Serena*, 9*.

89. It is methodologically important to separate this writing from Toland's later works and thus from the changes in his attitude. Only in *Christianity not Mysterious* can Toland be regarded as a 'critical Deist' in the above-mentioned sense; later he moves further and further away from this transitional position. M.C.Jacob's rejection of the designation 'Deist' for Toland (*Newtonian Ideology*, 307) affects only his middle and late phases.

90. *Christianity*, 6.

91. Op.cit., 14f., cf. 38, 146.

92. Both quotations, op.cit., 38.

93. 482 and n.69.

94. Op.cit., XVI.

95. Op.cit., 15.

96. Toland hopes for the support of the grace of God in his plans, op.cit., XV – we are reminded of Herbert's experience of revelation, cf. 189 above.

97. Op.cit., 133.

97a. C.L.Becker, *Heavenly City*, passim, esp. 29ff., has already drawn attention to this in saying that the 'philosophers' were more heavily dependent on 'medieval Christian thought' than is usually believed.

98. Op.cit., 40. Cf. also op.cit., 41f.: 'Whoever reveals any thing that is, whoever tells us something we did not know before, his Words must be intelligible, and the Matter possible. This Rule holds good, let God or Man be the Revealer.'

99. Op.cit., 133.

100. Gawlick, in *Reimarus*, 27, stresses that this was logical on the basis of rationalism. In the introduction to Toland, *Christianity*, 12f., in this context he speaks of an 'irrefutable basic conviction'; however, in *Reimarus*, 37, he gives reasons why 'rationalism disappeared from theology'.

101. Op.cit., 145f.

102. Introduction to *Christianity*, 11*. Lechler, op.cit., 193, already pointed out 'that the author essentially thinks in supranaturalistic terms by having no suspicions about the direct intervention of a higher power in the regularity of things, provided only that a rational aim is intended and that there is scant use of miracle'. Troeltsch, op.cit., 447, differs, wrongly supposing that Locke's supranaturalism has completely disappeared with Toland.

103. 'Now whatever is contrary to Reason can be no Miracle', op.cit., 150; cf. 151, 155f.

104. Op.cit., 152ff.

105. Op.cit., 150.

106. Op.cit., 46-49.

107. Op.cit., 23.

108. Op.cit., 46. Cf. also 36: 'To believe the Divinity of Scripture, or the sense of any Passage thereof, without rational Proofs, and an evident Consistency, is a blameable Credulity.'

109. '...if they read the sacred Writings with that Equity and Attention that is due to meer Humane Works: Nor is there any different Rule to be follow'd in the Interpretation of Scripture from what is common to all other Books', op.cit., 49.

Toland leaves open his attitude to patristic allegorical or typological exegesis, op.cit., 119ff., but we can recognize that he has reservations about it.

110. Op.cit., 50, cf. 52.

111. Op.cit., 54.

112. Part II, IV, op.cit., 58ff.

113. In the sense of discursive thought, cf. the quotation op.cit., 482 n.67.

114. Op.cit., 59.

115. Op.cit., 60.

116. Op.cit., 63.

117. Hunt, *Religious Thought*, I, 436f., points out that Toland borrows from Which-cote in his understanding of 'mystery'.

118. Op.cit., 67.

119. Op.cit., 70.

120. Part III, ch.I, 68ff.

121. Part III, ch.III, 90ff.

122. Op.cit., 108.

123. Op.cit., 158.

124. Part III, V, op.cit., 158ff.

125. Here we already have intimations of Toland's later special conception, see below, 303f.

126. Op.cit., 168.

127. Op.cit., 176; the word is also made to catch the eye by being printed in small capitals.

128. Lechler, op.cit., 209, judged otherwise, and put this work along with others by Toland in the appendix to his account.

129. The last two letters in the collection, addressed to an unknown recipient, in a respectful argument discuss with Spinoza the theme of matter and movement; they fall outside the scope of this work. However, it should be noted that Toland's natural philosophy is an integral part of his thought and his whole attitude. Formerly it was often seen as an early episode in the history of dialectical materialism (this was also the reason for the German edition by E.Pracht, *Briefe an Serena*, 1959. But his view – again recently put forward by Sabetti, *Toland*, passim – that Toland was an atheist, has been rejected by Gawlick, op.cit., 14ff., with good reasons). M.C.Jacob has recently demonstrated at length (following references by F.Heinemann, op.cit., 55f., and G.Aquilecchia, 'Nota su John Toland traduttore di Giordano Bruno', *English Miscellany* 9, 1958, 77-86) the connecting links with Giordano Bruno's hylo-zooic natural philosophy, which can be traced back to Hermetic roots (for this and its effects, not least in England, cf. F.A.Yates, *Giordano Bruno and the Hermetic Tradition*, 1964; id., *The Rosicrucian Enlightenment*, 1972). However, this was rationalized by Toland. Cf. also Sabetti, *Toland*, esp. 175ff., and above all C.Giuntini, 'Toland e Bruno: ermetismo "revoluzionario"?', *RF(T)* 66, 1975, 199-235, who demonstrates how Toland uses the theories of Bruno, stripped of their magical and astrological features, to construct the 'superstition-critical' system of a 'natural religion' directed against the Newtonians. The pantheism which emerges in Toland's last writing, *Pantheisticon*, 1720, is a final additional step. For the theme, in addition to J.Berthold, *John Toland und der Monismus der Gegenwart*, 1876, and H.Metzger, *Attraction Universelle et religion naturelle chez quelques commentateurs anglais de Newton*, 1938, 106-10, cf. P.Casini, 'Toland e l'attività della materia', *RCSF* 22, 1967, 24-53 (= *L'universo-macchina. Origini della filosofia newtoniana*, 1969, 205-37), who points out that in these two letters Toland is attacking Newton's view of 'absolute' space and 'absolute' time in order to counter his influence among the moderates and apologists, op.cit. 41f. (In *L'universo-macchina*, 224f., he stresses even more strongly Toland's political aim: his polemic against Newton was aimed at winning over the ruling

classes to the freethinking deistic standpoint.) For his influence on French materialism see also L.G.Grocker, 'Toland et le matérialisme de Diderot', *RHLF* 53, 1953, 289-95.

130. 'Serena' is a pseudonym for the consort of Frederick I, whom Toland visited in 1701 and again in 1702 in connection with his political mission of handing over the Acts of Succession to the Princess Sophie of Hanover, the mother of the Queen, cf. above all F.Heinemann, 'Toland and Leibniz', *PhRev* 54, 1945, 437-57 = *Beiträge zur Leibniz-Forschung* (ed. Schischkoff), 1947, 193-212; also Gawlick, Introduction to Toland, *Letters to Serena*, 5*; M.C.Jacob, *Newtonian Ideology*, 314f.

131. Op.cit., 1-18.

132. Op.cit., 19-68.

133. Op.cit., 69-130.

134. In a letter to an unnamed German nobleman, printed in Heinemann, *John Toland*, 42f. (Brit.Lib.Add.MSS 4465, fol.7); cf. also Gawlick, Introduction to *Letters*, 19 n.9.

135. We again have the constant theme of Humanistic scholarly criticism. Again 'priests' are singled out as the authors of many prejudices, among them above all the pulpit preachers (the orthodox clergy are excepted, but this is evidently a *captatio benevolentiae*), op.cit., 8.

136. Op.cit., 16.

137. Toland sought to enlarge on this point in his apology *Vindicius Liberius*, 1702, 103ff., but did not correct it throughout; cf. the quotation in Gawlick, Introduction to *Christianity*, 32 n.57.

138. Motzo Dentice di Accadia, *GCFI*, 1934, 84 = *Preilluminismo*, 189.

139. Op.cit., 40.

140. Op.cit., 45.

141. Op.cit., 19, 56, 66.

142. Op.cit., Introduction, 11.

143. In op.cit., 66, we find the striking comment: "'tis impossible that God shou'd lie; and what he has reveal'd, tho not in every thing falling under our Comprehension, must yet be true and absolutely certain'! However, this is consistent with the positional theology mentioned above.

144. See above, 298.

145. Op.cit., 71.

146. Motzo Dentice di Accadia, *GCFI*, 1934, 84 = *Preilluminismo*, 189.

147. Op.cit., 127.

148. Op.cit., 128f. Redwood, *Reason, Ridicule and Religion*, 142, indicates further outlines for books on superstition and kindred themes in Toland's manuscripts; the printed books give only part of his complete view.

149. *Nazarenus: or Jewish, Gentile, and Mahometan Christianity*, 1718 (second edition; it contains only corrections of misprints as compared with the first impression which appeared in the same year). After Mossner, *Bishop Butler*, 66, above all E.Hirsch, *Geschichte der neuern evangelischen Theologie* I, 1949, ⁵1975, 304-6 and Motzo Dentice di Accadia, *GCFI* 1934, 78-80 = *Preilluminismo*, 182-5, have indicated the significance of this writing for the history of theology; M.Wiener, 'John Toland and Judaism', *HUCA* 16, 1941, 215-42, writes from the Jewish standpoint. This work was produced in 1710 as the autograph preserved in Vienna shows, cf. Ricuperati, op.cit., 638. Mosheim, *Vindiciae*, already refuted it in detail.

150. According to Acts 24.5, cf. op.cit. 26.

151. In the original version Toland mainly made the apostle Paul responsible for this falsification of (Jewish) Christianity, which was originally pure, because of his influences from the Gentile world, cf. Ricuperati, op.cit., 640. This view is hardly recognizable any more in the printed version.

152. Op.cit., V.

153. Toland blames Luther for having wrongly rejected the Epistle of James: 'yea and by Works a man is justify'd', op.cit., XIIIf. M.Wiener, op.cit., 221, also quotes the passage.

154. Op.cit., 42f.

155 'as being oblig'd by an eternal and national covenant to the Law of Moses', op.cit., 62.

156. Whom Toland paraphrases at this point almost in Lockean terms: 'that Faith signifies the belief of one God, a persuasion of the truth of Christ's doctrine, and the inward sanctification of the mind'. op.cit., 64.

157. Op.cit., 65.

158. Op.cit., 69f.

159. Op.cit., 78ff.

160. Cf. op.cit., X.

161. Op.cit., 14ff., 20ff.

162. He therefore gives it the sub-title 'Jewish, Gentile and Mahometan Christianity'. One is reminded of the parable of the Ring, which already appears in Boccacio and was later taken up by Lessing.

163. *An Account of an Irish Manuscript of the Four Gospels with A Summary of the Ancient Irish Christianity...*, 1718.

164. *Two Problems concerning The Jewish Nation and Religion.* Cf. here also Wiener, op.cit., 233ff.

165. For the general theme cf. M.Wiener, op.cit; Reventlow, op.cit.

166. Also in this paper, 6; cf. also *Nazarenus*, XI, 64; in *Origines Judaicae*,161, 172f., etc.

167. At one point, *Nazarenus*, 63f., Toland indicates that the sacrificial legislation in the Old Testament has only secondary significance; he refers to Jeremiah, Ezekiel and Joel. Cf. also Wiener, op.cit., 230.

168. *Two Problems*, 8.

169. Now easily accessible in the new English-German edition by H.Mainusch: *Gründe für die Einbürgerung der Juden in Grossbritannien und Irland*, 1965. For the content see also the editor's introduction, 9-30, and Reventlow, op.cit.

170. *J.Tolandi Dissertationes Duae, Adeisidaemon et Origines Judaicae.* Including *Origines Judaicae, sive, Strabonis de Moyse et Religione Judaica Historia*, facsimile reprint 1970, cf. Reventlow, ibid.

171. Cf. the sub-title *In qua Dissertatione probatur, Livium Historicum in Sacris, Prodigiis, & Ostentis Romanorum enarrandis, haudquaquam fuisse credulum aut superstitiosum...*

172. *GCFI*, 1934, 86 = *Preilluminismo*, 191f.

173. *Adeisidaemon*, 68-70.

174. Op.cit., 71.

175. *Nec unicum tantum Numen praetendebat Moses Strabonicus, sed ejusmodi cultum ac sacrificandi modum tradere pollicebatur, quae neque sumtibus, neque divinis afflatibus, neque ullis absurdis actionibus cultores distraheret... sola Naturae lex, decem comprehensa praeceptis, absque omni rituum apparatu... solleniter illis demandata est, ac duabus lapideis Tabulis...*, op.cit., 157f. For the bias of this writing and its polemic against Toland in this respect through J. de la Faye, *Defensio religionis nec non Mosis et gentis judaicae, etc.*, 1709, cf. Ricuperati, op.cit., 663ff. There is a list of writings against Toland in Trinius, *Freydenker Lexicon*, 487ff.

176. Op.cit., 159.

177. Cf. esp. Wiener, op.cit.

178. *The Court of the Gentiles: or a Discourse touching the Original of Human Literature,*

both Philologie and Philosophie, from the Scriptures and Jewish Church, four vols, 1669-76. Cf. F.Manuel, *Isaac Newton Historian*, 1963, 95.

179. Cf. above, 316f.

180. Cf. Wiener, op.cit., 236ff.; also H.Graf Reventlow, 'Das Arsenal der Bibelkritik des Reimarus', in *Reimarus*, (44-65) 55. However, a correction should be made on the basis of Toland's own information: Preface to *Tetradymus*, III: this is a work from Toland's 'later years'.

181. He himself mentions (Preface, III) the work of the Helmstadt orientalist H.von der Hardt, *Ephemerides Philologicae*, 1703, 90, written about the same time, in which the same theory emerges. This is a sign of his universal reading.

182. Op.cit., 6f.

183. Op.cit., Preface, II.

184. Here, then, he is a pure 'rationalist' in the terms defined by Heinemann. Of the other writings collected in the *Tetradymus*, the second, *Clidophorus: or of the Exoteric and Esoteric Philosophy*, (61-100) is of interest. In it Toland continues on a parallel level his search for the pure, original cult-free truth which he thinks that he can find here in the arcane discipline of ancient philosophy, because that philosophy adapted itself only outwardly to popular prejudices and established religions. (For the distinction between esoteric and exoteric philosophy cf. already *Letters to Serena*, 56f., 114-16). The fourth: *Mangoneutes*, (137-226) is a defence of the *Nazarenus* against various attacks.

185. After some more incidental remarks in *The Life of John Milton*, 1698, which brought heavy polemic down on him. He planned a detailed defence against them.

186. *Amyntor, or, a Defence of Milton's Life*, 1699. E.Hirsch, op.cit., has similarly drawn particular attention to this.

187. Outwardly this gives a somewhat ambiguous impression as a result of Toland's position under Lord Harley (since 1705), who had gone over to the party of the 'new Tories' (cf. D.Ogg, *England*, 444. For Lord Harley, cf.A. McInnes, *Robert Harley, Puritan Politician*, 1970); cf. Heinemann, op.cit., 46ff. The Toland biography which is still needed would have to go into the complicated relationships.

188. Op.cit., 20-41.

189. Op.cit., 47f., cf. 56f.

190. Op.cit., 49ff.

191. Op.cit., 57f.

192. Op.cit., 59.

193. Op.cit., 60ff.

194. E.Hirsch, op.cit., draws attention to this.

195. In the writing *Pantheisticon*, 1720. Cf. recently also M.C.Jacob, *Toland*, and Sabetti, *Toland*, esp. 223ff.; he puts the work in the context of an older rationalist and pantheistic system of Toland's.

196. The Freiburg philosophical dissertation by A.Seeber, *John Toland als politischer Schriftsteller*, 1933, did not yet have the background information which F.Heinemann (in part) and M.C.Jacob (now in more detail) offer, above all from material in the British Library. From this it has become clear that Toland's political position on the extreme wing of the Whigs and his membership of a republican Masonic club was closely connected with his religious attitude (cf. already Heinemann, op.cit., 53f.; for his connections with an early Masonic association see M.C.Jacob, 'An Unpublished Record of a Masonic Lodge in England:1710', *ZRGG* 22, 1970, 168-171; id., *Newtonians*, 216ff. Cf. also id., 'Newtonianism and the Origins of the Enlightenment. A Reassessment', *Eighteenth Century Studies* 11, 1977, 1-25). This attitude increasingly developed from a rationalistic Christianity to what was at first still a Christian natural religion, and then turned into an explicit pantheism, cf. Jacob, op.cit., esp.325ff. For the theme cf. also Casini, op.cit., 29ff.

197. For Shaftesbury, after T.Fowler, *Shaftesbury and Hutcheson*, 1882 (xerographic reprint, nd) and the one-sided German idealist C.F.Weiser, *Shaftesbury und das deutsche Geistesleben*, 1916 (reprinted 1969), cf.above all the more recent monographs by L.Bandini, *Shaftesbury: Etica e religione*, 1930; R.L.Brett, *The Third Earl of Shaftesbury*, 1951 (though this is primarily concerned with the significance of Shaftesbury for literary aesthetics; another work of similarly literary-critical interest is E.Wolff, *Shaftesbury und seine Bedeutung für die englische Literatur des 18.Jahrhunderts*, 1960 [for criticism of Brett cf. id., 13]); and S.Grean, *Shaftesbury's Philosophy of Religion and Ethics*, 1967; also specifically on the theme, A.O.Aldridge, *Shaftesbury and the Deist Manifesto*, 1951 (wrongly, I feel, condemned by Grean, op.cit., Preface, XIII and 265, n.10 as obscure – cf. also the review by R.L.Brett, *RESt* NS 4, 1953, 78f.); specifically on his ethics, L.Zani, *L'Etica di Lord Shaftesbury*, 1954. Moreover, there are numerous articles and sections in general accounts of the history of philosophy. Shaftesbury's works are available in a collection which he made himself: *Characteristics of Men, Manners, Opinions, Times* (First edition 1711, a further ten editions in the eighteenth century [I have used the sixth edition, 1738, three vols] – cf. Grean, op.cit., 281; new edition by J.M.Robertson, 1900, reprinted 1963, 1964). There is a detailed account of the history of the origin of the collection in Horst Meyer, *Limae labor: Untersuchungen zur Textgenese und Druckgeschichte von Shaftesbury's 'The Moralists'*, two vols, EHS R.XIV, Vol.63/1-2, 1978, bibliography, 789-804. Important unprinted material has been edited by B.Rand, *The Life, Unpublished Letters, and Philosophical Regimen of Anthony, Earl of Shaftesbury*, 1900 (xerographic reprint, nd); cf. F.A.Uehlein, *Kosmos und Subjektivität. Lord Shaftesbury's Philosophical Regimen*, 1976. *The Second Characters, or the Language of Forms* (ed. B.Rand, 1914), is irrelevant to the theme.

198. Even in the eighteenth century verdicts on him differed widely. He appears with Tindal on the title-page of the apologetic *Cure of Deism*, 1736, as one of the two *Oracles of Deism*, and the 'Deistic Confession of Faith' in Skelton, *Deism Revealed*, [1]1749, [2]1751 (two vols) is firmly stamped with Shaftesbury's principles (in op.cit., I, 32, his name is mentioned along with Collins, Toland and Tindal among the chief Deists, similarly in Leland, *View*, I, 77ff.); moreover in the same year J.Brown brought out a special counterblast *Essays on the Characteristics of Shaftesbury*. However, others defended him as orthodox (e.g. G.W.Rabener, *Antoni Comitis Shaftsburii cogitationes argutae de laude*, 1750). Cf. also Leland, *View*, I, 86ff.; Trinius, *Freydenker Lexikon*, 410f. Here it should be remembered, however, that the term 'Deist' was often used imprecisely by orthodox apologetic (cf. also Gawlick, in Lechler, VII; *Reimarus*, 18, etc.). Of modern commentators, Aldridge, *Manifesto*, 302, etc., sees him decidedly as a Deist because of his anti-Biblicism ('the one element which conclusively separates a latitudinarian Christian from a deist is a strong current of anti-Biblicism', op.cit, 357). Bandini, op.cit., 39, also asserts: 'Shaftesbury appartiene al movimento deista', but limits this considerably in what follows. Most scholars tend rather to reject this classification, cf. e.g. E.Wolff, op.cit., 14; Grean, op.cit., 59, 63: 'he was a Deist with a difference'. Cf. also Gestrich, 'Deismus', *TRE* 8, 400: 'The deistic thinking of... the Third Earl of Shaftesbury... is also singular.' Grean sees the difference between Shaftesbury and Deism proper in his stress on feeling and the visionary element, in place of deistic rationalism, op.cit., 35., cf. also 258.

199. *The Platonic Renaissance in England*, 157ff.

200. For the rendering of Shaftesbury's own title ASKEMATA (in Greek) by *Regimen*, cf. Rand, op.cit., X; E.Albee, review, in *PhRev* 12, 1903, (452-4), 452 is more critical.

201. E.Albee, op.cit., similarly in *PhRev* 25, 1916, 182, rejects it as a mere collection of material and therefore as insignificant for Shaftesbury's own philosophy; W.E.Alderman, 'Shaftesbury and the Doctrine of Moral Sense in the Eighteenth Century', *PMLA* 46, 1931, (1087-94) 1094 n.35, recalls that because it was only printed in 1900 it cannot have any bearing on Shaftesbury's contemporary influence.

202. E.A.Tiffany, 'Shaftesbury as Stoic', *PMLA* 38, 1923, 642-84 (Aldridge, *Manifesto*, 332 and passim, agrees). Rand himself also thought: 'He is the greatest Stoic of modern times', op.cit., XII. Cf. also V.Schönfeld, *Die Ethik Shaftesburys*, Diss. phil.Giessen, 1920, esp. 65ff.

203. Cf. Wolff, op.cit., 9ff.; Grean, op.cit.7: 'Shaftesbury's philosophy is a complicated fusion of Stoic and Platonic thought.'

204. Cf. Schönfeld, op.cit., 65; Grean, op.cit., 5f.

205. For its equally emotional preaching and its influence cf. also R.S.Crane, 'Suggestions toward a Genealogy of the "Man of Feeling"', *JELH* 1, 1934, 205-30.

206. As is well known, Shaftesbury's first publication was an edition of Whichcote's sermons with a preface of his own: *Select Sermons of Dr. Whichcot*, 1698.

207. So especially Wolff, op.cit., passim.

208. Scholars are fond of quoting his comment in *Characteristics* I, 189 (when not indicated otherwise, the edition by Robertson is quoted): 'The most ingenious way of becoming foolish is by a system'. However, it should again be remembered that polemic against scholastic philosophy is a favourite Humanist theme, cf. the context I, 188.

209. For his influence on German Idealism cf. Weiser, op.cit., and on the French Enlightenment, D.Schlegel, *Shaftesbury and the French Deists*, 1956.

210. F.H.Heinemann, 'The Philosopher of Enthusiasm. With material hitherto unpublished', *RIPh* 6, 1952, 294-322. However, his interpretation of the term 'enthusiasm' in Shaftesbury (op.cit., 299) is still too provisional, see below.

211. Cf. S.von Lempicki, 'Shaftesbury und der Irrationalismus', *StPh* 2, 1937, 19-110. For true and false 'enthusiasm' according to Shaftesbury cf. id., 53.

212. *JELH* 20, 1953, 267-99; cf. also id., 'Shaftesbury and the Age of Sensibility', in *Studies in Criticism and Aesthetics 1660-1800*, Festschrift S.H.Monk, ed. H. Anderson and J.S.Shea, 1967, 73-92.

213. This closer definition is missing in Tuveson; it will be important to us in later discussion.

214. Cf. II, 105f.: 'being thus... convinced the more still of my own being and of this self of mine "that" 'tis a real self drawn out and copied from another principal and original self (the Great One of the world), "I endeavour to be really one with it as far as I am able. I consider that...to this body there is an order, to this order a mind; that to this general mind each particular one must have relation, as being of like substance...and more like still, if it co-operates with it to general good..."' – In a detailed investigation of the *Philosophical Regimen*, Uehlein, *Kosmos*, had stressed this as the basic idea of Shaftesbury's ethical and philosophical system: as the embodiment of the ethical attitude proclaimed by Shaftesbury, 'virtue' is the combination of a rational grasp of the totality of the cosmos and the deliberate incorporation of the moral existence of man in the harmony of this totality. Shaftesbury found the nearest approximation to this ideal in the Stoa.

215. To this degree the reference by Schönfeld, op.cit., 47, to the Stoic *homologoumenos tei physei zen* (Cleanthes) is substantially correct.

216. Op.cit., 276.

217. Cf. already Fowler, op cit., 76-83; Schönfeld, op.cit., 21 n.2, points out that the expression,which only appears once in the text (I, 262), occurs often in the marginal notes of the editions which Shaftesbury himself prepared (*An Inquiry*, Book I, Part III, secs. 1,2,3; ⁶1738, II, 40ff.) which Robertson unfortunately leaves out, also in the index ⁶1738, II fol. Ee 2 – similarly deleted by Robertson); cf. also Grean, op.cit., 201. – Cf. also W.E.Alderman, *PMLA* 46, 1931, 1087-94. – G.W.Trianosky, 'On the Obligation to be Virtuous. Shaftesbury and the Question: Why be Moral?', *JHP* 16, 1978, 289-300, makes a further distinction between the obligation to observe

moral rules of life given on the basis of the 'moral sense' and an obligation independent of that incurred by the acceptance of a moral code.

218. Tuveson, op.cit., 279f.

219. II, 135; cf. also Bandini, XIIf.; Grean, op.cit., 240. On the other hand Shaftesbury thinks that a critical development of these natural capacities is absolutely necessary before an appropriate taste can develop, II, 257. Cf. also the distinction between innate ideas about the concepts of good and evil (which he rejects) and the 'passion or affection towards society', the innate social drives (which he defends), *Life, Letters*, ed. Rand, 415.

220. Tuveson, op.cit., 275.

221. Cf. Berkeley's charge that he is 'without one grain of religion', in Grean, op.cit., 98. For his own verdict cf. op.cit., 107f.

222. Religion, too, is an innate human capacity: 'He is not only born to virtue, friendship, honesty, and faith; but to religion, piety, adoration, and a generous surrender of his mind to whatever happens from that Supreme Cause or order of things, which he acknowledges entirely just and perfect', II, 295. For Shaftesbury God is for the most part impersonal and immanent, cf. Grean, op.cit., 26.

223. II, 129.

224. Op.cit., 32f. and n.35.

225. Cf. above, 422 n.87.

226. 'So that beauty, said I, and good with you, Theocles, I perceive, are still one and the same. "'Tis so", said he', II, 128. Cf. also II, 268f.

227. I, 27.

228. Op.cit., 36.

229. Op.cit., 35. Cf. also id., 'Self-Interest and Public Interest in Shaftesbury's Philosophy', *JHP* 2, 1964, 37-45.

230. II, 57.

231. D.F.Norton, 'Shaftesbury and Two Scepticisms', *Fil.* 19, 1968, 713-24 points out that Shaftesbury distinguishes between the two forms of scepticism: he regards epistemological scepticism in Bayle's sense as appropriate, wheras he strictly rejects ethical scepticism along the lines of Hobbes and Locke.

232. *Life, Letters*, ed. Rand, 138f. – Cf. also above, 578 n.214.

233. II, 178. However, taste needs further education, cf. II, 257; Aldridge, *Manifesto*, 336.

234. I, 261ff.

235. The basic view here that man is by nature a social being (in contrast to Hobbes' theory that the primal state was one of the war of all against all) corresponds to the basic attitude which L.Whitney calls 'primitivism', cf. *Primitivism and the Idea of Progress*, 1934 reprinted 1965, esp. 27ff. Whitney demonstrates that Shaftesbury says little new here, but only takes up earlier lines. Cf. also her article 'Thomas Blackwell, A Disciple of Shaftesbury', *PQ* 5, 1926, 196-211. Also W.E.Alderman, 'Shaftesbury and the Doctrine of Benevolence in the Eighteenth Century', in *Transactions of the Wisconsin Academy of Science, Arts and Letters* 16, 1931, 137-59; Grean, op.cit., 137ff.

236. Cf. Aldridge, *Manifesto*, 309.

237. Evidently a dig at the doctrine of original sin.

238. I, 263.

239. I, 264; cf. also Aldridge, op.cit., 309f.

240. Cf. Grean, op.cit., 64.

241. I, 264. In this connection the criticism of Locke contained in the letter to M.Ainsworth is also important. He censures Locke's voluntaristic concept of God: 'morality, justice, enquiry depend only on law and will, and God indeed is a perfect free agent in his sense; that is, free to anything, that is however ill: for if He wills

it, it will be made good; virtue may be vice, and vice virtue in its turn, if he pleases.' *Life, Letters* , ed. Rand, 404. Cf. also 416.

242. Cf. Aldridge, *Manifesto*, 365.

243. I, 266ff.; cf. already 247. For the discussion of this problem, which was widespread at the time, and other advocates of Shaftesbury's view, especially B.Hoadly, cf. Aldridge, op.cit., 304ff. For the problem in general cf. Grean, op.cit., 184ff.

244. Cf. Grean, op.cit., XIII, 229ff., and the passages cited there.

245. II, 92.

246. II, 181-94.

247. See above, 568 n.31.

248. II, 189.

249. Shaftesbury asserts that they were expelled for leprosy (!): 'It can scarce be said in reality, from what appears in Holy Writ, that their retreat was voluntary.' For his theory Shaftesbury refers to Tacitus, Justin and (by way of Marsham) to Manetho, II, 190 n.1.

250. II, 191; cf.n.2.Here too there is a reference (probably taken over by Tindal, see below, 326f.) to Ezek.20.25 and the laws given by God contradicting his real will, cf. above, 579f. n.241. At another point Shaftesbury writes: 'That they had certainly in religion, as in everything else, the least good-humour of any people in the world is apparent', II, 227; cf. I, 22. At a third point (I, 184) he calls the Jews 'people who of all human kind were the most grossly selfish, crooked and perverse.' Here the antisemitic tradition which derives from the Middle Ages again comes through strongly, but it has religious rather than popular motivation. According to Shaftesbury, 'good humour' and cheerfulness should be the most important positive characteristics of true religion, cf. I, 17,24; II, 217 and Grean, op.cit.,30f. Whereas with the charge of 'ill-humour' or melancholy, which is virtually synonymous with 'enthusiasm' (I, 17), the Jews are condemned as a people (as emerges from I, 22f., especially in New Testament times), the first kings of Israel and particular David (because of his dancing before the ark, I Sam.6) are mentioned as examples of cheerfulness in worship, II, 227f.; however, the note (228 n.6) stresses the exhibitionist character of this dance and gives the impression of ambiguity. Cf. also Aldridge, *Manifesto*, 360.

251. I, 230.

252. II, 193.

253. II, 227.

254. I, 229ff.

255. I, 230.

256. I, 193.

257. I, 231.

258. Ibid.

259. Given Shaftesbury's principles of wit and humour (cf. Grean, op.cit., 120ff.), his comments in *Advice to an Author*, where he wants to allow room for 'Religion, as by law established', as for heraldry, in which normal standards do not apply (I, 233), could be reckoned as part of his favourite kind of irony. However, in the *Miscellaneous Reflections* he says, evidently quite seriously, that he submits with full confidence to the views established by law (II, 201). There is already doubt about this in Stephen, *History*, II, 19.

260. This is precisely what was required in theory by Hobbes, see above, 221 and 538 n.199. In this sense Shaftesbury can honestly declare that he has acted and spoken 'as just conformists to the lawful church', II, 352; cf. also II, 18. Leland, *View*, I, 100, already indicated the exact agreement with Hobbes on this point, and he has

been followed by other commentators, cf. Aldridge, *Manifesto*, 346f. There is certainly no special dependence. For the theme cf. also Grean, op.cit., 114f.

261. Therefore Aldridge, *Manifesto*, 367, refers, probably rightly, to a statement in the *Philosophical Regimen* (*Life, Letters*, ed. Rand, 29) where he advises him not to disturb the opinions and religious rites of the simple people: 'How should they know?... Wilt thou teach them? If not, what does thou teach them in this other way, but impiety and atheism?' In I, 14, Shaftesbury follows J.Harrington in just the same way in his view "tis necessary a people should have a public leading in religion. For to deny the magistrate a worship, or take away a national church, is as mere enthusiasm as the notion which sets up persecution.' There is a formula in II, 365, which sounds very like Hobbes: if there is a kind of divine embassy (the clergy – here Shaftesbury uses ironically a high-faluting fashionable title for their spiritual office claimed by one of his church opponents, cf. II, 364f.), then it is not otherwise 'but through the magistrate and by the prince of sovereign power here on earth, that these gentlemen agents are appointed, distinguished, and set over us'. Here Locke's humility in the *Reasonableness* is replaced by aristocratic self-awareness. He spoke on the problem in most detail in II, 219ff. Following a parable which is meant to show how easily a society can be convinced even of views which are directly contrary to reality, he speaks of the means which any authority has at its disposal for forcing any particular faith on its subjects, so that mere birth can decide on whether a person is Christian, Moslem or Jew. Therefore 'there can be no rational belief but where comparison is allowed, examination permitted, and a sincere toleration established' (II, 220). Nevertheless Shaftesbury accords priority to the belief ordained by the authorities: 'If the belief be in any measure consonant to truth and reason, it will find as much favour in the eyes of mankind as truth and reason need desire.' Cf. also I, 14: 'For to deny the magistrate a worship, or take away a national church, is a mere enthusiasm as the notion which sets up persecution. Despite some difficulties in respect of the 'speculations or mysteries' it contains, reasonable people will 'conform the better with what their interest, in conjunction with their good-humour, inclines them to receive as credible, and observe as their religious duty and devotional task', above all 'in order to be more sociable'! Here are the typical maxims of an enlightened Anglican of the upper class! Aldridge, *Manifesto*, 367f., is essentially right on this point. After I, 19f., of course this adaptation can be purely external (under Moslem or Roman rule).

262. The expression 'religion, as by law established', is the official term in Whig propaganda!

263. II, 17-20, 34, 53, 85, 103, 105, 238.

264. II, 201.

265. See above, 258f., 269.

266. I, 84ff.

267. According to the *Letter concerning Enthusiasm* this relates to the appearance of the 'French prophets'; cf. also II, 200 n.3.

268. II, 87.

269. II, 89.

270. Cf. Aldridge, *Manifesto*, 361.

271. '...God witnessing for himself', not 'men for God', II, 90.

272. II, 91.

273. See above, 312.

274. II, 227ff.

275. Cf. above, 580 n.250.

276. II, 228.

277. II, 230f.

278. *Manifesto*, 360.

279. II, 232 and n.2.

280. Its author Chillingworth is here introduced as 'a famed controversial divine of our Church', II, 354.

281. In this figure one can easily recognize a spokesman for Shaftesbury's own views, which he defends against High Church zealots, cf. Aldridge, *Manifesto*, 346.

282. II, 355.

283. I, 97.

284. Ibid.

285. Aldridge, *Manifesto*, 363, points out that the passage quoted in I, 97 is noted in Shaftesbury's index under 'Scripture, Judgement of'. In the *Miscellaneous Reflections* Shaftesbury deals openly with the Bible.

286. II, 297.

287. II, 298.

288. II, 302.

289. "Tis true, indeed, that as to critical learning and the examination of originals, texts, glosses, various readings, styles, compositions, manuscripts, compilements, editions, publications, and other circumstances such as are common to the sacred books with all other writings and literature, this we have confidently asserted to be a just and lawful study,' II, 352.

290. II, 307f.

291. Cf. Kraus, *Geschichte*, 29f.

292. As an example of such text-critical observations which affect the content Shaftesbury cites Luke 1.1-4 (evidently taking up Leclerc, cf. Aldridge, *Manifesto*, 363); II, 307 n.2.

293. II, 358ff.

294. *Manifesto*, 364.

295. Cf. esp. I, 240, 277; II, 19.

296. Cf. above, 578 n.209.

297. II, 202ff.

298. II, 203. A last remnant of the attempt to anchor his own view ('sceptic') in the New Testament can be recognized here. However, the way in which Paul is sought as a key witness for this is perverse; in the Enlightenment, by contrast he was usually criticized as the first theologaster.

299. Here he is probably thinking above all of the influence of Aristotelianism on the university theology of the seventeenth century – somewhat of an anachronistic topical reference (cf. II, 207: 'being fallen thus from remote antiquity to later periods'), and, as we saw, a favourite theme of Humanist polemic against contemporary scholasticism.

300. II, 212ff.

301. See above, 312.

302. II, 181f.

303. II, 183f.

304. II, 186.

305. *Manifesto*, 345ff.

306. Cf. C.Mullett, *Religion*, 462-74; G.L.Cherry, 'The Legal and Philosophical Position of the Jacobites', *JMH* 22, 1950, 309-21; D.Bahlman, *The Moral Revolution*; G.M.Trevelyan, *The English Revolution 1688-1689* (reprinted 1963), esp. 175ff.

307. Cf. also L.M.Hawkins, *Allegiance in Church and State: The Problem of the Non-Jurors in the English Revolution*, 1928.

308. Cf., however, recently G.V.Bennett, 'King William and the Episcopate', in *Essays in Modern English Church History*, ed.G.V.Bennett & J.D.Walsh, 1966, 104-31, who warns against the customary all too schematic judgment of William III's policy of appointments. For events in church politics between 1689 and 1714 cf. also id.,

'Conflict in the Church', in *Britain after the Glorious Revolution, 1689-1714*, ed. G.Holmes, 155-75. He regretfully comments: 'There is no satisfactory history of the Church for this period', op.cit., 174.

309. Cf. G.Burnet, *History* II, 347, etc.; C.Hill, *The Century of Revolution, 1603-1714*, 1961 (⁶1966), 291f.

310. For the discord between the two on the occasion of Toland's appointment to a position under R.Harley, the statesman outlawed as a Whig apostate (cf. above, 576 n.187), cf. Heinemann, *John Toland and the Age of Reason*, 50ff.

311. This was already recognized very aptly by the contemporary Whig propagandist M.Tindal (see further below) in his pamphlet directed against the High Churchmen, *New High-Church Turn'd Old Presbyterian*, 1709.

312. Cf. G.V.Bennett, *The Tory Crisis in Church and State, 1688-1730: The Career of Francis Atterbury, Bishop of Rochester*, 1975.

313. Cf. N.Sykes, *Church and State in England in the XVIIIth Century*, 1934, 298, 301f.

314. J.Toland writes in 1710: 'We in England are divided into Whigs and Tories. The First are Zealous Sticklers for Civil Liberty, and Sworn Enemies to Ecclesiastical Tyranny. The latter do not willingly admit of any Toleration in Matters of Religion; or of any Check upon the Will of the Sovereign,' *Mr. Toland's Reflections on Dr. Sacherverell's Sermon Preach'd at St. Paul's, Nov.5, 1709*, 1710, 3; cf.Aldridge, *Manifesto*, 348.

315. *England in the Reigns of James II and William III*, (1955), ²1957, 529.

316. Cf. esp. *Manifesto*, 352.

317. Facsimile reprint ed. G.Gawlick, 1967.

318. Cf. the introduction to *Christianity* by G.Gawlick, op.cit., 5*-38*, and the literature mentioned there, 39*-43*. Also C.Motzo Dentice di Accadia, 'La supremacia dello stato', *GCFI* 17, 2.ser., Vol.4, 1936, (225-55) 225-234 = id., *Preilluminismo*, 239-51; Casini, *Introducione*, 106ff. – For further political pamphlets by Tindal cf. Gawlick, op.cit., nn.7,12,13,14, on pp.441.

319. I have used the fourth edition of 1709. For the content cf. also Aldridge, *Manifesto*, 348f.; Motzo Dentice, op.cit., 225ff.; Sina, *Ragione*, 622ff.

320. Op.cit., V.

321. 'Nothing made so much way for the Reformation, as Henry VIII's depriving the Clergy of so great a Part of their Powers and Riches,' op.cit., 215.

322. Op.cit., 303.

323. J.H.Plumb, *The Growth of Political Stability in England, 1675-1725*, 1967, ch.5, 'The Rage of Party', 129ff., esp. 134ff., 152.

324. Cf. also the basic work by K.Feiling, *A History of the Tory Party*, 1924 (third reprint 1965).

325. 'None can have a juster Esteem for all her Clergy, who, according to the Doctrine of the best-constituted Church, disown all Independency,' op.cit., 303.

326. Op.cit., LXXXIV; cf. also 303.

327. Therefore J.H.Plumb, op.cit., n.2, is probably wrong in seeing Shaftesbury as isolated in his attitude during the reign of Queen Anne.

328. 'that there's no Divine Commission which parcels the Earth into particular Governments, or any Family or Person that has an immediate Commission from Heaven to rule the Whole or any Part of it...' op.cit., 2. 'A Father is so far from acquiring such an Arbitrary Power over his Child, by being instrumental in giving him Life...', op.cit., 4, and especially: '...if Government of the whole Earth was given to Adam first, and after him to the eldest Son of the eldest Branch, as the Makers of this Hypothesis assert...', op.cit., 6. Filmer's theories were therefore still alive in certain circles after 1700, despite Locke's disputing of them.

329. *State of Nature*, cf. op.cit., 11; Tindal, too, derives the original freedom of the

individual from the law of nature and associates it with the individual right to the realization of happiness, op.cit., 10.

330. 'Men are naturally free', op.cit., 6.

331. Op.cit., 4 (there is also a reference here to the traditional objection based on the inequality of children, cf. above, 272).

332. 'And as the Laws derive their Authority from the present Government, so this owes its obliging Power not to any Compacts of the People in former Ages, but to the Consent of the present Generation...' op.cit., 7.

333. 'So that the Government, the present as well as the past, has no other Origin than the Consent of the Partys concerned; all expressly or tacitly, collectively or singly, agreeing to it', op.,cit., 8.

334. 'And consequently all Power, by the express or tacit Consent of the Partys concern'd, must be at first lodged in the Majority, who may...keep it in their own hands, or else intrust it with whom they think fit...', op.cit., 6f.

335. The existence of the secret Calves' Head Club, to which Toland belonged (cf. Heinemann, *John Toland*, 52f.), shows that the republican ideas of the Commonwealth period still survived underground. Here the ideas of Milton played a special part, cf. Sensabaugh, *Milton*.

336. 'A Limited Monarch', op.cit., 275. On the other hand there is a warning against the danger of absolutism (under Charles II), which has been overcome, op.cit., 275.

337. 'To punish the Evil, the Immoral, the Vicious, and reward the Good, the Moral, the Virtuous', op.cit., 12.

338. Tindal, very much like Locke, sees in eudaemonism a natural-law presupposition of social life: 'God by implanting in Man that only innate and inseparable Principle of seeking his own Happiness... has given him a Right, or rather has made it his Duty to do all that's necessary to that End', op.cit., 10.

339. Op.cit., 12f., cf 18f. – here we find the same limits to tolerance as in Locke, with the same reasons for them.

340. 'that all being under an indispensable Obligation to worship God after the manner they think most agreeable to his Will, and in all Religious Matters whatever to follow the Dictates of their Consciences, none cou'd make over the Right of judging for himself, since that wou'd cause his religion to be absolutely at the disposal of another,' op.cit., 14. Cf. also 66: '... a Power over the Conscience or Mind of Man, 'tis no less than usurping upon the Prerogative of God himself.' This separation of the private sphere of the conscience as being untouchable by the state is reminiscent of Hobbes: however, according to Tindal, among the Free Churches (not in the state church, see below) the conscience of church members is also normative for the outward forms of worship.

341. Op.cit., 15; cf.23.

342. Evidently Tindal also owes this to Locke, cf. above, 280ff.

343. All men have a right 'to form what Clubs, Companys or Meetings they think fit, either for Business or Pleasure, which the Magistrate, as long as the Publick sustains no Damage, cannot hinder without manifest Injustice,' op.cit., 15.

344. 'No man's Religion, like his Lands, descends from Father to Son, but every one, when capable, is to chuse his own Church. And the only Motive that is to determine him is the saving of his own Soul: for as he is oblig'd ... to join himself with that Church which he judges will best conduce to it; so the same Reason... will oblige him to leave that Church...', op.cit., 23f.

345. Op.cit., 24f.

346. Op.cit., 19. The same principle is put forward by B.Ibbot, 'The Nature and Extent of the Office of the Civil Magistrate', in *The Pillars of Priestcraft and Orthodoxy Shaken*, ed. R.Baron, I, [2]1768, 204-44.

347. 'And there can be no manner of pretence why those Christian Religious Assemblys which are not of the Magistrate's Persuasion, may not maintain themselves by that Natural Right by which all other have done it, from their first Existence to this very day,' op.cit., 29.

348. In his account, this is the High Church position, op.cit., 30. It corresponds exactly with E.Gibson's own interpretation of Anglican law in the introduction to his *Codex Juris Ecclesiae Anglicani*, XIX, cited by Sykes, *Church and State*, 299.

349. Op.cit., 31.

350. Ch.1: 'That there cannot be two Independent Powers in the same Society', op.cit., 33ff.

351. Op.cit., 37.

352. The death penalty inflicted on a citizen by the secular authorities robs the church of a member to whom it has an independent legal claim; conversely church excommunication prevents the person affected from exercising a civil profession, as he is avoided by all his fellow citizens, and so on (op.cit., 37f.).

353. Nor should they receive it; that is not changed in any way by the short period under Harley's Tory ministry (cf. Burnet, *History*, VI, 8ff.; G.M.Trevelyan, *England under Queen Anne*, III, 1934 [reprinted 1948], 61ff.; Feiling, *History*, 424ff.), in which Atterbury was made Bishop and the Canterbury Synod was called into lively activity. Its quest for authority independent of the state was never fulfilled, and in connection with the Bangor controversy of 1717 its sessions were complete discontinued by a forced postponement for a century and a half. For the history of the two Synods of York and above all Canterbury and the relationship between state and church in England cf. Sykes, *State and Church*, esp. ch.VII, 284-331.

354. In fact the name of the 'great' Erastus is mentioned with respect, op.cit., 107, and the publication of his work *De Excommunicatione* in London, 1689, was celebrated as a pious action, op.cit., LXII. For the acceptance of particular ideas of Hobbes, and the nevertheless fundamental gulf between his basic views and Toland's attitude cf. also Aldridge, *Manifesto*, 349, though he overlooks Tindal's 'Parliamentary Erastianism'.

355. Op.cit., LXXXIII; cf. 210: 'But this Reason will make the Parliament, not only then but always, better Judges (than the clergy) of Religion.'

356. 'As wanting none of its due Rights and Privileges', ibid. In this sense Tindal gives his work the title 'The Rights of the Christian Church asserted...': he wants to defend the democratic church against the priestly usurping of its rights.

357. Op.cit., 155. Cf. also op.cit., 176: '...in the Beginning the Government of the Holy Church had altogether a Democratical Form.'

358. Op.cit., 156.

359. C.Garbett, *Church and State in England*, 1950, 86ff.

360. Cf. the title *Erastianism Triumphant*, op.cit., 86. Cf. also Laski, see below, n.366: also B.Williams, *The Whig Supremacy, 1714-1760*, ²1962, 68: 'But at no time in our history was the Anglican church, both in England and in Ireland, so completely Erastian and so entirely subservient to the purposes of civil government as in the eighteenth century.'

361. Ibid.

362. R.H.Murray, *The Political Consequences of the Reformation*, 1926, 263ff., demonstrates this unity of thinking on scripture (which still comes from the Middle Ages) by Sir Thomas Smith, *De Republica Anglorum*, 1583 (1584).

363. Op.cit., 173.

364. The latter is particularly important: 'Cujus est destruere ejus est condere, and so vice versa, is a certain Maxim,' op.cit., 236.

365. Op.cit., 237, cf. also 126. This thesis is also taken over by Shaftesbury, cf. *Characteristics* II, 365.

366. Cf. H.J.Laski, *Political Thought in England. Locke to Bentham*, 1920 (reprinted 1955), 82: 'So that the Erastianism of the eighteenth century goes deep enough to make the Church no more than a moral police department of the State.'

367. Op.cit., 21.

368. Op.cit., 112f.

369. Op.cit., 120.

370. Cf. his pamphlet *New High Church*.

371. Cf. Garbett, op.cit., 59ff.

372. Ch.IV, 122ff., cf. esp. 147, 174: 'There is no particular Form of Church Government of Divine Appointment, but that 'tis of a mutable nature, and ought to be chang'd according to circumstances.'

373. Op.cit., 124.

374. Op.cit., 135ff.

375. Op.cit., 152f.

376. Op.cit., 149f.

377. Op.cit., 153.

378. In a letter to M.Ainsworth, *Life, Letters*, ed. Rand, 403, Shaftesbury gives his assent indirectly to Tindal's ideas of church order, but he evidently often used him elsewhere, cf. Aldridge, *Manifesto*, 348ff.

379. In addition to the work discussed mention should also be made here of *An Essay concerning the Laws of Nations and the Rights of Sovereigns*, 1693; *An Essay concerning the Power of the Magistrate and the Rights of Mankind in Matters of Religion*, 1697 (both in a collected volume: *Four Discourses on the Following Subjects...*, 1709).

380. E.g. op.cit., 216, 255, 296.

381. Op.cit., 296.

382. E.g. 270.

383. Op.cit., 96f.

384. Op.cit., 269.

385. The principles of B.Hoadly in his polemic against the High Churchmen are very similar: *A Preservative against the Principles and Practices of the Non-Jurors both in Church and State*, 1716 (for the content cf. H.J.Laski, *Political Thought*, 74ff.; N.Sykes, *Church and State*, 290ff.), which provided the occasion for the famous Bangor controversy.

385a. For these developments cf. also G.V.Bennett, 'Conflict in the Church', in G.Holmes (ed.), *Britain after the Glorious Revolution 1689-1714*, 1969, 155-75.

386. 'The Final Phase of Divine Right Theory in England, 1688-1702', *EHR* 77, 1962, 638-58. Cf. also id., *Anglican Reaction to the Revolution of 1688*, 1962, esp. 65ff., 80ff.

387. *The Divine Right of the Revolution Scripturally and Rationally Evinced and Applied*, 1793 (first appeared 1706). Cf. also Straka, *Final Phase*, 657 n.2; *Anglican Reaction*, 112. There is a copy in Dr Williams's Library, London.

388. Cf. Ogg, *England*, 227.

389. Op.cit., 29ff., quotation 34. Here, too, the reason for the appeal to the authority of the Old Testament is an apologia for the *status quo*, now made in reverse: (cf. e.g. V: 'to establish all loyal subjects in the firm belief of the just right her Majesty has to the crown'). The controversy with Filmer is always in the foreground here; one of the ironical arguments against the acceptance of a *ius divinum* of the linear succession in primogeniture is that in that case, rule over the world should have to have descended from Adam to his oldest son, namely Cain (V, 16). The patriarchal narratives then give numerous examples of the younger son and not the oldest becoming the heir (e.g. Isaac, Jacob, Joseph, 17ff.). David, morally dubious, but a good king because of his faithfulness to Yahweh, and chosen by God, can be the type for the now legitimate monarchs of England in both respects; Fleming puts

forward the principle that 'they (these properties) are applicable, materially considered... to all rightly constituted Christian kingdoms, but especially to ours,' 59. By contrast, Jeroboam becomes the type of the apostate James II, 44ff.

390. In *A Collection of State Tracts, publish'd on the Occasion of the Late Revolution of 1688 and During the Reign of King William III, 1705-7*, I, 640-56; cf. Straka, op.cit., 642 n.3, on 641.

391. Cf. Feiling, *History*, 363.

392. H.Sacheverell, *A Discourse Showing the Dependence of Government upon Religion*, 1702.

393. For the events e.g. Burnet, *History*, V, 435ff.; Feiling, *History*, 416f.; Bennett, *Conflict*, 170f.; G.Holmes, *The Trial of Dr Sacheverell*, 1973.

394. The name goes back to W.Molyneux in a letter to Locke, as a designation for Toland, *Works of John Locke*, IX, 405; it was then popularized above all by A.Collins, see below. Cf. also G.Gawlick, Introduction to Toland, *Christianity*, 17, and nn.41-43. J.Redwood, *Reason, Ridicule and Religion*, marks out the broader horizon against which the emergence of the Deists is to be seen (cf. also the Preface, 10), though his survey is necessarily very general.

395. Furthermore, Lechler was aware of the problem, cf. *Geschichte*, XLIIf., though he did not have the means for an adequate solution. Still, he has made a good start on it.

396. *Priestcraft in Perfection: Or, a Detection of the Fraud of Inserting and Continuing this Clause The Church hath Power to Decree Rites and Ceremonys, etc*, 1710 (second and third editions in the same year).

397. Their motives were thus by no means as noble as Gawlick makes them out to be: 'The incisive criticism which the Deists made of the church belief of their time, sometimes expressed very abruptly, arose out of the sensibility of their moral awareness, which could not accept the harshness of various biblical and theological doctrines.' Preface to Lechler, *Geschichte*, XX. Like their opponents, they had much more concrete and selfish reasons for their polemic, which should therefore be evaluated in a much more matter-of-fact way. J.H.Plumb, *The Growth of Political Stability in England 1675-1725*, 1967, has described the political background to events which led to the gradual establishment of Whig Rule. For the role of the Bible, especially the Old Testament, in this period the comment by C.J.Sommerville, 'Religious Typologies and Popular Religion in Restoration England', *ChH* 45, 1976, (32-41) 34f., is typical; surveying the popular religious literature of the time, he makes the statistical comment that with the growth of the appeal to history, nature and reason, there was a clear decline in quotations from the Old Testament and a shift to the New.

398. Simply because of the considerably longer period of his activity (up to his death in 1750) Gordon, who was the heir to Trenchard (who died as early as 1722) and even married the widow of his patron, is the more important of the two contestants. Cf. the investigation by J.M.Bulloch, 'Thomas Gordon, The "Independent Whig"', in *Aberdeen University Library Bulletin* 3, 1918, Nos.17,18 (also as an offprint), which is particularly important because of its wealth of bibliographical references, and on both figures, C.Robbins, *The Eighteenth Century Commonwealthman*, 115ff.

399. After some earlier pamphlets in 1719, cf. Bulloch, op.cit., 10f.

400. From 1721 to 1747; for the details cf. Bulloch, op.cit., 14f. I have used the sixth edition (three vols), 1736.

401. After the fifth edition the initials of the authors were given, cf. Bulloch, op.cit., 14.

402. Op.cit., I, 2.

403. Op.cit., 3.

404. Op.cit., 4.

405. Cf. above 583 n.325.

406. Op.cit,. 10.

407. Op.cit., 12. In the pamphlet published in 1720: *Priestianity, Or, A View of the Disparity between the Apostels and the Modern Inferior Clergy* (cf. Bulloch, op.cit., 16f. – I have used the original) Gordon compares the behaviour of the apostles with the unworthy behaviour of the modern clergy – the lower clergy, i.e. those with predominantly Tory inclinations.

408. Op.cit., 14f. This programme is carried through in respect of the struggle for power of the English clergy in the work by Sir Edmund Thomas, *A Short View of the Conduct of the English Clergy, So far as relates to Civil Affairs, From the Conquest to the Revolution*(1737), in *The Pillars of Priestcraft* ed. Baron, II.

409. No.11 (30 March 1720), op.cit., 82ff.

410. No.12 (6 April 1720), op.cit., 90ff.

411. 'The most Wicked of all Men', No.17 (11 May 1720), op.cit., 132ff. Cf. also the comment in *The Character of an Independent Whig* (originally published 1719, cf. Bulloch, op.cit., 11), printed e.g. in *A Collection of Tracts. By the Late John Trenchard, Esq., and Thomas Gordon, Esq.*, I, 1751, 312: 'The Clergy are the best or the worst of Men; and as the first cannot be too much honoured, the latter cannot be too much despised.'

412. No.40 (19 October 1720), op.cit., II, 73ff.; cf. also nos.62-64, op.cit., III, 71ff.

413. No.45 (23 November 1720), op.cit., II, 124ff.

414. No.18 (18 May 1720), op.cit., I, 141ff.

415. No.19 (25 May 1720), op. cit., 149ff.

416. No.26 (13 July 1720). ' Religion and Virtue consisting in doing good Actions, or in a Disposition to do them,' op.cit., 224. Cf. also op.cit., 165: 'Nothing is, or can be, pure Religion, but either what God commands and tells us he will accept, or what is dictated by eternal Reasons, which is the Law of Nature.'

417. 'Our saviour... instituted... a Religion without one Ceremony in it. The Religion of the Gospel is as pure from Fancies and Ceremonies, as from Pride and the Spirit of Dominion,' op.cit., 274.

418. No.34 (7 September 1720), op.cit., II, 14ff.; nos. 66-67, op.cit., III, 112ff.

419. Cf. Bulloch, op.cit.,16. Printed in *A Collection of Tracts*, II, 370-85.

420. Op.cit., 384.

421. 'The Church proved a Creature of the Civil Power, by Acts of Parliament, and the Oaths of the Clergy', no.13, (13 April 1720), op.cit., I, 99ff.

422. No.15 (27 April 1720), op.cit., I, 115ff.

423. No.14 (20 April 1720), op.cit., I, 108ff.

424. No.47 (7 December 1720), op.cit., II, 144ff.

425. No.48 (14 December 1720), op.cit., II, 154ff.

426. Cf. Feiling, *History*, 409.

427. Op.cit., III, 321ff.

428. Op.cit.,III, 341. The same charge also appears in *The Character*, 313.

429. Op.cit., III, 363. Here, however, the king is excused as having been lured astray by the High Churchmen of the time, op.cit., 365: cf. also *The Character*, op.cit., 313: 'Laud, who having got the Regal Power out of a weak Prince's hand into his own.'

430. Cf. above, n.411.

431. Op.cit., 312.

432. Op.cit., 326f. – Bulloch, op.cit., 23, also mentions an *Essay on Publick Sports and Diversions*, 1743, in which Gordon evidently sarcastically changes his demands into their opposite. (For an understanding of these charges cf. Bahlman, op.cit., 5.)

433. Op.cit., 318. The same polemic in ironical form also appears in *The Creed of an Independent Whig*, 370f.

434. No.4 (10 February 1720), op.cit., I, 23.

435. Ibid.

436. Cf. also op.cit., I, 68: 'To believe that Jesus Christ was the only Son of God, was the great Principle of the Christian Religion.'

437. Op.cit., I, 23: 'Nothing is plainer than the Law and the Gospel', op.cit., 25. Cf. esp. 9 (16 March 1720): 'Of the Clearness of Scripture', op.cit., I, 63ff.

438. No.6 (24 February 1720), op.cit., I, 38ff.

439. Op.cit., I, 38.

440. 'Almighty God will never require of us to see in the Dark, till he has given us new eyes; nor to believe any Article, or obey any Precept, till we understand him, and know what he means,' op.cit., I, 24. Cf. also no.35 (14 September 1720), op.cit., II, 24ff.

441. Op.cit., I, 67.

442. Op.cit., II, 24 – 'and the Means of Self-preservation'; Gordon also advocates a eudaimonistic ethic.

443. Op.cit., II, 28.

444. Op.cit., II, 32.

445. A.Trinius, *Freydenker Lexicon*, 22f. There 1714 is given as the year of appearance; in the reprint which I used in *The Pillars of Priestcraft*, IV, 1768, it is given as 1716. According to Whiston (Trinius) and Baron, the author is Francis Hare (later Bishop of Chichester).

446. Op.cit., 15f.

447. Op.cit., 16.

448. Op.cit., 17.

449. Op.cit., 18.

450. Op.cit., 19.

451. Op.cit., 48.

452. Op.cit., 49.

453. For Hare's previous actions as a political pamphleteer cf. N.Sykes, *Church and State*, 59. This previous activity rules out what at first sight might appear to be a possible interpretation of the polemical work as an argument for the Puritan ideal of scripture.

2. Forms of Apologetic

1. Its head even played a significant role at the English Court, see below.

2. Cf. e.g. T.Sprat, *History of the Royal Society (1667)*, ed. J.I.Cope and H.W.Jones, 1958; T.Birch, *History of the Royal Society of London*, four vols, 1756; H.Lyons, *The Royal Society 1660-1940*, 1944. Cf. also R.F.Jones, *Ancients and Moderns*, 170ff.

3. The biography with the most material is still that by D.Brewster, *Memoirs of the Life, Writings and Discoveries of Sir Isaac Newton*, two vols, 1855 (reprinted, ed. R.S.Westfall, 1965), though its perspective is limited and not unprejudiced. Cf. also L.T.More, *Isaac Newton: A Biography*, 1934 (reprinted 1962); E.N.da C.Andrade, *Sir Isaac Newton*, 1954 (also as a paperback edition), and most recently F.E.Manuel, *A Portrait of Sir Isaac Newton*, 1968. Cf. also Casini, *Introduzione*, 1-49.

4. A significant part of his literary remains, for almost two centuries in the possession of the Portsmouth family, was scattered to the winds by a sale in 1936 and only gathered together after the war in three places (Cambridge [England], Wellesley [Mass.] and principally Jerusalem) and made accessible for scholarly use. F.E.Manuel has above all dealt thoroughly with Newton's theological works: F.E. Manuel, *Isaac Newton Historian*, 1963; id., *The Religion of Isaac Newton*, 1974 (cf. also R.-D.Herrmann, 'The Religious and Metaphysical Thought of Isaac Newton', *JR* 56, 1976, 204-19); F.E.Manuel, *A Portrait*, 117ff. A small selection of theological manu-

scripts was published by H.McLachlan, *Sir Isaac Newton: Theological Manuscripts*, 1950. Cf. also G.S.Brett, 'Newton's Place in the History of Religious Thought', in *Sir Isaac Newton: A Bicentenary Evaluation of his Work*, 1928, 259-73 (unfortunately unusable because of inadequate acquaintance with the sources); E.W.Strong, 'Newton and God', *JHI* 13, 1952, 147-67; R.S.Westfall, *Science and Religion*, 193-220; K.D.Buchholtz, *Isaac Newton als Theologe*, 1965 (a well-informed survey of the most important basic positions of Newton relevant here, but limited to the state of research at the time of the first edition, 1954, without taking account of more recent secondary literature); F.Wagner, *Isaac Newton im Zwielicht zwischen Mythos und Forschung. Studien zur Epoche der Aufklärung*, 1976, esp. II, 32ff. There is an account of research (up to the year of the appearance of the article, but with notes of works in preparation), in I.B.Cohen, 'Newton in the Light of Recent Scholarship', *Isis* 51, 1960, 489-514 (for the theological works, 498ff.); cf. also the bibliography in id., *Introduction to Newton's 'Principia'*, 1971, 355-68, and the bibliographical survey by P.Gay, *The Enlightenment II: The Science of Freedom*, 1969, 610-21. Wagner, *Newton*, 59f., thinks that a final verdict on Newton's preoccupation with theological themes is impossible because of the dispersal of the literary remains.

5. In particular, the Unitarian H.McLachlan, *Religious Opinions*, has adopted this perspective, and it also underlies his choice of texts (see the previous note). For the theme cf. also Buchholtz, op.cit., 32ff.,36ff., 60ff.; Manuel, *Religion*, 57ff.

6. Cf. above, 547 nn.146-8.

7. Newton, like Locke, is significantly horrified at the consequences of an open confession of Anti-trinitarianism after the fashion of his disciples Whiston and Clarke.

8. Manuel, *Religion*, 53ff.

9. Yahuda MS.15.5, fol. 98 v, quoted by Manuel, op.cit., 55; as in Locke, in Newton, too, the content of this confession is: 'And the gospel is that Jesus is the Christ', McLachlan, *Theological Manuscripts*, 31.

10. R.-D.Herrmann, op.cit., rightly notes that Newton, too, had a 'metaphysic'.

10a. Cf. also J.Harrison, *The Library of Isaac Newton*, 1978, 19.

11. Cf. Manuel, *Isaac Newton Historian*, 97; id., *Religion*, 11. For Newton's religious rationalism and his argument for natural religion, which he identified with Christianity, cf. already R.S.Westfall, 'Isaac Newton, Religious Rationalist', *RR* 22, 1958, 155-70, who at the same time rejects William Law's old theory that Newton was a mystic and disciple of Jakob Boehme.

12. Cf.above, 306 n.178. F.Manuel has usefully referred to these connections, cf. the chapter 'Israel Vindicated' in his *Isaac Newton Historian*, 88ff. Cf. also the connection with so-called Euhemerism; Manuel, *The Eighteenth Century confronts the Gods*, 1959, esp. 112ff.

13. In the *Abstract of Chronology* (1725), in the *Chronology of Ancient Kingdoms Amended* (1728) and the *Original of Monarchies* (in Manuel, op.cit., 199-221).

14. J.Scaliger, *Opus novum de emendatione temporum*, 1583.

15. Cf. Manuel, *Religion*, 86ff. Compare especially the manuscript 'The Language of the Prophets' (extract in McLachlan, *Sir Isaac Newton: Theological Manuscripts*, 119-26).

16. Cf. Manuel, *Portrait*, ch.13, 264ff.: 'The Autocrat of Science' (also already in *Daed.* 97, 1968, 969-1001).

17. Cf. Manuel, *Portrait*, 119f.; *Religion*, 30f.

18. Newton's thesis in the *Seven Statements on Religion* (among the unpublished papers) has become famous: 'That Religion and Philosophy are to be preserved distinct. We are not to introduce divine revelations into Philosophy nor philosophical opinions into religion' (now reprinted in McLachlan, *Theological Manuscripts*, 58).

19. Cf. Buchholtz, op.cit., 66.

20. I.Newton, *Opera quae exstant omnia*, ed. S.Horsely, five vols, 1779-85 (reprinted 1964), III, 170-4 (cf. also I.Newton, *Principia*, ET A.Motte, ed. F.Cajori, 1934, II [⁵1962], 543-7; id., *Philosophiae naturalis principia mathematica*, third ed. in facsimile with variant readings, ed. A.Koyre and I.B.Cohen, 1972, II, 759-65. There is a reprint of the various manuscripts – with an English translation – in *Unpublished Scientific Papers of Isaac Newton*, ed. A.R.Hall and M.B.Hall, 1962 [reprinted 1979], 348-64; cf. also the fragment Ms.Add.3965, sect.13, fol.541r-542r and 545r-546r from the Portsmouth Collection in the Cambridge University Library, published by J.E.McGuire, 'Newton on Place, Time and God', *BJHS* 11, 1978, 114-29). In the third edition the wording of the *Scholium* has been slightly altered, cf. Koyre and Cohen, op.cit., critical apparatus. For the origin of the *Scholium* cf. Cohen, Introduction, op.cit., 240-5. For other manuscript versions cf. Manuel, *Religion*, 40 n.23. There are further comments on Newton's conception of God in Clarke's Latin translation of the *Opticks*, 1706, Quaestio XX. E.W.Strong, 'Newton's "Mathematical Way"', in *JHI* 12, 1951, (90-110) 101f., demonstrates that Newton's theory of space and time as the 'Sensorium of God' in his *Scholium* does not affect the two planes of his scientific system (the empirical and mathematical planes), but represents a third additional plane.

21. Behind the tradition founded by Bacon and Boyle we must recall here the old legacy of 'natural theology', which had retained a significant role in the forms of Western Christianity with a Humanist stamp, albeit in changing forms. This role also explains the consequences which the rise of modern science and the world view which it fundamentally changed inevitably had on the further development of the general cultural situation in the eighteenth century.

22. *Elegantissima haecce Solis, Planetarum & Cometarum compages non nisi consilio & dominio Entis intelligentis & potentis oriri potuit. Et si stellae fixae sint centra similium systematum, haec omnia, simili consilio constructa, suberunt Unius dominio...*, *Opera*, ed. Horsely, III, 171 = *Principia* ed. Koyre and Cohen, II, 760.

23. *Opera*, ed. Horsely, IV, 261f.

24. Similarly also in the well-known first letter to R.Bentley, *Opera*, ed. Horsely, IV, 429ff.

25. Manuel puts particular stress on this notion, which he also seeks to explain in psychological terms from Newton's youthful experiences as a 'quest for the father', cf. *Religion*, 17; cf. also *Portrait*, 32. Buchholtz, op.cit., 69, also rightly sees this confession as a central statement: it remains questionable, however, whether it goes with Newton's dissociation from Deism, which similarly recognized a personal God!

26. *Hic omnia regit, non ut Anima mundi, sed ut universorum Dominus. Et propter dominium suum, Dominus Deus* Pantocrator *dici solet. Nam Deus est vox relativa, & ad servos refertur... Deus summus est Ens aeternum, infinitum, absolute perfectum: sed Ens, utcunque perfectum, sine dominio, non est Dominus Deus. Dicimus enim Deus meus, Deus vester, Deus Israelis, Deus deorum, & Dominus dominorum; sed non dicimus Aeternus meus, Aeternus vester, Aeternus Israelis... Hae appellationes relationem non habent ad servos*, *Opera*, ed. Horsely, IV, 171f. = *Principia*, ed. Koyre and Cohen, II, 760f. – I. Hartill, 'The Faith of Newton', *JTVI* 78, 1946, 75-84, stresses Newton's personal faith. – Manuel, *Religion*, 75, emphasizes his 'anti-metaphysical bias'; F.E.L.Priestley, 'The Clarke-Leibniz Controversy', in *The Methodological Heritage of Newton*, ed. R.E.Butts and J.W.Davis, 1970, (34-56) 45ff., develops more precisely the contrast of this statement to the system of the 'great chain of Being'. On the other side it should be noted that Newton does not go into the historical course of revelation in the incarnation, but branches off into the cosmological hypothesis of the effect of the 'electrical and elastic' spirit, cf. Wagner, *Newton*, 54.

27. *Non est aeternitas & infinitas, sed aeternus & infinitus; non est duratio & spatium, sed durat & adest. Scholium generale*, *Opera*, ed. Horsely, III, 172 = *Principia*, ed. Koyre

and Cohen, II, 761. Cf. also *Optics*, Query 31, *Opera*, IV, 262: 'And yet we are not to consider the world as the body of God, or the several parts thereof as the parts of God. He is an uniform Being, void of organs, members or parts; and they are his creatures subordinate to him, and subservient to his will.' To this is attached a notion which is developed further in Query 28, according to which space could be the 'sensorium' of God (Newton imagines the 'sensorium' in a living being as a place of the inner perception of impressions communicated through the senses): 'Does it not appear from phaenomena, that there is a Being incorporeal, living, intelligent, omnipresent, who, infinite space, as it were in his sensory, sees the things themselves intimately...' *Opera*, ed. Horsely, IV, 238.

28. H.Metzger, *Attraction universelle*, 55ff.

29. M.Boas and R.Hall, 'Newton's "Mechanical Principles"', *JHI* 20, 1959, 167-78; H.Guerlac, *Newton et Epicure (Conférence donnée au Palais de la découverte le 2 Mars 1963 [Alençon])*, esp. 26ff.

30. Facsimile of the original edition (1756) in I.B.Cohen (ed.,), *Isaac Newton's Papers and Letters on Natural Philosophy*, 1958, 271-312.

31. Cf. also J.E.McGuire, 'Force, Active Principles and Newton's Invisible Realm', *Ambix* 15, 1968, 154-208. This more precise statement is a necessary corrective to the still widespread popular view that from the beginning Newton conceived of a 'clockwork universe' in which God had only the role of prime mover. Thus e.g. H.Butterfield, 'Newton and his Universe', in *The History of Science. Origins and Results of the Scientific Revolution*, 1951 (fifth reprint 1963), (77-86), 86; cf. also B.Willey, 'How the Scientific Revolution of the Seventeenth Century Affected other Branches of Thought', ibid., (87-96) 94. – On the other hand Newton did not simply take over Cudworth's view. Rather, he followed Cambridge Neoplatonism in working independently on ancient traditions, as his 'classical' scholia show, and arrived at the view that his natural philosophy had already been put forward by the ancients. Cf. J.E.McGuire and P.M.Rattansi, 'Newton and the "Pipes of Pan"', in *Notes and Records of the Royal Society* 21, 1966, 108-43. For an unpublished outline of a new version of the twenty-third question of the *Opticks* cf. also M.C.Jacob, *Newtonians*, 242ff.

32. S.L.Bethell, *The Cultural Revolution of the Seventeenth Century*, 1951 (reprinted 1963), 57ff. points out that Newton's view of the universe makes God superfluous as a factor in scientific thinking. That this drove theology out of science 'was the real revolution of the seventeenth century, a revolution from which we have not yet recovered,' op.cit., 63.

33. E.A.Burtt, *The Metaphysical Foundations of Modern Physical Science*, ^{2}1932 (reprinted 1967), has given a classical account of his relevance.

34. Burtt, op.cit., 223ff., has shown that even positivism cannot get by without metaphysics, even if it suppresses it into the sub-conscious.

35. Manuel, *Religion*, 49, thinks that towards the end of his life Newton himself sensed the growing independence of secular Newtonianism.

36. There is a survey of the main representatives in H.Metzger, op.cit. Cf. also P.Casini, *L'Universo*. Newton himself could still easily reconcile his voluntaristic conception of God with his scientific view of the world by a methodological separation of the two realms; he could not yet see the autonomy of his system. For the differences between Newton and Leibniz in this respect cf. M.R.Perl, 'Physics and Metaphysics in Newton, Leibniz and Clarke', *JHI*, 30, 1969, 507-26, esp. 523ff.

37. Cf. J.H.Monk, *Life of Richard Bentley*, two vols, ^{6}1833 (reprinted 1969); H.Metzger, op.cit., 79ff.; Casini, *L'universo*, 55ff.

38. For the first printings and further editions cf. A.T.Bartholomew and J.W.Clark, *Richard Bentley, D.D., A Bibliography*, 1908; for the content cf. A.Koyre, *From the Closed World to the Infinite Universe*, 1957, [164ff.]. In addition to the facsimile partial printing of the first edition (1963) in I.B.Cohen (ed.), *Isaac Newton's Papers*, 313-94,

I have used the edition in *The Works of R.B.*, ed. A.Dyce, 1836-38 (reprinted 1971), III, 1-200.

39. More exactly in a first addition to this Testament; cf. the wording in *The Works of the Honourable Robert Boyle*, ed. T.Birch, five vols, ²1772 (reprinted 1965), I, CLXVII. For the Boyle lectures and the following paragraphs cf. also Redwood, *Reason, Ridicule and Religion*, 103ff.; M.C.Jacob, *Newtonians*, 143ff.

40. For the details of its preparation, in addition to Monk, I, 37ff., cf. recently H.Guerlac and M.C.Jacob, 'Bentley, Newton and Providence', *JHI*, 30, 1969, 307-18; cf. also P.Miller, 'Bentley and Newton', in *Newton's Papers and Letters on Natural Philosophy*, ed. I.B.Cohen, 1958, 271-394. For Bentley's dependence on Locke cf. D.J.Allan, 'Locke and Bentley', *Locke Newsletter* 7, 1976, 55-77.

41. Sermons III-V (2 May 1692; 6 June 1692; 5 September 1692).

42. Sermons VI-VIII: they have the common title 'A Confutation of Atheism from the Origin and Frame of the World', *Works* III, 119.

43. Cf. Guerlac and Jacob, op.cit., 316ff.

44. Now in *Correspondence of Isaac Newton*, ed. H.W.Turnbull, III, 1961, 233.

45. Thus e.g. Guerlac and Jacob, op.cit., 31f.

46. Cf. e.g. Bentley's summary conclusion, op.cit., 200: 'For such an usefulness of things, or a fitness of means to ends, as neither proceeds from the necessity of their beings, nor can happen to them by chance, doth necessarily infer that there was an intelligent Being, which is the author and contriver of that usefulness.'

47. Thus Manuel, *Portrait*, 125, thinks, probably rightly, that Newton was 'genuinely pleased that Bentley had shown his system developed in the *Principia* to be so useful as a powerful weapon against atheism'. Cf. also Casini, *L'universo*, 62.

48. Manuel, *Religion*, 39.

49. J.G.Herder, *Älteste Urkunde des Menschengeschlechtes*, in *Werke*, ed. B.Suphan, VI, 1883 (reprinted 1967), 202.

50. Facsimile reprint 1964 (together with *A Discourse concerning the Unchangeable Obligation of Natural Religion*, 1706). Cf. also Metzger, *Attraction Universelle*, 115ff. For Clarke cf. also Casini, *Introduzione*, 84ff.

51. Cf. 595 n.70.

52. The work went through twelve editions up to 1754; I had a German translation ed. J.A.Fabricius, 1741. In addition Derham also wrote an *Astro-Theology; or a demonstration of the being and attributes of God from a survey of the Heavens*, 1715. For Derham cf. also Metzger, op.cit., 155ff.; Casini, *L'universo*, 149ff.

53. I used the edition by J.D.Titius, Leipzig 1755.

54. New editions: *The Leibniz-Clarke Correspondence*, ed. H.G.Alexander, 1956; *Correspondance Leibniz-Clarke présentée d'après les manuscrits originaux des bibliothèques de Hannovre et de Londres*, ed. A.Robert, 1957 (there is also a Russian edition, 1960). The correspondence is also contained in *Die philosophischen Schriften von G.W.Leibniz*, ed. C.J.Gerhard, VII, 1931, 347-440. See e.g. C.D.Broad, 'Leibniz' Last Controversy with the Newtonians', *Theoria*, 12, 1946, 143-68; A.Koyre and I.B.Cohen, 'The Case of the Missing Tanquam; Leibniz, Newton and Clarke', *Isis* 52, 1961, 555-66; id., 'Newton and the Leibniz-Clarke-Correspondence, with notes on Newton, Conti and Des Maizeaux', *AIHS* 15, 1962, 63-126; A.R. and M.B.Hall, 'Clarke and Newton', *Isis* 52, 1961, 583-5; M.R.Perl, op.cit.; F.E.L.Priestley, op.cit.; H.Erlichson, 'The Leibniz-Clarke Controversy', *AmJPh* 35, 1967, 89-98.

55. Cf. on this especially Priestley, op.cit., and D.Kubrin, 'Newton and the Cyclical Cosmos: Providence and the Mechanical Philosophy', *JHI* 28, 1967, 325-46. M.R.Perl, op.cit., seeks to demonstrate that Clarke did not understand Newton's mathematical and physical doctrines correctly, but this question is irrelevant here.

56. Cf.Priestley, op.cit., 44.

57. Priestley, op.cit., 52.

58. 1748 (reprinted 1968).

59. Cf. op.cit., 381f. He treats the first point as being immediately illuminating: 'a manifest contrivance immediately suggests a contriver'. The weakness of this argument was brought to light only much later, ultimately only by Kant. The second raises the question whether the innermost movements in the bodies, of which he speaks as an argument for God's continuing active presence, can in fact provide the same proof, for if there are physical explanations for these movements, a constant mover for them can be dispensed with. Leibniz already made this objection in substance against Clarke: in fact the Newtonian view of the world was also inappropriate for the notion of a cosmos shaped by God through history. Cf. also Priestley, op.cit., 51f.

60. *Telluris Theoria Sacra: orbis nostri originem & mutationes generales, quas aut jam subiit, aut subiturus est, complectens*, two vols., 1681-89.

61. The baroque title gives the whole content: *A New Theory of the Earth, from its Original, to the Consummation of all Things, wherein the Creation of the World in six Days, the Universal Deluge and the Great Conflagration, as laid down in the Holy Scriptures, are shewn to be perfectly agreeable to Reason and Philosophy. With a discourse concerning the Mosaick History of the Creation*, 1696. On p.3 we read: 'The Mosaick Creation is not a Nice and Philosophical account of the Origin of All Things, but an Historical and True Representation of the formation of our single Earth out of a confused Chaos, and of the successive and visible changes thereof each day, till it became the habitation of Mankind' (also quoted by Manuel, *Religion*, 37). Whiston's later work *Astronomical Principles of Religion, Natural and Revealed*, 1725, also has the same aim, of demonstrating not only natural religion but the truth of the biblical revelation of Jews and Christians from the insights into the system of the universe that have been gained (to compare 'the two great divine books', 133). Among the reasons which he gives at the end of his work for his belief in the truth of Jewish and Christian revelations (259-61), three at the beginning are: 'I. The Reveal'd Religion of the Jews and Christians lays the Law of Nature for its Foundation... II. Astronomy, and the rest of our certain Mathematick Sciences, do confirm the Accounts of Scripture... III. The ancientest and best Historical Accounts now known, do generally speaking, confirm the Accounts of Scripture', 259. For Whiston's two works cf. also H.Metzger, *Attraction Universelle*, 96ff.; Casini, *L'universo*, 83ff.; Redwood, *Reason, Ridicule and Religion*, 123f. Redwood, 249 n.64, is rightly amazed that so far there is no biography of Whiston, who is a very interesting figure.

62. Instead of this, John Woodward, *An Essay toward a Natural History of the Earth*, 1695, wanted to demonstrate the reliability of the biblical story of the Flood by fossil remains.

63. Whiston, *Astronomical Principles*, 243.

64. Outside the narrower circle of the Newtonians but influential in a similar direction was also the work by William Wollaston, *Religion of Nature Delineated*, 1724, which was read, among others, three times by Queen Caroline, cf. Mossner, *Bishop Butler*, 4.

65. He was therefore removed in 1710 from all his posts in Cambridge including the chair of Mathematics which he had taken in 1701 as Newton's successor. Cf. E.Duffy, ' "Whiston's Affair": The Trials of a Primitive Christian 1709-1714', *JEH* 27, 1976, 129-51.

66. Cf. also Francis Bacon, *The Advancement of Learning and New Atlantis*, Book I, 1.3 (new edition, 1951, 11): 'Let no man upon a weak conceit of sobriety or an illapplied moderation think or maintain, that a man can search too far, or be too well studied in the book of God's word, or in the book of God's works, divinity or philosophy...' For the theme of the two 'books' cf. also Manuel, *Religion*, 27ff.

67. Apart from discussions of his correspondence with Leibniz, the literature on

Clarke is sparse; from more recent times, apart from E.Albee, 'Clarke's Ethical Philosophy', *PhRev* 37, 1928, 304-27, 403-32, and E.Garin, 'Samuel Clarke e il razionalismo inglese del secolo XVIII', *Sophia* 2, 1934, 106-16, 294-304, 385-426 (cf. also id., *L'illuminismo inglese. I Moralisti*, 1941), one can mention only J.P.Ferguson, 'Dr Samuel Clarke. An Eighteenth-Century Heretic', 1976. Cf. also D.A.Pailin, 'Clarke, Samuel (1675-1729)', *TRE* 8, 1981, 90-2. For Clarke's metaphysical system cf. also J.Gay, 'Matter and Freedom in the Thought of Samuel Clarke', *JHI* 24, 1953, 85-105. Cf. also Casini, *L'universo*, 109-48; Sina, *Ragione*, 679ff., and Clarke's dispute with Collins over the immaterial nature and the immortality of the soul, R.Attfield, 'Clarke, Collins and Compounds', *JHP* 15, 1977, 45-54.

68. Reprint cf. 593 n.50 above.

69. Op.cit.

70. 'The supreme Cause and Author of all things must of necessity be a Being of infinite goodness, justice, and truth, and all other perfections, such as become the supreme Judge and Governor of the world', op.cit., 233.

71. 'From hence it follows, that though God is a most perfectly free Agent, yet he cannot but do always what is Best and Wisest in the whole.' Op.cit., 247. The title to this sub-thesis given in the margin runs: 'Of the Necessity of God's doing always what is Best and Fittest in the whole.'

72. 'Seldom does one encounter, even in the popular literature of philosophy or theology, so substantial a recantation presented as the triumphant concluding of an elaborate chain of argument', op.cit., 324.

73. Prop. XI, Demonstration, 221ff.

74. Prop. X, op.cit., 150ff.

75. Prop. IX, op.cit., 126ff.

76. Op.cit., 249. Albee, op.cit., 416, points out that this argument, which seeks to find a compromise between theology and philosophy, appears in quite a similar form in Cumberland and Leibniz.

77. Op.cit., 250; cf. also *Discourse*, 61f.

78. *Discourse*, 45f. Cf. further Albee, op.cit., 404ff.

79. R.Cumberland, *De legibus naturae disquisitio philosophica*, 1672.

80. For the connections cf. Garin, *Clarke*, 394ff.

81. He belongs in the broader sense to the group of Cambridge Platonists.

82. *Discourse*, Table of Contents, unpaginated.

83. Op.cit., 406f. Cf. also Garin, op.cit., 411.

84. Prop. IV, op.cit., 160ff.

85. 'But that now in this present World, the natural order of things is so perverted, that Vice often flourishes in great prosperity, and Virtue falls under the greatest calamities of Life.' Margin title, op.cit., 165, and Table of Contents.

86. Op.cit., 170ff.

87. Cf. also Garin, op.cit., 115.

88. Prop.V, 193ff. Through this third chain of argumentation the argument of the discourse falls into three inconsistent parts (so also Albee, op.cit., 431).

89. Prop. VI, 207ff.

90. Prop. VII, 241ff.

91. Prop. VIII and IX, 263ff. Here is the favourite argument among the Latitudinarians: 'The necessary Marks and Proofs of a Religion coming from God, are these... that the Doctrines it teaches, be all such, as, though not indeed discoverable by the bare Light of Nature, yet, when discovered by Revelation, may be consistent with, and agreeable to, sound and unprejudiced Reason,' op.cit., 265.

92. Prop. X, 266ff.

93. Prop. XI, 277ff.

94. Prop. XII, 285ff.

95. Prop. XIII, op.cit., 290ff.
96. Prop. XIV, 346ff.
97. Op.cit., 367.
98. Op.cit., 352.
99. Op.cit., 356.
100. Op.cit., 361.
101. Op.cit., 362f.
102. A basic feature of Lessing's essay *Die Erziehung des Menschengeschlechtes* is already suggested here, though the historical perspective is lacking.
103. Op.cit., 109.
104. 'Se dunque, come vuole il Tindal, il deista è tale in quanto ammette la rivelazione non perchè rivelata, ma perchè rationale, il Clarke lo fu pienamente', op.cit., 116.
105. Cf. above, 583 n.317. The sub-title runs 'or the Gospel a Republication of the Religion of Nature.' For the content cf. above, 374ff.
106. Cf. Garin, op.cit., 112.
107. *Christianity*, ch.14, op.cit., 353ff.
108. *Discourse*, 34. Cf. also Albee, op.cit., 404.
109. The view of M.C.Jacob, *Toland*, 308: 'Thus the Newtonian natural philosophy, far from leading to deism, offered... one of the most effective systems for the refutation of atheism devised during the seventeeth century', does not stand further examination and not just because of the false parallelism between Deism and atheism. In this respect a clear distinction must be made between Toland (especially in his late phase) and other Deists, like Tindal.
110. Accounts of research: A. Babolin, 'Il pensiero etico e religioso di Joseph Butler nella critica d'oggi', *RFNS* 63, 1971, 470-86; id., 'La Analogy of religion di Joseph Butler nella critica d'oggi', id., 64, 1972, 683-98; id., Introduzione, in *Opere*, see below, I, 3-29. Monographs: W.A.Spooner, *Bishop Butler*, 1900; A.E.Baker, *Bishop Butler*, 1923; Mossner, op.cit.; W.J.Norton, *Bishop Butler, Moralist and Divine*, 1938; A. Duncan-Jones, *Butler's Moral Philosophy*, 1952 (see also G.K.Riddle, 'The Place of Benevolence in Butler's Ethics', *PhQ*, 9, 1959, 356-62); R.A.Carlsson, *Butler's Ethics*, 1964; A.Jeffner, *Butler and Hume*. The biography with the fullest material is still that of T.Bartlett, *Memoirs of the Life, Character, and Writings of Joseph Butler*, 1839. Cf. also G.Gassmann, 'Butler, Joseph (1692-1752)', *TRE* 7, 1981, 496f. Earlier editions of his work: *The Works of ...J.B.*, ed. S.Halifax, two vols., 1884; ed. W.E.Gladstone, two vols, 1896 (also *Studies Subsidiary to the Works of Bishop Butler*, 1896); ed. J.H.Bernard, two vols., 1900; *The Analogy of Religion*, Introduction by E.C.Mossner, 1961. (At the time of working on this section unfortunately I usually had access only to the edition by Halifax.) There is a list of the numerous complete and partial editions in Babolin, in *Opere* I, 125-34. Italian translation: *Opere*, a cura di A.Babolin: I, *Corrispondenza. Sei sermoni, Allocuzioni*, 1971; II, *I quindici sermoni*; III, *L'analogia...*, 1969. For the secondary literature cf. Mossner, op.cit., bibliography, 241-5; Babolin, in *Opere* I, 134-44. Cf. esp. T.McPherson, 'The Development of Bishop Butler's Ethics', *Phil.* 23, 1948, 317-31; 24, 1949, 3-22; D.D.Raphael, 'Bishop Butler's View of Conscience', *Phil.* 24, 1949, 219-38; A.R.White, 'Conscience and Self-Love in Butler's Sermons', *Phil.* 27, 1952, 329-44; S.A.Grave, 'Butler's Analogy', *CambJourn* 6, 1952/53, 169-80; id., 'The Foundations of Butler's Ethics', *AJPh* 30, 1952, 73-89; K.Dick, 'Das Analogieprinzip bei John Henry Newman und seine Quelle in Joseph Butlers *Analogy*', in *Newman Studien*, ed. H.Fries and W.Becker, 5.F., 1962, 9-228; J.L.Murphy, 'A Rationalist Defence of Christianity', *AEcR* 148, 1963, 217-35, 315-36; P.Fuss, 'Sense and Reason in Butler's Ethics', *Dialogue*, 7, 1969, 180-93; J.Kleinig, 'Butler in a Cool Hour', *JHP* 7, 1969, 399-411; D.Galli, 'L'analogia della religione secondo J.Butler', *RSFil.* 24, 1971, 88-109; E.Garin, 'A proposito di Joseph Butler', *RCSF* 26, 1971, 336f.; B.Sza-

bados, 'Butler on Corrupt Conscience', *JHP* 14, 1976. 462-9. For its influence on German neology (through the translation by J.J.Spalding, 1756) cf. also R.Staats, 'Der theologiegeschichtliche Hintergrund des Begriffes "Tatsache"', *ZTK* 70, 1973, 316-45. Cf. also the extensive introduction by A.Babolin, *Opere* I, 3-122.

111. Cf. Mossner, op.cit., 79. M.Pattison already observed, 'Tendencies of Religious Thought in England, 1688-1750', in *Essays and Reviews*, ⁹1861, 254-329 (= Collection of British Authors, Vol.613, 1862, 229ff.), 286: 'It is no paradox to say that the merit of the Analogy lies in its want of originality.' (The fact that Butler has no quotations is no indication of his originality, *pace* Dick, *Analogieprinzip*, 29. Many of his ideas were more or less common opinion.)

112. It is therefore possible to pass over the numerous apologetic writings which appeared between Clarke and Butler, including the most famous of them, G.Berkeley's *Alciphron*, 1732.

113. For his influence on the young Newman cf. e.g. K.Dick, *Analogieprinzip*, 64ff., and passim; J.L.Murphy, 'The Influence of Bishop Butler on Religious Thought', *TS* 24, 1963, (361-401) 381ff.

114. The attempt by C.D.Broad, 'Butler as a Theologian', *HibJ* 21, 1923, 637-56 (also in id., *Religion, Philosophy and Physical Research*, 1953) as it were to rehabilitate him is hardly convincing today. His editor J.H.Bernard still observed in 1900: 'the Analogy is still one of the most important books which can be placed in the hand of a student; and the masterly statements of Christian doctrine in the first and fifth chapters of the Second Part are worthy of the deepest attention of the theologian.' Editor's introduction to the *Works*, I, XXV.

115. In this connection the division of the rationalistic period in England into two by M.Pattison is still helpful. He uses the year 1750 as a dividing line between an earlier period, in which 'the main endeavour was to show that there was nothing in the contents of the revelation which was not agreeable to reason', and a later period, in which 'the controversy was narrowed to what are usually called the"Evidences" or the historical proof of the genuineness and authenticity of the Christian records', op.cit., 260.

116. For the overall plan cf. Gladstone, in Butler, *Works* I, *Analogy*, Introduction, 16 n.1. There is a short list of contents for individual chapters in Mossner, op.cit., 83ff., and Dick, *Analogieprinzip*, 29ff.

117. He is also by no means the first to apply the principle of analogy, cf. Mossner, op.cit., 80f. He uses the analogy between nature and religion in the same way as Berkeley. For the special character of his use of the concept of analogy in contrast with the use of analogy in earlier Anglican theology, which still had a scholastic stamp, cf. also Bethell, *Cultural Revolution*, 66ff., and Dick, op.cit., esp. 55, who prefers to speak of 'a kind of univocity', in view of the universality of the scheme; cf. also 45ff.

118. In the introduction to the *Analogy* Butler similarly enumerates five points for the 'notion of religion in general and of Christianity', ed. Halifax, I, 10f. (ed. Gladstone, I, 17), which in part correspond with Herbert's *notitiae communes circa religionem*, cf. above, 188. Cf. also Jeffner, *Butler and Hume*, 89f.; Dick, *Analogieprinzip*, 53.

119. Cf. also Dick, *Analogieprinzip*, 36: '...that by natural religion Butler simply understands a natural morality whose expression consists in virtuous life and whose assurance lies in a righteousness of God which provides compensation in the beyond'.

120. Ch.6, directed against fatalism, can be passed over, as it is a digression in the context.

121. Cf. above, 254ff.

122. For the dependence of Butler's epistemology on Locke, cf. e.g. Murphy, *AEcR*, 317ff., and above all Jeffner, op.cit., 31ff.

123. 'There are two ways in which the subject of morals may be treated. One begins from inquiring into the abstract relations of things: the other from a matter of fact, namely what the particular nature of man is...' Preface to the *Sermons*, ed. Halifax, II, VIIIf. (ed. Gladstone, II, 5). – Cf. also Mossner, op.cit., 100: 'with the express aim of indicating to man his duty and of showing, not the theoretical reasonableness of religion, but its reasonableness in practice.'

124. '....that in this treatise I have argued upon the principles of others, not my own, and have omitted what I think true, and of the utmost importance, because by others thought unintelligible, or not true,' *Analogy*, Part Three, ch.VIII, ed. Halifax 303 (ed. Gladstone, 367). On the other hand it is surely misleading to assume that Butler could therefore have developed quite a different overall theology, *pace* Bernard, Editor's Introduction in *Works*, I, XXIf. His principle was fully in accord with the thought of his time.

125. Cf. Jeffner, op.cit., 85f., whose account has the attraction that he reduces Butler's (and Hume's) patterns of thought to logical mathematical formulae and thus makes them very vivid.

126. Jeffner, op.cit., 69.

127. The double meaning of the term 'nature' should be noted; for Butler it also has an eminently practical reference: 'not what science can disclose us of the laws of the cosmos, but a narrow observation of what men do in ordinary life', Pattison, op.cit., 294. Pattison simply overlooks the fact that these are not alternatives but that in Newton's train of thought the one follows the other.

128. Cf. Jeffner, op.cit., 108ff. For the influence of Newton and Butler cf. also already A.Baker, *Bishop Butler*, 10.

129. For this argument designated A 1 by Jeffner, see op.cit., 70ff.

130. Hume's criticism was already in effect a death blow to Butler's system, cf. Jeffner, op.cit., passim.

131. 'Probable evidence is essentially distinguished from demonstrative by this, that it admits of degrees; and of all variety of them, from the highest moral certainty, to the very lowest presumption', *Analogy*, Introduction, ed. Halifax, 1 (ed. Gladstone, 3).

132. Cf. also Jeffner, op.cit., 86.

133. Cf. esp. chs. IV, V.

134. *Analogy*, ed. Halifax, 153.

135. Murphy's argument at this point, *AEcR*, 22, goes somewhat wrong because of his estimation of Deism.

136. Op.cit., 154.

137. Here he uses in principle the 'general analogy argument', cf. Jeffner, on this special case, op.cit., 76.

138. Cf. Murphy, *AEcR*, 321ff.

139. There is an example of this way of arguing e.g. in Part II, ch.VI (ed. Halifax, 235f.), where Butler presupposes the case that some may find the arguments for Christianity extremely dubious: 'even this doubtful evidence will, however, put them into a general state of probation in the moral and religious sense'. For just as, if a person may have only the slightest doubt whether someone else is not perhaps his benefactor and he is not dependent on him for temporal advantage, he must feel particularly obliged towards such a person, so, if the evidence made Christianity or religion in general only the slightest bit credible or probable, this is an adequate reason for following it, 'because the apprehension that religion may be true does as really lay men under obligations, as a full conviction that it is true'.

140. Op.cit., Part II, ch. VII. Quotation ed. Halifax, 250.

141. Ed. Halifax, 273f.

142. Op.cit., 290 (ed. Gladstone, 351).

143. Ibid.

144. Conclusion, ed. Halifax, 315.

145. For the manner of arguing for miracles and prophecy cf. Jeffner, op.cit., 112ff.

146. Part II, ch. VII, ed. Halifax, 281 (ed. Gladstone, 340).

147. Butler also takes over the doctrine of verbal inspiration for the divinity of scripture for his proofs of Christ's divinity from miracles and prophecy; for the circular argument which arises here cf. Mossner, op.cit., 98f.

148. Thus, rightly, Murphy, *AEcR*, 318, 327f. This evaluation is, however, to be qualified by the observation that Butler again speaks of the mystery of God and to this extent preserves a religious dimension, cf. also Jeffner, op.cit., 191f., and Dick, op.cit., 42. That Butler at all events is 'profoundly interested in living religion' is only correct in a very limited way, within his rationalist and moralist limitations.

149. Here mention should be made especially of his *Fifteen Sermons Preached at the Rolls Chapel* (1726), now in *Works*, II; the preface to the Sermons and the dissertation 'On the Nature of Virtue' (second appendix to the *Analogy*) are now in *Works*, I (ed.Halifax, 328ff.). I have also used the edition of the *Sermons*, London 1828. A recent thorough investigation of Butler's ethical system on the basis of the Sermons can now be found in B.von Eckardt, *Ethik der Selbstliebe. Joseph Butlers Theorie der menschlichen Natur*, 1980.

150. He speaks of 'the moral fitness and unfitness of actions, prior to all will whatever; which I apprehend... to determine the Divine conduct', *Analogy*, ed. Halifax, 303 (ed. Gladstone, 367), and 'that there is, in the nature of things, an original standard of right and wrong in actions, independent upon all will, but which unalterably determines the will of God, to exercise that moral government over the world, which religion teaches...' op.cit., ed. Halifax, 304 (ed. Gladstone, 368).

151. Cf. Jeffner, op.cit., 210f.

152. Cf. the quotations in n.150 above.

153. Cf. A.E.Taylor, 'Some Features of Butler's Ethics', *Mind* 35, 1926, 273-300 (also in id., *Philosophical Studies*, 1930, 291-320), 283, cf. also 290. For the imbalance between the 'Full Naturalistic Thesis' and the predominance of conscience in Butler cf. also N.L.Sturgeon, 'Nature and Conscience in Butler's Ethics', *PhRev* 58, 1976, 316-56. Butler stresses, note to Sermon XII, *Sermons*, 1828 ed., 137: 'There are certain dispositions of mind, and certain actions, which are in themselves approved or disapproved by mankind, abstracted from the consideration of their tendency to the happiness or misery of the world; approved or disapproved by reflection, by that principle within, which is the guide of life, the judge of right and wrong.' T.McPherson, op.cit., sought to demonstrate that the two aspects follow one after the other chronologically in the development of Butler's ethics; the ethics derived from human nature is that of the Sermons, that from the ordering of the world is that of the *Analogy*. However, in the sentences quoted above, 598 n.123, from the preface to his Sermons, Butler sums up the two as complementary possibilities of deduction. For Butler's psychological moral theory cf. especially C.D.Broad, *Five Types of Ethical Theory*, 1930 (⁹1967), 55ff.; Duncan-Jones, op.cit., chs.2-4, 41ff.(on the conscience, ch.3, 69ff.); Jeffner, ch.2, 44f.; B.von Eckardt, *Ethik*, seeks to demonstrate a theory of man as a 'dynamic system' in the ethics developed by Butler in his Sermons, which ethically culminates in a 'dynamic theology of self-fulfilment' (15). In Butler self-love is virtually cultivated as the goal of a higher morality (cf. esp. 52ff.). In fact Butler shows not only that 'this our nature... is adapted to virtue' (*Sermons*, Preface, VII); self-love also leads without constraint, as a legitimate feeling, to the good of others (XVf., and Sermon XI). The transition does not need much effort (*pace* von Eckardt, 214ff.).

154. Op.cit., ch.7, 142ff.

155. Op.cit., ch. 7, sec.3, 148ff. Cf. also *Sermons*, Preface, VII: 'Thus nothing can possibly be more contrary to nature than vice...'

156. P.A.Carlsson, op.cit., stresses this connection with theology, but at the same time only touches on one side of Butler's thought.

157. For the theme cf. esp. Grave, *AJP*; Riddle, op.cit.; akin to this is the problem of the relationship between self-love and conscience; cf. L. Stephen, *English Thought*, II, 49f.; Taylor, op.cit., 294ff.; White. op.cit.; McPherson, op.cit.; and lastly Kleinig, op.cit., on the famous 'cool-hour' passage in Sermon XI, ed. Halifax, 150f. (ed. Gladstone, 206).

158. Conversely we now only have the apologetic demonstration that in all its statements Scripture does not contradict generally valid morality, on which reason has to judge: 'Reason can, and it ought to judge, not only of the meaning, but also of the morality and the evidence of revelation. First, It is the province of reason to judge of the morality of the Scripture; i.e. not whether it contains things different from what we should have expected from a wise, just and good Being... but whether it contains things plainly contradictory to wisdom, justice or goodness, to what the light of nature teaches us of God,' *Analogy*, Part II, Ch.III, ed. Halifax, 193.

159. Westfall, *Science and Religion*, 106.

159a. He is recalled especially by D.Greene, 'Augustinianism and Empiricism: A Note on Eighteenth-Century Intellectual History', *Eighteenth-Century Studies* 1, 1967, 33-68; id., 'The Via Media in an Age of Revolution: An Anglicanism in the Eighteenth Century', in *The Varied Pattern*, ed. P.Hughes and D.Williams, 1971, 297-320. However, Pope, Swift and Johnson are Christians in a different way from Newton and Boyle, Locke and Berkeley (against Greene, 'Augustinianism', 39). Greene's protest against the underestimation of the basic Christian attitude in England in the eighteenth century is justified, but does not do away with the 'Stoicism' (cf. 'Augustinianism', 62f.).

160. The secondary literature on Swift is very extensive. As bibliographies see D.M.Berwick, *The Reputation of Jonathan Swift, 1781-1882*, 1941; M.D.Clubb, 'The Criticism of Gulliver's "Voyage to the Houyhnhnms"', *SSLL* 1941, ed. H.Craig, 203-32; L.A.Landa and J.E.Tobin, *Jonathan Swift – A List of Critical Studies Published from 1895, to which is added, Remarks on Some Swift Manuscripts in the United States*, 1945; J.J.Statis, *A Bibliography of Swift Studies 1945-1965*, 1967; C.Lamont, 'A Checklist of Critical and Biographical Writings on Jonathan Swift, 1945-65', in A.A.Jeffares (ed.), *Fair Liberty was All his Cry. A Tercentenary Tribute*, 1967, 356-91. There are numerous collections of articles and book extracts on Swift; cf. especially M.P.Foster (ed.), *A Casebook on Gulliver among the Houyhnhnms*, 1961; J.Traugott (ed.), *Discussions of Jonathan Swift*, 1962; E.Tuveson (ed.), *Swift. A Collection of Critical Essays*, 1964; Jeffares, *Fair Liberty*; id. (ed.), *Swift. Modern Judgements*, 1968; B.Vickers (ed.), *The World of Jonathan Swift*, 1968; K.Williams (ed.), *Swift. The Critical Heritage*, 1970 (earlier criticism of Swift down to the beginning of the nineteenth century); C.J.Rawson, *Focus: Swift*, 1971; D.Donoghue (ed.), *Jonathan Swift: a Critical Anthology*, 1971. For the editions of his work cf. H.Teerinck, *A Bibliography of the Writings of Jonathan Swift*, second edition ed. A.H.Scouten, 1963. The modern standard editions are: *The Prose Works of Jonathan Swift*, ed. H.Davis, etc., 14 vols., 1939-68; *Correspondence*, ed. H.Williams, 5 vols, 1963-5; *Journal to Stella*, ed. H.Williams, 2 vols, 1948; *Poems*, ed. H.Williams, 3 vols, ²1958; *Collected Poems*, ed. J.Horrell, 2 vols, 1958.

161. Cf. D.Worcester, *The Art of Satire*, 1940; E.Leyburn, *Satiric Allegory: Mirror of Man*, 1956; N.Frye, *The Anatomy of Criticism*, 1957; R.Poulson,*The Fictions of Satire*, 1967; and specifically on Swift: J.M.Bullitt, *Jonathan Swift and the Anatomy of Satire: A Study of Satiric Technique*, 1953; R.C.Elliott, *The Power of Satire: Magic, Ritual, Art*, 1960; H.Davis, 'The Satire of Jonathan Swift' (1947), in id., *Jonathan Swift. Essays on his Satire and Other Studies*, 1964, 101-60; E.E.Rosenheim, Jr, *Swift and the Satirist's*

Art, 1963; C.J.Rawson, 'The Character of Swift's Satire', in id. (ed.), *Focus: Swift*, 17-75.

161a. The writing *A Discourse of the Contests and Dissentions Between the Nobles and the Commons in Athens and Rome* (ed. F.H.Ellis, 1967), which comes from the time of William III and is aimed at the Tory party, also combines both methods.

162. For the history of more recent research cf. M.Voigt, *Swift and the Twentieth Century*, 1964; also the introduction by E.Tuveson in id.(ed.), *Swift*, 1-14; by N.Jeffares, in id., *Swift*, 11-35.

163. His lengthy stay in England, 1707-14, during which as a man of letters he cultivated connections with the highest political circles and enjoyed social life in London to the full, was connected with a commission carried out on behalf of the Irish church. Cf. the most recent biography by I. Ehrenpreis, *Swift, The Man, His Works, And the Age*, II, 1967, 195ff.

164. Cf. e.g. E.Tuveson, 'The Dean as Satirist', *UTQ* 22, 1953, 368-75 = *Swift*, ed. Tuveson, 10-110; R.M.Frye, 'Swift's Yahoo and the Christian Symbols for Sin', *JHI* 15, 1953, 201-17 = *Casebook*, ed. Foster, 208-26; W.B.Ewald, Jr, *The Masks of Jonathan Swift*, 1954, 40-52; B.Hall, ' "An Inverted Hypocrite": Swift the Churchman', in Vickers (ed.), *World*, 38-68; Greene, 'Via Media'. – R.Quintana, 'Gulliver's Travels: The Satiric Intent and Execution', in McHugh and Edwards (eds.), *Swift*, (89-93) 88f., still had claimed: 'Swift has been very careful to touch as little as possible on matters of a religious nature.' For Swift's official activity as country clergyman and Dean of St Patrick's Cathedral in Dublin cf. L.A.Landa, *Swift and the Church of Ireland*, 1954; id., 'Jonathan Swift: "Not the Gravest of Divines"', in McHugh and Edwards (eds.), *Swift*, 38-60; for his state church politics cf. J.C.Beckett, 'Swift as Ecclesiastical Statesman', in *Essays in British and Irish History, in Honour of J.E.Todd*, 1949, 135-52 = Traugott (ed.), *Discussions*, 121-30 = Jeffares (ed.), *Fair Liberty*, 146-65. Cf. also R.B.McDowell, 'Swift as a Political Thinker', in McHugh and Edwards (eds.), *Swift*, 176-86.

165. Hall, op.cit., and Ewald, op.cit., are concerned with both.

166. For this cf. E.Pons, *Swift, les années de jeunesse et le conte du Tonneau*, 1932; M.Starkman, *Swift's Satire on Learning in A Tale of a Tub*, 1950; R.M.Adams, 'Swift and Kafka: Satiric Incongruity and the Inner Defeat of the Mind', in *Strains of Discord: Studies in Literary Openness*, 1958, 146-79; R.Paulson, *Theme and Structure in Swift's Tale of a Tub*, 1960 (and the discussions by H.Davis in *RESt* NS 12, 1961, 300-2; P.Harth, *MPh* 58, 1961, 282-5); P.Harth, *Swift and Anglican Rationalism: The Religious Background of a Tale of a Tub*, 1961; J.Traugott, 'A Tale of a Tub', in *Focus: Swift*, 76-120; D.Ward, *Jonathan Swift. An Introductory Essay*, 1973, 16-58.

167. The fourth journey here rightly holds the centre of attention. Cf. above all the views extracts of which are given in Foster, *Casebook* (the extracts given in F.Brady [ed.], *Twentieth Century Interpretations of Gulliver's Travels*, 1968, are sometimes very short) and most of the contributions in the collection by E.Tuveson, *Swift*. Also C.J.Rawson, *Gulliver and the Gentile Reader*, 1973, I, 1-32 (= *Essays ... in Honour of J.Butt*, 1968, 51-90). I found K.Williams, *Jonathan Swift and the Age of Compromise*, 1958, Ch.VII, 154ff., particularly important (there is also an extract in Tuveson, op.cit., 115-22; cf. also id., 'Gulliver's Voyage to the Houyhnhnms', *ELH* 18, 1951, 275-86 = Foster [ed.], *Casebook*, 193-203) and Rosenheim, *Swift*. W.A.Speck, *Swift*, 1969, provides a short introduction to the work as a whole.

168. For a long time (cf. E.Pons, *Swift*; R.Quintana, *The Mind and Art of Jonathan Swift*, 1936 [reprinted 1953, 1965], 86-96; Rosenheim, *Swift*, 54-66; Harth, op.cit., 2ff.) commentators have made it clear that the satire deals with two separate themes: the basic narrative describes abuses in religion, while the 'Digressions' concern themselves (up to Section IX, which is closely connected with VIII) with abuses in science. Both parts were also composed successively, cf. A.C.Guthkelch and D.N.Smith,

Introduction to Swift, *A Tale of a Tub*, ²1958; H.Davis, Introduction, in *Prose Works*, op.cit., I; Harth, op.cit., 6ff.

169. Harth, op.cit., 56, observes that this is so usual a convention in Anglican rationalism that it is impossible to work out a direct source for the fable. For the background cf. also D.Ward, *Swift*, 59ff.

170. Harth, op.cit., 57.

171. R.F.Jones, *Ancients and Moderns*.

172. R.Quintana, 'Two Paragraphs in A Tale of a Tub, Section IX', *MPH* 73, 1975, 15-32, stresses against B.Vickers, *Swift and the Baconian Ideal* (id. [ed.], *World*, 87-128), that in the two paragraphs Swift is not attacking Bacon but above all Descartes, in favour of traditional Aristotelian realism. Adams, *Swift and Kafka*, 147, observes that this debate was already almost out of fashion at the time the satire was composed; Swift's perspective in many respects points back to the previous century.

173. Cf. M.Nicolson and N.M.Mohler, 'The Scientific Backround of Swift's Voyage to Laputa', *Annals of Science* 2, 1937, 325-7.

174. Rosenheim, *Swift*, 101, is right in pointing out that it is too little to treat the fourth journey merely as satire: 'It must be seen... as the expression of answers to the kind of universal question which are the province not of the satiric but of the philosophic mind.' Cf. also ibid., 225.

175. A remark by W.M.Thackeray, *The English Humourists of the Eighteenth Century*, 1853, 38f., has become famous (cf. the extracts in Foster [ed.], *Casebook*, op.cit., 85f., and Traugott [ed.], *Discussions*, 14-21): 'As for the humour and conduct of this famous fable, I suppose there is no person who reads but must admire; as for the moral, I think it horrible, shameful, unmanly, blasphemous; and giant and great as this Dean is, I say we should hoot him...The reader of the fourth part of Gulliver's Travels is like the hero himself in this instance. It is Yahoo-language; a monster gibbering shrieks and gnashing imprecations against mankind, – tearing down all shreds of modesty, past all sense of manliness and shame; filthy in word, filthy in thought, furious, raging, obscene.'

176. Cf. also the judgment of G.Orwell, 'Politics vs. Literature: An Examination of Gulliver's Travels', in id., *Shooting an Elephant and Other Essays*, 1950, 53-76. One effect of this attitude is the psycho-analytical judgment in the Freudian sense in J.M.Murphy, *Jonathan Swift*, 1954, 432-48, and above all N.O.Brown, *From Life Against Death*, 1959, 179-201 = Tuveson (ed.), *Swift*, 31-54 = Traugott (ed.), *Discussion*, 92-104. Here the often discussed theme of Swifts so-called obscene poems has some relevance. Cf. also Ward, *Swift*, 130.

177. Like the *Sentiments of a Church-of-England Man*, the *Letter to a Young Gentleman lately entered into Holy Orders* and the Sermons (cf. also the *Letter from a Member of the House of Commons in Ireland concerning the Sacramental Text* against the Dissenters), cf. Hall, op.cit., and the introduction to the Sermons by L.A.Landa in *Prose Works*, IX, 97-137.

178. Especially, *An Argument To prove, That the Abolishing of Christianity in England, May, as Things now Stand, be attended with some Inconvenience, and perhaps not produce those many good Effects proposed thereby* (cf. also Rosenheim, *Swift*, 39ff.). It is uncertain whether *A project for the Advancement of Religion, and the Reformation of Manners* is meant ironically or seriously; the latter would presuppose a certain naivety on the part of Swift or the pessimistic attitude that an official encouragement of hypocrisy should be preferred to the increasing lack of commitment among the leading classes in the state.

179. Satirically described in the contempt which Gulliver describes on his final return for the friendly Portuguese captain and above all for his family; he can literally no longer stand the smell of his family. The earlier view, that the Houyhnhnms embodied an ideal of Swift's (a utopian one, thus e.g. still G.Sherburn, 'Errors

Concerning the Houyhnhnms', *MPh* 56, 1958, 92-97 = Foster [ed.], *Casebook*, 258-66, is untenable – J.L.Clifford, 'Gulliver's Fourth Voyage: "Hard " and "Soft" Schools of Interpretation', in L.S.Champion [ed.], *Quick Springs of Sense*, 1974, 33-49, terms this trend the 'hard' school of interpretation, further representatives there); cf. above all K.M.Williams, 'Gulliver's Voyage to the Houyhnhnms', *JELH* 18, 1951, 275-86 =Jeffares (ed.), *Swift*, 247-57 = Foster (ed.), *Casebook*, 193-203; S.H. Monk, 'The Pride of Lemuel Gulliver', *Sewanee Rev.* 63, 1955, 48-71 = Brady (ed.), *Interpretations*, 70-9; Rosenheim, *Swift*, esp. 216f. Cf. also Rawson, *Gulliver and the Gentle Reader*, 29ff.; Adams, *Swift and Kafka*, 165.

180. The earlier view of I.Ehrenpreis, 'The Origins of Gulliver's Travels', *PMLA* 62, 1957, 880-99; id., *The Personality of Jonathan Swift*, 1958 (reprinted 1969), 99-109, is exaggerated; he sought to see the Houyhnhnms specifically as a satire of the Deists (this is expressly rejected by Ehrenpreis in 'The Meaning of Gulliver's Last Voyage', *RELit* 3, 1962, 18-38 = *Swift*, ed. Tuveson, op.cit., 123-42). The view of T.O.Wedel, 'On the Philosophical Background of Gulliver's Travels', *SP* 23, 1926, 442-50 = Foster (ed.), *Casebook*, 87-94 = Brady (ed.), *Interpretations*, 23-54, is more apt; he sees as Swift's target the general Stoicism of the time. According to R.J.Dircks, 'Gulliver's Tragic Rationalism', *Criticism* 2, 1960, 134-49, the account of the Houyhnhnms is an ironical satire of the political and social principles of the Whigs, who appeal to Locke's philosophy.

181. Recently it has often been said that above all he is attacking quite inappropriate human pride.

182. Cf. the works mentioned above, 601 n.164; also the introduction by E.Tuveson to id., *Swift*, esp. 7,10f. G.Orwell's judgment, *Politics*, 62, seems absurd today: 'Swift shows no sign of having any religious beliefs, at least in any ordinary sense of the words.' For the use of the Yahoos as a symbol representing traditional Christian ideas of man's 'fleshly' sinfulness cf. R.M.Frye, 'Swift's Yahoo and the Christian Symbols for Sin', *JHI* 15, 1954, 201-17. For criticism, however, see also W.A.Murray, ibid., 599-601.

183. *Correspondence*, ed. Williams, III, 102-5.

184. The background to this distinction has become much clearer since R.S.Crane, 'The Houyhnhnms, the Yahoos, and the History of Ideas', in *Reason and Imagination: Studies in the History of Ideas, 1600-1800*, ed. J.A.Mazzeo, 1962, 231-53 = Brady (ed.), *Interpretation*, 80-88 = id., *The Idea of the Humanities and other Essays*, II, 1967, 261-82, has demonstrated that in rejecting the first definition mentioned Swift is referring specifically to Porphyrean logic, to which he had been introduced as an authority in Dublin College, during his time studying there, in the form of the *Institutio Logicae* of N.Marsh (1679, ²1681).

185. Swift himself rejects the charge that he is a misanthrope in his letter to Pope of 26 November 1725 (*Correspondence*, ed. Williams, III, 116-19): 'I tell you after all that I do not hate Mankind, it is vous autres who hate them because you would have them reasonable Animals, and are Angry for being disappointed.'

186. Cf. J.L.Baroll, III, 'Gulliver and the Struldbruggs', *PMLA* 73, 1958, 43-50.

187. Cf. E.Reiss, 'The Importance of Swift's Glubbdubdrib Episode', *JEGP* 59, 1960, 223-8.

188. Op.cit., 228.

189. Therefore B.Hall's criticism of Harth, in Vickers (ed.), *World*, 53f., for his theory that in the *Tale of a Tub* Swift stands in the line of 'Anglican rationalism' is unjustified, as one has to use the *Sermons* and above all *Gulliver's Travels* as evidence for Swift's later changes of mind.

190. Cf. M.Price, *To the Palace of Wisdom*, 1965, ch. VI, 'Swift: Order and Obligation', 180-240. For Swift's *Letter to a Young Gentleman*, cf. also Harth, op.cit., 32ff.

191. E.g. R.Quintana, *Mind*, 320f.; K.Williams, *Swift*, 204ff. – J.L.Clifford, 'Voyage',

calls this view the 'Soft' school of interpretation (he lists a number of representatives).

192. The first one to shatter the traditional view at this point was F.R.Leavis, 'The Irony of Swift', *Scrutiny* II, 1934, 364-78 = id., *Determinations*, 1934, 78-108 = id., *The Common Pursuit*, 1952, 73-87 = *Casebook*, ed. Foster, 204-7 (extract) = Traugott (ed.), *Discussions*, 35-43. Cf. also Rosenheim, *Swift*, op.cit., esp. 216f., 219. Also Rawson, *Gulliver and the Gentle Reader*, 30, whose view is that the Houyhnhnms are meant quite positively by Swift, but concedes that they are not meant as a model, as it is beyond question impossible for us to imitate them. 'But it is more important still to say that the Houyhnhnms are not a statement of what man ought to be so much as a statement of what he is not', op.cit., 51. Ward, *Swift*, 170ff., gives a balanced comment.

193. Thus rightly already Wedel, op.cit.; also K.Williams, 'Gulliver's Voyage to the Houyhnhnms', 247, etc.

194. Rawson, *Gulliver*, op.cit., 28f. Cf. also Ward, *Swift*, 128ff. (also on the role of the Houyhnhnms: Gulliver is given only the choice of positive or negative humanity: both Yahoos and Houyhnhnms are false images, not reality).

195. Rosenheim, *Swift*, 214, therefore calls this form of satire 'homiletic'; cf. also 216: 'And here it is vital that we remember the ultimately homiletic character of Swift's undertaking. His task... is to implant not affirmative conviction but an agonizing awareness of inadequacy and false pride within the minds of his audience.' For the purpose of the Gulliver Satire, to depict the split in human nature in all its ambivalence (here Swift was also referring to himself), cf. also W.B.Varnochan, *Lemuel Gulliver's Mirror for Man*, 1968, ch.3, 52-115.

196. This contradiction can also be demonstrated in Swift's relationship to Boling-broke as expressed in scattered comments in Swift's correspondence; this is in my view a theme which has still to be worked out (cf. the hints in Williams, *Swift*, 187ff., and Tuveson, Introduction, in Tuveson [ed.], *Swift*, 7). Cf. the General Index in Williams (ed.), *Correspondence*, V, 299f.

197. L.A.Landa, in Swift, *Prose Works*, IX, 101, describes it as a 'conservative adherence to simple and indisputable orthodoxy'.

198. Hall, op.cit., 45, complains: 'Modern literary criticism has produced many brilliant analyses of the surface of the satires, but is curiously silent about the assumptions behind them...'

199. Cf. J.Sutherland, *Background for Queen Anne*, 1939, 78-126; R.I.Cook, *Jonathan Swift as a Tory Pamphleteer*, 1967.

200. However, one should realize that the conservative form of Christian tradition still predominated in the parishes of the Anglican church; cf. also Quintana, *Swift, An Introduction*, 1955 (reprinted 1962, 1966), 154. Still, Swift's satires were addressed to educated people, and to them things looked quite different.

3. The Heyday of Deism

1. Cf. Lechler, *Geschichte*, 217-39; C.Motzo Dentice di Accadia, 'Il Deismo Inglese del settecento, S.2', *GCFI* 16, ser.2, vol.3, 1935, 323-43; id., *Preilluminismo*, 211-25; J.H.Broome, 'Une Collaboration: Collins et Desmaizeaux', *RLC* 30, 1956, 160-79; G.Gawlick, Introduction to Collins, *A Discourse of Free-Thinking*, 1713, facsimile reprint 1965; E.A.Bloom and L.D.Bloom, *Introduction to A Discourse concerning Ridicule and Irony in Writing (1729)*, reprinted 1970; J.O'Higgins, *Antony Collins: The Man and His Work*, 1970, list of the works of Collins, id., 243ff. Cf. also Sina, *Ragione*, 508ff. For Collins' hermeneutic, especially his understanding of Old Testament prophecy, see H.W.Frei, *The Eclipse of Biblical Narrative: A Study in Eighteenth and Nineteenth Century Hermeneutics*, 1974, 66-85.

2. Cf. Lechler, op.cit., 217ff.; O'Higgins, *Collins*, 3ff.

3. Cf. Gawlick, Introduction, 19f.; O'Higgins, *Collins*, 51ff. The second edition appeared in 1709.

4. Op.cit., 3.

5. Op.cit., 4.

6. O'Higgins has drawn attention to the parallel, *Collins*, 51f. For the connections between the two Deists cf. id., 13ff.

7. For the relationship of Collins to his teacher Locke cf. also the letter to Clarke quoted by Gawlick, op.cit., 34 n.6.

8. Op.cit., 24f.

9. Op.cit., 7ff.

10. Op.cit., 8.

11. Op.cit., 9f.

12. Op.cit., 14; cf. also the quotation in O'Higgins, *Collins*, 54.

13. Op.cit., 16.

14. Op.cit., 17f.

15. Quotations, op.cit., 18.

16. Op.cit., 15, 20. For Collins' relationship to Tillotson cf. also O'Higgins, *Collins*, 45-7.

17. However, to assume a specific dependence of Collins on Spinoza is unjustified. O'Higgins, *Collins*, 55; Collins, here stands rather in the broad stream of Humanist tradition.

18. *Demonstratio Evangelica*, 1690.

19. *Essay*, 21-23.

20. Op.cit., 23. O'Higgins, *Collins*, 55f., also takes the view that Collins did not in any way want to discredit the work as such.

21. *Essay*, 23ff.

22. Arguing against F.Gastrell, *Considerations concerning the Trinity*, 1696.

23. Op.cit., 42ff.

24. *A Vindication of the Divine Attributes, in some Remarks on his Grace the Archbishop of Dublin's Sermon intituled 'Divine Predestination consistent with the Freedom of Man's Will'*, 1710. For details cf. O'Higgins, *Collins*, 61ff.

25. Op.cit., 96.

26. This work went into five editions in all up to 1790. Cf. also the new impression, *Determinism and Freewill. Anthony Collins' A Philosophical Inquiry Concerning Human Liberty*, edited and annotated by J.O'Higgins, 1976.

27. For the details cf. O'Higgins, *Collins*, 69ff.; also Gawlick, Introduction, 20f.

28. Cf. also above, 587 n.393.

29. *Priestcraft in Perfection*, 1710 (two further editions appeared in the same year-I have used the third). Shortly afterwards Collins enlarged the pamphlet by a second one, *Reflections on 'Priestcraft in Perfection'*; both appeared anonymously. For the content and the problem of the tradition of the text of the Thirty-Nine Articles see the detailed account by O'Higgins, *Collins*, 132ff. In 1724, Collins returned to the theme in a more extensive work, *An Historical and Critical Essay on the Thirty-Nine Articles*.

30. 'Or, A Detection of the Fraud of Inserting and Continuing this Clause...'

31. 'the Scandal of this Popish Clause', 9, cf. also 14, is caused by the 'Forgerys of Priests', 46, whose goal has merely been 'to promote the Interest of the Clergy... by Fraud', 45.

32. Op.cit., 18f., 22.

33. 'some Chaplain or Corrector of the Press..., who has thus impos'd on his Lordship (the Archbishop) and the World', op.cit., 19.

34. On pp.6-8.

35. Op.cit., 6-8.

36. O'Higgins, too, thinks of the work that: 'It could have been written by a moderate puritan member of the Church of England', *Collins*, 143.

37. 'This blessed Martyr made no scruple to put a Falshood on the World', op.cit., 37.

38. 'How great a value we Protestants ought to set upon the Holy Scriptures, those inestimable Treasures of Wisdom and Knowledge... They have a universal Tradition to support them, infinitely beyond the Evidence of any other matter of fact, and have besides the demonstration of the Spirit and of Power. But I cannot express my sense better against the Authority of Priests, and for the Authority of the Scriptures than in the words of our incomparable Chillingworth' (there follows a quotation from *The Religion of Protestants*, ch.6, 56). For Collins' relationship to Chillingworth cf. also O'Higgins, *Collins*, 44, 50, etc. (see Index, s.v.).

39. Op.cit. For the various editions cf. Gawlick, Introduction, 29ff.

40. Cf. Gawlick, op.cit. 27f.

41. Cf. Gawlick, op.cit., 22 and n.20.

42. Cf. O'Higgins, *Collins*, 77 and n.7, 91f.

43. 'By Free-Thinking then I mean, The Use of the Understanding in endeavouring to find out the Meaning of any Proposition whatsoever, in considering the nature of the Evidence of or against it, and in judging of it according to the seeming Force or Weakness of the Evidence', op.cit., 5.

44. *Remarks upon a Late Discourse of Free-Thinking... by Phileleutherus Lipsiensis* (R.Bentley)(1713), in Bentley, *Works*, III, 288-474. For the content cf. already Lechler, op.cit., 233ff.

45. "Tis really no more than think and judge as you find; which every inhabitant of Bedlam practises every day...', op.cit., 297.

46. Cf. also Lechler, op.cit., 222.

47. Bentley, op.cit., 297, stresses the words 'any whatsoever' in Collins' definition: in fact Collins develops this notion further on the following pages.

48. *The Impositions of Priests*, op.cit., 8.

49. Op.cit., 10.

50. The stringency and inner order of which has often been criticized with very good reasons, cf. already Bentley, op.cit., and e.g. Lechler, op.cit., 233; O'Higgins, *Collins*, 81ff.

51. Op.cit., 32.

52. The abortive attempt at a definition of freethinking at the beginning, and the following discussion of the arguments pro (Section II) and contra (section III), evidently follows a scholastic pattern of disputation and seems very alien to the modern reader on this particular theme.

53. Third Argument, 35ff.

54. 'The Design of the Gospel was, by preaching, to set all Men upon Free-Thinking' (Sixth Argument, op.cit., 44).

55. By contrast, one should not take seriously the ironically formulated Fifth Argument in which Collins wants people like Sacheverell and Atterbury to be forced to work as missionaries abroad, and in the interest of freethinking in religious matters to have missionaries from Siam in England (op.cit., 41ff.).

56. In the text there is '6thly', an obvious misprint.

57. Op.cit., 46.

58. Op.cit., 52-56.

59. Op.cit., 57-61. Here Collins cites Jeremy Taylor, characteristically abbreviating him. He omits the qualification Taylor had made, that the fundamentalia were clearly transmitted in scripture; cf. Gawlick, op.cit., n. on 58,5, p.194*; O'Higgins, *Collins*,

86. In his answer Bentley immediately complained about the inaccuracy of this quotation. For the problem cf. also O'Higgins, *Collins*, 233.

60. On this O'Higgins, *Collins*, 86ff.; J.Grabe, *Spicilegium S.S.Patrum*, ²1700, I, 320; cf. the argument in Gawlick, op.cit., n. on 86,8, p.204*; J.Mill, *Prolegomena* to his *Novum Testamentum Graecum*, ed. L.Kusterus, 1710, 22ff., cf. ibid., n. on 87,5, and W.Beveridge, cf. ibid., note on 87,5.

61. Op.cit., 88ff. On this point Collins again refers to John Mill's critical edition of the text of the New Testament; for this cf. also A.Fox, *John Mill and Richard Bentley. A Study of the Textual Criticism of the New Testament, 1675-1729*, 1954.

62. Op.cit., 98f. The quotation is also used by O.Higgins, *Collins*, 88.

63. *Geschichte*, 222f.

64. On the other hand Collins again refers to representatives of rational Anglicanism, including Chillingworth (op.cit., 34, 75, 86, 177) and Jeremy Taylor (passim, cf. Gawlick, op.cit., Index of names, 231*), and Latitudinarians, especially Tillotson (cf. ibid., see O'Higgins, op.cit., 94), even though he partly deliberately puts their view on one side (cf. n.59 above).

65. In *Nouvelles Littéraires*, 24 April 1717, 271f., cf. in O'Higgins, *Collins*, 20f.

66. Op.cit., 56.

67. *Discourse*, 121ff.

68. Among them, in addition to those already mentioned, the following appear in a positive sense: e.g. Erasmus (124, 177), Henry More (48, 68, 78), Cudworth (48, 85, cf. also 62, 128), F.Bacon (104, 106 and esp. 169: 'My Lord Bacon show'd himself to be a great Free-thinker'); for the favourable verdict even on Hobbes (170, cf. 96, 104) cf. O'Higgins, Index, ad loc. The list in *Collins*, 177, is particularly illuminating. Here, as well as Erasmus, who stands at the beginning of this catalogue of Humanist saints, there are also the names of Descartes, Gassendi, Grotius, Hooker, Chillingworth, Falkland, Herbert of Cherbury, John Hales and also Milton, Wilkins and finally Locke. O'Higgins, *Collins*, 23ff., has referred to the catalogue of Collins' private library and the titles listed there as evidence of the wide range of literature he used.

69. It is no coincidence that for the 'Essay on the Thirty-Nine Articles' O'Higgins recalls the very similar attitude of Lord Brooke, *Collins*, 144 (for Brooke cf. above, 509 n.204).

70. O'Higgins, *Collins*, 92, thinks of the ancestors of freethinking mentioned by Collins in the *Discourse*, 121ff., which go from Socrates, Plato and Aristotle through Cicero, Seneca and Solomon to Bacon, Hobbes and Tillotson: 'It was certainly a mixed bag.' But his list is less the product of personal obscurity in Collins' thought (cf. O'Higgins, *Collins*, 92) than a representative testimony to the fluctuating spectrum of those who handed down the rationalist moralist tradition, which included both ancient Stoicism as revived in Humanism and the modern Puritans and Latitudinarians (despite their internal oppositions).

71. 'He still had links with what he considered to be the Protestant idea', O'Higgins, *Collins*, 84.

72. In his answer to the *Discourse* Bentley points out the weakness in its argument in respect of the significance of the text-critical variants in the New Testament, *Remarks*, 345ff. Elsewhere, too, Bentley can convincingly demonstrate Collins' lack of technical knowledge in the different areas he discusses and his amateur way of dealing with the facts; O'Higgins therefore judges that Bentley clearly demonstrated to Collins his dissatisfaction with the latter's academic standards. However, the fact that he never once attempts this in connection with the question of religious authority, to which Collins gives a central position (cf. O'Higgins, *Collins*, 83, 93) shows the weakness of the rationalist apologetic represented by Bentley, which had

much too much in common with the Deistic opposition in the presuppositions of its thought to have been able seriously to sustain such a line.

73. Op.cit., 115f.

74. Op.cit., 109; the ironical emphasis lies on the 'orthodox' and shows that his general formula 'priests' envisages the High Church party.

75. Similarly also O'Higgins, *Collins*, 91.

76. Cf. O'Higgins, *Collins*, 143f.

77. Cf. O'Higgins, *Collins*, 115ff.

78. *Discourse*, 35ff.

79. Cf. the numerous editions following one after another in close succession; for Collins' influence abroad cf. O'Higgins, *Collins*, 201ff.

80. *The Infallibility of Human Judgement, Its Dignity and Excellency. Being a New Art of Reasoning, and Discovering Truth, by reducing all disputable Cases in Philosophy, Morals, Politics, or Religion to general irresistible, and self-evident Truths*, 1713. I have used the second edition of 1721. According to Lechler, op.cit., 239 n.1, a fourth edition appeared in 1724 and according to Trinius, *Freydenker Lexicon*, 31, a fifth in 1725. There is brief mention of the content in Lechler, op.cit.

81. Op.cit., 2.

82. Op.cit., 6.

83. 'This Judgement of Man is an involuntary Faculty, acted upon by Objects and Determines, without an Consent of the Will; like a Mirror, which gives a true Image of every thing that can be brought to it...', op.cit., 6f.

84. Op.cit., 8.

85. Op.cit., 13.

86. 'This Judgement, Reason, Light of Nature, Conscience or common Sense, is one and the same Thing...', op.cit., 25; cf. also 59.

87. Op.cit., 25; cf. also 39: 'Physical and Metaphysical opinions, as well those tending to religion as Philosophy, are Results and Conclusions taken from the Discovery and Observation of certain Things seen, or Matters of Fact... Which Things and Matters come under the common Cognizance and Observation of all Mankind. Religion and Knowledge is not confin'd to any Persons, who have particular Faculties of perceiving, judging and improving thereby.' 40: 'In all other Religious and Philosophical Enquiries, as well as in these of the Being of GOD, and the Immortality of the Soul, the Things seen, and Matters done, are the same to the common Senses of Mankind, to one as well as to another.'

88. Op.cit., 26.

89. Op.cit., 42.

90. Op.cit., 53.

91. Cf. esp. op.cit., 59: 'The Understanding of Mankind consists of Apprehension, otherwise called Perception; Judgement and Will, otherwise call'd Resolution.' The errors of mankind lie in false apprehension, which precedes a judgment, or when the will resolves on an action without a previous judgment, or in contrast to it.

92. 'The Knowledge of the Being of GOD is the Effect of natural Reasoning on Things obvious to our Senses, discovering the World and Things contain'd to be the Production of some one just, wise, powerful, and perfect Being or Agent; and to this irresistible Conception or Idea we give the name of GOD,' op.cit., 61.

93. Cf. above, 594 n.65. – On Whiston cf. M.Farrell, *William Whiston*, 1981, on the debate about prophecy, 262ff.; cf. also Sina, *Ragione*, 530ff.

94. W.Whiston, *The Accomplishment of Scripture Prophecies. Being Eight Sermons Preached at the Cathedral Church of St.Paul in the year MDCCVII...*, 1708.

95. Op.cit., 1.

96. The rationalist justification is worth noting: 'A single and determinate sense of every Prophecy, is the only natural and obvious one; and no more can be admitted

without putting a force upon plain words, and no more assented to by the Minds of inquisitive Men, without a mighty bias upon their rational faculties,' op.cit., 13f.

97. Significantly Woolston, who argues in quite the reverse direction, appeals to the Fathers!

98. Op.cit., 67.

99. Op.cit., 68, 70.

100. Op.cit., 220ff.

101. Op.cit., 164ff.

102. Op.cit., 172ff.

103. Op.cit., 281ff.

104. Op.cit., 176ff.

105. Cf. e.g. Lechler, op.cit., 269ff.; O'Higgins, *Collins*, 155ff.; Frei, *Eclipse*, 66ff.; Redwood, *Reason, Ridicule and Religion*, 209ff. I have used the 1737 edition (the date of a 1739 edition is probably an error in Trinius, *Freydenker Lexicon*, 150).

106. Op.cit., I: Collins is now more moderate than in the *Discourse of Free-Thinking*.

107. Once again, at the conclusion, op.cit., 273ff., he praises his learning, but in his opinion this is not matched by his power of judgment, also because of his temperament.

108. Op.cit., 225; also quoted by Lechler,op.cit., 271 n.1.

109. Op.cit., 4.

110. Op.cit., 13f.

111. '...if the proofs for Christianity from the Old Testament be not valid; if the Arguments founded on those Books be not conclusive; and the Prophecies cited from thence be not fulfill'd; then has Christianity no just Foundation; for the Foundation, on which Jesus and his Apostles built it, is then invalid and false,' op.cit., 28.

112. Matt. 1.22f.; 2.15; 2.23; 11.14; 13.14.

113. Op.cit., 44.

114. Op.cit., 43ff.

115. Op.cit., 156ff.

116. 1727.

117. Ch. XII, 379ff.

118. Cf. O'Higgins, *Collins*, 157ff.

119. Frei, *Eclipse*, makes it clear that here Collins bases his work completely on the hermeneutical principles of his teacher Locke, who allows only sensation or reflexion as the two foundations of knowledge. There can be meaningful statements only in the words of the prophets taken in the literal sense; in that case they refer to their own time, and not to Jesus Christ. All other understandings (the allegorical or the typological sense) are arbitrary or absurd, and therefore similarly can produce no legitimate connection between the Old Testament prophecies and Jesus Christ. Collins tried to cast suspicion on the rules of typological interpretation along the lines of Surenhusius' discussion of the Old Testament texts in the New Testament, which he fundamentally misunderstood (W.Surenhusius, *Biblos katallages. Tractatus in quo secundum veterum Theologorum Hebraeorum, Formulas allegandi, et Modos interpretandi conciliantur Loca ex Vetero in Novum Testamentum allegata*, 1713. – However, Collins does not quote the original but the review by M.de la Roche, in *Memoirs of Literature*, VI, 1722, 115f.), op.cit., 53f.; cf. O'Higgins, *Collins*, 167f.

120. Op.cit., 78ff.

121. Op.cit., 87.

122. Collins' basis for this assertion is J.Clericus, *Historia Ecclesiastica*, 1716, 24f.

123. Op.cit., 82. With Dodwell, Collins therefore names Christianity 'mystical Judaism'.

124. For the problem cf. O'Higgins, *Collins*, 171ff.

125. Cf. also Lechler, *Geschichte*, 274.

126. For details cf. O'Higgins, *Collins*, 155ff. Lechler, op.cit., 275, had a much more favourable judgment on the quality of Collins' argument.

127. For the direct refutations cf. Trinius, *Freydenker Lexikon*, 155ff.; Lechler, *Geschichte*, 275ff.; O'Higgins, *Collins*, 174ff. Collins himself cites thirty-five refutations in the preface of the volume with which he replies to the attacks: *The Scheme of Literal Prophecy Considered*, 1726, Xff. (three of them, by Woolston, are in fact on his side, cf. O'Higgins, *Collins*, 174).

128. *The Reasoning of Christ and his Apostles, in their Defence of Christianity consider'd*, ²1726. For the content cf. Lechler, *Geschichte*, 277ff. Another work of Bullock is *Jesus Christ the Prophet whom Moses fore-told*, 1724 (²1725).

129. Cf. op.cit., especially the Preface.

130. Cf. above, 141ff.

131. *An Essay upon the Truth of the Christian Religion: Wherein its Real Foundation upon the Old Testament is Shewn*, 1725.

132. *A Defence of Christianity from the Prophecies of the Old Testament...*, 1725.

133. So above all J.Newcombe, *A Sermon preached before the University of Cambridge at St.Mary's Church*, 1724, but also S.Clarke, *A Discourse concerning the Connexion of the Prophecies in the Old Testament and the Application of them to Christ*, 1725, and S.Chandler.

134. *Defence*, 207ff.

135. W.Whiston, *A List of Suppositions and Affections in a late Discourse of the Grounds and Reasons, etc.*, 1724; id., *The Literal Accomplishment of Scripture Prophecies*, 1724; id., *A Supplement to the Literal Accomplishment, etc.*, 1725.

136. Above, 609 n.116.

137. *Scheme*, 147ff.

138. Cf. Lechler, op.cit., 282f. This writing and not the *Discourse* must be mentioned above all in this connection, *pace* H.J.Kraus, *Geschichte*, n. 6 on section 17, 514.

139. Cf. O'Higgins, *Collins*, 176.

140. One example of this is the work by S.Chandler, 'An Answer to a late Book entitled: A Discourse, etc.', in *A Vindication of the Christian Religion*, 1725, Part II. In it, Chandler stresses that Christianity is in no way only based on the prophecies of the Old Testament but *inter alia* on the teachings and miracles of Christ. Christ himself never referred to the Old Testament prophecies as proof of his mission and the apostles did so only to the Jews. The application of the Old Testament prophecies to Christ was always a difficult task for Christian theologians. On the relationship between Judaism and Christianity generally Chandler observes that the most important principles of religion, like the unity of God and his sole worship, are certainly common to both Christianity and Judaism, but that Judaism is a lesser form intended only as a preparation for the greater, for a limited time and a single people, laden with outward ceremonies and supported by what are usually only temporal promises and threats. Christianity is the higher religion which offers worship of God only in the Spirit and in truth, and is supported by eternal reward and punishments. The Deistic polemic against the Old Testament thus fell on fruitful ground within church circles, even where people at least formally held on to the whole Bible.

141. J.Green, *Letters to the Author of the 'Grounds and Reasons of the Christian Religion'*, 1726.

142. T.Lobb, *A Brief Defence of the Christian Religion*, 1726.

143. A.Collins, *A Letter to the Author of the Discourse of the Grounds and Reasons*(1726), 1737. Collins maintained his anonymity and therefore could reply fictitiously to it himself.

144. Op.cit., 32f.

145. Op.cit., 96.

146. Ibid.

147. Op.cit., 179.

148. *Scheme*, 425-33; cf. O'Higgins, *Collins*, 187.

149. O'Higgins, *Collins*, 199.

150. The *Discourse concerning Ridicule and Irony in Writing*, 1729, recently reprinted under his name, has been shown by O'Higgins, *Collins*, 196f., probably correctly, to have been wrongly attributed to him.

151. J.Rogers, *The Necessity of Divine Revelation and the Truth of the Christian Religion Asserted*, 1727.

152. A.Collins, *A Letter to Dr. Rogers...*, 1727.

153. *Letter*, 78f.

154. Op.cit., 82-84.

155. Op.cit., 105.

156. Op.cit., 80.

157. *Geschichte*, 289ff.

158. However, H.J.Hillerbrand, 'The Historicity of Miracles: The Early Eighteenth-Century Debate among Woolston, Annet, Sherlock, and West', *SR* 3, 1973/74, 132-51, has once again precisely described the course of the debate and worked out the hermeneutical principles of those involved. Cf. also Sina, *Ragione*, 600ff.

159. As Fellow of a Cambridge College (he was removed from this post in 1721 as a punishment). – For his life cf. the anonymous *Life*, written by an admirer, 1733. According to C.C.Woog, *De Vita et Scriptis Thomae Woolstonii*, 1743, 5, the author is Thomas Stackhouse (*narratum mihi fuit a non nemini*); according to Trinius, *Freydenker Lexicon*, 520, it was E.Curll. Woog, op.cit., provides some corrections and also lists Woolston's writings. Cf. also H.C.Lemker, *Historische Nachricht von T. Woolstons Schicksal, Schriften und Streitigkeiten*, 1740; A.Le Moine, *Dissertation historique sur les écrits de Mr.Woolston, sa condemnation et les écrits publiés par lui*, 1732. These writings indicate that the controversies surrounding Woolston also provoked lively involvement on the Continent.

160. The baroque sub-title says almost everything about the purpose and content of the work: *The Old Apology for the Truth of the Christian Religion revived, Wherein is shewn, Against the Jews, that Christ is the Prophet like Mose, doing all those Signs, Wonders and Judgements before and upon the Emperors and Empire of Rome which Moses wrought upon Pharaoh and Egypt,... And, Against the Gentiles, that God in Christ Jesus did manifest his Divine Authority to the Emperors and the Gentiles in the best and properest manner that can be imagined...'*

161. As we saw, this is the case for England. By contrast, in the American colonies typological thought continued to flourish for a long time, cf. above, 484 n.129.

162. Cf. above, 497 n.434.

163. Op.cit., 3.

164. Op.cit., 7.

165. 'And that deliverance of the Israelites out of Egypt, we own in General to be Typical of the Redemption of the World, and deliverance of the Church by Christ Jesus: Moses tells the Israelites, that a Prophet (meaning Christ) would the Lord their God raise unto them of their Brethren like unto him,' op.cit., 9. It is worth noting that there is another allusion to the theme of prophecy (again understood in a traditional way) in the quotation from Deut.18.18.

166. Strikingly, he limits himself to this.

167. Op.cit., 29f.

168. Op.cit., 85.

169. Op.cit., 34ff. Cf. also the corresponding reference to the Acts of Pilate, op.cit.,

265ff. He later published a separate work on the Epistle of Pilate, *Dissertatio de Pontii Pilati epistola circa res Jesu Christi gestas*, 1720.

170. Op.cit., 37.

171. Op.cit., 74ff.

172. Op.cit., 80.

173. Op.cit., 364ff.

174. Op.cit., 368f.

175. Op.cit., 374.

176. As Origen redivivus, who accuses modern theologians of having abandoned the truth which he taught, and as a foreigner who discovers in England the qualities of the despised Quakers, comparable with earliest Christianity – because they are adherents of allegorical exegesis.

177. *Origenis Adamantii Renati epistola ad Doctores, Whitbejum, Waterlandium, Whistonum, aliosque Litteratos huius seculi disputatores, circa fidem vere orthodoxam et scripturarum interpretationem*, 1720; *Origenis Adamantii Epistola secunda*, 1720; *A Letter to Dr. Bennett* (the severest critic of the Quakers) *upon this question, whether the People called Quackers be not the nearest of any other sect in Religion, resemble the primitive Christians in Principles and Practice? By Aristobulus*, 1720; *A second letter to Dr. Bennett in defence of the Apostles and primitive Fathers of the Church for their allegorical Interpretation of the Law of Moses, against the Ministers of the Letter and literal Commentators of his Age*, 1721.

178. See the previous note.

179. These include the pamphlets, six issues of which appeared in the form of a series: *Free-gift to the Clergy, Or, The Hireling Priests of what Denomination soever*, 1722 (*A Second, Third, Fourth*, till 1724), in which Woolston challenges the clergy 'to a Disputation on this Question, Whether The Hireling Preachers of this Age, who are all Ministers of the Letter, be not Worshippers of the Apocalyptical Beast, and Ministers of Anti-Christ?'

180. At many points a kind of love-hate relationship with his fellow clergy comes through, cf. e.g. *A Second Free-Gift*, 56: 'God forbid that the Clergy of this Church, whom I so dearly love, should be Antichrist's Ministers to do so great Wickedness. I had much rather do and suffer any things for my old Friends the Clergy, so well do I still love them, than that they should perpetrate such a horrid Villany...' Cf. also e.g. the dedication to the Moderator (cf. n.182 below), X, where Woolston declares that he was brought up among the clergy and has regarded his love for them as unchangeable. He therefore regrets all the more the break with them which has now taken place.

181. See above, 225ff.

182. *The Moderator between an Infidel and an Apostate...*, 1725.

183. Op.cit., 117ff., Woolston criticizes Luther severely for his championship of the literal sense.

184. Cf. *Moderator*, 23: 'The Inference that I make from all this is, that the only way of proving against the Jews, the Messiahship of our Jesus, is from his Completion of the Prophecies that went before of him. If the Truth of his Gospel can't be demonstrated by its Harmony to the Law of Moses; and the Divine Authority of the New Testament, by its Correspondence to the Old, we must give up the Cause of Christianity to them.'

185. *Moderator*, 44.

186. *Moderator*, 44ff.

187. *Discourse*, 31.

188. 'This is admirably reason'd!', *Moderator*, 46.

189. *Moderator*, 49.

190. 'and was I not convinced that the whole Story, in which there is no Sense according to the Letter, was but a Type and Figure of his Spiritual and Mystical

Death and Resurrection out of the Grave of the Letter of the Law and the Prophets, in which he has been buried..., I should believe it to be but an idle Tale', *Moderator*, 52f.

191. *A Discourse on the Miracles of our Saviour*, 1727 (I have used the sixth edition of 1729, cf. also in Lechler); *A Second Discourse, etc.*, 1727 (⁴1729); *A Third Discourse*, 1728 (⁴1729); *A Fourth Discourse*, 1728 (⁴1729); *A Fifth Discourse*, 1728 (³1729); *A Sixth Discourse*, 1729 (²1729). A *Defence of the Discourse* also appeared in two parts, 1729/30. For the enormous circulation of these works cf. Lechler, *Geschichte*, 294.

192. Cf. Lechler, *Geschichte*, 296.

193. One example of this procedure, the healing miracle by the pool of Bethesda (John 5) is given by Lechler, *Geschichte*, 296ff.

194. Cf. Hillerbrand, *The Historicity*, 135.

195. 1729. Thirteenth edition 1755, also in French and German translations, 1732 and 1751.

196. The first edition was apparently in 1744 (according to Leland, *View*, I, 270) or 1743 (thus Trinius, *Freydenker Lexicon*, 374). Because of the pseudonym, for a time T.Morgan was taken as the author. I have used a microfilm of the third edition, 1744 (in the preface Annet describes the second edition as a pirated edition full of mistakes).

197. For the debate cf. Leland, op.cit., 267ff., and especially Lechler, *History*, 311ff. and Hirsch, *Geschichte*, I, 315ff.; Redwood, *Reason, Ridicule and Religion*, 147ff.

198. On the apologetic side e.g. G.West, *Observations on the History and the Evidence of the Resurrection of Jesus Christ*, 1747 (third edition in the same year, German translation 1748, French translation 1757); on the Deist side e.g. T.Chubb (see below 00f.), with various works (e.g. *A Discourse on Miracles Considered as Evidences to prove the Divine Original of a Revelation*, 1741; *Of Miracles*, in *The Author's Farewell to his Readers*, sec.VIII, in *Posthumous Works*, 1748, II, 177-249).

199. *Resurrection*, 5.

200. Cf. above, 360ff.

201. Op.cit., 7.

202. Op.cit., 14.

203. "Tis founded on the eternal attributes of the Deity, and the invariable nature, reason and fitness of things', op.cit., 9.

204. Op.cit., 9f.

205. Op.cit., 14f.

206. Op.cit., 65.

207. Ibid.

208. Op.cit., 69.

209. Op.cit., 72.

210. 'What no man's senses ever discern'd, was never the object of any man's sense,' op.cit., 74.

211. Ibid.

212. Ibid.

213. Op.cit., 75.

214. Op.cit., 77.

215. Op.cit., 82.

216. Sub-title: 'or the Gospel, a Republication of the Religion of Nature' (further editions 1730, 1731, 1732, 1733. German translation by J.Lorenz Schmidt, 1741, together with the refutation by J.Foster, *The Usefulness, Truth and Excellency of the Christian Revelation...*, 1731, which is not, however, a real riposte as it makes natural religion the criterion almost in the same way as Tindal [short list of contents also in Trinius, *Freydenker Lexicon*, 283f.]). The work is described as Volume I on the title page. In fact before he died Tindal had prepared a second volume for publication,

but this never appeared, cf. Gawlick, op.cit., 35*f. I have used the facsimile edition, ed. G.Gawlick, 1967.

217. Gawlick, op.cit., 39*-43*, gives a bibliography. Cf. also his introduction to the new edition and Sina, *Ragione*, 630ff.

218. The fact that a new edition appeared in the United States as late as 1798 (cf. Gawlick, op.cit., 38 and n.41) indicates how late Deism continued to be an influence in the USA. The American Constitution and American church life even now show the cultural consequences of the Enlightenment.

219. There is a list in Trinius, *Freydenker Lexicon*, 465ff. Redwood, *Reason, Ridicule and Religion*, 145f., mentions a copy in the Bodleian with marginal notes by Waterland, but I have not seen this.

220. P.Skelton, *Ophiomaches; or, Deism revealed*, 1749, II, 344, called it 'the Bible of Deism'; cf. also the evidence cited in Gawlick, op.cit., n.1 on 44*.

221. Gawlick, op.cit., 5*.

222. Gawlick, op.cit., 6*.

223. Op.cit., 13.

224. Op.cit., 30 – one example of numerous similar formulations. Cf. e.g. also 'what is founded on the Nature of Things, and the immutable Relations they bear to one another', op.cit., 6.

225. Op.cit., 8.

226. Op.cit., 298.

227. Op.cit., 46.

228. Op.cit., 13.

229. In Gawlick's account, op.cit., 17*, it looks as though Tindal was the first to reverse the relationship of religion and morality; however, this reversal was already suggested in the Humanist tradition, and emerges clearly e.g. in Shaftesbury.

230. Op.cit., 14f.

231. Cf. also op.cit., 283.

232. Op.cit., 3; cf. also 125.

233. Op.cit., 5; cf. also 197; 397f.

234. 'that they who never heard of any external Revelation; yet if they knew from the Nature of Things what's fit for them to do, they know all that God will, or can require of them,' op.cit., 357; cf. also 394.

235. Cf. also the quotation from Augustine at the end: *Errare possum, haereticus esse nolo*, and Gawlick, op.cit., 13*.

236. Op.cit., 4.

237. Gawlick, op.cit., 14*f., points out that Tindal here in fact took up a formula of the Latitudinarian T.Sherlock and made it more radical.

238. Cf. Gawlick, op.cit., 28*f.

239. Chapter VIII follows with its comments on pagan and Jewish sacrificial practices (among other things he mentions circumcision as a superstitious practice, op.cit., 90ff.); the models are familiar from the time of Herbert of Cherbury, op.cit., 85ff.

240. Op.cit., 116.

241. Op.cit., 131. This reasoning is very interesting, because it draws attention to the metaphysical background to the whole approach of Enlightenment thought and its orientation on the creation narratives. Cf. also 133: 'If God can command some Things arbitrarily, we can't be certain, but that he may command all things so.' Chapter XI, 141ff., has an even fuller discussion of the problems.

242. Cf. esp. op.cit., 169ff.

243. Op.cit., 109; cf. also 431. The fact that he regards Congregationalism as apostolic and characteristic of early Christianity again shows his Puritan heritage. Cf. also Tindal's earlier comments, above 321f.

244. Op.cit., 121f., 136, 149f.

245. Op.cit., 23*.

246. Op.cit., 422. Cf. also the comments on the duties of the 'Common people', op.cit., 279ff., and chapter XIII, op.cit., 232ff. (cf. also above, 377f.).

247. For the very similar formulations in Locke and Shaftesbury cf. above, 261ff., and 581 n.261. On p.235 of his book Tindal comprehensively cites a comment in this connection.

248. Gawlick, op.cit., 27*f., relies on the distinction between theoretical and practical certainty in seeking to rob this objection of its force. But is not the 'Reality of moral awareness' itself a hypothesis (of post-Kantian Idealism), which overlooks social relationships and thus the relativity of all moral conceptions? (The consequence of this for Christians can only be to incorporate ethics into the specific relationship of faith to life and thus to the revealed will of God; it is likewise a part of historical reality.)

249. According to Tindal, 'human happiness' is the only goal of all religion, op.cit., 104; God requires nothing for himself, op.cit., 44ff. Religion consists essentially in acting for the common good: 'If Men, according to the best of their Understanding, act for their common Good, they then govern themselves by the same Rule God governs them... in being intirely govern'd by it, they have done all that God requires,' op.cit., 279.

250. G.Gawlick assesses Tindal's thought in a largely positive way (with the qualification that he refers to the philosophical significance of the Christian doctrine of reconciliation along Kantian lines, op.cit., 32*). It is impossible to enter into a detailed discussion of his presuppositions here, but that is implicit in the whole of my account. At all events, the 'reality of moral awareness' (op.cit., 28*) is not an adequate critical instrument for a judgment on revealed religion. Cf. also Gawlick's comments on religion and Christianity in *Der Deismus als Grundzug*, 37.

251. Note the abundant quotations which permeate the whole work, many of them from Latitudinarian theologians. The last chapter (op.cit., 353ff.), is devoted to a detailed discussion of Clarke's arguments; here Tindal very acutely points out the impossibility of reconciling natural religion and revelation in his account, and skilfully uses Clarke's arguments to justify his own view that only natural religion can be of value.

252. Chapter XIII, op.cit., 232ff.

253. In an interesting section of the fictitious conversation between his persons A and B (of whom A is the spokesman of the author and B elicits the decisive statements from A by his mild objections and questions) the problem is whether religion does not also have duties towards God as its content (op.cit., 278ff.). A introduces the theme by putting the rhetorical question whether it is not impossible that the one self-existent being, to whom all other beings owe their existence, should require something for himself from mankind, whom he had created; whether he gave them any other rule of life 'but to oblige them to act for their common Good? If then an Action is for their Good, is not that alone an infallible Test of its being approv'd by God?' This is followed by the statement which we already find hinted at in Shaftesbury, that if people only acted according to their best knowledge for their common good, they would have done all that God requires (cf. also 330). B in reply ventures to object that the common man may well be capable enough of knowing his duties towards his fellows, but does he know his duty to God as clearly? Here A replies with another series of rhetorical questions in which he stresses the love and reverence men must feel for the supreme Being and how this reverence is expressed above all in the highest conceptions that they can have of him 'and that the highest Honour and Worship they can render him, is solemnly to own him to be what he

is?' God defined in metaphysical terms cannot be the subject of real feeling; he is merely the point of projection at which an abstract world order is reflected.

254. Op.cit., 246f.

255. Op.cit., 247.

256. Ibid.

257. The duty of men towards God is 'to introduce into his Creation as much Happiness as they can', op.cit., 280.

258. It again seems like an echo of Locke's remarks when Tindal lists 'Peasants and Mechanicks, Men and Maid-servants' as members of the common folk, op.cit., 299.

259. Op.cit., 241. Cf. also 278. '...the Principles, on which Religion is founded, must be so obvious, that all men, even of the meanest Capacity, may from thence discern their Duty both to God and Man.'

260. He himself gives a detailed quotation from Locke with his comments to this effect, op.cit., 235.

261. Op.cit., 232, 284; cf.237f., 290-2.

262. Op.cit., 238f. It is characteristic of his way of proceeding that he takes this list from a work by Bishop Taylor. Evidently Tindal, too, is well instructed in matters of biblical exegesis as one can also see from his further remarks and biblical quotations throughout the chapter. We can find the same thing with most of the leading cultural figures of the time. The technical expressions mentioned in the list open up an interesting perspective on the contemporary state of interpretation, which was already on a far higher level than is usually assumed.

263. Tindal again quotes the famous Bentley, in order to have a witness above suspicion, op.cit., 324f.

264. Op.cit., 322f.

265. Op.cit., 323; there is also criticism of Chillingworth in op.cit., 241.

266. Op.cit., 233. Cf. also 316.

267. In ironic form, Tindal repeats the statements which could still be understood positively in Shaftesbury, as though the English clergy could be excluded from the usual charge against the pagan priests: 'Priests of other Religion, we know, will lie for Interest; but we can never suspect, that our own Priests, tho' they take the same Methods, act on the same Motives,' op.cit., 233, cf. also 282. Indeed English priests are even worse than foreign ones because of their zest for persecution, op.cit., 287. As he occasionally hints (op.cit., 299), here he has above all the 'High Church Clergy among the Reform'd' in mind.

268. Op.cit., 240: 'There's only a verbal Difference between a Lawmaker, and a sovereign Interpreter of Laws, to whose Interpretation all are oblig'd to submit.'

269. Op.cit., 243.

270. 'Ought we not to be certain, that the first Propagators of it cou'd not be impos'd on themselves, or wou'd not impose on Others? Or, in other Words, were infallible and impeccable?', ibid.

271. Op.cit., 243-5. Cf. also 263ff.

272. Here, too, Tindal refers to Locke, op.cit., 294. Cf. also 246.

273. 'must not our Reason tell us, that infinite Wisdom can have no Commands, but what are founded on the unalterable Reason of Things? And if God cou'd command at one Time for Commanding-sake in any one Point, he might do so in all Points, and Times; and consequently, that an arbitrary Will, which might change every Moment, wou'd govern all Things?', op.cit., 246f. The dilemmas which arose in the medieval dispute over universals (to which Ockham responded with his voluntarism), recur here.

274. Op.cit., 250ff.

275. Op.cit., 252f.

276. Op.cit., 256ff.
277. Op.cit., 267; cf. also 275f.
278. Op.cit., 271ff.
279. Op.cit., 268.
280. Op.cit., 269.
281. Op.cit., 276.
282. Op.cit., 283.
283. Op.cit., 297. Barbeyrac also points in the passage quoted to the exemplary character of Stoic morality; this above all gains Tindal's approval.
284. Op.cit., 258ff.
285. Op.cit., 262.
286. Op.cit., 287.
287. Op.cit., 326f.
288. Op.cit., 328.
289. Op.cit., 304. Cf. also the summary given by B, op.cit., 351. At another point Tindal can also take up a remark by Prideaux, according to whom nature and the reason of things are 'the Touchstone of All Religion', op.cit., 424f.
290. Gawlick, op.cit., 46* n.22, believes that Tindal is dependent here on T.Chubb *The Previous Question, with Regard to Religion* (in *A Collection of Tracts on Various Subjects*, 1730, [209-220] 215f. First published 1725). He has already said that from a practical point of view one can get by with such a criterion. This would fit in with the character of Tindal's work as a compendium.
291. Op.cit., 330.
292. Op.cit., 338.
293. Op.cit., 332ff.
294. Op.cit., 338, 340.
295. Op.cit., 340.
296. Op.cit., 345. Here one is again reminded of Locke, cf. above, 000f.
297. Op.cit., 340.
298. Cf. above, 92ff.
299. Op.cit., 344; cf. 349.
300. Op.cit., 345.
301. Op.cit., 342.
302. 'what the Nature of God, and the Nature of Things point out to all Men, who dare use their Reason, to be his Will, his immutable Will', op.cit., 247.
303. Cf. also op.cit., 421: 'that Religion was, and always must be invariably the same.' The static world-view underlying this is also expressed in questions like, 'Will any affirm, that the Nature of God is not eternally the same? Or that the Nature of Man is chang'd? Or that the Relations God and Man stand in to one another, are not always the same...?', op.cit., 426.
304. Even if in another connection he rejects the claim of the Latitudinarians that one can lay such foundations, see above.
305. Op.cit., 431.
306. For the form cf. also Gawlick, op.cit., 5*.
307. Here Tindal refers to a statement from the Bible: Heb.8.10f. = Jer.31.33f., op.cit., 295!

4. The Late Phase

1. *Geschichte*, 343ff. On Chubb cf. also Sina, *Ragione*, 655ff.
2. For a contemporary Life see the anonymous work *A Short and Faithful Account of the Life and Character of the Celebrated Mr. Thomas Chubb... in a Letter from a Gentleman of that City to his Friend in London*, 1747. Cf. also the autobiographical notes, 'The

Author's Account of Himself', in *Posthumous Works*, two vols., 1748, I, II-VIII. The only (partially satisfactory) modern monograph is by T.L.Bushell, *The Sage of Salisbury: Thomas Chubb, 1679-1747*, 1967. Unfortunately he does not give a comprehensive list of Chubb's works. But cf. Trinius, *Freydenker Lexicon*, 129ff.; S.Allibone (ed.), *A Critical Dictionary of English Literature and British and American Authors*, 1858 (reprinted 1965), I, 381; *NEBrit* 15, 1974, II, 913. Cf. also Motzo Dentice, *GCFI* 1935, 333-42 = *Preilluminismo*, 227-37.

3. *An Enquiry concerning the Use of Reason in Matters of Revelation*, in *A Collection of Tracts*, 165-7; *A Discourse concerning Reason, with Regard to Religion and Divine Revelation*, 1731; *The Sufficiency of Reason in Matters of Religion*, 1732 (appendix to *An Enquiry concerning the Grounds and Reasons on Which Two of Our Anniversary Solemnities are Founded*).

4. *The Previous Question; A Supplement to the Previous Question* (in *A Collection of Tracts*, 221-39); *An Enquiry into the Ground and Foundation of Religion*, 1740.

5. In *Posthumous Works*, II.

6. 'And now no one wrote more fluently than Chubb', Trinius, *Freydenker Lexicon*, 128.

7. Which Bushell does not even note!

8. In *Geschichte*, 346, there is a survey of contents, albeit incomplete, 346-58. Bushell, op.cit., 129ff., also quotes from it but with additions from the *Posthumous Works*, failing to note the changes in Chubb's basic views which had taken place in the meantime (for these cf. already Lechler, op.cit., 349!).

9. Op.cit., 357.

10. Chubb's ideas remind Bushell, op.cit., 17f., of the Cambridge Platonists. However this could be because both the Cambridge Platonists and the Deists belong in the wider context of the rational ethical movement; moreover, the fact that the Cambridge Platonists have a similar emotional tone to Chubb's remarks could be explained by his optimistic philosophical mood. However, Chubb does differ from them in the matter-of-fact didactic style of his book.

11. *True Gospel*, op.cit., 5,9.

12. His posthumous work *Concerning the Personal Character of Jesus Christ* (in *The Author's Farewell, Posthumous Works*, II, 253-98) differs. Bushell, op.cit., 130, who puts all Chubb's ideas on the same level because he does not note his inner development, includes his remarks here without further ado.

13. Op.cit., 1. Indirectly this also furthers human satisfaction in this world, since what serves as a preparation for the world to come usually also makes a person feel happy here, p.3.

14. 'Happiness is the proper object of desire to every intelligent dependent being, and misery is the proper object of their aversion and shunning,' op.cit., 15.

15. Op.cit., 16.

16. Op.cit., 16f.

17. Op.cit., 17.

18. Op.cit., 18, 104f.,140f. – Lechler, *Geschichte*, 348 n.2, recalls that these points correspond to the third, fourth and fifth of Herbert's articles (*notitiae communes*, see above 188). This example shows the basic unity of the Deistic movement in some of the main elements of its thought. In this particular respect Chubb is very conservative.

19. This is the definition of the 'moral law' in which Chubb follows contemporary practice (cf. also 28, 55, 107, etc.). Cf. also 'conformable to our natural notions of things', op.cit., 81, 121, a formula in which Chubb's marked dependence on Locke is evident. For this see also Bushell, op.cit., 18.

20. At this third point, too, one is struck by the way in which Chubb retains biblical notions which at this period already seem very old-fashioned, and are now

put forward predominantly only in orthodox circles. On the other hand, we can also point to some statements where he advocates an autonomous ethic in which, in accordance with Shaftesbury's ideas, virtue is its own reward, cf. Bushell, op.cit., 26. Chubb's thinking is not consistent to the last degree.

21. Cf. also op.cit.,20. Jesus taught no new law.

22. Op.cit., 21,28,30.

23. Op.cit., 21,29,30.

24. Op.cit., 22.

25. Op.cit., 20.

26. For his financial means cf. Bushell, op.cit., 10ff.

27. It is also striking that a series of responses to Chubb appeared anonymously, cf. the list in Trinius, *Freydenker Lexicon*, 138ff.

28. Cf. Bushell, op.cit., 93-95.

29. Op.cit., 51ff., cf. 44.

30. Cf. below.

31. Op.cit., 69ff.; quotation, 70.

32. Op.cit., 79. In Chubb's later, critical phase, things changed: in the posthumous treatise *Of a future state of existence to men* (in *The Author's Farewell, Posthumous Works,* I, 309-81), Chubb doubts the circumstances and witnesses of the resurrection.

33. Op.cit., 43.

34. Op.cit., 44.

35. Even today, a return to the proclamation of the historical Jesus is one of the favourite methods of Christianity with an ethical orientation.

36. Op.cit., 55.

37. Op.cit., 46.

38. Op.cit., 48f.

39. Op.cit., 118ff.

40. Op.cit., 142.

41. Op.cit., 32.

42. Op.cit., 112.

43. Op.cit., 115f. – Bushell, op.cit., 10, 20, recalls Spinoza's influence on Chubb (through Clarke). It is particularly evident at a point like this.

44. Op.cit., 152. The abhorrent moral behaviour of the Antinomians is also a warning against this false teaching, op.cit., 143f.

45. Op.cit., 150.

46. Op.cit., 146-8.

47. Op.cit., 164.

48. Op.cit., 102.

49. Op.cit., 17,102.

50. 'so in this every person is, and must be a volunteer', op.cit., 9.

51. Op.cit., 9-12, 60ff.

52. Op.cit., 180, cf. 129f.,134f.

53. Op.cit., 58.

54. Op.cit., 10, 58.

55. Op.cit., 66f.

56. Op.cit., 67.

57. Cf. also op.cit., 169ff.

58. Op.cit., 102.

59. Op.cit., 126f.

60. Op.cit., 138f.

61. Op.cit., 165.

62. Chubb judges the original institution of the ministries of deacon and bishop

by the apostles to have been a necessary measure, but the office of bishop was meant to be oversight over an individual community, op.cit., 85ff.

63. Op.cit., 170ff., 132ff., cf. 68f.

64. Op.cit., 85.

65. Once again the theme is taken up by Chubb in his posthumous writing *Of Divine Revelation in General* (in *The Author's Farewell*, sec.VI, *Posthumous Works*, II, 3-136), 131. Here Locke's list of occupations ('Shepherds and ploughmen, tinkers and coblers') also appears (noted by Lechler, *Geschichte*, 351 n.3, but without giving the volume number). Lechler, op.cit., 357f., overlooks this connection with Locke when he regards Chubb's account at this point as his very own.

66. Op.cit.

67. '...it must be a matter of uncertainty whether the revelation be divine, or not; because we have no rule to judge, and from which we may distinguish, with certainty, divine revelation from delusion...we have no criterion, no way by which we can distinguish, with certainty, divine visions from other visions, nor divine voices from other voices; therefore, it must be uncertain whether the revelation produced by them be divine, or not,' op.cit., 5.

68. Op.cit.,7f.

69. Op.cit., 13ff., 35ff. – As a contemporary example (obviously something that concerned him a great deal, as we can see from the constant repetition), Chubb mentions Methodism, which spread completely without any proof from miracles, op.cit., 44 n.

70. Op.cit., 83ff.

71. Op.cit., 91ff.

72. Op.cit., 93ff.

73. Op.cit., 101ff.

74. Op.cit., 110ff.

75. Op.cit., 112. Here one can think of what is said in *The True Gospel*.

76. Op.cit., 112 – the qualifications contained in this sentence (which are similarly made in connection with the Gospels as a whole) should be noted!

77. The honesty of Chubb's reason for this is very characteristic of him: 'which last, as it is what I do not understand, so thereby it is out of the reach of inquiry', op.cit., 72. Cf. the similar remark about Islam, op.cit., 35, 39f.

78. Op.cit., 73ff.

79. Op.cit., 64ff. 'And that the Christian revelation has been in evil case, as having been greatly corrupted and depraved, I think, abundantly appears from hence, viz. that, whilst it was running through the channels of oral and written tradition, it's pretended guardians have extracted the very mystery of iniquity from it,' op.cit., 66f.

80. Op.cit., 115ff.

81. 'according to some learned men', op.cit., 115. Chubb himself is proud that he is not one of them!

82. Op.cit.,128. 'If any thing is offered to us under the character of divine revelation, it calls for our most careful inspection, as well as our serious attention, lest we should be misled thereby', op.cit., 124.

83. Op.cit., 124.

84. Op.cit., 77f.

85. Op.cit., 78; cf. 76.

86. In op.cit., 131ff., he distinguishes between 'common sense' and 'Common honesty', but common sense and not learned knowledge is the judge of the latter, 133.

87. Op.cit., 129ff. Thus in a different form the polemic of Humanism against book learning continues.

88. Op.cit., 61, 80.
89. He refers to this for it, op.cit., 82f.
90. Op.cit., 41.
91. Op.cit., 41ff.
92. Op.cit., 53ff.
93. Op.cit., 60f.
94. Op.cit., 32f.
95. Op.cit., 40.
96. Op.cit., 44.
97. 'As to discipleship to Christ, I think myself concerned to imitate that excellent example he has sent me, and to follow those wholesome counsels or precepts he has given, or recommended to me', op.cit., 44.
98. Op.cit., 16ff.
99. Op.cit., 16.
100. 'surely, this cannot be done, but by wrestling with and conquering our most natural notices of a Deity', op.cit., 17.
101. Op.cit., 29 or 27f.
102. Op.cit., 20.
103. Op.cit., 21f.
104. Op.cit., 22f.
105. Op.cit., 24ff.
106. Op.cit., 18f.
107. 1738-1740. I have used the facsimile reprint 1969, ed. G.Gawlick. His introduction is at the same time the most detailed modern discussion (often sympathetic to Morgan). Cf. also already Lechler, *Geschichte*, 370-95; Hirsch, *Geschichte*, I, 331-8. List of writings in Trinius, *Freydenker Lexicon*, 369-75; ibid., 375-87, and *Erste Zugabe*, 52-57, for the writings which appeared against him.
108. Cf. the titles in Gawlick, 31*n.5.
109. Cf. Trinius, *Freydenker Lexicon*, 362-8.
110. C. Middleton, *A Letter to Dr. Waterland*,1731; id., *A Defence of the Letter to Dr. Waterland*, 1732; id., *Some Remarks on a Reply to the Defence...*, 1732; *Remarks on Some Observations, addressed to the Author of the Letter*, 1733.
111. Cf. *A Defence of the Letter*, 2.
112. Cf. ibid., 16.
113. 'That Moses having first persuaded himself that every thing he was doing was agreeable to the Will of God, thought it necessary above all things to instill the same Notion into the People', op.cit., 32.
114. Op.cit., 81f.
115. Op.cit., 36.
116. Op.cit., 13.
117. Cf. the titles in Trinius, op.cit.; the main arguments are in Lechler, op.cit., 388ff.
118. *The Divine Legation of Moses demonstrated on the Principles of a Religious Deist, from the omission of a future State of Rewards and Punishments in the Jewish Dispensation*, I-III, 1737-40. The title betrays Warburton's real argument; it is precisely the absence of expectation of rewards and punishments in the world to come that is a sign of the divine character of the Mosaic religion. Cf. also Lechler, *Geschichte*, 391ff.
119. Op.cit., I, VIII.
120. *Letter to Eusebius*, 28. Moreover, Gawlick, op.cit., 26*, recalls a reference in Morgan's *Physico-Theology: Or, a Philosophic-Moral Disquisition concerning Human Nature, Free Agency, Moral Government and Divine Providence* (1741), 224f., to W.Wollaston's *The Religion of Nature Delineated*, 1724, which belongs to the same school of ethical rationalism.

121. Op.cit., III, 150. Cf. also the definition of natural law, op.cit., I, 25.
122. Op.cit., I, 282.
123. Op.cit., I, 421ff.
124. Op.cit., I, 186ff.; Lechler, *Geschichte*, 371f.
125. For this cf. recently Gawlick, op.cit., 14*ff. Moreover, in this context both Lechler and Gawlick refer to the prayer which Morgan's 'Christian Deist' addresses to the creator and governor of the world, I, 426f. Cf. also his observations on prayer, I, 179ff.
126. Cf. above, 593 n.55.
127. Gawlick, op.cit., 29*.
128. See above, 341ff.
129. See above 550 n.195.
130. Op.cit., I, 27, cf. also 169, 179.
131. Op.cit., I, 144f.; cf. II, 22f.
132. Note again that he puts particular emphasis on Newton!
133. III, III.
134. III, 151ff.
135. II, 24; the conceptuality at this point is based on Locke's epistemology.
136. I, 392ff.
137. I, 439.
138. II, 25f.
139. I, 85f.; cf. 200.
140. Cf. above, 369ff.
141. Cf. above, 610 n.128.
142. I, 19, 42ff.; cf. also Gawlick, op.cit., 18*; *Letter to Eusebius*, 33, 35f.
143. I, 331f.
144. Gawlick, op.cit., 23*, notes it with some disapproval.
145. I, 230. Here we find the same theory of the history of religion which was already developed by Herbert of Cherbury in *De religione Gentilium*, cf. above 000ff.
146. I, 231ff.; cf. also II, 85f., 104f.
147. I, 237f., 239ff.
148. I, 241.
149. I, 242ff.
150. I, 249, cf. 257, 259, 265, etc.: II, 71: 'that this miraculously stupid People were always inspired and prepossessed with the Spirit of the Devil.'
151. I, 271.
152. Cf. also I, 52.
153. I, 42ff.
154. I, 125ff.
155. I, 103.
156. I, 104ff.
157. I, 198f.
158. I, 26f. However, the 'Christian Deist' at one point indicates that while Moses (and the prophets) had to adapt themselves to the condition of the people who had been corrupted by Egyptian superstition, he had in view a secret double meaning in all that he wrote which as well as the political sense intended for the crude notions of the people also included a true and reasonable meaning which could only be understood by those who were wiser, I, 249f.
159. See above, 284f.
160. I, 71.
161. I, 29.
162. I, 27.
163. Cf. above 124ff.

164. I, 54, 71, 119ff.

165. I, 334; cf. further I, 22, 299f.; II, 177ff.

166. I, 298f.; II, 176.

167. I, 306ff.; cf. II, 197ff.

168. I, 301f.,313f.

169. II, 107ff.

170. P.Bayle, 'David', in *Dictionnaire Historique et Critique*, third (fifth) edition 1738, II, 253ff., 908ff. (two versions). Cf. also W.Rex, 'Pierre Bayle: The Theology and Politics of the Article on David', *BHR* 24, 1962, 168-89; 25, 1963, 366-403 = id., *Essays on Pierre Bayle and the Religious Controversy*, 1965, 197ff.

171. The origin of the supposed name of the place (I Sam.19.18f., 22f.; 20.1) is presumably a scribal error (cf. F.Delitzsch, *Lese- und Schreibfehler im Alten Testament*, 1920, sec. 57b,) of which Morgan was as yet unaware.

172. I, 282.

173. I, 283ff.

174. I, 285.

175. I, 304f.

176. Cf. also I, 284. However, the prophets did not reach the heights of the Christian religion, I, 334f. For the theme of prophecy cf. also II, 160ff.

177. Cf. also II, 162.

178. I, 251ff. Cf. also III, 39ff.

179. III, 66, cf. 107.

180. 'In the first and purest Ages, before Luxury, Avarice and Ambition had taken Place, men lived with an intire, absolute Trust in, and Reliance upon God', III, 94.

181. III, 93.

182. J. Wellhausen, *Prolegomena to the History of Israel*, ET 1885. L.Perlitt, *Vatke and Wellhausen*, 1965, has not paid enough attention to these connections with the Enlightenment.

183. II, 68.

184. II, 69f.; cf. also II, 226.

185. Morgan wrote the second volume as a refutation of Leland's apology: *The Divine Authority of the Old and New Testament asserted*, 1739.

186. I, 251; cf. also above 401.

187. *A Collection of Tracts* etc, 1726, XXII. Gawlick, who draws attention to it, op.cit., 21 gives a wrong page number.

188. II, 129.

189. Leland referred particularly to his response to Tindal, *An Answer to a Late Book, intituled, Christianity as Old as the Creation*, 1733.

190. '...that in this sense, I am of no Religion at all; or which is the same thing, I am no implicit Believer, and cannot receive any historical Facts, especially such as are extraordinary and miraculous, as infallibly true,' op.cit., I, 411.

191. Ibid. It is very probable that this list influenced Chubb's posthumous work on religion.

192. I, 412.

193. I, 392.

194. I, 333.

195. I, 394.

196. 'And every Thing in Moses and the Prophets, relating to moral Truth and Righteousness, must be a Proof of this', op.cit., I, 33.

197. 'And thus far, Theophanes, I am a Christian, and at the same Time a Deist, or, if you please, this is my Christian Deism,' I, 394; cf. 165.

198. Cf. op.cit., I, 167: 'our Christian Prophet, who is the only Legislator in Matters of Religion.'

199. Cf. Gawlick, op.cit., 7f.

200. I, 98f.

201. II, 32f.

202. II, 65ff.

203. III, 141f.,310.

204. Lechler, *Geschichte*, 387; cf. W.Gass, *Geschichte der protestantischen Dogmatik*, 1862, III, 355; Cf.Gawlick, op.cit., 22

205. Gawlick, op.cit., 221.

206. Op.cit., I, 381, 387.

207. Gawlick, op.cit.,16

208. Cf. above 590 n.11.

209. It is not mentioned by Lechler. But cf. Trinius, *Freydenker Lexicon*, 327f. However, he had no information about its true publication date, since he gives it as 1736 and then is amazed at the note about the same work in the *Leipziger Gelehrten Zeitung* of 1734.

210. London 1733 (copy in the British Library).

211. Op.cit., 27.

212. Op.cit., 1-26.

213. Op.cit., 28.

214. Op.cit., 30, 43.

215. Op.cit., 29.

216. Op.cit., 30ff.

217. Op.cit., 35.

218. Op.cit., 35 n.g.

219. Op.cit., 35f.

220. All these observations are contained in a note on the original short entry which goes on for pages, n.(h) on 36-41.

221. Op.cit., 40f.

222. Op.cit., n.(i), 41-44.

223. Op.cit., 54, 52.

224. Op.cit., 55.

225. Op.cit., 60.

226. Op.cit., 61.

227. Which he says he learned from his mother who had died (and in whose memory he gave his speech in the hall of a London guild), op.cit., 64f. The key statement in it is: 'the Body is the Prison of the Soul'.

228. Op.cit., VI.

229. 1748. It had been preceded by the same author's *Dissertation on the Civil Government of the Hebrews*, 1740 (^{2}1745; German translation 1755 and 1756), cf. Lechler, *Geschichte*, 388, and Trinius, *Freydenker Lexicon*, 377f. In this work the author said even more explicitly that the real aim of the well-ordered Hebrew state, with its division of authority, was to guard against idolatry.

230. The author cites the *More Nebuchim* in respect of the purposes of the law mentioned there: direction in civil and political actions, the truths of faith and moral precepts, op.cit., 3f., and n.

231. 'A noble author', op.cit., 26; 27 n. goes on to give the name in connection with a quotation from *De Veritate*.

232. Op.cit., 27.

233. The apologist could generously overlook the fact that the theory of *ideae innatae* had become obsolete since Locke, as the content of ethical rationalism amounted to virtually the same thing.

234. Op.cit., 298.

235. *A Defence of Reveal'd Religion against the Exceptions of a late Writer, in his Book, Intituled, Christianity as Old as the Creation, &c.*, 1732.

236. *Geschichte*, 362: '...must be acknowledged to be masterly'.

237. Op.cit., 366.

238. *Defence*, 11.

239. Op.cit., 46, 113f., 150.

240. Op.cit., 48ff.

241. Op.cit., 229ff. Especially in this chapter the author refers to the epistemology of Locke ('the Glory of that Age, and the Instructor of the present', 236). In op.cit., 364f., he discusses the indispensible character of revelation specifically for the lower classes of the population.

242. Op.cit., 48.

243. Cf. also Lechler, *Geschichte*, 364.

244. Op.cit., 65ff.; this is against the view put forward e.g. by Shaftesbury.

245. Op.cit., 88f.

246. Op.cit., 90ff.

247. Op.cit., 116ff.

248. Chapter III, op.cit., 145ff.

249. Op.cit., 158ff.

250. Op.cit., 185.

251. Op.cit., 198.

252. Op.cit., 203.

253. Op.cit., 223.

254. Op.cit., 226f., cf. 336f.

255. Op.cit., 454.

256. Ibid.

257. Cf. N.Sykes, *Edmund Gibson. Bishop of London 1669-1748*, 1926.

258. (E.Gibson) *The Bishop of London's Pastoral Letter to the People of his diocese...*, 1728; *The Bishop of London's Second Pastoral Letter..*, 1730; *Third Pastoral Letter...*, 1731. N.Sykes, op.cit., 250, refers to the towering influence of Locke in this line of argument, which ends up by asserting that while natural reason is in principle capable of attaining to all necessary knowledge about God's being and properties and our moral duties, the mass of people are not capable of achieving the knowledge of the learned philosophers and therefore need revelation.

259. 1740 (I have used a copy from the University Library of Belfast).

260. Op.cit., 84ff. Cf. 93: 'And the Advantage of the Principle is, that the Rule of Action is now doubly secured, by its own Reasonableness, and by this demonstratively sure Addition.'

261. More accurately, an action together with the rational motivation for such an action: 'it is always a Reason taken from the Consideration of God for doin(g) what is right,' op.cit., 88. 'Religion consists in the Belief or Practice of any thing that is right, from the Consideration of God,' op.cit., 93.

262. Op.cit., 100.

263. Op.cit., 114.

264. Op.cit., 117.

265. Op.cit., 118.

266. David, guilty of many crimes, is again an example (in addition to the dispute between Paul and Barnabas and between Peter and Paul), op.cit., 126.

267. Op.cit., 127.

268. Op.cit., 128ff.

269. Op.cit., 134ff.

270. Op.cit., 202ff. There is exactly the same thing with Gibson, cf. N.Sykes, *Gibson*, 250.

271. *Der Deismus als Grundzug*, 36.

Conclusion

1. Cf. the three most recent works: J.Hart, *Viscount Bolingbroke: Tory Humanist*, 1966; I.Kramnik, *Bolingbroke and his Circle*, 1968; H.T.Dickinson, *Bolingbroke*, 1970.

2. For the connection between the historical legacy and contemporary theological developments in the USA, cf. e.g. J.C.Hough Jr, 'Theologie und Revolution in den Vereinigten Staaten', *VF* 17, 1972, 63-85.

3. Cf. Lechler, *Geschichte*, 447ff. For the influence of English literature in eighteenth-century Germany cf. now generally B.Fabian, 'English Books and Their Eighteenth-Century German Readers', in P.Korshin (ed.), *The Widening Circle: Essays on the Circulation of Literature in Eighteenth-Century Europe*, 1976, 119-75.

4. Cf. *Hermann Samuel Reimarus*.

5. Ed. G.Alexander, two vols, 1972.

6. For Wellhausen, who was very influential in this respect, see above, 623 n.182. However, as Perlitt, op.cit., has shown, it is impossible to demonstrate any direct influence of the Hegelian Vatke on Wellhausen. Rather, he must be put in a wider context in the history of ideas.

7. K.Schwarzwäller, 'Probleme gegenwärtiger Theologie und das Alte Testament', in *Probleme biblischer Theologie*, Festschrift G.von Rad, 1971, 479-93, gives a brilliant account of the consequences this has for modern theology.

Index

Anonymous,
De tribus impostoribus (ed.
G. Bartsch, trans R. Walter)
519 n.4
Anonymous,
Exceptions 547 n.146
Anonymous,
Life of Chubb 617 n.2
Anonymous,
Life of Mr Woolston 611 n.159
Anonymous,
Patriarcha non Monarcha 562 n.448
Anonymous,
Relation 503 n.69
Anonymous,
Theologia Deutsch (Latin trans.,
S. Castellio) 448 n.31
Theologia Deutsch (Latin trans.,
S. Franck) 448 n.31
Theologia Deutsch (ed. H. Mandel)
448 n.31
Theologia Deutsch (ed. H. Denck/
L. Haetzer) 448 n.31
Anonymous,
Whole Duty 543 n.76
Aaron, R. L.,
'Limits' 554 nn.264, 271
'Locke' 547 n.154, 550 n.195,
565f., n.536
Aarsleff, H.,
'Some Observations' 549 n.177,
554 n.264
Abelard, P.,
Introduction 426 n.148
Abrams, P.,
Introductions to Locke,
Two Tracts 547 nn.152, 153, 548,
549, 558 n.384, 560 n.409
Ackerman, T. F.,
'Two Concepts' 527 n.190
Adam, J.,
Evangelische 427 n.109

Adam, J./Roth, H. G./Krebs, M.
(eds.),
Quellen 443 n.2, 453 n.87, 456,
469 n.51
Adams, R. M.,
'Swift' 601 n.166, 602 n.172,
603 n.179
Adorno, F.,
'La crisi' 422 n.78
Ahlstrom, S. E.,
History 484 n.129
Albee, É.,
PhRev 12, 1903 577 nn.200, 201
PhRev 25, 1916 577 n.201
'Philosophy' 594 nn.67, 68,
595 nn.76, 78, 596 n.108
Alberti, R. von,
Staatsbewusstsein 419 n.49, 422 n.79
Alderman, W. E.,
'Shaftesbury and the Doctrine of
Benevolence' 579 n.235
'Shaftesbury' (*PMLA* 46, 1931)
577 n.201, 578 n.217
Aldridge, A. O.,
Manifesto 551 n.202, 579, 581, 582,
583, 585 n.354, 586 n.378,
597 nn.197, 198
Aldridge, J. W.,
Hermeneutics 435 n.4
Alexander, H. G. (ed.),
Leibniz/Clarke Correspondence
593 n.54
Alexander, R. W.,
'Myth' 528 n.35, 533 n.93c
Alexander IV,
Bulle Chartularium (ed. H. Denifle)
429 n.218
Algovin, K.,
'Citizen' 527 n.24
Allan, D. J.,
'Locke' 593 n.40

Allen, J. W.,
  Political Thought 476 n.1, 536 n.150
Allers, R.,
  Review of C. A. Viano,
    Locke 546 n.141
Allibone, S.,
  Dictionary 618 n.2
Allison, G. F.,
  Rise 489 n.232
Anagnine, E.,
  Pico 423 n.92, 424 nn.114, 122
Anderson, H./Shea, J. S. (eds.),
  Studies 578 n.212
Andrade, E. N. da C.,
  Newton 589 n.3
Andresen, C. (ed.),
  Handbuch 2, 444 n.6, 452,
    458 n.167, 510 n.220
Andrewes, L.,
  Catechistical Doctrine
  (in *Minor Works*) 491 n.267,
    497 n.419
  Minor Works (ed. Wilson-Bliss)
    491 n.267, 497, 498
  A Summary (in *Minor Works*) 144
  Tortura Torti (in *Minor Works*) 129,
    497 n.426
Angeleri, C.,
  Problema 416 nn.2, 10, 417 nn.14,
    18, 418 n.29
Angelo von Clareno,
  Historia 429 n.220
Annet, P.,
  Resurrection 372–4, 613
Anrich, G.,
  Bucer 466 n.5, 467, 474 n.157
  Strassbourg 473 n.127
  'Strassbourg Reformation'
    467 n.16
Aqua, G. dell'/Münster, L.,
  'Pico' 424 n.117a
Aquilecchia, G.,
  'Nota' 573 n.491
Arber, E.,
  Introductory Sketch 483 n.103,
    493 n.329
Aristotle,
  Ethics 273
Armour, R. S.,
  Baptism 451 nn.60, 64, 452 n.74,
    456 n.139, 457 n.158
Arnauld, A.,
  Histoire 555 n.304
Arnold, G.,
  Ketzerhistorie 453 n.85
Ashcraft, R.,
  'Faith' 547 nn.145, 149, 554, 555,
    556 n.32

Ashley, M.,
  Cromwell 504 n.88, 515 n.292
Ashton, R.,
  Civil War 502 n.63, 504 n.84a
  Puritanism 477 n.13
Aston, M. E.,
  'Lollardy and Sedition' 473 n.274,
    480 n.66
  'Lollardy and the
    Reformation' 434 n.274
Atterbury, F.,
  Letter 321
  Sermons 551 n.202
Attfield, R.,
  'Clarke' 595 n.67
Aubray, J.,
  Brief Lives (ed. A. Clark) 524 n.1
Audland, J.,
  Letter (in T. Camm/C. Marshall,
    ed., *Memory*) 540 n.34
  Particulars (in ibid.) 541 n.35
  Memory 540 n.22
Auer, A.,
  Frömmigkeit 437 n.27, 438 nn.30,
    33, 439 n.46, 441 nn.64, 79,
    442 n.83
  'Manetti' 419 n.44
Augustine,
  Confessions 420 n.58, 510 n.212
  De doctrina 41, 441 n.70
Augustijn, C.,
  'Ecclesiology' 436 n.8, 439 n.50
  'Erasmus von Rotterdam' 437 n.18
  'Erasmus, Desiderius' 437 n.18
Auksi, P.,
  'Sermons' 430 n.228, 431 n.238
Austin, E. M.,
  Ethics 269, 514 n.265
Aylmer, G. E. (ed.),
  Interregnum 553 n.93a
Aylmer, G. E.,
  Levellers 515 n.293
  'Unbelief' 566 n.5
Aynhoe, J.,
  Description 540 n.22

Babbage, B.,
  Puritanism 483 n.119
Babolin, A.,
  'Analogy' 596 n.110
  'Il pensiero' 596 n.110
  Introduction (to J. Butler,
    Opere) 596 n.110
Bacon, F.,
  Advancement 594 n.66
Bagshaw, E.,
  Great Question 548 n.164
  Necessity 548 n.164
  Second Part 548 n.164

Bahlmann, D.,
  Moral Revolution 539 n.3,
    582 n.306, 588 n.432
Bahner, W. (ed.),
  Renaissance 418 n.29
Bainton, R. H.,
  'Castellio' (in *Persecution and
    Liberty*) 463 n.236, 464 n.240,
    465 nn.241, 242
  Concerning Heretics 464 n.236,
    465 n.258
  'Continuity' 436 n.12
  Erasmus 437, 438 n.34, 441 nn.84,
    85, 442 nn.89, 90, 443 nn.107,
    108
  Ochino 449 n.36
  'Tradition' 464 n.236, 465 n.262
  'Wesen' 443 n.107
  'Wing' 443 n.1
Bainton, R./Becker, B./Valkhoff, M./
    van der Woude, S. (ed.),
  Castellioniana 463 n.236, 464 n.240,
    465 n.259
Baker, A. E.,
  Butler 596 n.110, 598 n.128
Baker, D. (ed.),
  Reform 480 n.70
Baker, H.,
  Image 423 n.99
  Wars of Truth 510 n.220, 511 n.235
Bakker de, W. J.,
  'Rothmann' 461 n.212
  Vroege theologie 461 n.213
Balthasar, K.,
  Geschichte 428 nn.190, 196
Bandini, L.,
  Shaftesbury 577 nn.197, 198,
    579 n.219
Bank, H.,
  Review of W. Euchner,
    Naturrecht 550 n.196
Barbers, M.,
  Toleranz 452 n.76, 453 n.89
Baring, G.,
  'Bibliography' 448 n.31
  Denck 446 n.12
Barker, A. E.,
  'Liberty' 507 n.150, 508 nn.174,
    176
  Milton 503 n.76, 505, 508, 509,
    518 n.351, 518f. n.357
  Milton's Divorce Tracts 507 n 150
  'Schoolmasters' 504 n.90
Barnes, R.,
  Vitae 110
Barnes, W. H. F.,
  'Rational Theology' 533 n.93c
Baron, H.,
  Crisis 419 nn.45, 48

'Erwachen' 420 n.66
'From Petrarch' 420 n.60
Literature 419 n.45
'Petrarch' 420 nn.57, 60, 421 n.62
'Renaissance' 416 n.2
Review of W. K. Ferguson,
  Renaissance 416 n.2
Baron, R. (ed.),
  Pillars 332, 333, 584 n.346,
    588 n.408
Barroll, J. L.,
  'Gulliver' 603 n.186
Barry, B.,
  'Warrender' 528 n.37
Barsel, J. J. van,
  Perkins 490 n.249
Bartholomew, A. T./Clark J. W.,
  Bentley 592 n.38
Bartlett, T.,
  Memoirs 596 n.110
Bass, H. J. (ed.),
  State 479 n.37
Bataillon, M.,
  Erasme 440 n.56
Baudouin, C. (tr.),
  De l'art de douter 464 n.236,
    465 n.254
Bauer, J.,
  'Reflections' 476 n.2
Bauer, J. B.,
  'Brüderlichkeit' 463 n.236
Bauer, K.,
  'Colet' 437 n.17
Baum, J. W.,
  Capito and Bucer 466 n.5, 467 n.20
Bauman, C.,
  Gewaltlosigkeit 444 n.3, 445 n.7,
    448 n.31, 450, 456
Baumer, F. L. van,
  Theory 486
Baumgartner, W.,
  Naturrecht 549 n.173, 564 n.490a
Baumrin, B. H. (ed.),
  Hobbes' Leviathan 529 n.41,
    530 n.51
Bayer, O.,
  Theologie 415 n.3
Bayle, P.,
  'David' 567 n.16, 623 n.170
Beachy, A. J.,
  Concept 451 n.62
Becker, B.,
  'Castellio' 463 n.236, 465 n.262
Becker, B. (ed.),
  Servet 463 n.236
Becker, B./Valkhoff, M. (eds.),
  L'impunité 464 n.236
Becker, C. L.,
  Heavenly City 571 n.85a, 572 n.97a

Becker, M. B.,
  'Individualism' 418 n.34
Beckett, J. C.,
  'Swift' 601 n.164
Bedford, R. D.,
  Defence 519 n.1, 520 nn.7, 9, 521,
    522 nn.25, 41, 524 nn.74, 78
Beek, M. van,
  Vocabulary 476 n.2, 481 n.88
Beer, E. S. de,
  'English Liberalism' 560 n.413,
    563 n.477
Bell, H.,
  Archbishop Laud 484 n.126
Bellardi, W.,
  Geschichte 472 n.109, 473 n.124
Bellarmine, R.,
  De summo 207
  Responsio 497 n.424
Bellussi, G. B.,
  'Considerazioni' 529 n.44
Bender, H. S.,
  Grebel 446 n.17, 448 n.29
  Leitbild 447 nn.20, 22, 449 n.38,
    451 n.58
  'Propheten' 445 n.12
  Review of F. Littell, *Anabaptist
    View* 449 n.44
  'Theology' 445 n.11
  'Vision' 450 n.50
  MennEnc 450 n.50
Bendix, R.,
  Weber 478 n.34
Bennet, J.,
  Browne 568 n.21
Bennett, G. V.,
  'Conflict' (in *Britain*, ed.
    G. Holmes) 582 n.308,
    586 n.385a
  'King William' (in *Essays*, ed.
    Bennett, G. V./Walsh, J. D.)
    582 n.308
  Tory Crisis 583 n.312
Bennett, G. V./Walsh, J. D. (eds.),
  Essays 582 n.308
Benrath, G. A.,
  Bibelkommentar 430 n.228, 431, 433
  Bibliography (in *VF*, 16, 1971)
    431 n.231, 432 n.254
  'Lehre' 444 n.6, 452, 458 n.167
  'Stand' (in *TLZ* 92, 1967)
    431 nn.228, 229, 432 nn.241, 254
  'Wyclif and Hus' 430 n.228,
    431 n.235, 432 n.254, 433 n.261
Benrath, G. A. (ed.),
  Wegbereiter 426 n.156, 434 n.278
Benrath, K.,
  Ochino 449 n.36

Bensing, M.,
  Müntzer 458 n.166
  Müntzer und der Thuringer Aufstand
    458 n.166
Benson, A. C.,
  Laud 484 n.124
Bentley, R.,
  Works (ed. A. Dyce) 592f. n. 38,
    593, 606, 607 n.72
Benz, E.,
  'Creator' 428 n.181
  Ecclesia 427f. n.177, 428, 429,
    430 nn.222, 226
  'Excerptsätze' 429
Bercovitch, S.,
  'Controversy' 484 n.127,
    497 nn.436, 437, 498 nn.453, 455
  'Typology' 484 n.127, 497 nn.436,
    437
Bergfried, U.,
  Verantwortung 449 n.43
Bergsten, T.,
  Hubmaier 446 n.13, 448 n.31
  'Pilgrim Marbeck' (*KHÅ* 57, 1957)
    444f. n.6, 445 n.10, 457
  'Pilgrim Marbeck' (*KHÅ* 58, 1958)
    444f. n.6, 445 n.10, 451 n.64
Berkeley, G.,
  Alciphron 596 n.110
Berlin, I.,
  'Hobbes' 528 n.34
Bernard, J. H.,
  Introduction to J. Butler,
    Works 597 n.114, 598 n.124
Bernhardt, J.,
  'Génèse' 530 n.59
  'Raison' 538 n.200a
Bernhofer-Pippert, E.,
  Denkweisen 450, 451 nn.54, 62,
    452 n.75
Berthold, J.,
  Toland 573 n.130
Berwick, D. M.,
  Swift 600 n.160
Bethell, S. L.,
  Cultural Revolution 489 n.232,
    592 n.33, 597 n.117
Bianca, M.,
  Dalla natura 528 n.33
Biddle, J. C.,
  'Infallibility' 548 nn.157, 162a, 549,
    555 n.281
  'Critique' 554 n.271
Bietenholz, P. G.,
  Basle 463 n.236
Billanovich, G.,
  'Petrarca' 420 n.60

Birch, J.,
Life of Tillotson 499 n.466,
544 nn.103, 105
Birch, T.,
History 589 n.2
Birell, T. A.,
Introduction to S. Patrick, *Brief
Account* 539 n.2
Bizer, E.,
Abendmahlsstreit 467 n.91
Introduction to H. Heppe,
Dogmatik 479 n.51
Black, J. B.,
Reign 486 n.170
Blanke, F.,
'Beobachtungen' 450 n.51
Brüder 446 n.17, 449 n.33
'Täufertum' 445 nn.7, 12, 446 n.17,
447 n.18
'Vorstufen' 446 n.17
'Wiedertäufer' 462 n.227
Blaschke, L.,
in *Blätter für Deutsche Philosophie*
1928 452 n.76
Blench, J. W.,
Preaching 476 n.8
Bloch, E.,
Müntzer 458 n.166
Bloom, E. A. and L. D.,
Introduction to A. Collins,
Discourse concerning Ridicule
604 n.1
Bloomfield, M.,
'Joachim' 427 n.164, 428 n.185
Blount, C.,
Miscellaneous Works 290–4, 567, 568
Philostratus 290, 567
Religio Laici 523 n.55, 567 n.9
Blumenberg, H.,
Legitimität 415 n.4
Boas, M./Hall, R.,
'Mechanical Principles' 592 n.29
Bobbio, N.,
Introduction to T. Hobbes, *Opere*
529 n.39
Locke 548 n.158, 552 n.243
Boehmer, H.,
Luther 136
'Münster' (in *Gesammelte Aufsätze*)
460 n.192
Bohatec, J.,
Budé 493 n.341
'Calvin' 493 n.341
Boisset, J.,
Sagesse 493 n.341
Bolde, S.,
Some Considerations 547 n.146,
556 n.305

Bonanate, U.,
Blount 566, 568 n.23, 569 n.46
I Puritani 484 n.122
Bondatti, P. G.,
Gioachinismo 429 n.202, 207
Bonnard, G.,
Controverse 483 n.117
Boor, F. de,
Simoniebegriff 430 n.228, 433 n.256
Borinski, L.,
Humanismus 487 n.170
'Lebensideale' 489 n.234
Bornkamm, H.,
Bucer 466 nn.2, 4, 467 nn.17, 18
'Erasmus' 439 n.49
Jahrhundert 439 n.49
Luther 492 n.297
Review of F. Blanke, *Brüder*
448 n.31
Borst, A.,
Katharer 425, 426
Bouchard, D. F.,
Milton 504 n.85
Boulanger, J.,
'Siecle' 418 n.24
Bourne, E. C. E.,
Anglicanism 481, 484 n.124,
493 n.330, 502, 503 n.68
Bourne, H. R. F.,
Life 552 n.226, 556 n.309,
557 n.339, 563, 564
Bouyer, L.,
Autour d'Erasme 435 n.6, 436 n.8
'Erasmus' 435 n.4
Bowle, J.,
Hobbes 562 nn.12, 14
Boyle, R.,
Works (ed. T. Birch) 593 n.39
Bracciolini, P.,
Epistolae (ed. T. Tonelli) 420 n.54
Bradford, J.,
Writings (ed. A. Townsend)
487 n.184, 492 n.313
Bradshaw, W.,
English Puritanism (ed.
R. C. Simmons) 483 n.119
Puritanism (ed. R. C. Simmons)
483 n.119
Brady, F.,
Interpretations 601 n.167, 603 n.179
Braghina, L.,
'Pico' 423 n.93a
Brailsford, H. N.,
Levellers 515, 517 n.322
Braithwaite, W. C.,
Beginnings 539 n.14, 540 nn.24, 25
Brandi, K.,
Rienzo 417 n.5

Brandt, F.,
  Hobbes 525 n.10
Brandt, R.,
  'Locke' 546 n.137a
  'Observations' 552 n.232
Brandt, R. (ed.),
  Locke Symposium 552 nn.221, 232
Bräuer, S.,
  'Forschung' 458 n.167
  'Müntzer' (*LuJ* 38, 1971) 444 n.2,
    458 n.165
  'Müntzer' (*ZdZ* 1975) 458 n.167,
    460 n.198
  Review of W. Elliger, *Müntzer*
    458 n.167
Brauer, S./Goertz, H.-J.,
  'Müntzer' 458 n.167
Braun, D.,
  Leviathan 197, 533 n.92
  De vera religione 519 n.1, 524 n.75
Brecht, H.,
  'Herkunft' 447 n.24
Brendler, G.,
  Täuferreich 462 n.227
Brendler, G. (ed.),
  Frühbürgerliche Revolution 449 n.33
Brett, G. S.,
  'Newton's Place' (in Newton, *A
    Bicentenary Evaluation*)
    590 n.4
Brett, R. L.,
  RESt NS IV, 1953 597 n.197
  Shaftesbury 597 n.197
Breward, I.,
  Perkins 476 n.6, 480 nn.71, 82,
    481 n.87, 490
Brewster, D.,
  Newton (ed. Westfall) 589 n.3
Brinton, H.,
  Preface to G. F. Nuttall, *Studies*
    540 n.17
Broad, C. D.,
  'Butler' 597 n.114
  'Controversy' 593 n.54
  Religion 593 n.54
  Types 599 n.153
Broadbent, E. H.,
  Church 447 n.14
Brockbank, E.,
  Burrough 540 n.24
Bromley, J. S./Kossmann, E. H. (ed.),
  Britain 434 n.274, 480 n.66
Broome, J. H.,
  'Collaboration' 604 n.1
Brown, J.,
  Essay 577 n.198
Brown, J. H.,
  'Note' 529 n.40
  'Hobbes' 529 n.40

Brown, K. C.,
  'Hobbes' Grounds' 531 n.59
Brown, K. C. (ed.),
  Hobbes Studies 528 n.34, 529 nn.41,
    49, 530 n.51, 531 n.67
Brown, N. O.,
  Life 602 n.176
Brown, S. M.,
  'Hobbes' 530 n.51
  Introduction to A. E. Taylor,
    Ethical Doctrine (in *Hobbes
    Studies*, ed. K. C. Brown)
    529 n.41
Browne, R.,
  Booke (in *Writings*, ed. A. Peel/
    L. H. Carlson) 130
  Treatise (in *Writings*, ed. ibid.) 130,
    134f., 141–3, 494, 498
  Writings, ed. ibid. 483 n.118, 494,
    498
Browne, T.,
  Enquiries 568 n.21
  Religio 568 n.21
  Works (ed. G. Keynes) 568 n.21
Brumm, U.,
  Puritanismus 479 nn.37, 47,
    484 nn.126, 128, 497 n.436
  Religose Typologie 497 n.436
Bucer, M.,
  Bericht 471 n.80, 472 nn.102, 103
  Briefwechsel (ed. M. Lenz) 466 n.6,
    473 n.123, 125
  Correspondance (ed.
    J. Pollet) 466 n.6
  Correspondance (ed. J. Rott) 466 n.4
  Das ym selbs (in DW 1) 468 nn.24,
    26, 472 n.113
  Dialogi 472 n.103
  Ephesians Commentary 75, 81,
    472 n.101, 473, 474
  Getrewe Warning (in DW 2)
    469 n.50, 470 n.59
  Gospels Commentary 74f., 471, 472
  Grund und Ursach (in DW 1)
    471 n.88, 472 n.111
  John Commentary 83–5, 469 nn.50,
    53, 470 n.68, 471 nn.74, 83,
    472 n.98
  Opera Latina (ed. F. Wendel=OL)
    466 n.5, 472 nn.155, 156, 475
  Psalms Commentary 75, 471 n.76
  De regno (in OL) 80, 83–5, 207,
    466 n.6
  Romans Commentary 77, 470,
    471 n.71
  Schriften (ed. R. Stupperich=DW)
    466 n.6, 468 nn.24, 27
  Seelsorge (in DW 7) 81, 82,
    475 n.172

Summary (in DW1) 468 n.24,
470 n.58, 472, 473
De Vera (Latin trans., in *Scripta
Anglicana*) 473 n.126
Wahrhaftiger Bericht (in DW 2)
471 nn.82, 99
Zephaniah Commentary 145, 148
Buchholtz, K. D.,
Newton 590, 591 n.25
Buck, A.,
Introduction to A. Buck (ed.),
Begriff 416 n.2, 418, 420 nn.52,
55
Geschichtsdenken 418 n.31
'Humanismus' 416 n.2
'Humanismus
(Forschungsbericht)' 419 n.47
'Humanismus im Mittelalter?'
420 n.55
'Problem' 421 n.62
'Rangstellung' 418 n.35, 419 n.36
Buddensieg, R.,
Introduction to J. Wyclif, *Sacrae
Scripturae* 431 n.230
Wyclif 431 n.230
Buisson, F.,
Castellion 436, 464 n.236,
465 nn.245, 254
Bullitt, J. M.,
Swift 600 n.161
Bulloch, J. M.,
'Gordon' 587, 588
Bullock, T.,
Jesus 610 n.128
Reasoning 610 n.128
Bünderlin, J.,
Berechnung 454 n.92
Einlayttung 454 n.92
Erklärung 454 n.92
Ursach (ET C. R. Forster/
W. Jerosch) 454 n.92
Buonaiuti, E.,
Gioacchino 426 n.164
Burckhardt, J.,
Cicerone 417 n.7
Kultur 9–13, 416 n.1, 417 nn.6, 11,
423 n.91
'Renaissance' 497 n.7
Burdach, K.,
Briefwechsel 417 n.5
Mittelalter 417 nn.5, 15
Reformation 417 nn.5, 15, 418 n.30
'Rienzo' 417 n.5
'Sinn' 417 n.5
Burkholder, G.,
'Nachfolge' 451 n.59
Burki, E. P.,
Notes 529 n.49

Burnet, G.,
History 538 n.2, 539 nn.5, 13,
583 n.309, 585 n.353, 587 n.393
Burnet, T.,
Archaeologiae Philosophicae 291
Theoria 340, 594 n.60
Burrage, C.,
Story 494 n.344
Burrough, E.,
Memorable Works 226, 227, 228
Burtt, E. A.,
Metaphysical Foundations 592 nn.32,
33
Bush, D.,
English Literature 510 n.224,
511 nn.238, 239
Bushell, T. L.,
Chubb 618, 619
Butler, J.
Analogy (1736) 345
Analogy (intro E. C. Mossner)
596 n.110
German trans. J. J. Spalding
596 n.110
Opere (ed. A. Babolin) 596 n.110
Works (ed. S. Halifax)
596 n.110, 597 n.118, 598, 599
Works (ed. W. E. Gladstone)
596 n.110, 597 n.118, 598, 599
Works (ed. J. H. Bernhard)
596 n.110
Butterfield, H.,
'Newton' (in *History of Science*)
592 n.31
Butts, R. E./Davis, J. W.,
Heritage 591 n.26

Caccamo, D.,
Eretici Italiani 463 n.230
'Ricerche' 463 n.230
Calder, I. M.,
'Attempt' 477 n.9
Calder, I. M. (ed.),
Activities 477 n.9
Calvin, J.,
Institutes 489 n.239
Camm, T./Marshall, C. (ed.),
Memory 540, 541 n.35
Campana, A.,
'Origin' 419 n.51
Campbell, W. E.,
Erasmus 484f. n.130
Canavero, A. T.,
'S. Agostino' 442 n.85a
Cantimori, D.,
Eretici Italiani 463
Cantimori, D. (ed.),
Per la storia 463 n.230, 464 n.236

Carabelli, G.,
  Tolandiana 570 n.60
Carlini, A.,
  'Herbert di Cherbury' 520 n.9
Carlson, L. H.,
  Martin Marprelate 483 n.117
  Introduction to R. Browne,
    Writings 494 n.344
Carlsson, R. A.,
  Butler's Ethics 596 n.110, 600 n.156
Caroll, R. T.,
  Stillingfleet 514 n.265
Carré, M. H.,
  'Cudworth' 514 n.265
Cartwright, T.,
  Cartwrightiana (ed. A. Peel/
    L. H. Carlson) 490 n.246
  Replie 489 n.233
  Short Catechism 120, 122
Casini, P.,
  Introduzione 566 n.3, 570 n.60,
    583 n.318, 589 n.2, 593 n.50
  'Toland' 573 n.130, 576 n.196
  L'universo 573 n.130, 592 nn.35, 37,
    593 nn.47, 52, 594 n.61, 595 n.67
Cassirer, E.,
  Individuum 10, 497 n.9
  Platonic Renaissance 590 n.220,
    577 n.109
Castellio, S.,
  De haereticis (ed. S. van der Woude)
    464 n.236
  (French Trans, *Traité de hérétiques*,
    ed. P. Olivet) 464 n.236
  De arte (in Cantimori, ed., *Storia*)
    464 n.236
  De arte (ed. Feist) 71, 465 n.254
  (ET in *Concerning Heretics*. ed.
    R. H. Bainton) 464 n.236,
    465 n.258
  (French trans., *De l'art*, by
    C. Baudouin) 464 n.236,
    465 n.254
Cattaneo, M. A.,
  'Alcune osservationi' 529 n.40
  'Hobbes' 528 n.33
  Il positivismo 530 n.50
Chambliss, J. J.,
  'Conduct' 553 n.243
Champion, L. S. (ed.),
  Quick Springs 603 n.179
Chandler, S.,
  Answer 610 n.140
  Defence 610 n.132
  Vindication 610 n.140
Charles I,
  Eikon Basilike 307

Chenu, M. D.,
  'Moines' 425 n.145
Cherry, C. (ed.),
  Religious Interpretations 498 n.437
Cherry, G. L.,
  'Position' 582 n.306
Cheyne, T. K.,
  Founders 415 n.5
Cheynell, F.,
  Chillingworthi Novissima 499 n.3
Chillingworth, W.,
  Answer 501 n.26
  Preface 500 n.12, 501 nn.28, 32
  Religion of Protestants 147, 149–52,
    500–2, 565 n.521
Christopherson, H. O.,
  Bibliographical Introduction
    546 n.138
Chrysostom, John,
  Adversus Judaeos 58
Chubb, T.,
  Collection 617 n.290, 618
  Discourse 613 n.198, 618 n.3
  Enquiry 618 nn. 3, 4
  Posthumous Works 613 n.198, 618,
    619, 620
  Previous Question 617 n.290,
    618 n.4
  Sufficiency 618 n.3
  True Gospel 384–91, 618–20
  article on Chubb: *NEBrit* 15, 1964
    618 n.2
Cicero, M. T.,
  De natura 12f., 419 n.36, 513 n.262
Clarke, S.,
  Connexion 593 n.50, 610 n.133
  Demonstration 339, 341–3, 594–5
  Discourse 341–4, 593 n.50, 595–6
Clasen, C. P.,
  Anabaptism 444 n.3, 445 n.11,
    449 n.38
Clebsch, W.,
  Protestants 485, 486, 487 n.171
Clemen, O. (ed.),
  Flugschriften 448 n.25, 450 nn.51,
    53
Clericus, J.,
  Historia 609 n.122
Clifford, J. L.,
  'Voyage' 603 nn.179, 191
Clifton, R.,
  'Fear' 500 n.14, 504 n.83a
Clive, H.,
  'Hobbes' 531 n.67
Clubb, M. D.,
  'Criticism' 600 n.160
Cohen, J. B.,
  Introduction to Newton's *Principia*
    590 n.4, 591 n.20

Newton 590 n.4
Coleman, F. M.,
  Hobbes 528 n.33
Colet, J.,
  Works (ed. J. H. Lupton) 436 n.16
Colie, R. L.,
  Light 510 n.220, 538 n.2
Collier, J.,
  History 486 n.163
Collins, A.,
  Determinism (ed. J. O'Higgins) 605 n.245
  Discourse (ed. G. Gawlick) 357–60, 606–8
  Discourse c. Ridicule 611 n.150
  Essay 354–5, 358
  Grounds 365–6, 609
  Inquiry 356
  Letter 610 n.143, 611
  Letter to Dr Rogers 611
  Priestcraft 587 n.396, 605 n.29
  Reflections 605 n.29
  Scheme 366–9, 606, 609–10
  Thirty-nine Articles 605 n.29
  Vindication 605 n.24
Collins, W. E. (ed.),
  Commemoration 484 n.124
  Lectures 502 n.67
Collinson, P.,
  'Authorship' 482 n.100
  'Beginnings' 492
  Grindal 474 n.155, 482 n.104
  'Jewish Purifyings' 493 n.327
  Movement 476 n.7, 477, 478 n.36, 479 n.53, 482 n.112, 483, 490 n.251, 492 n.324, 493 n.330
Colomer, E.,
  'Individuo' 423 n.95
  'Menschenbild' 423 n.99, 424 n.105a
Commers, R.,
  'Hobbes' 527 n.19
Conybeare, J.,
  Defence 407–9, 624 n.235, 625
Cook, R. I.,
  Swift 604 n.199
Coolidge, J. S.,
  Renaissance 488 nn.107, 108, 489 n.233, 492
Coppens, J.,
  'Erasme' 435 n.4
  'Erasmus' 436 n.8
  Ontwikkelingsgang 415 n.5, 525 n.8
  'Portrait' 440 n.56
Cordier, P. M.,
  Jean Pic 423 n.92
Cornelius, C. A.,
  Geschichte 446 n.17

Cornforth, M. (ed.),
  Essays 434 n.274
Costello, W. J.,
  Scholastic Curriculum 511 n.226
Cotman, I.,
  Private Men 499 n.1
Courvoisier, J.,
  La notion 472 n.109, 473, 474, 475 n.173
Coutts, A.,
  Denck 452 n.71
Cox, R.,
  Literature 492 nn.288, 300
  Locke 547 n.152, 549 nn.175, 177, 563 n.482
Cragg, G. R.,
  Church 539 n.2
  Freedom 488 n.207, 494 n.343, 502 n.66
  Great Persecution 540 n.21
  Puritanism 484 n.129, 510 n.221, 538f. n.2, 542 n.67, 543, 544 n.90, 570 nn.60, 65
  Reason 520 n.6, 566 n.5
Cragg, G. R. (ed.),
  Platonists 510 n.160
Craig, H. (ed.),
  'Criticism' 600 n.160
Craig, J.,
  Principia (ed. J. D. Titius) 555
Crane, R. S.,
  'Houyhnhnms' 603 n.184
  Idea 603 n.184
  'Suggestions' 578 n.205
Cranmer, T.,
  Opera (ed. A. Kuyper) 482 n.97
  Works (ed. J. E. Cox) 481 n.94, 492 n.310
Cranston, M.,
  Locke 547 nn.147, 148, 548 n.158, 549, 560 n.413
  in J. Locke, *Human Understanding* 546 n.138
Cranston, M./Peters, R. S. (eds.),
  'Disciples' 526 n.16
  Hobbes 524 n.3, 526 n.16, 528 n.37, 532 n.79
Creighton, M.,
  Art.'Jewel, John' 496 n.414
  'Position' 484 n.126
Cremeans, C. D.,
  Reception 479 n.54, 480 n.69, 483 n.116
Crippa, R.,
  Studi sulla coscienza 560 n.417
Crocco, A.,
  G. da Fiore 426 n.164, 428 n.179
Cronin, H. S.,
  'Conclusions' 434 n.278

Crous, E.,
  Lehren 547 n.145, 555 n.302a
Crowley, R.,
  Brief Discourse 101
Cudworth, R.,
  Treatise 513 n.265
  True Intellectual System (ed.
    T. Birch) 513 n.259, 514 nn.269,
    271
  True Intellectual System (ed.
    Harrison) 513 n.265
Culverwel, N.,
  Light (ed. J. Brown) 514 n.265
Cumberland, R.,
  De legibus 595 n.79
Cure of Deism see W. Smith
Curl, E.,
  Toland 570 n.60
Curtis, M. H.,
  'Conference' 483 n.118
  Oxford 511 n.226

Dahrendorf, W.,
  Lockes Kontroverse 542f. n.52
Dalgarno, M. T.,
  'Analysing Hobbes' 527 n.196
Daly, L. J.,
  Wyclif 430 n.228, 433
Daniel, S. H.,
  'Locke' 553 n.249
Dankbaar, W.,
  Bucer 466 n.4
Davies, E. T.,
  Episcopacy 488 nn.207, 210,
    496 n.414
  Political Ideas 488 n.207
Davies, G.,
  Early Stuarts 504 n.88, 515 n.292
Davies, H.,
  Free Churches 494 n.348
  Worship 476 n.8, 481 n.91,
    539f. n.14, 542 n.66
  Worship II 476 n.8
Davies, J. F.,
  Heresy 480 n.66
Davis, H.,
  Introduction to Swift, *Prose Works*
    601 n.166
  RESt NS 12, 1961 601 n.166
  Satire 600 n.161
  'Swift' 600 n.161
Davis, J. C.,
  'Levellers' 517 n.322
Davis, K. R.,
  Anabaptism 466 n.16, 448 n.32a,
    449 n.35, 450 n.45, 451 n.62
  'Anabaptism' 451 n.54
  'Erasmus' 448 n.25
  'Origins' 449 nn.32, 35, 450 n.45

Dawley, P. M.,
  Whitgift 481 n.82, 488 n.197
Deeley, A.,
  'Provision' 432 n.246
Dejung, C.,
  Wahrheit 452 n.76, 754 n.109
Delitzsch, F.,
  Lese und Schreibfehler 623 n.170
Delius, W.,
  Review of J. S. Coolidge,
    Renaissance 492 n.304
Demaus, R.,
  Tyndale 187
Demke, C. (ed.),
  Müntzer 458 n.167, 459 nn.176, 180
Denck, H.,
  'Bekenntnis' (in *Schriften*, ed.
    W. Fellmann/
    G. Baring) 451 n.63
  'Vom Gesetz Gottes' (in ibid.) 56,
    57
  Micah Commentary (in ibid.) 55,
    452 n.73
  Schriften (as above) 443 n.2,
    448 n.31, 450 n.55, 452 n.72, 455
  Widerruf (in ibid.) 53–55, 452 n.72
Denifle, H.,
  Evangelium 429
Deppermann, K.,
  Hoffman 461 n.208
  'Weg' 461 n.208
Derham, W.,
  Astro-theology 593 n.52
  Physico-thology 593 n.52
Dering, E.,
  'Sermon' (in C. J. Trinterud, ed.,
    Puritanism) 136–8, 496
Desmaizeaux, P.,
  Chillingworth 499 n.3
  Hales 499 n.3
  in J. Toland, *Collection* 570 n.60
  in J. Toland, *Miscellaneous
    Works* 570 n.60
Dethlefs, G.,
  'Wiedertäuferreich' 462 n.227
Detmer, H.,
  Anabaptistica 462 n.217a
  Bekenntnisse (in id., ed., *Zwei
    Schriften*) 462 n.221
Dick, K.,
  'Analogieprinzip' 596 nn.110, 111,
    597
Dickens, A. G.,
  'Ambivalent English
    Reformation' 480 n.66
  English Reformation 434 n.274,
    276 nn.5, 6, 480 n.66, 481 n.93,
    482 nn.100, 110, 485 n.130,
    486 n.158, 493 n.335

'Heresy' 434 n.274, 480 n.66
Lollards 434 n.274, 480 n.66
Review of G. Williams,
   Writers 445 n.11
Dickens, A. G. et al. (ed.),
   Background 480 n.66
Dickinson, H. T.,
   Bolingbroke 666 n.1
Diehl, W.,
   Bedeutung 472 n.109, 473 n.125
Diesselhorst, M.,
   Ursprünge 526 n.10
Diestel, L.,
   Geschichte 2, 416 n.6, 455 n.109,
   525 n.8
Dilthey, W.,
   'Auffassung' 10, 417 n.8
   'Weltanschauung' 436 n.10
Dircks, R. J.,
   'Tragic' 603 n.180
Dismer, R.,
   Geschichte 458 n.180, 460 n.189
Dixon, R. W.,
   History 482 nn.103, 105
Dod, J./Cleaver, R.,
   Catechism 122, 491 n.267, 492 n.293
Dohna, L. Graf, zu,
   Reformation S. 432 n.245
Dolfen, C.,
   Stellung 437 n.20
Donoghue, D. (ed.),
   Swift 600 n.160
Dörries, A.,
   'Erasmus' 439 n.49
Dovie, D.,
   Fraticelli 430 n.222
Doyle, P.,
   'Contemporary Background'
   533 n.90
Dress, W.,
   Mystik 424 n.126
Droz, E.,
   'Castellioniana' 464 n.236
Duff, A.,
   History 415 n.5
Duffield, G. E. (ed.),
   Calvin 479 n.51
Duffield, G. E.,
   Introduction to W. Tyndale, *Work*
   485 nn.130, 132
Duffy, E.,
   'Affair' 594 n.65
Dugmore, C. W./Duggan, C. (ed.),
   Studies 476 n.2, 481 n.87,
   492 n.286, 502 n.66
Dulles, A.,
   Princeps 424 n.118
Dülmen, von R.,
   Reformation 458 n.167, 463 n.227

Duncan-Jones, A.,
   Butler's Moral Philosophy 596 n.110,
   599 nn.153, 154, 600 n.155
   Laud 484 n.126
Dunham, W. H./Pargellis, S.,
   Complaint 482 n.115
Dunn, J.,
   'Politics' 561 n.142
   Political Thought 546 nn.141, 142,
   560 n.417
Dunn, W. P.,
   Browne 568 n.21
Durandus von Osca,
   Liber 426 n.156

Ebbinghaus, J.,
   Introduction to J. Locke, *Letter* 278,
   563, 564, 565
Ebeling, G.,
   'Significance' 2, 415
Ebert, K.,
   Handeln 458 n.167
   Theologie 458 n.167
Eckardt, B. von,
   Ethik 59 nn.149, 153
Eckert, W. P.,
   Erasmus 436 n.9, 437 n.18
Edelsbrunner, G.,
   Arnold von Brescia 426 n.163
Edwards, J.,
   Several Causes 547 n.145
   Socinianism 547 n.156
   Creed 547 n.146
Eels, H.,
   Bucer 466 n.5
Ehrenpreis, I.,
   'Meaning' 603 n.179
   'Origins' 603 n.179
   'Personality' 603 n.179
   Swift 601 n.163
Ehrle, F.,
   'Olivi' 430 nn.222, 226
   'Die Spiritualen' 429 n.220,
   430 nn.226, 227
Elliger, W.,
   Leben 458 n.167, 459, 460 n.197
   Müntzer 458 n.167, 460 n.191
   'Müntzer und das Altes
   Testament' 459 n.180
Elliott, J. H./Koenigsberger, H. G.
   (eds.),
   Diversity 534 n.106
Elliott, R. C.,
   Satire 601 n.161
Ellis, F. H. (ed.),
   Discourse 601 n.161a
Elton, G. R.,
   'England' 480 n.70
   'Reform' 480 n.70, 486 n.164

Emerson, E. H.,
  Puritanism 482 n.103
Emerton, E.,
  Defensor pacis 435 nn.265, 266
d'Entreves, A. P.,
  Contribution 488 n.207
  Hooker 488 n.207
Eppelsheimer, H. W.,
  Petrarca 421 n.63
Erasmus of Rotterdam,
  Enchiridion (ed. W. Welzig) 41, 46,
    437 nn.28, 29, 438 n.34,
    439 n.52, 440 n.56, 441,
    442 nn.85, 95
  De fide (ed. C. R. Thompson)
    434 n.1
  Vom freien Willen (German trans.
    O. Schumacher) 434 n.1
  Letters (ed. A. Flitner) 434 n.1
  Letters (ed. W. Kohler) 434 n.1
  De libero arbitrio (ed. J. von Walter)
    434 n.18
  Opera omnia (ed. J. Clericus=LB)
    434 n.1, 438
  Opera omnia (new ed.=K) 434 n.1,
    438
  Opuscula (ed. W. K. Ferguson)
    434 n.1
  Opus epistolarum (ed. P. S. Allen=
    Allen) 434 n.1, 437 n.21,
    438 n.36, 440 n.56, 442 n.86, 443
  Schriften (Lt.Germ. ed. W. Welzig)
    434 n.1, 438
  Werke, (ed. H. and A. Holborn=H)
    434 n.1, 438
Erastus,
  De excommunicatione 585 n.354
Erlichson, H.,
  'Controversy' 593 n.54
Etienne, J.,
  Spiritualisme 435 n.5, 440 n.56,
    442 n.93
Euchner, W.,
  'Locke' 546 n.142, 549 nn.173, 176
  Naturrecht 546, 549 n.176, 550,
    551 n.220, 552, 553 n.245,
    554 nn.253, 262, 561 n.442
  'Streit' (in *Politische
    Vierteljahresschrift* 3, 1962)
    546 n.142, 549 nn.173, 176
  in Locke J., *Zwei Abhandlungen*
    561 n.442, 562 n.471
Eusebius,
  Church History 497 nn.434, 436
Ewald, W. B.,
  Swift 601 nn.164, 165
Ewing, G. W. (ed.),
  Locke's *Reasonableness* 547 n.145

Fabian, B.,
  'Books' 626 n.3
Farr, W.,
  Wyclif 430 n.228, 433 nn.256, 263,
    434 nn.268, 269
Fast, H.,
  Bullinger 445 n.12
  'Dependence' 447, 448 nn.25, 27
  'Grebel' 447 n.17
  Art. 'Täufer' 447 n.18
  'Wahrheit' 446 n.17
  'Variation' 450 n.45
Fast, H. (ed.),
  Flügel 443 n.1, 445 n.8, 453 n.87,
    456
  Täufer II 443 n.2
Faye, J. de la,
  Defensio 575 n.175
Fazio, B.,
  Excellentia 13
Fearns, J.,
  Ketzer 425 nn.136, 154
  'Von Bruis' 425 n.130, 426
Feiling, K.,
  History 583 n.324, 585 n.353,
    587 nn.391, 393, 588 n.426
Feist-Hirsch, E.,
  'Castellio' 464 n.239
  Cotton 484 n.127, 498 n.453
Fellmann, W.,
  'Irenik' 451 n.56
Ferguson, W. K.,
  'Interpretation' 417 n.11
  Reinterpretation 416 n.2
  Renaissance 416 n.2
Fetscher, I.,
  Introduction to T. Hobbes,
    Leviathan 524 nn.2, 3, 525,
    526 n.17, 530 n.52
Ficino,
  Opera 422 n.80
Fienberg, S. P.,
  'Goodwin' 517 n.324
Figgis, J. N.,
  Divine Right 560 n.420
Filmer, R.,
  Anarchy (ed. P. Laslett) 272,
    560 n.424, 561, 563 n.476
  Aristotle's Politics (ed. ibid.)
    561 n.436
  H. Grotius' De Jure Belli (ed. ibid.)
    561 n.441
  Observations (ed. ibid.) 560 n.424
  Patriarcha (ed. ibid.) 271–3,
    536 n.125
  Patriarcha (in J. Locke, *Zwei
    Abhandlungen*, ed. H. Wilmanns)
    536 n.125, 560 n.417,
    563 nn.475–6

Finch, J. S.,
  Browne 568 n.21
Fisch, M. H.,
  Review of Rossi, *Vita* 519 n.1
Fischer, H. K.,
  'Kritische Beiträge' (in M. Weber,
    Ethik II) 478 nn.29, 34
Fischoff, E.,
  'Protestant Ethic' 478
Fischer, M. S.,
  Boyle 545 n.119
Fitzralph, R.,
  De pauperie 433 n.266
Fixler, M.,
  Milton 504 n.85, 507 n.141
Flasch, K.,
  Metaphysik 419 n.44
Fleming, R.,
  Divine Right 328, 586 nn.387, 389
Förschner, F.,
  Concordia 427 n.175
Förster, W.,
  Hobbes 494 n.354, 533 n.88,
    535 n.127, 536 n.126a
Forshall, J./Madden, J.,
  Bible 434 n.275
Forster, J.,
  Vane 539 n.12
Forster, M. P.,
  Casebook 600 n.160, 601 nn.164,
    166, 602 n.175, 603 n.179
Foster, C. R.,
  'Bünderlein' 454 n.92
  'Denck' 454 n.92
Foster, J.,
  Usefulness 613 n.216
Fowler, D. C.,
  'Trevisa' 434 n.275
Fowler, T.,
  Shaftesbury 577 n.197, 578 n.217
Fox, A.,
  Mill 607 n.60
Franck, S.,
  'Brief' 453 n.87
  Buch 444 n.2
  Geschichtsbibel 58, 444 n.2,
    455 n.109, 456
  Chronica-Abconterfayung 55
  Von Ketzern 453 n.85
  Kriegsbüchlein (ed. Klink) 444 n.2
  Paradoxa (ed. H. Ziegler) 444 n.2
  Paradoxa (new High German ed.
    S. Wollgast) 444 n.2, 453 nn.88,
    90, 454, 455
Frank, J.,
  Levellers 515 nn.287, 293,
    517 n.335, 518 nn.336, 339
Franklin, J. H.,
  Locke 562 n.469

Franz, G. (ed.),
  Wiedertäuferakten 443 n.2
Frederick, R. W. H.,
  Wyclif 431 n.229
Frei, H. W.,
  Eclipse 604 n.1, 609 nn.105, 119
Freiday, D.,
  The Bible 436 n.16, 485 nn.130, 133,
    488 n.207, 489 n.230
Frere, W. H.,
  Review of Pierce, *Historical
    Introduction* 483 n.117
Frere, W. H./Douglas, C. E. (eds.),
  Manifestoes 482 nn.114, 115,
    493 nn.315, 319
Freund, J.,
  Le dieu mortel 531
Freund, M.,
  Toleranz 483 n.121, 500 n.8,
    539 n.12
Friedmann, R.,
  Art, 'Anabaptists' 446 n.12
  'Conception' 445 n.12
  'Confession' 450 n.51
  'Doctrine', 451 n.57a, 454 n.90
  'Interpretations' 446 n.12
  Art. 'Keller, Ludwig' 446 n.14
  'Progress' 446 n.12
  Theology 444 n.3, 450 nn.45, 46,
    454 n.90
Friedmann, R. (ed.),
  Glaubensbekenntnisse 443 n.2
Fries, H./Becker, W. (eds.),
  Newman Studien 596 n.109
Friesen, A.,
  'Impulse' 437 n.19, 438 n.43
  'Müntzer in Marxist
    Thought' 458 n.166
  'Müntzer and the OT' 458 n.180,
    460 n.192, 461 n.207
  'Müntzerdeutung' 458 nn.166, 167
  Reformation 458 n.166
  'Social Revolution' 445 n.12
Friesen, A./Goertz, H. J. (eds.),
  Müntzer 458 nn.166, 167,
    460 n.198, 461 n.203
Fristedt, S. L.,
  Bible 434 n.275
Frye, N.,
  Anatomy 600 n.161
Frye, R. M.,
  'Swift' 600 n.164
  'Yahoo' 601 n.164
Fulke, W.,
  Declaration 129
Fulton, J. F.,
  Bibliography 545 n.119
  'Boyle' 545 n.119

Fürstenau, H.,
  Wiclif's Lehren 433 n.263
Fuss, P.
  'Sense' 596 n.110

Gäbler, U.,
  'Problem' 454 n.92
Gadamer, H. G.,
  Truth 415 n.3
Gairdner, J.,
  'Visitation' 481 n.93
Gale, T.,
  Court 306, 575 n.178
Galli, D.,
  'Analogia' 596 n.110
Gane, E. R.,
  'Exegetical' 481 n.96
  AUSS 493 n.327a
Garbett, C.,
  Church and State 585, 586 n.371
Gardiner, S.,
  De vera oboedientia 497 n.430
  Obedience (ed. P. Janelle) 497 n.430
Gardiner, S. R.,
  Civil War 477 n.14, 504 n.88,
    515 n.287
  Commonwealth 483 n.121, 504 n.88
Gardiner, S. R. (ed.),
  Documents 503 n.69
Garin, E.,
  'S. Agostino' 422 n.85a
  'Butler' 596 n.110
  'Clarke' 595, 596 n.106
  'Concetto' 418 n.31
  Convegno Internazionale I 423 n.93
  Dignitas 419 n.37
  Educazione 420 nn.53, 54
  Filosofi 419 n.47, 422 n.83
  Geschichte 420 nn.53, 54
  *Humanismus=Umanesimo=Italian
    Humanism* 15, 419 n.43,
    420 nn.53, 54, 421, 422 n.87
  Introduction to Pico, *De dignitate*
    422f. n.90
  'Il francescanesimo' 417 n.23
  Religious Thought 419 n.43
  'Ricerche' 422 n 76
Garrett, C. H.,
  'Exiles' 479 n.54, 482 n.100
Gass, W.,
  Geschichte 624 n.204
Gassendi, P.,
  Ad librum 521 n.23
Gassmann, G.,
  'Lehrentwicklung' 510 n.220
  'Butler' 596 n.110

Gastaldi, U.,
  Storia 444 n.3, 447 n.17, 448 n.27,
    452 n.64
Gastrell, F.,
  Considerations 605 n.22
Gauthier, D. P.
  Logic 530 n.50, 531 n.71
Gauthier, O.,
  'Why Ought One' 530 n.50
Gavre, H.,
  'Hobbes' 531 n.71
Gawlick, G.,
  'Abraham's Sacrifice' 524 n.71
  'Cicero' 521 n.15, 572 n.88
  'Contribution' 564 n. 491
  Art. 'Deismus' 519 n.6, 566 nn.2,
    5, 625 n.271
  Introductions
    to A. Collins, *Discourse* 604 n.1,
      605, 606
    to Herbert, *Dialogue* 519f. n.5,
      523
    to id., *De Religione Gentilium*
      519 n.5, 522 n.44, 523 nn.50,
      53
    to id., *De veritate* 519 nn.5, 11,
      521, 522
    to Morgan, *Moral Philosopher*
      621, 622, 623, 624
    to Tindal, *Christianity* 583 n.318,
      614, 615, 617 n.306
    to J. Toland, *Christianity*
      555 n.280, 566 n.5, 569–73,
      574 n.137, 587 n.394
    to id., *Letters to Serena* 570 n.60,
      572 n.88, 573 n.134
  'Reimarus' 481 n.84, 519 nn.6, 8,
    522 nn.37, 41, 566 n.2,
    571 nn.84, 85, 572 n.100,
    573 nn.129, 130, 577 n.198
  Preface to G. V. Lechler, *Geschichte*
    519 nn.6, 8, 566 nn.2, 5,
    577 n.198, 587 n.397
Gay, J.,
  'Clarke' 595 n.67
Gay, P.,
  Deism 567 n.14, 569 n.56
  Enlightenment 590 n.4
Gebhardt, E.,
  Italie 417 n.23
  Origines 417 n.23, 425 n.127
  Renaissance 417 n.23, 425 n.127
Gebhardt, G.,
  Stellung 436 n.8
Gee, H./Hardy, W. J. (ed.),
  Documents 483 n.119, 492 n.296,
    493 n.335, 502 n.63, 503 n.71
Gehrmann, S.,
  review in *Neue Polit.* 532 n.85

Gelder, H. A. E. van,
   Reformations 415 n.12, 424 n.125,
   435 n.6, 449 n.33, 480 n.60
George, C. H.,
   'Puritanism' 476 n.1, 477 n.15
George, C. H. and K.,
   Protestant Mind 476 nn.1, 4
George, E. A.,
   Seventeenth Century 510 n.220,
   514 nn.272, 281
Gerdes, H.,
   Luther 459 n.180
   'Weg' 459 n.180
Gerhardus von Borgo San Donnino,
   Introductoris 29
Germain, C. St.,
   Dialogus 179
Gerner, G. G.,
   'Folgerungen' 451 n.57a
   Gebrauch 450 nn.50, 51, 451 nn.55,
   61a
Gerritsen, J.,
   in P. Laslett,
   Observations 561 n.444
Gerson, J.,
   Oeuvres (ed. Glorieux) 441 n.77
Gert, B.,
   'Introduction', *T. Hobbes* 532 n.71
Gestrich, G.,
   'Deismus' 520 n.6
Gfrörer, A.
   Origo 520 n.8
Gibson, E.,
   Codex 585 n.348
   Pastoral Letter(s) 625 n.258
Gilby, A.,
   Dialogue 101, 497 n.432
   Fortress 102
Gillett, G. R. (ed.),
   Catalogue 504 n.87
Gilmore, M. P.,
   'Renaissance' 418 n.31
Gilmour, J. S. L.,
   'Blount' 566 n.7
Gilson, K.,
   Heloise 11, 418 n.25
   'Humanisme' 418 n.25
Giran, R. E.,
   Castellion 436 n.236
Giuntini, C.,
   Toland 570 n.60, 573 n.129,
   576 n.195
Gladstone, W. E.,
   in Butler, *Works* 597 n.116
   Studies 597 n.116
Glover, W. R.,
   'God' 201, 531 n.67
   'Human Nature' 531 n.67,
   533 n.89

Goen, C. C.,
   'Puritanism' 484 n.129
Goertz, H. J.,
   'Einweisung' 449 n.34
   Müntzer 458 n.167
   'Mystiker' 458 n.167
   Ordnung 444 n.5, 446 n.12,
   447 nn.19, 24, 448, 454 n.94,
   457 n.194, 458, 459, 460 nn.189,
   192, 461 n.199, 207
   'Schwerpunkt' 458 n.167
   Täufer 444 n.3, 445 n.11, 450 n.45,
   451 n.60, 454 n.99
Goertz, H. J. (ed.),
   Radikale Reformation 447 n.17,
   452 nn.67, 76, 461 n.212
   Umstrittenes Täufertum 461 n.208
Goeters, G.,
   Haetzer 448 n.31
Goeters, J. F. G.,
   'Vorgeschichte' 446 n.17
Goldbach, G.,
   'Denck' 451 n.56, 458 n.168
Goldsmith, M. M.,
   Hobbes 526 n.19, 531 n.71
Gooch, G. P.,
   Hobbes 526 n.14, 535 n.119
   Ideas 483 n.121
   Political Thought 525 n.4
Goodwin, J.,
   Anti-cavalierisme (in *Tracts*, ed.
   W. Haller) 180, 517 n.327
   Divine Authority (in ibid.) 182
Gordon, T.,
   Essay 588 n.432
   Priestianity 588 n.407
Gordon, T./Trenchard, J.,
   Collection of Tracts 330, 331, 587, 588
   Independent Whig 330–2, 587, 588
Gorham, G. C.,
   Gleanings 481 n.94
Gough, W. J.,
   Introduction to J. Locke, *Epistola*
   (ed. R. Klibansky/J. W. Gough)
   547 n.153, 556 n.332, 563 nn.488,
   490, 564 n.497, 565
Gould, G.,
   Documents 539 n.5
Grabe, J.,
   Spicilegium 607 n.60
Grace, W. J.,
   Ideas 504 n.85, 505 nn.96, 100
Grady II, R. C.,
   'Law' 532 n.78
   Political Obligation 528 n.33
Grane, L.,
   'Müntzer' 458 n.167, 459 n.180,
   460 n.190

Grave, S. A.,
 'Analogy' 596 n.110
 'Foundation' 596 n.110, 600 n.157
Gray, E. M.,
 Criticism 415 n.5
Grean, S.,
 Philosophy 597 nn.197, 198, 578,
  579, 580, 581 n.261
 'Self-interest' 579 n.229
Greaves, R. L.,
 'Bunyan' 489 n.236
Green, J.,
 Letters 610 n.141
Green, R. W. (ed.),
 Protestantism 477 n.17, 478 n.28
Green, V. H. H.,
 Renaissance 416 n.2
Greene, D.,
 'Augustinianism' 600 n.159a
 'Via media' 600 n.159a
Greenham, R.,
 Catechizing 491 n.266
Greenleaf, W. H.,
 'Hobbes' (in *Hobbes-Forschungen*,
  ed. R. Koselleck/R. Schnur)
  524 n.3, 526 n.11, 530 n.55,
  531 n.64
 Order 560 n.417
Greenslade, S. L.,
 Introduction to W. Tyndale, *Work*
  485 n.130
Greive, H.,
 'Kabbala' 424 n.114
Grendler, P. F.,
 'Concept' 419 n.51
Greschat, M.,
 'Anfänge' 467 nn.8, 10
 'Ansatz' 466 n.5, 467, 469 nn.29,
  46, 470 n.54, 475 n.163
 'Bucer' 467 n.13
 'Bücherverzeichnis' 467 n.20
Greschat, M. (ed.),
 Reformationszeit I 437 n.18,
  452 n.67, 458 n.167, 461 n.208
 Reformationszeit II 452 n.76,
  455 n.105a, 469 n.46
Greville, R. (Lord Brooke),
 Discourse (in W. Haller, *Tracts on
  Liberty*) 167, 168
 Nature (ed. V. da Sola Pinto)
  509 n.202, 510 n.212
Gritsch, E.,
 Reformer 458 nn.167, 168
Grocker, L. G.,
 'Toland' 537 n.130
Grolman, A. von,
 in *Blätter für Deutsche Philosophie*
  1928 452 n.76

Grotius, H.,
 De Jure Belli 274, 561 n.440
Grundig, C. G.,
 Geschichte 519 n.1
Gründler, O.,
 Gotteslehre 480 n.72
Grundmann, H.,
 Bewegungen 425, 426, 428
 'Biographie' 417 n.164
 Forschungen 427, 428 n.184
 Ketzergeschichte 425, 426 n.153
 Studien 426, 427, 428 nn.181, 188,
  429
Gualter, R.,
 Homélie 135, 495 n.392
Guerlac, H.,
 Newton 592 n.29
Guerlac, H./Jacob, M. C.,
 'Bentley' 593
Guggisberg, R.,
 Castellio 463f. n.236, 465 n.262
Güldner, G.,
 Toleranz-Problem 463 n.236,
  464 n.236
Gunneweg, A. H. J.,
 Understanding 416 n.1
Guthkelch, A. C./Smith, D. N.,
 Introduction to J. Swift, *Tale*
  601f. n.168
Guttmann, E.,
 Colloquia 442 n.92
Gysi, L.,
 Platonism 511 n.232, 514 nn.265,
  269

Haas, M.,
 'Sattler' 447 n.17
 'Täuferkirchen' 445 nn.6, 11,
  449 n.39
 'Täufertum' 445 n.6, 449 n.34
 'Weg' 447 n.17
Haas, M. (ed.),
 Täufer IV 443 n.2
Haeghen, F. van den (ed.),
 Bibliotheca Erasmiana 435 n.1
Hahn, C. U.,
 Geschichte 425 n.128
Hahn, F.,
 'Probleme' 415 n.3
Hahn, H. F.,
 Modern Research 415 n.5
Hale, J. R.,
 'Renaissance' 418 n.29
Hales, J.,
 Works (ed. J. Hailes) 152, 499 n.4,
  502 n.58
 Judgement (in *Works*, ed.
  Hailes) 502 n.58

Hall, A. R. & M. B.,
'Clarke' 593 n.54
Scientific Papers 591 n.20
Hall, B.,
'Calvin' 479 n.51
'Puritanism' 476 n.2, 481 n.87
Swift 601 nn.154, 155, 602 n.277,
603 n.189, 604 nn.191, 198
Hall, D. D.,
'Understanding' (in *State*, ed.
H. J. Bass) 479 nn.37, 40,
480 n.70, 481 n.80
Hall, J.,
Answer 503 n.75
Confutation 507 n.144
Defence 503 n.75
Episcopacie 503 nn.75, 77
Remonstrance 503 n.75
Hall, R./Woolhouse, R.,
'Forty Years' 546 n.140
Hall, T.,
'Possibilites' 448 n.25
Haller, W.,
Introduction to *Tracts on Liberty*
516 n.316
Introduction to *Leveller Tracts*, ed.
W. Haller/G. Davies 483 n.122
Liberty 476 n.7, 515 n.287,
516 n.315, 517
Rise 92, 476 n.7, 477 n.9,
479 nn.52, 53, 480 n.63,
481 n.90, 494 nn.343, 354,
503 n.69, 505 n.95, 509 n.200,
516 n.313
'Word' 517 n.323
Haller, W. (ed.),
Tracts on Liberty 504 n.287, 509,
516, 517, 518
Haller, W./Davies, G. (eds.),
Leveller Tracts 483 n.122, 518
Hancey, J. O.,
'Locke' 556 n.308a
Handschin, W.,
Petrarca 420 n.57
Handy, R. T.,
'Consciousness' 498 n.437
Hanford, J. H.,
'Milton' 504 n.91, 505 n.94
Milton Handbook 507 n.147
Hanning, R. W.,
Vision 497 n.433
Hardt, H. von der
Ephemerides 576 n.181
Hare, F.,
'Difficulties' (in *Pillars*, ed.
R. Baron) 332, 333
Harrison, J.,
Newton 590 n.10a

Harrison, R.,
Writings (ed. A. Peel/
L. H. Carlson) 483 n.118
Hart, J.,
Bolingbroke 626 n.1
Harth, D.,
Philologie 435 n.4
Harth, P.,
MPh 58, 1961 601 n.166
Swift 601 nn.166, 168, 602 nn.169,
170, 604 nn.189, 190
Hartill, J.,
'Faith' 591 n.26
Harvey, E.,
Bucer 466 n.4, 474 nn.154, 155,
475 n.159
Haskins, C. H.,
Renaissance 418 n.23
Haug, R. A.,
in Milton, *Prose Works*, ed.
D. H. Wolfe 506
Hawkins, L. M.,
Allegiance 582 n.307
Hearnshaw, J. C.,
Vane 539 n.12
Heckel, J.,
Cura religionis 498 n.445, 535 n.110
Hege, A.,
Denck 451 n.56, 452 n.71, 454 n.99
Hegler, A.,
'Franck' 453 n.88
Geist 452 n.76
Heinemann, F.,
'Toland' (*APh* 4, 1950) 570 n.60,
571, 573 nn.130, 134,
576 nn.187, 196
'Toland' (*PhRev* 54, 1945) 573 n.129
'Toland' (*RESt* 20, 1944 & *RESt* 25,
1949) 570 n.60
Heinemann, F. H.,
'Philosopher' 578 n.210
Heitmann, K.,
Fortuna 421 n.66
Helton, T. (ed.),
Renaissance 421 n.74
Henkel, J.,
Contributions 436 n.15
Henningsen, M.,
'Divine Right' 560 n.417
Hentze, W.,
Kirche 438 n.33
Hepburn, R.,
'Hobbes' 432 n.79
Heppe, H.,
Geschichte 490 nn.248, 249
Herbert of Cherbury, Edward, Lord,
Appendix (ed. G. Gawlick) 191
Autobiography (ed. S. Lee) 522 n.38

De Causis Errorum (ed. G. Gawlick)
  519 n.5
Dialogue (ed. ibid.) 191, 192, 193,
  519 n.5
Life 519 n.1
De religione Gentilium (ed. Gawlick)
  188–192, 519 n.5, 622 n.145
De Religione Laici (ed. ibid.) 190,
  191, 519 n.5
De Religione Laici (ed.
  H. R. Hutcheson) 519 n.2
De Religione Laici (ed.
  H. G. Wright) 523 n.55
De veritate (ed. G. Gawlick)
  186–190, 519 n.5
Herder, J. G.,
  Werke (ed. B. Suphan) 339,
  593 n.49
Herrmann, R.-D.,
  'Thought' 589 n.4, 590 n.10
Hershberger, G. F. (ed.),
  Recovery 444 n.3, 445 nn.7, 11,
  446 n.12, 451 n.57a, 454 n.90
  Studies 451 n.570, 454 n.90
  Theology 446 n.17, 454 n.90
Heyer, F.,
  Kirchenbegriff 444 n.4, 449 n.39
Heylin, P.,
  Antidotum Lincolniense 503 n.71
  Coale 503 n.71
  Cyprianus Anglicus 484 n.124,
  503 n.74
Hickeringill, E.,
  Priestcraft 321
Highfield, I. R. L.,
  Relations 432 n.246
Hill, C.,
  Antichrist 487 n.90
  'Bourgeois Revolution' 477 n.13
  Change 478 n.32
  'Lollards' 434 nn.274, 282
  Milton 504 nn.85, 91, 505,
  506 n.115, 507 nn.147, 150,
  508 n.180
  Problems 477 nn.9, 13
  Puritanism 477 nn.13, 15
  Revolution 477 n.13, 583 n.309
  Society 476 n.2, 477 n.13,
  481 nn.86, 88, 492 nn.286, 290,
  493 n.333
  World 503 n.70
Hill, S.,
  Solomon (in *Collection of State
  Tracts*) 328, 587 n.390
Hillerbrand, H. J.,
  'Anabaptism' 449 n.34
  Bibliographie=Bibliography 444 n.3
  Ethik 447 n.19, 456 n.141,
  457 n.152

Fellowship 452 n.76, 418 n.167
'Gegenwärtige Täuferforschung'
  450 nn.45, 46
'Historicity' 611 n.158, 613 n.194
'Origin' 447 n.23, 448 n.25
Review of J. Kiwiet, *Pilgram
  Marbeck* 447 n.19
'Täuferforschung' 446 n.12,
  449 n.37
Hillerdal, G.,
  Reason 448, 489 n.231
Himbury, D. M.,
  'Religious Belief' 517 n.322
Hinnant, C. H.,
  Hobbes 526 n.19
Hinneberg, P. (ed.),
  Kultur 444 n.6
Hinrichs, C.,
  Luther und Müntzer 459, 460
Hinton, R. W. K.,
  'Note on Dating' 562 n.446
Hirsch, E.,
  Geschichte 574 n.149, 576 nn.186,
  194, 613 n.197, 621 n.107
Hirsch-Reich, B.,
  'Bibliographie' 427 n.164
Hoadly, B.,
  Preservative 586 n.385
Hobbes, T.,
  De Cive (in *Opera Philosophica*, ed.
  W. Molesworth) 199, 209–14,
  527 n.18
  De Cive (German ed. G. Gawlick)
  209–14, 527 n.18, 534 n.96,
  535 n.121
  Elements of Law (ed. F. Tonnies)
  529 n.48
  English Works (ed.
  W. Molesworth=EW)
  527 n.24, 530 n.57
  De Homine (in *Opera Philosophica*,
  ed. W. Molesworth) 533
  De Homine (German ed.
  G. Gawlick) 527 n.23,
  534 nn.96, 102, 536
  Leviathan (in English Works, ed.
  W. Molesworth) 527 n.24
  Leviathan (ed. I. Fetscher) 206–8,
  214–19, 527 n.23, 531 n.61, 536,
  537
  Leviathan (ed. P. C. Mayer-Tasch)
  525 n.5
  Leviathan (ed. M. Oakeshott)
  206–8, 214–19, 527 nn.23, 40
  Man and Citizen (ed. B. Gert)
  532 n.71
  Opera Philosophica (ed.
  W. Molesworth=OL)
  527 n.18., 531 n.61, 533, 534

Vita (in *Opera Philosophica*, above)
533 nn.91, 93
Vom Burger (ed. G. Gawlick)
527 n.18, 535 nn.109, 127
Höffe, O. (ed.),
Hobbes 527 n.21
Klassiker I 524 n.1, 546 n.137a
Hoffmann, M.,
Erkenntnis 435 n.4, 436 n.11,
438 n.29, 439 nn.45, 51
Ordonnantie 461 n.208
Ordinance (in Williams, ed.,
Writers) 461 n.208
Holder-Egger, D.,
*Chronicle of Salimbene of
Parma* 429 n.201
Holeczek, H.,
Bibelphilologie 435 n.4, 485 n.133
Holl, K.,
'Luther' 444 nn.4, 6, 466 n.12,
447 nn.20, 22, 450 n.49
Hollinger, D. A.,
'P. Miller' 478 n.37, 479 n.47
Holmes, G. (ed.),
Britain 582f. n.308, 586 n.385a
Trial 587 n.394
Holsten, W.,
'Christentum' 467 n.10
Hood, F. C.,
Divine Politics 197, 528 n.32, 530,
531, 533 n.88
Hooker, R.,
Laws 116–18, 488–9
Laws (ed. W. Speed Hill) 116–18,
488–9
Hooper, J.,
Notae (ed. C. Hopf) 112–16, 126,
487–8
Writings (ed. S. Carr) 113, 487
Hoopes, R.,
Right Reason 510 n.220, 511 n.242
Hopf, C.,
Bucer 466 n.4, 471 n.89, 474, 475,
476 n.197
Horawitz, A./Hartfelder, K. (eds.),
Briefwechsel 466 n.8
Horsch, J.,
In *MennQR* 4–8, 1930–34 44 n.22,
450 n.51
Horst, I. B.,
Anabaptism 480 n.66
Hosmer, J. K.,
Vane 539 n.12
Hough, J. C.,
'Theologie' 626 n.2
Howell, W. S.,
Logic 479 n.42
Hrubi, F. R.,
'Leviathan' 526 n.19

Hubatsch, W. (ed.),
Wirkungen 458 n.167
Hubmaier, B.,
Schriften (ed. G. Westin/
T. Bergsten) 444 n.2
Huck, I. C.,
Joachim 426 n.164
Hudson, A.,
'Compilation' 434 n.272
Hudson, W. S.,
Cambridge 474 n.155, 482 n.104
'Mystical Religion' 518 n.349,
539 n.11, 540 nn.16, 17
Hudson, W. S. (ed.),
Nationalism 241
Huet, D.,
Demonstratio 305, 605 n.18
Hughes, M. Y.,
Perspectives 504 n.85
Hughes, P./Williams, D. (eds.),
Varied Pattern 600 n.159a
Huizinga, J.,
Erasmus 436 n.9, 437 n.18,
441 n.85
Herfstij 418 n.26
'Problem' 418 n.27
Humphrey, E. F.,
Nationalism 498 n.437
Humphrey, W. G.,
'Tillotson' 542 n.66, 544 n.109
Hundert, E. J.,
'Market Society' 562 n.472
Hungerland, G.,
'Hobbes' theory' 528 n.35
Hunt, E.,
Dean Colet 436 n.16
Hunt, J.,
Religious Thought 570 n.60,
573 n.117
Huntley, F. L.,
Browne 568 n.21
Hurley, M.,
'Scriptura' 430 n.228, 431, 432
Hutin, S.,
More 511 n.228
Introduction to H. More, *Opera
Omnia* 511 n.228
Hutten, U. von,
Epistolae, ed. A. Bomer 436 n.10
Hutton, W. H.,
Laud 484 n.124
Hyma, A.,
'Continental Origins' 481 n.73
'Erasmus' 437 n.17
'Life' 436 n.15, 437 nn.17, 18
Hyman, J. D.,
Chillingworth 499 n.3

Ibbot, B.,
    'Civil Magistrate' (in *Pillars*, ed.
    R. Baron) 584 n.346
Ignatius a Jesu,
    Narratio 565 n.518
Ilarino, G.,
    La eresie 425 nn.136, 140
    Ugo Speroni 426
Ilive, J.,
    Oration 404–5
Ilting, K. H.,
    Introduction to F. Tönnies, *Hobbes*
    529 n.41
    'Hobbes' 538 n.195
Innocent III,
    De Contemptu 13
Ireland, W. W.,
    Vane 539 nn.12, 13
Ives, I. W. (ed.),
    Revolution 516 n.315, 517 n.322a

Jacob, H.,
    Attestation 495 n.361
    Confession 133, 494 n.373
    Divine Beginning 133
    Exhortation 494 n.369
    Exposition 134, 494 n.358
    Reasons 131–3
    Supplication 495 n.368
Jacob, J. R.,
    Boyle 500 n.9a
Jacob, M. C.,
    'Masonic Lodge' 576 n.196
    'Newtonian Ideology' 570 n.60,
    572 n.89, 573 n.129, 576 nn.195,
    196, 594 n.109
    Newtonians 539 nn.1, 2, 542 n.66,
    571 n.63a, 576 n.196, 592 n.31,
    593 n.39
Jacoby, E. G.,
    'Anti-White' 526 n.10
Jacquod, J.,
    'S. Castellion' 464 n.236, 465 n.262
Jacquod, J./Jones, H. W. (eds.),
    White 525 n.10
James I,
    Book of Sports 124
    A more 139
James, D. G.,
    Life of Reason 547 n.149, 554, 555
James, S. V. (ed.),
    Puritans 478 n.37
Janelle, P.,
    Obedience 430
Jänicke, M.,
    Wissenschaft 531 n.68
Jansma, I. G.,
    Melchiorites 463 n.227

Javelet, R.,
    Image 419 n.39
Jayne, S.,
    Colet 436 n.16
Jeffares, A. N.,
    Fair Liberty 600 nn.160, 161,
    601 nn.162, 164
    Swift 600 nn.160, 161, 603 n.179
Jeffner, A.,
    Butler and Hume 545 n.118,
    596 n.110, 597 nn.118, 122, 598,
    599
Jeffs, R. (ed.),
    Revolution 483 n.120
Jenny, B.,
    'Täuferbekenntnis' 450 n.51,
    451 n.61, 456 n.139
Jewel, J.,
    Apologia 496 n.414
Joachim of Fiore,
    Adversus Judaeos (ed. A. Frugoni)
    427 n.164
    De articulis (ed. E. Buonaiuti)
    427 n.164
    Concordia 427 n.164, 428
    Expositio 427 n.164, 428 n.79
    Liber figurarum (ed. R. Tondelli)
    427 n.164
    Psalterium 427 n.164
    Tractatus (ed. E. Buonaiuti)
    427 n.164, 428 n.181
    Vaticinia 427 n.164
Ps-Joachim,
    Interpretatio 28, 428 n.197
Joachim Jungius Gesellschaft (ed.),
    Reimarus 520 n.6, 626 n.4
Joachimsen, P.,
    In *Blätter fur Deutsche Philosophie*
    1928 452 n.76
Johnson, H. J.,
    Review of F. S. McNeilly, *Anatomy*
    537 n.197
Johnson, P. J.,
    Doctrine 525 n.4, 533 n.90a,
    534 nn.94, 106
Jones, R. F.,
    Ancients 545 n.117, 589 n.2,
    602 n.171
Jones, R. M.,
    Mysticism 404 n.343
    Reformers 448 n.31, 463 n.234,
    539 n.12, 590 n.220
Jones, W. R. D.,
    Crisis 481 n.91
Jordan, W. K.,
    Development 483 483 n.121,
    500 n.8, 590 n.220
    'Thought' 483 n.121

Judson, M. A.,
  Parker 517 n.318

Kaczerowski, K.,
  Franck 444 n.2
Kaegi, W.,
  Castellio 463 n.236
  'Renaissanceforschung' 417 n.12,
  418 nn.18, 27
Kalivoda, R.,
  'Metaphysik' (in *Miscellanea
  Mediaevalia* II, ed. P. Wilpert)
  432 n.256
Kamen, H.,
  Intoleranz 500 n.8
Kaminsky, K.,
  'Wyclifism' 433 nn.263, 268,
  434 n.269
Karlstadt, A.,
  Sabbat 492 n.288
Karskens, M.,
  'Thomas Hobbes' 526 n.19
Käsemann, E.,
  'Exegese' 415 n.2
Kawerau, P.,
  Hoffmann 461 nn.208, 210
Keller, L.,
  Reformation 446 n.13, 448 n.28
Kendall, W.,
  Locke 549 n.178
Kerssenbroeck, H. von,
  Anabaptistici 462 n.217a
Kessler, E.,
  'Geschichtsdenken' 420 n.56,
  421 n.67
Kevan, E. F.,
  Grace 488 n.197, 490 nn.263, 264,
  491
King, P. Lord,
  Life 546 n.139, 552 nn.238, 240,
  554, 564
Kirchhoff, K.-H.,
  Reich 462 n.227
  Taüfer 463 n.227
  Utopia 463 n.227
Kirsch, G.,
  Erasmus 439 n.51
Kiwiet, J.,
  Marbeck 446 n.19, 457
  'Theologia' 448 n.31
Klassen, W.,
  Covenant 451 n.64, 456 n.143,
  457 nn.145, 150
  'Marpeck' 457 n.150
  Art 'Sabbatarier' 457 n.162
  Art 'Sabbatarian Anabaptists'
  457 n.162
Kleinig, J.,
  'Butler' 596 n.110, 600 n. 157

Kluge, D.,
  'Rechts' 462 n.217a
  'Vorbereitung' 462 n.217a
Knappen, M. M.,
  Puritanism 476 n.7, 479 n.51,
  480 n.70, 481 nn.90, 93, 482,
  483 nn.116, 119, 484 n.136,
  486 n.168, 487 n.194
  'W. Tyndale' 494 n.354
Knös, B.,
  'Encore G. Pléthon' 422 n.80
  'Pléthon' 422 n.80
Knoth, E.,
  Ubertino 430 n.225
Knott, E.,
  Charity 500 n.12, 500 n.37
Koch, K.,
  Studium pietatis 466 n.5, 467 nn.8,
  10, 468, 469, 470 nn.64, 65, 471,
  472 nn.109, 110, 474, 475 n.170,
  476 n.194
Kodalle, K. H.,
  Hobbes 525 nn.6, 7, 527 n.26, 528,
  530, 531, 532 n.86, 534 n.102,
  535, 536, 537
  'Schmitt' 531 n.71, 532 n.82
  'Subjektivitat' 532 n.84
Köhler, W.,
  'Geistesahnen' 465 n.242
  'Täufertum' (*ARG* 37.1940; 40.1943;
  41.1948) 446 n.12
  'Verantwortung' 450 n.50
  Art. 'Wiedertäufer' 448 n.25
  Zwingli and Luther 467 n.9
Kohls, E. W.,
  'Bedeutung' 439 n.45
  'Bucer' 467 n.100
  Lebensaufgabe 448 n.25
  Luther 435 n.5, 436 n.7, 437,
  438 n.42, 439 n.49
  'Position' 436 n.7
  Schule 467 nn.19, 20
  Theologie 435, 436 n.7, 439,
  440 n.56
Köhn, M.,
  'Bucer Bibliography' 466 n.5
Kolfhaus, W.,
  Christliches Leben 494 n.342
Koller, H. (ed.),
  Reformatio 432 n.245
Kommoss, R.,
  Franck 454 n.95
König, R.,
  Preface to R. Bendix, *Weber*
  478 n.34
Korshin, P. J. (ed.),
  Circle 626 n.3
Kortholt, C.,
  De Tribus Impostoribus 519 n.4

Koselleck, R./Schnur, R. (ed.),
  Hobbes-Forschungen 494 n.354,
    524 nn.2, 3, 531 n.67a,
    536 n.126a
Koster, L. de,
  Locke's Second Treatise 563 n.443
Kottich, R. G.,
  Lehre 521 n.14
Koyre, A.,
  'Franck' 452 n.76, 453 n.88
  Mystiques 452 n.76
  World 592 n.38
Koyre, A./Cohen, J. B.,
  'Missing Tanquam' 593 n.54
  'Newton' 593 n.54
Kraeling, E. G.,
  The Old Testament 415 n.5, 525 n.8
Krahn, C.,
  Dutch Anabaptism 461 nn.208, 211
Krahn, F.,
  'Prolegomena' 449 n.41
Kramnik, I.,
  Bolingbroke 626 n.1
Krapp, R. M.,
  Anglicanism 484 n.125, 499 nn.1, 3,
    500 nn.8, 9, 502 nn.59, 60
Kraus, H. J.,
  Geschichte 2, 4, 415 n.6, 416,
    610 n.138
Krebs, M., (ed.),
  Quellen 443 n.2
Kressner, H.,
  Ursprünge 96, 495 n.392
Kristeller, P. O.,
  'Aristotelian' 421 n.70
  'Averroism' 421 n.70
  Classics 418 n.32
  Eight Philosophers 419 n.51,
    420 n.57, 421 n.73
  'L'état' 422 n.82
  Ficino 85, 87, 418 n.35, 422
  'Humanist Learning' (in *Studies*)
    419 nn.51, 52
  'Movement' (in *Renaissance
    Thought*) 419 n.51
  'Pico' 424 n.117a
  'Platonism' (in *Facets*) 421 n.75
  Renaissance Thought Vol. I
    418 nn.30, 32, 420 n.54, 421,
    422 nn.84, 86
  Studies 418 n.32, 420 n.56
  'Tradition' (in *Renaissance Thought*)
    421 n.70
  Tradizione 418 n.32
  'View' (in *Renaissance*, ed.
    T. Helton) 421 n.74
Krook, D.,
  'Hobbes' 528 n.29

Kroon, M. de,
  'De christelijke overheid' 474 n.144
Krüger, F.,
  Bucer 440 n.61, 441 nn.62, 74,
    466 nn. 3, 5, 467 nn.11, 9, 468,
    469, 470, 472
Krüger, S.,
  HZ 180, 1955 433 n.265
Kubrin, D.,
  'Newton' 593 n.53
Kugler, F. (ed.),
  Geschichte 417 n.7
Kühler, W. J.,
  Geschiedenis I 461 nn.208, 211,
    462 n.226
Kühn, U.,
  Via charitatis 475 n.163
Kurze, D.,
  'Lollarden' 434 n.276
Kuss, O.,
  'Klarheit' 435 n.4, 439 n.49
Kwaad, G. C.,
  'Thomas Hobbes' 528 n.32

Lafer, C.,
  'Hobbes' 529 n.39
Laird, J.,
  Hobbes 537 n.186
Lambert, M. D.,
  Poverty 428 n.190
Lamont, C.,
  'Checklist' 600 n.160
Lamont, W. M.,
  Godly Rule 496 n.405a, 497 n.430,
    498 n.437a, 503 nn.73, 75
  Marginal Prynne 503 nn.72, 73
Lampe, G. W. H. (ed.),
  Cambridge History 435 n.4
Lamprecht, S. P.,
  Innate Ideas 514 n.269
Landa, L. A.,
  Introduction to the Sermons in
    Swift, *Prose Works* 602 n.177,
    604 n.197
  Swift 601 n.164
Landa, L. A./Tobin, J. E.,
  Swift 600 n.160
Lang, A.,
  'Butzer' 466 n.4, 480 n.57
  Evangelienkommentar 466 n.1,
    467 n.16, 468 nn.24, 25,
    469 nn.29, 46, 470 n.54, 471, 472,
    473 n.27
  Puritanismus 466 n.4, 467 n.16,
    474 n.158, 480 n.57, 482 n.160,
    490 nn.244, 250
  ZKG 48, 1929 474 n.156
Lanson, G.,
  'Questions' 566 n.4

Lantoine, A.,
  Toland 570 n.60
a Lasco, J.,
  Opera (ed. H. Kuyper) 482 n.97
Laski, H. J.,
  Political Thought 585 n.360,
  585 n.365, 586 n.385
Laslett, P.,
  'Filmer' 560, 561 n.418
  Observations 561 n.444
  in J. Locke, *Two Treatises*
  547 nn.152, 153, 550, 560 n.411,
  561 nn.442, 444
  Introduction to R. Filmer,
  Patriarcha 560, 561
Lau, F.,
  'Apokalyptik' 461 n.203
Laud, W.,
  Works (ed. Scott-Bliss) 502 nn.62,
  65
Laun, F. J.,
  'Bradwardin' 433 n.262
  'Prädestination' 433 n.262
Lavater, J. C.,
  De Ritibus 113
Leavis, F. R.,
  Determinations 604 n.192
  'Irony' 604 n.192
  Pursuit 604 n.192
Lechler, G. V.,
  Geschichte 432 n.242, 519 n.1,
  566 nn.2, 3, 568, 570 n.60,
  571 n.82, 572 n.102, 573 n.128,
  587 nn.395, 397, 604 n.1, 606,
  608 n.80, 609, 610, 611 n.157,
  613, 617 n.1, 618, 620 n.65,
  621 nn.117, 118, 622 nn.124, 125,
  624 nn.204, 219, 625, 626 n.3
  'Wyclif' 430 n.228
Lecler, J.,
  Geschichte 497 n.430
Leclerq, J.,
  'L'Exégèse' 431 n.233
  Pierre 426 nn.147, 148
Leeuwen von, H. G.,
  Certainty 500 n.18, 544 n.103
Lehmann, G.,
  in *Blätter für Deutsche Philosophie*
  1928 452 n.76
Lehmann, K.,
  'Horizont' 415 n.3
Leibniz, G. W.,
  Schriften (ed. C. J. Gerhardt)
  593 n.54
Leigh, W.,
  Queene Elizabeth 137, 138
Leland, J.,
  Answer 623 n.189
  Divine Authority 623 n.185

View 567 n.16, 569 n.46, 577 n.198,
  580 n.260, 613 n.197
Lemker, H. C.,
  Nachricht 611 n.159
Lemos, R. M.,
  Hobbes 526 n.19, 529 n.46,
  531 n.71, 561 n.443
Lempicki, S. von,
  'Shaftesbury' 578 n.211
LeMoine, A.,
  Dissertation 611 n.160
Lessing, G. E.,
  Erziehung 556 n.328, 596 n.102
Letwin, S. R.,
  'Christianity' 530 n.49
Levi, G. A.,
  'Pensiero' 420 n.59
Levy, M.,
  Sabbath 492
Leyburn, E.,
  Allegory 600 n.161
Leyden, W. von,
  Introduction to J. Locke, *Essay*
  549 n.172, 550 n.195, 551 n.220,
  552 n.223
  Review of C. A. Viano, *Locke*
  546 n.141
Lichtenstein, A.,
  More 510 nn.222, 223, 511, 512, 513
Liebing, H.,
  'Ausgänge' 416 n.14
  'Frage' (in *Autour de M. Servet*)
  464 n.239, 465
  Servet 465
  Schriftauslegung 464 n.239
Lienhard, M.,
  Anabaptism 444 n.3, 449 n.35
Lienhard, M./Willer, J.,
  Strassburg 472 n.109
Lightfoot, J.,
  Harmony 555 n.304
Lilburne, J.,
  Freedom 517 n.322
  Worke (in *Tracts*, ed. W. Haller)
  517 n.317
Lindberg, C. (ed.),
  Genesis 434 n.275
Lindeboom, J.,
  Franc-tireur 452 n.76, 456 n.132
  Stiefkinderen 465 n.261
Lindt, A./Deppermann, K.,
  Pietismus 454 n.90
Lippe, R. zur,
  'Bürgerliche' 532 n.77
Lips, J.,
  'Stellung' 535 nn.116, 117
Littauer, L.,
  Anschauungen 452 n.76, 453 n.109

Littell, F.,
  'Kirchenbegriff' 449 n.45
  Anabaptist View 440 n.42
Little, D.,
  Religion 476 nn.2, 6, 477 n.16,
    478 n.27, 480 n.58, 481 n.83
  'Weber' 478 n.27
Lloyd, W.,
  Sermon 545 n.17
Lobb, T.,
  Defence 610 n.142
Locher, G. W.,
  'Zwingli' 447 n.17, 480 n.69
  Reformation 444 n.3
Locke, G. L.,
  Tillotson 542 n.66, 543, 544 nn.103,
    105, 545
Locke, J.,
  Carta (ed. A. Waismann/
    R. Klibansky) 563 n.484
  Difference (in Lord King, *Life*)
    564 n.501
  Ecclesia (in Lord King, *Life*)
    564 n.495
  Epistola (ed. R. Klibanksy,
    J. W. Gough) 278–85,
    547 n.153, 563–6
  *Essay concerning Human
    Understanding* (ed.
    P. H. Nidditch) 254–9
  Essay concerning the Understanding
    (Draft B, ed. B. Rand) 231,
    552 n.224
  Essay on the Law of Nature (ed.
    W. von Leyden) 231, 552 n.224,
    248–53, 552
  Ethics 253, 552 n.240
  Human Understanding (ed.
    M. Cranston) 346, 354,
    546 n.138, 548 n.155, 570 n.59
  Letter (trans J. Ebbinghaus)
    563 n.484, 565
  Letter (ed. M. Montouri) 563 n.484
  Letter (trans W. Popple) 563 n.484,
    565
  Lettera (ed. R. Klibansky/
    E. de Marchi) 547 n.153,
    563 n.484
  Lettre (ed. R. Klibansky/R. Polin)
    563 n.484
  Reasonableness (in *Works*) 259–70,
    547 n.146, 556–9, 581 n.261
  Reasonableness
    (I. T. Ramsey) 260–70,
    347 n.146, 556–9
  Reasonableness (G. W. Ewing)
    547 n.146
  Third Letter (in *Works*) 548 n.155

  Toleration (in F. Bourne, *Life*)
    279–80, 563 n.490, 564
  Toleration (in C. A. Viano, ed.,
    Scritti) 279–80, 563 n.490, 564
  Tracts (ed. P. Abrams) 246–7, 279,
    548–9
  Treatises (ed. P. Laslett) 248, 274–7,
    536 nn.327, 372, 561–3
  Vindication (in *Works*) 260, 263, 270,
    547 n.147, 556 n.307, 557 n.332
  Works 546 n.138, 547 n.147,
    548 n.155, 556–9, 570 n.58,
    587 n.394
Loewenich, W. von
  'Selbstkritik' 455 n.102
Lohse, B.,
  Aussenseiter 458 n.167
  'Denck' 451 nn.63, 71
  'Müntzer' 458 n.166
  Review of W. Elliger, *Müntzer*
    458 n.167
  'Stellung' 445 n.11, 447 n.24
Long, P.,
  Summary Catalogue 546 n.139
Loofs, F.,
  Leitfaden (ed. K. Aland) 430 n.228,
    431 n.230, 434 n.262
Looss, S.,
  'Butzer' 466 n.5
Loretz, O./Stolz, W (ed.),
  Frage 415 n.1
Lorimer, P.,
  J. Knox 482 n.97, 487 n.194
Loserth, J.,
  Quellen 442 n.2, 452 n.65,
    457 nn.153, 158
Lovejoy, A.,
  Essays 556 n.325
  Great Chain 556 n.325
Lowance, M. L.,
  'Magnalia' 497 n.437
Lowde, J.,
  Discourse 526 n.12
Lowman, M.,
  Dissertation 634 n.229
  Ritual 407
Loyer, D.,
  'Hooker' 488 n.212a
Lubac, H. de,
  Exegese 431 n.233, 440 n.56, 441
  Pic 423, 424 n.104
Lubienski, Z.,
  Grundlagen 525 n.7
Lupton, J. H.,
  Colet 436 n.15
Luther, M.,
  Auslegung 492 n.288
  De servo arbitrio 439 n.49
  Tischreden 436 n.10, 439 n.51

Unterricht 492 n.288
Von weltlicher Obrigkeit 474 n.144
Lyon, T.,
Theory 500 n.8
Lyons, H.,
Royal Society 589 n.2
Lyons, W.,
Infallibility 360–2, 608

Mabbott, J. D.,
Locke 546 n.140, 560 n.411
Macdonald, H./Hargreaves, M.,
Thomas Hobbes 524 n.2
Mackie, J. L.,
Problems 546 n.141
Mackintosh, W. L.,
Laud 484 n.124
MacLaurin, C.,
Account 340, 594 n.49
MacPherson, C. B.,
Individualism 546 nn.143, 144,
556 n.311
'Man' (in *Hobbes-Studies*, ed.
K. C Brown) 528 n.34
Political Theory 528
Mahlmann, T.,
Review of K. Scholder,
Ursprünge 415 n.7
Mainusch, H.
Introduction to Toland, *Gründe*
575 n.169
Malherbe, M.,
'Hobbes' 526 n.19
Mallard, W.,
'Wyclif' 430 n.228, 431 nn.235, 236
Mancini, J./Crinella, G.,
Locke 546 n.140
Mandel, H.,
Introduction to T. Müntzer,
Theologia Deutsch 448 n.31
Mandelbaum, M.,
'Realism' 546 n.141, 551 n.217
Manet, P.,
Naissances 532 n.77, 538 n.87g,
534 n.106
Manenschijn, G.,
Moraalen 527 nn.21, 26
Manetti,
De dignitate 13f.
Manning, B.,
English People 504 n.83
'Levellers' 516 n.315
Politics 503 n.79, 517 n.322
'Religion and Politics' 503 n.79
Manselli, R.,
'Arnold von Brescia' 426 n.163
'Eresie' 426 n.147
'Il monaco' 426 n.150
Lectura 430 nn.223, 224

Manteuffel,T.,
Geburt 430 n.221
Manuel, F. E.,
Daed.97, 1948 590 n.16
Eighteenth Century 590 n.12
Newton Historian 576 n.76, 589 n.4,
590
Portrait 589 nn.3, 4, 590, 591,
592 n.35, 593 n.48, 595 n.67
Religion 568 n.31
Maouas, Y.,
'Essai' 536 n.157
Marbeck, P.,
Rechenschaft 457 n.152
Testamenterleutterung 61, 456 n.152
Verantwortung (ed. J. Loserth) 61,
467 n.148
Vermanung (ed. J. Loserth) 61,
457 n.148
Vermanung (ed. C. Hedge) 61,
457 n.149
Marböck, J. (ed.),
Aspekte der Brüderlichkeit 463 n.236
Marcel, R.,
'Les Découvertes' 437 n.17
'Marsile Ficin' 422 n.82
Marchant, R. A.,
Puritans 493 n.333
Marchi, E. de,
Introduction to J. Locke, *Lettera*
547 n.153, 548 nn.154, 158,
550 n.204, 552 n.232
Margolin, J. C.,
Douze Années 435 n.3
Erasmus 439 n.52
L'Idée 439 n.52
Quatorze Années 435 n.3
Maron, G.,
Individualismus 452
'T. Müntzer' 460 n.198
Marprelate, M.,
Epistle (ed. E. Arber) 222,
483 n.117, 493 n.331
Epitome (ed. id.) 483 n.117
Texts (ed. id.) 493 n.331
Texts (ed. W. Price) 483 n.117
Marriot, J.,
Crisis 503 n.70
Marsden, G. M.,
'P. Miller' 479
Marsh, N.,
Institutio 603 n.184
Marshall, J. S.,
R. Hooker 488 n.207, 489 n.231
Marsham, J.,
Canon 568 nn.31, 32
Marsilius of Padua,
Defensor Pacis (German-Latin ed. by

. W. Kunzmann and H. Kusch)
36, 433 n.265
Martelotti, G.,
De viris 421 n.67
Martin, A. von,
Religion 417 n.11
Martineau, J.,
Types 514 n.264
Martines, L.,
Social World 419 n.46
Masai, F.,
'Pléthon' 422 n.80
'Problème' 422 n.80
Mason, A. J.,
Church 499 nn.451, 466
Mason, D.,
Life 504 n.85, 519 n.358
Mather, C.,
Magnalia 497 n.437
Mau, R.,
'Müntzer' 459 nn.180, 182,
460 nn.187, 191
Maurer, W.,
'Luther' 444 n.4
Mazzeo, J. A. (ed.),
Reason 603 n.184
McCaughlin, R. E.,
'Schwenkfeld' 452 n.67
McConica, J. M.,
Humanists 480 n.60, 486 n.168
McDowell, R. B.,
'Swift' 601 n.164
McElwee, W.,
Fool 483 n.119
McFarlane, K. B.,
Wycliffe 430 n.228, 431 n.234, 432,
434
McGiffert, A. C.,
Protestant Thought 543 n.76
McGinn, D. J.,
Controversy 487 nn.197, 199
McGoldrick, J.,
Disciples 485
McGrath, P.,
Papists 486 n.170
McGuire, J. E./Ratansi, P. M.,
'Newton' (in *Notes and
Records*) 591 n.20, 592 n.31
McIlwain, C. H. (ed.),
Political Works 497 n.424
McInnes, A.,
Harley 576 n.187, 583 n.310
McKenzie, J. A.,
'Theology' 489 n.236
McKisack, M.,
Century 432
McLachlan, H. J.,
Religious Opinions 547 nn.147, 148,
590 n.5

Socinianism 499 n.1, 547 n.158
Theological Manuscripts 590
McNeill, J.,
History 480 n.67
'Left Wing' 443 n.1
McNeilly, F. S.,
Anatomy 526 n.11
McPherson, T.,
'Development' 596 n.110,
599 n.153, 600 n.157
Mead, S. E.,
Experiment 484 n.128
Mecenseffy, G. (ed.),
'Herkunft' 446 n.12
Österreich I & II 443 n.2
'Verständnis' 451 n.60
Meissenger, K. A.,
Erasmus 438 n.39
Melanchton, P.
Loci 482 n.99
Merrill, T.,
Perkins 490
Mersenne, P. M.,
Correspondance (ed. C. de Waard)
187, 521 n.23
Merton, E. S.
Browne 568 n.21
Mesnard, P.
'Le Caractère' 436 n.9
Mestwerdt, P.,
Anfänge 436 n.14
Metzger, H.,
Attraction universelle 573 n.130,
592, 593 nn.50, 52, 504 n.61
Meusel, A.,
Müntzer 458 n.166
Meyer, C. S.,
Elizabeth I 482 n.104
'Erasmus' 435 n.4
Meyer, H.,
Limae Labor 577 n.197
Michaelis, G.,
R. Hooker 488
Michelet, J.,
Histoire 416 nn.3, 4
Middleton, C.,
Defence 621
Letter 621 n.110
Observations 621 n.110
Remarks 621 n.110
Miles, L.,
Colet 436 n.16
Mill, J.,
Prolegomena (ed. L. Kusterns)
607 n.60
Miller, P.,
'Bentley' (in Cohen, I.B., ed.,
Newton's Papers) 593 n.40
Errand 478 n.37

'Marrow' 119, 123, 478 n.37,
   490 n.256, 491 n.288,
   492 nn.284, 285
Mind, 1939 478 n.37, 479,
   480 n.235
Mind, 1953 478 n.37
Orthodoxy 94, 479 n.38
'R. Williams' (in R. Williams,
   Complete Writings, ed. P. Miller)
   498 n.454
on him
   P. Miller and the American Mind
   479 n.37
Miller, P./Johnson, T.,
   Puritans 478 n.37
Milton, J.,
   Animadversions (in *Prose Works*, ed.
   D. M. Wolfe) 159, 503 n.44
   Apology (in ibid.) 161
   Areopagitica (in ibid) 156, 164, 165,
   166
   Comus (in *Works*, ed.
   F. A. Patterson) 156, 157, 158,
   506 n.99
   Considerations (in ibid.) 183
   Defensio (in ibid.) 505 n.104
   Doctrine (in *Prose Works*, ed.
   Wolfe) 151, 156, 162, 163
   Lycidas (in *Works*, ed. Patterson)
   156, 157
   Of Reformation 156
   Paradise Lost 156
   Paradise Regained 266
   Poems 156
   Prose Works, ed. D. M. Wolfe 503–6
   Reason (in ibid.) 159, 160,
   505 n.108, 507–9
   Scripture (in ibid.) 164, 509 n.187
   Tetrachordon (in ibid.) 133
   Treatise (in *Works*, ed. Patterson)
   182, 183
Milton, J. R.,
   'John Locke' 552 n.221
Mintz, S. I.,
   Hunting 526 n.12, 538 n.200
Missner, M.,
   'Hobbes' Method' 525 n.5a
Mitchell, W. F.,
   Pulpit Oratory 542 n.66
Mizuta, H.,
   List 524 n.2
Moeller, B. (ed.),
   Bauernkriegs-Studien 458 n.167
Mohler, L.,
   Bessarion 422 n.81
Molen, R. van der,
   'Anglican' 482 nn.100, 102
Møller, J.,
   Beginnings 485 nn.130, 137,

   486 nn.153, 167, 489 nn.236,
   237, 490 nn.240, 244
Molke, A./Tedeschi, J. A. (eds.),
   Renaissance 419 n.51
Molnar, A.,
   'Works' 431 n.228
   Valdensti 426 n.156
Monk, J. H.,
   Bentley 592 nn.37, 40, 593 n.40
Monk, S. H.,
   'Pride' 603 n.179
Monnerjahn, E.,
   Pico 423, 424
Monson, C.,
   'Locke' 549 n.176
Monteiro, J. P.,
   'Estado' 527 n.24
Moore, J. T.,
   'Development' 548 nn.154, 158
   'Language' 555 n.293, 559 n.399a
   'Moral' 555 n.301a
   'Toleration' 554 n.272
More, H.,
   Annotations 512 n.247
   Conjectura 512 n.250
   Divine Dialogues 512
   Enchiridion (in *Opera Omnia*)
   513 n.257
   Mystery 512 nn.249, 251
   Opera Omnia 511 n.228, 512,
   513 n.259
More, L. T.,
   Newton 589 n.3
Moreau, P. E.,
   'Loi divine' 529 n.47
Morgan, E. S.,
   Visible Saints 494 n.342
Morgan, I.,
   Godly Preachers 476 n.8
Morgan, T.,
   Collection 623 n.187
   Moral Philosophers (ed. G. Gawlick)
   395–404, 621–4
   Physico-Theology 397, 621, 622
Morris, B.,
   'Gauthier' 526 n.13, 530 n.50
Mosheim, J. L.,
   Vindiciae 570 n.60, 574 n.149
Mosse, G. L.,
   'Puritanism' 478 n.35, 479 n.46,
   480 n.73
Mossner, E. C.,
   Bishop Butler 520 n.6, 566 n.6,
   568 n.22, 569 n.56, 594 n.64,
   596 nn.110, 111, 597 n.117,
   598 n.123, 599
Motzo Dentice di Accadia, C.,
   'Il Deismo' (*GCFI* 15, 1934)
   570 nn.60, 62, 574, 575

'Il Deismo' (*GCFI* 16, 1935) 604 n.1
  Supremacia 583 nn.318, 319
  Preilluminismo 570 nn.60, 62, 574,
    575, 604 n.1, 618 n.2
Mourgeon, J.,
  La science 527 n.20
Mozley, J. F.,
  Tyndale 484
Muhlen, K.-H. zur,
  Nos extra nos 451 n.54
Mühlpfordt, G.,
  'Luther' 447 n.20
Müller, J.,
  Bucer 466 n.4, 467 n.10, 468 n.5,
    469, 470, 471, 472
  Introduction to M. Bucer, *Das ym
    selbs* (in DW) 468 n.26
Müller, L. (ed.),
  Glaubenserzeugnisse 443 n.2
Müntzer, T.,
  Entblössung (in *Werke, Kritische
    Ausgabe*) 64, 65, 66, 459, 460 n.197
  Fürstenpredigt (in ibid.) 66, 67,
    459 nn.174, 182, 461 n.199
  Schutzrede (in ibid.) 460
  Werke, Kritische Ausgabe (ed.
    P. Kirn/G. Franz) 444 n.2,
    457 n.165, 459 n.174
  Werke (ed. M. Bensing/R. Rüdiger)
    457 n.165
  Werke (ed. S. Barauer/W. Ullmann)
    457 n.165
Muff, M.,
  Kritik 570 n.61
Muir, K.,
  Milton 504 n.85
Muirhead, J. H.,
  Platonic Tradition 510 n.220,
    514 n.265
Mullett, C. F.,
  'Religion' 539 n.3, 582, n.306
  'Toleration' 539 n.5
Munz, P.,
  Place 488
Muralt, L. von,
  Review of J. Horsch 447 n.22,
    450 n.53
  Glaube 446 n.16, 488 n.25, 450 n.50
Murphy, J. L.,
  'Influence' 597 n.113
  'Rationalist Defence' 596 n.10,
    597 n.122, 598 nn.135, 138,
    599 n.148
Murphy, J. M.,
  Swift 602 n.176
Murray, R. H.,
  Political Consequences 585 n.362
Murray, W. A.,
  'Swift' 603 n.182

Muss-Arnold, W.,
  'Efforts' 482 n.98, 483 n.117

Nankinvell, J.,
  'Stillingfleet' 541 n.40
Nantes, R. de,
  Histoire 428 n.90
Napoli, G. di,
  'Contemptus' 418 n.35, 419 nn.41,
    43, 424 n.104
  Pico 423, 424
Neale, J. E.,
  'Acts' 482 n.104
  Elizabeth 1 482 n.104
  Essays 487 n.170
Nelson, J. H.,
  Hales 499 n.4
Nelson, N.,
  'Individualism' 418 n.34
Neumann, H.,
  Masse 463 n.227
New, J. F. H.,
  Anglican 481 n.81
Newald, R.,
  Erasmus 437 n.18
Newcombe, J.,
  Sermon 610 n.133
Newton, I.,
  Correspondence (ed.
    H. W. Turnbull) 593 n.44
  Opera (ed. S. Horsely) 591, 592
  Principia (ed. A. Koyre/
    J. B. Cohen) 397, 591, 592
  Principia (trans A. Motte, ed.
    F. Cajori) 591 n.20
Nicholl, H. P.,
  Toland 570 n.60
Nicoladoni, A.,
  Bünderlin 454 n.92
Nicolson, M./Nohler, N. M.,
  'Background' 602 n.173
Nidditch, P. H.,
  Locke Newsletter 546 n.138
Niebuhr, H. R.,
  Kingdom 498 n.437
Niesel, W.,
  'Ablehnung' 493 n.341
Niesert, J. (ed.),
  Urkundensammlung I 462 n.217a
Niethammer, F. J.,
  Streit 419 n.50
Nipperdey, T.,
  'Theologie' 458 n.167
Nitschke, A.,
  Welt 425 n.141
Nordström, J.,
  Medetid 418 n.24
Norton, D. F.,
  'Shaftesbury' 579 n.231

Norton, W. J.,
  Butler 596 n.109
Notestein, W.,
  English People 476 n.7
Nuttall, G. F.,
  Holy Spirit 510 n.244, 539 n.11,
    540 n.16
  Review of J. S. Coolidge,
    Renaissance 492 n.304
  Studies 540 nn.16f.
  Visible Saints 494 n.344, 354

Oakeshott, M.,
  Civil Association 528 n.37
  Introduction to T. Hobbes,
    Leviathan 527 nn.28, 30
  'Moral Life', in *Rationalism* 528,
    530 n.50
  'Obey God?' 530 n.50
Oberman, H. A.,
  Bradwardine 433 n.262
Oelrich, K. H.,
  Erasmus 437 n.19
Ogg, D.,
  England 539 n.3, 576 n.187,
    583 n.315, 586 n.388
O'Higgins, J.,
  Collins 604, 605, 606–8, 609–11
  'Tillotson' 542 n.66, 543 n.76,
    544 n.106,, 545 n.115
Olivecrona, K.,
  'Locke' 562 n.446
Olivi, P. J.,
  Postilla 30
Ollero, A.,
  'Hobbes' 529 n.39
Olsen, V. N.,
  New Testament 507 n.150
Orr, J.,
  English Deism 520 n.6, 568 n.22
Orr, R.,
  Reason 484 n.125, 499 nn.4, 11,
    500, 501
Orwell, G.,
  'Politics' 602 n.176
  Shooting 602 n.176
Overall, J.,
  Book 139, 145, 560 n.420
Ozment, S.,
  'Franck' 452 n.76,, 454 n.95
  Mysticism 452 n.56
  Reformation 472 n.109

Pacchi, A.,
  Bibliografia Hobbesiana 524 n.2
  Convenzione 525 f.n.10
Packull, W. O.,
  'Denck' 451 n.55
  'Entwicklung' 451 n.55

Mysticism 448 n.31, 451 n.55,
    454 nn.92, 99, 455 n.105
Pailin, D. A.,
  'Clarke' 595 n.67
Pantin, W. A.,
  Church 432 n.245
Pare, G. (ed. et al.),
  Renaissance 418 n.23
Parker, H.,
  Observations 305
Parker, H. B.,
  'J. Cotton' 484 n.127
Parker, M.,
  Correspondence (ed. Bruce/Perowny)
    482 n.105
Parker, T. M.,
  'Arminianism' 502 n.66
Parker, W. R.,
  Milton 504 n.85
Parry, G.,
  Locke 546 n.142, 551 n.221,
    556 n.311
Parry, R. H. (ed.),
  Civil War 504 n.88, 517 n.323
Passmore, J. A.,
  Cudworth 289, 295
Pastor, L.,
  Geschichte 417 n.13
Patrick, S.,
  Brief account (ed. T. A. Birell)
    538 n.2
Patrides, C. A.,
  'Note on Method' (in *Cambridge
    Platonists* 511 n.232
  Cambridge Platonists (ed.)
    510 n.220, 511, 512 n.252, 513,
    514 nn.270, 271
  'Reading List' (in ibid.) 511 n.232
Pattison, M.,
  'Tendencies' 596 n.111, 597 n.115,
    598 n.127
Pauck, W.,
  'Historiography' 448 n.32
  'Reich Gottes' 474 n.156,
    474f n.158, 475 n.181, 480 n.58
Pauley, W. C. de,
  Candle of the Lord 510 n.22,
    512 n.244, 514 n.272
Paulson, R.,
  'Theme' 601 n.166
Pawson, G. P. H.,
  Cambridge Platonists 510 n.220
Payne, J. B.,
  'Hermeneutics' 435 nn.2, 4,
    436 n.7, 437 n.27, 438, 439,
    440 n.55
Pearl, V.,
  Puritan Revolution 503 n.79

Pearson, S.,
　T. _Cartwright_ 479 n.54, 482 nn.112,
　113
Pearson, S. C. Sr.,
　Religion 555 n.299
Pease, T. C.,
　Movement 483 n.121, 517 nn.322,
　336
Pennington, D./Thomas K. (eds.),
　Puritans 565 n.5
Peremans, N.,
　Erasme et Bucer 468 n.23
Perkins, W.,
　Armilla 490 n.243
　Chain 121
　De praedestinationis modo 120,
　490 n.252
　Discourse (ed. T. Merill) 121
　Treatise (ed. T. Merill) 121
　Works (ed. J. Legate/C. Legge)
　490 nn.257, 260
Perl, M. R.,
　'Physics' 592 n.36, 593 nn.54, 55
Perlitt, L.,
　Vatke 623 n.182, 626 n.6
Petegorsky, D. W.,
　Democracy 515 n.288
Peters, R.,
　Hobbes 526 n.19, 535 n.121,
　536 n.139
Petrarch, F.,
　De contemptu 13
　De viris (ed. G. Martelloti) 15,
　421 n.67
　Le familiari (ed. V. Rossi) 420 n.60
　Rerum 15, 421 n.69
Pettit, N.,
　Heart 490 n.253
Peuckert, W. E.,
　Franck 452 n.107
Pfeiffer, G./Wenderhorst, A. (eds.),
　Fränkische Lebensbilder 455 n.107
Pfeiffer, R.,
　'Erasmus' 437 n.17
Philippen, L. J. M.,
　'Norbertus' 426 n.154
Philonenko, A.,
　'Hobbes' 527 n.21
Pico, G. della Mirandola,
　Briefe (ed. L. Dorez) 434 n.119
　Commento 423 nn.97, 424 n.113
　De Ente 423 nn.90, 93
　De dignitate (ed. B. Cicognani)
　422 n.90
　Disputationes (ed. E. Garin) 18f.
　Heptaplus (ed. id.) 423, 424 n.106
　Oratio (ed. id.) 17–19, 423 nn. 96,
　100, 424 nn.105–6

Pierce, W.,
　Hist Introduction 483 n.117
Pineas, R.,
　W. Tyndale 485 n.130
Pirenne, H.,
　'Tanchelin' 426 n.154
Plath, U.,
　Calvin 464 n.236
Plato,
　Republic 16
Plumb, J. H.,
　Growth 583 nn.323, 327, 587 n.397
Pocock, J. G. A.,
　'Constitution' 560 n.418a
　'Time' 534 n.106, 535 n.118a,
　536 n.138, 538 n.200a
Pocock, J. G. A. (ed.),
　Revolutions 477 n.13
Polin, R.,
　'Justice' 563 n.477
　Politique 526 n.14, 550 n.182,
　556 n.312, 563 n.477
Polishook, J. H.,
　R. Williams 484 n.127
Pollard, A. W./Redgrave, G. R.
　(eds.),
　Catalogue 486 n.169
Pomponazzi, P.,
　Tractatus 567 n.10
Pons, E.,
　Swift 601 n.166
Porter, H. C.,
　'Nose' 441 n.65, 507 n.150,
　509 n.198
　Reformation 481 n.82, 491 n.267,
　496 n.418, 511 n.227
Porter, H. C. (ed.),
　Puritanism 482 n.114, 483 n.16,
　487 n.171
Porter, J. W.,
　Rothmann 461 n.212, 462
Post, R. R.
　Devotion 436 n.15
　'Erasmus' 436 n.15
Poulson, R.,
　Fictions 600 n.161
Powicke, F. J.,
　Browne 483 n.118
　Cambridge Platonists 510 n.220,
　514 n.272, 515 n.281
Prall, S. E.,
　Puritan Revolution 503 n.82
Price, F. D.,
　'Diocese' 481 n.93
Price, J.,
　Walwins Wiles (in _Leveller Tracts_, ed.
　W. Haller/G. Davies) 381
Price, M.,
　Palace 604 n.190

Priestley, F. E. L.,
'Controversy' (in *Heritage*, ed.
R. E. Butts/J. W. Davies)
591 n.26, 593, 594 n.59
Primus, J. H.,
Controversy 481 n.93, 482 n.103,
487 n.184, 492 n.313,
493 nn.316, 317
Prynne, M.,
Antipathie 155
Discovery 503 n.69
Pusino, J.,
'Einfluss' 438 n.32

Quintana, R.,
'Gulliver's Travels' 601 n.164
Mind 601 n.167, 603 n.191
Swift 604 n.200
Tale 602 n.172

Rabener, G. W.,
Cogitationes 577 n.198
Rachfal, F.,
'Kalvinismus' (in M. Weber, *Ethik*
II) 478 n.29
Rabil, A., Jr,
Erasmus 535 n.4, 438 n.35,
450 n.55
Raber, K.,
Studien 452 n.76, 455 n.109, 456
Rack, H. D.,
'Boyle' 545 n.119
Rammstedt, O.,
Sekte 463 n.227
Ramsay, R. W.,
Ireton 516 n.305
Ramsey, I. T. (ed.),
Locke's Reasonableness 547 n.145,
556–9
Ranke, L. von,
Geschichte 447 n.20
Raphael, D. D.,
'View' 596 n.109
Raubenheimer, R.,
'Bucer' 467f. n.21
Rauche, G. A.,
Aspekte 553 n.243
Rawson, C. J.,
'Character' 601 n.161
'Gulliver' 601 n.166, 603 n.179,
604 n.194
Swift 600 n.160, 603 n.192
Ray, J.,
Discourses 339
Reale, M.,
'O legado' 529 n.39
Redwood, J. A.,
'Blount' 566 n.7

Redwood, J.,
Reason 526 n.12, 547 n.148,
587 n.394, 593 n.39, 609 n.105,
613 n.197, 614 n.219
Reeves, M.,
Influence 428, 429 n.207, 430
Rehm, W.,
'Renaissancekult' 417 n.12
Reik, M. M.,
Golden Lands 534 n.93c
Reimarus, H. S.,
Apologie (ed. G. Alexander) 412
Reinitz, R.,
'Argument' 484 n.127, 494 n.456
'Background' 484 n.127
Reiss, E.,
'Importance' 603 nn.187, 188
Remusat, C. de,
Lord Herbert 519 n.1
Renaudet, A.,
Etudes 435 n.6
'Message' 435 n.6
Rendtorff, T.,
'Bibelwissenschaft' 425 n.4
Glaube 563 n.488
Reventlow, H. Graf,
'Judaism' 570 n.60, 575 nn.165,
167
Reimarus 533 n.87, 576 n.180
Rex, W.,
'Bayle' 623 n.170
Essays 623 n.170
Richardson, R. C.,
Debate 477 nn.13, 14
Richey, R. E./Jones, D. G. (eds.),
Religion 484 n.129
Richmond, H. M.,
Milton 404 n.85, 505
Ricuperati, G.,
'Libertinismo' 570 n.60,
574 nn.149, 151, 575 n.75
Riddle, G. K.,
'Benevolence' 596 n.110, 600 n.157
Ridley, J.,
Cranmer 481 nn.93, 98
Ridley, N., Bishop,
Answer (in J. Bradford, *Writings*)
487 n.184, 492 n.313
Riedemann, P.,
'Rechenschaft' 456 n.146,
457 n.152
Ritschl, A.,
Geschichte 50, 446 n.15
'Widertäufer' 462 n.227
Ritschl, O.,
Dogmengeschichte III 466 n.5,
468 nn.27, 29, 473 n.127

Ritter, G.,
Review of D. Cantimori, *Häretiker*
463
Robbins, C.,
Commonwealthman 587 n.398
Robert, A. (ed.),
Correspondance Leibniz-Clarke
593 n.54
Robertson, D. B.,
Foundations 536 n.316
Robertson, G. C.,
Hobbes 524 n.1
Robinson, H.,
Zurich Letter I 480 nn.56, 68
Zurich Letters II 480 nn.56, 68
Robinson, H. (ed.),
Reformation 479 n.56
Robson, J. A.,
Wyclif 430 n.228, 431 n.232,
432 n.256, 433 n.262
Roche, M. de la,
Review of W. Surenhusius (in
Memoirs) 609 n.119
Röd, W.,
'Thomas Hobbes' 524 n.1
Rogers, G. A. J.,
'Locke' 552 n.221, 553 n.243
Rogers, J.,
Necessity 611 n.151
Rogge, J.,
'Wort und Geist' 459 n.180,
460 n.188
Rohr, J. von,
'Covenant' 489 n.236
Roll, H.,
'De slotel' 462 n.216
Rosenmeier, R.,
'Teacher' 484 n.127
Rosenheim, E. E.,
Swift 600 n.161, 601 n.168,
602 nn.178, 179, 603 n.179,
604 nn.192, 195
Ross, R./Schneider, H. H./
Waldmann, T.,
Hobbes 525 n.4, 531 n.70
Rossi, M.,
Alle fonti 520 nn.9, 10, 522 n.25
in *Transactions* 523 n.55
Chirbury 519–523
Rotermundt, R.,
Denken J. Lockes 549 n.179
Rothert, H.,
Reich 462 n.227
Rothmann, B.,
Bekenntnisse (in *Schriften*) 457 n.149
Bericht (in ibid.) 69
Restitution (in ibid.) 416 nn.216,
219

Schriften (ed. R. Stupperich)
444 n.2, 461, 462
Verborgenheit (in *Schriften*)
416 n.216
Rotondo, A.,
'Movimenti' 443 n.1
'Pietro Perna' 464 n.236
Rott, J.,
Correspondence 466 n.6
Routley, E.,
Religious Dissent 494 n.343, 539 n.5
Roux, L. (ed.),
Introduction to Hobbes, *Les
éléments*
529 n.48
Rowse, A. L.,
England 476 n.6, 477 n.16
Rüegg, W.,
Cicero 419 n.50, 420 n.53
Rupp, G.,
'Karlstadt' 492 n.288
Makers 485 n.132
Reformation 458 n., 167
'Word' 449 n.35
Russell, C. (ed.),
Origins 499 n.1, 500 n.10,
504 n.83a
Russo, F.,
Bibliografia 427 n.164
Gioacchino da Fiore 426 n.164
'Rassegna' 427 n.164
Ryan, J. K.,
'Smith' 514 n.272

Saage, R.,
Herrschaft 515 nn.287, 289
Sabetti, A.,
Toland 570 n.60, 571 n.64,
573 n.129
Sacheverell, H.,
Discourse 587 n.392
Saint-Thierry, W. of,
Cantica 13, 419 n.38
Saitta, G.,
Marsilio Ficino 422 n.82
Salimbene of Parma,
Chronicle (ed. D. Holder-Egger) 29,
429 n.201
Chronicle (German trans.
A. Doren) 29, 429 n.201
Saltmarsh, J.,
End 182, 518 n.350
Salutatii,
De laboribus 14
Salvateorelli, L.,
'Locke' 559 n.405
Sandeus, F.,
De regibus 419 n.41

Santinello, G.,
  'Erasmo' 437 n.17
Savignac, J.,
  in *Le Monde* 440 n.59
Scaliger, J.,
  Opus 590 n.14
Schäfer, R.,
  Bibelauslegung 415 n.5
Schauffele, W.,
  Täufer 444 n.3
Schedler, G.,
  'Hobbes' 527 n.19a
Schiavone, M.,
  Problemi 422 n.82
Schiess, T.,
  Briefwechsel 473 n.122
Schischkoff, G. (ed.),
  Beiträge 573 n.129
Schlegel, D.,
  Shaftesbury 578 n.209
Schlingensiepen, H.,
  'Erasmus' 435 n.4, 450 n.55
Schmeidel, B.,
  Introduction to Salimbene of
    Parma, *Chronicle*, ed. D. Holder-
    Egger 429 n.201
Schmid, M.,
  'Deismus' 571 n.82
Schmid, R.,
  'Müntzer' 458 n.166
Schmidt, K.,
  Religion 496 n.395, 498 n.437, 455,
    515 n.288
Schmidt, M.,
  'Andrewes' 496 n.418
  'Kirchenbegriff' 430 n.228, 432
  'Problematik' 476 n.2
  'Stillingfleet' 541 n.40
  'Wyclif' 430 n.228
Schmidt, M. A.,
  'Kirche' 433 n.266
Schmitt, C.,
  'Begriff' 201, 534 nn.95, 97
  Leviathan 527 n.22
  'Reformation' 524 n.3, 525 n.4,
    528 n.33, 531 nn.64, 68, 534, 535
  Staat 527 n.22,528 n.33, 534n.95
Schneider, H. W.,
  'Piety' 531 n.70
Schnur, R.,
  Individualismus 535 n.114
Schnur, R. (ed.),
  Staatsträson 532 n.84
Schöffler, H.,
  Abendland 492 n.286
Schochet, G. J.,
  Patriarchalism 560
Schonfeld, F.,
  Ethik 506, 507

Scholder, K.,
  Ursprünge 3–5
Scholem, G.,
  'Kabbala' 424 n.114
Scholz, H.,
  Religionsphilosophie 520 n.10
Scholz, R.,
  Ockham 433 n.266
Schornbaum, K. (ed.),
  Geschichte 463 n.2
  Quellen 463 n.2
Schottenloher, O.,
  Erasmus 436 n.17, 438 n.36
  'Lex naturae' 436, 439 n.52,
    440 nn.53, 54
  Review of E. W. Kohls, *Theologie*
    435 n.5, 436 n.7, 438 n.36,
    439 n.51
Schouls, P. A.,
  Imposition 546 n.141, 553 n.243,
    556 n.311, 563 n.482a
Schreiner, J. (ed.),
  Einführung 415 n.3
Schrenk, G.,
  Gottesreich 457 n.160, 489 n.237,
    536 n.138
Schubert, H. von,
  Wiedertäufer 462 n.227
Schulte-Nordholt, H.,
  Het Beeld 416 n.2, 418 n.29
Schultz, H.,
  Milton 519 n.357
Schultz, R.,
  'Anschauung' 473 n.127,
    474 nn.156, 158, 475 n.160
Schwarz, R.,
  'Müntzer' 457 n.165
  Theologie 458 n.167, 461 n.199
Schwarzwäller, K.,
  Sibboleth 437 n.49
  'Probleme' 676 n.7
Schwenckfeld, C.,
  Corpus 443 n.2, 452 n.69, 457 n.163
  Iudicium 457 n.158
Schwindt, A.,
  Denck 454 n.94
Scivoletto, M.,
  Fra Salimbene 429 n.201
Scrinium Erasmianum 436 nn.2, 3,
  437 nn.26, 439 n.52, 440 nn.54,
  59
Scripta Anglicana 473 n.126, 481 n.94
Seaver, P. S.,
  Review of J. S. Coolidge,
    Renaissance 492 n.304
Secret, F.,
  'Pico' 424 n.114
  Kabbalistes 424 n.114
  'Nouvelles' 424 n.117a

Seebass, G.,
  'Denck' 455 n.107
  Hut 459 n.177a, 460 n.189,
    463 n.228a
  Müntzers Erbe 443 n.2
Seeber, A.,
  Toland 576 n.196
Seeberg, R.,
  Dogmengeschichte 466 n.5, 467 n.13,
    468 n.24
Seebohm, F.,
  Reformers 437 n.17
Segall, H.,
  Defensor pacis 433 n.265
Séguenny, A.,
  'Exégèse' 455 n.109
  'Franck, Sebastian' 453 n.76
Seidlmayer, M.,
  Wege 420 n.57, 421 n.68
Selby-Bigge, L. A.,
  British Moralists 295, 296
Selge, K.-V.,
  Waldenser 426
Seliger, M.,
  'Locke's Natural Law' 550 n.182
Semprini, G.,
  'L'amore' 423 n.93a
  Convegno Internazionale 424 n.105a
  Filosofia 423 n.92
Seneca,
  Epistulae 420 n.59
Sensabaugh, G. G.,
  Milton 504 n.85, 584 n.335
Servetus,
  Dialogorum 463 n.225
Shaftesbury, A. A. C. Earl of,
  Characteristics (⁶1738) 577 n.197,
    578 n.217
  Characteristics (ed. J. M. Robertson)
    309–19, 577–82
  Life, Letters (ed. B. Rand)
    577 n.197, 579 nn.219, 241,
    581 n.261, 586 n.378
  Regimen (ed. B. Rand) 308,
    577 n.200
  Second Characters (ed. B. Rand)
    577 n.19703
Shapiro, B.,
  Wilkins 545 nn.117, 118
Shaw, H.,
  Levellers 516 n.315
Sherburn, G.,
  'Errors' 603 n.179
Sherlock, T.,
  Tryal 372, 613 n.195
Shipps, K.,
  'Political Puritan' 477 n.9
Shirley, F. J.,
  R. Hooker 488 nn.207, 213

Siegel, P. N.,
  'Humanism' 480 nn.60, 74,
    486 n.164
Sikes, G. A.,
  Vane 539 n.12
Simmons, R. C. (ed.),
  Puritanism 483 n.119
Simon, I.,
  Three Restoration Divines 542 nn.66,
    68, 543 n.76, 545 n.118
Simpkinson, C. H.,
  Laud 484 n.124
  'Religion' 505 n.67
Simpson, A.,
  Puritanism 481 n.80
Sina, M.,
  Ragione 499 nn.1, 3, 510 n.220,
    514 n.272, 519 n.1, 538 n.2,
    542 n.66, 548 n.153, 554 n.268,
    555 n.301a, 566 n.7, 567 n.9,
    570 n.60, 604 n.1, 617 n.1
Singh, R.,
  'J. Locke' 550 n.182
Sippel, T.,
  'Ursprung' 540 n.16
  Vorgeschichte 540 n.16
  Werdendes Quäkertum 540 n.16
Sirluck, E.,
  Introduction to J. Milton, *Prose
    Works*, II 504 n.85, 507 n.150,
    508 nn.173, 178, 509 n.197
Sisson, C. J.,
  Judicious Marriage 488 n.207
Skelton, P.,
  Deism 566 n.2, 577 n.198,
    614 n.220
Skinner, Q.,
  'Conquest' 533 n.93a
  'History' 533 n.93a, 535 n.115
  'Hobbes' 525 n.4, 526 n.16,
    533 n.93a
  'Ideological Context' 526 n.16,
    533 n.93a, 535 n.115
  Review article 531 n.66
Smalley, B.,
  'Bible' 432 n.255
  'Postilla' 433 n.258
  Study 431 n.233
Smectymnuus (Pseudonym),
  Answer 155, 504 n.86
Smirin, M. M.,
  Volksreformation 458 n.166
Smith, D. C.,
  'R. Browne' 483 n.118
Smith, H. S./Handy, R. T./Loescher,
  R. L.,
  Christianity 484 n.129

Smith, J.,
  Prophecy (in *Select Discourses*, ed.
    S. Patrick) 176, 514 n.273
  Righteousness (in ibid.) 175
  Superstition (in ibid.) 593 n.261
Smith, P.,
  Erasmus 437 n.18
Smith, T.,
  De Republica 585 n.362
Smithson, R. J.,
  Anabaptists 449 n.40
Smucker, D.,
  'Historiography' 445 n.11,
    446 n.16
Smyth, C. H.,
  Cranmer 471 n.89
Solt, L. F.,
  Saints 507 n.147, 517 n.323,
    518 n.348
Sommerville, C. J.,
  'Conversion' 489 n.236
  'Typologies' 587 n.397
Southgate, W. M.,
  Marian Exiles 479 n.54
Sozzi, B. T.,
  Petrarca 420 n.57
Spalding, J. C.,
  'Restitution' 486, 488 nn.200, 201
Speck, W. A.,
  Swift 601 n.167
Speer, H.,
  Review of W. Euchner, *Naturrecht*
    550 n.198
Spencer, J.,
  De legibus 568 n.31, 569
  Dissertatio 568 n.31
  Works (ed. L. Chappelow) 568 n.31
Spijker, W. van't,
  'Eenheid' 472 n.103
Spitz, L. W.,
  'Humanism' 467 n.13
  Renaissance 436 n.12, 441 n.71
Spooner, W. A.,
  Butler 596 n.110
Spragen, T. A.,
  World 526 n.10
Sprat, T.,
  History, ed. J. I. Cope/
    H. W. Jones 589 n.1
Sprunger, K. L.,
  'Ames' 479 n.42
Staats, R.,
  'Hintergrund' 596 n.110
Stacey, J.,
  Wyclif 430 n.228, 431 nn.230, 232,
    432 nn.242, 244, 434 nn.272, 276
Starkman, M.,
  Satire 601 n.166
Statis, J. J.,

  Bibliography 600 n.160
Stayer, J. H.,
  Anabaptists 458 n.167, 460 n.198,
    461 nn.208, 211, 462 n.226
  'Anfänge' 446 n.17
Stayer, J. M./Packull, W. O. (eds.),
  Anabaptists 444 n.3, 445 nn.11, 12,
    458 n.167, 446 n.12, 447 n.17,
    449 n.34
  'Kristallisationspunkt' 446 n.17
Stayer, J. M./Packull, W. O./
    Deppermann, K.,
  'Monogenesis' 446 n.12, 448 n.27,
    457 n.164a
Steck, K. G.
  Luther 444 n.4, 447 n.22, 450 n.54
Steinmetz, M.,
  Review of T. Müntzer, *Schriften*,
    ed. P. Kirn/G. Franz 457 n.168
  'Müntzerforschung' 457 n.168
Steinmetz, M./Brendler, G. (eds.),
  Weltwirkung 447 n.20, 449 n.33
Stephen, L.,
  English Thought 547 n.148,
    569 n.56, 580 n.259, 600 n.157
Stephens, W. P.,
  Holy Spirit 470 n.52, 471 n.80,
    472 n.111
Stillingfleet, E.,
  Discourse 570 n.58
  Irenicum 229–32
  Letter 566 n.6
  Origines Sacrae 233–5
Stimson, D.,
  'Wilkins' 545 n.117
Stoeffler, F.,
  Rise 120, 482 n.111, 490, 491 n.266
Straka, G.,
  Anglican Reaction 586 n.386
  'Final Phase' 586 nn.386, 387,
    587 n.390
Stranks, C. J.,
  Anglican Devotion 543 n.75
Strasser, O. E.,
  Pensée 474 nn.144, 147
Strauss, L.,
  Natural Right(=*Naturrecht*)
    528 n.37, 547 n.152, 549 nn.176,
    179, 550, 562 n.470
  'Doctrine' 550 n.186
  Political Philosophy 52 n.37
Strider, R. E. L.,
  R. Greville 509, 510
Strohl, H.,
  'Bucer' 467 n.10
  Review of J. Courvoisier, *La
    Notion* 472 n.109
  RHPR 10, 1930 474 n.156
  'Theologie' 470 n.64

'Un aspect' 474 n.156
Strong, E. W.,
  'Mathematical Way' 591 n.20
  'Newton' 590 n.4
Strype, J.,
  Life 482 n.105
Stuart, R. O.,
  Breaking 482 n.109, 490 n.249
Stubbs, P.,
  Anatomy 124
Stumpf, R.,
  'Hobbes' 524 n.2
Stupperich, R.,
  'Anschauungen' 472 nn.109, 110,
    473 n.129
  'Bucer' 466 n.5, 468 n.23
  'Butzerforschung' 466 nn.3, 7
  Erasmus 437 n.18
  Introduction to M. Bucer, *Schriften*
    (DW 1) 467 nn.12 14
  Introduction to M. Bucer, *Schriften*
    (DW 7) 473 n.126, 474 nn.141,
    144
  Introduction to B. Rothmann,
    Schriften 461 nn.212, 213,
    462 n.221
  Festschrift 466 n.5, 467 n.8
  Humanismus 468 n.23, 469 n.30
  'Kirche' 472 n.109
  'Schriftverständnis' 469 n.31
  Täufertum 462 n.216, 462 n.227,
    463 n.228
Sturgeon, N. L.,
  'Nature' 599 n.153
Suits, D. B.,
  'Hobbes' Argument' 528 n.33a
Summers, W. H.,
  Lollards 480 n.66
Surenhusius, W.,
  Tractatus 609 n.119
Sutherland, J.,
  'Background' 582
Sutherland, S. R.,
  'Religion' 530 n.49
Svendsen, K.,
  'Science' 507 n.150
Swift, J.,
  Collected Poems (ed. J. Horrell)
    600 n.160
  Correspondence (ed. H. Williams)
    600 n.160, 603 nn.183, 185,
    604 n.196
  Gulliver 351, 352
  Journal (ed. id.) 600 n.160
  Poems (ed. id.) 600 n.160
  Prose Works (ed. H. Davis)
    600 n.160
  Tub 351
Sykes, A. A.,

Essay 610 n.131
Principles 409–10, 625
Sykes, N.,
  Church 497 n.430, 499 n.466, 539,
    542 n.66, 568 n.385, 583 n.313,
    589 n.453
  Old Priest 497 n.430, 499 n.466
  'Sermons' 542 n.66
  Sheldon to Secker 538 n.2
  Gibson 625
Symylie, J.,
  'M. L. King' 498 n.437
Szabados, B.,
  'Butler' 596f. n.110

Taft, F. L.,
  Preface to J. Milton, *Apology* (in
    Prose Works ed. D. M. Wolfe)
Taft, F. L./Baizer, A.,
  'Legion' 503 n.80
Tanner, J. R.,
  Documents 483 n.119, 492 n.294
Tatnall, E. C.,
  'Wyclif' 430 n.228, 433 n.268
Tavard, G. H.,
  'Holy Church' 433 n.261
  Holy Writ 433 n.261
  Tradition 500 n.12, 535 n.107a
Tawney, R. H.,
  Religion 478 n.25
  Introduction to M. Weber,
    Protestant Ethic 478 n.25
Taylor, A. E.,
  'Ethical Doctrine' = *Hobbes-Studies*,
    ed. K. C. Brown = *Leviathan*,
    ed. B. H. Baumrin 529
  'Features' 599 n.153, 600 n.157
  Studies 599 n.153
Teerinck, H.,
  Bibliography (ed. A. H. Scouten)
    600 n.160
Teufel, E.,
  'Landräumig' 452 n.76, 456 n.137
  'Luther' 453 n.86
  'Täufertum' 446 n.12
Thackeray, W. M.,
  Humourists 602 n.175
Thiemann, R. F.,
  'Law' 460 n.189
Thode, H.,
  Franz von Assisi 417 n.23, 425 n.127
Thomas, E.,
  'Short view' (in *Pillars*, ed.
    R. Baron) 588 n.408
Thomas, K.,
  'Origins' 528 n.356, 533 n.90a
Thomas Aquinas,
  Summa 419 n.39
Thomason, G.,

Catalogue 504 n.87
Thompson, B.,
  'Bucer' 466 n.3
Thompson, M. P.,
  'Reception' 562 n.446a
Thomson, J. A. F.,
  Lollards 434 n.274, 480 n.66
Thomson, M. A.,
  History 539 n.5
Thomson, S. H.,
  Europe 482 n.104
  'Basis' 430 n.228, 432 n.256
Thornton, L. S.,
  R. Hooker 488
Tibi, R.,
  Review of W. Euchner, *Naturrecht*
  550 n.196
Tielsch, E. W.,
  Introduction to *Milton* 504 n.85,
  507 n.150, 509 n.189
Tiffany, E. A.,
  Shaftesbury 505
Tillotson, J.,
  Select Sermons 542 n.66
  Sermon 538 n.1
  Sermons (ed. Henry) 542 n.66
  Preface to J. Wilkins, *Principles*
  241, 242, 545
  Works (ed. T. Birch) 235–40, 542–5
  Works (ed. R. Barker) 235–40,
  542–5
Tillyard, E. M. W.,
  Milton 504 n.85
Tindal, M.,
  Christianity (ed. G. Gawlick) 321,
  327, 344, 374–84, 412, 583 n.318
  German trans. J. L. Schmidt
  613 n.216
  Four Discourses 586 n.378
  Laws of Nations 586 n.379
  New High Church 583 n.311,
  586 n.370
  Power of the Magistrate 586 n.379
  Rights 321–7, 583–6
Tjernagel, N. S. (ed.),
  Essays 487 n.171
Tocco, F.,
  Tribolazioni 429 n.220
Toffanin, G.,
  Che Chosa 11, 417 n.22
  La fine 417 n.22
  Religione 417 n.22
  Storia 417 n.22
Toland, J.,
  Adeisidaemon 305, 575
  Amyntor 546 n;186
  Christianity (ed. G. Gawlick)
  294–301, 569–73

Christentum (trans W. Lunde, intro.
  L. Zscharnack) 569 n.55
  Gründe (ed. H. Mainusch)
  575 n.169
  Letters to Serena (ed. E. Pracht)
  573 n.130
  Letters to Serena (ed.
  G. Gawlick) 301–3
  Milton 307, 576 n.185
  Nazarenus 303–304, 574–5
  Origines 305, 575
  Pantheisticon 573 n.130, 576 n.195
  Pantheisticon (German trans.
  L. Fensch) 576 n.195
  Pantheisticon 573 n.130, 576 n.195
  Reasons 505
  Reflections 583 n.314
  Tetradymus 306–7, 576
  Vindicius Liberius 574 n.137
Tönnies, F.,
  Thomas Hobbes 523 n.1, 528 n.33,
  534 n.104
Toon, P.,
  Puritans 481 n.91
Töpfer, B.,
  'Handschrift' 429, 430
  Reich 427, 428, 429 nn.200, 202
Torrance, T. F.,
  Kingdom 474 n.156
Torre, A. della,
  Storia 422 n.82
Tracy, J.,
  Erasmus 436 n.15, 437 n.17,
  441 n.77, 442 n.86
Traugott, J.,
  Discussions 560 n.160, 601 n.163,
  602 nn.175, 176, 604 n.192
  'Tale' 601 n.166
Travers, W.,
  Explicatio 103, 507 n.147
Treinen, H.,
  Studien 442 n.93
Trevelyan, G. M.,
  England 432 n.245, 585 n.353
  English Revolution 582 n.306
Trevor-Roper, H. R.,
  'T. Hobbes', in *Hist. Essays*
  525 n.429
  Laud 502 n.60, 508 nn.69, 71
Trianovsky, G. W.,
  'Obligation' 578 n.217
Trinius, J. A.,
  Freydenker Lexikon 570 n.60,
  575 n.175, 577 n.198, 589 n.445,
  608 n.80, 609 n.105, 610 n.127,
  613 nn.196, 216, 614 n.219,
  618 nn.2, 6, 619 n.27,
  621 nn.107, 109, 624 nn.209, 229

Trinkaus, C.,
  'Anticipation' 418 n.29
  Image 418 n.29, 420 nn.56, 57,
    421 nn.72, 72a, 422 n.83
Trinkaus, C./Oberman, H. (eds.),
  Holiness 418 n.29, 452 n.76
Trinterud, L. J. (ed.),
  'Origins' 96, 480 n.70, 486 n.151
  Puritanism 480 n.29, 452 n.76
  'Reappraisal' (ChH 1962) 485 n.133
Tripet, A.,
  Pétrarque 420 n.57
Troeltsch, E.,
  'Christentum' 444 n.6
  Deismus 566 n.1, 572 n.102
  Social Teaching 444 n.6, 446 nn.16,
    17, 494 n.347
Tulloch, J.,
  Theology 499, 510 n.220, 511,
    512 n.246, 514 nn.272, 281,
    538 n.2, 541 nn.40, 49
Turner, W.,
  Huntyng 101–12, 493 n.330
  Wolfe 493 n.330
Tuveson, E. L.,
  'Dean' 601 n.164
  Idea 498
  'Importance' 309, 579
  'Shaftesbury' 309, 578 n.212
  'Swift' 600 n.160, 601 nn.164, 166,
    602 n.176, 603 nn.180, 182,
    604 n.196 601 n.164
Tyacke, N. R. N.,
  Arminianism 499 n.1
  'Puritanism' 499 n.1, 500 n.10
Tyndale, W.,
  Answer (ed. H. Walter) 491 n.289
  Jonas (in *Doc. Treat.*) 106
  New Testament (ed. N. N. Wallis)
    106–107
  Pathway (in *Doctrinal Treatises*, ed.
    H. Walter) 106–107, 485 n.136
  Pentateuch (ed. J. I. Mombert) 106,
    107, 485 n.134, 486
  Practice (in *Expositions*, ed.
    H. Walter) 108
  Prologue to NT 1525, ed.
    A. W. Pollard 105, 488 n.130
  Prologue to NT 1531 (in *Doctr. Treat*)
    106
  Work (ed. S. L. Greenslade) 485
  Work (ed. G. E. Duffield) 485, 486
Tyrell, J.,
  Patriarcha non monarcha 562 n.448

Ubertino da Casale,
  Arbor 430 n.225
Uehlein, A.,
  Kosmos 577 n.197

Ullmann, B. L.,
  'Geschichtsverständnis' 459 n.176,
    460 n.192, 461 nn.199, 202
  'Ordo rerum' 459 n.177
  'Lehre' 461 n.199
  'Renaissance' 418 n.30
Unruh, B.,
  'Revolution' 445 n.12
Upham, C. W.,
  Vane 539 n.11
Urner, H.,
  'Taufe' 452 n.68
Ussher, J.,
  Annales 336

Vadian, J.,
  Gott 486 n.167
Valkhoff, M. F. (ed.),
  Conseil 464 n.236
Vasoli, C.,
  Introduction to Pico, *Opera*
    423 n.92
Venerabilis, Petrus,
  Epistola (ed. J. Fearns) 426 n.148
Verhuis, S. L.,
  Zeugnis 452
Vescovini, G. F.,
  Review of C. A. Viano, *Locke*
    546 n.141
Vialatoux, J.,
  La cité 526 n.20, 527 n.20
Viano, C. A.,
  Locke 546 n.141, 547 n.148,
    548 n.165, 551 n.217, 555 n.303,
    561 n.441, 563 n.490, 564 n.298
Vickers, B.,
  Swift 600 n.160, 602 n.172
  World 600 n.160, 601 n.164,
    603 n.189
Villey, P.,
  'L'Influence' 566 n.8
Viola, F.,
  Behemoth 527 n.21
  'Totalitarismo' 527 n.21
Viret, P.,
  Instruction 520 n.8
Vitalli, O.,
  Denck 451 n.56
Voegelin, E. (ed.),
  Revolution 560 n.417
Vogel, C. J. de,
  'Erasmus' 436 n.8, 438 n.36,
    439 n.46, 400 n.54
Vogler, B.,
  'Elsass' 472 n.109
Voight, G.,
  'Wiederbelebung' 421 n.62
Voigt, M.,
  Swift 601 n.162

Volz, H.,
'Müntzer' 458 n.165
Vooght, P. de,
'Sources' 430 n.228, 431 n.231
'Wyclif' 430 n.228, 431 nn.231, 232
Vossius, G. J.,
De Theologia 522 n.44

Waard, C. de (ed.),
Mersenne 521 n.23
Wade, I. O.,
Clandestine Organization 415 n.15,
566 n.4
Walker, D. P.,
Theology 520 n.9
Wagner, F.,
Newton 590 n.4, 591 n.26
Wallis, H. M.,
Laud 484 n.124
Walser, E.,
Florentinus 417 n.19
Gesammelte Studien 417 nn.12, 18,
418 n.27
Religion 417 n.20
Studien 417 n.21
Walsh, K.,
England 477 n.13
Walwyn, W.,
Just Defence (in *Leveller Tracts*, ed.
W. Haller/G. Davies) 181, 182,
518 n.338
Wisper (in ibid.) 518 n.339
Voice (in D. M. Wolfe, *Milton*) 181,
518
Walzer, M.,
'Puritanism' 478 n.27
Revolution 478 n.27
Warburton, W.,
Divine Legation 396, 621 n.118
Ward, D.,
Swift 601 n.166, 602 nn.169, 176,
604 nn.192, 194
Warnach, V. (ed.),
Hermeneutik 415 n.1
Warrender, H.,
Political Philosophy 529, 530
Watkin, E. I.,
Poets 512 n.246
Smith 514 n.272
Watkin, H. M. G.,
Church and State 543 n.106
Watkins, J. W. N.,
System 526 n.19, 529 n.39, 532 n.71
Watts, M. R.,
Dissenters I 494, 504 n.88,
515 n.289, 516 n.315
Weber, H. E.,
Reformation 466 n.5, 467 n.15,
459 n.29

Weber, K.,
Lucius Cary 499 n.5
Weber, M.,
Protestantische Ethik I 477 nn.17ff.,
478
Protestantische Ethik II 477 nn.17ff.,
478
Protestant Ethic (ET Talcott
Parsons) 477 n.17
Wedel, T. O.,
'Background' 603 n.179, 604 n.193
Wehr, G.,
'Müntzer' 459 n.174
Weigelt, H.,
'Franck' 452 n.76, 453 n.86,
454 n.95, 455
'Schwenkfeld' 452 n.67
Tradition 452 n.66
Weiser, C. F.,
Shaftesbury 306, 623 n.182
Weiss, U.,
'Rationalismus' 524 n.3
Wellhausen, J.,
Prolegomena 306, 623 n.182
Welsby, P. A.,
L. Andrewes 496 nn.417, 420
Welzel, H.,
Naturrecht 551 n.221
Wende, P.,
Probleme 504 n.88
Wendel, F.,
Introduction to M. Bucer, *Opera
Latina* 474 n.155, 475, 476 n.197
L'église 472 n.109, 473 n.124
Wendelborn, G.,
Verhältnis 432 n.255
TLZ 91, 1966 432 n.255
Wenger, J.,
'Biblizismus' 457 n.147
'Confession' 450 n.51
'Reformation' 447 n.17, 456 n.144
Wenger, J. C. (ed.),
Bekenntnis 457 n.147
Werkmeister, W. K. (ed., et al.),
Facets 418 n.31
West, G.,
Observations 613 n.98
West, W. M. S.,
'J. Hopper' (*BQ*, NS 15, 1954/55)
481 nn.92, 93, 487
'J. Hooper' (ibid., 1956) 481 nn.92,
96, 487 n.181
Westermann, C. (ed.),
Essays 415 n.1
Westfall, R. S.,
'Newton' 590 n.11
Science 545 nn.118, 120, 552 n.232,
568 n.21, 590 n.4, 600 n.159

Westin, G.,
 'Döparrörelsen' 444 n.6
 'Weg' 444 n.6
Whichcote, B.,
 Aphorisms (ed. W. R. Inge)
 511 n.227, 513 n.263
 Select Sermons (ed. A. A. C. Earl of
 Shaftesbury) 578 n.206
 Works 512–13
Whiston, W.,
 Accomplishment 362–4, 608, 609
 Astronomical Principles 594 nn.61,
 64
 Essay 364
 List 610 n.135
 Literal Accomplishment 610 n.135
 New Theory 340, 594 n.61
 Supplement 610 n.135
Whitaker, W. B.,
 Sunday 492 n.290
White, A. R.,
 'Conscience' 596 n.110, 600 n.157
White, B. R.,
 'Tradition' 494
Whitgift, J.,
 Works (ed. J. Ayre) 488, 497 n.481
Whiting, C. E.,
 Studies 539, 540
Whiting, J.,
 Persecution 540 n.21
Whitney, L.,
 'Blackwell' 579 n.235
 Primitivism 579 n.235
Whittingham, W.,
 Discourse 482 n.100
Wiener, J. H.,
 'Skinner' 533 n.93b
Wiener, M.,
 'Toland' 574 n.149, 575, 576 n.180
William of St Amour,
 Liber 429 n.209
Wilkins, J.,
 Principles 241–2, 249
Wilkinson, J. T.,
 1662– and After 539 n.5
Willey, B.,
 Background 510 n.220, 514 n.272,
 575 n.286
 English Moralists 510, n.220
 'Scientific Revolution' (in *History of
 Science*) 592 n.31
Williams, A.,
 Preface to Milton, *Tetrachordon*
 508 n.167
Williams, B.,
 Whig supremacy 585 n.360
Williams, C. H.,
 W. Tyndale 485 n.187

Williams, G.,
 Reformation 443 n.1, 461 n.211
Williams, G. (ed.),
 Writers 445 nn.7, 11, 453 n.87,
 461 n.208
Williams, G. H.,
 'Studies' 446 n.12
Williams, J.,
 Holy Table 503 n.71
Williams, K.,
 Heritage 600 n.160
 Swift 601 n.167, 603 n.191,
 604 n.196
 'Voyage' 601 n.167, 602 n.179,
 604 n.193
Williams, R.,
 Complete Writings (ed. P. Miller)
 498 n.454, 519 n.357
 Ministry (in *Complete Writings*)
 519 n.357
Willicock, J.,
 Vane 539 n.12
Willms, B.,
 Antwort 528 nn.35, 36, 532,
 535 n.120
 'Aspekte' 524 n.3
 'Vermessung' 524 n.3, 527,
 529 n.40, 531 n.64, 538 nn.195,
 196
 'Weg' 524 n.3, 526 n.14, 532 n.78
Wilson, F. P.,
 Review of J. S. Cooldige,
 Renaissance 492 n.304
Winkler, G.,
 Introduction to Erasmus, *Schriften*
 (ed. W. Welzig) 438 nn.37, 41,
 440 n.54, 442 n.94
Wiswedel, W.,
 'Glait' 457 n.163
 'Problem' 450
Wittwer, W. W.,
 Grundrechte 516 n.315, 517 n.320
Wolf, E.,
 'Botschaft' 416 n.13
Wolf, F. O.,
 Wissenschaft 527 n.13
Wolf, H. H.,
 Einheit 457 n.161, 489 n.238,
 494 n.342
Wolfe, D. M.,
 Introduction to Milton, *Prose Works*,
 Vol. I 503–6, 509 n.200
 Milton 504 n.85, 518 nn.341, 345
Wolfe, D. M. (ed.),
 Leveller Manifestoes 515
Wolff, E.,
 Shaftesbury 577 nn.197, 98, 578

Wollaston, W.,
  Religion 594 n.64, 621 n.120
Wollgast, S.,
  'Bermerkungen' 453 nn.90, 91
  Introduction to S. Franck, *Paradoxa* 435 n.90
  Franck 452 n.76
  Pantheismus 452 n.76, 453 n.89, 454 nn.95, 99, 455 n.109, 456 n.137
Wolter, H.,
  'Aufbruch' 425 n.145
Wood, T.,
  Discourse 482 nn.100, 102
Woodfield, R.,
  'Hobbes' 531 n.67
Woodhouse, A. S. P.,
  'Argument' 505 n.96
  Puritanism 515, 516, 516 nn.335, 336
Woodward, J.,
  Essay 594 n.62
Woog, C. C.,
  De Vita 611 n.160
Woolrych, A.,
  'Cromwell' 517 n.323
  'Puritanism' 517 n.3221
Woolston, T.,
  Defence 613 n.191
  Discourses 613 n.191
  Epistola 612 n.177
  Epistola Secunda 612 n.177
  Free Gift 612 n.179
  Letter 612 n.177
  Moderator 612
  Old Apology 370, 371, 611–12
  Second Letter 612 n.177
Worcester, D.,
  Satire 600 n.161
Workman, H. B.,
  Wyclif 430 n.228, 431 n.232, 432 nn.243, 251, 434
Woude, S. van der,
  Verguisd Geloof 463 n.236
Wray, F.,
  'Vermanung' 456 n.149
Wren, T. E.,
  Person Universe 534 n.93c
Wright-Henderson, P. A.,
  Life 545 n.117
Wyclif, J.,
  De civili dominio 433 n.261, 434 nn.270, 271
  De dominio divino (ed. R. L. Poole) 433 n.266
  De eucharistia 32, 431 n.236
  De officio regis 433 n.267
  Opera Latina (ed. Wyclif Society) 430 n.228

Opuscula (ed. S. H. Thomson) 32
Sacrae scripturae 430 n.228
Summa (ed. S. H. Thomson) 430 n.228
Tractatus (ed. A. Breck) 430 n.228
Trialogus (ed. G. Lechler) 430 n.228
English Works (ed. F. D. Matthew) 430 n.228
Select English Works (ed. T. Arnold) 430 n.228

Yarborough, S. A.,
  Henry Jacob 494 n.354
Yates, F. A.,
  Astraea 496 n.415a
  Bruno 573 n.129
  Rosicrucian 573 n.129
Yoder, J. H.,
  'Dissent' 446 n.17, 450 n.50
  'Evolution' 446 n.17, 450 n.51
  Täufertum I 446 n.17, 450 n.51
  Täufertum II 446 n.17, 450 nn.47, 51, 450 n.52, 456 n.139
  'Turning point' 450 n.51
Yolton, J. W.,
  Compass 546 n.141, 560 n.413, 561 n.442, 563 n.477
  JHP 6, 1968 559 n.384
  'Locke' 549 n.176, 550 n.182, 554 n.253
  Way of Ideas 546 n.141
Yolton, J. W. (ed.),
  J. Locke, Problems and Perspectives 547 n.145
Yule, G.,
  Independents 515 n.287, 517 n.326

Zaepernick, G.,
  'Welt' 454 n.90
Zagorin, P.,
  Court 483 n.118, 502 n.66
  History 483 n.118
Zani, L.,
  Etica 597 n.197
Zarone, G.,
  John Locke 550 n.179
Zielinski, T.,
  Cicero 420 n.53, 512 n.88
Ziff, L.,
  Puritanism 484 nn.126, 127
Zimmermann, T. P. C.,
  'Confession' 421 n.68
Zschäbitz, G.,
  'Stellung' 449 n.33
  Wiedertäuferbewegung 449 n.33
Zschäbisch, G./Franke, A.,
  Buch 432 n.245

Zscharnack, L.,
    Introduction to J. Locke,
        Reasonableness (trans C. Winckler)
        555 n.303
    Introduction to J. Toland,
        Christentum 569 n.55, 570 n.61

Zwingli, H.,
    von der Touf (in *Werke*) 456 n.139
    Ursache (in *Werke*) 456 n.139